ACCOUNTING CYCLE   (Chapters 3 and 4)

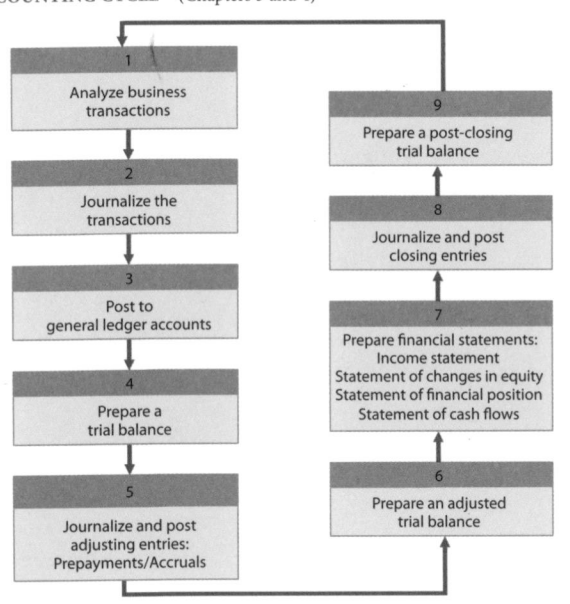

1. Analyze business transactions
2. Journalize the transactions
3. Post to general ledger accounts
4. Prepare a trial balance
5. Journalize and post adjusting entries: Prepayments/Accruals
6. Prepare an adjusted trial balance
7. Prepare financial statements: Income statement / Statement of changes in equity / Statement of financial position / Statement of cash flows
8. Journalize and post closing entries
9. Prepare a post-closing trial balance

INVENTORY   (Chapter 5)

Perpetual vs. Periodic Journal Entries (buyer)

Transaction	Perpetual	Periodic (Appendix 5A)
Purchase of merchandise	Dr. Merchandise Inventory Cr. Cash or Accounts Payable	Dr. Purchases Cr. Cash or Accounts Payable
Freight on merchandise purchased (FOB shipping point)	Dr. Merchandise Inventory Cr. Cash or Accounts Payable	Dr. Freight In Cr. Cash or Accounts Payable
Return of purchased merchandise	Dr. Cash or Accounts Payable Cr. Merchandise Inventory	Dr. Cash or Accounts Payable Cr. Purchase Returns and Allowances
Paying creditors on account within discount period	Dr. Accounts Payable Cr. Merchandise Inventory Cr. Cash	Dr. Accounts Payable Cr. Purchase Discounts Cr. Cash
Adjustment of inventory in accounting records to lower physical count amount (entry is opposite for higher amount)	Dr. Cost of Goods Sold Cr. Merchandise Inventory	No entry

Perpetual vs. Periodic Journal Entries (seller)

Transaction	Perpetual	Periodic (Appendix 5A)
Sale of merchandise	Dr. Cash or Accounts Receivable Cr. Sales Dr. Cost of Goods Sold Cr. Merchandise Inventory	Dr. Cash or Accounts Receivable Cr. Sales No entry
Freight on merchandise sold (FOB destination)	Dr. Freight Out Cr. Cash or Accounts Payable	Dr. Freight Out Cr. Cash or Accounts Payable
Return of sold merchandise (assuming resaleable)	Dr. Sales Returns and Allowances Cr. Cash or Accounts Receivable Dr. Merchandise Inventory Cr. Cost of Goods Sold	Dr. Sales Returns and Allowances Cr. Cash or Accounts Receivable No entry
Collection of account from customer within discount period	Dr. Cash Dr. Sales Discounts Cr. Accounts Receivable	Dr. Cash Dr. Sales Discounts Cr. Accounts Receivable
Period-end adjusting entry	No entry	Dr. Merchandise Inventory (ending) Dr. Cost of Goods Sold Dr. Purchase Returns and Allowances Dr. Purchase Discounts Cr. Merchandise Inventory (beginning) Cr. Purchases Cr. Freight In

INVENTORY   (Chapter 6)

Ownership of Merchandise

	FOB Shipping Point	FOB Destination
Goods purchased in transit	Buyer's (once shipped)	Seller's (until it reaches the buyer's destination)
Good sold in transit	Buyer's (once shipped)	Seller's (until it reaches the buyer's destination)

Inventory Cost Determination Methods

1. Specific identification: Used for goods that are not ordinarily interchangeable, or goods that have been produced and segregated for specific projects
2. Cost formulas: First-in, first-out (FIFO) or Average

Guidelines for Choice of Cost Formula

1. Choose method that corresponds to physical flow of goods.
2. Report inventory cost on the statement of financial position close to inventory's recent cost.
3. Use same method for all inventories having similar nature and usage.

Financial Statement Effects of Cost Determination Methods (during period of rising prices)

	Specific Identification	FIFO	Average
Income Statement			
Cost of goods sold	Variable	Lower	Higher
Gross profit	Variable	Higher	Lower
Profit	Variable	Higher	Lower
Statement of Financial Position			
Cash (pre-tax)	Same	Same	Same
Ending inventory	Variable	Higher	Lower
Retained earnings	Variable	Higher	Lower

Inventory Errors

Errors Made in Determining the Cost of Inventory

If Merchandise Inventory is:	Then Cost of Goods Sold is:	Then Gross Profit is:	Then Profit Before Income Tax is:	Then Retained Earnings is:
Overstated	Understated	Overstated	Overstated	Overstated
Understated	Overstated	Understated	Understated	Understated

Errors Made in Recording Purchase of Inventory

If purchase of inventory on account is recorded:	Then Merchandise Inventory is:	Then Cost of Goods Sold and Profit are:	Then Accounts Payable is:	Then Retained Earnings is:
Too early	Overstated	Unaffected	Overstated	Unaffected
Too late	Understated	Unaffected	Understated	Unaffected

Formula for Cost of Goods Sold (Periodic Inventory System—Appendix 5A)

Beginning Inventory + Cost of Goods Purchased = Cost of Goods Available for Sale − Ending Inventory = Cost of Goods Sold

INTERNAL CONTROL AND CASH   (Chapter 7)

Control Activities

Authorization of transactions and activities
Segregation of duties
Documentation
Physical controls
Independent checks of performance
Human resource controls

Calculation of Deposits in Transit

Deposits in transit at beginning of period + Deposits recorded in company's books this period − Deposits recorded on this period's bank statement = Deposits in transit at end of period

Calculation of Outstanding Cheques

Outstanding cheques at beginning of period + Cheques recorded in company's books this period − Cheques recorded on this period's bank statement = Outstanding cheques at end of period

Calculation of Unadjusted Cash Balance per Books

Adjusted cash balance per books or per bank from prior period + Cash receipts − Cash payments = Unadjusted cash balance per books at beginning of period

Bank Reconciliation

Bank	Books
Cash balance per bank statement (unadjusted)	Cash balance per books (unadjusted)
Add: Deposits in transit	Add: EFT collections and other deposits
Deduct: Outstanding cheques	Deduct: Service charges and other payments
Add (deduct): Bank errors	Add (deduct): Book errors
= Adjusted cash balance per bank	= Adjusted cash balance per books

Note: 1. Errors should be offset (added or deducted) on the side that made the error.
2. Adjusting journal entries should only be made on the books side.

STOP AND CHECK: (1) Do adjusted cash balances per bank and per books agree? (2) Does adjusted cash balance equal the balance in the general ledger Cash account after all adjusting journal entries have been made?

Debit and Credit Card Transactions (Chapters 7 and 8)

Debit Card	Bank Credit Card	Company Credit Card

Dr. Cash
  Cr. Sales
	Dr. Cash
	  Cr. Sales
		Dr. Accounts Receivable
		  Cr. Sales

Note: Debit and credit card fees are recorded as Bank Charges Expense during the bank reconciliation process. Normally no fees are charged for company credit cards.

RECEIVABLES   (Chapter 8)

Bad Debts

Transaction	Journal Entry
Record credit sales	Dr. Accounts Receivable Cr. Sales
Estimate bad debts	Dr. Bad Debts Expense Cr. Allowance for Doubtful Accounts
Write off uncollectible account	Dr. Allowance for Doubtful Accounts Cr. Accounts Receivable

Subsequent recovery	Dr. Accounts Receivable
	  Cr. Allowance for Doubtful Accounts
	Dr. Cash
	  Cr. Accounts Receivable

Notes Receivable

Transaction	Journal Entry
Issue notes receivable	Dr. Notes Receivable Cr. Cash or Accounts Receivable
Record interest	Dr. Cash or Interest Receivable Cr. Interest Revenue

Record honouring (collection) of notes receivable)	Dr. Cash
	  Cr. Notes Receivable
	  Cr. Interest Revenue and/or Interest Receivable

Estimate bad debts	Dr. Bad Debts Expense Cr. Allowance for Doubtful Notes

Record dishonouring of notes receivable (eventual collection assumed)	Dr. Accounts Receivable
	  Cr. Notes Receivable
	  Cr. Interest Revenue and/or Interest Receivable

Record dishonouring of notes receivable (eventual collection not assumed)	Dr. Allowance for Doubtful Notes
	  Cr. Notes Receivable
	  Cr. Interest Receivable (if any)

LONG-LIVED ASSETS   (Chapter 9)

Recording Depreciation and Amortization

Property, plant, and equipment	Dr. Depreciation Expense Cr. Accumulated Depreciation
Limited life intangible assets	Dr. Amortization Expense Cr. Accumulated Amortization

Calculation of Annual Depreciation Expense

Straight-line	$\dfrac{\text{Cost} - \text{Residual value}}{\text{Useful life (in years)}}$
Diminishing-balance	Carrying amount (cost – accumulated depreciation) at beginning of year × Depreciation rate (Straight-line rate × multiplier) Straight-line rate = 1 ÷ Useful life (in years)
Units-of-production	$\dfrac{\text{Cost} - \text{Residual value}}{\text{Estimated total units of activity}} \times$ Actual units of activity during year

Note: 1. If depreciation is calculated for partial periods, the straight-line and diminishing-balance methods must be adjusted for the relevant proportion of the year. Multiply annual depreciation expense by the number of months expired in the year divided by 12 months.
2. The total depreciation for the diminishing-balance method is limited to depreciable cost (cost – residual value).

Impairment Loss

Carrying amount (cost − accumulated depreciation) – Recoverable amount = Impairment loss

Dr. Impairment Loss
  Cr. Accumulated Depreciation (or Amortization, or asset if no contra account)

Derecognition of Property, Plant, and Equipment

1. Update depreciation for appropriate portion of current year	Dr. Depreciation Expense Cr. Accumulated Depreciation
2. Calculate carrying amount	Cost – Accumulated depreciation = Carrying amount
3. Calculate gain or loss	Proceeds – Carrying amount = Gain (loss)
4. Record disposal	Dr. Cash (or Receivable) Dr. Accumulated Depreciation Dr. Loss (or credit Gain) Cr. Property, Plant, and Equipment account

LIABILITIES   (Chapter 10)

Examples of Liabilities

Current Liabilities	Non-Current Liabilities
Bank indebtedness	Instalment notes payable
Accounts payable	Bonds payable
Sales tax payable	Finance lease liability
Property tax payable	Future income taxes
Salaries payable	Pension liabilities
Payroll deductions (such as CPP payable, EI payable, income tax payable, union dues payable)	
Employee benefits (such as CPP payable, EI payable, health insurance benefits payable)	
Short-term notes payable	
Current maturities of non-current debt	
Provisions and contingent liabilities (uncertain liabilities)	

Instalment Notes Payable—Payment Schedule

Payments	Interest Period	(A) Cash Payment	(B) Interest Expense	(C) Reduction of Principal	(D) Principal Balance
Fixed principal payments	Month	Variable B + C	D* × Annual Interest Rate × 1/12	Principal balance ÷ # of months	D* – C
Blended principal and interest	Month	Fixed B + C	D* × Annual Interest Rate × 1/12	A – B	D* – C

* From the prior period

Bonds Payable (Appendix 10A)

Premium	Market interest rate < Coupon interest rate
Face Value	Market interest rate = Coupon interest rate
Discount	Market interest rate > Coupon interest rate

Amortization of Bond Premium or Discount (Appendix 10A)

Continued on EP-4 at the end of the book

WileyPLUS

WileyPLUS is a research-based, online environment for effective teaching and learning.

The market-leading homework experience in *WileyPLUS* offers:

A Blank Sheet of Paper Effect

The *WileyPLUS* homework experience, which includes type-ahead for account title entry, imitates a blank sheet of paper format so that students use recall memory when doing homework and will do better in class, on exams, and in their professions.

A Professional Worksheet Style

The professional, worksheet-style problem layouts help students master accounting skills while doing homework that directly applies to the classroom and the real world.

The Opportunity to Catch Mistakes Earlier

Multi-part problems further help students focus by providing feedback at the part-level. Students can catch their mistakes earlier and access content-specific resources at the point of learning.

WileyPLUS includes a full ebook, interactive tutorials, assessment capabilities, and Blackboard integration.

STARR COMPANY
Trial Balance
June 30, 2014

	Debit	Credit
cal	$	
Cash		
Owner's Capital		
	$	$

Type-ahead feature for account title entry replaces drop-down menus.

www.wileyplus.com

FINANCIAL ACCOUNTING

TOOLS FOR BUSINESS DECISION-MAKING

Sixth Canadian Edition

Paul D. Kimmel Ph.D., CPA
University of Wisconsin—Milwaukee, Wisconsin

Jerry J. Weygandt Ph.D., CPA
University of Wisconsin—Madison, Wisconsin

Donald E. Kieso Ph.D., CPA
Northern Illinois University, DeKalb, Illinois

Barbara Trenholm MBA, FCA
University of New Brunswick, Fredericton, New Brunswick

Wayne Irvine CFA, CA
University of Calgary, Calgary, Alberta

WILEY

Dedicated to our students—past, present, and future.

Library and Archives Canada Cataloguing in Publication

Kimmel, Paul D., author

Financial accounting: tools for business decision-making / Paul D. Kimmel, Jerry J. Weygandt, Donald E. Kieso, Barbara Trenholm, Wayne Irvine.—Sixth Canadian edition.

Includes indexes.
ISBN 978-1-118-64494-2 (bound)

1. Accounting—Textbooks.   I. Weygandt, Jerry J., author   II. Kieso, Donald E., author   III. Trenholm, Barbara, author   IV. Irvine, Wayne, author   V. Title.

HF5636.K54 2013   657'.044   C2013-905152-X

Production Credits

Acquisitions Editor: Zoë Craig
Vice President and Publisher: Veronica Visentin
Director of Marketing: Joan Lewis-Milne
Marketing Manager: Anita Osborne
Editorial Manager: Karen Staudinger
Production Manager: Tegan Wallace
Developmental Editor: Daleara Jamasji Hirjikaka
Media Editor: Channade Fenandoe-Alli
Editorial Assistant: Luisa Begani
Interior Design and Cover: Joanna Vieira
Typesetting: Aptara
Cover Photo: ©istock.com/Chris Hepburn
Printing and Binding: Courier

Printed and bound in the United States of America

1 2 3 4 5 CC 18 17 16 15 14

WILEY

John Wiley & Sons Canada, Ltd.
5353 Dundas Street West, Suite 400
Toronto, ON, M9B 6H8 Canada

Visit our website at: www.wiley.ca

Your TEAM *FOR* SUCCESS
in Accounting

Wiley is your partner in accounting education. We want to be the first publisher you think of when it comes to quality content, reliable technology, innovative resources, professional training, and unparalleled support for your accounting classroom.

Your Wiley Accounting Team for Success is composed of three distinctive advantages that you won't find with any other publisher:

- Author commitment
- Wiley Faculty Network
- WileyPLUS

AUTHOR COMMITMENT
A Proven Author Team of Inspired Teachers

The Team for Success authors bring years of industry and academic experience, as well as a passion for teaching, to the development of their textbooks. This cohesive team brings continuity of writing style, pedagogy, and end-of-chapter material to each course so you and your students can seamlessly progress from introductory through advanced courses in accounting.

Collaboration. Innovation. Experience.

After decades of success as outstanding educators, Barbara Trenholm and Wayne Irvine, the authors of this book and part of the Wiley Accounting Team for Success, understand that teaching accounting goes beyond simply presenting information. The authors are truly effective because they know that teaching is about telling compelling stories in ways that make each concept come to life and help relate accounting concepts to real-world experiences.

They demonstrate an intangible ability to effectively deliver complex material so that it is clear and understandable while staying one step ahead of emerging global trends in business.

These authors work together throughout the entire process. The end result is a true collaboration where the authors bring their individual experience and talent to the development of every paragraph, page, and chapter, thus creating a well-rounded, thorough view on any given accounting topic.

Many Ways in One Direction

Our **Team for Success** has developed a learning system that addresses every learning style. Each year brings new insights, feedback, ideas, and improvements on how to deliver the material to every student with a passion for the subject in a format that gives them the best chance to succeed. The key to the team's approach is in understanding that, just as there are many different ways to learn, there are also many different ways to teach.

WILEY FACULTY NETWORK
A Team of Educators Dedicated to Your Professional Development

The Wiley Faculty Network (WFN) is a global group of seasoned accounting professionals who share best practices in teaching with their peers. Our Virtual Guest Lecture Series provides the opportunity you need for professional development in an on-line environment that is relevant, convenient, and collaborative. The quality of these seminars and workshops meets the strictest standards, so we are proud to offer valuable professional development credits to attendees.

With a number of faculty mentors in accounting, it's easy to find help with your most challenging curriculum questions—just ask our experts!

WileyPLUS
An Experienced Team of Support Professionals

The *WileyPLUS* account managers understand the time constraints of busy faculty who want to provide the best resources available to their students with minimal frustrations and planning time. They know how intimidating a new version of software can sometimes be, so they are sure to make the transition easy and painless.

Account managers act as your personal contact and expert resource for training, course set-up, and shortcuts throughout the *WileyPLUS* experience.

Your success as an educator directly correlates to student success, and that's our goal. The Wiley Accounting Team for Success truly strives for YOUR success! Partner with us today!

Barbara Trenholm, MBA, FCA, is a professor emerita at the University of New Brunswick, for which she continues to teach locally and internationally. Her teaching and educational leadership has been widely recognized. She is a recipient of the Leaders in Management Education Award, the Global Teaching Excellence Award, and the University of New Brunswick's Merit Award and Dr. Allan P. Stuart Award for Excellence in Teaching.

Professor Trenholm is a member of the boards of several public and private companies, including Plazacorp Retail Properties Ltd. She is a past board member of Atomic Energy of Canada Limited, the Canadian Institute of Chartered Accountants, and the Atlantic School of Chartered Accountancy and past president of the New Brunswick Institute of Chartered Accountants. She has also served as a chair of the Canadian Institute of Chartered Accountants Academic Research Committee, Interprovincial Education Committee, and Canadian Institute of Chartered Accountants/Canadian Academic Accounting Association Liaison Committee. She has served as a member of the Canadian Institute of Chartered Accountants Qualification Committee, International Qualifications Appraisal Board, and Education Reengineering Task Force and the American Accounting Association's Globalization Initiatives Task Force, in addition to numerous other committees at the international, national, and provincial levels of the profession.

She has presented at many conferences and published widely in the field of accounting education and standard setting in journals, including *Accounting Horizons, Journal of the Academy of Business Education, CAmagazine, CGA Magazine,* and *CMA Magazine.*

Wayne Irvine, CFA, CA, teaches accounting at the Haskayne School of Business, University of Calgary. Prior to his full-time academic career, Wayne worked for 12 years at Price Waterhouse in the audit group and as manager of the Calgary office's continuing education program.

Wayne has taught courses for both the CA School of Business and CMA Alberta and is involved in the new CPA professional education program.

In addition to other publishing projects, he has authored a number of case exams for the CA School of Business and published a case in *Accounting Perspectives.*

Wayne is a four-time recipient of the University of Calgary's Students' Union Teaching Excellence Award and the only member of his faculty to have been awarded a Hall of Fame Teaching award from that organization. He received the Chartered Accountants' Education Foundation teaching award in 2000, 2008, and 2011. In 2008 and 2012, he also won the Commerce Undergraduate Society Award for Outstanding Teaching and Learning and received a distinguished service award from the Institute of Chartered Accountants of Alberta in 2009.

Paul D. Kimmel, Ph.D., CPA, received his bachelor's degree from the University of Minnesota and his doctorate in accounting from the University of Wisconsin. He is an Associate Professor at the University of Wisconsin—Milwaukee, and has public accounting experience with Deloitte & Touche. He was the recipient of the UWM School of Business Advisory Council Teaching Award, the Reggie Taite Excellence in Teaching Award, and a three-time winner of the Outstanding Teaching Assistant Award at the University of Wisconsin. He is also a recipient of the Elijah Watts Sells Award for Honorary Distinction for his results on the CPA exam. He is a member of the American Accounting Association and the Institute of Management Accountants and has published articles in *Accounting Review, Accounting Horizons, Advances in Management Accounting, Managerial Finance, Issues in Accounting Education,* and *Journal of Accounting Education,* as well as other journals. His research interests include accounting for financial instruments and innovation in accounting education. He has published papers and given numerous talks on incorporating critical thinking into accounting education, and helped prepare a catalogue of critical thinking resources for the Federated Schools of Accountancy.

Jerry J. Weygandt, Ph.D., CPA, is the Arthur Andersen Alumni Emeritus Professor of Accounting at the University of Wisconsin—Madison. He holds a Ph.D. in accounting from the University of Illinois. Articles by Professor Weygandt have appeared in *Accounting Review, Journal of Accounting Research, Accounting Horizons, Journal of Accountancy,* and other academic and professional journals. Professor Weygandt is author of other accounting and financial reporting books and is a member of the American Accounting Association, the American Institute of Certified Public Accountants, and the Wisconsin Society of Certified Public Accountants. He has served on numerous committees of the American Accounting Association and as a member of the editorial board of *Accounting Review;* he also has served as President and Secretary-Treasurer of the American Accounting Association. In addition, he has been actively involved with the American Institute of Certified Public Accountants and has been a member of the Accounting Standards Executive Committee of that organization. He served on the FASB task force that examined the reporting issues related to accounting for income taxes and as a trustee of the Financial Accounting Foundation. Professor Weygandt has received the Chancellor's Award for Excellence in Teaching and the Beta Gamma Sigma Dean's Teaching Award. He is on the board of directors of M&I Bank of Southern Wisconsin. He is the recipient of the Wisconsin Institute of CPA's Outstanding Educator's Award and the Lifetime Achievement Award. In 2001, he received the American Accounting Association's Outstanding Accounting Educator Award.

Donald E. Kieso, Ph.D., CPA, received his bachelor's degree from Aurora University and his doctorate in accounting from the University of Illinois. He has served as chairman of the Department of Accountancy and is currently the KPMG Emeritus Professor of Accounting at Northern Illinois University. He has public accounting experience with Price Waterhouse & Co. and Arthur Andersen & Co. and research experience with the Research Division of the American Institute of Certified Public Accountants. He is a recipient of NIU's Teaching Excellence Award and four Golden Apple Teaching Awards. Professor Kieso is a member of the American Accounting Association, the American Institute of Certified Public Accountants, and the Illinois CPA Society. He has served as a member of the Board of Directors of the Illinois CPA Society, the AACSB's Accounting Accreditation Committees, and the State of Illinois Comptroller's Commission; as Secretary-Treasurer of the Federation of Schools of Accountancy; and as Secretary-Treasurer of the American Accounting Association. Professor Kieso is currently serving on the Board of Trustees and Executive Committee of Aurora University, and is a member of various other boards. From 1989 to 1993, he served as a charter member of the national Accounting Education Change Commission. He is the recipient of the Outstanding Accounting Educator Award from the Illinois CPA Society, the FSA's Joseph A. Silvoso Award of Merit, the NIU Foundation's Humanitarian Award for Service to Higher Education, the Distinguished Service Award from the Illinois CPA Society, and in 2003 an honorary doctorate from Aurora University.

The Sixth Canadian Edition expands our emphasis on student learning and improves upon a highly rated teaching and learning package in the following ways:

Continued Emphasis on Helping Students Learn Accounting Concepts

We have carefully scrutinized all chapter material to ensure that it helps students learn accounting concepts. We have added more explanations, examples, illustrations, and summaries throughout the text to better facilitate learning.

The Accounting Cycle

For many students, success in an introductory accounting course hinges on developing a sound conceptual understanding of the accounting cycle. In past editions, we have received positive feedback regarding the framework that we have used in Chapters 3 and 4. In this edition, we have expanded our use of this framework to include equation analysis in Chapter 3 as well as the closing process in Chapter 4. We also added diagrams describing the impact of original journal entries on adjusting journal entries in Chapter 4.

Missing in Action

We have added a new feature, *Missing in Action,* in Chapter 7 to illustrate how a missing control activity can result in errors or misstatements. We believe this feature, which is much broader than the former *Anatomy of a Fraud* boxes, will be effective in demonstrating the importance of internal controls to both accounting and non-accounting students.

Student-Friendly Companies

One of the goals of the financial accounting course is to orient students to the application of accounting principles and techniques in practice. Accordingly, we have expanded our practice of using numerous examples from real companies throughout the textbook to add more high-interest enterprises that we hope will increase student engagement. For example, we have changed our feature companies to Shoppers Drug Mart and Jean Coutu. References to these companies have been included throughout the textbook, including simplified financial statements in the chapter material where appropriate, ratio analysis, *Using the Decision Toolkit,* end-of-chapter assignments, and detailed financial statements in Appendices A and B at the end of the textbook.

IFRS and ASPE

The fifth Canadian edition was significantly rewritten to incorporate International Financial Reporting Standards (IFRS) and Accounting Standards for Private Enterprises (ASPE), which were still in their infancy at the time of writing the fifth edition. While the pace of change in standards has slowed somewhat, new standards continue to evolve and come into effect. As a result, this sixth edition has undergone a comprehensive updating, refinement, and consolidation of standard changes relevant to introductory accounting students, with a view to helping students succeed in a multiple GAAP world that will continue to change in the future.

Differences between IFRS and ASPE are highlighted throughout the chapter with an ASPE logo (ASPE) where applicable. Each chapter concludes with a *Comparing IFRS and ASPE* table to provide students with a quick summary of the key distinctions between the two sets of accounting standards. End-of-chapter material includes questions, exercises, and problems relevant to both sets of standards. In addition, a case in the Broadening Your Perspective section called *Comparing IFRS and ASPE* focuses specifically on ASPE. The Serial Case, in the same section, follows the development of a small, private company using ASPE at the beginning of the text that later converts to a publicly traded company using IFRS.

Critical Thinking

New to this edition is a critical thinking case in the Broadening Your Perspective section of each chapter. These cases challenge students to apply what they learn in the chapter to a less structured scenario and to think critically on their own to solve typical business problems and to analyze financial information.

Collaborative Learning Activities

Each chapter in this edition highlights one of the Broadening Your Perspective cases with the symbol 👤 indicating that the case can be assigned as a group activity. Detailed presentation material and facilitation notes are available online to help instructors engage students to get the most out of working together and supporting each other during the learning process.

Comprehensive Revisions

In addition to the above new features, this edition was subject to comprehensive updating to ensure that it continues to be relevant and fresh.

Our textbook includes more than 235 references to real-world companies. All of the company information was updated and replaced, as necessary. In addition, nearly half of the chapter-opening feature stories were replaced with new stories, while the remainder were updated. More than half of the *Accounting Matters!* insight boxes are new. The *All About You* feature was either replaced or updated in each chapter with new statistics and information applicable to today's student. The *Do It!* activities in this edition were also updated or replaced as required. These activities give students an opportunity to stop and actively test their understanding of the material as they read the chapter.

All hypothetical financial illustrations in the text and end-of-chapter material were reviewed to ensure that the numbers used were realistic. All of the end-of-chapter material was carefully reviewed and real company information updated or replaced, as required. Topical gaps in breadth and depth of coverage, as well as degree of difficulty, were identified and material added or replaced as required. In total, nearly half of the questions, brief exercises, exercises, problems, and cases in the end-of-chapter material either are new or were significantly modified.

New Supplements

Our extensive supplement package for both instructors and students was carefully reviewed and updated. New to the supplements available to students with this edition are problem walk-throughs and QR codes linking to quizzes that can be scanned on smart phones.

KEY FEATURES OF EACH CHAPTER

Chapter 1: The Purpose and Use of Financial Statements

- Feature story is about Shoppers Drug Mart and how accounting aids decision-making
- Identifies the users and uses of financial accounting information and forms of business organization—proprietorship, partnership, private corporation, and public corporation
- Describes the business activities—financing, investing, and operating activities—that affect companies
- Explains the content, purpose, and interrelationships of each of the financial statements—income statement, statement of changes in equity, statement of financial position, and statement of cash flows
- Uses financial statements of a hypothetical company (to keep it simple), followed by those for a real company, Shoppers Drug Mart (to make it relevant)
- Keeping an Eye on Cash describes how each of the business activities—financing, investing, and operating activities—affects cash
- Comparing IFRS and ASPE summarizes key differences in choice of accounting standards and financial statements
- All About You focuses on a student's personal annual report (resumé)
- Using the Decision Toolkit compares Shoppers Drug Mart's financial statements with those of Jean Coutu and their industry
- *Key changes*: Increased references to ethics. Added new illustrations to explain how common shares and retained earnings are calculated in the statement of changes in

equity and to reinforce the preparation order of financial statements. Expanded discussion of the differences between Shoppers Drug Mart's simplified statements included in the chapter and its real statements included in the appendix, including a brief introduction to accumulated other comprehensive income.

Chapter 2: A Further Look at Financial Statements

- Feature story is about Plazacorp Retail Properties, its users, and use of accounting standards
- Presents the classified statement of financial position
- Applies ratio analysis to Plazacorp, First Capital Realty, and their industry (working capital, current ratio, debt to total assets, earnings per share, and price-earnings ratios)
- Describes the conceptual framework of accounting
- Keeping an Eye on Cash discusses Apple's free cash flow
- Comparing IFRS and ASPE summarizes key differences in terminology, presentation of earnings per share, and application of the conceptual framework
- All About You introduces a personal statement of financial position
- Using the Decision Toolkit analyzes Canadian Tire's liquidity, profitability, and solvency and those of its industry
- *Key changes*: Updated terminology relating to investments. Moved coverage of accrued receivables and payables to Chapter 4. Expanded coverage of unearned revenues.

Chapter 3: The Accounting Information System

- Feature story is about BeaverTails' experiences with an accounting information system
- Covers transaction analysis, emphasizing the fundamentals while avoiding unnecessary detail
- Explains the first three steps in the accounting cycle, from journalizing to posting to preparation of the trial balance
- Keeping an Eye on Cash relates cash transactions to the operating, investing, and financing activities undertaken by a company
- Comparing IFRS and ASPE indicates that there are no significant differences in this chapter
- All About You feature discusses the importance of keeping track of (accounting for) personal documents and records
- Using the Decision Toolkit prepares a trial balance for lululemon athletica, and identifies on which financial statement each account would be presented
- *Key changes*: Study objectives for journalizing and posting now separated. Numbers used in Sierra Corporation accounting cycle example updated, and new transactions added for accounts payable and income tax. Added illustrations on debit and credit rules and the accounting equation to help students better understand the components of retained earnings. Accounting equation analysis included in the illustration of the recording process. First three steps of accounting cycle now positioned within entire accounting cycle.

Chapter 4: Accrual Accounting Concepts

- Feature story is about Western University's application of accrual accounting

- Explains revenue and expense recognition
- Emphasizes the difference between cash and accrual accounting
- Completes the accounting cycle, from adjusting entries to the closing process
- Keeping an Eye on Cash contrasts the calculation of profit and cash flows from operating activities
- Comparing IFRS and ASPE summarizes key differences in the frequency of adjusting entries and terminology
- All About You feature discusses revenue recognition, including motivations to misstate revenue
- Using the Decision Toolkit reviews the timing of recognizing revenue for Best Buy gift cards
- *Key changes*: Expanded criteria for, and discussion of, revenue and expense recognition criteria. Added a comparison of cash and accrual bases of accounting. Diagrams describing impact of original journal entries on adjusting journal entries and summaries included at the end of each adjusting entry section. Incorporated accounting equation into closing process. Deferred discussion of closing entries for comprehensive income (loss) until Chapter 12.

Chapter 5: Merchandising Operations
- Feature story is about Loblaw's initiatives to improve its process of getting products from its suppliers to its shelves
- Introduces merchandising concepts using perpetual inventory system (the periodic inventory system is presented in an appendix)
- Explains how to record purchases and sales of merchandise
- Presents single-step and multiple-step income statements
- Applies ratio analysis to Loblaw, Metro, and their industry (gross profit margin and profit margin)
- Keeping an Eye on Cash explains the cash conversion cycle
- Comparing IFRS and ASPE summarizes key differences in the classification of expenses on the income statement
- All About You compares shopping experiences on-line, in large chain stores, and in locally owned stores
- Using the Decision Toolkit compares Sobeys' profitability with that of Loblaw and Metro and their industry
- *Key changes*: Updated sales tax information. Clarified illustration of goods in transit. Added illustration of closing entries for inventory in periodic inventory system.

Chapter 6: Reporting and Analyzing Inventory
- Feature story is about lululemon's inventory management
- Explains how inventory quantities and ownership are determined
- Covers cost determination methods and their financial statement effects using perpetual inventory system (the periodic inventory system is presented in an appendix)
- Discusses effects of inventory errors on financial statements
- Outlines how to value and record inventory at the lower of cost and net realizable value

- Applies ratio analysis to lululemon athletica, Limited Brands, and their industry (inventory turnover and days in inventory)
- Keeping an Eye on Cash reviews impact of choice of cost determination method on cash flow
- Comparing IFRS and ASPE indicates that there are no significant differences in this chapter
- All About You is about inventory theft and loss prevention techniques
- Using the Decision Toolkit reviews Under Armour's inventory management and liquidity and that of its industry
- *Key changes*: Expanded discussion of goods in transit and clarified more specifically the nature of misstatements arising from errors in recording purchases of merchandise inventory as well as errors made when determining the cost of this inventory.

Chapter 7: Internal Control and Cash
- Feature story is about cash control at Nick's Steakhouse and Pizza
- Explains the nature of internal control activities and the limitations of internal control
- Identifies control activities over cash receipts and cash payments
- Discusses bank reconciliations in detail as a control feature
- Explains how cash is reported and managed
- Keeping an Eye on Cash explains how too much cash may not necessarily be a good thing
- Comparing IFRS and ASPE indicates that there are no significant differences in this chapter
- All About You feature helps identify how much cash a student will need to pay for a university education
- Using the Decision Toolkit reviews internal control issues at a local basketball association
- *Key changes*: Reorganized and refocused discussion on fraud. Changed the Anatomy of a Fraud boxes to Missing in Action boxes, which focus on the impact of missing internal controls. Explained how to calculate the unadjusted cash balance. Simplified references to bank fees and charges.

Chapter 8: Reporting and Analyzing Receivables
- Feature story is about Canadian Tire's receivables
- Presents the basics of accounts and notes receivable and bad debt estimation
- Explains statement presentation of receivables
- Identifies various ways to manage receivables
- Applies ratio analysis to Canadian Tire, Sears, and their industry (receivables turnover and average collection period)
- Keeping an Eye on Cash explains the impact of receivables management on profit and cash flow
- Comparing IFRS and ASPE indicates that there are no significant differences in this chapter
- All About You feature covers the advantages and disadvantages of credit cards

- Using the Decision Toolkit compares Canadian Tire's receivables management and liquidity with Walmart's, Sears's, and their industry
- *Key changes*: Added a review of accounts receivables transactions and separated the introduction to receivables from accounting for bad debts. Simplified the accounting for nonbank credit cards and their fees. Reordered the discussion of estimating uncollectible accounts, revised the aging schedule, and added general ledger accounts to show how accounts are affected. Clarified which notes are trade receivables, how notes are valued, and use of allowance for doubtful notes account, and added a new section comparing notes receivable and notes payable. Deleted concentration of credit risk discussion and sale and securitization of receivables.

Chapter 9: Reporting and Analyzing Long-Lived Assets

- Feature story is about WestJet's property and equipment
- Covers the acquisition and derecognition of property, plant, and equipment
- Reviews buy or lease decisions
- Explains the calculation and implications of using different depreciation methods
- Discusses the accounting for intangible assets and goodwill
- Reviews the reporting of long-lived assets
- Applies ratio analysis to WestJet, Air Canada, and their industry (return on assets, asset turnover, and profit margin)
- Keeping an Eye on Cash discusses the effect of depreciation on accrual-based profit and cash provided by operating activities
- Comparing IFRS and ASPE identifies differences in terminology, use of the revaluation and valuation models, impairment tests, and disclosure requirements
- All About You feature deals with the decision to buy, rent, or share a car
- Using the Decision Toolkit reviews and analyzes Transat A.T. Inc.'s long-lived assets in comparison to WestJet, Air Canada, and their industry
- *Key changes*: Repositioned discussion of asset retirement costs to determination of cost section. Rewrote leasing section to clarify distinction between operating and finance leases. Combined explanation and calculation of depreciation with other accounting issues related to depreciation, clarified explanations of depreciation methods, added a summary comparison of formulas, and expanded illustration of retirements. Removed discussion of exchanges of assets. Added sample journal entries, general ledger accounts, and equations to property, plant, and equipment and intangible assets sections. Added a summary of the different types of long-lived assets in the reporting section.

Chapter 10: Reporting and Analyzing Liabilities

- Feature story is about Canada Post's liabilities
- Covers current liabilities, including operating lines of credit, sales taxes, property taxes, payroll, short-term notes payable, current maturities of non-current debt, provisions, and contingencies
- Covers non-current liabilities, including instalment notes payable and bonds payable
- Applies effective-interest method of amortization to long-term instalment notes and bonds
- Reviews reporting and analysis of liabilities
- Applies ratio analysis to Canada Post, UPS, and their industry (debt to total assets and times interest earned)
- Keeping an Eye on Cash explores cash effects of debt and the importance of meeting debt covenants
- Comparing IFRS and ASPE summarizes key differences in the definition of probability used to record a contingent liability and in amortizing bond premiums and discounts
- All About You is about student loans
- Using the Decision Toolkit compares Canada Post's liquidity and solvency with Royal Mail's and their industry
- *Key changes*: Expanded discussion of the difference between provisions and contingencies. Condensed and moved detailed coverage of bonds to an appendix to the chapter.

Chapter 11: Reporting and Analyzing Shareholders' Equity

- Feature story is about Tim Hortons
- Discusses corporate form of organization
- Covers issues related to common and preferred shares, including reasons why companies repurchase their own shares
- Explains cash dividends, stock dividends, stock splits, and implications for analysis
- Describes the presentation of equity items in statement of financial position and statement of changes in equity (IFRS) or statement of retained earnings (ASPE)
- Applies ratio analysis to Tim Hortons, Second Cup, and their industry (payout ratio, dividend yield, earnings per share, and return on common shareholders' equity)
- Keeping an Eye on Cash discusses how much cash is enough in order to pay a cash dividend
- Comparing IFRS and ASPE summarizes key differences in issuing shares for noncash considerations, presentation of comprehensive income, the statement of changes in equity and statement of retained earnings, and presentation of earnings per share
- All About You is about investing in shares
- Using the Decision Toolkit compares Starbucks's dividend record and earnings performance with those of Tim Hortons and their industry
- *Key changes*: Increased emphasis on private corporations. Added a summary of the advantages and disadvantages of corporations. Deleted discussion of par value and treasury shares. Combined accounting for common and preferred share transactions into one section. Replaced detailed accounting for reacquisition of shares with a general overview and clarified discussion of how stock splits work. Added a summary of shareholders' equity

transactions and information about cumulative and noncumulative preferred dividends in earnings per share discussion. Condensed discussion about complex capital structures.

Chapter 12: Reporting and Analyzing Investments
- Feature story is about Scotiabank's management of investments
- Explains why companies purchase debt and equity securities as strategic or non-strategic investments
- Describes the various valuation models for non-strategic investments: fair value through profit or loss, fair value through other comprehensive income, amortized cost, and cost
- Describes the accounting for strategic investments, including the use of the equity and cost valuation models
- Discusses other comprehensive income, including the statement of comprehensive income, and accumulated other comprehensive income
- Explains how investments are reported on the financial statements under each of the valuation models used for non-strategic and strategic investments, including the different reporting requirements under IFRS and ASPE
- Introduces consolidation accounting for financial reporting purposes at a conceptual level
- Keeping an Eye on Cash explains how investment-related transactions are treated on the statement of cash flows
- Discusses the accounting for investments in bonds and compares it with bonds payable in a chapter appendix
- Comparing IFRS and ASPE explains differences in the use of the fair value through OCI model, accounting for investments in associates, amortization methods for bond investments, and consolidation of financial statements
- All About You discusses saving for a university education and discusses the benefits of savings options such as a tax-free savings account
- Using the Decision Toolkit explores the various ways of accounting for different types of investments
- *Key changes*: Revised first four study objectives to cover accounting models used for investments without reference to ASPE or IFRS so that coverage could focus on the theoretical basis for each model. How the models are then applied under ASPE and IFRS is now covered in a single study objective. IFRS coverage was updated to be consistent with IFRS 9.

Chapter 13: Statement of Cash Flows
- Feature story is about Teck Resources' cash flows
- Explains the purpose and content of the statement of cash flows
- Describes the preparation of the operating, investing, and financing activities of the statement of cash flows.

Splits the operating activities section into two parts, allowing the instructor to use the indirect approach, the direct approach, or both
- Applies ratio analysis to Teck and Freeport-McMoRan (cash current debt coverage, cash total debt coverage, and free cash flow)
- Keeping an Eye on Cash explains cash flow effects of different phases of the corporate life cycle
- Comparing IFRS and ASPE summarizes key differences in classification of activities
- All About You is about how students should save and some of the costs and opportunities of managing cash
- Using the Decision Toolkit calculates cash-based ratios and analyzes cash flows for Stantec
- *Key changes*: Updated definitions of operating, investing, and financing activities. Expanded explanations comparing direct and indirect methods of presentation for operating activities. Introduced coverage dealing with classification manipulations within the statement of cash flows. Added exercises and problems that consisted of more basic cash flow movements.

Chapter 14: Performance Measurement
- Feature story is about Hudson's Bay Company's business strategy, including its acquisitions and divestitures
- Discusses sustainable income, and implications of discontinued operations
- Demonstrates horizontal analysis, vertical analysis, and ratio analysis
- Applies ratio analysis to Hudson's Bay, Sears, and their industry (comprehensive analysis of all ratios)
- Discusses factors that can limit financial analysis, including alternative accounting policies, professional judgement, comprehensive income, diversification, inflation, and economic factors
- Keeping an Eye on Cash outlines the questions the statement of cash flows answers and analyzes Hudson's Bay's cash flows
- Comparing IFRS and ASPE summarizes key differences in reporting of earnings per share, comprehensive income, and segments
- All About You is about investing in the stock market
- Using the Decision Toolkit assesses the liquidity, profitability, and solvency of Goldcorp, Yamana Gold, and their industry
- *Key changes*: Deleted discussion of changes in accounting policies from sustainable income section. Clarified terminology used in horizontal and vertical analysis. Reordered profitability ratios to improve students' understanding of their relationship. Expanded coverage dealing with the relationship between key ratios such as return on assets and return on equity.

ACTIVE TEACHING AND LEARNING
SUPPLEMENTARY MATERIAL

KIMMEL'S INTEGRATED TECHNOLOGY SOLUTIONS:
HELPING TEACHERS TEACH AND STUDENTS LEARN

WileyPLUS

www.wiley.com/go/kimmelcanada

Financial Accounting, Sixth Canadian Edition, features a full line of teaching and learning resources. Driven by the same basic beliefs as the textbook, these supplements provide a consistent and well-integrated learning system. This hands-on, real-world package guides instructors through the process of active learning and gives them the tools to create an interactive learning environment. With its emphasis on activities, exercises, and the Internet, the package encourages students to take an active role in the course and prepares them for decision-making in a real-world context.

FOR INSTRUCTORS

In addition to the support instructors receive from the Wiley Faculty Network, we offer several useful supplements and resources on the book's companion website and in *WileyPLUS*. On these sites, instructors will find the Solutions Manual, PowerPoint presentations, Test Bank, Instructor's Manual, Computerized Test Bank, and other valuable teaching resources.

The supplements are prepared by subject matter experts and contributors who are often users of the text. Supplements are meticulously reviewed by the authors to ensure consistency with the textbook. Supplements like the test bank and the solutions manual are also rigorously checked to ensure accuracy.

FOR STUDENTS

Students will find selected support materials on the book's companion website and an expanded list of resources in *WileyPLUS* that will help them develop their conceptual understanding of class material and increase their ability to solve problems. In addition to other resources, students will find:

- PowerPoint Presentations
- Chart of Accounts
- Checklist of Key Figures
- Annual Reports
- Financial Statement Analysis Primer

ACKNOWLEDGEMENTS

During the course of development of the sixth Canadian edition of *Financial Accounting: Tools for Business Decision-Making*, the authors benefited from the feedback from instructors and students of financial accounting across the country, including many users of the previous editions of this text.

We particularly wish to express our appreciation to Peggy Wallace of Trent University. Four of the chapters in this textbook were prepared in collaboration with Peggy. We benefited greatly from her fresh insights and perspectives.

In addition, the constructive advice and attention to accuracy by the following contributors to the sixth edition text and supplements provided valuable input to the development of this edition.

Sally Anderson, *University of Calgary*

Angela Davis, *Booth University College*

Catriona Eigenfeldt, *Kwantlen Polytechnic University*

Robert Ducharme, *University of Waterloo*

Ilene Gilborn

Rosalie Harms, *University of Winnipeg*

Cecile Laurin, *Algonquin College*

Kayla Levesque, *Cambrian College*

Debbie Musil, *Kwantlen Polytechnic University*

Marie Sinnott, *College of New Caledonia*

Ruth-Ann Strickland, *Western University*

Amanda Wallace, *Nipissing University*

Peggy Wallace, *Trent University*

Jerry Zdril, *Kwantlen Polytechnic University*

We appreciate the exemplary support and commitment given us by the talented team at Wiley Canada, including Zoë Craig, Acquisitions Editor; Deanna Durnford, Supplements Coordinator; Channade Fenandoe-Alli, Media Editor; Daleara Hirjikaka, Developmental Editor; Anita Osborne, Marketing Manager; Karen Staudinger, Editorial Manager; Maureen Talty, General Manager, Higher Education; Luisa Begani, Editorial Assistant; Veronica Visentin, Vice President and Publisher; Tegan Wallace, Production Manager; and Carolyn Wells, Vice President, Marketing; in addition to all of Wiley's dedicated sales managers and representatives, who continue to work diligently to service your needs.

We also wish to specifically thank the many people who worked behind the scenes to improve the design and accuracy of this text, including the typesetting team at Aptara; Laurel Hyatt, copyeditor; Zofia Laubitz, proofreader; and Belle Wong, indexer.

It would not have been possible to write this text without the understanding of our employers, colleagues, students, family, and friends. Together, they provided a creative and supportive environment for our work.

We have tried our best to produce a text and supplement package that is error-free and that meets your specific needs. Suggestions and comments from users are encouraged and appreciated. Please don't hesitate to let us know of any improvements that we should consider for subsequent printings or editions. You can send us your thoughts and ideas by e-mailing KimmelAuthors@gmail.com.

Barbara Trenholm
Wayne Irvine

Student success is a team effort.

The Team for Success is focused on helping you get the most out of your accounting courses in the digital age.

Students
read it
Access the right amount of information for each course anytime, anywhere, on any device.

Students
see it
Illustrations and interactive tutorials bring the content to life and make accounting concepts easier to understand.

Students
do it
The *Do It!* exercises throughout the textbook will help students apply their understanding of accounting. The *WileyPLUS* homework experience imitates a blank sheet of paper using type-ahead for account entry, and helps students catch mistakes early by providing feedback at the part level.

Students
get it
The powerful combination of quality text, visual approach to learning, and highly intuitive homework experience supports the digital student workflow, preparing them for class, exams, and future study.

passion success
teaching
collaboration
expertise
passion collaboration
team teaching
passion for teaching
success expertise
collaboration passion

www.wileyteamforsuccess.ca

team *for* success

read it!

Feature Stories introduce chapter topics using real-world companies that are engaging to students.

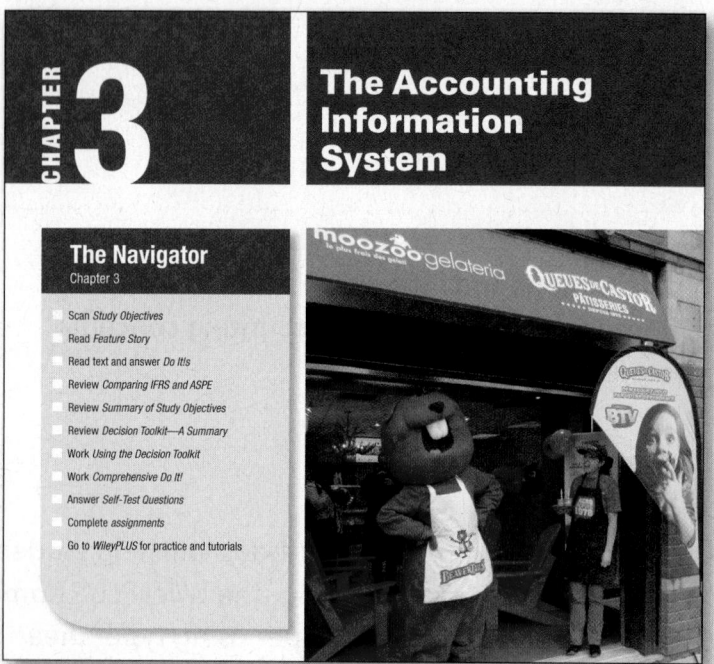

Extracts from real company financial statements appear throughout the book.

DANIER LEATHER INC.	
Statement of Financial Position (partial)	
June 30, 2013	
(in thousands)	
Shareholders' equity	
Share capital	$11,533
Contributed surplus	954
Retained earnings	43,422
	55,909

The Keeping an Eye on Cash feature
helps students understand the connections with, and the significance of, cash.

▪ Keeping an Eye on Cash

Can a company have too much cash? Yes, according to some, including Mark Carney, Governor of the Bank of England and former Governor of the Bank of Canada. In August 2012, Carney noted that Canadian corporations were "sitting on mountains of 'dead money'." The size of the Canadian "mountain" was approximately $600 billion in January 2012, with major Canadian companies such as Suncor Energy ($5.4 billion), George Weston (owner of Loblaw) ($3.5 billion), and Barrick Gold ($2.5 billion) holding significant amounts. Carney noted that Canadian companies should be investing their cash in new property, plant, and equipment or increasing the dividends paid to shareholders. In the United States, the cash mountain was nearly U.S. $1.5 trillion.

Tim Cook, CEO of Apple, informed shareholders at the 2013 annual meeting that he was actively pursuing what to do with the company's growing cash pile. At December 31, 2012, the pile of cash amounted to $137.1 billion (cash and cash equivalents). Possible uses of the cash included increasing the dividend paid to shareholders and buying back shares.

Is too much cash also a problem for small businesses, such as Sharon McCollick's company discussed earlier in the chapter? McCollick might think that she can never have too much cash in her business, but that isn't correct. Having large amounts of cash sitting in bank accounts that pay little or no interest is not an effective management strategy. Cash can be invested in interest-paying investments for the short or longer term. It can also be used to upgrade existing equipment or expand the business when the cash balances increase beyond what is required for normal business operations.

Accounting Matters insight boxes provide glimpses into how real companies make decisions using accounting information and how individuals use accounting information in their decision-making.

ACCOUNTING MATTERS!

NHL Signing Bonuses

Does hiring a top National Hockey League (NHL) player add value to the team? The owner and fans would say so. However, simply agreeing to sign a contract to play for a hockey team is not an economic event that results in an accounting transaction. Despite the team's perceived value rising by the hiring of top talent, a transaction is not recorded until the player starts playing and earns his salary . . . and hopefully generates additional revenue for the team, as well.

On the other hand, signing bonuses do result in an economic transaction and consequently are treated differently. When a player is given a signing bonus to sign with the team, he is paid cash at the time of signing and the team's assets, liabilities, and equities change. NHL signing bonuses can be significant, ranging from $1 million to $10 million over the last few years.

Missing in Action boxes in Chapter 7 help
illustrate how a missing internal control can result in errors or misstatements.

MISSING IN ACTION

Kevin Lin works in the IT department at Twillingate Inc. The company provides a MacBook Pro® to all salespeople when they join the company. The laptop must be returned to Kevin when a salesperson leaves. Kevin is responsible for managing the laptops. He tracks them using an Excel spreadsheet that includes the date purchased, serial number, date assigned to a salesperson, date returned by a salesperson, and any repair information. The spreadsheet is sent to the asset clerk in the accounting department every month. One day, Angela Liu, the new asset clerk, decided to verify Kevin's spreadsheet after learning that no one in accounting or IT had ever checked it. When Angela attempted to match the information on the spreadsheet to the physical laptops, she found that two employees had left the company without returning their laptops. In addition, a laptop was identified as being out for repairs for over a year and Kevin hadn't followed up with the repair company. Finally, a laptop listed as unassigned could not be located.

THE MISSING CONTROL
Independent Verification
The asset clerk should have verified Kevin's spreadsheet on a regular basis to ensure all of Twillingate's computer assets were accounted for.

read it!

All About You ▶ Paying for Your University Education

It is important that you consider how much cash you will need to pay for your university education. It is all about planning. Do you know the cost of your tuition? If you don't live at home, what are your costs of renting? Utilities, including your cell phone? Food? Entertainment? Clothing? Transportation? Once you have determined the costs that you will incur, how will you pay for them? Have you applied for every possible scholarship, grant, and bursary? Have you obtained a student loan from the Government of Canada? Do you have credit card debt? Do you have a line of credit? With proper planning, you can reduce the amount that you are going to have to borrow to complete your education.

The hard part about planning how much cash you need is that sometimes you have no idea! Your starting point is to track where your cash is coming from and where it is going. Track what you receive and spend during the course of a day, a week, a month, a term, and then a school year. Try accumulating all of the receipts for items purchased during the course of a week and put them in an envelope. At the end of the week, analyze the receipts to determine where the money has gone. Continue doing so for a month. Once you have reviewed all of the receipts for a whole month, attempt to categorize them by type of expenditure. Or you could try using an Excel spreadsheet to help you keep track and categorize. There are free apps that can help, such as My Student Budget Planner. The website GetSmarterAboutMoney.ca has many tools to help you determine what

An *All About You* feature and activity helps students to link accounting concepts and the lessons learned from real-life situations to some aspects of personal finance, such as applying for a student loan, using credit cards, and buying a car. These topics provide great opportunities for classroom discussion.

Useful summaries of how accounting standards apply to publicly traded companies using IFRS and private companies using ASPE review the material covered in each chapter.

comparing
IFRS and ASPE

Key Differences	International Financial Reporting Standards (IFRS)	Accounting Standards for Private Enterprises (ASPE)
Terminology	Leases that are essentially the purchase of an asset are called *finance leases*. *Depreciation* is used to describe cost allocation for property, plant, and equipment.	Leases that are essentially the purchase of an asset are known as *capital leases*. *Amortization* may be used instead of *depreciation* for property, plant, and equipment.
Models for valuing property, plant, and equipment	Choice of cost model or revaluation model.	Only cost model allowed.
Impairment requirements for property, plant, and equipment and intangible assets with finite lives	Must determine each year if indicators of impairment are present and, if so, perform an impairment test. Reversals of impairment losses are allowed.	Impairment tests differ between IFRS and ASPE. Reversals of impairment losses are not allowed.
Impairment requirements for intangible assets with indefinite lives and goodwill	Must perform impairment test annually. Impairment losses can be reversed on intangible assets with indefinite lives but cannot be reversed on goodwill.	If indicators of impairment are present, an impairment test must be performed. Reversals of impairment losses are not allowed.
Disclosure	Must provide a reconciliation of the opening and closing carrying amounts of each class of long-lived assets.	Reconciliation not required.

Summary of Study Objectives

1. **Identify and discuss the major characteristics of a corporation.** The major characteristics of a corporation are separate legal existence, limited liability of shareholders, transferable ownership rights, the ability to acquire capital, a continuous life, separation of corporation management from ownership, increased cost and complexity of government regulations, and the possibility of reduced corporate income tax.

   Corporations issue shares for sale to investors. The proceeds received from the issue of shares become the company's legal capital. Shares then trade among investors on the secondary stock market and do not affect the company's financial position.

2. **Record share transactions.** If only one class of shares is issued, they are considered to be common shares. When shares are issued for noncash goods or services in a company using IFRS, the fair value of the goods or services received is used to record the transaction if it can be reliably determined. If not, the fair value of the common shares is used. For a private company following ASPE, the more reliable of the two fair values should be used, which is usually also the fair value of the goods or services received.

   The accounting for preferred shares is similar to the accounting for common shares. Preferred shares have contractual provisions that give them preference over common shares for dividends and assets in the event of liquidation. Dividends are quoted as an annual rate (such as $5 preferred), but are normally paid quarterly.

   In addition, preferred shares may have other preferences, such as the right to convert, redeem, and/or retract. However, preferred shares do not have the right to vote—only common shares have voting rights.

3. **Prepare the entries for cash dividends, stock dividends, and stock splits, and understand their financial impact.** Entries for both cash and stock dividends are required at the declaration date and the payment or distribution date. There is no entry (other than a memo entry) for a stock split. The overall impact of a cash dividend is to reduce assets (cash) and shareholders' equity (retained earnings). Stock dividends increase common shares and affect assets, liabilities, or shareholders' equity in total. Stock splits also have no impact on assets, liabilities, or shareholders' equity. The number of shares increases with both stock dividends and stock splits.

4. **Indicate how shareholders' equity is presented in the financial statements.** In the shareholders' equity section of the statement of financial position for companies using IFRS, share capital, retained earnings, and accumulated other comprehensive income, if any, are reported separately. If additional contributed capital exists, then the caption "Contributed capital" is used for share capital (preferred and common shares) and additional contributed capital that may have been created from various sources. A statement of changes in equity explains the changes in each shareholders' equity account, and in total, for the reporting period. Notes to the financial statements explain details about authorized and issued shares, restrictions on retained earnings, and dividends in arrears, if there are any.

   For private companies reporting using ASPE, comprehensive income is not reported and a statement of changes in equity is not required. Instead, a statement of retained earnings is prepared that explains the changes in the retained earnings account for the reporting period. Changes to share capital and any other equity items are disclosed in the notes to the statements.

5. **Evaluate dividend and earnings performance.** A company's dividend record can be evaluated by looking at what percentage of profit it chooses to pay out in dividends, as measured by the dividend payout ratio (dividends divided by profit) and the dividend yield ratio (dividends per share divided by the share price).

   Earnings performance can be measured by two profitability ratios: earnings per share (profit less preferred dividends divided by the weighted average number of common shares) and the return on common shareholders' equity ratio (profit less preferred dividends divided by average common shareholders' equity).

Summaries are included to help students review the material just covered.

see it!

CONTENT FOR ALL LEARNING STYLES

In addition to a textbook consistently reviewed as very readable, over 50% of the textbook provides visual presentations and interpretations of content.

Transaction Analyses illustrations visually help students understand the impact of an accounting transaction.

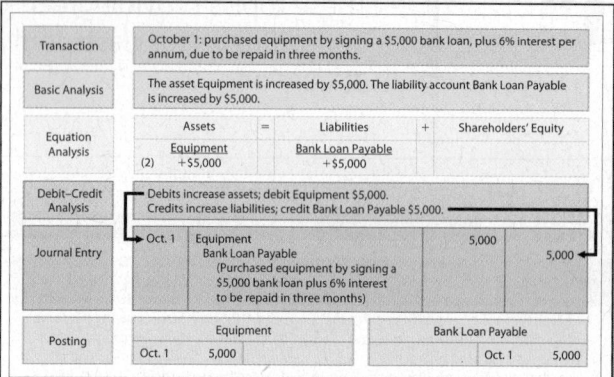

Accounting Equation Analyses appear in the margin next to key journal entries and reinforce the impact of the transaction on the accounting equation. They also report the cash effect of each transaction to reinforce understanding of the difference between cash effects and accrual accounting.

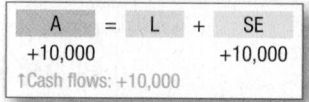

Infographics reinforce important textual concepts.

Illustrations are clearly identified and easy to review.

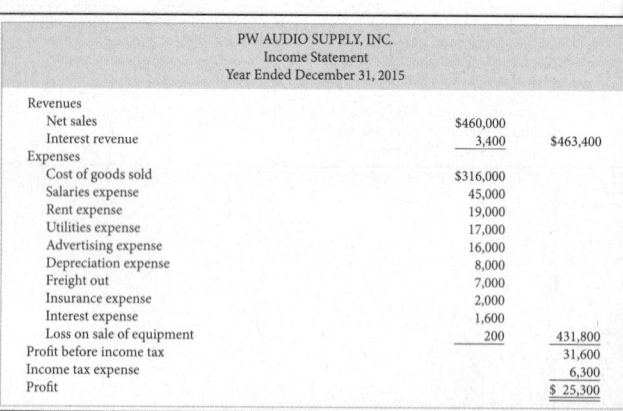

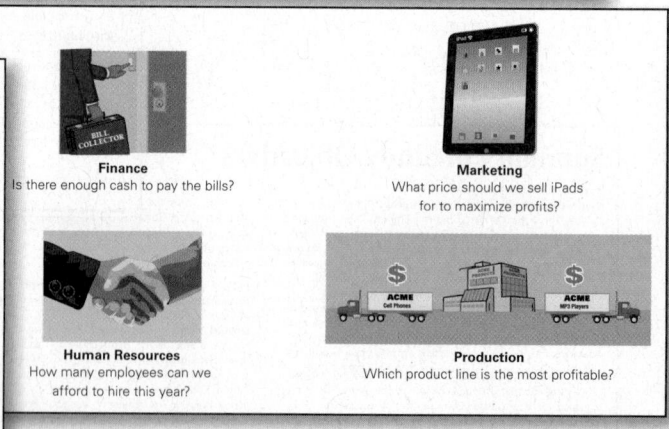

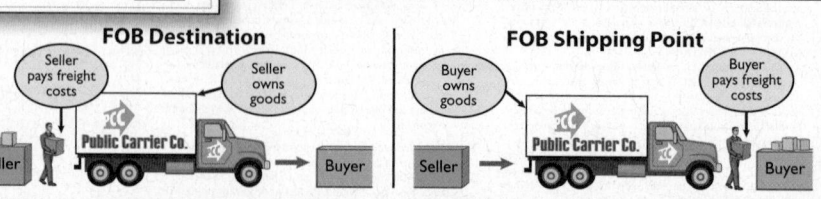

do it!

Clear **Do It!** exercises in the textbook narrative provide step-by-step applications of a concept at the precise moment students acquire the knowledge. Each Do It! in the textbook narrative includes a solution, an Action Plan, and a path of related brief exercises and exercises.

End-of-chapter **Questions**, **Brief Exercises**, two sets of **Problems**, and **Broadening Your Perspective Cases** are all keyed to learning objectives and provide students with further practice opportunities.

BEFORE YOU GO ON...

▶Do It! Closing Entries
The adjusted trial balance for Nguyen Corporation shows the following selected accounts: Dividends $500; Common Shares $30,000; Retained Earnings $12,000; Service Revenue $18,000; Rent Expense $1,500; Supplies Expense $500; Salaries Expense $8,000; and Income Tax Expense $1,000. (a) Prepare the closing entries at December 31. (b) What is the balance in the Income Summary and Retained Earnings accounts after closing?

Action Plan
- Close revenues and expenses into the Income Summary account.
- Stop and check your work: Is the balance in each individual revenue and expense account now zero? Does the balance in the Income Summary account equal the reported profit (loss)?
- Close the balance in the Income Summary account into the Retained Earnings account.
- Close the Dividends account into the Retained Earnings account. Do not close Dividends into the Income Summary account.
- Stop and check your work: Does the balance in the Retained Earnings account equal the ending balance reported in the financial statements?

Solution
(a)

Dec. 31	Service Revenue		18,000	
	Income Summary			18,000
	(To close revenue account)			
31	Income Summary		11,000	
	Rent Expense			1,500
	Supplies Expense			500
	Salaries Expense			8,000
	Income Tax Expense			1,000
	(To close expense accounts)			
31	Income Summary		7,000	
	Retained Earnings			7,000
	(To close income summary)			
31	Retained Earnings		500	
	Dividends			500
	(To close dividends)			

(b)

Income Summary				Retained Earnings			
	11,000		18,000			Beg. bal.	12,000
CE	7,000	Bal.	7,000	CE	500	CE	7,000
		End. bal.	0			End. bal.	18,500

Related Exercise Material: BE4-12, BE4-13, BE4-14, and E4-11.

Questions

(SO 1)	1.	What are current assets? Give four examples of current assets a company might have.	(SO 2)	13. Why can you compare the price-earnings ratio among different companies but not earnings per share?
(SO 1)	2.	What is meant by the term *operating cycle*?	(SO 2)	14. The **TD Bank** has a price-earnings ratio of 12 times, while **CIBC** has a price-earnings ratio of 10 times. Which company do investors appear
(SO 1)	3.	(a) Distinguish between current assets and non-current assets. (b) Distinguish between current assets and current liabilities. Why does showing		

Brief Exercises

BE2–1   The following are the major statement of financial position classifications:

1. Current assets
2. Long-term investments
3. Property, plant, and equipment
4. Intangible as

5. Current liabilities
6. Non-current liabilities
7. Share capital

Broadening Your Perspective

Financial Reporting: *Shoppers Drug Mart*

BYP3–1   The financial statements of **Shoppers Drug Mart** are presented in Appendix A at the end of this book. They contain the following selected accounts:

Accounts payable and accrued liabilities	Income tax expense
Accounts receivable	Inventory
Cash	Land
Dividends	Sales

Comprehensive Do It!

At October 31, 2015, the year-end trial balance for the Blizzard Snow Removal Corporation in Inuvik shows the following balances for selected accounts:

Prepaid insurance	$ 1,800
Equipment	15,000
Accumulated depreciation—equipment	3,000
Bank loan payable	10,000
Unearned revenue	2,100

Blizzard makes its adjusting entries annually. Analysis reveals the following additional data about these accounts:

1. Prepaid insurance is the cost of a one-year insurance policy, effective October 1, 2015.
2. The equipment was purchased on November 1, 2013, and is expected to have a useful life of five years.
3. The bank loan was signed on November 1, 2014, and is repayable in two years. Interest on this 6% loan is due on a monthly basis on the first day of each month.
4. Seven customers paid for the company's six-month, $300 snow removal service package in September. These customers were serviced in October after an early blizzard.
5. Snow removal services provided to other customers but not billed at October 31 totalled $1,500.
6. Income tax instalments have been made each month. Further calculations at year end determine that an additional $250 of income tax will be payable this year.

Instructions
Prepare the adjusting entries at October 31.

Action Plan
- Note that adjustments are being made annually.
- Before determining what adjustments are necessary, look at the amounts that are currently recorded in the accounts.
- After making adjustments, check that the balances in each T account reflect what you meant them to (even when T accounts are not required).
- Show your calculations.

Comprehensive Do It! problems at the end of each chapter apply the Do It! and address multiple topics.

passion success
teaching
collaboration
expertise
passion collaboration
team teaching
passion for teaching
success expertise
collaboration passion

get it!

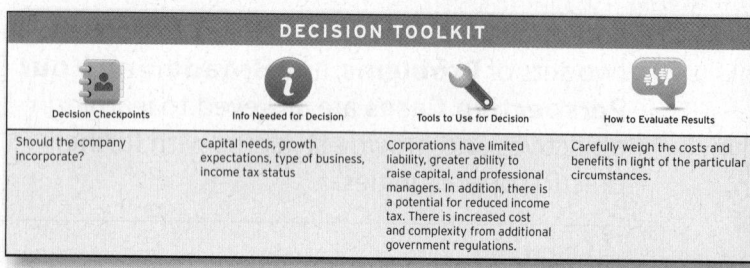

The Decision Toolkit and the **Decision Toolkit Summary** direct students to the tools and information they need when evaluating business issues.

Using the Decision Toolkit asks students to apply toolkit lessons to a financial statement analysis exercise. Suggested solutions are provided.

Critical Thinking Cases challenge students to apply what they learn in the chapter to a less structured scenario and to think critically on their own to solve typical business problems.

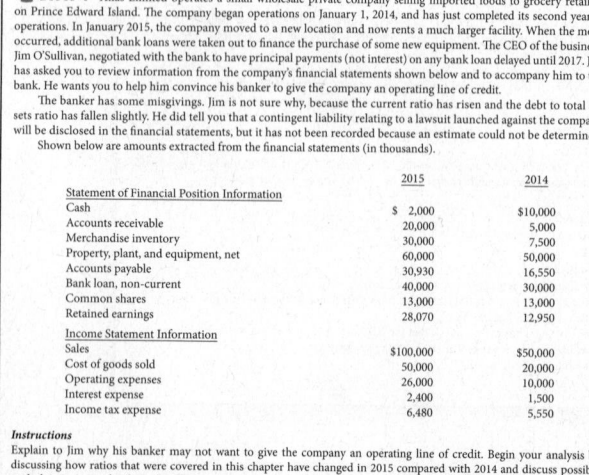

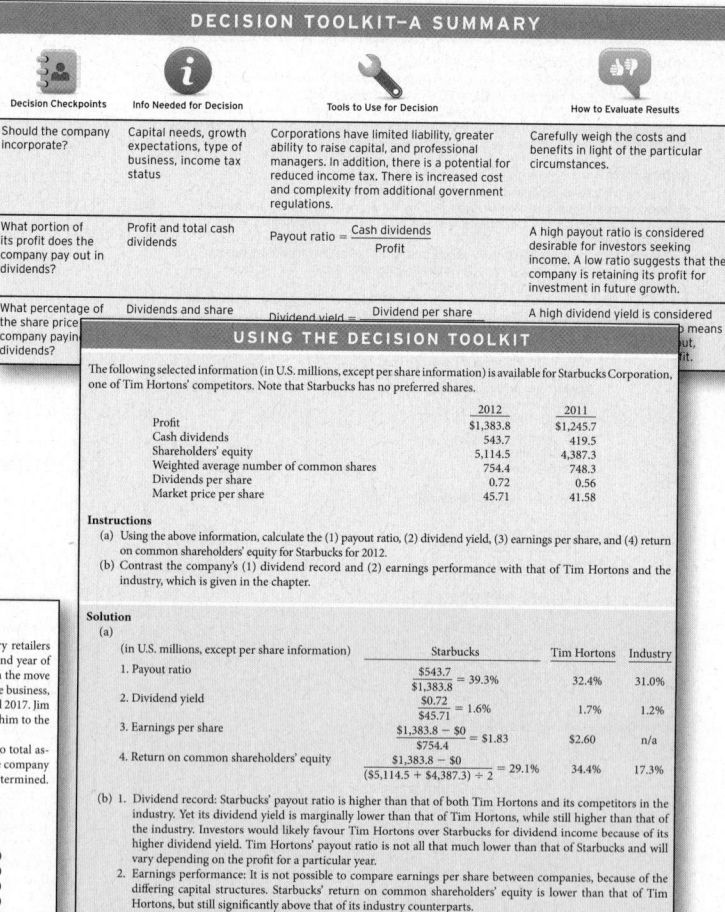

The symbol 👤 shown in this critical thinking case, or shown in other types of Broadening Your Perspective cases, include optional **Collaborative Learning Activities** to solve the case in a group environment.

What TYPE of learner are you?

Understanding each of these basic learning styles enables the authors to engage students' minds and motivate them to do their best work, ultimately improving the experience for both students and faculty.

	Intake: To take in the information	To make a study package	Text features that may help you the most	Output: To do well on exams
VISUAL	• Pay close attention to charts, drawings, and handouts your instructors use. • Underline. • Use different colours. • Use symbols, flow charts, graphs, different arrangements on the page, white spaces.	Convert your lecture notes into "page pictures." To do this: • Use the "Intake" strategies. • Reconstruct images in different ways. • Redraw pages from memory. • Replace words with symbols and initials. • Look at your pages.	The Navigator/Feature Story/Preview Infographics/Illustrations Accounting equation analyses Highlighted words Comprehensive Do It! Problem/Action Plan Questions/Exercises/Problems Financial Reporting problem Comparative Analysis problem	• Recall your "page pictures." • Draw diagrams where appropriate. • Practise turning your visuals back into words.
AURAL	• Attend lectures and tutorials. • Discuss topics with students and instructors. • Explain new ideas to other people. • Record your lectures. • Leave spaces in your lecture notes for later recall. • Describe pictures and visuals to somebody who was not in class.	You may take poor notes because you prefer to listen. Therefore: • Expand your notes by talking with others and with information from your textbook. • Record summarized notes and listen. • Read summarized notes out loud. • Explain your notes to another "aural" person.	Preview Accounting Matters! Insight Boxes Do It! Action Plan Summary of Learning Objectives Glossary Comprehensive Do It! Problem/Action Plan Self-Test Questions Questions/Exercises/Problems Financial Reporting problem Comparative Analysis problem Ethics Case	• Talk with the instructor. • Spend time in quiet places recalling the ideas. • Do extra assignments and attempt practice quizzes. • Say your answers out loud.
READING/ WRITING	• Use lists and headings. • Use dictionaries, glossaries, and definitions. • Read handouts, textbooks, and supplementary readings. • Use lecture notes.	• Write out words again and again. • Reread notes silently. • Rewrite ideas and principles in other words. • Turn charts, diagrams, and other illustrations into statements.	The Navigator/Feature Story/Study Objectives Preview Do It! Action Plan Summary of Learning Objectives Glossary/Self-Test Questions Questions/Exercises/Problems Financial Reporting problem Comparative Analysis problem Critical Thinking Case All About You Comprehensive Case	• Do extra assignments. • Practise with multiple-choice questions. • Write paragraphs, beginnings, and endings. • Write your lists in outline form. • Arrange your words into hierarchies and points.
KINESTHETIC	• Use all your senses. • Go to labs, take field trips. • Listen to real-life examples. • Pay attention to applications. • Use hands-on approaches. • Use trial-and-error methods.	You may take poor notes because topics do not seem concrete or relevant. Therefore: • Put examples in your summaries. • Use case studies and applications to help with principles and abstract concepts. • Talk about your notes with another "kinesthetic" person. • Use pictures and photographs that illustrate an idea.	The Navigator/Feature Story/Preview Infographics/Illustrations Do It! Action Plan Summary of Learning Objectives Comprehensive Do It! Problem/Action Plan Self-Test Questions Questions/Exercises/Problems Financial Reporting problem Comparative Analysis problem All About You	• Do extra assignments. • Role-play the exam situation.

Visit www.vark-learn.com and complete the Questionnaire to determine what type of learning style you have.

BRIEF CONTENTS

APPENDICES

CONTENTS

The Purpose and Use of Financial Statements

The **Navigator** is a learning system designed to prompt you to use the learning aids in the chapter and set priorities as you study.

The Navigator
Chapter 1

- [ ] Scan *Study Objectives*
- [ ] Read *Feature Story*
- [ ] Read text and answer *Do It!s*
- [ ] Review *Comparing IFRS and ASPE*
- [ ] Review *Summary of Study Objectives*
- [ ] Review *Decision Toolkit—A Summary*
- [ ] Work *Using the Decision Toolkit*
- [ ] Work *Comprehensive Do It!*
- [ ] Answer *Self-Test Questions*
- [ ] Complete *assignments*
- [ ] Go to *WileyPLUS* for practice and tutorials

Study Objectives give you a framework for learning the specific concepts that are covered in the chapter.

study objectives

After studying this chapter, you should be able to:

SO 1 Identify the uses and users of accounting.

SO 2 Describe the primary forms of business organization.

SO 3 Explain the three main types of business activity.

SO 4 Describe the purpose and content of each of the financial statements.

The **Feature Story** helps you picture how the chapter relates to the real world of accounting and business. You will find references to the story throughout the chapter.

Managing a Healthy Bottom Line

With more than 1,250 stores across the country, and sales in 2012 of nearly $10.8 billion, Shoppers Drug Mart Corporation is Canada's largest drug store chain, reaching 9 out of 10 Canadians.

Like many large companies, Shoppers started out small. Its origins can be traced to 1921, when Leon Koffler opened the first two Koffler drugstores in Toronto. In 1941, his son, Murray Koffler, took over the family-owned business. In 1962, Murray Koffler introduced a new concept in pharmacies by opening the first Shoppers Drug Mart. It featured self-service for customers and offered mass merchandising. Shoppers soon grew into a private corporation with 17 stores, each one owned by a pharmacist as an "Associate." Shoppers franchises stores to pharmacist-owners who can offer personal service to local communities and benefit from the buying power, brand name, and marketing expertise of Shoppers' head office.

Over the years, the company has continued to grow and innovate. In its first year in business, Shoppers created its own Life brand of private label health and beauty and other products. It now carries more than 7,500 private label products under several brand names. Shoppers expanded in 1971 into British Columbia and Alberta and the following year into Quebec, where the stores are called Pharmaprix. In 1985, it opened a food section in some stores. In 1991, it launched the HealthWATCH program, which provides patients counselling and advice on medications and health and wellness. In 2006, it purchased MediSystem Technologies Inc., a provider of pharmaceutical products and services to long-term care facilities in Ontario and Alberta. Shoppers opened its first Murale beauty boutique in 2008 and now has six luxury beauty destinations operating under the trademark Murale.

In 2001, Shoppers became a public corporation, issuing 30 million common shares at a price of $18 per share. That would have been a good investment for anyone who bought initial shares and held on to them, because in 2013, the Shoppers' board of directors and shareholders approved the company's purchase by Loblaw Companies Limited for $33.18 in cash plus 6/10ths of a Loblaw share for each Shoppers' share. That worked out to $61.54 per Shoppers' share. The $12.4-billion buyout, subject to federal government and court approval at the time of writing, merged Canada's largest drug store chain with Canada's largest grocery store chain, creating a company to better compete in the fast-changing retail business, focusing on health and nutrition. "We are delighted to partner with Loblaw to leverage our combined strengths. For our shareholders, this transaction provides significant and immediate value, as well as the ability to benefit from future upside by virtue of their continued ownership of shares in the combined company," said Domenic Pilla, President and Chief Executive Officer of Shoppers Drug Mart.

Shoppers will continue to operate as a separate division of Loblaw. Shoppers and Loblaw stores expected to sell each other's private-label products, expanding the choices for consumers.

How does a company like Shoppers Drug Mart decide to make all these moves in the hopes of boosting profitability? Whether creating its associate business model, becoming a public company, or diversifying into food and beauty products, Shoppers relies on one key tool: accounting.

And the way Shoppers communicates its accounting information to investors, lenders, suppliers, and other interested parties is through its financial statements.[1]

the navigator

<table>
<tr><td>

preview of CHAPTER | **1**

</td><td>

How do you start a business? How do you make it grow into a widely recognized brand name like Shoppers Drug Mart in our chapter-opening feature story? How do you determine whether your business is making or losing money? When you need to expand your operations, where do you get money to finance the expansion—should you borrow, issue shares, or use company funds? To be successful in business, countless decisions have to be made—and decisions require accounting information, as mentioned in our feature story.

The purpose of this chapter is to show you accounting's role in providing useful financial information for decision-making. The chapter is organized as follows:

</td></tr>
</table>

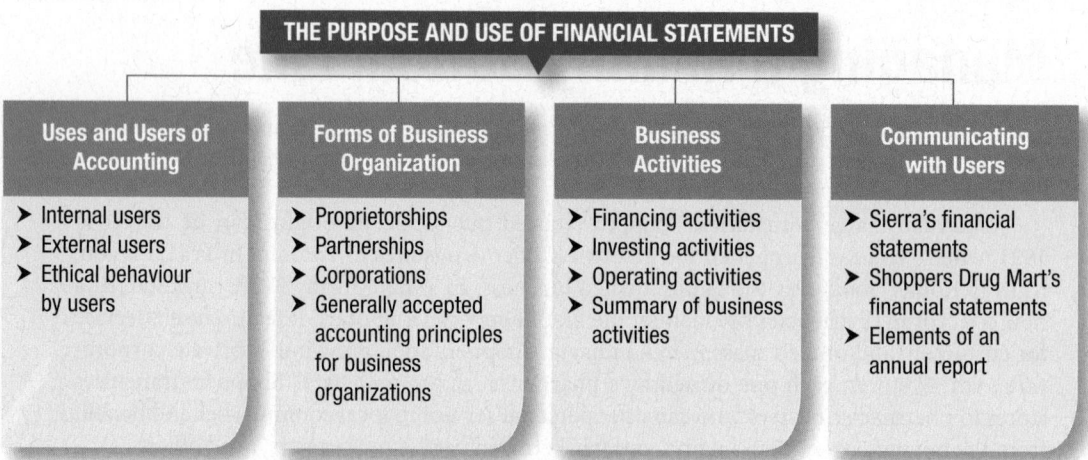

THE PURPOSE AND USE OF FINANCIAL STATEMENTS

Uses and Users of Accounting	Forms of Business Organization	Business Activities	Communicating with Users
➤ Internal users ➤ External users ➤ Ethical behaviour by users	➤ Proprietorships ➤ Partnerships ➤ Corporations ➤ Generally accepted accounting principles for business organizations	➤ Financing activities ➤ Investing activities ➤ Operating activities ➤ Summary of business activities	➤ Sierra's financial statements ➤ Shoppers Drug Mart's financial statements ➤ Elements of an annual report

Uses and Users of Accounting

Accounting is the information system that identifies and records the economic events of an organization, and then communicates them to a wide variety of interested users. Why does accounting matter to these users? The world's economic systems depend on highly transparent, reliable, and accurate financial reporting. Because of this, accounting has long been labelled "the language of business."

That's one of the reasons why so many Canadians, even those who do not plan on becoming accountants, study accounting. For example, Monique Leroux, president and CEO of Desjardins Group; Elizabeth Marshall, a senator; Zarin Mehta, president and executive director of the New York Philharmonic; George Melville, chairman and owner of Boston Pizza International; Syd Pallister, CFO of Gibbs-Delta Tackle; and Paul Sobey, president and CEO of Empire Company Limited, all have studied accounting in depth.

Whether you plan to become an accountant or not, a working knowledge of accounting will be relevant and useful in whatever role you assume as a user of accounting information. Whether you plan to own your own business, work for someone else in their business, or invest in a business, understanding accounting will be helpful to you. To demonstrate the value of accounting to you as an individual, each chapter includes an "All About You" feature and a related activity in the end-of-chapter material that links an accounting concept to your personal or business life.

Users of accounting information can be divided broadly into two types: internal users and external users. We will discuss each of these in the sections that follow.

INTERNAL USERS

Internal users of accounting information plan, organize, and run companies. They work for the company. These include finance directors, marketing managers, human resource personnel, production supervisors, and company officers.

In running a business, internal users must answer many important questions, as shown in Illustration 1-1.

Finance
Is there enough cash to pay the bills?

Marketing
What price should we sell iPads
for to maximize profits?

Human Resources
How many employees can we
afford to hire this year?

Production
Which product line is the most profitable?

▶Illustration 1-1
Questions asked by internal users

To answer these and other questions, users need detailed accounting information on a timely basis; that is, it must be available when it is needed. For internal users, accounting provides a variety of internal reports, such as financial comparisons of operating alternatives, projections of profit from new sales campaigns, analyses of sales costs, and forecasts of cash needs. In addition, companies present summarized financial information in the form of financial statements for both internal and external use.

EXTERNAL USERS

There are several types of external users of accounting information. Investors use accounting information to make decisions to buy, hold, or sell their ownership interest. Lenders, such as bankers, use accounting information to evaluate the risks of lending money. Other creditors, such as suppliers, use accounting information to decide whether or not to grant credit (sell on account) to a customer. **Investors, lenders, and other creditors** are considered to be the primary users of accounting information.

Some questions that investors, lenders, and other creditors may ask about a company are shown in Illustration 1-2.

> **Alternative Terminology** notes give synonyms that you may hear or see in the workplace and in this text.

Alternative Terminology
Investors are also known as *shareholders* and *creditors* are also known as *lenders*.

Investors
Should I purchase shares of this
company?

Lenders and Other Creditors
Will the company be able to pay
its debts as they come due?

▶Illustration 1-2
Questions asked by external users

In addition to investors, lenders, and other creditors, there are many other external users with a variety of information needs and questions. For example, potential employees use annual reports to learn about the company and evaluate job prospects. Labour unions use financial information to bargain for better salaries and benefits. And taxing authorities, such as the Canada Revenue Agency, use financial statements to assess a company's income tax.

ETHICAL BEHAVIOUR BY USERS

In order for financial information to have value to its users, whether internal or external, it must be prepared by individuals with high standards of ethical behaviour. Ethics in accounting is of the utmost importance to accountants and the decision makers who rely on the financial information they produce.

Fortunately, most individuals in business are ethical. Their actions are both legal and responsible. They consider the organization's interests when they make decisions. Accountants and other professionals have extensive rules of conduct to guide their behaviour with each other and the public. In addition, many companies today have codes of conduct that outline their commitment to ethical behaviour in their internal and external relationships.

To sensitize you to ethical situations and give you practice at solving ethical dilemmas, we highlight the importance of ethics in different ways in this text:

1. A number of the feature stories and other parts of the text discuss the central importance of ethical behaviour to financial reporting.
2. Many of the *Accounting Matters* boxes and marginal *Ethics Notes* highlight ethics situations and issues in actual business settings.
3. Every chapter includes an *Ethics Case* in the end-of-chapter material that simulates a business situation and asks you to put yourself in the position of a key decision maker.

> **Do It! exercises** prompt you to stop and practice the key points you have just studied before you go further in your reading of the text. *Related exercise material* tells you which Brief Exercises (BE) and Exercises (E) at the end of the chapter have similar study objectives.

BEFORE YOU GO ON...

▶ Do It! Users of Accounting Information

The following is a list of questions that may be asked by different users of accounting information:

1. Will I be able to obtain enough cash to finance this month's cash shortfall?

2. Will the company be able to repay my loan when it comes due?

3. What was the labour cost for the production of 1,000 board feet of lumber?

4. Will the company stay in business long enough to service the products I buy from it?

5. Will the company's share price go up or down in the near future?

(a) Identify the type of user that would most likely ask each of the above questions from the following list of possible users: chief financial officer, customers, investors, lenders, or production manager.

(b) Indicate whether the user you chose is an internal or external user.

Action Plan

- Understand the difference between internal and external users: Internal users work for the company; external users do not.
- Understand the types of information internal and external users require to make decisions.

Solution

	(a) Type of User	(b) Internal or External User
1.	Chief financial officer	Internal
2.	Lenders	External
3.	Production manager	Internal
4.	Customers	External
5.	Investors	External

Related Exercise Material: BE1-1 and E1-1.

Forms of Business Organization

Businesses can be organized in different ways and the accounting standards they use can vary depending on the type of organization. There are three common forms of business organization: proprietorships, partnerships, and corporations.

STUDY OBJECTIVE 2
Describe the primary forms of business organization.

PROPRIETORSHIPS

When you graduate, you might decide to start your own business. If you do, you may choose to set up a proprietorship. A **proprietorship** is a business owned by one person. It is often called a "sole" proprietorship because the owner has no partners.

The proprietorship form of business organization is simple to set up and gives the owner control over the business. In most cases, only a relatively small amount of money (capital) is needed to start in business as a proprietorship. The owner (the proprietor) receives any profits, suffers any losses, and is personally liable (responsible) for all debts of the business. This is known as unlimited liability.

There is no legal distinction between the business as an economic unit and the owner. Accordingly, the life of the proprietorship is limited to the life of the owner. The business profits are reported as self-employment income and taxed on the owner's personal income tax return. However, for accounting purposes, the business records of the proprietorship must be kept separate from those related to the owner's personal activities.

The separation of business and personal records is known in its simplest form as the reporting entity concept. The **reporting entity concept** requires that the economic activity that can be identified with a particular company be kept separate and distinct from the activities of the owner and of all other economic entities. This concept applies not only to proprietorships, but also to partnerships and corporations, which are discussed in the next sections.

Small service businesses such as hair salons, plumbers, and mechanics are often proprietorships, as are many farms and small retail stores.

PARTNERSHIPS

Another possibility after graduating would be for you to join forces with other individuals to form a partnership. A **partnership** is a business owned by more than one person. In most respects, a partnership is similar to a proprietorship except that there is more than one owner. Partnerships are often formed because one person does not have enough economic resources to start or expand the business, or because partners bring unique skills or other resources to the partnership.

Partnerships are normally formalized in a written partnership agreement that outlines the formation of the partnership, partners' contributions, how profits and losses are shared, provisions for withdrawals of assets and/or partners, dispute resolution, and partnership liquidation. Although there are advantages to working with others, there are also disadvantages. Each partner generally has unlimited liability for all debts of the partnership, even if one of the other partners created the debt. However, there are certain situations where partnerships can be formed with limited liability for selected partners.

Similar to a proprietorship, the profits of the partnership are reported as self-employment income and taxed on each partner's personal income tax return. In addition, the reporting entity concept requires that partnership records be kept separate from each partner's personal activities.

Partnerships are typically used to organize professional service businesses, such as the practices of lawyers, doctors, architects, engineers, and accountants.

CORPORATIONS

As a third alternative after graduating, you might choose to form a business as a corporation. A **corporation** is a business organized as a separate legal entity owned by shareholders. Shoppers Drug Mart in our opening feature story is a corporation. As an investor in a corporation such as Shoppers

Alternative Terminology
Shares are also known as *stock*.

Drug Mart, you receive shares to indicate your ownership claim. It is often possible for individuals to become owners of shares (shareholders) by investing relatively small amounts of money.

Suppose that you are one of Shoppers Drug Mart's shareholders. The amount of cash that you have in your personal bank account and the balance you owe on your personal car loan are not reported in Shoppers Drug Mart's financial statements. Similar to proprietorships and partnerships, you and the company are separate reporting entities under the reporting entity concept.

Since a corporation is a separate legal entity, its life is indefinite. That means it continues on regardless of who owns its shares. It is not affected by the withdrawal, death, or incapacity of an owner, as is the case in a proprietorship or partnership. Consequently, buying shares in a corporation, especially a large corporation, is often more attractive than investing in a proprietorship or partnership because shares are easier to sell.

There are other factors that need to be considered when deciding which organizational form of business to choose. As we discussed earlier, if you choose to organize as a proprietorship or partnership, you are personally liable for all debts of the business. Shareholders are not responsible for corporate debts unless they have personally guaranteed them. So most shareholders enjoy limited liability since they only risk losing the amount they have invested in the company's shares.

All of these advantages taken together—indefinite life, ease of transferring ownership, and limited liability—can make it easier for corporations, especially large corporations, to raise capital (cash) compared with proprietorships and partnerships.

Proprietors and partners pay personal income tax on their respective shares of the profits, while corporations pay income tax as separate legal entities on any corporate profits. Corporations may receive a more favourable income tax treatment than other forms of business organization. Because of the wide variety of income tax issues that apply to different companies in different jurisdictions, you would be wise to seek professional advice on taxation matters before choosing any form of business organization.

Although the combined number of proprietorships and partnerships in Canada is more than the number of corporations, the revenue produced by corporations is far greater. Most of the largest companies in Canada—for example, Bombardier, Loblaw, Manulife Financial, Royal Bank, and Suncor—are corporations. Recently, the top 50 of Canada's largest corporations each reported annual revenues ranging from $11 billion to $51 billion.

Corporations such as these are publicly traded. That is, their shares are listed on Canadian, or other, stock exchanges such as the Toronto Stock Exchange (TSX). **Public corporations** are required to distribute their financial statements to investors, lenders, other creditors, other interested parties, and the general public. Shoppers Drug Mart is currently a public corporation. Its financial statements are readily available on its own website, as well as that of the System for Electronic Document Analysis and Retrieval (SEDAR), which posts financial statements for all public corporations in Canada. We have also included Shoppers Drug Mart's financial statements in Appendix A at the back of this textbook for your easy reference.

In addition to public corporations like Shoppers Drug Mart, there are **private corporations**. Private corporations also issue shares, but they do not make them available to the general public nor are they traded on public stock exchanges. These shares are often said to be "closely held." Consequently, many private corporations, especially small ones, do not have the same advantages of raising capital as do large corporations. For example, a small, local incorporated business would likely have as much difficulty raising funds as would a proprietorship or partnership.

There are some large private corporations, however, such as the Irving Group of Companies, the Jim Pattison Group, and McCain Foods. Some of these private corporations can equal the size of a public corporation. For example, Canada's top-earning private corporation reported annual revenue nearly equal to that of Canada's top-earning public corporation. Like proprietorships and partnerships, private companies almost never distribute their financial statements publicly. There is no requirement to do so as there is for public corporations, and most private corporations do not wish to disclose financial information to their competitors and the wider populace.

Many businesses start as proprietorships or partnerships and eventually incorporate. As the feature story pointed out, Shoppers Drug Mart began as a proprietorship in 1921 with two small operator-owned pharmacies in Toronto called Koffler Drug Stores. By 1962, the company had grown to 17 pharmacies and was renamed Shoppers Drug Mart. It subsequently became a private corporation and in 2001 became a public corporation. It is possible that Shoppers Drug Mart may revert to a private corporation after it is acquired by Loblaw. At the time of writing, it is anticipated that this acquisition will be completed early in 2014.

Because most Canadian business is transacted by corporations, this book focuses on the corporate form of organization. We will discuss the accounting for both publicly traded and private corporations in this textbook.

GENERALLY ACCEPTED ACCOUNTING PRINCIPLES FOR BUSINESS ORGANIZATIONS

How do businesses decide on the amount of financial information to disclose? In what format should financial information be presented? The answers to these questions can be found in accounting rules and practices that are recognized as a general guide for financial reporting purposes.

These rules and practices are referred to as **generally accepted accounting principles**, commonly abbreviated as GAAP. GAAP include broad policies and practices as well as rules and procedures that have substantive authoritative support and agreement about how to record and report economic events.

Generally accepted accounting principles can differ depending on the form of business organization. Publicly traded corporations must use International Financial Reporting Standards (IFRS), a set of global accounting standards developed by the International Accounting Standards Board. Private corporations, whose users can have different needs than publicly traded corporations, have a choice between using IFRS or Accounting Standards for Private Enterprises (ASPE), developed by the Canadian Accounting Standards Board.

Most private corporations choose to use ASPE, although there are exceptions. For example, McCain Foods Ltd. is a private company that chose to use IFRS instead of ASPE. It felt that IFRS was a more appropriate option for it given its size and global presence, as it has operations on six continents. We will learn more about IFRS and ASPE for corporations in Chapter 2.

As proprietorships and partnerships are private companies (even though they are not private *corporations*), these companies generally follow ASPE for external financial reporting purposes. However, proprietorships and partnerships often prepare financial statements only for the internal use of the owner(s), in which case they don't have to follow any particular set of accounting standards.

Alternative Terminology
Accounting principles are also commonly known as *accounting standards* or *accounting policies*.

The **ASPE** icon indicates that there is a reporting difference for private companies following Accounting Standards for Private Enterprises, compared with those companies following IFRS.

The **Accounting Matters!** perspectives give examples of how accounting is used in various business situations.

ACCOUNTING MATTERS!

What's in a Company Name?

How can you tell whether a company is a corporation or not? Corporations in Canada and the United States are identified by "Ltd." ("Ltée" in French), "Inc.," "Corp.," or in some cases, "Co." following their names. These abbreviations can also be spelled out. In Brazil and France, the letters used are "SA" (Sôciedade Anonima, Société Anonyme); in Japan, "KK" (Kabushiki Kaisha); in the Netherlands, "NV" (Naamloze Vennootschap); in Italy, "SpA" (Societá per Azioni); and in Sweden, "AB" (Aktiebolag).

In the United Kingdom, public corporations are identified by "plc" (public limited company), while private corporations are denoted by "Ltd." The same designations in Germany are "AG" (Aktiengesellschaft) for public corporations and "GmbH" (Gesellschaft mit beschränkter Haftung) for private corporations. There are no name distinctions between public and private corporations in Canada.

BEFORE YOU GO ON...

▶ Do It! Business Organizations

In choosing the right organizational form for your business, you must consider the characteristics of each. Choose from the characteristics listed below for each of ownership, liability, life, ease of raising capital, and income tax, and match the characteristic with

(continued)

the form of business organization—proprietorship, partnership, or corporation—they are normally associated with:

(a) Ownership: Choose among "one individual," "two or more individuals," or "many shareholders"

(b) Liability: Choose between "limited" or "unlimited"

(c) Life: Choose between "limited" or "indefinite"

(d) Ease of raising capital: Choose among "hard," "easier," or "easiest"

(e) Income tax: Choose between "paid by individual(s)" or "paid by entity"

Action Plan
- Understand the characteristics of each type of business organization.

Solution

	Proprietorship	Partnership	Corporation
(a) Ownership	One individual	Two or more individuals	Many individuals
(b) Liability	Unlimited	Unlimited	Limited
(c) Life	Limited	Limited	Indefinite
(d) Ease of raising capital	Hard	Easier	Easiest
(e) Income tax	Paid by individual	Paid by individuals (partners)	Paid by entity (corporation)

Related Exercise Material: BE1-2 and E1-2.

Business Activities

STUDY OBJECTIVE 3

Explain the three main types of business activity.

All businesses are involved in three types of activity: financing, investing, and operating. For example, Shoppers Drug Mart needed **financing** in 2012 to expand its operations, so it borrowed money from outside sources. It then **invested** the cash in new drugstores, as well as expanding and remodelling others. This helped Shoppers increase its **operating** activities and improve sales.

Let's now look at these three types of business activity in more detail.

FINANCING ACTIVITIES

It takes money to make money. The two primary ways of raising outside funds for corporations are (1) borrowing money (debt financing) and (2) issuing (selling) shares (equity financing) in exchange for cash.

Shoppers Drug Mart can borrow money in a variety of ways. The persons or companies that Shoppers owes money to are called lenders or creditors, one of the key user groups of accounting information. Amounts owed to lenders and other creditors—in the form of debt and other obligations—are called **liabilities**.

Specific names are given to different types of liabilities, depending on their source. For instance, Shoppers Drug Mart may have received funds from an operating line of credit with its bank. An operating line of credit is a pre-arranged bank loan for a maximum amount that allows a company to draw more money than there is on hand in its bank account. When a company uses its operating line of credit to cover cash shortfalls and overdraws its bank account, it results in a liability called **bank indebtedness**.

Shoppers Drug Mart may also have a short-term **loan payable** to a bank (also known as a note payable) for the money borrowed to purchase racks and display cabinets, for example. It may have

long-term debt, which can include **mortgages payable**, **bonds payable**, **finance lease obligations**, and other types of debt securities borrowed for longer periods of time.

A corporation may obtain equity financing by selling shares of ownership to investors. Shoppers Drug Mart first issued common shares to the general public in 2001 when it became a publicly traded corporation and listed its shares for sale on the TSX. **Common shares** is the term used to describe the amount paid by investors for shares of ownership in a company. Even if Shoppers becomes a private corporation after its acquisition by Loblaw, it will still have common shares. Its shares will, however, be owned by Loblaw rather than the general public. Common shares are just one class or type of shares (collectively known as **share capital**) that a company can issue.

Companies can also use cash for financing activities, such as repaying debt or repurchasing shares from investors. Shoppers Drug Mart did both in 2012. The claims of lenders and other creditors differ from those of shareholders. If you loan money to a company, you are one of its lenders or other creditors. In loaning money, you specify a repayment schedule; for example, payment at the end of each month. In addition, interest is normally added to the amount due or overdue. As a lender or other creditor, you have a legal right to be paid at the agreed time. In the event of nonpayment, you may force the company to sell assets to pay its debts.

Shareholders have no claim to corporate resources until the claims of lenders and other creditors are satisfied. If you buy a company's shares instead of loaning it money, you have no legal right to expect any payments until all of its lenders and other creditors are paid. Also, once shares are issued, the company has no obligation to buy them back, although it may choose to do so. On the other hand, debt obligations must be repaid.

Many companies pay shareholders a return on their investment on a regular basis, as long as there is enough cash to cover required payments to lenders and other creditors. Payments to shareholders are called **dividends** and are normally in the form of cash, although they can also take other forms. Shoppers Drug Mart paid a dividend of $1.06 per share to its shareholders in 2012.

INVESTING ACTIVITIES

After a company raises money through financing activities, it then uses that money for investing activities. Investing activities involve the purchase (or sale) of long-lived assets that a company needs in order to operate. **Assets** are resources that a company owns or controls. Every asset is capable of providing future economic benefits that can be short- or long-lived. Investing activities generally involve long-lived assets. For example, furniture, equipment, computers, vehicles, buildings, and land are all examples of long-lived assets that result from investing activities. Together, they are referred to as **property, plant, and equipment**, or "property and equipment," as Shoppers Drug Mart calls this asset category.

Other examples of long-lived assets include goodwill and intangible assets. **Goodwill** results from the acquisition of another company when the price paid is higher than the value of the purchased company's net identifiable assets. **Intangible assets** are assets that do not have any physical substance themselves but represent a privilege or a right granted to, or held by, a company. Examples of intangible assets include patents, copyrights, and trademarks.

Cash is one of the more important assets owned by Shoppers Drug Mart, or any other business. If a company has excess cash that it does not need in the short term, it might choose to invest it in debt securities (such as bonds) or equity securities (such as shares) of other corporations or organizations—these are called **investments**. Many students misunderstand the term *investing activities*, thinking the term means "investments" only. However, in the context of a business activity, investing activities means investing in the long-lived assets necessary to run the company and not just purchasing an investment on which to earn a return for the long term, such as interest or dividends.

OPERATING ACTIVITIES

Once a business has the finances and has made the investments it needs to get started, it can begin its operations. For example, Shoppers Drug Mart sells prescription and non-prescription drugs, as well as health and beauty aids and household products. We call the amounts earned from the sale of these goods **revenue**. In accounting language, revenues are increases in economic benefits—normally an increase in an asset but sometimes a decrease in a liability—that result from the sale of a product or service in the normal course of business.

Alternative Terminology
Property, plant, and equipment is also known as *capital assets* or *fixed assets*.

Alternative Terminology
Revenue is also known as *income*.

Revenues come from different sources and are identified by various names. For instance, Shoppers Drug Mart's main source of revenue is the money it earns from the sale of prescription and other products to consumers—it calls this revenue "sales." However, companies may also earn interest revenue on excess cash held as investments and rental income from unused space. Sources of revenue that are common to many businesses are **sales revenue, service revenue, interest revenue**, and **rent revenue**.

When Shoppers Drug Mart sells a prescription to a customer who has a drug plan, such as Blue Cross, it does not immediately receive all of the cash for the sale. Instead, it must send a bill to Blue Cross for the amount covered by the drug plan and then wait for Blue Cross to pay the amount owed. This right to receive money in the future is called an **account receivable**. Accounts receivable are assets because they will result in a future benefit—cash—when the amounts owed are eventually collected.

We first mentioned the term *assets* in the investing activities section above. A company's long-lived assets, such as property, plant, and equipment, are purchased through investing activities. Other assets—typically with shorter lives—result from operating activities, such as short-term trading investments and accounts receivable. Companies also have other types of receivables, such as interest receivable, rent receivable, and income tax receivable (also known as "deferred tax assets") that is due from the federal government.

Supplies are another example of a short-term asset used in day-to-day operations, as is inventory, which is described next. Before Shoppers Drug Mart can sell products to its customers, it must first buy prescription drugs, health-care aids, cosmetics, household items, and other goods. Items such as these that are held for future sale to customers result in an asset called inventory or **merchandise inventory**. When the goods (inventory) are sold, they are no longer an asset with future benefits but an expense. More specifically, the cost of the inventory sold is an expense called cost of goods sold. In accounting language, **expenses** are the costs of assets that are consumed or services that are used in the process of generating revenues. As we will learn in Chapter 4, expenses are related to assets and liabilities. When an expense is incurred, an asset will decrease or a liability will increase.

There are many kinds of expenses and they are identified by various names, depending on the type of asset consumed or service used. For example, Shoppers Drug Mart keeps track of these types of expenses: **cost of goods sold, operating and administrative expenses, interest expense**, and **income tax expense**. Shoppers' operating and administrative expenses item is a summary of individual expense accounts such as salaries, advertising, utilities, professional fees, rent, depreciation (the allocation of the cost of using property and equipment), amortization (the allocation of the cost of intangible assets), and other costs associated with running the business.

Short-term liabilities may result from some of these expenses. This occurs, for example, when Shoppers Drug Mart purchases drugs on credit (on account) from pharmaceutical companies (suppliers). The obligations to pay for these goods are called **accounts payable**. It may also have **interest payable** on the outstanding (unpaid) liability amounts owed to various lenders and other creditors, **dividends payable** to shareholders, **salaries payable** to employees, **property tax payable** to the municipal and/or provincial governments, and **sales tax payable** to the provincial and federal governments. **Income tax payable** (also known as "deferred tax liabilities") is an example of another liability that is payable to the government.

To determine whether it earned a profit, Shoppers Drug Mart compares the revenues earned in a period with the expenses incurred in that same period. The goal of every business is to sell a good or service for a price that is greater than the cost of producing or purchasing the good or providing the service, plus the cost of operating the business. This means that revenues should, ideally, be greater than the expenses incurred to generate the revenue. When revenues are more than expenses, a **profit** results, as shown in Illustration 1-3. Profit is also commonly known as *net earnings* or *net income*. In particular, companies following ASPE tend to use the term *net income*.

▸Illustration 1-3
Determination of profit (loss)

| Revenues | − | Expenses | = | Profit (Loss) |

Shoppers Drug Mart's revenues exceeded its expenses and it reported a profit of $608,481 thousand for the year ended December 29, 2012. When the opposite happens—that is, when expenses exceed revenues—a **loss** (also known as a net loss) results.

SUMMARY OF BUSINESS ACTIVITIES

To summarize our discussion in this section, there are three types of business activities that companies engage in: (1) financing, (2) investing, and (3) operating, as shown in Illustration 1-4.

►Illustration 1-4
Business activities

Financing Activities   Investing Activities   Operating Activities

1. **Financing activities** include borrowing cash from lenders by issuing debt, or conversely, using cash to repay debt. Cash can also be raised from shareholders by issuing shares, or paid to shareholders by repurchasing shares or distributing dividends.
2. **Investing activities** include purchasing and disposing of long-lived assets such as property, plant, and equipment and purchasing and selling long-term investments.
3. **Operating activities** result from day-to-day operations and include revenues and expenses and related accounts such as receivables, supplies, inventory, and payables.

BEFORE YOU GO ON...

►Do It! Business Activities

Classify each of the following items as (a) a financing, investing, or operating activity, and (b) an asset, liability, share capital, revenue, or expense.

1. An amount paid to an employee for work performed

2. An amount earned from providing a service

3. An issue of common shares

4. A truck that is purchased

5. An amount owed to a bank

Action Plan

- Classify each item based on its economic characteristics.
- Understand the differences among financing, investing, and operating activities.
- Understand the distinctions among assets, liabilities, share capital, revenues, and expenses.

Solution

	(a)	(b)
1.	Operating activity	Expense (salary expense)
2.	Operating activity	Revenue (service revenue)
3.	Financing activity	Share capital (common shares)
4.	Investing activity	Asset (truck—property, plant, and equipment)
5.	Financing activity	Liability (bank loan payable)

Related Exercise Material: BE1-3, BE1-4, E1-3, and E1-4.

the navigator

Communicating with Users

You will recall that we learned about internal and external users of accounting information earlier in this chapter. Users, especially external users, are interested in a company's assets, liabilities, and shareholders' equity, including revenues and expenses. For external reporting purposes, it is customary to arrange this information in four different financial statements that are the backbone of financial reporting.

1. **Income statement**: An income statement reports revenues and expenses to show how successfully a company performed during a period of time.
2. **Statement of changes in equity**: A statement of changes in equity shows the changes in each component of shareholders' equity (usually common shares and retained earnings), as well as total equity, during a period of time.
3. **Statement of financial position**: A statement of financial position presents a picture of what a company owns (its assets), what it owes (its liabilities), and the resulting difference (its shareholders' equity) at a specific point in time.
4. **Statement of cash flows**: A statement of cash flows shows where a company obtained cash during a period of time and how that cash was used.

Additional information is reported in **notes to the financial statements** that are cross-referenced to the four statements. These explanatory notes clarify information presented in the financial statements and provide additional detail. They are essential to understanding a company's financial performance and position.

While the above four financial statements are the statements most commonly provided by publicly traded companies, there are other financial statements. For example, a statement of comprehensive income must be prepared when a publicly traded company reports other comprehensive income earned from certain items. In addition, private corporations prepare a statement of retained earnings instead of a statement of changes in equity. We will wait until later chapters to illustrate these statements.

Financial statements must be produced annually, as well as quarterly, by public corporations. Financial statements are often produced monthly as well for internal use. An accounting time period that is one year in length is called a **fiscal year**.

Alternative Terminology
Quarterly financial statements are also called *interim* financial statements.

ACCOUNTING MATTERS!

Fiscal Year Ends

Nearly 75% of Canadian companies use December 31 for their fiscal year end. Why does every company not use December 31 as its accounting year end? Many companies choose to end their accounting year when their inventory or operations are at a low. This is advantageous because gathering accounting information requires a lot of time and effort from managers. They would rather do it when they are not too busy operating the business. Also, inventory is easier and less costly to count when it is low. Some companies whose year ends differ from December 31 are lululemon (Sunday closest to the end of January), Jean Coutu (Saturday closest to the end of February), CoolBrands (August 31), and Shoppers Drug Mart (Saturday closest to the end of December). Most governments use March 31 for their fiscal year end.

SIERRA'S FINANCIAL STATEMENTS

We will now look at the financial statements of a fictitious marketing agency, a service company called Sierra Corporation, to introduce you to the four primary financial statements: the income statement, statement of changes in equity, statement of financial position, and statement of cash flows.

Income Statement

The **income statement** reports the success or failure of the company's operations for a period of time—annually, quarterly, and/or monthly, as we mentioned in the previous section. In our example that follows, Sierra Corporation formed the company on October 1. It has been in operation for one month only, the month ended October 31, 2015, and reports its results monthly. To indicate that Sierra's income statement reports the results of operations for a period of one month, its statement is dated "Month Ended October 31, 2015."

The income statement lists the company's revenues first and then its expenses. We will learn about the order in which expenses can be listed in later chapters. For now, we have simply listed expenses in order of magnitude—that is, from the largest to the smallest. Expenses are deducted from revenues to determine profit (or loss) before income tax. Income tax expense is usually shown separately, immediately following the profit (or loss) before income tax line. Finally, profit (or loss) is determined by deducting the income tax expense.

A sample income statement for Sierra Corporation is shown in Illustration 1-5.

<aside>
Alternative Terminology
The *income statement* is also commonly known as the *statement of earnings* or *statement of profit and loss*.
</aside>

SIERRA CORPORATION Income Statement Month Ended October 31, 2015		
Revenues		
Service revenue		$20,600
Expenses		
Salaries expense	$6,000	
Supplies expense	1,500	
Rent expense	900	
Depreciation expense	83	
Insurance expense	50	
Interest expense	25	
Total expenses		8,558
Profit before income tax		12,042
Income tax expense		1,800
Profit		$10,242

<aside>
▶**Illustration 1-5**
Income statement

Helpful Hint
The heading of every statement identifies the company, the type of statement, and the time period covered by the statement. Sometimes another line is added to indicate the unit of measure. When it is used, this fourth line usually indicates that the data are presented in thousands or in millions.
</aside>

Note that cents are not included in the dollar figures recorded in financial statements. It is important to understand, however, that cents should be and are used in recording transactions in a company's internal accounting records. It is only for financial reporting purposes that financial statement amounts are normally rounded to the nearest dollar, thousand dollars, or million dollars, depending on the size of the company. For example, Shoppers Drug Mart rounds amounts in its financial statements to the nearest thousand dollars. External reporting condenses and simplifies information so that it is easier for the reader to understand.

It also really does not matter whether the data in the statements are listed in two columns, as they are for Sierra Corporation, or in one column. Companies use a variety of presentation formats, depending on their preference and what they think is easiest for the reader to understand.

Why are financial statement users interested in a company's profit? Investors are interested in a company's past profit because these numbers provide information that may help predict future profits. Investors buy and sell shares based on their beliefs about the future performance of a company. If you believe that Sierra will be even more successful in the future, and that this success will translate into a higher share price, you should buy Sierra's shares.

Like investors, lenders and other creditors also use the income statement to predict the future. When a bank loans money to a company, it does this because it believes it will be repaid in the future. If it thought it was not going to be repaid, it would not loan the money. Thus, before making the loan, the bank's loan officer must try to predict whether the company will stay in business long enough, and be profitable enough, to repay the loan and any interest charges. Thus, reporting recurring and increasing profits will make it easier for Sierra to raise additional cash either by borrowing or by issuing shares.

DECISION TOOLKIT

Decision Checkpoints	Info Needed for Decision	Tools to Use for Decision	How to Evaluate Results
Are the company's operations profitable?	Income statement	The income statement indicates the success or failure of the company's operating activities by reporting its revenues and expenses.	If the company's revenues exceed its expenses, it will report a profit; otherwise it will report a loss.

Statement of Changes in Equity

Every chapter presents useful information about how decision makers use financial statements. **Decision Toolkits** summarize discussions of key decision-making contexts and techniques.

The **statement of changes in equity** shows the changes in total shareholders' equity for the period, as well as the changes in each component of shareholders' equity during the period. It starts with the account balances at the beginning of the period and ends with the account balances at the end of the period. The time period is the same as for the income statement—for the year, quarter, or month.

The ownership interest in a company is known as **shareholders' equity**. In its simplest form, total shareholders' equity includes (1) share capital and (2) retained earnings. It can also include other types of accounts, such as accumulated other comprehensive income, that we will discuss later in this, and other, chapters.

Share capital represents amounts contributed by the shareholders in exchange for shares of ownership. If there is only one type of shares issued, it is called common shares. We will learn about another class of shares, called preferred shares, in Chapter 11. Together, these two classes of shares—common and preferred—combine to form the company's share capital.

The statement of changes in equity starts with the beginning balance of share capital—common shares, in Sierra's case. This is zero for Sierra Corporation because it just began operations at the beginning of the month, October 1. The statement then goes on to add any changes in share capital due to new shares issued (or to deduct any changes in share capital due to shares repurchased) during the period to arrive at the ending balance of share capital, as shown in equation format below.

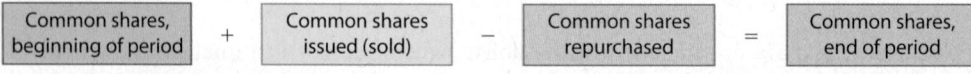

Common shares, beginning of period + Common shares issued (sold) − Common shares repurchased = Common shares, end of period

Retained earnings represent the cumulative profit that has been retained in the corporation. In other words, it is the profit that has not been paid out to shareholders that has accumulated since the company's date of incorporation. If retained earnings are negative—that is, there have been more losses than profits—it is known as a **deficit**.

In addition to showing the changes in share capital during the period, the statement of changes in equity also shows the amounts and causes of changes in retained earnings. The column for retained earnings starts with the beginning balance of retained earnings. Just as Sierra's beginning common shares balance was nil because it only began operations on October 1, so too is its beginning retained earnings balance. The profit for the period is added and dividends (if any) are deducted from the beginning balance to calculate the retained earnings at the end of the period, as shown in equation format below.

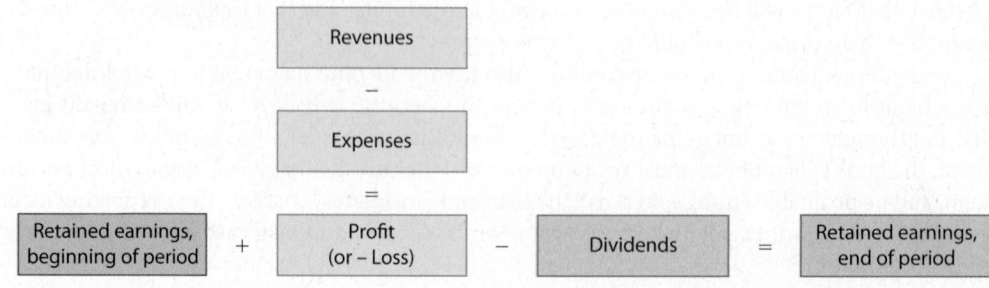

Revenues

−

Expenses

=

Retained earnings, beginning of period + Profit (or − Loss) − Dividends = Retained earnings, end of period

If a company has a loss, it is deducted (rather than added) to arrive at the ending balance of retained earnings. It is important to understand that dividends are not reported as an expense in the income statement. They are not an expense incurred to generate revenue. Instead, dividends are a distribution of retained earnings to shareholders and reported in the statement of changes in equity.

Illustration 1-6 presents Sierra Corporation's statement of changes in equity.

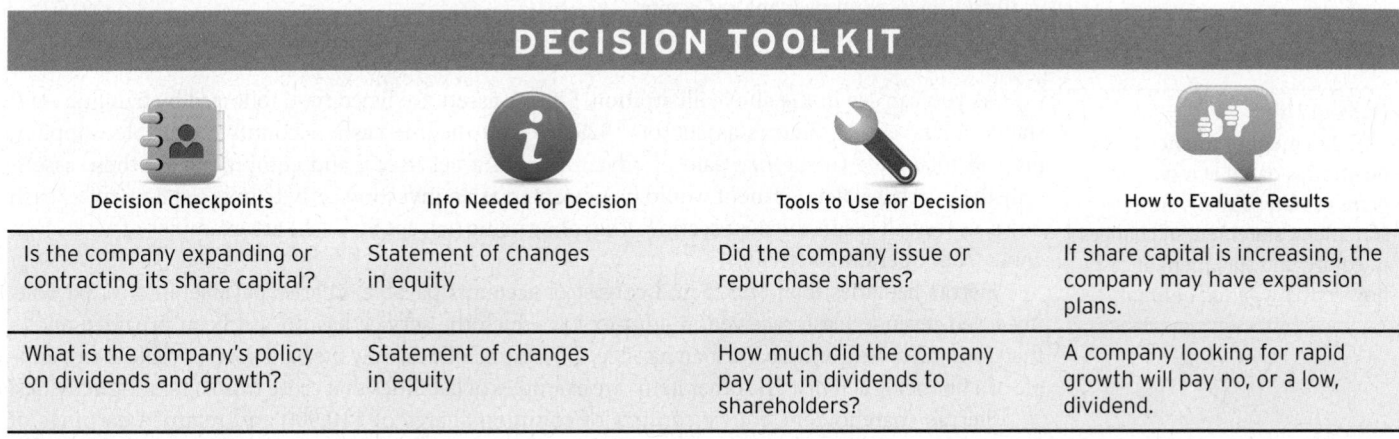

SIERRA CORPORATION
Statement of Changes in Equity
Month Ended October 31, 2015

	Common Shares	Retained Earnings	Total Equity
Balance, October 1	$ 0	$ 0	$ 0
Issued common shares	10,000		10,000
Profit		10,242	10,242
Dividends		(500)	(500)
Balance, October 31	$10,000	$ 9,742	$19,742

▶Illustration 1-6
Statement of changes in equity

Note that this statement adds both vertically (down; see "Total Equity" column) and horizontally (across; see "Balance, October 31" row).

By monitoring the statement of changes in equity for a publicly traded corporation, financial statement users can evaluate the use of equity for financing purposes. From this statement, they can determine the amount of shares that were issued during the period, for example. More importantly, the statement of changes in equity allows users to monitor a company's dividend payment practices. If Sierra is profitable, at the end of each period it must decide what portion of its profits to pay to shareholders through dividends. In theory, it could pay all of its current period profit, but few companies choose to do this. Why? Because they want to retain part of the profits in the business so the company can expand when it chooses to.

DECISION TOOLKIT

Decision Checkpoints	Info Needed for Decision	Tools to Use for Decision	How to Evaluate Results
Is the company expanding or contracting its share capital?	Statement of changes in equity	Did the company issue or repurchase shares?	If share capital is increasing, the company may have expansion plans.
What is the company's policy on dividends and growth?	Statement of changes in equity	How much did the company pay out in dividends to shareholders?	A company looking for rapid growth will pay no, or a low, dividend.

Statement of Financial Position

The **statement of financial position** reports assets and claims to those assets at a specific point in time. This statement is also commonly known as the balance sheet, especially for those companies following ASPE, and we will use these two terms interchangeably in this textbook.

Claims to assets are subdivided into two categories: claims of lenders and other creditors and claims of shareholders. As noted earlier, claims of lenders and other creditors are called liabilities. Claims of shareholders, the owners of the company, are called shareholders' equity. This relationship is shown below in equation format and is known as the basic **accounting equation**.

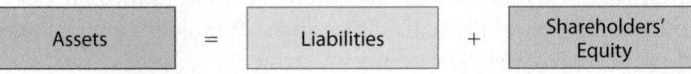

The relationship is where the name *balance sheet* comes from. Assets must be in balance with the claims to the assets. The right-hand side of the equation—the liabilities and equities—also shows how the assets have been financed (through debt by borrowing from lenders or other creditors or through equity by investments from shareholders [share capital] or profits retained in the company [retained earnings]).

Sierra's statement of financial position is shown in Illustration 1-7.

▶Illustration 1-7
Statement of financial position

SIERRA CORPORATION Statement of Financial Position October 31, 2015	
Assets	
Cash	$ 7,400
Accounts receivable	15,200
Supplies	1,000
Prepaid insurance	550
Equipment	4,917
Total assets	$29,067
Liabilities and Shareholders' Equity	
Liabilities	
Accounts payable	$ 1,500
Salaries payable	2,000
Interest payable	25
Unearned revenue	800
Bank loan payable	5,000
Total liabilities	9,325
Shareholders' equity	
Common shares	10,000
Retained earnings	9,742
Total shareholders' equity	19,742
Total liabilities and shareholders' equity	$29,067

Helpful Hint
The statement of financial position is dated at a *specific point in time*. The income statement, statement of changes in equity, and statement of cash flows cover a *period of time*.

As you can see in the above illustration, Sierra's assets are listed first, followed by liabilities and shareholders' equity. Sierra's assets total $29,067 and include cash, accounts receivable, supplies, prepaid insurance (insurance paid in advance but not yet used), and equipment. Of these assets, only the purchase of equipment would be presented as an investing activity in the statement of cash flows, as we will see in the next section. The other items (except for cash) are examples of assets that come from operating activities.

Sierra's liabilities total $9,325 and consist of accounts payable, salaries payable, interest payable, unearned revenue (cash received in advance for which the service has not yet been provided and is therefore still owed), and a bank loan payable. Of these liabilities, only the bank loan payable is an example of a financing activity. The other items are examples of liabilities that arose from operating activities.

Sierra's shareholders' equity consists of common shares of $10,000 and retained earnings of $9,742, for total shareholders' equity of $19,742. Note that Sierra's total liabilities and total shareholders' equity equal its total assets of $29,067.

The items listed in the statement of financial position can be ordered in different ways. For example, Sierra presents its assets first, followed by liabilities and shareholders' equity. Some companies present these items in a different order, to better represent the nature of their business. We will learn more about how to order items within the statement of financial position in Chapter 2.

Lenders and other creditors analyze a company's statement of financial position to determine the likelihood that they will be repaid. They carefully evaluate the nature of the company's assets and liabilities. For example, does the company have assets that could easily be sold, if required, to repay its debts? Do the company's assets exceed its liabilities in both the short and long terms?

Managers use the statement of financial position to determine whether inventory is adequate to support future sales and whether cash on hand is sufficient for immediate cash needs. Managers also look at the relationship between total liabilities and shareholders' equity to determine whether they have the best proportion of debt and equity financing.

DECISION TOOLKIT

 Decision Checkpoints	 Info Needed for Decision	 Tools to Use for Decision	 How to Evaluate Results
Does the company rely mainly on debt or on equity to finance its assets?	Statement of financial position	The statement of financial position reports the company's resources and claims to those resources. There are two types of claims: liabilities and shareholders' equity.	Compare the amount of liabilities as a percentage of total assets with the amount of shareholders' equity as a percentage of total assets to determine whether the company relies more on lenders and other creditors or on shareholders for its financing.

Statement of Cash Flows

The main function of a **statement of cash flows** is to provide financial information about the cash receipts and cash payments of a business for a specific period of time. To help investors, lenders and other creditors, and others in their analysis of a company's cash position, the statement of cash flows reports the effects on cash of a company's (1) operating activities, (2) investing activities, and (3) financing activities during the period of time.

Recall from earlier in the chapter that operating activities result from transactions that create revenues and expenses. Investing activities involve the purchase or sale of long-lived resources such as property, plant, and equipment that a company needs to operate and the purchase or sale of investments in long-term securities. Financing activities involve borrowing (or repaying) long-term debt from (to) lenders and issuing (or repurchasing) shares or distributing dividends to shareholders.

Operating activities are normally presented first in the statement of cash flows, followed by investing and financing activities. In addition, the statement shows the net increase or decrease in cash during the period, and the cash amount at the end of the period.

The statement of cash flows for Sierra is shown in Illustration 1-8. Note that the positive numbers in the illustration indicate cash inflows. Numbers in parentheses indicate cash outflows.

▶Illustration 1-8
Statement of cash flows

SIERRA CORPORATION Statement of Cash Flows Month Ended October 31, 2015		
Operating activities		
Cash receipts from operating activities	$ 6,200	
Cash payments for operating activities	(8,300)	
Net cash used by operating activities		$ (2,100)
Investing activities		
Purchase of equipment	$ (5,000)	
Net cash used by investing activities		(5,000)
Financing activities		
Issue of common shares	$10,000	
Borrowing of bank loan	5,000	
Payment of dividend	(500)	
Net cash provided by financing activities		14,500
Net increase in cash		7,400
Cash, October 1		0
Cash, October 31		$ 7,400

In the above illustration, Sierra's statement of cash flows shows that overall cash increased by $7,400 during the month. This increase resulted primarily because financing activities provided cash of $14,500. Operating activities did not generate enough cash to fund investing activities of $5,000 during the period. In fact, operating activities used $2,100 of cash rather than generating any cash. Consequently, the company had to generate cash from its financing activities to cover the use of $2,100 cash by its operating activities and $5,000 cash by its investing activities.

For now, you should not worry too much about where the numbers came from. Our intention is only to introduce this statement briefly at this point. We will learn more about the preparation of the statement of cash flows in Chapter 13.

DECISION TOOLKIT

 Decision Checkpoints	 Info Needed for Decision	 Tools to Use for Decision	How to Evaluate Results
Does the company generate enough cash from operating activities to fund its investing activities?	Statement of cash flows	The statement of cash flows shows the amount of cash provided or used by operating activities, investing activities, and financing activities.	Compare the amount of cash provided by operating activities with the amount of cash used by investing activities. Any deficiency in cash from operating activities must be made up with cash provided by financing activities.

> You will find a section called **Keeping an Eye on Cash** in each chapter to help you understand the importance of cash.

■ Keeping an Eye on Cash

Understanding where its cash comes from and where it goes is critical for a company. The statement of cash flows provides answers to these simple but important questions: (1) Where did cash come from during the period? (2) How was cash used during the period? (3) What was the change in the cash balance during the period?

The statement of cash flows answers these questions by summarizing cash flows as operating, investing, or financing activities. A user of this statement can then determine the amount of cash provided (or used) by operating activities, the amount of cash provided (or used) for investing purposes, and the amount of cash provided (or used) by financing activities.

Operating activities are activities the company performs to generate profits. It is desirable for operating activities to provide cash (positive balance) rather than use cash (negative balance). A positive source of cash from operating activities can help pay for investments to grow the business.

Investing activities include the purchase or sale of long-lived assets used in operating the business, or the purchase or sale of long-term investment securities. For most growing companies, investing activities use cash rather than provide cash, because growing companies purchase or replace more assets than they dispose of.

Financing activities include borrowing or repaying money, issuing or repurchasing shares, and paying dividends. For most growing companies, financing activities provide cash rather than use cash. Most growing companies have to borrow money or issue shares rather than being able to repay financing. As companies mature, they are able to repay financing and this balance becomes negative (cash used) more often than positive.

Relationships between the Statements

Because the results on some statements are used as data for other statements, the statements are said to be interrelated (related to each other). These interrelationships are evident in Sierra's financial statements.

1. The statement of changes in equity depends, in part, on the results of the income statement. Sierra reported profit of $10,242 for the month, as shown in Illustration 1-5. This amount is added to the beginning amount of retained earnings as part of the process of determining ending retained earnings—one of the components of total shareholders' equity shown in the statement of changes in equity in Illustration 1-6.
2. The statement of financial position and statement of changes in equity are interrelated. Note the ending balances of each component of shareholders' equity—common shares, $10,000, and retained earnings, $9,742—as well as total shareholders' equity of $19,742 at the end of the month reported on the statement of changes in equity in Illustration 1-6. These are reported in the shareholders' equity section of the statement of financial position in Illustration 1-7.
3. The statement of cash flows and the statement of financial position are also interrelated. The statement of cash flows presented in Illustration 1-8 shows how the cash account changed during the period by stating the amount of cash at the beginning of the period, the sources and uses of cash during the month, and the amount of cash at the end of the period, $7,400. The ending amount of cash shown on the statement of cash flows agrees with the amount of cash shown in the assets section of the statement of financial position in Illustration 1-7.

Study these interrelationships carefully. To prepare financial statements, you must understand the sequence in which these amounts are determined and how each statement affects the next. Because each financial statement depends on information contained in another statement, financial statements must be prepared in the following order: (1) income statement; (2) statement of changes in equity; (3) statement of financial position; and (4) statement of cash flows, as illustrated visually below:

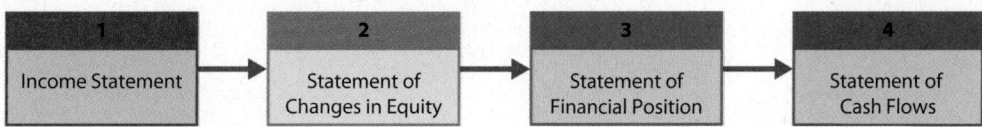

SHOPPERS DRUG MART'S FINANCIAL STATEMENTS

The same relationships that you observed among the financial statements of Sierra Corporation can be seen in the 2012 simplified financial statements of Shoppers Drug Mart Corporation, presented in Illustration 1-9.

Shoppers Drug Mart's actual financial statements are presented in Appendix A at the end of the book. If you compare Shoppers Drug Mart's actual financial statements with those presented in Illustration 1-9, you will notice some similarities and differences that we would like to clarify for you below.

1. *Statement titles:* Shoppers Drug Mart uses different titles in some of its actual financial statements than we have used in this textbook and in Illustration 1-9 on the following page. As explained earlier in this chapter, there are a number of statement titles that mean the same thing: statement of earnings is how Shoppers refers to its income statement, statement of changes in shareholders' equity is how Shoppers refers to its statement of changes in equity, and balance sheet is how Shoppers refers to its statement of financial position.
2. *Consolidated financial statements:* Shoppers Drug Mart presents consolidated financial statements. This means that the financial results include not only Shoppers but also all the companies it owns or controls. Although the financial results of these companies are consolidated (combined) for reporting purposes, individual accounting records and financial statements are also produced for each specific company. In order to accurately assess the

SHOPPERS DRUG MART CORPORATION
Income Statement
Year Ended December 29, 2012
(in thousands)

Revenues		
Sales		$10,781,848
Expenses		
Cost of goods sold	$6,609,229	
Operating and administrative expenses	3,291,698	
Finance expenses	57,595	
Total expenses		9,958,522
Profit before income tax		823,326
Income tax expense		214,845
Profit		$ 608,481

SHOPPERS DRUG MART CORPORATION
Statement of Changes in Equity
Year Ended December 29, 2012
(in thousands)

	Share Capital	Retained Earnings	Accumulated Other Comprehensive Income (Loss)	Other	Total Equity
Balance, January 1	$1,481,720	$2,806,078	$(30,214)	$10,246	$4,267,830
Repurchase of common shares	(55,635)				(55,635)
Profit		608,481			608,481
Dividends		(219,793)			(219,793)
Other comprehensive loss			(4,978)		(4,978)
Other changes to equity	5,230	(278,418)		610	(272,578)
Balance, December 29	$1,431,315	$2,916,348	$(35,192)	$10,856	$4,323,327

SHOPPERS DRUG MART CORPORATION
Statement of Financial Position
December 29, 2012
(in thousands)

Assets

Cash		$ 104,529
Accounts receivable		469,683
Inventory		2,148,484
Property and equipment		1,717,993
Goodwill		2,572,707
Intangible assets		339,972
Other assets		120,353
Total assets		$7,473,721

Liabilities and Shareholders' Equity

Liabilities		
Bank indebtedness	$ 170,927	
Accounts payable and accrued liabilities	1,206,748	
Income taxes payable	17,994	
Dividends payable	54,180	
Long-term debt	696,807	
Other liabilities	1,003,738	
Total liabilities		$3,150,394
Shareholders' equity		
Share capital	$1,431,315	
Retained earnings	2,916,348	
Accumulated other comprehensive loss	(35,192)	
Other equity items	10,856	
Total shareholders' equity		4,323,327
Total liabilities and shareholders' equity		$7,473,721

SHOPPERS DRUG MART CORPORATION
Statement of Cash Flows
Year Ended December 29, 2012
(in thousands)

Operating activities		
Cash receipts from operating activities	$10,805,503	
Cash payments for operating activities	(9,888,687)	
Net cash provided by operating activities		$916,816
Investing activities		
Acquisition of property and equipment	$ (203,535)	
Acquisition or development of intangible assets	(54,385)	
Business acquisitions	(129,454)	
Acquisition of other assets	(7,700)	
Net cash used by investing activities		(395,074)
Financing activities		
Repurchase of common shares	$ (333,747)	
Repayment of debt	(4,797)	
Payment of dividends	(218,732)	
Other	21,497	
Net cash used by financing activities		(535,779)
Net decrease in cash		(14,037)
Cash, January 1		118,566
Cash, December 29		$ 104,529

performance and financial position of each company, it has to be possible to distinguish each company's activities from the transactions of any other company, even if the companies are related. This is another application of the reporting entity concept.

3. *Fiscal year:* Shoppers Drug Mart's fiscal year ends on the Saturday closest to the end of December. Consequently, its year end does not fall on the same date each year. For example, its 2012 year end was December 29, 2012, while its 2011 year end was December 31, 2011.

4. *Comparative statements:* Public corporations are required to present their financial statements for at least two fiscal years. Financial statements that cover more than one period are called comparative statements and assist users in comparing the financial position and performance of one accounting period with that of the prior period(s).

5. *Unit of measure:* The numbers are reported in thousands of dollars on Shoppers Drug Mart's financial statements; that is, the last three zeros (000) are omitted in both Illustration 1-9 and Shoppers Drug Mart's actual financial statements.

6. *Condensed statements:* The statements included in Illustration 1-9 have been condensed and simplified to assist your learning—but they may look complicated to you anyway. Do not be alarmed by this. By the end of the book, you will have a lot of experience in reading and understanding financial statements such as these, and they will no longer look so complicated.

Income Statement

Take a look at the simplified version of Shoppers Drug Mart's income statement presented in Illustration 1-9. While Sierra is a service company, providing services to earn its revenue, Shoppers Drug Mart is a retail company. It sells products to earn its revenue.

For 2012, Shoppers Drug Mart reported sales of $10,781,848 thousand. As was mentioned earlier, Shoppers Drug Mart reports its numbers in thousands of dollars. Thus, Shoppers' total sales revenue is $10,781,848,000 and not $10,781,848. It then subtracts a variety of expenses related to operating the business. These expenses, totalling $9,958,522 thousand, include cost of goods sold, operating and administrative expenses, and finance expenses. Interest expense is commonly known as finance expense, as Shoppers uses in its income statement.

Total expenses are deducted from revenue to determine profit before income tax of $823,326 thousand. After subtracting the income tax expense of $214,845 thousand, the company reports a profit for the year ended December 29, 2012, of $608,481 thousand.

Statement of Changes in Equity

Shoppers Drug Mart presents information next about its shareholders' equity in the simplified statement of changes in equity in Illustration 1-9. This statement shows the changes in Shoppers Drug Mart's share capital and retained earnings. During the year, Shoppers repurchased $55,635 thousand of its own common shares. This, in addition to $5,230 thousand of other changes to its share capital, resulted in a balance at the end of the year of $1,431,315 thousand. Shoppers' retained earnings was increased by profit of $608,481 thousand and decreased by the payment of dividends of $219,793 thousand. This, in addition to $278,418 thousand of other changes to retained earnings, resulted in a balance at the end of the year of $2,916,348 thousand. Note that the profit figure in the retained earnings column is the same as the profit reported on the income statement, as indicated with a ① in Illustration 1-9. Regardless of the order the financial statements are presented in, the income statement must be prepared first, because the profit (or loss) for the period is needed to prepare the statement of changes in equity.

Shoppers Drug Mart's statement of changes in equity also includes a column for accumulated other comprehensive income (loss), as well as other items that affect shareholders' equity. Companies such as Shoppers Drug Mart reporting under IFRS may have complex items that are similar to revenues and expenses but, due to their nature, are not used to determine profit. Rather, they determine **other comprehensive income**. If a company has other comprehensive income (or loss) during the period, it is added to (or deducted from in the case of a loss) a shareholders' equity account called **accumulated other comprehensive income**. Similar to the retained earnings account, which accumulates profit over time, the accumulated other comprehensive income account is also a shareholders' equity account that accumulates other comprehensive income over time.

We will learn more about other comprehensive income and accumulated other comprehensive income in Chapter 11. We will also learn about differences in how changes that affect shareholders' equity, including other comprehensive income, affect public and private corporations in that chapter.

Statement of Financial Position

Shoppers Drug Mart's statement of financial position shown in Illustration 1-9 includes the types of assets mentioned in this chapter: cash, accounts receivable, inventory, property and equipment, goodwill, intangible assets, and other types of assets.

Similarly, its liabilities include bank indebtedness (amounts owed to the bank), accounts payable and accrued liabilities (we will learn about accrued liabilities in Chapter 2), income taxes payable, dividends payable to shareholders, and long-term debt, as well as other types of liabilities.

Shopper Drug Mart's statement of financial position shows that total assets equal $7,473,721 thousand and total liabilities equal $3,150,394 thousand at December 29, 2012. The ending balances of Shoppers Drug Mart's share capital, retained earnings, accumulated other comprehensive income, and other items taken from the statement of changes in equity agree to (are equal to) the same items shown in the shareholders' equity section of the statement of financial position. Follow the arrow marked with a ② in Illustration 1-9 to confirm that the total shareholders' equity of $4,323,327 thousand reported in the statement of changes in equity as at December 29, 2012, agrees to the total shareholders' equity presented in the statement of financial position at the same date. Note also that total liabilities and total shareholders' equity equal total assets of $7,473,721.

You can see that Shoppers Drug Mart relies more on equity financing than debt. It has 37% more total shareholders' equity than it has total liabilities. As you learn more about financial statements, we will discuss how to interpret the relationships and changes in financial statement items.

Statement of Cash Flows

Shoppers Drug Mart's cash decreased by $14,037 thousand in 2012. The reasons for the increase in cash can be determined by examining the statement of cash flows in Illustration 1-9.

As Shoppers Drug Mart was renovating its existing stores and adding more of them, it consequently spent considerable cash—$395,074 thousand—on investing activities. For example, it spent $203,535 thousand on new property and equipment and $129,454 thousand for business acquisitions (of new stores). Note that the cash provided by operating activities—$916,816 thousand—was enough to finance all of Shoppers' investing activities. The remainder was used to repurchase common shares and repay the bank and other lenders. In addition, Shoppers paid $218,732 thousand of dividends to its shareholders. The net result of the sources and uses of cash during the year was a decrease in cash of $14,037 thousand.

This increase in cash is added to the opening balance of $118,566 thousand to result in an ending cash balance of $104,529 thousand. Trace the ending balance of cash reported in the statement of cash flows to the ending balance reported in the statement of financial position, as indicated by the arrow marked with a ③ in Illustration 1-9.

ELEMENTS OF AN ANNUAL REPORT

Public corporations must produce an **annual report** each year. The annual report is a document that includes useful nonfinancial information about the company, as well as financial information. Nonfinancial information may include the company's mission, goals and objectives, products, and people.

Financial information normally includes a management discussion and analysis (often abbreviated as MD&A), a statement of management responsibility for the financial statements, an auditors' report, the financial statements introduced in this chapter that are reported for at least two years, explanatory notes to the financial statements, and a historical summary of key financial ratios and indicators. No analysis of a company's financial situation and prospects is complete without a review of each of these items.

BEFORE YOU GO ON...

▶ Do It! Financial Statements

CSU Corporation began operations on January 1, 2015. The following account information is available for CSU Corporation on December 31, 2015: service revenue $22,200, accounts receivable $4,000, accounts payable $2,000, rent expense $9,000, bank loan payable $5,000, common shares $10,000, equipment $16,000, insurance expense $1,000, supplies $1,800, interest expense $200, cash $4,800, income tax expense $1,800, and dividends $600. Using this information, prepare an income statement, statement of changes in equity, statement of financial position, and statement of cash flows for the year.

For the operating activities section of the statement of cash flows, cash receipts from operating activities were $18,200 and cash payments for operating activities were $11,800. For the investing activities section, cash of $16,000 was paid for the purchase of the equipment. For the financing activities section, cash of $5,000 was received from the bank loan and $10,000 from the issue of common shares. Cash of $600 was paid for dividends.

Action Plan

- Classify each account into the following categories: revenues, expenses, dividends, assets, liabilities, and shareholders' equity.
- Report revenues and expenses for the period in the income statement.
- Start with opening balances and show the amounts and causes of the changes in share capital and retained earnings for the period to determine ending balances in the statement of changes in equity.
- Present assets and claims to those assets (liabilities and shareholders' equity) at a specific point in time in the statement of financial position.
- Show the changes in cash for the period, classified as operating, investing, or financing activities in the statement of cash flows.
- Remember that the income statement, statement of changes in equity, and statement of cash flows cover a period of time, while the statement of financial position is reported at a specific point in time.

Solution

See next page.

> You will find a section called **Comparing IFRS and ASPE** at the end of each chapter to help you understand the differences in reporting for companies using IFRS, compared with those using ASPE.

comparing
IFRS and ASPE

Key Differences	International Financial Reporting Standards (IFRS)	Accounting Standards for Private Enterprises (ASPE)
Accounting standards	Publicly traded corporations must use IFRS; private corporations can choose to use IFRS or ASPE.	Private corporations can choose to use IFRS or ASPE. Once the choice is made, it must be applied consistently. Proprietorships and partnerships generally follow ASPE.
Terminology	The balance sheet is more commonly known as the statement of financial position and net income as profit under IFRS.	The statement of financial position is more commonly known as the balance sheet and profit as net income under ASPE.
Statement of changes in equity vs. statement of retained earnings	A statement of changes in equity must be presented that shows the changes in all components of shareholders' equity (for example, share capital and retained earnings).	A statement of retained earnings is presented that shows the change in only one component—retained earnings—of shareholders' equity.

the navigator

Helpful Hint
The arrows in this illustration show the relationships among the four financial statements.

Solution

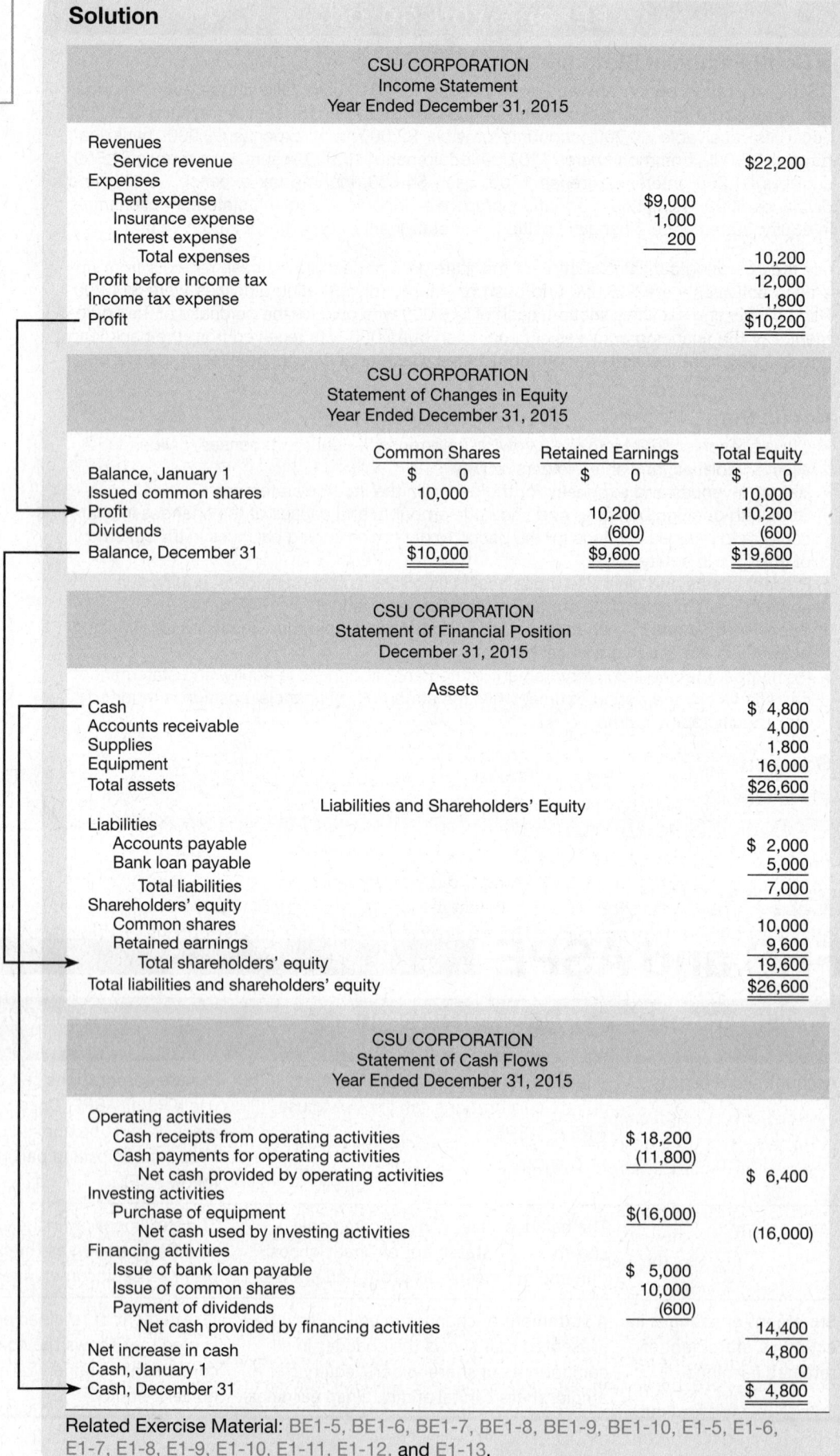

CSU CORPORATION
Income Statement
Year Ended December 31, 2015

Revenues		
Service revenue		$22,200
Expenses		
Rent expense	$9,000	
Insurance expense	1,000	
Interest expense	200	
Total expenses		10,200
Profit before income tax		12,000
Income tax expense		1,800
Profit		$10,200

CSU CORPORATION
Statement of Changes in Equity
Year Ended December 31, 2015

	Common Shares	Retained Earnings	Total Equity
Balance, January 1	$ 0	$ 0	$ 0
Issued common shares	10,000		10,000
Profit		10,200	10,200
Dividends		(600)	(600)
Balance, December 31	$10,000	$9,600	$19,600

CSU CORPORATION
Statement of Financial Position
December 31, 2015

Assets	
Cash	$ 4,800
Accounts receivable	4,000
Supplies	1,800
Equipment	16,000
Total assets	$26,600
Liabilities and Shareholders' Equity	
Liabilities	
Accounts payable	$ 2,000
Bank loan payable	5,000
Total liabilities	7,000
Shareholders' equity	
Common shares	10,000
Retained earnings	9,600
Total shareholders' equity	19,600
Total liabilities and shareholders' equity	$26,600

CSU CORPORATION
Statement of Cash Flows
Year Ended December 31, 2015

Operating activities		
Cash receipts from operating activities	$ 18,200	
Cash payments for operating activities	(11,800)	
Net cash provided by operating activities		$ 6,400
Investing activities		
Purchase of equipment	$(16,000)	
Net cash used by investing activities		(16,000)
Financing activities		
Issue of bank loan payable	$ 5,000	
Issue of common shares	10,000	
Payment of dividends	(600)	
Net cash provided by financing activities		14,400
Net increase in cash		4,800
Cash, January 1		0
Cash, December 31		$ 4,800

Related Exercise Material: BE1-5, BE1-6, BE1-7, BE1-8, BE1-9, BE1-10, E1-5, E1-6, E1-7, E1-8, E1-9, E1-10, E1-11, E1-12, **and** E1-13.

All About You ▶ Your Personal Annual Report

You probably have already prepared a resumé and used it to find a job. In some ways, your resumé is like a company's annual report. Its purpose is to enable others to evaluate your past, in an effort to predict your future.

A resumé is your opportunity to create a positive first impression. It is important that it be impressive, but it should also be accurate. In order to increase their job prospects, some people are tempted to inflate their resumés by overstating the importance of some past accomplishments or positions.

Consider the skills that you have acquired from part-time or vacation employment or volunteering. These could include dealing with difficult people, improving your interpersonal skills, meeting work-related deadlines and responsibilities, and mastering time management skills. Experts suggest that, while you are at school, you should use the time to build up your "human capital"; that is, to develop the job skills that will enable you to have a rewarding career.

Surveys of human resource professionals have found that an online profile can play an important part in the evaluation of your skills and experience. This applies to professional networks such as LinkedIn as well as social network sites, such as Facebook or Twitter. Your online profile should not conflict with your resumé and it should give a professional view of you.

> The **All About You** feature helps you link real-life situations to the accounting concepts in each chapter. An **All About You Activity** is included in the Broadening Your Perspective section of the end-of-chapter material.

Some Facts

- Office Team, a leading staffing firm, made the following suggestions to make the best use of network profiles:
  - Highlight your key skills and experience.
  - Limit access to pictures and any other material that could be embarrassing.
  - Keep your profile up to date and complete.
  - Include a personal photo; it can be casual, but must look professional.
- BackCheck, a Vancouver company that provides pre-employment screening for employers, has checked over 3 million resumés and found that one-quarter (25%) appeared to contain omissions, exaggerations, or falsehoods. Human resource professionals state that the major areas in which resumés are embellished or exaggerated are education, experience, responsibilities, work dates, and salaries.
- Do not be tempted to lie on your resumé. Don't change dates, add false information, or suggest that you have graduated from school, when you have not. Potential employers can check with your university or college to confirm your qualifications and they can check with your former employers about your previous employment history. Increasingly, too, your profile on the Internet can be used to verify information on your resumé.[2]

What Do You Think?

You and your friend are in your last year of university. You are both interviewing for positions at an accounting firm. A number of years ago, your friend was convicted of driving without a licence and has a police record. He has neglected to include this information on his application and has asked you not to mention or disclose this information. You know that many of the accounting firms do a background check before hiring prospective employees. You would really like to work for this accounting firm. Should you tell on your friend?

YES—The accounting firm is going to be performing a background check, which may include a police record check, and it is important that they know about the situation in advance. It would be best if you could somehow convince your friend to be forthright and disclose this information himself. If your friend were honest, the accounting firm is much more likely to consider your friend's (and your) application for employment. This would eliminate your need to have to disclose this information.

NO—It is not your place to disclose personal information about other applicants to the accounting firm unless you are asked specifically by the firm whether you know anything of relevance regarding his application. It is likely that as a condition of employment, the accounting firm will perform a background check, which may include a police record check, and therefore it would find out this information without your disclosure. It would be best, however, if you could convince your friend to personally disclose this information himself.

Summary of Study Objectives

1. **Identify the uses and users of accounting.** The purpose of accounting is to provide useful information for decision-making. There are two types of groups who use accounting information: internal users and external users. Internal users work for the business and need accounting information to plan, organize, and run operations. The primary external users are investors and lenders and other creditors. Investors (existing and potential shareholders) use accounting information to help decide whether to buy, hold, or sell shares. Lenders (such as bankers) and other creditors (such as suppliers) use accounting information to evaluate the risk of loaning money or granting credit to a business.

2. **Describe the primary forms of business organization.** There are three types of business organizations: proprietorships, partnerships, and corporations. A proprietorship is a business owned by one person. A partnership is a business owned by two or more people. A corporation is a separate legal entity whose shares provide evidence of ownership. Corporations can be public, which means their shares are available to the general public, or private, which means their shares are closely held.

    Generally accepted accounting principles are a common set of guidelines, which can differ depending on the form of business organization, that are used to record and report economic events. Public corporations follow International

Financial Reporting Standards (IFRS) and private corporations have the choice of using IFRS or Accounting Standards for Private Enterprises (ASPE). Proprietorships and partnerships generally use ASPE.

3. **Explain the three main types of business activity.** Financing activities involve collecting the necessary funds (through debt or equity) to support the business. Investing activities involve acquiring the resources (such as property, plant, and equipment) that are needed to run the business. Operating activities involve putting the resources of the business into action to generate a profit.

4. **Describe the purpose and content of each of the financial statements.** The income statement presents the revenues and expenses of a company for a specific period of time. The statement of changes in equity summarizes the changes in shareholders' equity that have occurred for a specific period of time. The statement of financial position reports the assets, liabilities, and shareholders' equity of a business at a specific date. The statement of cash flows summarizes information about the cash inflows (receipts) and outflows (payments) for a specific period of time. Notes to the financial statements add explanatory detail where required. The financial statements are included in an annual report, along with nonfinancial and other financial information.

Glossary

Accounting The process of identifying, recording, and communicating the economic events of a business to interested users of the information. (p. 4)

Accounting equation The equation that states that Assets = Liabilities + Shareholders' Equity. (p. 17)

Assets The resources owned or controlled by a business that provide future economic benefits. (p. 11)

Corporation A business organized as a separate legal entity having ownership divided into transferable shares held by shareholders. (p. 7)

Deficit A negative balance in retained earnings as a result of accumulated losses from the prior and current periods exceeding the profits. (p. 16)

Dividends The distribution of retained earnings from a corporation to its shareholders, often in the form of cash. (p. 11)

Expenses The decrease in economic benefits that result from the costs of assets consumed or services used in ongoing operations to generate revenue. (p. 12)

Financing activities Activities that include (1) borrowing (or repaying) cash to lenders, and (2) issuing (or reacquiring) shares or paying dividends to investors. (p. 13)

Fiscal year An accounting period that is one year long. (p. 14)

Generally accepted accounting principles (GAAP) A general guide, having substantial authoritative support, that describes how economic events should be recorded and reported for financial reporting purposes. (p. 9)

Income statement (also known as statement of earnings or statement of profit and loss) A financial statement that presents the revenues and expenses and resulting profit or loss of a company for a specific period of time. (p. 15)

Investing activities Activities that include purchasing and disposing of long-lived assets such as property, plant, and equipment and long-term investments. (p. 13)

Liabilities The debts and obligations of a business. Liabilities are claims of lenders and other creditors on the assets of a business. (p. 10)

Loss (also known as net loss) The amount by which expenses are more than revenues. The opposite of profit. (p. 12)

Operating activities Activities that result from day-to-day operations and include revenues and expenses and related accounts such as receivables, supplies, inventory, and payables. (p. 13)

Partnership A business owned by more than one person. (p. 7)

Profit (also known as net income or net earnings) The amount by which revenues are more than expenses. (p. 12)

Proprietorship   A business owned by one person. (p. 7)

Reporting entity concept   The concept that economic activity that can be identified with a particular company must be kept separate and distinct from the activities of the owner(s) and of all other economic entities. (p. 7)

Retained earnings   The amount of accumulated profit (less losses, if any), from the prior and current periods, that has been kept in the corporation for future use and not distributed to shareholders as dividends. (p. 16)

Revenue   (also known as income) The increase in economic benefits that result from the operating activities of a business, such as the sale of a product or provision of a service. (p. 11)

Share capital   Shares representing the ownership interest in a corporation. If only one class of shares exists, it is known as common shares. (p. 11)

Shareholders' equity   The shareholders' claim on total assets, represented by the investments of the shareholders (share capital) and undistributed earnings (retained earnings) generated by the company. (p. 16)

Statement of cash flows   A financial statement that provides information about the cash inflows (receipts) and cash outflows (payments) for a specific period of time. (p. 19)

Statement of changes in equity   A financial statement that summarizes the changes in total shareholders' equity, as well as each component of shareholders' equity, for a specific period of time. (p. 16)

Statement of financial position   (also known as balance sheet) A financial statement that reports the assets, liabilities, and shareholders' equity at a specific date. (p. 17)

DECISION TOOLKIT

Decision Checkpoints	Info Needed for Decision	Tools to Use for Decision	How to Evaluate Results
Are the company's operations profitable?	Income statement	The income statement indicates the success or failure of the company's operating activities by reporting its revenues and expenses.	If the company's revenues exceed its expenses, it will report a profit; otherwise it will report a loss.
Is the company expanding or contracting its share capital?	Statement of changes in equity	Did the company issue or repurchase shares?	If share capital is increasing, the company may have expansion plans.
What is the company's policy on dividends and growth?	Statement of changes in equity	How much did the company pay out in dividends to shareholders?	A company looking for rapid growth will pay no, or a low, dividend.
Does the company rely mainly on debt or on equity to finance its assets?	Statement of financial position	The statement of financial position reports the company's resources and claims to those resources. There are two types of claims: liabilities and shareholders' equity.	Compare the amount of liabilities as a percentage of total assets with the amount of shareholders' equity as a percentage of total assets to determine whether the company relies more on lenders and other creditors or on shareholders for its financing.
Does the company generate enough cash from operating activities to fund its investing activities?	Statement of cash flows	The statement of cash flows shows the amount of cash provided or used by operating activities, investing activities, and financing activities.	Compare the amount of cash provided by operating activities with the amount of cash used by investing activities. Any deficiency in cash from operating activities must be made up with cash provided by financing activities.

> **Using the Decision Toolkit** cases ask you to use information from financial statements to make financial decisions. Before you study the solution, we encourage you to think about how the questions related to the decision would be answered.

USING THE DECISION TOOLKIT

The Jean Coutu Group (PJC) Inc. is the second-largest pharmacy chain in Canada and Shoppers Drug Mart's number one competitor. Assume that you are reviewing the financial information of each company to determine if you should invest in Shoppers Drug Mart or Jean Coutu.

Instructions

(a) Which financial statements should you review before you invest?

(b) What should each of these financial statements tell you? Which financial statement will you likely be most interested in?

(c) Jean Coutu's fiscal year end is the Saturday closest to the end of February. Shoppers Drug Mart's fiscal year end is the Saturday closest to the end of December. Will it be possible to compare these companies' financial statements since they have different fiscal year ends?

(d) Simplified financial statements for Jean Coutu follow. More detailed financial statements are included in Appendix B at the end of this textbook. What broad comparisons can you make between Shoppers Drug Mart and Jean Coutu by reviewing their financial statements?

THE JEAN COUTU GROUP (PJC) INC.
Income Statement
Year Ended March 2, 2013
(in millions)

	2013	2012
Revenues		
Sales	$2,468.0	$2,463.2
Other revenues	619.5	291.9
Total revenues	3,087.5	2,755.1
Expenses		
Cost of goods sold	2,169.0	2,184.3
General and operating expenses	247.5	237.6
Depreciation and amortization expense	31.7	30.4
Finance expenses	2.0	1.0
Total expenses	2,450.2	2,453.3
Profit before income tax	637.3	301.8
Income tax expense	78.9	71.8
Profit	$ 558.4	$ 230.0

THE JEAN COUTU GROUP (PJC) INC.
Statement of Changes in Equity
Year Ended March 2, 2013
(in millions)

	Share Capital	Retained Earnings	Accumulated Other Comprehensive Income	Other	Total Equity
Balance, beginning of year	$559.7	$ 88.6	$ 0	$ 0.9	$ 649.2
Issued common shares	6.5			(1.0)	5.5
Repurchase of common shares	(29.1)	(52.6)		(1.2)	(82.9)
Profit		558.4		0.8	559.2
Dividends		(60.8)			(60.8)
Other comprehensive income		(0.2)	40.8		40.6
Balance, end of year	$537.1	$533.4	$40.8	$ (0.5)	$1,110.8

THE JEAN COUTU GROUP (PJC) INC.
Statement of Financial Position
March 2, 2013
(in millions)

Assets

Trade and other receivables	$ 199.6	$ 206.5
Inventories	190.1	166.2
Property and equipment	359.5	361.1
Goodwill	36.0	36.0
Intangible assets	195.0	186.9
Other assets	412.5	116.1
Total assets	$1,392.7	$1,072.8

Liabilities and Shareholders' Equity

Liabilities		
Bank overdraft	$ 21.6	$ 5.0
Trade and other payables	225.2	230.6
Income taxes payable	18.5	23.2
Long-term liabilities	15.8	163.8
Other liabilities	0.8	1.0
Total liabilities	281.9	423.6
Shareholders' equity		
Share capital	537.1	559.7
Retained earnings	533.4	88.6
Accumulated other comprehensive income	40.8	
Other equity items	(0.5)	0.9
Total shareholders' equity	1,110.8	649.2
Total liabilities and shareholders' equity	$1,392.7	$1,072.8

THE JEAN COUTU GROUP (PJC) INC.
Statement of Cash Flows
Year Ended March 2, 2013
(in millions)

Operating activities		
Cash receipts from operating activities	$2,474.9	$2,463.2
Cash payments for operating activities	(2,251.1)	(2,218.2)
Net cash provided by operating activities	223.8	245.0
Investing activities		
Acquisition of property and equipment	(20.9)	(24.9)
Acquisition of intangible assets	(16.1)	(22.7)
Proceeds from disposal of Rite Aid	82.8	22.0
Sale of other assets	20.2	8.7
Net cash provided (used) by investing activities	66.0	(16.9)
Financing activities		
Repurchase of common shares	(81.0)	(127.3)
Repayment of debt	(149.8)	(34.9)
Payment of dividends	(60.8)	(53.8)
Other	(14.8)	(0.6)
Net cash used by financing activities	(306.4)	(216.6)
Net increase (decrease) in cash	(16.6)	11.5
Bank overdraft, beginning of year	(5.0)	(16.5)
Bank overdraft, end of year	$ (21.6)	$ (5.0)

Solution

(a) Before you invest, you should investigate the income statement, statement of changes in equity, statement of financial position, and statement of cash flows for each company. In addition, the notes to the financial statements should be carefully reviewed.

(b) The income statement shows a company's revenues and expenses and overall profitability for the current period. The statement of changes in equity shows any changes in share capital as well as the impact that the current period's profit and dividends have on the company's retained earnings. The statement of financial position reveals the company's financial position and the relationship between assets, liabilities, and shareholders' equity. Finally, the statement of cash flows reveals where the company is getting and spending its cash. This is especially important for a company that wants to grow.

Investors would probably be most interested in the income statement because it shows past performance and this can give an indication of future performance.

(c) Shoppers Drug Mart's fiscal year will overlap Jean Coutu's for 10 months (March through December). If there have been no substantial changes to the economy that would affect their business during the two-month period that Jean Coutu's financial results cover but Shoppers Drug Mart's do not (or vice versa), it really does not matter when each company's fiscal year ends. It is more important that we compare what each company was able to achieve within an equivalent period of time—whether it be one year, six months, or one quarter.

If, however, a major change does occur in the intervening period (the period where the statements do not overlap), such a change would likely reduce the usefulness of a comparison of the two companies' financial statements.

(d) Many interesting comparisons can be made between the two companies. Jean Coutu is much smaller, less than one-fifth of the asset size of Shoppers Drug Mart. For example, Jean Coutu has total assets of $1,392.7 million versus $7,473.7 million for Shoppers Drug Mart. Jean Coutu also has lower revenue—total revenues of $3,087.5 million versus $10,781.8 million for Shoppers Drug Mart. Jean Coutu reported profit for its current fiscal year of $558.4 million, compared with Shoppers Drug Mart's profit of $608.5 million. Despite Jean Coutu being less than one-fifth the size of Shoppers Drug Mart, it produced nearly the same (92%) profit so it is managing its revenues and expenses wisely.

The two companies' statements of cash flows show Jean Coutu reporting a bank overdraft (bank-indebtedness) and Shoppers Drug Mart a positive cash balance at the end of the current fiscal year.

While these comparisons are useful, these basic measures are not enough to determine whether one company will be a better investment than the other. In later chapters, you will acquire more tools to help you compare the relative profitability and financial health of these, and other, companies.

the navigator

Comprehensive Do It!

The **Comprehensive Do It!** is a final review before you begin your homework. **Action Plans** give you tips about how to approach the problem, and the **Solution** provided demonstrates both the form and content of complete answers.

Jeff Andringa, a former university hockey player, started Ice Camp Ltd., a hockey camp for children from ages 6 to 16. Eventually he would like to expand and open hockey camps across the country. Jeff has asked you to help him prepare financial statements at the end of his first year of operations. He tells you the following facts about his business activities.

In order to get the business off the ground, he decided to incorporate and follow IFRS. He sold common shares to himself on January 3, 2015, raising $5,000 through the sale of 500 of these shares. In addition, the company borrowed $10,000 from a local bank. A used bus for transporting kids was purchased for $12,000 cash. Hockey nets and other miscellaneous equipment were purchased with $1,500 cash. The company earned camp tuition of $100,000 during the year but has collected only $90,000 of this amount so far. Thus, at the end of the year it was still owed $10,000. The company rents time at a local rink. Total ice rental costs during the year were $14,000, insurance was $6,000, salaries were $20,000, and administrative expenses totalled $7,000—all of which were paid in cash. The company incurred $800 in interest expense on the bank loan, which it still owed at the end of the year. The company also owes $10,440 in income tax. The company paid Jeff dividends of $35,000 rather than salary during the year.

The balance in the corporate bank account at December 31, 2015, was $9,500 ($5,000 + $10,000 − $12,000 − $1,500 + $90,000 − $14,000 − $6,000 − $20,000 − $7,000 − $35,000).

Instructions

Prepare an income statement, statement of changes in equity, and statement of financial position for the year.

Action Plan
- On the income statement, show revenues and expenses for a period of time.
- On the statement of changes in equity, show the changes in share capital and retained earnings for a period of time.
- On the statement of financial position, report assets, liabilities, and shareholders' equity at a specific date.

Solution to Comprehensive Do It!

ICE CAMP LTD.
Income Statement
Year Ended December 31, 2015

Revenues		
Camp tuition revenue		$100,000
Expenses		
Salaries expense	$20,000	
Ice rental expense	14,000	
Administrative expense	7,000	
Insurance expense	6,000	
Interest expense	800	
Total expenses		47,800
Profit before income tax		52,200
Income tax expense		10,440
Profit		$ 41,760

ICE CAMP LTD.
Statement of Changes in Equity
Year Ended December 31, 2015

	Common Shares	Retained Earnings	Total Equity
Balance, January 1	$ 0	$ 0	$ 0
Issued common shares	5,000		5,000
Profit		41,760	41,760
Dividends		(35,000)	(35,000)
Balance, December 31	$5,000	$ 6,760	$11,760

ICE CAMP LTD.
Statement of Financial Position
December 31, 2015

Assets	
Cash	$ 9,500
Accounts receivable	10,000
Bus	12,000
Equipment	1,500
Total assets	$33,000

Liabilities and Shareholders' Equity	
Liabilities	
Interest payable	$ 800
Income tax payable	10,440
Bank loan payable	10,000
Total liabilities	21,240
Shareholders' equity	
Common shares	5,000
Retained earnings	6,760
Total shareholders' equity	11,760
Total liabilities and shareholders' equity	$33,000

the navigator

WileyPLUS   Self-Test Questions, Brief Exercises, Exercises, Problems: Set A, and many more components are available for practice in *WileyPLUS*.

Self-Test Questions

Answers are at the end of the chapter.

Quiz Yourself

(SO 1) 1. Which statement about users of accounting information is *incorrect*?
(a) Management is an internal user.
(b) Investors are internal users.
(c) Lenders and other creditors are external users.
(d) The Canada Revenue Agency is an external user.

(SO 1) 2. Who are the primary users of accounting information?
(a) Labour unions
(b) Customers
(c) Employees
(d) Investors, lenders, and other creditors

(SO 2) 3. In which of the following area(s) do corporations have an advantage over partnerships and proprietorships?
(a) Raising capital
(b) Unlimited legal life
(c) Limited liability
(d) All of the above

(SO 2) 4. Which of the following statements is correct in distinguishing between a private corporation and a public corporation?
(a) Only public corporations issue shares; private corporations do not.
(b) Private corporations issue shares but do not make them available to the general public.
(c) Both private and public corporations must make their financial statements available to the general public.
(d) Both public and private corporations must use IFRS for financial reporting purposes.

(SO 3) 5. Which is *not* one of the three primary business activities?
(a) Financing
(b) Planning
(c) Operating
(d) Investing

(SO 3) 6. Which of the following is *not* an example of a financing activity?
(a) Borrowing money from a bank
(b) Repaying money to a bank

(c) Selling goods on credit
(d) Paying dividends

(SO 3) 7. Operating activities include all of the following *except*:
(a) Purchasing goods for resale
(b) Performing services
(c) Paying employee salaries
(d) Purchasing a cash register

(SO 4) 8. Which financial statement reports assets, liabilities, and shareholders' equity?
(a) Income statement
(b) Statement of changes in equity
(c) Statement of financial position
(d) Statement of cash flows

(SO 4) 9. Financial statements must be prepared in the following order:
(a) (1) Income statement, (2) statement of cash flows, (3) statement of changes in equity, and (4) statement of financial position.
(b) (1) Statement of changes in equity, (2) income statement, (3) statement of cash flows, and (4) statement of financial position.
(c) (1) Statement of financial position, (2) income statement, (3) statement of changes in equity, and (4) statement of cash flows.
(d) (1) Income statement, (2) statement of changes in equity, (3) statement of financial position, and (4) statement of cash flows.

(SO 4) 10. As at December 31, Stoneland Corporation has assets of $35,000 and shareholders' equity of $15,000. What are the liabilities for Stoneland Corporation as at December 31?
(a) $15,000
(b) $20,000
(c) $35,000
(d) $50,000

the navigator

Questions

The financial results of real companies are included in the end-of-chapter material. These company names are shown in **red**.

(SO 1) 1. What is accounting?

(SO 1) 2. Distinguish between internal and external users of accounting information.

(SO 1) 3. What kinds of questions might internal users of accounting information want answered? External users?

(SO 1) 4. Why is ethics as important to accountants as it is to the decision makers who rely on financial information?

(SO 2) 5. Identify the advantages and disadvantages of each of the following forms of business organization: (a) proprietorship, (b) partnership, (c) private corporation, and (d) public corporation.

(SO 2) 6. Identify the similarities and differences between a public corporation and a private corporation.

(SO 2) 7. (a) Identify the financial reporting standards a public and a private corporation may use. (b) Why do you think they differ?

(SO 2) 8. Explain how the reporting entity concept applies to business organizations.

(SO 3) 9. Explain the following terms and give an example of each: (a) asset, (b) liability, (c) shareholders' equity, (d) revenues, and (e) expenses.

(SO 3) 10. Distinguish between operating, investing, and financing activities.

(SO 3) 11. Give two examples of each kind of business activity: (a) operating, (b) investing, and (c) financing.

(SO 3) 12. Name two local companies that provide services and generate service revenue. Name two local companies that sell products and generate sales revenue.

(SO 4) 13. What is a fiscal year end? Why does a company's fiscal year not always end on December 31?

(SO 4) 14. André is puzzled reading **Air Canada**'s financial statements. He notices that the numbers have all been rounded to the nearest million. He thought financial statements were supposed to be accurate and wonders what happened to the rest of the money. Respond to André's concern.

(SO 4) 15. The basic accounting equation is Assets = Liabilities + Shareholders' Equity. Replacing words with dollar amounts, what is **Shoppers Drug Mart**'s accounting equation at December 29, 2012? Shoppers' simplified financial statements can be found in Illustration 1-9 within this chapter.

(SO 4) 16. What are the primary components explained in a statement of changes in equity? What types of items generally increase each component? What types of items generally decrease each component?

(SO 4) 17. (a) What is the purpose of the statement of cash flows? (b) What are the three main categories of activities included in the statement?

(SO 4) 18. Why is a statement of financial position prepared as at a specific point in time, while the other financial statements cover a period of time?

(SO 4) 19. How are each of the following pairs of financial statements related?
(a) Income statement and statement of changes in equity
(b) Statement of changes in equity and statement of financial position
(c) Statement of financial position and statement of cash flows

(SO 4) 20. Identify the four financial statements used by corporations using (a) IFRS and (b) ASPE.

Brief Exercises

BE1–1 The following list presents different types of evaluations made by various users of accounting information:

Identify users of accounting information.
(SO 1)

1. Determining if the company respected income tax regulations
2. Determining if the company pays reasonable salaries
3. Determining if the company can pay for purchases made on account
4. Determining if a marketing proposal will be cost-effective
5. Determining if the company's profit will result in a share price increase
6. Determining if the company should use debt or equity financing

(a) Beside each user of accounting information listed in the left-hand column of the table that follows, write the number of the evaluation above (1 to 6) that the user would most likely make.

(b) Indicate if the user is internal or external. The first item has been done for you as an example.

	(a) Type of Evaluation	(b) Type of User
Investor	5	External
Marketing manager		
Creditor		
Chief financial officer		
Canada Revenue Agency		
Labour union		

Identify forms of business organization.

(SO 2)

BE1–2 Match each of the following forms of business organization—(1) proprietorship, (2) partnership, (3) public corporation, or (4) private corporation—with the set of characteristics that best describes it.

(a) _____ Simple to set up; founder retains control

(b) _____ Separate legal entity; shares closely held

(c) _____ Easier to transfer ownership and raise funds; no personal liability

(d) _____ Shared control; increased skills and resources

(e) _____ Issues shares; can choose to follow IFRS or ASPE accounting standards

Classify items by activity.

(SO 3)

BE1–3 Classify each item by type of business activity—operating (O), investing (I), or financing (F).

(a) _____ Cash received from customers

(b) _____ Dividends paid to shareholders

(c) _____ Common shares issued to investors

(d) _____ Money borrowed from a bank

(e) _____ Purchase of an office building

(f) _____ Salaries paid

Identify business activity and effect on cash.

(SO 3)

BE1–4 For each of the following items, indicate (a) the type of business activity—operating (O), investing (I), or financing (F)—and (b) whether it increased (+), decreased (–), or had no effect (NE) on cash. The first one has been done for you as an example.

	(a) Type of Activity	(b) Cash Effect
1. Sold goods on account.	O	NE
2. Borrowed money from a bank.		
3. Purchased inventory for cash.		
4. Provided a service for cash.		
5. Paid salaries in cash.		
6. Purchased a delivery truck for cash.		

Use accounting equation.

(SO 4)

BE1–5 Use the accounting equation to answer these independent questions:

(a) The shareholders' equity of Sansom Corporation is $120,000. Its total liabilities are $55,000. What is the amount of Sansom's total assets?

(b) The liabilities of Houle Corporation are $170,000. Houle's share capital is $100,000 and its retained earnings are $90,000. What is the amount of Houle's total assets?

(c) The total assets of Pitre Limited are $150,000. Its share capital is $50,000 and its retained earnings are $25,000. What is the amount of its total liabilities?

(d) The total assets of Budovitch Inc. are $500,000 and its liabilities are equal to half its total assets. What is the amount of Budovitch's shareholders' equity?

Use accounting equation.

(SO 4)

BE1–6 At the beginning of the year, Lam Ltd. had total assets of $800,000 and total liabilities of $500,000. Use this information to answer each of the following independent questions.

(a) If Lam's total assets increased by $150,000 during the year and total liabilities decreased by $80,000, what is the amount of shareholders' equity at the end of the year?

(b) During the year, Lam's total liabilities decreased by $50,000. The company reported a profit of $50,000, sold additional shares for $75,000, and paid no dividends during the year. What is the amount of total assets at the end of the year?

(c) If Lam's total assets decreased by $80,000 during the year and shareholders' equity increased by $110,000, what is the amount of total liabilities at the end of the year?

Identify financial statement.

(SO 4)

BE1–7 Indicate which statement—income statement (IS), statement of financial position (SFP), statement of changes in equity (SCE), or statement of cash flows (SCF)—you would examine to find each of the following items:

(a) _____ Sales revenue

(b) _____ Supplies

(c) _____ Dividends

(d) _____ Cash provided by operating activities

(e) _____ Total liabilities

(f) _____ Cash used for financing activities

(g) _____ Salaries expense

(h) _____ Common shares issued during the year

Identify assets, liabilities, and shareholders' equity.

(SO 4)

BE1–8 Indicate whether each of these items is an asset (A), a liability (L), or shareholders' equity (SE):

(a) _____ Accounts receivable

(b) _____ Salaries payable

(c) _____ Equipment
(d) _____ Office supplies
(e) _____ Common shares
(f) _____ Bank loan payable
(g) _____ Retained earnings
(h) _____ Cash

BE1-9 Determine whether each transaction would increase (+), decrease (−), or have no effect (NE) on each the following components found in the statement of changes in equity: share capital, retained earnings, and total shareholders' equity. The first one has been done for you as an example.

Determine effect of transactions on shareholders' equity.
(SO 4)

	Share Capital	Retained Earnings	Total Shareholders' Equity
(a) Profit	NE	+	+
(b) Issue of common shares			
(c) Dividends paid to shareholders			
(d) Cash			
(e) Loss			
(f) Issue of long-term debt			

BE1-10 Go-Ahead Limited began the year with common shares of $100,000 and retained earnings of $350,000. During the year, it issued an additional $25,000 of common shares, reported a profit of $75,000, and paid dividends of $5,000.
(a) Calculate the ending balances of (1) common shares, (2) retained earnings, and (3) total shareholders' equity.
(b) Explain how your answer would change if the company had reported a loss of $75,000 rather than a profit.

Calculate ending equity balances.
(SO 4)

Exercises

E1-1 **Facebook, Inc.** is a public corporation and has been one of the world's most active social networking sites. Its revenue is generated primarily from advertising.

Identify users of accounting information.
(SO 1)

Instructions
(a) Identify two internal users of Facebook's accounting information. Write a question that each user might try to answer by using accounting information.
(b) Identify two external users of Facebook's accounting information. Write a question that each user might try to answer by using accounting information.

E1-2 Consider the following statements.

Identify forms of business organization.
(SO 2)

	Proprietorship	Partnership	Public Corporation	Private Corporation
1. No personal liability	F	F	T	T
2. Owner(s) pay(s) personal income tax on company profits				
3. Generally easiest form of organization to raise capital				
4. Ownership indicated by shares				
5. Required to issue quarterly financial statements				
6. Owned by one person				
7. Limited life				
8. Usually easiest form of organization to set up				
9. Required to use IFRS as its accounting standards				
10. Shares are closely held				

Instructions
Indicate if each of the statements listed in the left-hand column of the table above is normally true (T) or false (F) for each of the following types of business organization: proprietorship, partnership, public corporation, and private corporation. The first one has been done for you as an example.

Classify business
activities.
(SO 3)

E1–3   Consider the following business activities.

	Type of Activity
1. Cash receipts from customers paying for daily ski passes	O
2. Payments made to purchase additional snow-making equipment	_____
3. Payments made to repair the grooming machines	_____
4. Receipt of funds from the bank to finance the purchase of the additional snow-making equipment	_____
5. Issue of shares to raise funds for a planned expansion	_____
6. Repayment of a portion of the loan from the bank (see #4)	_____
7. Payment of interest on the bank loan	_____
8. Payment of salaries to the employees who operate the ski lifts	_____
9. Receipt of a grant from the government for training a group of disabled skiers	_____
10. Payment of dividend to shareholders	_____

Instructions
Classify each of the above items by type of business activity: operating (O), investing (I), or financing (F). The first one has been done for you as an example.

Identify business
activity and effect
on cash.
(SO 3)

E1–4   Consider the following business activities.

	(a) Type of Activity	(b) Cash Effect
1. Purchase of goods for resale	O	–
2. Purchase of equipment	_____	_____
3. Borrowed money from a bank	_____	_____
4. Purchase of long-term investment	_____	_____
5. Sale of merchandise to customers	_____	_____
6. Issue of common shares	_____	_____
7. Sale of long-term investment	_____	_____
8. Payment of dividends	_____	_____
9. Repayment of money owed to bank	_____	_____
10. Payment of interest on money borrowed from bank	_____	_____

Instructions
(a) For each of the above items, indicate the type of business activity—operating (O), investing (I), or financing (F).
(b) Indicate whether each of the above items would increase (+) or decrease (–) cash. Assume all items are cash transactions. The first one has been done for you as an example.

Identify financial
statement.
(SO 4)

E1–5   Consider the following typical accounts and statement items.

1. _____ Cash	9. _____ Accounts receivable
2. _____ Profit	10. _____ Interest expense
3. _____ Service revenue	11. _____ Cash provided by operating activities
4. _____ Common shares	12. _____ Cash used by investing activities
5. _____ Sales	13. _____ Bank loan payable
6. _____ Dividends	14. _____ Equipment
7. _____ Merchandise inventory	15. _____ Retained earnings
8. _____ Income tax expense	

Instructions
Indicate on which statement(s)—income statement (IS), statement of financial position (SFP), statement of changes in equity (SCE), and/or statement of cash flows (SCF)—you would find each of the above accounts or items. Note that there may be more than one correct statement for some of the above.

Calculate accounting
equation and profit.
(SO 4)

E1–6   K-Os Corporation reported the following selected information for the two years ended December 31:

	2015	2014
Total assets	$520,000	$440,000
Total liabilities	350,000	290,000

Instructions
(a) Calculate total shareholders' equity at December 31, 2014 and 2015.
(b) Calculate the change in total shareholders' equity for the year ended December 31, 2015.
(c) K-Os's shareholders' equity consists only of common shares and retained earnings. Using the change in total shareholders' equity calculated in (b) above, calculate the profit or loss for the year ended December 31, 2015, assuming:
   1. K-Os issued no common shares during the year and paid no dividends.
   2. K-Os issued no common shares during the year and paid dividends of $5,000.

3. K-Os issued $25,000 of additional common shares during the year and paid no dividends.
4. K-Os issued $10,000 of additional common shares during the year and paid dividends of $5,000.

E1-7   Summaries of selected data from the financial statements of two corporations follow. Both companies have just completed their first year of operations.

Determine missing amounts.
(SO 4)

	Lumber Inc.	Trucking Inc.
Income statement		
Total revenues	$1,000,000	$ [7]
Total expenses	[1]	250,000
Profit	150,000	50,000
Statement of changes in equity		
Total shareholders' equity, beginning of year	0	0
Common shares, beginning of year	0	0
Issue of shares	100,000	[8]
Common shares, end of year	[2]	20,000
Retained earnings, beginning of year	0	0
Profit	[3]	[9]
Dividends	[4]	10,000
Retained earnings, end of year	100,000	40,000
Total shareholders' equity, end of year	[5]	[10]
Statement of financial position		
Total assets	1,050,000	[11]
Total liabilities	850,000	150,000
Total shareholders' equity	[6]	[12]

Instructions
Determine the missing amounts for [1] to [12]. Note that you may not be able to solve each item in numerical order.

E1-8   The following amounts (in thousands) were taken from the December 31 statements of financial position of **Maple Leaf Foods Inc.**:

Calculate accounting equation and profit.
(SO 4)

	2012	2011
Total assets	$3,243,696	$2,940,459
Total liabilities	2,285,697	2,010,346

Instructions
(a) How much is Maple Leaf Foods' shareholders' equity at December 31, 2012 and 2011?
(b) Write Maple Leaf Foods' accounting equation for each year.
(c) Calculate the change in total shareholders' equity for the year ended December 31, 2012.
(d) Assume that Maple Leaf Foods had the following changes to its shareholders' equity in 2012: dividends of $22,229 thousand, and other shareholders' equity items of $(65,181) thousand. How much profit did it report in 2012?

E1-9   The following list of accounts, in alphabetical order, is for Aventura Inc. at November 30, 2015:

Classify accounts and prepare statement of financial position.
(SO 4)

_____	Accounts payable	$ 26,200
_____	Accounts receivable	19,500
_____	Bank loan payable	34,000
_____	Buildings	100,000
_____	Cash	20,000
_____	Common shares	20,000
_____	Equipment	30,000
_____	Income tax payable	6,000
_____	Land	44,000
_____	Merchandise inventory	18,000
_____	Mortgage payable	97,500
_____	Retained earnings	48,500
_____	Supplies	700

Instructions

(a) For each of the above accounts, identify whether it is an asset (A), liability (L), or shareholders' equity (SE) item.

(b) Prepare a statement of financial position at November 30.

Classify accounts and prepare income statement.
(SO 4)

E1-10   The following selected accounts and amounts (in millions) were taken from the February 2, 2013, financial statements of **Reitmans (Canada) Limited**.

_____ Administrative expenses	$ 47.4
_____ Cost of goods sold	372.1
_____ Dividends	52.1
_____ Finance expenses	1.3
_____ Finance income	5.6
_____ Income tax expense	8.5
_____ Selling and distribution expenses	550.2
_____ Sales	1,000.5

Instructions

(a) For each of the above accounts, identify whether it is a revenue (R) or expense (E) account or an account that is not reported on the income statement (NR).

(b) Prepare an income statement for the year.

Prepare an income statement and statement of changes in equity.
(SO 4)

E1-11   The following information is for Kon Inc. for the year ended December 31, 2015:

Common shares, Jan. 1	$20,000
Common shares issued during year	10,000
Retained earnings, Jan. 1	58,000
Office expense	1,600
Dividends	5,000
Rent expense	12,400
Service revenue	61,000
Utilities expense	2,400
Salaries expense	30,000
Income tax expense	3,000

Instructions

Prepare an income statement and statement of changes in equity for the year.

Calculate profit and prepare statements of changes in equity and financial position.
(SO 4)

E1-12   Sea Surf Campground, Inc. is a public camping ground in Ocean National Park. It has the following financial information as at December 31, 2015:

Camping revenue	$168,000
Accounts payable	5,000
Bank loan payable	50,000
Cash	7,500
Equipment	119,000
Income tax expense	10,000
Dividends	12,000
Operating expenses	130,000
Supplies	2,500
Common shares, Jan. 1	30,000
Common shares issued during year	10,000
Retained earnings, Jan. 1	18,000

Instructions

(a) Determine profit for the year.

(b) Prepare a statement of changes in equity and a statement of financial position for the year.

Interpret financial information.
(SO 4)

E1-13   Consider each of the following independent situations:

1. The statement of changes in equity of Yu Corporation shows dividends of $70,000, while profit for the year was $75,000.

2. The statement of cash flows for Surya Corporation shows that cash provided by operating activities was $10,000; cash used by investing activities was $100,000; and cash provided by financing activities was $120,000.

3. Naguib Ltd.'s statement of financial position reports $200,000 of total liabilities and $250,000 of shareholders' equity.

4. Rijo Inc. has total assets of $100,000 and no liabilities.

Instructions
For each company, write a brief interpretation of these financial facts. For example, you might discuss the company's financial health or what seems to be its growth philosophy.

Problems: Set A

P1–1A Financial decisions made by users often depend on one financial statement more than the others. Consider each of the following independent, hypothetical situations:

Identify users of accounting information. (SO 1)

1. The South Face Inc. is considering extending credit to a new customer. The credit terms would require the customer to pay within 30 days of receiving goods.
2. An investor is considering purchasing the common shares of Orbite Online, Inc. The investor plans on holding the investment for at least five years.
3. Caisse d'Économie Base Montréal is thinking about extending a loan to a small company. The company would be required to make interest payments at the end of each month for three years, and to repay the loan at the end of the third year.
4. The chief financial officer of Tech Toy Limited is trying to determine whether the company is generating enough cash to increase the amount of dividends paid to shareholders in this, and future, years. He needs to be sure that Tech Toy will still have enough cash to expand operations when needed.

Instructions
(a) Identify the key user(s) in each situation and determine whether they are internal or external users.
(b) State whether the user(s) you identified in (a) would be most interested in the income statement, statement of financial position, or statement of cash flows to make their decision. Choose only one financial statement in each case, and briefly give reasons for your choice.

P1–2A Five independent situations follow:

Determine forms of business organization and accounting standards. (SO 2)

1. Three computer science professors have formed a business to expand wireless access for computers. Each has contributed an equal amount of cash and knowledge to the venture. While their plans look promising, they are concerned about the legal liabilities that their business might confront.
2. Joseph LeBlanc, a student looking for summer work, has opened a bicycle rental shop in a small shed on the Trans Canada Trail system.
3. Robert Steven and Tom Cheng each owned a snowboard manufacturing business and have now decided to combine their businesses. They expect that in the coming year they will need to raise funds to expand their operations.
4. Darcy Becker, Ellen Sweet, and Meg Dwyer recently graduated with business degrees, with majors in accounting. Friends since childhood, they have decided to start an accounting practice.
5. Hervé Gaudet wants to rent storage lockers in airports across the country. His idea is that customers will be able to leave their luggage at the airport if they have a long layover so they can explore the local surroundings without being burdened with luggage. This will require the rental of space in each airport as well as the hiring of employees and other operating costs.

Instructions
(a) In each of the above situations, explain what form of organization the business is likely to take: proprietorship, partnership, public corporation, or private corporation. Give reasons for your choice.
(b) Indicate which type of accounting standards—IFRS or ASPE—each of the business organizations you identified in (a) is most likely to use for external reporting purposes.

P1–3A All companies are involved in three types of activities: operating, investing, and financing. The names and descriptions of corporations in several different industries follow:

Identify business activities. (SO 3)

Indigo Books & Music—book retailer
High Liner Foods—processor and distributor of seafood products
Mountain Equipment Co-op—outdoor equipment retailer
Ganong Bros. —maker of candy
Royal Bank—banking and financial service provider

Instructions
(a) For each of the above corporations, provide a likely example of (1) one of its operating activities, (2) one of its investing activities, and (3) one of its financing activities.
(b) Which of the activities that you identified in (a) are common to most corporations? Which activities are not?

Classify accounts.
(SO 4)

P1–4A Slipstream Ltd. reports the following list of accounts, in alphabetical order:

	(a)	(b)
Accounts payable	L	SFP
Accounts receivable		
Bank loan payable		
Cash		
Common shares		
Equipment		
Income tax expense		
Income tax payable		
Interest expense		
Office expense		
Prepaid insurance		
Rent expense		
Repair and maintenance expense		
Salaries payable		
Service revenue		
Vehicles		

Instructions

(a) Classify each account as an asset (A), liability (L), share capital (SC), revenue (R), or expense (E) item. The first one has been done for you as an example.

(b) Identify on which financial statement(s)—income statement (IS), statement of changes in equity (SCE), and/or statement of financial position (SFP)—each account would be reported. Note that there may be more than one correct statement for some of the above. The first one has been done for you as an example.

Prepare accounting equation.
(SO 4)

P1–5A Craft Carpentry Limited reports the following statement of financial position accounts, in alphabetical order:

Accounts payable	$ 6,400	L
Accounts receivable	10,800	A
Bank loan payable	9,000	L
Cash	1,250	A
Common shares	1,000	SE
Equipment	19,400	A
Income tax payable	2,000	L
Interest payable	100	L
Prepaid insurance	600	A
Retained earnings	12,250	SE
Salaries payable	1,000	L
Supplies	1,200	A
Unearned revenue	1,500	L

Instructions

(a) Classify each account as an asset (A), liability (L), or shareholders' equity (SE) item.

(b) Calculate total assets, total liabilities, and total shareholders' equity and prepare Craft Carpentry's accounting equation.

(c) Craft Carpentry's retained earnings was $2,250 at the beginning of the year. The company reported revenues of $72,000, expenses of $50,000, and dividends of $12,000 during the year. Prepare a calculation that proves how retained earnings of $12,250 at the end of the year were determined.

Determine missing amounts; answer questions.
(SO 4)

P1–6A Selected information (in millions) is available for **Sears Canada Inc.** and **Canadian Tire Corporation, Limited** for a recent fiscal year:

	Sears	Canadian Tire
Beginning of year		
Total assets	$ [1]	$12,338.8
Total liabilities	1,638.7	[4]
Total shareholders' equity	1,092.0	4,409.0

End of year

Total assets	2,479.1	[5]
Total liabilities	[2]	8,417.8
Total shareholders' equity	1,076.4	[6]
Changes during year in shareholders' equity	–	–
Repurchase of shares	0.1	225.0
Dividends	101.9	97.7
Total revenues	4,511.1	11,451.0
Total expenses	[3]	10,951.8
Other decreases in shareholders' equity	14.8	10.9

Instructions

(a) Determine the missing amounts for [1] to [6].

(b) Which company has a higher proportion of debt financing at the end of its fiscal year? Of equity financing?

(c) Sears's year end is the last Saturday in January. Canadian Tire's year end is the last Saturday in December. How might these differing year-end dates affect your comparison in (b)?

P1–7A On June 1, 2015, One Planet Cosmetics Corp. was formed. Its assets, liabilities, share capital, revenues, expenses, and dividends as at June 30 follow:

Prepare financial statements.
(SO 4)

Cash	$ 6,000	Service revenue	$12,000
Accounts receivable	4,000	Supplies expense	1,200
Supplies	1,400	Interest expense	800
Equipment	32,000	Office expense	1,500
Accounts payable	2,300	Utilities expense	1,300
Bank loan payable	14,000	Income tax expense	700
Common shares	25,000	Salaries expense	3,400
Dividends	1,000		

Instructions

(a) Prepare an income statement, statement of changes in equity, and statement of financial position for the month.

(b) Explain why it is necessary to prepare the financial statements in the order listed in (a).

P1–8A Selected financial information follows for Maison Corporation for the year ended December 31, 2015:

Prepare statement of cash flows; comment on adequacy of cash.
(SO 4)

Cash, Jan. 1	$ 12,000
Cash dividends paid	10,000
Cash paid to purchase equipment	35,000
Cash payments for operating activities	120,000
Cash receipts from operating activities	140,000
Cash received from issue of long-term debt	20,000
Cash received from issue of shares	20,000

Instructions

(a) Classify each of the above items, except for cash at the beginning of the year, as an operating, investing, or financing activity.

(b) Prepare a statement of cash flows for Maison Corporation for the year.

(c) Comment on the adequacy of cash provided by operating activities to fund the company's investing activities.

P1–9A Incomplete financial statements for Baxter, Inc. follow.

Calculate missing amounts; explain statement interrelationships.
(SO 4)

BAXTER, INC.	
Income Statement	
Year Ended November 30, 2015	
Revenues	$90,000
Operating expenses	[1]
Profit before income tax	30,000
Income tax expense	6,000
Profit	$ [2]

BAXTER, INC.
Statement of Changes in Equity
Year Ended November 30, 2015

	Common Shares	Retained Earnings	Total Equity
Balance, December 1, 2014	$ 0	$ 0	$ 0
Issued common shares	12,000		[5]
Profit		[3]	[6]
Dividends		(10,000)	(10,000)
Balance, November 30, 2015	$12,000	$ [4]	$ [7]

BAXTER, INC.
Statement of Financial Position
November 30, 2015

Assets		Liabilities and Shareholders' Equity	
Cash	$ 5,000	Liabilities	
Accounts receivable	10,000	Accounts payable	$ [10]
Land	[8]	Bank loan payable	50,000
Buildings	60,000	Total liabilities	84,000
Equipment	25,000	Shareholders' equity	
Total assets	$ [9]	Common shares	[11]
		Retained earnings	[12]
		Total shareholders' equity	[13]
		Total liabilities and shareholders' equity	$110,000

Instructions

(a) Calculate the missing amounts for [1] to [13]. Note that you may not be able to solve each item in numerical order.

(b) Explain (1) the sequence for preparing the financial statements, and (2) the interrelationships between the income statement, statement of changes in equity, and statement of financial position.

Prepare corrected statement of financial position; identify financial statements for ASPE.
(SO 4)

P1–10A   GG Corporation, a private corporation, was formed on July 1, 2015. On July 31, Guy Gélinas, the company's president, prepared the following statement of financial position:

GG CORPORATION
Statement of Financial Position
July 31, 2015

Assets		Liabilities and Shareholders' Equity	
Cash	$ 20,000	Accounts payable	$ 34,000
Accounts receivable	50,000	Boat loan payable	40,000
Merchandise inventory	36,000	Common shares	50,000
Boat	24,000	Retained earnings	6,000
	$130,000		$130,000

Guy admits that his knowledge of accounting is somewhat limited and is concerned that his statement of financial position might not be correct. He gives you the following additional information:

1. The boat actually belongs to Guy Gélinas, not to GG Corporation. However, because Guy thinks he might take customers out on the boat occasionally, he decided to list it as an asset of the company. To be consistent, he also included as a liability of the company the personal bank loan that he took out to buy the boat.

2. Included in the accounts receivable balance is $10,000 that Guy personally loaned to his brother five years ago. Guy included this in the receivables of GG Corporation so that he wouldn't forget that his brother owes him money.

3. Guy's statements didn't balance. To make them balance, he adjusted the Common Shares account until assets equalled liabilities and shareholders' equity.

Instructions

(a) Identify any corrections that should be made to the statement of financial position and explain why.

(b) Prepare a corrected statement of financial position. (*Hint*: To get the balance sheet to balance, adjust Common Shares).

(c) What other financial statements should GG Corporation prepare, assuming it follows Accounting Standards for Private Enterprises?

Problems: Set B

P1–1B   Financial decisions made by users often depend on one financial statement more than the others. Consider each of the following independent, hypothetical situations:

1. An Ontario investor is considering purchasing the common shares of Fight Fat Ltd., which operates 13 fitness centres in the Toronto area. The investor plans on holding the investment for at least three years.
2. Comeau Ltée is considering extending credit to a new customer. The terms of the credit would require the customer to pay within 45 days of receipt of the goods.
3. The chief financial officer of Private Label Corporation is trying to determine whether the company is generating enough cash to increase the amount of dividends paid to shareholders in this, and future, years. She needs to ensure that there will still be enough cash to expand operations when needed.
4. Drummond Bank is considering extending a loan to a small company. The company would be required to make interest payments at the end of each month for five years, and to repay the loan at the end of the fifth year.

Identify users of accounting information.
(SO 1)

Instructions
(a) Identify the key user(s) in each situation and determine whether they are internal or external users.
(b) State whether the user(s) you identified in (a) would be most interested in the income statement, statement of financial position, or statement of cash flows. Choose only one financial statement in each case, and briefly give reasons for your choice.

P1–2B   Five independent situations follow:

1. Dawn Addington, a student looking for summer work, has opened a vegetable stand along a busy local highway. Each morning, she buys produce from local farmers, then sells it in the afternoon as people return home from work.
2. Joseph Counsell and Sabra Surkis each own a bike shop. They have decided to combine their businesses and try to expand their operations to include skis and snowboards. They expect that in the coming year they will need funds to expand their operations.
3. Three chemistry professors have formed a business that uses bacteria to clean up toxic waste sites. Each has contributed an equal amount of cash and knowledge to the venture. The use of bacteria in this situation is experimental, and legal obligations could result.
4. Abdul Rahim has run a successful but small cooperative health and organic food store for over five years. The increased sales at his store have made him believe that the time is right to open a chain of health and organic food stores across the country. Of course, this will require a substantial investment for inventory and property, plant, and equipment, as well as for employees and other resources. Abdul has no savings or personal assets.
5. Mary Emery, Richard Goedde, and Jigme Tshering recently graduated with law degrees. They have decided to start a law practice in their hometown.

Determine forms of business organization and accounting standards.
(SO 2)

Instructions
(a) In each of the above situations, explain what form of organization the business is likely to take: proprietorship, partnership, public corporation, or private corporation. Give reasons for your choice.
(b) Indicate which type of accounting standards—IFRS or ASPE—that each of the business organizations you identified in (a) is most likely to use for external reporting purposes.

P1–3B   All companies are involved in three types of activities: operating, investing, and financing. The names and descriptions of corporations in several different industries follow:

Identify business activities.
(SO 3)

> **WestJet Airlines**—airline
> **University of Calgary Students' Union**—university student union
> **GlaxoSmithKline**— pharmaceutical manufacturer
> **Maple Leaf Sports & Entertainment**—professional sports company (including ownership of the Toronto Maple Leafs hockey team and Raptors basketball team)
> **Empire Company**—food retailer and real estate investments (including ownership of Sobeys)

Instructions
(a) For each of the above corporations, provide a likely example of (1) one of its operating activities, (2) one of its investing activities, and (3) one of its financing activities.
(b) Which of the activities that you identified in (a) are common to most corporations? Which activities are not?

Classify accounts.
(SO 4)

P1–4B   Gulfstream Inc. reports the following list of accounts, in alphabetical order:

	(a)	(b)
Accounts payable	L	SFP
Accounts receivable		
Bank loan payable		
Buildings		
Cash		
Common shares		
Cost of goods sold		
Equipment		
Income tax expense		
Income tax payable		
Interest expense		
Land		
Merchandise inventory		
Mortgage payable		
Office expense		
Prepaid insurance		
Salaries payable		
Sales		

Instructions
(a) Classify each account as an asset (A), liability (L), share capital (SC), revenue (R), or expense (E) item. The first one has been done for you as an example.
(b) Identify on which financial statement(s)—income statement (IS), statement of changes in equity (SCE), and/or statement of financial position (SFP)—each account would be reported. Note that there may be more than one correct statement for some of the above. The first one has been done for you as an example.

Prepare accounting equation.
(SO 4)

P1–5B   D&K Delivery Limited reports the following statement of financial position accounts, in alphabetical order:

Accounts payable	$10,800
Accounts receivable	16,400
Bank loan payable	40,000
Cash	11,250
Common shares	5,000
Income tax payable	2,000
Interest payable	400
Prepaid insurance	700
Retained earnings	42,250
Salaries payable	2,050
Supplies	1,250
Unearned revenue	2,500
Vehicles	75,400

Instructions
(a) Classify each account as an asset (A), liability (L), or shareholders' equity (SE) item.
(b) Calculate total assets, total liabilities, and total shareholders' equity and prepare D&K Delivery's accounting equation.
(c) D&K Delivery's retained earnings were $22,250 at the beginning of the year. The company reported revenues of $172,000, expenses of $140,000, and dividends of $12,000 during the year. Prepare a calculation that proves how retained earnings of $42,250 at the end of the year were determined.

Determine missing amounts; answer questions.
(SO 4)

P1–6B   Selected information is available for **Tim Hortons Inc.** and **Starbucks Corporation** for a recent fiscal year:

	Tim Hortons (in CAD millions)	Starbucks (in USD millions)
Beginning of year		
Total assets	$2,204.0	$ [4]
Total liabilities	[1]	2,973.1
Total shareholders' equity	1,154.4	4,387.3

End of year		
Total assets	2,284.2	[5]
Total liabilities	1,094.1	3,104.7
Total shareholders' equity	[2]	[6]
Changes during year in shareholders' equity	–	
Repurchase of shares	18.7	1.1
Dividends	[3]	543.7
Total revenues	3,123.8	13,604.6
Total expenses	2,716.0	12,219.9
Other decreases in shareholders' equity	222.9	112.7

Instructions
(a) Determine the missing amounts for [1] to [6].
(b) Which company has the higher proportion of debt financing at the end of its fiscal year? Of equity financing?
(c) Tim Hortons' year end is the Sunday nearest to the end of December. Starbucks' year end is the last Sunday in September. In addition, Tim Hortons reports its financial results in Canadian dollars and Starbucks reports in U.S. dollars. Is it appropriate to compare these two companies in (b)?

P1–7B   On May 1, 2015, Aero Flying School Ltd. was formed. Its assets, liabilities, share capital, revenues, expenses, and dividends as at May 31 follow:

Prepare financial statements.
(SO 4)

Cash	$ 5,300	Rent expense	$2,200
Accounts receivable	10,200	Repair and maintenance expense	700
Equipment	60,300	Fuel expense	3,300
Accounts payable	2,200	Office expense	2,300
Bank loan payable	22,000	Salaries expense	1,000
Service revenue	12,600	Income tax expense	600
Interest expense	100	Dividends	800
Common shares	50,000		

Instructions
(a) Prepare an income statement, statement of changes in equity, and statement of financial position for the month of May.
(b) Explain why it is necessary to prepare the financial statements in the order listed in (a).

P1–8B   Selected financial information follows for Furlotte Corporation for the year ended June 30, 2015:

Prepare statement of cash flows; comment on adequacy of cash.
(SO 4)

Cash, July 1	$ 40,000
Cash payments for operating activities	109,000
Cash paid for equipment	40,000
Repayment of long-term debt	15,000
Cash dividends paid	13,000
Cash receipts from operating activities	158,000

Instructions
(a) Classify each of the above items, except for cash at the beginning of the year, as an operating, investing, or financing activity.
(b) Prepare a statement of cash flows for Furlotte Corporation for the year.
(c) Comment on the adequacy of cash provided by operating activities to fund the company's investing activities.

P1–9B   Incomplete financial statements for Wu, Inc. follow:

Calculate missing amounts; explain statement interrelationships.
(SO 4)

WU, INC.	
Income Statement	
Year Ended August 31, 2015	
Service revenue	$85,000
Operating expenses	[1]
Profit before income tax	35,000
Income tax expense	9,000
Profit	$ [2]

WU, INC.
Statement of Changes in Equity
Year Ended August 31, 2015

	Common Shares	Retained Earnings	Total Equity
Balance, September 1, 2014	$25,000	$20,000	$ [5]
Issued common shares	10,000		[6]
Profit		[3]	[7]
Dividends		[4]	[8]
Balance, August 31, 2015	$35,000	$31,000	$[9]

WU, INC.
Statement of Financial Position
August 31, 2015

Assets		Liabilities and Shareholders' Equity	
Cash	$ [10]	Liabilities	
Accounts receivable	15,000	Accounts payable	$19,000
Land	20,000	Shareholders' equity	
Buildings	40,000	Common shares	[12]
Equipment	5,000	Retained earnings	[13]
Total assets	$ [11]	Total liabilities and shareholders' equity	$85,000

Instructions

(a) Calculate the missing amounts [1] to [13]. Note that you may not be able to solve each item in numerical order.

(b) Explain (1) the sequence for preparing and presenting the financial statements, and (2) the interrelationships between the income statement, statement of changes in equity, and statement of financial position.

Prepare corrected statement of financial position; identify financial statements for ASPE.
(SO 4)

P1–10B The Independent Book Shop Ltd. was formed on April 1, 2014. It is a small private corporation, run by Joanna Kay. On March 31, 2015, Joanna prepared the following income statement:

INDEPENDENT BOOK SHOP LTD.
Income Statement
Year Ended March 31, 2015

Revenues		
Accounts receivable	$23,000	
Service revenue	41,000	
Total revenues		$64,000
Expenses		
Rent expense	$12,000	
Office expense	5,000	
Vacation expense	4,000	
Total expenses		21,000
Profit before income tax		85,000
Income tax expense		5,000
Profit		$90,000

Joanna admits that her knowledge of accounting is somewhat limited and is concerned that her income statement might not be correct. She gives you the following additional information:

1. Included in the Service Revenue account is $3,000 of revenue that the company expects to earn in April 2015. Joanna included it in this year's statement so she wouldn't forget about it.

2. Joanna operates her business in a converted carriage house attached to her parents' downtown home. They do not charge her anything for the use of this building, but she thinks that if she paid rent it would have cost her about $12,000 a year. She included this amount in the income statement as Rent Expense because of the "opportunity cost."

3. To reward herself after a year of hard work, Joanna took a vacation to Greece. She used personal funds to pay for the trip, but she reported it as an expense on the income statement since it was her job that made her need the vacation.

Instructions

(a) Identify any corrections that should be made to the income statement and explain why.

(b) Prepare a corrected income statement.

(c) What other financial statements should the Independent Book Shop prepare, assuming it follows Accounting Standards for Private Enterprises?

Broadening Your Perspective

Financial Reporting: *Shoppers Drug Mart*

BYP1–1 Actual financial statements (rather than the simplified financial statements presented in the chapter) for **Shoppers Drug Mart** are presented in Appendix A at the end of this book.

Answer questions about financial statements. (SO 4)

Instructions

(a) What are the five financial statements that Shoppers Drug Mart includes in its financial statement package? Which ones were discussed in this chapter?

(b) Look at Shoppers Drug Mart's income statement (which it calls statement of earnings). Did its sales increase or decrease between 2012 and 2011? Did its profit (which it calls net earnings) increase or decrease between the two years? Are its sales and profit moving in the same direction (that is, both increasing or both decreasing)? If not, explain why not.

(c) Look at Shoppers Drug Mart's statement of financial position (which it calls balance sheet). Identify its total assets, total liabilities, and total shareholders' equity as at (1) December 29, 2012, and (2) December 31, 2011.

(d) Look at Shoppers Drug Mart's statement of changes in equity (which it calls statement of changes in shareholders' equity). What were the balances in its share capital and retained earnings accounts at the end of 2012? At the end of 2011? Do these amounts agree to the same balances reported in the shareholders' equity section of the statement of financial position?

(e) How much cash did Shoppers Drug Mart have at December 29, 2012? At December 31, 2011? Which financial statement(s) did you look at to answer this question?

Comparative Analysis: *Shoppers Drug Mart* and *Jean Coutu*

BYP1–2 The financial statements of **Jean Coutu** are presented in Appendix B following the financial statements for **Shoppers Drug Mart** in Appendix A.

Compare financial statements. (SO 4)

Instructions

(a) Based on the information in these financial statements, determine the following for each company:
1. Total assets, liabilities, and shareholders' equity at the end of the current and prior fiscal years
2. Sales and profit for the current and prior fiscal years

(b) Calculate the percentage change between the current and prior fiscal years for each company for the assets, liabilities, shareholders' equity, sales, and profit amounts determined in (a).

(c) What conclusions about the two companies can you draw from the data you determined in (b)?

(d) Jean Coutu's fiscal year end is the Saturday closest to the end of February. Shoppers Drug Mart's fiscal year end is the Saturday closest to the end of December. Knowing that the year ends of Shoppers Drug Mart and Jean Coutu are not the same, do you have any concerns about the comparisons you made in (c)?

Comparing IFRS and ASPE

BYP1–3 In Canada, public corporations are required to adopt International Financial Reporting Standards (IFRS) as accounting standards. Private corporations are given a choice, and must decide between two sets of accounting standards: Accounting Standards for Private Enterprises (ASPE) or IFRS.

Distinguish between public and private companies. (SO 1, 2)

Instructions

(a) What is the key difference between public and private companies?

(b) Who are the key users of public company financial statements? Who are the key users of private company financial statements?

(c) What is the difference between users of public company financial statements and users of private company financial statements?

(d) Why do you think public companies do not have a choice regarding which accounting standards they use?

(e) Why do you think private companies do have a choice regarding the accounting standards they use?

> Optional **collaborative learning activities** in each chapter are identified by an icon and allow you to practice solving problems with colleagues.

Critical Thinking Case

BYP1–4 Industrial Maids Service Ltd. (IMS) is a corporation based in Sarnia, Ontario that focuses on cleaning commercial properties, which is a very competitive business. Although IMS tries to recruit highly trained employees, it is not

Analyze income statement. (SO 4)

able to pay a very high hourly salary. Cleaning services are charged to clients by the hour and the average rate is $17 per hour. Some of the cleaning done by this company is performed with larger equipment that is repaired by the company. The average employee will work an entire shift at one client's premises.

Prestige Cleaning Services Inc. (PCS) also operates a cleaning service in Sarnia but this company focuses on residential cleaning and targets large homes in high-income areas. The company is owned by a former NHL star who is very effective at securing cleaning contracts. Most of the cleaning work done by this company occurs during the day and the company is able to attract experienced cleaning staff and pay them a higher salary. Cleaning services are charged to clients by the hour and the average rate is $30 per hour. The equipment used by this company is inexpensive. Most employees will clean two or three houses during a single shift so the company owns several vehicles.

Listed below are condensed income statements of the two corporations:

	IMS	PCS
Service revenue	$1,020,000	$900,000
Salaries expense	600,000	450,000
Rent expense	42,000	23,000
Other operating expenses	4,000	14,000
Interest expense	25,000	13,000
Profit before income tax	349,000	400,000
Income tax expense	87,250	100,000
Profit	$ 261,750	$300,000

Instructions

(a) How many hours of cleaning service did each company provide to its clients?
(b) What is the average rate of pay per hour that each company pays its employees?
(c) Which company do you think uses larger facilities? Why do you think this is?
(d) Why does PCS likely have higher other operating expenses than IMS?
(e) One of the companies financed its start up by taking out a higher amount of bank loan than the other company. Which company do you think this was? Both companies are charged the same rate of interest by their banks.
(f) What is the most significant factor that makes PCS more profitable than IMS?

Ethics Case

Discuss certification of financial statements.
(SO 1)

BYP1-5 Chief executive officers (CEOs) and chief financial officers (CFOs) of publicly traded companies are required to personally certify that their companies' financial statements and other financial information contain no untrue statements and do not leave out any important facts. Khan Corporation just hired a new management team, and its members say they are too new to the company to know whether the most recent financial reports are accurate or not. They refuse to sign the certification.

Instructions

(a) Who are the stakeholders in this situation?
(b) Should the CEO and CFO sign the certification? Explain why or why not.
(c) What are the CEO's and CFO's alternatives?

"All About You" Activity

Describe the elements of a personal annual report.
(SO 4)

BYP1-6 Every company needs to plan in order to move forward. Its top management must consider where it wants the company to be in three to five years. Like a company, you need to think about where you want to be in three to five years and you need to start taking steps now in order to get there. With some forethought, you can help yourself avoid a bad resumé, like the one described in the "All About You" feature in this chapter.

Instructions

(a) Where would you like to be working in three to five years? Describe your plan for getting there by identifying specific steps that you need to take.
(b) In order to get the job you want, you will need a resumé. Your resumé is the equivalent of a company's annual report. It needs to provide relevant and reliable information about your past and accomplishments so that employers can decide whether to "invest" in you. Do a search on the Internet to find a good resumé format. What are the basic elements of a resumé?
(c) A company's annual report provides information about its accomplishments. In order for investors to use the annual report, the information must be reliable; that is, users must have faith that the information is accurate and believable. How can you provide assurance that the information on your resumé is reliable?

Serial Case

BYP1-7   As part of the requirements of her university entrepreneurship program, Natalie Koebel had been operating "Cookie Creations," a proprietorship, on a part-time basis. The purpose of Cookie Creations was to provide lessons to whoever wished to learn how to make cookies. For the most part, these lessons took place in people's homes, schools, and community centres. Natalie provided all of the ingredients and utensils required to make cookies. As Natalie approaches her graduation from university, she is considering other opportunities available in addition to operating Cookie Creations.

Natalie's parents, Janet and Brian Koebel, have been operating Koebel's Family Bakery Ltd., a private corporation, for a number of years. They have been overwhelmed with the demand for their cupcakes. They have recently negotiated a contract with a national coffee shop to provide cupcakes on a weekly basis. They have also negotiated a long-term loan to purchase a new piece of equipment.

In anticipation of Natalie graduating, and in hope of spending a little more time away from the bakery, they have discussed with Natalie the possibility of her becoming one of the shareholders of Koebel's Family Bakery Ltd. In addition, Natalie would assume the full-time responsibility of administrator. Natalie could continue to provide cookie-making lessons; however, that would be done by Koebel's Family Bakery in future rather than by Natalie personally.

Identify form of business organization, accounting information, and business activities.
(SO 1, 2, 3)

> This **serial case** starts in this chapter and continues in each chapter of the book.

Instructions

(a) Discuss the benefits and weaknesses of each of these two forms of business organization, Cookie Creations and Koebel's Family Bakery Ltd.

(b) What form of generally accepted accounting principles do you anticipate each of these business organizations is using? Explain.

(c) As Koebel's Family Bakery begins to meet the demands of its new contractual commitment with the national coffee shop, what accounting information will Natalie need as administrator, and why? How often will she need this information?

(d) What types of users do you anticipate will use Koebel's Family Bakery's accounting information? What information will these users require?

(e) Identify one example of an operating activity, investing activity, and financing activity that Koebel's Family Bakery would likely be engaged in.

Answers to Self-Test Questions

1. b   2. d   3. d   4. b   5. b
6. c   7. d   8. c   9. d   10. b

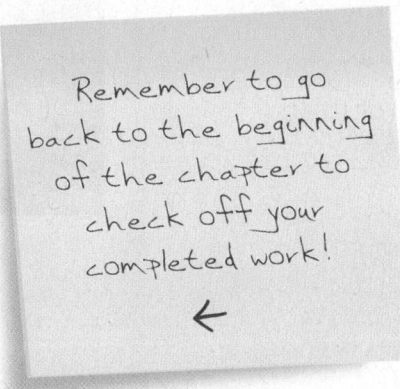

Remember to go back to the beginning of the chapter to check off your completed work!
←

Endnotes

[1]Shoppers Drug Mart Corporation 2012 annual report; "Shoppers Drug Mart Corporation Reports Strong Fourth Quarter Results," company news release, February 7, 2013; "Loblaw Companies Limited to Acquire Shoppers Drug Mart Corporation for $12.4 Billion in Cash and Stock," Shoppers Drug Mart news release, July 15, 2013; "Loblaw to Buy Shoppers Drug Mart for $12.4B," CBCnews.ca, July 15, 2013; "Shoppers Drug Mart Shareholders Approve Plan of Arrangement with Loblaw Companies Limited," Shoppers Drug Mart news release, September 12, 2013.

[2]Robert Half, Business Etiquette: *The New Rules in the Digital Age,* 2011. Suzanne Wintrob, "Don't Get Caught Lying on Your Resume," *Globe and Mail,* published June 16, 2010, updated August 23, 2012. Derek Abma, "Online Profiles Might Replace Resumes, Survey Indicates," Post media News, February 21, 2011. Sandra Oliver, "The Right Fit," *CA Magazine,* May 2013, p. 42.

A Further Look at Financial Statements

The Navigator
Chapter 2

- Scan *Study Objectives*
- Read *Feature Story*
- Read text and answer *Do It!s*
- Review *Comparing IFRS and ASPE*
- Review *Summary of Study Objectives*
- Review *Decision Toolkit—A Summary*
- Work *Using the Decision Toolkit*
- Work *Comprehensive Do It!*
- Answer *Self-Test Questions*
- Complete *assignments*
- Go to *WileyPLUS* for practice and tutorials

study objectives

After studying this chapter, you should be able to:

SO 1 Identify the sections of a classified statement of financial position.

SO 2 Identify and calculate ratios for analyzing a company's liquidity, solvency, and profitability.

SO 3 Describe the framework for the preparation and presentation of financial statements.

Real Values and International Standards

Plazacorp Retail Properties Ltd. is the owner of 347 shopping malls and strip plazas throughout Canada. Because the company's shares trade on the Toronto Stock Exchange, Plazacorp is a publicly accountable enterprise and must prepare its financial statements in accordance with International Financial Reporting Standards (IFRS). Such enterprises are required to make their financial statements available to current shareholders and to potential investors interested in purchasing the company's shares. In this way, investors, who are major users of the company's financial statements, can be informed about its financial activities.

Besides investors, other major users of Plazacorp's financial statements are bankers. The most significant asset on the company's statement of financial position is investment properties, consisting of the land and buildings used by retail tenants that pay rent to Plazacorp. When these investment properties are acquired, the company will finance part of their cost by borrowing money from a bank. This type of loan is called a mortgage because it is secured by land and buildings. This security or collateral can be seized by the bank if the company fails to make the required mortgage payments. Consequently, mortgages are the most significant liability that the company has—for example, at December 31, 2012, Plazacorp had $259 million in mortgages—and the bankers who provided these mortgages to the company are very interested in understanding the nature of the related security.

When financial statements are prepared, they must provide relevant and reliable information for all users of the financial statements, including both investors and bankers. IFRS provides the means of doing so. When Plazacorp and its competitors prepare financial statements using the same accounting standards, this makes their financial statements comparable. Being able to compare the profitability and financial position of competing companies is very important to investors. IFRS requires assets that will be used for more than one year, like investment properties, to be shown in a separate category on the statement of financial position known as non-current assets. Likewise, liabilities such as mortgages that will take a number of years to pay off are shown as non-current liabilities. This is done so that bankers can determine if there is enough security for the outstanding loans they have made to the company.

A number of assumptions and theoretical concepts are used to create accounting standards. For example, investment properties are purchased, at the time the cost and the fair value of the asset are equal. However, several years later, the fair value of the investment properties is likely to be very different from their cost. If the fair value is considerably higher than the cost of the property, should the cost or the fair value be reported on the statement of financial position? Under IFRS, companies can choose either cost or fair value. Many users may prefer to see the fair value of these assets because such information is considered to be relevant and up to date. On the other hand, the company may be reluctant to use this option because of the difficulty and cost involved in determining what fair value really is. Such a value may not be highly reliable. Plazacorp decided to report its investment properties at fair value because it best met the needs of the users of its financial statements.[1]

the navigator

<table>
<tr><td>preview of CHAPTER 2</td><td>In this chapter, we take a closer look at the statement of financial position and introduce some useful ways for evaluating the information provided by the financial statements. We also examine the financial reporting concepts underlying the preparation and presentation of financial statements, including those used by publicly accountable enterprises such as Plazacorp discussed in our feature story, as well as those used by private companies.</td></tr>
</table>

The chapter is organized as follows:

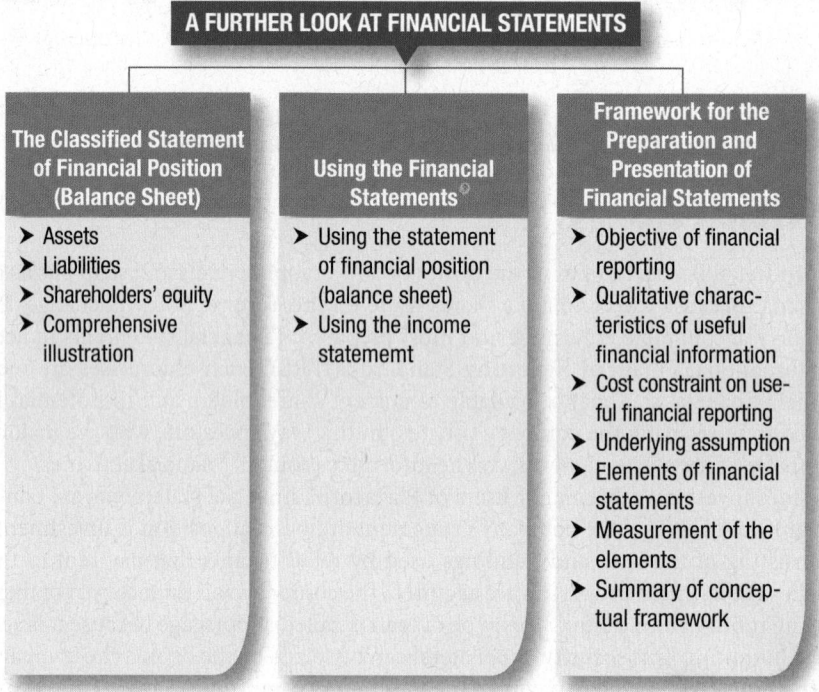

The Classified Statement of Financial Position (Balance Sheet)

STUDY OBJECTIVE 1
Identify the sections of a classified statement of financial position.

In Chapter 1, we introduced four financial statements: the statement of financial position, income statement, statement of changes in equity, and statement of cash flows. In this section, we will look at the statement of financial position in more detail and introduce standard statement classifications.

The statement of financial position, also commonly known as the balance sheet, presents a snapshot of a company's financial position—its assets, liabilities, and shareholders' equity—at a point in time. In Chapter 1, individual asset, liability, and equity items were listed in no particular order in the statement of financial position. To improve users' understanding of a company's financial position, companies group similar types of assets and similar types of liabilities together. A classified statement of financial position generally contains the standard classifications, ordered as shown in Illustration 2-1.

▶Illustration 2-1

Statement of financial position classifications

Assets	Liabilities and Shareholders' Equity
Current assets	Current liabilities
Investments	Non-current liabilities
Property, plant, and equipment	Shareholders' equity
Intangible assets	Share capital
Goodwill	Retained earnings

These classifications or groupings help readers of the financial statements determine such things as (1) whether the company has enough assets to pay its debts as they come due and (2) the claims of short-term and long-term creditors and lenders on the company's total assets. The classifications can be ordered as shown in Illustration 2-1 or in reverse order. In the sections that follow, we explain each of these classifications and ordering possibilities.

ASSETS

Assets are the resources that a company owns or controls that will provide future economic benefits. Assets include those resources whose benefits will be realized within one year (current assets) and those resources whose benefits will be realized over more than one year (non-current assets).

Current Assets

Current assets are assets that are expected to be converted into cash or will be sold or used up within one year of the company's financial statement date or its operating cycle, whichever is longer.

The **operating cycle** of a company is the average period of time it takes for a business to pay cash to obtain products or services and then receive cash from customers for these products or services. In a merchandising business, this means the time it takes to purchase inventory, pay cash to suppliers, sell the inventory on account, and then collect cash from customers. In a service business, this is the time it takes to pay employees, provide services on account, and then collect the cash from customers. For most businesses, the operating cycle is less than a year but for some businesses, such as vineyards or airplane manufacturers, the operating cycle is longer than a year. For the purposes of this textbook, we will assume companies use one year to determine whether an asset is current or non-current.

Common types of current assets include:

1. Cash
2. Trading investments
3. Accounts receivable
4. Notes receivable, including loans receivable
5. Merchandise inventory
6. Supplies
7. Prepaid expenses

You are already familiar with cash, which includes not only cash on hand but cash in banks or other financial institutions. We will briefly discuss each of the other common types of current assets in the above list. **Trading investments** are investments in debt securities such as bonds of another company, or equity securities such as shares of another company, that are bought with the intention of selling the investments after a short period of time in order to earn a profit from their price fluctuations. We will learn more about trading investments in Chapter 12.

Accounts receivable are amounts owed to the company by customers who purchased products or services on credit (on account) and are normally supported with an invoice. Other types of receivables can arise from amounts owed to the company for interest, sales tax, rent, and like items. Normally they are not supported by an invoice and must sometimes be estimated. These types of receivables are often called **accrued revenues**, and arise when payments for revenues earned by the company have not yet been received in cash. We will learn more about accrued revenues in Chapter 4.

Notes receivable are amounts owed to the company by customers or others that are supported by a written promise to repay. Loans receivable are a type of note receivable.

Merchandise inventory refers to goods held for sale to customers. As we saw in the case of Shoppers Drug Mart in Chapter 1, its inventory consists of goods such as prescription drugs, health-care aids, cosmetics, and household items. **Supplies** include consumable items like office supplies (such as paper, toner, pens) and cleaning supplies. They are a current asset because we expect that these will be used up by the business within the year.

Prepaid expenses represent the cost of expenses like rent and insurance paid in advance of use. They are current assets because they reflect unused benefits such as office space and insurance coverage available for future use during the year.

While total current assets must be disclosed, there is no prescribed order for current assets to be presented on the statement of financial position. North American companies normally list current assets in the order in which they are expected to be converted into cash; that is, in their order of liquidity. Some international companies list current assets in the reverse order of liquidity.

Current assets are shown in a simplified Illustration 2-2 for Empire Company Limited. Note that Empire calls its statement of financial position "balance sheet," as do many companies.

►Illustration 2-2
Current assets section

| EMPIRE COMPANY LIMITED
Balance Sheet (partial)
May 4, 2013
(in millions)	
Current assets	
Cash and cash equivalents	$ 455.2
Accounts receivable	381.7
Inventories	900.8
Prepaid expenses	86.2
Loans and other receivables	136.5
Total current assets	1,960.4

We have already learned about most of these accounts in Chapter 1, except for "cash equivalents," which is a new term. Cash equivalents are short-term, highly liquid investments with very little risk that can be easily sold. We will learn more about cash equivalents in Chapter 7.

Non-Current Assets

Alternative Terminology
The terms *non-current* and *long-term* are used interchangeably in this text.

Non-current assets are not expected to be converted into cash, sold, or used up by the business within one year of the financial statement date or its operating cycle. In other words, non-current assets consist of all assets that are not classified as current assets.

Common types of non-current assets include:

1. Investments
2. Property, plant, and equipment
3. Intangible assets and goodwill
4. Other assets

Long-term investments include (1) multi-year investments in debt securities (for example, loans, notes, bonds, or mortgages) that management intends to hold to earn interest; and (2) equity securities (for example, shares) of other companies that management plans to hold for many years to generate investment revenue or for strategic reasons. These assets are classified as long-term because they are not readily marketable or because management is not intending to sell the investment and convert it into cash within one year. Often, long-term investments are referred to only as *investments*. If the word "investment" is used without any modifier (trading or long-term), it is assumed to be long-term. We will learn more about long-term investments in Chapter 12.

As an example, BlackBerry reports only long-term debt investments in the partial statement of financial position (which it calls balance sheet) shown in Illustration 2-3. In the notes to the financial statements, it describes these investments as consisting of commercial paper, treasury bills, government notes, corporate notes and bonds, asset-backed securities, as well as other types of investments. Note that when these financial statements were issued, the company had not yet changed its name to BlackBerry and was reporting under its former name of Research In Motion.

►Illustration 2-3
Investments section

| RESEARCH IN MOTION LIMITED
Balance Sheet (partial)
March 2, 2013
(in USD thousands)	
Long-term investments	$221

Property, plant, and equipment are tangible assets with relatively long useful lives that are currently being used in operating the business. This category includes land, buildings, equipment, and furniture.

Alternative Terminology
Property, plant, and equipment are sometimes called *capital assets* or *fixed assets.*

Although the order of property, plant, and equipment items can vary among companies, these items are normally listed in the statement of financial position in their order of permanency. That is, land is usually listed first as it has an indefinite life, and is followed by the asset with the next longest useful life, normally buildings, and so on.

Most companies record their property, plant, and equipment at cost. However, as was mentioned in the feature story, some companies may choose to record these assets at fair value instead. This is known as the **revaluation model**. This is often used in the real estate industry but seldom applied by other industries. For example, Plazacorp, introduced in our feature story, uses the revaluation model. We will discuss the revaluation model in Chapter 9, but until then, we will assume the use of cost unless otherwise indicated.

Property, plant, and equipment, except land, have estimated useful lives over which they are expected to generate revenues. Because these assets benefit future periods, their cost is allocated over their estimated useful lives through a process called **depreciation**. Companies calculate depreciation by systematically assigning a portion of the asset's cost to depreciation expense each year (rather than expensing the full cost in the year the asset was purchased). We will learn how to calculate depreciation in Chapters 4 and 9.

Only assets with estimated useful lives are depreciated. Land also generates revenue, but its estimated useful life is considered to be infinite as land does not usually wear out or lose its value. Consequently, the cost of land is never depreciated.

Assets that are depreciated should be reported on the statement of financial position at cost less their accumulated depreciation. Accumulated depreciation shows the amount of depreciation taken so far over the *life of the asset*. It is a **contra asset account**; that is, its balance is subtracted from the balance of the asset that it relates to. The difference between cost and accumulated depreciation is referred to as the **carrying amount**, also commonly known as net book value or just simply book value.

Clothing retailer Reitmans details in a note to the financial statements, its property, plant, and equipment—which it calls property and equipment because it does not own a plant—as shown in Illustration 2-4. Note that, except for land, all of Reitmans' property and equipment are depreciated. This company also has leasehold improvements, which are long-lived additions or renovations made to leased property that Reitmans rents in large shopping centres.

REITMANS (CANADA) LIMITED
Balance Sheet Information (partial)
February 2, 2013
(in thousands)

Reitmans (CANADA) LIMITED

	Cost	Accumulated Depreciation	Carrying Amount
Property and equipment			
Land	$ 5,860	$ -	$ 5,860
Buildings and improvements	53,149	22,467	30,682
Fixtures and equipment	166,756	85,936	80,820
Leasehold improvements	189,730	101,961	87,769
	$415,495	$210,364	$205,131

▶Illustration 2-4
Property, plant, and equipment section

Many companies have assets that cannot be seen but are valuable. **Intangible assets** are noncurrent assets that do not have physical substance and that represent a privilege or a right granted to, or held by, a company. Examples of intangible assets include patents, copyrights, franchises, trademarks, trade names, and licences that give the company an exclusive right of use for a specified period of time.

Intangible assets are normally divided into two groups for accounting purposes: those with definite useful lives and those with indefinite useful lives. Similar to buildings and equipment, the cost of intangible assets with definite useful lives is allocated over these future periods through the use of amortization. Amortization of intangible assets is the same as depreciation for property, plant, and equipment, even though a different term is used.

IFRS for publicly traded companies recommends the use of the term *depreciation* to refer to the allocation of cost over the useful lives of depreciable property, plant, and equipment and the term *amortization* to refer to the allocation of the cost of certain kinds of intangible assets. In contrast, Accounting Standards for Private Enterprises recommend the use of the term *amortization* to allocate the cost of both property, plant, and equipment and intangible assets. To complicate matters further, some publicly traded companies use the terms *depreciation* and *amortization* interchangeably. Regardless of what term is used, the cost of property, plant, and equipment and intangible assets with definite useful lives is allocated over these useful lives.

You will recall that land, which has an indefinite useful life, is not depreciated. Similarly, intangible assets with indefinite lives are not amortized. We will learn more about depreciating and amortizing both tangible and intangible long-lived assets in Chapter 9.

An asset that is similar to an intangible asset and is usually discussed along with intangibles is goodwill. Goodwill results from the acquisition of another company when the price paid for the company is higher than the fair value of the purchased company's net identifiable assets (net means the value of the assets less the value of the liabilities as both are typically obtained and assumed when buying a company). Goodwill is a calculated amount—simply the difference between the price paid for the company and the fair value of the assets less liabilities acquired from the purchased company. The difference, which is goodwill, represents a value not attributable to any recorded asset or liability and relates to something intangible like the reputation of the company and the quality of its employees.

Goodwill is similar to intangible assets in that it has no physical substance and will generate future value. It differs from intangible assets in that it cannot be separated from the company and sold—it is determined in relation to the acquired company as a whole. The only way it can be sold is to sell the acquired company. Goodwill is not amortized and is reported separately from other intangibles.

Illustration 2-5 shows, in a note to the financial statements, how Shaw Communications reports its goodwill and intangible assets, which consist of various rights and licences.

► Illustration 2-5
Intangible assets and goodwill section

SHAW COMMUNICATIONS INC. Statement of Financial Position Information (partial) August 31, 2012 (in millions)	**Shaw)**
Intangibles	
Broadcast rights and licenses	$6,675
Program rights and advances	253
Goodwill	715
Wireless spectrum licenses	191
Other intangibles	236

Alternative Terminology
Deferred income tax is also called *future income tax.*

Some companies also report other types of assets that do not fit neatly into any of the above classifications. These can include non-current receivables, deferred income tax assets, and property held for sale, among many other items. Deferred income tax assets represent the income tax that is expected to be recovered in a later year or years due to deductions that a company is able to take when preparing its *future* corporate income return.

Other assets are usually separately reported so that users can get a better idea of their nature and are accompanied by an explanatory note to the financial statements. Because these types of assets vary widely in practice, they are not illustrated here.

LIABILITIES

Liabilities are obligations that result from past transactions. Similar to assets, they are also classified as current (due within one year) and non-current (due after more than one year).

Current Liabilities

Current liabilities are obligations that are to be paid or settled within one year of the company's statement date or its operating cycle, whichever is longer. As with current assets, companies use a period longer than one year if their operating cycle is longer than one year. For the purposes of this textbook, we will assume an operating cycle equal to, or shorter than, one year.

Common examples of current liabilities include:

1. Bank indebtedness
2. Accounts payable
3. Unearned revenue
4. Notes payable, including bank loans payable
5. Current maturities of long-term debt

You may recall from Chapter 1 that **bank indebtedness** is a short-term loan from a bank, typically occurring when a company uses an operating line of credit to cover cash shortfalls. **Accounts payable** represents amounts owed by the company to suppliers for purchases made on credit (account). They are usually supported by an invoice. Other types of payables can arise from amounts owed by the company for salaries, interest, sales tax, rent, income tax, and similar items. They are normally not supported by an invoice and may have to be estimated because of this. These types of payables are often called **accrued payables** and arise when expenses incurred by the company have not yet been paid in cash. We will learn more about accrued expenses and payables in Chapter 4.

Unearned revenue represents cash received in advance from a customer before revenue is earned. For example, an airline would receive cash from passengers to purchase their tickets in advance of the flight. It is recorded as a current liability because the airline has an obligation to provide the flight in the future.

Notes payable are amounts owed, often to banks but also to suppliers or others, that are supported by a written promise to repay. Amounts owed to banks are usually known as bank loans payable. It is common to refer to notes and loans interchangeably, and we will do so in this text. Notes can be current or non-current. When a company has a non-current or long-term note or loan payable (such as a five-year bank loan), a portion of the loan is often repayable each year. The portion of the payment due to be made sometime during the next year is classified as **current maturities of long-term debt**. The remainder of the loan is classified as a non-current liability.

Similar to current assets, North American companies often list current liabilities in the order in which they are expected to be paid; that is, in their order of liquidity by due date. However, for many companies, the items in the current liabilities section are arranged according to an internal company custom rather than a prescribed rule. And some international companies list current liabilities in a reverse order of liquidity, similar to current assets.

The current liabilities section from the statement of financial position of Sears Canada is shown in Illustration 2-6.

SEARS CANADA INC. Statement of Financial Position (partial) February 2, 2013 (in millions)	**Sears·**
Current liabilities	
Accounts payable and accrued liabilities	$548.3
Unearned revenue	197.5
Income and other taxes payable	33.9
Current portion of long-term obligations	5.2
Total current liabilities	784.9

▶Illustration 2-6
Current liabilities section

Users of financial statements look closely at the relationship between current assets and current liabilities. This relationship is important in evaluating a company's ability to pay its current liabilities. We will talk more about this later in the chapter when we learn how to use the information in the statement of financial position.

Non-Current Liabilities

Obligations that are expected to be paid or settled after one year are classified as **non-current liabilities**, or, as they are commonly known, long-term liabilities.

Examples of non-current liabilities include:

1. Notes payable, including bank loans payable, mortgages payable, and bonds payable
2. Lease obligations
3. Pension and benefit obligations
4. Deferred income tax liabilities

We discussed notes payable in the current liabilities section above. **Mortgages payable** are similar to long-term notes but have property (such as a house or a building) pledged as security for the loan. **Bonds payable** are used by large corporations and governments to borrow large sums of money. **Lease obligations** include amounts to be paid in the future on long-term rental contracts used for equipment or other property. **Pension and benefit obligations** are amounts companies owe past and current employees for retirement benefits. **Deferred income tax liabilities** represent income tax related to the current year's profit that is expected to be paid in a later year or years when a company prepares its *future* corporate income return.

Non-current liabilities reported in the statement of financial position are normally accompanied by extensive notes to the financial statements that describe the nature and terms of the obligation and other relevant details. For example, disclosure for a long-term mortgage payable would include the maturity date, interest rate, and any security pledged to support it. Non-current liabilities will be discussed in detail in Chapter 10.

In Illustration 2-7, TELUS reported non-current liabilities of $9,239 million on a recent statement of financial position. There is no generally prescribed order for reporting non-current liabilities.

▶ **Illustration 2-7**
Non-current liabilities section

TELUS CORPORATION Statement of Financial Position (partial) December 31, 2012 (in millions)	
Non-current liabilities	
Long-term debt	$5,711
Other long-term liabilities	1,904
Deferred income taxes	1,624
	9,239

Additional detail about its liabilities was reported by TELUS in the notes to its financial statements. There it indicated that its long-term debt consisted of notes, commercial paper, debentures, and bonds, and it gave details about the amounts, interest rates, and maturity dates. Its other long-term liabilities comprise liabilities for pensions and post-retirement benefits, as well as other items.

SHAREHOLDERS' EQUITY

Shareholders' equity is divided into two parts: share capital and retained earnings. As was mentioned in Chapter 1, some companies may include other parts in the shareholders' equity section, such as accumulated other comprehensive income. We will learn more about accumulated other comprehensive income in Chapters 11 and 12.

Share Capital

Alternative Terminology
Share capital is also commonly known as *capital stock*.

As we learned in Chapter 1, shareholders purchase shares in a company by investing cash (or other assets). When the company receives these assets, it issues ownership certificates to these investors in the form of common or preferred shares. If preferred shares are issued in addition to common shares, the total of all classes of shares issued is classified as, or titled, **share capital**. Quite often, companies have only one class of shares and the title is simply "common shares." International companies often call these ordinary shares.

Retained Earnings

The cumulative profits that have been retained for use in a company are known as **retained earnings**. Recall from Chapter 1 that the changes during the year (or period) to both share capital and retained earnings are detailed on the statement of changes in equity. The ending balances of share capital and retained earnings, determined on the statement of changes in equity, are combined and reported as shareholders' equity on the statement of financial position.

The shareholders' equity section of Danier Leather's statement of financial position is shown in Illustration 2-8. In addition to share capital and retained earnings, Danier Leather also reports contributed surplus, which is commonly known as **additional contributed capital**. Additional contributed capital represents amounts contributed by shareholders (in addition to share capital) as a result of certain types of equity transactions. We will learn more about it in Chapter 11.

▶Illustration 2-8
Shareholders' equity section

DANIER LEATHER INC. Statement of Financial Position (partial) June 30, 2013 (in thousands)	
Shareholders' equity	
Share capital	$11,533
Contributed surplus	954
Retained earnings	43,422
	55,909

COMPREHENSIVE ILLUSTRATION

All of the standard classifications discussed above are illustrated in a comprehensive statement of financial position for a hypothetical company called Frenette Corporation in Illustration 2-9.

▶Illustration 2-9
Classified statement of financial position in order of liquidity

FRENETTE CORPORATION Statement of Financial Position October 31, 2015			
Assets			
Current assets			
Cash		$ 6,600	
Trading investments		2,000	
Accounts receivable		7,000	
Merchandise inventory		4,000	
Supplies		2,100	
Prepaid insurance		400	
Total current assets			$ 22,100
Long-term investments			7,200
Property, plant, and equipment			
Land		$40,000	
Buildings	$75,000		
Less: Accumulated depreciation	15,000	60,000	
Equipment	$24,000		
Less: Accumulated depreciation	5,000	19,000	
Total property, plant, and equipment			119,000
Goodwill			3,100
Total assets			$151,400

(continued)

Liabilities and Shareholders' Equity		
Liabilities		
Current liabilities		
Accounts payable	$ 2,100	
Salaries payable	1,600	
Interest payable	450	
Unearned revenue	900	
Bank loan payable	11,000	
Current portion of mortgage payable	1,000	
Total current liabilities		$ 17,050
Non-current liabilities		
Mortgage payable	$10,300	
Total non-current liabilities		10,300
Total liabilities		27,350
Shareholders' equity		
Common shares	$74,000	
Retained earnings	50,050	
Total shareholders' equity		124,050
Total liabilities and shareholders' equity		$151,400

Illustration 2-9 uses the common practice among North American companies of classifying the items on the statement of financial position in order of liquidity (from the most to the least liquid). Accounting standards do not prescribe the order in which items are presented in the statement of financial position. As was mentioned earlier in the chapter, international companies often present items in this statement using a reverse order of liquidity. Some Canadian companies, especially financial institutions and real estate companies, use this reverse-liquidity order format as well. Plazacorp, our feature company in this chapter, presents items in its statement of financial position in this manner.

Statements prepared using a reverse-liquidity order usually show assets first followed by shareholders' equity and liabilities. The assets section starts with non-current assets, followed by current assets. Non-current assets include goodwill and intangible assets; property, plant, and equipment; and long-term investments, which are normally grouped under a non-current heading. This differs from the separate disclosure of non-current assets without a heading that is more usual in North America, as we saw in Illustration 2-9. Within the current assets section, items are listed in reverse order of liquidity; that is, cash is normally shown last. Items within the property, plant, and equipment section are normally listed in order of permanency, similar to that shown in Illustration 2-9.

Shareholders' equity is shown next, followed by liabilities. The liabilities section presents non-current liabilities before current liabilities, and current liabilities are listed in reverse order of liquidity similar to current assets.

This difference in ordering assets and liabilities is summarized in Illustration 2-10.

▶Illustration 2-10

Order of items presented in the statement of financial position

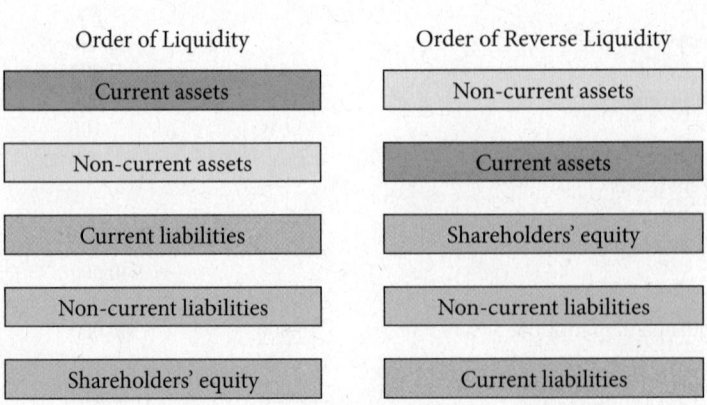

Companies are allowed to choose how to order items so they can provide information that is most useful to their users. For your assignments, it is recommended that you use the standard order used by most North American companies—that is, in order of decreasing liquidity—unless specifically instructed to do otherwise.

▶Do It! Statement of Financial Position Classifications

The following selected accounts were taken from a company's statement of financial position:

_____ Accounts payable
_____ Accounts receivable
_____ Accumulated depreciation—buildings
_____ Bank loan payable (due in 6 months)
_____ Buildings
_____ Cash
_____ Common shares
_____ Goodwill
_____ Income tax payable
_____ Interest payable
_____ Land
_____ Merchandise inventory
_____ Mortgage payable (due in 10 years)
_____ Notes receivable (due in 3 months)
_____ Prepaid insurance
_____ Retained earnings
_____ Salaries payable
_____ Sales taxes payable
_____ Supplies
_____ Trading investments
_____ Unearned revenue
_____ Vehicles

Classify each of the above accounts as current assets (CA), non-current assets (NCA), current liabilities (CL), non-current liabilities (NCL), or shareholders' equity (SE).

Action Plan

- Understand the differences between each broad statement classification: assets, liabilities, and shareholders' equity.
- Determine if asset and liability items are current or non-current by assessing whether the item is likely to be realized, paid, or settled within one year.

Solution

CL	Accounts payable
CA	Accounts receivable
NCA	Accumulated depreciation—buildings
CL	Bank loan payable (due in 6 months)
NCA	Buildings
CA	Cash
SE	Common shares
NCA	Goodwill
CL	Income tax payable
CL	Interest payable
NCA	Land
CA	Merchandise inventory
NCL	Mortgage payable (due in 10 years)
CA	Notes receivable (due in 3 months)
CA	Prepaid insurance
SE	Retained earnings
CL	Salaries payable
CL	Sales taxes payable
CA	Supplies
CA	Trading investments
CL	Unearned revenue
NCA	Vehicles

Related Exercise Material: BE2-1, BE2-2, BE2-3, BE2-4, E2-1, E2-2, E2-3, E2-4, and E2-5.

the navigator

Using the Financial Statements

In Chapter 1, we briefly discussed how the financial statements give information about a company's financial position and performance. In this chapter, we continue this discussion by showing you specific tools, such as ratio analysis, that can be used to analyze two of the financial statements—the statement of financial position and income statement—in order to make a more meaningful evaluation of a company.

Ratio analysis expresses the relationships between selected items of financial statement data. Liquidity, solvency, and profitability ratios are the three general types of ratios that are used to analyze financial statements, as shown in Illustration 2-11.

▸Illustration 2-11

Ratio classifications

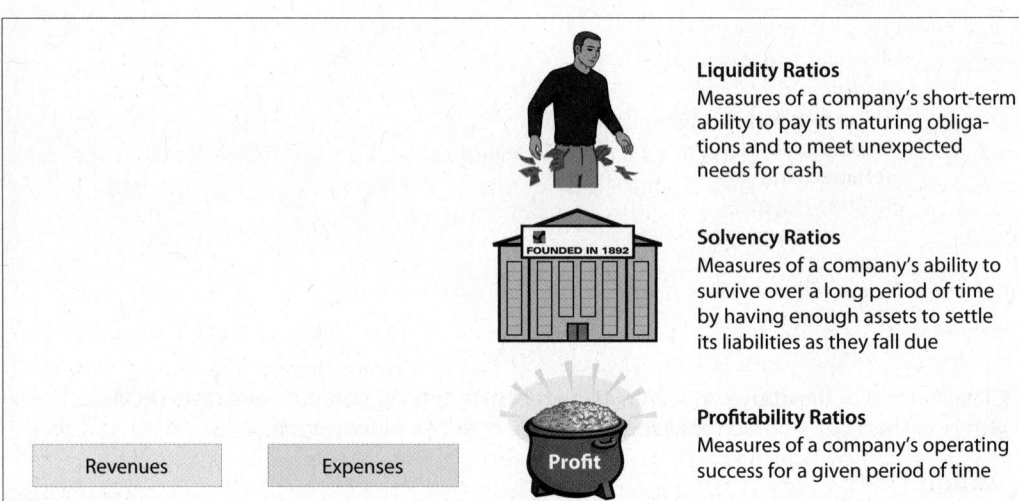

Liquidity Ratios
Measures of a company's short-term ability to pay its maturing obligations and to meet unexpected needs for cash

Solvency Ratios
Measures of a company's ability to survive over a long period of time by having enough assets to settle its liabilities as they fall due

Profitability Ratios
Measures of a company's operating success for a given period of time

Ratios can give clues about underlying conditions that may not be easy to see when the items of a particular ratio are examined separately. Since a single ratio by itself is not very meaningful, in this and later chapters we will use the following comparisons wherever possible:

1. **Intracompany comparisons** covering two or more periods for the same company
2. **Intercompany comparisons** based on comparisons with a competitor in the same industry
3. **Industry average comparisons** based on average ratios for particular industries with specific company ratios

In the following sections, we will introduce some examples of liquidity, solvency, and profitability ratios, using Plazacorp Retail Properties Ltd.'s statement of financial position and income statement.

To broaden our analysis to include an intercompany comparison, we will then compare Plazacorp's ratios for two years with those of one of its competitors, First Capital Realty Inc. Finally, we will compare ratios for Plazacorp and First Capital Realty with those from their industry.

USING THE STATEMENT OF FINANCIAL POSITION (BALANCE SHEET)

You can learn a great deal about a company's financial health by evaluating the relationships between its various assets and liabilities. A condensed statement of financial position for Plazacorp with comparative data for two fiscal years is shown in Illustration 2-12.

PLAZACORP RETAIL PROPERTIES LTD. Statement of Financial Position December 31 (in millions)		

Assets	2012	2011
Non-current assets	$599.8	$525.1
Current assets	7.5	25.2
Total assets	$607.3	$550.3
Liabilities and Shareholders' Equity		
Liabilities		
Non-current liabilities	$300.0	$317.4
Current liabilities	56.1	34.1
Total liabilities	356.1	351.5
Shareholders' equity	251.2	198.8
Total liabilities and shareholders' equity	$607.3	$550.3

▶Illustration 2-12

Plazacorp statement of financial position

As we mentioned earlier in the chapter, Plazacorp presents its statement of financial position in a reverse-liquidity order, although its shareholders' equity section is not positioned as shown in Illustration 2-10. Recall that companies have the option of presenting the information in their financial statements in a way that best meets the needs of their users.

Liquidity

Suppose you are a contractor entering into an arrangement to renovate some of the properties operated by Plazacorp. You would be concerned about Plazacorp's liquidity—its ability to pay obligations that are expected to become due within the next year. You would use liquidity ratios to look closely at the relationship of its current assets to its current liabilities. **Liquidity ratios** measure a company's short-term ability to pay its maturing obligations (usually its current liabilities), and to meet unexpected needs for cash. We will look at two examples of liquidity measures in this chapter—working capital and the current ratio—and others in later chapters.

Working Capital. One measure of liquidity is **working capital**, which is the difference between current assets and current liabilities. When working capital is positive, there is a greater likelihood that the company will be able to pay its liabilities. When working capital is negative, a company may have to borrow money; otherwise, short-term creditors may not be paid.

Illustration 2-13 shows the calculation of working capital for Plazacorp for 2012 and 2011, and compares it with that of First Capital Realty. Note that detailed calculations are not included for either First Capital Realty or the industry—just the results for comparison purposes.

WORKING CAPITAL = CURRENT ASSETS − CURRENT LIABILITIES		
($ in millions)	2012	2011
Plazacorp	$7.5 − $56.1 = $(48.6)	$25.2 − $34.1 = $(8.9)
First Capital Realty	$12.8	$(276.6)
Industry average	n/a	n/a

▶Illustration 2-13

Working capital

Plazacorp reported negative working capital in both 2012 and 2011, which means that its current liabilities exceeded its current assets. Note, however, that the fact that its working capital is negative does not mean that this company is nearing bankruptcy. It obtains monthly cash flows from tenant rent payments that are sufficient to meet its current obligations and some of its current liabilities consist of unearned revenues from rent collected in advance. Unearned revenues are not liabilities that have to be settled with cash. First Capital Realty, on the other hand, improved its working capital because it obtained a higher amount of cash during the year when it sold off some of its properties.

When industry averages are not available for the ratios that we calculate in this text, such as working capital, this is indicated by "n/a" (not available).

Current Ratio.   An important liquidity ratio is the **current ratio**, which is calculated by dividing current assets by current liabilities. The current ratio is a more dependable indicator of liquidity than working capital because it measures the relative relationship between current assets and current liabilities and therefore makes comparisons between smaller companies like Plazacorp and larger companies like First Capital Realty possible. Furthermore, two companies with the same amount of working capital may have significantly different current ratios.

The 2012 and 2011 current ratios for our two companies and the industry average are shown in Illustration 2-14.

▸Illustration 2-14
Current ratio

($ in millions)	CURRENT RATIO = $\dfrac{\text{CURRENT ASSETS}}{\text{CURRENT LIABILITIES}}$	
($ in millions)	2012	2011
Plazacorp	$\dfrac{\$7.5}{\$56.1} = 0.1{:}1$	$\dfrac{\$25.2}{\$34.1} = 0.7{:}1$
First Capital Realty	1.0:1	0.5:1
Industry average	0.9:1	2.0:1

What does the ratio actually mean? The 2012 current ratio of 0.1:1 means that for every dollar of current liabilities, Plazacorp has 10 cents of current assets. It is interesting to note that some industries tend to have much lower current ratios than we would expect. Although a general belief regarding the current ratio is that it should exceed a value of at least 1 to 1, we have to understand that this ratio will be different for companies in different industries. It is therefore more worthwhile to compare the ratios of competitors within an industry than the ratios of companies operating in different industries. Compared with a company that produces and sells inventory, real estate companies will not have inventories and since most tenants pay rent on time, their accounts receivable will be very low. Furthermore, since cash flows from rent are very predictable, large cash reserves are not needed. Therefore, compared with companies that sell inventory, a real estate company will have much lower current assets and this is the major reason for the lower current ratios we see above.

The current ratio is only one measure of liquidity. It does not take into account the composition of the current assets. For example, a satisfactory current ratio may not reveal that a portion of the current assets can be tied up in uncollectible accounts receivable or slow-moving inventory. The composition of the assets matters because a dollar of cash is more easily available to pay current liabilities falling due than is a dollar of inventory. For example, suppose a company's cash balance declined while its inventory increased by an even greater amount. To finance this increase in inventory, the company obtained long-term bank loans. Consequently, current assets will rise. If inventory increased because the company was having difficulty selling it, then the current ratio, which is rising, would not fully reflect the reduction in the company's liquidity. We will look at these effects in more detail in later chapters.

DECISION TOOLKIT

Decision Checkpoints

Info Needed for Decision

Tools to Use for Decision

How to Evaluate Results

Decision Checkpoints	Info Needed for Decision	Tools to Use for Decision	How to Evaluate Results
Can the company meet its short-term obligations?	Current assets and current liabilities	Working capital = Current assets − Current liabilities	A higher amount indicates liquidity.
		Current ratio = $\dfrac{\text{Current assets}}{\text{Current liabilities}}$	A higher ratio suggests favourable liquidity.

Solvency

Now suppose that, instead of being a short-term creditor, you are interested in either buying Plazacorp's shares or making a long-term loan to the company. Investors and long-term lenders are interested in a company's long-run solvency—its ability to pay interest as it comes due and to repay the face value of debt at maturity. **Solvency ratios** measure a company's ability to survive over a long period of time by having enough assets to settle its liabilities as they fall due.

Debt to Total Assets. The **debt to total assets** ratio is one source of information about long-term debt-paying ability. It measures the percentage of assets that are financed by lenders and other creditors rather than by shareholders. Financing provided by lenders and creditors (debt) is riskier than financing provided by shareholders (equity) because debt and the related interest must be repaid at specific points in time, whether the company is performing well or not. On the other hand, equity does not have to be repaid and there is no requirement for companies to pay dividends.

The debt to total assets ratio is calculated by dividing total debt (both current and non-current liabilities) by total assets. The higher the percentage of debt to total assets, the greater is the risk that the company may be unable to pay its debts as they come due. The ratios of debt to total assets for Plazacorp, First Capital Realty, and the industry average are shown in Illustration 2-15.

> **Helpful Hint**
> Some users evaluate solvency using a ratio of debt divided by shareholders' equity. The lower this "debt to equity" ratio, the better a company's solvency.

▶ Illustration 2-15
Debt to total assets

DEBT TO TOTAL ASSETS = $\dfrac{\text{TOTAL LIABILITIES}}{\text{TOTAL ASSETS}}$		
($ in millions)	2012	2011
Plazacorp	$\dfrac{\$356.1}{\$607.3} = 58.6\%$	$\dfrac{\$351.5}{\$550.3} = 63.9\%$
First Capital Realty	55.4%	58.7%
Industry average	65.0%	71.0%

The 2012 ratio for Plazacorp means that approximately 59 cents of every dollar that the company invested in assets was provided by its lenders and other creditors. Plazacorp's ratio improved (fell) in 2012. The same decrease occurred for First Capital Realty and the industry overall. During the recent recession, many real estate companies had debt levels that were too high and the decrease that we see above reflects the industry's desire to have lower levels of debt relative to assets. The higher the ratio, the higher the amount of interest expense that a company will incur. If liabilities are too high, there is a lower equity "cushion" available to lenders and other creditors if the company becomes insolvent (unable to pay its debts). Thus, from the lenders' and other creditors' point of view, a high ratio of debt to total assets is undesirable and they would view the ratios of the two companies above as favourable when compared with the industry average.

DECISION TOOLKIT

 Decision Checkpoints	 Info Needed for Decision	 Tools to Use for Decision	 How to Evaluate Results
Can the company meet its long-term obligations?	Total debt and total assets	Debt to total assets = $\dfrac{\text{Total liabilities}}{\text{Total assets}}$	A lower percentage suggests favourable solvency.

■ **Keeping an Eye on Cash**

In the statement of cash flows, cash provided by operating activities is intended to indicate the company's cash-generating capability. Analysts have noted, however, that cash provided by operating activities fails to take into account the fact that a company must invest in new property, plant, and equipment (capital expenditures) just to maintain its current level of operations. A company must also try to maintain dividends at current levels to satisfy investors.

A solvency measurement that offers additional insight regarding a company's cash-generating ability is free cash flow. Free cash flow describes the cash remaining from operating activities after adjusting for capital expenditures and dividends paid.

Consider the following example: For the year ended September 29, 2012, Apple Inc. generated almost U.S. $51 billion in cash flow from its operations but spent only U.S. $10 billion on new property, plant, and equipment. Its free cash flow was over U.S. $40 billion. When such a large amount of free cash flow is generated by a company and it cannot find ways to spend it by increasing capital expenditures, shareholders begin to demand dividend payments, which is exactly what Apple did just before releasing its September 29, 2012, financial statements. The company paid over U.S. $2 billion in dividends during the 2012 fiscal year. Some shareholders still felt that even more dividends should have been paid out given the large amount of free cash flow.

USING THE INCOME STATEMENT

Plazacorp generates profits for its shareholders by earning rent from tenants. The income statement reports how successful it is at generating profit from its rental operations. Illustration 2-16 shows a condensed and simplified income statement for Plazacorp, with comparative data for two recent fiscal years.

►Illustration 2-16
Plazacorp's income statement

PLAZACORP RETAIL PROPERTIES LTD. Income Statement Year Ended December 31 (in millions)		
	2012	2011
Sales revenue	$ 59.4	$55.6
Other revenues	48.7	30.5
Total revenues	108.1	86.1
Operating expenses	30.1	25.7
Finance expenses	16.7	20.7
Other expenses		0.2
Total expenses	46.8	46.6
Profit before income tax expense	61.3	39.5
Income tax expense	14.2	10.5
Profit	$ 47.1	$29.0

PLAZA

Profitability

Existing and potential investors, lenders, and other creditors are interested in a company's profitability. **Profitability ratios** measure a company's operating success for a specific period of time. We will look at two examples of profitability ratios in this chapter: earnings per share and the price-earnings ratio.

Earnings per Share.   **Earnings per share (EPS)** measures the profit earned on each common share. Accordingly, earnings per share is reported only for common shareholders. It is calculated by dividing the profit available to the common shareholders by the weighted average number of common shares.

Unless a company has preferred shares, the profit available to common shareholders will be the same as the profit reported on a company's income statement. If a company has preferred shares, preferred share dividends must be deducted from profit. We will learn more about how to calculate profit available to common shareholders and the weighted average number of shares in Chapter 11.

Shareholders usually think in terms of the number of shares they own—or plan to buy or sell— so reducing profit to a per-share amount gives a useful number for determining the investment return. In fact, earnings per share is such an important measure that it must be presented in the financial statements for publicly traded companies. It is the only ratio with this requirement. Private corporations reporting under Accounting Standards for Private Enterprises are not required to report earnings per share.

The earnings per share for both Plazacorp and First Capital Realty are shown below in Illustration 2-17.

EARNINGS PER SHARE = $\dfrac{\text{PROFIT AVAILABLE TO COMMON SHAREHOLDERS}}{\text{WEIGHTED AVERAGE NUMBER OF COMMON SHARES}}$		
	2012	2011
Plazacorp	$0.68	$0.46
First Capital Realty	$2.08	$3.27
Industry average	n/a	n/a

► Illustration 2-17
Earnings per share

Comparisons of earnings per share are not very meaningful among companies, because of the wide variation in the number of shares issued by each company and because some companies use financing structures with different levels of debt and equity. This is why there is no industry average for earnings per share in Illustration 2-17.

Price-Earnings Ratio.   Although we cannot compare the earnings per share of two companies, we can use this amount to calculate a ratio that is comparable. This is the **price-earnings (P-E) ratio**. The price-earnings ratio is a frequently quoted statistic that measures the ratio of the stock market price of each common share to its earnings per share. It is calculated by dividing the market price per share by earnings per share.

We should note that we have classified the price-earnings ratio as a profitability ratio for simplicity in this chapter. In later chapters, we will learn that the P-E ratio is not really a measure of "corporate" profitability but rather a profitability ratio used by investors for valuation purposes.

The market price of Plazacorp's shares at year end was $4.95 and $4.65, respectively, for 2012 and 2011. If we take these prices and divide them by the earnings per share amounts for each applicable year from Illustration 2-17, we can determine the price-earnings ratios as shown in Illustration 2-18.

PRICE-EARNINGS RATIO = $\dfrac{\text{MARKET PRICE PER SHARE}}{\text{EARNINGS PER SHARE}}$		
	2012	2011
Plazacorp	$\dfrac{\$4.95}{\$0.68}$ = 7.3 times	$\dfrac{\$4.65}{\$0.46}$ = 10.1 times
First Capital Realty	9.6 times	7.2 times
Industry average	5.0 times	4.6 times

► Illustration 2-18
Price-earnings ratio

The price-earnings ratio shows what investors expect of a company's future profitability. This ratio will be higher if investors think that current profit levels will increase and it will be lower if investors think that profits will decline.

In 2012, Plazacorp recorded an increase in the value of some of its properties and this increased profit. As these properties were not actually sold for cash, the share price did not rise to reflect this and the price-earnings ratio fell because the denominator rose but not the numerator. First Capital Realty had a similar event but it was recorded in 2011, causing a major increase in profit in that year.

In 2012, a similar increase was not recorded so earnings per share fell, with very little change to the share price, which resulted in an increase in the price-earnings ratio.

Both Plazacorp and First Capital Realty's price-earnings ratios exceeded that of the industry average in both years. It is difficult to compare these two companies with the industry average as not all companies in this industry use the revaluation model and adjust the value of their properties to fair value each year.

ACCOUNTING MATTERS!

Using Ratios to Make Investment Decisions

Benjamin Graham was an economist who taught finance at Columbia University. In 1949 he authored one of the most famous books on investing, called *The Intelligent Investor*, in which he urged investors to buy stable, profitable companies when their share prices were low. He also thought that the company's current ratio should be greater than 2 : 1, indicating that the company had good liquidity, which gave it a margin of safety. One of Graham's students was Warren Buffett, who bought shares in a company called Berkshire Hathaway in 1962 for just over $11 per share. He used that company to invest in other companies. By early 2013, one Berkshire Hathaway share was worth over $160,000, making Warren Buffet the second-richest U.S. citizen, behind Bill Gates, the co-founder of Microsoft.[2]

DECISION TOOLKIT

Decision Checkpoints	Info Needed for Decision	Tools to Use for Decision	How to Evaluate Results
How does the company's profit compare with previous years?	Profit available to common shareholders and weighted average number of common shares	Earnings per share = $\dfrac{\text{Profit available to common shareholders}}{\text{Weighted average number of common shares}}$	A higher measure suggests improved performance. Values should not be compared across companies.
How does the market see the company's prospects for future profitability?	Market price per share and earnings per share	Price-earnings ratio = $\dfrac{\text{Market price per share}}{\text{Earnings per share}}$	A high ratio suggests the market expects good performance, although it may also suggest that shares are overvalued.

BEFORE YOU GO ON...

▶ Do It! Ratio Analysis

Selected financial information is available for Drummond Inc.

	2015	2014
Current assets	$ 72,000	$ 60,800
Total assets	400,000	341,000
Current liabilities	40,000	38,000
Total liabilities	180,000	150,000
Profit	90,000	40,000
Weighted average number of common shares	90,000	50,000
Market price per common share	12	8

Drummond has no preferred shares, so profit is equal to the profit available to common shareholders.

(a) Calculate the (1) current, (2) debt to total assets, (3) earnings per share, and (4) price-earnings ratios for each year.

(b) Based on the ratios calculated in part (a), state whether there was an improvement or deterioration in liquidity, solvency, and profitability for Drummond in 2015.

Action Plan

- Use the formula for the current ratio: current assets ÷ current liabilities.
- Use the formula for debt to total assets: total liabilities ÷ total assets.
- Use the formula for earnings per share: profit available to common shareholders ÷ weighted average number of common shares.
- Understand that higher is better for liquidity and profitability ratios and lower is better for certain solvency ratios, like debt to total assets.

Solution

(a)

	2015	2014	Comparison
1. Current ratio	$ 72,000 ÷ $40,000 = 1.8:1	$60,800 ÷ $38,000 = 1.6:1	Improved
2. Debt to total assets ratio	$180,000 ÷ $400,000 = 45.0%	$150,000 ÷ $341,000 = 44.0%	Deteriorated
3. Earnings per share	$90,000 ÷ 90,000 = $1.00	$40,000 ÷ 50,000 = $0.80	Improved
4. Price-earnings ratio	$12 ÷ $1 = 12 times	$8 ÷ $0.80 = 10 times	Improved

(b) Liquidity: The current ratio increased from 1.6:1 in 2014 to 1.8:1 in 2015. This would be viewed as an improvement, depending on how the composition of its current assets (such as receivables and inventories) changed.

Solvency: The debt to total assets ratio increased from 44% in 2014 to 45% in 2015. This would be viewed as a deterioration as the company has a higher debt, as a percentage of its assets, to repay in the future.

Profitability: Both the earnings per share and price-earnings ratios increased between 2014 and 2015. Both would be viewed as an improvement. Investors are viewing Drummond's potential to generate future profits favourably, as indicated by the price-earnings ratio.

Related Exercise Material: BE2-5, BE2-6, BE2-7, E2-6, E2-7, and E2-8.

the navigator

Framework for the Preparation and Presentation of Financial Statements

How do Plazacorp and First Capital Realty decide on the type of financial information to disclose? What format should they use? How should they measure assets, liabilities, revenues, and expenses? These and all other companies get guidance from a standardized framework for the preparation and presentation of financial statements called the conceptual framework for financial reporting. Standard-setting bodies, in consultation with the accounting profession and business community, determine this framework.

According to standard setters, the **conceptual framework** is "a coherent system of interrelated objectives and fundamentals that can lead to consistent standards and that prescribes the nature, function, and limits of financial accounting statements." In other words, the conceptual framework

STUDY OBJECTIVE 3

Describe the framework for the preparation and presentation of financial statements.

of accounting guides decisions about what to present in financial statements, alternative ways of reporting economic events, and appropriate ways of communicating this information.

Not every country uses the same conceptual framework or set of accounting standards. They can, and do, differ significantly from country to country. This lack of uniformity has arisen over time because of differences in legal systems, in processes for developing standards, in government requirements, and in economic environments.

The International Accounting Standards Board (IASB)—the standard-setting body responsible for developing International Financial Reporting Standards—was formed to reduce these areas of difference and unify global standard setting. Currently, more than 125 countries either require or permit the use of IFRS. This includes Canada, which adopted IFRS in 2011. Most remaining major economies have established timelines to converge with, or to make a decision to adopt, IFRS in the near future. This includes Canada's most significant trading partner, the United States, which is evaluating whether to eventually adopt IFRS as the required set of standards for U.S. publicly traded companies or to simply incorporate parts of IFRS into U.S standards. In the meantime, accounting standard setters for the IASB and its U.S. equivalent, the Financial Accounting Standards Board (FASB), are working closely together to minimize the differences in their standards.

One initiative under way by the IASB is a project to update the conceptual framework. Some of the key conceptual framework items we will cover in this chapter include:

- Objective of general purpose financial reporting
- Qualitative characteristics of useful financial information
- Underlying assumption
- Elements of financial statements
- Measurement of the elements of financial statements

There are other portions of the conceptual framework that will be discussed in future accounting courses. For the purpose of this textbook, we will concentrate on the sections outlined above.

We must note that the work to update the conceptual framework is being completed in phases. At the time of writing, the first two components described above—the objective and qualitative characteristics—had been finalized. Work on the other sections of the conceptual framework outlined above was suspended in 2010 but began again in early 2013 and had yet to be finalized at the time of writing. Consequently, some of the specific definitions for elements of the financial statements may change slightly after this textbook is published, but these changes will not change the basic meaning of the elements of financial statements for our purposes.

The conceptual framework is fundamentally similar for publicly traded companies in Canada reporting under IFRS and private companies reporting under ASPE. While there are some differences, the Accounting Standards Board—the Canadian accounting standard setter—has committed to update the conceptual framework for private companies to remain consistent with the IASB conceptual framework. It does not believe that the differences between publicly accountable companies and private companies justify different conceptual frameworks.

OBJECTIVE OF FINANCIAL REPORTING

The **objective of financial reporting** is to provide financial information about a company that is useful to existing and potential investors, lenders, and other creditors in making decisions about providing resources to the company. Those decisions involve buying, selling, or holding equity and debt instruments and providing or settling loans and other forms of credit. Although a wide variety of users rely on financial reporting, investors, lenders, and other creditors are identified as the main users of financial reporting. You will recall that we discussed these and other users and their needs in Chapter 1.

Financial information about a company is provided by general purpose financial statements that strive to meet the needs of all users. These statements provide information about the company's economic resources and the claims against these resources. Financial statements also provide information about the effects of transactions and other events that change a company's economic resources and claims. Both types of information provide useful input for decisions made by external users about providing resources to the company.

Financial statements are prepared using the **accrual basis of accounting**. Under the accrual basis of accounting, the effects of transactions on a company's economic resources and claims are recorded in the period when a transaction occurs and not when cash is received or paid. For example, a law firm would record revenue in the accounting period when the legal services are provided to the client and not necessarily in the accounting period when the client pays for the services. We will learn about the accrual basis of accounting in the next two chapters.

QUALITATIVE CHARACTERISTICS OF USEFUL FINANCIAL INFORMATION

The qualitative characteristics of useful financial information identify the types of information that are likely to be most useful to existing and potential investors, lenders, and other creditors in making their decisions. The qualitative characteristics are divided into those that are fundamental and those that are enhancing.

Fundamental Qualitative Characteristics

The two fundamental qualitative characteristics of useful financial information are (1) relevance and (2) faithful representation. To be useful for decision-making, information must be relevant and faithfully represent the proper meaning of that information.

Accounting information has **relevance** if knowledge of it will influence a user's decision. Relevant information may have predictive value, confirmatory value, or both. Financial information has **predictive value** if it helps users make predictions about future events. Financial information has **confirmatory value** if it helps users confirm or correct their previous predictions or expectations. For example, information about a company's sales for the current year can be used as a basis to help predict sales in one or more future years. It can also be compared with sales predictions that were made in past years. The results of such comparisons can help a user to confirm or correct the processes that were used to make these previous predictions.

Materiality is an important component of relevance. Information is considered material if its omission or misstatement could influence the decisions of users. Materiality and relevance are both defined in terms of what influences or makes a difference to a decision maker. A decision not to disclose certain information may be made, say, because users have no need for that kind of information (it is not relevant) or because the amounts involved are too small to make a difference (they are not material). Magnitude by itself, without regard to the nature of the item and the circumstances in which the judgement has to be made, is not generally a sufficient basis for a materiality judgement. For example, if a government official receives a bribe, the amount involved may not be significant but because of its nature, knowledge of the bribe will affect decisions that users of that information will make.

For accounting information to be useful, it must not only be relevant but it must represent economic reality; that is, it must be a **faithful representation** of what really exists or happened. Often this requires accountants to report the economic substance rather than the legal form of an event. For example, if a company sells a product to a customer but agrees to buy it back at a later date, there really is no sale (the product was simply loaned to the customer), and to faithfully represent this event, no sale would be recorded. To provide a faithful representation, information must be **complete** (nothing important was omitted), neutral (not biased toward one position or another), and **free from material error**.

Complete, unbiased, and factual information that is faithfully represented is critical in financial reporting. Of course, perfection is seldom, if ever, achievable. Consequently, faithful representation does not necessarily mean accuracy in all respects. For example, as we will learn in later chapters, estimates are required in accounting, and estimates may not be accurate. However, a representation of an estimate can be faithful if the amount is described as being an estimate, the nature and limitations of the estimating process are explained, and no errors have been made in the process used to develop the estimate.

ACCOUNTING MATTERS!

Getting the Numbers Right

On November 4, 2011, Poseidon Concepts Ltd. shares began trading on the Toronto Stock Exchange. The Calgary-based corporation rented fluid holding tanks to companies engaged in horizontal drilling of oil and gas wells. The company's shares began trading at just over $11 and management planned to pay out more than $1 of dividends per share annually. This meant that, even if the share price did not change, an investor would receive a return on his or her investment of almost 10% per year. Since the dividend was attractive to investors and because the company was expected to grow rapidly, more shares were sold to the public at $13 each in February 2012. Following this, the share price rose to over $16 per share.

In its income statement for the nine months ending September 30, 2012, Poseidon reported revenues of over $148 million, which was more than triple the revenue reported in the same nine-month period in 2011. However, a new expense was recorded for the first time on those financial statements. This was bad debt expense and it represents the value of accounts receivable that are determined to be uncollectible. The bad debt expense was over $9 million. When investors saw this, the share price plunged by more than 60%.

On November 27, 2012, a class action lawsuit was launched against the company claiming that some of the revenues should not have been recorded. On December 27, 2012, the board of directors appointed a special committee to investigate this issue and suspended all dividend payments. After an internal investigation, the company announced on February 13, 2013, that more than $95 million of the revenue reported should not have been recorded. On the following day, Poseidon shares ceased trading. At that time, the shares had a value of $0.27 each. By May 17, 2013, the shares were delisted from the Toronto Stock Exchange and the company's assets were up for sale.

Accounting problems like the one at Poseidon have made it clear that those who prepare financial statements must get the numbers right in order to provide relevant and faithfully represented information that is useful to external users.[3]

Enhancing Qualitative Characteristics

In addition to the two fundamental qualities of relevance and faithful representation, the conceptual framework also describes four enhancing qualities of useful information. These are (1) comparability, (2) verifiability, (3) timeliness, and (4) understandability.

In accounting, **comparability** results when users can identify and understand similarities in, and differences among, items. **Consistency**, although related to comparability, does not mean the same thing. Instead, consistency aids comparability when a company uses the same accounting principles and methods from year to year or when companies with similar circumstances use the same accounting principles. Therefore, if a company prepares financial statements on a consistent basis each year, the financial statements from each of those years will be comparable. If all companies within an industry use the same accounting principles, their financial statements will become more comparable. This does not mean that a company can never change from one accounting principle to another. Companies can change accounting principles, but only if the change is required by the standard setters or if the change will result in more relevant information for decision-making.

Information has **verifiability** if different knowledgeable and independent users can reach consensus that the information is faithfully represented. Verifiability can be determined by verifying an amount directly; for example, by counting cash. It can also be determined by checking the inputs to a formula and recalculating the outputs. Public accountants perform audits of financial statements to verify their accuracy.

For accounting information to be relevant, it must have **timeliness**. That is, it must be available to decision makers before it loses its ability to influence decisions. For example, regulators require that public companies listed on major stock exchanges provide their financial statements to investors within 90 days of their year end.

Information has the quality of **understandability** if it is classified, characterized, and presented clearly and concisely. Understandable information means that users with a reasonable knowledge of business can interpret the information and comprehend its meaning.

Applying the enhancing qualitative characteristics is an iterative process that does not have to follow a prescribed order. In addition, sometimes one enhancing qualitative characteristic may have to be given less emphasis in order to maximize another qualitative characteristic. For example, a new financial reporting standard may improve relevance or faithful representation in the longer term while comparability of results with prior periods is sacrificed in the shorter term.

COST CONSTRAINT ON USEFUL FINANCIAL REPORTING

The **cost constraint** is a pervasive constraint that ensures that the value of the information provided in financial reporting is greater than the cost of providing it. That is, the benefits of financial reporting information should justify the costs of providing and using it.

For example, to achieve completeness, which we discussed along with the fundamental qualitative characteristic of faithful representation, accountants could record or disclose every financial event that occurs and every uncertainty that exists. However, providing additional information increases costs, and the benefits of providing this information, in some cases, may be less than the costs.

UNDERLYING ASSUMPTION

A key assumption—the going concern assumption—creates a foundation for the accounting process. The **going concern assumption** assumes that a company will continue to operate for the foreseeable future. Of course, some businesses do fail. However, if a business has a history of profitable operations and access to financial resources, it is reasonable to assume that it will continue operating long enough to carry out its existing objectives and commitments.

The going concern assumption has important implications in accounting. If a company is assumed to be a going concern, then reporting assets, such as equipment, as non-current makes sense because those assets are expected to be used for more than one year. Without the going concern assumption, we would be assuming that the business is in the process of shutting down and is selling all of its assets as soon as possible. In that case, the equipment would be a current asset so the going concern assumption is essential to the way we record items in the financial statements.

ELEMENTS OF FINANCIAL STATEMENTS

Financial statements portray the financial effects of transactions and other events by grouping them into broad categories or classes according to their economic characteristics. These broad classes are termed the **elements of financial statements**, which include **assets**, **liabilities**, **equity**, **income** (including gains), and **expenses** (including losses).

Because these elements are so important and are often interrelated, they must be precisely defined and universally measured and applied. You were briefly introduced to these definitions in Chapter 1. We will summarize them in Illustration 2-19 and will discuss these definitions in more detail in later chapters.

▶Illustration 2-19
Elements of financial statements

Assets An asset is a resource controlled by the company as a result of past events and from which future economic benefits are expected to flow to the company.

Liabilities A liability is a present obligation of the company arising from past events, the settlement of which is expected to result in an outflow from the company of resources embodying economic benefits.

Equity Equity is the residual interest in the assets of the company after deducting all its liabilities.

Income Income includes both revenue and gains. Revenue arises in the course of the ordinary activities of the company while gains may or may not arise from ordinary activities. Income is the increase in economic benefits during the accounting period in the form of inflows or enhancements of assets or decreases of liabilities that result in increases in equity, other than those relating to contributions from equity participants.

Expenses Expenses include losses as well as those expenses that arise from ordinary activities of the company. Losses may or may not arise from ordinary activities. Expenses are decreases in economic benefits during the accounting period in the form of outflows or depletions of assets or incurrence of liabilities that result in decreases in equity, other than those relating to distributions to equity participants.

MEASUREMENT OF THE ELEMENTS

Using the objective of financial reporting, the qualitative characteristics, and the underlying assumption described in the previous sections, standard setters have developed foundational principles that describe which, when, and how the elements of financial statements should be recognized, measured, and reported. These foundational principles are known as generally accepted accounting principles (GAAP), which were introduced to you in Chapter 1. In Canada, "generally accepted" means that these principles are widely recognized and have authoritative support through the Canadian and provincial business corporations acts and securities legislation.

Generally accepted accounting principles related to the *recognition* of the elements of financial statements will be introduced in Chapter 4. In this chapter, we introduce two bases of *measurement*— historical cost and fair value. These are more commonly referred to as "measurement bases" rather than "principles," although both terms can be, and are, used interchangeably. It is worth noting that, although we discuss only two bases of measurement here, a number of different measurement models are used to different degrees and in varying combinations in financial statements.

Alternative Terminology
The words *principles, standards, policies, models,* and *bases* are used interchangeably in accounting.

Historical Cost

The **cost basis of accounting** states that assets and liabilities should be recorded at their cost at the time of acquisition. This is true not only at the time when the item is purchased, but also during the time that an asset or liability is held.

For example, if a company were to purchase land for $3 million, it would be recorded and reported on the statement of financial position at $3 million at the time of purchase. But what would the company do if by the end of the next year the land had increased in value to $4 million? The answer is that under historical cost, the land would still be reported at $3 million. In this particular case, cost is the most **relevant** value because the land is intended for use in the business. It is not being held for resale. The land will continue to be reported at cost until either it is sold or the **going concern assumption** is no longer valid.

Fair Value

The **fair value basis of accounting** states that certain assets and liabilities should be recorded and reported at fair value (the price that would be received to sell an asset or paid to transfer a liability). It is worth noting that at the acquisition date, cost and fair value are generally the same. It is only as time passes that these two values diverge and fair value may become a more useful measure than cost for certain types of assets and liabilities. For example, certain investment securities held for trading are reported at fair value because market price information is readily available for these types of assets and they are intended to be sold, in which case the fair value is more relevant for users' needs.

In choosing between cost and fair value, two fundamental qualitative characteristics that make financial information useful for decision-making are applied: relevance and faithful representation. Recall that in our chapter-opening feature story Plazacorp chose to use fair value because it felt it was a more **relevant** measure for its income-producing properties.

In determining which basis of measurement to use, the factual nature of the cost figures must be weighed against the relevance of the fair value figures. In general, standard setters require that most assets be recorded using historical cost because fair values may not always be representationally faithful. That is, cost is the more faithful representation because it can be easily verified and is neutral. Only in situations where assets are actively traded, such as investment securities or investment properties in certain industries such as the real estate industry, is the fair value basis of accounting applied.

SUMMARY OF CONCEPTUAL FRAMEWORK

As we have seen, the conceptual framework for developing sound reporting practices starts with the objective of financial reporting—providing financial information that is useful for decision-making. Financial information is provided by general purpose financial statements that are prepared using the accrual basis of accounting. Qualitative characteristics help ensure that the information provided in these statements is useful. A key assumption—the going concern assumption—underlies the preparation of financial statements. The elements of the financial statements define the main terms used in the financial statements and measurement bases describe how the elements of financial statements should be measured and reported.

The conceptual framework is summarized in Illustration 2-20.

Objective of Financial Reporting		

Qualitative Characteristics of Useful Financial Information		
Fundamental Qualitative Characteristics	Enhancing Qualitative Characteristics	Constraint
1. Relevance • Predictive value • Confirmatory value • Materiality 2. Faithful representation • Complete • Neutral • Free from material error	1. Comparability 2. Verifiability 3. Timeliness 4. Understandability	1. Cost

▶ Illustration 2-20
Summary of conceptual framework

Underlying Assumption—Going Concern	

Elements of Financial Statements	Measurement of the Elements
1. Assets 2. Liabilities 3. Equity 4. Revenue 5. Expenses	1. Historical cost 2. Fair value

BEFORE YOU GO ON...

▶ Do It! Conceptual Framework

The following is an alphabetized list of the qualitative characteristics, assumption, and measurement bases found in the conceptual framework for financial reporting.

1. Comparability
2. Cost constraint
3. Historical cost
4. Fair value
5. Faithful representation
6. Going concern
7. Relevance
8. Timeliness
9. Understandability
10. Verifiability

Match each item above with a description below.

(a) _____ The qualitative characteristic that the use of the same accounting principles enables evaluation of one company's results relative to another company's.

(b) _____ The qualitative characteristic for describing information that indicates that the information makes a difference in a decision.

(c) _____ The basis of measurement that assets are reported at the cost incurred to acquire the item.

(d) _____ The qualitative characteristic that the value of information should exceed the cost of preparing it.

(e) _____ The qualitative characteristic that presents a true and transparent picture of what really exists or happened.

(continued)

(f) _____ The qualitative characteristic that information can be recalculated and determined to be without errors or omissions.

(g) _____ The qualitative characteristic that information is available before it loses its ability to influence decisions.

(h) _____ The assumption that a company will continue to operate for the foreseeable future.

(i) _____ The qualitative characteristic that informed users are able to interpret information and comprehend its meaning.

(j) _____ The basis of measurement that assets are reported at the price that would be received if the item was sold.

Action Plan

- Understand the fundamental and enhancing qualitative characteristics of accounting information:
  - Fundamental: relevance and faithful representation.
  - Enhancing: comparability, verifiability, timeliness, and understandability.
  - Constraint: cost.
- Understand the underlying assumption of the accounting process: going concern.
- Understand the choice between how the elements of financial statements are measured: historical cost or fair value.

Solution

(a) 1   (b) 7   (c) 3   (d) 2   (e) 5   (f) 10   (g) 8   (h) 6   (i) 9   (j) 4

Related Exercise Material: BE2-8, BE2-9, BE2-10, E2-9, and E2-10.

comparing
IFRS and ASPE

Key Differences	International Financial Reporting Standards (IFRS)	Accounting Standards for Private Enterprises (ASPE)
Terminology	The term *depreciation* refers to the allocation of the cost of depreciable tangible assets over their useful lives. The term *amortization* refers to the allocation of the cost of certain kinds of intangible assets over their useful lives.	The term *amortization* is used for the allocation of the cost of both depreciable tangible assets and certain kinds of intangible assets over their useful lives.
Earnings per share	Required to present in financial statements	Not required to present in financial statements
Conceptual framework for financial reporting	Still under development	Same general framework currently under development by international and U.S. standard setters anticipated to be applied to private enterprises when complete

By now you should be comfortable with how to prepare a company's statement of financial position. Perhaps it is time to look at your personal statement of financial position. Similar to a corporate statement, a personal statement of financial position reports what you own and what you owe.

What are the items of value that you own—your personal assets? Some of your assets are liquid—cash and items of value that can be easily converted into cash. Others, such as vehicles, jewellery, art, electronics, real estate, and some types of investments, may be less liquid. Some assets, such as investments and real estate, tend to increase in value over time, thereby increasing your personal equity. Other assets, such as vehicles and computers, tend to fall in value, thereby decreasing your personal equity.

What are the amounts you owe—your personal liabilities? These liabilities may be either current (to be repaid within 12 months) or non-current (not to be paid until more than a year from now). Student loans, vehicle loans, credit card bills, and mortgages are all examples of liabilities.

Your personal equity is the difference between your total assets and your total liabilities. A person may have a high equity position but still have financial difficulties because of a shortage of cash. You can increase your equity in various ways, including increasing your savings, decreasing your spending, and increasing the value of your investments. Your personal equity is not money that is available for use. Rather it is an indication of your net assets (assets less liabilities) or financial position at a specific point in time.

Some Facts

- The average debt load of Canadians between ages 18 to 24 at the end of 2012 was $71,628 (up $3,030 or 4.4% from the previous year). The average debt load of Canadians between 25 and 44 was $137,259 (up $1,654 or 1.2%).
- Credit card companies continue to charge interest on outstanding balances of around 20%. Department store cards are closer to 30%. During the fourth quarter of 2012, credit card debt per Canadian household was approximately $3,637.
- Mortgage interest rates have never been lower. Banks are encouraging prospective homeowners to purchase homes at interest rates as low as 3%.
- A survey conducted on behalf of the Canadian Institute of Chartered Accountants indicated that one half of respondents identified reducing debt and minimizing interest payments as a priority. Approximately 6 in 10 respondents purchased only what they could afford. This means that 40% of Canadians are purchasing more than they can afford![4]

What Do You Think?

Should you prepare a personal statement of financial position?

YES In order to attain your financial goals, you need to know where you are starting from. The personal statement gives you an idea of how much debt you have in relation to the amount of assets you have accumulated (your personal debt to total assets ratio). The personal statement gives you a benchmark that will allow you to measure your progress toward your financial goals.

NO Your present financial position is dramatically different from what it will look like in the future. To date you have no debt and only purchase what you can afford. After graduation, you will have a job, or a better job, and you will not have to pay back any loans outstanding.

Summary of Study Objectives

1. *Identify the sections of a classified statement of financial position.* In a classified statement of financial position, assets are classified as current or non-current assets. In the non-current asset category, they are further classified as investments; property, plant, and equipment; intangible assets and goodwill; or other assets. Liabilities are classified as either current or non-current. There is also a shareholders' equity section, which shows share capital and retained earnings, among other equity items if any exist.

2. *Identify and calculate ratios for analyzing a company's liquidity, solvency, and profitability.* Liquidity ratios, such as working capital and the current ratio, measure a company's short-term ability to pay its maturing obligations and meet unexpected needs

for cash. Solvency ratios, such as debt to total assets, measure a company's ability to survive over a long period by having enough assets to settle its liabilities as they fall due. Profitability ratios, such as earnings per share and the price-earnings ratio, measure a company's operating success for a specific period of time.

3. *Describe the framework for the preparation and presentation of financial statements.* The key components of the conceptual framework are (1) the objective of financial reporting; (2) qualitative characteristics of useful financial information, which include fundamental and enhancing characteristics and the cost constraint; (3) the going concern assumption underlying the accounting process; (4) elements of the financial statements; and (5) measurement of the elements of financial statements.

Glossary

Accounts payable   Amounts owed to suppliers for purchases made on credit (on account). (p. 59)

Accounts receivable   Amounts owed by customers who purchased products or services on credit (on account). (p. 55)

Bank indebtedness   A short-term loan up to a maximum amount pre-arranged with a bank to cover cash shortfalls. (p. 59)

Comparability   An enhancing qualitative characteristic of useful information that enables users to identify and understand similarities in, and differences among, items. (p. 74)

Conceptual framework   A coherent system of interrelated elements that guides decisions about what to present in financial statements, alternative ways of reporting economic events, and appropriate ways of communicating this information. (p. 71)

Contra asset account   An account that is offset against (reduces) an asset account on the statement of financial position. (p. 57)

Cost basis of accounting   A basis of measurement that states that assets and liabilities should be recorded and reported at their cost at the time of acquisition, as well as during the time the asset is held. (p. 76)

Cost constraint   The constraint that the costs of obtaining and providing information should not be higher than the benefits that are gained by providing it. (p. 75)

Current assets   Cash and other resources that it is reasonable to expect will be converted into cash, or will be sold or used up within one year of the company's financial statement date or its operating cycle, whichever is longer. (p. 55)

Current liabilities   Obligations that will be paid or settled within one year of the company's financial statement date or its operating cycle, whichever is longer. (p. 59)

Current maturities of long-term debt   The portion of a non-current or long-term loan that is repayable in the current year. (p. 59)

Current ratio   A measure of liquidity used to evaluate a company's short-term debt-paying ability. It is calculated by dividing current assets by current liabilities. (p. 66)

Debt to total assets   A measure of solvency showing the percentage of total financing that is provided by lenders and other creditors. It is calculated by dividing total liabilities by total assets. (p. 67)

Earnings per share (EPS)   A measure of profitability showing the profit earned by each common share. It is calculated by dividing profit available to common shareholders by the weighted average number of common shares. (p. 68)

Elements of financial statements   A set of definitions of basic terms in accounting, such as assets, liabilities, equity, revenues, and expenses. (p. 75)

Fair value basis of accounting   A basis of measurement that states that assets should be reported at their fair value (price to sell). (p. 76)

Faithful representation   A fundamental qualitative characteristic describing information that represents economic reality. It must be complete, neutral, and free from material error. (p. 73)

Going concern assumption   The assumption that the business will remain in operation for the foreseeable future. (p. 75)

Intangible assets   Assets of a long-lived nature that do not have physical substance but represent a privilege or a right granted to, or held by, a company. (p. 57)

Liquidity ratios   Measures of a company's short-term ability to pay its maturing obligations (usually current liabilities) and to meet unexpected needs for cash. (p. 65)

Long-term investments   (also known as investments) Investments in debt securities intended to be held for many years to earn interest, and (2) equity securities of other companies held to generate investment revenue or held for strategic reasons. (p. 56)

Merchandise inventory   (also known as inventory) Goods held for sale to customers. (p. 55)

Non-current assets   (also known as long-term assets) Assets that are not expected to be converted into cash, sold, or used up by the business within one year of the statement date or its operating cycle. (p. 56)

Non-current liabilities (also known as long-term liabilities) Obligations that are not expected to be paid or settled within one year or the company's operating cycle. (p. 60)

Notes payable (also known as loans payable) Amounts owed to suppliers, banks, or others that are supported by a written promise to repay. (p. 59)

Notes receivable (also known as loans receivable) Amounts owed by customers or others that are supported by a written promise to repay. (p. 55)

Objective of financial reporting The provision of information about a company's financial position, performance, and changes in financial position that is useful to existing and potential investors, lenders, and other creditors in making decisions about providing resources to the company. (p. 72)

Operating cycle Average period of time it takes for a business to pay cash to obtain products or services and then receive cash from customers for these products or services. This can be one year or longer, depending on the type of business. (p. 55)

Prepaid expenses Costs paid in advance of use (such as rent and insurance). (p. 55)

Price-earnings (P-E) ratio A profitability measure of the ratio of the market price of each common share to the earnings per share. It reflects investors' beliefs about a company's future profit potential. (p. 69)

Profitability ratios Measures of a company's operating success for a specific period of time. (p. 68)

Property, plant, and equipment Tangible assets of a long-lived nature that are being used to operate the business. (p. 57)

Relevance A fundamental qualitative characteristic describing information that makes a difference in a decision. It should have predictive value, confirmatory value, or both, and be material. (p. 73)

Solvency ratios Measures of a company's ability to survive over a long period of time by having enough assets to settle its liabilities as they fall due. (p. 67)

Supplies Consumable items used in running a business, such as office and cleaning supplies. (p. 55)

Timeliness An enhancing qualitative characteristic of useful information that means that information is available to decision-makers in time to be capable of influencing their decisions. (p. 74)

Trading investments Investments in debt securities or equity securities of other companies that are bought with the intention of selling them after a short period of time in order to earn a profit from their price fluctuations. (p. 55)

Understandability An enhancing qualitative characteristic of useful information that means that information is clearly and concisely classified, characterized, and presented. (p. 74)

Unearned revenue Cash received when a customer pays in advance of being provided with a service or product. (p. 59)

Verifiability An enhancing qualitative characteristic of useful information that means that different knowledgeable and independent users could reach consensus, although not necessarily complete agreement, that the information is a faithful representation. (p. 74)

Working capital A measure of liquidity used to evaluate a company's short-term debt-paying ability. It is calculated by subtracting current liabilities from current assets. (p. 65)

DECISION TOOLKIT—A SUMMARY

 Decision Checkpoints	 Info Needed for Decision	 Tools to Use for Decision	 How to Evaluate Results
Can the company meet its short-term obligations?	Current assets and current liabilities	Working capital = Current assets − Current liabilities	A higher amount indicates liquidity.
		Current ratio = $\dfrac{\text{Current assets}}{\text{Current liabilities}}$	A higher ratio suggests favourable liquidity.
Can the company meet its long-term obligations?	Total debt and total assets	Debt to total assets = $\dfrac{\text{Total liabilities}}{\text{Total assets}}$	A lower percentage suggests favourable solvency.
How does the company's profit compare with previous years?	Profit available to common shareholders and weighted average number of common shares	Earnings per share = $\dfrac{\text{Profit available to common shareholders}}{\text{Weighted average number of common shares}}$	A higher measure suggests improved performance. Values should not be compared across companies.
How does the market see the company's prospects for future profitability?	Market price per share and earnings per share	Price earnings ratio = $\dfrac{\text{Market price per share}}{\text{Earnings per share}}$	A high ratio suggests the market expects good performance, although it may also suggest that shares are overvalued.

the navigator

USING THE DECISION TOOLKIT

Condensed and simplified financial statements with comparative data for Canadian Tire Corporation, Limited for the years ended December 29, 2012, and December 31, 2011, are shown below.

CANADIAN TIRE CORPORATION, LIMITED Balance Sheet December 29 (in millions)		
	2012	2011
Assets		
Current assets	$ 7,789.0	$ 6,993.4
Long-term receivables and other assets	681.2	668.9
Long-term investments	182.7	128.2
Goodwill and intangible assets	1,089.9	1,110.0
Investment property	95.1	72.4
Property and equipment	3,343.5	3,365.9
Total assets	$13,181.4	$12,338.8
Liabilities and Shareholders' Equity		
Liabilities		
Current liabilities	$ 4,624.1	$ 4,153.0
Long-term debt	2,336.0	2,347.7
Long-term deposits	1,111.8	1,102.2
Other long-term liabilities	345.9	326.9
Total liabilities	8,417.8	7,929.8
Shareholders' equity		
Share capital	688.0	710.5
Other equity items	1.2	12.1
Retained earnings	4,074.4	3,686.4
Total shareholders' equity	4,763.6	4,409.0
Total liabilities and shareholders' equity	$13,181.4	$12,338.8

CANADIAN TIRE CORPORATION, LIMITED Income Statement Year Ended December 29 (in millions)		
	2012	2011
Operating revenue	$11,427.2	$10,387.1
Total expenses	10,784.6	9,775.9
Profit before income tax	642.6	611.2
Income tax expense	143.4	144.2
Profit	$ 499.2	$ 467.0

Additional information:
- Canadian Tire's profit is the same as its profit available to common shareholders. The weighted average number of shares was 81.4 million in both 2012 and 2011. The share price was $69.11 at the end of 2012, and $65.90 at the end of 2011.
- Industry averages are as follows: current ratio, 1.4:1 in 2012 and 1.5:1 in 2011; debt to total assets, 25.9% in 2012 and 24.2% in 2011; and price-earnings ratio, 14.1 times in 2012 and 12.3 times in 2011. Industry averages are not available for earnings per share.

Instructions

(a) Calculate Canadian Tire's current ratio for both fiscal years. Discuss the company's liquidity generally, and compared with the industry.

(b) Calculate Canadian Tire's debt to total assets for both fiscal years. Discuss the company's solvency generally, and compared with the industry.

(c) Calculate Canadian Tire's earnings per share and price-earnings ratio for both fiscal years. Discuss the company's profitability generally, and compared with the industry.

Solution

(a) <u>Liquidity</u>
Current ratio (in millions)

	Canadian Tire	Industry
2012	$7,789.0 ÷ $4,624.1 = 1.7:1	1.4:1
2011	$6,993.4 ÷ $4,153.0 = 1.7:1	1.5:1

Based on the current ratio, Canadian Tire's liquidity appears strong as its current ratio exceeds that of the industry.

(b) <u>Solvency:</u>
Debt to total assets (in millions)

	Canadian Tire	Industry
2012	$8,417.8 ÷ $13,181.4 = 63.9%	25.9%
2011	$7,929.8 ÷ $12,338.8 = 64.3%	24.2%

Canadian Tire's solvency remained almost unchanged in 2012. However, its reliance on debt financing is higher (worse) than that of the industry in both years. In contrast to what we observed with Canadian Tire's liquidity, which was above the industry average, its solvency is below average.

(c) <u>Profitability</u>
Earnings per share (in millions)

	Canadian Tire	Industry
2012	$499.2 ÷ 81.4 = $6.13	n/a
2011	$467.0 ÷ 81.4 = $5.74	n/a

Price-earnings ratio

	Canadian Tire	Industry
2012	$69.11 ÷ $6.13 = 11.3 times	14.1 times
2011	$65.90 ÷ $5.74 = 11.5 times	12.3 times

Canadian Tire's profitability improved in 2012 as its earnings per share rose. However, the share price did not rise as much as the earnings per share and this is why the price-earnings ratio fell slightly. One reason for the decline in this ratio likely reflects investors' concerns about Canadian Tire's ability to continue to improve its profitability in the future. This concern was not reflected in the industry averages, which exceeded Canadian Tire's price-earnings ratio in each year.

the navigator

Comprehensive Do It!

The following accounts and amounts are taken from the financial statements of the Paloma Corporation for the year ended January 31, 2015:

Accounts payable	$ 1,558,000
Accounts receivable	1,204,000
Accumulated depreciation—buildings	300,000
Accumulated depreciation—equipment	200,000
Bank loan payable (due within one year)	2,000
Buildings	2,000,000
Cash	170,000
Common shares	3,000,000
Cost of goods sold	11,800,000
Dividends	74,000
Equipment	500,000
Goodwill	304,000
Income tax expense	90,000
Interest expense	84,000
Land	178,000
Long-term investments	350,000
Merchandise inventory	2,970,000
Mortgage payable	1,016,000
Operating expenses	2,476,000
Prepaid expenses	156,000
Retained earnings, February 1, 2014	1,480,000
Sales	14,800,000

Additional information:

$250,000 of the mortgage is due within the current year. There were no changes in common shares during the year.

Instructions

Prepare an income statement, statement of changes in equity, and statement of financial position for Paloma Corporation.

Action Plan
- Identify which accounts should be reported on each statement. Then determine which classification (current assets, non-current assets, current liabilities, non-current liabilities, or shareholders' equity on the statement of financial position; or in revenues or expenses on the income statement) each account should be reported in.
- Prepare the statements in this order: (1) income statement, (2) statement of changes in equity, and (3) statement of financial position.
- The income statement covers a period of time. In preparing the income statement, first list revenues, and then expenses. List expenses in order of size—from largest to smallest. Report income tax expense separately.
- The statement of changes in equity covers the same period of time as the income statement. This statement calculates the ending balance in common shares by adding any changes to common shares to the opening common shares amount. The ending balance in retained earnings is calculated by adding profit (from the income statement) to, and deducting dividends from, the opening retained earnings amount.
- The statement of financial position is prepared at a specific point in time. In preparing a classified statement of financial position, list items in order of their liquidity in the current classifications and in order of their permanency in the non-current classifications.

Solution to Comprehensive Do It!

PALOMA CORPORATION Income Statement Year Ended January 31, 2015		
Sales		$14,800,000
Expenses		
Cost of goods sold	$11,800,000	
Operating expenses	2,476,000	
Interest expense	84,000	
Total expenses		14,360,000
Profit before income tax		440,000
Income tax expense		90,000
Profit		$ 350,000

PALOMA CORPORATION Statement of Changes in Equity Year Ended January 31, 2015			
	Common Shares	Retained Earnings	Total Equity
Balance, February 1, 2014	$3,000,000	$1,480,000	$4,480,000
Profit		350,000	350,000
Dividends		(74,000)	(74,000)
Balance, January 31, 2015	$3,000,000	$1,756,000	$4,756,000

PALOMA CORPORATION Statement of Financial Position January 31, 2015			
Assets			
Current assets			
Cash		$ 170,000	
Accounts receivable		1,204,000	
Merchandise inventory		2,970,000	
Prepaid expenses		156,000	
Total current assets			$4,500,000
Investments			350,000
Property, plant, and equipment			
Land		$ 178,000	
Buildings	$2,000,000		
Less: Accumulated depreciation	(300,000)	1,700,000	
Equipment	$ 500,000		
Less: Accumulated depreciation	(200,000)	300,000	2,178,000
Goodwill			304,000
Total assets			$7,332,000
Liabilities and Shareholders' Equity			
Liabilities			
Current liabilities			
Accounts payable		$1,558,000	
Bank loan payable		2,000	
Current portion of mortgage payable		250,000	
Total current liabilities			$1,810,000
Non-current liabilities			
Mortgage payable ($1,016,000 − $250,000)			766,000
Total liabilities			2,576,000
Shareholders' equity			
Common shares		$3,000,000	
Retained earnings		1,756,000	4,756,000
Total liabilities and shareholders' equity			$7,332,000

WileyPLUS   Self-Test, Brief Exercises, Exercises, Problems: Set A, and many more components are available for practice in *WileyPLUS*.

Self-Test Questions

Answers are at the end of the chapter.

Quiz Yourself

(SO 1) 1. In a classified statement of financial position, assets are usually classified by North American companies in this order:
(a) current assets; investments; property, plant, and equipment; and intangible assets.
(b) current assets; intangible assets; property, plant, and equipment; and investments.
(c) property, plant, and equipment; current assets; investments; and intangible assets.
(d) intangible assets; property, plant, and equipment; investments; and current assets.

(SO 1) 2. In a classified statement of financial position, the following selected current assets are usually classified by North American companies in this order:
(a) accounts receivable, cash, prepaid insurance, and merchandise inventory.
(b) cash, merchandise inventory, accounts receivable, and prepaid insurance.
(c) cash, accounts receivable, merchandise inventory, and prepaid insurance.
(d) prepaid insurance, merchandise inventory, accounts receivable, and cash.

(SO 1) 3. International companies often list current assets by:
(a) importance.
(b) permanence.
(c) liquidity.
(d) reverse liquidity.

(SO 2) 4. Which of the following is *not* an indicator of a company's profitability?
(a) Current ratio
(b) Earnings per share
(c) Profit
(d) Price-earnings ratio

(SO 2) 5. Which of the following ratios is the best indicator of a company's ability to pay current liabilities?
(a) Price-earnings ratio
(b) Current ratio
(c) Debt to total assets
(d) Earnings per share

(SO 2) 6. Which of the following ratios is the best indicator of a company's ability to survive over the long term?
(a) Price-earnings ratio
(b) Current ratio

(c) Debt to total assets
(d) Earnings per share

(SO 2) 7. The following ratios are available for Bachus Inc. and Newton Ltd.

	Current Ratio	Debt to Total Assets	Earnings per Share
Bachus	2.0:1	75.5%	$3.50
Newton	1.5:1	40.3%	$2.75

Compared with Newton, Bachus has:
(a) higher liquidity, higher solvency, and higher profitability.
(b) lower liquidity, higher solvency, and higher profitability.
(c) higher liquidity, lower solvency, and higher profitability.
(d) higher liquidity and lower solvency, but profitability cannot be compared based on the information provided.

(SO 3) 8. Which of the following is *not* a fundamental or enhancing qualitative characteristic of useful financial information?
(a) Accrual basis of accounting
(b) Relevance
(c) Faithful representation
(d) Comparability

(SO 3) 9. What accounting constraint allows a company to ignore the conceptual framework if the cost of providing the information is greater than the benefit?
(a) Comparability
(b) Verifiability
(c) Cost
(d) Relevance

(SO 3) 10. The cost basis of accounting states that:
(a) the benefits should exceed the costs of providing information.
(b) cost is more relevant than fair value.
(c) assets should be reported at their fair value.
(d) assets should be reported at their historical cost.

the navigator

Questions

(SO 1) 1. What are current assets? Give four examples of current assets a company might have.

(SO 1) 2. What is meant by the term *operating cycle*?

(SO 1) 3. (a) Distinguish between current assets and non-current assets. (b) Distinguish between current assets and current liabilities. Why does showing these items as current in nature matter?

(SO 1) 4. (a) What are current liabilities? (b) Give four examples of current liabilities a company might have.

(SO 1) 5. (a) Distinguish between current liabilities and non-current liabilities. (b) Explain how a bank loan can sometimes be classified as both a current liability and a non-current liability.

(SO 1) 6. Identify the two components of shareholders' equity normally found in a corporation and indicate the purpose of each.

(SO 1) 7. Explain what it means to present a statement of financial position in order of liquidity, as is done by many North American companies, compared with presenting it in an order of reverse liquidity, as is done by many international companies.

(SO 2) 8. Explain what each of the following classes of ratios measures and give an example of each: (a) liquidity ratios, (b) solvency ratios, and (c) profitability ratios.

(SO 2) 9. Why is the current ratio a better measure of liquidity than working capital?

(SO 2) 10. "The current ratio should not be used as the only measure of liquidity, because it does not take into account the composition of the current assets." Explain what this statement means.

(SO 2) 11. Dong Corporation has a debt to total assets ratio of 45%, while its competitor, Du Ltd., has a debt to total assets ratio of 55%. Based on this information, which company is more solvent? Why?

(SO 2) 12. Jonathan Baird, the founder of Waterboots Inc., needs to raise $500,000 to expand his company's operations. He has been told that raising the money through debt by obtaining a bank loan will increase the riskiness of his company much more than by raising the money by issuing common shares. He doesn't understand why this is true. Explain it to him.

(SO 2) 13. Why can you compare the price-earnings ratio among different companies but not earnings per share?

(SO 2) 14. The **TD Bank** has a price-earnings ratio of 12 times, while **CIBC** has a price-earnings ratio of 10 times. Which company do investors appear to favour?

(SO 2) 15. Explain why increases in earnings per share, price-earnings, and current ratios are considered to be signs of improvement in a company's financial health, but an increase in the debt to total assets ratio is considered to be a sign of deterioration.

(SO 3) 16. (a) Describe the conceptual framework and explain how it helps financial reporting. (b) Is the conceptual framework applicable to publicly traded companies reporting using IFRS, to private companies using ASPE, or to both?

(SO 3) 17. (a) What is the objective of financial reporting? (b) Who are the main users that rely on this objective?

(SO 3) 18. Explain how the going concern assumption supports the classification of assets and liabilities as current and non-current.

(SO 3) 19. Identify and explain the two fundamental qualitative characteristics of useful financial information.

(SO 3) 20. How is materiality related to the fundamental qualitative characteristic of relevance?

(SO 3) 21. Identify and explain the four enhancing qualitative characteristics of useful financial information. Is there a prescribed order for applying these enhancing characteristics?

(SO 3) 22. Explain how the cost constraint relates to the quality of completeness.

(SO 3) 23. What are the elements of financial statements?

(SO 3) 24. Identify and explain the two bases used to measure the elements of financial statements.

(SO 3) 25. Explain how the qualitative characteristics of relevance and faithful representation relate to the cost and fair value bases of accounting.

Brief Exercises

BE2–1 The following are the major statement of financial position classifications:

Classify accounts.
(SO 1)

1. Current assets
2. Long-term investments
3. Property, plant, and equipment
4. Intangible assets
5. Current liabilities
6. Non-current liabilities
7. Share capital
8. Retained earnings

Classify each of the following selected accounts by writing in the number of its appropriate classification above:

(a) _____ Accounts payable
(b) _____ Accounts receivable
(c) _____ Accumulated depreciation
(d) _____ Buildings
(e) _____ Cash
(f) _____ Patents
(g) _____ Dividends
(h) _____ Income tax payable
(i) _____ Long-term investments

(j) _____ Land
(k) _____ Merchandise inventory
(l) _____ Common shares
(m) _____ Supplies
(n) _____ Mortgage payable, due in 20 years
(o) _____ Current portion of mortgage payable
(p) _____ Prepaid insurance
(q) _____ Unearned revenue

Prepare current assets section.
(SO 1)

BE2–2   A list of current assets for Swann Limited includes the following: accounts receivable $14,500; cash $16,400; merchandise inventory $9,000; supplies $4,200; and prepaid insurance $3,900. Prepare the current assets section of the statement of financial position.

Prepare property, plant, and equipment section.
(SO 1)

BE2–3   A list of financial statement items for Shum Corporation includes the following: accumulated depreciation—buildings $33,000; accumulated depreciation—equipment $25,000; buildings $110,000; equipment $70,000; and land $65,000. Prepare the property, plant, and equipment section of the statement of financial position.

Prepare current liabilities section.
(SO 1)

BE2–4   Hirjikaka Inc. reports the following current and non-current liabilities: accounts payable $22,500; salaries payable $3,900; interest payable $5,200; unearned revenue $900; income tax payable $6,400; mortgage payable (due within the year) $5,000; mortgage payable (due in more than one year) $50,000. Prepare the current liabilities section of the statement of financial position.

Calculate ratios and evaluate liquidity.
(SO 2)

BE2–5   **Indigo Books & Music Inc.** reported the following selected information for the years ended March 31, 2012, and April 2, 2011 (in thousands):

	2012	2011
Total current assets	$453,629	$336,980
Total current liabilities	229,503	235,365

(a) Calculate the working capital and current ratio for each year.
(b) Was Indigo's liquidity stronger or weaker in 2012 compared with 2011?

Calculate ratios and evaluate solvency.
(SO 2)

BE2–6   Convenience store operator **Alimentation Couche-Tard Inc.** reported the following selected information for the years ended April 29, 2012, and April 24, 2011 (in U.S. $ millions):

	2012	2011
Current assets	$1,337.4	$1,242.2
Non-current assets	3,115.8	2,684.0
Current liabilities	1,566.8	977.4
Non-current liabilities	711.8	969.4

(a) Calculate the debt to total assets ratio for each year.
(b) Was the company's solvency stronger or weaker in 2012 compared with 2011?

Calculate ratios and evaluate profitability.
(SO 2)

BE2–7   The following information is available for **Leon's Furniture Limited** for the years ended December 31 (in thousands, except for share price):

	2012	2011
Profit available to common shareholders	$46,782	$56,666
Weighted average number of common shares	70,033	69,969
Share price	$12.99	$12.40

(a) Calculate the earnings per share and the price-earnings ratio for each year.
(b) Indicate whether profitability improved or deteriorated in 2012.

Identify components of conceptual framework.
(SO 3)

BE2–8   Presented below is a chart showing selected portions of the conceptual framework. Fill in the blanks from (a) to (f).

Qualitative Characteristics		Constraint	Underlying Assumption	Measurement of the Elements
Fundamental Qualitative Characteristics	Enhancing Qualitative Characteristics			
Relevance	Comparability	(d)	(e)	Cost
(a)	(b)			(f)
	Timeliness			
	(c)			

BE2–9 The following selected items relate to the qualitative characteristics of useful financial information discussed in this chapter:

Identify qualitative characteristics.
(SO 3)

1. Comparability
2. Completeness
3. Confirmatory value
4. Cost constraint
5. Faithful representation
6. Freedom from error or bias
7. Materiality
8. Neutrality
9. Predictive value
10. Relevance
11. Timeliness
12. Understandability
13. Verifiability

Match each characteristic to one of the statements below:

(a) _____ Information that has predictive value, confirmatory value, and is material is said to have this fundamental qualitative characteristic.
(b) _____ Information that is complete, neutral, and reasonably free of error is said to have this fundamental qualitative characteristic.
(c) _____ This enhancing qualitative characteristic requires that similar companies should apply the same accounting principles to similar events for successive accounting periods.
(d) _____ This quality results in information that has nothing important omitted.
(e) _____ This constraint requires that the value of the information presented should be greater than the cost of providing it.
(f) _____ Public accountants perform audits to determine this enhancing qualitative characteristic.
(g) _____ This quality requires that information cannot be selected to favour one position over another.
(h) _____ This enhancing qualitative characteristic describes information that a reasonably informed user can interpret and comprehend.
(i) _____ When information provides a basis for forecasting profits for future periods, it is said to have this quality.
(j) _____ This quality describes information that confirms or corrects users' prior expectations.
(k) _____ This enhancing qualitative characteristic requires that information be available to decision makers before it loses its ability to influence their decisions.
(l) _____ Faithful representation means that information is complete, neutral, and this third quality.
(m) _____ This quality allows items of insignificance that would not likely influence a decision not to be disclosed.

BE2–10 For each of the situations discussed below, choose a basis of measurement to use and explain why.

Identify bases of measurement.
(SO 3)

(a) Sosa Ltd. is a real estate company that purchases and holds land for eventual sale to developers.
(b) Mohawk Inc. is a manufacturing company that purchased land on which it plans to construct a new plant next year. It expects the value of the land to rise rapidly over the next few years.

Exercises

E2–1 The following are the major statement of financial position classifications:

Classify accounts.
(SO 1)

1. Current assets
2. Long-term investments
3. Property, plant, and equipment
4. Intangible assets
5. Current liabilities
6. Non-current liabilities
7. Shareholders' equity

Instructions

Classify each of the following selected accounts taken from TELUS Corporation's statement of financial position by writing in the number of the appropriate classification above:

(a) _____ Accounts payable and accrued liabilities   (h) _____ Goodwill
(b) _____ Accounts receivable   (i) _____ Income and other taxes payable
(c) _____ Accumulated depreciation   (j) _____ Income and other taxes receivable
(d) _____ Buildings and leasehold improvements   (k) _____ Inventories
(e) _____ Common shares   (l) _____ Land
(f) _____ Current maturities of long-term debt   (m) _____ Long-term debt
(g) _____ Dividends payable   (n) _____ Prepaid expenses

Prepare assets section. (SO 1)

E2–2 The assets (in thousands) that follow were taken from the December 31, 2012, balance sheet for **Big Rock Brewery Inc.**:

Accounts receivable	$ 2,358	Intangible assets	$ 128
Accumulated depreciation—buildings	827	Inventories	3,892
Accumulated depreciation—machinery and equipment	6,480	Land	2,516
Accumulated depreciation—mobile equipment	149	Machinery and equipment	20,800
Accumulated depreciation—office furniture	140	Mobile equipment	645
Buildings	11,070	Office furniture	310
Cash	4,281	Prepaid expenses and other	364

Instructions

Prepare the assets section of the statement of financial position.

Prepare liabilities and equity sections. (SO 1)

E2–3 The liabilities and shareholders' equity items (in thousands) that follow were taken from the March 31, 2012, balance sheet for **Saputo Inc.**:

Accounts payable and accrued liabilities	$ 571,814
Bank loans payable (current)	166,631
Common shares	629,606
Deferred income taxes payable (non-current)	156,632
Income taxes payable	163,996
Long-term debt	379,875
Other long-term liabilities	54,486
Retained earnings	1,467,108

Instructions

Prepare the liabilities and shareholders' equity sections of the statement of financial position.

Prepare statement of financial position. (SO 1)

E2–4 These items are taken from the financial statements of Summit Ltd. at December 31, 2015:

Accounts payable	$ 14,050	Interest expense	$ 4,750
Accounts receivable	13,780	Interest payable	1,600
Accumulated depreciation—buildings	45,600	Land	54,000
Accumulated depreciation—equipment	17,770	Long-term investments	30,000
Service revenue	73,040	Mortgage payable	95,000
Buildings	128,800	Operating expenses	48,680
Cash	15,040	Prepaid insurance	390
Common shares	50,000	Retained earnings, Jan. 1	66,520
Equipment	62,400	Supplies	740
Income tax expense	5,000		

Instructions

(a) Calculate profit and the ending balance of retained earnings at December 31, 2015. It is not necessary to prepare a formal income statement or statement of changes in equity.

(b) Prepare a statement of financial position. Assume that $13,600 of the mortgage payable will be paid in 2016.

E2–5 These financial statement items are for Batra Corporation at year end, July 31, 2015:

Prepare financial
statements.
(SO 1)

Salaries expense	$44,700	Supplies expense	$ 900
Utilities expense	2,600	Dividends	12,000
Equipment	35,900	Depreciation expense	3,000
Accounts payable	4,220	Retained earnings, Aug. 1, 2014	17,940
Service revenue	81,100	Rent expense	10,800
Rent revenue	18,500	Income tax expense	5,000
Common shares	10,000	Supplies	1,500
Cash	5,060	Trading investments	20,000
Accounts receivable	17,100	Bank loan payable (due Dec. 31, 2015)	21,800
Accumulated depreciation—equipment	6,000	Interest expense	2,000
Interest payable	1,000		

Additional information:
Batra started the year with $6,000 of common shares and issued additional shares for $4,000 during the year.

Instructions
Prepare an income statement, statement of changes in equity, and statement of financial position for the year.

E2–6 The chief financial officer (CFO) of Padilla Corporation requested that the accounting department prepare a preliminary statement of financial position on December 20, 2015. He knows that certain debt agreements with its lenders require the company to maintain a current ratio of at least 2:1 and wants to know how the company is doing. The preliminary statement of financial position follows:

Calculate ratios and
evaluate liquidity.
(SO 2)

PADILLA CORPORATION
Statement of Financial Position
December 20, 2015

Assets		Liabilities		
Current assets		Current liabilities		
Cash	$ 25,000	Accounts payable	$20,000	
Accounts receivable	30,000	Salaries payable	20,000	$ 40,000
Prepaid insurance	5,000	Non-current liabilities		
Total current assets	60,000	Bank loan payable		80,000
Equipment	200,000	Total liabilities		120,000
Total assets	$260,000	Shareholders' equity		
		Common shares	$90,000	
		Retained earnings	50,000	140,000
		Total liabilities and shareholders' equity		$260,000

Instructions
(a) Calculate the current ratio based on the data in the preliminary statement of financial position.
(b) Based on the results in part (a), the CFO requested that $20,000 of the cash be used to pay off the balance of the accounts payable account on December 21. Calculate the current ratio after this payment is made, assuming there are no further changes to current assets and current liabilities.
(c) Is it ethical for the CFO to recommend this action?

E2–7 Huntingdon Capital Corp. is a competitor of Plazacorp and First Capital Realty. Huntingdon reported the following selected information (in millions):

Calculate ratios and
comment on liquidity
and solvency.
(SO 2)

	2012	2011
Current assets	$103.5	$ 77.3
Non-current assets	217.8	422.5
Current liabilities	30.8	78.0
Non-current liabilities	114.8	218.2

Instructions
(a) Calculate the working capital, current ratio, and debt to total assets ratio for each year.
(b) Did Huntingdon's liquidity and solvency improve or worsen during 2012?
(c) Using the data in the chapter, compare Huntingdon's liquidity and solvency with that of Plazacorp, First Capital Realty, and the industry for 2012 and 2011.

Calculate ratios and evaluate profitability.
(SO 2)

E2–8 The following information is available for **Cameco Corporation** for the year ended December 31 (in thousands, except share price):

	2012	2011
Profit available for common shareholders	$264,583	$449,844
Weighted average number of common shares	395,234	394,662
Share price	$19.59	$18.41

Instructions
(a) Calculate the earnings per share and price-earnings ratio for each year.
(b) Based on your calculations above, how did the company's profitability change from 2012 to 2011?

Identify qualitative characteristics.
(SO 3)

E2–9 Here are some fundamental and enhancing qualitative characteristics of useful financial information:

1. Comparability
2. Completeness
3. Confirmatory value
4. Faithful representation
5. Freedom from error or bias
6. Materiality

7. Neutrality
8. Predictive value
9. Relevance
10. Timeliness
11. Understandability
12. Verifiability

Instructions
Match each characteristic to one of the following statements, using the numbers 1 to 12.

(a) _____ Accounting information cannot be selected, prepared, or presented to favour one set of interested users over another.

(b) _____ Accounting information must be available to decision makers before it loses its ability to influence their decisions.

(c) _____ Accounting information is prepared on the assumption that users have a reasonable understanding of accounting and general business and economic conditions.

(d) _____ Accounting information provides a basis to evaluate a previously made decision.

(e) _____ Accounting information includes everything it needs to and nothing important is omitted. This is an important component of faithful representation.

(f) _____ Accounting information helps users make predictions about the outcome of past, present, and future events.

(g) _____ Accounting information about one company can be evaluated against the accounting information from another company.

(h) _____ Accounting information is included if its omission or misstatement could influence the economic decisions of users. This is an important component of relevance.

(i) _____ All the accounting information that is necessary to faithfully represent economic reality is included.

(j) _____ Accounting information can be determined to be free of material error.

(k) _____ Accounting information is included if it will make a difference in users' decisions.

(l) _____ Accounting information about a company can be confirmed by two or more users to be a faithful representation.

Identify assumption or principle.
(SO 3)

E2–10   Marietta Corp. had the following reporting issues during the year:

1. Land with a cost of $208,000 that is intended to be used by the company as a building site was reported at its fair value of $260,000.
2. A surplus parcel of land with a cost of $150,000 intended for resale in the near future is reported at its fair value of $160,000.
3. The president of Marietta, Deanna Durnford, decided it wasn't necessary to classify assets and liabilities as current and non-current as she expects to operate the company only for another 10 years.

Instructions
For each of the above situations, identify (a) the assumption or principle involved, and (b) whether it is being followed correctly or has been violated.

Problems: Set A

Classify accounts.
(SO 1)

P2–1A   You are provided with the following selected balance sheet accounts for entertainment retailer **HMV Group plc**:

Accumulated depreciation
Cash
Common (ordinary) shares
Current income tax payable

Current income tax recoverable
Interest-bearing loans and borrowings (current)
Interest-bearing loans and borrowings (non-current)
Inventories
Investments
Plant, equipment, and vehicles
Trade and other payables
Trade and other receivables
Trademarks

Instructions
Identify the balance sheet (statement of financial position) category for classifying each account. For example, accumulated depreciation should be classified as a contra asset in the property, plant, and equipment section of HMV's balance sheet.

P2-2A The following items are from the assets section of **WestJet Airlines Ltd.**'s December 31, 2012, statement of financial position (in thousands):

Prepare assets section.
(SO 1)

Accounts receivable	$ 37,576
Accumulated depreciation—aircraft	1,127,889
Accumulated depreciation—buildings	20,025
Accumulated depreciation—ground property and equipment	79,052
Accumulated depreciation—leasehold improvements	5,536
Accumulated depreciation—spare engines and parts	44,713
Aircraft	2,605,277
Buildings	135,924
Cash	1,459,822
Ground property and equipment	136,167
Inventory	35,595
Intangible assets	50,808
Leasehold improvements	16,538
Other assets	297,899
Prepaid expenses, deposits, and other	101,802
Spare engines and parts	146,422

Instructions
(a) Identify the statement of financial position category in which each of the above items should be classified.
(b) Prepare the assets section of the statement of financial position.

P2-3A The following items are from the liability and shareholders' equity sections of **WestJet Airlines Ltd.**'s December 31, 2012, statement of financial position (in thousands):

Prepare liabilities and equity sections.
(SO 1)

Accounts payable and accrued liabilities	$460,003
Advance ticket sales	480,947
Current portion of long-term debt	199,044
Deferred income tax (long-term)	356,748
Long-term debt	574,139
Other current liabilities	47,859
Other long-term liabilities	155,570
Other shareholders' equity items	64,110
Retained earnings	793,296
Share capital	614,899

Instructions
(a) Identify the statement of financial position category in which each of the above items should be classified.
(b) Prepare the liabilities and equity sections of the statement of financial position.
(c) If you completed P2-2A, compare the total assets in P2-2A with the total liabilities and shareholders' equity in P2-3A. Do these two amounts agree?

Prepare financial statements; discuss relationships.
(SO 1)

P2–4A   These items are taken from the financial statements of Mbong Corporation for the year ended December 31, 2015:

Retained earnings, Jan. 1	$105,000	Depreciation expense	$ 6,200
Utilities expense	2,000	Accounts receivable	14,200
Equipment	66,000	Insurance expense	2,200
Accounts payable	8,300	Salaries expense	37,000
Buildings	72,000	Accumulated depreciation—equipment	17,600
Cash	5,200	Income tax expense	6,000
Salaries payable	3,000	Supplies	200
Common shares	34,200	Supplies expense	1,000
Dividends	5,000	Bank loan payable, due 2018	15,000
Service revenue	81,700	Trading investments	20,000
Prepaid insurance	2,000	Accumulated depreciation—buildings	18,000
Repair and maintenance expense	2,800	Interest expense	1,500
Land	40,000	Interest revenue	500

Additional information:

1. Mbong started the year with $30,000 of common shares and issued $4,200 more during the year.
2. $1,500 of the bank loan payable is due to be repaid within the next year.

Instructions
(a) Prepare an income statement, statement of changes in equity, and statement of financial position for the year.
(b) Explain how each financial statement is related to the others.

Calculate ratios and comment on liquidity, solvency, and profitability.
(SO 2)

P2–5A   The financial statements of Johanssen Inc. are presented here:

JOHANSSEN INC.
Income Statement
Year Ended December 31, 2015

Sales		$2,218,500
Expenses		
Cost of goods sold	$1,012,500	
Operating expenses	906,000	
Interest expense	98,000	2,016,500
Profit before income tax		202,000
Income tax expense		42,000
Profit		$ 160,000

JOHANNSSEN INC.
Statement of Financial Position
December 31, 2015

Assets		
Current assets		
Cash	$ 60,100	
Trading investments	54,000	
Accounts receivable	207,800	
Merchandise inventory	125,000	$ 446,900
Property, plant, and equipment		625,300
Total assets		$1,072,200

Liabilities and Shareholders' Equity		
Current liabilities		
Accounts payable	$100,000	
Income tax payable	15,000	
Current portion of mortgage payable	27,500	$ 142,500
Mortgage payable		310,000
Total liabilities		452,500
Shareholders' equity		
Common shares	$307,630	
Retained earnings	312,070	619,700
Total liabilities and shareholders' equity		$1,072,200

Additional information:

1. Profit available to common shareholders was $160,000.
2. The weighted average number of common shares was 40,000.
3. The share price at December 31 was $35.

Instructions

(a) Calculate the following values and ratios for 2015. We provide the results for 2014 for comparative purposes.

    1. Working capital (2014: $260,500)
    2. Current ratio (2014: 1.6:1)
    3. Debt to total assets (2014: 31.5%)
    4. Earnings per share (2014: $3.15)
    5. Price-earnings ratio (2014: 7.5 times)

(b) Using the information in part (a), discuss the changes in liquidity, solvency, and profitability between 2015 and 2014.

P2–6A Selected financial statement data for a recent year for Chen Corporation and Caissie Corporation, two competitors, are as follows:

Calculate ratios and comment on liquidity, solvency, and profitability.
(SO 2)

	Chen	Caissie
Sales revenue	$1,800,000	$620,000
Cost of goods sold	1,175,000	340,000
Operating expenses	283,000	98,000
Interest expense	10,000	4,000
Income tax expense	85,000	35,400
Current assets	407,200	190,400
Non-current assets	532,000	139,700
Current liabilities	166,325	133,700
Non-current liabilities	108,500	40,700
Share price	25	15
Weighted average number of common shares	76,000	62,000

Instructions

(a) Calculate working capital and the current ratio for each company. Comment on their relative liquidity.
(b) Calculate the debt to total assets ratio for each company. Comment on their relative solvency.
(c) Calculate the profit, earnings per share, and price-earnings ratio for each company. Assume that the profit you calculate equals the profit available to common shareholders. Comment on the two companies' relative profitability.

P2–7A Selected financial data for a recent year for two clothing competitors, **Le Château Inc.** and **Reitmans (Canada) Limited**, are presented here (in thousands, except share price):

Calculate ratios and comment on liquidity, solvency, and profitability.
(SO 2)

	Le Château	Reitmans
Current assets	$132,223	$301,374
Total assets	220,210	594,555
Current liabilities	47,382	86,914
Total liabilities	80,412	139,537
Profit (loss) available to common shareholders	(8,717)	26,619
Share price	$4.08	$12.39
Weighted average number of common shares	25,659	65,188

Instructions

(a) For each company, calculate the following values and ratios. Where available, industry averages are included in parentheses.

    1. Working capital (n/a)
    2. Current ratio (2.0:1)
    3. Debt to total assets (24.0%)
    4. Earnings per share (n/a)
    5. Price-earnings ratio (19.3 times)

(b) Compare the liquidity, solvency, and profitability of the two companies and their industry.

P2–8A Selected ratios for Pitka Corporation are as follows:

Comment on liquidity, solvency, and profitability.
(SO 2)

	2015	2014	2013
Working capital	$10,000	$25,000	$35,000
Current ratio	1.1:1	1.2:1	1.2:1
Debt to total assets	34.2%	42.3%	40.0%
Earnings per share	$3.50	$3.15	$3.40
Price-earnings ratio	5.7 times	5.1 times	5.5 times

Instructions

(a) Identify if the change in each value or ratio is an improvement or deterioration between (1) 2013 and 2014, and (2) 2014 and 2015.

(b) Briefly discuss the change in Pitka's liquidity, solvency, and profitability over the three-year period.

Discuss financial reporting objective, qualitative characteristics, and elements.
(SO 3)

P2–9A   Bobby Young is the accountant for the Blazers, a new professional hockey team. He has just finished preparing the financial statements for the team's first year end, which falls on December 31, 2015. The chief financial officer (CFO) of the team is Bucky Ryan and he has just reviewed the financial statements and made the following requests of Bobby:

1. Because the team's bank has asked to have a final copy of the financial statements by January 15, 2016, Bobby recorded the utilities expense for December 2015 based on an estimate because he normally receives the utility bill three weeks after the month the bill pertains to. Bucky wants this removed from the financial statements because it is not a "solid" number based on an invoice.

2. The team has bought a small building near the arena. The area has recently been selected by the city for some significant development and consequently the value of the property has risen 15% in the past year. Bobby has not shown this increase in value on the financial statements but Bucky would like him to do so.

3. The team recently signed Wayne Crosby to play next year. Upon signing, the team paid Wayne a "no strings attached" signing bonus. Bobby recorded this as an expense but Bucky would like him to record it as an asset since it relates to a future period.

Instructions

(a) What is the objective of financial reporting? Do Bucky's suggestions for what should be reported on the financial statements meet the objective of financial reporting? Explain.

(b) For each of the items covered above, determine if the proposed changes enhance or diminish the qualitative characteristics of the team's financial statements and whether it is dealing with these items in a manner that is consistent with the definitions for elements of financial statements.

Discuss bases of measurement.
(SO 3)

P2–10A   In 2011, when publicly traded companies in Canada adopted IFRS, real estate companies were given the choice of using cost or fair value to account for their real estate portfolios. This was not an easy decision for real estate companies to make as there were advantages and disadvantages to each choice. In the end, while many companies chose to revalue their real estate portfolios to fair value, others chose cost.

Instructions

(a) Identify the advantages and disadvantages of each of the two bases of measurement: cost and fair value.

(b) Speculate as to why a company might choose to adopt the fair value basis of accounting for its real estate portfolio. What impact do you think this will have on the elements of its financial statements?

(c) Speculate as to why a company might choose to adopt the cost basis of accounting for its real estate portfolio. What impact do you think this will have on the elements of its financial statements?

(d) Do you believe you could effectively compare the financial statements of two competing companies using different bases of measurement?

Problems: Set B

Classify accounts.
(SO 1)

P2–1B   You are provided with the following selected balance sheet accounts for **L'Oréal Group SA**, the world's largest beauty products company:

Accumulated amortization—patents and trademarks
Accumulated depreciation—industrial machinery and equipment
Bank overdraft
Cash
Common (ordinary) shares
Current borrowings and debts
Income tax payable (current)
Industrial machinery and equipment

Inventories
Investments
Land
Non-current borrowings and debts
Patents and trademarks
Prepaid expenses
Trade accounts payable
Trade accounts receivable

Instructions

Identify the balance sheet (statement of financial position) category for classifying each account. For example, accumulated amortization—patents and trademarks should be classified as a contra asset in the intangible assets section of L'Oreal's balance sheet.

P2–2B The following items are from the assets section of Devon Limited's December 31, 2015, statement of financial position:

Prepare assets section.
(SO 1)

Accounts receivable	$ 4,145
Accumulated amortization—patents	10,190
Accumulated depreciation—buildings	22,470
Accumulated depreciation—equipment	85,900
Buildings	53,150
Cash	97,625
Equipment	166,750
Goodwill	42,425
Patent	29,415
Land	5,860
Trading investments	71,630
Merchandise inventory	93,320
Prepaid expenses	25,950

Instructions

(a) Identify the statement of financial position category in which each of the above assets should be classified.

(b) Prepare the assets section of the statement of financial position.

P2–3B The following items are from the liability and shareholders' equity sections of Devon Limited's December 31, 2015, statement of financial position:

Prepare liabilities and
equity sections.
(SO 1)

Accounts payable	$ 2,900
Current portion of mortgage payable	3,570
Mortgage payable	71,430
Retained earnings	338,290
Common shares	39,225
Unearned revenue	16,295

Instructions

(a) Identify the statement of financial position category in which each of the above items should be classified.

(b) Prepare the liabilities and equity sections of the statement of financial position.

(c) If you completed P2–2B, compare the total assets in P2–2B with the total liabilities and shareholders' equity in P2–3B. Do these two amounts agree?

P2–4B These items are taken from financial statements of Beaulieu Limited for the year ended December 31, 2015:

Prepare financial
statements; discuss
relationships.
(SO 1)

Cash	$ 8,000
Buildings	80,000
Accumulated depreciation—buildings	12,000
Accounts receivable	7,500
Prepaid insurance	250
Equipment	32,000
Accumulated depreciation—equipment	19,200
Accounts payable	9,550
Salaries payable	3,000
Common shares	20,000
Income tax expense	5,000
Long-term investments	20,000
Retained earnings, Jan. 1	34,000
Dividends	3,500
Service revenue	80,500
Depreciation expense	5,400
Insurance expense	2,400
Salaries expense	33,000
Utilities expense	3,700
Interest expense	8,000
Interest revenue	500
Land	50,000
Mortgage payable	80,000

Additional information:

1. Beaulieu started the year with $15,000 of common shares and issued $5,000 more during the year.

2. $10,000 of the mortgage payable is due to be repaid within the next year.

Instructions

(a) Prepare an income statement, statement of changes in equity, and statement of financial position for the year.

(b) Explain how each financial statement is related to the others.

Calculate ratios and comment on liquidity, solvency, and profitability.
(SO 2)

P2–5B   The financial statements of Fast Corporation are presented here:

FAST CORPORATION
Income Statement
Year Ended December 31, 2015

Sales		$706,000
Expenses		
Cost of goods sold	$420,000	
Operating expenses	144,000	
Interest expense	10,000	574,000
Profit before income taxes		132,000
Income tax expense		35,400
Profit		$ 96,600

FAST CORPORATION
Statement of Financial Position
December 31, 2015

Assets

Current assets		
Cash	$ 23,100	
Trading investments	34,800	
Accounts receivable	86,200	
Merchandise inventory	109,750	$253,850
Property, plant, and equipment		465,300
Total assets		$719,150

Liabilities and Shareholders' Equity

Current liabilities		
Accounts payable	$134,200	
Income tax payable	10,350	
Current portion of mortgage payable	12,000	$156,550
Mortgage payable		132,000
Total liabilities		288,550
Shareholders' equity		
Common shares	$100,000	
Retained earnings	330,600	430,600
Total liabilities and shareholders' equity		$719,150

Additional information:

1. Profit available to common shareholders was $96,600.
2. The weighted average number of common shares was 40,000.
3. The share price at December 31 was $30.

Instructions

(a) Calculate the following values and ratios for 2015. The results for 2014 are provided for comparative purposes.
 1. Working capital (2014: $78,000)
 2. Current ratio (2014: 1.4:1)
 3. Debt to total assets (2014: 51.5%)
 4. Earnings per share (2014: $1.35)
 5. Price-earnings ratio (2014: 10.8 times)

(b) Using the information in part (a), discuss the changes in liquidity, solvency, and profitability between 2014 and 2015.

P2-6B Selected financial statement data for a recent year for Belliveau Corporation and Shields Corporation, two competitors, are as follows:

Calculate ratios and comment on liquidity, solvency, and profitability.
(SO 2)

	Belliveau	Shields
Sales revenue	$450,000	$890,000
Cost of goods sold	260,000	620,000
Operating expenses	130,000	59,000
Interest expense	6,000	10,000
Income tax expense	10,000	65,000
Current assets	180,000	700,000
Non-current assets	600,000	800,000
Current liabilities	75,000	300,000
Non-current liabilities	190,000	200,000
Share price	2.50	6.00
Weighted average number of common shares	200,000	200,000

Instructions
(a) Calculate working capital and the current ratio for each company. Comment on their relative liquidity.
(b) Calculate the debt to total assets ratio for each company. Comment on their relative solvency.
(c) Calculate the profit, earnings per share, and price-earnings ratio for each company. Assume that the profit you calculate equals the profit available to common shareholders. Comment on the two companies' relative profitability.

P2-7B Selected financial data for a recent year for two discount retail chains, **Walmart Stores, Inc.** and **Target Corporation**, are presented here (in U.S. $ millions, except for share price):

Calculate ratios and comment on liquidity, solvency, and profitability.
(SO 2)

	Walmart	Target
Current assets	$ 59,940	$16,388
Total assets	203,105	48,163
Current liabilities	71,818	14,031
Total liabilities	121,367	31,605
Profit available to common shareholders	16,999	2,999
Share price	69.95	61.15
Weighted average number of common shares	3,374	657

Instructions
(a) For each company, calculate the following values and ratios. Where available, industry averages have been included in parentheses.
  1. Working capital (n/a)
  2. Current ratio (1.8:1)
  3. Debt to total assets (16.9%)
  4. Earnings per share (n/a)
  5. Price-earnings ratio (18.6 times)
(b) Compare the liquidity, solvency, and profitability of the two companies and their industry.

P2-8B Selected ratios for Giasson Corporation are as follows:

Comment on liquidity, solvency, and profitability.
(SO 2)

	2015	2014	2013
Working capital	$47,000	$53,000	$50,000
Current ratio	1.5:1	1.7:1	2.0:1
Debt to total assets	25.4%	25.5%	20.0%
Earnings per share	$0.86	$1.29	$1.00
Price-earnings ratio	4.7 times	5.1 times	5.5 times

Instructions
(a) Identify if the change in each value or ratio is an improvement or deterioration between (1) 2013 and 2014, and (2) 2014 and 2015.
(b) Briefly discuss the change in Giasson's liquidity, solvency, and profitability over the three-year period.

P2-9B Brenda Chan is the new accountant for a small private company called Ace Construction Limited. She has recently prepared the year-end financial statements for the company. Brenda's boss, Virginia Schwirtz, who is the chief executive officer (CEO), has asked her to make three changes to the financial statements as follows:

Discuss financial reporting objective, qualitative characteristics, and elements.
(SO 3)

1. Remove an expense and its related liability that Brenda recorded for damages expected to be paid from a lawsuit due to a poorly done construction job a few months ago. Virginia believes that, although it is highly likely that Ace will have to pay for these damages, because a final agreement about the exact amount of these damages will not be agreed to until next month, nothing relating to this issue should be recorded in the financial statements or disclosed in the notes to the financial statements.

2. Just prior to the end of the year, Ace signed a contract to build a new arena for the city for a fixed fee of $80 million. As long as the company can build the facility for less than this amount, the company will make a profit. Since the value of the contract is fixed and because the city has always paid its bills on time, Virginia wants the revenue for this contract to be recorded in the current year because that was when the contract was signed.

3. The company has a chequing account that is allowed to go into an overdraft (negative) position. When the balance falls into an overdraft, the bank begins to charge interest on that amount as if it were a bank loan, which in essence it is. Since there is no due date on such a balance, Virginia would like the loan to be reported as a non-current liability.

Instructions

(a) What is the objective of financial reporting? Are Brenda's or Virginia's actions consistent with these objectives? Explain.

(b) For each of the items covered above, determine if the proposed changes enhance or diminish the qualitative characteristics of the company's financial statements and whether the company is dealing with these items in a manner that is consistent with the definitions for elements of financial statements.

Identify bases of measurement.
(SO 3)

P2–10B   The following are hypothetical situations that require the choice of one of the two bases of measurement: cost or fair value.

1. You purchase your textbooks at the university bookstore to use during the term, but plan on selling them at the end of the term.
2. You purchase a new iPad and plan on never parting with it, at least not until a new model comes out.
3. You purchase software for your computer under a special deal that allows you to upgrade it whenever a new version is released.
4. You purchase a used car.
5. You purchase land, which you eventually hope to build a home on.

Instructions

(a) Identify the advantages and disadvantages of each of the two bases of measurement: cost and fair value.

(b) For each of the above situations, identify which basis of measurement would be the most appropriate to choose, and explain why.

Broadening Your Perspective

Financial Reporting: *Shoppers Drug Mart*

Answer questions about statement of financial position.
(SO 1)

BYP2–1   The financial statements of **Shoppers Drug Mart** are presented in Appendix A at the end of this book.

Instructions

(a) What were the balances of Shoppers Drug Mart's total current assets and total assets at the end of 2012 and 2011?

(b) In what order are Shoppers Drug Mart's current assets listed? Non-current assets?

(c) What were the balances of Shoppers Drug Mart's total current liabilities and total liabilities at the end of 2012 and 2011?

(d) In what order are its current liabilities listed? Non-current liabilities?

Comparative Analysis: *Shoppers Drug Mart and Jean Coutu*

Calculate ratios and comment on liquidity, solvency, and profitability.
(SO 2)

BYP2–2   The financial statements of **Jean Coutu** are presented in Appendix B following the financial statements for **Shoppers Drug Mart** in Appendix A.

Instructions

(a) For each company, calculate or find the following ratios and values for the most recent fiscal year. Industry averages, where available, are shown in parentheses.
   1. Working capital (n/a)
   2. Current ratio (1.4:1)
   3. Debt to total assets (30.6%)
   4. Earnings per share (n/a)
   5. Price-earnings ratio (the year-end share price was $42.80 for Shoppers Drug Mart and $15.78 for Jean Coutu) (42.0 times)

(b) Based on your findings for part (a), discuss the relative liquidity, solvency, and profitability of the two companies and their industry.

Comparing IFRS and ASPE

BYP2–3   McCain Foods Limited is a large multinational private company generating in excess of $6 billion in sales. It pro-
duces both frozen and non-frozen food products and makes one-third of the frozen French fries produced worldwide. It has
manufacturing operations on six continents, sales operations in over 160 countries, and employs more than 20,000 people.

*Discuss qualitative
characteristics of ac-
counting information
for private and public
companies.
(SO 3)*

Most private companies choose to use ASPE. However, some private companies like McCain have adopted IFRS.
Because the company is so large, it treats itself for reporting purposes like a public company.

Instructions

(a) McCain has numerous subsidiaries located throughout the globe. How would this type of multinational structure
motivate McCain to choose IFRS?

(b) Why would users of McCain's financial statements want them prepared using IFRS? Try to relate the users' needs to
the four qualitative characteristics of accounting information: relevance, faithful representation, comparability, and
understandability.

(c) It is often assumed that only large private companies would choose to adopt IFRS and small companies would avoid
IFRS. Why do you think that is? Can you think of reasons why a small private company would want to adopt IFRS?

Critical Thinking Case

BYP2–4   Kenmare Architects Ltd. (KAL) was incorporated and commenced operations on January 1, 2014. Sheila
Kenmare, the company's only employee, consults with various clients and uses expensive equipment to complete her work.
When the company was formed, Sheila bought 10,000 common shares but at the beginning of 2015, another 1,000
common shares were sold to Sheila's mother.

*Analyze income
statement.
(SO 1, 2)*

In addition to selling shares, KAL received financing from Sheila's Uncle Harry in the form of a loan that was taken out
on January 1, 2014. Her uncle required the company to pay only the interest on the loan and no principal in 2014, which
KAL did. However, he wanted both interest and a portion of the principal to be paid during 2015. These payments were made
evenly throughout 2015. Harry was surprised when Sheila paid down more of the loan balance in 2015 than he asked her to.

The following shows the financial statements of the company for the past two years:

KENMARE ARCHITECTS LTD.
Income Statement
Year Ended December 31

	2015	2014
Service revenue	$120,000	$100,000
Salaries expense	74,000	59,000
Rent and other office expenses	20,000	20,000
Depreciation expense	12,000	12,000
Interest expense	2,700	3,600
Profit before income tax	11,300	5,400
Income tax	3,390	1,890
Profit	$ 7,910	$ 3,510

KENMARE ARCHITECTS LTD.
Statement of Financial Position
December 31

	2015	2014
Cash	$ 9,000	$ 22,000
Accounts receivable	37,000	9,000
	46,000	31,000
Equipment	84,000	84,000
Accumulated depreciation	(24,000)	(12,000)
	60,000	72,000
	$106,000	$103,000
Accounts payable	$ 29,580	$ 14,490
Current portion of loan payable	4,000	8,000
	33,580	22,490
Loan payable	26,000	52,000
	59,580	74,490
Common shares	35,000	25,000
Retained earnings	11,420	3,510
	46,420	28,510
	$106,000	$103,000

Instructions

(a) When the company was formed, how much did Sheila pay for her shares? How much did her mother pay for her shares?

(b) At the end of 2014, what portion of the loan did Uncle Harry want paid off in 2015? How much of the loan was actually paid off in 2015? What was the total amount of cash received by Harry in 2014 and 2015?

(c) Calculate the current ratio for each year. Has the company's liquidity improved?

(d) Calculate the debt to total assets ratio for each year. Did the company's solvency improve? What effect did the change in this ratio have on the income statement?

(e) Calculate the earnings per share of the company for each year. Why do you think that the earnings per share changed in 2015?

(f) Assume that the price Sheila paid for her shares was the share price throughout 2014. Using that price, determine the value of the price-earnings ratio for that year. Assume that the price Sheila's mother paid for her shares was the share price throughout 2015. Using that price, determine the price-earnings ratio for 2015. Why do you think the value of this ratio changed? Do you think that the share price change was justified?

(g) What was the major reason for the company to sell shares in 2015?

Ethics Case

Discuss early implementation of accounting standards. (SO 3)

BYP2–5　Kathy Onishi, the controller at Redondo Corporation, a private corporation, discussed with Redondo's vice-president of finance the possibility of switching from ASPE to IFRS. She said it would result in a better comparison of the company's financial condition and profit with its competitors. Furthermore, some bankers preferred to see financial statements prepared under IFRS. When the vice-president determined that switching would decrease reported profit for the year, he strongly discouraged Kathy from implementing IFRS.

Instructions

(a) Who are the stakeholders in this situation?

(b) What, if any, are the ethical considerations in this situation?

(c) What could Kathy gain by adopting IFRS? Who might be affected by a decision not to adopt it?

"All About You" Activity

Prepare personal statement of financial position. (SO 1)

BYP2–6　As discussed in the "All About You" feature presented in this chapter, in order to evaluate your own financial situation, you need to prepare a personal statement of financial position. Assume that you have gathered the following information:

Amount owed on student loan (non-current)	$20,500
Balance in chequing account	1,500
Amount paid for vehicle	3,000
Student fees due in three months' time	2,300
Amount paid for laptop and accessories	750
Amount paid for clothes and furniture	4,500
Balance owed on credit card	900
Balance owed on loan from parents	2,400

Instructions

(a) Using the information provided above, prepare a personal statement of financial position. Instead of shareholders' equity, use personal equity or deficit. Calculate the debt to total assets ratio.

(b) Can you prepare your own personal statement of financial position? What is your debt to total assets ratio? How does your ratio compare with the one you calculated in part (a)?

Serial Case

(*Note:* This serial case was started in Chapter 1 and will continue in each chapter.)

Answer questions about sources of financial information. (SO 2, 3)

BYP2–7

After graduating from university and investigating the opportunities available to her, Natalie chooses to work for Koebel's Family Bakery Ltd. She begins the process of familiarizing herself with the business operation and all of the information that is generated to enable her parents to run their business on a day-to-day basis.

While at a trade show, Natalie is introduced to Gerry Richards, operations manager of Biscuits, a national food retailer and publicly traded company. After much discussion, Gerry asks Natalie (acting for Koebel's Family Bakery Ltd.) to consider being Biscuits' major supplier of oatmeal chocolate chip cookies. He provides Natalie with the most recent copy of Biscuits' financial statements. He anticipates that Koebel's Family Bakery will need to provide Biscuits with approximately 1,500 dozen cookies a week. Koebel's Family Bakery is to provide a monthly invoice to Biscuits and will be paid approximately 30 days from the date the invoice is received in its Toronto office.

Natalie is thrilled with the offer; however, she is concerned that taking on this additional contractual commitment along with the one that has just recently been negotiated for providing cupcakes will be too much for Koebel's Family Bakery to handle.

Instructions

Natalie has come to you for advice and asks the following questions.

(a) Gerry Richards has provided me with a full set of Biscuits' financial statements. Can you please identify each financial statement included in this package and explain what type of information each one provides?

(b) How do I know that the information included in the financial statements is verifiable and prepared on a timely basis?

(c) I would like to be sure that Biscuits will be able to pay Koebel's Family Bakery's invoices. How can I determine if Biscuits has enough cash to meet its current liabilities? Are there any ratios or financial information I should look at to obtain that information?

(d) Is Biscuits profitable? Are there any ratios or financial information I should look at specifically to obtain that information?

(e) Does Biscuits have any non-current debt? If so, is Biscuits able to pay off both its debt and the related interest on its debt? Are there any ratios or financial information I should look at specifically to obtain that information?

(f) If Koebel's Family Bakery were to sign a contract committing to provide 1,500 dozen cookies a week, what other factors should be considered before accepting the contract?

Answers to Self-Test Questions

1. a   2. c   3. d   4. a   5. b
6. c   7. d   8. a   9. c   10. d

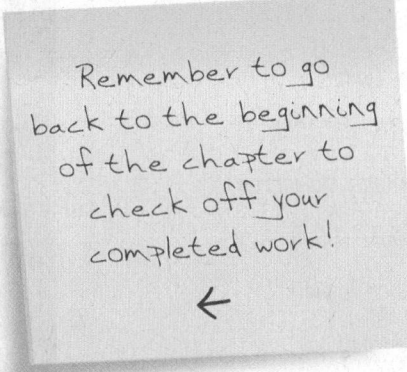

Remember to go back to the beginning of the chapter to check off your completed work!

←

Endnotes

[1]Plazacorp Retail Properties Ltd. 2012 Annual Report. Plazacorp corporate website, www.plaza.ca.

[2]Benjamin Graham, *The Intelligent Investor*, New York: Harper Business, 2003, p. 367. Alex Cuadros, Bloomberg News, "Warren Buffet Is Once Again the World's Third-Richest Person," *Financial Post*, March 22, 2013. Matthew J. Belvedere, "Buffet's Berkshire Stock: 'Bull' Gabelli vs. 'Bear' Kass," CNBC.com, May 3, 2013.

[3]"Poseidon Concepts Corp., Poseidon Concepts Ltd., Poseidon Concepts Limited Partnership and Poseidon Concepts Inc.: CCAA Filing," PricewaterhouseCoopers website, http://www.pwc.com/ca/en/car/poseidon/index.jhtml, updated July 4, 2013. Tim Kiladze, "Poseidon Concepts Dropped from TSX," *The Globe and Mail*, April 18, 2013. Barry Critchley, "Poseidon Concepts Dives to 27¢ from $16.03 in Less Than Five Months," *Financial Post*, February 14, 2013.

[4]Linda Nguyen, "Seniors Piling on Debt Faster Than Any Other Age Group," Canadian Press, February 14, 2013. Garry Marr, "High Credit Card Rates Costing Canadians a Fortune," *Financial Post*, March 30, 2013. Tamsin McMahon, "Half of Canadians Are Worried about Their Finances," *Maclean's* magazine, January 24, 2013. "Worried Canadians Increasingly Cautious about Their Money: CICA Survey," CICA news release, January 22, 2013.

The Accounting Information System

The Navigator
Chapter 3

- [ ] Scan *Study Objectives*
- [ ] Read *Feature Story*
- [ ] Read text and answer *Do It!s*
- [ ] Review *Comparing IFRS and ASPE*
- [ ] Review *Summary of Study Objectives*
- [ ] Review *Decision Toolkit—A Summary*
- [ ] Work *Using the Decision Toolkit*
- [ ] Work *Comprehensive Do It!*
- [ ] Answer *Self-Test Questions*
- [ ] Complete *assignments*
- [ ] Go to *WileyPLUS* for practice and tutorials

the
navigator

study objectives

After studying this chapter, you should be able to:

SO 1 Analyze the effects of transactions on the accounting equation.

SO 2 Define debits and credits and explain how they are used to record transactions.

SO 3 Journalize transactions.

SO 4 Post transactions.

SO 5 Prepare a trial balance.

Learning to Handle the Dough

For generations, grandmothers in Grant Hooker's family would make a pastry of flattened, whole-wheat dough as a special treat, called a BeaverTails® pastry, which became a staple with Mr. Hooker's own kids.

In 1978, Mr. Hooker sold the family secret to the public for the first time at a music festival and agricultural fairs in the Ottawa Valley. The crowd loved it. Mr. Hooker trademarked the name "BeaverTails" and built his own booth in Ottawa's Byward Market in 1980 to sell them full-time. However, sales weren't as swift as at the fairs.

Undaunted, Mr. Hooker secured permission to sell BeaverTails pastries on the Rideau Canal during Ottawa's Winterlude festival. Within three years, BeaverTails Canada Inc. had the contract to sell all the food on the Rideau Canal and employed 450 people. The business continued to grow; BeaverTails began franchising in 1990 and now includes more than 80 outlets across Canada, with additional locations in Saudi Arabia, Japan, and Colorado's ski country. The original Byward Market location made headlines in 2009 when U.S. President Barack Obama dropped in for a BeaverTails pastry during his first official visit to Ottawa.

At first, keeping track of the money was straightforward for Mr. Hooker and didn't require a formal accounting system. It was merely a matter of staying on top of how much was owed to suppliers and staff, and in rent and utilities. Mr. Hooker, who has no formal business training, got along fine simply managing the chequebook.

But this changed with franchising. "We weren't just selling products to people for cash, putting the cash in the bank, and then writing cheques for what we owed," says Mr. Hooker. "We were into receivables; people owed us money." The company also had liabilities—in the form of a bank loan.

Mr. Hooker hired a firm to set up an accounting system for the business, an experience he describes as a "rude awakening" that cost him approximately $200,000. One of the accounting staff members was negligent, and the company's accounts weren't balanced properly.

"I realized how much improper accounting could cost me and how, if I didn't understand accounting, I'd have to trust somebody," Mr. Hooker says. He hired another accountant to rebuild the accounting system, working closely with him to learn how it worked.

The breakthrough point for him, he says, was in understanding that "cash is a debit." Assets (from the statement of financial position) and expenses (from the income statement) have normal debit balances. Liabilities and shareholders' equity (from the statement of financial position) and revenues (from the income statement) have normal credit balances. To increase the amount in an account, an entry has to be the same sign, he adds. In other words, only debits increase debit accounts and credits increase credit accounts.

Now that he understands the basics of the accounting system, Mr. Hooker monitors it very closely. He insists his accountant provide him with "TAMFS"—timely, accurate, monthly financial statements. "That is an absolute necessity any time a business grows to where the owner puts his trust in somebody else to handle the money," he says.[1]

the
navigator

<table>
<tr><td>preview of
CHAPTER</td><td>3</td></tr>
</table>

As indicated in the feature story, an accounting information system that produces timely and accurate financial information is a necessity for a company like BeaverTails. The purpose of this chapter is to explain and illustrate the features of an accounting information system. The chapter is organized as follows:

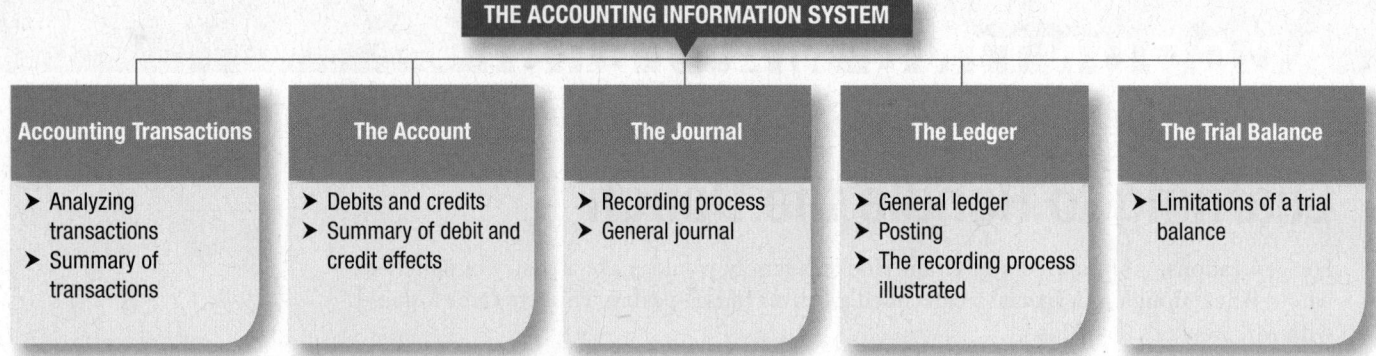

THE ACCOUNTING INFORMATION SYSTEM

Accounting Transactions	The Account	The Journal	The Ledger	The Trial Balance
➤ Analyzing transactions ➤ Summary of transactions	➤ Debits and credits ➤ Summary of debit and credit effects	➤ Recording process ➤ General journal	➤ General ledger ➤ Posting ➤ The recording process illustrated	➤ Limitations of a trial balance

Accounting Transactions

STUDY OBJECTIVE 1
Analyze the effects of transactions on the accounting equation.

The system of collecting and processing transaction data and communicating financial information to decision makers is known as the **accounting information system**. Accounting information systems vary widely. Some factors that shape these systems are the type of business and its transactions, the size of the company, the amount of data, and the information that management and others need. For example, as indicated in the feature story, BeaverTails did not need a formal accounting system when it first began. However, as the business and the number and type of transactions grew, an organized accounting information system became essential.

An accounting information system begins with determining what relevant transaction data should be collected and processed. Not all events are recorded and reported as accounting transactions. Only those events that cause changes in assets, liabilities, or shareholders' equity should be recorded. For example, suppose a new employee is hired. Should this event be recorded in the company's accounting records? The answer is "no." While the hiring of an employee will lead to a future accounting transaction (the payment of salary after the work has been completed), no accounting transaction has occurred at this point.

An **accounting transaction** occurs when assets, liabilities, or shareholders' equity items change as a result of an economic event. Illustration 3-1 summarizes the process that is used to decide whether or not to record economic events.

▸Illustration 3-1
Transaction identification process

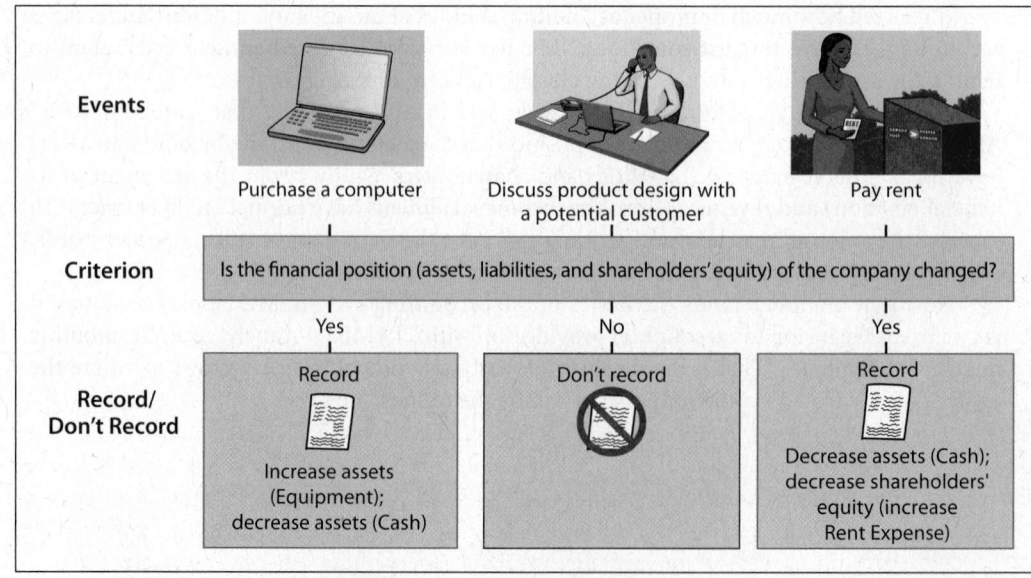

ACCOUNTING MATTERS!

NHL Signing Bonuses

Does hiring a top National Hockey League (NHL) player add value to the team? The owner and fans would say so. However, simply agreeing to sign a contract to play for a hockey team is not an economic event that results in an accounting transaction. Despite the team's perceived value rising by the hiring of top talent, a transaction is not recorded until the player starts playing and earns his salary . . . and hopefully generates additional revenue for the team, as well.

On the other hand, signing bonuses do result in an economic transaction and consequently are treated differently. When a player is given a signing bonus to sign with the team, he is paid cash at the time of signing and the team's assets, liabilities, and equities change. NHL signing bonuses can be significant, ranging from $1 million to $10 million over the last few years.

ANALYZING TRANSACTIONS

In Chapter 1, you learned about the accounting equation:

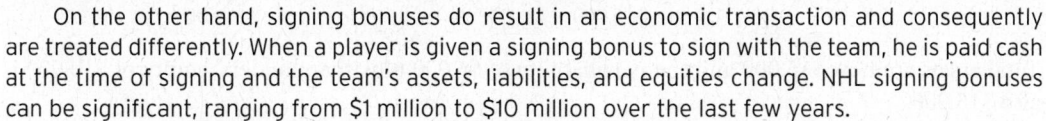

| Assets | = | Liabilities | + | Shareholders' Equity |

In this chapter, you will learn how to analyze transactions for their effect on each component of the accounting equation—assets, liabilities, and shareholders' equity. Remember that the accounting equation must always balance, so each transaction will have a dual (double-sided) effect on the equation. For example, if an individual asset is increased, there must be either a corresponding decrease in another asset, an increase in a specific liability, and/or an increase in shareholders' equity.

Note that two or more items could be affected when analyzing the accounting equation. Assume that services of $200 have been provided, for which $50 has been received in cash and the remainder is owed on account. An asset (cash) would increase by $50, a different asset (accounts receivable) would increase by $150, and shareholders' equity (service revenue) would increase by $200.

Chapter 1 presented the financial statements for Sierra Corporation for its first month of operations, October 2015. You should review these financial statements at this time. To illustrate the effects of economic events on the accounting equation, we will now examine some of the events that affected Sierra Corporation in its first month of operations and were ultimately reported on its financial statements in Chapter 1 in Illustrations 1-5, 1-6, 1-7, and 1-8.

Transaction (1): Investment by Shareholders.   On October 1, cash of $10,000 was invested in Sierra Corporation in exchange for 10,000 common shares. This transaction results in an equal increase in assets and shareholders' equity. There is an increase of $10,000 in the asset account Cash and an increase of $10,000 in the shareholders' equity account Common Shares.

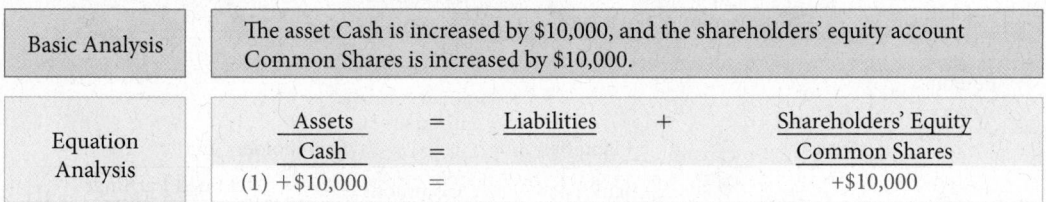

Basic Analysis	The asset Cash is increased by $10,000, and the shareholders' equity account Common Shares is increased by $10,000.

	Assets	=	Liabilities	+	Shareholders' Equity
Equation Analysis	Cash	=			Common Shares
	(1) +$10,000	=			+$10,000

The two sides of the accounting equation remain equal after this transaction. Note that investments by shareholders are not recorded as revenue, but as common shares of the corporation.

Transaction (2): Purchase of Equipment.   Also on October 1, Sierra borrowed $5,000 from Scotiabank to purchase equipment. It promised to repay the bank loan, plus 6% interest per annum (year), in three months. This transaction results in an equal increase in assets and liabilities: Equipment (an asset) increases by $5,000 and the liability Bank Loan Payable increases by $5,000. The specific effect of this transaction and the cumulative effect of the first two transactions are:

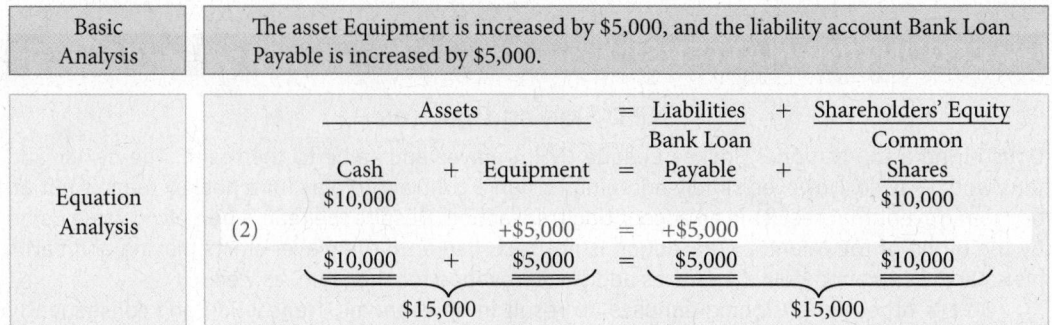

| Basic Analysis | The asset Equipment is increased by $5,000, and the liability account Bank Loan Payable is increased by $5,000. |

		Assets			=	Liabilities	+	Shareholders' Equity
						Bank Loan		Common
Equation Analysis		Cash	+	Equipment	=	Payable	+	Shares
		$10,000						$10,000
	(2)			+$5,000	=	+$5,000		
		$10,000	+	$5,000	=	$5,000		$10,000
				$15,000			$15,000	

Total assets are now $15,000 and the new liability of $5,000 plus shareholders' equity of $10,000 is also $15,000.

Transaction (3): Payment of Rent.   On October 2, Sierra Corporation paid its office rent for the month of October in cash, $900. To record this transaction, Cash is decreased by $900 and Rent Expense is increased by $900. Rent is an expense incurred by Sierra in its effort to generate revenues. Expenses decrease retained earnings, which in turn decrease shareholders' equity. You will recall from earlier chapters that shareholders' equity consists of common shares (which is one type of share capital) and retained earnings. Retained earnings are increased by revenues and decreased by expenses and dividends.

We have expanded our accounting equation in Illustration 3-2 to show the detailed components of shareholders' equity.

▶Illustration 3-2
Expanded accounting equation

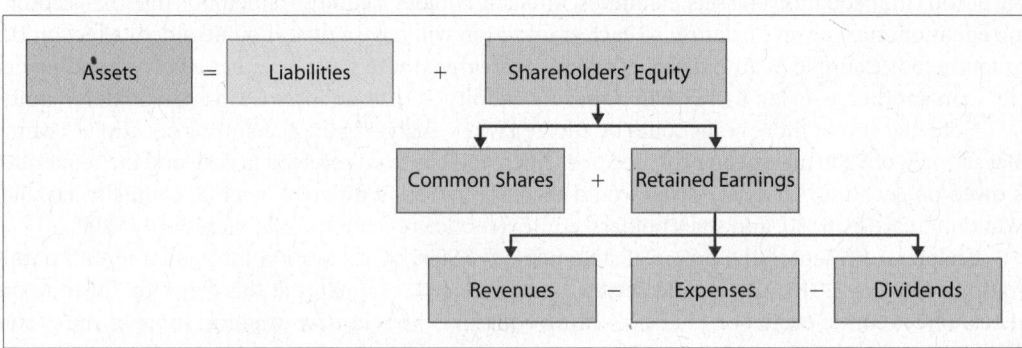

We will use this expansion of the components of shareholders' equity and retained earnings in our tabular accounting equations that follow. As there is not enough room to use specific account names for each individual revenue and expense account in the expanded accounting equation shown below, they will be summarized under the column headings Revenues (abbreviated as "Rev."), Expenses (abbreviated as "Exp."), and Dividends (abbreviated as "Div.").

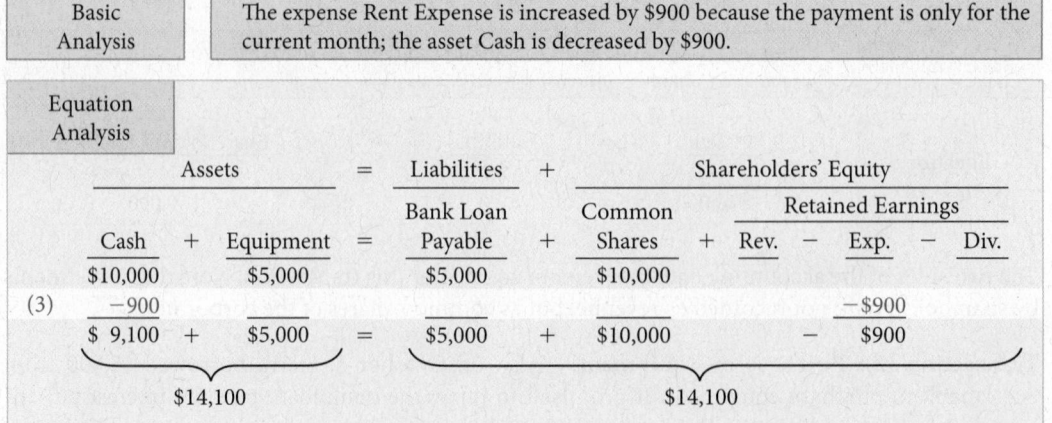

| Basic Analysis | The expense Rent Expense is increased by $900 because the payment is only for the current month; the asset Cash is decreased by $900. |

Equation Analysis											

	Assets			=	Liabilities	+			Shareholders' Equity			
					Bank Loan		Common			Retained Earnings		
	Cash	+	Equipment	=	Payable	+	Shares	+	Rev.	−	Exp.	−	Div.
	$10,000		$5,000		$5,000		$10,000					
(3)	−900										−$900	
	$ 9,100	+	$5,000	=	$5,000	+	$10,000			−	$900	
		$14,100						$14,100				

As mentioned above, expenses reduce retained earnings and ultimately shareholders' equity. Therefore, this transaction reduces both assets and shareholders' equity by $900, keeping the equation in balance.

Transaction (4): Purchase of Insurance. On October 5, Sierra paid $600 for a one-year insurance policy effective October 1 that expires next year on September 30. This results in a transaction because one asset was exchanged for another. The asset Cash is decreased by $600. The asset Prepaid Insurance (abbreviated as "Pre. Ins.") is increased by $600 because the payment is for more than the current month. Payments of expenses that will benefit more than one accounting period are assets and are identified as prepaid expenses or prepayments. We will learn more about how to account for prepayments in the next chapter.

As shown, the balance in total assets did not change; one asset account decreased by the same amount by which another increased.

Basic Analysis	The asset Prepaid Insurance is increased by $600 because the payment extends to more than the current month; the asset Cash is decreased by $600.

Equation Analysis

	Assets			=	Liabilities	+		Shareholders' Equity			
					Bank Loan		Common		Retained Earnings		
	Cash +	Pre. Ins. +	Equipment =		Payable +		Shares +	Rev. −	Exp. −	Div.	
	$9,100		$5,000		$5,000		$10,000		$900		
(4)	−600	+$600									
	$8,500 +	$600 +	$5,000 =		$5,000 +		$10,000		− $900		
		$14,100						$14,100			

Transaction (5): Hiring of New Employees. On October 7, Sierra hired four new employees to begin work on Monday, October 12. Each employee will receive a weekly salary of $500 for a five-day (Monday–Friday) workweek, payable every two weeks. Employees will receive their first paycheques on Friday, October 23. There is no effect on the accounting equation because the company's assets, liabilities, and shareholders' equity have not changed. An accounting transaction has not occurred because the employees have not yet worked; at this point, there is only an agreement that the employees will begin work on October 12. (See transaction 10 for the first payment of salaries.)

Transaction (6): Purchase of Supplies on Account. On October 9, Sierra purchased advertising supplies on account from Aero Supply Corp. for $2,500. The account is due in 30 days. This transaction is referred to as a purchase "on account" or "on credit." Instead of paying cash, the company incurs a liability, usually an account payable, by promising to pay cash in the future.

Assets are increased by this transaction because supplies represent a resource that will be used in the future in the process of providing services to customers. Liabilities are increased by the amount due to Aero Supply. The asset Supplies (abbreviated as "Sup.") is increased by $2,500, and the liability Accounts Payable (abbreviated as "A/P") is increased by the same amount. The Bank Loan Payable account has also been abbreviated as "L/P" (indicating a Loan Payable) due to space limitations in the equation analysis below. The effect on the equation is:

Basic Analysis	The asset Supplies is increased by $2,500; the liability Accounts Payable is increased by $2,500.

Equation Analysis

	Assets				=	Liabilities		+		Shareholders' Equity			
									Common		Retained Earnings		
	Cash +	Sup. +	Pre. Ins. +	Equipment =		A/P +	L/P +		Shares +	Rev. −	Exp. −	Div.	
	$8,500		$600	$5,000			$5,000		$10,000		$900		
(6)		+$2,500				+$2,500							
	$8,500 +	$2,500 +	$600 +	$5,000 =		$2,500 +	$5,000 +		$10,000		− $900		
		$16,600								$16,600			

Transaction (7): Services Performed on Account.   On October 13, Sierra performed $20,000 of advertising services for Copa Ltd. Sierra sent Copa a bill for these services, asking for payment within 30 days.

Companies often provide services "on account" or "on credit." Instead of receiving cash, the company receives a different type of asset, an account receivable. Accounts receivable represent the right to receive payment at a future date.

Revenue, however, is earned when services are performed. Therefore, revenue is recorded when services are performed, even though cash has not been received. Because revenue increases retained earnings—a shareholders' equity account—both assets and shareholders' equity are increased by this transaction.

In this transaction, Accounts Receivable (abbreviated as "A/R") is increased by $20,000 and Service Revenue is increased by the same amount. The new balances in the equation are:

Basic Analysis	The asset Accounts Receivable is increased by $20,000. The revenue account Service Revenue is increased by $20,000.

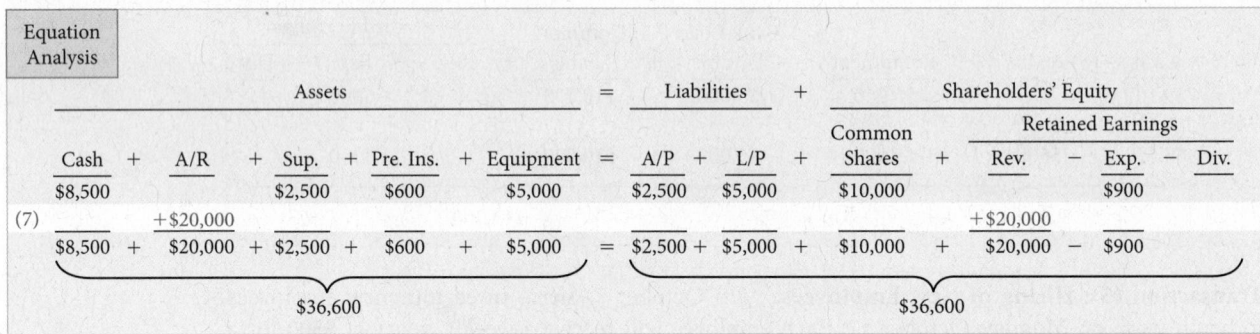

Transaction (8): Receipt of Cash in Advance from Customer.   On October 19, Sierra received a $1,200 cash advance from R. Knox, a client, for advertising services that are not expected to be completed until November. Revenue should not be recorded until the work has been performed. However, since cash was received before performing the advertising services, Sierra has a liability for the work due. We call this liability unearned revenue.

Note that the word *unearned* indicates that this is a liability account rather than a revenue account. Although many liability accounts have the word *payable* in their title, not all do. Unearned Revenue is a liability account even though the word *payable* is not used.

This transaction results in an increase to Cash (an asset) of $1,200 and an increase in Unearned Revenue (a liability) by the same amount:

Basic Analysis	The asset Cash is increased by $1,200; the liability Unearned Revenue is increased by $1,200 because the service has not been provided yet.

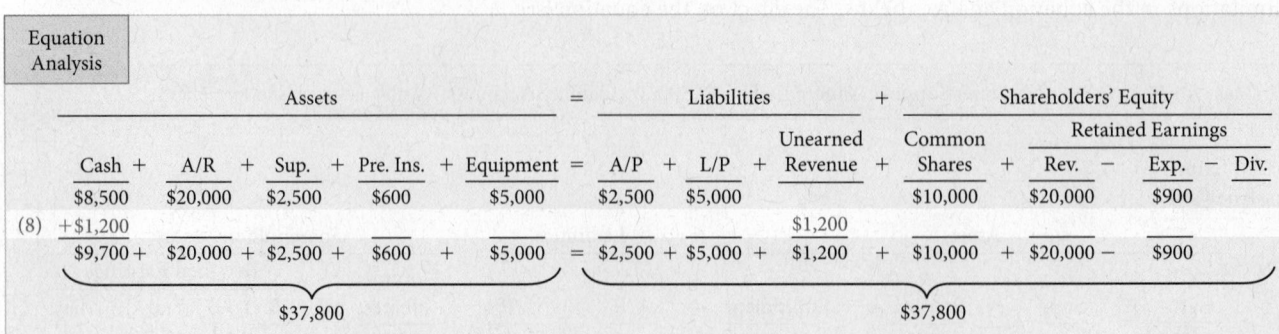

Transaction (9): Payment on Account.   On October 22, Sierra made a partial payment of $1,000 on the amount it owed for the supplies purchased from Aero Supply on October 9. Recall that the supplies and an account payable from this transaction were recorded earlier in transaction 6, when the supplies were purchased. Supplies should not be recorded again when the cash is paid. Rather,

Accounts Payable is decreased by $1,000 and Cash is decreased by the same amount. The new balances in the accounting equation are:

Basic Analysis	The liability Accounts Payable is decreased by $1,000; the asset Cash is decreased by the same amount.

Equation Analysis

	Assets					=	Liabilities			+	Shareholders' Equity			
									Unearned		Common		Retained Earnings	
	Cash +	A/R +	Sup. +	Pre. Ins. +	Equipment =		A/P +	L/P +	Revenue +		Shares +	Rev. −	Exp. −	Div.
	$9,700	$20,000	$2,500	$600	$5,000		$2,500	$5,000	$1,200		$10,000	$20,000	$900	
(9)	−1,000						−1,000							
	$8,700 +	$20,000 +	$2,500 +	$600 +	$5,000 =		$1,500 +	$5,000 +	$1,200 +		$10,000 +	$20,000 −	$900	

$36,800 = $36,800

Transaction (10): Payment of Salaries. Employees worked two weeks, earning $4,000 in salaries (4 employees × $500/week × 2 weeks), and were paid on October 23. Salaries are an expense similar to rent because they are a cost of generating revenues. While the act of hiring the employees in transaction 5 did not result in an accounting transaction, the payment of the employees' salary is a transaction because assets and expenses are affected. Cash is decreased by $4,000 and Salaries Expense is increased by $4,000 (which reduces retained earnings, which in turn reduces shareholders' equity, by $4,000):

Basic Analysis	The expense Salaries Expense is increased by $4,000; the asset Cash is decreased by $4,000.

Equation Analysis

	Assets					=	Liabilities			+	Shareholders' Equity			
									Unearned		Common		Retained Earnings	
	Cash +	A/R +	Sup. +	Pre. Ins. +	Equipment =		A/P +	L/P +	Revenue +		Shares +	Rev. −	Exp. −	Div.
	$8,700	$20,000	$2,500	$600	$5,000		$1,500	$5,000	$1,200		$10,000	$20,000	$ 900	
(10)	−4,000												−4,000	
	$4,700 +	$20,000 +	$2,500 +	$600 +	$5,000 =		$1,500 +	$5,000 +	$1,200 +		$10,000 +	$20,000 −	$4,900	

$32,800 = $32,800

Transaction (11): Payment of Dividend. On October 26, Sierra paid a $500 cash dividend. Dividends are a distribution of retained earnings rather than an expense—they are not incurred to generate revenue. Cash is decreased by $500 and Dividends is increased by $500, which reduces both retained earnings and shareholders' equity:

Basic Analysis	Dividends is increased by $500; the asset Cash is decreased by $500.

Equation Analysis

	Assets					=	Liabilities			+	Shareholders' Equity			
									Unearned		Common		Retained Earnings	
	Cash +	A/R +	Sup. +	Pre. Ins. +	Equipment =		A/P +	L/P +	Revenue +		Shares +	Rev. −	Exp. −	Div.
	$4,700	$20,000	$2,500	$600	$5,000		$1,500	$5,000	$1,200		$10,000	$20,000	$4,900	
(11)	−500													−$500
	$4,200 +	$20,000 +	$2,500 +	$600 +	$5,000 =		$1,500 +	$5,000 +	$1,200 +		$10,000 +	$20,000 −	$4,900 −	$500

$32,300 = $32,300

Transaction (12): Collection on Account.   On October 30, Copa paid Sierra $5,000 of the amount owing on its account. Recall that an account receivable and the revenue from this transaction were recorded earlier in transaction 7, when the service was provided. Revenue should not be recorded again when the cash is collected. Rather, Cash is increased by $5,000 and Accounts Receivable is decreased by $5,000, bringing the balance in this account to $15,000—the amount still owing from Copa. Total assets and total liabilities and shareholders' equity are unchanged, as shown:

Basic Analysis	The asset Cash is increased by $5,000. The asset Accounts Receivable is decreased by $5,000.

Equation Analysis

			Assets			=		Liabilities			+		Shareholders' Equity			
										Unearned		Common		Retained Earnings		
	Cash +	A/R +	Sup. +	Pre. Ins. +	Equipment =		A/P +	L/P +	Revenue +		Shares +	Rev. −	Exp. −	Div.
	$4,200	$20,000	$2,500	$600	$5,000		$1,500	$5,000	$1,200		$10,000	$20,000	$4,900	$500
(12)	+5,000	−5,000												
	$9,200 +	$15,000 +	$2,500 +	$600 +	$5,000 =		$1,500 +	$5,000 +	$1,200 +		$10,000 +	$20,000 −	$4,900 −	$500

$32,300 $32,300

Transaction (13): Payment of Income Tax.   On October 30, Copa paid a monthly income tax instalment of $1,800. Cash is decreased by $1,800 and Income Tax Expense is increased by $1,800, which in turn decreases retained earnings and shareholders' equity by $1,800:

Basic Analysis	The expense Income Tax Expense is increased by $1,800; the asset Cash is decreased by $1,800.

Equation Analysis

			Assets			=		Liabilities			+		Shareholders' Equity			
										Unearned		Common		Retained Earnings		
	Cash +	A/R +	Sup. +	Pre. Ins. +	Equipment =		A/P +	L/P +	Revenue +		Shares +	Rev. −	Exp. −	Div.
	$ 9,200	$15,000	$2,500	$600	$5,000		$1,500	$5,000	$1,200		$10,000	$20,000	$4,900	$500
(13)	−1,800												−1,800	
	$7,400 +	$15,000 +	$2,500 +	$600 +	$5,000 =		$1,500 +	$5,000 +	$1,200 +		$10,000 +	$20,000 −	$6,700 −	$500

$30,500 $30,500

SUMMARY OF TRANSACTIONS

The transactions of Sierra Corporation are summarized in Illustration 3-3 to show their cumulative effect on the accounting equation. The transaction numbers, the specific effects of each transaction, and the final balances are indicated. Remember that event 5—the hiring of employees—did not result in a transaction, so no entry is included for that event.

	Assets					=	Liabilities			+	Shareholders' Equity			
									Unearned		Common	Retained Earnings		
	Cash +	A/R +	Sup. +	Pre. Ins. +	Equipment =		A/P +	L/P +	Revenue +		Shares +	Rev. −	Exp. −	Div.
(1)	+$10,000										+$10,000			
(2)					+5,000			+$5,000						
(3)	−900												−$ 900	
(4)	−600			+$600										
(6)			+$2,500				+$2,500							
(7)		+$20,000										+$20,000		
(8)	+1,200								+$1,200					
(9)	−1,000						−1,000							
(10)	−4,000												−4,000	
(11)	−500													−$500
(12)	+5,000	−5,000												
(13)	−1,800												−1,800	
	$7,400 +	$15,000 +	$2,500 +	$600 +	$5,000 =		$1,500 +	$5,000 +	$1,200 +		$10,000 +	$20,000 −	$6,700 −	$500
			$30,500							$30,500				

▶Illustration 3-3
Tabular summary of transactions

The illustration demonstrates that (1) each transaction must be analyzed for its effect on the three primary components of the accounting equation (assets, liabilities, and shareholders' equity), and (2) the two sides of the equation must always be equal.

DECISION TOOLKIT

Decision Checkpoints	Info Needed for Decision	Tools to Use for Decision	How to Evaluate Results
Has an accounting transaction occurred?	Details of the event	Accounting equation	Determine the effect, if any, on assets, liabilities, and shareholders' equity.

BEFORE YOU GO ON...

▶Do It! Analyze Transactions

Selective transactions made by Virmari Corporation for the month of August follow:

1. Common shares were issued to shareholders for $25,000 cash.

2. Equipment costing $7,000 was purchased on account.

3. Services amounting to $8,000 were performed for customers. Of this amount, $2,000 was received in cash and $6,000 is due on account.

4. Rent was paid for the month, $850.

5. Customers owing $6,000 on account paid $4,000 of the balance due (see transaction 3).

6. Dividends of $1,000 were paid to shareholders.

Prepare a tabular analysis that shows the effects of these transactions on the accounting equation.

(continued)

Action Plan

- Analyze the effects of each transaction on the accounting equation.
- Remember that a change in an asset will require a change in another asset, a liability, or shareholders' equity in order to keep the accounting equation in balance.

Solution

	Cash	+	Accounts Receivable	+	Equipment	=	Accounts Payable	+	Common Shares	+	Revenues	−	Expenses	−	Dividends
(1)	+$25,000								+$25,000						
(2)					+$7,000	=	+$7,000								
(3)	+2,000		+$6,000								+$8,000				
(4)	−850												−$850		
(5)	+4,000		−4,000												
(6)	−1,000														−$1,000
	$29,150 +		$2,000	+	$7,000	=	$7,000	+	$25,000	+	$8,000	−	$850	−	$1,000

Assets = Liabilities + Shareholders' Equity

Accounts Receivable, Equipment under Assets. Accounts Payable under Liabilities. Common Shares, Retained Earnings (Revenues − Expenses − Dividends) under Shareholders' Equity.

$38,150 = $38,150

Related Exercise Material: BE3-1, BE3-3, E3-1, E3-2, E3-4, and E3-8.

The Account

STUDY OBJECTIVE 2
Define debits and credits and explain how they are used to record transactions.

Instead of using a tabular summary like the one in Illustration 3-3 for Sierra Corporation, an accounting information system uses accounts. An **account** is an individual accounting record of increases and decreases in a specific asset, liability, or shareholders' equity item. For example, Sierra Corporation has separate accounts for cash, accounts receivable, accounts payable, service revenue, salaries expense, and so on.

In its simplest form, an account consists of three parts: (1) the title of the account, (2) a left or debit side, and (3) a right or credit side. Because the alignment of these parts of an account resembles the letter T, it is referred to as a **T account**. The basic form of an account is shown in Illustration 3-4.

▶Illustration 3-4
Basic form of T account

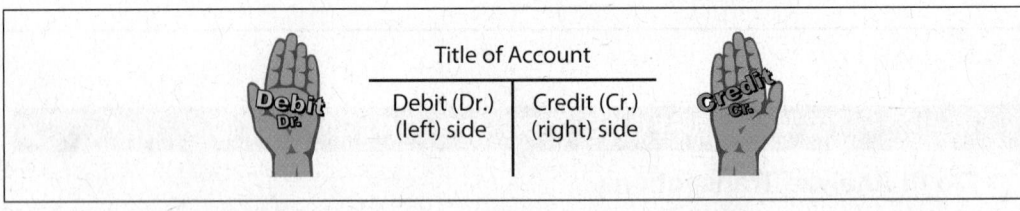

Title of Account

Debit (Dr.) (left) side | Credit (Cr.) (right) side

Alternative Terminology
A *T account* is also known as a *general ledger account*.

The actual account form used in practice looks different from the above T account. As shown below, it is designed with six columns that include information in addition to the two debit and credit columns included in T accounts.

TITLE OF ACCOUNT					
Date	Explanation	Ref.	Debit	Credit	Balance

Because of its simplicity, the T account is used for teaching purposes and will be used throughout this textbook instead of the more formal six-column account form shown above.

DEBITS AND CREDITS

The term **debit** means left, and the term **credit** means right. These terms are commonly abbreviated as Dr. for debit and Cr. for credit. Debits and credits are merely directional signals used in the recording process to describe where entries are made in the accounts. For example, the act of entering an amount on the left side of an account is called **debiting** the account, and making an entry on the right side is **crediting** the account. When the totals of the two sides are compared, an account will have a debit balance if the total of the debit amounts recorded exceeds the total of the credit amounts recorded. Conversely, an account will have a credit balance if the credit amounts exceed the debits.

When we record transactions, two or more accounts are affected and their balances change. We use debits and credits to explain the effect of these changes. At all times, the debit movement in the accounts must equal the credit movement in the accounts. The equality of debits and credits is the basis for the **double-entry accounting system**, in which the dual (two-sided) effect of each transaction is recorded in appropriate accounts. This system provides a logical method for recording transactions and ensuring that amounts are recorded accurately. If every transaction is recorded with equal debits and credits, then the sum of all the debits to the accounts must equal the sum of all the credits.

The following diagram will help us understand how debit and credit effects apply to the accounting equation:

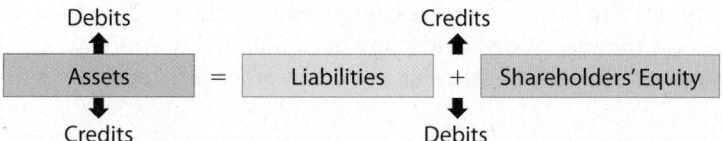

Beginning on the left-hand side of the accounting equation (asset accounts), we can see that increases in asset accounts are recorded by debits. The converse is also true: decreases in asset accounts are recorded by credits. If we cross to the right-hand side of the equation, it must follow that increases and decreases in liabilities and shareholders' equity have to be recorded opposite from increases and decreases in assets. Thus, increases in liabilities and shareholders' equity are recorded by credits and decreases by debits.

We will apply debit and credit procedures to T accounts for each component of the accounting equation—assets, liabilities, and shareholders' equity—in the following sections.

> **Helpful Hint**
> Debits and credits do not always mean "increases" and "decreases." While debits do increase certain accounts (such as assets), they decrease other accounts (such as liabilities).

Assets and Liabilities

If we look at the accounting equation, we note that assets are on the left side of the equation. Consequently, **asset accounts normally show debit (left-side) balances**. Increases in assets must be entered on the left or debit side of a T account while decreases in assets must be entered on the right or credit side. Debits to a specific asset account should exceed credits to that account, which results in a normal debit balance. It was a breakthrough for Mr. Hooker in the feature story when he learned that assets, such as cash, are normally debits.

Knowing an account's normal balance may help when you are trying to identify errors. For example, a credit balance in an asset account such as Land would indicate a recording error. Occasionally, however, an abnormal balance may be correct. The Cash account, for example, will have a credit balance if the bank allows a company to overdraw its bank balance. If the Cash account has a credit balance, it is called "bank indebtedness" and reported as a current liability rather than as a current asset. We will learn more about cash and bank indebtedness in Chapter 7. In addition, contra asset accounts, such as Accumulated Depreciation, have a normal credit balance.

As we mentioned earlier, because assets are on the opposite side of the accounting equation from liabilities, increases and decreases in assets are recorded opposite from increases and decreases in liabilities. Consequently, **liability accounts normally show credit (right-side) balances**. Increases in liability accounts must be entered on the right or credit side of a T account while decreases in liability accounts must be entered on the left or debit side. Credits to a specific liability account should exceed debits to that account, which results in a normal credit balance.

> **Helpful Hint**
> The normal balance of an account is always on its increase side.

The effects that debits and credits have on assets and liabilities and their normal balances are as follows:

Assets		Liabilities	
Debit for increase	Credit for decrease	Debit for decrease	Credit for increase
Normal balance			Normal balance

Shareholders' Equity

All asset and liability accounts have the same debit/credit rule procedures. That is, all asset accounts are increased by debits and decreased by credits. All liability accounts are increased by credits and decreased by debits. However, shareholders' equity consists of different components, and they do not all move in the same direction. You will recall from Illustration 3-2 earlier in the chapter that shareholders' equity is usually composed of common shares (one type of share capital) and retained earnings. Retained earnings can be further subdivided into revenues and expenses (which make up profit) and dividends; these components are then added to (in the case of profit) or deducted from (in the case of dividends) any beginning balance in retained earnings. In the following sections, we will look at how debit and credit procedures apply to each of these equity components.

Increases in Shareholders' Equity.   Common shares and retained earnings both increase shareholders' equity. Common shares are issued in exchange for cash and other assets received from shareholders when they invest in the business. Retained earnings are the portion of shareholders' equity that has been accumulated through the profitable operation of the company. Retained earnings (and shareholders' equity in turn) are increased by revenues.

Consequently, the common shares, retained earnings, and revenue accounts are increased by credits and decreased by debits. **The normal balance in these accounts is a credit balance.** This, and the effects that debits and credits have on them, is shown below:

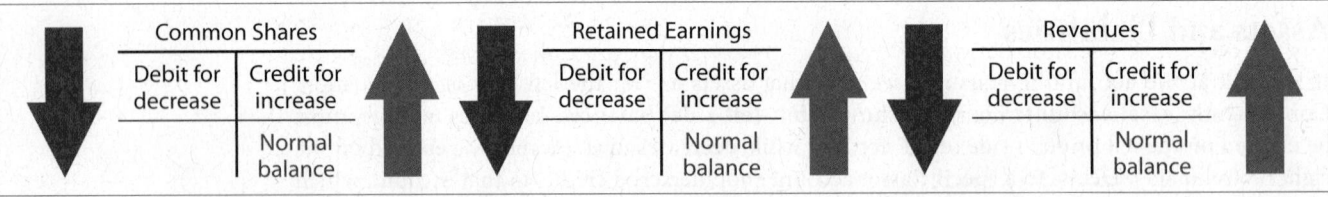

Common Shares		Retained Earnings		Revenues	
Debit for decrease	Credit for increase	Debit for decrease	Credit for increase	Debit for decrease	Credit for increase
	Normal balance		Normal balance		Normal balance

Decreases in Shareholders' Equity.   Expenses and dividends both decrease retained earnings (which in turn decreases shareholders' equity). Expenses, along with revenues, combine to determine profit. Since expenses are the negative factor in the calculation of profit, and revenues are the positive factor, it is logical that the increase and decrease sides of expense accounts should be the reverse of revenue accounts. Thus, expense accounts are increased by debits and decreased by credits.

Dividends are a distribution to shareholders of retained earnings, which reduces retained earnings. If retained earnings are decreased by debits, it follows that increases in the dividends account are recorded with debits. Credits to the dividends account are unusual, but might be used to correct a dividend recorded in error, for example.

Because expense and dividend accounts are increased by debits, **the normal balance in these accounts is a debit balance.** This, and the effects that debits and credits have on them, is shown below:

SUMMARY OF DEBIT AND CREDIT EFFECTS

Illustration 3-5 summarizes the debit and credit effects on the expanded accounting equation.

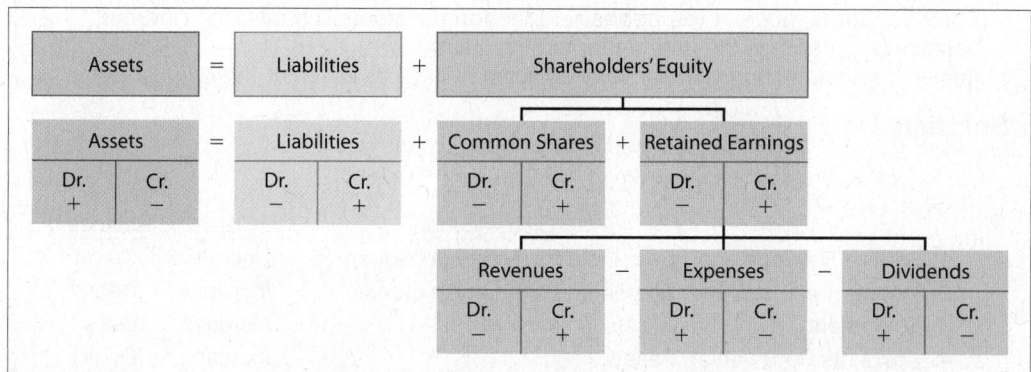

►Illustration 3-5
Summary of debit and credit rules for expanded accounting equation

Assets, on the left-hand side of the accounting equation, are increased by debits. Liabilities and shareholders' equity, on the other side of the equation, are increased by credits. As we learned earlier, shareholders' equity is further divided into at least two components: common shares and retained earnings. Since shareholders' equity is increased by credits, both of these accounts—common shares and retained earnings—are also increased by credits.

Retained earnings can be further subdivided into revenues and expenses (revenues and expenses combine to determine profit) and dividends, which add to or reduce any beginning balance in retained earnings. Since revenues increase retained earnings and shareholders' equity, increases in revenue accounts are recorded by credits. Expenses and dividends decrease retained earnings, and thus shareholders' equity. Decreases in shareholders' equity are recorded by debits. Because expenses and dividends decrease shareholders' equity, increases in each of these accounts are recorded by debits.

Like the basic accounting equation, the expanded equation must always be in balance (total debits must equal total credits). Study Illustration 3-5 carefully. It will help you understand the fundamentals of the double-entry accounting system.

BEFORE YOU GO ON...

►Do It! Debits and Credits

Lin Limited has the following selected accounts:

1. Service Revenue
2. Income Tax Expense
3. Equipment
4. Accounts Receivable
5. Accumulated Depreciation

6. Unearned Revenue
7. Accounts Payable
8. Common Shares
9. Salaries Expense
10. Dividends

(continued)

(a) Indicate whether each of the above accounts is an asset, liability, or shareholders' equity account. If the account is an asset or liability, indicate its statement of financial position classification. If it is a shareholders' equity account, indicate what specific type it is (share capital, revenue, expense, or dividends).

(b) Indicate whether a debit would increase or decrease each account.

(c) Identify the normal balance.

Action Plan

- Classify each account into its place in the expanded accounting equation.
- Apply the debit and credit rules. Remember that assets are increased by debits, and liabilities and shareholders' equity are increased by credits. Don't forget that the individual components of shareholders' equity do not all move in the same direction.
- Note an exception for contra asset accounts. Even though they are assets, contra asset accounts move in the opposite direction as assets. That is, their normal balance is a credit as they are deducted from assets.
- Remember that the normal balance of an account is on its increase side.

Solution

Account	(a) Classification	(b) Debit Effect	(c) Normal Balance
1. Service Revenue	Shareholders' equity (revenue)	Decrease	Credit
2. Income Tax Expense	Shareholders' equity (expense)	Increase	Debit
3. Equipment	Assets	Increase	Debit
4. Accounts Receivable	Assets	Increase	Debit
5. Accumulated Depreciation	Assets (contra asset)	Decrease	Credit
6. Unearned Revenue	Liabilities	Decrease	Credit
7. Accounts Payable	Liabilities	Decrease	Credit
8. Common Shares	Shareholders' equity (share capital)	Decrease	Credit
9. Salaries Expense	Shareholders' equity (expense)	Increase	Debit
10. Dividends	Shareholders' equity (dividends)	Increase	Debit

Related Exercise Material: BE3-2, BE3-3, BE3-4, E3-3, E3-4, and E3-8.

The Journal

STUDY OBJECTIVE 3
Journalize transactions.

While the tabular accounting equation is helpful to understand the effects that transactions have on the accounts, it is not a practical way to keep track of the many transactions companies have. Consequently, a more formalized recording process is used to record transactions.

RECORDING PROCESS

The procedures used in the recording process are part of what is called the **accounting cycle**—a series of nine steps to record transactions and prepare financial statements. We will introduce four of these steps in this chapter and the remaining five steps in the next chapter. Illustration 3-6 presents steps 1 to 4 on the following page.

We have already discussed, in the first section of this chapter, the first step of the accounting cycle. Recall that each transaction must be analyzed to determine if it has an effect on the accounts. Evidence of the transaction comes from a **source document**, such as a sales slip, cheque, bill, or cash register tape. In the beginning, as described in our feature story, Grant Hooker used cheques to begin the recording process for BeaverTails. This evidence of the transaction is

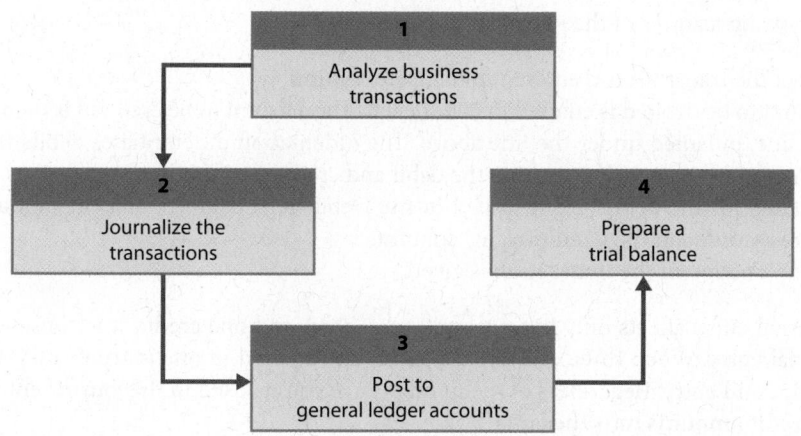

►Illustration 3-6
The accounting cycle—Steps 1–4

analyzed to determine the effect on specific accounts. Deciding whether a transaction has occurred, and if so what to record, is the most critical point in the accounting process.

GENERAL JOURNAL

In the second step of the accounting cycle, the transaction information is recorded as a journal entry in the general journal (a book of original entry). Transactions are recorded in chronological order (by date) in a journal before continuing the recording process (which is step 3 of the accounting cycle). For each transaction, the journal shows the debit and credit effects on specific accounts. Companies may use various kinds of journals, but every company has the most basic form of journal, a **general journal**.

The general journal makes several contributions to the recording process:

1. It discloses the complete effect of a transaction in one place, including an explanation and, where applicable, identification of the source document.
2. It provides a chronological record of transactions.
3. It helps to prevent and locate errors, because the debit and credit amounts for each entry can be quickly compared.

Entering transaction data in the general journal is known as **journalizing**. To illustrate the technique of journalizing, let's look at the first transaction of Sierra Corporation. On October 1, common shares were issued in exchange for $10,000 cash. In tabular equation form, this transaction appeared in our earlier discussion as follows:

Assets	=	Liabilities	+	Shareholders' Equity
Cash	=			Common Shares
(1) +$10,000	=			+$10,000

This transaction would be recorded in the general journal as follows:

> In the margins next to key journal entries are **equation analyses** that summarize the effects of the transaction on the accounting equation (A = L + SE) and cash flows.

GENERAL JOURNAL			
Date	Account Titles and Explanation	Debit	Credit
2015 Oct. 1	Cash	10,000	
	Common Shares		10,000
	(Issued common shares)		

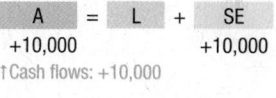

A	=	L	+	SE
+10,000				+10,000

↑Cash flows: +10,000

Note the following features of the journal entry:

1. The date of the transaction is entered in the Date column.
2. The account to be debited is entered first at the left. The account to be credited is then entered on the next line, indented under the line above. The indentation differentiates debits from credits and decreases the chance of switching the debit and credit amounts by mistake.
3. The amounts for the debits are recorded in the Debit (left) column, and the amounts for the credits are recorded in the Credit (right) column.
4. A brief explanation of the transaction is given.

If a journal entry affects only two accounts, one debit and one credit, it is considered to be a simple journal entry. When three or more accounts are required in one journal entry, the entry is called a compound entry. Regardless of the number of accounts used in the journal entry, **the total debit and credit amounts must be equal.**

In assignments when specific account titles are given, they should be used in journalizing. When account titles are not given, you should create account titles that identify the nature and content of each account. Ambiguous or multiple account titles with similar names can lead to incorrect financial reporting. For example, a company could use any one of these account titles for recording the cost of delivery trucks: Automobiles, Delivery Trucks, Trucks, or Vehicles. However, if it uses more than one of these account titles, it will not be able to easily determine the total cost of its delivery trucks.

Once the company chooses the specific account title to use (say, Vehicles), all future transactions related to that account should be recorded in the Vehicles account. Note that an account title itself should not contain explanations or descriptions (such as Vehicles Purchased).

Although explanations are an important part of each journal entry, you may omit them unless otherwise instructed in your homework assignments because including an explanation in an assignment simply involves copying the information from the problem to your assignment.

BEFORE YOU GO ON...

▶ Do It! Record Transactions

You will recall that a tabular accounting equation was prepared in an earlier Do It! in this chapter (at the end of the Accounting Transactions/Summary of Transactions section found in Study Objective 1) for Virmari Corporation. Virmari's transactions are reproduced here for your convenience, with transaction dates included:

Aug.	1	Common shares were issued to shareholders for $25,000 cash.
	4	Equipment costing $7,000 was purchased on account.
	9	Services amounting to $8,000 were performed for customers. Of this amount, $2,000 was received in cash and $6,000 is due on account.
	10	Rent was paid for the month, $850.
	29	Customers owing $6,000 on account paid $4,000 of the balance due (see Aug. 9 transaction).
	30	Dividends of $1,000 were paid to shareholders.

Record the above transactions in the general journal.

Action Plan

- Refer back to the tabular accounting equation in the original Do It! to review the effects of each transaction on the accounting equation.
- Apply the debit and credit rules to increases and decreases in the accounts.
- Choose an appropriate account name for each transaction (including revenue and expense transactions, which did not include account names in the prior Do It!).
- Record the transactions in the general journal in good format. Recall that debits are normally recorded first, followed by credits, which are indented.

Solution

GENERAL JOURNAL

Date	Account Titles and Explanations	Debit	Credit
Aug. 1	Cash	25,000	
	Common Shares		25,000
	(Issued common shares for cash)		
4	Equipment	7,000	
	Accounts Payable		7,000
	(Purchased equipment on account)		
9	Cash	2,000	
	Accounts Receivable	6,000	
	Service Revenue		8,000
	(Performed services for cash and credit)		
10	Rent Expense	850	
	Cash		850
	(Paid monthly rent)		
29	Cash	4,000	
	Accounts Receivable		4,000
	(Collected amounts owing on account)		
30	Dividends	1,000	
	Cash		1,000
	(Paid dividends to shareholders)		

Related Exercise Material: BE3-5, BE3-6, BE3-7, E3-5, E3-6, and E3-8.

The Ledger

The third step in the accounting cycle is to transfer the journal entries recorded in the general journal to the appropriate accounts in the general ledger. The entire group of accounts maintained by a company is referred to as the ledger. The ledger keeps all the information about changes in specific account balances in one place.

GENERAL LEDGER

Companies may use various kinds of ledgers, but every company has a general ledger. A **general ledger** contains all the asset, liability, shareholders' equity, revenue, and expense accounts. Each account has a number so that it is easier to identify. A company can use a loose-leaf binder or card file for the ledger, with each account kept on a separate sheet or card. A column in spreadsheet software can also be used as a general ledger account, but most companies today use a computerized accounting system where the entries from the journal are automatically recorded in the ledger by the software.

The ledger is often arranged in the order in which accounts are presented in the financial statements, beginning with the statement of financial position accounts. The asset accounts come first, followed by liability accounts, and then shareholders' equity accounts, including share capital, retained earnings, and dividend accounts, followed by revenue and expense accounts. Of course, in a computerized accounting system, the accounts can easily be rearranged in whatever order is wanted.

Most companies list their ledger accounts in a **chart of accounts**. The chart of accounts is the framework for the accounting database. It lists the accounts and the account numbers that identify where the accounts are in the ledger. The numbering system that is used to identify the accounts can be quite sophisticated or pretty simple. Similar to the ledger, the chart of accounts usually starts with the statement of financial position accounts, followed by the income statement accounts.

STUDY OBJECTIVE 4
Post transactions.

The chart of accounts for Sierra Corporation is shown in Illustration 3-7. Accounts shown in red are used in this chapter; accounts shown in black are explained in later chapters. The four-digit numbering system allows room for new accounts to be created as needed during the life of the business.

▶ Illustration 3-7

Chart of accounts

SIERRA CORPORATION—CHART OF ACCOUNTS									
Assets		**Liabilities**		**Shareholders' Equity**		**Revenues**		**Expenses**	
1000	Cash	3000	Accounts Payable	4000	Common Shares	5000	Service Revenue	7000	Salaries Expense
1100	Accounts Receivable	3100	Salaries Payable	4500	Retained Earnings			7100	Supplies Expense
1500	Supplies	3200	Interest Payable	4600	Dividends			7500	Rent Expense
1550	Prepaid Insurance	3300	Unearned Revenue					7600	Depreciation Expense
2000	Equipment	3400	Bank Loan Payable					8200	Insurance Expense
2010	Accumulated Depreciation—Equipment							8400	Interest Expense
								9000	Income Tax Expense

POSTING

The procedure of transferring journal entries from the general journal to the general ledger accounts is called **posting**. This phase of the recording process accumulates the effects of journalized transactions in the individual accounts. Posting involves transferring information from the general journal to the general ledger. For example, the date and amount shown on the first line of a general journal entry is entered in the debit column of the appropriate account in the general ledger. The same is done for the credit side of the entry—the date and amount are entered in the credit column of the general ledger account.

Posting should be done in chronological order. That is, all the debits and credits of one journal entry should be posted before going on to the next journal entry. Posting should also be done on a timely basis—at least monthly—to ensure that the general ledger is up to date. In a computerized accounting system, posting is usually performed by software simultaneously after each journal entry is prepared.

The first three steps in the accounting cycle—analyze, journalize, and post transactions—occur repeatedly in every company, whether a manual or a computerized accounting system is used. However, the first two steps—the analysis and entering of each transaction—must be done by a person even when a computerized system is used. The basic difference between a manual and computerized system is in the last step (Step 3) in the recording process—posting the information (and in some of the subsequent steps in the accounting cycle that we will learn about later). In a computerized system, Step 3 is done automatically by the computer. In order to understand how this happens, we need to understand manual approaches to the recording process, which is what we will focus on in this chapter.

ACCOUNTING MATTERS!

Computerized Accounting Systems

Organizations of all shapes and sizes use computerized accounting systems. Cathy Love, the administrator of Bryony House, a Halifax women's shelter, agrees. "We really need our computerized system to track our accounts in detail," she says. The shelter users the popular small-business accounting software, Simply Accounting. In addition, the shelter's fundraising activities are tracked in detail using custom donation software. The shelter's staff have found that the more easily and quickly they can get the information they need, the more time they have to do their main work with the women who come for help.

BEFORE YOU GO ON...

▶ Do It! Post Transactions

The following selected journal entries are included in Ahair Ltd.'s general journal:

May	1	Cash	20,000	
		Common Shares		20,000
		(Issued common shares)		
	4	Equipment	4,800	
		Accounts Payable		4,800
		(Purchased equipment on account)		
	6	Supplies	600	
		Cash		600
		(Purchased supplies)		

Post the journal entries to the general ledger.

Action Plan

- Posting involves transferring the journalized debits and credits to specific T accounts in the general ledger.
- Ledger accounts should be arranged in statement order.
- Determine the ending balances of each ledger account by netting (calculating the difference between) the total debits and credits.

Cash						Accounts Payable				
May	1	20,000	May	6	600			May	4	4,800
Bal.		19,400								

Supplies				Common Shares			
May	6	600			May	1	20,000

Equipment			
May	4	4,800	

Related Exercise Material: BE3-8, BE3-9, BE3-10, E3-7, E3-8, and E3-9.

the navigator

THE RECORDING PROCESS ILLUSTRATED

The following transaction analyses show the basic steps in the recording process using the transactions for the month of October for Sierra Corporation. A basic analysis, equation analysis, and debit–credit analysis are done before the journalizing and posting of each transaction. Study these transaction analyses carefully. Doing so will help you understand the journal entries discussed in this chapter, as well as more complex journal entries described in later chapters.

▶ Transaction (1)

Investment by shareholders

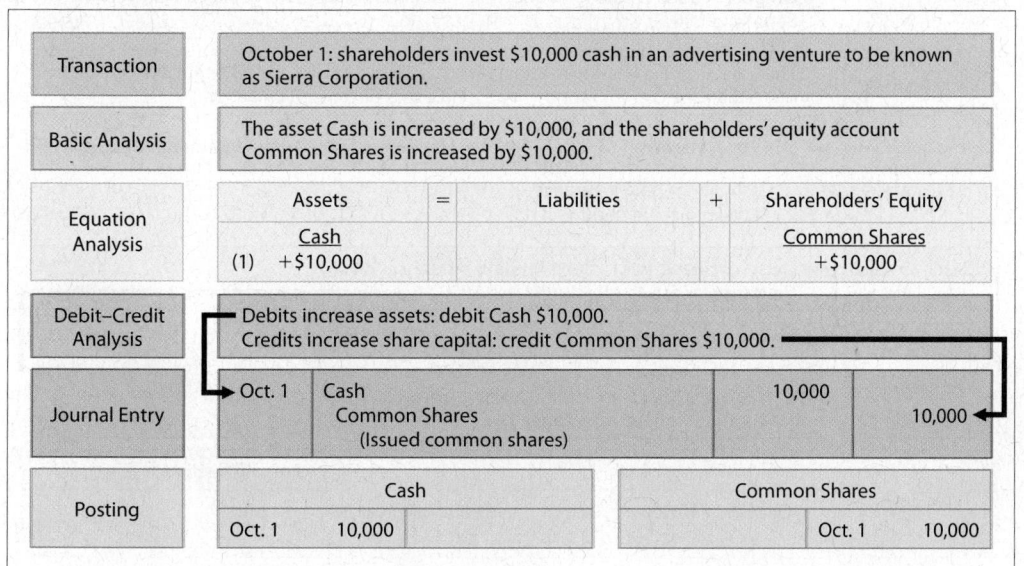

▸ **Transaction (2)**
Purchase of equipment

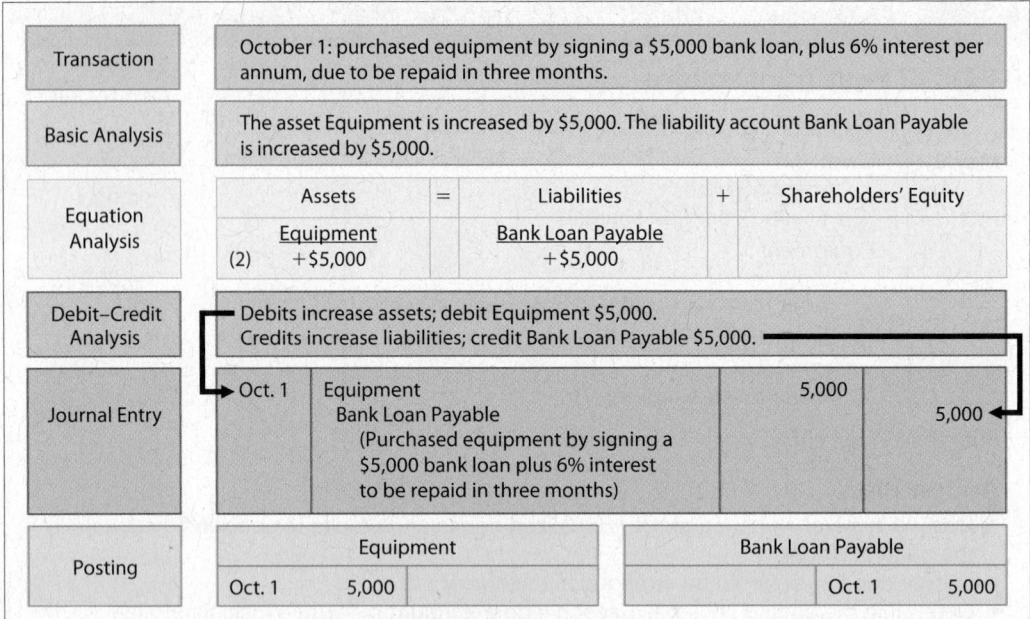

Transaction	October 1: purchased equipment by signing a $5,000 bank loan, plus 6% interest per annum, due to be repaid in three months.
Basic Analysis	The asset Equipment is increased by $5,000. The liability account Bank Loan Payable is increased by $5,000.

	Assets	=	Liabilities	+	Shareholders' Equity
Equation Analysis	Equipment		Bank Loan Payable		
(2)	+$5,000		+$5,000		

Debit–Credit Analysis	Debits increase assets; debit Equipment $5,000. Credits increase liabilities; credit Bank Loan Payable $5,000.

Journal Entry	Oct. 1	Equipment
		    Bank Loan Payable
		      (Purchased equipment by signing a
		      $5,000 bank loan plus 6% interest
		      to be repaid in three months)
			5,000	5,000

Posting	Equipment		Bank Loan Payable	
	Oct. 1 5,000			Oct. 1 5,000

▸ **Transaction (3)**
Payment of rent

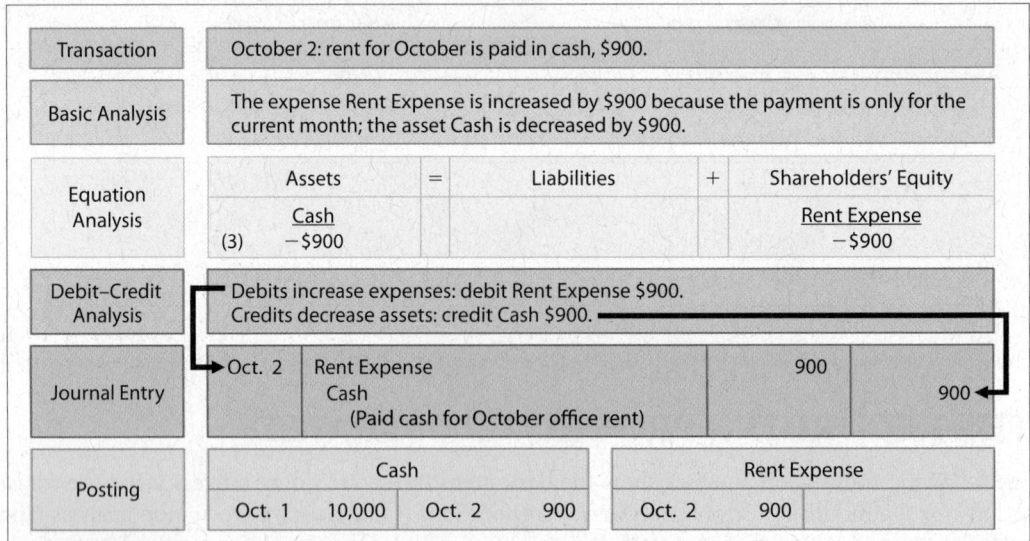

Transaction	October 2: rent for October is paid in cash, $900.
Basic Analysis	The expense Rent Expense is increased by $900 because the payment is only for the current month; the asset Cash is decreased by $900.

	Assets	=	Liabilities	+	Shareholders' Equity
Equation Analysis	Cash				Rent Expense
(3)	−$900				−$900

Debit–Credit Analysis	Debits increase expenses: debit Rent Expense $900. Credits decrease assets: credit Cash $900.

Journal Entry	Oct. 2	Rent Expense
		    Cash
		      (Paid cash for October office rent)
			900	900

Posting	Cash		Rent Expense	
	Oct. 1 10,000	Oct. 2 900	Oct. 2 900	

▸ **Transaction (4)**
Purchase of insurance

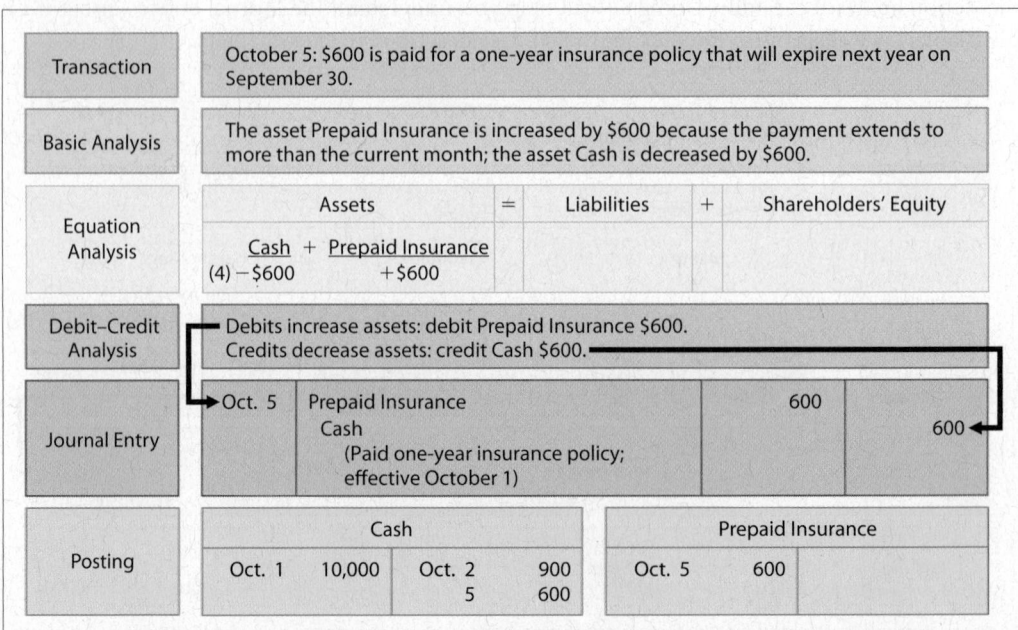

Transaction	October 5: $600 is paid for a one-year insurance policy that will expire next year on September 30.
Basic Analysis	The asset Prepaid Insurance is increased by $600 because the payment extends to more than the current month; the asset Cash is decreased by $600.

	Assets	=	Liabilities	+	Shareholders' Equity
Equation Analysis	Cash + Prepaid Insurance				
(4)	−$600 +$600				

Debit–Credit Analysis	Debits increase assets: debit Prepaid Insurance $600. Credits decrease assets: credit Cash $600.

Journal Entry	Oct. 5	Prepaid Insurance
		    Cash
		      (Paid one-year insurance policy;
		      effective October 1)
			600	600

Posting	Cash		Prepaid Insurance	
	Oct. 1 10,000	Oct. 2 900 5 600	Oct. 5 600	

▶ Transaction (5)

Hiring of new employees

Transaction	October 7: hired four employees to begin work on Monday, October 12. Each employee is to receive a weekly salary of $500 for a five-day workweek (Monday–Friday), payable every two weeks—first payment to be made on Friday, October 23.
Basic Analysis	An accounting transaction has not occurred. There is only an agreement that the employees will begin work on October 12. Thus, a debit–credit analysis is not needed because there is no accounting entry. (See transaction of October 23 for first entry.)

▶ Transaction (6)

Purchase of supplies on account

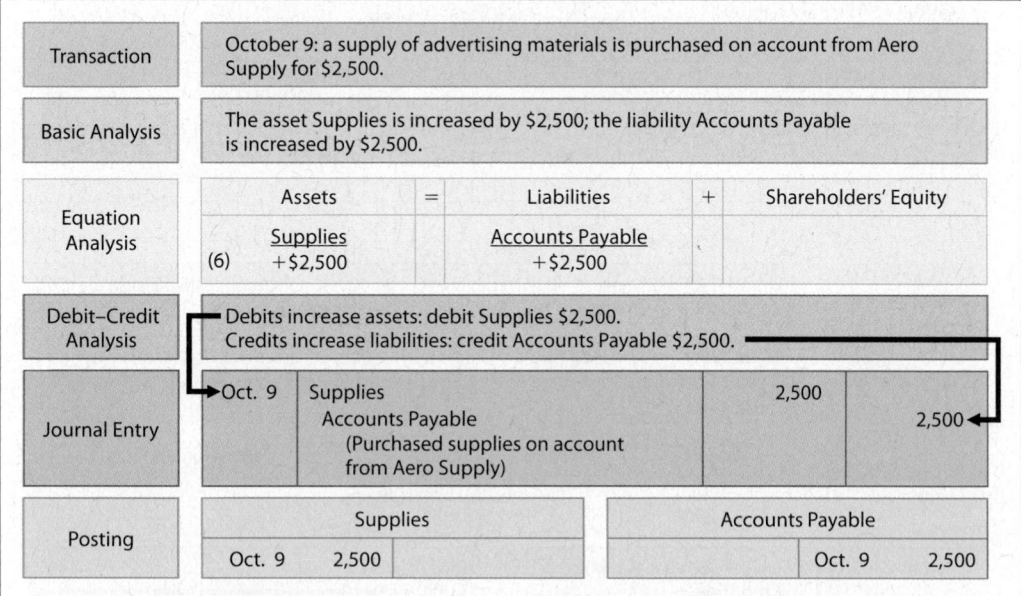

▶ Transaction (7)

Services performed on account

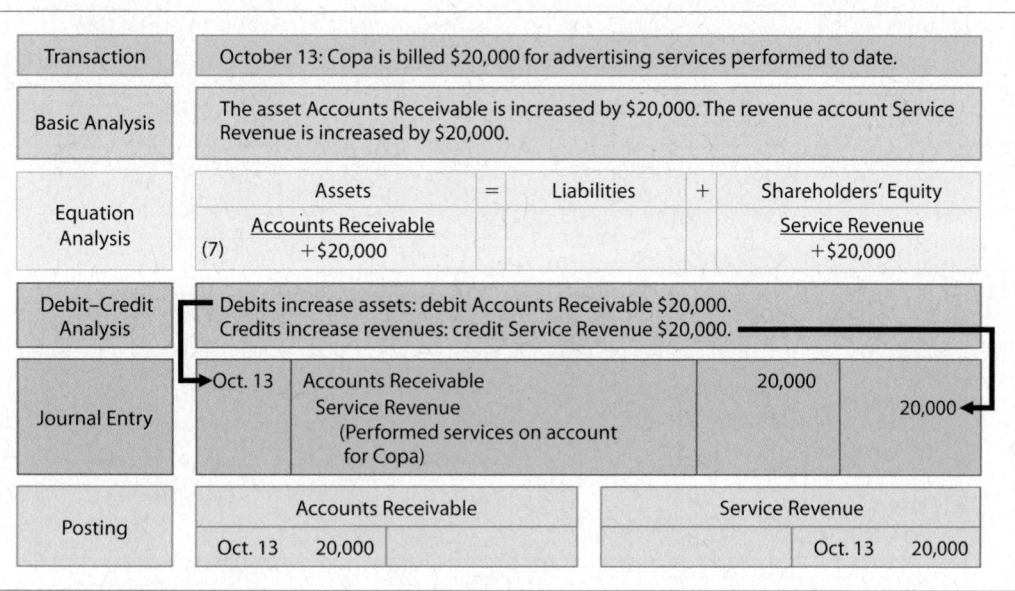

▶ **Transaction (8)**
Receipt of cash in advance
from customer

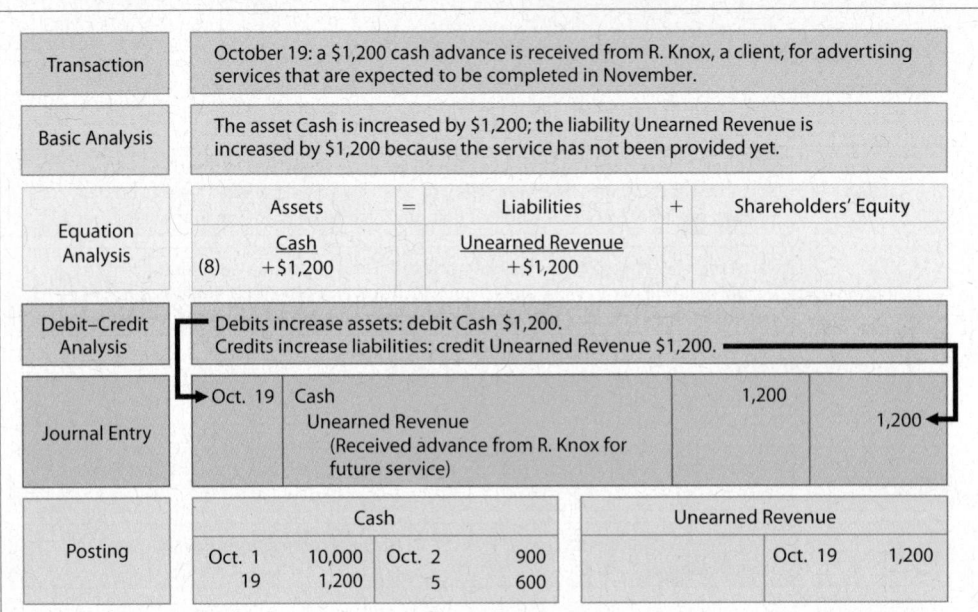

Transaction	October 19: a $1,200 cash advance is received from R. Knox, a client, for advertising services that are expected to be completed in November.
Basic Analysis	The asset Cash is increased by $1,200; the liability Unearned Revenue is increased by $1,200 because the service has not been provided yet.

Equation Analysis	Assets	=	Liabilities	+	Shareholders' Equity
	Cash		Unearned Revenue		
(8)	+$1,200		+$1,200		

Debit–Credit Analysis	Debits increase assets: debit Cash $1,200. Credits increase liabilities: credit Unearned Revenue $1,200.

Journal Entry	Oct. 19	Cash		1,200	
		Unearned Revenue			1,200
		(Received advance from R. Knox for future service)			

Posting

Cash					Unearned Revenue		
Oct. 1	10,000	Oct. 2	900			Oct. 19	1,200
19	1,200	5	600				

▶ **Transaction (9)**
Payment on account

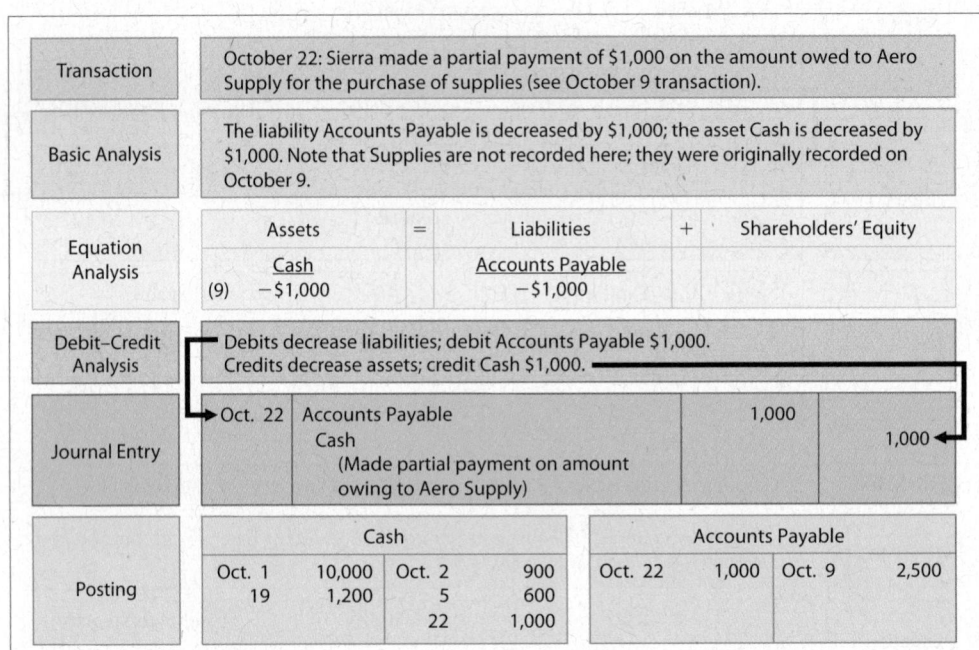

Transaction	October 22: Sierra made a partial payment of $1,000 on the amount owed to Aero Supply for the purchase of supplies (see October 9 transaction).
Basic Analysis	The liability Accounts Payable is decreased by $1,000; the asset Cash is decreased by $1,000. Note that Supplies are not recorded here; they were originally recorded on October 9.

Equation Analysis	Assets	=	Liabilities	+	Shareholders' Equity
	Cash		Accounts Payable		
(9)	−$1,000		−$1,000		

Debit–Credit Analysis	Debits decrease liabilities; debit Accounts Payable $1,000. Credits decrease assets; credit Cash $1,000.

Journal Entry	Oct. 22	Accounts Payable		1,000	
		Cash			1,000
		(Made partial payment on amount owing to Aero Supply)			

Posting

Cash					Accounts Payable			
Oct. 1	10,000	Oct. 2	900		Oct. 22	1,000	Oct. 9	2,500
19	1,200	5	600					
		22	1,000					

▶ **Transaction (10)**
Payment of salaries

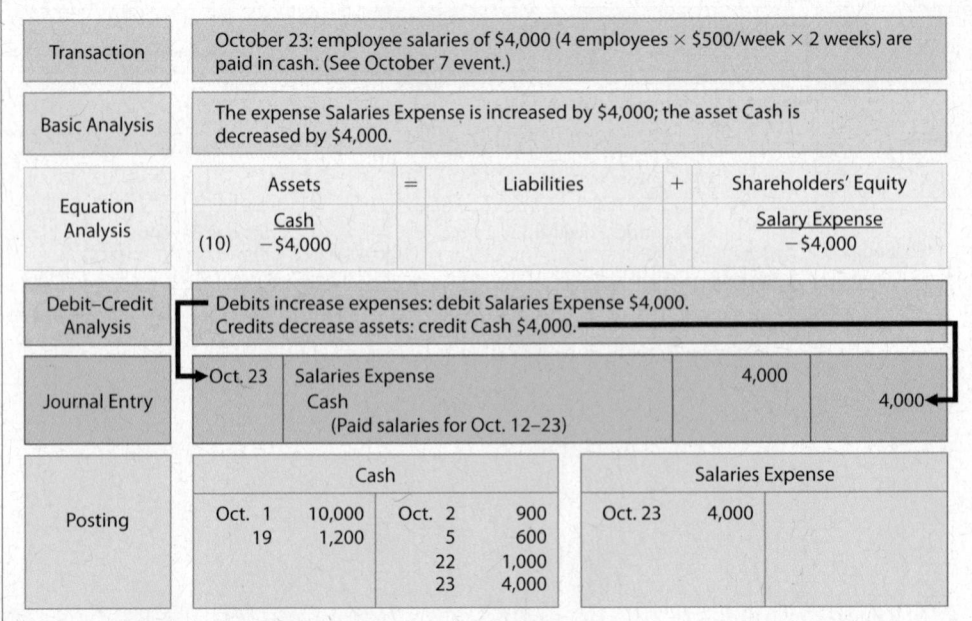

Transaction	October 23: employee salaries of $4,000 (4 employees × $500/week × 2 weeks) are paid in cash. (See October 7 event.)
Basic Analysis	The expense Salaries Expense is increased by $4,000; the asset Cash is decreased by $4,000.

Equation Analysis	Assets	=	Liabilities	+	Shareholders' Equity
	Cash				Salary Expense
(10)	−$4,000				−$4,000

Debit–Credit Analysis	Debits increase expenses: debit Salaries Expense $4,000. Credits decrease assets: credit Cash $4,000.

Journal Entry	Oct. 23	Salaries Expense		4,000	
		Cash			4,000
		(Paid salaries for Oct. 12–23)			

Posting

Cash					Salaries Expense		
Oct. 1	10,000	Oct. 2	900		Oct. 23	4,000	
19	1,200	5	600				
		22	1,000				
		23	4,000				

Transaction	October 26: Sierra paid a $500 cash dividend to shareholders.
Basic Analysis	Dividends is increased by $500; the asset Cash is decreased by $500.

Equation Analysis	Assets	=	Liabilities	+	Shareholders' Equity
	Cash				Dividends
(11)	−$500				−$500

Debit–Credit Analysis	Debits increase dividends: debit Dividends $500.
	Credits decrease assets: credit Cash $500.

Journal Entry	Oct. 26	Dividends		500	
		Cash			500
		(Paid cash dividend)			

Posting

Cash					Dividends		
Oct. 1	10,000	Oct. 2	900	Oct. 26	500		
19	1,200	5	600				
		22	1,000				
		23	4,000				
		26	500				

Transaction	October 30: received $5,000 in cash from Copa in partial payment of its account. (See October 13 transaction.)
Basic Analysis	The asset Cash is increased by $5,000. The asset Accounts Receivable is decreased by $5,000. Note that Service Revenue is not recorded here; it was originally recorded on October 13 when the service was performed.

Equation Analysis	Assets		=	Liabilities	+	Shareholders' Equity
	Cash	+ Accounts Receivable				
(13)	+$5,000	−$5,000				

Debit–Credit Analysis	Debits increase assets: debit Cash $5,000.
	Credits decrease assets: credit Accounts Receivable $5,000.

Journal Entry	Oct. 30	Cash		5,000	
		Accounts Receivable			5,000
		(Received partial payment on account from Copa)			

Posting

Cash					Accounts Receivable			
Oct. 1	10,000	Oct. 2	900	Oct. 13	20,000	Oct. 30	5,000
19	1,200	5	600				
30	5,000	22	1,000				
		23	4,000				
		26	500				

Transaction	October 30: paid $1,800 income tax instalment for October.
Basic Analysis	The expense account Income Tax Expense is increased by $1,800; the asset account Cash is decreased by $1,800.

Equation Analysis	Assets	=	Liabilities	+	Shareholders' Equity
	Cash				Income Tax Expense
(13)	−$1,800				−$1,800

Debit–Credit Analysis	Debits increase expenses; debit Income Tax Expense $1,800.
	Credits decrease assets; credit Cash $1,800.

Journal Entry	Oct. 30	Income Tax Expense		1,800	
		Cash			1,800
		(Paid income tax instalment for October)			

Posting

Cash					Income Tax Expense		
Oct. 1	10,000	Oct. 2	900	Oct. 30	1,800		
19	1,200	5	600				
30	5,000	22	1,000				
		23	4,000				
		26	500				
		30	1,800				

The general journal for Sierra Corporation for the month of October is summarized below.

SIERRA CORPORATION			
General Journal			
Date	Account Titles and Explanation	Debit	Credit
2015			
Oct. 1	Cash	10,000	
	Common Shares		10,000
	(Issued common shares)		
1	Equipment	5,000	
	Bank Loan Payable		5,000
	(Purchased equipment by signing a $5,000 bank loan plus 6% interest to be repaid in three months)		
2	Rent Expense	900	
	Cash		900
	(Paid cash for October office rent)		
5	Prepaid Insurance	600	
	Cash		600
	(Paid one-year insurance policy; effective October 1)		
9	Supplies	2,500	
	Accounts Payable		2,500
	(Purchased supplies on account from Aero Supply)		
13	Accounts Receivable	20,000	
	Service Revenue		20,000
	(Performed services on account for Copa)		
19	Cash	1,200	
	Unearned Revenue		1,200
	(Received advance from R. Knox for future service)		
22	Accounts Payable	1,000	
	Cash		1,000
	(Made partial payment on amount owing to Aero Supply)		
23	Salaries Expense	4,000	
	Cash		4,000
	(Paid salaries for Oct. 12–23)		
26	Dividends	500	
	Cash		500
	(Paid cash dividend)		
30	Cash	5,000	
	Accounts Receivable		5,000
	(Received partial payment on account from Copa)		
30	Income Tax Expense	1,800	
	Cash		1,800
	(Paid income tax instalment for October)		

The general ledger for Sierra Corporation follows.

SIERRA CORPORATION							
General Ledger							
Cash					**Unearned Revenue**		
Oct.	1	10,000	Oct.	2	900		Oct.	19	1,200
	19	1,200		5	600				
	30	5,000		22	1,000				
				23	4,000				
				26	500	**Bank Loan Payable**		
				30	1,800		Oct.	1	5,000
Bal.		7,400							

		Accounts Receivable					Common Shares		
Oct.	13	20,000	Oct.	30	5,000		Oct.	1	10,000
Bal.		15,000							

		Supplies				Dividends	
Oct.	9	2,500		Oct.	26	500	

		Prepaid Insurance				Service Revenue		
Oct.	5	600			Oct.	13	20,000

		Equipment				Salaries Expense	
Oct.	1	5,000		Oct.	23	4,000	

		Accounts Payable					Rent Expense	
Oct.	22	1,000	Oct.	9	2,500	Oct.	2	900
			Bal.		1,500			

		Income Tax Expense	
Oct.	30	1,800	

■ Keeping an Eye on Cash

The Cash general ledger account shown on the previous page and reproduced below, including transaction numbers, reflects all of the inflows and outflows of cash that occurred for Sierra Corporation during October.

		Cash						
Oct.	1	10,000	(1)	Oct.	2	900	(3)
	19	12,000	(8)		5	600	(4)
	30	5,000	(12)		22	1,000	(9)
					23	4,000	(10)
					26	500	(11)
					30	1,800	(13)
Bal.		7,400					

The Cash account and the recorded cash transactions indicate why cash changed during October. However, to make this information useful for analysis, it is summarized in a statement of cash flows. As we learned in Chapter 1, the statement of cash flows classifies each transaction as an operating activity, an investing activity, or a financing activity. A user of this statement can then determine the amount of cash provided by operating activities, the amount of cash used for investing activities, and the amount of cash provided by financing activities.

Operating activities are the types of activities the company performs to generate profits. Transactions 3, 4, 8, 9, 10, 12, and 13 relate to cash received or spent to directly support its operations.

Investing activities include the purchase or sale of long-lived assets used in operating the business, or the purchase or sale of long-term investments. Although Sierra did purchase equipment, it was not purchased for cash but rather with a bank loan payable. This is considered to be a noncash type of investing activity and consequently is not included in the Cash account above.

The primary types of *financing activities* are borrowing (and paying back) money, issuing shares, and paying dividends. The financing activities of Sierra Corporation are transactions 1 and 11. It also signed a bank loan payable to purchase the equipment mentioned above, which is considered to be a noncash financing activity.

The Trial Balance

The fourth step in the accounting cycle is to prepare a trial balance. A **trial balance** is a list of general ledger accounts and their balances at a specific time. It is prepared at the end of an accounting period, which is usually monthly, but could also be quarterly or annually. For Sierra Corporation, we have assumed that its accounting period is one month for illustrative purposes.

In the trial balance, the accounts are listed in the order in which they appear in the ledger, with debit balances listed in the left column and credit balances in the right column. The totals of the two columns must be equal.

The main purpose of a trial balance is to prove (check) that the debits equal the credits after posting. That is, the sum of the debit account balances must equal the sum of the credit account balances. If the debit and credit totals don't agree, the trial balance can help uncover errors in journalizing and posting. For example, the trial balance will not balance if a debit or credit amount is unequal in a journal entry, or if the amount is transferred incorrectly to the general ledger from a journal entry. If the trial balance does not balance, then the error must be located and corrected before proceeding.

A trial balance is also useful in the preparation of financial statements, as will be explained in the next chapter. The procedure for preparing a trial balance is as follows:

1. List the account titles and their balances in the same order as in the general ledger (which is usually in financial statement order). Debit balances should be entered in the debit column and credit balances in the credit column.
2. Total the debit column and the credit column.
3. Ensure that the debit and credit column totals are equal (agree).

The trial balance prepared from the general ledger of Sierra Corporation shown earlier is presented in Illustration 3-8 below. Note that the total debits, $37,700, equal the total credits, $37,700.

SIERRA CORPORATION Trial Balance October 31, 2015		
	Debit	Credit
Cash	$ 7,400	
Accounts receivable	15,000	
Supplies	2,500	
Prepaid insurance	600	
Equipment	5,000	
Accounts payable		$ 1,500
Unearned revenue		1,200
Bank loan payable		5,000
Common shares		10,000
Dividends	500	
Service revenue		20,000
Salaries expense	4,000	
Rent expense	900	
Income tax expense	1,800	
	$37,700	$37,700

You might wonder why there is no retained earnings account included in the above trial balance. When a trial balance is first prepared, it is important to understand that the retained earnings account balance that is listed on the trial balance is not the retained earnings balance at the end of the period; rather, it is the retained earnings balance at the beginning of the period. In Sierra's case, its beginning retained earnings balance is zero as this is its first month of operations; accounts with zero balances are not normally included in a trial balance.

Why is the beginning balance used for the retained earnings account rather than the ending balance, as is the case in all the other accounts listed? Recall that retained earnings at the beginning of a period plus revenues less expenses and dividends for the period gives us retained earnings at the end of the period. If a trial balance lists revenues, expenses, and dividend account balances, the retained earnings balance has not yet been updated for these items and must therefore represent the balance in retained earnings at the beginning of the period. We will learn how to update retained earnings at the end of the accounting period in the next chapter.

LIMITATIONS OF A TRIAL BALANCE

Although a trial balance reveals many types of errors in the recording process, it does not prove that all transactions have been recorded or that the general ledger is correct. Errors may exist even though the trial balance column totals agree. For example, the trial balance may balance even when:

1. a transaction is not journalized,
2. a correct journal entry is not posted,
3. a journal entry is posted twice,
4. incorrect accounts are used in journalizing or posting, or
5. errors that cancel each other's effect are made in recording the amount of a transaction.

In other words, as long as equal debits and credits are posted, even to the wrong account or in the wrong amount, the total debits will equal the total credits. Nevertheless, despite its limitations, the trial balance is a useful screen for finding many errors.

Ethics Note
When they evaluate an accounting system, auditors consider errors and irregularities to be different. An error is the result of an unintentional mistake. As such, it is neither ethical nor unethical. An irregularity, on the other hand, is an intentional misstatement, which is generally viewed as unethical.

BEFORE YOU GO ON...

▶ Do It! Preparing a Trial Balance

Koizumi Kollections Ltd. has the following alphabetical list of accounts and balances at July 31, 2015:

Accounts payable	$33,700	Equipment	$ 35,700
Accounts receivable	71,200	Income tax expense	12,000
Bank loan payable	49,500	Land	51,000
Buildings	86,500	Operating expenses	93,100
Cash	3,200	Service revenue	171,100
Common shares	99,400	Unearned revenue	3,000
Dividends	4,000		

Each of the above accounts has a normal balance. Prepare a trial balance, rearranging the accounts in normal ledger (financial statement) order.

Action Plan

- Reorder the accounts as they would normally appear in the general ledger: statement of financial position accounts are listed first (assets, liabilities, and shareholders' equity), and then income statement accounts (revenues and expenses).
- Determine whether each account has a normal debit or credit balance.
- List the amounts in the appropriate debit or credit column.
- Total the trial balance columns. Total debits must equal total credits or a mistake has been made.

(continued)

Solution

KOIZUMI KOLLECTIONS LTD.
Trial Balance
July 31, 2015

	Debit	Credit
Cash	$ 3,200	
Accounts receivable	71,200	
Land	51,000	
Buildings	86,500	
Equipment	35,700	
Accounts payable		$ 33,700
Unearned revenue		3,000
Bank loan payable		49,500
Common shares		99,400
Dividends	4,000	
Service revenue		171,100
Operating expenses	93,100	
Income tax expense	12,000	
	$356,700	$356,700

Related Exercise Material: BE3-11, BE3-12, BE3-13, E3-9, E3-10, E3-11, and E3-12.

DECISION TOOLKIT

 Decision Checkpoints	 Info Needed for Decision	 Tools to Use for Decision	How to Evaluate Results
How do you determine that debits equal credits?	All general ledger account balances	Trial balance	List the account titles and their balances, total the debit and credit columns, and verify equality.

comparing
IFRS and ASPE

Key Differences	International Financial Reporting Standards (IFRS)	Accounting Standards for Private Enterprises (ASPE)
No significant differences		

In this chapter, you learned about the features of accounting information systems that help companies keep track of their important financial information. As you know, each company is an economic entity and its daily transactions create a large amount of financial information and documents. Although you are not a company, you are an economic entity and each day you, too, enter into a variety of economic transactions. And just as they do for companies, some of these transactions produce important financial documents that you need to keep track of.

Individuals vary in the way they keep track of this information. Some of us are meticulous with record keeping, while others pay little attention to their financial affairs. Most of us really should regularly set aside time to keep our financial records up to date and in order.

What are some of the documents and records in your life? Suppose you had 10 minutes to collect your most important possessions and flee to safety. Would you know where to find your vital personal papers? Are they in one place or scattered about your home?

Some Facts

- Some examples of your personal documents and records might include:
  - Identification records (birth certificate, driver's licence, passport, social insurance card, health card)
  - Bank account statements and loan information
  - Titles, deeds, and registrations for property and vehicles owned and any lease (rental) agreements
  - Credit card statements and receipts
  - Employment information
  - Income tax information (copies of past returns, assessment notices, and proof of tax payment)
- You can keep financial and personal records in filing cabinets, on your computer, or in a safety deposit box at a bank. On your computer, keep encrypted or password-protected lists of your financial and personal information and where it is stored. You should also make a backup copy of items on your computer and store the backup off site.
- Watch out for identify theft. Experts offer the following tips to reduce the likelihood of your being a target.
  - Protect your Social Insurance Number. Don't use it as identification. When someone requests your Social Insurance Number, ask why before providing the number.
  - Never provide personal information or banking information by texting or e-mail.
  - Subscribe to the highest level of privacy on your social media accounts.
  - Carry only the identification you need.
  - Keep your access codes, usernames, passwords, and PINs secret. Don't share your e-mail or social media passwords.
  - Protect your computer and its information by installing security software.
  - Review your bank statements and credit card statements regularly.
  - Remove mail from your mailbox promptly.
  - Pay attention to your billing cycle on all invoices that you receive (such as cell phone bills and telephone bills). Follow up missing invoices and statements or suspicious transactions.[2]

What Do You Think?

Do you really need to take the time to organize your financial documents?

YES — Everyone engages in personal and financial transactions each day. For a variety of reasons, we need to maintain documentation of these transactions and ensure that these documents are not lost or stolen.

NO — I lead a relatively uncomplicated life, and I can usually find the documents that I need when I require them. There is little risk that these documents will be lost or stolen.

Summary of Study Objectives

1. *Analyze the effects of transactions on the accounting equation.* Each business transaction has a dual effect on the accounting equation: assets = liabilities + shareholders' equity. For example, if an individual asset is increased, there must be a corresponding decrease in another asset, or increase in a specific liability, or increase in shareholders' equity.

2. *Define debits and credits and explain how they are used to record transactions.* The terms *debit* and *credit* are synonymous with *left* and *right*. Assets, expenses, and dividends are increased by debits and decreased by credits. The normal balance of these accounts is a debit balance (the increase side). Liabilities, common shares, retained earnings, and revenues are increased by credits and decreased by debits. The normal balance of these accounts is a credit balance (the increase side).

3. *Journalize transactions.* The initial record of a transaction is entered in a general journal. The journal discloses in one place the complete effect of a transaction, provides a chronological record of transactions, and helps prevent or locate errors because the debit and credit amounts for each entry can be readily compared.

4. *Post transactions.* Posting is the process of transferring journal entries from the general journal to the general ledger. This accumulates the effects of the journalized transactions in the individual ledger accounts.

5. *Prepare a trial balance.* A trial balance is a list of accounts and their balances at a specific time. The main purpose of the trial balance is to prove the mathematical equality of debits and credits after posting. A trial balance also can help uncover errors in journalizing and posting and is useful in preparing financial statements.

Glossary

Account   An individual accounting record of increases and decreases in a specific asset, liability, or shareholders' equity item. (p. 114)

Accounting cycle   A series of nine steps followed by accountants to record transactions and prepare financial statements. The first four steps were introduced in this chapter: analyzing transactions (step 1), journalizing transactions (step 2), posting transactions (step 3), and preparing a trial balance (step 4). (p. 118)

Accounting information system   The system of collecting and processing transaction data and communicating financial information to interested parties. (p. 106)

Accounting transaction   An economic event that is recorded in the financial statements because it involves an exchange that affects assets, liabilities, or shareholders' equity. (p. 106)

Chart of accounts   A list of a company's accounts and account numbers that identify where the accounts are in the general ledger. (p. 121)

Credit   The right side of an account. (p. 115)

Debit   The left side of an account. (p. 115)

Double-entry accounting system   A system that records the dual effect of each transaction in appropriate accounts. (p. 115)

General journal   The book of original entry in which transactions are recorded in chronological order. (p. 119)

General ledger   The book of accounts that contains a company's asset, liability, and shareholders' equity, revenue, and expense accounts. (p. 121)

Posting   The procedure of transferring journal entries to the general ledger accounts. (p. 122)

T account (also known as a general ledger account)   The basic form of an account, with a debit (left) side and a credit (right) side showing the effect of transactions on the account. (p. 114)

Trial balance   A list of general ledger accounts and their balances at a specific time, usually at the end of the accounting period. (p. 130)

DECISION TOOLKIT—A SUMMARY

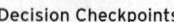 Decision Checkpoints	 Info Needed for Decision	 Tools to Use for Decision	 How to Evaluate Results
Has an accounting transaction occurred?	Details of the event	Accounting equation	Determine the effect, if any, on assets, liabilities, and shareholders' equity.
How do you determine that debits equal credits?	All general ledger account balances	Trial balance	List the account titles and their balances, total the debit and credit columns, and verify equality.

USING THE DECISION TOOLKIT

lululemon athletica inc. is one of Canada's leading designers and suppliers of athletic wear. lululemon reports the following list of accounts, in alphabetical order. All accounts have normal balances.

LULULEMON ATHLETICA INC.
List of Accounts
February 3, 2013
(in USD thousands)

Accounts payable	$ 31,077
Accounts receivable	6,351
Cash	590,179
Common shares	221,934
Cost of goods sold expense	607,532
Goodwill and intangible assets	30,201
Income tax expense	109,965
Income taxes payable	39,637
Inventories	155,222
Non-current liabilities	30,422
Other non-current assets	19,185
Other current liabilities	62,643
Other operating expenses	875
Other revenue	4,957
Other shareholders' equity items	21,090
Prepaid expenses and other current assets	35,301
Property and equipment	214,639
Retained earnings, beginning of year	373,719
Sales revenue	1,370,358
Selling, general, and administrative expenses	386,387

Instructions

(a) Prepare a trial balance for lululemon, reordering the accounts in financial statement order.

(b) On the trial balance, identify on which financial statement (FS) each account should be reported. Write "SFP" beside the accounts that should be shown on the statement of financial position, "IS" beside those that should be shown on the income statement, and "SCE" beside those that should be shown on the statement of changes in equity. (*Note*: Some accounts may be shown on more than one statement.)

Solution

LULULEMON ATHLETICA INC.
Trial Balance
February 3, 2013
(in USD thousands)

	(a)		(b)
	Debit	Credit	FS
Cash	$ 590,179		SFP
Accounts receivable	6,351		SFP
Inventories	155,222		SFP
Prepaid expenses and other current assets	35,301		SFP
Property and equipment	214,639		SFP
Goodwill and intangible assets	30,201		SFP
Other non-current assets	19,185		SFP
Accounts payable		$ 31,077	SFP
Income taxes payable		39,637	SFP
Other current liabilities		62,643	SFP
Non-current liabilities		30,422	SFP
Common shares		221,934	SFP, SCE
Other shareholders' equity items		21,090	SFP, SCE

(*continued*)

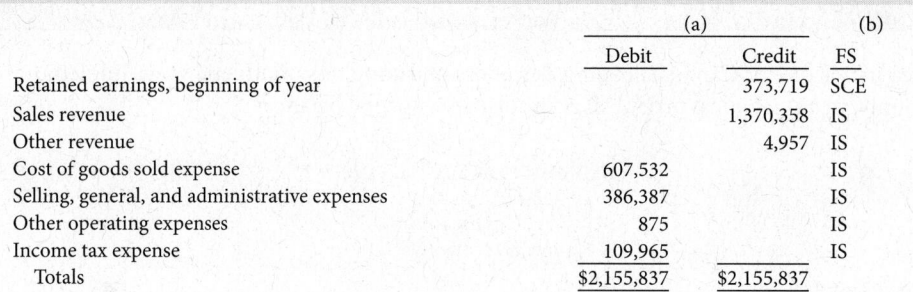

	(a)		(b)
	Debit	Credit	FS
Retained earnings, beginning of year		373,719	SCE
Sales revenue		1,370,358	IS
Other revenue		4,957	IS
Cost of goods sold expense	607,532		IS
Selling, general, and administrative expenses	386,387		IS
Other operating expenses	875		IS
Income tax expense	109,965		IS
Totals	$2,155,837	$2,155,837	

Comprehensive Do It!

Campus Laundry Ltd. opened on September 1, 2015. During the first month of operations, the following transactions occurred:

Sept. 1 Shareholders invested $20,000 cash in the business when 10,000 common shares were issued by the company.

3 Paid $1,000 cash for rent for the month of September.

4 Purchased washers and dryers for $25,000, paying $10,000 in cash and borrowing $15,000 from the bank for six months, at 8% interest per annum.

7 Paid $1,200 for a one-year insurance policy.

15 Paid employee salaries of $2,500.

15 Performed services on account for a nearby restaurant, $6,200.

21 Paid a $700 cash dividend to shareholders.

29 Cash receipts for laundry services performed throughout the month were $5,000.

30 Paid employee salaries of $2,500.

30 Owed utilities of $1,200 at the end of the month.

30 Paid monthly income tax instalment of $600.

Instructions

(a) Journalize the above transactions.

(b) Open T accounts and post the transactions.

(c) Prepare a trial balance.

(d) Prepare an income statement, statement of changes in equity, and statement of financial position.

Action Plan

• Make separate journal entries for each transaction.

• In journalizing, make sure debits equal credits, use specific account titles taken from the chart of accounts, and provide an appropriate explanation of the journal entry.

• Arrange the general ledger in financial statement order, beginning with the statement of financial position accounts.

• Prepare a trial balance that lists accounts in the order in which they appear in the ledger.

• In the trial balance, list debit balances in the left column and credit balances in the right column. Check the accuracy of your work. Total debits must equal total credits.

• Prepare the income statement first, paying attention to the order that accounts are listed in.

• Prepare the statement of changes in equity second and determine how each shareholders' equity account balance has changed during the period.

• Prepare the statement of financial position last, paying attention to the categories and order in which accounts are listed. Ensure that total assets equal total liabilities plus equity.

Solution to Comprehensive Do It!

(a)

Date		Account Titles and Explanation	Debit	Credit
2015				
Sept.	1	Cash	20,000	
		Common Shares		20,000
		(Issued common shares)		
	3	Rent Expense	1,000	
		Cash		1,000
		(Paid September rent)		
	4	Equipment	25,000	
		Cash		10,000
		Bank Loan Payable		15,000
		(Purchased laundry equipment for cash and a bank loan, due in six months, at 8% interest)		
	7	Prepaid Insurance	1,200	
		Cash		1,200
		(Paid one-year insurance policy)		
	15	Salaries Expense	2,500	
		Cash		2,500
		(Paid salaries)		
	15	Accounts Receivable	6,200	
		Service Revenue		6,200
		(To record revenue for laundry services provided)		
	21	Dividends	700	
		Cash		700
		(Paid a $700 cash dividend)		
	29	Cash	5,000	
		Service Revenue		5,000
		(To record collection for laundry services provided)		
	30	Salaries Expense	2,500	
		Cash		2,500
		(Paid salaries)		
	30	Utilities Expense	1,200	
		Accounts Payable		1,200
		(To record utilities due in October)		
	30	Income Tax Expense	600	
		Cash		600
		(Paid income tax instalment for month)		

(b)

Cash					
Sept.	1	20,000	Sept.	3	1,000
	29	5,000		4	10,000
				7	1,200
				15	2,500
				21	700
				30	2,500
				30	600
Bal.		6,500			

Accounts Receivable		
Sept.	15	6,200

Common Shares		
	Sept.	1	20,000

Dividends		
Sept.	21	700

Service Revenue		
	Sept.	15	6,200
		29	5,000
	Bal.		11,200

(continued)

Prepaid Insurance				Salaries Expense		
Sept.	7	1,200		Sept.	15	2,500
					30	2,500
Equipment				Bal.		5,000
Sept.	4	25,000				
				Utilities Expense		
Accounts Payable				Sept.	30	1,200
	Sept.	30	1,200			
				Rent Expense		
Bank Loan Payable				Sept.	3	1,000
	Sept.	4	15,000			
				Income Tax Expense		
				Sept.	30	600

(c)

CAMPUS LAUNDRY LTD.
Trial Balance
September 30, 2015

	Debit	Credit
Cash	$ 6,500	
Accounts receivable	6,200	
Prepaid insurance	1,200	
Equipment	25,000	
Accounts payable		$ 1,200
Bank loan payable		15,000
Common shares		20,000
Dividends	700	
Service revenue		11,200
Salaries expense	5,000	
Utilities expense	1,200	
Rent expense	1,000	
Income tax expense	600	
	$47,400	$47,400

(d)

CAMPUS LAUNDRY LTD.
Income Statement
Month Ended September 30, 2015

Revenues		
Service revenue		$11,200
Expenses		
Salaries expense	$5,000	
Utilities expense	1,200	
Rent expense	1,000	7,200
Profit before income tax		4,000
Income tax expense		600
Profit		$ 3,400

CAMPUS LAUNDRY LTD.
Statement of Changes in Equity
Month Ended September 30, 2015

	Common Shares	Retained Earnings	Total Equity
Balance, September 1	$ 0	$ 0	$ 0
Issued common shares	20,000		20,000
Profit		3,400	3,400
Dividends		(700)	(700)
Balance, September 30	$20,000	$2,700	$22,700

CAMPUS LAUNDRY LTD.
Statement of Financial Position
September 30, 2015

Assets

Current assets		
Cash	$ 6,500	
Accounts receivable	6,200	
Prepaid insurance	1,200	$13,900
Property, plant, and equipment		
Equipment		25,000
Total assets		$38,900

Liabilities and Shareholders' Equity

Current liabilities		
Accounts payable	$ 1,200	
Bank loan payable	15,000	$16,200
Shareholders' equity		
Common shares	$20,000	
Retained earnings	2,700	22,700
Total liabilities and shareholders' equity		$38,900

the navigator

WileyPLUS   **Self-Test, Brief Exercises, Exercises, Problems: Set A, and many more components are available for practice in *WileyPLUS*.**

Self-Test Questions

Answers are at the end of the chapter.

Quiz Yourself

(SO 1) 1. Which of the following events would *not* be recorded in the accounting records?
(a) Purchased equipment on account.
(b) Obtained permission to purchase land from the board of directors.
(c) Issued common shares.
(d) Paid a dividend to shareholders.

(SO 1) 2. When cash is received in advance of performing a service, the effects on the accounting equation are:
(a) an increase in assets and a decrease in shareholders' equity.
(b) an increase in assets and an increase in shareholders' equity.
(c) an increase in assets and an increase in liabilities.
(d) an increase in liabilities and an increase in shareholders' equity.

(SO 2) 3. Debits normally:
(a) increase both assets and liabilities.
(b) decrease both assets and liabilities.
(c) increase assets and decrease liabilities.
(d) decrease assets and increase liabilities.

(SO 2)   4. Which accounts normally have debit balances?
   (a) Assets, expenses, and revenues
   (b) Assets, expenses, and retained earnings
   (c) Assets, liabilities, and dividends
   (d) Assets, dividends, and expenses

(SO 3)   5. Which of these statements about journalizing is true?
   (a) Journal entries must be prepared after the trial balance is prepared.
   (b) Journal entries must be prepared after transactions have been analyzed to determine their effect on the accounts.
   (c) Journal entries don't involve amounts, they just note in narrative form the details of a transaction.
   (d) If a journal entry affects more than two accounts, it is known as a simple journal entry.

(SO 3)   6. Which of these statements about a general journal is *false*?
   (a) It is not a book of original entry.
   (b) It provides a chronological record of transactions.
   (c) It helps to locate errors because the debit and credit amounts for each entry can be quickly compared.
   (d) It discloses the complete effect of a transaction in one place.

(SO 4)   7. A general ledger:
   (a) contains only asset and liability accounts.
   (b) should show accounts in alphabetical order.

   (c) is a collection of the entire group of accounts maintained by a company.
   (d) provides a chronological record of transactions.

(SO 4)   8. Posting:
   (a) normally occurs before journalizing.
   (b) transfers general ledger transaction data to the general journal.
   (c) is an optional step in the accounting cycle.
   (d) transfers general journal entries to general ledger accounts.

(SO 5)   9. A trial balance:
   (a) is a list of accounts with their balances at a specific time.
   (b) proves that transactions have been correctly journalized.
   (c) will not balance if a correct journal entry is posted twice.
   (d) proves that all transactions have been recorded.

(SO 5)   10. A trial balance will not balance if:
   (a) a journal entry to record a cash sale is posted twice.
   (b) the purchase of supplies on account is debited to Supplies and credited to Cash.
   (c) a $100 cash dividend is debited to Dividends for $1,000 and credited to Cash for $100.
   (d) a $450 payment on account is debited to Accounts Payable for $45 and credited to Cash for $45.

Questions

(SO 1)   1. What is an accounting information system? Describe some of the factors that may impact the design of a company's information system.
(SO 1)   2. Why are some events recorded as accounting transactions but others are not?
(SO 1)   3. Which of the following events should be recorded in the accounting records? Explain your answer in each case.
   (a) The company wins an award as one of the top 50 companies in Canada to work for.
   (b) Supplies are purchased on account.
   (c) A shareholder dies.
   (d) The company pays a cash dividend to its shareholders.
   (e) A local lawyer agrees to provide legal services to the company for the next year.
(SO 1)   4. Can a business enter into a transaction that affects only the left side of the accounting equation? If so, give an example.
(SO 1)   5. What is the effect of each of the following transactions on the expanded accounting equation?
   (a) Paid cash for janitorial services.
   (b) Purchased equipment on account.

   (c) Issued common shares to investors in exchange for cash.
   (d) Paid income tax.
   (e) Collected an account receivable.
(SO 2)   6. Natalie Boudreau, an introductory accounting student, believes debit balances are favourable and credit balances are unfavourable. Is Natalie correct? Discuss.
(SO 2)   7. Given that both liabilities and shareholders' equity are on the same side of the accounting equation, why is it that all liability accounts are increased by credits but all shareholders' equity accounts are not?
(SO 2)   8. For each of the following accounts, indicate (a) whether the account would have a normal debit or credit balance, and (b) the appropriate statement classification (income statement, statement of changes in equity, statement of financial position) for each.
   1. Accounts Receivable
   2. Accounts Payable
   3. Equipment
   4. Dividends

5. Supplies
6. Service Revenue
7. Unearned Revenue
8. Income Tax Expense
9. Prepaid Rent
10. Bank Loan Payable

(SO 2) 9. For the following transactions, identify the account to be debited and the account to be credited:
(a) Supplies are purchased on account
(b) Payment of an amount owing to a supplier
(c) Cash is borrowed from the bank
(d) Employees are paid salaries in cash
(e) Cash is received from a customer in advance
(f) An expense is paid in advance
(g) Services are performed on account
(h) A customer's account is collected
(i) A dividend is paid to shareholders
(j) Income tax is paid

(SO 2) 10. For each account listed below, indicate whether it generally will have debit entries only, credit entries only, or both debit and credit entries:
(a) Cash
(b) Accounts Receivable
(c) Dividends
(d) Accounts Payable
(e) Service Revenue
(f) Salaries Expense
(g) Unearned Revenue

(SO 3) 11. (a) What is a general journal? (b) How does the journal facilitate the recording process?

(SO 3) 12. Explain why the format of the following items in a journal entry are important: (a) including a date, (b) recording debit entries first, (c) indenting credit entries, and (d) including a brief explanation.

(SO 3) 13. Meghan is recording the purchase of a truck in a journal entry and can't decide what account title to use for the truck. She is thinking about using "Truck Purchased," but she also likes the account titles "Mack Truck" or "Big Rig," which better represent the type of truck the company purchased. Give Meghan advice about choosing an account title to use in a journal entry.

(SO 3, 4) 14. An efficiency expert who was reviewing the steps in the accounting cycle suggested dropping the general journal and recording and summarizing transactions directly into the general ledger instead. Comment on this suggestion.

(SO 3, 4) 15. Does it matter how frequently transactions are posted from the general journal to the general ledger? Explain.

(SO 4) 16. (a) What is a general ledger? (b) In what order are accounts usually arranged in a general ledger?

(SO 4) 17. (a) What is a chart of accounts and why is it important? (b) How does numbering the accounts help?

(SO 4) 18. Arrange the following accounts in their normal order in a chart of accounts: cash, common shares, dividends, income tax expense, prepaid insurance, service revenue, supplies, unearned revenue.

(SO 5) 19. (a) What is a trial balance? (b) From what source document(s) is it prepared?

(SO 5) 20. Does it matter in which order accounts are listed in the trial balance?

(SO 5) 21. On a trial balance, why does the retained earnings balance shown relate to the beginning of the period rather than the end of the period?

(SO 5) 22. Two students are discussing the use of a trial balance. They wonder whether the following errors, each considered separately, would prevent the trial balance from balancing. What would you tell the students?
(a) The bookkeeper debited Supplies for $750 and debited Accounts Payable for $750 for the purchase of supplies on account.
(b) Cash collected on account was debited to Cash for $1,000 and credited to Service Revenue for $1,000.
(c) A journal entry recording the payment of dividends was posted to the general ledger as a debit to the Dividends account of $650 and a credit to the Cash account of $560.

(SO 5) 23. Identify and describe the first four steps in the accounting cycle.

Brief Exercises

BE3–1 Presented below are a number of economic events. Prepare a tabular analysis of the effects of the above transactions on the expanded accounting equation.

Analyze effects of transactions. (SO 1)

1. Purchased supplies on account, $250.
2. Provided a service on account, $500.
3. Paid salaries expense, $300.
4. Issued common shares in exchange for cash, $5,000.
5. Paid a cash dividend to shareholders, $400.
6. Received cash from a customer who had previously been billed for services provided, $500 (see item 2).
7. Paid account owed to supplier, $250 (see item 1).
8. Paid for insurance in advance, $100.
9. Received cash in advance from a customer for services to be performed in the future, $300.
10. Performed the service that the customer previously paid for (see item 9).

Indicate debit and credit effects and statement classification.
(SO 2)

BE3–2 For each of the following accounts, indicate the (a) effect of a debit or credit on the account, (b) normal balance, and (c) appropriate statement classification (income statement, statement of changes in equity, and/or statement of financial position). Note that there may be more than one statement classification in some cases.

1. Accounts payable
2. Advertising expense
3. Service revenue
4. Accounts receivable
5. Unearned revenue
6. Cash
7. Dividends
8. Common shares
9. Prepaid insurance
10. Equipment
11. Retained earnings
12. Income tax expense

Prepare basic analysis, equation analysis, and debit–credit analysis.
(SO 1, 2)

BE3–3 Selected transactions for Ing Corporation for the month of June are presented below. For each transaction, prepare a (a) basic analysis, (b) equation analysis, and (c) debit–credit analysis.

June	1	Issued common shares to shareholders in exchange for $2,500 cash.
	2	Purchased supplies on account for $250.
	12	Billed J. Kronsnoble $300 for welding work done.
	22	Received cash from J. Kronsnoble for work billed on June 12.
	25	Hired an employee to start work on July 2.
	28	Received cash of $200 from K. Jones as a deposit for welding work to be done in July.
	29	Paid for supplies purchased on June 2.
	30	Paid $100 for income tax.

Indicate debit–credit analysis.
(SO 2)

BE3–4 Riko Corporation has the following selected transactions:

1. Issued common shares to shareholders in exchange for $5,000.
2. Paid rent in advance for six months, $2,100.
3. Paid administrative assistant $500 salary.
4. Billed clients $1,200 for services provided.
5. Received $900 from clients for services provided in item 4 above.
6. Purchased $500 of supplies on account.
7. Paid supplier amount owing, $500.
8. Borrowed $1,000 cash from the bank.

For each transaction, indicate (a) the basic type of account debited and credited (asset, liability, shareholders' equity), (b) the specific account debited and credited, and (c) whether the specific account is increased or decreased to record this transaction. Use the following format, in which the first one has been done for you as an example:

| | Account Debited | | | Account Credited | | |
	(a) Basic Type	(b) Specific Account	(c) Effect	(a) Basic Type	(b) Specific Account	(c) Effect
Transaction						
1.	Asset	Cash	Increase	Shareholders' equity	Common Shares	Increase

Record transactions.
(SO 3)

BE3–5 Journalize the transactions given in BE3–1.

Record transactions.
(SO 3)

BE3–6 Journalize the transactions for Ing Corporation given in BE3–3.

Record transactions.
(SO 3)

BE3–7 Journalize the transactions for Riko Corporation given in BE3–4.

Determine missing amounts in ledger.
(SO 4)

BE3–8 Fill in the missing amounts from the following T accounts.

Accounts Receivable				Accounts Payable				Sales		
Aug. 10	17,500					Aug. 5	(c)		Aug. 10	50,000
15	6,500					18	3,400	Aug. 12	500	
		Aug. 23	(a)	Aug. 29	5,800				15	45,000
Bal.	9,000					Bal.	3,600		Bal.	(c)
Sept. 5	(b)					Sept. 12	7,700		Sept. 5	(f)
		Sept. 15	8,000	Sept. 23	5,900			Sept. 25	450	
Bal.	5,000					Bal.	(d)		Bal.	99,000

BE3–9 Using T accounts, post the journal entries in BE3–6 to the general ledger.

Post journal entries.
(SO 4)

BE3–10 Selected transactions are presented in journal entry form below. For each entry, (a) provide an explanation of the transaction, and (b) using T accounts, post the journal entries to the general ledger.

Post journal entries.
(SO 4)

GENERAL JOURNAL			
Date	Account Titles	Debit	Credit
May 5	Accounts Receivable	3,200	
	Service Revenue		3,200
12	Cash	1,900	
	Accounts Receivable		1,900
15	Supplies	200	
	Accounts Payable		200
20	Cash	2,000	
	Service Revenue		2,000
25	Salaries Expense	2,500	
	Cash		2,500
28	Accounts Payable	200	
	Cash		200
30	Income Tax Expense	750	
	Cash		750

BE3–11 From the ledger balances given below, listed in alphabetical order, prepare a trial balance for Carland Inc. at June 30, 2015. All accounts have a normal debit or credit balance.

Prepare trial balance.
(SO 5)

Accounts payable	$ 3,000	Income tax expense	$ 400
Accounts receivable	4,000	Rent expense	1,000
Accumulated depreciation —equipment	3,600	Retained earnings	12,650
Cash	4,400	Salaries expense	4,000
Common shares	10,000	Service revenue	7,600
Dividends	200	Trading investments	6,000
Equipment	17,000	Unearned revenue	150

BE3–12 Different types of posting errors are identified in the following table. For each error, indicate (a) whether the trial balance will balance (yes or no), (b) the amount of the difference if the trial balance will not balance, and (c) the trial balance column (debit or credit) that will have the larger total. Consider each error separately. Use the following form, in which error 1 is given as an example:

Identify effects of posting errors on trial balance.
(SO 5)

Error	(a) In Balance	(b) Difference	(c) Larger Column Total
1. A $1,200 debit to Supplies was posted as a $2,100 debit.	No	$900	Debit
2. A $1,000 credit to Cash was posted twice as two credits to Cash.			
3. A $5,000 debit to Dividends was posted to the Common Shares account.			
4. A journal entry debiting Cash and crediting Service Revenue for $2,500 was not posted.			
5. The collection of $500 cash on account was posted as a debit of $500 to Cash and a credit of $500 to Accounts Payable.			
6. The payment of $1,000 on an account payable owed to the insurance company was posted as a debit to the Insurance Expense account. No credit was posted.			

BE3–13 An inexperienced bookkeeper prepared the following trial balance. She finished with a huge sigh of relief because she was able to balance the trial balance. (a) Is the trial balance correct? (b) If you answered "no" in (a), prepare a correct trial balance, assuming all accounts have a normal debit or credit balance.

Prepare corrected trial balance.
(SO 5)

BOURQUE LIMITED
Trial Balance
December 31, 2015

	Debit	Credit
Cash	$10,000	
Accounts receivable	6,500	
Supplies	3,500	
Accounts payable	1,500	
Unearned revenue	2,200	
Common shares	5,000	
Retained earnings	13,000	
Dividends		$ 4,500
Service revenue		20,000
Salaries expense		9,100
Office expense		4,400
Supplies expense		1,200
Rent expense		2,000
Income tax expense		500
	$41,700	$41,700

Exercises

Analyze effects
of transactions.
(SO 1)

E3–1   Selected transactions for Green Lawn Care Ltd. follow:

1. Issued common shares to shareholders in exchange for $5,000 cash.
2. Purchased $250 of supplies on account.
3. Billed customers $2,500 for services performed.
4. Paid a $100 dividend to shareholders.
5. Received $1,800 cash from customers billed in transaction 3.
6. Purchased equipment for $3,500, paying $500 cash and signing a bank loan in payment.
7. Performed services for $1,200 cash.
8. Paid full amount owing for supplies purchased in transaction 2.
9. Paid $750 in salaries to employees.
10. Paid $600 for insurance coverage in advance.

Instructions
Prepare a tabular analysis of the effects of the above transactions on the expanded accounting equation.

Analyze effects
of transactions.
(SO 1)

E3–2   Wong Computer Corporation entered into these transactions during the month of May:

1. Purchased computers on account for $8,000 from Dell.
2. Paid $1,600 for rent for the month of May.
3. Provided computer services for $3,800 on account.
4. Paid Ontario Hydro $300 cash for utilities used in May.
5. Issued common shares to Li Wong in exchange for an additional $20,000 investment in the business.
6. Paid Dell for computers purchased in transaction 1.
7. Purchased a one-year accident insurance policy for $500 cash.
8. Received $3,000 cash in partial payment of the account in transaction 3.
9. Paid Li Wong a $500 dividend.
10. Paid income tax of $250 for the month.

Instructions
(a) Prepare a tabular analysis of the effects of the above transactions on the expanded accounting equation.
(b) Calculate profit for the month.

E3–3   You are presented with the following alphabetical list of items, selected from the financial statements of **Saputo Inc.**:

Accounts payable and accrued liabilities	Income taxes payable
Bank loan payable	Interest expense
Cash	Inventories
Dividends	Prepaid expenses
Dividends payable	Receivables
Furniture, machinery, and equipment	Revenues
General and administrative expenses	Trademarks
Goodwill	
Income tax expense	

Instructions

For each of the above accounts, identify the following:

(a) the type of account (assets, liabilities, share capital, dividends, revenues, expenses);

(b) the normal balance of the account; and

(c) on which financial statement (income statement, statement of changes in equity, statement of financial position) Saputo would likely report the account.

E3–4   Selected transactions for the Decorators Mill Ltd., an interior decorator corporation in its first month of business, are as follows:

March	2	Issued common shares for $11,000 cash.
	4	Purchased used car for $1,000 cash and $9,000 on account, for use in the business.
	10	Billed customers $2,300 for services performed.
	13	Paid $225 cash to advertise business opening.
	25	Received $1,000 cash from customers billed on March 10.
	27	Paid amount owing for used car purchased on March 4.
	30	Received $700 cash from a customer for services to be performed in April.
	31	Paid dividends of $500 to shareholders.

Instructions

For each of the above transactions, prepare a (a) basic analysis, (b) equation analysis, and (c) debit–credit analysis.

E3–5   Data for the Wong Computer Corporation were presented in E3–2.

Instructions

Journalize the transactions.

E3–6   Data for the Decorators Mill Ltd. were presented in E3–4.

Instructions

Journalize the transactions.

E3–7   The journal entries for the Decorators Mill were prepared in E3–6.

Instructions

Post the journal entries to T accounts.

E3–8   Selected transactions for the Basler Corporation during its first month in business are presented below:

Sept.	1	Issued common shares for $20,000 cash.
	2	Performed $9,000 of services on account for a customer.
	4	Purchased equipment for $12,000, paying $5,000 in cash and borrowing the balance from the bank.
	10	Purchased $500 of supplies on account.
	25	Received $4,500 cash in advance for architectural services to be provided next month.
	30	Paid account owing for supplies (see September 10 transaction).
	30	Collected $5,000 on account owing from customer (see September 2 transaction).

Instructions

For each of the above transactions, do the following:

(a) Prepare a basic analysis.

(b) Prepare an equation analysis.

(c) Prepare a debit–credit analysis.

(d) Journalize the transaction.

(e) Using T accounts, post the journal entry to the general ledger.

Post journal entries and prepare trial balance.

(SO 4, 5)

E3–9   Selected transactions from the general journal of Kang, Inc. for its first month of operations are presented here:

GENERAL JOURNAL

Date		Account Titles	Debit	Credit
Aug.	1	Cash	3,000	
		Common Shares		3,000
	7	Cash	1,800	
		Service Revenue		1,800
	11	Equipment	4,000	
		Cash		1,500
		Bank Loan Payable		2,500
	14	Accounts Receivable	1,450	
		Service Revenue		1,450
	16	Cash	900	
		Unearned Revenue		900
	28	Cash	700	
		Accounts Receivable		700
	30	Salary Expense	2,000	
		Cash		2,000
	31	Dividends	500	
		Cash		500

Instructions

(a) Prepare an explanation for each of the journal entries listed above.
(b) Using T accounts, post the journal entries to the general ledger.
(c) Prepare a trial balance at August 31, 2015.

Prepare trial balance.

(SO 5)

E3–10   The following is the general ledger for Holly Corp.:

GENERAL LEDGER

	Cash					Common Shares		
Oct.	1	2,000	Oct.	5	400		Oct. 1	2,000
	9	650		12	1,500			
	15	5,000		16	300			
	20	500		30	1,250			
				30	500			

	Accounts Receivable					Dividends	
Oct.	6	800	Oct. 20	500	Oct. 16	300	
	20	1,940					

	Supplies			Service Revenue		
Oct.	5	400		Oct.	6	800
					9	650
					20	1,940

	Equipment			Salaries Expense	
Oct.	2	2,000	Oct. 30	500	

	Accounts Payable					Advertising Expense	
Oct. 12	1,500	Oct.	2	2,000	Oct. 28	400	
			28	400			

	Income Tax Payable			Rent Expense	
		Oct. 31	180	Oct. 30	1,250

	Bank Loan Payable			Income Tax Expense	
		Oct. 15	5,000	Oct. 31	180

Instructions

(a) Prepare an explanation for each ledger posting that was made above.

(b) Prepare a trial balance at October 31, 2015.

E3–11 The following is a list of accounts for Speedy Delivery Service, Inc. at July 31, 2015:

Prepare trial balance and financial statements.

(SO 5)

Accounts payable	$ 9,500	Interest expense	$ 3,600
Accounts receivable	14,000	Bank loan payable, due 2017	39,000
Accumulated depreciation	21,400	Prepaid insurance	200
—equipment			
Cash	8,000	Rent expense	9,000
Common shares	38,000	Repairs and maintenance expense	5,700
Equipment	99,000	Retained earnings, Aug. 1, 2014	20,850
Depreciation expense	9,700	Salaries expense	25,000
Dividends	800	Salaries payable	800
Vehicles expense	4,750	Service revenue	75,000
Income tax expense	3,000	Trading investments	20,000
Insurance expense	1,800		

Additional information:

During the year, the company issued common shares for $11,000.

Instructions

(a) Prepare a trial balance.

(b) Prepare an income statement, statement of changes in equity, and statement of financial position for the year.

(c) If you did not know the retained earnings amount in the trial balance, could you have prepared the financial statements in (b)?

E3–12 The bookkeeper for Castle's Equipment Repair Corporation made these errors in journalizing and posting:

Analyze errors and their effects on trial balance.

(SO 5)

1. A credit posting of $400 to Accounts Receivable was omitted.
2. A debit posting of $750 for Prepaid Insurance was debited to Insurance Expense.
3. A collection on account of $100 was journalized and posted as a $100 debit to Cash and a $100 credit to Service Revenue.
4. A credit posting of $500 to Accounts Payable was made twice.
5. A cash purchase of supplies for $250 was journalized and posted as a $250 debit to Supplies and a $25 credit to Cash.
6. A debit of $465 to Advertising Expense was posted as $456.

Instructions

For each error, indicate:

(a) whether the trial balance will balance (yes or no),

(b) the amount of the difference if the trial balance will not balance, and

(c) the trial balance column (debit or credit) that will have the larger total.

Consider each error separately. Use the following format, in which the first error is given as an example:

	(a)	(b)	(c)
			Larger
Error	In Balance	Difference	Column Total
1.	No	$400	Debit

Problems: Set A

P3–1A On April 1, Adventures Travel Agency, Inc. began operations. The following transactions were completed during the month:

Analyze effects of transactions.

(SO 1)

1. Issued common shares for $24,000 cash.
2. Obtained a bank loan for $7,000.
3. Paid $11,000 cash to buy equipment.
4. Paid $1,200 cash for April office rent.
5. Paid $1,450 for supplies.
6. Purchased $600 of advertising in the *Daily Herald*, on account.
7. Earned $18,000 for services performed: cash of $2,000 was received from customers, and the balance of $16,000 was billed to customers on account.
8. Paid $400 dividends to shareholders.

9. Paid the utility bill for the month, $2,000.
10. Paid *Daily Herald* the amount due in transaction 6.
11. Paid $40 of interest on the bank loan obtained in transaction 2.
12. Paid employees' salaries, $6,400.
13. Received $12,000 cash from customers billed in transaction 7.
14. Paid income tax, $1,500.

Instructions

(a) Prepare a tabular analysis of the effects of the above transactions on the expanded accounting equation.
(b) Calculate total assets, liabilities, and shareholders' equity at the end of the month and total profit for the month.

Analyze transactions and prepare financial statements.
(SO 1)

P3–2A On July 31, 2015, the general ledger of Hills Legal Services Inc. showed the following balances: Cash $4,000; Accounts Receivable $1,500; Supplies $500; Equipment $5,000; Accounts Payable $4,100; Common Shares $3,500; and Retained Earnings $3,400. During August, the following transactions occurred:

Aug. 3 Collected $1,200 of accounts receivable due from customers.
      5 Received $1,300 cash for issuing common shares to new investors.
      6 Paid $2,700 cash on accounts payable owing.
      7 Earned fees of $6,500, of which $3,000 was collected in cash and the remainder was due on account.
      12 Purchased additional equipment for $1,200, paying $400 in cash and the balance on account.
      14 Paid salaries, $3,500, rent, $900, and advertising expenses, $275, for the month of August.
      18 Collected the balance of the fees earned on August 7.
      20 Paid dividends of $500 to shareholders.
      24 Billed a client $1,000 for legal services provided.
      26 Received $2,000 from Laurentian Bank; the money was borrowed on a bank loan payable that is due in six months.
      27 Signed an engagement letter to provide legal services to a client in September for $4,500. The client will pay the amount owing after the work has been completed.
      28 Received the utility bill for the month of August in the amount of $275; it is not due until September 15.
      31 Paid income tax for the month, $500.

Instructions

(a) Beginning with the July 31 balances, prepare a tabular analysis of the effects of the August transactions on the expanded accounting equation.
(b) Prepare an income statement, a statement of changes in equity, and a statement of financial position for August.

Identify normal balance and statement classification.
(SO 2)

P3–3A You are presented with the following alphabetical list of selected items from the financial statements of **Danier Leather Inc.:**

Accounts payable and accrued liabilities	Income tax payable
Accounts receivable	Interest expense
Buildings	Inventories
Cash	Land
Common shares, beginning of year	Prepaid expenses
Cost of sales	Retained earnings, beginning of year
Furniture and equipment	Sales
Income tax expense	Selling, general, and administrative expenses

Instructions

(a) For each of the above accounts, identify (1) whether the account is increased by a debit or a credit and (2) the normal balance of the account.
(b) For each of the above accounts, indicate (1) the appropriate classification (current assets, non-current assets, current liabilities, non-current liabilities, share capital, dividends, revenues, expenses), and (2) on which financial statement (income statement, statement of changes in equity, statement of financial position) the company would likely report the account.

Analyze and record transactions.
(SO 1, 2, 3)

P3–4A You are presented with the following transactions for Paddick Enterprises Ltd. for the month of February:

Feb. 2 Purchased supplies on account, $600.
      3 Purchased equipment for $10,000 by signing a bank loan due in three months.
      6 Earned service revenue of $50,000. Of this amount, $30,000 was received in cash. The balance was on account.
      13 Paid $500 in dividends to shareholders.
      18 A customer paid $2,000 in advance for services to be performed next month.
      20 Paid the amount owing for the supplies purchased on February 2.
      23 Collected $20,000 of the amount owing from the February 6 transaction.

24   Paid office expenses for the month, $22,000.
27   Recorded salaries due to employees for work performed during the month, $14,000.
28   Paid interest of $50 on the bank loan signed on February 3.

Instructions

(a) For each of the above transactions, prepare a (1) basic analysis, (2) equation analysis, and (3) debit–credit analysis.

(b) Prepare journal entries to record each of the above transactions.

P3–5A   The Adventure Miniature Golf and Driving Range, Inc. opened on May 1. The following selected events and transactions occurred during May:

Record transactions.
(SO 3)

May   1   Issued common shares for $120,000 cash.
4   Purchased Henry's Golf Land for $270,000. The price consists of land $125,000; buildings $100,000; and equipment $45,000. Paid cash of $100,000 and signed a mortgage payable for the balance.
4   Paid $1,500 for a one-year insurance policy; coverage begins next month.
5   Advertised the opening of the driving range and miniature golf course, paying advertising expenses of $800.
6   Purchased golf clubs and other equipment for $9,000 on account from Titleist Corporation.
18   Received $8,800 from customers for golf fees earned.
20   Paid dividends of $1,000 to shareholders.
22   Received $1,200 from a school board that paid for students' golf lessons that will be given in June.
29   Paid Titleist Corporation in full for equipment purchased on May 6.
30   Paid $800 of interest on the mortgage payable.
30   Paid salaries of $3,400.

Instructions

Journalize the May transactions.

P3–6A   During the first month of operations, the following events and transactions occurred for Virmani Architects Inc.:

Record and post
transactions.
(SO 3, 4)

Apr.   1   Invested cash of $10,000 and equipment of $6,000 in the company in exchange for common shares.
1   Hired a secretary-receptionist at a monthly salary of $1,900.
2   Paid office rent for the month, $950.
3   Purchased architectural supplies on account from Halo Ltd., $1,900.
10   Completed blueprints on a carport and billed client $900.
13   Received $800 cash advance from a client for the design of a new home.
20   Received $1,500 for services performed for a client.
21   Received $500 from client for work completed and billed on April 10.
23   Received April's telephone bill for $135; due May 15. (*Hint:* Use the Office Expense account for telephone services.)
30   Paid secretary-receptionist for the month, $1,900.
30   Paid 50% ($950) of the amount owed to Halo Ltd. on account (see April 3 transaction).
.30   Paid $500 dividend.

Instructions

(a) Journalize the transactions.

(b) Using T accounts, post the April journal entries to the general ledger.

(c) After the accountant finished journalizing and posting the above transactions, he complained that this process took too much time. He thought it would be more efficient to omit the journal entry step in the accounting cycle and record the transactions directly in the general ledger. Explain to the accountant whether you think this is a good idea or not, and why.

P3–7A   On February 28, 2015, the Star Theatre, Inc.'s general ledger showed Cash $15,000; Land $85,000; Buildings $77,000; Equipment $20,000; Accounts Payable $12,000; Mortgage Payable $118,000; Common Shares $40,000; and Retained Earnings $27,000. During the month of March, the following events and transactions occurred:

Record and post trans-
actions; prepare trial
balance.
(SO 3, 4, 5)

Mar.   2   Received three movies to be shown during the first three weeks of March. The film rental was $27,000. Of that amount, $10,000 was paid in cash and the remainder will be paid on March 12. (*Hint:* Star Theatre uses the account Rent Expense to record film rentals).
2   Hired M. Brewer to operate concession stand. Brewer agrees to pay Star Theatre 15% of gross receipts, payable on the last day of each month, for the right to operate the concession stand. (*Hint:* Star Theatre uses the account Concession Revenue to record concessions earned.)
5   Ordered three additional movies, to be shown the last 10 days of March. The film rental cost will be $300 per night.
9   Received $16,300 from customers for admissions. (*Hint:* Star Theatre uses the account Fees Earned to record revenue from admissions.)
12   Paid balance due on the movies rented on March 2.
13   Paid the accounts payable owing at the end of February.
19   Paid advertising expenses, $950.

20   Received $16,600 from customers for admissions.
23   Received the movies ordered on March 5 and paid rental fee of $3,000 ($300 × 10 nights).
25   Received $18,400 from customers for admissions.
27   Paid salaries of $4,200.
30   Received statement from M. Brewer, showing gross concession receipts of $16,600, and the balance due to Star Theatre of $2,490 ($16,600 × 15%) for March. Brewer paid half of the balance due and will remit the remainder on April 5.
30   Paid $1,250 of the balance due on the mortgage, as well as $750 of interest on the mortgage.
30   Paid $3,000 for the monthly income tax instalment.

Instructions
(a) Using T accounts, enter the beginning balances in the ledger as at February 28.
(b) Journalize the March transactions.
(c) Post the March journal entries to the ledger.
(d) Prepare a trial balance at March 31.

Record and post
transactions; prepare
trial balance.
(SO 3, 4, 5)

P3–8A Pamper Me Salon Inc.'s general ledger at April 30, 2015, included the following: Cash $5,000; Supplies $500; Equipment $24,000; Accounts Payable $2,100; Bank Loan Payable $10,000; Unearned Revenue (from gift certificates) $1,000; Common Shares $5,000; and Retained Earnings $11,400. The following events and transactions occurred during May:

May   1   Paid rent for the month of May, $1,000.
       4   Paid $1,100 of the account payable at April 30.
       7   Issued gift certificates for future services for $1,500 cash.
       8   Received $1,200 cash from customers for services performed.
      14   Paid $1,200 in salaries to employees.
      15   Received $800 in cash from customers for services performed.
      15   Customers receiving services worth $700 used gift certificates in payment.
      21   Paid the remaining accounts payable from April 30.
      22   Received $1,000 in cash from customers for services performed.
      22   Purchased supplies of $700 on account. All of these were used during the month.
      25   Received a bill for advertising for $500. This bill is due on June 13.
      25   Received and paid a utilities bill for $400.
      29   Received $1,700 in cash from customers for services performed.
      29   Customers receiving services worth $600 used gift certificates in payment.
      31   Interest of $50 was paid on the bank loan.
      31   Paid $1,200 in salaries to employees.
      31   Paid income tax instalment for the month, $150.

Instructions
(a) Using T accounts, enter the beginning balances in the general ledger as at April 30.
(b) Journalize the May transactions.
(c) Post the May journal entries to the general ledger.
(d) Prepare a trial balance as at May 31.

Prepare trial balance.
(SO 5)

P3–9A You are presented with the following alphabetical list of accounts and balances (in thousands) for Taggar Enterprises Inc. at June 30, 2015:

Accounts payable	$ 1,500	Income tax payable	$ 100
Accounts receivable	3,000	Interest expense	100
Accumulated depreciation—buildings	4,000	Land	7,400
Accumulated depreciation—equipment	1,000	Long-term investments	3,550
Buildings	15,000	Merchandise inventory	5,100
Cash	1,800	Mortgage payable, due 2021	15,000
Common shares	5,000	Office expense	3,300
Cost of goods sold	13,700	Prepaid insurance	900
Equipment	3,000	Retained earnings, July 1, 2014	6,250
Income tax expense	1,000	Sales	25,000

Instructions
(a) Prepare a trial balance at June 30, sorting each account balance into the debit column or the credit column.
(b) If debits equal credits in Taggar's trial balance, do you have reasonable assurance that no errors exist? Explain.

Prepare financial
statements.
(SO 5)

P3–10A   Refer to the trial balance for Taggar Enterprises Inc. prepared in P3–9A. In addition to this information, note that during the year, common shares in the amount of $2,000 were issued and $1,250 of the mortgage is currently due.

Instructions
Prepare an income statement, statement of changes in equity, and statement of financial position for the year.

P3-11A The following trial balance of Cantpost Ltd., at the end of its first year of operations, June 30, 2015, does not balance:

Prepare corrected trial balance.

(SO 5)

	Debit	Credit
Cash		$ 1,241
Accounts receivable	$ 2,630	
Supplies	860	
Equipment	3,000	
Accumulated depreciation —equipment	600	
Accounts payable		2,665
Unearned revenue	1,200	
Common shares		1,000
Retained earnings, June 30, 2015		2,365
Dividends	800	
Service revenue		8,440
Salaries expense	3,400	
Office expense	910	
Depreciation expense	600	
Income tax expense	365	
	$14,365	$15,711

Each of the listed accounts has a normal balance per the general ledger. However, each account may not have been listed in the appropriate debit or credit column, or may not belong in the trial balance at all. In addition, an examination of the general ledger and general journal reveals the following errors:

1. Cash received from a customer on account was debited for $570, and Accounts Receivable was credited for the same amount. The actual collection was for $750.
2. The purchase of equipment on account for $360 was recorded as a debit to Supplies for $360 and a credit to Accounts Payable for $360.
3. Services were performed on account for a client for $890. Accounts Receivable was debited for $890 and Service Revenue was credited for $89.
4. A transposition (reversal of digits) error was made when copying the balance in the Salaries Expense account. The correct balance should be $4,300.
5. A payment for rent in the amount of $1,000 was neither recorded nor posted.

Instructions
Prepare the correct trial balance.

Problems: Set B

P3-1B On May 1, Marty's Repair Shop, Inc. commenced operations. The following transactions were completed during the month:

Analyze effects of transactions.

(SO 1)

1. Issued common shares for $28,000 cash.
2. Paid $1,280 for May office rent.
3. Purchased equipment for $16,000, paying $4,000 cash and signing a bank loan payable for the balance.
4. Purchased supplies on account, $700.
5. Received $4,200 from customers for repair services provided.
6. Paid for supplies purchased in transaction 4.
7. Paid May telephone bill of $200.
8. Provided repair services on account to customers, $3,600.
9. Paid employee salaries, $2,000.
10. Received $700 in advance for repair services to be provided next month.
11. Collected $1,600 from customers for services billed in transaction 8.
12. Paid $500 dividends to shareholders.
13. Paid $80 of interest on the bank loan obtained in transaction 3.
14. Paid income tax of $600.

Instructions
(a) Prepare a tabular analysis of the effects of the above transactions on the expanded accounting equation.
(b) Calculate total assets, liabilities, and shareholders' equity at the end of the month and total profit for the month.

Analyze transactions and prepare financial statements.
(SO 1)

P3–2B The general ledger of Corso Care Corp., a veterinary company, showed the following balances on August 31, 2015: Cash $4,500; Accounts Receivable $1,800; Supplies $350; Equipment $6,500; Accounts Payable $3,200; Common Shares $2,500; and Retained Earnings $7,450. During September, the following transactions occurred:

Sept.	1	Paid the accounts payable owing at August 31.
	1	Paid $1,200 rent for September.
	3	Collected $1,450 of accounts receivable due from customers.
	4	Hired a part-time office assistant at $50 per day to start work the following week, on Monday, September 7.
	5	Received $2,300 cash for issuing common shares to new investors.
	8	Purchased additional equipment for $2,050, paying $700 in cash and the balance on account.
	14	Billed $500 for veterinary services provided.
	15	Paid $300 for advertising expenses.
	25	Received $2,500 from Canadian Western Bank; the money was borrowed on a loan payable due in nine months.
	25	Sent a statement reminding a customer that money was still owed from August.
	28	Earned revenue of $4,500, of which $3,000 was received in cash. The balance is due in October.
	29	Paid part-time office assistant $750 for working 15 days in September.
	30	Incurred utility expenses for the month on account, $175.
	30	Paid dividends of $500 to shareholders.
	30	Paid income tax for the month, $350.

Instructions

(a) Beginning with the August 31 balances, prepare a tabular analysis of the effects of the September transactions on the expanded accounting equation.

(b) Prepare an income statement, a statement of changes in equity, and a statement of financial position for September.

Identify normal balance and statement classification.
(SO 2)

P3–3B You are presented with the following alphabetical list of selected items from the financial statements of **Reitmans (Canada) Limited**:

Administrative expenses	Income tax payable
Buildings	Inventories
Cost of goods sold	Mortgage payable, due November 2017
Dividends	Prepaid expenses
Finance income	Retained earnings, beginning of year
Fixtures and equipment	Sales
Goodwill	Trade and other receivables
Income tax expense	Trade payables

Instructions

(a) For each of the above accounts, identify (1) whether the account is increased by a debit or a credit and (2) the normal balance of the account.

(b) For each of the above accounts, indicate (1) the appropriate classification (current assets, non-current assets, current liabilities, non-current liabilities, share capital, dividends, revenues, expenses), and (2) on which financial statement (income statement, statement of changes in equity, statement of financial position) the company would likely report the account.

Analyze and record transactions.
(SO 1, 2, 3)

P3–4B You are presented with the following transactions for the Dankail Corporation for the month of January:

Jan.	2	Issued $10,000 of common shares for cash.
	5	Provided services on account, $2,500.
	6	Obtained a bank loan for $30,000.
	7	Paid $40,000 to purchase a hybrid car to be used solely in the business.
	9	Received a $5,000 deposit from a customer for services to be provided in the future.
	12	Billed customers $20,000 for services performed during the month.
	19	Paid $500 to purchase supplies.
	20	Provided $1,500 of services for the customer who paid in advance on January 9.
	23	Collected $5,000 owing from customers from the January 12 transaction.
	26	Received a bill for utilities of $125, due February 26.
	29	Paid rent for the month, $1,500.
	31	Paid $4,000 of salaries to employees.
	31	Paid interest of $300 on the bank loan from the January 6 transaction.
	31	Paid income tax for the month, $3,600.

Instructions

(a) For each of the above transactions, prepare a (1) basic analysis, (2) equation analysis, and (3) debit–credit analysis.

(b) Prepare journal entries to record the above transactions.

P3–5B   The Mountain Biking Corp. opened on April 1. The following selected events and transactions occurred during April: Record transactions. (SO 3)

Apr.	1	Issued common shares for $100,000 cash.
	3	Purchased an out-of-use ski hill costing $370,000, paying $60,000 cash and signing a bank loan payable for the balance. The $370,000 purchase price consisted of land $204,000; buildings $121,000; and equipment $45,000.
	8	Purchased advertising space of $1,800 on account.
	10	Paid salaries to employees, $2,800.
	13	Hired a park manager at a salary of $4,000 per month, effective May 1.
	14	Paid $5,500 for a one-year insurance policy.
	17	Paid $600 of dividends to shareholders.
	20	Received $10,600 in cash from customers for admission fees.
	30	Paid $1,800 on account for the advertising purchased on April 8.
	30	Paid $2,000 of interest on the bank loan.
	30	Paid an income tax instalment of $800.

Instructions

Journalize the April transactions.

P3–6B   During the first month of operations, the following events and transactions occurred for Astromech Accounting Services Inc.: Record and post transactions. (SO 3, 4)

May	1	Issued common shares for $20,000 cash.
	1	Paid office rent of $950 for the month.
	4	Hired a secretary-receptionist at a salary of $2,000 per month. She started work the same day.
	4	Purchased $750 of supplies on account from Read Supply Corp.
	11	Completed an income tax assignment and billed client $2,725 for services provided.
	12	Received $3,500 in advance on a management consulting engagement.
	15	Received $2,350 for services completed for Arnold Corp.
	20	Received $1,725 from client for work completed and billed on May 11.
	22	Paid one third of balance due to Read Supply Corp. (See May 4 transaction.)
	25	Received a $275 telephone bill for May, to be paid next month. (*Hint:* Use the Office Expense account to record telephone services.)
	29	Paid secretary-receptionist $2,000 salary for the month.
	29	Paid monthly income tax instalment, $300.
	29	Paid $250 dividend.

Instructions

(a) Journalize the transactions.

(b) Using T accounts, post the May journal entries to the general ledger.

(c) After the accountant finished journalizing and posting the above transactions, she complained that this process took too much time. She thought it would be more efficient to omit the journal entry step in the accounting cycle and record the transactions directly in the general ledger. Explain to the accountant whether you think this is a good idea or not, and why.

P3–7B   On March 31, 2015, the Lake Theatre, Inc.'s general ledger showed Cash $6,000; Land $100,000; Buildings $80,000; Equipment $25,000; Accounts Payable $5,000; Mortgage Payable $125,000; Common Shares $50,000; and Retained Earnings $31,000. During the month of April, the following events and transactions occurred: Record and post transactions; prepare trial balance. (SO 3, 4, 5)

Apr.	2	Paid film rental fee of $800 on first movie. (*Hint:* Lake Theatre uses the account Rent Expense to record film rentals.)
	3	Paid advertising expenses, $620.
	3	Hired Thoms Limited to operate concession stand. Thoms agrees to pay the Lake Theatre 20% of gross concession receipts, payable monthly, for the right to operate the concession stand. (*Hint:* Lake Theatre uses the account Concession Revenue to record concessions earned.)
	6	Ordered two additional films at $750 each.
	11	Received $1,950 from customers for admissions. (*Hint:* Lake Theatre uses the account Fees Earned to record revenue from admissions.)
	16	Paid $2,000 of the balance due on the mortgage. Also paid $850 in interest on the mortgage.
	17	Paid $2,800 of the accounts payable.
	20	Received one of the films ordered on April 6 and was billed $750. The film will be shown in April.
	25	Received $7,300 from customers for admissions.

26   Paid salaries, $1,900.

27   Prepaid $700 rental fee on special film to be run in May. (*Hint:* Use the account Prepaid Rent to record rental fees paid in advance.)

30   Received statement from Thoms showing gross concession receipts of $5,600 and the balance due to the Lake Theatre of $1,120 ($5,600 × 20%) for April. Thoms paid half of the balance due and will remit the remainder on May 5.

30   Paid $1,000 for the monthly income tax instalment.

Instructions

(a) Using T accounts, enter the beginning balances in the ledger as at March 31.

(b) Journalize the April transactions.

(c) Post the April journal entries to the ledger.

(d) Prepare a trial balance at April 30.

Record and post transactions; prepare trial balance.
(SO 3, 4, 5)

P3–8B   KG Spring Skating School Inc. had the following account balances as at April 30, 2012: Cash $23,000; Equipment $2,000; Accounts Payable $500; Unearned Revenue (for advance registration fees) $17,500; Common Shares $1,000; and Retained Earnings $6,000. The following events and transactions occurred during May:

May   4   Paid for ice time for first two weeks of the May school, $7,200. (*Hint:* Use the account Rent Expense to record ice rentals.)

9   Paid accounts payable outstanding at April 30.

11   Booked ice with the city for the July session. It will cost $14,400.

11   Received and paid a bill for $500 for advertising of the May skating school.

15   Paid coaches and assistant coaches, $1,000.

18   Paid for ice time for second two weeks of the May school, $7,200.

21   Received a bill for Internet service for $100. This invoice is due on June 15. (*Hint:* Use the account Office Expense to record Internet costs.)

29   Last day of May session. All of the advance registration fees have now been earned.

29   Paid $200 cash for supplies used immediately.

29   Received advance registrations for the next four-week skating session in July, $2,200.

29   Purchased gifts for volunteers who helped out during May session, $300. (*Hint:* Use the account Advertising Expense to record gifts.)

29   Paid coaches and assistant coaches, $1,000.

31   Paid income tax instalment for the month, $1,100.

Instructions

(a) Using T accounts, enter the beginning balances in the general ledger as at April 30.

(b) Journalize the May transactions.

(c) Post the May journal entries to the general ledger.

(d) Prepare a trial balance as at May 31.

Prepare trial balance.
(SO 5)

P3–9B   You are presented with the following alphabetical list of accounts and balances (in thousands) for Asian Importers Limited as at January 31, 2015:

Account	Amount	Account	Amount
Accounts payable	$ 46,300	Goodwill	$ 7,600
Accounts receivable	30,200	Income tax expense	14,000
Accumulated depreciation—buildings	13,000	Interest expense	2,150
Accumulated depreciation—equipment	3,600	Land	42,500
Buildings	39,500	Merchandise inventory	74,250
Bank loan payable (due 2018)	10,050	Mortgage payable	19,750
Cash	6,000	Office expense	67,750
Common shares	32,900	Other current liabilities	12,200
Cost of goods sold	244,200	Prepaid insurance	3,950
Dividends	1,850	Retained earnings, February 1, 2014	37,050
Equipment	10,900	Sales	370,000

Instructions

(a) Prepare a trial balance, sorting each account balance into the debit column or the credit column.

(b) If debits equal credits in Asian's trial balance, do you have reasonable assurance that no errors exist? Explain.

Prepare financial statements.
(SO 5)

P3–10B   Refer to the trial balance for Asian Importers prepared in P3–9B. In addition to this information, note that during the year, common shares in the amount of $12,900 were issued and $6,300 of the mortgage is currently due.

Instructions

Prepare an income statement, statement of changes in equity, and statement of financial position for the year.

P3–11B The following trial balance of Messed Up Ltd., at the end of its first year of operations, May 31, 2015, does not balance:

Prepare corrected trial balance.
(SO 5)

	Debit	Credit
Cash	$ 2,997	
Accounts receivable	2,630	
Equipment	9,200	
Accumulated depreciation—equipment	4,200	
Accounts payable	4,600	
Common shares	4,250	
Retained earnings, May 31, 2015		$ 2,147
Service revenue		14,529
Salaries expense		8,150
Advertising expense		1,132
Depreciation expense		2,100
Insurance expense		600
Income tax expense		400
	$27,877	$29,058

Each of the listed accounts has a normal balance per the general ledger. However, each account may not have been listed in the appropriate debit or credit column, or may not belong in the trial balance at all. An examination of the general ledger and general journal reveals the following errors:

1. Prepaid Insurance, Accounts Payable, and Income Tax Expense were each understated by $100.
2. A transposition (reversal of digits) error was made in Service Revenue. Based on the posting made, the correct balance was $14,259.
3. A $750 dividend paid to shareholders was debited to Salaries Expense and credited to Cash.
4. A $120 collection on account was recorded as a debit to Accounts Payable and a credit to Accounts Receivable.
5. A $2,000 bank loan was signed in exchange for the purchase of equipment. The transaction was neither journalized nor posted.

Instructions
Prepare the correct trial balance.

Broadening Your Perspective

Financial Reporting: *Shoppers Drug Mart*

BYP3–1 The financial statements of **Shoppers Drug Mart** are presented in Appendix A at the end of this book. They contain the following selected accounts:

Analyze the effects of transactions.
(SO 1)

Accounts payable and accrued liabilities	Income tax expense
Accounts receivable	Inventory
Cash	Land
Dividends	Sales

Instructions
(a) Identify the type (assets, liabilities, or shareholders' equity) of account for each of the above. For any shareholders' equity accounts, indicate whether the account is a dividend, revenue, or expense.
(b) What is the increase (debit or credit) and decrease (debit or credit) side for each account? What is the normal balance for each account?
(c) Identify the probable other account(s) in each transaction listed below and the effect on that (those) other account(s) when:
   1. Dividends are paid.
   2. Income tax is paid.
   3. Inventory is purchased on account.
   4. Land is purchased by signing a bank loan payable.
   5. Sales are made on account.
(d) In which financial statement (statement of earnings, statement of changes in shareholders' equity, or balance sheet) is each account included?

Comparative Analysis: *Shoppers Drug Mart and Jean Coutu*

Prepare expanded accounting equation.
(SO 2)

BYP3–2 The financial statements of **Jean Coutu** are presented in Appendix B following the financial statements for **Shoppers Drug Mart** in Appendix A.

Instructions

(a) Using Shoppers Drug Mart's financial statements, put the total amount classifications provided for assets, liabilities, and shareholders' equity into the accounting equation format as at December 29, 2012. In other words, insert the appropriate total amounts for total assets = total liabilities + total shareholders' equity. Further break down shareholders' equity into its total component parts.

(b) Using Jean Coutu's financial statements, put the total amount classifications provided for assets, liabilities, and shareholders' equity into the accounting equation format as at March 2, 2013. Further breakdown shareholders' equity into its total component parts. (*Hint:* Use the statement of changes in equity.)

Comparing IFRS and ASPE

Understand the accounting information system.
(SO 1, 3, 4)

BYP3–3 **CREIT (Canadian Real Estate Investment Trust)** is a real-estate property management company. Its properties include retail, office, and industrial centres across Canada and in the U.S. It is a publicly accountable enterprise whose shares trade on the Toronto Stock Exchange.

First Pro Shopping Centres, which operates under the banner "Smartcentres," is also a real-estate property management company. First Pro Shopping Centres is a privately held company and holds properties across Canada, with a concentration in Ontario.

Instructions

(a) One of the companies mentioned above prepares its financial statements using International Financial Reporting Standards (IFRS), while the other uses Accounting Standards for Private Enterprises (ASPE). Which company reports under IFRS? Why?

(b) Are the users of the financial statements of each company listed above different? Do you think this influences the type of accounting standards that each company uses?

(c) In light of your answer to (b) above, which company is more likely to have the more sophisticated accounting information system? Explain.

(d) Could either of the companies mentioned above maintain accounting records without using a journal or a ledger? Would this be efficient?

Critical Thinking Case

Analyze and record transactions; prepare financial statements; answer questions.
(SO 1, 2, 3, 4, 5)

BYP3–4 Melissa Young had always been encouraged by her accounting professor to apply her accounting skills as much as possible. When her uncle asked her to prepare his accounting records for a company he owns, called Uncle Bob's Repairs Ltd., she readily agreed.

The company has two employees who repair and service all computers used by four large companies in the area. Melissa spoke to her professor who suggested that, due to the size of the business, she could record the company's transactions on a spreadsheet with the column headings representing the names of accounts that would appear in order on the income statement and statement of financial position. Each row of the spreadsheet could act like a journal entry. In addition, each column could act like a T account showing all debit and credit entries to an account. Melissa could add up the columns on the spreadsheet to determine the balance in each account at the end of the year. She could then build her financial statements on the spreadsheet by referencing the amounts for each item or category on the financial statements from the column totals.

Her uncle gave her the following information regarding its first year of operations, ending August 31, 2015:

1. When the corporation was formed on September 1, 2014, common shares were sold to Uncle Bob for $10,000 cash.
2. Uncle Bob added up all of the invoices the company issued to its customers and the total came to $229,400. All of these were issued on credit.
3. The company received $190,000 cash from customers when they paid their invoices.
4. The company rents a small repair shop for $3,500 per month. The shop was rented for the full year and all rent was paid in cash. In addition, the landlord required the company to pay one month's rent in advance.
5. Salaries to employees totalled $120,000 for the year and were paid in cash.
6. Uncle Bob determined from a review of numerous invoices that the office expenses for the year were $36,400. Of these, all were paid except $4,000 that was still owing.
7. In late August 2015, a new customer approached the company and signed a contract for service to be done to its computers starting in October 2015. The customer paid the company $2,000 in advance to secure the service.
8. Uncle Bob estimated that given the profit earned by the company this year, income tax expense should be $6,200 but this would not have to be paid for another two months.
9. The company paid Uncle Bob a dividend amounting to $1,000 at the end of the year.

Instructions

(a) Prepare a tabular analysis of the effects of the above transactions on the expanded accounting equation. If you have access to spreadsheet software, prepare the analysis on a spreadsheet as suggested. If not, prepare the analysis manually as shown in the chapter.

(b) Do you think that a spreadsheet could be used as described above and replace the requirement to journalize and post transactions? Explain.

(c) Prepare an income statement, statement of changes in equity, and statement of financial position for the year.

(d) There were seven transactions that affected cash. Which of these related to operating activities? What was their total effect? What would Uncle Bob think about the operating cash flow? Which cash flows would be considered financing activities? Did the company need these cash flows?

(e) The company could not borrow any money from a bank to help start operations. Why do you think this happened?

(f) If the income taxes were due next week, would the company be able to pay them?

(g) Why does the company have to pay income tax? Should Uncle Bob pay tax on any of the profit earned by the company?

Ethics Case

BYP3–5 Ron Hollister is a member of a group of students who have been given an accounting assignment by their professor. Ron is responsible for the portion of the assignment that requires the preparation of the trial balance and the financial statements. The assignment is due within an hour and Ron is working alone. All he has to do is complete his part of the assignment and hand the entire document in for grading. He has just prepared the trial balance and found out that it does not balance. The total credits are greater than the total debits by $810.

Without telling the other members of the group, Ron forces the trial balance to balance by adding $810 to the general and administrative expense because it was the largest expense and he hoped no one would notice the difference. He wished that he had a few more hours to find out why the trial balance did not balance, but he knows he can't miss the deadline for handing in the assignment.

Discuss ethical issues related to trial balance errors.
(SO 5)

Instructions

(a) Who are the stakeholders in this situation?

(b) What ethical issues are involved?

(c) What are Ron's alternatives?

(d) Would your answer change if Ron was a professional accountant and was preparing financial statements for a public company?

"All About You" Activity

BYP3–6 In this chapter, you learned the features of accounting information systems that companies use to keep track of their important financial information. Let's now apply these same concepts to your personal financial information.

Discuss personal accounting systems.
(SO 1, 3)

Instructions

(a) Why is it important that you develop a system to maintain and keep your personal and financial records up to date?

(b) How would you organize such a system for yourself?

(c) What would you do if you lost your wallet with your credit cards and identification inside?

Serial Case

(*Note:* This is a continuation of the serial case from Chapters 1 and 2.)

BYP3–7 On June 1, 2014, Natalie becomes both a shareholder and chief administrator of operations of Koebel's Family Bakery Ltd. After much discussion with her parents, Janet and Brian, Natalie decides not to accept the Biscuits retail chain's offer to supply oatmeal chocolate chip cookies. At this point, Natalie believes that it is best to focus on providing Coffee Beans, the national coffee shop, with all of its cupcake requirements. After becoming comfortable with Coffee Beans' contractual commitment and determining the extent of oven space available, Natalie and Koebel's Family Bakery can then reconsider the Biscuits offer.

Record and post transactions; prepare trial balance.
(SO 3, 4, 5)

Natalie obtains a copy of Koebel's Family Bakery Ltd.'s trial balance at June 30 to become familiar with the organization's accounting records.

KOEBEL'S FAMILY BAKERY LTD.
Trial Balance
June 30, 2014

	Debit	Credit
Cash	$ 39,004	
Accounts receivable	5,900	
Merchandise inventory	16,250	
Supplies	1,875	
Prepaid insurance	12,000	
Land	100,000	

(*continued*)

	Debit	Credit
Buildings	165,000	
Accumulated		
depreciation—buildings		$137,500
Equipment	42,000	
Accumulated		
depreciation—equipment		14,000
Vehicles	52,500	
Accounts payable		3,540
Unearned revenue		100
Bank loan payable		22,500
Mortgage payable		53,200
Common shares		300
Retained earnings		66,788
Dividends	30,000	
Rent revenue		6,000
Sales		638,768
Sales returns and allowances	5,000	
Cost of goods sold	102,386	
Salaries expense	287,532	
Freight out	18,000	
Utilities expense	12,000	
Advertising expense	9,000	
Property tax expense	5,950	
Interest expense	5,299	
Income tax expense	33,000	
Total	$942,696	$942,696

While a number of transactions have already been recorded and posted for the month of June, there are other transactions listed below that have not yet been recorded in the accounting records:

June	2	A one-year insurance policy is purchased for $15,360. This policy represents property insurance on the buildings and equipment for the period June 1, 2014 to June 30, 2015. (The balance in the Prepaid Insurance account represents a one-year vehicle-insurance policy on a delivery truck, recorded in the Vehicles account, purchased on January 1.)
	5	Natalie attends to the receipt of advertising supplies. 5,000 brochures were purchased on account from Nakhooda Printing for $2,500. (*Hint:* Use the Supplies account.)
	16	Koebel's Family Bakery purchases baking equipment for $2,520 cash to accommodate the production of cupcakes. (*Hint:* Use the Equipment account.)
	18	Natalie's good friend is getting married in July and wants Koebel's Family Bakery to provide a wedding cake and cupcakes for the wedding celebration. A $500 cash deposit is received in advance.
	19	Natalie teaches a cookie-making class that was booked a number of months ago. A $100 deposit had been received in advance and is included in the Unearned Revenue account. $300 is collected in cash at the end of the class, representing the remaining balance due.
June	20	The first order for the preparation of 200 dozen miniature cupcakes is received from Coffee Beans. Natalie supervises the preparation of these cupcakes. She ensures that there are adequate amounts of baking ingredients on hand and that the order is appropriately filled.
	23	200 dozen cupcakes are delivered to the Coffee Beans warehouse in Calgary. An invoice of $2,040 for the preparation of these cupcakes is included.
	27	A $100 invoice for use of Natalie's cell phone is received. The cell phone is used exclusively for Koebel's Family Bakery's business. The invoice is for services provided in June and is due on July 15. (*Hint:* Use the Utilities Expense account.)
	30	Natalie receives her first paycheque from Koebel's Family Bakery, $3,250.
	30	250 dozen cupcakes are delivered to the Coffee Beans warehouse in Calgary. An invoice of $2,550 for the preparation of these cupcakes is included.

Instructions

(a) Using T accounts, enter the opening balances in the general ledger as at June 30.

(b) Journalize the above transactions.

(c) Post the journal entries to the general ledger.

(d) Prepare an updated trial balance at June 30.

Answers to Self-Test Questions

1. b   2. c   3. c   4. d   5. b
6. a   7. c   8. d   9. a   10. c

Remember to go back to the beginning of the chapter to check off your completed work!

←

Endnotes

[1] "History," company website, www.beavertailsinc.com; Philip Fine, "A Sweet Story of Success," *The Montreal Gazette*, February 7, 2013, p. A28; "Canada's BeaverTails Travels to Switzerland for the World Economic Forum," company news release, January 15, 2011.

[2] "Protect Yourself against Identify Theft," Canada Revenue Agency, www.cra-arc.gc.ca/E/pub/tg/rc284/rc284-09e.pdf, retrieved May 17, 2013; Katherine Scarrow, "Young more Susceptible to Fraud than Old. Surprised?," *Globe and Mail*, March 5, 2012, updated September 10, 2012; "How to Protect Yourself from Identity Theft," Canada Post, http://www.canadapost.ca/cpo/mr/assets/pdf/aboutus/identitytheft_en.pdf, retrieved May 21, 2013.

Comprehensive Case: Chapters 1–3

Software Advisors Limited was organized on January 1, 2015. The company plans to use the following chart of accounts:

1000	Cash	4500	Retained Earnings
1100	Accounts Receivable	5000	Service Revenue
1200	Supplies	7000	Advertising Expense
1300	Prepaid Insurance	7100	Salaries Expense
2000	Equipment	7200	Interest Expense
3000	Accounts Payable	7300	Office Expense
3100	Bank Loan Payable	7400	Rent Expense
4000	Common Shares	9000	Income Tax Expense

Record and post transactions; prepare trial balance and financial statements.
(SO 3, 4, 5)

The company had the following transactions in the month of January:

January	2	Issued 1,000 common shares for $15 each.
	3	Borrowed $50,000 from the bank on a long-term loan.
	4	Finalized the lease for office space and paid the first month's rent of $3,000.
	5	Purchased $40,000 of equipment for $20,000 cash and $20,000 on account.
	10	Paid for an advertisement in a local paper, $500.
	11	Purchased supplies on account, $1,000.
	13	Paid for several advertising spots on the local radio station, $3,000.
	15	Paid employees $7,500 for the first two weeks of work.
	17	Summarized and recorded the billings to clients for the first two weeks of January. Billings totalled $15,000. These amounts are due by the 10th of the next month.
	20	Paid $1,000 for the current month's office expenses.
	24	Received $10,000 from clients in partial settlement of accounts billed on the 17th.
	30	Paid annual insurance policy with coverage up to February 1, 2016, for $6,000.
	30	Summarized and recorded the billings to clients for the last two weeks of January. Billings totalled $18,000. These amounts are due by the 28th of the next month.
	31	Paid employees $7,500 for the last two weeks of work.
	31	Made a payment to the bank of $300 for interest on the bank loan and $700 to pay on the amount owing for the bank loan.
	31	Paid Canada Revenue Agency $1,200 for an income tax instalment.

Instructions

(a) Journalize the January transactions.
(b) Set up T accounts and post the journal entries prepared in (a).
(c) Prepare a trial balance at January 31.
(d) Prepare an income statement, statement of changes in equity, and statement of financial position for January.

Accrual Accounting Concepts

the navigator

study objectives

After studying this chapter, you should be able to:

SO 1 Explain when revenues and expenses are recognized and how this forms the basis for accrual accounting.

SO 2 Describe the types of adjusting entries and prepare adjusting entries for prepayments.

SO 3 Prepare adjusting entries for accruals.

SO 4 Prepare an adjusted trial balance.

SO 5 Prepare closing entries and a post-closing trial balance.

School's Out, Time to Balance the Books

At Western University in London, Ontario, as at campuses across the country, classes for most students start in September and end in April. Likewise, the university's fiscal year end is April 30. So essentially, the university closes its books at the same time the students do. This cohesion helps the university to satisfy the criteria needed to recognize revenues and expenses at the appropriate time when services are performed and expenses incurred, respectively.

However, many students at Western take intersession courses. They pay their course fees before the year end of April 30, but the courses don't start until May or later. "We would get intersession fees and other fees in advance of our year end, so there is a deferral there," says Carter Scott, Western's controller. The university defers the recognition of that revenue until the following accounting period, the one in which it provides the teaching services.

Another example of the deferral of revenue is the advance fees students pay for residence admission to hold their spot for the coming year. The university defers recognition of this revenue until the start of the academic year in September, when the students move into the residences.

Research activities provide another example. Western receives more than $150 million per year in external revenues for research projects, making research an integral part of the university's activities. "In a lot of cases, granting agencies' year ends are in March, so they send the funds in at the beginning of March," Mr. Scott points out. "For any faculty member who gets a grant, it's deferred until they start expending it, because it's restricted for that purpose. Restricted revenues for which the related expenses have not been incurred are reported as unearned revenue on the university's balance sheet." The grant money is matched against expenses incurred over the course of the research project, which could go on for years.

Expenses, too, must be recorded in the year in which they were incurred. "Post-employment benefits, at most universities, are a very large number that you accrue for," Mr. Scott explains. Other expenses that would have to be accrued at year end include vacation pay, outstanding salary for the approximately 3,800 full-time faculty and staff members, and utility bills.

"Accrual accounting is considered the most appropriate method of financial reporting because revenues and expenses are recognized in the period to which they relate, regardless of whether there has been a receipt or payment of cash," Mr. Scott explains. "A more meaningful picture of financial position and operations is provided under accrual accounting than on a cash flow basis."

Recording revenues and expenses in the correct period is a challenge, but one that must be met to best reflect the various activities of a large university like Western.[1]

the navigator

preview of
CHAPTER | 4

In Chapter 3, we examined the first four steps of the accounting cycle, which included the recording process up to and including the preparation of the trial balance. Although we prepared financial statements directly from the trial balance in that chapter, additional steps are necessary to properly update the accounts before the financial statements are prepared.

In this chapter, we introduce you to the accrual basis accounting concepts that guide the recognition of revenue and expenses in the appropriate time period. We will also describe the remaining steps in the accounting cycle.

The chapter is organized as follows:

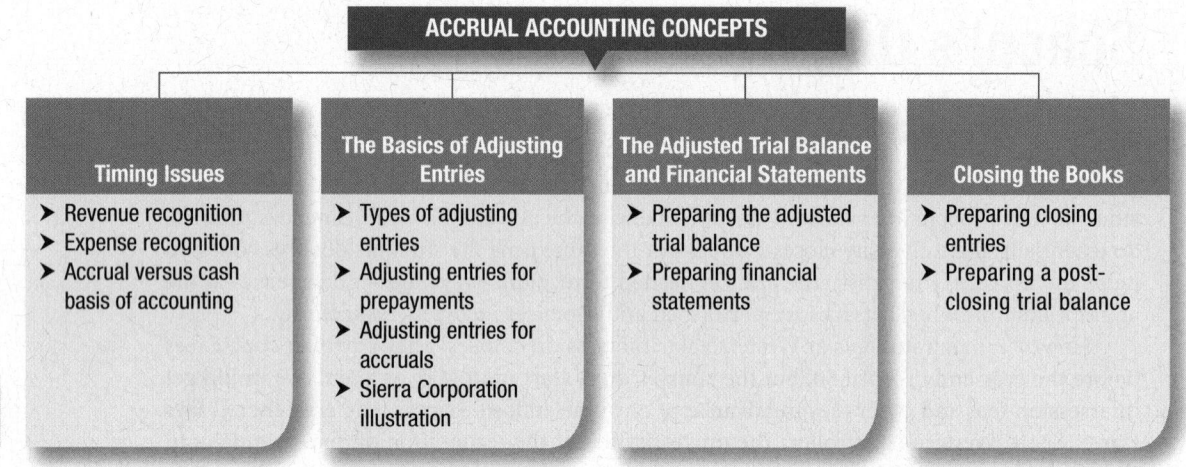

Timing Issues

STUDY OBJECTIVE 1

Explain when revenues and expenses are recognized and how this forms the basis for accrual accounting.

Accounting would be simple if we could wait until a company ended its operations to prepare its financial statements. As the following anecdote shows, if we waited until then we could easily determine the amount of lifetime profit earned:

A grocery store owner from the old country kept his accounts payable on a spindle, accounts receivable on a notepad, and cash in a box. His daughter, an accountant, chided him: "I don't understand how you can run your business this way. How do you know what you've earned?"

"Well," the father replied, "when I arrived in Canada 40 years ago, I had nothing but the clothes I was wearing. Today your sister is a doctor, your brother is a teacher, and you are an accountant. Your mother and I have a nice car, a well-furnished house, and a cottage at the lake. We have a good business and everything is paid for. So, you add all that together, subtract the clothes, and there's your profit."

Although the grocer may be correct in his evaluation of how to calculate profit over his lifetime, most companies need more immediate feedback about how well they are doing. For example, management needs monthly reports on financial results, publicly traded corporations present quarterly and annual financial statements to shareholders, and the Canada Revenue Agency requires these businesses to file monthly sales tax reports and annual income tax returns.

Consequently, accounting divides the economic life of a business into artificial time periods. Accounting time periods are generally one month, one quarter (three months), or one year. You will recall from Chapter 1 that accounting time periods of one year are known as a fiscal year; shorter time periods are known as **interim periods**.

Many accounting transactions affect more than one of these arbitrary time periods. For example, we saw in the feature story that research grants received by faculty at Western University can span multiple years. We also saw how Western collects intersession course fees in one fiscal year but delivers the courses in the next fiscal year. Determining the amount of revenue and expenses to report in a particular accounting period can be difficult. Accounting standards are therefore necessary to determine when we should recognize revenues and expenses.

REVENUE RECOGNITION

Revenue is generally considered to be earned (recognized) when goods or services are exchanged for cash or claims to cash (such as accounts receivable), which results in an increase in future economic benefits, as we learned in Chapter 2. You will also recall from our discussion of the elements of financial statements in Chapter 2 that revenues arise in the course of "ordinary" activities, such as the sale of merchandise in a merchandising company or the provision of services in a service company. Revenues can also arise from other activities, such as rent revenue, investment income (from sources such as interest or dividends), and gains on sale.

Alternative Terminology
Revenue is also known as *income*.

Although companies expect to receive cash in exchange for goods sold or services performed, it is *not* the receipt of cash that dictates when revenue is recognized. Rather, **revenue recognition** occurs when three conditions are met:

1. the sales or performance effort is substantially complete,
2. the revenue amount is determinable (measurable), and
3. the collection of the revenue is reasonably assured.

In a merchandising company, revenue is recognized (recorded) when the merchandise is sold (normally at the point of sale). In a service company, revenue is recognized (recorded) at the time the service is performed. Regardless of whether cash is received at the point of sale or delivery of service or expected to be received at some point in future, the revenue is recognized when earned; that is, when the above three conditions have been met.

To illustrate, assume a consulting company provided services to a client on account after doing a detailed credit check. The services were performed in September. In October, the company sent the client an invoice, and in November, the company received payment from the client. In what month should the revenue be recorded by the consulting company? The answer is September because that was when the service was performed and consequently the revenue was earned. An asset account, Accounts Receivable, would be increased, as would a revenue account, Service Revenue. At that time, the amount of the revenue could be measured because, even though an invoice had not been prepared, the price would have been known and agreed to by both parties. Furthermore, the revenue and any related accounts receivable are likely to be collected.

The International Accounting Standards Board and Financial Accounting Standards Board in the United States have a joint project under way to clarify the principles for recognizing revenue and to develop a common revenue standard for the two bodies. This project is in the process of being finalized at the time of writing and is expected to become effective for reporting periods commencing January 1, 2017.

DECISION TOOLKIT

Decision Checkpoints	 Info Needed for Decision	 Tools to Use for Decision	 How to Evaluate Results
At what point should the company record revenue?	Need to understand the nature of the company's business, in particular when the sales or performance effort is considered to be complete.	Revenue should be recorded when earned; that is, when the sales or performance effort is complete, the revenue amount determined, and collection anticipated.	Recognizing revenue too early overstates current period revenue; recognizing it too late understates current period revenue.

EXPENSE RECOGNITION

Recall from Chapter 2 that expenses are the costs of assets that are consumed or services used in a company's ordinary business activities. Expenses are tied to changes in assets and liabilities. When an expense is incurred, an asset will decrease or a liability will increase. Consequently, just as revenues are related to increases in future economic benefits, expenses are related to decreases in future economic benefits.

Expense recognition is linked to revenue recognition when there is a direct association between the expenses incurred and the generation of revenue. This is commonly known as **matching** as the effort (expenses) is matched with the results (revenues). And, similar to revenue recognition, expense recognition is not tied to the payment of cash. Expenses are recognized when incurred regardless of whether cash is paid or not.

Consider again the consulting business mentioned in the last section. During the month of September, company employees provided services to a client. Because of this, the company owes these employees salaries. This obligation creates an increase in a liability, Salaries Payable (or a decrease in an asset, Cash), and a corresponding increase in an expense, Salaries Expense. In this case and in the case of Western University, described in our feature story, the expenses were recognized in the same month as the revenues because the expenses were incurred at the same time and contributed to the earning of the revenue. This does not mean that revenues and expenses are always recognized at the same time.

Sometimes, it is not possible to directly associate expenses with revenue. For example, if a company rented office space, each month the rent would be due and this would increase a liability, Rent Payable (or decrease an asset, Cash) and increase an expense, Rent Expense, even if the company earned no revenue in a particular month. It is also difficult to match interest expense with the revenue this finance cost might help earn. Other examples include costs that help generate revenue over multiple periods of time, such as the depreciation of long-lived assets such as equipment. We will learn more about allocating expenses such as these later in this chapter.

DECISION TOOLKIT

Decision Checkpoints	Info Needed for Decision	Tools to Use for Decision	How to Evaluate Results
At what point should the company record expenses?	Need to understand the nature of the company's business and whether the expense can be directly associated with revenue.	Expenses are recognized when assets are decreased or when liabilities are increased. Often expenses can be directly associated with revenues; that is, the effort (expense) should be matched with the result (revenue).	Recognizing expenses too early overstates current period expenses; recognizing them too late understates current period expenses.

ACCRUAL VERSUS CASH BASIS OF ACCOUNTING

The combined application of revenue recognition and expense recognition results in accrual basis accounting. **Accrual basis accounting** means that transactions affecting a company's financial statements are recorded in the periods in which the events occur, rather than when the company actually receives or pays cash. This means recognizing revenues when they are earned rather than only when cash is received. Likewise, expenses are recognized in the period in which goods (such as supplies) are consumed or services (such as employees' labour) are used, rather than only when cash is paid.

An alternative to the accrual basis is the cash basis. Under **cash basis accounting**, revenue is recorded only when cash is received, and an expense is recorded only when cash is paid. Cash basis accounting seems appealing because of its simplicity, but it can result in misleading information for decision-making because it leaves a time gap between the matching of efforts (expenses) with results (revenues).

Suppose that you own a painting company called Colours Paint Barn and you paint a building complex during year 1. In year 1, you incur and pay total expenses of $50,000, which includes the cost of the paint and your employees' salaries. You bill your customer $80,000 at the end of year 1, but you are not paid until year 2. On an accrual basis, you would report the revenue during the period when it is earned—year 1. The expenses would be recognized (recorded) in the period in which the revenues were earned. Thus, your profit for year 1 would be $30,000, and no revenue or expense from this project would be reported in year 2. The $30,000 of profit reported for year 1 provides a useful indication of the profitability of your efforts during that period.

If, instead, you were reporting on a cash basis, you would report expenses of $50,000 in year 1 and revenues of $80,000 in year 2. In year 1 there would be a loss of $50,000, while profit for year 2 would be $80,000.

Illustration 4-1 compares the accrual-based results with the cash-based results for Colours Paint Barn.

▶Illustration 4-1

Accrual versus cash basis accounting

	Year 1		Year 2	
Activity	Purchased paint, painted building complex, paid employees		Received payment for work done in year 1	
Accrual basis	Revenue	$ 80,000	Revenue	$ 0
	Expense	50,000	Expense	0
	Profit	$ 30,000	Profit	$ 0
Cash basis	Revenue	$ 0	Revenue	$80,000
	Expense	50,000	Expense	0
	Loss	$(50,000)	Profit	$80,000

While total profits are the same over the two-year period ($30,000), cash basis measures are not very informative about the results of your efforts during year 1 or year 2. The total overall profit of $30,000 is the result of a loss of $50,000 in year one and a big swing in profit to $80,000 in year 2. As Carter Scott, the controller of Western University in our feature story, said, "Accrual accounting is considered the most appropriate method of financial reporting because revenues and expenses are recognized in the period to which they relate, regardless of whether there has been a receipt or payment of cash. A more meaningful picture of financial position and operations is provided under accrual accounting than on a cash flow basis."

The following schedule summarizes the differences between when revenues and expenses are recognized under the accrual and cash bases of accounting.

	ACCRUAL BASIS OF ACCOUNTING	CASH BASIS OF ACCOUNTING
Revenue is recognized	When earned	When received
Expense is recognized	When incurred (goods are consumed or services used)	When paid

As we learned in Chapter 2, the accrual basis of accounting forms part of the conceptual framework and is required for the preparation of financial statements. Although different accounting standards are sometimes used in other countries, the accrual basis of accounting is central to all of these standards. The cash basis of accounting is not permitted for use in Canada, or in other countries, except in certain circumstances.

ACCOUNTING MATTERS!

Recognizing Revenues and Expenses from the Sale of iPhones

In the past, electronics giant Apple Inc. was required to spread the revenues and product costs from its iPhone sales over a two-year period following the sale of the phone. It was argued that since Apple was obligated to provide software updates after the phone was sold, it should spread the revenue and expenses over the same period. However, since the company received full payment upfront, the cash flows from iPhones significantly exceeded the revenue reported from iPhone sales in each accounting period. It also meant that the rapid growth of iPhone sales was not fully reflected in Apple's income statement.

New accounting requirements, which were adopted by Apple in 2010, changed the way the company accounted for revenue and expenses from the sale of its iPhone and similar products. Now, Apple recognizes revenues and expenses at point of sale—when the iPhone is delivered to the customer. Once the new accounting standard was adopted and applied to prior periods, Apple's revenues from iPhone sales ended up being 17% higher, and its cost of goods sold 10% higher, in 2009 than previously reported.[2]

BEFORE YOU GO ON...

▶Do It! Accrual Basis and Cash Basis Accounting

During the year ended December 31, 2015, Jomerans Corp. collected $125,000 cash from customers, of which $30,000 was for services provided in 2014. At December 31, 2015, customers owed $19,500 for services provided in 2015. Calculate the revenue for 2015 using (a) the cash basis of accounting, and (b) the accrual basis of accounting.

Action Plan
- For the cash basis of accounting, revenue is equal to the cash received.
- For the accrual basis of accounting, report revenue in the period in which it is earned, not when it is collected.
- Under the accrual basis of accounting, cash collected in 2015 for revenue earned in 2014 should not be included in the 2015 revenue.
- Under the accrual basis of accounting, amounts still owing by customers at the end of 2015 for services provided in 2015 should be included in the 2015 revenue.

Solution

(a) Revenue using the cash basis of accounting	$125,000
(b) Cash received from customers in 2015	$125,000
Deduct: Collection of 2014 receivables	(30,000)
Add: Amounts owing at December 31, 2015	19,500
Revenue using the accrual basis of accounting	$114,500

Related Exercise Material: BE4-1, BE4-2, E4-1, and E4-2.

The Basics of Adjusting Entries

For revenues to be recorded in the period in which they are earned, and for expenses to be recorded when incurred, we may have to record **adjusting entries** to update accounts at the end of the accounting period. Adjusting entries ensure that revenue recognition and expense recognition are properly applied and make it possible to produce up-to-date and relevant financial information at the end of the accounting period.

You will recall that we learned the first four steps of the accounting cycle in Chapter 2. Adjusting entries form the next step—Step 5—of the cycle, as shown in Illustration 4-2.

STUDY OBJECTIVE 2

Describe the types of adjusting entries and prepare adjusting entries for prepayments.

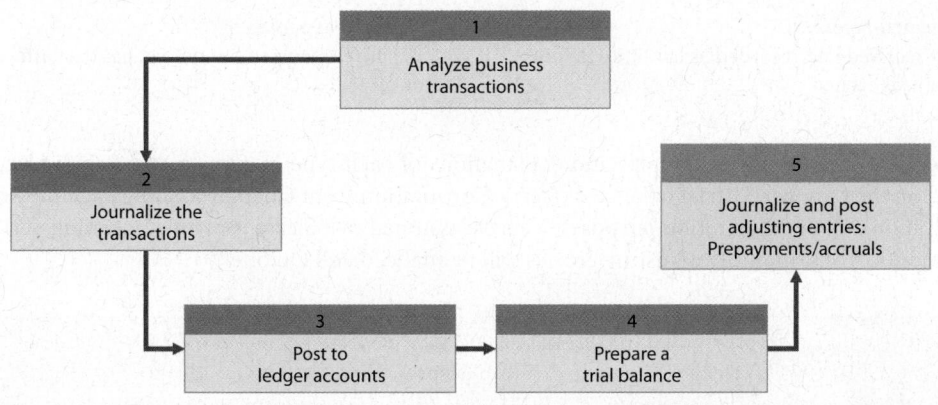

▶Illustration 4-2
The accounting cycle—Steps 1–5

Adjusting entries are necessary because the trial balance—the first pulling together of the transaction data—may not contain complete and up-to-date data. This is true for several reasons:

1. Some events are not recorded daily, because it would not be useful or efficient to do so. Examples are the use of supplies and the earning of salaries by employees.
2. Some costs are not recorded during the accounting period, because these costs expire with the passage of time rather than as a result of recurring daily transactions. Examples include rent, insurance, and depreciation.
3. Some items may be unrecorded. An example is a utility service bill that will not be received until the next accounting period. The bill, however, covers services delivered in the current accounting period.

Adjusting entries are required every time financial statements are prepared. For public corporations, this means at least quarterly as they are required to issue quarterly financial statements. For private corporations, this means at least annually although many companies may choose to record adjusting entries more frequently.

Preparing adjusting entries requires an understanding of the company's operations and the interrelationship of accounts and can be a long and detailed process. For example, to accumulate the adjustment data for supplies, a company may need to count its remaining supplies. It may also need to prepare supporting schedules of insurance policies, rental agreements, and other contractual commitments.

In addition, adjustment data are often not available until after the end of the period. For example, telephone and other bills will not be received until after the month end or year end. In such cases, the data are gathered as soon as possible after the end of the period and adjusting entries are made, but they are still dated at the period end (in other words, the statement of financial position date).

Each account in the trial balance will need to be analyzed to see if it is complete and up to date. Because many of the amounts listed in the trial balance are incomplete until adjusting entries are prepared, this trial balance is commonly referred to as an **unadjusted trial balance**, which simply means it was prepared before adjusting entries have been made.

TYPES OF ADJUSTING ENTRIES

Adjusting entries can be classified as either prepayments or accruals. Each of these classes has two subcategories, as follows:

PREPAYMENTS	ACCRUALS
Prepaid expenses Expenses paid in cash and recorded as assets before they are used	**Accrued revenues** Revenues earned but not yet received in cash or recorded
Unearned revenues Cash received and recorded as liabilities before revenue is earned	**Accrued expenses** Expenses incurred but not yet paid in cash or recorded

Subsequent sections give examples and explanations of each type of adjustment. Each example is based on the October 31 trial balance of Sierra Corporation from Chapter 3, shown again below in Illustration 4-3. For illustration purposes, we have assumed that Sierra uses an accounting period of one month. Thus, monthly adjusting entries will be made, dated October 31.

▶ Illustration 4-3
Unadjusted trial balance

SIERRA CORPORATION Trial Balance October 31, 2015		
	Debit	Credit
Cash	$ 7,400	
Accounts receivable	15,000	
Supplies	2,500	
Prepaid insurance	600	
Equipment	5,000	
Accounts payable		$ 1,500
Unearned revenue		1,200
Bank loan payable		5,000
Common shares		10,000
Dividends	500	
Service revenue		20,000
Salaries expense	4,000	
Rent expense	900	
Income tax expense	1,800	
	$37,700	$37,700

Note that when a trial balance has no preceding adjective in its title, such as "adjusted" trial balance or "post-closing" trial balance (both of which we will learn about in subsequent sections), it is assumed to be an unadjusted trial balance.

ADJUSTING ENTRIES FOR PREPAYMENTS

Alternative Terminology
Prepayments are also known as *deferrals*.

Prepayments increase current assets such as prepaid expenses and also affect certain types of non-current assets such as buildings and equipment. A prepayment can also be received rather than paid, in which case the prepayment increases current liabilities such as unearned revenue. We will look at each of these types of prepayments—prepaid expenses and unearned revenues—in the next sections.

Prepaid Expenses

Costs that are paid for in cash before they are used are recorded as **prepaid expenses**. When such a cost is incurred, an asset (prepaid) account is increased (debited) to show the service or benefit that will be received in the future and cash is decreased (credited). In a few cases, the asset is purchased on account, but ultimately cash is paid.

Prepaid expenses are costs that expire either with the passage of time (such as insurance) or through use (such as supplies). It is not practical to record the expiration of these costs on a daily basis. Instead, we record these expired costs when financial statements are prepared. At each statement date, adjusting entries are made for two purposes: (1) to record the expenses (expired costs) applicable to the current accounting period, and (2) to show the remaining amounts (unexpired costs) in the asset accounts.

The original journal entry to record a prepaid expense normally involves a debit to an asset (prepaid expenses) account and a credit to the Cash account. It can also involve a credit to a payable account, instead of Cash. An adjusting entry for prepaid expenses is required to recognize the expense and reduction of the asset (prepaid expenses). Consequently, adjusting entries for prepaid expenses result in an increase (a debit) to an expense account and a decrease (a credit) to an asset (prepaid expenses) account, as shown below.

> **Helpful Hint**
> A cost can be an asset or an expense. If the cost has future benefits (that is, the benefits have not yet expired), it is an asset. If the cost has no future benefits (that is, the benefits have expired), it is an expense.

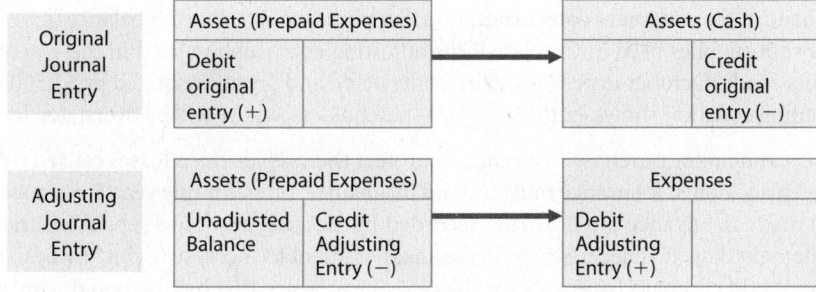

Until prepaid expenses are adjusted, assets are overstated and expenses are understated. If expenses are understated, then profit and shareholders' equity will be overstated.

In the following sections, we will look at three examples of prepaid expenses, beginning with supplies.

Supplies.   The purchase of supplies, such as paper and envelopes, results in an increase (a debit) to an asset (Supplies) account. During the accounting period, supplies are used. Rather than record supplies expense as the supplies are used, supplies expense is recognized at the end of the accounting period. At that time, the company must count the remaining supplies. The difference between the balance in the supplies (asset) account and the actual cost of supplies on hand gives the supplies used (an expense) for that period.

Recall from Chapter 3 that Sierra Corporation purchased supplies costing $2,500 on October 9. This is an example of a prepayment made on account, rather than by cash. The payment was recorded by increasing (debiting) the asset account Supplies and increasing (crediting) the liability account Accounts Payable. The Supplies account therefore shows a balance of $2,500 in the October 31 trial balance. A count at the close of business on October 31 reveals that $1,000 of supplies are still on hand. Thus, the cost of supplies used is $1,500 ($2,500 − $1,000).

The following illustration outlines the basic analysis, similar to that shown in Chapter 3, used to determine the appropriate adjusting entry to record and post. Note that the debit–credit rules you learned in Chapter 3 also apply to adjusting and other types of journal entries.

▶Adjustment (1)
Prepaid expenses—supplies

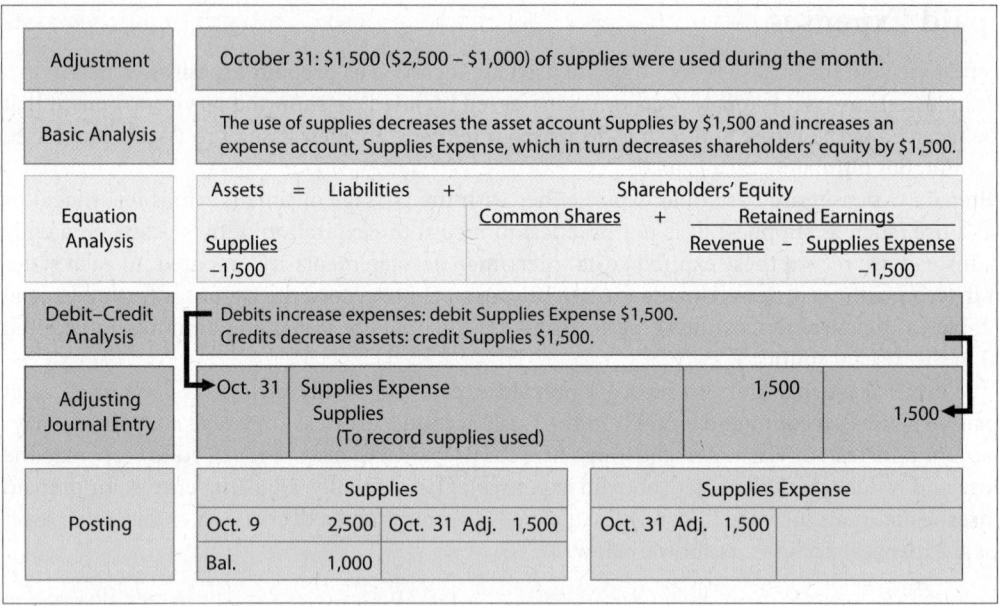

After adjustment, the asset account Supplies shows a balance of $1,000, which is equal to the cost of supplies on hand at the statement date. In addition, Supplies Expense shows a balance of $1,500, which equals the cost of supplies used in October. If the adjusting entry (abbreviated in the T account above as "Adj.") is not made, October expenses will be understated and profit overstated by $1,500. Moreover, as the accounting equation shows, both assets and shareholders' equity will be overstated by $1,500.

Insurance.   Companies purchase insurance to protect themselves from losses caused by fire, theft, and unforeseen accidents. Insurance must be paid in advance, often for one year. Insurance payments (premiums) made in advance are normally recorded in the asset account Prepaid Insurance. At the financial statement date, it is necessary to make an adjustment to increase (debit) Insurance Expense and decrease (credit) Prepaid Insurance for the cost of insurance that has expired during the period.

On October 5, Sierra Corporation paid $600 for a one-year insurance policy. Coverage began on October 1. The payment was recorded by increasing (debiting) Prepaid Insurance when it was paid. This account shows a balance of $600 in the October 31 trial balance. An analysis of the insurance policy reveals that $50 of insurance expires each month ($600 ÷ 12 months). The expiration of the prepaid insurance would be recorded as follows:

▶Adjustment (2)
Prepaid expenses—insurance

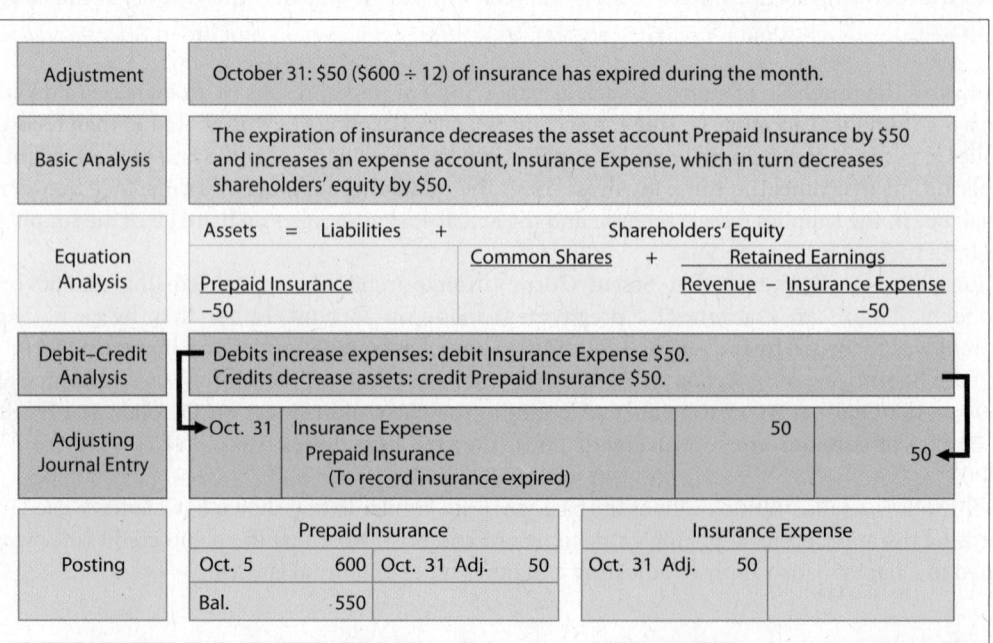

After adjustment, the asset Prepaid Insurance shows a balance of $550, which represents the cost that applies to the remaining 11 months of insurance coverage (11 × $50). At the same time, the balance in Insurance Expense is equal to the insurance cost that was used in October. If this adjustment is not made, October expenses will be understated and profit overstated by $50. Moreover, both assets and shareholders' equity will be overstated by $50.

Depreciation. A company typically owns a variety of assets that have long lives, such as buildings and equipment. Each one is recorded as an asset, rather than as an expense, in the year it is acquired because these long-lived assets provide a service for many years. The period of service is called the **useful life**.

From an accounting standpoint, the acquisition of certain types of long-lived assets is essentially a long-term prepayment for services. Similar to other prepaid expenses, there is a need to recognize the cost that has been used (an expense) during the period and to report the unused cost (an asset) at the end of the period. **Depreciation** is the process of allocating the cost of a long-lived or non-current asset, such as buildings and equipment, to expense over its useful life. Only assets with specified useful lives are depreciated. We call them *depreciable assets*. When an asset, such as land, has an unlimited useful life, it is not depreciated.

While the term *depreciation* is normally used in relation to property, plant, and equipment, the term *amortization* is used in relation to intangible assets. These terms mean the same thing—the allocation of the cost of a long-lived asset to expense over its useful life. We will learn about amortizing intangible assets in Chapter 9. As was mentioned in Chapter 2, some companies use the term *amortization* in place of *depreciation*, especially private companies reporting under ASPE.

One point about depreciation is very important to understand: depreciation is an allocation concept, not a valuation concept. That is, we depreciate an asset to allocate its cost to the periods over which we use it. We are not trying to record a change in the actual value of the asset.

Calculation of Depreciation. A common practice for calculating depreciation expense for a period of time is to divide the cost of the asset by its useful life. This is known as the **straight-line method of depreciation**. Of course, at the time an asset is acquired, its useful life is not known with any certainty. It must therefore be estimated. Because of this, depreciation is an estimate rather than a factual measurement of the cost that has expired.

Sierra Corporation purchased equipment that cost $5,000 on October 1. If its useful life is expected to be five years, annual depreciation is $1,000 ($5,000 ÷ 5). Illustration 4-4 shows the formula to calculate depreciation expense in its simplest form. The formula to calculate straight-line depreciation will be refined to include residual value at the end of the useful life in Chapter 9, and other methods of depreciation will also be introduced at that time.

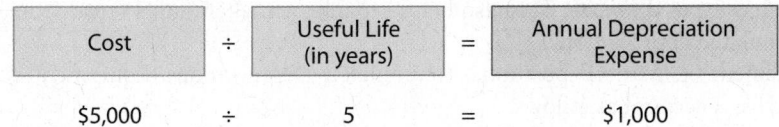

▶Illustration 4-4
Formula for straight-line depreciation

Of course, if you are calculating depreciation for partial periods, the annual expense amount must be adjusted for the portion of the year that the asset was used. For example, if we wish to determine the depreciation for one month, we would multiply the annual result by one-twelfth as there are 12 months in a year. For Sierra Corporation, depreciation on the equipment is estimated to be $83 per month ($1,000 × 1/12). Accordingly, depreciation for October is recognized as follows:

▸Adjustment (3)
Prepaid expenses—depreciation

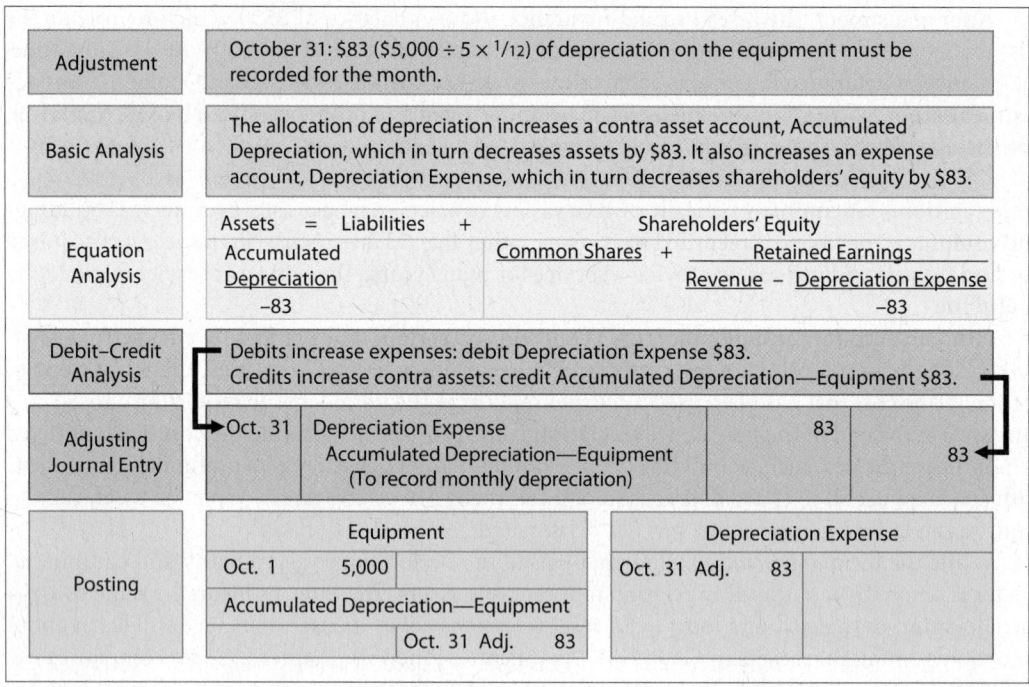

Adjustment	October 31: $83 ($5,000 ÷ 5 × $^1/_{12}$) of depreciation on the equipment must be recorded for the month.		
Basic Analysis	The allocation of depreciation increases a contra asset account, Accumulated Depreciation, which in turn decreases assets by $83. It also increases an expense account, Depreciation Expense, which in turn decreases shareholders' equity by $83.		

Equation Analysis

Assets	=	Liabilities	+	Shareholders' Equity		
Accumulated Depreciation				Common Shares +		Retained Earnings
					Revenue −	Depreciation Expense
−83						−83

Debit–Credit Analysis	Debits increase expenses: debit Depreciation Expense $83. Credits increase contra assets: credit Accumulated Depreciation—Equipment $83.	

Adjusting Journal Entry	Oct. 31	Depreciation Expense	83	
		Accumulated Depreciation—Equipment		83
		(To record monthly depreciation)		

Posting

Equipment			Depreciation Expense	
Oct. 1 5,000			Oct. 31 Adj. 83	
Accumulated Depreciation—Equipment				
	Oct. 31 Adj. 83			

The balance in the Accumulated Depreciation account will increase by $83 each month until the asset is fully depreciated in five years. Accumulated depreciation represents the cumulative total of the depreciation expense since the asset was purchased, less any reductions when assets are sold (which we will learn about in Chapter 9).

As in the case of other prepaid expenses, if this adjusting entry is not made, depreciation expense will be understated and profit overstated by $83. Total assets and shareholders' equity will also be overstated by $83.

Helpful Hint
Every contra account has increases, decreases, and normal balances that are opposite to those of the account it relates to.

Statement Presentation of Depreciation.   As we learned in Chapter 2, a contra account is an account that is offset against (deducted from) a related account on the income statement or statement of financial position. Accumulated Depreciation—Equipment is a **contra asset account**. That means it is offset against an asset account, Equipment, on the statement of financial position. Its normal balance is a credit—the opposite of the normal debit balance of its related account, Equipment.

There is a simple reason for using a separate contra account instead of decreasing (crediting) Equipment: using this account discloses both the original cost of the equipment and the total estimated cost that has expired to date. This also helps separate actual amounts (cost) from estimated amounts (accumulated depreciation).

In the statement of financial position, Accumulated Depreciation—Equipment is deducted from the related asset account as follows:

Equipment	$5,000
Less: Accumulated depreciation—equipment	83
Carrying amount	4,917

The difference between the cost of a depreciable asset and its related accumulated depreciation is referred to as the **carrying amount** of that asset. The carrying amount is also commonly known as net book value, or simply book value. In the above illustration, the equipment's carrying amount at the statement of financial position date is $4,917. Be sure to understand that, except at acquisition, the asset's carrying amount and its fair value (the price at which it could be sold) are two different amounts. As noted earlier, the purpose of depreciation is not to state an asset's value, but to allocate its cost over time.

The following summarizes the accounting for prepaid expenses.

PREPAID EXPENSES				
Original Transaction	Examples	Reasons for Adjustment	Accounts before Adjustment	Adjusting Entry
Expenses paid in cash and recorded as assets before they are used	Insurance, supplies, advertising, rent, depreciation	Prepaid expenses recorded in asset accounts have been used	Expenses understated; Assets overstated	Dr. Expense Cr. Asset

Unearned Revenue

When cash is received in advance for items like rent, magazine subscriptions, and customer deposits—received for services that will be provided in the future—it results in **unearned revenues**. Cash is increased (debited) and the liability account Unearned Revenue increased (credited) to recognize that the company has received cash in advance and has an obligation to provide a service in the future, or refund the cash. Airlines, such as Air Canada, treat cash received from the sale of tickets as unearned revenue until the flight service is provided. Similarly, tuition fees received by universities before the academic session begins are considered unearned revenue, as at Western University in our feature story.

Alternative Terminology
Unearned revenues are also called *deferred revenues.*

Unearned revenues are the opposite of prepaid expenses. Indeed, unearned revenue on the books of one company is likely to be a prepaid expense on the books of the company that has made the advance payment. For example, if identical accounting periods are assumed, your landlord will have unearned rent revenue when you (the tenant) have prepaid rent.

It is not practical to make daily journal entries as the revenue is earned. Instead, recognition of earned revenue is delayed until the adjustment process. At that time, an adjusting entry is then made to record the revenue that has been earned during the period and to show the liability that remains at the end of the accounting period.

As shown below, the original journal entry to record unearned revenues results in an increase (debit) to the asset (cash) and an increase (credit) to the liability (unearned revenue). The subsequent adjusting entry results in a decrease (debit) to the liability (unearned revenue) account and an increase (credit) to a revenue account.

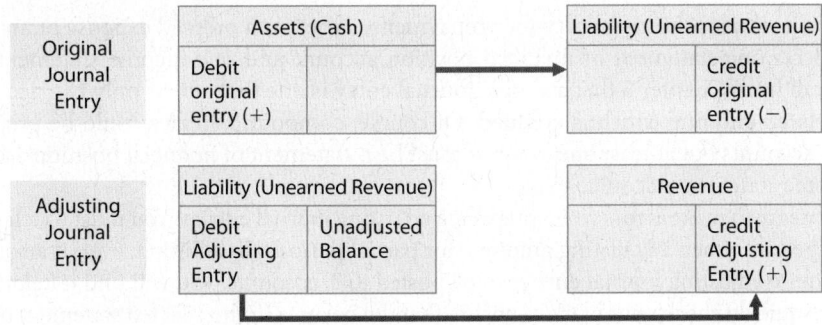

Typically, until the adjustment is made, liabilities are overstated and revenues are understated. If revenues are understated, then profit and shareholders' equity are also understated.

Returning to our example, we note that Sierra Corporation received $1,200 on October 19 from R. Knox for advertising services expected to be completed in the next month, November. The payment was credited to Unearned Revenue, and this liability account shows a balance of $1,200 in the October 31 trial balance. From a review of the work performed by Sierra for Knox during October, it is determined that $400 worth of work was done in October.

After adjustment, the liability Unearned Revenue shows a balance of $800, which represents the remaining advertising services expected to be performed in the future. At the same time, Service Revenue shows total revenue earned in October of $20,400. If this adjustment is not made, revenues and profit will be understated by $400. Moreover, liabilities will be overstated by $400 and shareholders' equity will also be understated by that amount.

▸Adjustment (4)
Unearned revenues—services

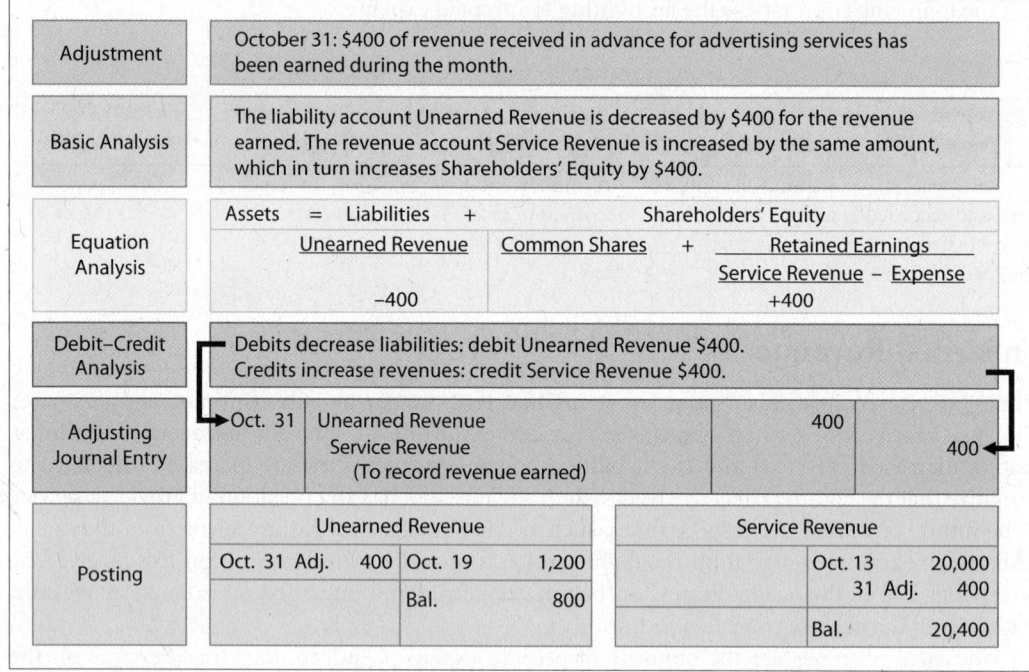

The following summarizes the accounting for unearned revenues.

UNEARNED REVENUE				
Original Transaction	Examples	Reasons for Adjustment	Accounts before Adjustment	Adjusting Entry
Cash received and recorded as liabilities before revenue is earned	Rent, magazine subscriptions, customer deposits for future service	Unearned revenues recorded in liability accounts have been earned	Liabilities overstated; Revenues understated	Dr. Liability Cr. Revenue

Note that each simple adjusting entry for prepayments, whether a prepaid expense or an unearned revenue, affects one statement of financial position account and one income statement account. You will recall from Chapter 3 that a simple journal entry is one that affects only two accounts, one which is debited and one which is credited. Of course, compound entries could be prepared that affect more accounts but at least one account must be a statement of financial position account and one an income statement account.

It is very easy to make errors when preparing adjusting journal entries. You must watch your dates carefully, especially when calculating amounts for partial periods. In addition, even if an assignment does not require adjusting journal entries to be posted to T accounts, you will find it helpful to use a T account to quickly check your work to ensure that the balance in the affected statement of financial position account actually says what you intended it to say after the entry has been recorded and posted.

BEFORE YOU GO ON...

▸Do It! Adjusting Entries for Prepayments

Hammond, Inc.'s general ledger includes these selected accounts on March 31, 2015, before adjusting entries are prepared:

	Debit	Credit
Prepaid rent	$ 3,600	
Supplies	2,800	
Equipment	24,000	
Accumulated depreciation—equipment		$5,750
Unearned revenue		9,200

An analysis of the accounts shows the following:

1. Three months of rent ($1,200 per month) were paid in advance on March 1.

2. Supplies on hand total $800 on March 31, 2015.

3. The equipment was purchased April 1, 2013, and is estimated to have a useful life of eight years.

4. Half of the unearned revenue was earned in March.

Prepare the adjusting entries for March, assuming entries are made monthly.

Action Plan

- Make sure you prepare adjustments for the appropriate time period.
- Adjusting entries for prepaid expenses require a debit to an expense account and a credit to an asset (or contra asset) account.
- Adjusting entries for unearned revenues require a debit to a liability account and a credit to a revenue account.

Solution

1.	Mar. 31	Rent Expense	1,200	
		Prepaid Rent		1,200
		(To record rent used: $3,600 ÷ 3)		
2.	31	Supplies Expense	2,000	
		Supplies		2,000
		(To record supplies used: $2,800 – $800)		
3.	31	Depreciation Expense	250	
		Accumulated Depreciation—Equipment		250
		(To record monthly depreciation: $24,000 ÷ 8 × $\frac{1}{12}$)		
4.	31	Unearned Revenue	4,600	
		Service Revenue		4,600
		(To record revenue earned: $9,200 × $\frac{1}{2}$)		

Related Exercise Material: BE4-3, BE4-4, BE4-5, E4-3, E4-4, E4-6, E4-7, and E4-8.

the navigator

ADJUSTING ENTRIES FOR ACCRUALS

The second category of adjusting entries is **accruals**. Adjusting entries for accruals are required in order to record revenues earned, or expenses incurred, in the current accounting period. Unlike prepayments, accruals have not been recognized through daily entries and thus are not yet reflected in the accounts. Until an accrual adjustment is made, the revenue account (and the related asset account), or the expense account (and the related liability account), is understated. Thus, adjusting entries for accruals will increase both a statement of financial position account and an income statement account.

There are two types of adjusting entries for accruals: accrued revenues and accrued expenses. We now look at each type in more detail.

Accrued Revenues

Accrued revenues are revenues that have been earned but not yet received in cash or recorded. Accrued revenues may accumulate (accrue) with the passing of time, as in the case of interest revenue, or they may result from services that have been performed but not yet billed or collected, such as fees. The former are unrecorded because they do not involve daily transactions. The latter may be unrecorded because only a portion of the total service has been provided and the client will not be billed until the service has been completed. Therefore the recording of accrued revenues is not initiated like most revenue-carrying transactions by creating a sales invoice.

STUDY OBJECTIVE 3
Prepare adjusting entries for accruals.

Helpful Hint
For accruals, there may have been no prior entry, and the accounts requiring adjustment may both have zero balances prior to adjustment.

Alternative Terminology
The process of accruing revenue is also referred to as *accruing a receivable* because both are created in the same entry.

Since accrued revenues have not previously been recorded, an adjusting entry is required for two purposes: (1) to show the receivable that exists at the end of the period, and (2) to record the revenue that has been earned during the period. Until the adjustment is made, both assets and revenues are understated. Consequently, profit and shareholders' equity will also be understated.

As shown below, an adjusting entry for accrued revenues results in an increase (a debit) to an asset account and an increase (a credit) to a revenue account.

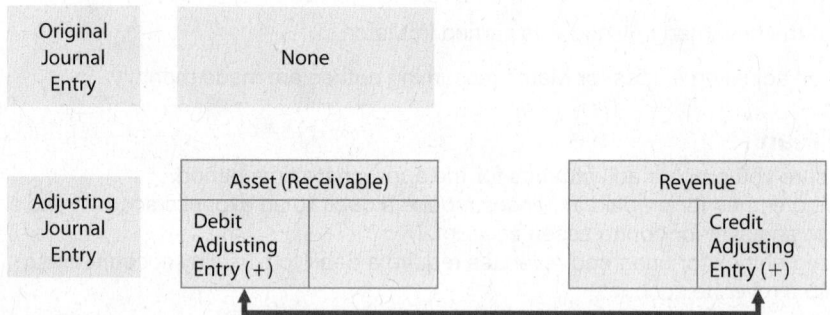

In October, Sierra Corporation earned $200 for advertising services that were not billed to clients before October 31. Because these services have not been billed, they have not yet been recorded.

► Adjustment (5)
Accrued revenues—accounts receivable

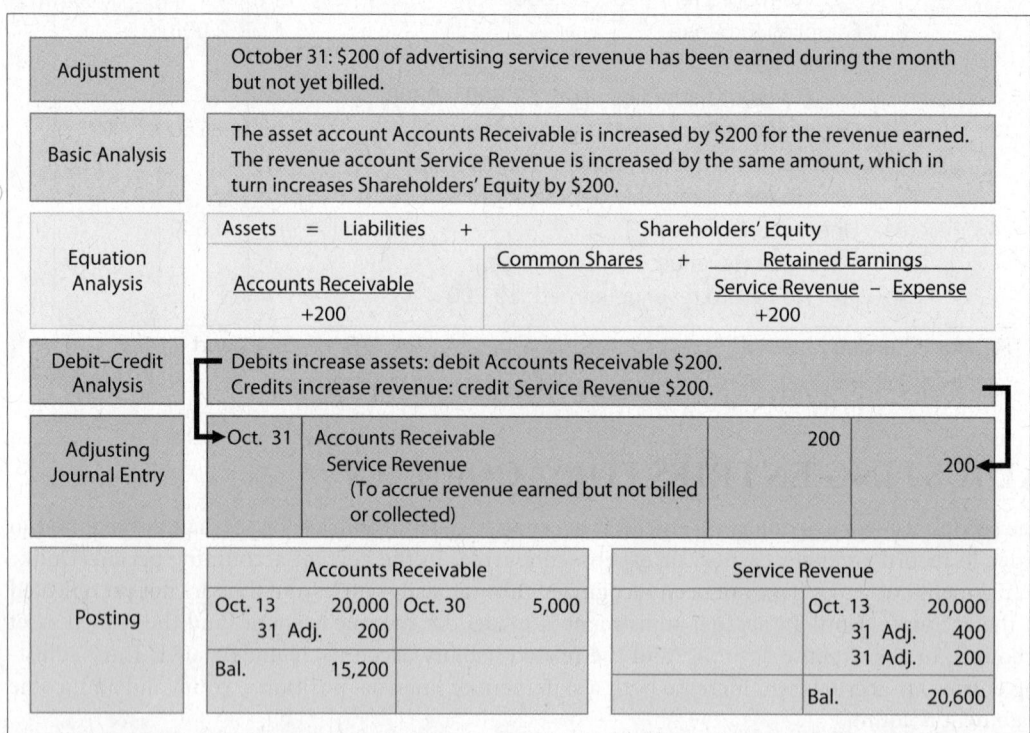

The asset Accounts Receivable shows that $15,200 is owed by clients at the statement of financial position date. The balance of $20,600 in Service Revenue represents the total revenue earned during the month. If the adjusting entry is not made, revenues and profit on the income statement, and assets and shareholders' equity on the statement of financial position, will be understated.

In the next accounting period, cash will be collected from clients for services provided in October, as well as for services provided in November. When this occurs, the entry to record the collection should recognize that $200 of the revenue was earned in October and has already been recorded in the October 31 adjusting entry and should not be re-recorded. For example, assume that $2,500 of revenue is collected from clients on November 6. Of this amount, $2,300 relates to services provided for cash in the first week of November, and $200 is for the services provided in October on account. The collection of cash from clients will be recorded as follows:

Nov. 6	Cash	2,500	
	Accounts Receivable		200
	Service Revenue		2,300
	(To record collection of account and cash receipts from services provided)		

A	=	L	+	SE
+2,500				+2,300
−200				

↑Cash flows: +2,500

Some accountants prefer to reverse accrual entries at the beginning of a new accounting period rather than try to remember what entries had been made in the prior period. A reversing entry is made at the beginning of the next accounting period. It is the exact opposite of the adjusting entry made in the previous period. The accrual is reversed to ensure that revenue is not recorded a second time when the invoice is prepared. The preparation of reversing entries is an optional accounting procedure that is not a required step in the accounting cycle and will not be discussed here.

The following summarizes the accounting for accrued revenue.

ACCRUED REVENUE				
Original Transaction	Examples	Reasons for Adjustment	Accounts before Adjustment	Adjusting Entry
None	Interest, rent, services performed but not yet collected	Revenues have been earned but not yet received in cash or recorded	Assets understated; Revenues understated	Dr. Asset Cr. Revenue

Accrued Expenses

Accrued expenses are expenses incurred but not yet paid or recorded. Interest, rent, salaries, property tax, and income tax are common examples of accrued expenses. Accrued expenses result from the same factors as accrued revenues. In fact, an accrued expense on the books of one company is an accrued revenue to another company. For example, the $200 accrual of service revenue for Sierra Corporation discussed above is an accrued expense for the client that received the service.

Since accrued expenses have not previously been recorded, an adjusting entry is required for two purposes: (1) to record the obligations that exist at the end of the period, and (2) to recognize the expenses that apply to the current accounting period. Until the adjustment is made, both liabilities and expenses are understated. Consequently, profit and shareholders' equity are overstated.

An adjusting entry for accrued expenses results in an increase (debit) to an expense account and an increase (credit) to a liability account, as shown below.

Alternative Terminology
The process of accruing an expense is also referred to as *accruing a payable* because both are created in the same entry.

Original Journal Entry	None		

Adjusting Journal Entry	Expense		Liability	
	Debit Adjusting Entry (+)			Credit Adjusting Entry (+)

We now look in more detail at some specific types of accrued expenses, beginning with accrued interest.

Helpful Hint
To make interest easier to understand, this chapter uses a simplified method of interest calculation using months instead of days. In reality, interest is calculated by multiplying the annual interest amount by a ratio that uses the exact number of days in the interest period divided by the number of days in a year.

Interest. Sierra Corporation signed a bank loan for $5,000 on October 1, repayable in three months. The bank loan accrues interest at an annual rate of 6%. **Interest rates are always expressed in annual terms.** The amount of the interest accumulation is determined by three factors: (1) the principal amount, or face value, of the loan ($5,000 for Sierra); (2) the interest rate, which is always expressed as an annual rate (6% for Sierra); and (3) the length of time that the loan is outstanding (unpaid) (three months for Sierra).

Interest is sometimes due monthly, and sometimes at maturity when the principal amount is due. In this instance, interest is due on the $5,000 bank loan at its due date, three months in the future. The total interest due at that time will be $75 ($5,000 × 6% × 3/12), or $25 for one month. Note that the time period is expressed as a fraction of a year.

The formula for calculating interest, including how it applies to Sierra Corporation for the month of October, is shown in Illustration 4-5.

▶ **Illustration 4-5**
Formula for calculating interest

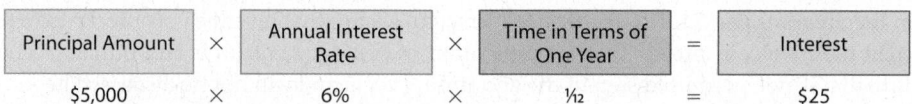

The accrual of interest at October 31 is reflected as follows:

▶ **Adjustment (6)**
Accrued expenses—interest

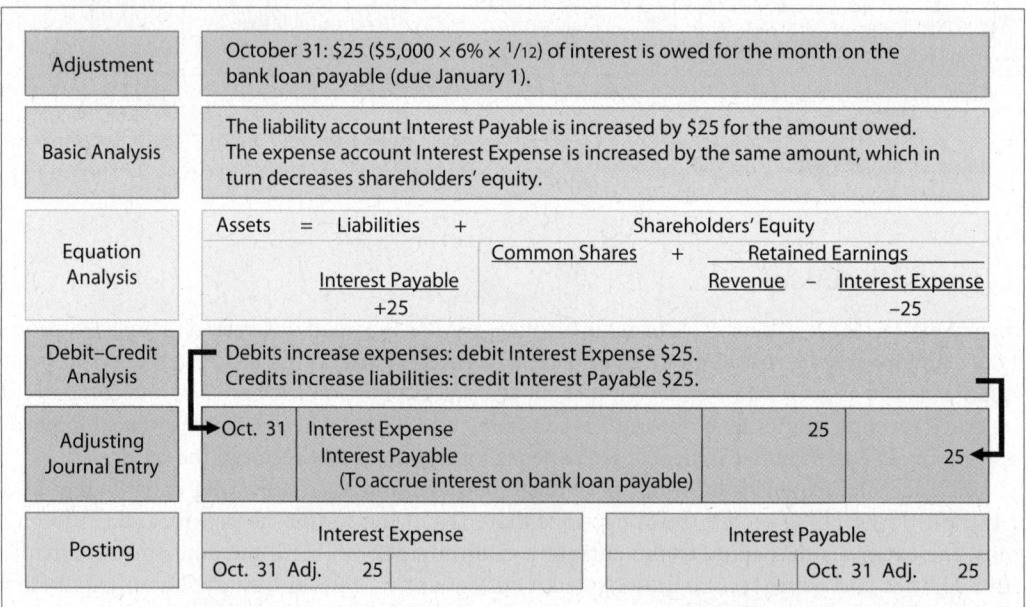

Interest Expense shows the interest charges for the month of October. The amount of interest owed at the statement date is shown in Interest Payable. It will not be paid until the bank loan comes due on January 1, 2016. The Interest Payable account is used, instead of crediting Bank Loan Payable, to disclose the two different types of obligations—interest and principal—in the accounts and statements. If this adjusting entry is not made, liabilities and expenses will be understated and profit and shareholders' equity will be overstated.

Since this is a three-month note, Sierra will also need to make identical adjustments at the end of November and December to accrue for interest expense incurred in each of these months. After the three adjusting entries have been posted, the balance in Interest Payable will be $75 ($25 × 3). The following entry is made on January 1, 2016, when the loan and interest are paid:

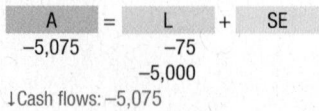

	A	=	L	+	SE
	−5,075		−75		
			−5,000		

↓ Cash flows: −5,075

Jan. 1	Interest Payable	75	
	Bank Loan Payable	5,000	
	Cash		5,075
	(To record payment of bank loan and interest)		

This entry does two things: (1) it eliminates the liability for Interest Payable that was recorded in the October 31, November 30, and December 31 adjusting entries; and (2) it eliminates the bank loan payable. Notice also that the account Interest Expense is not included in this entry, because the full amount of interest incurred was accrued in previous months.

Salaries. Some types of expenses, such as employee salaries, are paid for after the services have been performed and require an accrual adjustment when financial statements are prepared. For example, at its year end, Western University, described in our feature story, accrues salary and vacation pay for approximately 3,500 faculty and staff.

At Sierra Corporation, salaries are paid every two weeks. Sierra's four employees were last paid on October 23 for the period October 12–23. The next payment of salaries will not occur until November 6. As shown on the calendar below, there are five working days that remain unpaid for October (October 26–30).

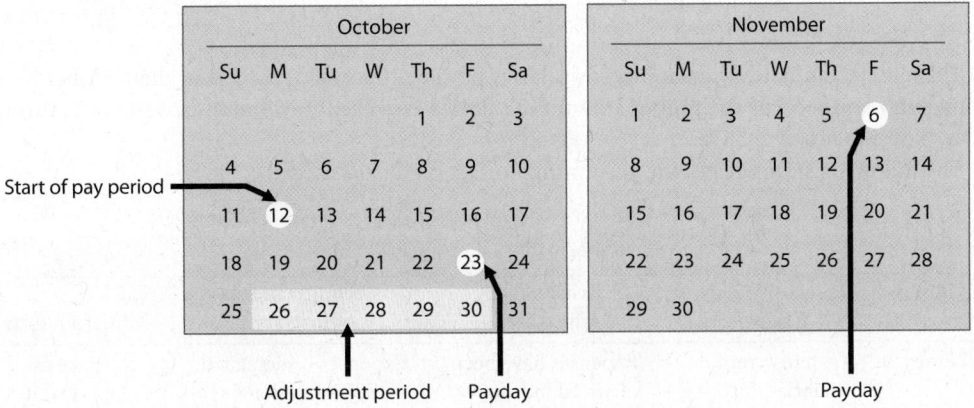

At October 31, the salaries for these five days (Monday, October 26 through Friday, October 30) represent an accrued expense and related liability for Sierra. As the four employees each receive a salary of $500 a week for a five-day workweek from Monday to Friday, or $100 a day, accrued salaries at October 31 are $2,000 (5 days × $100/day × 4 employees).

▶ Adjustment (7)
Accrued expenses—salaries

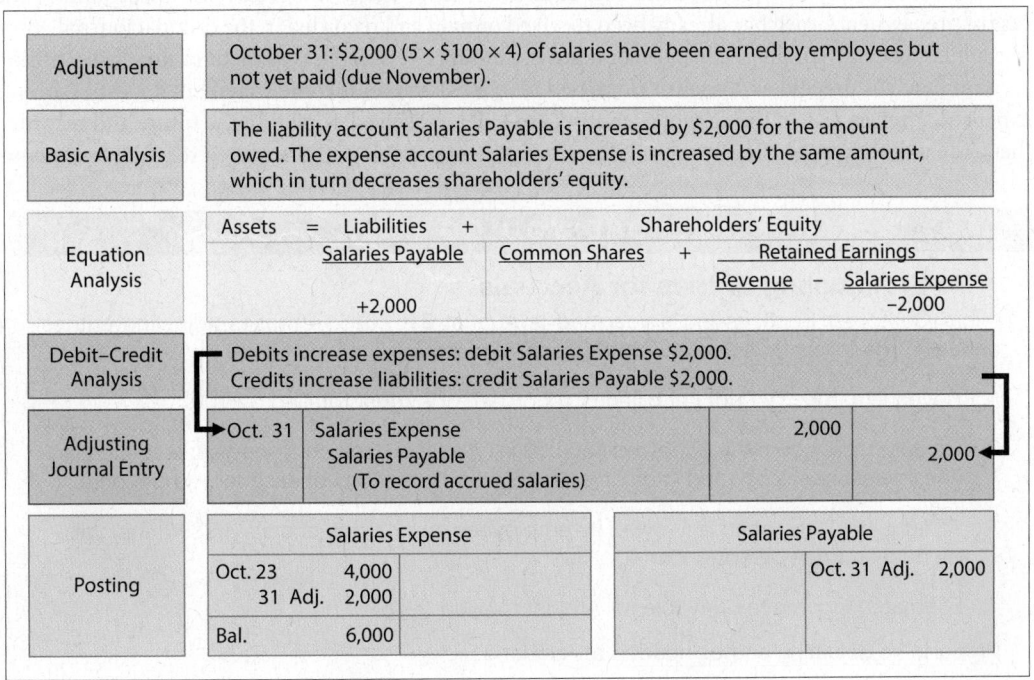

After this adjustment, the balance in Salaries Expense of $6,000 (15 days × $100/day × 4 employees) is the actual salary expense for October for the period October 12–31. The balance in Salaries Payable of $2,000 is the amount of the liability for salaries owed as at October 31. If the $2,000 adjustment for salaries is not recorded, Sierra's expenses and liabilities will be understated by $2,000. Profit and shareholders' equity will be overstated by $2,000.

At Sierra Corporation, salaries are payable every two weeks. Consequently, the next payday is November 6, when total salaries of $4,000 will again be paid. The payment consists of $2,000 of salaries payable at October 31 plus $2,000 of salaries expense for November 2–6 (5 days × $100/day × 4 employees). Therefore, the following entry is made on November 6:

A	=	L	+	SE
−4,000		−2,000		−2,000

↓Cash flows: −4,000

Nov. 6	Salaries Payable (Oct. 26–30)	2,000	
	Salaries Expense (Nov. 2–6)	2,000	
	Cash		4,000
	(Paid salaries for Oct. 26–Nov. 6)		

This entry eliminates the liability for salaries payable that was recorded in the October 31 adjusting entry and records the proper amount of salaries expense for Monday, November 2, through Friday, November 6, inclusive.

The following summarizes the accounting for accrued expenses.

ACCRUED EXPENSES				
Original Transaction	Examples	Reasons for Adjustment	Accounts before Adjustment	Adjusting Entry
None	Interest, rent, salaries, income tax	Expenses have been incurred but not yet paid in cash or recorded	Expenses understated; Liabilities understated	Dr. Expense Cr. Liability

Note that each adjusting entry for accruals, whether an accrued revenue or an accrued expense, affects at least one statement of financial position account and at least one income statement account, similar to adjusting entries for prepayments.

It is also important to understand that adjusting entries **never** involve the Cash account. In the case of prepayments, cash has already been received or paid and recorded in the original journal entry. The adjusting entry simply reallocates, or adjusts, amounts between a statement of financial position account (such as prepaid expenses or unearned revenues) and an income statement account (such as expenses or revenues). In the case of accruals, cash will be received or paid in the future and recorded then. The adjusting entry simply records the receivable or payable and the related revenue or expense.

BEFORE YOU GO ON...

▶Do It! Adjusting Entries for Accruals

Micro Computer Services Inc.'s year end is August 31, 2015. It makes adjusting entries annually. The following selected information is available:

1. Revenue earned but not yet billed or recorded for August totalled $1,100.

2. On July 1, the company borrowed $30,000 from a local bank on a one-year loan payable. The interest rate is 5% and interest is payable on the first day of each following month.

3. At August 31, the company owed its employees for one day of salary ($800) that will be paid on Friday, September 4.

4. Estimated income tax payable for August totalled $275.

Prepare the adjusting entries needed at August 31.

Action Plan

- Remember that accruals are entries that initially record a revenue or expense that was not previously recorded. Therefore, the adjustment pattern is different from the pattern for prepayments, which adjust items that were recorded earlier.
- Adjusting entries for accrued revenues require a debit to a receivable account and a credit to a revenue account.
- Adjusting entries for accrued expenses require a debit to an expense account and a credit to a liability account.
- Recall that interest rates are always stated as an annual rate.

Solution

1. Aug. 31	Accounts Receivable		1,100	
	Service Revenue			1,100
	(To accrue revenue earned but not billed or collected)			
2.	31	Interest Expense	125	
		Interest Payable		125
		(To record accrued interest for the month of August: $30,000 × 5% × 1/12)		
3.	31	Salaries Expense	800	
		Salaries Payable		800
		(To record accrued salaries)		
4.	31	Income Tax Expense	275	
		Income Tax Payable		275
		(To record accrued income taxes)		

Related Exercise Material: BE4-5, BE4-6, BE4-7, BE4-8, BE4-9, E4-5, E4-6, E4-7, and E4-8.

SIERRA CORPORATION ILLUSTRATION

The summary of the adjusting entries described in this chapter for Sierra Corporation on October 31 is presented below in the general journal.

GENERAL JOURNAL			
Date	Account Titles and Explanation	Debit	Credit
2015 Oct. 31	Supplies Expense	1,500	
	Supplies		1,500
	(To record supplies used)		
31	Insurance Expense	50	
	Prepaid Insurance		50
	(To record insurance expired)		
31	Depreciation Expense	83	
	Accumulated Depreciation—Equipment		83
	(To record monthly depreciation)		
31	Unearned Revenue	400	
	Service Revenue		400
	(To record revenue earned)		
31	Accounts Receivable	200	
	Service Revenue		200
	(To accrue revenue earned but not billed or collected)		
31	Interest Expense	25	
	Interest Payable		25
	(To accrue interest on bank loan payable)		
31	Salaries Expense	2,000	
	Salaries Payable		2,000
	(To record accrued salaries)		

The above adjusting journal entries are then posted to the general ledger, as shown below. Note that adjusting entries are denoted with Adj. (an abbreviation for adjustment) in the general ledger accounts to distinguish the adjusting entries from the monthly transaction entries that were posted in Chapter 3. As you review the general ledger, notice that the adjustments are highlighted in colour.

Note also that an account for retained earnings has been added in the general ledger. Because this is Sierra's first month of operations, there is no balance in the Retained Earnings account. Although accounts with a zero balance are not normally included in the general ledger, we have added it here to make it easier to prepare the statement of changes in equity in the next section. In addition, we will need to use this account again in the section on closing entries later in this chapter.

GENERAL LEDGER

Cash

Oct.	1	10,000	Oct.	2	900
	19	1,200		5	600
	30	5,000		22	1,000
				23	4,000
				26	500
				30	1,800
Bal.		7,400			

Bank Loan Payable

		Oct. 1	5,000

Common Shares

		Oct. 1	10,000

Accounts Receivable

Oct.	13	20,000	Oct. 30	5,000	
	31 Adj.	200			
Bal.		15,200			

Retained Earnings

		Oct. 1	0

Supplies

Oct.	9	2,500	Oct. 31 Adj.	1,500
Bal.		1,000		

Dividends

Oct.	26	500	

Prepaid Insurance

Oct.	5	600	Oct 31 Adj.	50
Bal.		550		

Service Revenue

		Oct. 13	20,000
		31 Adj.	400
		31 Adj.	200
		Bal.	20,600

Equipment

Oct.	1	5,000	

Salaries Expense

Oct.	23	4,000	
	31 Adj.	2,000	
Bal.		6,000	

Accumulated Depreciation—Equipment

	Oct. 31 Adj.	83

Supplies Expense

Oct.	31 Adj.	1,500	

Accounts Payable

Oct.	22	1,000	Oct. 9	2,500
			Bal.	1,500

Rent Expense

Oct.	2	900	

Salaries Payable

	Oct. 31 Adj.	2,000

Depreciation Expense

Oct.	31 Adj.	83	

(continued)

Interest Payable				Insurance Expense		
	Oct. 31 Adj.	25	Oct. 31 Adj.	50		

Unearned Revenue				Interest Expense		
Oct. 31 Adj.	400	Oct. 19	1,200	Oct. 31 Adj.	25	
		Bal.	800			

				Income Tax Expense		
				Oct. 30	1,800	

The Adjusted Trial Balance and Financial Statements

After all adjusting entries have been journalized and posted, another trial balance is prepared from the general ledger accounts. This trial balance is called an **adjusted trial balance**. It shows the balances of all accounts at the end of the accounting period, including those that have been adjusted. Because the accounts contain all the data that are needed for financial statements, the adjusted trial balance is the main source for the preparation of financial statements.

The preparation of the adjusted trial balance and financial statements form the next two steps of the accounting cycle, as shown in Illustration 4-6.

STUDY OBJECTIVE 4
Prepare an adjusted trial balance.

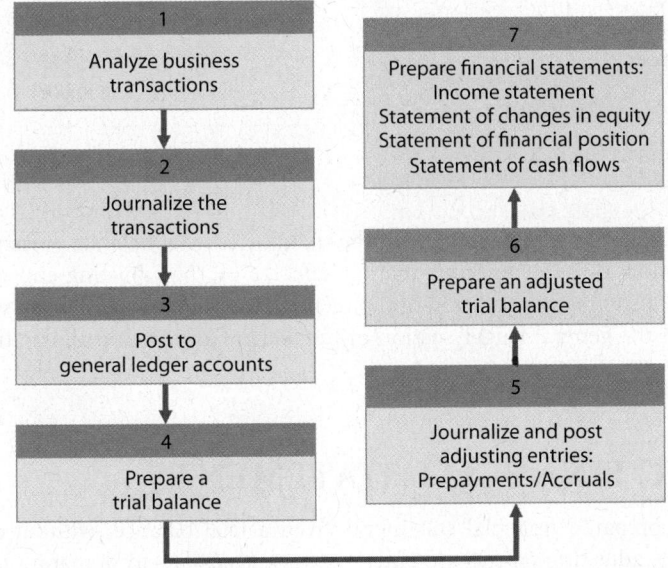

▶ Illustration 4-6
The accounting cycle—Steps 1–7

PREPARING THE ADJUSTED TRIAL BALANCE

The procedures for preparing an adjusted trial balance are the same as those described in Chapter 3 for preparing an unadjusted trial balance. An adjusted trial balance, similar to an unadjusted trial balance, lists the accounts in the general ledger and proves that the totals of the debit and credit balances in the ledger are equal after all adjustments have been recorded and posted.

The adjusted trial balance for Sierra Corporation is presented in Illustration 4-7 and has been prepared from the general ledger accounts shown in the previous section.

▸Illustration 4-7
Adjusted trial balance

	Debit	Credit
SIERRA CORPORATION		
Adjusted Trial Balance		
October 31, 2015		
Cash	$ 7,400	
Accounts receivable	15,200	
Supplies	1,000	
Prepaid insurance	550	
Equipment	5,000	
Accumulated depreciation—equipment		$ 83
Accounts payable		1,500
Salaries payable		2,000
Interest payable		25
Unearned revenue		800
Bank loan payable		5,000
Common shares		10,000
Retained earnings		0
Dividends	500	
Service revenue		20,600
Salaries expense	6,000	
Supplies expense	1,500	
Rent expense	900	
Depreciation expense	83	
Insurance expense	50	
Interest expense	25	
Income tax expense	1,800	
	$40,008	$40,008

Compare the adjusted trial balance with the unadjusted trial balance presented earlier in the chapter in Illustration 4-3. The amounts that are affected by the adjusting entries are highlighted in colour. You will also note the addition of the retained earnings account, even with a nil balance, as we discussed in the general ledger section of the Sierra Corporation Illustration earlier in this chapter.

PREPARING FINANCIAL STATEMENTS

In Chapter 3, we prepared financial statements from a trial balance, without adjusting entries. However, in reality, adjusting entries are almost always necessary to prepare financial statements under the accrual basis of accounting. Therefore, you should always prepare financial statements from an adjusted trial balance, never from an unadjusted trial balance.

In Illustration 4-8, we use the adjusted trial balance to prepare Sierra's financial statements. As we learned in prior chapters, the income statement is prepared first using the revenue and expense accounts. The statement of changes in equity is prepared next, using the common shares, retained earnings, and dividends accounts, and the profit (or loss) reported in the income statement. The statement of financial position is the third statement prepared, using the asset, liability, and shareholders' equity accounts. Note that shareholders' equity on the statement of financial position includes the ending common shares and retained earnings account balances as reported in the statement of changes in equity.

▶Illustration 4-8
Preparation of the financial statements from the adjusted trial balance

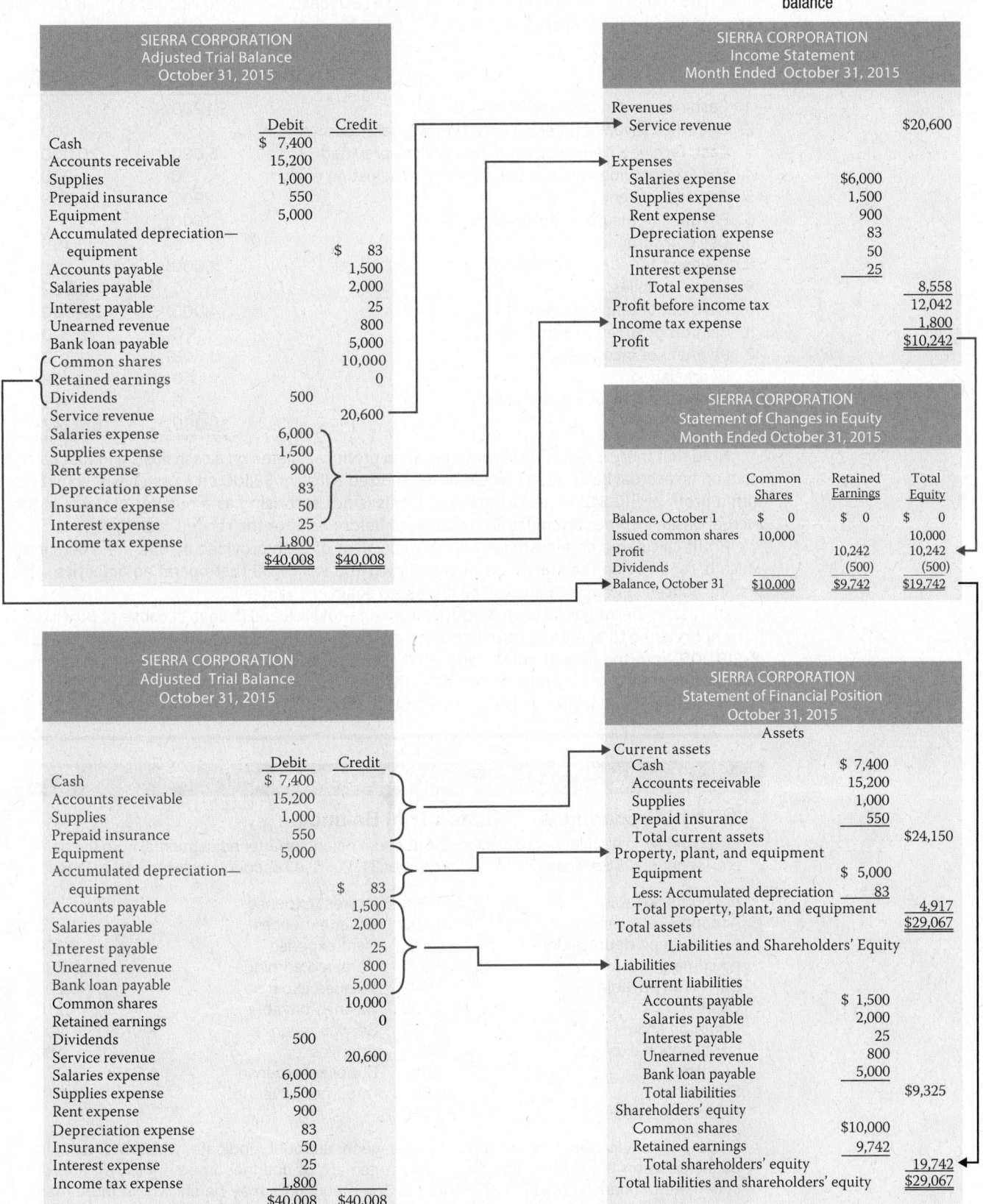

SIERRA CORPORATION
Adjusted Trial Balance
October 31, 2015

	Debit	Credit
Cash	$ 7,400	
Accounts receivable	15,200	
Supplies	1,000	
Prepaid insurance	550	
Equipment	5,000	
Accumulated depreciation—equipment		$ 83
Accounts payable		1,500
Salaries payable		2,000
Interest payable		25
Unearned revenue		800
Bank loan payable		5,000
Common shares		10,000
Retained earnings		0
Dividends	500	
Service revenue		20,600
Salaries expense	6,000	
Supplies expense	1,500	
Rent expense	900	
Depreciation expense	83	
Insurance expense	50	
Interest expense	25	
Income tax expense	1,800	
	$40,008	$40,008

SIERRA CORPORATION
Income Statement
Month Ended October 31, 2015

Revenues		
Service revenue		$20,600
Expenses		
Salaries expense	$6,000	
Supplies expense	1,500	
Rent expense	900	
Depreciation expense	83	
Insurance expense	50	
Interest expense	25	
Total expenses		8,558
Profit before income tax		12,042
Income tax expense		1,800
Profit		$10,242

SIERRA CORPORATION
Statement of Changes in Equity
Month Ended October 31, 2015

	Common Shares	Retained Earnings	Total Equity
Balance, October 1	$ 0	$ 0	$ 0
Issued common shares	10,000		10,000
Profit		10,242	10,242
Dividends		(500)	(500)
Balance, October 31	$10,000	$9,742	$19,742

SIERRA CORPORATION
Adjusted Trial Balance
October 31, 2015

	Debit	Credit
Cash	$ 7,400	
Accounts receivable	15,200	
Supplies	1,000	
Prepaid insurance	550	
Equipment	5,000	
Accumulated depreciation—equipment		$ 83
Accounts payable		1,500
Salaries payable		2,000
Interest payable		25
Unearned revenue		800
Bank loan payable		5,000
Common shares		10,000
Retained earnings		0
Dividends	500	
Service revenue		20,600
Salaries expense	6,000	
Supplies expense	1,500	
Rent expense	900	
Depreciation expense	83	
Insurance expense	50	
Interest expense	25	
Income tax expense	1,800	
	$40,008	$40,008

SIERRA CORPORATION
Statement of Financial Position
October 31, 2015

Assets		
Current assets		
Cash	$ 7,400	
Accounts receivable	15,200	
Supplies	1,000	
Prepaid insurance	550	
Total current assets		$24,150
Property, plant, and equipment		
Equipment	$ 5,000	
Less: Accumulated depreciation	83	
Total property, plant, and equipment		4,917
Total assets		$29,067
Liabilities and Shareholders' Equity		
Liabilities		
Current liabilities		
Accounts payable	$ 1,500	
Salaries payable	2,000	
Interest payable	25	
Unearned revenue	800	
Bank loan payable	5,000	
Total liabilities		$9,325
Shareholders' equity		
Common shares	$10,000	
Retained earnings	9,742	
Total shareholders' equity		19,742
Total liabilities and shareholders' equity		$29,067

Keeping an Eye on Cash

We learned earlier in this chapter the difference between accrual and cash basis accounting. If we were to compare Sierra's profit calculated on a cash basis with profit calculated on an accrual basis, we would have the following:

	Profit (Loss)	
	Cash Basis	Accrual Basis
1. Cash received in advance from customer	$ 1,200	$ 0
2. Unearned revenue received in (1) that was later earned	0	400
3. Cash received from customers for services provided	5,000	20,000
4. Services provided on account recorded in adjusting entry	0	200
5. Payment of rent	(900)	(900)
6. Payment of insurance in advance	(600)	0
7. Use of insurance	0	(50)
8. Payment for supplies purchased on account	(1,000)	
9. Use of supplies	0	(1,500)
10. Payment of employee salaries	(4,000)	(4,000)
11. Salaries incurred, but not paid	0	(2,000)
12. Payment of income tax	(1,800)	(1,800)
13. Depreciation	0	(83)
14. Interest cost incurred, but not paid	0	(25)
Profit (loss)	$(2,100)	$10,242

Note that there is quite a difference between profit calculated on a cash basis and that calculated on an accrual basis. Sierra would have reported a loss of $2,100 on a cash basis, compared with a profit of $10,242 on an accrual basis. This is not surprising as a number of items in the accrual-based income statement are recognized before or after the related cash flow.

Profit calculated on a cash basis is the equivalent of cash provided by operating activities, which is reported on the statement of cash flows. You will recall that operating activities were first introduced in Chapter 1 and will be discussed again in Chapter 13.

Of course, Sierra has to have a positive cash flow overall and it does because of other cash flows not relating to operating (profit-related) activities in October. For example, it received cash of $10,000 from the sale of shares and used cash of $500 to pay dividends. These amounts, combined with the cash used for operating activities (cash basis loss), result in Sierra's final cash balance in its general ledger of $7,400 (−$2,100 + $10,000 − $500).

BEFORE YOU GO ON...

▶ Do It! Preparing an Adjusted Trial Balance

Listed below, in alphabetical order, are the account balances (after adjustments) from the general ledger of KS Services Limited at December 31, 2015. All accounts have normal balances.

Accounts payable	$ 4,660	Interest expense	$ 50
Accounts receivable	9,600	Other expenses	1,675
Accumulated depreciation—		Rent expense	16,800
equipment	5,200	Retained earnings	3,700
Bank loan payable	1,000	Salaries expense	30,700
Cash	1,100	Salaries payable	710
Common shares	5,000	Service revenue	67,200
Depreciation expense	2,600	Supplies	180
Dividends	1,000	Supplies expense	475
Equipment	20,800	Unearned revenue	1,010
Income tax expense	3,500		

Prepare the adjusted trial balance. Beside each account, indicate whether it should be included on the income statement (IS), statement of changes in equity (SCE), and/or statement of financial position (SFP). (Note: Some accounts may be shown on more than one statement.)

Action Plan

- The title of the adjusted trial balance includes the name of the company, the type of trial balance, and the date.
- Accounts are listed in the same order as in an unadjusted trial balance: assets, liabilities, shareholders' equity, revenues, and expenses.
- Apply the debit–credit rules to determine normal balances and list the amounts in the correct columns.
- Ensure that total debits equal total credits.
- Use the trial balance order of the accounts to help you identify which accounts should be reported on the income statement, statement of changes in equity, and/or statement of financial position.

Solution

KS SERVICES LIMITED
Adjusted Trial Balance
December 31, 2015

	Debit	Credit	Statement
Cash	$ 1,100		SFP
Accounts receivable	9,600		SFP
Supplies	180		SFP
Equipment	20,800		SFP
Accumulated depreciation—equipment		$ 5,200	SFP
Bank loan payable		1,000	SFP
Accounts payable		4,660	SFP
Salaries payable		710	SFP
Unearned revenue		1,010	SFP
Common shares		5,000	SFP & SCE
Retained earnings		3,700	SFP & SCE
Dividends	1,000		SCE
Service revenue		67,200	IS
Depreciation expense	2,600		IS
Rent expense	16,800		IS
Salaries expense	30,700		IS
Supplies expense	475		IS
Interest expense	50		IS
Other expenses	1,675		IS
Income tax expense	3,500		IS
	$88,480	$88,480	

Related Exercise Material: BE4-10, BE4-11, E4-7, E4-8, E4-9, and E4-10.

Closing the Books

In previous chapters, you learned that revenue and expense accounts and the dividends account are subdivisions of retained earnings, which is reported in the shareholders' equity section of the statement of financial position. Because revenues, expenses, and dividends relate to activities over a particular accounting period, they are considered **temporary accounts**. In contrast, all statement of financial position accounts are considered **permanent accounts** because their balances are carried forward into future accounting periods. For example, if a company has cash at the end of the year, that cash balance will also exist at the beginning of the next year, so it is a permanent account. The following table identifies the accounts in each category.

STUDY OBJECTIVE 5
Prepare closing entries and a post-closing trial balance.

TEMPORARY	PERMANENT
All expense accounts	All asset accounts
All revenue accounts	All liability accounts
Dividends account	All shareholders' equity accounts

PREPARING CLOSING ENTRIES

At the end of the accounting period, the temporary account balances are transferred to the permanent shareholders' equity account Retained Earnings through the preparation of closing entries. **Closing entries** formally record in the general journal and the ledger the transfer of the balances in the revenue, expense, and dividends accounts to the Retained Earnings account, thereby updating that account to its end-of-period balance. In Illustration 4-7, you will note that Retained Earnings has an adjusted balance of zero. Until the closing entries are made, the balance in Retained Earnings will be its balance at the beginning of the period. For Sierra, this is zero because it is Sierra's first year of operations. After closing entries are recorded and posted, the balance in Retained Earnings is the end-of-period balance. This ending balance in the general ledger account will now be the same as the ending balance reported on the statement of changes in equity in the retained earnings column and on the statement of financial position in the shareholders' equity section.

In addition to updating Retained Earnings to its ending balance, closing entries produce a zero balance in each temporary account. As a result, these accounts are ready to accumulate data about revenues, expenses, and dividends for the next accounting period. Permanent accounts are not closed because the future benefits relating to assets and the obligations relating to liabilities still exist.

When closing entries are prepared, each revenue and expense account could be closed directly to Retained Earnings. This is common in computerized accounting systems where the closing process occurs automatically when it is time to start a new accounting period. For our purposes, this practice can result in too much detail in the Retained Earnings account. Accordingly, the revenue and expense accounts are first closed to another temporary account, **Income Summary**. Only the resulting total amount (profit or loss) is transferred from this account to the Retained Earnings account. Illustration 4-9 illustrates the closing process.

▶Illustration 4-9
Closing process

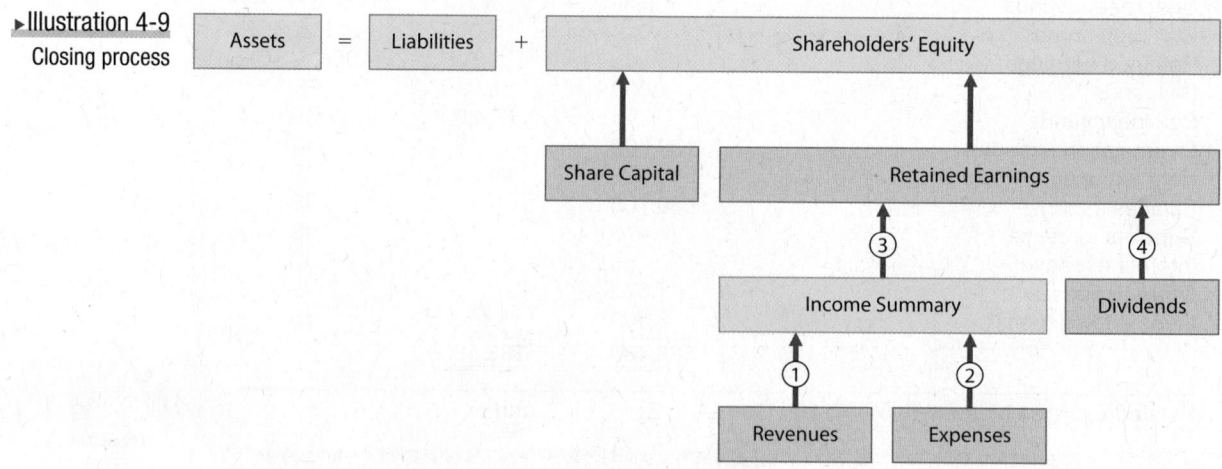

To prepare closing entries, four steps are necessary:

1. To close revenue accounts: Debit each individual revenue account for its balance, and credit Income Summary for total revenues. After this, all revenue accounts will have zero balances.
2. To close expense accounts: Debit Income Summary for total expenses, and credit each individual expense account for its balance. After this, all expense accounts will have zero balances.
3. To close Income Summary: Debit Income Summary for the balance in the account (or credit it if there is a loss), and credit (debit) Retained Earnings. After this, the Income Summary account balance is zero.
4. To close the Dividends account: Debit Retained Earnings for the balance in the Dividends account, and credit Dividends, thereby bringing the balance in this account to zero. Do not close Dividends to the Income Summary account along with expenses. Dividends are not expenses and do not affect profit; they are a distribution of retained earnings.

Journalizing and posting closing entries is a required step in the accounting cycle—step 8, as shown in Illustration 4-10 on the following page.

Step 8 is done after financial statements have been prepared. Closing entries are generally recorded and posted only at the end of a company's annual accounting period. Closing entries can be prepared directly from the general ledger or the adjusted trial balance. If we were to prepare closing

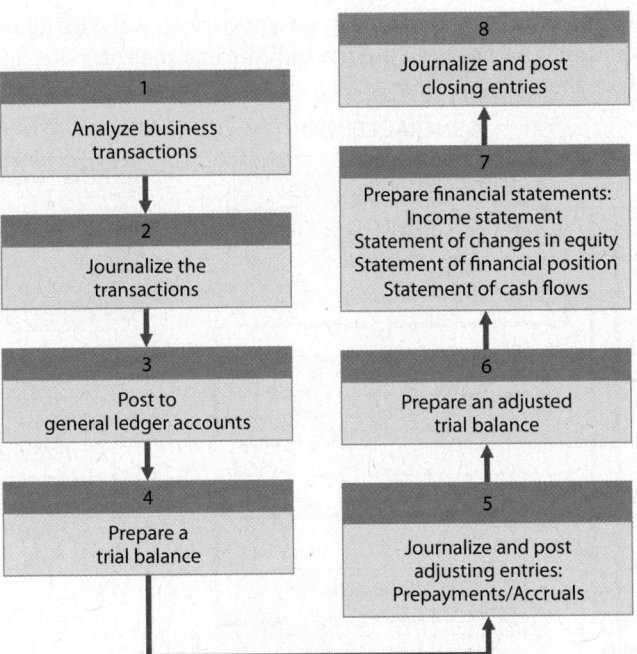

▸Illustration 4-10
The accounting cycle—Steps 1–8

entries for Sierra Corporation, we would likely use the adjusted trial balance presented earlier in the chapter in Illustration 4-7. In Sierra's case, all temporary accounts (Dividends, Service Revenue, and its seven different expense accounts) must be closed.

Even though Retained Earnings is not a temporary account, it will also be involved in the closing process. Remember that the Retained Earnings balance presented in the adjusted trial balance is the beginning balance, not the ending balance. This permanent account is not closed, but the profit (loss) and dividends for the period must be transferred into Retained Earnings through closing entries to update the account to its ending balance.

Sierra's general journal showing its closing entries follows.

GENERAL JOURNAL			
Date	Account Titles and Explanation	Debit	Credit
	Closing Entries		
2015	(1)		
Oct. 31	Service Revenue	20,600	
	Income Summary		20,600
	(To close revenue account)		
	(2)		
31	Income Summary	10,358	
	Salaries Expense		6,000
	Supplies Expense		1,500
	Rent Expense		900
	Depreciation Expense		83
	Insurance Expense		50
	Interest Expense		25
	Income Tax Expense		1,800
	(To close expense accounts)		
	(3)		
31	Income Summary	10,242	
	Retained Earnings		10,242
	(To close profit to retained earnings)		
	(4)		
31	Retained Earnings	500	
	Dividends		500
	(To close dividends to retained earnings)		

Sierra's general ledger showing the posting of the above closing entries follows. Note that in the general ledger the notation "CE" has been used to indicate that the entry is a closing entry (CE).

GENERAL LEDGER

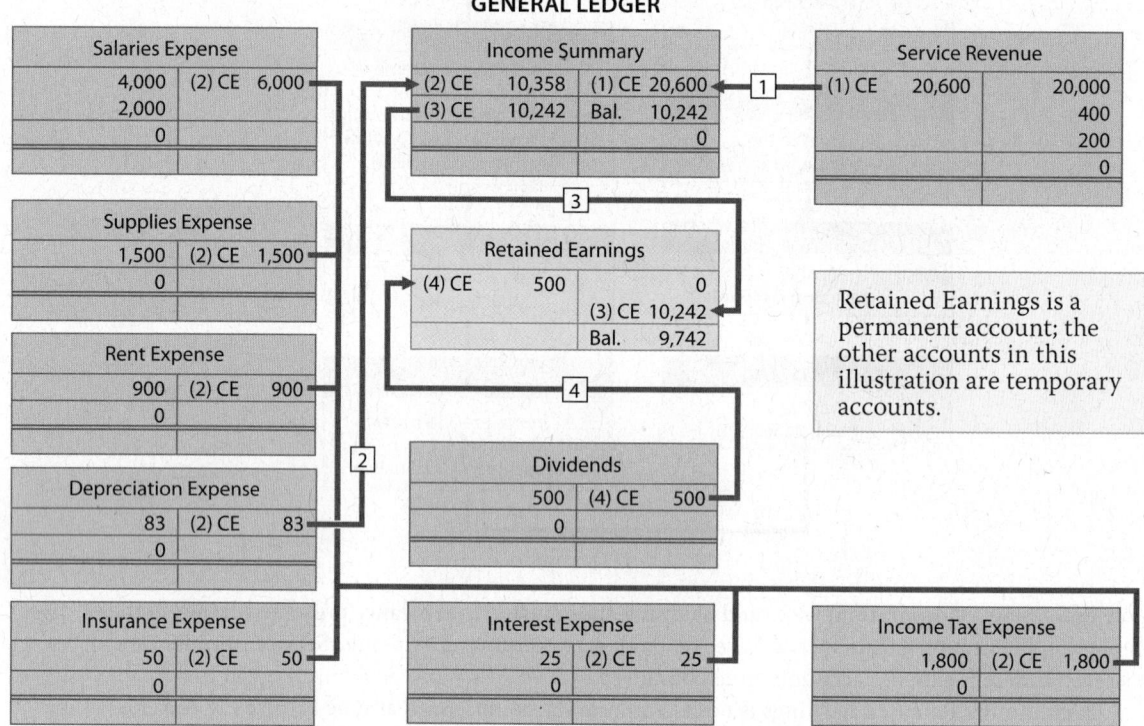

It is important to check your work after the closing entries are posted.

1. The balance in the Income Summary account, immediately before the final closing entry to transfer the balance to the Retained Earnings account (entry 3 above), should equal the profit (or loss) reported in the income statement.
2. All temporary accounts (revenues, expenses, income summary, and dividends) should have zero balances.
3. The balance in the Retained Earnings account should equal the ending balance reported in the statement of changes in equity and statement of financial position.

ACCOUNTING MATTERS!

Closing the Books

Most companies work very hard to prepare adjusting and closing entries as soon as possible so that their financial statements can be released promptly. World-class companies can close their books within five days. David Smith, corporate controller of Atomic Energy of Canada Limited (AECL), notes that when he first started working at the company, it took 10 days to close the books. Today, AECL closes its books in four days. Like other world-class companies, "AECL's ability to do a quick close gives management sufficient time to analyze the results to make informed and timely decisions," says Mr. Smith.

PREPARING A POST-CLOSING TRIAL BALANCE

After all closing entries are journalized and posted, another trial balance, called a post-closing trial balance, is prepared from the ledger. We have learned about the unadjusted and adjusted trial balances so far. The third and last trial balance is the **post-closing trial balance**, which lists all permanent accounts and their balances after closing entries are journalized and posted. The purpose of this trial balance is to prove the equality of the permanent account balances that are carried forward into the next annual accounting period. Since all temporary accounts will have zero balances, the post-closing trial balance will contain only permanent—statement of financial position—accounts. Illustration 4-11 shows Sierra Corporation's post-closing trial balance.

▶Illustration 4-11

Post-closing trial balance

SIERRA CORPORATION Post-Closing Trial Balance October 31, 2015		
	Debit	Credit
Cash	$ 7,400	
Accounts receivable	15,200	
Supplies	1,000	
Prepaid insurance	550	
Equipment	5,000	
Accumulated depreciation—equipment		$ 83
Accounts payable		1,500
Salaries payable		2,000
Interest payable		25
Unearned revenue		800
Bank loan payable		5,000
Common shares		10,000
Retained earnings		9,742
	$29,150	$29,150

Preparation of a post-closing trial balance is the last step—step 9—in the accounting cycle. The entire accounting cycle is shown in Illustration 4-12 for your information and review.

▶Illustration 4-12

Steps in the accounting cycle

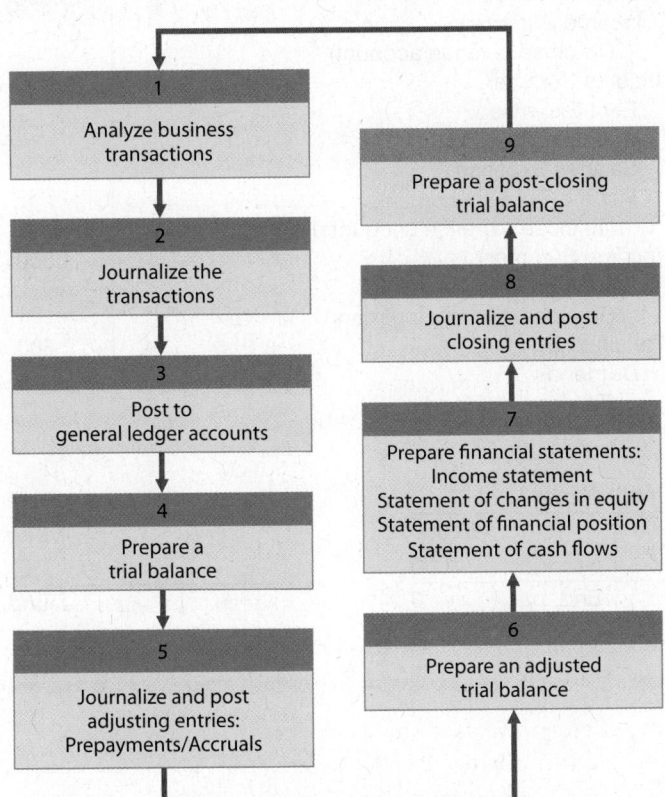

The accounting cycle begins with the analysis of business transactions and ends with the preparation of a post-closing trial balance. The steps are done in sequence and are repeated in each accounting period.

Steps 1 to 3 may occur daily during the accounting period, as we learned in Chapter 3, although some companies post monthly rather than daily to the general ledger. Steps 4 to 7 are done on a periodic basis, such as monthly, quarterly, or annually. Steps 8 and 9, closing entries and a post-closing trial balance, are usually prepared only at the end of a company's annual accounting period.

BEFORE YOU GO ON...

▶Do It! Closing Entries

The adjusted trial balance for Nguyen Corporation shows the following selected accounts: Dividends $500; Common Shares $30,000; Retained Earnings $12,000; Service Revenue $18,000; Rent Expense $1,500; Supplies Expense $500; Salaries Expense $8,000; and Income Tax Expense $1,000. (a) Prepare the closing entries at December 31. (b) What is the balance in the Income Summary and Retained Earnings accounts after closing?

Action Plan

* Close revenues and expenses into the Income Summary account.
* Stop and check your work: Is the balance in each individual revenue and expense account now zero? Does the balance in the Income Summary account equal the reported profit (loss)?
* Close the balance in the Income Summary account into the Retained Earnings account.
* Close the Dividends account into the Retained Earnings account. Do not close Dividends into the Income Summary account.
* Stop and check your work: Does the balance in the Retained Earnings account equal the ending balance reported in the financial statements?

Solution

(a)	Dec. 31	Service Revenue	18,000	
		Income Summary		18,000
		(To close revenue account)		
	31	Income Summary	11,000	
		Rent Expense		1,500
		Supplies Expense		500
		Salaries Expense		8,000
		Income Tax Expense		1,000
		(To close expense accounts)		
	31	Income Summary	7,000	
		Retained Earnings		7,000
		(To close income summary)		
	31	Retained Earnings	500	
		Dividends		500
		(To close dividends)		

(b)

Income Summary			
	11,000		18,000
CE	7,000	Bal.	7,000
		End. bal.	0

Retained Earnings			
		Beg. bal.	12,000
CE	500	CE	7,000
		End. bal.	18,500

Related Exercise Material: BE4-12, BE4-13, BE4-14, and E4-11.

comparing
IFRS and ASPE

Key Differences	International Financial Reporting Standards (IFRS)	Accounting Standards for Private Enterprises (ASPE)
Frequency of adjusting entries	Public companies must release quarterly financial statements so adjusting entries have to be made at least quarterly, although many will record adjusting entries every month.	Private companies usually release financial statements to their banker(s) and shareholder(s), along with certain financial information to the Canada Revenue Agency on an annual basis, so adjusting entries may be made only at year end, although many will record adjusting entries more frequently.
Terminology	The term *depreciation* refers to the allocation of the cost of depreciable tangible assets over their useful lives. The term *amortization* refers to the allocation of the cost of certain kinds of intangible assets over their useful lives.	The term *amortization* is used for the allocation of the cost of both depreciable tangible assets and certain kinds of intangible assets over their useful lives.

the navigator

In this chapter, you learned about the three conditions that must be met before revenue can be recognized. You also learned that expenses should be recognized when the effort (expense) can be matched with the result (revenue).

Management and employees who keep track of accounting information may be motivated to overstate revenues and understate expenses. Some of these motivations include the need to increase profitability, the need for a company to obtain a bank loan, or the desire of an employee to obtain a larger bonus at the end of an accounting cycle. Intentional misstatement of revenues and/or expenses is referred to as fraudulent financial reporting.

Management (and accountants) must put in place systems of internal control that will prevent fraudulent financial reporting from occurring. These controls can prevent overstatement of revenue and understatement of expenses and include appropriate authorization of transactions, maintaining adequate documentation, and ensuring that all transactions recorded are appropriately authorized. You will learn more about internal controls in Chapters 6 and 7.

Some Facts

- Research in the United States found that there were 347 alleged cases of public company fraudulent financial reporting from 1998 to 2007. The most common fraud technique involved improper revenue recognition followed by understatement of expenses that were inappropriately recorded as assets. The most common motivations for committing the fraud included increasing share price, bolstering financial performance, and the desire to increase management compensation. This same research found that companies that engaged in fraudulent financial reporting often experienced bankruptcy after the fraud was discovered.
- In 2009, Garth Drabinsky and Myron Gottlieb, the founders of Live Entertainment Inc. (Livent), a Canadian public company, were sentenced to five years and four years in jail, respectively, for fraudulent financial reporting. At its peak in the 1990s, Livent was North America's largest live theatre company. The fraud occurred as a result of overstatement of revenues and understatement of expenses on financial statements from 1990 to the first quarter of 1998.
- Fraud as a result of financial statement misrepresentation can also occur when private companies are filing their corporate tax returns. The intention is to understate revenues and overstate expenses to ensure that the company pays minimum amounts of corporate income tax.[3]

What Do You Think?

Over the course of the summer, you operate your own landscaping business. You began your business last summer and have been successful in getting contracts to cut grass on a weekly basis. Most of these contracts begin in mid-April and are completed in mid-October. You are using your parents' old lawn mower and it is reaching the end of its useful life. It is the end of the summer and your local hardware store has a ride-on lawn mower with a snowplow attachment on sale. With the purchase of this lawn mower and plow attachment you could continue to operate your business over the winter. You have approached the bank to lend you money. The bank has requested that you provide a comparative income statement to the end of August. You are thinking that you will record as revenue all of the contract revenue you have earned to the end of August as well as the anticipated contract revenue that you expect to earn to the end of October. You will not record the expenses you expect to incur because you want to maximize the amount of profit your income statement reflects.

Should you be recording all of your revenue to the end of October even though it is only the end of August?

YES—The only way that you will be able to continue operating your business is to obtain the loan from the bank. The only way the bank will lend you the money is if your income statement reflects the maximum amount of profit you will earn to the end of August.

NO—If the bank determines that you are manipulating your income statement, it is unlikely to lend you the money. As well, the bank will likely ask that you prepare a cash budget to the end of October on which you could include all of the anticipated revenues you expect to earn and expenses you expect to incur.

Summary of Study Objectives

1. *Explain when revenues and expenses are recognized and how this forms the basis for accrual accounting.* Revenue is recognized (recorded) when goods or services are exchanged for cash or claims to cash, which results in an increase in future economic benefits. Expenses are recognized (recorded) when assets are consumed or services used, which results in a decrease in future economic benefits. By following revenue and expense recognition criteria, events are recorded in the period when they arise. This is known as the accrual basis of accounting.

2. *Describe the types of adjusting entries and prepare adjusting entries for prepayments.* There are two general types of adjusting entries: prepayments and accruals. Prepayments are either prepaid expenses or unearned revenues. Adjusting entries for prepayments record the portion of the prepayment that applies to the expense incurred or revenue earned in the current accounting period. The adjusting entry for prepaid expenses results in an increase (debit) to an expense account and a decrease (credit) to an asset account. The adjusting entry for unearned revenues results in a decrease (debit) to a liability account and an increase (credit) to a revenue account.

3. *Prepare adjusting entries for accruals.* Adjusting entries for accruals are required in order to record the revenues and expenses that apply to the current accounting period and that have not been recognized through daily entries. Accruals are either accrued revenues or accrued expenses. The adjusting entry for accrued revenues results in an increase (debit) to an asset account and an increase (credit) to a revenue account. The adjusting entry for accrued expenses results in an increase (debit) to an expense account and an increase (credit) to a liability account.

4. *Prepare an adjusted trial balance.* An adjusted trial balance is a trial balance that shows the balances of all accounts at the end of an accounting period, including those that have been adjusted. An adjusted trial balance facilitates the preparation of the financial statements.

5. *Prepare closing entries and a post-closing trial balance.* One purpose of closing entries is to update the Retained Earnings account to its end-of-period balance. A second purpose is to make all temporary accounts (revenue, expense, and dividend accounts) begin the new period with a zero balance. To accomplish this, entries are made to close each individual revenue and expense account to a temporary summary account called Income Summary. The Income Summary account is then closed to the Retained Earnings account. The Dividends account is also closed to Retained Earnings.

A post-closing trial balance lists only permanent accounts (statement of financial position accounts) and the balances that are carried forward to the next accounting period. The purpose of the post-closing trial balance, as with other trial balances, is to prove the equality of total debits and total credits.

the navigator

Glossary

Accrual basis accounting An accounting basis in which transactions that change a company's financial statements are recorded in the periods in which the events occur, rather than in the periods in which the company receives or pays cash. (p. 164)

Accrued expenses Expenses incurred but not yet paid in cash that are recorded at the end of the period by an adjusting entry. (p. 177)

Accrued revenues Revenues earned but not yet received in cash that are recorded at the end of an accounting period by an adjusting entry. (p. 175)

Adjusted trial balance A list of accounts and their balances after all adjustments have been made. (p. 183)

Adjusting entries Journal entries made at the end of an accounting period to update the accounts to ensure the proper recognition of revenues and expenses. (p. 167)

Carrying amount (also known as book value) The difference between the cost of a depreciable asset and its accumulated depreciation. (p. 172)

Cash basis accounting An accounting basis in which revenue is recorded only when cash is received, and an expense is recorded only when cash is paid. (p. 165)

Closing entries Entries at the end of an accounting period to transfer the balances of temporary accounts (revenues, expenses, and dividends) to the permanent shareholders' equity account Retained Earnings. (p. 188)

Depreciation (also known as amortization) The process of allocating the cost of a depreciable asset (for example, buildings and equipment) over its useful life. (p. 171)

Expense recognition The process of recording an expense when there is a decrease in future economic benefits related to a decrease in an asset or an increase in a liability in the course of ordinary activities that can be measured reliably. When there is a direct association between the expenses incurred and the generation of revenue, expenses (effort) are matched with revenues (results). (p. 164)

Income summary A temporary account used in closing revenue and expense accounts. (p. 188)

Permanent accounts   Statement of financial position accounts whose balances are carried forward to the next accounting period. (p. 187)

Post-closing trial balance   A list of permanent accounts and their balances after closing entries have been journalized and posted. (p. 190)

Prepaid expenses   Expenses that are generally paid in cash and recorded as assets before they are used. (p. 169)

Revenue recognition   The concept that revenue is generally considered to be earned (recognized) when goods or services are exchanged for cash or claims to cash (such as accounts receivable), which results in an increase in future economic benefits. In addition, three conditions must be met: (1) the sales or performance effort substantially complete, (2) revenue amount determinable, and (3) collection reasonably assured. (p. 163)

Straight-line method of depreciation   A depreciation method in which depreciation expense is calculated as the cost of an asset divided by its useful life. (p. 171)

Temporary accounts   Revenue, expense, and dividend accounts whose balances are transferred to Retained Earnings at the end of an accounting period. (p. 187)

Unadjusted trial balance   A list of accounts and their balances before adjusting entries have been made. (p. 168)

Unearned revenues   Cash that is received before revenue is earned and is therefore recorded as a liability until it is earned. (p. 173)

Useful life   The length of service of a depreciable asset. (p. 171)

DECISION TOOLKIT—A SUMMARY

 |  |  |

Decision Checkpoints	Info Needed for Decision	Tools to Use for Decision	How to Evaluate Results
At what point should the company record revenue?	Need to understand the nature of the company's business, in particular when the sales or performance effort is considered to be complete.	Revenue should be recorded when earned—that is, when the sales or performance effort is complete, the revenue amount determined, and collection anticipated.	Recognizing revenue too early overstates current period revenue; recognizing it too late understates current period revenue.
At what point should the company record expenses?	Need to understand the nature of the company's business and whether the expense can be directly associated with revenue.	Expenses are recognized when assets are decreased or when liabilities are increased. Often expenses can be directly associated with revenues; that is, the effort (expense) should be matched with the result (revenue).	Recognizing expenses too early overstates current period expenses; recognizing them too late understates current period expenses.

USING THE DECISION TOOLKIT

Gift cards are among the hottest marketing tools in merchandising today. A gift card is a plastic card, similar to a credit card, with a magnetic strip on the back, which is loaded with a cash value when it is purchased. Customers purchase these cards and give them to someone as a gift for later use.

Although gift cards are popular with marketing executives, they raise accounting questions about when revenue should be recognized. Take, for example, Best Buy, whose gift cards range in value from $25 to $500. Suppose that Robert Jacobs purchases a $100 gift card at Best Buy on December 24, and gives it to his wife, Laurel Jones, as a present on December 25. On January 3, Laurel uses the card to purchase $100 worth of merchandise from Best Buy. When do you think Best Buy should recognize revenue and why?

Solution

According to revenue recognition criteria, revenue should be recognized when the sales or performance effort is complete, the revenue amount determined, and collection anticipated.

In this particular case, revenue should be recorded when Best Buy provides the goods. Although the revenue amount was determined when the gift card was sold, and obviously collection was assured on that date as well, the sales or performance effort is not complete until the merchandise is sold. It is also at that time that the expense (cost of goods sold) would be recognized to match with the revenue.

Thus, when Best Buy receives cash in exchange for the gift card on December 24, it should increase (debit) an asset, Cash, and increase (credit) a liability, Unearned Revenue, for $100. On January 3, when Laurel exchanges the card for merchandise, Best Buy should recognize revenue and eliminate the balance in the Unearned Revenue account by debiting Unearned Revenue and crediting Sales Revenue, for $100. Best Buy sells a significant number of gift cards and reported unearned revenue from the sale of gift cards of U.S. $456 million in a recent year.

Comprehensive Do It!

At October 31, 2015, the year-end trial balance for the Blizzard Snow Removal Corporation in Inuvik shows the following balances for selected accounts:

Prepaid insurance	$ 1,800
Equipment	15,000
Accumulated depreciation—equipment	3,000
Bank loan payable	10,000
Unearned revenue	2,100

Blizzard makes its adjusting entries annually. Analysis reveals the following additional data about these accounts:

1. Prepaid insurance is the cost of a one-year insurance policy, effective October 1, 2015.
2. The equipment was purchased on November 1, 2013, and is expected to have a useful life of five years.
3. The bank loan was signed on November 1, 2014, and is repayable in two years. Interest on this 6% loan is due on a monthly basis on the first day of each month.
4. Seven customers paid for the company's six-month, $300 snow removal service package in September. These customers were serviced in October after an early blizzard.
5. Snow removal services provided to other customers but not billed at October 31 totalled $1,500.
6. Income tax instalments have been made each month. Further calculations at year end determine that an additional $250 of income tax will be payable this year.

Instructions

Prepare the adjusting entries at October 31.

Action Plan
- Note that adjustments are being made annually.
- Before determining what adjustments are necessary, look at the amounts that are currently recorded in the accounts.
- After making adjustments, check that the balances in each T account reflect what you meant them to (even when T accounts are not required).
- Show your calculations.

Solution to Comprehensive Do It!

	GENERAL JOURNAL		
Date	Account Titles and Explanation	Debit	Credit
	Adjusting Entries		
Oct. 31	Insurance Expense	150	
	Prepaid Insurance		150
	(To record insurance expired: $1,800 × ¹⁄₁₂)		
31	Depreciation Expense	3,000	
	Accumulated Depreciation—Equipment		3,000
	(To record annual depreciation: $15,000 ÷ 5 = $3,000)		
31	Interest Expense	50	
	Interest Payable		50
	(To accrue interest on the bank loan: $10,000 × 6% × ¹⁄₁₂)		
31	Unearned Revenue	350	
	Service Revenue		350
	(To record revenue earned: $300 ÷ 6 mos. × 7)		
31	Accounts Receivable	1,500	
	Service Revenue		1,500
	(To accrue revenue earned but not billed or collected)		
31	Income Tax Expense	250	
	Income Tax Payable		250
	(To accrue income tax payable)		

WileyPLUS

Self-Test, Brief Exercises, Exercises, Problems: Set A, and many more components are available for practice in *WileyPLUS*.

Self-Test Questions

Answers are at the end of the chapter.

Quiz Yourself

(SO 1) 1. A company gave a price quote for a possible service to a client in February, performed the required service for the client in March, sent an invoice to the client in April, and received payment in May. In which month should the revenue be recognized?
(a) February
(b) March
(c) April
(d) May

(SO 1) 2. Which one of the following statements is *false*?
(a) Companies record events that change their financial statements in the period in which events occur, even if cash was not exchanged.
(b) Companies recognize revenue in the period in which it is earned.
(c) Expenses are related to decreases in future economic benefits.
(d) Companies record revenue only when they receive cash, and record expense only when they pay out cash.

(SO 2) 3. The unadjusted trial balance shows Supplies $1,350 and Supplies Expense $0. If $600 of supplies are on hand at the end of the period, the adjusting entry is
(a) Supplies   600
       Supplies Expense   600
(b) Supplies Expense   600
       Supplies   600
(c) Supplies   750
       Supplies Expense   750
(d) Supplies Expense   750
       Supplies   750

(SO 2) 4. In early September, a university received $6 million from students for tuition in advance relating to the four-month fall term covering the period September 1 to December 31. When the cash was received, the Unearned

Revenue account was credited for the full amount. What adjusting journal entry should the university record on September 30 when preparing financial statements for that month?

(a) Tuition Revenue | 1,500,000 |
    Unearned Revenue | | 1,500,000
(b) Unearned Revenue | 1,500,000 |
    Tuition Revenue | | 1,500,000
(c) Unearned Revenue | 4,500,000 |
    Tuition Revenue | | 4,500,000
(d) Cash | 1,500,000 |
    Tuition Revenue | | 1,500,000

(SO 3) 5. A company has a three-month, $6,000 bank loan payable, signed on January 1 at an interest rate of 4%. Interest is due at maturity. What adjusting entry should the company make at the end of January if it prepares adjusting entries monthly?

(a) Interest Expense | 20 |
    Interest Payable | | 20
(b) Interest Expense | 60 |
    Interest Payable | | 60
(c) Interest Expense | 20 |
    Cash | | 20
(d) Interest Receivable | 20 |
    Interest Revenue | | 20

(SO 3) 6. Kathy Kiska earned a salary of $400 since she was last paid in mid-September and will be paid on October 1. The adjusting entry for Kathy's employer at September 30 is:

(a) Salaries Expense | 400 |
    Salaries Payable | | 400
(b) Salaries Expense | 400 |
    Cash | | 400
(c) Salaries Payable | 400 |
    Cash | | 400
(d) No entry is required.

(SO 4) 7. Which statement about the adjusted trial balance is *incorrect*?
(a) An adjusted trial balance proves the equality of the total debit balances and total credit balances in the ledger after all adjustments are made.
(b) The adjusted trial balance is the main source for the preparation of financial statements.
(c) The adjusted trial balance is prepared after the closing entries have been journalized and posted.
(d) The adjusted trial balance is prepared after the adjusting entries have been journalized and posted.

(SO 4) 8. The Retained Earnings balance in an unadjusted trial balance is $10,000. Profit for the period is $2,500 and dividends are $500. The Retained Earnings account balance in the adjusted trial balance will be:
(a) $9,500
(b) $10,000
(c) $12,000
(d) $12,500

(SO 5) 9. Which of the following accounts will have a zero balance after closing entries have been journalized and posted?
(a) Service Revenue
(b) Supplies
(c) Unearned Revenue
(d) Accumulated Depreciation

(SO 5) 10. Which type of account will appear in the post-closing trial balance?
(a) Permanent accounts
(b) Temporary accounts
(c) Income statement accounts
(d) The dividend account

Questions

(SO 1) 1. Why are adjusting entries needed? Include in your explanation a description of the recognition criteria that relate to adjusting the accounts.

(SO 1) 2. Tony Galego, a lawyer, accepts a legal engagement in March, does the work in April, bills the client $8,000 in May, and is paid in June. If Galego's law firm prepares monthly financial statements, when should it recognize revenue from this engagement? Why?

(SO 1) 3. In completing the engagement in question 2, Tony Galego incurs expenses that are specifically related to this engagement as follows: none in March, $4,500 in April, and none in May and June. How much expense should be deducted from revenue in the month(s) when the revenue is recognized? Why?

(SO 1) 4. How does the cash basis of accounting differ from the accrual basis of accounting? Which basis gives more useful information for decision-making? Why?

(SO 2) 5. The name "prepaid expense" implies that this type of account is an expense account and belongs on an income statement. However, these accounts actually appear on the statement of financial position as assets. Explain (a) why prepaid expense items are assets, and (b) why they require adjustment at the end of each period.

(SO 2) 6. The name "unearned revenue" implies that this type of account is a revenue account and belongs on an income statement. However, these accounts actually appear on the statement of financial position as liabilities. Explain (a) why unearned revenue items are liabilities, and (b) why they require adjustment at the end of each period.

(SO 2)   7. "Depreciation is a process of valuation that results in the reporting of the fair value of the asset." Do you agree? Explain.

(SO 2)   8. Explain the difference between (a) depreciation expense and accumulated depreciation, and (b) cost and carrying amount.

(SO 2)   9. What is a contra asset account? Why do we use a contra asset account to record accumulated depreciation instead of directly reducing the depreciable asset account?

(SO 2, 3)   10. "An adjusting entry affects at least one statement of financial position and one income statement account." Do you agree? Why or why not?

(SO 2, 3)   11. Adjusting entries for prepayments *always* include the Cash account, and adjusting entries for accruals *never* include the Cash account. Do you agree? Why or why not?

(SO 2, 3)   12. The original journal entry must first be examined before an adjusting entry for a prepayment can be prepared. Why is this not also the case for an adjusting entry for an accrual?

(SO 3)   13. A company makes an accrued revenue adjusting entry for $780 and an accrued expense adjusting entry for $510. How much was profit overstated or understated prior to these adjusting entries? Explain.

(SO 3)   14. Reactor Corp. has incurred utility costs for the month of December, but the utility company does not send out its bills until the 15th of the following month. Reactor does not plan on recording the utility costs until it receives the bill on January 15. Assuming Reactor prepares adjusting entries monthly, when should it record these costs—in December or in January? Identify the date of the entry you believe should be used and which accounts should be debited and credited.

(SO 4)   15. Why is it appropriate to prepare financial statements directly from an adjusted trial balance but not from an unadjusted trial balance?

(SO 2, 3, 5)   16. How do adjusting journal entries differ from transaction entries recorded on a daily basis? How do closing journal entries differ from adjusting journal entries?

(SO 4, 5)   17. Explain how an unadjusted trial balance, adjusted trial balance, and post-closing trial balance are similar, and how they differ. How often, and when, should each one be prepared?

(SO 4, 5)   18. Why is the retained earnings balance on the unadjusted trial balance the same amount that appears on the adjusted trial balance? Why is the retained earnings balance on an adjusted trial balance different from the amount that appears on the post-closing trial balance?

(SO 5)   19. What are two reasons for recording closing entries?

(SO 5)   20. Why is the account Dividends not closed with the expense accounts?

(SO 5)   21. Identify whether the Income Summary account would be debited or credited when making each of the four closing entries, assuming the company has (a) profit for the year, and (b) a loss for the year.

(SO 5)   22. Which steps in the accounting cycle may be done daily, which steps are done on a periodic basis (monthly or quarterly), and which steps are usually done only at the company's fiscal year end?

Brief Exercises

Indicate impact on cash and profit.
(SO 1)

BE4–1   Transactions that affect cash do not necessarily affect profit. Identify the impact, if any, of each of the following transactions on cash and profit. The first transaction has been completed for you as an example.

	Cash	Profit
(a) Purchased supplies for cash, $100	−$100	$0

(b) Made an adjusting entry to record use of $75 of the supplies in (a).
(c) Performed services on account, $1,000.
(d) Received $800 from customers in payment of their account in (c).
(e) Purchased equipment for cash, $5,000.
(f) Made an adjusting entry to record depreciation of equipment in (e), $1,000.
(g) Obtained a $1,000 bank loan.
(h) Made an adjusting entry to accrue interest on the loan in (g), $50.
(i) Received $500 cash for services to be provided in the future.
(j) Made an adjusting entry relating to the amount received in (i) to show that $200 of the services had now been provided.
(k) Made an adjusting entry to record utilities incurred but not yet paid, $250.

Calculate revenue on accrual and cash bases.
(SO 1)

BE4–2   Blindleia Care Corporation had the following selected transactions in September:

1. Collected $200 cash from customers for services provided in August.
2. Collected $500 cash from customers for services provided in September.

3. Billed customers $600 for services provided in September.
4. Provided $100 services to customers who paid in advance in August.
5. Received $100 from customers in advance for services to be provided in October.

(a) Calculate revenue for the month of September using the accrual basis of accounting.
(b) Calculate revenue for the month of September using the cash basis of accounting.

BE4–3 Sain Advertising Ltd.'s opening trial balance on January 1 shows Supplies $1,500. On May 1, the company purchased additional supplies for $4,800 on credit. On December 31, there are $2,300 of supplies on hand.
(a) Prepare the journal entry to record the purchase of supplies on May 1.
(b) Calculate the amount of supplies used during the year.
(c) Prepare the adjusting entry required at December 31.
(d) Using T accounts, enter the opening balances in the affected accounts, post the journal entries in (a) and (c), and indicate the adjusted balance in each account.

Prepare and post transaction and adjusting entries for supplies.
(SO 2)

BE4–4 On January 2, 2015, the Claymore Corporation purchased a delivery truck for $50,000 cash. The company uses straight-line depreciation and estimates that the truck will have a five-year useful life. The company has a December 31 year end and adjusts its accounts annually.
(a) Prepare the journal entry to record the purchase of the delivery truck on January 2.
(b) Prepare the adjusting entries required on December 31, 2015 and 2016.
(c) Indicate the statement of financial position presentation of the delivery truck at December 31, 2015 and 2016.

Prepare transaction and adjusting entries for depreciation; show statement presentation.
(SO 2)

BE4–5 On June 1, 2015, Bere Ltd. pays $6,000 to Marla Insurance Corp. for a one-year insurance policy. Both companies have fiscal years ending December 31 and adjust their accounts annually.
(a) Record the June 1 transaction on the books of (1) Bere and (2) Marla.
(b) Calculate the amount of insurance that expired during 2015 and the unexpired cost at December 31.
(c) Prepare the adjusting entry required on December 31 by (1) Bere and (2) Marla.
(d) Post the above entries and indicate the adjusted balance in each account.

Prepare and post transaction and adjusting entries for insurance.
(SO 2, 3)

BE4–6 The total weekly payroll for Classic Auto Repairs Ltd. is $5,000 ($1,000 per day). The payroll is paid every Monday for employee salaries earned during the previous five-day workweek (Monday through Friday, inclusive). Salaries were last paid on Monday, November 28. This year the company's year end, November 30, falls on a Wednesday. Salaries will be paid next on Monday, December 5.
Prepare the journal entries to record each of the following:
(a) Payment of the salaries on November 28
(b) The adjustment to accrue salaries at November 30
(c) Payment of the salaries on December 5

Prepare transaction and adjusting entries for salaries.
(SO 3)

BE4–7 Zieborg Maintenance Corp. has a $375 monthly contract with Crispy Treat Inc. for general maintenance services. Zieborg invoices Crispy on the first of the month for services that it provided in the previous month. Crispy must then pay for these services by the 10th of the following month. Zieborg has a November 30 year end and prepares adjusting entries monthly.
(a) Prepare any adjusting entry required on November 30 by Zieborg.
(b) Given your entry in (a), will Zieborg also need to record a journal entry on December 1 when it invoices Crispy for services provided in November? Why or why not?
(c) Zieborg receives $375 from Crispy on January 10 for services provided in November. Prepare Zieborg's journal entry.

Prepare adjusting and subsequent entries for accrued revenue.
(SO 3)

BE4–8 On July 1, 2015, Nakhooda Limited purchased a truck for $40,000, paying $10,000 cash and signing a 6% six-month bank loan payable for the remainder.
Prepare the journal entries to record each of the following:
(a) The purchase of the truck on July 1
(b) The accrual of interest at year end, December 31, assuming interest has not previously been accrued
(c) Repayment of the interest and the loan on January 1, 2016

Prepare adjusting and subsequent entries for interest.
(SO 3)

BE4–9 Fill in the missing amounts in the following income tax schedule for the Ducharme Corporation. Assume that 2013 was the company's first year of operations.

Determine missing amounts for income tax.
(SO 3)

	2013	2014	2015
Income tax expense	$2,600	$3,600	$ (c)
Income tax payable	(a)	500	700
Income tax paid	2,200	(b)	4,200

Prepare adjusted trial balance.
(SO 4)

BE4–10   The Oromocto Corporation reports the following adjusted account balances, shown in alphabetical order, at the end of its fiscal year, February 28, 2015:

Accounts payable	$13,000		Income tax payable	$ 50
Accounts receivable	28,000		Insurance expense	3,500
Accumulated depreciation—equipment	5,400		Prepaid insurance	2,500
Cash	8,000		Rent expense	6,000
Common shares	20,000		Retained earnings	21,000
Depreciation expense	4,400		Salaries payable	3,000
Dividends	2,000		Salaries expense	16,400
Equipment	23,450		Supplies	1,000
Fees earned	39,500		Supplies expense	4,000
Income tax expense	300		Utilities expense	2,400

Prepare an adjusted trial balance at February 28.

Prepare financial statements.
(SO 4)

BE4–11   Refer to the data in BE4–10 for Oromocto Corporation. During the year ended February 28, 2015, common shares were issued for $5,000. Prepare (a) an income statement, (b) a statement of changes in equity, and (c) a statement of financial position.

Prepare closing entries.
(SO 5)

BE4–12   Refer to the data in BE4–10 for Oromocto Corporation. Prepare the closing journal entries.

Prepare and post closing entries.
(SO 5)

BE4–13   The income statement for Regina Cleaning Services Ltd. for the year ended November 30 shows Service Revenue $126,000; Salaries Expense $90,000; Repairs and Maintenance Expense $15,000; and Income Tax Expense $4,200. The statement of changes in equity shows an opening balance for Retained Earnings of $50,000 and Dividends $5,000.
(a) Calculate the profit or loss for the year.
(b) Prepare the closing journal entries.
(c) Using T accounts, post the closing entries, and determine the ending balances.

Identify post-closing trial balance accounts.
(SO 5)

BE4–14   The following selected accounts appear in the adjusted trial balance for **Maple Leaf Foods Inc.** Identify which accounts would be included in Maple Leaf Foods' post-closing trial balance.
(a) Accounts receivable
(b) Interest expense
(c) Prepaid expenses
(d) Dividends
(e) Depreciation expense
(f) Accounts payable and accruals
(g) Cost of goods sold
(h) Retained earnings
(i) Accumulated depreciation
(j) Income tax expense

Exercises

Identify point of revenue recognition.
(SO 1)

E4–1   The following independent situations require professional judgement to determine when to recognize revenue from the transactions:
(a) **WestJet** sells you a non-refundable one-way airline ticket in September for your flight home at Christmas.
(b) You pay for a one-year subscription to **Maclean's Magazine** in March.
(c) The **Toronto Blue Jays** sell season tickets to games in the Rogers Centre. The season begins in April and ends in October. You purchase your tickets in February.
(d) The **RBC Financial Group** loans you money in August. The loan and the interest are repayable in full in November.
(e) In August, you order a sweater from **Sears** using its on-line catalogue. The sweater arrives in September and you charge it to your Sears credit card. You receive and pay the Sears bill in October.

Instructions
Identify when revenue should be recognized in each situation.

E4–2   In its first year of operations, Athabasca Corp. earned $52,000 in service revenue. Of that amount, $8,000 was on account and the remainder, $44,000, was collected in cash from customers.

The company incurred various expenses totalling $31,000, of which $27,500 was paid in cash. At year end, $3,500 was still owing on account. In addition, Athabasca prepaid $2,000 for insurance coverage that covered the last half of the first year and the first half of the second year. Athabasca expects to owe $3,000 of income tax when it files its corporate income tax return after year end.

Calculate profit on accrual and cash bases.
(SO 1)

Instructions
(a) Calculate the first year's profit under the accrual basis of accounting.
(b) Calculate the first year's profit under the cash basis of accounting.
(c) Which basis of accounting (accrual or cash) gives the most useful information for decision makers? Explain.

E4–3   Action Quest Games Inc. adjusts its accounts annually. The following information is available for the year ended December 31, 2015:

Prepare and post transaction and adjusting entries for prepayments.
(SO 2)

1. Purchased a one-year insurance policy on June 1, for $1,800 cash.
2. Paid $6,500 on August 31 for five months' rent in advance.
3. On September 4, received $3,600 cash in advance from a corporation to sponsor a game each month for a total of nine months for the most improved students at a local school.
4. Signed a contract for cleaning services starting December 1, for $1,000 per month. Paid for the first two months on November 30. (*Hint:* Use the account Prepaid Cleaning to record prepayments.)
5. On December 5, received $1,500 in advance from a gaming club. Determined that on December 31, $475 of these games had not yet been played.

Instructions
(a) For each of the above transactions, prepare the journal entry to record the initial transaction.
(b) For each of the above transactions, prepare the adjusting journal entry that is required on December 31. (*Hint:* Use the account Sponsorship Revenue for item 3 and Repairs and Maintenance Expense for item 4.)
(c) Post the journal entries in parts (a) and (b) to T accounts and determine the final balance in each account balance. (*Note:* Posting to the Cash account is not required.)

E4–4   Acadia Inc. owns the following long-lived assets:

Prepare adjusting entries for depreciation; calculate carrying amount.
(SO 2)

Asset	Date Purchased	Cost	Estimated Useful Life
Vehicles	Jan. 1, 2012	$28,000	7 years
Equipment	July 1, 2013	12,000	3 years
Furniture	Jan. 1, 2015	10,000	5 years

Instructions
(a) Prepare depreciation adjusting entries for each asset for the year ended December 31, 2015, assuming the company adjusts its accounts annually.
(b) For each asset, calculate its accumulated depreciation and carrying amount at December 31, 2015.

E4–5   Greenock Limited has the following information available for accruals for the year ended December 31, 2015. The company adjusts its accounts annually.

Prepare adjusting and subsequent entries for accruals.
(SO 3)

1. The December utility bill for $425 was unrecorded on December 31. Greenock paid the bill on January 11.
2. Greenock is open seven days a week and employees are paid a total of $3,500 every Monday for a seven-day (Monday–Sunday) workweek. December 31 is a Thursday, so employees will have worked four days (Monday, December 28—Thursday, December 31) that they have not been paid for by year end. Employees will be paid next on January 4.
3. Greenock signed a $45,000, 5% bank loan on November 1, 2014, due in two years. Interest is payable on the first day of each following month.
4. Greenock receives a fee from Pizza Shop next door for all pizzas sold to customers using Greenock's facility. The amount owing for December is $300, which Pizza Shop will pay on January 4. (*Hint:* Use the Fees Earned account.)
5. Greenock rented some of its unused warehouse space to a client for $6,000 a month, payable the first day of the following month. It received the rent for the month of December on January 2.

Instructions
(a) For each situation, prepare the adjusting entry required at December 31. Round all calculations to the nearest dollar.
(b) For each situation, prepare the journal entry to record the subsequent cash transaction in 2016.

Prepare transaction and adjusting entries.
(SO 2, 3)

E4–6 The CCBC Corporation had the following post-closing trial balance at the beginning of its fiscal year, July 1, 2015:

	Debit	Credit
Cash	$ 4,400	
Accounts receivable	6,550	
Supplies	1,200	
Equipment	15,000	
Accumulated depreciation—equipment		$ 4,500
Unearned revenue		2,500
Common shares		5,000
Retained earnings		15,150
Totals	$27,150	$27,150

During the month of July, the following selected transactions took place:

July	2	Paid $1,500 for two months' rent in advance for July and August.
	7	Purchased $200 of supplies on account.
	14	Collected half of outstanding accounts receivable.
	15	Borrowed $1,000 from the bank at an interest rate of 5%.
	21	Received $1,000 cash from a customer for services to be provided in August.
	28	Provided $1,500 of services to a customer on account.

Additional information:

1. At July 31, the company had provided $800 of services for a client that it had not billed or recorded.
2. Supplies on hand at July 31 were $500.
3. The equipment has a 10-year useful life.
4. Interest is due on the bank loan on the first day of each following month, beginning August 1.
5. As at July 31, the company owed $2,500 to its employees for the month just ended.
6. As at July 31, the company had earned $2,000 of revenue that had been paid in advance.

Instructions
(a) Record the July transactions.
(b) Prepare adjusting entries at July 31, assuming the company prepares adjusting entries monthly. Round all calculations to the nearest dollar.

Prepare adjusting entries.
(SO 2, 3)

E4–7 On March 31, 2015, Easy Rental Agency Inc.'s trial balance included the following unadjusted account balances. The company's year end is December 31 and it adjusts its accounts quarterly.

	Debit	Credit
Prepaid insurance	$14,400	
Supplies	2,800	
Equipment	21,600	
Accumulated depreciation—equipment		$ 5,400
Unearned revenue		9,600
Loan payable		20,000
Rent revenue		30,000
Salaries expense	14,000	

An analysis of the accounts shows the following:

1. The equipment, which was purchased on January 1, 2014, is estimated to have a useful life of four years.
2. One-third of the unearned rent revenue is still unearned at the end of the quarter.
3. The loan payable has an interest rate of 6%. Interest is paid on the first day of each following month and was last paid March 1, 2015.
4. Supplies on hand total $850 at March 31.
5. The one-year insurance policy was purchased for $14,400 on January 1.
6. Income tax is estimated to be $3,200 for the quarter.

Instructions

Prepare the quarterly adjusting entries required at March 31, 2015.

E4–8 A partial adjusted trial balance follows for Nolet Ltd. at January 31, 2015. The company's fiscal year end is December 31 and it makes adjustments monthly.

Analyze adjusted data.
(SO 2, 3, 4)

	Debit	Credit
Supplies	$ 700	
Prepaid insurance	1,600	
Equipment	7,200	
Accumulated depreciation—equipment		$3,660
Income tax payable		800
Unearned revenue		750
Service revenue		2,000
Depreciation expense	60	
Insurance expense	400	
Supplies expense	950	
Income tax expense	1,800	

Instructions

(a) If $1,600 was received in December and these services were performed as expected in January, what was the balance in Unearned Revenue at January 1? Assume there were no other transactions that affected Unearned Revenue during this period.
(b) If the amount in the Depreciation Expense account is the depreciation for one month, when was the equipment purchased? Assume that there have been no purchases or sales of equipment since this original purchase.
(c) If the amount in Insurance Expense is the amount of the January 31 adjusting entry, and the original insurance premium was for one year, what was the total premium and when was the policy purchased?
(d) If the amount in Supplies Expense is the amount of the January 31 adjusting entry, and $750 of supplies were purchased in January, what was the balance in Supplies on January 1?
(e) If $1,800 was recorded as payable in December and $2,000 of income tax was paid in January, what was the balance in Income Tax Payable at January 1?

E4–9 Fraser Valley Services Ltd. reports the following adjusted account balances, shown in alphabetical order, at the end of its fiscal year, August 31, 2015:

Prepare adjusted trial balance.
(SO 4)

Accounts payable	$ 2,800	Interest expense	$ 1,500
Accounts receivable	18,225	Interest payable	1,500
Accumulated depreciation—equipment	5,905	Prepaid insurance	3,450
Bank loan payable, due September 1, 2018	25,000	Rent expense	15,000
Cash	11,430	Rent payable	1,250
Common shares	5,000	Retained earnings	5,400
Depreciation expense	2,275	Salaries expense	19,200
Dividends	600	Salaries payable	2,200
Equipment	25,600	Service revenue	54,275
Income tax expense	2,000	Supplies	3,400
Income tax payable	1,500	Supplies expense	1,750
Insurance expense	1,100	Unearned revenue	700

Instructions

Prepare an adjusted trial balance.

E4–10 The adjusted trial balance for Fraser Valley Services Ltd. was prepared in E4–9. During the year, the company issued common shares for $1,000.

Prepare financial statements.
(SO 4)

Instructions

Prepare (a) an income statement, (b) a statement of changes in equity, and (c) a statement of financial position.

E4–11 The adjusted trial balance for Fraser Valley Services Ltd. was prepared in E4–9.

Prepare closing entries and post-closing trial balance.
(SO 5)

Instructions

(a) Prepare the closing entries at August 31.
(b) Prepare a post-closing trial balance.

Problems: Set A

Calculate profit on cash and accrual bases.
(SO 1)

P4–1A   Your examination of the records of Southlake Corp. shows the company collected $187,800 in cash from customers and paid $109,400 in cash for operating costs in its first year of operations. If Southlake followed the accrual basis of accounting, it would report the following year-end balances in selected accounts:

Accounts payable	$ 3,000
Accounts receivable	8,400
Accumulated depreciation	24,600
Income tax payable	15,800
Prepaid insurance	3,000
Unearned revenue	2,800

Instructions
(a) Calculate Southlake's profit on a cash basis for the year.
(b) Calculate Southlake's profit on an accrual basis for the year. (*Hint*: Start with the profit calculated on a cash basis in (a) and then adjust for prepayments and accruals.)
(c) Which basis of accounting do you recommend Southlake use? Why?

Prepare transaction and adjusting entries for prepayments.
(SO 2)

P4–2A   Ouellette Corporation began operations on January 2. Its year end is December 31, and it adjusts its accounts annually. Selected transactions for the current year follow:

1. On January 2, purchased supplies for $4,100 cash. A physical count at December 31 revealed that $700 of supplies were still on hand.
2. Purchased a vehicle for $45,000 on April 1, paying $5,000 cash and signing a $40,000 bank loan for the balance. The vehicle is estimated to have a useful life of five years.
3. Purchased a $3,600, one-year insurance policy for cash on August 1. The policy came into effect on that date.
4. Received a $1,600 advance cash payment from a client on November 9 for services to be provided in the future. As at December 31, half of these services had been completed.
5. On December 1, the company rented additional office space for a six-month period starting on December 1 for $1,200 each month. It paid rent for the months of December and January in advance on this date.

Instructions
(a) For each of the above situations, prepare the journal entry for the original transaction.
(b) For each of the above situations, prepare any adjusting entry required at December 31.

Prepare adjusting and subsequent entries for accruals.
(SO 3)

P4–3A   Zheng Corporation had the following selected transactions in the month of March. The company adjusts its accounts monthly.

1. The company has an 8%, $12,000 bank loan payable due in one year. Interest is payable on the first day of each following month.
2. At the end of March, the company earned $250 interest on its investments. The bank deposited this amount in Zheng's cash account on April 1.
3. Zheng has five employees who each earn $200 a day. Salaries are normally paid on Fridays for work completed Monday through Friday of the same week. Salaries were last paid on Friday, March 27. March 31 falls on a Tuesday this year. Salaries will be paid next on Friday, April 3.
4. At the end of March, the company owed the utility company $550 and the telephone company $200 for services received during the month. These bills were paid on April 10. (*Hint:* Use the Office Expense account for the telephone services.)
5. At the end of March, Zheng has earned service revenue of $3,000 that it has not yet billed. It bills its clients for this amount on April 4. On April 30, it collects $2,000 of this amount due.

Instructions
(a) For each of the above situations, prepare the adjusting journal entry required at March 31.
(b) For each of the above situations, prepare the journal entry to record the subsequent cash transaction in April.

Prepare transaction and adjusting entries.
(SO 2, 3)

P4–4A   The following independent events for New Age Theatre Ltd. during the year ended November 30, 2015, require a journal entry or an adjusting journal entry, or both. The company adjusts its accounts annually.

1. On June 1, 2014, the theatre purchased vehicles for $80,000 cash. The vehicles' estimated useful life is five years.
2. The theatre has eight plays each season. This year's season starts in October 2015 and ends in May 2016 (one play per month). Season tickets sell for $320. On October 1, 400 season tickets were sold for the 2015–2016 season. The theatre credited Unearned Revenue for the full amount received on October 1 and uses a Ticket Revenue account to record revenue earned from season tickets.
3. Supplies on hand amounted to $1,000 at the beginning of the year. On February 17, additional supplies were purchased for cash at a cost of $2,100. At the end of the year, a physical count showed that supplies on hand amounted to $500.

4. On June 1, 2015, the theatre borrowed $100,000 from the Bank of Montreal at an interest rate of 6%. The principal is to be repaid in one year. The interest is payable on the first day of each following month.

5. The New Age Theatre rents a portion of its facilities for $400 a month to a local dance club that uses the space for rehearsals. On November 2, the club's treasurer accidentally sent a cheque for only $200 for the November rent. She promised to send a cheque in December for the balance when she returned from vacation. On December 4, the theatre received a $600 cheque for the balance owing from November plus all of December's rent.

6. The total weekly payroll is $7,000, paid every Monday for employee salaries earned during the prior seven-day week (Sunday to Saturday). Salaries were last paid (and recorded) on Monday, November 30, and will be paid next on Monday, December 7.

7. Upon reviewing its income tax calculations on November 30, the theatre noted that an additional $1,250 of income tax was owed. This additional amount was paid on December 29.

Instructions

(a) Prepare the journal entry to record the original transaction for items 1, 2, 3, 4, and 5.

(b) Prepare the year-end adjusting entry required for items 1 through 7 on November 30.

(c) Record the subsequent cash transactions in December for (1) the interest paid on December 1 (item 4), (2) the cheque received on December 4 (item 5), (3) the payroll paid on December 7 (item 6), and (4) the income tax paid on December 29 (item 7).

P4–5A   A review of the ledger of Chance Corporation at July 31, 2015, produces the following unadjusted data for the preparation of annual adjusting entries:

Prepare adjusting entries.
(SO 2, 3)

1. Prepaid Insurance, July 31 unadjusted balance, $11,700: The company has separate insurance policies on its building and its vehicles. Policy B4564 on the building was purchased on December 1, 2013, for $10,800. The policy has a term of two years. Policy A2958 on the vehicles was purchased on February 1, 2015, for $4,500. This policy has a term of 18 months.

2. Buildings, July 31 unadjusted balance, $444,000: The company owns two buildings. The first was purchased on September 1, 2001, for $252,000 and has an estimated 30-year useful life. The second was purchased on May 1, 2009, for $192,000 and has an estimated 40-year useful life.

3. Unearned Revenue, July 31 unadjusted balance, $51,000: The selling price of a magazine subscription is $50 for 12 monthly issues. A review of subscription contracts reveals the following:

Subscription Date	Number of Subscriptions Sold
November 1, 2014	220
February 1, 2015	310
May 1, 2015	490
	1,020

4. Salaries Payable, July 31 unadjusted balance, $0: There are nine salaried employees. Salaries are paid every Monday for the previous six-day workweek (Monday to Saturday). Six employees receive a salary of $625 each per week, and three employees earn $750 each per week. July 31 is a Friday.

Instructions

(a) Prepare a calculation to show why the unadjusted balance in the Prepaid Insurance account is $11,700 and why the unadjusted balance in the Unearned Revenue account is $51,000.

(b) Prepare the adjusting journal entries required at July 31. (*Hint:* Use the account Subscription Revenue for item 3.)

P4–6A   Near the end of its first year of operations, December 31, 2015, Creative Designs Ltd. approached the local bank for a $20,000 loan and was asked to submit financial statements prepared on an accrual basis. Although the company kept no formal accounting records, it did maintain a record of cash receipts and payments. The following information is available for the year ended December 31:

Convert cash to accrual basis; prepare financial statements.
(SO 1, 2, 3, 4)

	Cash Receipts	Cash Payments
Issue of common shares	$ 20,000	
Fees earned	157,600	
Equipment		$ 35,400
Supplies		6,800
Rent		20,000
Insurance		3,840
Income tax		6,000
Advertising		6,800
Salaries		59,800
Office expense		1,800
Dividends		10,000
	$177,600	$150,440

Additional information:

1. Fees from design work earned but not yet collected amounted to $2,400.
2. The equipment was purchased at the beginning of January and has an estimated six-year useful life.
3. Supplies on hand on December 31 were $1,260.
4. Rent payments included a $1,500 per month rental fee and a $2,000 deposit that is refundable at the end of the two-year lease. (*Hint:* Use the Prepaid Rent account for the refundable deposit.)
5. The insurance was purchased on February 1 for a one-year period expiring January 31, 2016.
6. Salaries earned for the last four days in December and to be paid in January 2016 amounted to $3,050.
7. At year end, it was determined that an additional $7,000 is owed for income tax.

Instructions

(a) Calculate the cash balance at December 31.
(b) Prepare an accrual-based (1) income statement, (2) statement of changes in equity, and (3) statement of financial position.

Prepare and post
adjusting entries;
prepare adjusted trial
balance.
(SO 2, 3, 4)

P4–7A The following is River Tours Limited's unadjusted trial balance at its year end, November 30, 2015. The company adjusts its accounts annually.

	Debit	Credit
Cash	$ 1,800	
Accounts receivable	2,640	
Supplies	965	
Prepaid rent	2,400	
Prepaid insurance	7,320	
Equipment	13,440	
Accumulated depreciation—equipment		$ 3,360
Boats	140,400	
Accumulated depreciation—boats		46,800
Accounts payable		1,925
Unearned revenue		14,000
Bank loan payable		54,000
Common shares		10,000
Retained earnings		27,225
Fees earned		110,575
Salaries expense	69,560	
Repairs and maintenance expense	11,170	
Rent expense	13,200	
Interest expense	3,465	
Advertising expense	825	
Income tax expense	700	
	$267,885	$267,885

Additional information:

1. The insurance policy has a one-year term beginning April 1, 2015. At that time, a premium of $7,320 was paid.
2. The equipment has an estimated useful life of 8 years. The boats have an estimated useful life of 12 years.
3. A physical count shows $300 of supplies on hand at November 30.
4. The bank loan payable has a 7% interest rate. Interest is paid on the first day of each following month.
5. Deposits of $1,400 each were received for advance tour reservations from 10 school groups. At November 30, all of these deposits have been earned.
6. Employees are owed a total of $500 at November 30.
7. A senior citizens' organization that had not made an advance deposit took a river tour for $1,250. This group was not billed until December for the services provided.
8. Additional advertising costs of $260 have been incurred, but the bills have not been received by November 30.
9. On November 1, the company paid $2,400 rent in advance for November and December.
10. Income tax payable for the year is estimated to be an additional $300 beyond that recorded to date.

Instructions

(a) Prepare T accounts, and enter the unadjusted trial balance amounts.
(b) Prepare and post the adjusting journal entries required at November 30.
(c) Prepare an adjusted trial balance at November 30.

P4–8A   On October 31, 2015, the Alou Equipment Repair Corp.'s post-closing trial balance was as follows. The company adjusts its accounts monthly.

Complete accounting cycle through to preparation of financial statements.
(SO 2, 3, 4)

	Debit	Credit
Cash	$15,580	
Accounts receivable	15,820	
Supplies	4,000	
Equipment	18,000	
Accumulated depreciation—equipment		$ 3,600
Accounts payable		4,600
Salaries payable		1,000
Unearned revenue		1,000
Common shares		10,000
Retained earnings		33,200
	$53,400	$53,400

During November, the following transactions were completed:

Nov.	9	Paid $2,200 to employees for salaries due, of which $1,000 is for October salaries payable and $1,200 for November.
	12	Issued common shares for $5,000.
	13	Received $12,400 cash from customers in payment of accounts.
	19	Received $11,400 cash for services performed in November.
	20	Purchased supplies on account, $600.
	21	Paid creditors $4,600 of accounts payable due.
	23	Paid November rent, $600.
	23	Paid salaries, $2,400.
	27	Performed services on account, $3,800.
	28	Paid a cash dividend, $500.
	30	Received $1,100 from customers for services to be provided in the future.

Adjustment data for the month:

1. Supplies on hand are $1,000.
2. Accrued salaries payable are $1,000.
3. The equipment has an estimated useful life of five years.
4. Unearned revenue of $800 was earned during the month.
5. Income tax payable is estimated to be $1,100.

Instructions

(a) Prepare T accounts, and enter the opening balances at November 1.
(b) Prepare and post the November transaction entries.
(c) Prepare a trial balance at November 30.
(d) Prepare and post the adjusting journal entries for the month.
(e) Prepare an adjusted trial balance at November 30.
(f) Prepare (1) an income statement, (2) a statement of changes in equity, and (3) a statement of financial position.

P4–9A   Refer to the data for Alou Equipment Repair Corp. in P4–8A. Assume that Alou closes its books monthly.

Prepare and post closing entries; prepare post-closing trial balance.
(SO 5)

Instructions

(a) Prepare the closing journal entries.
(b) Post the closing entries to the T accounts prepared in P4–8A.
(c) Prepare a post-closing trial balance at November 30.

Prepare adjusted trial balance, closing entries, and post-closing trial balance.
(SO 4, 5)

P4–10A Accounts from the adjusted trial balance at September 30, 2015, are listed in alphabetical order below for Ozaki Corp.:

Accounts payable	$ 4,460	Income tax payable	$ 200
Accounts receivable	8,435	Interest expense	105
Accumulated depreciation—equipment	750	Interest payable	105
Bank loan payable	7,800	Rent expense	1,500
Cash	3,250	Retained earnings	2,600
Common shares	7,000	Salaries expense	13,840
Depreciation expense	750	Salaries payable	840
Dividends	700	Supplies	1,265
Equipment	15,040	Supplies expense	485
Fees earned	22,485	Unearned revenue	550
Income tax expense	600	Utilities expense	820

Instructions

(a) Prepare an adjusted trial balance.

(b) Prepare the closing journal entries.

(c) Prepare a post-closing trial balance at September 30.

Prepare and post adjusting entries; prepare adjusted trial balance and financial statements; assess financial performance.
(SO 2, 3, 4)

P4–11A The following is the unadjusted trial balance for Rainbow Lodge Ltd. at its year end, May 31, 2015. The company adjusts its accounts monthly.

	Debit	Credit
Cash	$ 6,400	
Accounts receivable	11,800	
Supplies	4,880	
Prepaid insurance	4,550	
Land	106,370	
Buildings	168,000	
Accumulated depreciation—buildings		$ 16,800
Furniture	33,600	
Accumulated depreciation—furniture		13,440
Accounts payable		8,140
Unearned revenue		17,500
Mortgage payable, due in 2019		126,000
Common shares		60,000
Retained earnings		41,580
Dividends	2,000	
Rent revenue		200,320
Salaries expense	98,700	
Utilities expense	26,600	
Interest expense	9,240	
Insurance expense	3,640	
Advertising expense	1,000	
Income tax expense	7,000	
	$483,780	$483,780

Additional information:

1. An annual insurance policy was purchased for the first time on October 1, 2014, for $10,920 cash.
2. A count of supplies shows $1,340 of supplies on hand on May 31.
3. The buildings have an estimated useful life of 20 years.
4. The furniture has an estimated useful life of five years.
5. Customers must pay a $100 deposit if they want to book a room in advance during the peak period. An analysis of these bookings indicates that 175 deposits were received and credited to Unearned Revenue. By May 31, 25 of the deposits were earned.
6. On May 25, a local business contracted with Rainbow Lodge to rent one of its housekeeping units for four months, starting June 1, at a rate of $2,800 per month. An advance payment equal to one month's rent was paid on May 25 and credited to Rent Revenue.
7. On May 31, Rainbow Lodge has earned $1,780 of rent revenue from customers who are currently staying at the inn. The customers will only pay the amount owing when they check out in early June.
8. Salaries of $1,590 are unpaid at May 31.
9. The mortgage interest rate is 8%. Interest has been paid to May 1; the next payment is due June 1.

10. The May utility bill of $2,240 has not yet been recorded or paid.
11. Additional income tax is estimated to be $1,000.
12. During the month of May, $4,000 of common shares were issued. (*Note*: This has already been recorded.)

Instructions
(a) Prepare T accounts, and enter the trial balance amounts.
(b) Prepare and post the adjusting journal entries for the month.
(c) Prepare an adjusted trial balance at May 31.
(d) Prepare (1) an income statement, (2) a statement of changes in equity, and (3) a statement of financial position for the year.
(e) A friend of yours is considering investing in the company and asks you to comment on the company's operations and financial position. Is the company performing well or not? Does the financial position look healthy or weak? Use specific information from the financial statements to support your answer.

P4–12A Refer to the data for Rainbow Lodge Ltd. in P4–11A.

Instructions
(a) Prepare the closing journal entries.
(b) Post the closing entries to the T accounts prepared in P4–11A.
(c) Prepare a post-closing trial balance at May 31.

Prepare and post closing entries; prepare post-closing trial balance.
(SO 5)

Problems: Set B

P4–1B Your examination of the records of Northland Corp. shows the company collected $78,100 in cash from customers and paid $53,900 in cash for operating costs in its first year of operations. If Northland followed the accrual basis of accounting, it would report the following year-end balances in selected accounts:

Calculate profit on cash and accrual bases.
(SO 1)

Accounts payable	$ 905
Accounts receivable	1,450
Accumulated depreciation	8,625
Income tax payable	4,600
Prepaid insurance	810
Unearned revenue	700

Instructions
(a) Calculate Northland's profit on a cash basis for the year.
(b) Calculate Northland's profit on an accrual basis for the year. (*Hint*: Start with the profit calculated on a cash basis in (a) and then adjust for prepayments and accruals.)
(c) Which basis of accounting do you recommend Northland use? Why?

P4–2B Bourque Corporation began operations on January 2. Its year end is December 31, and it adjusts its accounts annually. Selected transactions for the current year follow:

Prepare transaction and adjusting entries for prepayments.
(SO 2)

1. On January 2, purchased supplies for $2,100 cash. A physical count at December 31 revealed that $550 of supplies were still on hand.
2. Purchased equipment for $20,000 cash on March 1. The equipment is estimated to have a useful life of five years.
3. Purchased a one-year, $5,040 insurance policy for cash on June 1. The policy came into effect on that date.
4. On November 15, received a $1,275 advance cash payment from three clients for services to be provided in the future. As at December 31, work had been completed for two of the clients ($425 each).
5. On December 15, the company paid $2,500 rent in advance for the next month (January).

Instructions
(a) For each of the above situations, prepare the journal entry for the original transaction.
(b) For each of the above situations, prepare any adjusting journal entry required at December 31.

P4–3B Hangzhou Corporation had the following selected transactions in the month of November. The company adjusts its accounts monthly.

Prepare adjusting and subsequent entries for accruals.
(SO 3)

1. Hangzhou has a biweekly payroll of $6,000. Salaries are normally paid every second Monday for work completed for the two preceding weeks. Employees work a five-day week, Monday through Friday. Salaries were last paid Monday, November 23, and will be paid next on Monday, December 7.
2. The company has a 7%, $20,000 bank loan payable due September 1 of the next year. Interest is payable on the first day of each following month.

3. At the end of November, Hangzhou has $1,000 of invoices for services provided to customers that have not yet been sent. It mails these invoices on December 1, and collects the amounts due on December 21.
4. At the end of November, the company earned $10 interest on the cash in its bank account. The bank deposited this amount in the company's cash account on December 1.
5. At the end of November, it was estimated that the company owed $1,000 of income tax. This amount was paid on December 18.

Instructions

(a) For each of the above situations, prepare the adjusting journal entry required at November 30.
(b) For each of the above situations, prepare the journal entry to record the subsequent cash transaction in December.

Prepare transaction and adjusting entries.
(SO 2, 3)

P4–4B The following independent events for Repertory Theatre Ltd. during the year ended December 31, 2015, require a journal entry or an adjusting journal entry, or both. The company adjusts its accounts annually.

1. Supplies on hand amounted to $1,500 at the beginning of the year. On March 1, additional supplies were purchased for $5,250 cash. At the end of the year, a physical count showed that supplies on hand amounted to $1,000.
2. The theatre owns a truck that was purchased on January 2, 2015, for $120,000. The truck's estimated useful life is four years.
3. The theatre has nine plays each season, which starts in September 2015 and ends in May 2016 (one play per month). Season tickets sell for $360. On August 21, 600 season tickets were sold for the upcoming 2015–2016 season. The theatre credited Unearned Revenue for the full amount received on August 21 and uses a Ticket Revenue account to record revenue earned from season tickets.
4. On June 1, the theatre borrowed $30,000 from La Caisse Populaire Desjardins at an interest rate of 6%, to be repaid in one year. The interest is payable on the first day of each following month.
5. The total weekly payroll is $9,000, paid every Monday for employee salaries earned during the prior six-day workweek (Tuesday to Sunday). This year, December 31 falls on a Thursday. Salaries were last paid (and recorded) on Monday, December 28, and will be paid next on Monday, January 4.
6. Repertory Theatre rents a portion of its facilities for $600 a month to a local seniors' choir that uses the space for rehearsals. The choir's treasurer was ill during December, and on January 6, the theatre received a cheque for both the amount owing for the month of December and the rent for the month of January.
7. Upon reviewing its books on December 31, the theatre noted that a telephone bill for the month of December had not yet been received. A call to Aliant determined that the telephone bill was for $1,125. The bill was paid on January 12. (*Hint:* Use the Office Expense account for telephone services.)

Instructions

(a) Prepare the journal entry to record the original transaction for items 1, 2, 3, and 4.
(b) Prepare the year-end adjusting entry required for items 1 through 7 on December 31.
(c) Record the subsequent cash transaction in January for (1) the interest paid on January 1 (item 4), (2) payment of the payroll on January 4 (item 5), (3) receipt of the rent on January 6 (item 6), and (4) payment of the telephone bill on January 12 (item 7).

Prepare adjusting entries.
(SO 2, 3)

P4–5B A review of the ledger of Greenberg Corporation at October 31, 2015, produces the following unadjusted data for the preparation of annual adjusting entries:

1. Prepaid Advertising, October 31 unadjusted balance, $14,160: The company has two advertising contracts in two trade magazines that publish monthly, with the first advertisement running in the month following the month in which the contract is signed. Contract A650 was signed February 1 to run in 12 magazine issues, starting March 1 for $520 per month. Contract B974 was signed June 1 to run in 16 magazine issues starting July 1 for $495 per month.
2. Unearned Revenue, October 31 unadjusted balance, $303,000: The company began subleasing office space in its new building on September 1. At October 31, the company had the following rental contracts that are paid in full for the entire term of the lease.

Date	Term (in months)	Monthly Rent	Number of Leases
Sept. 1	6	$4,500	5
Oct. 1	6	7,000	4

3. Bank Loan Payable, October 31 unadjusted balance, $90,000: This represents a one-year, 8% bank loan signed on April 1. Interest is payable at maturity.
4. Vehicles, October 31 unadjusted balance, $39,000: The company owns a delivery truck, purchased for $39,000 on April 1, 2014. The truck has a five-year useful life.

Instructions

(a) Prepare a calculation to show why the unadjusted balance in the Prepaid Advertising account is $14,160 and why the unadjusted balance in the Unearned Revenue account is $303,000.
(b) Prepare the adjusting journal entries required at October 31.

P4–6B The Radical Edge Ltd., a ski tuning and repair shop, opened November 1, 2014. Although the company did not keep any formal accounting records, it did maintain a record of cash receipts and payments. The following information is available at the end of the first ski season, April 30, 2015:

Convert cash to accrual basis; prepare financial statements.
(SO 1, 2, 3, 4)

	Cash Receipts	Cash Payments
Issue of common shares	$20,000	
Ski and snowboard repair services	66,500	
Repair equipment		$47,040
Rent		4,550
Insurance		2,760
Advertising		920
Utility bills		1,900
Salaries		7,200
Income tax		6,000
	$86,500	$70,370

Additional information:

1. At the end of April, customers owe The Radical Edge $1,440 for services they have received and not yet paid for.
2. The repair equipment was purchased at the beginning of November and has an estimated useful life of eight years.
3. On November 1, the company began renting space at a cost of $650 per month on a one-year lease. As required by the lease contract, the company paid the last month's (October 2015) rent in advance.
4. The insurance policy was purchased November 1 and is effective for one year.
5. At April 30, $4,240 is owed for unpaid salaries.
6. At April 30, it was determined that an additional $800 is owed for income tax.

Instructions
(a) Calculate the cash balance at April 30.
(b) Prepare an accrual-based (1) income statement, (2) statement of changes in equity, and (3) statement of financial position for the six months ended April 30.

P4–7B The following is Ortega Limo Service Ltd.'s unadjusted trial balance at its year end, December 31, 2015. The company adjusts its accounts annually.

Prepare and post adjusting entries; prepare adjusted trial balance.
(SO 2, 3, 4)

	Debit	Credit
Cash	$ 4,600	
Accounts receivable	8,220	
Supplies	2,500	
Prepaid insurance	3,600	
Prepaid rent	2,300	
Vehicles	58,000	
Accumulated depreciation—vehicles		$ 14,500
Furniture	16,000	
Accumulated depreciation—furniture		4,000
Unearned revenue		3,600
Bank loan payable, due September 1, 2019		27,475
Common shares		5,000
Retained earnings		7,600
Dividends	3,800	
Service revenue		115,600
Salaries expense	57,000	
Rent expense	12,650	
Repairs and maintenance expense	4,690	
Interest expense	2,415	
Income tax expense	2,000	
	$177,775	$177,775

Additional information:

1. The insurance policy has a one-year term beginning March 1, 2015. At that time, a premium of $3,600 was paid.
2. A physical count of supplies at December 31 shows $570 of supplies on hand.
3. The vehicles were purchased on January 2, 2014, and have an estimated useful life of four years.
4. The furniture was purchased on July 2, 2012, and has an estimated useful life of 10 years.
5. Service revenue earned but not billed or recorded at December 31 is $1,750.
6. Interest on the 7% bank loan is paid on the first day of each following quarter (January 1, April 1, July 1, and October 1).

7. One of Ortega's customers paid $3,600 in advance for a six-month contract at the rate of $600 per month. The contract began on November 1 and Ortega credited Unearned Revenue at the time.
8. Drivers' salaries total $230 per day. At December 31, three days of salaries are unpaid.
9. On December 1, Ortega paid $2,300 ($1,150 per month) for the December 2015 and January 2016 rent in advance.
10. Income tax for the year is estimated to be $2,850. The company has paid $2,000 in income tax instalments to date.

Instructions
(a) Prepare T accounts and enter the trial balance amounts.
(b) Prepare and post the adjusting journal entries required at December 31.
(c) Prepare an adjusted trial balance at December 31.

Complete accounting cycle through to preparation of financial statements.
(SO 2, 3, 4)

P4–8B   On August 31, 2015, the Rijo Equipment Repair Corp.'s post-closing trial balance was as follows. The company prepares adjusting entries monthly.

	Debit	Credit
Cash	$ 9,760	
Accounts receivable	7,440	
Supplies	1,600	
Equipment	30,000	
Accumulated depreciation— equipment		$ 3,000
Accounts payable		6,200
Salaries payable		1,400
Unearned revenue		800
Common shares		20,000
Retained earnings		17,400
	$48,800	$48,800

During September, the following transactions were completed:

Sept.	4	Paid employees $2,200 for salaries due, of which $1,400 was for August salaries payable and $800 for September.
	6	Received $5,400 cash from customers in payment of accounts.
	11	Received $8,800 cash for services performed in September.
	12	Sold common shares for $5,000.
	17	Purchased supplies on account, $2,000.
	21	Paid creditors $7,000 of accounts payable due.
	24	Paid September and October rent, $2,000 ($1,000 per month).
	25	Paid salaries, $2,200.
	26	Performed services on account, $1,600.
	27	Received $1,300 from customers for services to be provided in the future.
	28	Paid a cash dividend, $500.
	28	Paid income tax for the month, $600.

Adjustment data for the month:

1. Supplies on hand total $800.
2. Accrued salaries payable are $1,600.
3. Accrued service revenue for $600.
4. The equipment has a useful life of 10 years.
5. Unearned revenue of $800 has been earned.

Instructions
(a) Prepare T accounts, and enter the opening balances at September 1.
(b) Prepare and post the September transaction entries.
(c) Prepare a trial balance at September 30.
(d) Prepare and post the adjusting journal entries for the month.
(e) Prepare an adjusted trial balance at September 30.
(f) Prepare (1) an income statement, (2) a statement of changes in equity, and (3) a statement of financial position.

Prepare and post closing entries; prepare post-closing trial balance.
(SO 5)

P4–9B   Refer to the data for Rijo Equipment Repair Corp. in P4–8B. Assume that Rijo closes its books monthly.

Instructions
(a) Prepare the closing journal entries.
(b) Post the closing entries to the T accounts prepared in P4–8B.
(c) Prepare a post-closing trial balance at September 30.

P4-10B Accounts from the adjusted trial balance at December 31, 2015, are listed in alphabetical order below for Grant Advertising Agency Limited:

Accounts payable	$ 4,800	Insurance expense	$ 1,600
Accounts receivable	19,750	Interest expense	700
Bank loan payable	10,000	Interest payable	700
Cash	11,000	Prepaid insurance	800
Common shares	20,000	Rent expense	7,200
Depreciation expense	13,200	Retained earnings	10,400
Dividends	2,000	Salaries expense	13,625
Equipment	66,000	Salaries payable	1,625
Accumulated depreciation—equipment	39,600	Trading investments	10,850
Fees earned	60,600	Supplies	1,265
Income tax expense	7,000	Supplies expense	5,935
Income tax payable	7,000	Unearned revenue	6,200

Prepare adjusted trial balance, closing entries, and post-closing trial balance. (SO 4, 5)

Instructions
(a) Prepare an adjusted trial balance.
(b) Prepare the closing journal entries.
(c) Prepare a post-closing trial balance at December 31.

P4-11B The following is the unadjusted trial balance for Rocky Mountain Resort Inc. at its year end, August 31, 2015. The company adjusts its accounts annually.

Prepare and post adjusting entries; prepare adjusted trial balance and financial statements; assess financial performance. (SO 2, 3, 4)

	Debit	Credit
Cash	$ 38,820	
Supplies	6,990	
Prepaid insurance	12,720	
Land	70,000	
Buildings	290,000	
Accumulated depreciation—buildings		$ 87,000
Furniture	57,200	
Accumulated depreciation—furniture		22,880
Accounts payable		13,000
Unearned revenue		71,000
Mortgage payable, due 2019		120,000
Common shares		40,000
Retained earnings		72,000
Dividends	10,000	
Rent revenue		497,000
Salaries expense	306,000	
Utilities expense	75,200	
Repairs and maintenance expense	28,250	
Interest expense	7,700	
Income tax expense	20,000	
	$922,880	$922,880

Additional information:

1. The one-year insurance policy was purchased on May 31 for $12,720.
2. A count of supplies on August 31 shows $1,380 of supplies on hand.
3. The buildings have an estimated useful life of 50 years.
4. The furniture has an estimated useful life of 10 years.
5. Customers must pay a $200 deposit if they want to book a cottage during the peak period. An analysis of these bookings indicates 355 deposits were received and credited to Unearned Revenue. Only 45 of these deposits have not been earned by August 31.
6. Salaries of $1,680 were unpaid at August 31.
7. The August utility bill of $3,120 has not yet been recorded or paid.
8. On August 25, a local business contracted with Rocky Mountain to rent one of the cottages for six months, starting October 1, at a rate of $3,000 per month. An advance payment equal to two months' (October and November) rent was received on August 31 and credited to Rent Revenue.
9. The mortgage interest rate is 7%. Interest has been paid to August 1; the next payment is due September 1.
10. Income tax payable is estimated to be $2,000.
11. During the month of May, $5,000 of common shares were issued. (*Note*: This has already been recorded.)

Instructions

(a) Prepare T accounts, and enter the trial balance amounts.

(b) Prepare and post the adjusting journal entries for the year.

(c) Prepare an adjusted trial balance at August 31.

(d) Prepare (1) an income statement, (2) a statement of changes in equity, and (3) a statement of financial position.

(e) A friend of yours is considering investing in the company and asks you to comment on the results of operations and financial position. Is the company performing well or not? Does the financial position look healthy or weak? Use specific information from the financial statements to support your answer.

Prepare and post closing entries; prepare post-closing trial balance.
(SO 5)

P4–12B   Refer to the data for Rocky Mountain Resort Inc. in P4–12B.

Instructions

(a) Prepare the closing journal entries.

(b) Post the closing entries to the T accounts prepared in P4–12B.

(c) Prepare a post-closing trial balance at August 31.

Broadening Your Perspective

Financial Reporting: *Shoppers Drug Mart*

Analyze adjusting entries and prepare closing entries.
(SO 2, 3, 5)

BYP4–1   The financial statements of **Shoppers Drug Mart** are presented in Appendix A at the end of this book.

Instructions

(a) Review Shoppers Drug Mart's balance sheet at December 29, 2012.

   1. Identify two accounts presented on this statement that may have been used in an adjusting entry for prepayments. Identify the statement of earnings account most likely involved in each adjusting entry.

   2. Identify two accounts presented on this statement that may have been used in an adjusting entry for accruals. Identify the statement of earnings account most likely involved in each adjusting entry.

(b) Using Shoppers Drug Mart's statement of earnings, reconstruct the summary closing journal entries for revenues and expenses for the year ended December 29, 2012. (*Note:* You may combine current and deferred income tax as one income tax expense account and amount for the purpose of preparing closing entries.)

Comparative Analysis: *Shoppers Drug Mart* and *Jean Coutu*

Discuss types of adjusting entries.
(SO 2, 3)

BYP4–2   The financial statements of **Jean Coutu** are presented in Appendix B following the financial statements for **Shoppers Drug Mart** in Appendix A.

Instructions

(a) Shoppers Drug Mart has a current asset called Prepaid Expenses and Deposits reported on its balance sheet, as does Jean Coutu (called Prepaid Expenses). Explain what this account likely represents and whether it would likely require adjusting entries at year end. If so, identify the type of adjusting entry (prepayment or accrual) that would most likely be required and the income statement account most likely involved.

(b) Shoppers Drug Mart has a current liability called Income Taxes Payable reported on its balance sheet, as does Jean Coutu. Explain what this account likely represents and whether it would likely require adjusting entries at year end. If so, identify the type of adjusting entry (prepayment or accrual) that would most likely be required and the income statement account most likely involved.

Comparing IFRS and ASPE

Compare accounting cycles.
(SO 2, 3, 4, 5)

BYP4–3   **First Capital Realty Inc.** and **First Pro Shopping Centres** are both real estate development companies, specializing in shopping centres. However, First Capital Realty is a public company using IFRS and First Pro Shopping Centres is a private company using ASPE. Because First Capital Realty is a publicly traded company, it is required to release quarterly financial statements to its shareholders. First Pro Shopping Centres only releases its financial statements annually to its bankers and for the purposes of its annual tax filings.

Instructions

(a) Compare and contrast the steps in the accounting cycle for each company. Would you expect there to be any significant differences? Explain.

(b) Based upon what you have read in the first four chapters of this text, identify any reporting differences you would expect to see in the two companies' financial statements.

Critical Thinking Case

BYP4–4   Janice Tamagi is the accountant for Thin Dime Ltd., which retails low-priced household products through over 20 retail stores across Canada. The company's year end is December 31 and Janice is preparing the financial statements for the current year end. At this time, tension between management and staff is extremely high because a new collective agreement with the union representing most of the company's retail staff is being renegotiated. Management is pleading with the union representatives to reduce their request for a salary increase, claiming that the company simply cannot afford it. Janice showed the draft financial statements with a profit before income tax of $2.8 million to her boss, Anna Chen, who is the corporate controller. The reported profit had increased by 10% compared with the prior year. After reviewing the statements and discussing them with Janice, Anna asked her to do the following:

Analyze effect of estimates on prepayments and accruals.
(SO 2, 3)

1. Most of the furniture and fixtures owned by the company are depreciated over a 12-year life and depreciation expense this year was $600,000. Anna wants the useful life to be revised to 8 years, which would result in a revised depreciation expense of $900,000. Janice believes that it is possible for these assets to have a useful life of anywhere from 8 to 12 years.
2. One of the company's stores will probably be shut down next spring. The final decision to do so has not yet been made. If the store is to be shut down, severance pay for the employees who work there would be $400,000. Anna would like this amount accrued as salary expense in the current financial statements because it is highly likely to occur.
3. When Janice was preparing the financial statements, there were a few office expenses that related to December that she had not yet received the invoices for. For example, none of the stores had received their utility bills yet for the month of December. Because the financial statements had to be finalized promptly due to the negotiations with the union, Janice estimated the amount of these bills and recorded them in December. The total amount of this accrual was $150,000. Anna felt that it was more prudent to accrue $230,000 rather than $150,000 just to be safe.
4. At the end of every year, the management team always received a bonus of $200,000, which Janice recorded as bonus expense in the income statement. Anna believes that since this amount has been paid in each of the preceding five years, it is really just a form of regular salary for these employees and is suggesting that it be shown within salary expense, with no bonus expense showing on the income statement this year.

Instructions
(a) Prepare the journal entries to adjust the financial statements as Anna has proposed.
(b) If Janice records these entries, what will the profit before income tax for the current year now be?
(c) Why do you think Anna suggested that the useful lives of furniture and fixtures be reduced?
(d) Do you think that it is appropriate to accrue an expense for the store closure? Why or why not?
(e) Do you think that the increase in the office expense accrual is justified? Why was it done?
(f) Is it appropriate to classify the management bonus to salary expense? Why or why not?

Ethics Case

BYP4–5   Sundream Travel Agency Ltd. is a company that sells vacation packages and has a new Chief Executive Officer (CEO) who is reviewing the draft December 31 year-end financial statements prepared by the company's controller. On these statements, the current assets total $400,000 while the current liabilities total $210,000, which results in a current ratio of 1.9:1. Several months ago, the company obtained some new bank financing that requires it to maintain a current ratio of at least 2:1. After reviewing the statements, the CEO suggests that the controller change the financial statements for two transactions.

Discuss ethics when making adjustments.
(SO 1, 2, 3)

The first transaction involves a vacation package that was sold to a ski club. The vacation starts in two months' time, in early March, and the club has paid $12,000 in advance for the trip. Since the cash has been received, the CEO suggests that the credit relating to this transaction be shown in sales revenue.

The second transaction relates to an accrual of $3,000 for December interest expense that is not due until early January. The CEO suggests that this accrual should not be made since the interest is not due until next year.

Instructions
(a) Who are the stakeholders in this situation?
(b) How will agreeing to the CEO's request have an impact on the financial statements?
(c) Is the CEO acting in an ethical manner? Why?
(d) In what way does the existence of accounting standards enhance ethical behaviour?

"All About You" Activity

BYP4–6   In this chapter, you learned the three conditions that must be met before revenue can be recognized. In any organization, there is always a risk that fictitious revenue may be recorded before it is earned.

Discuss when revenue should be recognized.
(SO 1)

Assume that you are a sales clerk in a shoe store. Your job is to sell products to prospective customers; once they are sold, you enter the transaction in the cash register. The selling price of all shoes to be sold is preprogrammed in the register by head office. The transactions recorded in the cash register provide the basis on which revenue is recorded in the accounting records. A sale is not processed and recorded until payment (whether by cash, debit card, or credit card) is appropriately authorized. You are paid a weekly salary and a percentage commission based on the sales that you have personally made.

Instructions

(a) When does the shoe store record revenue? How is each condition of revenue recognition met before revenue is recorded?

(b) What would be your incentive to overstate the recording of revenues?

(c) How is the shoe store preventing you from overstating revenues?

Serial Case

(*Note*: This is a continuation of the serial case from Chapters 1 through 3.)

Prepare and post adjusting journal entries; prepare adjusted trial balance.
(SO 2, 3, 4)

BYP4–7 Natalie reviews the updated trial balance prepared in Chapter 3. She recalls from her introductory accounting class that there are some adjustments that need to be prepared. She gathers up as much information as she can to enable the following adjusting journal entries to be prepared on June 30, Koebel's Family Bakery's year end:

1. A count reveals that $600 worth of advertising brochures, recorded in the Supplies account, have been distributed during the month of June.

2. Depreciation is to be recorded on the building for the year. The building was purchased 26 years ago and has an estimated useful life of 30 years.

3. Depreciation is to be recorded on the equipment for the year. The equipment was purchased three years ago at a cost of $42,000 and has an estimated useful life of six years. Recall as well that there was new baking equipment purchased on June 16 at a cost of $2,520. One month's depreciation is to be recorded on this equipment; its useful life is six years.

4. Depreciation is to be recorded on the delivery truck, recorded in the Vehicles account. The delivery truck was purchased on January 1 at a cost of $52,500 and has an estimated useful life of five years.

5. Interest on the bank loan and mortgage payable was last paid on June 25. Interest accrued on the five days remaining in June is $55.

6. One month's worth of the 12-month property insurance policy purchased for $15,360 on June 2 has expired.

7. Six months' worth of the prepaid vehicle insurance has also expired. Recall that this insurance was purchased on January 1 for an annual cost of $12,000.

8. At the end of June, heat and electricity on the building, $1,025, was owed. Amounts are to be paid by July 15. (*Hint*: Use the Utilities Expense account).

9. During the last week of June an unexpected order was received from Biscuits to prepare 750 dozen oatmeal chocolate chip cookies. The order was filled and an invoice was prepared, $1,600. This invoice was not included in the accounting records at June 30.

10. Salaries for employees were paid on June 30. There were two part-time employees working in the bake shop on June 30 who forgot to submit their timesheets for that day. They both worked an eight-hour shift and were paid $13 an hour.

Instructions

(a) Prepare T accounts and enter the unadjusted June 30 trial balance amounts from BYP 3–7 in Chapter 3.

(b) Prepare the adjusting journal entries required at June 30.

(c) Post the adjusting journal entries to the T accounts.

(d) Prepare an adjusted trial balance at June 30, 2014.

Answers to Self-Test Questions

1. b	2. d	3. d	4. b	5. a
6. a	7. c	8. b	9. a	10. a

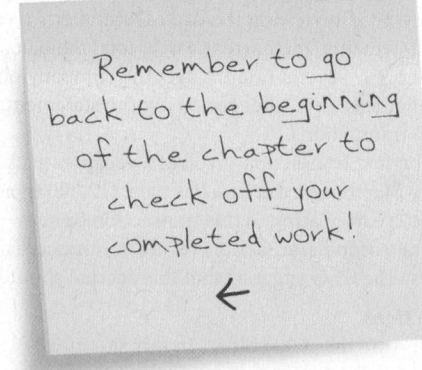

Remember to go back to the beginning of the chapter to check off your completed work!

←

Endnotes

[1]*The University of Western Ontario Combined Financial Statements*, April 30, 2012; "Facts & Figures 2011-12," university website, www.uwo.ca.

[2]Apple 2010 Annual Report; Apple Three-Year Financial History, as Revised (both taken from Apple's website http://investor.apple.com/financials.cfm).

[3]Mark Beasley, et al., *Fraudulent Financial Reporting 1998-2007: An Analysis of U.S. Public Companies*, COSO (Committee of Sponsoring Organizations of the Treadway Commission), May 2010, http://www.coso.org/documents/COSOFRAUDSTUDY2010_001.pdf; Janet McFarland, "Theatre Impresario Garth Drabinsky's Apology Stops Short of Confession to Fraud," *Globe and Mail*, October 24, 2012; Janet McFarland, "Drabinsky Loses Bid to Appeal Fraud Conviction," *Globe and Mail*, March 29, 2012, updated September 6, 2012; Barbara Shecter, "Curtain to Rise Again for Livent at OSC," *National Post*, March 13, 2013.

Comprehensive Case: Chapters 1–4

At June 30, 2015, the end of its most recent fiscal year, Red River Computer Consultants Ltd.'s post-closing trial balance was as follows:

Record and post transaction, adjusting, and closing journal entries; prepare adjusted trial balance and financial statements.
(SO 2, 3, 4, 5)

	Debit	Credit
Cash	$5,230	
Accounts receivable	1,200	
Supplies	690	
Accounts payable		$ 400
Unearned revenue		1,120
Common shares		3,600
Retained earnings		2,000
	$7,120	$7,120

The company underwent a major expansion in July. New staff was hired and more financing was obtained. Red River conducted the following transactions during July 2015, and adjusts its accounts monthly.

July 2   Issued $50,000 of common shares for cash.
3   Purchased liability insurance coverage for a year, $3,600.
3   Paid the first two (July and August 2015) months' rent for an annual lease of office space for $4,000 per month. (*Hint*: Use the Prepaid Rent account.)
6   Purchased $3,800 of supplies for cash.
7   Purchased equipment, paying $4,000 cash and signing a two-year bank loan for $20,000. The equipment has a four-year useful life. The bank loan has a 6% interest rate which is payable on the first day of each following month.
9   Visited client offices and agreed on the terms of a consulting project. Red River will invoice the client, Connor Productions, on the 20th of each month for work performed.
10   Collected $1,200 on account from Milani Brothers Ltd. This client was invoiced in June when the service was provided to them.
13   Completed services for Fitzgerald Enterprises. This client paid $1,120 in advance last month. All services relating to this payment are now completed. (*Hint*: Use the Fees Earned account.)
14   Paid a utility bill of $400. This related to June utilities that were accrued at the end of June.
16   Met with a new client, Thunder Bay Technologies. Received $12,000 cash in advance for future work to be performed.
18   Paid semi-monthly salaries for $11,000.
20   Invoiced Connor Productions for $28,000 of consulting fees provided on account. (*Hint*: Use the Fees Earned account.)
20   Received an invoice for legal advice, $2,200. The amount is not due until August 15. (*Hint*: Use the Professional Fees Expense account.)
23   Completed the first phase of the project for Thunder Bay Technologies. Recognized $10,000 of revenue from the cash advance previously received (see July 16 transaction).
27   Received $15,000 cash from Connor Productions in partial payment of the invoice issued on July 20.
31   Prepared adjusting entries for the following:
- Expiry of insurance coverage (see July 3 transaction)
- Adjustment of prepaid rent (see July 3 transaction)
- Supplies used, $1,250 (see July 6 transaction)
- Equipment depreciation (see July 7 transaction)
- Accrual of interest on bank loan (see July 7 transaction)
- Salaries for the second half of July, $11,000, to be paid on August 1
- Estimated utilities expense for July, $800 (invoice to be received in August)
- Income tax for July, $1,200, to be paid in August

Instructions
(a) Record the above transactions and adjusting journal entries.
(b) Prepare T accounts and post the general and adjusting journal entries.
(c) Prepare an adjusted trial balance as at July 31.
(d) Prepare (1) an income statement, (2) a statement of changes in equity, and (3) a statement of financial position.
(e) Prepare and post closing journal entries to the T accounts set up in part (b).
(f) Red River needs to maintain a current ratio of 2.5:1 in order to maintain its financial standing with its bankers. Calculate the current ratio. Has it achieved the 2.5-to-1 benchmark?

Merchandising Operations

The Navigator
Chapter 5

- ☐ Scan *Study Objectives*
- ☐ Read *Feature Story*
- ☐ Read text and answer *Do It!s*
- ☐ Review *Comparing IFRS and ASPE*
- ☐ Review *Summary of Study Objectives*
- ☐ Review *Decision Toolkit—A Summary*
- ☐ Work *Using the Decision Toolkit*
- ☐ Work *Comprehensive Do It!*
- ☐ Answer *Self-Test Questions*
- ☐ Complete *assignments*
- ☐ Go to *WileyPLUS* for practice and tutorials

the navigator

study objectives

After studying this chapter, you should be able to:

SO 1 Identify the differences between service and merchandising companies.

SO 2 Prepare entries for purchases under a perpetual inventory system.

SO 3 Prepare entries for sales under a perpetual inventory system.

SO 4 Prepare a single-step and a multiple-step income statement.

SO 5 Calculate the gross profit margin and profit margin.

SO 6 Prepare entries for purchases and sales under a periodic inventory system and calculate cost of goods sold (Appendix 5A).

Going with the Flow

Loblaw Companies Limited, Canada's largest grocery chain, has more than 1,000 corporate and franchised stores across the country. Its banners include Loblaws, Real Canadian Superstore, No Frills, Provigo, Zehrs, and Atlantic Superstore. With thousands of products, including those from its own labels such as President's Choice and "no name," managing inventory—most of which is perishable—is key to operations.

Until recently, Loblaw's supply chain—the process of getting products from suppliers to store shelves—was based on a "stock and ship" model, which focused on product storage. Inventory was replenished based on warehouse shipment data. In other words, Loblaw used historical information to plan future shipments. This sometimes resulted in the company's warehouses overflowing while its store shelves were understocked. By the time a tub of yogourt appeared in a store dairy case, for example, it could already be two thirds of the way toward its best-before date. The company estimated that its outdated supply chain process cost it tens of millions of dollars because some competitors could get food to customers faster, fresher, and cheaper.

In 2007, Loblaw launched a five-year, multimillion-dollar plan to transform its supply chain from "stock and ship" to a "flow" model, where products would be ordered, stored, shipped, and shelved based on customer demand. Loblaw found efficiencies in every step of this inventory flow.

One change was to combine inefficient regional supply chains into one national one. The company established four regional centres that would coordinate transportation, including using Loblaw's massive fleet of trucks, the largest in Canada. It reduced the number of distribution centres from 30 to 23, eliminated costly outside storage facilities, and created a single warehouse management system.

Loblaw implemented software that integrates the function of forecasting product demand with replenishing items. The company also worked closely with suppliers to change the way food and other products are shipped to regional centres and individual stores. For example, some suppliers now package and ship items that are ready to be shelved without the need for warehouse staff to repackage and relabel them. This transformation isn't just for perishables, as Loblaw improved how it manages inventory sold under its Joe Fresh clothing brand. It's important to stock the latest styles, which are constantly changing.

In addition to its supply chain project, Loblaw plans to move to a perpetual inventory system, where upgraded information technology will allow it to track the value of its inventory in real time. At the end of 2012, its inventory was valued at more than $2 billion, accounting for about one third of the company's current assets.

Loblaw spent about $63 million on investments in information technology and its supply chain in 2012 alone. But the grocer has seen a strong return on investment. It estimates it saves up to $5 million a year thanks to improvements in such areas as labour efficiency, which increased by 5%. The company also reduced receiving time by approximately 25%, resulting in fresher products on its shelves. Having fresher items not only increases sales to customers wanting better-tasting food, but it also reduces shrinkage—the loss of inventory that plagues every retailer's bottom line—due to expired items that can no longer be sold.[1]

the navigator

preview of
CHAPTER

5

The first four chapters of this text focused mostly on service companies, like the fictional Sierra Corporation. In this and the next chapter, we turn our attention to merchandising companies. Merchandising is one of the largest and most influential industries in Canada. Merchandising companies such as Loblaw buy and sell merchandise for profit rather than perform a service. In this chapter, you will learn the basics of accounting for merchandising transactions. You will also learn how to prepare and analyze the income statement for a merchandising company.

The chapter is organized as follows:

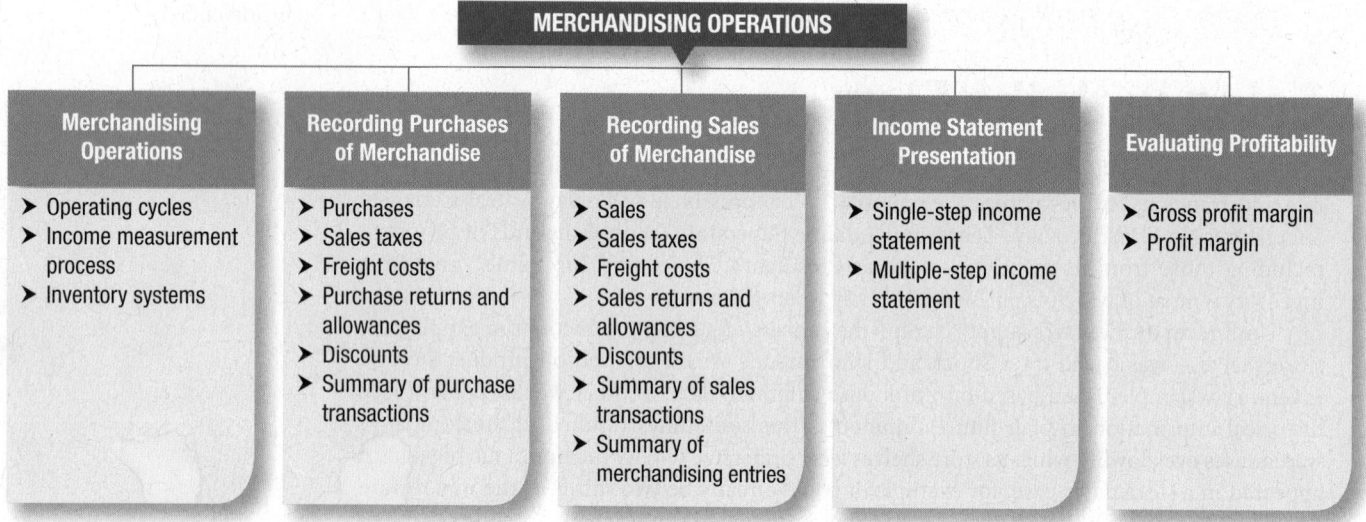

MERCHANDISING OPERATIONS

Merchandising Operations	Recording Purchases of Merchandise	Recording Sales of Merchandise	Income Statement Presentation	Evaluating Profitability
➤ Operating cycles ➤ Income measurement process ➤ Inventory systems	➤ Purchases ➤ Sales taxes ➤ Freight costs ➤ Purchase returns and allowances ➤ Discounts ➤ Summary of purchase transactions	➤ Sales ➤ Sales taxes ➤ Freight costs ➤ Sales returns and allowances ➤ Discounts ➤ Summary of sales transactions ➤ Summary of merchandising entries	➤ Single-step income statement ➤ Multiple-step income statement	➤ Gross profit margin ➤ Profit margin

Merchandising Operations

STUDY OBJECTIVE 1

Identify the differences between service and merchandising companies.

Merchandising involves purchasing products (inventory) to resell to customers. Inventory for a merchandising company can consist of many different items. For example, in a Loblaw store, fresh fruit, canned goods, President's Choice frozen entrees, Joe Fresh clothes, cosmetics, and over-the-counter medications are just a few of the inventory items on hand. These items have two common characteristics: (1) Loblaw owns them, and (2) they are in a form ready for sale to customers. Thus, only one inventory classification, **merchandise inventory** or just inventory, is needed to describe the many different items that make up the total inventory.

Merchandising companies that purchase and sell directly to consumers are called **retailers**. Merchandising companies that sell to retailers are known as **wholesalers**. Companies that produce goods for sale to wholesalers (or others) are called **manufacturers**.

A manufacturing company also has inventory, but differs from a merchandising company in that some of its inventory may not yet be ready for sale. Its inventory has the same first characteristic as inventory for a merchandising company: the company owns it. However, this inventory is not in a form ready for sale to customers; rather, it is in the process of production for sale to customers.

As a result, inventory is usually classified into three categories by manufacturing companies: raw materials, work in process, and finished goods. **Raw materials** are the basic goods and materials that are on hand and will be used in production but have not yet been sent into production. **Work in process** is that portion of inventory on which production has started but is not yet complete. **Finished goods** inventory is manufactured items that are completed and ready for sale.

Our focus in this chapter is primarily on merchandising inventory. Manufacturing inventory will be discussed in more detail in a managerial accounting course.

OPERATING CYCLES

The steps in the accounting cycle for a merchandising company are the same as the steps for a service company. However, the **operating cycle**—the time it takes to go from cash to cash in producing revenues—is usually longer for a merchandising company than it is for a service company. In a service company, the company performs services for cash or for an account receivable (which eventually results in cash when the account receivable is collected). In a merchandising company, the company first has to purchase merchandise for cash or an account payable before it can sell it for cash or an account receivable.

Illustration 5-1 contrasts the operating cycles of service and merchandising companies, assuming purchases and sales are made on account.

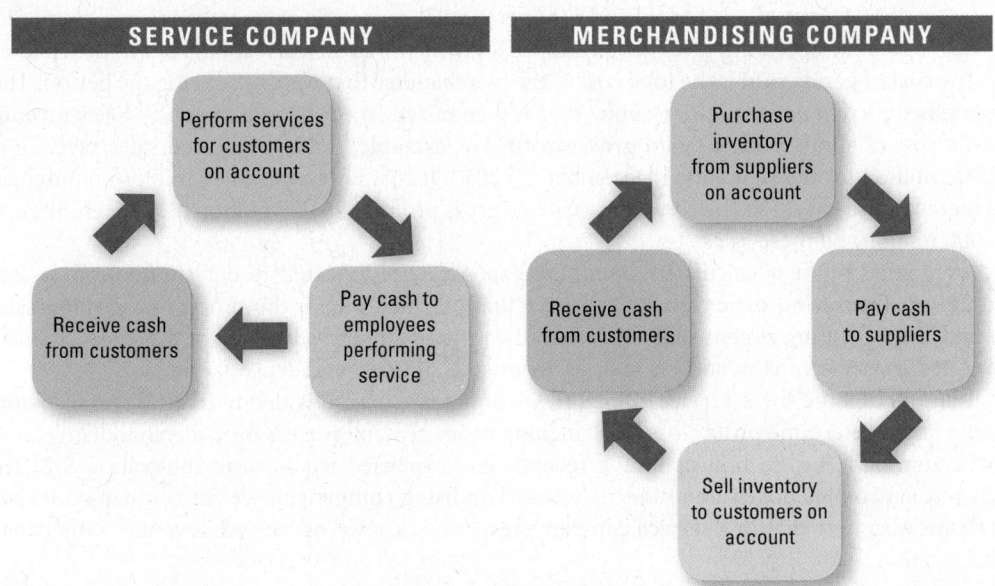

▶Illustration 5-1
Operating cycles

■ Keeping an Eye on Cash

The operating cycle for a merchandising company, as explained above, is the amount of time between buying inventory on account from suppliers and collecting cash from the customers who bought the inventory. In a typical operating cycle, a merchandising company purchases inventory on credit, which increases accounts payable. The company then sells that inventory on credit, which increases accounts receivable. Afterwards, it pays cash for its accounts payable, and collects cash from its accounts receivable. The amount of time between the outlay of cash and the collection of cash is known as the cash conversion cycle. Note that the company may be required to pay its suppliers before collecting the cash from its customers. As a result, the merchandising company may have to borrow cash in order to meet all of its obligations.

A short cash conversion cycle implies that the company needs to finance its inventory and accounts receivable for only a short period of time. Merchandising companies such as Canadian Tire or Loblaw do a significant portion of cash sales. Thus they have greater liquidity and their conversion cycles are shorter than those of companies that sell on account. A long cash conversion cycle indicates lower liquidity, thus less cash is available at any point in time. The lower the liquidity, the longer period of time over which a company must finance its inventory and accounts receivable.

Examples of the cash conversion cycles for three grocers and one bookseller are presented below:

Loblaw Companies Limited	−20 days
Metro Inc.	6 days
Sobeys Inc.	−18 days
Indigo Books & Music Inc.	42 days

Both Loblaw and Sobeys have negative cash conversion cycles because they sell their inventory faster and collect cash from sales faster than they pay off their payables. Metro pays its payables much quicker than Loblaw and Sobeys, while Indigo, due to the nature of its inventory, which is mainly books, takes much longer to sell its inventory than the grocery store companies.

INCOME MEASUREMENT PROCESS

Measuring profit for a merchandising company is basically the same as for a service company. That is, profit (or loss) results when expenses are deducted from revenues. In a merchandising company, the main source of revenue is from the sale of merchandise, which is often referred to simply as **sales revenue** or just sales. As we learned in Chapter 1, revenue is also called "income," especially by international companies that operate outside of Canada.

Unlike expenses for a service company, expenses for a merchandising company are divided into two categories: (1) cost of goods sold and (2) operating expenses. Some merchandising companies may also have non-operating revenues and expenses, which we will learn about later in the chapter.

Alternative Terminology
Gross profit is also called *gross margin*.

The **cost of goods sold** is the total cost of the merchandise that was sold during the period. This expense is directly related to the revenue that is recognized from the sale of goods. Sales revenue less the cost of goods sold is called **gross profit**. For example, Loblaw reported sales revenue of $32,000 million for the year ended December 29, 2012. It cost Loblaw $24,000 million to purchase this merchandise to sell, so the company earned a gross profit of $8,000 million ($32,000 million − $24,000 million) on these sales.

After gross profit is calculated, operating expenses are deducted to determine profit before income tax. **Operating expenses** are expenses that are incurred in the process of earning sales revenue. The operating expenses of a merchandising company include many of the same expenses found in a service company, such as salaries, insurance, utilities, and depreciation.

Then, as is done for a service company, income tax expense is deducted from profit before income tax to determine profit (loss). The income measurement process for a merchandising company, assuming it has no non-operating revenue and expenses, is shown in Illustration 5-2. The items in the two blue boxes are unique to a merchandising company; a service company does not use them. Also note that in a service company, revenue is known as "service revenue" rather than "sales revenue."

▶Illustration 5-2
Income measurement process for a merchandising company

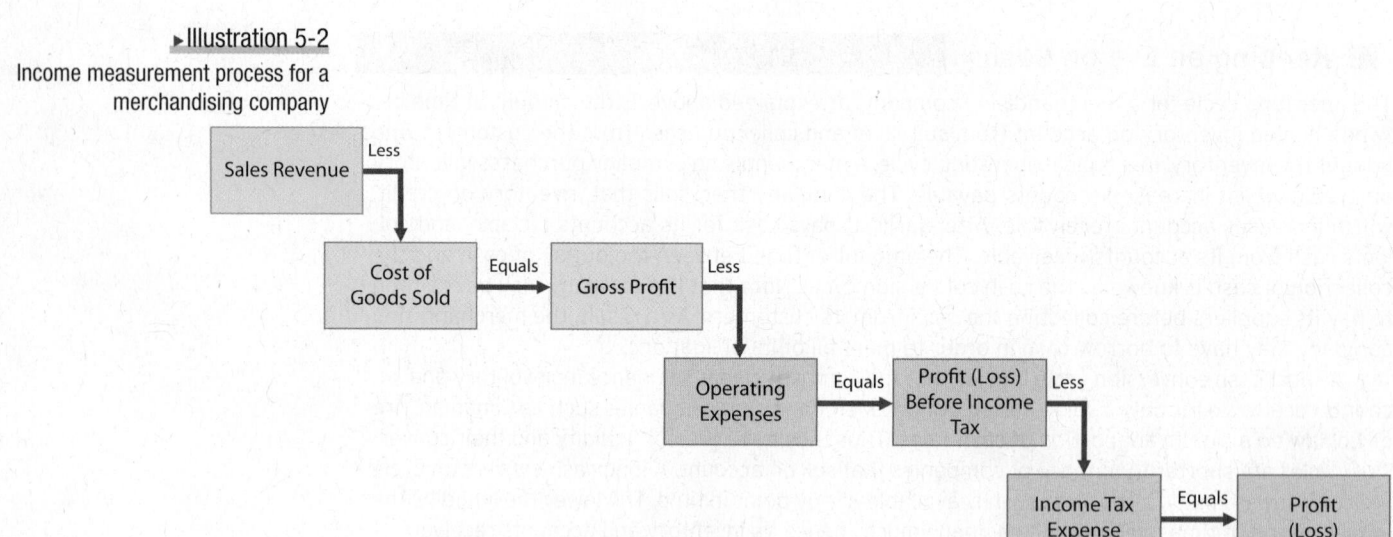

INVENTORY SYSTEMS

A merchandising company keeps track of its inventory to determine what is available for sale (inventory) and what has been sold (cost of goods sold). The flow of costs for a merchandising company is as follows: What you have on hand at the beginning of the period plus what you purchase during the period gives you the total goods you have available for sale during the period. Or, in accounting terms, *beginning inventory* plus the *cost of goods purchased* equals the *cost of goods available for sale*. As goods are sold, they are assigned to *cost of goods sold*. (We will learn how to assign these costs in Chapter 6.) Those goods that are not sold by the end of the accounting period represent what's left, or in accounting terms, *ending inventory*. Ending inventory (unsold goods) is reported as merchandise inventory, a current asset on the statement of financial position. The cost of goods sold (goods sold) is reported as cost of goods sold expense on the income statement.

Illustration 5-3 describes these relationships.

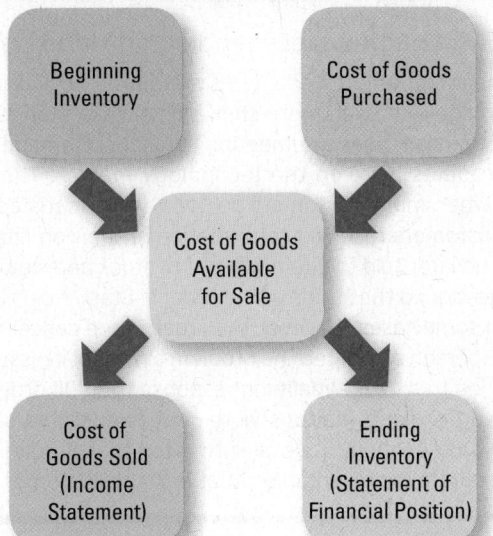

One of two systems is used to account for inventory and the cost of goods sold: a **perpetual inventory system** or a **periodic inventory system**.

Perpetual Inventory System

In a **perpetual inventory system**, detailed records are maintained for the cost of each product that is purchased and sold. These records continuously—perpetually—show the quantity and cost of the inventory purchased, sold, and on hand. For example, a Ford auto dealership keeps separate inventory records for each automobile, truck, and van on its lot and showroom floor.

When inventory items are purchased under a perpetual inventory system, the purchased item is recorded by debiting (increasing) the Merchandise Inventory account. When merchandise inventory is later sold, the cost of the goods that have just been sold (the original purchase cost of the merchandise) is obtained from the inventory records. This cost is transferred from the account Merchandise Inventory (an asset) to the account Cost of Goods Sold (an expense). **Under a perpetual inventory system, the cost of goods sold and the reduction in inventory—both its quantity and cost—are recorded each time a sale occurs.** As a result, the Merchandise Inventory account reflects the amount of ending inventory on hand. This helps make it possible for management to monitor merchandise availability and maintain optimum inventory levels.

Inventory is usually the largest current asset for a merchandiser. Effective control over the merchandise on hand is an important feature of a perpetual inventory system. Since the inventory records show the quantities that should be on hand, the merchandise can be counted at any time to see whether the amount actually on hand matches the inventory records. Any differences that are found can be investigated and adjusted, if required.

To adjust for any inventory shortages, the Cost of Goods Sold account would be debited and the Merchandise Inventory account credited. Although the "missing" inventory has not been sold, the Cost of Goods Sold account is debited because inventory losses are considered part of the cost of selling the goods. The missing inventory must be removed from the Merchandise Inventory account so that the account reflects the actual amount of inventory on hand.

To adjust for inventory overages, the Merchandise Inventory account would be debited and the Cost of Goods Sold account would be credited.

For control purposes, a physical inventory count is always taken at least once a year and ideally more often, under the perpetual inventory system. We will learn more about counting inventory in the next chapter.

Managing Merchandise on Hand

Retailers have long faced customer anger when items are out of stock, but the rise of on-line shopping and social media has made that even more challenging. Take Staples Canada, for example. Its president said that its biggest challenges are meeting consumer demand for e-commerce, and the stranglehold that Apple products have on the technology market. Those two issues came face to face in December 2012, when many customers posted their dissatisfaction with Staples Canada via Facebook and Twitter. Customers received confirmation of their on-line orders for an advertised special on Apple TV only to be later told the item was out of stock and would not be restocked before Christmas. If a customer questioned the status of the order, a Staples service representative advised the customer to cancel it. In some cases, however, the orders were cancelled without the customer's knowledge. A Staples spokesperson attributed the problem to a website issue. "The on-line promotion was extremely popular and led to an overwhelming response to fulfill orders." Unfortunately, due to on-line system challenges, order confirmations were sent to customers even though Staples did not have the item in stock. One unhappy customer tweeted that Staples should invest in a better inventory system. "This was a totally preventable situation," the customer wrote.[2]

Periodic Inventory System

In a **periodic inventory system**, detailed inventory records of the merchandise on hand are not kept throughout the period. As a result, **the cost of goods sold is determined only at the end of the accounting period**—that is, periodically—when a physical inventory count is done to determine the cost of the goods on hand. First, the physical inventory count determines the quantities on hand, and then costs are assigned to these quantities. As was mentioned earlier, we will learn how to assign costs to quantities in Chapter 6.

In a periodic inventory system, the cost of the goods on hand (ending inventory) must be determined at the end of the accounting period before we can calculate the cost of the goods sold during the period. To determine the cost of goods sold under a periodic inventory system, the following steps are necessary:

1. Beginning inventory: Determine the cost of goods on hand at the beginning of the accounting period (beginning inventory). Note that this is the same amount as the previous accounting period's ending inventory.
2. Cost of goods available for sale: Add the cost of goods purchased to the beginning inventory. The total is the **cost of goods available for sale** during the period.
3. Ending inventory: Determine the cost of goods on hand at the end of the accounting period (ending inventory) from the physical inventory count. Subtract the ending inventory from the cost of goods available for sale. The result is the cost of goods sold.

How do companies decide whether to use a perpetual or periodic inventory system? They compare the cost of the detailed record keeping that is required for a perpetual inventory system with the benefits of having the additional information about, and control over, their inventory. The widespread availability of computerized perpetual inventory software and optical scanners has enabled the majority of companies to enjoy the benefits of perpetual inventory systems at a reasonable cost.

Some small businesses find it unnecessary or uneconomical to invest in a perpetual inventory system. Managers of these businesses can, in most cases, find other ways to control merchandise and manage day-to-day operations using a periodic inventory system.

Because the perpetual inventory system is widely used, we illustrate it in this chapter. The periodic inventory system is described in the appendix to this chapter.

BEFORE YOU GO ON...

▶Do It! Inventory Calculations

Michelle's Music Limited has 10 WAVE® Music System III units on hand at January 1. Each unit cost $325. Michelle's purchased 20 units during the year for a total cost of $7,000. Twenty-five units were sold during the year at a cost of $342 each and a selling price of $579 each. (a) Determine the following amounts in both units and dollars: (1) beginning inventory on January 1, (2) cost of goods purchased, (3) cost of goods available for sale, (4) cost of goods sold, and (5) ending inventory on December 31. (b) The company uses a periodic inventory system. The year-end physical inventory count showed 5 WAVE® music systems on hand. Does the physical inventory count agree with your calculations in part (a)(5)?

Action Plan

- Remember the formulas:
   Beginning inventory + cost of goods purchased = cost of goods available for sale.
   Cost of goods available for sale − ending inventory = cost of goods sold.
- The selling price affects sales revenue but not the cost of goods sold or inventory, which are carried at cost.

Solution

(a)

		Units		Dollars
1.	Beginning inventory	10	(10 × $325)	$ 3,250
2.	Cost of goods purchased	20		7,000
3.	Cost of goods available for sale	30		10,250
4.	Cost of goods sold	(25)	(25 × $342)	(8,550)
5.	Ending inventory	5		$ 1,700

(b) Yes, the physical inventory count of five units in ending inventory does agree with the calculations in part (a). If there was a shortage, an entry debiting Cost of Goods Sold and crediting Merchandise Inventory would be made for an amount relating to the cost of the units that should be on hand.

Related Exercise Material: BE5-1, BE5-2, and E5-1.

Recording Purchases of Merchandise

Purchases of merchandise for resale are recorded in the Merchandise Inventory account. The purchase cost is increased by freight costs in certain circumstances and decreased by any purchase returns, allowances, and discounts. The net result of all of these costs is known as the **cost of goods purchased.** We will discuss each of these components of the cost of goods purchased in the next sections.

STUDY OBJECTIVE 2

Prepare entries for purchases under a perpetual inventory system.

PURCHASES

Inventory purchases can be made for cash or credit (on account). The buyer normally records purchases when the goods are transferred from the seller to the buyer. A record, whether written or electronic, should support every purchase as the record provides evidence of the transaction.

A cash register receipt indicating the items purchased and amounts paid should support cash purchases. Cash purchases are recorded by a debit (increase) to the Merchandise Inventory account and a credit (decrease) to the Cash account.

A purchase invoice that includes the total purchase price and other relevant information should support credit purchases. The buyer does not prepare a separate **purchase invoice**. Instead, the seller prepares an invoice. The original copy of the invoice goes to the buyer to be used as a purchase invoice. The seller keeps a copy that is used as a sales invoice.

In addition, in many larger companies, when orders are placed with a supplier, credit purchases are documented by a **purchase order** that details the types, quantities, and agreed prices for products or services the seller will provide to the buyer. This purchase order is later matched up with the purchase invoice to ensure that proper quantity of goods ordered was actually received and at the proper price. Credit purchases are recorded by a debit (increase) to the Merchandise Inventory account and a credit (increase) to the Accounts Payable account.

To illustrate the recording of purchases on account, let's assume that PW Audio Supply, Inc. (the seller) prepares an invoice for the sale of speakers to Sauk Stereo Ltd. (the buyer) on May 4 in the amount of $3,800. The terms of the sale are 2/10, n/30, FOB shipping point. We will discuss what these terms mean in detail in the next few sections.

Sauk Stereo would make the following entry to record the purchase of merchandise:

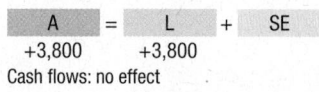

+3,800   +3,800

Cash flows: no effect

May 4	Merchandise Inventory	3,800	
	Accounts Payable		3,800
	(To record goods purchased on account from PW		
	Audio Supply, terms 2/10, n/30, FOB shipping point)		

Only merchandise purchased for the purpose of selling to customers is recorded in the Merchandise Inventory account. For example, Loblaw would record purchases of fresh produce, frozen food, household goods, clothes, and anything else it purchased for resale to customers by debiting (increasing) the Merchandise Inventory account. Purchases of assets that the company will use rather than resell, such as supplies and equipment, are recorded as increases to specific asset accounts rather than as increases to the Merchandise Inventory account. For example, Loblaw would increase the Supplies account to record the purchase of cash register receipt paper or materials that it uses to make shelf signs.

SALES TAXES

Most merchandising and service companies collect sales taxes on the goods they sell and the services they provide. Sales taxes in Canada include the Goods and Services Tax (GST), which is a federal sales tax, and the Provincial Sales Tax (PST). Several provinces, including Ontario and the Atlantic provinces, combine the GST and PST into a single Harmonized Sales Tax (HST). At the time of writing, GST was 5% and PST varied, depending on the province or territory, from 0% to 9.975%. For those provinces using an HST system, the rates can be as high as 15%.

When merchandising companies purchase goods for resale, they pay GST or HST on the cost of the goods. However, GST or HST does not form part of the cost of the merchandise because companies can get back any GST or HST they pay on purchases (by offsetting it against the GST or HST they collect from customers). Generally, retailers do not pay PST on purchases of goods for resale, as they are exempt for this purpose.

Sales taxes add much complexity to the accounting process, as not all goods and services are taxable. The accounting transactions described in this chapter are therefore presented without the added complication of sales taxes. We will learn more about sales taxes in Chapter 10.

FREIGHT COSTS

The sales/purchase invoice should indicate whether the seller or the buyer pays the cost of transporting the goods to the buyer's place of business. Freight terms state who pays the freight charges (shipping costs) and who is responsible for the risk of loss or damage to the merchandise during transit. Freight terms can vary, but are often expressed as either FOB destination or FOB shipping point. The letters FOB mean "free on board" until the point where ownership is transferred.

FOB (free on board) destination means that the seller is responsible for delivering the goods to the destination. The seller pays the freight costs for transporting the goods to the buyer's destination and is responsible for any loss or damage that occurs along the way.

FOB (free on board) shipping point means that the buyer is responsible for the freight costs from the shipping point to the buyer's destination (normally the buyer's place of business). The buyer is also responsible for any loss or damage that occurs along the way. In other words, the buyer owns the goods at the point of shipping even though the goods will not arrive at the buyer's destination for several days, weeks, or even months.

Illustration 5-4 shows these shipping terms.

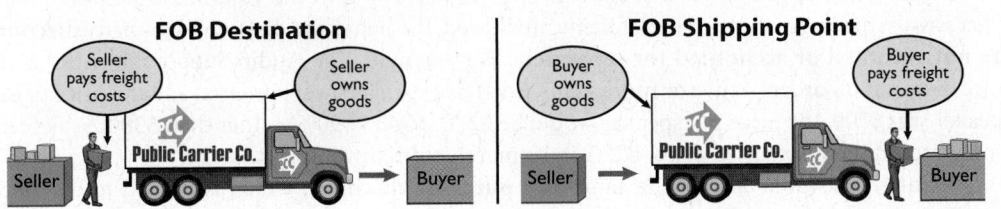

▶Illustration 5-4
Freight terms

We mentioned earlier in the Purchases section that the terms of the sale of the speakers from PW Audio Supply to Sauk Stereo were FOB shipping point. This means that the buyer (Sauk Stereo) paid the freight charges from the shipping point (likely PW Audio Supply's place of business) to the destination (Sauk Stereo's place of business) and recorded this freight by debiting (increasing) its Merchandise Inventory account. Why? **The cost of inventory not only includes the purchase cost but also includes other costs incurred to transport the inventory and make it ready for sale.** As a result, any freight paid by the buyer is recorded as part of the cost of the merchandise purchased.

Assume that upon delivery of the goods on May 4, Sauk Stereo (the buyer) pays Public Carrier Co. $150 for freight charges. The entry on Sauk Stereo's books is:

> **Helpful Hint**
> The buyer only pays freight when the shipping terms are FOB shipping point.

May 4	Merchandise Inventory	150	
	Cash		150
	(To record payment of freight on goods purchased)		

A	=	L	+	SE
+150				
−150				

↓Cash flows: −150

In contrast, if the freight terms had been FOB destination rather than FOB shipping point, the seller (PW Audio Supply) would have paid the freight costs. Sauk Stereo would have no entry to record and PW Audio Supply would record the freight costs it paid on outgoing merchandise as an operating expense. We will learn how to record freight costs incurred by the seller later in the chapter.

PURCHASE RETURNS AND ALLOWANCES

A buyer may be dissatisfied with the merchandise received. The goods may be damaged or defective, of inferior quality, or might not fit the buyer's specifications. In such cases, the buyer may return the goods to the seller. The buyer will receive a cash refund if the purchase was made for cash. Credit is given if the purchase was made on account.

Alternatively, the buyer may choose to keep the merchandise if the seller is willing to give an allowance (deduction) from the purchase price. These types of transactions are known as **purchase returns and allowances.** In both cases, the result is a decrease in the cost of goods purchased.

Assume that Sauk Stereo returned goods costing $300 to PW Audio Supply on May 8. Because these goods were originally sold on account, Sauk Stereo will receive a credit (rather than cash) from PW Audio Supply for the return of this merchandise. The entry by Sauk Stereo for the returned merchandise is:

May 8	Accounts Payable	300	
	Merchandise Inventory		300
	(To record return of goods to PW Audio Supply)		

A	=	L	+	SE
−300		−300		

Cash flows: no effect

Sauk Stereo increased the Merchandise Inventory and Accounts Payable accounts when the goods were originally purchased. Sauk Stereo therefore decreases the Merchandise Inventory and Accounts Payable accounts when it returns the goods, or when it is granted an allowance.

DISCOUNTS

The purchase terms for inventory items can include one or more discounts that are available to the buyer if certain activities occur. For example, Loblaw receives allowances from certain sellers for volume (quantity) purchases and purchase discounts.

A **quantity discount** gives a reduction in price according to the volume of the purchase. In other words, the larger the number of items purchased, the better the discount. **Quantity discounts are not recorded or accounted for separately.** For example, PW Audio Supply may offer a 10% price discount on orders of five or more items. So, if five speakers were ordered and the price of each speaker was $300, the price per speaker would be $270 ($300 × 90%) rather than $300. Sauk Stereo would record the discounted price, $270, in its merchandise inventory account.

Quantity discounts are not the same as a **purchase discount**, which is offered to encourage customers to pay the amount owed early. A purchase discount offers advantages to both parties: the purchaser saves money, and the seller is able to shorten its operating cycle by converting accounts receivable into cash earlier.

Purchase discounts are noted on the invoice through credit terms. These terms specify the amount of the purchase discount and the time period during which it is offered. They also indicate the date by which the purchaser is expected to pay the full invoice price. In the invoice prepared by PW Audio Supply for the sale of speakers, the credit terms were 2/10, n/30, which is read "two-ten, net thirty." This means that a 2% cash discount may be taken on the invoice price, less ("net of") any returns or allowances, if payment is made within 10 days of the invoice date (the discount period). Otherwise, the invoice price, less any returns or allowances, is due 30 days from the invoice date.

Not every seller offers purchase discounts, although they are common in certain industries. When the seller chooses not to offer a discount for fast payment, credit terms will specify only the maximum time period for paying the balance due. For example, the period may be stated as n/30, meaning that the net amount must be paid in 30 days.

Purchase discounts are recorded separately in the accounting records. When an invoice is paid within the discount period, the amount of the discount decreases the cost recorded in the Merchandise Inventory account.

To illustrate, assume Sauk Stereo pays the balance due of $3,500 (gross invoice price of $3,800 less purchase returns and allowances of $300) on May 14, the last day of the discount period. **Note that discounts are not taken on freight costs, especially if the products were carried by an independent shipper.** The discount is $70 ($3,500 × 2%), and the amount of cash paid by Sauk Stereo is $3,430 ($3,500 − $70). The entry to record the May 14 payment by Sauk Stereo is:

A	=	L	+	SE
−3,430		−3,500		
−70				

↓ Cash flows: −3,430

May 14	Accounts Payable	3,500	
	Cash		3,430
	Merchandise Inventory		70
	(To record payment to PW Audio Supply within discount period)		

If Sauk Stereo failed to take the discount and instead made full payment of $3,500 on June 3 (30 days after the date of sale), Sauk Stereo would make the following entry rather than the one shown above:

A	=	L	+	SE
−3,500		−3,500		

↓ Cash flows: −3,500

June 3	Accounts Payable	3,500	
	Cash		3,500
	(To record payment to PW Audio Supply with no discount taken)		

A merchandising company should take advantage of all available purchase discounts. Passing up the discount may be viewed as paying interest for use of the money. For example, if Sauk Stereo passed up the discount, it would be paying 2% for the use of $3,500 for 20 days. This equals an annual interest rate of 36.5% (2% × 365 ÷ 20). It would be better for Sauk Stereo to borrow at bank interest rates, which are substantially lower than 36.5%, than lose the discount.

Because of the importance of taking purchase discounts, some companies prepare journal entries to track the discounts not taken, or lost. Consequently, there are other ways to record discounts than shown in this section. These will be discussed in an intermediate accounting course.

SUMMARY OF PURCHASE TRANSACTIONS

A summary of the effect of the previous purchase transactions on Merchandise Inventory is provided in the following T account (with transaction descriptions in parentheses). Sauk Stereo originally purchased $3,800 worth of inventory for resale. It paid $150 in freight charges. It then returned $300 worth of goods. Finally, it received a $70 discount off the balance owed because it paid within the discount period. This results in a balance in the Merchandise Inventory account of $3,580, as follows:

		Merchandise Inventory			
(Purchase)	May 4	3,800	May 8	300	(Purchase return)
(Freight)	4	150	14	70	(Purchase discount)
	Bal.	3,580			

The $3,580 amount in the Merchandise Inventory account represents the **cost of the goods purchased**. The cost of goods purchased includes the cost of the merchandise, increased by any freight costs incurred if the shipping terms are FOB shipping point, and decreased by any purchase returns and allowances and purchase discounts.

BEFORE YOU GO ON...

▶ Do It! Purchase Transactions

On September 2, Brighthouse Corp. buys merchandise on account from Junot Inc. for $1,500, terms 2/10, n/30, FOB shipping point. The appropriate company pays freight charges of $75 on September 4 from the point of shipping to the destination. On September 8, Brighthouse returns $200 of the merchandise to Junot. On September 11, Brighthouse pays the total amount owing. Record the transactions on Brighthouse's books.

Action Plan

- Purchases of goods for resale are recorded in the asset account Merchandise Inventory when a perpetual inventory system is used.
- Examine freight terms to determine which company pays the freight charges. Freight charges paid by the buyer increase the cost of the merchandise inventory.
- The Merchandise Inventory account is reduced by the cost of merchandise returned.
- Calculate purchase discounts using the net amount owing for purchases (purchases less any purchase returns and allowances). Do not calculate purchase discounts on freight.
- Reduce the Merchandise Inventory account by the amount of the purchase discount.

Solution

Brighthouse (Buyer)

Sept. 2	Merchandise Inventory		1,500	
	Accounts Payable			1,500
	(To record goods purchased on account from Junot, terms 2/10, n/30, FOB shipping point)			
4	Merchandise Inventory		75	
	Cash			75
	(To record freight paid on goods purchased)			
8	Accounts Payable		200	
	Merchandise Inventory			200
	(To record return of goods to Junot)			
11	Accounts Payable ($1,500 − $200)		1,300	
	Merchandise Inventory ($1,300 × 2%)			26
	Cash ($1,300 − $26)			1,274
	(To record payment to Junot within discount period)			

Related Exercise Material: BE5-3, BE5-4, BE5-5, E5-2, E5-3, E5-4, E5-6, and *E5-13.

the navigator

Recording Sales of Merchandise

STUDY OBJECTIVE 3

Prepare entries for sales under a perpetual inventory system.

You will recall from Chapter 2, when we discussed the elements of the financial statements, that revenue is recorded (recognized) when there is an increase in assets such as the receipt of cash or increase in accounts receivable as a result of the performance of a service or delivery of goods. For a merchandising company, revenue will normally be recognized when earned. This occurs when the ownership of the merchandise is transferred from the seller to the buyer and the buyer assumes the risks of owning the merchandise. At this point, the sales transaction is completed and the selling price is established.

We will discuss how to record sales revenue, including sales taxes, freight costs, sales returns and allowances, and sales discounts, in the next sections.

SALES

To record sales revenue, an asset (typically cash or accounts receivable) account is debited (increased) and the sales revenue account is credited (also increased). Alternatively, if a customer had previously paid in advance, a liability (unearned revenue) account is debited (decreased) and the sales revenue account credited (increased).

Similar to purchase transactions, every sales transaction—whether for cash or credit—should be supported by a record—whether written or electronic—that provides evidence of the sale. Cash register tapes provide evidence of cash sales. A **sales invoice** provides support for a credit sale.

While only one journal entry is required to record the purchase of merchandise, **two journal entries are required to record each sale in a perpetual inventory system**. The first entry records the sales revenue: Cash (or Accounts Receivable, if it is a credit sale) is increased by a debit and Sales is increased by a credit for the selling (invoice) price of the goods. The second entry records the cost of the merchandise sold: Cost of Goods Sold is increased by a debit and Merchandise Inventory is decreased by a credit for the cost of the goods. As a result, at all times Merchandise Inventory will show the amount of inventory that is (should be) on hand.

To illustrate a credit sales transaction, we will continue to use PW Audio Supply's sale of $3,800 of merchandise on May 4 to Sauk Stereo that was illustrated earlier in the purchases section. Assume the merchandise cost PW Audio Supply $2,400 when it was originally purchased. The sale is recorded as follows:

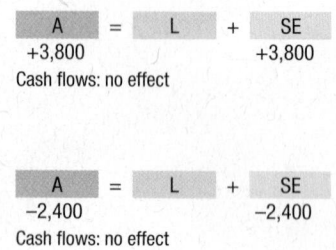

	A	=	L	+	SE				
	+3,800				+3,800				

Cash flows: no effect

A	=	L	+	SE
−2,400				−2,400

Cash flows: no effect

May 4	Accounts Receivable	3,800	
	Sales		3,800
	(To record credit sale to Sauk Stereo, terms 2/10, n/30, FOB shipping point)		
4	Cost of Goods Sold	2,400	
	Merchandise Inventory		2,400
	(To record cost of merchandise sold to Sauk Stereo)		

For internal decision-making purposes, merchandising companies may use more than one sales account. For example, PW Audio Supply may decide to keep separate sales accounts for its major product lines, rather than a single combined sales account. This enables company management to monitor sales trends more closely and respond in a more strategic way to changes in sales patterns. For example, if sales of wireless speakers are increasing while sales of powered speakers are decreasing, the company should re-evaluate both its advertising and pricing policies on each of these items to ensure that they are optimal.

On the income statement presented to external users, most merchandising companies provide only a single sales figure—the sum of all of their individual sales accounts. This is done for two reasons. First, providing detail on all of the individual sales accounts would make the income statement much longer. Second, companies generally do not want their competitors to know the details of their operating results.

SALES TAXES

Merchandising companies collect sales taxes on the goods they sell. You will recall from earlier in the chapter that sales taxes can include GST or HST.

When a company collects sales taxes from selling a product or service, these **sales taxes are not recorded as revenue**. The sales taxes are collected on behalf of the federal and provincial governments, and must be periodically remitted to these authorities. Sales taxes that are collected from selling a product or service are recorded as a liability until they are paid to the government. Further discussion of sales taxes is deferred until Chapter 10.

FREIGHT COSTS

As discussed earlier in the chapter, freight terms on the sales invoice—FOB destination and FOB shipping point—indicate who is responsible for shipping costs. If the terms are FOB destination, the seller assumes the responsibility for delivering the goods to their intended destination. Freight costs incurred by the seller on outgoing merchandise are an operating expense to the seller. These costs are debited to the account Freight Out or Delivery Expense. When the seller pays the freight charges, the seller will usually set a higher invoice price for the goods to cover the cost of shipping.

> **Helpful Hint**
> The seller only pays freight when the shipping terms are FOB destination.

In PW Audio Supply's sale of electronic equipment to Sauk Stereo, the freight terms (FOB shipping point) indicate that Sauk Stereo (the buyer) must pay the cost of shipping the goods from the shipping point (likely PW Audio Supply's place of business) to their destination (Sauk Stereo's place of business). PW Audio Supply makes no journal entry to record the cost of shipping, since the buyer, not the seller, incurred this cost.

If the freight terms had been FOB destination, PW Audio Supply would have paid the freight costs and prepared a journal entry to record the cost as an operating expense, as shown below:

May 4	Freight Out	150	
	Cash		150
	(To record payment of freight on goods sold)		

A = L + SE
−150   −150
↓Cash flows: −150

SALES RETURNS AND ALLOWANCES

We now look at the "flip side" of purchase returns and allowances, as these are recorded as **sales returns and allowances** on the books of the seller. When customers (buyers) return goods, or are given price reductions, the seller will either return cash to the buyer, or reduce the buyer's accounts receivable if the goods were originally purchased on credit.

Just as a sale requires two entries in a perpetual inventory system, so too do returns and allowances. PW Audio Supply prepares the two separate journal entries shown below to record the $300 credit for goods returned by Sauk Stereo. The first entry records a debit (increase) to the Sales Returns and Allowances account and a credit (decrease) to the Accounts Receivable account for the $300 selling price. Note that if the sales return had been for a cash sale, Cash would be credited instead of Accounts Receivable.

The Sales Returns and Allowances account is a **contra revenue account** to Sales. The normal balance of the Sales Returns and Allowances account is a debit. A contra account is used to disclose the amount of sales returns and allowances. A debit (decrease) recorded directly to Sales would hide the percentage of total sales that ends up being lost through sales returns and allowances. It could also distort comparisons between total sales in different accounting periods.

This information is important to management. Excessive returns and allowances suggest the possibility of inferior merchandise, inefficiencies in filling orders, errors in billing customers, or mistakes in the delivery or shipment of goods.

The second journal entry required to record a sales return in a perpetual inventory system debits (increases) the Merchandise Inventory account (assuming a $140 cost) and credits (decreases) the Cost of Goods Sold account.

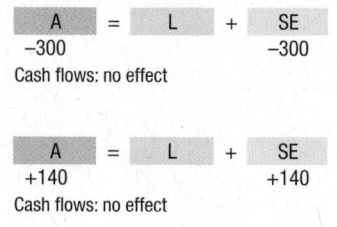

May 8	Sales Returns and Allowances	300	
	Accounts Receivable		300
	(To record return of goods by Sauk Stereo)		
8	Merchandise Inventory	140	
	Cost of Goods Sold		140
	(To record cost of merchandise returned by Sauk Stereo)		

The second entry shown above assumes that the merchandise is not damaged; it can be resold so the amount is restored to inventory. If the merchandise is not resaleable and is discarded, a second entry is not made. Since the goods are defective and cannot be resold, the seller cannot increase its Merchandise Inventory and the original cost of goods sold recorded is still the correct amount. A second entry is also not required when the seller gives the buyer an allowance. Giving a customer a sales allowance does not change the cost of the goods sold; it only changes the amount of revenue earned on the sale.

DISCOUNTS

When quantity discounts and sales discounts are given on invoice prices, they affect the seller, as well as the buyer. No separate entry is made to record a **quantity discount**. Sales are recorded at the invoice price—whether it is the full retail price, a sale price, or a volume discount price.

Like a purchase discount, the seller may offer the buyer a cash discount for quick payment of the balance due. From the seller's point of view, this is called a **sales discount** and is offered on the invoice price less sales returns and allowances, if any.

Although no new account is added to record purchase discounts in a perpetual inventory system—the discount is recorded as a reduction in the Merchandise Inventory account—a new account, called Sales Discounts, is added to record sales discounts. Like the account for sales returns and allowances, Sales Discounts is a **contra revenue account** to Sales. Its normal balance is a debit. This account is used, instead of debiting Sales, so that management can monitor if customers are taking advantage of cash discounts.

For PW Audio Supply, the sales discount is $70 ([$3,800 − $300] × 2%). The entry to record the cash receipt of $3,430 ($3,800 − $300 − $70) on May 14 from Sauk Stereo within the discount period is:

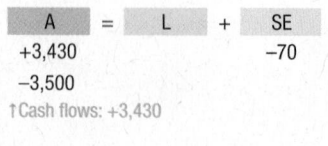

May 14	Cash	3,430	
	Sales Discounts	70	
	Accounts Receivable		3,500
	(To record collection from Sauk Stereo within discount period)		

If a customer does not take the discount, PW Audio Supply debits (increases) the Cash account for $3,500 and credits (decreases) the Accounts Receivable account for the same amount, as shown below:

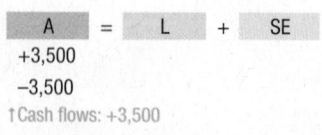

June 3	Cash	3,500	
	Accounts Receivable		3,500
	(To record collection from Sauk Stereo with no discount taken)		

SUMMARY OF SALES TRANSACTIONS

PW Audio Supply sold merchandise for $3,800, and $300 of it was later returned. A sales discount of $70 was granted as the invoice was paid within the discount period. In contrast to the purchase transactions illustrated earlier in the chapter, which affected only one account, Merchandise Inventory, sales transactions are recorded in different accounts. A summary of the effects of these transactions is provided in the following T accounts.

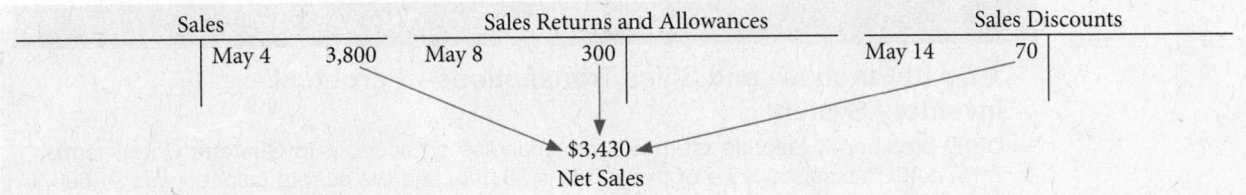

These three accounts combine to determine net sales. Illustration 5-5 shows the formula for the calculation of net sales.

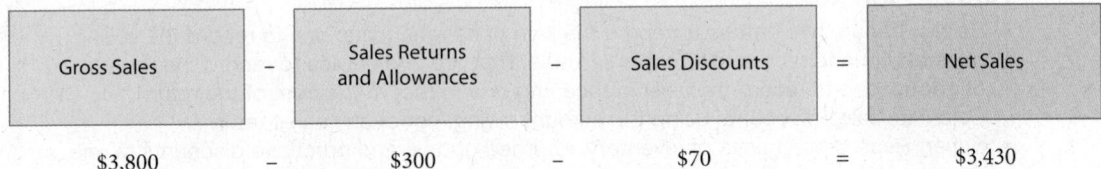

Gross Sales	–	Sales Returns and Allowances	–	Sales Discounts	=	Net Sales
$3,800	–	$300	–	$70	=	$3,430

Total sales, before deducting any sales returns and allowances and sales discounts, are known as **gross sales.** Gross sales less returns and allowances and discounts are called **net sales.** The calculation of net sales is the same whether the company uses a perpetual or a periodic inventory system. Note that freight paid by the seller is recorded as an operating expense and does not affect net sales.

SUMMARY OF MERCHANDISING ENTRIES

In the previous two sections, we have explained the journal entries made to record purchases and sales of merchandise. The following is a summary of the entries for merchandising accounts in a perpetual inventory system:

	Transactions	Recurring Journal Entries	Debit	Credit
Purchases	Purchasing merchandise for resale.	Merchandise Inventory Cash or Accounts Payable	XX	XX
	Paying freight costs on merchandise purchased FOB shipping point.	Merchandise Inventory Cash	XX	XX
	Receiving purchase returns or allowances from suppliers.	Cash or Accounts Payable Merchandise Inventory	XX	XX

	Paying creditors on account within discount period.	Accounts Payable
		    Merchandise Inventory
		    Cash
			XX	XX
				XX

	Paying creditors on account after discount period.	Accounts Payable Cash	XX	XX

Sales	Selling merchandise to customers.	Cash or Accounts Receivable
		    Sales
		Cost of Goods Sold
		    Merchandise Inventory
			XX
			
			XX
				XX
				
				XX

	Giving sales returns or allowances to customers.	Sales Returns and Allowances
		    Cash or Accounts Receivable
		Merchandise Inventory
		    Cost of Goods Sold
			XX
			
			XX
				XX
				
				XX

	Paying freight costs on sales, FOB destination.	Freight Out Cash	XX	XX
	Receiving payment on account from customers within discount period.	Cash Sales Discounts Accounts Receivable	XX XX	XX
	Receiving payment on account from customers after discount period.	Cash Accounts Receivable	XX	XX

BEFORE YOU GO ON...

▶ Do It! Purchase and Sales Transactions—Perpetual Inventory System

On September 4, Lalonde Ltée sells merchandise on account to Guerette Corp., terms 2/10, n/45. The selling price of the goods is $3,000, and the cost to Lalonde was $1,600. On September 8, goods with a selling price of $600 and a cost of $280 are returned for credit and restored to inventory. On September 13, Lalonde receives payment in full from Guerette. Record the transactions on the books of both companies, assuming a perpetual inventory system is used.

Action Plan

- Seller: Prepare two entries to record the sale of merchandise: one to record the selling price and one to record the cost of the sale. Prepare two entries to record the return of goods: one to record the selling price and one to record the cost of the return. Calculate sales discounts using the amount owing, net of any sales returns.
- Buyer: Record purchases of inventory, returned goods, and purchase discounts in one account—Merchandise Inventory. Calculate purchase discounts using the amount owing, net of any purchase returns.

Solution

Lalonde Ltée (Seller)

Sept.	4	Accounts Receivable	3,000	
		Sales		3,000
		(To record credit sale to Guerette, terms 2/10, n/45)		
	4	Cost of Goods Sold	1,600	
		Merchandise Inventory		1,600
		(To record cost of goods sold to Guerette)		
	8	Sales Returns and Allowances	600	
		Accounts Receivable		600
		(To record credit granted for receipt of returned goods from Guerette)		
	8	Merchandise Inventory	280	
		Cost of Goods Sold		280
		(To record cost of goods returned from Guerette)		
	13	Cash ($2,400 − $48)	2,352	
		Sales Discounts ([$3,000 − $600] × 2%)	48	
		Accounts Receivable ($3,000 − $600)		2,400
		(To record collection from Guerette within discount period)		

Guerette Corp. (Buyer)

Sept.	4	Merchandise Inventory	3,000	
		Accounts Payable		3,000
		(To record goods purchased on account from Lalonde, terms 2/10, n/45)		
	8	Accounts Payable	600	
		Merchandise Inventory		600
		(To record return of goods to Lalonde)		
	13	Accounts Payable ($3,000 − $600)	2,400	
		Merchandise Inventory ([$3,000 − $600] × 2%)		48
		Cash ($2,400 − $48)		2,352
		(To record payment to Lalonde within discount period)		

Related Exercise Material: BE5-4, BE5-6, E5-2, E5-3, E5-5, E5-6, and *E5-13.

Income Statement Presentation

Merchandisers use the classified statement of financial position introduced in Chapter 2, but add a merchandise inventory account in the current assets section of the statement.

Two different forms of the income statement are widely used by merchandising companies. One is the **single-step income statement**. It has this name because only one step—subtracting total expenses (except for income tax expense) from total revenues—is required for determining profit before income tax. A second form of the income statement is the **multiple-step income statement**. This statement gets its name because it shows multiple steps in determining profit before income tax. We will look at each of these statement forms in the following sections.

STUDY OBJECTIVE 4
Prepare a single-step and a multiple-step income statement.

SINGLE-STEP INCOME STATEMENT

In a **single-step income statement**, all data are classified into two categories: (1) revenues and (2) expenses. Revenues include both operating and non-operating revenues and gains (for example, interest revenue). Expenses include cost of goods sold, operating expenses, and non-operating expenses and losses (for example, interest expense). Income tax expense is usually disclosed separately from the other expenses in a single-step income statement.

Illustration 5-6 shows a single-step income statement for PW Audio Supply, Inc., using assumed data.

PW AUDIO SUPPLY, INC.		
Income Statement		
Year Ended December 31, 2015		
Revenues		
Net sales	$460,000	
Interest revenue	3,400	$463,400
Expenses		
Cost of goods sold	$316,000	
Salaries expense	45,000	
Rent expense	19,000	
Utilities expense	17,000	
Advertising expense	16,000	
Depreciation expense	8,000	
Freight out	7,000	
Insurance expense	2,000	
Interest expense	1,600	
Loss on disposal	200	431,800
Profit before income tax		31,600
Income tax expense		6,300
Profit		$ 25,300

Illustration 5-6
Single-step income statement—perpetual inventory system

Private companies following ASPE do not have to list their expenses in any particular order. Companies following IFRS must classify expenses by either their nature or function. Classifying expenses by **nature** means that expenses are reported according to their natural classification (such as salaries, transportation, depreciation, advertising).

To classify expenses by **function** means that expenses are reported according to the activity (business function) for which they were incurred (for example, cost of goods sold, administrative expenses, and selling expenses). Although expenses can be listed in any order within each classification, as we have done in past chapters, we have listed expenses in order of magnitude—from largest to smallest. Illustration 5-6 shown above presents PW Audio Supply's expenses by function.

We should note that while cost of goods sold is a separate account for a merchandising company classifying expenses by function, cost of goods sold can be shown in several components when classifying expenses by nature. This is typically done by showing the purchases of merchandise inventory and the changes in merchandise inventory during the period on two separate lines in the income statement.

Administrative expenses relate to general operating activities such as management, accounting, and legal matters. **Selling expenses** are associated with making sales. They include advertising expenses as well as the expenses of completing the sale, such as delivery and shipping expenses.

Companies can choose between classifying expenses by nature or function, depending on whichever provides information that is more relevant. If a company chooses to present its expenses by function, it must also disclose additional information on the nature of certain expenses such as depreciation and employee benefits expense.

The single-step income statement is the form we have used in the text so far. There are two main reasons for using the single-step form: (1) a company does not realize any profit until total revenues exceed total expenses, so it makes sense to divide the statement into these categories; and (2) the single-step form is simple and easy to read. Regardless of the simplicity of the single-step format, the majority of Canadian companies use the multiple-step form of income statement. We will learn why in the next section.

MULTIPLE-STEP INCOME STATEMENT

The **multiple-step income statement** is so named because it shows several steps in determining profit (or loss). It is often considered more useful because it highlights the components of profit separately. Loblaw, our feature company in this chapter, uses the multiple-step form of income statement.

The multiple-step income statement shows five main steps:

Operating Activities

1. Net sales: Sales returns and allowances and sales discounts are subtracted from gross sales to determine net sales.
2. Gross profit: Cost of goods sold is subtracted from net sales to determine gross profit.
3. Profit from operations: Operating expenses are deducted from gross profit to determine profit from operations.
4. Non-operating revenues and expenses: The results of activities that are not related to operations are added (as other revenues) or subtracted (as other expenses) to determine profit before income tax.
5. Profit: Income tax expense is subtracted from profit before income tax to determine profit (loss).

The first three steps involve the company's principal operating activities. The fourth step distinguishes between **operating and non-operating** activities and is only necessary if the company has non-operating activities. The last step is the same step shown in a single-step statement. We will now look more closely at the components of a multiple-step income statement using assumed data for PW Audio Supply.

Net Sales

The multiple-step income statement for a merchandising company begins by presenting sales revenues. The two contra revenue accounts, Sales Returns and Allowances and Sales Discounts, are deducted from gross sales in the income statement to arrive at net sales. The sales revenues section of the income statement is presented here.

Sales revenue		
Sales		$480,000
Less: Sales returns and allowances	$12,000	
Sales discounts	8,000	20,000
Net sales		460,000

This presentation shows the key aspects of the company's main revenue-producing activities. Many companies condense this information and report only the net sales figure in their income statement.

Gross Profit

Earlier in the chapter, you learned that the cost of goods sold is deducted from net sales to determine **gross profit**. Based on the sales data presented above (net sales of $460,000) and an assumed cost of goods sold amount of $316,000, the gross profit for PW Audio Supply is $144,000, calculated as follows:

Net sales	$460,000
Cost of goods sold	316,000
Gross profit	144,000

It is important to understand what gross profit is—and what it is not. Gross profit represents the **merchandising profit** of a company. Because operating expenses have not been deducted, it is not a measure of the overall profit of a company. Nevertheless, management and other users closely watch the amount and trend of gross profit. We will learn how to express gross profit as a rate in the next section and compare this rate on an intracompany, intercompany, and industry basis to determine the effectiveness of a company's purchasing and pricing policies.

Profit from Operations

Profit from operations, or the results of the company's normal operating activities, is calculated by subtracting operating expenses from gross profit.

At PW Audio Supply, assumed operating expenses totalling $114,200 have been classified by nature rather than by function, as shown below. You will recall our discussion in the single-step income statement section about classifying operating expenses by either nature or function. This is required whether a company uses the single- or multiple-step format.

After subtracting operating expenses from gross profit, PW Audio Supply's profit from operations is determined to be $29,800, as shown below:

Gross profit		$144,000
Operating expenses		
Salaries expense	$45,000	
Rent expense	19,000	
Utilities expense	17,000	
Advertising expense	16,000	
Depreciation expense	8,000	
Freight out	7,000	
Insurance expense	2,000	
Loss on disposal	200	114,200
Profit from operations		29,800

Reporting profit from operations as a separate number from overall profit helps users in understanding the profitability of the company's continuing operations or typical business activities.

Non-operating (Other) Revenues and Expenses

Non-operating items consist of other revenues, as well as other expenses, that are not related to the company's main operations.

Examples of other revenues include interest revenue, rent revenue (if the company's main activity is not rentals), and investment revenue. In addition, gains that are infrequent or unusual are normally reported in this section. Examples of other expenses include finance (interest) costs. Losses that are infrequent and unusual are also reported in this section.

When a company has non-operating revenues and expenses, they are presented in the income statement right after "profit from operations." The distinction between operating and non-operating activities is crucial to many external users of financial data. Profit from operations is viewed as sustainable and therefore long-term, and non-operating activities are viewed as nonrecurring and therefore short-term. When forecasting next year's income, analysts put the most weight on this year's profit from operations as it has more **predictive value** and they put less weight on this year's non-operating activities.

PW Audio Supply's non-operating activities, using assumed data, are presented below. Depending on whether the non-operating activities result in a net increase (other revenues exceed other expenses) or net decrease (other expenses exceed other revenues), they are added to or deducted from the profit from operations. The result is profit before income tax.

Profit from operations		$29,800
Other revenues and expenses		
Interest revenue	$3,400	
Interest expense	1,600	1,800
Profit before income tax		31,600

If there are no non-operating activities, profit from operations will be the same as profit before income tax.

Profit

Profit is the final outcome of all the company's operating and non-operating activities. PW Audio Supply's profit is $25,300 after deducting its income tax expense of $6,300:

Profit before income tax	$31,600
Income tax expense	6,300
Profit	$25,300

In Illustration 5-7, we bring together all the steps above in a comprehensive multiple-step income statement for PW Audio Supply. Note that the profit in Illustrations 5-7 (multiple-step) and 5-6 (single-step) is the same. The differences between the two income statements are the amount of detail displayed and the order of presentation.

▸Illustration 5-7

Multiple-step income statement— perpetual inventory system

PW AUDIO SUPPLY, INC.
Income Statement
Year Ended December 31, 2015

Sales revenue		
Sales		$480,000
Less: Sales returns and allowances	$12,000	
Sales discounts	8,000	20,000
Net sales		460,000
Cost of goods sold		316,000
Gross profit		144,000
Operating expenses		
Salaries expense	$45,000	
Rent expense	19,000	
Utilities expense	17,000	
Advertising expense	16,000	
Depreciation expense	8,000	
Freight out	7,000	
Insurance expense	2,000	
Loss on disposal	200	114,200
Profit from operations		29,800
Other revenues and expenses		
Interest revenue	$ 3,400	
Interest expense	1,600	1,800
Profit before income tax		31,600
Income tax expense		6,300
Profit		$ 25,300

BEFORE YOU GO ON...

▶ Do It! Multiple-Step Income Statement Amounts

Tyrone Inc. reported the following selected information:

Administrative expenses	$ 200,000
Cost of goods sold	1,238,000
Income tax expense	23,000
Interest expense	4,000
Rent revenue	36,000
Sales	1,820,000
Sales returns and allowances	170,000
Sales discounts	30,000
Selling expenses	122,000

Calculate the following amounts for Tyrone Inc.: (a) net sales, (b) gross profit, (c) profit from operations, (d) profit before income tax, and (e) profit.

Action Plan

- Recall the formula for net sales: Sales – sales returns and allowances – sales discounts.
- Recall the formula for gross profit: Net sales – cost of goods sold.
- Separate relevant accounts into operating (selling and administrative expenses) and non-operating (other revenues and expenses).
- Recall the formula for profit from operations: Gross profit – operating expenses.
- Recall the formula for profit before income tax: Profit from operations + other revenue – other expenses.
- Recall the formula for profit: Profit before income tax – income tax expense.

Solution

(a) Net sales: $1,820,000 − $170,000 − $30,000 = $1,620,000

(b) Gross profit: $1,620,000 (from part (a)) − $1,238,000 = $382,000

(c) Profit from operations: $382,000 (from part (b)) − ($200,000 + $122,000) = $60,000

(d) Profit before income tax: $60,000 (from part (c)) + $36,000 − $4,000 = $92,000

(e) Profit: $92,000 (from part (d)) − $23,000 = $69,000

Related Exercise Material: BE5-7, BE5-8, BE5-9, E5-7, E5-8, E5-9, and E5-10.

the navigator

Evaluating Profitability

In Chapter 2, we learned about two profitability ratios: earnings per share and the price-earnings ratio. We add two more examples of profitability ratios in this chapter: the gross profit margin and profit margin, which take into account the impact of inventory. Inventory has a significant effect on a company's profitability because cost of goods sold is usually the largest expense on a merchandising company's income statement.

STUDY OBJECTIVE 5
Calculate the gross profit margin and profit margin.

GROSS PROFIT MARGIN

When a company's gross profit is expressed as a percentage, this number is called the **gross profit margin**. It is calculated by dividing the amount of gross profit by net sales. For PW Audio Supply, the gross profit margin is 31.3% ($144,000 ÷ $460,000). This means that PW Audio Supply earns a gross profit of $0.31 for every $1 of net sales that is earned. The gross profit margin is generally considered more informative than the gross profit amount because the margin expresses a relationship between gross profit and net sales rather than a simple amount expressed in dollars. For example, a gross profit amount of $1 million may sound impressive, but if it is the result of sales of $100 million, the company's gross profit margin is only 1%. In other words, there was only $0.01 of gross profit available to cover operating expenses for every $1 of net sales.

In the following illustration, we will calculate the gross profit margin for Loblaw, and a major competitor, Metro. The gross profit margins for Loblaw, Metro, and their industry for two recent fiscal years are presented in Illustration 5-8.

▶Illustration 5-8
Gross profit margin

GROSS PROFIT MARGIN $= \dfrac{\text{GROSS PROFIT}}{\text{NET SALES}}$		
($ in millions)	2012	2011
Loblaw	$\dfrac{(\$31{,}604 - \$24{,}185)}{\$31{,}604} = 23.5\%$	$\dfrac{(\$31{,}250 - \$23{,}894)}{\$31{,}250} = 23.5\%$
Metro	18.4%	18.1%
Industry average	23.3%	23.4%

Loblaw's gross profit margin did not change in 2012 compared with 2011 and the company's gross profit margin is close to the industry average. Loblaw (and the rest of the industry) tends to have a greater portion of its sales from non-grocery items than Metro. The gross profit on these items tends to be higher and this contributes to a higher gross profit than that experienced at Metro.

DECISION TOOLKIT

 Decision Checkpoints	 Info Needed for Decision	 Tools to Use for Decision	 How to Evaluate Results
Is the price of goods keeping pace with changes in the cost of inventory?	Gross profit and net sales	Gross profit margin $= \dfrac{\text{Gross profit}}{\text{Net sales}}$	If the ratio decreases over time, it suggests the company is not passing on increases in inventory costs to its customers by raising prices as fast as costs are rising. It can also mean that the company is reducing prices when costs have not fallen to the same extent.

PROFIT MARGIN

Like gross profit, profit is often expressed as a percentage of sales. The **profit margin** measures the percentage of each dollar of sales that results in profit. It is calculated by dividing profit by net sales for the period.

What is the difference between gross profit margin and profit margin? Gross profit margin indicates how much higher the selling price is than the cost of goods sold. Profit margin indicates how well the selling price covers all expenses (including the cost of goods sold). A company can improve its profit margin by increasing its gross profit margin, by controlling its operating and other expenses, by earning other revenues, or by experiencing a decrease in the income tax rate.

Profit margins for Loblaw, Metro, and the industry average are presented in Illustration 5-9.

►Illustration 5-9
Profit margin

	PROFIT MARGIN = $\dfrac{\text{PROFIT}}{\text{NET SALES}}$	
($ in millions)	2012	2011
Loblaw	$\dfrac{\$650}{\$31,604} = 2.1\%$	$\dfrac{\$769}{\$31,250} = 2.5\%$
Metro	4.1%	3.4%
Industry average	0.7%	0.7%

Although Loblaw had a higher gross profit ratio, as shown in Illustration 5-8, it had a lower profit margin than Metro. This is primarily due to Metro's reputation for controlling its operating costs, which caused Metro's profit margin to rise in 2012 while Loblaw's fell slightly. However, Loblaw has generated more profit margin than the industry average.

Both the gross profit margin and profit margin are **profitability measures** that vary according to the specific industry. Businesses with a high turnover of inventory, such as food stores, generally experience lower gross profit and profit margins. Low-turnover businesses, such as computer manufacturers (Apple, for example), have higher gross profit and profit margins. In general, the higher the gross profit margin and profit margin, the better.

ACCOUNTING MATTERS!

Determining the Cost of an iPad

It is important for companies to pay close attention to their costs, as cost is one of the biggest drivers of profitability. Research firm IHS estimates that the cost of manufacturing Apple's iPad mini is U.S. $188 for materials and another $10 for manufacturing. When the mini first went on sale, the suggested retail price of U.S. $329 was for the base model with Wi-Fi and 16 gigabytes of memory. The addition of memory adds a small incremental cost. The parts used in the manufacture of the 7.9-inch touch-sensitive display cost approximately $80 and represent about 43% of the total cost of materials. This means that Apple is most likely generating a gross profit of U.S. $131 for an iPad mini. This translates into a gross profit margin of 40% on the base model.

That doesn't mean that Apple is making 43% of profit, of course. There are development costs, marketing, and other operating expenses to take into account before arriving at its profit margin. Nonetheless, its profitability on this item would appear to be healthy, based on these estimates.[3]

DECISION TOOLKIT

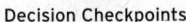 Decision Checkpoints	Info Needed for Decision	Tools to Use for Decision	How to Evaluate Results
Is the company maintaining an adequate margin between sales and expenses?	Profit and net sales	Profit margin = $\dfrac{\text{Profit}}{\text{Net sales}}$	A higher ratio suggests a favourable return on each dollar of sales.

BEFORE YOU GO ON...

▶ Do It! Calculate and Evaluate Profitability

Sports-R-Us Corporation reported the following information:

($ in thousands)	2015	2014
Net sales	$1,347	$1,331
Cost of goods sold	863	853
Operating expenses	439	407
Income tax expense	15	24

(a) Calculate the gross profit margin and profit margin for each of 2014 and 2015.

(b) Did Sports-R-Us's profitability improve or decline in 2015?

Action Plan

- Calculate gross profit and profit.
- Calculate the gross profit margin by dividing gross profit by net sales.
- Calculate the profit margin by dividing profit by net sales.
- A higher gross profit margin and profit margin indicate improved profitability.

Solution ($ in thousands)

(a) Gross profit

2015: $1,347 − $863 = $484

2014: $1,331 − $853 = $478

Profit

2015: $1,347 − $863 − $439 − $15 = $30

2014: $1,331 − $853 − $407 − $24 = $47

	2015	2014
Gross profit margin	$\dfrac{\$484}{\$1,347} = 35.9\%$	$\dfrac{\$478}{\$1,331} = 35.9\%$
Profit margin	$\dfrac{\$30}{\$1,347} = 2.2\%$	$\dfrac{\$47}{\$1,331} = 3.5\%$

(b) Sports-R-Us's gross profit margin remained unchanged in 2015. However, its profit margin declined. It appears that the company has good control of its cost of goods sold but needs to review its operating expenses, which appear to have increased faster than sales.

the navigator

Related Exercise Material: BE5-10, BE5-11, E5-6, E5-9, E5-10, and E5-11.

APPENDIX 5A—Periodic Inventory System

STUDY OBJECTIVE 6

Prepare entries for purchases and sales under a periodic inventory system and calculate cost of goods sold.

As described in this chapter, there are two basic systems of accounting for inventory: (1) the perpetual inventory system and (2) the periodic inventory system. In the chapter, we focused on accounting for inventory in a perpetual system. In this appendix, we discuss and illustrate the periodic system.

In both perpetual and periodic systems, revenues from the sale of merchandise are recorded when sales are made. However, one key difference between the two systems is the point at which the cost of goods sold is calculated and recorded. In a periodic system, on the date of sale, the cost of the merchandise sold is not recorded. While the *cost of goods sold is determined each time a sale is made in a perpetual inventory system, it is only determined at the end of each period in a periodic inventory system.*

Furthermore, in a periodic system, purchases of merchandise are recorded in the temporary Purchases expense account rather than the permanent Merchandise Inventory asset account. Also, in a periodic system, purchase returns and allowances, purchase discounts, and freight costs on purchases are recorded in separate temporary expense, or expense-related, accounts. Consequently, if a periodic system is used, the Merchandise Inventory account shown in an unadjusted trial balance represents the beginning inventory balance, which is the ending balance from the prior period.

To illustrate the recording of merchandise transactions under a periodic inventory system, we will use purchase and sale transactions between PW Audio Supply, Inc. (the seller) and Sauk Stereo Ltd. (the buyer), as illustrated for the perpetual inventory system earlier in this chapter. You will recall that PW Audio Supply sold speakers to Sauk Stereo on May 4 in the amount of $3,800. The terms of the sale are 2/10, n/30, FOB shipping point.

RECORDING PURCHASES OF MERCHANDISE

Sauk Stereo records the $3,800 purchase of merchandise from PW Audio Supply on May 4 as follows:

May 4	Purchases	3,800	
	Accounts Payable		3,800
	(To record goods purchased on account from PW Audio Supply, terms 2/10, n/30, FOB shipping point)		

A	=	L	+	SE
		+3,800		−3,800

Cash flows: no effect

The Purchases account is a temporary expense account reported on the income statement. Its normal balance is a debit.

Freight Costs

The freight terms for Sauk Stereo's purchase of merchandise are FOB shipping point, which means that the buyer pays the freight costs. Upon delivery of the goods, Sauk Stereo pays Public Carrier Co. $150 for freight charges on its purchases from PW Audio Supply. The entry on Sauk Stereo's books is as follows:

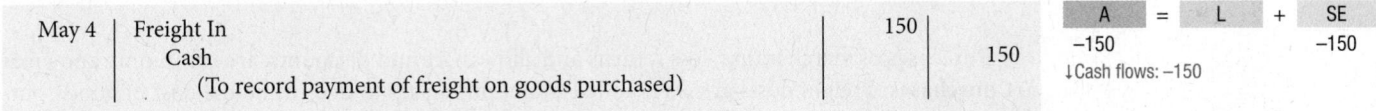

May 4	Freight In	150	
	Cash		150
	(To record payment of freight on goods purchased)		

A	=	L	+	SE
−150				−150

↓Cash flows: −150

Like Purchases, Freight In is a temporary expense account whose normal balance is a debit. Just as freight was part of the cost of the merchandise inventory in a perpetual inventory system, **freight is part of the cost of goods purchased** in a periodic inventory system. The cost of goods purchased includes any freight charges incurred in bringing the goods to the buyer. As a result, freight in is added to net purchases to determine the cost of goods purchased.

Purchase Returns and Allowances

When $300 of merchandise is returned to PW Audio Supply, Sauk Stereo prepares the following entry to recognize the return:

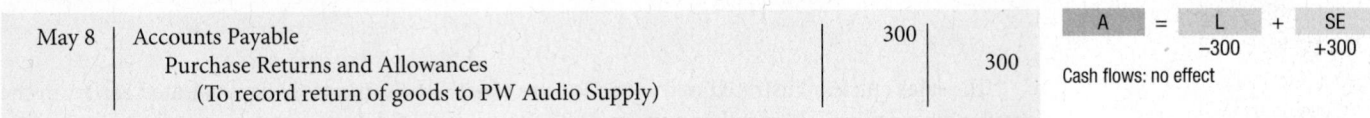

May 8	Accounts Payable	300	
	Purchase Returns and Allowances		300
	(To record return of goods to PW Audio Supply)		

A	=	L	+	SE
		−300		+300

Cash flows: no effect

Purchase Returns and Allowances is a temporary account whose normal balance is a credit. It is a **contra expense account** whose balance is subtracted from the Purchases account.

Purchase Discounts

Recall that the invoice terms were 2/10, n/30. On May 14, Sauk Stereo pays the balance due on account to PW Audio Supply of $3,500 ($3,800 − $300), less the 2% cash discount allowed by PW Audio Supply for payment within 10 days. Note that freight costs are not subject to a purchase discount. Purchase discounts apply on the invoice cost of the merchandise purchased, less any returns. In this case, the purchase discount is $70, calculated as follows: ($3,800 − $300) × 2% = $70.

The payment and discount are recorded by Sauk Stereo as follows:

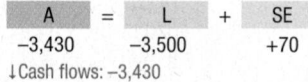

A	=	L	+	SE
−3,430		−3,500		+70

↓Cash flows: −3,430

May 14	Accounts Payable	3,500	
	Cash		3,430
	Purchase Discounts		70
	(To record payment to PW Audio Supply within discount period)		

Purchase Discounts is a temporary account whose normal balance is a credit. Like Purchase Returns and Allowances, it is a contra expense account subtracted from the Purchases account.

As was mentioned earlier, a temporary expense account is used in each of the above transactions to record purchases of merchandise instead of the Merchandise Inventory account used in a perpetual inventory system. The Purchases and Freight In accounts are debited rather than Merchandise Inventory in the first two entries, and Purchase Returns and Allowances and Purchase Discounts are credited in the last two entries rather than Merchandise Inventory. These temporary accounts are needed for calculating the cost of goods purchased at the end of the period, as shown in Illustration 5A-1.

►Illustration 5A-1

Formula for cost of goods purchased

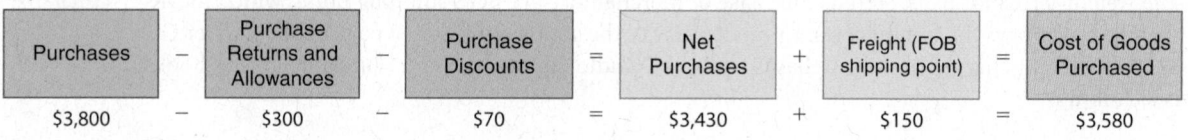

Purchases	−	Purchase Returns and Allowances	−	Purchase Discounts	=	Net Purchases	+	Freight (FOB shipping point)	=	Cost of Goods Purchased
$3,800	−	$300	−	$70	=	$3,430	+	$150	=	$3,580

Purchases of merchandise, less returns and allowances and discounts, are commonly known as **net purchases**. Freight costs are then added to net purchases to determine the cost of goods purchased. Note that the cost of goods purchased, $3,580, is the same in a periodic inventory system as it is in a perpetual inventory system, as shown in the Summary of Purchase Transactions section later in this appendix.

RECORDING SALES OF MERCHANDISE

The sale of $3,800 of merchandise to Sauk Stereo on May 4 is recorded by the seller, PW Audio Supply, as follows:

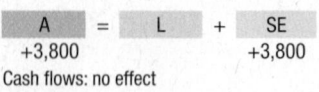

A	=	L	+	SE
+3,800				+3,800

Cash flows: no effect

May 4	Accounts Receivable	3,800	
	Sales		3,800
	(To record credit sale to Sauk Stereo, terms 2/10, n/30, FOB shipping point)		

The sales entries illustrated in this section are exactly the same as those illustrated earlier in the chapter for a perpetual inventory system, with one exception. In a perpetual inventory system, two journal entries are made for each transaction. The first entry records the accounts receivable and sales revenue, as illustrated above. The second journal entry records the cost of the sale by transferring the inventory to the Cost of Goods Sold account.

In a periodic inventory system, there is only one journal entry made at the time of the sale (the entry to record the sales revenue). The cost of the sale is not recorded. Instead, as discussed earlier, the cost of goods sold is determined by calculation at the end of the period.

Freight Costs

Freight costs incurred by the seller on outgoing merchandise are an operating expense to the seller. There is no distinction in accounting for these costs between a perpetual and periodic inventory system. Under both systems, these costs are debited to the Freight Out or Delivery Expense account.

You will recall that Sauk Stereo (the buyer) paid the shipping costs in our sales illustration, so PW Audio Supply (the seller) doesn't need to make a journal entry at this point.

Sales Returns and Allowances

When Sauk Stereo returns merchandise on May 8, PW Audio Supply records the $300 sales return as follows:

May 8	Sales Returns and Allowances	300	
	Accounts Receivable		300
	(To record return of goods by Sauk Stereo)		

A = L + SE
−300 −300
Cash flows: no effect

Just as we observed that only one entry is needed when sales are recorded in a periodic inventory system, one entry is also all that is needed to record a return. In a perpetual inventory system, two entries are needed to record the sales return and its cost.

Sales Discounts

On May 14, PW Audio Supply receives a payment of $3,430 ($3,800 − $300 − $70) on account from Sauk Stereo. Because the payment was received within the discount period, the sales discount of $70 ([$3,800 − $300] × 2%) reduces the cash received. PW Audio Supply records the collection of the account as follows:

May 14	Cash	3,430	
	Sales Discounts	70	
	Accounts Receivable		3,500
	(To record collection from Sauk Stereo within discount period)		

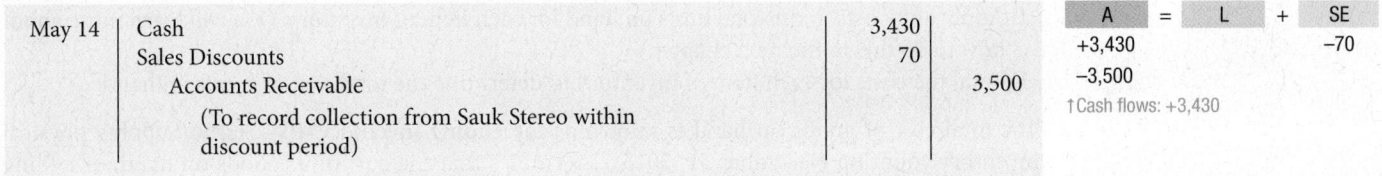

A = L + SE
+3,430 −70
−3,500
↑Cash flows: +3,430

All of the above accounts combine to determine net sales. The formula for net sales was shown in Illustration 5-5 in the chapter, and has been reproduced in Illustration 5A-2 for convenience.

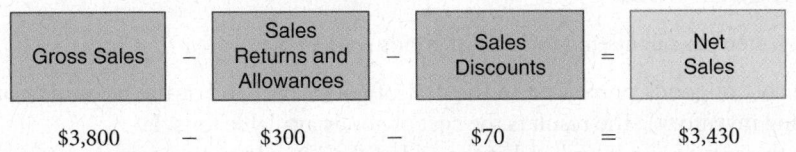

Gross Sales	−	Sales Returns and Allowances	−	Sales Discounts	=	Net Sales
$3,800	−	$300	−	$70	=	$3,430

▶Illustration 5A-2
Formula for net sales

CALCULATING COST OF GOODS SOLD

As was mentioned earlier, calculating the cost of goods sold is different in a periodic inventory system than in a perpetual inventory system. In a periodic inventory system, there is no running account (continuous updating) of changes in cost of goods sold and inventory as there is in a perpetual inventory system. The cost of goods sold for the period and the balance in ending inventory are calculated at the end of the period.

To calculate the cost of goods sold in a periodic inventory, three steps are required:

1. Calculate the cost of goods purchased.
2. Determine the cost of goods on hand (ending inventory) at the end of the accounting period.
3. Calculate the cost of goods sold by adding the cost of opening inventory to the cost of goods purchased to arrive at goods available for sale and then subtract the ending inventory from that amount.

We will discuss each of these steps in the following sections.

Cost of Goods Purchased

Earlier in this appendix, we used four accounts—Purchases, Freight In, Purchase Returns and Allowances, and Purchase Discounts—to record the purchase of inventory. These four accounts combine to determine the cost of goods purchased. You may find it helpful to review the formula to calculate cost of goods purchased shown earlier in Illustration 5A-1.

Using assumed data for PW Audio Supply, the calculation of net purchases and the cost of goods purchased is as follows:

Purchases		$325,000
Less: Purchase returns and allowances	$10,400	
Purchase discounts	6,800	17,200
Net purchases		307,800
Add: Freight in		12,200
Cost of goods purchased		320,000

Cost of Goods on Hand

To determine the cost of the inventory on hand, PW Audio Supply must take a physical inventory. Taking a physical inventory involves these procedures:

1. Count the units on hand for each item of inventory.
2. Apply unit costs to the total units on hand for each item of inventory. (We will learn more about how to do this in the next chapter.)
3. Total the costs for each item of inventory to determine the total cost of goods on hand.

The total cost of goods on hand is known as the ending inventory. PW Audio Supply's physical inventory count on December 31, 2015, determines that the cost of its goods on hand, or ending inventory, is $40,000. This ending inventory amount will be used to calculate the cost of goods sold, as shown in the next section.

Cost of Goods Sold

There are two steps in calculating the cost of goods sold:

1. Add the cost of goods purchased to the cost of goods on hand at the beginning of the period (beginning inventory). The result is the cost of goods available for sale.
2. Subtract the cost of goods on hand at the end of the period (ending inventory) from the cost of goods available for sale. The result is the cost of goods sold.

The ending inventory at December 31, 2015, was given above as $40,000. We will assume that PW Audio Supply's ending inventory at December 31, 2014 (which is the same as its beginning inventory at January 1, 2015) is $36,000. Using this information and the cost of goods purchased determined above, we can determine PW Audio Supply's cost of goods available for sale and cost of goods sold as follows:

Merchandise inventory, January 1			$ 36,000
Purchases		$325,000	
Less: Purchase returns and allowances	$10,400		
Purchase discounts	6,800	17,200	
Net purchases		307,800	
Add: Freight in		12,200	
Cost of goods purchased			320,000
Cost of goods available for sale			356,000
Merchandise inventory, December 31			40,000
Cost of goods sold			316,000

In summary, the cost of goods purchased is added to the beginning inventory to determine the cost of goods available for sale. Ending inventory is then deducted from the cost of goods available for sale to determine the cost of goods sold. In other words, what you have on hand at the beginning of the period, plus what you purchase during the period, gives you the total goods available for sale during the period. Subtract what you have not sold, and you are left with the amount that must have been sold.

Illustration 5A-3 presents this as a formula and inserts the relevant data for PW Audio Supply.

▶ Illustration 5A-3
Formula for cost of goods sold

ADJUSTING ENTRY AT PERIOD END

It is important to remember that when using a periodic inventory system, no entries are posted to the Merchandise Inventory account during the period. Because the Merchandise Inventory account does not reflect an up-to-date balance and because the Cost of Goods Sold account does not have any balance as it was not used during the period, we need to record an adjusting entry at the end of each period to update the amounts in these accounts.

In the adjusting entry shown below for PW Audio, the Merchandise Inventory account is debited for the ending inventory amount of $40,000 that was determined when counting items at the end of the period and credited for the beginning inventory amount of $36,000. Cost of Goods Sold is also debited for $316,000, the amount we calculated above, and the balances of any purchase-related accounts are brought to zero as these amounts are now allocated to Cost of Goods Sold:

Dec. 31	Merchandise Inventory (ending)	40,000	
	Cost of Goods Sold	316,000	
	Purchase Returns and Allowances	10,400	
	Purchase Discounts	6,800	
	Merchandise Inventory (beginning)		36,000
	Purchases		325,000
	Freight in		12,200
	(To allocate purchase-related accounts and change in Merchandise Inventory to Cost of Goods Sold)		

A	=	L	+	SE
+40,000				−316,000
−36,000				−10,400
				−6,800
				+325,000
				+12,200

Cash flows: no effect

COMPARISON OF ENTRIES—PERPETUAL VS. PERIODIC

The periodic inventory system's entries for purchases and sales are shown in Illustration 5A-4 next to those that were illustrated earlier in the chapter under the perpetual inventory system. Having these entries side by side should help you compare the differences. The entries that are different in the two inventory systems are highlighted in red.

ENTRIES ON SAUK STEREO'S BOOKS (BUYER)

Transaction		Perpetual Inventory System			Periodic Inventory System		
May 4	Purchase of merchandise on credit	Merchandise Inventory Accounts Payable	3,800	3,800	Purchases Accounts Payable	3,800	3,800
4	Freight costs on purchases	Merchandise Inventory Cash	150	150	Freight In Cash	150	150
8	Purchase returns and allowances	Accounts Payable Merchandise Inventory	300	300	Accounts Payable Purchase Returns and Allowances	300	300
14	Payment on account with a discount	Accounts Payable Cash Merchandise Inventory	3,500	3,430 70	Accounts Payable Cash Purchase Discounts	3,500	3,430 70

ENTRIES ON PW AUDIO SUPPLY'S BOOKS (SELLER)

Transaction		Perpetual Inventory System			Periodic Inventory System		
May 4	Sale of merchandise on credit	Accounts Receivable Sales	3,800	3,800	Accounts Receivable Sales	3,800	3,800
		Cost of Goods Sold Merchandise Inventory	2,400	2,400	No entry		
8	Return of merchandise sold	Sales Returns and Allowances Accounts Receivable	300	300	Sales Returns and Allowances Accounts Receivable	300	300
		Merchandise Inventory Cost of Goods Sold	140	140	No entry		
14	Cash received on account with a discount	Cash Sales Discounts Accounts Receivable	3,430 70	3,500	Cash Sales Discounts Accounts Receivable	3,430 70	3,500
Dec. 31	Period-end adjustment	No entry			Merchandise Inventory (ending) Cost of Goods Sold Purchase Returns and Allowances Purchase Discounts Merchandise Inventory (beginning) Purchases Freight in	40,000 316,000 10,400 6,800	36,000 325,000 12,200

▶ Illustration 5A-4

Comparison of entries under perpetual and periodic inventory systems

INCOME STATEMENT

Once cost of goods sold is calculated in a periodic inventory system, gross profit, operating expenses, non-operating items, profit before income tax, and profit are reported in a multiple-step or single-step income statement in the same way as they are in a perpetual inventory system. The only reporting difference in a multiple-step income statement is that the cost of goods sold section has more detail in a periodic inventory system than in a perpetual inventory system (see red highlighted text in Illustration 5A-5). Compare Illustration 5A-5 with the multiple-step income statement shown in Illustration 5-7 for a perpetual inventory system where only one line is reported for the cost of goods sold.

PW AUDIO SUPPLY INC.
Income Statement
Year Ended December 31, 2015

Sales revenue			
Sales			$480,000
Less: Sales returns and allowances		$ 12,000	
Sales discounts		8,000	20,000
Net sales			460,000
Cost of goods sold			
Merchandise inventory, January 1		$ 36,000	
Purchases	$325,000		
Less: Purchase returns and allowances	10,400		
Purchase discounts	6,800		
Net purchases	307,800		
Add: Freight in	12,200		
Cost of goods purchased		320,000	
Cost of goods available for sale		356,000	
Merchandise inventory, December 31		40,000	
Cost of goods sold			316,000
Gross profit			144,000
Operating expenses			
Salaries expense		$ 45,000	
Rent expense		19,000	
Utilities expense		17,000	
Advertising expense		16,000	
Depreciation expense		8,000	
Freight out		7,000	
Insurance expense		2,000	
Loss on disposal		200	114,200
Profit from operations			29,800
Other revenues and expenses			
Interest revenue		$ 3,400	
Interest expense		1,600	1,800
Profit before income tax			31,600
Income tax expense			6,300
Profit			$ 25,300

Using the periodic inventory system does not affect the content of the statement of financial position. As in the perpetual system, the ending balance of merchandise inventory is reported in the current assets section, and at the same amount.

BEFORE YOU GO ON...

►Do It! Purchase and Sales Transactions—Periodic Inventory System

On September 4, Lalonde Ltée sells merchandise on account to Guerette Corp., terms 2/10, n/45. The selling price of the goods is $3,000. On September 8, goods with a selling price of $600 are returned for credit and restored to inventory. On September 13, Lalonde receives payment in full from Guerette. Record the transactions on the books of both companies, assuming a periodic inventory system is used.

Action Plan

- Seller: Prepare only one entry to record the sale and do not record the cost of the sale. Prepare only one entry to record the return of goods and do not record the cost of the return. Calculate sales discounts using the amount owing, net of any sales returns.
- Buyer: Record purchases of inventory, returned goods, and purchase discounts in separate accounts. Calculate purchase discounts using the amount owing, net of any purchase returns.

Solution

Lalonde Ltée (Seller)

Sept. 4	Accounts Receivable		3,000	
	Sales			3,000
	(To record credit sale to Guerette, terms 2/10, n/45)			
8	Sales Returns and Allowances		600	
	Accounts Receivable			600
	(To record credit granted for receipt of returned goods from Guerette)			
13	Cash ($2,400 − $48)		2,352	
	Sales Discounts ([$3,000 − $600] × 2%)		48	
	Accounts Receivable ($3,000 − $600)			2,400
	(To record collection from Guerette within discount period)			

Guerette Corp. (Buyer)

Sept. 4	Purchases		3,000	
	Accounts Payable			3,000
	(To record goods purchased on account from Lalonde, terms 2/10, n/45)			
8	Accounts Payable		600	
	Purchase Returns and Allowances			600
	(To record return of goods to Lalonde)			
13	Accounts Payable ($3,000 − $600)		2,400	
	Purchase Discounts ([$3,000 − $600] × 2%)			48
	Cash ($2,400 − $48)			2,352
	(To record payment to Lalonde within discount period)			

Related Exercise Material: *BE5-12, *BE5-13, *BE5-14, *BE5-15, *BE5-16, *E5-12, *E5-13, *E5-14, and *E5-15.

comparing
IFRS and ASPE

Key Differences	International Financial Reporting Standards (IFRS)	Accounting Standards for Private Enterprises (ASPE)
Income statement	Expenses must be classified by nature or by function.	Expenses can be classified in any manner the company finds useful.

All About You ▶ More About Shopping

In this chapter, you learned about merchandising companies and how to complete the accounting transactions that give managers the information they need to run a successful business. There are many challenges in retail operations. For example, retailers must recognize the needs of their customers and ensure the availability of inventory. You will have noticed that the retail business is constantly changing as retailers try to attract you as a customer. Brand-new stores open, or old stores reopen in new locations or under a new name. Sometimes stores go out of business. In an increasingly competitive environment, retailers must provide an enjoyable customer experience and attempt to sell their products at competitive prices. In this competitive environment, many retailers recognize that their customers are using the Internet to help make purchase decisions.

Some Facts

- According to a recent study, approximately 88% of Canadians use the Internet and 91% of Canadians in the 18- to 34-year-old age group have made on-line purchases. Even if a final purchase is made at a retail store, the Internet plays an important role in obtaining product information before the final purchase is made. Shoppers expect prices, terms of sale, and return policies to be consistent whether purchasing from a website or at a store.

- Showrooming, a relatively new concept, occurs when customers browse for products in retail stores before searching for the same product on-line to find the lowest price. A smart phone application enables you to scan the barcode of the item you wish to purchase and then directs you to a store or website that sells the goods at the lowest price.

- Word of mouth is still the most powerful force in influencing a purchase decision. Two thirds of Canadians surveyed said that recommendations from family and friends have the greatest influence when they go shopping.

- About 7% of Canadians are reviewing on-line classified sites such as Kijiji and Craigslist at least once a day. Another 17% visit these sites once or twice a week. Many retailers are providing ads on these sites to direct on-line shoppers to their websites.

- Surveys indicate that the vast majority of coupons are clipped from weekend newspaper inserts; however, digital coupon use is growing. Many retailers are making coupons available on-line to entice shoppers to visit their stores.

- Despite the increase in on-line shopping, many Canadians still prefer to shop in person. Those consumers like to touch the product they are buying and like to take the product home immediately. They don't like to pay for costs of shipping, don't like the inconvenience of returning a product they bought on-line, and don't like to give their credit card information on-line.

What Do You Think?

The number and profitability of chain-owned stores is growing. Should you support a locally owned store instead? Should you always shop where the price is lowest, even if the store is part of a chain? Should you only shop at chain stores that have an on-line store?

YES It is important to support local businesses. I like the personal service and the fact that all of the profits stay in the community. I also like to see what I am buying before I purchase a product and want the ability to discuss the merits of purchasing the product with a real person.

NO With the pressure on my budget, I have to find the best deals. This includes buying from the cheapest sources, whether from a website or from a chain-owned store.[4]

Summary of Study Objectives

1. **Identify the differences between service and merchandising companies.** A service company performs services. It has service or fee revenue and operating expenses. A merchandising company sells goods. It has sales revenue, cost of goods sold, and gross profit in addition to operating expenses. Both types of company may also report non-operating items and each would report income tax expense.

2. **Prepare entries for purchases under a perpetual inventory system.** The Merchandise Inventory account is debited for all purchases of merchandise and for freight costs if those costs are paid by the buyer (shipping terms FOB shipping point). It is credited for purchase discounts, and purchase returns and allowances.

3. **Prepare entries for sales under a perpetual inventory system.** When inventory is sold, two entries are required: (1) Cash or Accounts Receivable is debited and Sales is credited for the selling price of the merchandise, and (2) Cost of Goods Sold is debited and Merchandise Inventory is credited for the cost of inventory items sold. Contra revenue accounts are used to record sales returns and allowances and sales discounts. Two journal entries are also required for sales returns so that both the selling price and the cost of the returned merchandise are recorded. Freight costs paid by the seller (shipping terms FOB destination) are recorded as an operating expense.

4. **Prepare a single-step and a multiple-step income statement.** In a single-step income statement, all data (except for income tax expense) are classified under two categories—revenues or expenses—and profit before income tax is determined in one step. Income tax expense is separated from the other expenses and reported separately after profit before income tax to determine profit (loss).

   A multiple-step income statement shows several steps in determining profit. Step 1 deducts sales returns and allowances and sales discounts from gross sales to determine net sales. Step 2 deducts the cost of goods sold from net sales to determine gross profit. Step 3 deducts operating expenses (which can be classified by nature or by function) from gross profit to determine profit from operations. Step 4 adds or deducts any non-operating items to determine profit before income tax. Finally, step 5 deducts income tax expense to determine profit (loss).

5. **Calculate the gross profit margin and profit margin.** The gross profit margin, calculated by dividing gross profit by net sales, measures the gross profit earned for each dollar of sales. The profit margin, calculated by dividing profit by net sales, measures the profit earned for each dollar of sales. Both are measures of profitability that are closely watched by management and other interested parties.

6. **Prepare entries for purchases and sales under a periodic inventory system and calculate cost of goods sold (Appendix 5A).** The periodic inventory system differs from the perpetual inventory system in that separate temporary accounts are used in the periodic system to record (1) purchases, (2) purchase returns and allowances, (3) purchase discounts, and (4) freight costs that are paid by the buyer (shipping terms FOB shipping point). The formula for cost of goods purchased is as follows: Purchases – purchase returns and allowances – purchase discounts = net purchases; and net purchases + freight in = cost of goods purchased.

   Both systems use temporary accounts to record (1) sales, (2) sales returns and allowances, and (3) sales discounts. However, in a periodic inventory system, only one journal entry is made to record a sale of merchandise as the cost of goods sold is not recorded throughout the period. Instead, the cost of goods sold is determined at the end of the period.

   To determine the cost of goods sold, first calculate the cost of goods purchased, as indicated above. Then, calculate the cost of goods sold as follows: Beginning inventory + cost of goods purchased = cost of goods available for sale; and cost of goods available for sale – ending inventory = cost of goods sold.

   At the end of the period, the Merchandise Inventory account is adjusted to reflect its proper balance as determined from the inventory count results. The change in this account is allocated to the Cost of Goods Sold account as are the balances in the Freight In and Purchases account and any related contra accounts.

Glossary

Contra expense account An account that is offset against (reduces) an expense account on the income statement. Examples include purchase returns and allowances and purchase discounts. (p. 245)

Contra revenue account An account that is offset against (reduces) a revenue account on the income statement. Examples include sales returns and allowances and sales discounts. (p. 233)

Cost of goods available for sale The sum of beginning inventory and the cost of goods purchased. (p. 226)

Cost of goods purchased The sum of net purchases and freight in. (p. 227)

Cost of goods sold The total cost of merchandise sold during the period. In a perpetual inventory system, it is calculated and recorded for each sale. In a periodic inventory system, it is calculated at the end of the accounting period by deducting ending inventory from the cost of goods available for sale. (p. 224)

FOB (free on board) destination Freight terms indicating that the seller will pay for the shipping costs of the goods until they arrive at their destination (normally the buyer's place of business). (p. 228)

FOB (free on board) shipping point Freight terms indicating that the seller is responsible for the goods only until they reach their shipping point (normally the seller's place of business). The buyer will pay for the shipping costs of the goods from the shipping point until they arrive at their destination. (p. 228)

Function A method of organizing expenses on the income statement by way of the activity (business function) for which they were incurred (such as cost of goods sold, administrative, and selling). (p. 237)

Gross profit Sales revenue less cost of goods sold. (p. 224)

Gross profit margin Gross profit expressed as a percentage of sales. It is calculated by dividing gross profit by net sales. (p. 241)

Gross sales Total sales before deducting any sales returns and allowances and sales discounts. (p. 235)

Multiple-step income statement An income statement that shows several steps to determine profit or loss. (p. 237)

Nature A method of organizing expenses on the income statement by way of their natural classification (such as salaries, transportation, depreciation, and advertising). (p. 237)

Net purchases Purchases less purchase returns and allowances and purchase discounts. (p. 246)

Net sales Gross sales less sales returns and allowances and sales discounts. (p. 235)

Operating expenses Expenses incurred in the process of earning sales revenue. They are deducted from gross profit to arrive at profit from operations. (p. 224)

Periodic inventory system An inventory system in which detailed records are not maintained and the ending inventory and cost of goods sold are determined only at the end of the accounting period. (p. 226)

Perpetual inventory system A detailed inventory system in which the quantity and cost of each inventory item is maintained. The records continuously show the inventory that should be on hand and the cost of the items sold. (p. 225)

Profit from operations The results of a company's normal operating activities. It is calculated as gross profit less operating expenses. (p. 239)

Profit margin Profit expressed as a percentage of net sales. It is calculated by dividing profit by net sales. (p. 242)

Purchase discount A price reduction, based on the invoice price less any returns and allowances, claimed by a buyer for early payment of a credit purchase. (p. 230)

Purchase returns and allowances A return of goods for cash or credit, or a deduction granted by the seller on the selling price of unsatisfactory merchandise. (p. 229)

Quantity discount A price reduction that reduces the invoice price and is given to the buyer for volume purchases. (p. 230)

Sales discount A price reduction that is based on the invoice price less any returns and allowances and is given by a seller for early payment of a credit sale. (p. 234)

Sales returns and allowances A return of goods or reduction in price of unsatisfactory merchandise. (p. 233)

Sales revenue The main source of revenue in a merchandising company. (p. 224)

Single-step income statement An income statement that shows only one step (revenues less expenses) in determining profit (or loss). (p. 237)

DECISION TOOLKIT—A SUMMARY

 Decision Checkpoints	 Info Needed for Decision	 Tools to Use for Decision	 How to Evaluate Results
Is the price of goods keeping pace with changes in the cost of inventory?	Gross profit and net sales	Gross profit margin $= \dfrac{\text{Gross profit}}{\text{Net sales}}$	If the ratio decreases over time, it suggests the company is not passing on increases in inventory costs to its customers by raising prices as fast as costs are rising. It can also mean that the company is reducing prices when costs have not fallen to the same extent.
Is the company maintaining an adequate margin between sales and expenses?	Profit and net sales	Profit margin $= \dfrac{\text{Profit}}{\text{Net sales}}$	A higher ratio suggests a favourable return on each dollar of sales.

the navigator

USING THE DECISION TOOLKIT

The following selected information is available for Sobeys Inc.:

(in $ millions)	2012	2011
Net sales	$16,022	$15,738
Cost of goods sold	12,148	11,893
Net income	335	325

Instructions

(a) Loblaw is approximately twice the size of Sobeys (based on net sales) and Metro is somewhat smaller than Sobeys. Can a comparison of the financial results of these three companies be meaningful?

(b) Calculate the gross profit margin and profit margin for Sobeys for 2012 and 2011.

(c) Using the ratios calculated in part (b), compare the gross profit margin and profit margin with that of Loblaw, Metro, and their industry found in Illustrations 5-8 and 5-9 in the chapter.

Solution

(a) It does not matter that Loblaw is larger than Sobeys and Metro. Ratio analysis puts each company's financial information into the same perspective for a comparison. It is the relationship between the amounts that is meaningful.

(b) **Gross profit margin:**

(in $ millions)	2012	2011
Sobeys	$\dfrac{(\$16{,}022 - \$12{,}148)}{\$16{,}022} = 24.2\%$	$\dfrac{(\$15{,}738 - \$11{,}893)}{\$15{,}738} = 24.4\%$
Loblaw	23.5%	23.5%
Metro	18.4%	18.1%
Industry average	23.3%	23.4%

Profit margin:

(in $ millions)	2012	2011
Sobeys	$\dfrac{\$335}{\$16{,}022} = 2.1\%$	$\dfrac{\$325}{\$15{,}738} = 2.1\%$
Loblaw	2.1%	2.5%
Metro	4.1%	3.4%
Industry average	0.7%	0.7%

(c) Sobeys' gross profit margin shows a marginal decrease between 2011 and 2012. Both Loblaw's and the industry average were stable, suggesting that any price increases were passed along to customers. Metro's gross margin ratio, on the other hand, reflects a small increase.

All three companies reported a significantly higher profit margin than the industry average. Despite a stable gross margin ratio, Loblaw's profit margin decreased by approximately 0.5 percentage points. This decrease may be attributable to the increase in selling, general, and administrative expenses between 2011 and 2012. In 2011, Metro reported closure costs of $20.5 million that negatively affected the profit margin. No closure costs were incurred in 2012.

the navigator

Comprehensive Do It!

The adjusted trial balance at December 31, 2015, for Dykstra Inc. follows:

DYKSTRA INC. Adjusted Trial Balance December 31, 2015		
	Debit	Credit
Cash	$ 4,500	
Accounts receivable	11,100	
Merchandise inventory	29,000	
Prepaid insurance	2,500	
Land	150,000	
Buildings	500,000	
Accumulated depreciation—buildings		$ 40,000
Equipment	95,000	
Accumulated depreciation—equipment		18,000
Accounts payable		10,600
Property tax payable		4,000
Bank loan payable—short-term		25,000
Mortgage payable		551,000
Common shares		70,000
Retained earnings		61,000
Dividends	10,000	
Sales		536,800
Sales returns and allowances	6,700	
Sales discounts	5,000	
Cost of goods sold	363,400	
Administrative expenses	111,500	
Selling expenses	19,600	
Interest expense	4,600	
Interest revenue		2,500
Income tax expense	6,000	
	$1,318,900	$1,318,900

Additional information:
- $21,000 of the mortgage is due within the next year.
- Dykstra issued $5,000 of common shares during the year.

Instructions
Assuming Dykstra uses a perpetual inventory system, prepare a multiple-step income statement, statement of changes in equity, and statement of financial position for the year.

Action Plan
- Prepare the income statement in steps:
  1. Sales less sales returns and allowances and sales discounts equals net sales.
  2. Net sales less cost of goods sold equals gross profit.
  3. Gross profit less operating expenses (classified by function in this case as selling and administrative expenses) equals profit from operations.
  4. Profit from operations plus non-operating revenues and gains or minus expenses and losses equals profit before income tax.
- Prepare the statement of changes in equity showing the movement in common shares, retained earnings, and total equity.
- Prepare the statement of financial position ensuring that merchandise inventory is a current asset.

Solution to Comprehensive Do It!

DYKSTRA INC.
Income Statement
Year Ended December 31, 2015

Sales		$536,800
Less: Sales returns and allowances	$ 6,700	
Sales discounts	5,000	11,700
Net sales		525,100
Cost of goods sold		363,400
Gross profit		161,700
Operating expenses		
Administrative expenses	$111,500	
Selling expenses	19,600	131,100
Profit from operations		30,600
Other revenues and expenses		
Interest revenue	$ 2,500	
Interest expense	4,600	(2,100)
Profit before income tax		28,500
Income tax expense		6,000
Profit		$ 22,500

DYKSTRA INC.
Statement of Changes in Equity
Year Ended December 31, 2015

	Common Shares	Retained Earnings	Total Equity
Balance, January 1	$65,000	$61,000	$126,000
Issue of common shares	5,000		5,000
Profit		22,500	22,500
Dividends		(10,000)	(10,000)
Balance, December 31	$70,000	$73,500	$143,500

DYKSTRA INC.
Statement of Financial Position
December 31, 2015

Assets

Current assets			
Cash		$ 4,500	
Accounts receivable		11,100	
Merchandise inventory		29,000	
Prepaid insurance		2,500	
Total current assets			$ 47,100
Property, plant, and equipment			
Land		$150,000	
Buildings	$500,000		
Less: Accumulated depreciation	40,000	460,000	
Equipment	$ 95,000		
Less: Accumulated depreciation	18,000	77,000	
Total property, plant, and equipment			687,000
Total assets			$734,100

Liabilities and Shareholders' Equity		
Liabilities		
Current liabilities		
Accounts payable	$ 10,600	
Property tax payable	4,000	
Bank loan payable	25,000	
Mortgage payable—current portion	21,000	
Total current liabilities		$ 60,600
Non-current liabilities		
Mortgage payable		530,000
Total liabilities		590,600
Shareholders' equity		
Common shares	$ 70,000	
Retained earnings	73,500	143,500
Total liabilities and shareholders' equity		$734,100

the navigator

WileyPLUS | Self-Test, Brief Exercises, Exercises, Problems: Set A, and many more components are available for practice in *WileyPLUS*.

Note: All questions, exercises, and problems below with an asterisk (*) relate to material in Appendix 5A.

Self-Test Questions

Answers are at the end of the chapter.

Quiz Yourself

(SO 1)   1. Which of the following statements is true?
  (a) The operating cycle for a merchandising company is usually longer than that of a service company.
  (b) Cost of goods available for sale equals the total of cost of goods purchased and ending inventory.
  (c) A merchandising company usually has three different types of inventory: raw materials, work in process, and finished goods.
  (d) It is not necessary to perform a physical inventory count in a perpetual inventory system.

(SO 2)   2. A $1,000 purchase of merchandise inventory is made on June 12, terms 2/10, n/30. On June 16, merchandise costing $150 is returned. What amount will be paid if payment is made in full on June 21? On July 11?
  (a) $980 and $1,000
  (b) $833 and $850
  (c) $850 and $1,000
  (d) $833 and $980

(SO 2)   3. Enrage Inc. purchased merchandise for $310 on May 12, terms 1/10, n/30, FOB shipping point. On May 12, freight costs of $25 were also paid

by the company. On May 15, Enrage returned merchandise costing $10. On May 21, the company paid the amount owing. What is the ending balance in the Merchandise Inventory account related to these transactions, if Enrage uses a perpetual inventory system?
  (a) $300.00
  (b) $318.50
  (c) $322.00
  (d) $325.00

(SO 2, 3)   4. When goods are shipped with the freight terms FOB shipping point in a perpetual inventory system:
  (a) the buyer pays the freight costs and debits Merchandise Inventory.
  (b) the buyer pays the freight costs and debits Freight In.
  (c) the seller pays the freight costs and debits Cost of Goods Sold.
  (d) the seller pays the freight costs and debits Freight Out.

(SO 3)   5. To record the sale of goods for cash in a perpetual inventory system:
(a) only one journal entry is necessary to record the
cost of goods sold and reduction of inventory.
(b) only one journal entry is necessary to record
the receipt of cash and the sales revenue.
(c) two journal entries are necessary: one to record the receipt of cash and sales revenue for
the selling price, and one to record the cost of
the goods sold and reduction of inventory.
(d) two journal entries are necessary: one to
record the receipt of cash and reduction of inventory for the selling price, and one to record
the cost of the goods sold and sales revenue.

(SO 3)   6. Which of the following is a contra revenue
account that normally has a debit balance?
(a) Sales
(b) Sales Returns and Allowances
(c) Cost of Goods Sold
(d) Freight Out

(SO 4)   7. Net sales are $500,000; cost of goods sold is
$325,000; selling expenses are $10,000; administrative expenses are $40,000; other revenue is
$15,000; and income tax expense is $8,000. What
is the gross profit?
(a) $175,000
(b) $140,000
(c) $132,000
(d) $125,000

(SO 4)   8. Which of the following appears on both a single-
step and multiple-step income statement?
(a) Gross profit
(b) Profit from operations
(c) Merchandise inventory
(d) Profit before income tax

(SO 5)   9. Which of the following would affect the gross
profit margin?
(a) An increase in interest expense
(b) A decrease in depreciation expense
(c) An increase in cost of goods sold
(d) A decrease in freight out

(SO 5)   10. Net sales are $400,000; cost of goods sold is
$310,000; operating expenses are $60,000; other
revenue is $10,000; and income tax expense is
$8,000. What are the gross profit margin and
profit margin?
(a) 7.5% and 8.0%
(b) 8.0% and 22.5%
(c) 22.5% and 8.0%
(d) 25.0% and 8.0%

(SO 6)   *11. When goods are purchased for resale by a company using a periodic inventory system:
(a) purchases are debited to Merchandise
Inventory.
(b) purchases are debited to Purchases.
(c) purchases are debited to Cost of Goods Sold.
(d) purchases are debited to Finished Goods
Inventory.

(SO 6)   *12. Beginning inventory is $45,000; purchases are
$460,000; purchase returns and allowances are
$30,000; freight in is $7,500; and ending inventory is $65,000. What is the cost of goods sold
under a periodic inventory system?
(a) $447,500
(b) $417,500
(c) $410,000
(d) $372,500

Questions

(SO 1)   1. (a) What is meant by the term *operating cycle*?
(b) Why is the normal operating cycle for a
merchandising company likely to be longer
than that of a service company?

(SO 1)   2. (a) Explain the income measurement process in
a merchandising company. (b) How does income
measurement differ between a merchandising
company and a service company?

(SO 1)   3. Suppose you are starting a company that sells
used clothes. What factors would you consider
in determining whether to use a perpetual or
periodic inventory system?

(SO 1)   4. Song Yee wonders why a physical inventory
count is necessary in a perpetual inventory system. After all, the accounting records show how
much inventory is on hand. Explain why a physical inventory count is required in a perpetual
inventory system.

(SO 2)   5. Why are purchases of merchandise for resale
not recorded in the same account as purchases
of other items, such as supplies or equipment?
Would it not be better to use one account to
record all these purchases?

(SO 2)   6. Butler's Roofing Ltd. received an invoice for a
purchase of merchandise for $10,000, terms
1/10, n/30. (a) Calculate the cost of missing this
purchase discount to Butler's Roofing. (b) Should
it take advantage of the cash discount offered or
not? Explain.

(SO 2, 3)   7. Inventory was purchased on credit in April and
paid for in May. It was sold in June. In which
month should the company record the sale as
revenue and in which month should the company record the cost of goods sold as expense?

(SO 2, 3)   8. (a) Distinguish between FOB shipping point
and FOB destination. (b) What freight term will

result in a debit to Merchandise Inventory by the buyer? A debit to Freight Out by the seller?

(SO 2, 3) 9. Explain why purchase returns are credited directly to the Merchandise Inventory account but sales returns are not debited directly to the Sales account.

(SO 2, 3) 10. (a) Distinguish between a quantity discount, a purchase discount, and a sales discount. (b) Explain how each kind of discount is recorded.

(SO 3) 11. If merchandise is returned and restored to inventory, the Cost of Goods Sold account is credited. However, if merchandise is returned but not restored to inventory (because it is not resaleable), Cost of Goods Sold is not credited. Why not?

(SO 3) 12. As the end of Agnew Inc.'s fiscal year approached, it became clear that the company had excess inventory. Belden Glass, the head of marketing and sales, ordered his sales staff to "add 20% more units to each order that you ship. The customers can always ship the extra back next year if they decide they don't want it. We've got to do it to meet this year's sales goal." Discuss the implications of Belden's order.

(SO 4) 13. Distinguish between a single-step and a multiple-step income statement for a merchandising company.

(SO 4) 14. Which type of income statement—single-step or multiple-step—does **Shoppers Drug Mart** use? You can find its financial statements in Appendix A at the back of this textbook.

(SO 4) 15. (a) What is the difference between classifying expenses in an income statement by nature or by function? (b) Does this classification apply only to a single-step income statement, to a multiple-step income statement, or both?

(SO 4) 16. **Shoppers Drug Mart**'s biggest competitor, after **Jean Coutu**, is the **Katz Group**. Its Canadian stores include Rexall Drug Stores, Guardian, Medicine Shoppe, and Pharma Plus Drugmart, among others. Katz is a private company, while Shoppers and Jean Coutu are publicly traded companies. How might Katz's expenses reported on its income statement differ from those presented by Shoppers and Jean Coutu?

(SO 4) 17. Why is interest expense reported as a non-operating expense and not as an operating expense on a multiple-step income statement?

(SO 5) 18. Explain the difference, if any, between gross profit margin and profit margin.

(SO 5) 19. What factors affect a company's gross profit margin; that is, what can cause the gross profit margin to increase and what can cause it to decrease?

(SO 5) 20. Identify two types of companies that you would expect to have a high gross profit margin and two types of companies that you would expect to have a low gross profit margin.

(SO 6) *21. Identify the accounts that are added to or deducted from purchases in a periodic inventory system to determine the cost of goods purchased. For each account, indicate (a) whether its balance is added or deducted and (b) what its normal balance is.

(SO 6) *22. How is the cost of goods sold calculated and recorded in a periodic inventory system? In a perpetual inventory system?

(SO 6) *23. What differences would be found on an income statement prepared for a company using a periodic inventory system, compared with a company using a perpetual inventory system?

Brief Exercises

BE5–1 The operating cycles of three different companies are shown below.

Company	Operating Cycle (in days)
A	40
B	72
C	99

Compare operating cycles. (SO 1)

(a) Which company has the most efficient operating cycle? (b) Identify which of the three companies is most likely a service company, a merchandising company, and a manufacturing company.

BE5–2 Selected information from the income measurement process for a service company and a merchandising company is shown below.

Determine missing amounts for income measurement process. (SO 1)

Company	Sales or Service Revenue	Cost of Goods Sold	Gross Profit	Operating Expenses	Profit before Income Tax	Income Tax Expense	Profit
A	$100	$ 0	$ 0	$65	$ [1]	$ 9	$[2]
B	100	[3]	60	[4]	35	[5]	26

(a) Determine the missing amounts [1] through [5]. (b) Identify which of the two companies—A or B—is a service company and which is a merchandising company. Explain why you made the choices you did.

Determine balance in Merchandise Inventory account.
(SO 2)

BE5–3 At the beginning of the year, Point Claire Shipping Ltd., a company that has a perpetual inventory system, had $25,000 of merchandise inventory. During the year, inventory costing $100,000 was purchased. Of this, $12,000 was returned to the supplier and a 5% discount was taken on the remainder. Freight costs incurred by the company for merchandise purchases amounted to $2,400. The cost of goods sold during the year was $93,000. Determine the balance in the Merchandise Inventory account at the end of the year.

Record purchase and sales transactions.
(SO 2, 3)

BE5–4 On August 24, Pocras Corporation purchased merchandise on account from Wydell Inc. The selling price of the goods is $900 and the cost of goods sold is $590. Both companies use perpetual inventory systems. Record the above transactions on the books of both companies.

Record purchase transactions.
(SO 2)

BE5–5 Prepare the journal entries to record the following purchase transactions in Xtra Inc.'s books. Xtra uses a perpetual inventory system.

Jan. 2   Xtra purchased $15,000 of merchandise from Fundy Corp., terms 2/10, n/45, FOB destination.
     5   The appropriate company paid freight costs of $300.
     6   Xtra returned $2,000 of the merchandise purchased on January 2, because it was not needed.
    11   Xtra paid the balance owed to Fundy.

Record sales transactions.
(SO 3)

BE5–6 Refer to BE5–5 and prepare the journal entries to record the following sales transactions in Fundy Corp.'s books. Fundy uses a perpetual inventory system.

Jan. 2   Fundy sold $15,000 of merchandise to Xtra Inc., terms 2/10, n/45, FOB destination. The cost of the merchandise sold was $11,250.
     5   The appropriate company paid freight costs of $300.
     6   Xtra returned $2,000 of the merchandise purchased from Fundy on January 2, because it was not needed. The cost of the merchandise returned was $1,500, and it was restored to inventory.
    11   Fundy received the balance due from Xtra.

Calculate amounts from income statement.
(SO 4)

BE5–7 Saguenay Limited reports the following information: sales $650,000; sales returns and allowances $25,000; sales discounts $55,000; cost of goods sold $320,000; administrative expenses $100,000; selling expenses $25,000; other revenues $20,000; other expenses $30,000; and income tax expense $25,000. Assuming Saguenay uses a multiple-step income statement, calculate the following: (a) net sales, (b) gross profit, (c) profit from operations, (d) profit before income tax, and (e) profit.

Identify placement of items on income statement.
(SO 4)

BE5–8 Explain where each of the following items would appear on (a) a single-step income statement and (b) a multiple-step income statement where expenses are classified by nature: depreciation expense, cost of goods sold, freight out, income tax expense, interest expense, interest revenue, rent revenue, salaries expense, sales, sales discounts, and sales returns and allowances.

Identify classification of expenses on income statement.
(SO 4)

BE5–9 A company presented its income statement using the following format:

Sales revenue	$x
Cost of goods sold	x
Gross profit	x
Administrative expenses	x
Selling expenses	x
Profit from operations	x
Other revenues and expenses	x
Profit before income tax	x
Income tax expense	x
Profit	x

(a) Is this company using a single- or multiple-step form of income statement? (b) Is it classifying its expenses by nature or by function? Explain.

Calculate profitability ratios and comment.
(SO 5)

BE5–10 In 2015, Modder Corporation reported net sales of $250,000, cost of goods sold of $137,500, operating expenses of $50,000, and income tax expense of $20,000. In 2014, it reported net sales of $200,000, cost of goods sold of $114,000, operating expenses of $40,000, other revenues of $10,000, and income tax expense of $15,000. (a) Calculate the gross profit margin and profit margin for each year. (b) Comment on Modder's changing profitability.

Calculate profitability ratios and comment.
(SO 5)

BE5–11 In 2012, **Canadian Tire Corporation** reported sales revenue of $11,427.2 million, cost of goods sold of $7,929.3 million, and profit of $499.2 million. In 2011, it reported sales revenue of $10,387.1 million, cost of goods sold of $7,326.4 million, and profit of $467.0 million. (a) Calculate the gross profit margin and profit margin for each year. (b) Comment on Canadian Tire's changing profitability.

*BE5–12 From the information in BE5–5, prepare the journal entries to record the purchase transactions on Xtra Inc.'s books, assuming a periodic inventory system is used instead of a perpetual inventory system.

Record purchase transactions.
(SO 6)

*BE5–13 From the information in BE5–6, prepare the journal entries to record the sales transactions on Fundy Corp.'s books, assuming a periodic inventory system is used instead of a perpetual inventory system.

Record sales transactions.
(SO 6)

*BE5–14 Bassing Corp. uses a periodic inventory system and reports the following information: sales $750,000; sales returns and allowances $75,000; sales discounts $25,000; purchases $425,000; purchase returns and allowances $11,000; purchase discounts $9,000; freight in $10,000; freight out $18,000; beginning inventory $60,000; and ending inventory $100,000. Assuming Bassing uses a multiple-step income statement, calculate (a) net sales, (b) net purchases, (c) cost of goods purchased, (d) cost of goods sold, and (e) gross profit.

Calculate amounts from income statement.
(SO 6)

*BE5–15 Halifax Limited reported the following selected data for the year ended December 31, 2015: purchases $195,000; purchase returns and allowances $6,600; purchase discounts $20,400; freight in $5,250; freight out $11,250; beginning inventory $105,000; and ending inventory $120,000. (a) Prepare the cost of goods sold section for Halifax in a multiple-step income statement. (b) Explain how the remainder of Halifax's income statement would differ, if at all, if it used a perpetual inventory system.

Prepare cost of goods sold section.
(SO 6)

*BE5–16 At the end of the year, Tunnel Mountain Resorts Ltd., a company that has a periodic inventory system, had the following account balances on its unadjusted trial balance: Merchandise Inventory $30,000, Purchases $262,000, Purchase Discounts $4,000, Freight in $7,000. The inventory count at the end of the year determined that the inventory on hand at that time cost $24,000. Record the adjusting journal entry that would be made at the end of the year to update the Merchandise Inventory and Cost of Goods Sold accounts.

Prepare period-end adjusting entry for periodic system.
(SO 6)

Exercises

E5–1 Listed below are selected companies, accompanied by a brief description of their business:

1. **Toys "R" Us, Inc.** sells toys.
2. **Fasken Martineau Dumoulin LLP** is a law firm.
3. **Atlantic Grocery Distributors Ltd.** distributes food products to grocery stores.

Distinguish between service and merchandising companies.
(SO 1)

Instructions

(a) Identify whether the primary type of business for each of the above companies is as a service company, merchandiser (retailer) company, or merchandiser (wholesaler) company.

(b) Comment on how the operating cycles and income measurement processes of each of the above companies might differ, if at all.

E5–2 Listed below are selected examples of transactions related to the purchase and sale of merchandise inventory. Assume a perpetual inventory system is in use.

Identify debit and credit effects of inventory transactions.
(SO 2, 3)

1. Purchase of $3,500 of inventory for cash.
2. Purchase of $4,000 of inventory on account, terms 2/10, n/45.
3. Payment of $400 cash for freight on purchase of inventory (FOB shipping point).
4. Return of $750 of inventory to seller for credit on account.
5. Payment of amount owed for purchase of $3,500 of inventory, terms 2/10, n/30, paid within discount period.
6. Sale of inventory on account, terms n/30. Selling price $10,000; cost of sale $4,000.
7. Payment of $600 cash for freight on sale of inventory (FOB destination).
8. Return of unwanted inventory from buyer for credit on account. Selling price $1,000; cost of sale $400. Goods restored to inventory for future resale.
9. Return of damaged inventory from buyer for cash. Selling price $750; cost of sale $300. Goods not resaleable are discarded.
10. Receipt of payment ($6,000) from customer on account, terms n/30.

Instructions

For each of the above transactions, indicate: (a) the basic type (asset, liability, revenue, or expense) of each account to be debited and credited; (b) the specific name of the account(s) to debit and credit (for example, Merchandise Inventory); and (c) whether each account is increased (+) or decreased (–) and by what amount. The first one has been done for you as an example.

	Account Debited			Account Credited		
	(a)	(b)	(c)	(a)	(b)	(c)
	Basic Type of Account	Specific Account	Amount	Basic Type of Account	Specific Account	Amount
1.	Asset	Merchandise Inventory	+$3,500	Asset	Cash	–$3,500

Record and post purchase and sales transactions.
(SO 2, 3)

E5–3 On September 1, the beginning of its fiscal year, Campus Office Supply Ltd. had an inventory of 10 calculators at a cost of $20 each. The company uses a perpetual inventory system. During September, the following transactions occurred:

Sept. 2 Purchased 75 calculators for $20 each from Digital Corp. on account, terms n/30.
10 Returned two calculators to Digital for $40 credit because they did not meet specifications.
11 Sold 26 calculators for $30 each to Campus Book Store, terms n/30.
14 Granted credit of $30 to Campus Book Store for the return of one calculator that was not ordered. The calculator was restored to inventory.
21 Sold 30 calculators for $30 each to Student Card Shop, terms 1/10, n/30.
29 Paid Digital the amount owing.
30 Received payment in full from the Student Card Shop.

Instructions
(a) Record the September transactions.
(b) Create T accounts for the Merchandise Inventory and Cost of Goods Sold accounts. Post the opening balances and the September transactions.
(c) Determine the ending balances in both dollars and quantities.

Record purchase transactions.
(SO 2)

E5–4 Olaf Corp. uses a perpetual inventory system. The company had the following inventory transactions in April:

Apr. 3 Purchased merchandise from DeVito Ltd. for $28,000, terms 1/10, n/30, FOB shipping point.
6 The appropriate company paid freight costs of $700 on the merchandise purchased on April 3.
7 Purchased supplies on account for $5,000.
8 Returned damaged merchandise to DeVito and was given a purchase allowance of $3,500. The merchandise was repaired by DeVito and returned to inventory for future resale.
30 Paid the amount due to DeVito in full.

Instructions
(a) Record the above transactions in Olaf's books.
(b) Assume that Olaf paid the balance due to DeVito on April 12 instead of April 30. Prepare the journal entry to record this payment on Olaf's books.

Record sales transactions.
(SO 3)

E5–5 Refer to the information in E5–4 for Olaf Corp. and the following additional information:

1. The cost of the merchandise sold on April 3 was $19,000.
2. The cost of the merchandise returned on April 8 was $2,300.
3. DeVito uses a perpetual inventory system.

Instructions
(a) Record the transactions in the books of DeVito.
(b) Assume that DeVito received the balance due from Olaf on April 12 instead of April 30. Prepare the journal entry to record this collection on DeVito's books.

Record purchase and sales transactions; calculate gross profit.
(SO 2, 3, 5)

E5–6 The following merchandise transactions occurred in December. Both companies use a perpetual inventory system.

Dec. 3 Pictou Ltd. sold $18,000 of merchandise to Thames Corp., terms 2/10, n/30, FOB shipping point. The cost of the merchandise sold was $10,000.
7 Shipping costs of $450 were paid by the appropriate company.
8 Thames returned unwanted merchandise to Pictou. The returned merchandise has a sales price of $1,200, and a cost of $650. It was restored to inventory.
11 Pictou received the balance due from Thames.

Instructions
(a) Record the above transactions in the books of Pictou.
(b) Record the above transactions in the books of Thames.
(c) Calculate the gross profit earned by Pictou on the above transactions.

Classify accounts.
(SO 4)

E5–7 The following list of accounts is from the adjusted trial balance for Swirsky Corporation:

Accounts payable	Equipment	Prepaid insurance
Accounts receivable	Income tax expense	Property tax payable
Accumulated depreciation	Interest expense	Salaries payable
Administrative expenses	Interest payable	Sales
Buildings	Land	Sales discounts
Cash	Merchandise inventory	Sales returns and allowances
Common shares	Mortgage payable	Unearned revenue

Instructions

For each account, identify whether it should be reported on the statement of financial position or income statement. Also specify where the account should be classified. For example, Accounts Payable would be classified under current liabilities on the statement of financial position.

E5–8 The following selected accounts from the Blue Door Corporation's general ledger are presented below for the year ended December 31, 2015:

Prepare income statement.

(SO 4)

Advertising expense	$ 55,000
Common shares	250,000
Cost of goods sold	1,085,000
Depreciation expense	125,000
Dividends	150,000
Freight out	25,000
Income tax expense	70,000
Insurance expense	15,000
Interest expense	70,000
Interest revenue	30,000
Merchandise inventory	67,000
Rent revenue	24,000
Retained earnings	535,000
Salaries expense	675,000
Sales	2,400,000
Sales discounts	8,500
Sales returns and allowances	41,000
Unearned revenue	8,000

Instructions

(a) Prepare a single-step income statement.

(b) Prepare a multiple-step income statement.

(c) Are the expenses classified by nature or function in the list of accounts above? Explain.

E5–9 Income statement information is presented here for two companies:

Determine missing amounts and calculate profitability ratios.

(SO 4, 5)

	Young Ltd.	Rioux Ltée
Sales	$99,000	$ [6]
Sales returns and allowances	[1]	5,000
Net sales	89,000	100,000
Cost of goods sold	58,750	[7]
Gross profit	[2]	40,000
Operating expenses	19,500	[8]
Profit from operations	[3]	18,000
Other revenues	750	0
Other expenses	0	2,000
Profit before income tax	[4]	[9]
Income tax expense	2,300	[10]
Profit	[5]	12,800

Instructions

(a) Calculate the missing amounts for items [1] to [10].

(b) Calculate the gross profit margin and profit margin for each company.

E5–10 Montmorency Ltée reported the following condensed income statement data (in thousands) for the year ended August 31, 2015:

Prepare income statement; calculate profitability ratios.

(SO 4, 5)

Administrative expenses	$ 670
Cost of goods sold	4,030
Income tax expense	560
Net sales	7,090
Other expenses	270
Selling expenses	260

Instructions

(a) Prepare a multiple-step income statement.

(b) Are the expenses classified by nature or function in the list of accounts above?

(c) Calculate the gross profit margin and profit margin.

Calculate profitability ratios and comment.
(SO 5)

E5-11 **Best Buy Co., Inc.** reported the following selected information for its three most recent fiscal years (in U.S. $ millions):

	2012	2011	2010
Net sales	$50,705	$49,747	$49,694
Cost of goods sold	38,132	37,197	37,534
Profit from operations	1,085	2,374	2,235
Profit (loss)	(1,231)	1,003	1,317

Instructions

(a) Calculate the gross profit margin and profit margin for Best Buy for each of the three years.
(b) Comment on whether the ratios have improved or deteriorated over the last three years.
(c) Recalculate the profit margin for the three years using operating income instead of profit. Does this result in a different trend than you saw in part (a)? If yes, what might be the reason for this change?

Record purchase and sales transactions.
(SO 6)

*E5-12 Data for Olaf Corp. and DeVito Ltd. are presented in E5-4 and E5-5.

Instructions

Repeat the requirements for E5-4 and E5-5, assuming a periodic inventory system is used instead of a perpetual inventory system.

Record purchase and sales transactions.
(SO 2, 3, 6)

*E5-13 Duvall Ltd. and Pele Ltd. incurred the following merchandise transactions in June.

June	10	Duvall sold $5,000 of merchandise to Pele, terms 1/10, n/30, FOB shipping point. The merchandise cost Duvall $3,000 when it was originally purchased.
	11	Freight costs of $250 were paid by the appropriate company.
	12	Duvall received damaged goods returned by Pele for credit. The goods were originally sold for $500; the cost of the returned merchandise was $300. The merchandise was not returned to inventory.
	19	Duvall received full payment from Pele.

Instructions

(a) Prepare journal entries for each transaction in the books of Duvall Ltd., assuming (1) a perpetual inventory system is used, and (2) a periodic inventory system is used.
(b) Prepare journal entries for each transaction for Pele Ltd., assuming (1) a perpetual inventory system is used, and (2) a periodic inventory system is used.

Determine missing amounts.
(SO 6)

*E5-14 Below are the cost of goods sold sections for the most recent two years for two companies using a periodic inventory system:

	Company 1		Company 2	
	Year 1	Year 2	Year 1	Year 2
Beginning inventory	$ 200	$ [5]	$1,000	$ [14]
Purchases	1,500	[6]	[10]	8,550
Purchase returns and allowances	50	100	200	400
Purchase discounts	30	50	150	100
Net purchases	[1]	1,800	7,210	[15]
Freight in	130	[7]	[11]	550
Cost of goods purchased	[2]	[8]	7,800	[16]
Cost of goods available for sale	[3]	2,300	[12]	[17]
Ending inventory	[4]	350	1,250	1,500
Cost of goods sold	1,480	[9]	[13]	[18]

Instructions

Fill in the numbered blanks to complete the cost of goods sold sections.

Prepare income statement.
(SO 6)

*E5-15 The following selected information is presented for Lively Limited for the year ended February 28, 2015. Lively uses a periodic inventory system.

Accounts receivable	$ 32,500	Purchases	$ 273,000
Administrative expenses	120,900	Purchase discounts	39,000
Common shares	85,000	Purchase returns and allowances	20,800
Dividends	42,000	Sales	435,500
Freight in	8,450	Sales discounts	27,300
Income tax expense	9,300	Sales returns and allowances	15,600
Interest expense	7,800	Selling expenses	9,100
Merchandise inventory, Mar. 1, 2014	54,600	Unearned revenue	4,500
Merchandise inventory, Feb. 28, 2015	79,300		

Instructions

(a) Prepare a multiple-step income statement.

(b) Prepare the year-end adjusting entry that would be made to update the Merchandise Inventory and Cost of Goods Sold accounts.

Problems: Set A

P5–1A The Breeze Hair Salon Inc. began operations six months ago. The salon's main business is hair styling and other hair treatment services. The salon also purchases and sells all of the products it uses, plus hair accessories such as hair extensions and jewellery. The sale of the products, while secondary to the salon's main business, still constitutes a significant amount of revenue. Most sales are paid by the salon's customers with cash, or paid for by debit and bank credit cards, which are considered to be equivalent to cash.

Identify appropriate inventory system.
(SO 1)

    The salon purchases its products from a local wholesaler, on credit terms of n/30 days. Normally, the salon purchases a two-month supply of products at a time. Karen, the manager of the salon, is not comfortable with a high level of accounts payable so the salon pays the wholesaler much earlier than 30 days if it has cash on hand.

    When the salon's accounting system was set up, a perpetual inventory system was established to track the products sold. Staff have been complaining to Karen that it is time-consuming to scan each product sold. Both the staff and customers are finding the additional time it takes to scan products to be frustrating, especially when the salon is busy.

    Karen had a physical inventory count performed after the salon's first six months of operations. When the quantities of merchandise determined at the physical count were compared with the quantities per the perpetual system, there were a number of discrepancies.

    Karen has noticed that the salon often runs out of the more popular products. She also noticed that while some items sell fast, others seem to collect dust. To get rid of these slow-moving products, the salon has to mark down the selling prices of its products, which is affecting the company's cash flow and gross profit.

Instructions

(a) Explain to Karen what an operating cycle is and why the salon is having problems with its cash flow and gross profit.

(b) Make a recommendation about what inventory system the salon should use and explain why.

(c) Explain to Karen the reasons for conducting an inventory count and advise her on the required frequency of counts.

P5–2A Phantom Book Warehouse Ltd. distributes hardcover books to retail stores. At the end of May, Phantom's inventory consists of 175 books purchased at $18 each. Phantom uses a perpetual inventory system.

Record purchase and sales transactions.
(SO 1, 2, 3)

    During the month of June, the following merchandise transactions occurred:

June	1	Purchased 140 books on account for $18 each from Reader's World Publishers, terms n/45.
	3	Sold 150 books on account to The Book Nook for $22 each, with a cost of $18, terms 2/10, n/45.
	5	Received a $180 credit for 10 books returned to Reader's World Publishers.
	8	Sold 80 books on account to Read-A-Lot Bookstore for $25 each, with a cost of $18, terms 2/10, n/45.
	9	Issued a $300 credit memorandum to Read-A-Lot Bookstore for the return of 12 damaged books. The books were determined to be no longer saleable and were destroyed.
	11	Purchased 130 books on account for $15 each from Read More Publishers, terms n/45.
	12	Received payment in full from The Book Nook.
	17	Received payment in full from Read-A-Lot Bookstore.
	22	Sold 125 books on account to Reader's Bookstore for $25 each, with an average cost of $15, terms 2/10, n/45.
	25	Granted Reader's Bookstore a $375 credit for 15 returned books. These books were restored to inventory.
	29	Paid Reader's World Publishers in full.

Instructions

(a) Is the Phantom Book Warehouse a retailer or a wholesaler? Explain.

(b) Record the June transactions for Phantom. (Record transactions to the nearest cent.)

(c) Create a T account for the Merchandise Inventory account. Post the opening balance and June transactions, and calculate the June 30 balance in the account.

(d) Determine the number of books Phantom has on hand on June 30. What is the average cost of these books on June 30? (*Hint:* Divide the ending balance in the Merchandise Inventory account calculated in part (c) and divide it by the number of books on hand at June 30. Round your answer to the nearest cent.)

Record purchase and sales transactions.
(SO 2, 3)

P5–3A   Presented here are selected transactions for Norlan Inc. during September of the current year. Norlan uses a perpetual inventory system.

Sept.	2	Purchased equipment on account for $25,000, terms n/30, FOB destination.
	3	Freight charges of $625 were paid by the appropriate party on the September 2 purchase of equipment.
	4	Purchased merchandise on account from Hillary Corp. at a cost of $65,000, terms 1/15, n/30, FOB shipping point.
	5	Purchased supplies for $4,000 cash.
	7	Freight charges of $1,600 were paid by the appropriate party on the September 4 purchase of merchandise.
	8	Returned damaged goods costing $5,000 that were originally purchased from Hillary on September 4. Received a credit on account.
	9	Sold merchandise costing $15,000 to Fischer Limited for $20,000 on account, terms 2/10, n/30, FOB destination.
	10	Freight charges of $375 were paid by the appropriate party on the September 9 sale of merchandise.
	17	Received the balance due from Fischer.
	18	Paid Hillary the balance due.
	20	Purchased merchandise for $6,000 cash.
	22	Sold inventory costing $20,000 to Kun-Tai Inc. for $27,000 on account, terms n/30, FOB shipping point.
	23	Freight charges of $500 were paid by the appropriate party on the September 22 sale of merchandise.
	28	Kun-Tai returned merchandise sold for $10,000 that cost $7,500. The merchandise was restored to inventory.

Instructions
(a) Record the September transactions on Norlan's books.
(b) Assume that Norlan did not take advantage of the 1% purchase discount offered by Hillary Corp. and paid Hillary on Oct. 3 instead of September 18. Record the entry that Norlan would make on Oct. 3 and determine the cost of missing this purchase discount to Norlan.

Record and post purchase and sales transactions; prepare trial balance.
(SO 2, 3)

P5–4A   At the beginning of the current golf season, on April 1, 2015 the general ledger of In the Pines Golf Shop showed Cash $6,000; Merchandise Inventory $2,500; Common Shares $5,100; and Retained Earnings $3,400. In the Pines Golf Shop uses a perpetual inventory system.
The following transactions occurred in April:

Apr.	3	Purchased golf bags, clubs, and balls on account from Balata Corp. for $4,600, terms 1/10, n/30, FOB shipping point.
	6	Freight of $120 was paid by the appropriate party on the April 3 purchase from Balata.
	9	Received a $200 purchase allowance from Balata for returned merchandise.
	10	Sold merchandise on account to members for $5,020, terms n/30. The cost of the merchandise sold was $2,010.
	12	Paid Balata in full.
	14	Received payments on account from members, $2,125.
	16	Purchased golf shoes, sweaters, and other accessories on account from Arrow Sportswear Limited for $1,300, terms 2/10, n/30.
	17	Received a $100 credit from Arrow Sportswear for returned merchandise.
	20	Sold merchandise on account to members for $3,200, terms n/30. The cost of the merchandise sold was $1,285.
	24	Paid Arrow Sportswear in full.
	27	Granted an $85 sales allowance to a member for soiled clothing. No merchandise was returned.

Instructions
(a) Prepare T accounts and enter the opening balances.
(b) Record and post the April transactions for In the Pines Golf Shop. Round all calculations to the nearest dollar.
(c) Prepare a trial balance as at April 30.

Record and post transactions and prepare partial financial statements.
(SO 2, 3, 4)

P5–5A   Eagle Hardware Store Ltd. completed the following merchandising transactions in the month of May 2015. At the beginning of May, Eagle's ledger showed Cash $7,000; Accounts Receivable $1,500; Merchandise Inventory $3,500; Common Shares $8,000; and Retained Earnings $4,000. Eagle Hardware uses a perpetual inventory system.

May	1	Purchased merchandise on account from Depot Wholesale Supply Ltd. for $5,800, terms 1/10, n/30, FOB shipping point.
	3	Freight charges of $145 were paid by the appropriate party on the merchandise purchased on May 1.

4   Sold merchandise on account to Shep Ltd. for $3,500, terms 2/10, n/30, FOB destination. The cost of the merchandise was $2,100.

7   Freight charges of $90 were paid by the appropriate party on the May 4 sale.

8   Received a $200 credit from Depot Wholesale Supply when merchandise was returned.

9   Paid Depot Wholesale Supply in full.

11   Purchased supplies for $400 cash.

14   Received payment in full from Shep Ltd. for merchandise sold on account on May 4.

15   Collected $1,000 of the accounts receivable outstanding at the beginning of the month. All accounts were originally sold on terms of n/30, with no sales discounts.

18   Purchased merchandise from Harlow Distributors Inc. for $2,000, terms n/30, FOB destination.

21   Freight of $50 was paid by the appropriate party on the May 18 purchase of merchandise.

22   Sold merchandise to various customers for $6,500 cash. The cost of the merchandise was $3,900.

29   Paid a $100 cash refund to customers for returned merchandise. The cost of the returned merchandise was $60. It was restored to inventory.

31   A physical inventory count was taken and determined that there was $5,100 of inventory on hand. Prepare any adjustment required.

Instructions

(a) Prepare T accounts and enter the opening balances.

(b) Record and post the May transactions for Eagle Hardware Store.

(c) Prepare a partial multiple-step income statement for the month ended May 31, through to gross profit.

(d) Prepare the current assets section of the statement of financial position as at May 31.

P5–6A The adjusted trial balance of Club Canada Wholesale Inc. contained the following accounts at December 31, the company's year end:

Prepare single- and multiple-step income statements.
(SO 4)

CLUB CANADA WHOLESALE INC.
Adjusted Trial Balance
December 31, 2015

	Debit	Credit
Cash	$ 8,875	
Accounts receivable	17,600	
Notes receivable	30,000	
Merchandise inventory	92,400	
Supplies	3,780	
Land	72,000	
Buildings	197,000	
Accumulated depreciation—buildings		$ 93,575
Equipment	83,500	
Accumulated depreciation—equipment		33,400
Accounts payable		57,500
Unearned revenue		7,550
Income tax payable		3,500
Mortgage payable		86,000
Common shares		20,000
Retained earnings		139,675
Sales		922,360
Sales returns and allowances	17,745	
Sales discounts	4,615	
Cost of goods sold	692,100	
Administrative expenses	116,115	
Selling expenses	5,900	
Interest expense	8,830	
Interest revenue		2,400
Income tax expense	15,500	
	$1,365,960	$1,365,960

Instructions

(a) Prepare a single-step income statement.

(b) Prepare a multiple-step income statement.

(c) Compare the two statements and comment on the usefulness of each one.

(d) Are the expenses in the statements classified by nature or by function? Explain.

Record and post adjusting entries; prepare adjusted trial balance and financial statements.
(SO 4)

P5–7A   The unadjusted trial balance of Mesa Inc., at the company's year end of December 31, follows:

MESA INC.
Trial Balance
December 31, 2015

	Debit	Credit
Cash	$ 17,000	
Accounts receivable	31,700	
Merchandise inventory	28,750	
Supplies	2,940	
Prepaid insurance	3,000	
Land	30,000	
Buildings	150,000	
Accumulated depreciation—buildings		$ 24,000
Equipment	45,000	
Accumulated depreciation—equipment		18,000
Accounts payable		33,735
Unearned revenue		4,000
Mortgage payable		147,100
Common shares		13,000
Retained earnings		31,425
Dividends	2,000	
Sales		265,770
Sales returns and allowances	2,500	
Sales discounts	3,275	
Cost of goods sold	171,225	
Salaries expense	30,950	
Utilities expense	5,100	
Interest expense	8,090	
Income tax expense	5,500	
	$537,030	$537,030

Additional information and adjustment data:

1. The 12-month insurance policy was purchased and was effective February 1, 2015.
2. There was $750 of supplies on hand on December 31.
3. Depreciation expense for the year is $6,000 for the buildings and $4,500 for the equipment.
4. Salaries of $750 are accrued and unpaid at December 31.
5. Accrued interest expense at December 31 is $735.
6. Unearned revenue of $975 is still unearned at December 31. On the sales revenue that was earned, the cost of goods sold was $2,000.
7. Of the mortgage payable, $9,800 is payable next year.
8. Income tax of $500 is due and unpaid.
9. A physical count of inventory indicates $23,800 on hand at December 31.
10. Common shares of $3,000 were issued during the year.

Instructions
(a) Prepare T accounts and enter the trial balance amounts.
(b) Record and post the adjusting entries, assuming the company adjusts its accounts annually.
(c) Prepare an adjusted trial balance at December 31.
(d) Prepare a multiple-step income statement, statement of changes in equity, and statement of financial position for the year.

Calculate profitability ratios and comment.
(SO 5)

P5–8A   Data for Club Canada Wholesale Inc. are presented in P5–6A.

Instructions
(a) Calculate the profit margin and gross profit margin.
(b) The vice-president of marketing and director of human resources have proposed that the company change its compensation of the sales force to a commission basis rather than paying a fixed salary. Given the extra incentive, they expect net sales to increase by 15%. They estimate that gross profit will increase by $27,000, operating expenses by $13,500, and income tax expense by $2,700. Non-operating expense is not expected to change. Calculate the expected new gross profit and profit amounts. (*Hint*: You do not need to prepare a formal income statement.)
(c) Calculate the revised gross profit margin and profit margin, using the information you calculated in part (b). Comment on the effect that this plan would have on profitability and evaluate the merit of this proposal.

P5-9A Psang Inc. purchases its merchandise inventory on credit and uses a perpetual inventory system. The company commenced operations on January 1, 2015, and during 2015 purchased merchandise costing $300,000. Of this amount, 80% was paid in 2015 with the balance paid in 2016. The company sold 90% of its inventory for $540,000 on credit. Of this amount, 70% was collected in 2015 with the rest collected in 2016. Operating expenses of $120,000 were incurred in 2015 and all were paid by the end of the year. The income tax rate is 30% and all income taxes relating to 2015 were paid in 2016. The following table indicates key amounts on the 2015 financial statements:

Calculate amounts and assess profitability.
(SO 4, 5)

	2015
Income statement data	
Sales	[1]
Cost of goods sold	[2]
Gross profit	[3]
Operating expenses	[4]
Profit before income tax	[5]
Income tax expense	[6]
Profit	[7]
Statement of financial position data	
Accounts receivable	[8]
Merchandise inventory	[9]
Accounts payable	[10]
Income tax payable	[11]

Instructions
(a) Calculate the balances for Sales and Accounts Receivable (items 1 and 8 above).
(b) Calculate the balances for Cost of Goods Sold, Merchandise Inventory, and Accounts Payable (items 2, 9, and 10 above).
(c) Calculate the gross profit, the balance in Operating Expenses, and the profit before income tax (items 3, 4, and 5 above).
(d) Calculate the balances for Income Tax Expense, profit, and Income Tax Payable (items 6, 7, and 11 above).
(e) Calculate the gross profit margin and profit margin for the company. All companies in this industry sell their products at approximately the same price and incur income tax at the same rate. If the company's gross profit margin and profit margin are higher than the industry average, what are the most likely explanations for this?

P5-10A The following selected information is available for **Danier Leather Inc.** for three fiscal years (in thousands):

Calculate ratios and comment.
(SO 5)

	2012	2011	2010
Current assets	$ 60,965	$ 58,948	$ 54,836
Current liabilities	11,748	12,838	17,958
Revenue	148,219	157,621	164,217
Cost of goods sold	71,513	71,352	77,438
Profit	4,003	7,568	7,219

Instructions
(a) Calculate the current ratio, gross profit margin, and profit margin for each year.
(b) Comment on whether the ratios have improved or deteriorated over the three years.
(c) Compare the 2012 ratios calculated in part (a) with the following industry averages: current ratio 2.0:1; gross profit margin 37.4%; and profit margin 6.1%. Are Danier Leather's ratios better or worse than those of its industry?

*P5-11A Data for Phantom Book Warehouse Ltd. are presented in P5-2A.

Record purchase and sales transactions; discuss inventory systems.
(SO 1, 6)

Instructions
(a) Record the June transactions on Phantom Book Warehouse's books, assuming it uses a periodic inventory system instead of a perpetual inventory system. (Record transactions to the nearest cent.)
(b) Identify the advantages and disadvantages of Phantom Book Warehouse using a periodic inventory system instead of a perpetual inventory system.

*P5-12A Data for Norlan Inc. are presented in P5-3A.

Record purchase and sales transactions.
(SO 6)

Instructions
(a) Record the September transactions on Norlan's books, assuming it uses a periodic inventory system instead of a perpetual inventory system.
(b) Assume that Norlan did not take advantage of the 1% purchase discount offered by Hillary Corp. and paid Hillary on Oct. 3 instead of September 18. Record the entry that Norlan would make on Oct. 3 and determine the cost of missing this purchase discount to Norlan.

Record and post
purchase and sales
transactions; prepare
trial balance.
(SO 6)

*P5–13A   Data for the In the Pines Golf Shop are presented in P5–4A.

Instructions

(a) Prepare T accounts and enter the opening balances.

(b) Record and post the April transactions for In the Pines Golf Shop, assuming it uses a periodic inventory system instead of a perpetual inventory system. The inventory count on April 30 determined that merchandise costing $4,857 was on hand. Round all calculations to the nearest dollar.

(c) Prepare an unadjusted trial balance as at April 30.

(d) Prepare the adjusting journal entry needed at the end of the period to update the Merchandise Inventory and Cost of Goods Sold accounts.

Prepare partial income
statement; calculate
gross profit.
(SO 5, 6)

*P5–14A   You have been provided with the following selected accounts for Feisty Ltd. for the year ended April 30, 2015:

Inventory, May 1, 2014	$ 600,000	Interest expense	$ 30,000
Purchases	5,900,000	Interest income	20,000
Accounts receivable	780,000	Accounts payable	600,000
Sales	9,300,000	Administrative expenses	810,000
Purchase discounts	40,000	Selling expenses	150,000
Freight in	120,000	Cash	160,000
Land	900,000	Common shares	200,000
Sales returns and allowances	250,000		

Feisty conducted a physical inventory count on April 30, 2015. Inventory on hand at that date was determined to be $700,000.

Instructions

(a) Prepare a partial multiple-step income statement for the year ended April 30, 2015, through to gross profit.

(b) Prepare the period-end adjusting journal entry to update the Cost of Goods Sold and Merchandise Inventory accounts.

(c) Calculate the gross profit margin. If the industry average gross profit margin is 30%, how does Feisty's gross profit margin compare?

Prepare financial
statements.
(SO 6)

*P5–15A   Andrea's Athletic Wear Inc.'s unadjusted trial balance amounts (prior to recording the adjusting entry to update Merchandise Inventory and Cost of Goods Sold accounts) appear in alphabetical order as follows on December 31, 2015, the end of its fiscal year:

Accounts payable	$129,450	Merchandise inventory, Jan. 1	$ 60,750
Accounts receivable	66,300	Mortgage payable	187,500
Accumulated depreciation—buildings	77,700	Prepaid insurance	3,600
Accumulated depreciation—equipment	64,350	Property tax payable	7,200
Administrative expenses	271,350	Purchases	602,400
Buildings	285,000	Purchase discounts	33,750
Cash	25,500	Purchase returns and allowances	9,600
Common shares	112,500	Retained earnings	102,900
Dividends	12,000	Salaries payable	5,250
Equipment	165,000	Sales	955,500
Freight in	8,400	Sales discounts	22,500
Income tax expense	24,000	Sales returns and allowances	12,000
Interest expense	15,600	Selling expenses	11,250
Land	112,500	Unearned revenue	12,450

Additional information:

1. Andrea's Athletic Wear uses a periodic inventory system.

2. A physical inventory count determined that merchandise inventory on December 31, 2015, was $108,900.

3. Of the mortgage payable, $18,750 is due in the next year.

4. Common shares of $37,500 were issued during the year.

Instructions

Prepare a multiple-step income statement and statement of changes in equity for 2015, and statement of financial position as at December 31.

Problems: Set B

P5–1B   The Fashion Palace Inc. sells a variety of home decorating merchandise, including pictures, small furniture items, dishes, candles, and area rugs. The company uses a periodic inventory system and counts inventory once a year. Most customers use the option to purchase on account and many take more than a month to pay. The company does not have any specific credit terms for its regular customers.

Identify appropriate inventory system. (SO 1)

  The general manager of The Fashion Palace, Rebecca Sherstabetoff, believes the company needs a bank loan because the accounts payable have to be paid long before the accounts receivable are collected. The bank manager is willing to give The Fashion Palace a loan but wants monthly financial statements.

  Rebecca has also noticed that, while some of the company's merchandise sells very quickly, other items do not. Sometimes she wonders just how long some of those older items have been in stock. She has observed that the company seems to run out of some merchandise items on a regular basis. And she is wondering how she is going to find someone with the time to count the inventory every month so that monthly financial statements can be prepared for the bank. She has come to you for help.

Instructions

(a) Explain to Rebecca what an operating cycle is and why the company is having problems paying its bills.

(b) Make a recommendation about what inventory system the company should use and explain why.

(c) Explain to Rebecca the reasons for conducting an inventory count and advise her on the required frequency of counts.

P5–2B   Travel Warehouse Ltd. distributes suitcases to retail stores. At the end of June, Travel Warehouse's inventory consisted of 30 suitcases purchased at $45 each. Travel Warehouse uses a perpetual inventory system. During the month of July, the following merchandising transactions occurred:

Record purchase and sales transactions. (SO 1, 2, 3)

July	2	Purchased 55 suitcases on account for $45 each from Trunk Manufacturers Ltd., terms 2/10, n/30.
	3	Received a $225 credit from Trunk Manufacturers after returning five suitcases because they were damaged.
	6	Sold 50 suitcases on account to Satchel World Inc. for $80 each, with a cost of $45, terms 2/15, n/45.
	7	Issued a $400 credit for five suitcases returned by Satchel World because they were the wrong model. The suitcases were returned to inventory.
	9	Sold five suitcases—this time the right model number—on account to Satchel World Inc. for $90 each, with a cost of $45, terms 2/15, n/45.
	11	Paid Trunk Manufacturers the balance owing.
	13	Sold 25 suitcases on account to The Going Concern, Limited for $80 each, with a cost of $45, terms 2/15, n/45.
	16	Purchased 70 suitcases on account for $3,500 from Holiday Manufacturers, terms n/45.
	17	Issued an $800 credit for ten suitcases returned by The Going Concern because they were damaged. These suitcases were not restored to inventory.
	20	Received payment in full from Satchel World for all transactions.
	27	Received payment in full from The Going Concern.

Instructions

(a) Is Travel Warehouse a retailer or a wholesaler? Explain.

(b) Record the July transactions for Travel Warehouse. (Record transactions to the nearest cent.)

(c) Create a T account for the Merchandise Inventory account. Post the opening balance and July transactions, and calculate the July 31 balance in the account.

(d) Determine the number of suitcases Travel Warehouse has on hand on July 31. What is the average cost of these suitcases on July 31? (*Hint:* Divide the ending balance in the Merchandise Inventory account calculated in part (c) and divide it by the number of suitcases on hand at July 31. Round your answer to the nearest cent.)

P5–3B   Presented here are selected transactions for Shaoshi Inc. during October of the current year. Shaoshi uses a perpetual inventory system.

Record purchase and sales transactions. (SO 2, 3)

Oct.	1	Purchased merchandise on account from Micron Ltd. at a cost of $65,000, terms 1/15, n/30, FOB shipping point.
	1	Freight charges of $1,600 were paid by the appropriate party on the October 1 purchase of merchandise.
	5	Returned for credit $7,000 of damaged goods purchased from Micron on October 1.
	8	Sold the remaining merchandise purchased from Micron to Guidant Corp. for $100,000 on account, with a cost of $59,600, terms 2/10, n/30, FOB destination.
	9	Freight charges of $2,300 were paid by the appropriate party on the October 8 sale of merchandise.

10   Guidant returned damaged merchandise that was purchased on October 8 for a $4,000 credit on account. The merchandise originally cost $2,384 and was not restored to inventory.

12   Purchased supplies for $5,000 cash.

15   Purchased merchandise for $7,500 cash.

17   Received the balance owing from Guidant.

20   Purchased equipment on account for $45,000.

28   Sold merchandise for $30,000 on account to Deux Ltée, terms 2/10, n/30, FOB shipping point. The merchandise had a cost of $18,000.

29   Freight charges of $750 were paid by the appropriate party on the October 28 sale of merchandise.

30   Paid Micron the balance owing.

31   Deux returned some of the merchandise that was purchased on October 28 for a $5,000 credit on account. The merchandise originally cost $3,000 and was restored to inventory.

Instructions

(a) Record the October transactions on Shaoshi's books.

(b) Assume that Shaoshi took advantage of the 1% purchase discount offered by Micron Ltd. and paid Micron on October 14 rather than October 30. Record the entry that Shaoshi would make on October 14 and determine the cost of missing this purchase discount to Shaoshi.

Record and post purchase and sales transactions; prepare trial balance.
(SO 2, 3)

P5–4B   At the beginning of the current tennis season, on April 1, the general ledger of Grand Slam Tennis Shop showed Cash $8,000; Merchandise Inventory $5,400; Common Shares $6,000; and Retained Earnings $7,400. Grand Slam Tennis Shop uses a perpetual inventory system.

The following transactions occurred in April:

Apr.   2   Purchased racquets and balls from Roberts Inc. for $4,900, terms 2/10, n/30, FOB shipping point.

3   The appropriate party paid $120 freight on the purchase from Roberts on April 2.

7   Received credit of $100 from Roberts for a damaged racquet that was returned.

11   Paid Roberts in full.

13   Purchased tennis shoes from Niki Sports Ltd. for $920 cash, FOB shipping point.

16   The appropriate party paid $15 freight on the purchase from Niki on April 13.

17   Purchased supplies for $1,300 cash from Discount Supplies Limited.

18   Received a $110 cash refund from Niki Sports for damaged merchandise that was returned.

20   Sold merchandise to members for $6,800 on account, terms n/30. The cost of the merchandise was $4,080.

21   Some of the merchandise purchased on April 20, with a sales price of $1,000 and a cost of $600, was returned by members. It was restored to inventory.

23   Sold merchandise to members for $5,600, terms n/30. The cost of the merchandise was $3,360.

25   Received cash payments on account from members, $8,000.

28   Granted a $150 sales allowance on account to a member for slightly torn tennis clothing. No merchandise was returned.

30   Purchased equipment for use in the business from DomCo Ltd. for $3,600, terms n/45.

Instructions

(a) Prepare T accounts and enter the opening balances.

(b) Record and post the April transactions for Grand Slam Tennis. Round all calculations to the nearest dollar.

(c) Prepare a trial balance as at April 30, 2015.

Record and post transactions and prepare partial financial statements.
(SO 2, 3, 4)

P5–5B   Nisson Distributing Ltd. completed the following merchandising transactions in the month of April. At the beginning of April, Nisson's general ledger showed Cash $4,000; Accounts Receivable $3,500; Merchandise Inventory transactions $2,500; Common Shares $5,000; and Retained Earnings $5,000. Nisson uses a perpetual inventory system.

Apr.   2   Purchased merchandise on account from Kai Supply Corp. for $8,900, terms 1/15, n/30, FOB shipping point.

3   The appropriate party paid $225 freight on the April 2 purchase from Kai Supply.

5   Sold $11,600 of merchandise on account to Kananaskis Supply Ltd., terms 2/10, n/30, FOB destination. The cost of the merchandise was $7,540.

9   The appropriate party paid $290 freight on the April 5 sale of merchandise to Kananaskis Supply.

10   Issued a $1,600 credit for merchandise returned by Kananaskis Supply. The merchandise originally cost $1,030 and was returned to inventory.

11   Purchased merchandise on account from Pigeon Distributors Limited for $4,200, terms 1/10, n/30, FOB destination.

12   The appropriate party paid $100 freight on the April 11 purchase from Pigeon Distributors.

13   Received a $300 credit for merchandise returned to Pigeon Distributors.

14   Received the balance owing from Kananaskis Supply.

17   Paid Kai Supply in full.

20   Paid Pigeon Distributors in full.

23   Sold merchandise for $6,400 cash. The cost of the merchandise was $5,200.

24   Made a $400 cash refund for damaged merchandise returned from the April 23 purchase. The cost of the merchandise returned was $260 and it was not restored to inventory.

27   Purchased merchandise from Tipsea Inc. for $6,100 cash.

30   Received a $500 refund for merchandise that was returned to Tipsea from the April 27 cash purchase.

Instructions

(a) Prepare T accounts and enter the opening balances.

(b) Record and post the April transactions for Nisson.

(c) Prepare a partial multiple-step income statement for the month ended April 30, through to gross profit.

(d) Prepare the current assets section of the statement of financial position as at April 30.

P5–6B   The adjusted trial balance of Brigus Wholesale Ltd. contained the following accounts at November 30, the company's fiscal year end:

Prepare single- and multiple-step income statements.
(SO 4)

BRIGUS WHOLESALE LTD.
Adjusted Trial Balance
November 30, 2015

	Debit	Credit
Cash	$ 50,200	
Accounts receivable	71,400	
Notes receivable	50,000	
Merchandise inventory	90,400	
Supplies	3,000	
Land	120,000	
Buildings	204,000	
Accumulated depreciation—buildings		$ 34,000
Equipment	96,000	
Accumulated depreciation—equipment		48,000
Accounts payable		97,000
Income tax payable		31,000
Unearned revenue		6,000
Mortgage payable		102,000
Common shares		60,000
Retained earnings		180,000
Sales		1,700,600
Sales returns and allowances	8,400	
Sales discounts	7,500	
Cost of goods sold	1,095,000	
Administrative expenses	341,340	
Selling expenses	86,200	
Interest expense	7,400	
Interest revenue		3,240
Income tax expense	31,000	
	$2,216,840	$2,261,840

Instructions

(a) Prepare a single-step income statement.

(b) Prepare a multiple-step income statement.

(c) Compare the two statements and comment on the usefulness of each one.

(d) Are the expenses in the statements classified by nature or by function? Explain.

Record and post adjusting entries; prepare adjusted trial balance and financial statements.
(SO 4)

P5–7B The unadjusted trial balance of Fashion Centre Ltd. contained the following accounts at November 30, the company's fiscal year end:

FASHION CENTRE LTD.
Trial Balance
November 30, 2015

	Debit	Credit
Cash	$ 22,000	
Accounts receivable	30,600	
Merchandise inventory	27,500	
Supplies	1,650	
Prepaid insurance	1,800	
Long-term investments	37,000	
Equipment	26,800	
Accumulated depreciation—equipment		$ 10,720
Accounts payable		34,400
Unearned revenue		3,000
Bank loan payable		35,000
Common shares		16,400
Retained earnings		30,000
Dividends	10,000	
Sales		248,500
Sales returns and allowances	4,600	
Sales discounts	4,520	
Cost of goods sold	157,000	
Salaries expense	32,600	
Rent expense	13,850	
Interest expense	4,000	
Advertising expense	2,100	
Income tax expense	2,000	
	$378,020	$378,020

Additional information and adjustment data:

1. The 12-month insurance policy was purchased on August 1.
2. There is $950 of supplies on hand at November 30.
3. Depreciation expense for the year is $5,360 on the equipment.
4. Salaries of $1,210 are unpaid at November 30.
5. Accrued interest expense at November 30 is $175.
6. Of the unearned revenue, $2,400 has been earned by November 30. The cost of goods sold incurred in earning this sales revenue is $1,560.
7. Of the bank loan payable, $5,000 is to be paid in the next year; the remainder is long-term.
8. Income tax of $1,100 is due and unpaid.
9. A physical count of inventory indicates $25,000 on hand at November 30.
10. Common shares of $5,000 were issued during the year.

Instructions
(a) Prepare T accounts and enter the trial balance amounts.
(b) Record and post the adjusting entries, assuming the company adjusts its accounts annually.
(c) Prepare an adjusted trial balance at November 30.
(d) Prepare a multiple-step income statement, statement of changes in equity, and statement of financial position for the year.

Calculate profitability ratios and comment.
(SO 5)

P5–8B Data for Brigus Wholesale Ltd. are presented in P5–6B.
Instructions
(a) Calculate the profit margin and gross profit margin.
(b) The vice-president of marketing and director of human resources have proposed that the company change its compensation of the sales force to a commission basis rather than paying a fixed salary. Given the extra incentive, they expect net sales to increase by 10%. They estimate that gross profit will increase by $60,000, operating expenses by $32,000, and income tax expense by $4,000. Non-operating expense is not expected to change. Calculate the expected new gross profit and profit amounts. (*Hint*: You do not need to prepare a formal income statement.)
(c) Calculate the revised gross profit margin and profit margin, using the information you calculated in part (b). Comment on the effect that this plan would have on profitability and evaluate the merit of this proposal.

P5–9B Tsang Inc. purchases its merchandise inventory on credit and uses a perpetual inventory system. The company began operations on January 1, 2015, and during 2015 purchased merchandise costing $200,000. Of this amount, 75% was paid in 2015 with the balance paid in 2016. The company sold 80% of its inventory for $400,000 on credit. Of this amount, 80% was collected in 2015 with the rest collected in 2016. Operating expenses of $140,000 were incurred in 2015 and all were paid by the end of the year. The income tax rate is 30% and all income taxes relating to 2015 were paid in 2016. The following table indicates key amounts on the 2015 financial statements:

Calculate amounts and assess profitability.
(SO 4, 5)

	2015
Income statement data	
Sales	[1]
Cost of goods sold	[2]
Gross profit	[3]
Operating expenses	[4]
Profit before income tax	[5]
Income tax expense	[6]
Profit	[7]
Statement of financial position data	
Accounts receivable	[8]
Merchandise inventory	[9]
Accounts payable	[10]
Income tax payable	[11]

Instructions

(a) Calculate the balances for Sales and Accounts Receivable (items 1 and 8 above).

(b) Calculate the balances for Cost of Goods Sold, Merchandise Inventory, and Accounts Payable (items 2, 9, and 10 above).

(c) Calculate the gross profit, the balance in Operating Expenses, and the profit before income tax (items 3, 4, and 5 above).

(d) Calculate the balances for Income Tax Expense, profit, and Income Tax Payable (items 6, 7, and 11 above).

(e) Calculate the gross profit margin and profit margin for the company. All companies in this industry sell their products at approximately the same price and incur income tax at the same rate. If the company's gross profit margin and profit margin are lower than the industry average, what are the most likely explanations for this?

P5–10B The following selected information is available for **Volvo Group**, headquartered in Sweden, for three fiscal years (in SEK [Swedish krona] millions):

Calculate ratios and comment.
(SO 5)

	2012	2011	2010
Current assets	152,751	172,659	147,139
Current liabilities	131,105	143,679	124,059
Net sales	303,647	310,367	264,749
Cost of goods sold	235,085	236,685	201,797
Profit	11,258	18,115	11,212

Instructions

(a) Calculate the current ratio, gross profit margin, and profit margin for each year.

(b) Comment on whether the ratios have improved or deteriorated over the three years.

(c) Compare the 2012 ratios calculated in part (a) with the following industry averages: current ratio 0.9:1; gross profit margin 13.5%; and profit margin (3.8)%. Are Volvo's ratios better or worse than those of its industry?

*P5–11B Data for Travel Warehouse Ltd. are presented in P5–2B.

Record purchase and sales transactions; discuss inventory systems.
(SO 1, 6)

Instructions

(a) Record the July transactions on Travel Warehouse's books, assuming it uses a periodic inventory system instead of a perpetual inventory system. (Record transactions to the nearest cent.)

(b) Identify the advantages and disadvantages of Travel Warehouse using a periodic inventory system instead of a perpetual inventory system.

*P5–12B Data for Shaoshi Inc. are presented in P5–3B.

Record purchase and sales transactions.
(SO 6)

Instructions

(a) Record the October transactions on Shaoshi's books, assuming it uses a periodic inventory system instead of a perpetual inventory system.

(b) Assume that Shaoshi took advantage of the 1% purchase discount offered by Micron Ltd. and paid Micron on October 14 rather than October 30. Record the entry that Shaoshi would make on October 14 and determine the cost of missing this purchase discount to Shaoshi.

Record and post purchase and sales transactions; prepare trial balance.
(SO 6)

*P5–13B   Data for Grand Slam Tennis Shop are presented in P5–4B.

Instructions
(a) Prepare T accounts and enter the opening balances.
(b) Record and post the April transactions for Grand Slam Tennis Shop, assuming it uses a periodic inventory system instead of a perpetual inventory system. The inventory count on April 30 determined that merchandise costing $4,209 was on hand. Round all calculations to the nearest dollar.
(c) Prepare an unadjusted trial balance as at April 30.
(d) Prepare the adjusting journal entry needed at the end of the period to update the Merchandise Inventory and Cost of Goods Sold accounts.

Prepare partial income statement; calculate gross profit.
(SO 5, 6)

*P5–14B   You have been provided with the following selected accounts for Severn Limited for the year ended June 30, 2015:

Inventory, July 1, 2014	$ 520,000
Purchases	6,280,000
Accounts receivable	660,000
Sales	7,800,000
Purchase returns and allowances	240,000
Freight in	80,000
Administrative expenses	740,000
Land	1,400,000
Sales discounts	100,000
Interest expense	20,000
Interest revenue	40,000
Accounts payable	540,000
Selling expenses	120,000
Cash	500,000
Common shares	300,000

Severn conducted a physical inventory count on June 30, 2015. Inventory on hand at that date was determined to be $600,000.

Instructions
(a) Prepare a partial multiple-step income statement for the year ended June 30, 2015, through to gross profit.
(b) Prepare the period-end adjusting journal entry to update the Cost of Goods Sold and Merchandise Inventory accounts.
(c) Calculate the gross profit margin. If the industry average gross profit margin is 26%, how does Severn's gross profit margin compare?

Prepare financial statements.
(SO 6)

*P5–15B   The Goody Shop Ltd.'s unadjusted trial balance amounts (prior to recording the adjusting journal entry to update Merchandise Inventory and Cost of Goods Sold) appear in alphabetical order as follows on November 30, 2015, the end of its fiscal year:

Administrative expenses	$230,100	Merchandise inventory, Dec. 1, 2014	$ 34,360
Accounts payable	32,310	Mortgage payable	106,000
Accounts receivable	13,770	Prepaid insurance	4,500
Accumulated depreciation—buildings	61,200	Property tax payable	3,500
Accumulated depreciation—equipment	19,880	Purchases	684,700
Buildings	175,000	Purchase discounts	16,000
Cash	8,500	Purchase returns and allowances	3,315
Common shares	26,000	Retained earnings	82,800
Dividends	5,000	Salaries payable	8,500
Equipment	57,000	Sales	989,000
Freight in	5,060	Sales discounts	15,000
Income tax expense	10,000	Sales returns and allowances	10,000
Income tax payable	6,000	Selling expenses	8,200
Interest expense	11,315	Unearned revenue	3,000
Land	85,000		

Additional information:

1. The Goody Shop uses a periodic inventory system.
2. A physical inventory count determined that merchandise inventory on November 30, 2015, was $37,350.
3. Of the mortgage payable, $5,300 is due in the next year.
4. Common shares of $25,000 were issued during the year.

Instructions
Prepare a multiple-step income statement, statement of changes in equity, and statement of financial position for the year.

Broadening Your Perspective

Financial Reporting: *Shoppers Drug Mart*

BYP5–1   The financial statements of **Shoppers Drug Mart** are presented in Appendix A at the end of this book.

Instructions

(a) Is Shoppers Drug Mart a service company, merchandising company, or manufacturing company? Explain.

(b) Does Shoppers Drug Mart classify its operating expenses on its income statement by nature or by function? Explain.

(c) Are any non-operating revenues or expenses included in Shoppers Drug Mart's income statement? If so, identify the accounts included.

(d) Calculate Shoppers Drug Mart's gross profit margin for 2012 and 2011.

(e) Calculate Shoppers Drug Mart's profit margin for 2012 and 2011.

(f) Comment on the trend in Shoppers Drug Mart's gross profit margin and profit margin.

Answer questions about income statement; calculate profitability ratios and comment.
(SO 1, 4, 5)

Comparative Analysis: *Shoppers and Jean Coutu*

BYP5–2   The financial statements of **Jean Coutu** are presented in Appendix B following the financial statements for **Shoppers Drug Mart** in Appendix A.

Instructions

(a) Determine the following values for each company as follows:

1. Percentage change in sales revenue for Jean Coutu and for Shoppers for the most recent year shown.

2. Percentage change in operating income for the most recent year shown.

3. Gross profit margin.

4. Profit margin.

(b) What conclusions about the relative profitability of the two companies can be drawn from these data?

Calculate profitability ratios and comment.
(SO 5)

Comparing IFRS and ASPE

BYP5–3   Country Coffee Limited is a restaurant chain specializing in fresh, ready-to-serve coffee. Country Coffee is owned by its sole founder, who began the chain over 20 years ago. Today the business has expanded to 25 corporate locations and 30 franchise locations across Canada.

Country Coffee faces fierce competition from various other chains specializing in coffee. Happy Coffee Inc. is a major competitor that has successfully built a chain of over 500 restaurants. Happy Coffee enjoys strong brand recognition and customer loyalty in the Canadian market.

The founder of Country Coffee would like to compare his chain's results with those of Happy Coffee. Happy Coffee is publicly traded and prepares its financial statements in accordance with IFRS, whereas Country Coffee uses ASPE. The following are condensed versions of income statements for Happy Coffee and Country Coffee for the year ended December 31, 2015:

Compare income statement formats and ratios.
(SO 4, 5)

HAPPY COFFEE INC.		
Income Statement		
Year Ended December 31, 2015		
(in millions)		
Revenues		
Sales		$2,536
Operating expenses		
Cost of goods sold	$1,619	
General and administrative expenses	417	2,036
Profit from operations		500
Other revenues and expenses		
Interest expense		24
Profit before income tax		476
Income tax expense		95
Profit		$ 381

COUNTRY COFFEE LIMITED
Income Statement
Year Ended December 31, 2015
(in millions)

Revenues		
Sales		$84
Operating expenses		
Merchandise inventory purchased	$25	
Changes in merchandise inventory	5	
Rent	15	
Salaries	10	
Depreciation	9	
Utilities	3	
Advertising	2	
Insurance	1	70
Profit from operations		14
Other revenues and expenses		
Interest expense		1
Profit before income tax		13
Income tax expense		3
Profit		$10

Instructions

(a) What is the main difference between the income statement presentation of Country Coffee and of Happy Coffee?

(b) Are these two formats acceptable under both ASPE and IFRS? Which of these methods requires a greater degree of judgement? Which of these two formats do you prefer and why?

(c) How will this difference affect the comparability of the two income statements?

(d) Will the use of different presentation formats impact the comparability of the gross profit margin and the profit margin of Country Coffee and Happy Coffee? Why or why not?

(e) What options does Country Coffee have if it wants to improve the comparability of its financial results with those of Happy Coffee?

Critical Thinking Case

Analyze the effect of errors on ratios.
(SO 2, 3, 5)

BYP5–4 Peshawar Retailers Ltd. is a small corporation that has operated for two years. In early 2015, the CEO of the company, Nazir Kumar, signed an employment contract with the company that allowed him to earn a bonus if he increased Peshawar's gross profit margin by more than 3%. The draft income statement for 2015 has just been prepared and is shown below.

	2015	2014
Net sales	$113,000	$80,000
Cost of goods sold	62,000	48,000
Gross profit	51,000	32,000
Operating expenses	21,000	8,000
Profit from operations	30,000	24,000
Income tax expense	9,000	7,200
Profit	$ 21,000	$16,800
Gross profit margin	45.1%	40.0%

The board of directors is about to meet and determine if Nazir is to be awarded his bonus. As one of the board members, you are surprised to receive an anonymous letter supposedly from a member of the accounting department that indicates that the CEO asked the staff member to do the following during 2015:

1. Record purchase returns of $7,000 as an increase of sales revenue.
2. Record freight of $5,000 paid on purchases of merchandise as an operating expense.
3. Record sales returns of $6,000 as an operating expense.

Instructions

(a) Assuming that the staff member is correct, determine if the CEO is eligible for his bonus.

(b) Did the adjustments requested by the CEO affect the profit margin?

(c) Based on the above, was any harm done to any users of the financial statements because of the adjustments made?

Ethics Case

Discuss ethics of timing purchase discounts.
(SO 2)

BYP5–5 Rita Pelzer was just hired as the assistant controller of Zaz Stores Ltd., a retail company. Among other things, the payment of all invoices is centralized in one of the departments Rita will manage. Her main responsibilities are to maintain the company's credit rating by paying all bills when they are due and to take advantage of all cash discounts.

Jamie Caterino, the former assistant controller, who has been promoted to controller, is training Rita in her new duties. He instructs Rita that she is to continue the practice of preparing all cheques for the amount due less the discount and to date the cheques the last day of the discount period. "But," Jamie continues, "we always hold the cheques at least four days beyond the discount period before mailing them. That way we get another four days of interest on our money. Most of our creditors need our business and don't complain. And, if they scream about our missing the discount period, we blame it on Canada Post. We've only lost one discount out of every hundred we take that way. I think everybody does it. By the way, welcome to our team!"

Instructions

(a) What are the ethical considerations in this case?

(b) Which stakeholders are harmed or benefited?

(c) Should Rita continue the practice started by Jamie? Does she have any choice?

"All About You" Activity

BYP5-6   Suppose that after you graduate with a business degree, you take a job as a manager of a local bookstore. You have been hired to expand the business and you recognize that there are many competitors in the bookstore industry. Your competitors enable customers to purchase books on-line at competitive prices. You are faced with a choice of either setting up an on-line website where your customers can order directly from you or opening up a new store where customers can come in, browse the shelves, and purchase what they require. Assume that you expect that net sales will remain the same despite the choice of alternative. Your objective is to maximize profit.

Distinguish between costs included in gross profit margin and profit margin.
(SO 5)

Instructions

(a) Consider both alternatives. Which alternative do you think would present a higher gross profit margin?

(b) Consider both alternatives. Which alternative do you think would present a higher profit margin?

(c) What other considerations would you have to take into account before proceeding with one of these two alternatives?

Serial Case

(*Note*: This is a continuation of the serial case from Chapters 1 through 4.)

BYP5-7   Natalie and her parents, Janet and Brian, are anxious to examine and analyze the updated financial statements. Natalie has obtained a copy of the financial statements of a major competitor, a public company, and has been able to determine a number of their ratios: the current ratio is 2:1, the gross profit margin is 75%, and the profit margin is 15%.

Record and post adjusting journal entries, prepare an adjusted trial balance and financial statements, calculate ratios and comment.
(SO 4, 5)

The following information represents additional adjustment data that must be recorded to enable the preparation of Koebel's year-end financial statements. Koebel's uses a perpetual inventory system.

1. The physical count of inventory indicates $18,000 on hand at June 30.
2. Of the bank loan payable, $7,500 is to be paid in the next year; the remainder is non-current.
3. Of the mortgage payable, $5,000 is to be paid in the next year; the remainder is non-current.
4. Natalie estimates that an additional $937 of corporate income tax is owed at June 30.

Instructions

(a) Record any required adjusting entries from the above data.

(b) Post to T accounts updated in Chapter 4.

(c) Prepare an adjusted trial balance at June 30.

(d) Prepare a multiple-step income statement for the year ended June 30.

(e) Calculate the ending retained earnings for the year.

(f) Prepare a statement of financial position as at June 30.

(g) Calculate the current ratio, gross profit margin, and profit margin for the year. Compared with Koebel's major competitor, are Koebel's Family Bakery's ratios better or worse than their competitor? Why do you expect there is a difference between Koebel's Family Bakery's ratios and those of its major competitor?

Answers to Self-Test Questions

1. a	2. b	3. c	4. a	5. c
6. b	7. a	8. d	9. c	10. c
*11. b	*12. b			

Remember to go back to the beginning of the chapter to check off your completed work! ←

Endnotes

[1]"Helping Loblaw Achieve High Performance Through Supply Chain Transformation," Accenture case study, 2013; Canadian Press, "Loblaws Claims Supply Chain Overhaul Successful," *Canadian Manufacturing*, March 1, 2012; "Loblaw Wins Top Supply Chain Award," *Canadian Grocer*, January 18, 2012; Kathleen Lau, "Loblaw Hungry for Improved IT Supply Chain," *Computing Canada*, February 20, 2008; "Loblaw, Targeting Wal-Mart Like Efficiency, Still Battling Supply Chain Re-Design Woes," *Supply Chain Digest*, January 26, 2006; Loblaw Companies Limited 2012 annual report.

[2]Ellen Roseman, "Staples Confirms Online Orders, Apologizes, after Stock Runs Out," *Toronto Star*, December 22, 2012; Paul Lungren, "JVS Panelists Take Close Look at Retail Sector," *Canadian Jewish News*, May 17, 2013; Mia Pearson, "Social Media Plays Growing Role into Online Retailing," *Globe and Mail*, May 17, 2012, updated September 10, 2012.

[3]Arik Hesseldahl, "Teardown Shows Apple iPad Mini costs at Least $188 to Build," All Things D, November 3, 2012, retrieved from http://allthingsd.com/20121103/teardown-shows-apple-ipad-mini-costs-at-least-188-to-build, April 12, 2013; Salvador Rodriguez, "The $329 iPad Mini Costs $198 to Make, Study Says," *Los Angeles Times*, November 5, 2012; Mark Prigg, "The REAL Cost of Your £269 iPad Mini? £117, According to an Online Site Which Ripped One Apart," *The Daily Mail*, November 5, 2012.

[4]PwC, "Demystifying the Online Shopper: 10 Myths of Multichannel Retailing, 2012," www.pwc.com/gx/en/retail-consumer/retail-consumer-publications/global-multi-channel-consumer-survey/index.jhtml, accessed May 30, 2013. Michele Sexsmith, "Today's Trends in Online Shopping," *Canadian Retailer*, summer 2012, pp. 22-25. J.C. Williams Group, "Online Shoppers and Buyers—White Paper," February 2013, http://www.jcwg.com/contents_supporters/library_files/Canada%20Post%20Online%20Shoppers%20and%20Buyers%20White%20Paper.pdf, accessed May 30, 2013.

Comprehensive Case: Chapters 3–5

Record and post general, adjusting, and closing entries; prepare trial balances and financial statements. (SO 2, 3, 4)

Heritage Furniture Limited reports the following information for the 11 months of the year in its February 28, 2015, trial balance:

HERITAGE FURNITURE LIMITED
Trial Balance
February 28, 2015

	Debit	Credit
Cash	$ 65,000	
Accounts receivable	350,000	
Merchandise inventory	2,750,000	
Supplies	7,500	
Prepaid rent	5,000	
Equipment	145,000	
Accumulated depreciation—equipment		$ 29,000
Accounts payable		1,550,000
Unearned revenue		35,000
Bank loan payable—non-current		450,000
Common shares		200,000
Retained earnings		550,500
Dividends	50,000	
Sales		5,479,400
Sales returns and allowances	107,000	
Sales discounts	65,000	
Cost of goods sold	3,843,900	

	Debit	Credit
Advertising expense	$ 75,000	
Freight out	180,000	
Office expense	26,000	
Rent expense	55,000	
Salaries expense	360,000	
Travel expense	12,500	
Utilities expense	20,000	
Interest expense	27,000	
Income tax expense	150,000	
	$8,293,900	$8,293,900

Heritage Furniture incurred the following transactions for the month of March. The company uses a perpetual inventory system.

Mar. 1 Received $125,000 on account from a major customer.
2 Paid a supplier an amount owing of $200,000, taking the full discount, terms 2/10, n/30.
5 Purchased merchandise from a supplier, $300,000, terms 2/10, n/30, FOB destination.
6 Recorded cash sales, $285,000. The cost of goods sold for these sales was $200,000.
7 Returned scratched merchandise to the supplier from the March 5 purchase, $25,000.
8 The appropriate company paid freight for the March 5 purchase, $7,500.
9 Sold $200,000 of merchandise on account, terms 2/10, n/30, FOB destination. The cost of goods sold was $140,000.
9 The appropriate company paid freight for the March 9 sale, $5,000.
12 Ordered custom merchandise for a local designer totalling $50,000. Received $12,500 as a deposit.
13 Accepted returned merchandise from the sale on March 9, $20,000. The cost of the goods returned to inventory was $14,000.
14 Paid for the merchandise purchased on March 5, net of merchandise returns on March 7.
16 Paid salaries of $45,000.
19 Received payment of merchandise sold on March 9, net of merchandise returns on March 13.
20 Recorded cash sales, $255,000. The cost of goods sold for these sales was $179,000.
27 Paid salaries of $50,000.
30 Paid rent, $5,000.

Adjustment and additional data:

1. Accrued $10,000 for utilities, $10,000 for salaries, and $9,000 for interest on the bank loan.
2. Recorded depreciation on equipment, which has an expected useful life of 10 years.
3. Recorded an additional $50,000 of income tax payable.
4. Common shares of $1,000 were issued during the year.
5. $45,000 of the bank loan is due to be repaid in the next year.

Instructions
(a) Prepare T accounts and enter the opening balances.
(b) Record and post the March transactions on Heritage Furniture's books.
(c) Prepare a trial balance as at March 31, 2015.
(d) Record and post adjusting entries for the year ended March 31, 2015, assuming adjusting entries are made annually.
(e) Prepare an adjusted trial balance as at March 31, 2015.
(f) Prepare a multiple-step income statement, statement of changes in equity, and statement of financial position for the year ended March 31, 2015.
(g) Prepare and post closing entries.
(h) Prepare a post-closing trial balance as at March 31, 2015.

Reporting and Analyzing Inventory

The Navigator
Chapter 6

- [ ] Scan *Study Objectives*
- [ ] Read *Feature Story*
- [ ] Read text and answer *Do It!s*
- [ ] Review *Comparing IFRS and ASPE*
- [ ] Review *Summary of Study Objectives*
- [ ] Review *Decision Toolkit—A Summary*
- [ ] Work *Using the Decision Toolkit*
- [ ] Work *Comprehensive Do It!*
- [ ] Answer *Self-Test Questions*
- [ ] Complete *assignments*
- [ ] Go to *WileyPLUS* for practice and tutorials

study objectives

After studying this chapter, you should be able to:

SO 1 Describe the steps in determining inventory quantities.

SO 2 Apply the methods of cost determination using specific identification, FIFO, and average cost under a perpetual inventory system.

SO 3 Explain the effects on the financial statements of choosing each of the inventory cost determination methods.

SO 4 Identify the effects of inventory errors on the financial statements.

SO 5 Demonstrate the presentation and analysis of inventory.

SO 6 Apply the FIFO and average cost inventory cost determination methods under a periodic inventory system (Appendix 6A).

the navigator

lululemon athletica Stretches Inventory Levels

Most retailers try to have just the right amount of inventory on hand. Too much inventory can result in increased storage costs and excess merchandise that must be sold at a discount, resulting in inventory writedowns or write offs. Too little inventory can result in lost sales and disappointed customers.

Some retailers, however, deliberately carry too little inventory in order to create demand. This has long been a strategy of lululemon athletica inc., which designs and sells yoga, athletic, and lifestyle clothing and gear. Founded by surfer, skater, and snowboarder Chip Wilson, lululemon opened its first store in Vancouver in 2000. It developed a niche following among yoga enthusiasts who gravitated toward its stretchy, technical fabrics. It now has more than 200 stores in Canada, the United States, and countries such as Australia and Hong Kong. The stores are corporate-owned or franchised.

By carrying lower quantities than needed to supply customer demand, lululemon enticed customers to return to the store to check product availability, or to make impulse buys of in-stock items. With a more limited supply, the retailer notes that it also avoids excess inventory levels, which could result in discounted prices and "could impair the strength and exclusivity of our brand."

Despite the price of its merchandise (around $100 for yoga pants) and the absence of reduced-price sales, lululemon developed a loyal following of customers who appreciated its unique designs and materials, quality, and customer service. Revenues continued to increase even when the stores carried limited inventory in some products.

But in early 2013, lululemon experienced an inventory shortage that was not deliberate. The company identified quality issues with "luon," a proprietary fabric used in its clothing that resulted in a recall of women's yoga pants because they were too see-through. The recall amounted to 17% of its total supply of women's yoga pants. The company charged a $17.5-million inventory provision to cost of sales. Meanwhile, it had to wait 90 days before replacement products were back on the shelves.

Other factors have put pressure on inventory. lululemon is moving beyond yoga and athletic gear into a lifestyle brand, creating further demand for its products that look at home on the streets and not just in the gym. The retailer's popularity in the United States is also growing, and lululemon now ships to more than 50 countries around the world through its website. At the same time, the company has experienced problems with forecasting product demand, and finding overseas suppliers who can meet quality standards.

The company seems to have changed its inventory strategy, moving away from deliberate shortages. After its yoga pant recall, it launched a marketing and social media campaign to keep customers informed of the quality issues and inventory timeline. It also revamped its quality control process and ramped up production at its overseas factories to handle demand.

lululemon was able to weather its inventory storm. In the first quarter of 2013, for example, despite the product recall and inventory shortages, revenues increased by 21% from the same period in 2012, from $285.7 million to $345.8 million. Its gross profit increased 9% in that time. Analysts expected even stronger sales in the rest of 2013.[1]

the navigator

In the previous chapter, we discussed the accounting for merchandise transactions. In this chapter, we first explain the procedures for determining inventory quantities. We then discuss three cost determination methods—specific identification; first-in, first-out (FIFO); and average cost—that can be used to assign amounts to the cost of goods sold and the cost of inventory on hand. We also discuss the effects that these cost determination methods and inventory errors can have on a company's financial statements. We conclude with a discussion of the presentation of inventory on the statement of financial position and the introduction of a new liquidity measure called inventory turnover, which is used to analyze inventory.

The chapter is organized as follows:

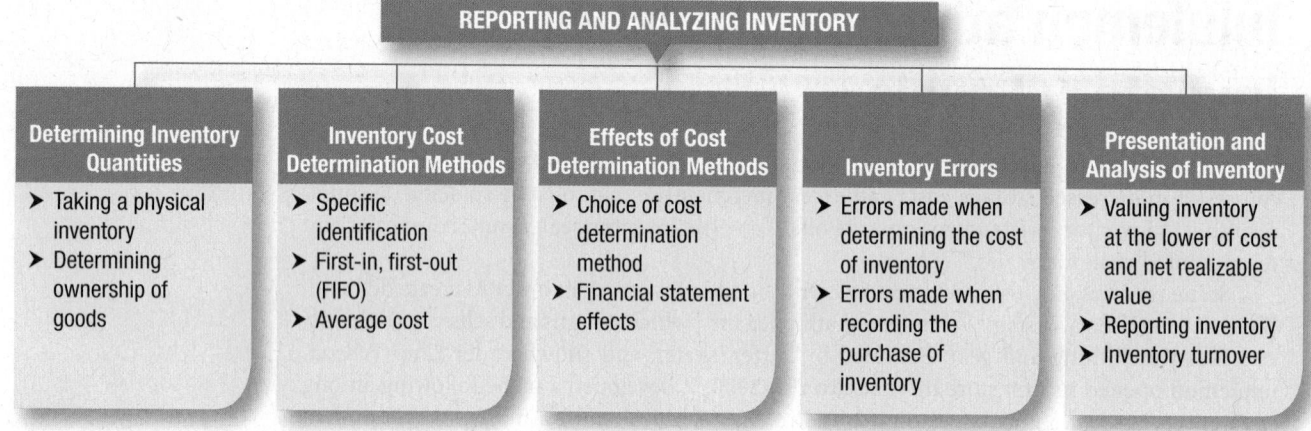

Determining Inventory Quantities

Whether they are using a perpetual or periodic inventory system, companies need to determine their inventory quantities at the end of each accounting period by physically counting their inventory.

You will recall from Chapter 5 that a perpetual inventory system continuously (perpetually) updates the inventory accounting records to show the quantity and cost of inventory that *should* be on hand. That does not mean that perpetual accounting records reflect what *is actually* on hand. Even if the accounting records are continuously updated, companies that use a perpetual inventory system must still physically count inventory at year end for two purposes: (1) to check the accuracy of their perpetual inventory records and (2) to determine the amount of inventory lost due to shrinkage or theft.

In a periodic inventory system, inventory quantities are not updated on a continuous basis. Companies that use a periodic inventory system must therefore take a physical inventory to determine the ending inventory (inventory on hand) at the end of each accounting period. Once the ending inventory amount is determined, this amount is then used to calculate the cost of goods sold for the period.

Determining inventory quantities, whether in a perpetual or periodic inventory system, involves two steps: (1) taking a physical inventory of goods on hand and (2) determining the ownership of goods.

TAKING A PHYSICAL INVENTORY

Taking a physical inventory involves counting, weighing, or measuring each kind of inventory on hand. In many companies, taking a physical inventory is a formidable task. For example, clothing retailers such as lululemon, mentioned in our chapter-opening feature story, have hundreds of different inventory items. An inventory count is generally more accurate when a limited number of, or no, goods are being sold or received during the counting. Consequently, companies often count inventory when the business is slow or when it is not open. And since most companies count their inventory at the end of the fiscal year, their year ends may coincide with slower periods. For example, lululemon's year end is the Sunday closest to January 31—following the holiday sales season when inventories are normally at their lowest level.

In order to reduce the number of errors discovered during an inventory count, a company should ensure that it has a good system of internal control. **Internal control** is a process designed to help an organization achieve reliable financial reporting, effective and efficient operations, and compliance with relevant laws and regulations. Internal control procedures for counting inventory include the following:

1. The counting should be done by employees who do not have responsibility for the custody or record-keeping of the inventory as this would mean that they are checking the work that they have been responsible for.
2. The validity of each inventory item should be established during the count. This means the counter should (a) check that the items actually exist; (b) determine the quantity of each item on hand; and (c) note the condition of the items, paying attention to any evidence of spoilage or damage that could affect the sales value. In many companies, particularly those in the technology industry, inventory obsolescence is also an issue.
3. A second count should be performed by another employee or auditor. Since counting should take place in teams of two, both members count the item. In the event the two counts don't arrive at the same quantity, a third count is required.

After the physical inventory is taken, the quantity of each kind of product is then multiplied by its cost to determine the total inventory cost. There are several ways to determine the cost of each product and these will be explained later in the chapter when we discuss the methods of inventory cost determination.

ACCOUNTING MATTERS!

Counting Inventory—Every Day

As previously mentioned, one reason why most companies count their inventory at year end is to determine the quantities on hand for financial reporting purposes. Additionally, they want to identify inventory lost through shrinkage, theft, and/or obsolescence. There is also a business reason for counting inventory, particularly if the company does not use a perpetual inventory system. By counting the inventory, the company will determine if inventory needs to be ordered. If the company uses a periodic inventory system, then management may count the inventory more frequently. Dollarama Inc. provides a good example.

Dollarama is a family business that started in Montreal as S. Rossy Inc. in 1910. It has grown since that time to become Canada's largest dollar store chain. Each of the approximately 700 store locations generates $2.3 million in sales from the 4,000 plus items in inventory. The maximum sales price of any item in the store at the time of writing is $2. Until recently, the only way Dollarama could determine whether it needed to order more inventory was to count it. Store employees counted 10 to 15 product items every day and manually tracked the quantities on cards. Store managers used this information to decide whether or not they needed to order more of a particular item. If more items were required, they sent an e-mail to head office and received them two weeks later. It took about 27 days to count all of the product items in inventory.

Counting inventory is a very labour-intensive process and there is no guarantee that the store will not run out of a popular item. For more than 15 years, Dollarama got by with a manual inventory system, but technology and competition caught up with it. In 2012, Dollarama completed a transformation of its inventory system from manual to electronic, and from periodic to perpetual. It put bar codes on every item and installed electronic scanners at the checkout counters. The scan data is now the primary source of information for stock replenishment.[2]

DETERMINING OWNERSHIP OF GOODS

When we take a physical inventory, we need to consider the ownership of goods. To determine who owns the inventory, two questions must be answered: (1) Do all of the goods included in the count belong to the company? (2) Does the company own any goods that were not included in the count such as in transit items?

Goods in Transit

Goods in transit at the end of the period (on board a truck, train, ship, or plane) make determining ownership a bit more complicated. The company may have purchased goods that have not yet been received, or it may have sold goods that have not yet been delivered. To arrive at an accurate count, ownership of these goods must be determined.

The rule to follow is straightforward. **Goods in transit should be included in the inventory of the company that has legal title to the goods.** As we learned in Chapter 5, legal title, or ownership, is determined by the terms of the sale. If the shipping terms are FOB destination, the seller has legal title to the goods while they are in transit. If the shipping terms are FOB shipping point, the buyer has legal title to the goods while they are in transit. These terms are important in determining the exact date when a purchase or sale should be recorded and what items should be included in inventory, even if the items are not physically present at the time of the inventory count.

The following table illustrates the transfer of ownership (legal title) when inventory is shipped. Assume that Magna (the seller) sells auto parts to General Motors (GM) (the buyer) and ships the parts on December 28. The parts do not reach GM until January. Both companies count their inventory on December 31. Depending on the shipping terms (FOB destination or FOB shipping point), an adjustment (indicated in red text) will need to be made to the inventory count results. The auto parts would not be counted if they are in transit but should be included in the final inventory balance if they are owned at that time.

Shipping Terms	Magna (Seller)	General Motors (Buyer)
FOB destination	Inventory belongs to Magna (seller) until it reaches GM's (buyer's) destination	Inventory belongs to GM (buyer) when it reaches GM's destination
FOB shipping point	Inventory belongs to Magna (seller) until shipped	Inventory belongs to GM (buyer) once shipment leaves Magna (seller)

Consigned Goods

In some lines of business, it is customary to hold goods belonging to other parties and sell them, for a fee, without ever taking ownership of the goods. These are called **consigned goods**. Under a consignment arrangement, the holder of the goods (called the *consignee*) does not own the goods. Ownership remains with the individual or company that wants to sell the goods (called the *consignor*) until the goods are actually sold to a customer. Because the consignee does not own consigned goods, the goods should not be included in the consignee's physical inventory count. Conversely, the consignor should include in its inventory any of its merchandise that is being held by the consignee.

For example, artists often display their paintings and other works of art in galleries on consignment. In such cases, the art gallery does not take ownership of the art—it still belongs to the artist. Therefore, if an inventory count is taken, any art on consignment should not be included in the art gallery's inventory. When the art sells, the gallery then takes a commission and pays the artist the remainder. Many craft stores, second-hand clothing stores, used sporting goods stores, and antique dealers sell goods on consignment to avoid the risk of purchasing an item they will not be able to sell.

Other Situations

Sometimes goods are not physically on the premises because a customer takes them home *on approval*. Goods on approval should be added to the physical inventory count because they still belong to the seller. The customer will either return the item or decide to buy it at some point in the future.

In other cases, goods are sold but the seller is holding them for alteration, or until the customer picks up the goods. These goods should not be included in the physical count, because legal title to ownership has passed to the customer.

Damaged or unsaleable goods should also be separated during the physical count and would normally not be counted if they had no value. In this case, any loss arising from the damage would be recorded. We will discuss this situation later in the chapter.

Summary

You will recall from Chapter 5 that purchases of merchandise should be recorded when ownership (title) of the merchandise passes from the seller to the buyer. In practice, however, purchases are usually recorded when the merchandise is received because it is difficult for buyers to identify exactly when the title legally passes to them. That is why some companies do not include goods in transit when initially performing their inventory count. Later, adjustments are made to the inventory count results to update both the quantities and amounts of unrecorded purchases and sales that are in transit, on consignment, or for other valid reasons.

BEFORE YOU GO ON...

▶ Do It! Rules of Ownership

The LaSalle Fashion House Corporation completed its inventory count at year end, August 31. It arrived at a total inventory amount of $400,000 after counting everything currently on hand in its warehouse. How will the following additional information affect the inventory count and cost?

1. Goods costing $30,000 and held on consignment for McQueen Dress Inc. were included in the inventory.

2. LaSalle's purchase of goods for $20,000 was in transit from Montreal as at August 31 (terms FOB shipping point) and not included in the count.

3. LaSalle sold inventory for $36,000 that cost $24,000 when purchased. The items were in transit to a customer in Vancouver as at August 31 (terms FOB destination) and not included in the count.

Action Plan

- Apply the rules of ownership to goods held on consignment:
  - Goods held on consignment **for** another company are not included in inventory.
  - Goods held on consignment **by** another company are included in inventory.
- Apply the rules of ownership to goods in transit:
  - FOB destination: Goods sold or purchased and shipped FOB destination will belong to the seller until they reach their destination.
  - FOB shipping point: Goods sold or purchased and shipped FOB shipping point belong to the buyer after they have been shipped.

Solution

Original count	$400,000
1. Consigned goods held at LaSalle for McQueen	(30,000)
2. Goods in transit (Purchases FOB shipping point)	20,000
3. Goods in transit (Sales FOB destination)	24,000
Adjusted count	$414,000

Related Exercise Material: BE6-1, BE6-2, E6-1, and E6-2.

Inventory Cost Determination Methods

STUDY OBJECTIVE 2

Apply the methods of cost determination using specific identification, FIFO, and average cost under a perpetual inventory system.

The physical inventory count we discussed in the last section determines the quantities on hand. If the perpetual inventory records reflect different quantities, these are adjusted to reflect the count results. Companies must then apply unit costs to the quantities to determine the total cost of the inventory. How do we determine what unit cost to apply?

Furthermore, how do we determine what cost to apply when we record the cost of merchandise sold in the accounting records throughout the period? The journal entries related to purchases and sales of merchandise were first illustrated in Chapter 5. At that time, however, you were either told the cost of the goods sold, or it was assumed, for simplicity, that all inventory items had the same unit cost. In practice, though, a company often purchases different items of inventory at different costs on different dates and from different suppliers. The cost per unit of acquiring inventory can therefore be different every time there is a purchase.

Entries to record purchases of merchandise do not show the unit cost of each item of merchandise that was acquired. The account Merchandise Inventory is simply debited for the total cost paid for all the units together, and Cash or Accounts Payable is credited. The entry to record the sales price is also not directly affected by the unit cost. Cash or Accounts Receivable is debited and the Sales account is credited for the sales price of the merchandise sold, not its unit cost.

However, the unit cost is needed in order to prepare the entry to record the cost of goods sold and remove the cost of the items sold from inventory. Because units of the same inventory item are typically purchased at different prices, it is necessary to determine which unit costs to use in the calculation of the cost of the goods sold. One method—specific identification—uses the actual physical flow of the goods to determine cost. We will look at this method next.

SPECIFIC IDENTIFICATION

The **specific identification method** tracks the actual physical flow of the goods in a perpetual inventory system. Each item of inventory is marked, tagged, or coded with its specific unit cost so that, at any point in time, the cost of the ending inventory and the cost of the goods sold can be determined.

Assume, for example, that Jaguar Canada buys three different cars at a cost of $77,200 for an XK coupe, $82,500 for an XK convertible, and $88,400 for an XKR coupe. During the month, two cars are then sold at the selling price of $96,500 for the XK coupe and $109,200 for the XKR coupe. At December 31, the XK convertible is still on hand. The cost of goods sold is therefore $165,600 ($77,200 + $88,400) and the ending inventory is $82,500. This determination is possible because it was easy to track the actual physical flow of these three inventory items, as shown in Illustration 6-1.

Specific identification is appropriate and required for goods that are not ordinarily interchangeable, and for goods that are produced and segregated for specific projects. It is used most often in situations involving a relatively small number of costly items that are easily distinguishable by their physical characteristics, serial numbers, or special markings. Examples include some types of jewellery, artwork, pianos, and automobiles. Specific identification is also suitable for many types of special orders.

While specific identification works well when a company sells high-unit-cost items that can be clearly identified from purchase through to sale, there are also disadvantages to using this method. Not surprisingly, it can be time-consuming and expensive to apply and not practical in many situations, which is why most companies in Canada do not use this method.

Another disadvantage of this method is that it may allow management to manipulate profit if items are not distinguishable from each other. To see how, assume that Jaguar Canada also sells automobile parts. It has 15 fuel pumps in stock, for which it paid between $235 and $275 when

▶Illustration 6-1

Specific identification

FOR SALE
PRICE
$105,600
Cost: $82,500

SOLD
$109,200
Cost: $88,400

SOLD
$96,500
Cost: $77,200

they were purchased. They sell for $500. If the company wanted to maximize its profit just before its year end, management could choose to sell the units with the lowest cost at $235 to deduct from revenues of $500. Or, it could minimize profit by selecting the highest-cost item at $275.

The requirement that the specific identification method be used only for goods that are not ordinarily interchangeable is an attempt to ensure that management does not use this method to manage profit. Consequently, many companies like Jaguar Canada use the specific identification method to track the cost of their automobile inventory while using another method to determine the cost of their parts inventory.

FIRST-IN, FIRST-OUT (FIFO)

Because the specific identification method is only suitable for certain kinds of inventories, other methods of cost determination are available to choose from. Two common inventory cost determination methods are first-in, first-out (FIFO) and average cost. We will explain FIFO first in this section, and then average cost in the next section. The **first-in, first-out (FIFO) cost method** assumes that the earliest (oldest) goods purchased are the first ones to be sold. This does not necessarily mean that the oldest units are in fact sold first, only that the cost of the oldest units is recognized first in cost of goods sold. Although the cost determination method chosen by a company does not have to match the actual physical movement of merchandise, it should correspond as closely as possible. FIFO generally does this because it is good business practice to sell the oldest units on hand first.

To illustrate the application of FIFO in a perpetual inventory system, we will assume that The Tee-Shirt Corporation has the following information for one of its products, the University Soccer Shirt, as shown in Illustration 6-2.

THE TEE-SHIRT CORPORATION University Soccer Shirt					
Date	Explanation	Units	Unit Cost	Total Cost	Balance in Units
Jan. 1	Beginning inventory	100	$10	$ 1,000	100
Apr. 15	Purchases	200	11	2,200	300
May 1	Sales	(150)			150
Aug. 24	Purchases	300	12	3,600	450
Sept. 10	Sales	(400)			50
Nov. 27	Purchases	400	13	5,200	450
		450		$12,000	

► Illustration 6-2
Inventory data for the University Soccer Shirt

Perpetual inventory schedules start with inventory on hand at the beginning of the year for each product. The schedule is updated for the quantity and cost of merchandise purchased and sold throughout the year. For example, we note in Illustration 6-2 that there were 100 units of merchandise costing $10 each on hand at the beginning of the year at a cost of $1,000 and 200 units of additional merchandise at $11 each that were purchased on April 15 at a cost of $2,200. This resulted, as of April 15, in 300 units available for sale at a total cost of $3,200 ($1,000 + $2,200) as shown in the partial inventory schedule below:

Date	Purchases Units	Purchases Cost	Purchases Total	Cost of Goods Sold Units	Cost of Goods Sold Cost	Cost of Goods Sold Total	Balance Units	Balance Cost	Balance Total
Jan. 1							100	$10	$1,000
Apr. 15	200	$11	$2,200				100 200	10 11	} 3,200

On May 1, the date of the first sale, we will apply the FIFO method to determine whether the 150 units that were sold cost $10, $11, or a mix of both amounts. The cost must be determined on this date so that the Cost of Goods Sold account can be debited and the Merchandise Inventory account credited for the cost of this sale. Note that the sale must also be recorded on this same date, which is done by debiting Cash or Accounts Receivable and crediting Sales. Although the sales price is required to record this entry, the above table does not include information about the sales price, as this is not needed to determine the *cost* of the goods sold or the *cost* of the ending inventory.

Under FIFO, the cost of the oldest goods on hand before each sale is allocated to the cost of goods sold under the assumption that they were sold first. Accordingly, the cost of goods sold on May 1 is assumed to consist of all 100 units of the January 1 beginning inventory and 50 units of the items purchased on April 15. This leaves 150 units of the April 15 purchase at a cost of $11 per unit remaining in ending inventory. In the table below, we have added this information (highlighted in red) to the inventory schedule that we started above.

Date	Purchases			Cost of Goods Sold			Balance		
	Units	Cost	Total	Units	Cost	Total	Units	Cost	Total
Jan. 1							100	$10	$1,000
Apr. 15	200	$11	$2,200				100	10	} 3,200
							200	11	
May 1				100	$10	} $1,550	150	11	1,650
				50	11				

After additional purchases are made on August 24, the cost of goods available for sale on this date now consists of 150 units at $11 each costing $1,650 and 300 units at $12 each costing $3,600, for a total of 450 units available for sale costing $5,250 ($1,650 + $3,600). This is shown below in the continuation of the perpetual inventory schedule:

Date	Purchases			Cost of Goods Sold			Balance		
	Units	Cost	Total	Units	Cost	Total	Units	Cost	Total
Jan. 1							100	$10	$1,000
Apr. 15	200	$11	$2,200				100	10	} 3,200
							200	11	
May 1				100	$10	} $1,550	150	11	1,650
				50	11				
Aug. 24	300	12	3,600				150	11	} 5,250
							300	12	

On September 10, when 400 units are sold, the cost of goods sold is assumed to consist of the oldest units available for sale consisting of the 150 remaining units purchased on April 15 at $11 each costing $1,650, and 250 units purchased on August 24 at $12 each costing $3,000. The cost of goods sold for this sale is $4,650 ($1,650 + $3,000). This leaves 50 units in ending inventory at a cost of $12 per unit, or $600 in total, as shown below:

Date	Purchases			Cost of Goods Sold			Balance		
	Units	Cost	Total	Units	Cost	Total	Units	Cost	Total
Jan. 1							100	$10	$1,000
Apr. 15	200	$11	$2,200				100	10	} 3,200
							200	11	
May 1				100	$10	} $1,550	150	11	1,650
				50	11				
Aug. 24	300	12	3,600				150	11	} 5,250
							300	12	
Sept. 10				150	11	} 4,650	50	12	600
				250	12				

After a purchase of 400 units on November 27, the ending inventory is 450 units consisting of 50 units at $12 costing $600 from the August 24 purchase and 400 units at $13 costing $5,200 from the November 27 purchase, for a total cost of $5,800 ($600 + $5,200). This transaction is included below in Illustration 6-3, completing the inventory schedule shown in sections above.

Date	Purchases Units	Cost	Total	Cost of Goods Sold Units	Cost	Total	Balance Units	Cost	Total
Jan. 1							100	$10	$1,000
Apr. 15	200	$11	$ 2,200				100 / 200	10 / 11	3,200
May 1				100 / 50	$10 / 11	$1,550	150	11	1,650
Aug. 24	300	12	3,600				150 / 300	11 / 12	5,250
Sept. 10				150 / 250	11 / 12	4,650	50	12	600
Nov. 27	400	13	5,200				50 / 400	12 / 13	5,800
	900		$11,000	550		$6,200			

▶Illustration 6-3
Perpetual inventory schedule—FIFO

Check: $6,200 + $5,800 = $12,000 ($1,000 + $11,000)

As at November 27, the total cost of goods sold is $6,200 and the ending inventory is $5,800. A useful check against calculation errors is to check whether the total of the cost of goods sold and ending inventory equals the total cost of goods available for sale of $12,000 (beginning inventory of $1,000 + purchases of $11,000).

In summary, FIFO assumes that the first goods purchased are the first ones sold. This method always takes into consideration the order of selling. As a result, FIFO assumes that the last goods purchased are still in ending inventory.

Whether a periodic or perpetual inventory system is used, FIFO will always result in the same cost of goods sold and ending inventory amounts. Recall from Chapter 5 that a key difference between these two inventory systems arises when the cost of goods available for sale (beginning inventory plus the cost of goods purchased) is allocated to the cost of goods sold and ending inventory. Under a perpetual inventory system, the cost of goods available for sale is allocated to the cost of goods sold as each item is sold. Under a periodic inventory system, the allocation is made only at the end of the period, with the cost of goods sold then calculated by deducting the ending inventory from the cost of goods available for sale.

The same costs will always be first in, and therefore first out, whether the costs are allocated throughout the accounting period as in the perpetual inventory system or at the end of the accounting period as in the periodic inventory system. The periodic inventory system using FIFO is demonstrated in Appendix 6A.

AVERAGE COST

The **average cost method** recognizes that it is not possible to measure a specific physical flow of inventory when the goods available for sale are homogeneous or non-distinguishable. Consider, for example, a fuel storage tank at a gas station. When the tank is refilled with gas that costs more than the gas that is currently in the tank, the gas mixes. As the gas is being sold, it is impossible to tell which batch of gas at which cost is being pumped and which batch of gas at which cost remains in the tank.

Under the average cost method, the allocation of the cost of goods available for sale between cost of goods sold and ending inventory is made based on the **weighted average unit cost** of the merchandise available for sale. The calculation of this amount is shown in the formula below in Illustration 6-4.

▶Illustration 6-4
Calculation of weighted average
unit cost

| Cost of Goods Available for Sale | ÷ | Units Available for Sale | = | Weighted Average Unit Cost |

Note that the weighted average unit cost is *not* calculated by taking a simple average of the costs of each purchase, but by weighting the quantities purchased at each unit cost. This is done by dividing the cost of goods available for sale by the units available for sale at the date of each purchase. Consequently, a new average is calculated, or "moves," after each purchase (or purchase return). Because of this, when using the average cost method for perpetual inventory systems, we often refer to this as a *moving* average cost method.

We will use the same information provided in Illustration 6-2 for The Tee-Shirt Corporation to prepare a perpetual inventory schedule using the average cost method so that you can compare the similarities and differences between the FIFO and average cost methods. In the partial perpetual inventory schedule below, note that the beginning inventory of 100 units at $10 each costing $1,000 and the April 15 purchase of 200 units at $11 each costing $2,200 combine to total 300 units available for sale at a total cost of $3,200 ($1,000 + $2,200).

Using the formula shown in Illustration 6-4, the weighted average unit cost on April 15 is $10.67 ($3,200 ÷ 300) (highlighted in red in the table below). Accordingly, the unit cost of the 150 units sold on May 1 is shown at $10.67, and the total cost of goods sold is $1,600 (150 × $10.67). This unit cost is used in costing the units sold until another purchase (or a purchase return) is made, and a new unit cost must then be calculated.

Date	Purchases			Cost of Goods Sold			Balance		
	Units	Cost	Total	Units	Cost	Total	Units	Cost	Total
Jan. 1							100	$10.00	$1,000.00
Apr. 15	200	$11.00	$2,200.00				300	10.67	3,200.00
May 1				150	$10.67	$1,600.00	150	10.67	1,600.00

On August 24, after 300 units costing $12 each are purchased for $3,600, a total of 450 units costing $5,200 ($1,600 + $3,600) are on hand. This results in a new average cost per unit of $11.56 ($5,200 ÷ 450). This new cost is used to calculate the cost of the September 10 sale and the units still on hand after the sale, as shown in the continuation of the inventory schedule below:

Date	Purchases			Cost of Goods Sold			Balance		
	Units	Cost	Total	Units	Cost	Total	Units	Cost	Total
Jan. 1							100	$10.00	$1,000.00
Apr. 15	200	$11.00	$2,200.00				300	10.67	3,200.00
May 1				150	$10.67	$1,600.00	150	10.67	1,600.00
Aug. 24	300	12.00	3,600.00				450	11.56	5,200.00
Sept. 10				400	11.56	4,622.22	50	11.56	577.78

A new unit cost will be calculated again after the November 27 purchase of 400 units for $5,200. After this purchase, there are 450 units on hand with a total cost of $5,777.78 ($577.78 + $5,200). This results in a new average cost of $12.84 ($5,777.78 ÷ 450), which will be used until another purchase is made (in the following year, in The Tee-Shirt Corporation's case).

These transactions, which complete the perpetual inventory schedule for the average cost method, are shown in Illustration 6-5 below.

As at November 27, therefore, the total cost of goods sold is $6,222.22 and the total ending inventory is $5,777.78. The total of these amounts should agree with the cost of goods available for sale, $12,000 ($6,222.22 + $5,777.78). This is a useful check, or proof, of the accuracy of your calculations.

In practice, average unit costs may be rounded to the nearest cent, or even to the nearest dollar. This illustration used the exact unit cost amounts in its calculations, as would a computerized

Date	Purchases			Cost of Goods Sold			Balance		
	Units	Cost	Total	Units	Cost	Total	Units	Cost	Total
Jan. 1							100	$10.00	$1,000.00
Apr. 15	200	$11.00	$ 2,200.00				300	10.67	3,200.00
May 1				150	$10.67	$1,600.00	150	10.67	1,600.00
Aug. 24	300	12.00	3,600.00				450	11.56	5,200.00
Sept. 10				400	11.56	4,622.22	50	11.56	577.78
Nov. 27	400	13.00	5,200.00				450	12.84	5,777.78
	900		$11,000.00	550		$6,222.22			

Check: $6,222.22 + $5,777.78 = $12,000 ($1,000 + $11,000)

▶Illustration 6-5
Perpetual inventory schedule—
average cost

schedule, even though the unit costs have been rounded to the nearest digit for presentation in Illustration 6-5. However, it is important to remember that this is a method of allocating costs and not a method to track actual costs. Using four digits, or even cents, suggests a false level of accuracy.

In summary, this cost determination method uses the average cost of the goods that are available for sale to determine the cost of goods sold and ending inventory. When a perpetual inventory system is used, the average unit cost is determined after each purchase (or purchase return). When a periodic inventory system is used, the average unit cost is determined once at the end of the accounting period. Because of the different times when the average unit cost is determined in a perpetual and periodic inventory system, different amounts can result for the cost of goods sold and ending inventory in each system when using the average cost method. The use of the average cost method in a periodic inventory system will be explained in Appendix 6A.

BEFORE YOU GO ON...

▶Do It! FIFO and Average Cost—Perpetual System

The inventory records of Ag Implement Inc. show the following data for the month of March:

Date	Explanation	Units	Unit Cost	Total Cost
Mar. 1	Beginning inventory	4,000	$3	$12,000
10	Purchases	6,000	4	24,000
19	Sales	(8,000)		
22	Purchases	5,000	5	25,000
28	Sales	(5,500)		
		1,500		$61,000

Determine the cost of goods sold and ending inventory under a perpetual inventory system using the (a) FIFO and (b) average cost methods.

Action Plan

- For FIFO, allocate the first costs to the cost of goods sold at the date of each sale. The latest costs will be allocated to the goods on hand (ending inventory).
- For average cost, determine the weighted average unit cost (cost of goods available for sale ÷ number of units available for sale) after each purchase. Multiply this cost by the number of units sold to determine the cost of goods sold, and by the number of units on hand to determine the cost of ending inventory.
- Prove that the cost of goods sold and ending inventory equal the cost of goods available for sale.

(continued)

Solution

(a) FIFO—Perpetual

Date	Purchases			Cost of Goods Sold			Balance		
	Units	Cost	Total	Units	Cost	Total	Units	Cost	Total
Mar. 1							4,000	$3	$12,000
10	6,000	$4	$24,000				4,000 6,000	3 4	}36,000
19				4,000 4,000	$3 4	}$28,000	2,000	4	8,000
22	5,000	5	25,000				2,000 5,000	4 5	}33,000
28				2,000 3,500	4 5	}25,500	1,500	5	7,500
	11,000		$49,000	13,500		$53,500			

Check: $53,500 + $7,500 = $61,000 ($12,000 + $49,000)

(b) Average Cost—Perpetual

Date	Purchases			Cost of Goods Sold			Balance		
	Units	Cost	Total	Units	Cost	Total	Units	Cost	Total
Mar. 1							4,000	$3.00	$12,000
10	6,000	$4	$24,000				10,000	3.60	36,000
19				8,000	$3.60	$28,800	2,000	3.60	7,200
22	5,000	5	25,000				7,000	4.60	32,200
28				5,500	4.60	25,300	1,500	4.60	6,900
	11,000		$49,000	13,500		$54,100			

Check: $54,100 + $6,900 = $61,000 ($12,000 + $49,000)

Related Exercise Material: BE6-3, BE6-4, BE6-5, BE6-6, *BE6-14, *BE6-15, E6-3, E6-4, E6-5, E6-6, E6-7, *E6-15, and *E6-16.

the navigator

Effects of Cost Determination Methods

STUDY OBJECTIVE 3

Explain the effects on the financial statements of choosing each of the inventory cost determination methods.

Each of the cost determination methods—specific identification, FIFO, and average cost—is acceptable for use by both publicly traded companies and private companies. However, there are guidelines that limit the choice of the method by management. We will discuss guidelines that influence the choice of the appropriate cost determination method and the impact these choices can have on the financial statements in the sections that follow.

CHOICE OF COST DETERMINATION METHOD

If companies have goods that are not ordinarily interchangeable, or goods that have been produced and segregated for specific projects, they must use the specific identification method to determine the cost of their inventory. Otherwise, they can choose to use either FIFO or average cost.

Canadian companies that use FIFO include Jean Coutu, Magna International, Maple Leaf Foods, and Saputo. However, the majority use the average cost method to determine the cost of their inventories, including Canadian Tire, Loblaw, and Sears Canada.

How should a company choose between FIFO and average cost? It should consider the following guidelines in making its choice:

1. Choose a method that corresponds as closely as possible to the physical flow of goods.
2. Report an inventory cost on the statement of financial position that is close to the inventory's recent cost.
3. Use the same method for all inventories having a similar nature and usage in the company.

After a company chooses a method of determining the cost of its inventory, that method should be used consistently from one period to the next. You will recall, from Chapter 2, that **comparability** of financial statements over successive time periods is an important enhancing characteristic of accounting information. Using FIFO in one year and average cost in the next year would make it difficult to compare the profit for the two years.

This is not to say that a company can never change from one method to another. However, a change in the method of cost determination can only occur if the nature and use of the inventory changes and a different method would result in a more reliable and more relevant presentation in the financial statements. Such a change is unusual with respect to inventories. We will learn more about changing accounting policies in Chapter 14.

FINANCIAL STATEMENT EFFECTS

Inventory affects both the statement of financial position and the income statement since ending inventory is included as a current asset on the statement of financial position and cost of goods sold is included as an expense on the income statement. Cost of goods sold also affects gross profit and profit, which in turn will affect retained earnings in the statement of changes in equity as well as in the shareholders' equity section of the statement of financial position. We will look at the impact of inventory on both the income statement and the statement of financial position in the next two sections.

Income Statement Effects

To understand the impact of the FIFO and average cost methods on the income statement, we will now examine their effects on The Tee-Shirt Corporation. The condensed income statements in Illustration 6-6 use the amounts we determined for cost of goods sold after applying the FIFO and average cost methods earlier in the chapter. This illustration also assumes that The Tee-Shirt Corporation sold its 550 units for $11,500, had operating expenses of $2,000, and is subject to an income tax rate of 30%.

▶ Illustration 6-6

Comparative effects of inventory cost methods

THE TEE-SHIRT CORPORATION Condensed Income Statements		
	FIFO	Average Cost
Sales	$11,500	$11,500
Cost of goods sold	6,200	6,222
Gross profit	5,300	5,278
Operating expenses	2,000	2,000
Profit before income tax	3,300	3,278
Income tax expense (30%)	990	983
Profit	$ 2,310	$ 2,295

The sales and operating expense figures are the same under both FIFO and average cost. But the cost of goods sold amounts are different. This difference is because of the unit costs that are allocated under each cost method. Each dollar of difference in cost of goods sold results in a corresponding dollar difference in profit before income tax. For Tee-Shirt, there is a $22 difference between the FIFO and average cost amounts for cost of goods sold. A fixed percentage (30%) applied to determine income tax expense results in a difference in profit between the two methods of $15.

In periods of changing prices, the choice of inventory cost method can have a significant impact on profit. In a period of inflation (rising prices), as is the case for Tee-Shirt, FIFO produces higher profit because cost of goods sold is composed of the lowest cost units and this in turn will maximize profit. As Illustration 6-6 shows, FIFO reports the highest profit ($2,310) and average cost the lowest ($2,295). This difference is not very large for Tee-Shirt, because prices are changing slowly. The more prices change, the larger this difference will be.

If prices are falling, the results from the use of FIFO and average cost are reversed: FIFO will report the lowest profit and average cost the highest. If prices are stable, both cost methods will report the same results.

Compared with FIFO, the average cost method will result in more recent costs being reflected in the cost of goods sold. This will better identify or match current costs with current revenues and result in a better measurement of profit on the income statement. Of course, the specific identification method provides the best match of costs and revenues, as it exactly matches each cost with the revenue it generates.

Statement of Financial Position Effects

One advantage of FIFO is that the costs allocated to ending inventory will approximate the inventory items' current (replacement) cost because the most recent purchases are assumed to be in ending inventory. For example, for Tee-Shirt, 400 of the 450 units in the ending inventory have a cost under FIFO at the most recent November 27 unit cost of $13. Since management needs to replace inventory when it is sold, a value that approximates the replacement cost is helpful for decision-making. That is why one of the guidelines in choosing an inventory cost method is to "report an inventory cost on the statement of financial position that is close to the inventory's recent cost." FIFO provides a more relevant ending inventory value on the statement of financial position than does average cost.

By extension, one limitation of the average cost method is that in a period of inflation the average cost results in older costs being included in ending inventory. For example, the average cost of Tee-Shirt's ending inventory, $12.84, includes the $10 unit cost of the beginning inventory as well as the cost of some of its earlier purchases. The understatement becomes greater over extended periods of inflation if the inventory includes goods that were purchased in one or more earlier accounting periods.

Summary of Effects of Cost Determination Methods

The effects of each of the three major cost determination methods are summarized below in Illustration 6-7.

▶Illustration 6-7
Effects of cost determination methods

Specific Identification	FIFO	Average Cost
• Exactly matches costs and revenues on the income statement.	• Ending inventory on the statement of financial position includes the most current costs (closest to replacement cost).	• Cost of goods sold on the income statement includes more current costs than FIFO.
• Tracks the actual physical flow.	• Approximates the physical flow of most retailers.	• Smooths the effects of price changes by assigning all units the same average cost.

The key financial statement differences that will result from using the three cost determination methods during a period of rising prices are summarized in Illustration 6-8. These effects will be the inverse if prices are falling and the same for all three methods if prices are constant. In all cases, it does not matter whether a company uses the perpetual or periodic inventory system.

▶Illustration 6-8
Summary of financial statement effects of cost determination methods during a period of rising prices

	Specific Identification	FIFO	Average Cost
Income statement			
Cost of goods sold	Variable	Lower	Higher
Gross profit	Variable	Higher	Lower
Profit	Variable	Higher	Lower
Statement of financial position			
Cash	Same	Same	Same
Ending inventory	Variable	Higher	Lower
Retained earnings	Variable	Higher	Lower

It is also worth remembering that all three methods will give exactly the same result over the life cycle of the business or its product. **That is, the allocation between the cost of goods sold and ending inventory may vary annually, but it will produce the same cumulative results over time.** Although much has been written about the impact of the choice of inventory cost determination method on a variety of performance measures, in reality there is little real economic distinction among the methods over time.

■ Keeping an Eye on Cash

We have seen that both inventory on the statement of financial position and cost of goods sold on the income statement are affected by the choice of cost determination method. It is very important to understand, however, that the choice of method does *not* affect cash flow. All three methods of cost determination—specific identification, FIFO, and average cost—produce exactly the same cash flow before income tax.

Why is that? Sales and purchases are not affected by the method of inventory cost determination. The only thing that is affected is the allocation of the cost of goods available for sale between the cost of goods sold and ending inventory—which does not involve cash.

Let's consider this further. When a company records its sales, it uses the same selling price regardless of whether it uses specific identification, FIFO, or average cost. It doesn't change its selling price based on its cost determination method. So cash receipts from cash sales, or collections of sales on account, are unchanged.

When a company records purchases of its merchandise for resale, it pays the same for the merchandise regardless of its method of cost determination. So cash payments for purchases, or payments on account, are unchanged.

In a perpetual inventory system, cost of goods sold is recorded by debiting the Cost of Goods Sold account and crediting the Merchandise Inventory account. There is no cash involved in this entry. The only accounts affected by the choice of cost determination method are inventory and retained earnings (and related amounts such as current assets, total assets, and total shareholders' equity) on the statement of financial position and cost of goods sold (and related amounts such as gross profit, profit before income tax, income tax, and profit) on the income statement.

DECISION TOOLKIT

 Decision Checkpoints	 Info Needed for Decision	 Tools to Use for Decision	 How to Evaluate Results
What is the impact of the choice of inventory cost determination method?	Are prices increasing, or are they decreasing?	Income statement and statement of financial position effects	In periods of rising prices, profit and inventory are higher under FIFO than average cost. FIFO results in the best measure of ending inventory on the statement of financial position. The average cost method provides opposite results—profit and inventory are lower compared with FIFO—but can smooth the impact of changing prices. Specific identification's impact on the financial statements will vary, depending on the actual cost. This method results in the best allocation of costs to revenues on the income statement.

BEFORE YOU GO ON...

▶ Do It! Cost Method Effects on Income Statements

On July 31, UFirst Inc. had the following merchandise transactions:

July 1   Beginning inventory, 2 units @ $75 each
      7   Purchases, 4 units @ $80 each
     19   Sales, 5 units @ $180 each
     25   Purchases, 6 units @ $100 each

(a) Calculate UFirst's cost of goods sold and ending inventory for the month of July assuming the use of (1) FIFO and (2) average cost in a perpetual inventory system.

(b) Prepare comparative income statements for each cost method, assuming operating expenses of $300 and an income tax rate of 25%.

Action Plan

- Recall that FIFO allocates the earliest costs to the cost of goods sold at the date of each sale.
- Recall that the average cost method uses a weighted average unit cost to determine the cost of goods sold at the date of each sale. For this method, use unrounded numbers in your calculations but round to the nearest cent for presentation purposes in an inventory schedule.
- In preparing comparative income statements, note that while the cost of goods sold will change between methods, the sales figure does not.

Solution

(a) (1) FIFO

Date	Purchases			Cost of Goods Sold			Balance		
	Units	Cost	Total	Units	Cost	Total	Units	Cost	Total
July 1							2	$75	$150
7	4	$ 80	$320				2	75	} 470
							4	80	
19				2	$75	} $390	1	80	80
				3	80				
25	6	100	600				1	80	} 680
							6	100	

Check: $390 + $680 = $1,070 ($150 + $320 + $600)

(a) (2) Average Cost

Date	Purchases			Cost of Goods Sold			Balance		
	Units	Cost	Total	Units	Cost	Total	Units	Cost	Total
July 1							2	$75.00	$150.00
7	4	$ 80.00	$320.00				6	78.33	470.00
19				5	$78.33	$391.67	1	78.33	78.33
25	6	100.00	600.00				7	96.91	678.33

Check: $391.67 + $678.33 = $1,070 ($150 + $320 + $600)

(b)

UFIRST INC. Condensed Income Statements		
	FIFO	Average Cost
Sales (5 × $180)	$900	$900
Cost of goods sold	390	392
Gross profit	510	508
Operating expenses	300	300
Profit before income tax	210	208
Income tax expense (25%)	52	52
Profit	$158	$156

Related Exercise Material: BE6-7, E6-3, E6-6, E6-7, and E6-12.

the navigator

Inventory Errors

Errors relating to inventory can arise in a number of ways. One type of error arises when the quantity or costs assigned to inventory are incorrect. This type of error is rarely corrected until the next time inventory is counted, so the financial statements of the current period will be misstated. In other words, when the Merchandise Inventory account is incorrect, the Cost of Goods Sold account is also incorrect because the cost of goods available for sale is allocated between the Merchandise Inventory account and the Cost of Goods Sold account. A second type of error occurs when the purchase of inventory is recorded incorrectly and this will cause an error in the Merchandise Inventory account and the Accounts Payable account.

STUDY OBJECTIVE 4
Identify the effects of inventory errors on the financial statements.

ERRORS MADE WHEN DETERMINING THE COST OF INVENTORY

Consider an example where a company has opening inventory of $20,000 and purchased inventory of $40,000 during 2014 for a total cost of goods available for sale of $60,000. If the correct cost of ending inventory is $15,000, this would mean that the cost of goods sold for the year would be $45,000 ($60,000 − $15,000). However, assume that an error in quantities or costs was made in determining the cost of inventory at the end of 2014 and the amount calculated was only $12,000 rather than correct amount of $15,000. In this case, cost of goods sold for 2014 would be $48,000 ($60,000 − $12,000), rather than the correct amount of $45,000.

An error made in determining the cost of inventory at the end of one period will also result in an error in the following period. As you know, the ending inventory of one period automatically becomes the beginning inventory of the next period. Consequently, **an error in ending inventory of the current period will have a reverse effect on profit of the next accounting period** if it is not found and corrected.

Because of the $3,000 understatement in ending inventory at the end of 2014 ($12,000 instead of $15,000), cost of goods sold in 2014 is overstated by $3,000 ($48,000 instead of $45,000). In addition, because the inventory balance was wrong at the end of 2014, it is also wrong at the beginning of 2015. If purchases made in 2015 were $68,000, the goods available for sale will be $80,000 ($12,000 + $68,000) when it really should be $83,000 ($15,000 + $68,000). Assuming that the cost of inventory on hand is determined correctly at the end of 2015 at $23,000, then the cost of goods sold would be determined as $57,000 ($80,000 − $23,000) when it really should be $60,000 ($83,000 − $23,000). Notice that the overstatement of cost of goods sold in 2014 is reversed by the understatement of cost of goods sold in 2015. Inventory errors relating to ending inventory will reverse in the following year as long as the inventory count is done correctly at the end of that subsequent year. Illustration 6-9 illustrates the following effects:

	2014		2015	
	Incorrect	Correct	Incorrect	Correct
Sales	$80,000	$80,000	$90,000	$90,000
Cost of goods sold	48,000	45,000	57,000	60,000
Gross profit	32,000	35,000	33,000	30,000
Operating expenses	10,000	10,000	20,000	20,000
Profit before income tax	22,000	25,000	13,000	10,000
	($3,000)		$3,000	
Gross profit	Profit understated		Profit overstated	

SAMPLE COMPANY
Extracts from Income Statements

The combined profit before income tax for two years is correct because the errors cancel each other out.

►Illustration 6-9
Effects of inventory errors on income statement for two years

The following table summarizes the effect of errors made when determining the cost of inventory:

If Merchandise Inventory is:	Then Cost of Goods Sold is:	Then Gross Profit is:	Then Profit Before Income Tax is:	Then Retained Earnings is:
Overstated	Understated	Overstated	Overstated	Overstated
Understated	Overstated	Understated	Understated	Understated

Note that the effect on the statement of financial position is balanced. In other words, the overstatement or understatement error in the Merchandise Inventory account equals the overstatement or understatement error in the Retained Earnings account. This, however, ignores the effect on income tax caused by the inventory error.

ERRORS MADE WHEN RECORDING THE PURCHASE OF INVENTORY

Another type of error that can affect the financial statements occurs when a purchase is recorded incorrectly. This will cause the Merchandise Inventory and Accounts Payable accounts to be misstated.

Consider an example where an accountant has recorded an inventory purchase on credit one day before year end for $5,000. The inventory, however, was in transit with terms FOB destination so the purchase should not be recorded until the inventory is received and that will not occur until the following year. This purchase was added to the inventory count results. Because of this error, the Merchandise Inventory account and the Accounts Payable account are both overstated.

The following table summarizes the effect of purchase errors, ignoring any income tax effects.

If purchase of inventory is recorded:	Then Merchandise Inventory is:	Then Cost of Goods Sold and Profit are:	Then Accounts Payable is:	Then Retained Earnings is:
Too early	Overstated	Unaffected	Overstated	Unaffected
Too late	Understated	Unaffected	Understated	Unaffected

BEFORE YOU GO ON...

▶ Do It! Inventory Errors

On June 30, 2015, Wang Ltd.'s year end, it counted $800,000 of inventory. During the count, inventory costing $20,000 was counted twice. This count did not include $100,000 of goods in transit from Laughlin Inc. that were purchased on June 29 on account and shipped to Wang FOB shipping point. Wang recorded the purchase on July 2 when the goods were received. (a) Determine the correct June 30 inventory amount. (b) Identify any accounts that are in error at June 30, and state the amount and direction (understated or overstated) of the error. You can ignore income tax effects. (c) Prepare the journal entry(ies) to correct any errors identified in part (b) for the year ended June 30, 2015. (d) If the errors were not corrected immediately, explain how they would eventually be corrected during the year ended June 30, 2016.

Action Plan

- For each error, use the income statement relationships to determine the error's impact on income statement accounts.
- For each error, use the accounting equation to determine the error's impact on statement of financial position accounts.
- For each error, record a journal entry to reverse the impact made by the error.

Solution

(a) By counting inventory twice, an assumption will be made that inventory costing $20,000 was on hand rather than sold, so Cost of Goods Sold will be understated.

However, with regard to the goods in transit, because these were not sold, the failure to include them in the determination of ending inventory will have no impact on cost of goods sold as these items were not available to be sold or counted.

(b) When inventory was counted twice, that error overstates the Merchandise Inventory account balance and, as mentioned above, understates the Cost of Goods Sold account balance. By not recording the inventory in transit, the Merchandise Inventory account is understated as is the Accounts Payable account balance.

The following table summarizes the effect of these errors on the statement of financial position using (U) for understated and (O) for overstated:

	Assets	=	Liabilities	+	Shareholders' equity
Count error	O $20,000	=	no effect	+	O $20,000
Purchase error	U $100,000	=	U $100,000	+	no effect

(c) June 30	Cost of Goods Sold	20,000	
	Merchandise Inventory		20,000
	(To correct for an overstatement in ending inventory arising from an error made when counting inventory)		
June 30	Merchandise Inventory	100,000	
	Accounts Payable		100,000
	(To record merchandise received on July 2, FOB shipping point)		

(d) During the following year ended June 30, 2016, when an inventory count is performed, the count team will notice that the balance in the Merchandise Inventory account is $20,000 higher than the amount on hand and will take steps to ensure that the error is corrected at that time. Also during the year ended June 30, 2016, when the invoice for the goods in transit is received from Laughlin Inc., the inventory purchase will be recorded and the Merchandise Inventory and Accounts Payable accounts adjusted for the effect of this purchase. Therefore, the two journal entries recorded on part (c) above will eventually be recorded but in the wrong year, in essence reversing the effect of the error but in a subsequent year.

Related Exercise Material: BE6-8, BE6-9, E6-8, and E6-9.

the navigator

Presentation and Analysis of Inventory

Presenting inventory appropriately on the financial statements is important for merchandising companies because the Merchandise Inventory account is usually the largest current asset on the statement of financial position while the largest expense on the income statement is cost of goods sold. For example, lululemon, introduced in our feature story, reported inventory of $155,222 thousand in 2012, which represented 14.8% of its total current assets. lululemon's cost of goods sold of $607,532 thousand is 61.1% of total expenses on its income statement.

In addition, these reported numbers are critical for analyzing a company's effectiveness in managing its inventory. In the next sections, we will discuss issues that are related to the presentation and analysis of inventory.

STUDY OBJECTIVE 5
Demonstrate the presentation and analysis of inventory.

VALUING INVENTORY AT THE LOWER OF COST AND NET REALIZABLE VALUE

Before presenting inventory on the financial statements, we must first ensure that it is properly valued. While a company would hope to sell its merchandise for more than it cost, in some cases this is not possible when inventory is damaged or is becoming obsolete. Furthermore, the prices of some goods can drop dramatically with a change in season—few people want to buy a snow blower in the summer. And, in some industries, such as the commodities industry, prices are significantly affected by changes in supply and demand.

For example, in a recent year, purchasing managers at Ford decided to make a large purchase of palladium, a precious metal used in vehicle emission devices. They made this large purchase because they feared a future shortage. The shortage did not materialize, and by the end of the year, the price of palladium had plummeted. Ford's inventory was then worth $1 billion less than its original cost. Do you think Ford's inventory should have been stated at cost or at its $1-billion lower fair value?

As you probably reasoned, when this situation occurs, the cost basis of accounting is no longer followed. **Assets should not be carried in excess of amounts expected to be realized from their sale or use.** Consequently, when the net realizable value of inventory is lower than its cost, inventory is written down to its net realizable value. This is called the **lower of cost and net realizable value (LCNRV) rule.** For a merchandising company, **net realizable value (NRV)** is the selling price, less any costs required to make the goods ready for sale.

The lower of cost and net realizable value rule is applied to the inventory at the end of the accounting period and results in an adjusting journal entry if NRV is lower than cost. To apply this rule, the following steps must be followed:

1. Determine the cost of the inventory, using specific identification, FIFO, or average cost.
2. Determine the net realizable value of the inventory.
3. Compare the two values—cost and net realizable value—determined in steps 1 and 2. Determine if net realizable value is lower than cost.
4. If net realizable value is lower than cost, adjust and report inventory on the financial statements at NRV rather than cost.

To illustrate the application of the LCNRV rule, assume that at March 31, 2015, New-2-You Autos Limited has the following inventory of used motor vehicles with costs and net realizable values as indicated:

	Cost	NRV	LCNRV
Vehicle A	$16,000	$15,500	$15,500
Vehicle B	14,500	15,300	14,500
Vehicle C	14,800	14,500	14,500
Vehicle D	13,200	14,800	13,200
Vehicle E	11,500	11,400	11,400
Total inventory	$70,000	$71,500	$69,100

In the above example, we compare the cost of each used motor vehicle with its net realizable value and choose the lower amount. The lower of these two amounts, or LCNRV, is listed in the third column. For example, the NRV of $15,500 is the lower amount for Vehicle A, whereas the cost of $14,500 is the lower amount for Vehicle B. This comparison would continue for the remaining vehicles (C through E) in inventory until the total value using the lower of cost and NRV rule is determined. In this example, the lower of cost or net realizable value is $69,100.

The lower of cost and net realizable value rule should be applied to individual inventory items, rather than total inventory. In certain cases, it can be applied to groups of similar items. This may be the case with items of inventory relating to the same product line that has similar purposes or uses. The story of BlackBerry's first-generation PlayBook tablets found later in this section is a good example of applying the lower of cost and net realizable value rule to a product group.

After the lower of cost and net realizable value has been determined—whether using individual inventory items or groups of inventory—the next step is to use the net realizable value, if it is lower than cost at the end of the accounting period, to adjust and report inventory. If New-2-You Autos uses a perpetual inventory system, an adjusting journal entry is required to write the inventory down by $900 ($70,000 − $69,100) as follows:

Alternative Terminology
Lower of cost and net realizable value is also called *lower of cost and market.*

Mar. 31	Cost of Goods Sold	900	
	Merchandise Inventory		900
	(To record decline in inventory value from original cost of $70,000 to net realizable value of $69,100)		

A	=	L	+	SE
−900				−900

Cash flows: no effect

The Cost of Goods Sold account is directly debited in the above entry for the loss, even though no merchandise was sold. This is because a decline in the value of inventory is considered to be an overall cost of buying and selling merchandise, and is therefore reported as the cost of goods sold rather than as a non-operating "other revenues and expenses" item. The Merchandise Inventory account is credited directly also to reflect the net realizable value of the inventory. There are other acceptable methods of recording a decline in inventory value, which will be discussed in an intermediate accounting course.

When the circumstances that previously caused inventories to be written down below cost no longer exist, or when there is clear evidence of an increase in net realizable value because of changed economic circumstances, the amount of the writedown is reversed. This occurs, for example, when an item of inventory that is carried at net realizable value, because its selling price had declined, is still on hand in a subsequent period and its selling price has increased. Reversals do not occur very often.

ACCOUNTING MATTERS!

Inventory Challenges

Waterloo, Ontario–based BlackBerry (formerly known as Research In Motion) provides wireless hardware, software, and services worldwide and is well known for its BlackBerry smart phones. To enter the growing tablet market, in 2011 BlackBerry launched its PlayBook tablet. It originally sold for $399. But sales were very slow, and the tablets piled up in inventory. During a six-month period in 2011, BlackBerry's inventory tripled from U.S. $94 million to U.S. $298 million. In November 2011, management announced the selling price on the first-generation PlayBook would be reduced to $199. This announcement provided support for speculation that the company had more PlayBooks in inventory than it could sell at full retail price. The estimated cost of a PlayBook was $205. At the new selling price of $199, BlackBerry needed to write down its PlayBook inventory by approximately $6 per tablet.[3]

REPORTING INVENTORY

Ending inventory is reported in the current assets section of the statement of financial position at its lower of cost and net realizable value. Most companies do not separately disclose the cost and net realizable value of their inventory—they simply state that it is recorded at the lower of cost and net realizable value. For example, lululemon, our feature story company, discloses the following in the notes to its financial statements: "Inventories, consisting of finished goods and raw materials, are stated at the lower of cost and market value. Cost is determined using weighted-average costs."

In addition to the basis of valuation, the following information related to inventory should also be disclosed in the financial statements or the notes to the statements: (1) the total amount of inventory; (2) the cost of goods sold; (3) the method of cost determination (specific identification, FIFO, or average cost); and (4) the amount of any writedown to net realizable value or reversals of previous writedowns, including the reason why the writedown was reversed.

In the significant accounting policy note for inventories, lululemon notes that it periodically reviews inventories and "makes provisions as necessary to appropriately value obsolete or damaged goods." In addition "the Company accrues for inventory shrinkage based on historical trends from actual physical inventory counts. Inventory shrinkage estimates are made to reduce the inventory value for lost or stolen items."

There are no significant differences at the introductory accounting level in the valuation or reporting of inventory between publicly traded companies reporting under IFRS and private companies reporting under ASPE. There are a few differences regarding specialized types of inventories that will be covered in an intermediate accounting course.

INVENTORY TURNOVER

A delicate balance must be kept between having too little inventory and too much inventory. Two ratios that can help a company manage its inventory levels are the inventory turnover and days in inventory ratios.

The **inventory turnover** ratio measures the number of times, on average, that inventory is sold ("turned over") during the period. It is calculated as the cost of goods sold divided by the average inventory. Whenever a ratio compares an account balance from the statement of financial position, such as inventory, with an account balance from the income statement, such as cost of goods sold, the account balance from the statement of financial position must be averaged. These averages are determined by adding the beginning and ending balances together and then dividing the result by two. Averages are used to ensure that the amount used for a statement of financial position account balance in a ratio is equal to the average balance throughout the period covered by the income statement account.

A complement to the inventory turnover ratio is the **days in inventory** ratio. It converts the inventory turnover into a measure of the average age of the inventory. It is calculated as 365 days divided by the inventory turnover ratio.

We will illustrate the calculation of the inventory turnover and days in inventory ratios for lululemon for three recent fiscal years using the following data (in thousands):

	2012	2011	2010
Cost of goods sold	$607,532	$431,569	$316,757
Inventory	155,222	104,097	57,469

Using the amounts shown above, Illustration 6-10 presents the inventory turnover and days in inventory ratios for lululemon. We also include, for comparison purposes, the ratios for Limited Brands Inc., and their industry. Limited Brands owns La Senza and other apparel retailers that compete against lululemon.

In general, a company that is managing its inventory effectively will have a higher than average inventory turnover ratio and a lower than average days in inventory ratio because this indicates

▶Illustration 6-10
Inventory turnover and days in inventory

$$\text{INVENTORY TURNOVER} = \frac{\text{COST OF GOODS SOLD}}{\text{AVERAGE INVENTORY}}$$

$$\text{DAYS IN INVENTORY} = \frac{\text{365 DAYS}}{\text{INVENTORY TURNOVER}}$$

($ in thousands)		2012	2011
lululemon	Inventory turnover	$\dfrac{\$607,532}{(\$155,222 + \$104,097) \div 2}$ = 4.7 times	$\dfrac{\$431,569}{(\$104,097 + \$57,469) \div 2}$ = 5.3 times
	Days in inventory	$\dfrac{365 \text{ days}}{4.7 \text{ times}}$ = 78 days	$\dfrac{365 \text{ days}}{5.3 \text{ times}}$ = 69 days
Limited Brands	Inventory turnover	6.1 times	6.2 times
	Days in inventory	60 days	59 days
Industry	Inventory turnover	4.6 times	4.0 times
	Days in inventory	79 days	91 days

that the company can sell its inventory faster than average. The ratios in Illustration 6-10 show that lululemon's inventory turnover decreased between 2011 and 2012 while Limited Brands' remained stable. In both years, Limited Brands' ratios indicate that it is turning its inventory over faster than lululemon. The reduced inventory turnover (and increase in days in inventory) for lululemon was due primarily to a strategic decision taken by management to have sufficient inventory on hand to meet demand. Consequently, lululemon's ratios are now very similar to the industry average. Overall, however, our analysis suggests that Limited Brands is more efficient in its inventory management than lululemon.

Both the inventory turnover and days in inventory ratios are liquidity ratios. Along with the current ratio, which was introduced in Chapter 2, these ratios are important in evaluating a company's liquidity, namely its ability to pay obligations that are expected to come due in the next year. Inventory is a significant component of the current ratio and a high level of inventory will result in a high current ratio. But if the inventory is not turning over very quickly, this will result in an "artificially" high current ratio.

Consequently, the current ratio should never be interpreted on its own. It should always be interpreted along with the inventory turnover ratio, as a high current ratio could mean good liquidity, or it could be artificially inflated by slow-moving inventory. Slow-moving inventory results in higher balances in the inventory account, which could also lead to excessive carrying costs (interest, storage, insurance, and taxes) or obsolete inventory.

Many companies have moved to streamline their supply chain operations, which include purchasing inventory and transporting it to the desired destination. One way of managing the amount of inventory on hand is to use a **just-in-time** approach. Rather than order large quantities of an inventory item, particularly one that is not in high demand, a company places a purchase order when the item is needed to fulfill a specific customer order. The company is then able to record the receipt and sale of the inventory item at or about the same time. This has the effect of reducing inventory quantities on hand. It also positively affects the inventory liquidity ratios.

DECISION TOOLKIT

Decision Checkpoints	Info Needed for Decision	Tools to Use for Decision	How to Evaluate Results
How long is an item in inventory?	Cost of goods sold; beginning and ending inventory	$$\text{Inventory turnover} = \frac{\text{Cost of goods sold}}{\text{Average inventory}}$$ $$\text{Days in inventory} = \frac{365 \text{ days}}{\text{Inventory turnover}}$$	A higher inventory turnover or lower days in inventory suggests efficiency, and that management is reducing the amount of inventory on hand relative to sales.

BEFORE YOU GO ON...

▶ Do It! Lower of Cost and Net Realizable Value

E-Efficiency Inc. sells three different types of home heating stoves (wood, gas, and pellet). The cost and net realizable value of its inventory of stoves are as follows at March 31, the company's year end:

	Cost	NRV
Wood	$250,000	$280,000
Gas	84,000	79,000
Pellet	112,000	101,000
Total inventory	$446,000	$460,000

(continued)

(a) What amount should E-Efficiency report for its inventory on its statement of financial position? (b) Prepare any journal entry required to record the inventory at its proper value.

Action Plan
- Compare the cost and NRV. Choose the lower value.
- Prepare a journal entry, if required, to adjust cost to net realizable value if it is lower.

Solution

(a)

	Cost	NRV	LCNRV
Wood	$250,000	$280,000	$250,000
Gas	84,000	79,000	79,000
Pellet	112,000	101,000	101,000
Total inventory	$446,000	$460,000	$430,000

E-Efficiency should report its inventory at the lower of cost and net realizable value of $430,000.

(b)

Mar.	31	Cost of Goods Sold ($446,000 – $430,000)	16,000	
		Merchandise Inventory		16,000
		(To record decline in inventory value from original cost of $446,000 to net realizable value of $430,000)		

the navigator

Related Exercise Material: BE6-10, BE6-11, BE6-12, E6-10, E6-11, and E6-12.

APPENDIX 6A—INVENTORY COST DETERMINATION METHODS IN PERIODIC SYSTEM

Both of the inventory cost determination methods—FIFO and average cost—described in the chapter for a perpetual inventory system may be used in a periodic inventory system. To show how to use each of these methods in a periodic system, we will use the data below for The Tee-Shirt Corporation's University Soccer Shirt.

THE TEE-SHIRT CORPORATION					
University Soccer Shirt					
Date		Explanation	Units	Unit Cost	Total Cost
Jan.	1	Beginning inventory	100	$10	$ 1,000
Apr.	15	Purchases	200	11	2,200
Aug.	24	Purchases	300	12	3,600
Nov.	27	Purchases	400	13	5,200
		Total	1,000		$12,000

The details shown above are the same as those shown earlier in the chapter, except that the sales information has been omitted. In the periodic inventory system, we ignore the different dates of each of the sales because we are not recording cost of goods sold at those times. Instead we make the allocation **at the end of a period** and assume that the entire pool of costs is available for allocation at that time.

The Tee-Shirt Corporation had a total of 1,000 units available for sale during the period. The total cost of these units was $12,000. A physical inventory count at the end of the year determined that 450 units remained on hand. Using these amounts, Illustration 6A-1 shows the formula for calculating cost of goods sold that we first learned in Chapter 5.

Beginning Inventory	+	Cost of Goods Purchased	=	Cost of Goods Available for Sale	–	Ending Inventory	=	Cost of Goods Sold
100 units	+	900 units	=	1,000 units	–	450 units	=	550 units
$1,000	+	$11,000	=	$12,000	–	?	=	?

►Illustration 6A-1
Formula for cost of goods sold

If we apply this formula to the unit numbers, we can determine that 550 units must have been sold during the year. The total cost (or "pool of costs") of the 1,000 units available for sale was $12,000. However, we don't know yet how much of the cost of goods available for sale to allocate to ending inventory and to cost of goods sold. We will demonstrate the allocation of this pool of costs using FIFO and average cost in the next sections.

FIRST-IN, FIRST-OUT (FIFO)

The allocation of the cost of goods available for sale at The Tee-Shirt Corporation under FIFO is shown in Illustration 6A-2.

►Illustration 6A-2
Periodic system—FIFO

COST OF GOODS AVAILABLE FOR SALE					
Date		Explanation	Units	Unit Cost	Total Cost
Jan.	1	Beginning inventory	100	$10	$ 1,000
Apr.	15	Purchases	200	11	2,200
Aug.	24	Purchases	300	12	3,600
Nov.	27	Purchases	400	13	5,200
		Total	1,000		$12,000

STEP 1: ENDING INVENTORY				STEP 2: COST OF GOODS SOLD	
Date	Units	Unit Cost	Unit Total		
Nov. 27	400	$13	$5,200	Cost of goods available for sale	$12,000
Aug. 24	50	12	600	Less: Ending inventory	5,800
Total	450		$5,800	Cost of goods sold	$ 6,200

Once we know the number of units in ending inventory, we assume it is composed of the most recent purchases made. In this example, 450 units are on hand and since the last purchase was for 400 units at $13 on November 27, this "layer" of inventory is assumed to be in the ending inventory balance. The remaining 50 units are then assumed to come from the next most recent purchase, which is a layer of units purchased at $12, on August 24.

Once the cost of the ending inventory is determined, the cost of goods sold is calculated by subtracting the ending inventory (the cost of the units not sold) from the cost of all goods available for sale (the pool of costs).

The cost of goods sold can also be separately calculated as shown below by including in that amount the cost of the oldest 550 units. Do this by taking the cost of the oldest layer of inventory costs and adding the costs of subsequent layers purchased in order of purchase date until the total cost of the oldest 550 units is determined. Note that of the 300 units purchased on August 24, only 250 units are assumed to have been sold. This agrees with our calculation of the cost of the ending inventory, where 50 of these units were assumed unsold and thus included in ending inventory.

Helpful Hint
Note the sequencing of the allocation: (1) Calculate ending inventory, and (2) determine cost of goods sold.

Date		Units	Unit Cost	Total Cost of Goods Sold
Jan.	1	100	$10	$1,000
Apr.	15	200	11	2,200
Aug.	24	250	12	3,000
Total		550		$6,200

Because of the potential for calculation errors, we recommend that the cost of goods sold amounts be separately calculated and proven in your assignments. The cost of goods sold and ending inventory totals can then be compared with the cost of goods available for sale to check the accuracy of the calculations. It would be as follows for The Tee-Shirt Corporation: $6,200 + $5,800 = $12,000. You will recall that we also did a similar check of our numbers under the perpetual inventory system.

Although the calculation format may differ, **the results under FIFO in a periodic inventory system are the same as in a perpetual inventory system**. (See Illustration 6-3 where, similarly, the ending inventory is $5,800 and the cost of goods sold is $6,200.) Under both inventory systems, the first costs in are the ones assigned to cost of goods sold and the last costs in are the ones assigned to ending inventory.

AVERAGE COST

When using a periodic system, the weighted average cost is calculated in the same manner that we used for a perpetual inventory system: by dividing the cost of goods available for sale by the units available for sale. However, with a periodic system, because we do not record cost of goods sold for each sale, we only calculate the average cost at the end of a period rather than after each purchase or purchase return, as shown in Illustration 6A-3.

▶Illustration 6A-3
Calculation of weighted average unit cost

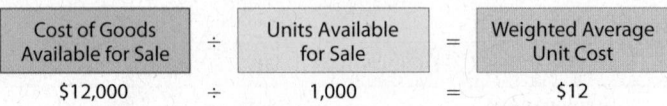

Cost of Goods Available for Sale	÷	Units Available for Sale	=	Weighted Average Unit Cost
$12,000	÷	1,000	=	$12

The weighted average unit cost, $12 in this case, is then applied to the units on hand to determine the cost of the ending inventory. The allocation of the cost of goods available for sale at The Tee-Shirt Corporation using the average cost method is shown in Illustration 6A-4.

▶Illustration 6A-4
Periodic system—Average

COST OF GOODS AVAILABLE FOR SALE				
Date	Explanation	Units	Unit Cost	Total Cost
Jan. 1	Beginning inventory	100	$10	$ 1,000
Apr. 15	Purchases	200	11	2,200
Aug. 24	Purchases	300	12	3,600
Nov. 27	Purchases	400	13	5,200
	Total	1,000		$12,000

STEP 1: ENDING INVENTORY			STEP 2: COST OF GOODS SOLD	
$12,000 ÷ 1,000 = $12			Cost of goods available for sale	$12,000
Units	Unit Cost	Total Cost	Less : Ending inventory	5,400
450	$12	$5,400	Cost of goods sold	$ 6,600

We can verify the cost of goods sold under the average cost method by multiplying the units sold by the weighted average unit cost (550 × $12 = $6,600). And, again, we can prove our calculations by ensuring that the total of the cost of goods sold and ending inventory equals the cost of goods available for sale ($6,600 + $5,400 = $12,000).

The results from applying the average cost method under the periodic inventory system should be compared with Illustration 6-5 shown earlier in the chapter, which presents the results from applying the average cost method under a perpetual inventory system. Notice that under a periodic inventory system, the ending inventory of $5,400 and cost of goods sold of $6,600 are not the same as the values calculated under a perpetual inventory system. This is because in a perpetual system, a new (moving) average is calculated with each purchase or purchase return. In a periodic system, the same weighted average is used to calculate the cost of goods sold for all the units sold during the period.

BEFORE YOU GO ON...

▶ Do It! FIFO and Average Cost—Periodic System

The accounting records of Baker's Dozen Company show the following data:

Apr.	1	Beginning inventory	5,000 units at $3
	12	Purchases	8,000 units at $5
	26	Sales	11,000 units at $9

Determine (a) the cost of goods available for sale, and (b) the cost of goods sold and ending inventory under a periodic inventory system using (1) FIFO, and (2) average cost.

Action Plan

- Ignore the selling price in allocating cost.
- Calculate the number of units available for sale, cost of goods available for sale, and the ending inventory in units.
- Determine the cost of ending inventory first. Calculate cost of goods sold by subtracting ending inventory from the cost of goods available for sale for each cost method.
- Understand the difference between FIFO and average cost.
- Check your work: Prove the cost of goods sold separately and then check that cost of goods sold plus ending inventory equals the cost of goods available for sale.

Solution

(a) Total units available for sale = 5,000 + 8,000 = 13,000
Cost of goods available for sale = (5,000 × $3) + (8,000 × $5) = $55,000
Ending inventory = 5,000 + 8,000 − 11,000 = 2,000 units

(b) (1) FIFO

Ending inventory	Units	Unit Cost	Total Cost
Apr. 30	2,000	$5	$10,000

Cost of goods sold: $55,000 − $10,000 = $45,000

Proof of cost of goods sold:

	Units	Unit Cost	Total Cost
Apr. 1	5,000	$3	$15,000
Apr. 12	6,000	5	30,000
	11,000		$45,000

Check: $45,000 + $10,000 = $55,000

(b) (2) Average Cost

Weighted average unit cost: $55,000 ÷ 13,000 = $4.23
Ending inventory: 2,000 × $4.23 = $8,461.54
Cost of goods sold: $55,000 − $8,461.54 = $46,538.46
Proof of cost of goods sold: 11,000 × $4.23 = $46,538.46
Check: $46,538.46 + $8,461.54 = $55,000

Related Exercise Material: *BE6-13, *BE6-14, *BE6-15, *E6-13, *E6-14, *E6-15, and *E6-16.

comparing
IFRS and ASPE

Key Differences	International Financial Reporting Standards (IFRS)	Accounting Standards for Private Enterprises (ASPE)
No significant differences.		

All About You ▶ Inventory Shrinkage

In this chapter, you learned about determining inventory quantities using a perpetual and periodic inventory tracking system. You also looked at three different cost determination methods. Retailers must control both the quantities and costs of inventory to enable them to generate profit. Profitability will ensure a retailer's continuing long-term viability.

Employee theft, customer theft, inventory counting mistakes, and inventory obsolescence are all issues that have a direct impact on a retailer's profit. It is therefore important that the retailer's accounting information system provide information about the inventory quantities on hand at any point in time, both to identify possible losses and to determine when more inventory needs to be purchased. It is also important that adequate controls be in place to ensure that inventory is appropriately costed and tracked for age and condition. Inventory management system software is being used extensively. The software provides benefits that include providing up-to-date perpetual inventory records, managing inventory gross profit margins by type of product, evaluating inventory turnover by type of product, and evaluating inventory obsolescence. These integrated systems also allow sales staff to respond to customer queries about product availability on a timely basis.

Some Facts

- A Statistics Canada survey on fraud in business found that 57% of retail businesses had experienced some kind of fraud. Of these frauds, 19% were committed by employees and the remainder by non-employees. The most common type of fraud committed by employees was asset misappropriation (theft of company cash, supplies, equipment, and inventory). The most common type of non-employee fraud was return fraud (the return of stolen merchandise or the return of stolen merchandise using counterfeit receipts to obtain a monetary refund).
- Employee theft can be partially prevented by pre-employment screenings. About three in five Canadian retailers perform pre-employment screening. Only 29% of retailers request a police background check.
- Two of the most popular types of inventory stolen are ladieswear and cosmetics, including fragrance. Because this inventory can be of significant value, it is also much more likely to be subject to criminal activity.
- Retailers have put in place several types of controls over their inventory. These include closed-circuit TV, DVR recording systems, observation mirrors over cash registers, security guards who control traffic flow, frequent (weekly, monthly) inventory counts that are reconciled to perpetual accounting records, frequent review of inventory management reports, staff monitoring of change rooms, and alarms on merchandise.
- Monitoring inventory via inventory management system software is the most important way to prevent inventory loss, inventory obsolescence, and damaged product loss. New monitoring technology promises to provide up-to-date information about inventory quantities and costing. The technology will also allow retailers to identify what products are being purchased to help make restocking decisions as well as identify the nature of the customer making the purchase. This same monitoring technology allows customers to access product information using computers in the retail store.[4]

What Do You Think?

Suppose you own a number of specialty boutiques selling mid-level, as well as expensive, locally sourced designer clothing and accessories. You have been experiencing significant losses of accessories at your stores. You suspect that it is a combination of employee and customer theft. Assuming it would be cost-effective, would you install video cameras to monitor both employees and customers?

YES— Most employees and customers are honest. However, some will steal if they are given the opportunity. Management has a responsibility to employ reasonable, cost-effective approaches to safeguard company assets.

NO— The use of video technology to monitor employees and customers sends a message of distrust. You may alienate your employees. Cameras might also reduce the welcoming atmosphere for your customers, who might find them offensive.

Summary of Study Objectives

1. Describe the steps in determining inventory quantities. The steps are (1) taking a physical inventory of goods on hand and (2) determining the ownership of goods in transit, on consignment, and in similar situations.

2. Apply the methods of cost determination using specific identification, FIFO, and average cost under a perpetual inventory system. Costs are allocated to the cost of goods sold account each time that a sale occurs in a perpetual inventory system. The cost is determined by specific identification, or by using the first-in, first-out (FIFO) or average cost methods.

Specific identification is used for goods that are not ordinarily interchangeable. This method tracks the actual physical flow of goods, allocating the exact cost of each merchandise item to cost of goods sold and ending inventory.

The FIFO cost method assumes a first-in, first-out cost flow for sales. Cost of goods sold consists of the cost of the earliest goods purchased. Ending inventory consists of the cost of the most recent goods purchased.

The average cost method is used for goods that are homogeneous or non-distinguishable. Under this method, a new weighted (moving) average unit cost is calculated after each purchase or purchase return and applied to the number of units sold (and as a result, to the number of units remaining in ending inventory).

3. Explain the effects on the financial statements of choosing each of the inventory cost determination methods. Specific identification results in an exact match of costs and revenues on the income statement. When prices are rising, the average cost method results in a higher cost of goods sold and lower profit than FIFO. The average cost method therefore results in a better allocation on the income statement of more current (recent) costs with current revenues than does FIFO. In the statement of financial position, FIFO is considered to be better because it results in an ending inventory that is closest to current (replacement) value. All three methods result in the same cash flow before income tax.

4. Identify the effects of inventory errors on the financial statements. Ignoring the effects of income tax, an error made in determining the quantities and/or cost of inventory at the end of the year will also affect cost of goods sold. If ending inventory is overstated, cost of goods sold will be understated and this in turn will cause profit to be overstated. Therefore, an error that overstates inventory will also overstate profit and after recording closing entries, the overstatement in profit will be reflected as an overstatement in retained earnings. In the following period, the overstatement in inventory will flow into cost of goods sold and overstate cost of goods sold and understate profit, thereby reversing the effect of the prior period error. As long as the cost of inventory at the end of this subsequent period is determined properly, the reversal of the error will mean that both inventory and retained earnings are not misstated at that time.

If an error is made by recording an inventory purchase in a period preceding the actual purchase, both inventory and accounts payable will be overstated; if the purchase has actually occurred but is not recorded or counted, then both inventory and accounts payable will be understated.

5. Demonstrate the presentation and analysis of inventory. Inventory is valued at the lower of its cost and net realizable value, which results in the recording of an increase in cost of goods sold and a reduction in inventory when the net realizable value is less than cost.

Ending inventory is reported as a current asset on the statement of financial position at the lower of cost and net realizable value. Cost of goods sold is reported as an expense on the income statement.

The inventory turnover ratio is a measure of liquidity. It is calculated by dividing the cost of goods sold by average inventory. It can be converted to days in inventory by dividing 365 days by the inventory turnover ratio. In general, a higher inventory turnover and lower days in inventory ratio is desired.

6. Apply the FIFO and average cost inventory cost determination methods under a periodic inventory system (Appendix 6A). Under the FIFO cost method, the cost of the most recent goods purchased is allocated to ending inventory. Cost of goods sold is calculated by deducting ending inventory from the cost of goods available for sale (or proven by applying the cost of the earliest goods on hand to determine the cost of goods sold).

Under the average cost method, the total cost of goods available for sale during the period is divided by the units available for sale during the same period to calculate a weighted average cost per unit. This unit cost is then applied to the number of units remaining in inventory to calculate the ending inventory. Cost of goods sold is calculated by deducting ending inventory from the cost of goods available for sale (or proven by applying the unit cost to the units sold to determine the cost of goods sold).

Each of these cost methods is applied in the same cost flow order as in a perpetual inventory system. The main difference is that in a perpetual inventory system, the cost is determined at the date of each sale, while in a periodic inventory system, the cost is determined only at the end of the period.

Glossary

Average cost method An inventory cost method that assumes that the goods available for sale are homogeneous or non-distinguishable. The cost of goods sold and ending inventory are determined using an average cost, calculated by dividing the cost of the goods available for sale by the units available for sale. (p. 293)

Consigned goods   Goods shipped by a consignor, who retains ownership, to a party called the consignee, who holds the goods for sale. (p. 288)

Days in inventory   A liquidity measure of the average number of days that inventory is held. It is calculated as 365 days divided by the inventory turnover ratio. (p. 306)

First-in, first-out (FIFO) cost method   An inventory cost method that assumes that the costs of the earliest (oldest) goods acquired are the first to be recognized as the cost of goods sold. The costs of the latest goods acquired are assumed to remain in ending inventory. (p. 291)

Internal control   A process designed to help an organization achieve reliable financial reporting, effective and efficient operations, and compliance with relevant laws and regulations. (p. 287)

Inventory turnover   A liquidity measure of the number of times, on average, that inventory is sold during the period. It is calculated by dividing the cost of goods sold by the average

inventory. Average inventory is calculated by adding the beginning and ending inventory balances and dividing the result by two. (p. 306)

Lower of cost and net realizable value (LCNRV)   A basis for stating inventory at the lower of its original cost and its net realizable value at the end of the period. (p. 304)

Net realizable value (NRV)   The selling price of an inventory item, less any costs required to make the item saleable. (p. 304)

Specific identification method   An inventory cost determination method used when goods are distinguishable and not ordinarily interchangeable. It follows the actual physical flow of goods, and individual items are specifically costed to arrive at the cost of goods sold and cost of the ending inventory. (p. 290)

Weighted average unit cost   The average cost of inventory weighted by the number of units purchased at each unit cost. It is calculated as the cost of goods available for sale divided by the number of units available for sale. (p. 293)

DECISION TOOLKIT—A SUMMARY

 Decision Checkpoints	 Info Needed for Decision	 Tools to Use for Decision	 How to Evaluate Results
What is the impact of the choice of inventory cost determination method?	Are prices increasing, or are they decreasing?	Income statement and statement of financial position effects	In periods of rising prices, profit and inventory are higher under FIFO than average cost. FIFO results in the best measure of ending inventory on the statement of financial position. The average cost method provides opposite results—profit and inventory are lower compared with FIFO—but can smooth the impact of changing prices. Specific identification's impact on the financial statements will vary, depending on the actual cost. This method results in the best allocation of costs to revenues on the income statement.
How long is an item in inventory?	Cost of goods sold; beginning and ending inventory	$$\text{Inventory turnover} = \frac{\text{Cost of goods sold}}{\text{Average inventory}}$$ $$\text{Days in inventory} = \frac{365 \text{ days}}{\text{Inventory turnover}}$$	A higher inventory turnover or lower days in inventory suggests efficiency, and that management is reducing the amount of inventory on hand relative to sales.

the navigator

USING THE DECISION TOOLKIT

Under Armour, Inc. specializes in the development, marketing, and distribution of athletic apparel designed to keep athletes cool and dry in any and every athletic activity. Unlike lululemon, which sells primarily through its own stores, Under Armour generates most of its net revenue from product sales through national, regional, independent, and specialty retailers. It is one of lululemon athletica's key competitors in Canada, although it offers a broader range of athletic clothing than lululemon.

Selected financial information for Under Armour, Inc. (in U.S. $ thousands) for three recent fiscal years follows:

	2012	2011	2010
Cost of goods sold	$955,624	$759,848	$533,420
Merchandise inventory	319,286	324,409	215,355
Current assets	903,598	689,663	555,850
Current liabilities	252,228	183,607	149,147

Selected industry ratios:

	2012	2011
Inventory turnover	4.6 times	4.0 times
Days in inventory	79 days	91 days
Current ratio	2.0:1	2.1:1

Instructions

(a) Under Armour uses FIFO. Assume prices have risen over the last two years. If Under Armour used the average cost method instead of FIFO, would its cost of goods sold and its inventory values be higher or lower than currently reported?

(b) Do each of the following:
1. Calculate the inventory turnover and days in inventory for 2012 and 2011.
2. Calculate the current ratio for each of 2012 and 2011.
3. Evaluate Under Armour, Inc.'s inventory management and overall liquidity over the most recent two years and in comparison with its industry.

Solution

(a) If Under Armour used the average cost method rather than FIFO during a period of rising prices, its cost of goods sold would be higher and its inventory lower than currently reported.

(b) (in U.S. $ thousands)

1.

	2012	2011
Inventory turnover	$\dfrac{\$955,624}{(\$319,286 + \$324,409) \div 2} = 3.0$ times	$\dfrac{\$759,848}{(\$324,409 + \$215,355) \div 2} = 2.8$ times
Days in inventory	$\dfrac{365 \text{ days}}{3.0 \text{ times}} = 122$ days	$\dfrac{365 \text{ days}}{2.8 \text{ times}} = 130$ days

2.

	2012	2011
Current ratio	$\$903,598 \div \$252,228 = 3.6{:}1$	$\$689,663 \div \$183,607 = 3.8{:}1$

3. Under Armour's inventory turnover shows a slight improvement between 2011 and 2012. Consequently, the number of days in inventory decreased by 8 days. The company's inventory turnover, however, is much lower than the industry average and this is why its days in inventory is much higher than the average. This may be due to the fact that Under Armour sells most of its inventory to retailers rather than directly to consumers and has to have higher levels of inventory on hand to meet their needs. The current ratio is quite strong compared with the industry average.

the navigator

Comprehensive Do It!

Englehart Ltd. uses a perpetual inventory system. The company has the following inventory data available for the month of March:

Date	Explanation	Units	Unit Cost/Price	Total Cost
Mar. 1	Beginning inventory	200	$4.30	$ 860
10	Purchases	500	4.50	2,250
15	Sales	(500)	9.00	
20	Purchases	400	4.75	1,900
25	Sales	(400)	9.00	
30	Purchase	300	5.00	1,500
		500		$6,510

Instructions

Determine the cost of goods sold for March and the cost of the ending inventory at March 31 using (a) FIFO and (b) average cost. (For average, use unrounded numbers in your calculations but round to the nearest cent for presentation purposes in your answer.)

Action Plan

- In a perpetual system, cost of goods sold is determined at the date of each sale. Inventory records maintain running balances of the ending inventory on hand.
- For FIFO, allocate the first costs to the cost of goods sold at each sale date.
- For average cost, calculate the weighted average unit cost (the cost of goods available for sale ÷ the number of units available for sale) after each purchase. Multiply the unit cost by the number of units sold to determine the cost of goods sold.
- Check your work: Prove that the cost of goods sold plus the ending inventory equals the cost of goods available for sale.

Solution to Comprehensive Do It!
(a) FIFO

Date	Purchases			Cost of Goods Sold			Balance		
	Units	Cost	Total	Units	Cost	Total	Units	Cost	Total
Mar. 1							200	$4.30	$ 860
10	500	$4.50	$2,250				200	4.30	} 3,110
							500	4.50	
15				200	$4.30	} $2,210	200	4.50	900
				300	4.50				
20	400	4.75	1,900				200	4.50	} 2,800
							400	4.75	
25				200	4.50	} 1,850	200	4.75	950
				200	4.75				
30	300	5.00	1,500				200	4.75	} 2,450
							300	5.00	
	1,200		$5,650	900		$4,060			

Check: $4,060 + $2,450 = $6,510 ($860 + $5,650)

(b) Average Cost

Date	Purchases			Cost of Goods Sold			Balance		
	Units	Cost	Total	Units	Cost	Total	Units	Cost	Total
Mar. 1							200	$4.30	$ 860.00
10	500	$4.50	$2,250.00				700	4.44	3,110.00
15				500	$4.44	$2,221.43	200	4.44	888.57
20	400	4.75	1,900.00				600	4.65	2,788.57
25				400	4.65	1,859.05	200	4.65	929.52
30	300	5.00	1,500.00				500	4.86	2,429.52
	1,200		$5,650.00	900		$4,080.48			

Check: $4,080.48 + $2,429.52 = $6,510 ($860 + $5,650)

WileyPLUS **Self-Test, Brief Exercises, Exercises, Problems: Set A, and many more components are available for practice in *WileyPLUS*.**

Note: All questions, exercises, and problems below with an asterisk (*) relate to material in Appendix 6A.

Self-Test Questions

Quiz Yourself

Answers are at the end of the chapter.

(SO 1) 1. A physical inventory count is normally taken:
(a) in a periodic inventory system.
(b) in a perpetual inventory system.
(c) at the end of the company's fiscal year.
(d) All of the above.

(SO 1) 2. As a result of a physical inventory count, Railway Ltd. determined that it had inventory of $120,000 on hand at December 31. This count did not take into consideration the following: (1) Rogers Consignment Inc. currently has goods costing $24,000 on its sales floor that belong to Railway but are being sold on consignment by Rogers. The selling price of these goods is $34,500. (2) Railway purchased $10,000 of goods that were shipped on December 27, FOB shipping point, and that are expected to be received by Railway on January 3. What is the correct amount of inventory that Railway should report on December 31?
(a) $120,000
(b) $130,000
(c) $144,000
(d) $154,000

(SO 2) 3. The specific identification method should only be used if the inventory consists of:
(a) homogeneous, nondistinguishable goods.
(b) non-interchangeable, distinguishable goods.
(c) high-priced, low-volume goods.
(d) low-priced, high-volume goods.

(SO 2) 4. Madoc Inc. uses a perpetual inventory system and has the following beginning inventory, purchases, and sales in March:

		Units	Unit Cost	Total Cost
March 1	Beginning inventory	10,000	$ 9	$ 90,000
9	Purchases	12,000	10	120,000
12	Sales	(20,000)		
18	Purchases	7,000	11	77,000

What is the weighted average cost per unit after the last purchase on March 18? (Round the average unit cost to the nearest cent.)
(a) $9.55
(b) $9.90
(c) $10.00
(d) $10.67

(SO 2) 5. Based on the data in question 4, what is the cost of goods sold using the FIFO cost method for the month of March?
(a) $95,000
(b) $97,000
(c) $190,000
(d) $192,000

(SO 3) 6. In periods of declining prices, the average cost method will result in:
(a) a gross profit that is higher than FIFO.
(b) a gross profit that is lower than FIFO.
(c) the same gross profit as FIFO.
(d) a negative gross profit.

(SO 4) 7. Lavigne Ltd. purchased $12,500 of inventory on credit from Mouton Ltée. Mouton shipped the inventory on December 21, 2014, FOB shipping point. Lavigne did not record the purchase until January 2015, when the inventory was received. What are the effects of this error on the 2014 inventory balance and the 2014 accounts payable balance?
(a) An understatement and an overstatement
(b) An overstatement and an understatement
(c) An overstatement and an overstatement
(d) An understatement and an understatement

(SO 4) 8. On December 31, 2014, Hall Corporation over-stated its inventory by $15,000 when performing the inventory count. No errors were made one year later when inventory was counted. What is the effect on Hall's shareholders' equity at December 31, 2014, and December 31, 2015?
(a) Overstated at December 31, 2014, and under-stated at December 31, 2015
(b) Overstated at December 31, 2014, and prop-erly stated at December 31, 2015
(c) Understated at December 31, 2014, and understated at December 31, 2015
(d) Under at December 31, 2014, and properly stated at December 31, 2015

(SO 5) 9. Avonlea Corp. had inventory at a cost of $5,000 and a net realizable value of $4,750 at the end of 2014. At the end of 2015, it had inventory at a cost of $6,000 and a net realizable value of $6,500. The amounts that should be reported for inventory at the end of 2014 and 2015, respec-tively, are:

(a) $5,000 and $6,000.
(b) $5,000 and $6,500.
(c) $4,750 and $6,000.
(d) $4,750 and $6,500.

(SO 5) 10. If a company's cost of goods sold is $120,000, its beginning inventory is $15,000, and its end-ing inventory is $25,000, what are its inventory turnover and days in inventory?
(a) 0.2 times and 1,825 days
(b) 4.8 times and 76 days
(c) 6 times and 61 days
(d) 8 times and 46 days

(SO 6) *11. Kam Ltd. has the following units and costs, and uses a periodic inventory system:

			Units	Unit Cost	Total Cost
Jan.	1	Beginning inventory	8,000	$11	$ 88,000
June	19	Purchases	13,000	12	156,000
Nov.	9	Purchases	5,000	13	65,000
			26,000		$309,000

If 9,000 units are on hand at December 31, what is the cost of the ending inventory using FIFO?
(a) $100,000
(b) $113,000
(c) $196,000
(d) $209,000

(SO 6) *12. Based on the data in question 11, what is the cost of goods sold (rounded to the nearest thousand dollars) using the average cost method?
(a) $105,000
(b) $107,000
(c) $202,000
(d) $204,000

Questions

(SO 1) 1. Your friend Tom Wetzel has been hired to help take the physical inventory in Kikujiro's Hardware Store. Explain to Tom how to do this job, giving him specific instructions for determining the inventory quantities that Kikujiro's has legal title over.

(SO 1) 2. What is internal control? How does it apply to taking a physical inventory count?

(SO 1) 3. Janine Ltd. ships merchandise to Fastrak Corporation on December 30. The merchandise reaches Fastrak on January 5. Indicate the terms of sale (FOB shipping point or FOB destination) that will result in the goods being included in (a) Janine's December 31 inventory and (b) Fastrak's December 31 inventory.

(SO 1) 4. Explain whether each of the following should be included in the inventory of Kingsway Inc.: (a) consigned goods held by a craft shop for sale on Kingsway's behalf, (b) goods taken home on approval by a Kingsway customer, and (c) goods sold but held for alteration by Kingsway.

(SO 2) 5. Distinguish between the three methods of deter-mining cost for inventories: specific identification,

FIFO, and average cost. Give an example of a type of inventory for which each method might be used.

(SO 2) 6. Which of the three inventory cost determina-tion methods assumes that goods available for sale are identical? Which assumes that the first goods purchased are the first to be sold? Which matches the actual physical flow of merchandise?

(SO 2) 7. Explain why a new weighted average unit cost must be calculated after each purchase when using the average cost method in a perpetual inventory system but not after each sale.

(SO 3) 8. What are the guidelines that a company should consider when choosing among the three meth-ods of determining cost for inventories: specific identification, FIFO, and average cost?

(SO 3) 9. Which inventory cost method—FIFO or average cost—provides the better measure of cost of goods sold on the income statement? The better measure of ending inventory on the statement of financial position? Explain.

(SO 3) 10. Compare the financial effects (ignore income tax) of using the FIFO and average inventory cost methods during a period of declining prices on (a) cash (pre-tax), (b) ending inventory, (c) cost of goods sold, (d) profit, and (e) retained earnings.

(SO 4)   11. If an error in counting ending inventory in one year will have the reverse effect in the following year, will this error need to be corrected when it is discovered? Explain.

(SO 4)   12. Mila Ltd.'s ending inventory at December 31, 2014, was understated by $5,000. Assuming that this error is not detected, what effect will it have on (a) 2014 profit before income tax, (b) 2014 retained earnings, (c) 2014 total shareholders' equity, (d) 2015 profit before income tax, (e) 2015 retained earnings, and (f) 2015 total shareholders' equity?

(SO 4)   13. Shediac Inc. purchased inventory from Bathurst Corp. four days prior to Shediac's year end. Bathurst shipped the goods to Shediac FOB destination two days before year end but Shediac did not receive the goods until the following year. The inventory clerk recorded the purchase of the inventory on credit prior to the year-end inventory count by debiting inventory and crediting accounts payable. Shediac performs a physical inventory count each year-end and makes any required adjustments. What overall effect will this error have on the components of the accounting equation—assets, liabilities, and shareholders' equity—at Shediac's year end (a) prior to any adjustment for the inventory count results, and (b) after any adjustment?

(SO 5)   14. Explain the meaning of (a) cost and (b) net realizable value, and explain (c) when the lower of cost and net realizable value rule should be used to value inventory.

(SO 5)   15. Why is the Cost of Goods Sold account debited in the journal entry to record a decline in

inventory value under the lower of cost and net realizable value rule even though no merchandise has been sold?

(SO 5)   16. Would an increase in the days in inventory ratio from one year to the next be viewed as an improvement or a deterioration in how efficiently a company manages its inventory?

(SO 5)   17. What are the consequences for a company when its inventory turnover ratio is (a) too high and (b) too low?

(SO 2, 6)*18. Your classmate does not understand the difference between the perpetual and periodic inventory systems. "The same cost methods are used in both systems," he says, "and a physical inventory count is required in both systems. So what's the difference?" Explain to your confused classmate how the perpetual and periodic inventory systems differ.

(SO 6)   *19. In a periodic inventory system, the ending inventory is counted and costed. This number is then used to calculate cost of goods sold. Emad asks, "Why can't you determine the cost of goods sold first instead of going through all of these steps?" Explain this to Emad.

(SO 2, 6)*20. Explain why, when a company uses FIFO with a periodic inventory system, the cost of goods sold and ending inventory costs are the same as they would be had FIFO been used with a perpetual system.

(SO 2, 6)*21. Explain why, when a company uses average cost method with a periodic inventory system, the cost of goods sold and ending inventory costs are different from the amounts calculated when using the average cost method with a perpetual inventory system.

Brief Exercises

BE6–1   Helgeson Inc. identifies the following items as possibly belonging in its physical inventory count. For each item, indicate whether or not it should be included in the inventory.
(a) Goods shipped on consignment by Helgeson to another company
(b) Goods held on consignment by Helgeson from another company
(c) Goods in transit to a customer, shipped FOB shipping point
(d) Goods in transit to Helgeson from a supplier, shipped FOB destination
(e) Goods in transit to a customer, shipped FOB destination
(f) Goods in transit to Helgeson from a supplier shipped FOB shipping point

Identify items in inventory.
(SO 1)

BE6–2   The Village Hat Shop Limited counted the entire inventory in its store on August 31 and arrived at a total inventory cost of $66,000. The count included $6,000 of inventory held on consignment for a local designer; $500 of inventory that was being held for customers who were deciding if they actually wanted to purchase the merchandise; and $1,000 of inventory that had been sold to customers but was being held for alterations. There were two shipments of inventory received on September 1. The first shipment cost $5,000. It had been shipped on August 29, terms FOB destination. The second shipment cost $3,750, plus freight charges of $250. It had been shipped on August 28, terms FOB shipping point. Neither of these shipments was included in the August 31 count. Calculate the correct cost of the inventory on August 31.

Calculate inventory cost.
(SO 1)

BE6–3   On January 3, Piano Corp. purchased three portable electronic keyboards for $600 each. On January 20, it purchased two more of the same model keyboards for $475 each. During the month, it sold two keyboards; one was purchased on January 3 and the other was purchased on January 20. (a) Calculate the cost of goods sold and ending inventory for the month using specific identification. (b) Explain how management could manipulate profit, if it wished to, using this method.

Apply specific identification.
(SO 2)

Apply perpetual FIFO.
(SO 2)

BE6–4   Akshay Limited uses the FIFO cost method in a perpetual inventory system. Fill in the missing amounts for items [1] to [18] in the following perpetual inventory schedule:

Date		Purchases			Cost of Goods Sold			Balance		
		Units	Cost	Total	Units	Cost	Total	Units	Cost	Total
Apr.	1							15	$18	$270
	6	30	[1]	$450				[2]	[3]	
								[4]	[5]	[6]
	9				15	[7]				
					10	[8]	[9]	[10]	[11]	[12]
	14	[13]	12	144				[14]	[15]	
								[16]	[17]	[18]

Apply perpetual average cost.
(SO 2)

BE6–5   Akshay Limited uses the average cost method in a perpetual inventory system. Fill in the missing amounts for items [1] to [13] in the following perpetual inventory schedule. (Use unrounded numbers in your calculations but round to the nearest cent for presentation purposes in your answer.)

Date		Purchases			Cost of Goods Sold			Balance		
		Units	Cost	Total	Units	Cost	Total	Units	Cost	Total
Apr.	1							15	$18	$270
	6	30	[1]	$450				[2]	[4]	[3]
	9				25	[5]	[6]	[7]	[9]	[8]
	14	[10]	12	144				[11]	[13]	[12]

Apply perpetual FIFO and average cost.
(SO 2)

BE6–6   Battery Limited uses a perpetual inventory system. The inventory records show the following data for its first month of operations:

Date		Explanation	Units	Unit Cost	Total Cost	Balance in Units
Aug.	2	Purchases	250	$7	$1,750	250
	3	Purchases	500	10	5,000	750
	10	Sales	(300)			450
	15	Purchases	900	12	10,800	1,350
	25	Sales	(325)			1,025

Calculate the cost of goods sold and ending inventory using (a) FIFO and (b) average cost. (For average, use unrounded numbers in your calculations but round to the nearest cent for presentation purposes in your answer.)

Discuss different cost methods.
(SO 3)

BE6–7   Interactive.com just started business and is trying to decide which inventory cost method—FIFO or average cost—to use. Assuming prices are falling, as they often do in the information technology sector, answer the following questions for Interactive.com:
(a) Which method will result in having higher ending inventory? Will this method also result in an ending inventory value that is closer to replacement cost? Explain.
(b) Which method will result in the higher cost of goods sold? Will this method also result in the most current cost of goods sold matched against revenue? Explain.
(c) What guidelines are important for Interactive.com to consider as it tries to select the most appropriate inventory cost method?

Determine effect of inventory error.
(SO 4)

BE6–8   DuPlessis Corporation incorrectly recorded $25,000 of goods held on consignment for another company as a purchase during the year ended December 31, 2015. The physical inventory count, which included the consigned goods, agreed with the perpetual inventory accounting records at year end. What effect, if any, will this error have on total assets, liabilities, and shareholders' equity at December 31, 2015, assuming the error is not detected before year end?

Determine effect of inventory error for two years.
(SO 4)

BE6–9   In its year-end physical inventory count, Tire Track Corporation forgot to count tires it had stored outside its warehouse in a trailer. As a result, ending inventory was understated by $7,000. Assuming that this error was not subsequently discovered and corrected, what is the impact of this error on assets, liabilities, and shareholders' equity at the end of the current year? At the end of the next year?

Determine LCNRV valuation.
(SO 5)

BE6–10   Hawkeye Video Centre Ltd. accumulates the following cost and net realizable value data at December 31:

Inventory Categories	Cost	NRV
High definition camcorders	$11,000	$10,200
Cameras	9,000	9,500
DVD players	14,000	12,800

(a) Calculate the lower of cost and net realizable value for Hawkeye's inventory.
(b) Prepare the entry needed to adjust Hawkeye's inventory value to the lower of cost or net realizable value at December 31.

BE6–11 The cost of Piper Music Inc.'s inventory at December 31, 2014, is $54,700. Its net realizable value on the same date is $52,500. (a) Prepare the adjusting journal entry required, if any, to record the decline in value of the inventory, assuming Piper Music uses a perpetual inventory system. (b) If Piper Music has the same inventory on hand at December 31, 2015, with a net realizable value of $55,000, what amount should it report its inventory at on that date?

Record LCNRV valuation.
(SO 5)

BE6–12 The following information is available for **Canadian Tire Corporation**:

	2012	2011	2010
Inventory	$ 1,503	$ 1,449	$ 933
Net sales	11,427	10,387	9,213
Cost of goods sold	7,929	7,326	6,422

Calculate inventory turnover and days in inventory.
(SO 5)

(a) Calculate the inventory turnover and days in inventory ratios for 2012 and 2011. (b) Did Canadian Tire's inventory management improve or deteriorate in 2012?

*****BE6–13** In its first month of operations, Queensland Inc. made three purchases of merchandise in the following sequence: (1) 370 units @ $9 each, (2) 700 units @ $12 each, and (3) 800 units @ $11 each. A physical inventory count determined that there were 600 units on hand at the end of the month. Assuming Queensland uses a periodic inventory system, calculate the cost of the ending inventory and cost of goods sold using (a) FIFO and (b) average cost. (For average, use unrounded numbers in your calculations but round to the nearest cent for presentation purposes in your answer.)

Apply periodic FIFO and average cost.
(SO 6)

*****BE6–14** G-Mac Corporation reports the following inventory data for the month of January:

Apply periodic FIFO.
(SO 2, 6)

Date		Explanation	Units	Unit Cost	Total Cost
Jan	1	Beginning inventory	15	$4.50	$ 67.50
	15	Purchases	18	5.00	90.00
	27	Purchases	13	4.50	58.50
			46		$216.00

A physical inventory count determined that there were 15 units on hand at the end of January.
(a) Calculate the cost of the ending inventory and cost of goods sold under FIFO, assuming G-Mac uses a periodic inventory system. (Round your answers to the nearest cent.)
(b) Would your answers to part (a) differ if G-Mac used a perpetual inventory system? Explain.
(c) Five of the 15 units on hand that were purchased on January 15, were damaged and had no resale value. Prepare the entry to reflect the damaged inventory under FIFO and a periodic inventory system.

*****BE6–15** At the beginning of the year, Seller Ltd. had 700 units with a cost of $4 per unit in its beginning inventory. The following inventory transactions occurred during the month of January:

Record transactions under perpetual and periodic FIFO.
(SO 2, 6)

Jan. 3 Sold 500 units on account for $6 each.
9 Purchased 1,000 units on account for $4 per unit.
15 Sold 800 units for cash at $8 each.

Prepare journal entries assuming that Seller Ltd. uses FIFO (a) under a perpetual inventory system and (b) under a periodic inventory system.

Exercises

E6–1 Shippers Ltd. had the following inventory situations to consider at January 31, its year end:

Identify items in inventory.
(SO 1)

1. Goods held on consignment for Boxes Unlimited since December 22
2. Goods shipped on consignment to Rinehart Holdings Ltd. on January 5
3. Goods that are still in transit and were shipped to a customer FOB destination on January 29
4. Freight costs due on goods in transit from item 3 above
5. Goods that are still in transit and were shipped to a customer FOB shipping point on January 29
6. Goods that are still in transit and were purchased FOB destination from a supplier on January 25
7. Goods that are still in transit and were purchased FOB shipping point from a supplier on January 25

Instructions

Identify which of the above items should be included in inventory. If an item should not be included in inventory, state where it should be recorded.

Determine correct
inventory amount.
(SO 1)

E6–2   Gatineau Bank is considering giving Novotna Corporation a short-term bank loan. Before doing so, it decides that further discussions with Novotna's accountant may be desirable. One area of particular concern is the inventory account, which according to a recent physical inventory count has a balance of $285,000 at December 31. This count agreed with the accounting records. Discussions with the accountant reveal the following:

1. Novotna sold goods costing $35,000 to India-based Moghul Company, FOB destination, on December 28. The goods are not expected to arrive in India until January 12. The goods were not included in the physical inventory count, because they were not in the warehouse.
2. The physical inventory count did not include goods costing $95,000 that were shipped to Novotna, FOB shipping point, on December 27 and were still in transit at year end.
3. Novotna received goods costing $28,000 on January 2. The goods were shipped FOB shipping point on December 26 by Cellar Corp. The goods were not included in the physical inventory count.
4. Novotna sold goods costing $49,000 to United Kingdom–based Sterling of Britain Ltd., FOB shipping point, on December 30. The goods were received by Sterling on January 8. They were not included in Novotna's physical inventory count.
5. On December 31, Schiller Corporation had $30,500 of goods held on consignment for Novotna. The goods were not included in the physical inventory count.
6. Included in the physical inventory count were $15,000 of parts for outdated products that the company had not been able to sell. It is unlikely that these obsolete parts will have any other use.

Instructions

(a) Determine the correct inventory amount on December 31.
(b) Explain why having an accurate inventory count is important to the bank in assessing whether to give Novotna a short-term bank loan or not.

Answer questions about
specific identification.
(SO 2, 3)

E6–3   On February 28, Discount Electronics Ltd. has three home entertainment systems left in stock. The purchase dates, serial numbers, and cost of each of the three systems are as follows:

Date		Serial Number	Cost
Jan.	2	#1012	$800
Feb.	1	#1045	740
	28	#1056	680

All three systems are priced to sell at $1,300. By March 31, two systems had been sold and one system remained in inventory.

Instructions

(a) Explain how Discount Electronics would use specific identification to determine the cost of goods sold and the cost of the ending inventory.
(b) Explain how Discount Electronics could manipulate its profit using specific identification by "selectively choosing" which home entertainment system to sell to the two customers in the month of March. What would Discount Electronics' cost of goods sold and gross profit be if the company wished to minimize profit? To maximize profit? Ignore income tax.
(c) What guidelines should Discount Electronics consider when deciding whether to use specific identification or one of the other cost methods to determine the cost of its inventory?

Apply perpetual FIFO.
(SO 2)

E6–4   Ohsweken Outdoor Stores Inc. uses a perpetual inventory system and has a beginning inventory, as at April 1, of 150 tents. This consists of 50 tents at a cost of $210 each and 100 tents at a cost of $225 each. During April, the company had the following purchases and sales of tents:

Date	Purchases		Sales	
	Units	Unit Cost	Units	Unit Price
Apr. 3			75	$400
10	200	$275		
17			250	400
24	300	290		
30			200	400

Instructions

(a) Determine the cost of goods sold and the cost of the ending inventory using FIFO.
(b) Calculate Ohsweken Outdoors's gross profit and gross profit margin for the month of April.
(c) Is the gross profit determined in part (b) higher or lower than it would be if Ohsweken Outdoors had used the average cost method? Explain.

E6–5 Basis Furniture Ltd. uses a perpetual inventory system and has a beginning inventory, as at June 1, of 500 bookcases at a cost of $125 each. During June, the company had the following purchases and sales of bookcases:

Apply perpetual average cost.
(SO 2)

		Purchases		Sales	
Date	Units	Unit Cost	Units	Unit Price	
June 6	1,200	$127			
10			1,000	$200	
14	1,800	128			
16			1,600	205	
26	1,000	129			

Instructions

(a) Determine the cost of goods sold and the cost of the ending inventory using the average cost method. (Use unrounded numbers in your calculations but round to the nearest cent for presentation purposes in your answer.)

(b) Calculate Basis Furniture's gross profit and gross profit margin for the month of June.

(c) Is the gross profit determined in part (b) higher or lower than it would be if Basis Furniture had used FIFO? Explain.

E6–6 Lakshmi Ltd. uses the perpetual inventory system and reports the following inventory transactions for the month of June:

Apply perpetual FIFO and average cost; compare effects.
(SO 2, 3)

Date	Explanation	Units	Unit Cost	Total Cost
June 1	Beginning inventory	150	$5	$ 750
12	Purchases	230	6	1,380
15	Sale	(250)		
16	Purchases	450	7	3,150
23	Purchases	150	8	1,200
27	Sales	(570)		

Instructions

(a) Determine the cost of goods sold and the cost of the ending inventory using (1) FIFO and (2) average cost. Ignore the effect of income tax. (For average, use unrounded numbers in your calculations but round to the nearest cent for presentation purposes in your answer.)

(b) Which cost method results in the higher cost of goods sold? Why?

(c) Which cost method results in the higher profit? Why?

(d) Which cost method results in the higher ending inventory? Why?

(e) Which cost method results in the higher cash flow? Why?

E6–7 Glenmount Inc. is trying to determine whether to use the FIFO or average cost method. The accounting records show the following selected inventory information:

Apply perpetual FIFO and average cost; compare effects.
(SO 2, 3)

	Purchases			Cost of Goods Sold			Balance		
Date	Units	Cost	Total	Units	Cost	Total	Units	Cost	Total
Oct. 2	9,000	$12	$108,000						
15	15,000	14	210,000						
29				22,000					

The company accountant has prepared the following partial income statement to help management understand the financial statement impact of each cost determination method.

	FIFO	Average Cost
Sales	$525,000	$525,000
Cost of goods sold	_____	_____
Gross profit	_____	_____
Operating expenses	200,000	200,000
Profit before income tax	_____	_____
Income tax expense (30%)	_____	_____
Profit	_____	_____

Instructions

(a) Complete the perpetual inventory schedule shown above, assuming the use of the FIFO cost method.

(b) Complete the perpetual inventory schedule shown above, assuming the use of the average cost method. (Use unrounded numbers in your calculations but round to the nearest cent for presentation purposes in your answer.)

(c) Fill in the missing information in the blanks shown in the income statements above.

(d) Explain whether the comparative profits of each cost method determined in part (c) will be expected to increase, decrease, or not change if (1) costs fall, and (2) costs remain stable.

Determine effects of inventory errors for two years
(SO 4)

E6–8   Seles Hardware Limited reported the following amounts for its cost of goods sold and merchandise inventory:

	2015	2014
Cost of goods sold	$168,000	$154,000
Ending inventory	37,000	30,000

Seles made two errors: (1) ending inventory for 2015 was overstated by $2,000 and (2) ending inventory for 2014 was understated by $4,000.

Instructions

(a) Calculate the correct ending inventory and cost of goods sold amounts for each year.

(b) Describe the impact of the error on (1) cost of goods sold, (2) profit before income tax, (3) assets, (4) liabilities, and (5) total shareholders' equity for each of the two years.

(c) Explain why it is important that Seles Hardware correct these errors as soon as they are discovered.

Correct partial income statements and calculate gross profit.
(SO 4)

E6–9   Aruba Inc. reported the following partial income statement data for the years ended December 31, 2015, and 2014:

	2015	2014
Sales	$265,000	$250,000
Cost of goods sold	205,000	194,000
Gross profit	60,000	56,000

Merchandise inventory was reported in the current financial position at $44,000, $52,000, and $49,000 at the end of 2013, 2014, and 2015, respectively. The ending inventory amounts for 2013 and 2015 are correct. However, the ending inventory at December 31, 2014, is understated by $8,000.

Instructions

(a) Prepare correct income statements for 2014 and 2015 through to gross profit.

(b) What is the cumulative effect of the inventory error on total gross profit for these two years?

(c) Calculate the gross profit margin for each of these two years, before and after the correction.

Record LCNRV valuation.
(SO 5)

E6–10   Calabogie Camera Shop Ltd. reports the following cost and net realizable value information for its inventory at December 31:

	Units	Unit Cost	Unit NRV
Cameras:			
Sony	4	$175	$160
Canon	8	150	152
Light Meters:			
Gossen	12	135	139
Seconic	10	115	110

Instructions

(a) Determine the lower of cost and net realizable value of the ending inventory.

(b) Prepare the adjusting journal entry required, if any, to record the lower of cost and net realizable value of the inventory assuming Calabogie Camera Shop uses a perpetual inventory system.

(c) A physical inventory count at December 31 found that two of the Canon cameras were badly damaged. It was determined they had no resale value. Prepare the adjusting entry required, if any, to record the damaged cameras.

Calculate inventory turnover, days in inventory, and gross profit margin.
(SO 5)

E6–11   The following information is available for **Gildan Activewear Inc.**, headquartered in Montreal, for three recent fiscal years (in U.S. $ thousands):

	2012	2011	2010
Inventory	$ 553,068	$ 568,311	$ 332,542
Net sales	1,948,253	1,725,712	1,311,463
Cost of goods sold	1,552,128	1,288,106	947,206

Instructions

(a) Calculate the inventory turnover, days in inventory, and gross profit margin for 2012 and 2011.

(b) Based on the ratios calculated in part (a), did Gildan's liquidity and profitability improve or deteriorate in 2012?

E6–12 The following comparative cost information is available for Kingswood Limited:

Determine effect of cost methods on liquidity. (SO 3, 5)

	Average Inventory	Cost of Goods Sold
FIFO	$222,500	$750,000
Average cost	227,500	735,000

Kingswood's current assets are $450,000, exclusive of inventory. Its current liabilities are $350,000.

Instructions
(a) Calculate Kingswood's inventory turnover ratio assuming (1) FIFO and (2) average cost is used to determine the cost of the ending inventory.
(b) Calculate Kingswood's current ratio assuming (1) FIFO and (2) average cost is used to determine the cost of the ending inventory.
(c) Does one cost method result in better measure of liquidity than the other for Kingswood? Explain.

*E6–13 Mawmey Inc. uses a periodic inventory system. Its records show the following for the month of May, with 15 units on hand at May 31:

Apply periodic FIFO and average cost. (SO 6)

Date		Explanation	Units	Unit Cost	Total Cost
May	1	Beginning inventory	30	$10	$300
	12	Purchases	50	12	600
	14	Purchases	20	15	300
		Total			

Instructions
Determine the cost of the ending inventory and cost of goods sold using (a) FIFO and (b) average cost. (For average, use unrounded numbers in your calculations but round to the nearest cent for presentation purposes in your answer.)

*E6–14 Lakshmi Ltd. reports the following inventory transactions in a periodic inventory system for the month of June. A physical inventory count determined that 225 units were on hand at the end of the month.

Apply periodic FIFO and average cost. (SO 6)

Date		Explanation	Units	Unit Cost	Total Cost
June	1	Beginning inventory	150	$5	$ 750
	12	Purchases	230	6	1,380
	16	Purchases	450	7	3,150
	23	Purchases	150	8	1,200

Instructions
(a) Determine the cost of the ending inventory and cost of goods sold using (1) FIFO and (2) average cost. (For average, use unrounded numbers in your calculations but round to the nearest cent for presentation purposes in your answer.)
(b) For item 2 of part (a), explain why the average unit cost is not $6.50 [($5 + $6 + $7 + $8) ÷ 4].
(c) By how much do the results for part (a) differ from E6–6, where the same information was used in a perpetual inventory system? Why?

*E6–15 Powder, Inc. sells an Xpert snowboard that is popular with snowboard enthusiasts. The following information shows Powder's purchases and sales of Xpert snowboards during November:

Apply perpetual and periodic FIFO and average cost. (SO 2, 6)

Date		Transaction	Units	Unit Cost	Unit Sales Price
Nov.	1	Beginning inventory	30	$295	
	5	Purchases	25	300	
	12	Sales	(42)		$460
	19	Purchases	40	305	
	22	Sales	(50)		470
	25	Purchases	30	310	
			33		

Instructions
(a) Determine the cost of goods sold and ending inventory using (1) FIFO and (2) average cost, assuming Powder uses a perpetual inventory system. (For average, use unrounded numbers in your calculations but round to the nearest cent for presentation purposes in your answer.)
(b) Determine the cost of goods sold and ending inventory using (1) FIFO and (2) average cost, assuming Powder uses a periodic inventory system. (For average, use unrounded numbers in your calculations but round to the nearest cent for presentation purposes in your answer.)

Record transactions in perpetual and periodic inventory systems.
(SO 2, 6)

*E6–16 Refer to the data provided for Powder, Inc. in E6–15.

Instructions

(a) Prepare journal entries to record purchases and sales for Powder in a perpetual inventory system using (1) FIFO and (2) average cost.

(b) Prepare journal entries to record purchases and sales for Powder in a periodic inventory system using (1) FIFO and (2) average cost.

Problems: Set A

Identify items in inventory.
(SO 1)

P6–1A Kananaskis Limited is trying to determine the amount of its ending inventory as at February 28, the company's year end. The accountant counted everything in the warehouse in early March, which resulted in an ending inventory amount of $150,000. However, the accountant was not sure how to treat the following transactions, so he did not include them in the count. He has asked for your help in determining whether or not the following transactions should be included in inventory:

1. Feb. 1 Kananaskis shipped $1,800 of inventory on consignment to Banff Corporation. By February 28, Banff had sold half of this inventory for Kananaskis.

2. 15 Kananaskis received $800 of inventory on consignment from Craft Producers Ltd. By February 28, Kananaskis had not sold any of this inventory.

3. 19 Kananaskis was holding merchandise that had been sold to a customer on February 19 but needed alteration before the customer would take possession. The merchandise cost $980 and alterations cost $120. The customer plans to pick up the merchandise on March 2 after the alterations are complete.

4. 23 Kananaskis shipped goods FOB shipping point to a customer. The merchandise cost $560. The appropriate party paid the freight costs of $70. The receiving report indicates that the goods were received by the customer on March 2.

5. 24 Kananaskis purchased goods FOB shipping point from a supplier. The merchandise cost $750. The appropriate party paid the freight costs of $80. The goods were shipped by the supplier on February 26 and received by Kananaskis on March 3.

6. 25 Kananaskis purchased goods FOB destination from a supplier. The merchandise cost $1,500. The appropriate party paid the freight costs of $150. The goods were shipped by the supplier on February 27 and received by Kananaskis on March 4.

7. 27 Kananaskis shipped goods FOB destination costing $1,900 to a customer. The appropriate party paid the freight costs of $200. The receiving report indicates that the customer received the goods on March 7.

8. Mar. 5 Kananaskis had $1,260 of inventory isolated in the warehouse. The inventory is designated for a customer who has requested that the goods not be shipped until March 5.

Instructions

(a) For each of the above situations, specify whether the item should be included in ending inventory, and if so, at what amount. For each item that is not included in ending inventory, indicate who owns it and what account, if any, it should have been recorded in.

(b) Calculate the revised ending inventory amount.

Apply specific identification.
(SO 2)

P6–2A Dean's Sales Ltd., a small Ford dealership, has provided you with the following information with respect to its vehicle inventory for the month of April. The company uses the specific identification method.

Date		Explanation	Model	Serial #	Unit Cost/Price
Apr.	1	Beginning inventory	Focus	C81362	$22,000
			Mustang	G62313	27,000
			Flex	X3892	29,000
			F-150	F1883	23,000
			F-150	F1921	27,000
	8	Sales	Focus	C81362	24,000
			Mustang	G62313	30,000
	12	Purchases	Mustang	G71811	28,000
			Mustang	G71891	26,000
			Flex	X4212	28,000
			Flex	X4214	29,000
			Escape	E21202	27,000
	18	Sales	Mustang	G71891	31,000
			Flex	X3892	32,000
			F-150	F1921	30,500
			Escape	E21202	30,000
	23	Purchases	Focus	C81528	25,000
			Escape	E28268	28,000

Instructions

(a) Determine the cost of goods sold and ending inventory for the month of April.

(b) Determine the gross profit for the month of April.

(c) Discuss whether the specific identification method is likely the most appropriate cost determination method for Dean's Sales.

P6–3A Sandoval Skateshop Ltd. reports the following inventory transactions for its skateboards for the month of April. The company uses a perpetual inventory system.

Apply perpetual FIFO and answer questions about effects.
(SO 2, 3)

Date		Explanation	Units	Unit Cost	Total Cost
Apr.	1	Beginning inventory	30	$50	$1,500
	6	Purchases	15	45	675
	9	Sales	(35)		
	14	Purchases	20	40	800
	20	Sales	(25)		
	28	Purchases	20	35	700

Instructions

(a) Determine the cost of goods sold and cost of ending inventory using FIFO.

(b) Assume that Sandoval wants to change to the average cost method. What guidelines must it consider before making this change?

(c) If the company does change to the average cost method and prices continue to fall, would you expect the cost of goods sold and ending inventory amounts to be higher or lower than these amounts when using FIFO?

P6–4A Information for Sandoval Skateshop Ltd. is presented in P6–3A. Use the same inventory data and assume that the company uses the perpetual inventory system.

Apply perpetual average cost and discuss errors.
(SO 2, 4)

Instructions

(a) Determine the cost of goods sold and cost of ending inventory using average cost. (Use unrounded numbers in your calculations but round to the nearest cent for presentation purposes in your answer.)

(b) When the company counted its inventory at the end of April, it counted only 24 skateboards on hand. What journal entry, if any, should the company make to record this shortage?

(c) If the company had not discovered this shortage, identify what accounts would be overstated or understated and by what amount.

P6–5A Save-Mart Centre Inc. began operations on May 1 and uses a perpetual inventory system. During May, the company had the following purchases and sales for one of its products:

Apply perpetual FIFO and average cost; compare effects.
(SO 2, 3)

		Purchases		Sales	
Date		Units	Unit Cost	Units	Unit Price
May	1	12	$100		
	3			8	$250
	8	10	110		
	13			8	275
	15	6	115		
	20			6	300
	27			4	325

Instructions

(a) Determine the cost of goods sold and cost of ending inventory using (1) FIFO and (2) average cost. Ignore the effect of income tax. (For average, use unrounded numbers in your calculations but round to the nearest cent for presentation purposes in your answer.)

(b) What guidelines should Save-Mart consider in choosing between the FIFO and average cost methods?

(c) Which cost method produces the higher gross profit and profit?

(d) Which cost method produces the higher ending inventory valuation?

(e) Which cost method produces the higher cash flow?

P6–6A You are provided with the following information for Amelia Inc., which purchases its inventory from a supplier for cash and has only cash sales. Amelia uses the average cost method in a perpetual inventory system. Increased competition has recently reduced the price of the product.

Record transactions using perpetual average cost; apply LCNRV.
(SO 2, 5)

Date		Explanation	Units	Unit Cost/Price
Apr.	1	Beginning inventory	50	$ 8
	6	Purchases	110	9
	8	Sales	(140)	12
	15	Purchases	120	7
	20	Sales	(110)	10
	27	Purchases	20	6

Instructions

(a) Prepare all journal entries for the month of April for Amelia, the buyer. (Use unrounded numbers in your calculations but round to the nearest cent for presentation purposes in your answer.)

(b) Determine the ending inventory amount for Amelia.

(c) On April 30, Amelia learns that the product has a net realizable value of $5 per unit. What amount should ending inventory be valued at on the April statement of financial position?

Determine effects of inventory error for two years.
(SO 4, 5)

P6–7A In its physical inventory count at its February 28, 2014, year end, The Orange Sprocket Corporation included inventory that was being held for another company to sell on consignment. The merchandise was sold in the next year and inventory was correctly stated at February 28, 2015.

Instructions

Ignoring income tax, indicate the effect of this error (overstated, understated, or no effect) on each of the following at year end:

	2015	2014
(a) Cash		
(b) Cost of goods sold		
(c) Profit		
(d) Retained earnings		
(e) Ending inventory		
(f) Gross profit margin ratio (40%)		
(g) Inventory turnover ratio (10 times)		

Determine effects of inventory errors for multiple years.
(SO 4, 5)

P6–8A The records of Kmeta Inc. show the following data for the years ended July 31:

	2015	2014	2013
Income statement:			
Sales	$340,000	$320,000	$300,000
Cost of goods sold	233,000	220,000	209,000
Operating expenses	68,000	64,000	64,000
Statement of financial position:			
Merchandise inventory	40,000	40,000	24,000

After the company's July 31, 2015, year end, the accountant discovers two errors:

1. Ending inventory on July 31, 2013, was actually $33,000, not $24,000. Kmeta owned goods held on consignment at another company that were not included in the inventory account.

2. Kmeta purchased $15,000 of goods from a supplier on July 30, 2014, with shipping terms FOB destination. Although it did not receive the goods until August 4, 2014, the goods were included in the July 31, 2014, year-end inventory. The purchase was then recorded properly on August 4, 2014.

Instructions

(a) For each of the three years, prepare both incorrect and corrected income statements through to profit before income tax.

(b) What is the combined (total) impact of these errors on retained earnings (ignoring any income tax effects) for the three years before correction? After correction?

(c) Calculate both the incorrect and corrected inventory turnover ratios for 2015 and 2014.

Determine and record LCNRV.
(SO 5)

P6–9A Tascon Corporation sells coffee beans, which are sensitive to price fluctuations. The following inventory information is available for this product at December 31, 2014:

Coffee Bean	Units	Unit Cost	Net Realizable Value
Coffea arabica	13,000 bags	$5.60	$5.55
Coffea robusta	5,000 bags	3.40	3.50

(a) Calculate Tascon's inventory at the lower of cost and net realizable value.

(b) Prepare any journal entry required to record the LCNRV, assuming that Tascon uses a perpetual inventory system.

(c) Assume that Tascon still holds this inventory a year later and that it has recovered from its decline in value; that is, the coffee's net realizable value exceeds its cost. Should Tascon carry its inventory at December 31, 2015, at cost, net realizable value, or some other value? Explain.

P6–10A You have been provided with the following information regarding Love Paper Ltd.'s inventory for June, July, and August.

Record and present LCNRV valuation for multiple periods. (SO 5)

	Paper Inventory (in tonnes)	Cost/Tonne	NRV/Tonne
June 30	6,000	$790	$850
July 31	6,700	850	815
August 31	5,500	815	790

Instructions

(a) Calculate the cost and net realizable value of Love Paper's paper inventory at (1) June 30, (2) July 31, and (3) August 31.

(b) Prepare any journal entry necessary to record the LCNRV of the paper inventory at (1) June 30, (2) July 31, and (3) August 31. Assume that Love Paper uses a perpetual inventory system.

(c) Are there any differences in recording LCNRV for companies reporting using ASPE rather than IFRS?

P6–11A The following information is available for **The Coca-Cola Company** (in U.S. $ millions):

Calculate ratios and comment on liquidity. (SO 5)

	2012	2011	2010
Cost of goods sold	$19,053	$18,216	$12,693
Inventories	3,264	3,092	2,650
Current assets	30,328	25,497	21,579
Current liabilities	27,821	24,282	18,508

In the notes to its financial statements, Coca-Cola disclosed that it uses the FIFO and average cost methods to determine the cost of its inventory.

The industry averages for the inventory turnover, days in inventory, and current ratios are as follows:

	2012	2011
Inventory turnover	7.8 times	7.4 times
Days in inventory	47 days	49 days
Current ratio	1.2:1	1.1:1

Instructions

(a) Calculate Coca-Cola's inventory turnover, days in inventory, and current ratios for 2012 and 2011. Comment on the company's liquidity over the two years, and in comparison with the industry.

(b) What might be the reason that Coca-Cola uses more than one cost method to determine the cost of its inventory?

P6–12A The following information is available for **Tim Hortons Inc.** and **Starbucks Corporation**, and their industry, for a recent year:

Compare ratios; comment on liquidity and profitability. (SO 5)

	Tim Hortons	Starbucks	Industry Average
Inventory turnover	16.1 times	5.3 times	24.4 times
Current ratio	1.3:1	1.9:1	1.2:1
Gross profit margin	11.9%	56.3%	37.6%
Profit margin	18.3%	10.4%	10.4%

Instructions

(a) Comment on the liquidity of the two companies in comparison with each other, and the industry.

(b) Comment on the profitability of the two companies in comparison with each other, and the industry.

Apply periodic FIFO and average cost.
(SO 6)

*P6–13A   Kane Ltd. had a beginning inventory on January 1 of 25 units of product SXL at a cost of $160 per unit. During the year, purchases were as follows:

	Units	Unit Cost	Total Cost
Mar. 15	70	$150	$10,500
July 20	50	145	7,250
Sept. 4	45	135	6,075
Dec. 2	10	125	1,250

Kane uses a periodic inventory system. At the end of the year, a physical inventory count determined that there were 20 units on hand.

Instructions

(a) Determine the cost of goods available for sale.
(b) Determine the cost of the ending inventory and the cost of the goods sold using (1) FIFO and (2) average cost. (Use unrounded numbers in your calculation of the average unit cost but round to the nearest cent for presentation purposes in your answer.)

Prepare partial financial statements and assess effects.
(SO 5, 6)

*P6–14A   Data for Kane Ltd. are presented in P6–13A. Assume that Kane sold product SXL for $200 per unit during the year.

Instructions

(a) Prepare a partial income statement through to gross profit for each of the two cost methods: (1) FIFO and (2) average cost.
(b) Show how inventory would be reported in the current assets section of the statement of financial position for (1) FIFO and (2) average cost.
(c) Which cost method results in the lower inventory amount for the statement of financial position? The lower gross profit amount for the income statement?

Apply perpetual and periodic FIFO.
(SO 2, 6)

*P6–15A   You are provided with the following information about Lynk Inc.'s inventory for the month of August:

Date		Description	Units	Unit Cost
Aug.	1	Beginning inventory	50	$90
	4	Purchase	180	92
	10	Sale	(160)	
	18	Purchase	70	94
	25	Sale	(100)	
	28	Purchase	40	95

Instructions

(a) Calculate the cost of ending inventory and cost of goods sold using FIFO in (1) a periodic inventory system, and (2) a perpetual inventory system.
(b) Compare your results for items 1 and 2 of part (a), commenting particularly on any differences or similarities between the two inventory systems.

Apply perpetual and periodic average cost.
(SO 2, 6)

*P6–16A   You are provided with the following information about Apple River Inc.'s inventory for the month of November:

Date		Explanation	Units	Unit Cost
Nov.	1	Beginning inventory	100	$20
	4	Purchase	500	21
	11	Sale	(450)	
	16	Purchase	750	22
	20	Sale	(800)	
	27	Purchase	600	23

Instructions

(a) Calculate the ending inventory and cost of goods sold using the average cost method in (1) a perpetual inventory system, and (2) a periodic inventory system. (Use unrounded numbers in your calculations but round to the nearest cent for presentation purposes in your answer.)
(b) Compare your results for items 1 and 2 of part (a), commenting specifically on any differences or similarities between the two inventory systems.

Problems: Set B

P6–1B Banff Limited is trying to determine the value of its ending inventory as at February 28, the company's year end. The accountant counted everything that was in the warehouse in early March, which resulted in an ending inventory amount of $112,000. However, the accountant was not sure how to treat the following transactions, so she did not include them in the count, with the exception of item 8. She has asked for your help in determining whether or not the following transactions should be included in inventory:

Identify items in inventory.
(SO 1)

1. Feb. 1 Banff received $1,800 of inventory on consignment from Kananaskis Limited. By February 28, Banff had sold half of this inventory for Kananaskis.
2.   5 Banff shipped $1,200 of inventory on consignment to a Jasper craft shop. By February 28, the craft shop had sold half of this inventory for Banff.
3.   20 Banff purchased goods FOB shipping point from a supplier. The merchandise cost $1,500. The appropriate party paid the freight costs of $150. The goods were shipped by the supplier on February 22 and received by Banff on March 1.
4.   23 Banff shipped goods FOB shipping point to a customer. The merchandise cost $1,600. The appropriate party paid the freight costs of $80. The receiving report indicates that the customer received the goods on March 1.
5.   24 Banff purchased goods FOB destination from a supplier. The merchandise cost $700. The appropriate party paid the freight costs of $35. The goods were shipped by the supplier on February 26 and received by Banff on March 2.
6.   25 Banff shipped goods FOB destination to a customer. The merchandise cost $800. The appropriate party paid the freight costs of $90. The receiving report indicates that the customer received the goods on March 3.
7.   27 A customer took goods home "on approval" from Banff. The merchandise cost Banff $1,300. The customer is going to let Banff know whether it wants the merchandise before March 4.
8.   28 Banff had damaged goods set aside in the warehouse because they were not saleable. These goods were included in the inventory count at their original cost of $800.

Instructions
(a) For each of the above situations, specify whether the item should be included in ending inventory, and if so, at what amount. For each item that is not included in ending inventory, indicate who owns it and what account, if any, it should have been recorded in.
(b) Calculate the revised ending inventory amount.

P6–2B The Piano Studio Ltd. has provided you with the following information with respect to its piano inventory for the month of August. The company uses the specific identification method.

Apply specific identification.
(SO 2)

Date	Explanation	Supplier	Serial #	Unit Cost/Price
Aug. 1	Beginning inventory	Yamaha	YH6318	$1,500
		Suzuki	SZ5716	1,100
		Suzuki	SZ5828	1,600
		Kawai	KG1268	1,500
		Kawai	KG1520	600
		Steinway	ST8411	2,600
		Steinway	ST0944	2,200
10	Sales	Suzuki	SZ5828	2,700
		Kawai	KG1520	1,000
15	Purchases	Yamaha	YH4418	1,300
		Yamaha	YH5632	1,600
18	Sales	Yamaha	YH4418	2,100
		Steinway	ST0944	3,700
22	Purchases	Suzuki	SZ6132	1,800
		Suzuki	SZ6148	1,600
26	Sales	Suzuki	SZ6132	2,900
		Yamaha	YH6318	2,500
		Yamaha	YH5632	2,600

Instructions

(a) Determine the cost of goods sold and ending inventory for the month of August.

(b) Determine the gross profit for the month of August.

(c) Discuss whether the specific identification method is likely the most appropriate cost determination method for the Piano Studio.

Apply perpetual FIFO and answer questions about effects.
(SO 2, 3)

P6–3B   BigFishTackle Co. Ltd. reports the following inventory transactions for its fishing rods for the month of April. The company uses a perpetual inventory system.

Date	Explanation	Units	Unit Cost	Total Cost
Apr. 1	Beginning inventory	50	$230	$11,500
6	Purchases	35	240	8,400
9	Sales	(55)		
14	Purchases	40	245	9,800
20	Sales	(50)		
28	Purchases	30	250	7,500

Instructions

(a) Determine the cost of goods sold and cost of ending inventory using FIFO.

(b) Assume that BigFishTackle wants to change to the average cost method. What guidelines must it consider before making this change?

(c) If the company does change to the average cost method and prices continue to rise, would you expect the cost of goods sold and ending inventory amounts to be higher or lower than these amounts when using FIFO?

Apply perpetual average cost and discuss errors.
(SO 2, 4)

P6–4B   Information for BigFishTackle Co. Ltd. is presented in P6–3B. Use the same inventory data and assume that the company uses the perpetual inventory system.

Instructions

(a) Determine the cost of goods sold and cost of ending inventory using average cost. (Use unrounded numbers in your calculations but round to the nearest cent for presentation purposes in your answer.)

(b) When the company counted its inventory at the end of April, it counted only 49 rods on hand. What journal entry, if any, should the company make to record this shortage?

(c) If the company had not discovered this shortage, identify what accounts would be overstated or understated and by what amount.

Apply perpetual FIFO and average cost; compare effects.
(SO 2, 3)

P6–5B   Family Appliance Mart Ltd. began operations on May 1 and uses a perpetual inventory system. During May, the company had the following purchases and sales for one of its products:

	Purchases		Sales	
Date	Units	Unit Cost	Units	Unit Price
May 1	110	$19		
6	140	22		
11			200	$35
14	80	23		
21			100	40
27	50	25		

Instructions

(a) Determine the cost of goods sold and cost of ending inventory using (1) FIFO and (2) average cost. Ignore the effect of income tax. (For average, use unrounded numbers in your calculations but round to the nearest cent for presentation purposes in your answer.)

(b) What guidelines should Family Appliance Mart consider in choosing between the FIFO and average cost methods?

(c) Which cost method produces the higher gross profit and profit?

(d) Which cost method produces the higher ending inventory valuation?

(e) Which cost method produces the higher cash flow?

P6–6B You are provided with the following information for Geo Inc., which purchases its inventory from a supplier on account. All sales are also on account. Geo uses the FIFO cost method in a perpetual inventory system. Increased competition has recently decreased the price of the product.

Record transactions using perpetual FIFO; apply LCNRV.
(SO 2, 5)

Date	Explanation	Units	Unit Cost Price
Oct. 1	Beginning inventory	60	$14
5	Purchases	100	13
8	Sales	(130)	20
15	Purchases	35	12
20	Sales	(50)	16
26	Purchases	15	11

Instructions
(a) Prepare all journal entries for the month of October for Geo, the buyer.
(b) Determine the ending inventory amount for Geo.
(c) On October 31, Geo learns that the product has a net realizable value of $10 per unit. What amount should ending inventory be valued at on the October 31 statement of financial position?

P6–7B In its physical inventory count at its March 31, 2014, year end, Backspring Corporation excluded inventory that was being held on consignment for Backspring by another company. The merchandise was sold in the next year and the inventory was correctly stated at March 31, 2015.

Determine effects of inventory error for two years.
(SO 4, 5)

Instructions
Ignoring income tax, indicate the effect of this error (overstated, understated, or no effect) on each of the following at year end:

	2015	2014
(a) Cash	_____	_____
(b) Cost of goods sold	_____	_____
(c) Profit	_____	_____
(d) Retained earnings	_____	_____
(e) Ending inventory	_____	_____
(f) Gross profit margin ratio (30%)	_____	_____
(g) Inventory turnover ratio (8 times)	_____	_____

P6–8B The records of Pelletier Inc. show the following data for the years ended July 31:

Determine effects of inventory errors for multiple years.
(SO 4, 5)

	2015	2014	2013
Income statement:			
Sales	$320,000	$312,000	$300,000
Cost of goods sold	187,000	203,000	170,000
Operating expenses	52,000	52,000	50,000
Statement of financial position:			
Merchandise inventory	37,000	24,000	37,000

After the company's July 31, 2015, year end, the controller discovers two errors:

1. Ending inventory at the end of 2013 was actually $27,000, not $37,000. Pelletier included goods held on consignment for another company that were mistakenly included in the 2013 inventory account.
2. Pelletier purchased $5,000 of goods from a supplier on July 30, 2014, with shipping terms FOB destination. Although it did not receive the goods until August 4, 2014, Pelletier included the goods in the July 31, 2014, year-end inventory. The purchase was then recorded properly on August 4, 2014.

Instructions
(a) For each of the three years, prepare both the incorrect and corrected income statements through to profit before income tax.
(b) What is the combined (total) impact of the errors on retained earnings (ignoring any income tax effects) for the three years before correction? After correction?
(c) Calculate both the incorrect and corrected inventory turnover ratios for each of 2015 and 2014.

Determine and record LCNRV.
(SO 5)

P6–9B Flin Flon Limited sells three products whose prices are sensitive to price fluctuations. The following inventory information is available for these products at March 31, 2014:

Product	Units	Unit Cost	Net Realizable Value
A	25	$ 7	$ 7
B	30	6	8
C	60	11	10

Instructions

(a) Calculate Flin Flon's inventory at the lower of cost and net realizable value.
(b) Prepare any journal entry required to record the LCNRV, assuming that Flin Flon uses a perpetual inventory system.
(c) Assume that Flin Flon still holds product C a year later and that it has recovered its decline in value and that the net realizable value of product C is now $11. Should Flin Flon carry its inventory of product C at March 31, 2015, at cost, net realizable value, or some other value? Explain.

Record and present LCNRV valuation for multiple periods.
(SO 5)

P6–10B You have been provided with the following information regarding R-Steel Inc.'s inventory for March, April, and May.

	Steel Inventory (in tonnes)	Cost/Tonne	NRV/Tonne
March 31	3,000	$725	$740
April 30	2,500	715	710
May 31	2,800	725	725

Instructions

(a) Calculate the cost and net realizable value of R-Steel's inventory at (1) March 31, (2) April 30, and (3) May 31.
(b) Prepare any journal entry required to record the LCNRV of the steel inventory at (1) March 31, (2) April 30, and (3) May 31. Assume that R-Steel uses a perpetual inventory system.
(c) Are there any differences in recording LCNRV for companies reporting using ASPE rather than IFRS?

Calculate ratios and comment on liquidity.
(SO 5)

P6–11B The following information is available for **PepsiCo, Inc.** (in U.S. $ millions):

	2012	2011	2010
Cost of goods sold	$31,291	$31,593	$26,575
Inventories	3,581	3,827	3,372
Current assets	18,720	17,441	17,569
Current liabilities	17,089	18,154	15,892

In the notes to its financial statements, PepsiCo disclosed that it uses the FIFO and average cost methods to determine the cost of the majority of its inventory.

The industry averages for the inventory turnover, days in inventory, and current ratios are as follows:

	2012	2011
Inventory turnover	7.8 times	7.4 times
Days in inventory	47 days	49 days
Current ratio	1.2:1	1.1:1

Instructions

(a) Calculate PepsiCo's inventory turnover, days in inventory, and current ratios for 2012 and 2011. Comment on the company's liquidity over the two years, and in comparison with the industry.
(b) What might be the reason that PepsiCo uses more than one cost method to determine the cost of its inventory?

Compare ratios; comment on liquidity and profitability.
(SO 5)

P6–12B **Magna International Inc.** is Canada's top manufacturer of auto parts and systems. Its top competitor is **Dana Holdings Inc.** The following information is available for these two competitors and their industry, for a recent year:

	Magna	Dana	Industry Average
Inventory turnover	12.9 times	8.2 times	9.0 times
Current ratio	1.4:1	2.2:1	1.5:1
Gross profit margin	11.6%	13.5%	17.2%
Profit margin	3.6%	3.7%	4.6%

Instructions

(a) Comment on the liquidity of the two companies in comparison with each other, and the industry.

(b) Comment on the profitability of the two companies in comparison with each other, and the industry.

(c) It would appear from the above ratios that the inventory turnover ratio may have an impact on the current ratio. Please explain why.

*P6–13B Steward Inc. had a beginning inventory on January 1 of 400 units of product MLN at a cost of $18 per unit. During the year, purchases were as follows:

	Units	Unit Cost	Total Cost
Feb. 20	1,200	$19	$22,800
May 5	1,000	21	21,000
Aug. 12	1,200	20	24,000
Dec. 8	600	22	13,200

Steward uses a periodic inventory system. At the end of the year, a physical inventory count determined that there were 400 units on hand.

Apply periodic FIFO and average cost. (SO 6)

Instructions

(a) Determine the cost of goods available for sale.

(b) Determine the cost of the ending inventory and the cost of goods sold using (1) FIFO and (2) average cost. (Use unrounded numbers in your calculation of the average unit cost but round to the nearest cent for presentation purposes in your answer.)

*P6–14B Data for Steward Inc. are presented in P6–13B. Assume that Steward sold product MLN for $40 per unit during the year.

Prepare partial financial statements and assess effects. (SO 5, 6)

Instructions

(a) Prepare a partial income statement through to gross profit for each of the two cost methods: (1) FIFO and (2) average cost.

(b) Show how inventory would be reported in the current assets section of the statement of financial position for (1) FIFO and (2) average cost.

(c) Which cost method results in the higher inventory amount for the statement of financial position? The higher gross profit amount on the income statement?

*P6–15B You are provided with the following information about Bear River Inc.'s inventory for the month of May:

Apply perpetual and periodic FIFO. (SO 2, 6)

Date	Description	Units	Unit Cost
May 1	Beginning inventory	15,000	$2.30
6	Purchase	40,000	2.35
11	Sale	(30,000)	
14	Purchase	50,000	2.40
21	Sale	(65,000)	
27	Purchase	40,000	2.45

Instructions

(a) Calculate the ending inventory and cost of goods sold using FIFO in (1) a perpetual inventory system, and (2) a periodic inventory system.

(b) Compare your results for items 1 and 2 of part (a), commenting specifically on any differences or similarities between the two inventory systems.

*P6–16B You are provided with the following information about Lahti Inc.'s inventory for the month of October.

Apply perpetual and periodic average cost. (SO 2, 6)

Date	Description	Units	Unit Cost
Oct. 1	Beginning inventory	50	$24
9	Purchase	125	26
15	Sale	(150)	
20	Purchase	70	27
29	Sale	(55)	

Instructions

(a) Calculate the cost of ending inventory and cost of goods sold using average cost in (1) a perpetual inventory system, and (2) a periodic inventory system. (Use unrounded numbers in your calculations but round to the nearest cent for presentation purposes in your answer.)

(b) Compare your results for items 1 and 2 of part (a), commenting specifically on any differences or similarities between the two inventory systems.

Broadening Your Perspective

Financial Reporting: *Shoppers Drug Mart*

Answer questions
about inventories.
(SO 3, 5)

BYP6-1   The financial statements of **Shoppers Drug Mart** are presented in Appendix A at the end of this book.

Instructions

(a) What amounts did Shoppers report for total inventories in its balance sheet at the end of 2012 and 2011?

(b) Calculate the change in the dollar amount of total inventories between 2012 and 2011 and the percentage change. Next, calculate inventory as a percentage of current assets for each of the two years. Comment on the results.

(c) Shoppers uses the first-in, first-out method. What guidelines do you think influenced Shoppers' choice of cost method?

(d) Refer to Note 9, Cost of goods sold in the financial statements. Did Shoppers write down its inventories to net realizable value in either 2012 or 2011? If so, reproduce the journal entry for the most recent year that Shoppers likely made.

Comparative Analysis: *Shoppers Drug Mart* and *Jean Coutu*

Calculate liquidity
ratios and comment.
(SO 5)

BYP6-2   The financial statements of **Jean Coutu** are presented in Appendix B following the financial statements for **Shoppers Drug Mart** in Appendix A.

Instructions

(a) Calculate the current ratio for each company for 2012.

(b) Calculate the inventory turnover and days in inventory ratios for each company for 2012.

(c) The 2012 industry average for the current ratio was 1.4:1, the inventory turnover was 7.7 times, and the days in inventory was 47 days. What conclusions about each company's liquidity in 2012 can you draw based on your results in parts (a) and (b) and the industry averages?

Comparing IFRS and ASPE

Compare effects of
different inventory
systems and methods.
(SO 1, 2, 3)

BYP6-3   Gibson Lumber Limited is a small sawmill operation, servicing Atlantic Canada. It is a privately traded company, using ASPE. Gibson does not have a sophisticated costing system for its inventory. It estimates the cost of its inventory using the periodic average cost method and performs a physical count at year end. The physical count is also performed using estimation techniques, such as measuring the piles of finished lumber and scaling the log piles.

Global Lumber Inc., an international lumber company, is a publicly traded company using IFRS that has just expanded into Atlantic Canada. It has a sophisticated inventory system including bar codes on each piece of lumber produced, along with detailed records of production costs. It uses the FIFO cost method under a perpetual inventory system.

Lumber prices are controlled by a commodity market and have been increasing slightly over the past year.

Instructions

(a) Are there any specific differences related to the use of the two different accounting standards—ASPE and IFRS—that financial analysts should consider when evaluating the management of inventory by Gibson and Global?

(b) Would the use of the two different inventory systems—periodic and perpetual—affect the comparison of the financial statements of each company? If so, explain how.

(c) Would the use of the two different cost methods—average cost and FIFO—affect the comparison of the financial statements of each company? If so, explain how.

Critical Thinking Case

BYP6–4   On December 1, 2015, Athabasca Building Supplies Ltd. (ABS) purchased Dunbar Doors Inc. (DDI) from Kevin Osepchuk. This is the first time that ABS has operated in the door business and the company welcomed the opportunity to sell doors to existing customers. When DDI was acquired, ABS also agreed to take over a DDI loan with the Royal Dominion Bank. The loan has a limit equal to 80% of the Merchandise Inventory account balance at year end pertaining to doors. The loan has been held with that bank for a number of years and is currently at $200,000. The bank requires verification of the inventory balance at the end of every year. As part of the deal to acquire DDI, Kevin agreed to serve as the new manager of ABS's Door Division and to receive a bonus equal to 10% of the operating profit of that division.

    You are a student who is helping ABS prepare its year-end financial statements. At the inventory count on December 31, you noticed that the employees counting the inventory at that time found that there were 800 doors on hand. ABS uses the perpetual average cost method.

    In looking at the company's inventory records, you discover that 2,600 doors were purchased from DDI on December 1 at a cost of $310 each. Later in the month, 800 doors were purchased from a U.S. supplier at CAD$240 each and shortly after, 600 doors were purchased from China at CAD$190 each. Finally, on the last day of the year, 100 more doors were purchased at CAD$200 but these were in transit on December 31 with terms FOB destination. The only sale for the month occurred when 3,200 doors were sold at $400 each to a contractor developing the largest condominium project in the area. All sales occurred after the purchase of the doors from China. Kevin supervised the count and determined the cost of the ending inventory. He calculated the ending inventory to be 900 doors at $310 each. He added 100 doors to the amount counted because of the doors in transit. Kevin earned a bonus of $16,700 in December.

Instructions

(a) Determine the cost of goods available for sale in December.
(b) Determine the cost of ending inventory at December 31.
(c) Based on the above, should there be an adjustment to Kevin's bonus?
(d) Does this adjustment have any other implications?
(e) What do you think about Kevin's actions?
(f) Assume that the decrease in the cost of doors from China is indicative of future trends in the industry and that the cost savings will be passed along to customers through price reductions that will decrease the selling price of a door to $240. Will that have any impact on the December financial statements?

Determine errors in recording inventory and writedowns. (SO 4, 5)

Ethics Case

BYP6–5   You are provided with the following information for Swag Diamonds Ltd. Swag only carries one brand and size of diamond—all are identical. Each batch of diamonds purchased is carefully coded and marked with its purchase cost.

Apply specific identification and average cost; answer questions. (SO 2, 3)

Mar. 1	Beginning inventory is 140 diamonds at a cost of $500 per diamond.
3	Purchased 200 diamonds at a cost of $540 each.
5	Sold 170 diamonds for $800 each.
10	Purchased 340 diamonds at a cost of $570 each.
25	Sold 500 diamonds for $850 each.

Instructions

(a) Assuming that Swag Diamonds uses the specific identification method, do the following:
    1. Show how Swag Diamonds could maximize its gross profit for the month by selecting which diamonds to sell on March 5 and March 25.
    2. Show how Swag Diamonds could minimize its gross profit for the month by selecting which diamonds to sell on March 5 and March 25.
(b) Who are the stakeholders in this situation? Is there anything unethical in choosing which diamonds to sell in a month?
(c) Assuming that Swag Diamonds uses a perpetual inventory system and the average cost method, how much gross profit would Swag Diamonds report? (Round the average unit cost to the nearest cent—two decimal places.)
(d) Which method of cost determination—specific identification or average cost—should Swag Diamonds select? Explain.

"All About You" Activity

BYP6–6   In the "All About You" feature in this chapter, you learned about inventory control. Suppose, after graduating, that you accept a job as a manager for a retail store that sells high-end and mid-level cameras and photographic equipment. The equipment is purchased from other countries and is subject to currency fluctuation.

Identify internal controls; adjust inventory; discuss method of cost determination. (SO 1, 2)

Instructions

(a) Identify some control measures that you think should be in place in your store to safeguard the inventory.

(b) Assume the store uses a perpetual inventory system. Do you think that taking a physical inventory count once a year is adequate? If not, how often do you think a physical inventory count should be taken? Identify any accounts that would be affected by an adjusting journal entry to update the inventory for any shortages or overages.

(c) Which cost determination method would you recommend that the store use? Why? Would you recommend that the store use the same method for both the cameras and small items such as picture frames? Why or why not?

Serial Case

(*Note:* This is a continuation of the serial case from Chapters 1 through 5.)

Apply perpetual FIFO and average; compare effects.
(SO 2, 3)

BYP6–7 The manager of Kzinski Supply Corp. has approached Koebel's Family Bakery to become the exclusive Canadian distributor of deluxe European mixers. Koebel's will pay Kzinski for its purchases of mixers in Canadian dollars. However, Kzinski uses euros as its primary currency, which means that the purchase price converted to Canadian dollars will change each time a mixer is purchased. The current cost of a mixer is $550 and Koebel's would propose to sell each mixer for $995. Natalie, Janet, and Brian believe that the mixers are top of the line and that, because these mixers are not available in Canada, many of their customers would be interested in purchasing this product.

Natalie believes that at the beginning of each month there should be at least three mixers in inventory. It takes approximately three weeks for the mixers to come from Europe and it is best to have an adequate supply of mixers on hand ready to be sold.

Currently, all inventory at Koebel's is accounted for using the average cost method in a perpetual inventory system. Natalie remembers that there is another cost method, FIFO, that can be used to determine the cost of inventory. Because this is a new type of inventory, she wonders if FIFO would make the accounting a little easier and better reflect ending inventory and cost of goods sold.

The following transactions occur between the months of July and October 2014:

July	4	Three deluxe mixers are purchased on account and received from Kzinski Supply for $1,650 ($550 each), FOB destination, terms n/30.
	14	One deluxe mixer is sold for $995 cash.
	25	Amounts owing to Kzinski Supply from the July 4 purchase are paid.
August	1	One deluxe mixer is purchased on account and received from Kzinski Supply for $568, FOB destination, terms n/30.
	27	Two deluxe mixers are sold for a total of $1,990 cash.
	29	Amounts owing to Kzinski Supply from the August 1 purchase are paid.
September	4	Three deluxe mixers are purchased on account and received from Kzinski Supply for $1,692 ($564 each), FOB destination, terms n/30.
	12	Three mixers are sold on account for a total of $2,985.
	29	Amounts owing to Kzinski Supply from the September 4 purchase are paid.
October	3	Three deluxe mixers are purchased on account and received from Kzinski Supply for $1,722 ($574 each), FOB destination, terms n/30.
	27	One deluxe mixer is sold for $995 cash.

Instructions

(a) Prepare a perpetual inventory schedule, assuming use of the FIFO cost method.

(b) Using the information you prepared in (a), prepare journal entries to record each transaction.

(c) Prepare a perpetual inventory schedule, assuming use of the average cost method.

(d) Using the information you prepared in (c), prepare journal entries to record each transaction.

(e) Calculate and compare the gross profit margin, assuming the use of the (1) FIFO, and (2) average cost method.

(f) What guidelines should Natalie consider when deciding which inventory cost method to use?

Answers to Self-Test Questions

1. d	2. d	3. b	4. d
5. c	6. a	7. b	8. b
9. c	10. c	*11. b	*12. c

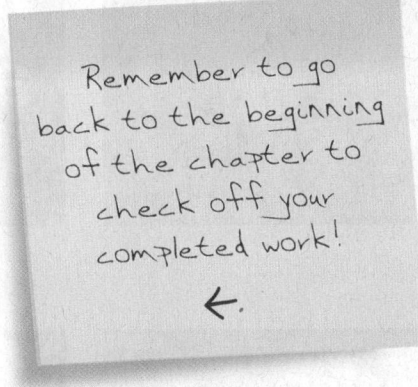

Remember to go back to the beginning of the chapter to check off your completed work!

Endnotes

[1]"Lululemon: Shares Tumble over Leadership Void and Inventory Problems," *Canadian Business*, June 11, 2013; Hollie Shaw, "Lululemon Shares Plunge as CEO Christine Day to Step Down," *Financial Post*, June 10, 2013; Shelley DuBois, "Lululemon: The Downside of Selling Hot Pants," CNNMoney.com, March 22, 2013; The Canadian Press, "Lululemon Recalls Pants for Being See-Through," CBC.ca, March 19, 2013; Hollie Shaw, "Has Lululemon Been Performing Below its Earnings Potential?," *Financial Post*, December 4, 2012; Marina Strauss, "Lululemon's Problem? Customers Can't Get Enough," The *Globe and Mail*, March 17, 2011; lululemon athletica inc. 2012 Annual Report; lululemon corporate website, www.lululemon.com.

[2]John Daly, "A Man and His Merchandise," *Globe and Mail Report on Business*, April 2012, pp. 25–30; James Cowan, "Retail: The Genius of Dollarama," *Canadian Business*, April 7, 2011; Dollarama 2012 annual report.

[3]David Milstead, "Inventory Overhang Casts a Shadow over RIM," *The Globe and Mail*, November 22, 2011, p. B16; Charles Arthur, "PlayBook Writeoff Means RIM's Tablet Has Been a $1.5bn Mistake," Technology Blog, Guardian.co.uk, December 5, 2011; Canadian Press, "RIM PlayBook Sales Hurt Earnings Targets," CBCNews.com, December 2, 2011.

[4]A. Taylor-Butts and S. Perreault, "Fraud Against Businesses in Canada," Statistics Canada, December 2009. Motorola Solutions, "Transforming the Customer Experience with RFID," 2013. Accessed May 30, 2013. PWC, "Stealing Retailer's Thunder: PWC Estimates Canadian Retailers are Losing over $10 Million a Day to Shrinkage," Toronto, October 31, 2012. Accessed May 30, 2013. Marjo Johne, "Sports Chek Sprints into Digital," The Globe and Mail," May 23, 2013, Accessed June 8, 2013.

CHAPTER 7

Internal Control and Cash

study objectives

After studying this chapter, you should be able to:

SO 1 Describe the primary components of an internal control system.

SO 2 Apply the key control activities to cash receipts and payments.

SO 3 Prepare a bank reconciliation.

SO 4 Explain the reporting and management of cash.

the navigator

Controlling Cash at Nick's

Nick Petros, the founder of Nick's Steakhouse and Pizza in Calgary, came to Canada from Greece at age 17 with no money and speaking no English. For 25 years, he worked his way up in the restaurant industry, as a dishwasher, busboy, waiter, maître d', and then manager. In 1979, armed with a collection of his mother's homemade recipes, he opened his own restaurant. Nick's youngest child, Mark, and his wife, Michelle, took over the business in 2000, but Nick is still a welcome presence in the restaurant, greeting customers old and new.

Located across the street from McMahon Stadium, home to the CFL's Calgary Stampeders, Nick's has become a Calgary family tradition. The restaurant has more than 70 full- and part-time employees including servers, bartenders, and delivery drivers. On a busy Friday or Saturday evening, around a dozen servers and bartenders serve as many as 1,200 people in the 7,000-square-foot (650-square-metre) restaurant and bar, with more guests on the patios in the summer. Mark Petros says his point-of-sale (POS) system helps him keep track of the orders, inventory, and money.

After taking a table's order, servers enter the items into one of six computer terminals throughout the restaurant. The computer is preprogrammed with the price of each item and the server simply presses a labelled button, for example, "Caesar salad" or "lasagna," to enter an order. The POS system sends the order information to the bar, salad station, or line cooks and uses the information to track inventory. The servers collect payment from their tables. At the end of a shift, the POS system provides an employee report that itemizes the credit card, debit card, and cash sales that the server owes.

The bartenders and servers have a cash float of $400. The hosting staff also has a float to use for pickup orders and in case the servers need change for large bills. Mr. Petros explains, "When an employee with a float starts the shift, he or she makes sure that the cash on hand is equal to the float plus any orders taken so far that day. At the end of their shift, the same calculation is done to see if it balances out. If it does not balance, the employee is responsible for the missing money."

Similarly, before the bartenders start their shift, they have to count the beer in the fridges and note the levels in partially full bottles of alcohol. Everything must correspond to the POS system. For example, if three beers are missing from the fridge, three beers should have been entered in the system. If they weren't, the bartender is responsible.

"There's never a discrepancy," says Mr. Petros. If there ever is one, he adds, it's easy to find the problem, usually an error in pushing a button or entering information.

While cash is an obvious concern for internal control, Mr. Petros estimates that, at most, 10% of sales are paid for in cash, with the majority of customers paying by credit or debit card. Mr. Petros makes a cash deposit at the bank every day.

While there are fewer cash transactions than in the past, cash control remains crucial to a business like Nick's Steakhouse and Pizza. Fortunately, with an internal system in place and the help of the latest technology, cash can be controlled reliably.

the navigator

<table>
<tr><td>preview of
CHAPTER 7</td><td>Cash is the lifeblood of any company. Large and small companies alike must guard it carefully. Even companies that are successful in every other way can go bankrupt if they fail to manage their cash. In this chapter, we explain the essential features of an internal control system and describe how these controls apply to cash receipts and cash payments. We then explain how cash is reported in the financial statements, and describe ways to manage and monitor cash.</td></tr>
</table>

The chapter is organized as follows:

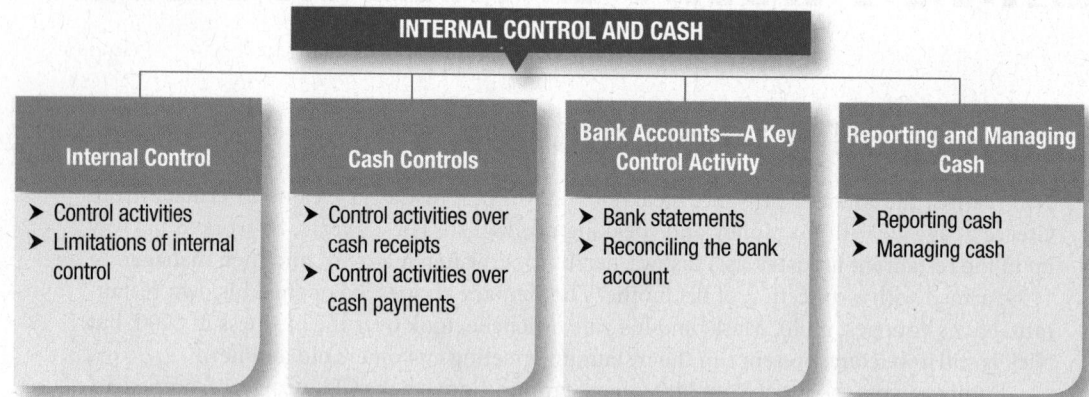

Internal Control

STUDY OBJECTIVE 1
Describe the primary components of an internal control system.

You were first introduced to the need for internal control in Chapter 6. As mentioned in that chapter, **internal control** consists of all the related methods and measures adopted within a company to help it achieve reliable financial reporting, effective and efficient operations, and compliance with relevant laws and regulations. Internal controls are also used to prevent and/or detect errors, which can give rise to unintentional misstatements in the financial statements. They also play a key role in the prevention and detection of intentional errors, misstatements, and stealing as a result of such things as occupational (employee) fraud.

Good internal control systems have the following five primary components:

- **Control environment:** It is the responsibility of management to make it clear that the organization values integrity, and that unethical activity will not be tolerated (often referred to as "setting the tone at the top").
- **Risk assessment:** Companies must identify and analyze the various factors that create risk for the business and determine how to best manage these risks.
- **Control activities:** To reduce the occurrence of unintentional and intentional errors, management must design policies and procedures to address the specific risks faced by the company.
- **Information and communication:** The internal control system must capture and communicate all pertinent information to the appropriate internal and external users.
- **Monitoring:** Internal control systems must be monitored periodically for their adequacy. To be effective, significant deficiencies must be communicated to those in authority, such as management and the board of directors.

CONTROL ACTIVITIES

Each of the five components of an internal control system is important. However, we will now focus on one of these components in particular: control activities. These activities form the backbone of a company's efforts to address the risks it faces. The specific control activities that are used by a company will vary depending on management's assessment of these risks. This assessment is also heavily influenced by the size and nature of the company.

Control activities that apply to most companies include the following:

- Authorization of transactions and activities
- Segregation of duties

- Documentation
- Physical controls
- Independent checks of performance
- Human resource controls

Each of these control activities is explained in the following sections.

Authorization of Transactions and Activities

An essential characteristic of internal control is the assignment of responsibility to specific employees. This control activity is most effective when **only one person is authorized to perform a specific task**.

To illustrate, assume that the cash in the cash register at the end of the day is $100 short of the cash rung up on the cash register. If only one person has operated the register, it is easy to identify who is responsible for the error. If two or more individuals have used the same register, it may be impossible to determine who is responsible for the error unless each person uses a separate cash drawer or passcode, or has their own employee report. For example, individual employee reports are produced for each staff member at Nick's Steakhouse and Pizza described in the feature story.

Establishing responsibility is significantly easier when there is a system for proper authorization. For example, the automated systems that are used by companies typically require passwords to ensure that only authorized personnel access the system. They also enable the company to assign responsibility for certain functions to a specific employee. This is the case at Nick's, where each employee has his or her own number to access the point-of-sale (POS) system. Another example of assigning responsibility is the common practice of requiring a supervisor to reverse a cashier's entry errors. The supervisor must insert a key or type a password to authorize the correction.

In addition, it is important that the right level of individual or the right department develop the internal control policies. For example, the vice-president of finance, not the vice-president of sales, should be responsible for establishing policies for credit sales because the vice-president of sales may be motivated to maximize sales—even to customers with poor credit ratings—in order to maximize sales commissions. A strong internal control policy for credit sales should also require written credit approval for sales transactions above a certain value. For example, sales on account amounting to more than $1,000 would require written credit approval.

MISSING IN ACTION

Marie St. Claire was the office manager at a medium-sized wholesaling business. When her boss retired, Marie was asked to take on some of his responsibilities, which included approval of all accounts payable invoices for payments. Realizing that no one would question her authority, Marie incorporated two businesses: one that performed office cleaning duties and another that performed courier services. She then printed up invoices from these two companies addressed to her employer. She approved the invoices for payment and then collected the cheques after they were mailed to a post office box number that she put on the invoices.

THE MISSING CONTROL

Authorization of Transactions and Activities
Marie was allowed to authorize transactions by herself with no one verifying whether the expenditure was reasonable or within company policies.

> Missing in Action boxes are introduced in this chapter to illustrate how a missing control activity can result in errors or misstatements.

Segregation of Duties

Segregation of duties is essential in a system of internal control because the responsibility for related activities should be assigned to different individuals. **When the same individual is responsible for related activities, the potential for errors increases.** In general, the following categories of activities should be separated from one another: authorization of transactions and activities (which was covered above), recording of transactions, and custody of assets.

As an example, consider what could happen if all purchasing activities—placing the orders, recording the transactions, and approving the payments—were carried out by one individual. That person could receive a bribe (a kickback) to buy merchandise at an inflated price from a dishonest supplier. The employee could record the transaction and approve payment without ever being discovered. The employee could also make up fictitious invoices from a hypothetical company, record the invoices, and approve them for payment. If the employee had access to the merchandise, she could approve the purchase of merchandise and then steal it. When the responsibilities for approving orders and payments, receiving, and recording are assigned to different individuals, the risk of such abuses is much lower. Segregation of duties also reduces the risk of unintentional errors such as recording the incorrect number of items received or the discount taken on the purchase of inventory.

Just as purchase activities must be segregated, the same is true for sales-related activities such as approving credit for customers, shipping goods, and preparing and recording invoices. For example, a salesperson could make sales at unauthorized prices to increase sales commissions, a shipping clerk could ship goods to himself or herself, or a billing clerk could understate the amount billed for sales made to friends and relatives. These abuses are less likely to occur when the sales tasks are divided: salespersons make the sale only after another employee checks the customer's credit, shipping department employees ship the goods based on the sales order, and billing department employees prepare the sales invoice after comparing the sales order with the report of goods shipped.

In small businesses, where it is more challenging to segregate duties, it is important that the owner and manager be actively involved in the business. They provide the oversight needed to ensure that the internal controls are working as intended. For example, Mark Petros of Nick's makes a daily bank deposit, which minimizes the opportunity for employees to misappropriate cash. He, or his delegate, should also review the bank reconciliation on a monthly basis and compare it with the daily sales reports. We will discuss the importance of bank reconciliations as a key control activity later in this chapter.

In summary, segregation of duties means that responsibilities should be divided up so that errors are detected before the financial statements are prepared. In other words, verification of an employee's work by another employee helps to ensure the accuracy of the accounting records. This activity also significantly reduces the risk that one person can both commit a fraud and cover it up.

MISSING IN ACTION

Tim Chan is the operations manager at a distribution centre for a sports equipment business. The company implemented a new perpetual inventory system for the first time that provided management with the amount of inventory that should always be on hand. Tim was assigned to count the inventory once a month and compare the count with the perpetual inventory records to identify damaged and obsolete items. Tim found counting to be time-consuming so he asked one of the distribution clerks in the warehouse to do the count and send him a report. Tim reviewed the report and signed off the count adjustments based on the information provided by the clerk. The clerk appeared to be doing a good job so Tim never followed up or counted the inventory. However, when the external auditors performed the year-end count, they found that the perpetual inventory records for composite hockey sticks and professional sport team jerseys were higher than the physical inventory count.

THE MISSING CONTROL

Segregation of Duties
The distribution clerk, who had access to the physical inventory, should not be responsible for the monthly counts. Tim was asked to perform the inventory counts because he didn't work in the warehouse or the purchasing department.

Documentation

Documents provide evidence that transactions and events have occurred at specified times with specified amounts. At Nick's, the point-of-sale system and employee reports provide documentation for the sale and the amount of cash received. Similarly, in other businesses a shipping document indicates that goods have been shipped and a sales invoice indicates that the customer has been billed for the goods. If a signature (or initials) is added to a document, it also becomes possible to identify the individual who is responsible for the transaction or event.

A key internal control for documentation is the use of prenumbered documents (such as receipts and cheques). The prenumbering can be done either electronically (with electronically generated documents) or manually. Prenumbering helps prevent a transaction from being recorded more than once or, conversely, from not being recorded at all.

A second key control is the requirement that **original documents** (source documents) required for accounting entries be promptly forwarded to the accounting department to help ensure timely and accurate recording of the transaction. Photocopies should not be used to record transactions as this increases the risk of duplicate entries and payments. For example, most companies now require employees to submit the actual boarding passes, together with the invoice from the airline or travel agent, when claiming travel expenses. The boarding pass provides evidence that the employee did take the scheduled flight and reduces the risk of reimbursing the employee more than once or for a flight that was later cancelled and not taken.

MISSING IN ACTION

Sophia and Tamra are sales representatives for their company. They both travel a great deal and complete expense reports to obtain reimbursements of their travel expenses from the company. One day, Sophia realized that the accounting department would accept photocopies of invoices relating to travel. Sophia went to Tamra's desk and noticed several invoices for an out-of-town trip Tamra had just taken. Sophia photocopied the invoices and submitted them as her own expenses. She received a reimbursement cheque for these costs. She did this 18 times during the year.

THE MISSING CONTROL

Documentation
The company should only accept original invoices when processing expense reimbursements.

A good internal control system can require the use of two or more of the specific control activities in a particular situation. For example, documentation is the missing control activity in the above Missing in Action box. In addition, all expense reports should be approved (authorization of transactions and activities) by someone in authority to ensure only authorized travel is claimed. The scenarios described in this, and other, Missing in Action boxes in this chapter only focus on the main control activity.

Physical Controls

Physical controls can be used to safeguard assets and enhance the reliability of accounting records. Physical controls include the controls shown in Illustration 7-1.

►Illustration 7-1
Physical controls

Safes, vaults, and safety deposit boxes for cash and business papers

Locked warehouses and storage cabinets for inventories and records

Computer facilities that require a password, fingerprint, or eyeball scan

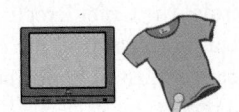

Alarms to prevent break-ins

Television monitors and garment sensors to deter theft

Time clocks for recording time worked

In addition to the physical controls shown above, a company should ensure that assets are adequately insured.

MISSING IN ACTION

Monique and Chantal are roommates who both work at a local bar. Sometimes they work the same shift. When employees begin their shift, they are supposed to swipe their employee cards at a time clock to register the time they arrived at work. Employees must do the same when they leave at the end of their shift. Quite often, Monique, who spends a lot of time with her boyfriend, will arrive at the bar late. If Chantal knows that Monique will be late, she will swipe Monique's card along with her own card. Sometimes, Chantal leaves the bar early because she has another part-time job. Rather than swiping her card when she leaves early, Chantal asks Monique to swipe her card for her later in the evening. They have been swiping each other's cards for more than eight months.

THE MISSING CONTROL

Physical Controls

Time clocks should be placed where they can be easily observed to prevent employees from "punching in or out" with someone else's time card.

Independent Checks of Performance

The four control activities that we just discussed—authorization of transactions and activities, segregation of duties, documentation, and physical controls—must be reviewed independently and frequently. Independent review is necessary because employees can forget or intentionally fail to follow internal controls, or they might become careless if there is no one to observe and evaluate their performance. These reviews should take place internally and externally, as described below.

Internal Reviews.   Independent internal reviews are especially useful in comparing accounting records with existing assets to ensure that nothing has been stolen. The beer count at the beginning of each shift by the bartender in the feature story about Nick's Steakhouse and Pizza is an example. Another example is the reconciliation by an independent person of the cash balance per books with the cash balance per bank. As mentioned earlier, we will learn more about bank reconciliations later in this chapter.

For independent internal reviews to be beneficial, three measures are recommended:

1. The review should be done periodically and sometimes on a surprise basis.
2. The employee performing the review should be independent of the personnel responsible for the information.
3. Discrepancies and exceptions should be reported to a management-level employee who can take appropriate corrective action.

It is very important that reviews be done on a regular basis in order to be an effective control.

In large companies, internal auditors often perform an independent review of control activities. **Internal auditors** are company employees who evaluate the effectiveness of the company's system of internal control. They periodically review the activities of departments and individuals to determine whether prescribed internal controls are being followed.

If a company lists its shares on a public stock exchange in Canada, a management report addressed to shareholders is included in the annual report that explains that management is responsible for the system of internal controls. The Chief Executive Officer (CEO) and Chief Financial Officer (CFO) must also provide certification regarding the effectiveness of internal controls. Any identified control weaknesses of significance must be reported in the Management Discussion and Analysis (MD&A) section of the annual report.

External Reviews.   It is useful to contrast independent *internal* reviews with independent *external* reviews. **External auditors** perform an important type of external review. They, in contrast to internal auditors, are independent of the company. They are professional accountants hired by a company to report on whether or not the company's financial statements fairly present its financial position and results of operations.

All public companies, including Shoppers Drug Mart, are required to have an external audit. A copy of Shoppers' auditors' report is included in Appendix A. As you will see in the report, external auditors plan and perform an audit to obtain reasonable assurance that the financial statements do not have any significant errors.

In addition, as part of the company's governance processes, the independent audit committee of the board of directors is responsible for reviewing the company's internal control systems to ensure that they are adequate to result in fair, complete, and accurate financial reporting.

MISSING IN ACTION

Kevin Lin works in the IT department at Twillingate Inc. The company provides a MacBook Pro® to all salespeople when they join the company. The laptop must be returned to Kevin when a salesperson leaves. Kevin is responsible for managing the laptops. He tracks them using an Excel spreadsheet that includes the date purchased, serial number, date assigned to a salesperson, date returned by a salesperson, and any repair information. The spreadsheet is sent to the asset clerk in the accounting department every month. One day, Angela Liu, the new asset clerk, decided to verify Kevin's spreadsheet after learning that no one in accounting or IT had ever checked it. When Angela attempted to match the information on the spreadsheet to the physical laptops, she found that two employees had left the company without returning their laptops. In addition, a laptop was identified as being out for repairs for over a year and Kevin hadn't followed up with the repair company. Finally, a laptop listed as unassigned could not be located.

THE MISSING CONTROL

Independent Verification
The asset clerk should have verified Kevin's spreadsheet on a regular basis to ensure all of Twillingate's computer assets were accounted for.

Human Resource Controls

Control measures in this area can include the following:

1. **Conducting thorough background checks.** Many believe that the most important and inexpensive measure any company can take to reduce employee theft and fraud is for the human resources department to conduct thorough background checks. For example, Loblaw weeds out prospective employees with criminal records in an effort to reduce the number of items vanishing from its stores. After the company introduced this policy, 7.5% of job applicants were eliminated.
2. **Bonding of employees who handle cash.** Bonding means having insurance protection against theft of assets by dishonest employees. This is often referred to as "fidelity" insurance. Fidelity insurance contributes to the safeguarding of cash in two ways. First, the insurance company carefully screens all individuals before adding them to the policy and may reject risky applicants. Second, bonded employees know that the insurance company will vigorously prosecute all offenders so they have an incentive to act honestly. Common fidelity insurance claims arise from employee dishonesty, embezzlement, forgery, robbery, computer fraud, wire transfer fraud, counterfeiting, and other criminal acts.
3. **Rotating employees' duties and requiring employees to take vacations.** These measures are designed to deter employees from attempting thefts, since they will not be able to permanently conceal their improper actions, especially if the company has difficulty segregating duties. For example, if a manager can approve both the hiring of staff and the hours they work, then requiring that manager to take a vacation will allow their replacement to determine if any fictitious employees are on the payroll. Many employee thefts have been discovered when the employee was on vacation or assigned to a new position.

MISSING IN ACTION

Tom Rollins is the supervisor of the payroll department for a company that operates a number of drilling rigs. He has the ability to approve staff hiring and salary levels, to set employees up in the accounting system, to enter information relating to hours worked, and to sign payroll cheques. Tom is a very popular employee who has been with the company for over 20 years. He has resisted requests to pay employee salaries directly through the bank, preferring instead to hand out pay-cheques every two weeks to each employee. He has never taken a vacation since he was promoted to his present position nearly five years ago. One afternoon, just after the payroll cheques were printed but not yet signed by Tom, he collapsed from a mild heart attack. While Tom recuperated at home, his boss signed all of the payroll cheques and then distributed them to employees. She noticed, however, that there was a cheque for an employee she did not recognize. When she checked the records, she found that the employee had been on the payroll for almost five years. Later investigation revealed that the unknown employee was Tom's ex-wife.

THE MISSING CONTROL

Human Resources
If Tom had been required to take a vacation more frequently, such a fraud might have been prevented or detected sooner.

LIMITATIONS OF INTERNAL CONTROL

No matter how well it is designed and operated, a company's system of internal control can only provide **reasonable assurance** that assets are properly safeguarded and that the accounting records are accurate and reliable. The concept of reasonable assurance is based on the belief that the costs of establishing control activities should not be more than their expected benefit.

To illustrate, consider shoplifting losses in retail stores. Such losses could be completely eliminated by having a security guard stop and search customers as they leave the store. Store managers have concluded, however, that the cost of doing so, along with the negative effects on customers' goodwill, outweighs the benefits achieved of reduced theft. Instead, stores have attempted to "control" shoplifting losses by using less costly procedures such as (1) posting signs saying, "We reserve the right to inspect all packages" and "All shoplifters will be prosecuted"; (2) using hidden TV cameras and store detectives to monitor customer activity; and (3) using sensor equipment at exits.

The size of the business may impose limitations on internal control. In a small company, for example, it may be difficult to apply segregation of duties and independent internal verification because of the small number of employees. In situations such as this, it is often necessary for the owner or management to assume the responsibility of performing or supervising incompatible functions. For example, at a small gas station, it is not unusual for a cashier to receive the cash and also prepare and make the night deposit at the bank. If the cash register tape is not locked, and the cashier could therefore tamper with the sales recorded in the cash register, it may be necessary for the owner to make the nightly bank deposits.

The human element is an important factor in every system of internal control. A good system can become ineffective as a result of lack of training, employee fatigue, carelessness, or indifference. For example, a receiving clerk may not bother to count goods received or just "fudge" the count, resulting in the wrong amount of inventory being added to the records.

Occasionally, two or more individuals may work together to get around prescribed control activities. Such collusion can significantly lessen the effectiveness of internal control because it eliminates the protection expected from segregating the employees' duties. If a supervisor and a cashier collaborate to understate cash receipts and steal the shortfall, the system of internal control may be defeated (at least in the short run). The act of collusion is also known as fraud.

Fraud is an intentional act to misappropriate (steal) assets or misstate financial statements. In its 2012 *Report to the Nations on Occupational Fraud and Abuse*, the Association of Certified Fraud Examiners (ACFE) reports that an organization loses approximately 5% of its annual revenues to fraudulent activities committed by its own employees. Asset misappropriation (for example, theft of cash or other assets) accounted for approximately 87% of the reported cases. Corruption and billing schemes pose a significant risk to organizations as this type of occupational (employee) fraud represented 50% of the reported fraud and abuse cases. Another key finding in the ACFE report was the size of losses suffered by small businesses. These organizations, which typically have fewer internal controls, suffered the largest average losses. In fact, smaller businesses often suffered larger losses than bigger businesses.

DECISION TOOLKIT

Decision Checkpoints	 Info Needed for Decision	 Tools to Use for Decision	 How to Evaluate Results
Are the company's financial statements supported by adequate internal controls?	Auditor's report, statement of management responsibility, management discussion and analysis	Control activities include (1) authorizing transactions and activities, (2) segregating duties, (3) documenting transactions, (4) employing physical controls, (5) independently checking performance, and (6) applying human resource controls	If there is any indication that these or other controls are lacking, the financial statements could contain errors.

BEFORE YOU GO ON...

▶ Do It! Control Activities

In each of the following situations, identify the appropriate control activity and state whether it has been supported or violated:

(a) The purchasing department orders, receives, and pays for merchandise.

(b) All cheques are prenumbered and accounted for.

(c) The internal auditor performs surprise cash counts.

(d) Extra cash is kept locked in a safe that can only be accessed by the head cashier and supervisor.

(e) Each cashier has his own cash drawer.

(f) The company's controller received a plaque for distinguished service because he had not taken a vacation in five years.

Action Plan

- Understand each of the control activities: authorization of transactions and activities, segregation of duties, documentation, physical controls, independent checks of performance, and human resource controls.

Solution

(a) Violation of segregation of duties

(b) Support of documentation procedures

(c) Support of independent performance checks

(d) Support of physical controls

(e) Support of authorization of transactions and activities

(f) Violation of human resource controls (employees should take vacations)

Related Exercise Material: BE7-1, BE7-2, BE7-3, BE7-4, E7-1, E7-2, E7-3, and E7-4.

the navigator

Cash Controls

Because cash is easily concealed and transported, it is highly susceptible to theft. In addition, because of the large volume of cash transactions, errors may easily occur in recording these transactions. To safeguard cash and to ensure the accuracy of the accounting records, effective control activities are essential.

Before we apply the control activities we learned in the last section to cash, let's first look at what cash is, and is not. **Cash** consists of coins, currency (paper money), cheques, money orders, and money on hand or on deposit in a bank or similar depository. The general rule is that if the bank will accept it for deposit, it is cash.

Cash does *not* include postdated cheques (cheques payable in the future), stale-dated cheques (cheques that will not be honoured because they are more than six months old), or returned cheques (cheques lacking sufficient funds). Because postage stamps or IOUs from employees are not the current medium of exchange or acceptable at face value on deposit, they are not considered cash either and are recorded as Supplies (postage stamps) and Advances to Employees (IOU's from employees).

You may wonder if debit and credit cards are, or are not, cash. The answer is: "It depends." Debit card transactions and bank credit card transactions, such as Visa and MasterCard, are considered cash, because banks accept them as deposits. On the other hand, nonbank credit card transactions, such as from using a Sears credit card, are not. We will learn more about nonbank credit card transactions in Chapter 8. Debit and credit cards—whether bank or nonbank—are used far more frequently than cash today, as Mark Petros mentioned in the chapter-opening feature story.

ACCOUNTING MATTERS!

What Is Cash?

The way people have paid for transactions has changed over the centuries. Did you know that the first metal coins date back to 610-560 BC? Coins continue to be in use today, of course, but these are changing as well. For example, in 2012, the Royal Canadian Mint announced it would no longer make pennies and that the coin would be withdrawn from circulation.

A form of paper money first appeared in 1685. Paper money has also undergone many changes in design, denomination, and paper composition. Canada, for example no longer has $1 and $2 bills (which were replaced with the "loonie" and "toonie" coins).

In the 1970s, debit and credit cards made their debut. By 2010, 94% of Canadians had a debit card. Further refinements to these cards include the introduction of the Visa debit card, which functions as a debit card when used in an ATM but can also be used as a credit card when making on-line purchases.

What's next? Paper cheques will soon be a thing of the past—at least for some. The Government of Canada has announced that individuals and businesses will no longer receive cheques from it in the mail after April 1, 2016. Instead, direct deposits will be used to make any Government payments. The cost to write a cheque is approximately $0.82, while the cost of a direct deposit is only $0.13.

New digital forms of money such as PayPal have appeared. The MasterCard PayPass card or enabled device operates on radio frequencies so it isn't necessary to insert the card in a point-of-sale terminal. Biometric digital payment systems will allow transactions to occur when you put your finger on the pad. As these digital forms of payment gain more acceptance, businesses will need to adapt their accounting and internal control processes to effectively control and manage their "cash" transactions.

CONTROL ACTIVITIES OVER CASH RECEIPTS

Cash receipts come from a variety of sources: cash sales; cheques received either at the time of sale or at a later date by mail; the receipt of interest, rents, and dividends; investments by shareholders; bank loans; and proceeds from the sale of assets. The internal control procedures relating to cash receipts will vary from one company to another depending on the nature of their business. To illustrate some of these control activities, we will cover ones used in a typical service or merchandising business.

Over-the-Counter Receipts

As we saw with Nick's Steakhouse and Pizza in our feature story, most businesses receive payment with cash, credit cards, or debit cards. Staff members who operate cash registers are given a float to make change for customers who pay cash. All sales must be entered into the register through point-of-sale software, which not only records the sale at the proper price but updates inventory records at the same time. Often the sale can be recorded simply by scanning the bar code on merchandise.

At the end of a shift, staff members must ensure that the cash in the register is equal to the float plus the cash sales that were recorded on the system. A supervisor (not the cashier) should access the system to determine the amount and type of sales recorded at that register so that cashiers cannot understate the sales reported if they have taken any cash. Employees must also ensure that the receipts are on hand for sales made by debit or credit cards and that these match sales that were recorded with this type of payment.

Let's assume that an employee steals the cash received from a customer and does not record the sale in the cash register. How will this theft be detected? After all, the cash collected from sales in the cash register will still equal the sales recorded. In this case, other internal control procedures, such as those used to control inventory, may detect the theft, particularly if inventory is counted frequently. The count results will reveal a lower amount of inventory on hand than is shown in the point-of-sale system. The frequency of inventory counts depends on the type and cost of inventory. For example, the bar staff count the beer every shift at Nick's because of beer's cost and susceptibility to theft. A large box store, on the other hand, may count non-perishable items such as canned goods weekly or monthly. Thus it would take longer for the theft to be detected. Therefore some companies use security cameras to monitor staff to ensure that all sales are recorded in the system.

Not all businesses have converted to point-of-sale technology either for cost or other reasons. When a business doesn't use point-of-sale technology, the possibility of unintentional and intentional errors increases. For example, a staff member must manually enter the sales price into the register rather than having the prices preprogrammed in the system. This can lead to an unintentional error such as entering the price as $5.49 rather than the correct price of $9.45. It also provides the opportunity for the staff member to record the sale at a lower price for friends. Finally, because inventory is not automatically updated, intentional and unintentional errors may not be located until inventory is counted at a much later date.

Generally, internal control over cash receipts is more effective when **cash receipts are deposited intact into the bank account on a daily basis or are made by electronic funds transfer.** An authorized employee, such as the head cashier or general manager, should make bank deposits.

Electronic Receipts

Electronic funds transfer (EFT) is a way of transferring money electronically from one bank account to another without any paper money changing hands. Debit and credit card transactions, mentioned earlier, are examples of electronic funds transfers. Another example is when customers use on-line banking to pay their accounts. When a customer pays his or her account, the cash is instantly transferred from the customer's bank account to the company's bank account.

Electronic funds transfers normally result in better internal control since company employees are not required to handle cash (or cheques, which will be discussed in the next section). This does not mean that recording errors or the opportunities for fraud are eliminated. For example, without proper authorization and segregation of duties, an employee might be able to redirect electronic collections into a personal bank account and conceal the theft with fraudulent accounting entries.

Cheque Receipts

Although the use of cheques has diminished, recent statistics from the Canadian Payments Association indicate that, although only 4% of all payments are made with cheques, they represent 40% of the value of all banking transactions. This makes sense as companies don't want to pay credit card fees on large-value transactions. For example, when you buy a new car, the dealer will want to receive a cheque, not your credit card. We will discuss the fees charged by banks when credit cards are used later in this chapter.

When a cheque is received at the time of the sale, it will be included in the cash register and form part of an employee's reconciliation of daily sales. When a cheque is received in the mail, it is usually accompanied by a remittance advice, which is the detachable part of the sales invoice that customers are asked to send back with their cheque. Mailroom clerks will send the remittance advices to the accountants responsible for recording cash receipts while sending the cheques to someone who will deposit them at the bank. The person making the bank deposit should have no record-keeping duties. In this way, accountants cannot intercept a cheque and record its receipt to cover up a theft. The person making the bank deposit will receive a bank-stamped deposit slip. Each day, an independent employee can then compare the amount of cash deposited per the deposit slip with the amount of cash receipts recorded that day to ensure that funds deposited were also recorded.

Illustration 7-2 shows examples of how the control activities explained earlier apply to cash receipts.

▶Illustration 7-2

Application of control activities to cash receipts

Control Activities over Cash Receipts

Authorization	Segregation of Duties	Documentation	Physical Controls	Independent Checks of Performance	Human Resource Controls
Authorize only designated personnel to handle cash receipts.	Have different individuals recording cash receipts and handling cash.	Use remittance advices, cash register tapes, and deposit slips or confirmations.	Store cash in safes and bank vaults with limited access; use cash registers.	Have supervisors count cash receipts daily; have an accountant compare total receipts with bank deposits daily.	Conduct background checks; bond personnel who handle cash; require employees to take vacations.

CONTROL ACTIVITIES OVER CASH PAYMENTS

Cash is disbursed for a variety of reasons, such as to pay expenses, to settle liabilities, or to purchase assets. Generally, control activities over cash payments are more effective when **payments are made by cheque or by electronic funds transfer, rather than in cash**. Other control procedures (such as petty cash funds, which are not discussed here) are put in place for the few payments that cannot be made by cheque (for example, postage).

Good control for cheques includes having them signed by at least two authorized employees. The cheque signers should carefully review the supporting documentation for the payment before signing the cheque. There should be a clear segregation of duties between the cheque-signing function and the accounts payable function to ensure that accountants cannot record invoices to companies they control and then sign cheques to pay these invoices. Cheques should be pre-numbered and all cheque numbers must be accounted for in the payment and recording process. Cheques should never be pre-signed and blank cheques and cheque-signing machines should be safeguarded.

Payments can also be made electronically. For example, when a company pays its employees' salaries using a direct deposit option, the cash is instantly transferred from the company's bank account to each employee's bank account. As we discussed in the cash receipts section, as long as there is proper authorization and segregation of duties, the use of EFT for cash payments will result in better internal control.

Examples of control activities applied to cash payments are shown in Illustration 7-3.

Control Activities over Cash Payments

Authorization	Segregation of Duties	Documentation	Physical Controls	Independent Checks of Performance	Human Resource Controls
Authorize only designated personnel to sign cheques or approve electronic payments.	Have different individuals approve and make payments; ensure cheque signers do not record cash payments.	Use prenumbered cheques and account for them in sequence; ensure each cheque has an approved invoice.	Store cash in safes and bank vaults with limited access; restrict access to blank cheques and signing machines; use electronic payments when possible.	Compare cheques with invoices; reconcile the bank statement monthly.	Conduct background checks; bond personnel who handle cash; require employees to take vacations.

▶Illustration 7-3

Application of control activities to cash payments

BEFORE YOU GO ON...

▶Do It! Control Activities over Cash Receipts

At Hamburger Heaven Restaurant, six employees working behind the counter share two cash registers. The owner says, "In an ideal situation, one person would be designated to ring in orders for each cash register, but when we get swamped, we all have to work together to keep things running smoothly." The prices of most items are preprogrammed into the cash register. At the end of the day, each register generates a sales report and one of the employees will count the cash in both registers, and after subtracting the float, will compare the total with the sales report. Then the employee puts the cash in an unlocked drawer in the office.

Identify any violations of control activities over cash receipts at this restaurant.

Action Plan

• Understand the application of each of the control activities to cash receipts: authorization of transactions and activities, segregation of duties, documentation, physical controls, independent checks of performance, and human resource controls.

Solution

Because more than one person can use the same cash register, the authorization of transactions and activities control has been violated. If there is a cash shortage in the register at the end of the day, it will not be possible to determine who is responsible for it.

Segregation of duties has also been violated. Staff members who ring up the sale on the cash register and have access to cash should not be the ones to check the cash receipts against the sales report. They could choose to not ring up a sale and pocket the cash instead.

Finally, physical controls are weak because cash should be deposited in a bank promptly, preferably as a night deposit.

Related Exercise Material: BE7-3, BE7-4, E7-3, and E7-4.

the navigator

Bank Accounts—A Key Control Activity

Several of the control activities discussed in the previous section involved the use of a bank—depositing cash on a regular basis, comparing cash receipts with bank deposit totals, and preparing monthly bank reconciliations. **In other words, the use of a bank contributes significantly to good internal control over cash.**

A company can control its cash by using a bank to safeguard its cash, cheques received and written, and electronic funds received and paid. The use of a bank minimizes the amount of currency that must be kept on hand. In addition, control is strengthened because a second record is maintained of all bank transactions, which can then be compared with the company's records. The

STUDY OBJECTIVE 3

Prepare a bank reconciliation.

bank regularly provides the company with a record of its bank transactions, which allows the company to reconcile the Cash account to the bank's records.

BANK STATEMENTS

Each month, the bank provides a bank statement showing the company's bank transactions and balances. For example, in Illustration 7-4, the statement for Laird Ltd. shows the following: (1) dates; (2) a description of each transaction; (3) the amounts deducted (**debited**) from the bank account (for example, cheques and other payments); (4) the amounts added (**credited**) to the bank account (for example, deposits and other receipts); and (5) the account balance after each transaction.

▶Illustration 7-4

Bank statement

Your branch address:

505 King Street
Fredericton, NB E3N 1E7

Business Banking Statement

For the period ending April 30, 2015

Business Banking

Your Branch
Fredericton Main Office
Transit number: 0123

**For questions about your
statement call** (506) 453-0280

Direct Banking
1-800-363-9992

**Easier, more personalized ABM
banking.**
Now you can select your personal
preferences including "My Usual Fast Cash"
and language options.

Visit bmo.com/abm to learn more about our
new ABM facilities.

Summary of account

Account	Opening balance ($)	Total amounts deducted ($)	+ Total amounts added ($)	Closing balance ($) on April 30, 2015
Interest Chequing Account # 0123 4567-890	13,256.90	11,719.70	13,069.53	14,606.73

Transaction details

Date	Description	Amounts deducted from account (debits)	Amounts added to account (credits)	Balance ($)
	Owner: LAIRD LTD. 500 QUEEN STREET FREDERICTON, NB E3B 5C2			
Apr 1	Opening balance			13,256.90
2	Deposit at BR. 0123		4,276.85	17,533.75
3	EFT, collection from M. Trask		2,137.50	19,671.25
6	Cheque, No. 436	1,185.79		18,485.46
7	Cheque, No. 439	3,260.00		15,225.46
13	Cheque, No. 441	2,420.00		12,805.46
14	Deposit at BR. 0123		425.60	13,231.06
16	Direct deposit, G. Jones		4,649.68	17,880.74
21	Returned cheque—NSF	425.60		17,455.14
21	NSF fee	40.00		17,415.14
23	Deposit at BR. 0098		1,579.90	18,995.04
26	EFT, payment of salaries	3,563.40		15,431.64
28	EFT, payment to Manulife Insurance	659.91		14,771.73
30	Debit and credit card fees	120.00		14,651.73
30	Bank service charges	45.00		14,606.73

BMO Bank of Montreal
A part of BMO Financial Group

At first glance, it may appear that the debits and credits reported on the bank statement are backward. How can amounts deducted from a bank account, like a cheque, be a debit? And how can amounts added to a bank account, like a deposit, be a credit? Debits and credits are not really backward. Cash is an asset account for the company. Assets are increased by debits (such as for cash receipts) and decreased by credits (such as for cash payments). Cash accounts for the bank, however, are liabilities because the bank is only holding the cash for the company. The company can

Helpful Hint
What to the bank is a *credit* is to the company a *debit*, and vice versa.

request it at any time. Liabilities are increased by credits and decreased by debits. When a company deposits money into its bank account, the bank's liability to the company increases. When a company writes a cheque or makes an electronic payment, the bank pays out this amount and decreases (debits) its liability to the company.

Amounts Deducted from a Bank Account (Debits)

Amounts deducted from a bank account include cheques and other payments. A cheque is a written order signed by an employee with signing authority that instructs the bank to pay a specific sum of money to a designated recipient (payee).

A common deduction in a company's bank account relates to the return of a previously deposited customer's cheque. A customer's cheque is said to bounce (is not honoured) when the customer does not have enough money in her bank account to cover the cheque. When this occurs, the customer's bank marks the cheque **NSF (not sufficient funds) cheque**, or **returned cheque**, and returns it to the depositor's bank. The bank then debits (decreases) the depositor's account, as shown by the notation, "Returned cheque—NSF" on the bank statement in Illustration 7-4 in the amount of $425.60 on April 21.

Note that the company previously deposited this cheque on April 14. Because the deposit was credited (added) to the bank account on April 14 and the cheque was not honoured, it must be debited (deducted) by the bank (see April 21 transaction). The bank returns the NSF cheque to the depositor as notification of the charge.

The company (depositor) will then advise the customer who wrote the NSF cheque that the payment was declined and that payment is still owed on the account. In addition, as the company's bank generally charges a service charge for processing a returned cheque, the company usually passes this on to the customer by adding the charged amount to the customer's account balance. You can see that the Bank of Montreal charged Laird a $40 NSF fee on April 21. In summary, the overall effect of an NSF cheque to the depositor is to create an account receivable and to reduce the cash in the depositor's bank account.

Many companies pay their employees' salaries using a direct deposit option. Laird pays its salaries this way. You can see the notation "EFT, payment of salaries" on April 26 in the bank statement in Illustration 7-4. When employee salaries are paid this way, the cash is automatically transferred from the company's bank account to each employee's bank account. It isn't necessary for the employee to hold an account at the company's bank for the transfer to be processed.

Other disbursements may appear on the bank statement. For example, pre-authorized payments relating to loans and insurance paid on a recurring basis are often made electronically. In Illustration 7-4, the notation "EFT, payment to Manulife Insurance" tells us that Laird authorized its insurance company to electronically withdraw the insurance premium on April 28.

Because the company initiated the transaction for salaries, and the transaction for the payment to Manulife, it can record them before receiving the bank statement. As we will learn later when we discuss deposits, sometimes a company will have to receive the bank statement before recording the transaction because another party initiated it. For example, a company won't know its customers have paid their accounts electronically until it receives the bank statement and supporting documentation.

You will recall that we discussed debit and bank credit cards earlier in this chapter. Companies are willing to pay a fee for the almost instantaneous transfer of cash that occurs when a customer uses debit and bank credit cards. Some banks deduct debit and credit card fees from the company's bank account daily and others monthly, depending on the terms of the debit and credit card agreements. We have assumed a monthly service charge for debit and credit card fees for Laird. You can see the fees of $120 related to these transactions were removed from Laird's bank account on April 30.

Note that banks do not bill companies for their fees. Rather, the bank deducts this amount directly from the company's bank account. In addition to service charges such as the NSF fee and debit and credit card fees discussed above, banks also deduct a service charge for the account services they provide. For example, $45 was deducted directly by the bank from Laird's account on April 30 for this purpose. Bank service charges vary widely depending on what kind of plan the company has with its bank.

Amounts Added to a Bank Account (Credits)

Deposits to a company's bank account can be made by an authorized employee, and documented by a deposit slip. Deposits can also be made by direct deposit, through an automated banking machine, or through an electronic funds transfer if the company allows customers to pay their accounts on-line. For example, in Illustration 7-4 Laird electronically collected $2,137.50 from a customer on April 3 in payment of an account. Another customer made a deposit directly to Laird's bank account on April 16 for $4,649.68.

In cases of electronic collections and direct deposits from customers, the company is often unaware of the collection until the bank statement is received. Why? When a customer pays his or her account using on-line banking or other electronic means, the cash is instantly transferred from the customer's bank account to the company's bank account. The primary evidence of these electronic cash receipts will be a line on the bank statement showing the amount, a reference number, and the name or account number of the person paying. Consequently, electronic receipts such as these are normally recorded directly from the bank statement.

Other additions to a company's bank account by the bank include any interest earned on the account balance and proceeds from operating lines of credit and bank loans. No separate notification is usually given for these amounts either.

RECONCILING THE BANK ACCOUNT

Although the bank and the company keep independent records of the company's chequing account, you might assume that the balances in both sets of records will always agree. In fact, the two balances are seldom the same because many transactions are not recorded at the same time on both records. It is therefore necessary to identify any differences between the bank statement and the company's accounting records whenever the bank statement is received and ensure that the reasons for the differences are acceptable. Reconciling the bank account is the process used to determine whether these differences are acceptable or not.

The lack of agreement between the balances has two causes:

1. **Time lags** that prevent one of the parties from recording the transaction in the same period as the other party
2. **Errors** by either party in recording transactions

Except in electronic banking transactions, time lags occur often. For example, several days may pass between the time a company mails a supplier a cheque and the date the supplier presents the cheque to the bank for payment. Cheques recorded by a company that have not yet cleared (been paid by) the bank are called **outstanding cheques**.

Similarly, when a company uses the bank's night depository to make its deposits, there will be a difference of one day (or more, if holidays intervene) between the time the receipts are recorded by the company and the time they are recorded by the bank. Deposits recorded by the company that have not yet been recorded by the bank are called **deposits in transit**.

Errors can also occur. The frequency of errors depends on how effectively the company and bank have implemented internal controls. Bank errors are infrequent. However, either party could accidentally record a $450 cheque as $45 or $540. In addition, the bank might mistakenly charge a cheque to the wrong account if the code is missing or if the cheque cannot be scanned. Direct deposits and electronic funds transfers also depend on the correct account being keyed into the system.

ACCOUNTING MATTERS!

Bank Errors

Bank errors may not occur as frequently as company errors, but they can still happen. Scotiabank's discount brokerage arm accidentally put $171 million of somebody else's money into a Toronto doctor's Scotiabank account. It took four months to find and correct the error. The red-faced bank admitted that many things went wrong—from posting the error to mistakes in reversals. And there are many more stories about banks making mistakes. However, they usually involve misplaced debits and rarely amounts as high as this.

Reconciliation Procedures

To get the most benefit from bank reconciliations, they should be prepared by an employee who has no other responsibilities related to cash. When the control activity of segregation of duties is not followed in preparing the reconciliation, cash embezzlements may go unnoticed. For example, a cashier who prepares the reconciliation can steal cash and hide the theft by misstating amounts on the reconciliation. In this way, the bank account would appear to reconcile with the company records and the theft would not be detected.

In reconciling the bank account, it is customary to reconcile the balance per the bank and the balance per the books to their adjusted (correct) cash balances. Both the books and the bank balance are likely to change as a result of the reconciliation process. The reconciliation is usually divided into two sections: one relating to the bank statement balance and one relating to the book balance. The starting point when preparing the reconciliation is to enter the balance per bank (found on the bank statement) and the balance per books (found in the Cash account in the general ledger) on the reconciliation. These are often called *unadjusted* balances, to distinguish them from the adjusted balances, which will be determined through the bank reconciliation process. Adjustments are then made to each balance so that any unrecorded transactions are accounted for, as shown in Illustration 7-5.

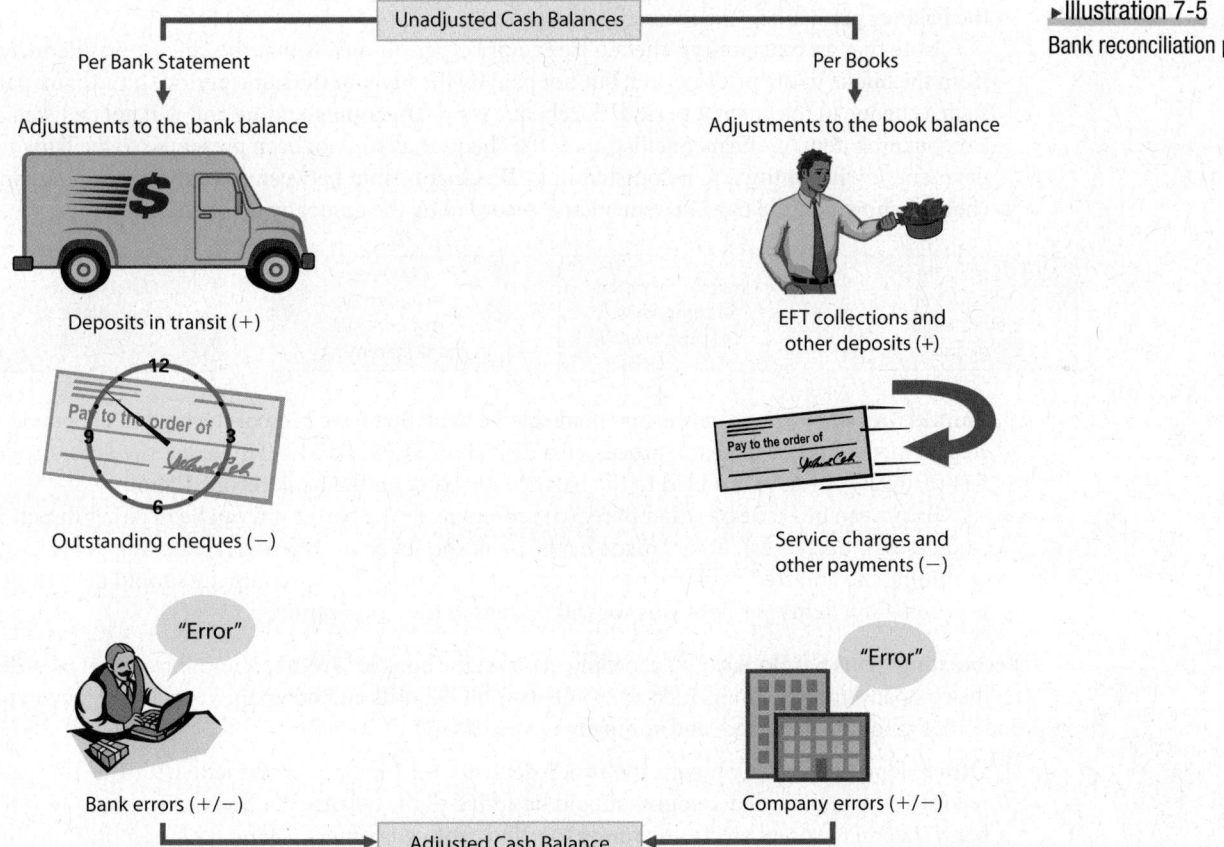

▶Illustration 7-5
Bank reconciliation procedures

The following steps reveal the major reconciling items that cause the difference between the two balances:

Reconciling Items per Bank. On the bank side of the reconciliation, the items to reconcile are deposits in transit (amounts added), outstanding cheques (amounts deducted), and bank errors (if any). By adjusting the bank balance for these items, we are bringing that balance up to date.

1. **Deposits in transit (+).** Compare the individual deposits on the bank statement with (1) the deposits in transit from the preceding bank reconciliation and (2) the deposits recorded in the books. Deposits in transit are already recorded on the company's books but have not yet been recorded by the bank because it does not know about them yet. Therefore, they must be added to the balance per bank in the reconciliation process.

Before determining the deposits in transit for the current period, you must check whether all deposits in transit that are outstanding from a prior period have cleared. For example, assume that Laird Ltd. used a night deposit slot to deposit $2,201.40 on Thursday, April 30. The bank will not receive or record this deposit until Friday, May 1. This amount would be treated as a deposit in transit at the end of April and would be added to the balance per bank in the reconciliation process. However, this outstanding deposit will clear the bank in May and will therefore no longer be a deposit in transit at the end of May. As at the end of May, this amount will have been recorded by both the company and the bank. The relationship between deposits in transit, deposits shown on the bank statement, and deposits recorded by the company is shown below:

Deposits in transit at beginning of period	+	Deposits recorded in company's books this period	−	Deposits recorded on this period's bank statement	=	Deposits in transit at end of period

2. **Outstanding cheques** (−). Compare the paid cheques shown on the bank statement or returned with the bank statement with (a) cheques outstanding from the preceding bank reconciliation and (b) cheques issued by the company. Outstanding cheques are already recorded on the company's books but have not yet cleared the bank account. Therefore, they must be deducted from the balance per bank in the reconciliation process.

Note that an outstanding cheque from a prior period means that the cheque was deducted from the books in the prior period, but not paid by the bank in the same period. If the bank paid such a cheque in the current period, the cheque is no longer outstanding and will not be listed as a reconciling item on the reconciliation. If the cheque has still not been presented to the bank for payment, it will continue to be outstanding. The relationship between outstanding cheques and cheques shown on the bank statement and recorded by the company is shown below:

Outstanding cheques at beginning of period	+	Cheques recorded in company's books this period	−	Cheques recorded on this period's bank statement	=	Outstanding cheques at end of period

3. **Bank errors** (+/−). Note any errors made by the bank that have been discovered in the previous steps. For example, if the bank processed a deposit of $1,693 as $1,639 in error, the difference of $54 ($1,693 − $1,639) is added to the balance per bank on the bank reconciliation.

Errors can be made by either party (the company or the bank) and can be in either direction (increases or decreases). Errors made by the bank should be included as reconciling items in determining the adjusted cash balance per bank. Errors made by the company should be included as reconciling items per books, as we will discuss in the next section.

Reconciling Items per Books.   Reconciling items on the book side relate to amounts not yet recorded on the company's books and include adjustments from deposits and other amounts added, payments and other amounts deducted, and company errors (if any).

1. **Other deposits** (+). Compare the other deposits on the bank statement with the company records. Any unrecorded amounts should be added to the balance per books. For example, if the bank statement shows electronic funds transfers from customers paying their accounts on-line, these amounts should be added to the balance per books on the bank reconciliation to update the company's records unless they had previously been recorded by the company.

2. **Other payments** (−). Similarly, any unrecorded other payments should be deducted from the balance per books. For example, if the bank statement shows service charges (such as debit and credit card fees and other bank service charges), this amount is deducted from the balance per books on the bank reconciliation to make the company's records agree with the bank's records. Normally, the company will already have recorded electronic payments. However, if this has not been the case, then these payments must be deducted from the balance per books on the bank reconciliation to make the company's records agree with the bank's records.

3. **Book errors** (+/−). Note any errors made by the depositor that have been discovered in the previous steps. For example, the company wrote cheque No. 439 to a supplier in the amount of $3,260 on April 7 but the accounting clerk recorded the cheque amount as $3,620. The error of

$360 ($3,620 − $3,260) is added to the balance per books because the company reduced the balance per books by $360 too much when it recorded the cheque as $3,620 instead of $3,260. Make sure that you include only errors made by the company, not the bank, as reconciling items in determining the adjusted cash balance per books.

Bank Reconciliation Illustrated

The bank statement for Laird Ltd. was shown in Illustration 7-4. It shows an unadjusted balance per bank of $14,606.73 on April 30, 2015. On this date, the unadjusted cash balance per books is $4,387.55.

From the steps described above, the following reconciling items for the bank can be determined:

1. **Deposits in transit** (+): After comparing the deposits recorded in the books with the deposits listed in the bank statement, it was determined that the April 30 deposit of $2,201.40 was not recorded by the bank until May 1. $2,201.40
2. **Outstanding cheques** (−): After comparing the cheques recorded in the books with the cheques listed in the bank statement, it was determined that three cheques were outstanding: No. 437, $3,000.00; No. 438, $1,401.30; and No. 440, $1,502.70.   5,904.00
3. **Bank errors** (+/−): None

Reconciling items per books are as follows:

1. **Other deposits** (+): Unrecorded electronic receipts from customers on account on April 3 and 16 determined from the bank statement: $2,137.50 + $4,649.68. $6,787.18
2. **Other payments** (−): The electronic payments on April 26 and 28 were previously recorded by the company when they were initiated. Unrecorded charges determined from the bank statement are as follows:

Returned cheque plus NSF fee on April 21 ($425.60 + $40)	465.60
Debit and credit card fees on April 30	120.00
Bank service charges on April 30	45.00

3. **Company errors** (+): Cheque No. 439 was correctly written by Laird for $3,260 and was correctly paid by the bank on April 7. However, it was recorded as $3,620 on Laird's books.   360.00

The bank reconciliation follows:

LAIRD LTD. Bank Reconciliation April 30, 2015		
Cash balance per bank statement		$14,606.73
Add: Deposits in transit		2,201.40
		16,808.13
Less: Outstanding cheques		
No. 437	$3,000.00	
No. 438	1,401.30	
No. 440	1,502.70	5,904.00
Adjusted cash balance per bank		$10,904.13
Cash balance per books		$ 4,387.55
Add: Electronic receipts from customers on account		
M. Trask	$2,137.50	
G. Jones	4,649.68	
Error in recording cheque No. 439 ($3,620 − $3,260)	360.00	7,147.18
		11,534.73
Less: Returned (NSF) cheque plus		
service charge ($425.60 + $40)	$ 465.60	
Debit and credit card fees	120.00	
Bank service charges	45.00	630.60
Adjusted cash balance per books		$10,904.13

Bank Reconciliation Journal Entries

The bank reconciliation shown above is only the first step in the reconciliation process. The reconciliation is not complete until the company books are adjusted to agree with the adjusted (correct) cash balance. The depositor must record each reconciling item that arises from determining the adjusted cash balance per books. If these items are not journalized and posted, the Cash account will not show the correct balance.

The adjusting entries for Laird Ltd.'s bank reconciliation at April 30 are as follows:

Electronic Receipts on Account.   A payment of an account by a customer is recorded in the same way, whether the cash is received through the mail or electronically. The entry is:

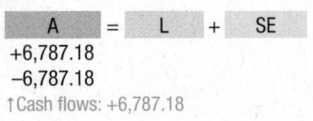

Apr. 30	Cash	6,787.18	
	Accounts Receivable		6,787.18
	(To record electronic collection of accounts for M. Trask, $2,137.50 and G. Jones, $4,649.68)		

In some cases, the company will have already recorded these transactions. Some companies monitor their bank account on-line daily in order to track changes in their account. Other companies, such as Laird, wait until the bank statement is received to record transactions such as these. When this transaction is posted, note that Laird would post the receivable collection to each individual account in its subsidiary ledger as well as in total to the Accounts Receivable control account.

Book Error.   An examination of the general journal shows that the incorrectly recorded cheque, No. 439, was a payment on account to a supplier. The correcting entry is:

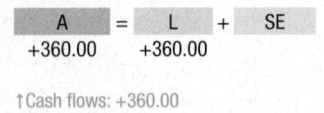

Apr. 30	Cash	360.00	
	Accounts Payable		360.00
	(To correct error in recording cheque No. 439)		

NSF Cheque.   As indicated earlier, a cheque returned for not sufficient funds (NSF) along with the related service charge becomes an account receivable to the depositor. The entry is:

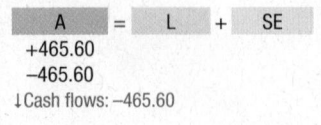

Apr. 30	Accounts Receivable ($425.60 + $40)	465.60	
	Cash		465.60
	(To re-establish accounts receivable for NSF cheque, and related service charge)		

Bank Charges Expense.   Fees for processing debit and credit card transactions are normally debited to the expense account Bank Charges, as are bank service charges. We have chosen to combine and record these in one journal entry below, although they also could be journalized separately.

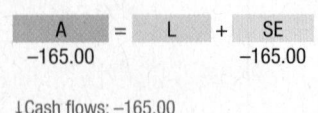

Apr. 30	Bank Charges Expense	165.00	
	Cash		165.00
	(To record charges for debit and credit card fees [$120] and bank service charges [$45])		

Our presentation assumes that all adjustments are made at the end of the month. In practice, a company may also make journal entries during the month as it receives information from the bank regarding its account, or as the company checks its bank account balances on-line.

After the entries are posted, the Cash account will appear as in the T account that follows. The adjusted cash balance of $10,904.13 shown in the ledger should agree with the adjusted cash balance per books in the bank reconciliation shown earlier.

	Cash				
Apr. 30 Bal.	4,387.55		Apr. 30	465.60	
30	6,787.18		30	165.00	
30	360.00				
Apr. 30 Bal.	10,904.13				

What entries does the bank make? **The bank cannot correct your errors on its books and you cannot correct the bank's errors on your books.** If any bank errors are discovered in preparing the reconciliation, the bank should be notified so it can make the necessary corrections on its records. The bank does not make any entries for deposits in transit or outstanding cheques. Only when these items reach the bank will it record them.

BEFORE YOU GO ON...

▶ Do It! Bank Reconciliation

The Cash account of the Oakville Athletic Association showed an unadjusted cash balance of $32,666 on December 31. The bank statement as at that date showed a balance of $36,168. After comparing the bank statement with the company records, the following information was determined.

1. Deposits in transit as at December 31 amounted to $7,286.

2. Cheques issued in December but still outstanding at the end of the month amounted to $6,000. Cheques still outstanding from the month of November totalled $560.

3. The bank made a mistake in recording a U.S. dollar payment received from a customer, overstating the Canadian funds received by $56.

4. Electronic receipts from customers in payment of their accounts totalled $4,699. These receipts have not yet been recorded by the company.

5. The company made an error in recording a customer's deposit in payment of its account. The company recorded the collection of the account as $209, when it should have been $290. The bank correctly recorded the deposit as $290.

6. The bank returned an NSF cheque in the amount of $478 that Oakville had deposited on December 20. The cheque was a payment on a customer's account.

7. The bank debited Oakville's account for service charges of $130. Of this amount, $45 was for processing the NSF cheque (see item 6 above), $30 for bank service charges, and $55 related to debit and credit card fees.

Prepare a bank reconciliation and any required journal entries for Oakville at December 31.

Action Plan

- Prepare the bank reconciliation in two sections: one for the bank and one for the company.
- Determine which reconciling items each side knows about and adjust the other side accordingly.
- Be careful when you determine the direction of an error correction.
- Prepare journal entries only for the book side, not the bank side.
- The adjusted cash balances must agree with each other when complete, and with the general ledger account after the journal entries are posted.

(continued)

Solution

OAKVILLE ATHLETIC ASSOCIATION
Bank Reconciliation
December 31

Cash balance per bank statement		$36,168
Add: Deposits in transit		7,286
		43,454
Less: Outstanding cheques ($6,000 + $560)	$6,560	
Error correction relating to U.S. dollar receipts	56	6,616
Adjusted cash balance per bank		$36,838
Cash balance per books		$32,666
Add: Electronic receipts from customers on account	$4,699	
Deposit error correction ($290 − $209)	81	4,780
		37,446
Less: NSF cheque ($478 + $45)	$523	
Bank service charges	30	
Debit and credit card fees	55	608
Adjusted cash balance per books		$36,838

Dec. 31	Cash		4,699	
	Accounts Receivable			4,699
	(To record electronic receipts on account)			
31	Cash		81	
	Accounts Receivable			81
	(To correct deposit error)			
31	Accounts Receivable		523	
	Cash			523
	(To re-establish accounts receivable for NSF cheque and related service charge)			
31	Bank Charges Expense		85	
	Cash			85
	(To record bank service charges [$30] and debit and credit card fees [$55])			

Check:

		Cash			
Dec. 31	Unadj. bal.	32,666	Dec. 31		523
31		4,699	31		85
31		81			
Dec. 31	Adj. bal.	36,838			

Related Exercise Material: BE7-5, BE7-6, BE7-7, BE7-8, BE7-9, BE7-10, BE7-11, E7-5, E7-6, E7-7, and E7-8.

Reporting and Managing Cash

STUDY OBJECTIVE 4

Explain the reporting and management of cash.

Business owners such as Mark Petros of Nick's and company managers must perform a difficult balancing act to manage cash. On one hand, it is critical to ensure that enough cash is available to pay bills as they come due, buy goods, and take advantage of opportunities as they present themselves. On the other hand, cash itself is an unproductive asset unless it is invested in other assets (such as investments; inventory; and property, plant, and equipment). So it is critical that management know at all times exactly how much cash there is, and how much cash is needed to fund future plans. In the next two sections, we will look at how cash is reported and will identify ways to manage and monitor cash.

REPORTING CASH

Cash is reported in two different financial statements: the statement of financial position and the statement of cash flows. The statement of financial position reports the amount of cash available at a specific point in time. The statement of cash flows shows the sources and uses of cash during a period of time. These two statements are linked because the ending cash amount reported on the statement of cash flows agrees with the cash amount reported on the statement of financial position. The statement of cash flows was introduced in Chapter 1 and will be discussed in detail in Chapter 13.

Because it is the most liquid asset owned by a company, cash is listed first in the current assets section of the statement of financial position, although the reverse order of liquidity can be used under IFRS. Many companies combine cash with cash equivalents. **Cash equivalents** are short-term, highly liquid (easily sold) trading investments that are subject to an insignificant risk of changes in value. Examples of cash equivalents include debt investments such as government treasury bills (T-bills) that mature in 90 days or less, money market funds, and 90-day bank term deposits.

Some companies may be in a cash deficit or overdraft position at year end. Bank overdrafts occur when a cheque is written for more than the amount in the bank account. This, in effect, is a short-term loan from the bank. Most companies have overdraft protection up to a certain amount with their banks. In an overdraft situation, the cash account will show a credit balance in the general ledger and is reported as a current liability called **bank indebtedness**. This is because the bank has the right to request funds from the company to cover the overdraft (demand) at any time.

Bank overdrafts are deducted from cash and cash equivalents. In summary, cash equivalents include:

A company may have cash that is not available for general use because it is restricted for a special purpose. For example, landfill companies are often required to maintain a fund of restricted cash to ensure that they will have adequate resources to cover closing and cleanup costs at the end of a landfill site's useful life. Cash that has a restricted use should be reported separately on the statement of financial position as **restricted cash**. Restricted cash may be reported as a current or non-current asset, depending on when the cash will be required.

Banks commonly require borrowers to maintain minimum cash balances when making loans to customers. These minimum balances, called **compensating balances**, provide the bank with support for the loans in the event the borrower fails to make a payment. Compensating balances are a form of restricted cash and are reported as a current or non-current asset depending on the term (length) of the loan.

Illustration 7-6 shows how Timmins Technology presents its cash.

TIMMINS TECHNOLOGY CORP. Statement of Financial Position (partial) December 31, 2015	
Current assets	
Cash and cash equivalents	$59,500,000
Restricted cash	6,850,000
Non-current assets	
Compensating cash balance	2,500,000

▶Illustration 7-6
Presentation of cash

Timmins provides further information about the restricted cash in the notes to the financial statements. The company received customer deposits for high-tech equipment to be manufactured and shipped in the next 12 months. The contracts require Timmins to hold the deposits (totalling

$6,850,000) in a separate bank account that cannot be used until the equipment is shipped. In addition, Timmins borrowed $50 million from the bank for expansion activities over the next five years. The bank requires Timmins to hold a compensating balance of 5% of the outstanding loan at all times.

MANAGING CASH

Many companies struggle, not because they cannot generate sales, but because they cannot manage their cash. A real-life example of this is a clothing manufacturing company owned by Sharon McCollick. McCollick gave up a stable, high-paying marketing job to start her own company. Soon she had more clothing orders than she could fill. Yet she found herself on the brink of financial disaster: her company could generate sales, but it was not collecting cash fast enough to support its operations. To survive, a business must have cash.

To understand cash management, consider the operating cycle of Sharon McCollick's clothing manufacturing company. First, it purchases cloth. Let's assume that it purchases the cloth on credit provided by the supplier, so the company owes its supplier money. Next, employees make the cloth into clothing. Now the company also owes its employees money. Then, it sells the clothing to retailers, on credit. McCollick's company will have no money to pay suppliers or employees until it collects money from its customers.

Ensuring that a company has sufficient cash to meet its needs is one of the greatest challenges its faces as it deals with the ebb and flow of cash. Any company can improve its chances of having adequate cash by following basic principles of cash management:

1. **Increase the speed of collection on receivables.** Money owed to Sharon McCollick by her customers is money that she needs as soon as possible. The faster customers pay her, the faster she can use those funds. Thus, rather than have an average collection period of 30 days, she may want an average collection period of 20 days. However, any attempt to force her customers to pay earlier must be carefully weighed against the possibility that she may anger or alienate them. Perhaps her competitors are willing to provide a 30-day grace period. As noted in Chapter 5, a common way to encourage customers to pay more quickly is to offer cash discounts for early payments under such terms as 2/10, n/30.

2. **Keep inventory levels low.** Maintaining a large inventory of cloth and finished clothing is costly. It ties up large amounts of cash to carry the inventory, as well as warehouse space. In addition, inventory can quickly become obsolete if it is held for a long period. Many companies routinely use techniques to reduce their inventory on hand, thus conserving their cash. Of course, if McCollick has inadequate inventory, she will lose sales. The proper level of inventory is an important decision, as we learned in Chapter 6.

3. **Delay payment of liabilities.** By keeping track of when bills are due, McCollick's company can avoid paying bills too early. Let's say her supplier allows 30 days for payment. If she pays in 10 days, she has lost the use of cash for 20 days. Therefore, she should use the full payment period, but she should not "stretch" payment past the point that could damage her credit rating (and future borrowing ability).

4. **Plan the timing of major expenditures.** To maintain operations or to grow, all companies must make major expenditures that normally require some form of outside financing. In order to increase the likelihood of obtaining outside financing, McCollick should carefully consider the timing of major expenditures in light of her company's operating cycle. If at all possible, expenditures should be made when the company normally has excess cash—usually during the off-season when inventory is low.

5. **Invest idle cash.** Cash on hand earns nothing. Excess cash should be invested, even if it is only overnight. Many businesses, such as McCollick's clothing company, are seasonal. During her slow season, if she has excess cash, she should invest it. To avoid an immediate cash crisis, however, it is very important that these investments be liquid and risk-free. A liquid investment has a market in which someone is always willing to buy or sell the investment. A risk-free investment means there is no concern that the party will default on its promise to pay its principal and interest.

For example, using excess cash to purchase shares in a small company because you heard that it was probably going to increase in value in the near term is inappropriate. First, the shares of small companies are often illiquid. Second, if the shares suddenly decrease in value, you might be forced to sell them at a loss in order to pay your bills as they come due. A common liquid, risk-free investment (albeit at a lower rate of interest) is treasury bills or money market funds.

6. **Prepare a cash budget.** A cash budget is a critical tool, showing anticipated cash flows over a one- or two-year period. It can show when additional financing will be necessary well before the actual need arises. Conversely, it can indicate when excess cash will be available for the repayment of debts, for investments, or for other purposes.

Because cash is so vital to a company, applying these principles of cash management to plan the company's cash needs is essential for any business. In a large company, one or more employees will be assigned responsibility for managing cash.

■ Keeping an Eye on Cash

Can a company have too much cash? Yes, according to some, including Mark Carney, Governor of the Bank of England and former Governor of the Bank of Canada. In August 2012, Carney noted that Canadian corporations were "sitting on mountains of 'dead money'." The size of the Canadian "mountain" was approximately $600 billion in January 2012, with major Canadian companies such as Suncor Energy ($5.4 billion), George Weston (owner of Loblaw) ($3.5 billion), and Barrick Gold ($2.5 billion) holding significant amounts. Carney noted that Canadian companies should be investing their cash in new property, plant, and equipment or increasing the dividends paid to shareholders. In the United States, the cash mountain was nearly U.S. $1.5 trillion.

Tim Cook, CEO of Apple, informed shareholders at the 2013 annual meeting that he was actively pursuing what to do with the company's growing cash pile. At December 31, 2012, the pile of cash amounted to $137.1 billion (cash and cash equivalents). Possible uses of the cash included increasing the dividend paid to shareholders and buying back shares.

Is too much cash also a problem for small businesses, such as Sharon McCollick's company discussed earlier in the chapter? McCollick might think that she can never have too much cash in her business, but that isn't correct. Having large amounts of cash sitting in bank accounts that pay little or no interest is not an effective management strategy. Cash can be invested in interest-paying investments for the short or longer term. It can also be used to upgrade existing equipment or expand the business when the cash balances increase beyond what is required for normal business operations.

DECISION TOOLKIT

 Decision Checkpoints	 Info Needed for Decision	 Tools to Use for Decision	 How to Evaluate Results
Is all of the company's cash available for general use?	Statement of financial position and notes to financial statements	Does the company report any cash as being restricted?	A restriction on the use of cash limits management's ability to use those resources for general obligations. This should be considered when assessing liquidity.
Is the company able to manage its cash effectively?	Terms of collection/payment for receivables and payables, inventory turnover rate, length of operating cycle, and cash budget (typically available only to management)	Assess the collection period, inventory on hand, when bills are paid, and whether cash discounts are available and taken. A cash budget can determine when additional cash is needed or is available for investment.	If receivables and inventory are not being sold and collected on a timely basis, liquidity is affected.

BEFORE YOU GO ON...

▶Do It! Presentation of Cash

Bay Resorts Limited reported the following selected items on May 31, 2015:

Accounts receivable	$29,000
Bank indebtedness	10,000
Cash in bank	12,300
Cash (restricted for an upcoming plant expansion in the next few years)	50,000
Compensating balance (for a non-current loan)	5,000
Debt investment (treasury bills, due in 30 days)	1,500
Equity investment (in common shares)	4,000
Postage stamps	50

(a) Calculate Bay Resorts' cash and cash equivalents.

(b) Identify where each of the above items not included in cash and cash equivalents should be reported on the statement of financial position.

Action Plan

- Understand the definition of cash equivalents: short-term, highly liquid trading investments − bank indebtedness.
- Understand the classifications on the statement of financial position.

Solution

(a)

Cash in bank	$12,300
Add: Debt investment	1,500
Less: Bank indebtedness	10,000
Cash and cash equivalents	$ 3,800

(b)

Accounts receivable	Accounts receivable (current asset)
Cash (restricted for an upcoming plant expansion)	Restricted cash (non-current asset)
Compensating balance (for a non-current loan)	Restricted cash (non-current asset)
Equity investment (in common shares)	Investments (likely non-current asset)
Postage stamps	Supplies (current asset)

Related Exercise Material: BE7-12, BE7-13, E7-9, and E7-10.

comparing
IFRS and ASPE

Key Differences	International Financial Reporting Standards (IFRS)	Accounting Standards for Private Enterprises (ASPE)
	No significant differences.	

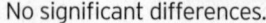

All About You ▶ Paying for Your University Education

It is important that you consider how much cash you will need to pay for your university education. It is all about planning. Do you know the cost of your tuition? If you don't live at home, what are your costs of renting? Utilities, including your cell phone? Food? Entertainment? Clothing? Transportation? Once you have determined the costs that you will incur, how will you pay for them? Have you applied for every possible scholarship, grant, and bursary? Have you obtained a student loan from the Government of Canada? Do you have credit card debt? Do you have a line of credit? With proper planning, you can reduce the amount that you are going to have to borrow to complete your education.

The hard part about planning how much cash you need is that sometimes you have no idea! Your starting point is to track where your cash is coming from and where it is going. Track what you receive and spend during the course of a day, a week, a month, a term, and then a school year. Try accumulating all of the receipts for items purchased during the course of a week and put them in an envelope. At the end of the week, analyze the receipts to determine where the money has gone. Continue doing so for a month. Once you have reviewed all of the receipts for a whole month, attempt to categorize them by type of expenditure. Or you could try using an Excel spreadsheet to help you keep track and categorize. There are free apps that can help, such as My Student Budget Planner. The website GetSmarterAboutMoney.ca has many tools to help you determine what it is costing you to attend university and what the expected cost will be as you complete your degree.

Remember that it is all about setting goals. If your goal is to complete your degree with little debt, then a plan will help you determine how you are going to minimize the amount of money that you have to borrow.

Some Facts

- In Canada, 40% of students have no debt when they graduate from university. Statistics Canada indicates that the remaining 60% who graduate with student debt will have approximately $27,000 of debt they will have to pay back.
- The easiest way to save money while going to university is to live at home. Studies show that, if you live at home, a four-year university degree will cost approximately $33,000 (this includes tuition, books, transportation, and entertainment). If you live away from home, it will cost $67,000 (which includes additional costs for food and housing).
- Every year, $70 million in scholarships, grants, and bursaries is set aside in Canada—$7 million of which goes unclaimed.
- If you buy a specialty coffee for $4 every day, it will cost you $1,460 a year. Spend $10 a day at the specialty coffee shop and you have accumulated approximately the cost of a term's full-time tuition.
- A recent Statistics Canada study indicated that the more a student worked during the school year, the more likely it was that their GPA would suffer.[1]

What Do You Think?

You are taking a full course load this term. You had a great job over the previous summer and would really like to have the same job next summer. Your employer has asked that you work part-time over the course of the term. This will guarantee that you can return to your job next summer. Should you accept the part-time job?

YES As long as you are able to keep up with your course work, then having the part-time job will help to pay for your education as well as guarantee lots of good work experience.

NO Your first priority is to finish up your education and do the very best you can in all of the courses that you are taking. You will have time enough after you graduate and get a job to repay all of your student loans.

Summary of Study Objectives

1. *Describe the primary components of an internal control system.* Internal control systems have the following components: the control environment, risk assessment, control activities, information and communication, and monitoring. Control activities include the authorization of transactions and activities, segregation of duties, documentation, physical controls, independent performance checks, and human resource controls.

2. *Apply the key control activities to cash receipts and payments.* Control activities over cash receipts include (a) designating only personnel such as cashiers to handle cash; (b) assigning the duties of receiving cash, recording cash, and having custody of cash to different individuals; (c) obtaining remittance advices for mail receipts, cash register tapes for over-the-counter receipts, and deposit slips or confirmations for bank deposits; (d) using company safes and bank vaults to store cash, with access limited to authorized personnel, and using cash registers in executing over-the-counter receipts; (e) depositing all cash intact daily in the bank account or using EFT; (f) making independent daily counts of register receipts and daily comparisons of total receipts with total deposits; and (g) conducting background checks, bonding personnel who handle cash, and requiring employees to take vacations.

   Control activities over cash payments include (a) making all payments by cheque or by EFT; (b) having only specified individuals authorized to sign cheques; (c) assigning to different individuals the duties of approving items for payment, paying the items, and recording the payments; (d) using prenumbered cheques and accounting for all cheques; (e) storing each cheque in a safe or vault with access restricted to authorized personnel, and using electronic methods to print amounts on cheques; (f) comparing each cheque or EFT with the approved invoice before initiating payment, and making monthly reconciliations of bank and book balances; and (g) conducting background checks, bonding personnel who handle cash, and requiring employees to take vacations.

3. *Prepare a bank reconciliation.* In reconciling the bank account, it is customary to reconcile the balance per books and the balance per bank to their adjusted balances. Reconciling items for the bank include deposits in transit, outstanding cheques, and any errors made by the bank. Reconciling items for the books include unrecorded amounts added to or deducted from the bank account and any errors made by the company. Adjusting entries must be made for all items required to reconcile the balance per books to the adjusted cash balance.

4. *Explain the reporting and management of cash.* Cash is usually listed first in the current assets section of the statement of financial position. Cash restricted for a special purpose is reported separately as a current asset or as a non-current asset, depending on when the cash is expected to be used. Compensating balances are a form of restriction on the use of cash and are reported as a current or non-current asset depending on the term of the restriction.

   The six principles of cash management are to (a) accelerate the collection of receivables, (b) keep inventory levels low, (c) delay the payment of liabilities, (d) plan the timing of major expenditures, (e) invest idle cash, and (f) prepare a cash budget.

Glossary

Cash Resources that consist of coins, currency, cheques, money orders, debit card slips, and bank credit card slips that are acceptable at face value on deposit in a bank or similar institution. (p. 350)

Cash equivalents Short-term, highly trading liquid investments that can be easily sold, net of any bank overdrafts repayable on demand. (p. 363)

Compensating balance A minimum cash balance required by a bank in support of a bank loan. (p. 363)

Deposits in transit Amounts deposited and recorded by the depositor that have not yet been recorded by the bank. (p. 356)

NSF (not sufficient funds) cheque (also known as a returned cheque) A cheque that is not paid by a bank, because there are insufficient funds in the bank account of the customer who wrote the cheque. (p. 355)

Outstanding cheques Cheques issued and recorded by a company that have not yet been paid (cleared) by the bank. (p. 356)

Restricted cash Cash that is not available for general use, but instead is restricted for a particular purpose. (p. 363)

DECISION TOOLKIT—A SUMMARY

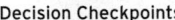

Decision Checkpoints

Info Needed for Decision

Tools to Use for Decision

How to Evaluate Results

Decision Checkpoints	Info Needed for Decision	Tools to Use for Decision	How to Evaluate Results
Are the company's financial statements supported by adequate internal controls?	Auditor's report, statement of management responsibility, management discussion and analysis	Control activities include (1) authorizing transactions and activities, (2) segregating duties, (3) documenting transactions, (4) employing physical controls, (5) independently checking performance, and (6) applying human resource controls.	If there is any indication that these or other controls are lacking, the financial statements could contain errors.
Is all of the company's cash available for general use?	Statement of financial position and notes to financial statements	Does the company report any cash as being restricted?	A restriction on the use of cash limits management's ability to use those resources for general obligations. This should be considered when assessing liquidity.
Is the company able to manage its cash effectively?	Terms of collection/payment for receivables and payables, inventory turnover rate, length of operating cycle, and cash budget (typically available only to management)	Assess the collection period, inventory on hand, when bills are paid, and whether cash discounts are available and taken. A cash budget can determine when additional cash is needed or is available for investment.	If receivables and inventory are not being sold and collected on a timely basis, liquidity is affected.

the navigator

USING THE DECISION TOOLKIT

Sparks Basketball (SB) is a not-for-profit organization whose main purpose is to promote healthy living through sports activity. Its members are basketball associations throughout the province, for which SB provides a variety of services. These services include insurance coverage, the organization of provincial tournaments, and discounts from sponsor organizations. It is a volunteer organization with an independent board of directors, and one paid position—that of executive director. While the executive director was on parental leave, SB's vice-president of finance, John Stevens, filled this position.

Unfortunately, some financial irregularities occurred while Mr. Stevens was acting as executive director. As the acting executive director, Mr. Stevens was responsible for paying invoices, making deposits, signing cheques along with SB's president, completing the bank reconciliation, and preparing financial statements for the annual general meeting.

An irregularity arose when it was discovered that the president's signature had been forged on several cheques. It was also determined that Mr. Stevens handled all deposits and cash payments by himself for a national basketball tournament hosted by SB. He had promised to have an independent treasurer for the tournament but did not get one. He also coached a basketball team in a nearby city, and had full access to the team's bank account. During this time, to save on bank fees, Mr. Stevens had also stopped having the bank return SB's cancelled cheques.

A forensic accountant was brought in to investigate further. He discovered many problems. The financial records were a mess, and there was almost no paper trail for many of the expenditures that were made. There were instances of "double dipping"—where one individual was reimbursed several times for the same expense claim. There were also several cheques made out to the team coached by Mr. Stevens. There was even a cheque where the payee's name had been scratched out and Mr. Stevens' name was inserted.

(continued)

Instructions

(a) Identify the main weakness in control activities at Sparks Basketball.

(b) Discuss what steps should be taken to ensure that this situation does not happen again.

(c) Discuss the trade-off between implementing an extensive internal control system and the cost of having such a system for a volunteer organization that has limited funds.

Solution

(a) The main control weakness at SB was the lack of segregation of duties. While the executive director was on parental leave, one person was responsible for all financial matters. There was also no review of Mr. Stevens' work, enabling him to make fraudulent transactions without anyone knowing about them.

(b) SB should require proper segregation of duties. Although it is often difficult to have proper segregation of duties in a not-for profit organization such as this, at least two people should be involved in all financial transactions. SB should require monthly bank reconciliations to be prepared by someone other than the executive director. The cancelled cheques should be returned each month so that they can be reviewed as well. In addition, independent checks of performance could be done by having someone from the board of directors review transactions and financial statements regularly.

(c) Implementation of extensive control systems can be expensive. Not-for-profit organizations must carefully choose what control measures are most important for their specific needs. However, the value of some control activities, such as segregation of duties, often offsets the cost, as it would have for SB. In addition, the organization should use as many free controls as it can. Examples include proper screening of possible volunteers and employees, written policies for how transactions should be processed, and a requirement that employees and volunteers sign a formal statement of ethical guidelines.

the navigator

Comprehensive Do It!

The Winnipeg Arts Society reports the following selected information with regard to cash at June 30:

From last month's bank reconciliation, at May 31:
Adjusted cash balance $34,080

From the general ledger Cash account:
Cash receipts, June 34,000
Cash payments, June 39,520

From the bank:

	Amounts Deducted (Debits)	Amounts Added (Credits)	Balance
WINNIPEG ARTS SOCIETY Bank Statement June 30			
Opening balance, June 1			35,380
Deposits		30,496	65,876
Cheques cleared	36,200		29,676
EFT, payment of insurance	1,000		28,676
NSF cheque ($310 + $40 service charge)	350		28,326
Bank service charges	24		28,302
Credit card fees	30		28,272
EFT, collection from Zukata		70	28,342

Additional information:
1. All cash receipts were deposited in the bank account. All cash payments were made by cheque.
2. There was a deposit in transit of $1,200 at May 31 that the bank recorded in June.
3. There were $1,500 of outstanding cheques at the end of May.
4. The pre-authorized EFT for insurance has already been recorded.
5. The NSF cheque was for $310, from Massif Corp., a customer, in payment of its account. The bank charged a $40 processing fee.
6. The EFT collection of $70 was incorrectly deposited by the bank to the society's account. It should have been deposited to the account of the Winnipeg Arts Council, a different organization with a similar name.

Instructions
(a) Calculate the unadjusted cash balance per books at June 30, prior to reconciliation.
(b) Calculate the (1) deposits in transit and (2) outstanding cheques at June 30.
(c) Prepare a bank reconciliation at June 30.
(d) Prepare any adjusting journal entries required from the reconciliation.

Action Plan
- The adjusted cash balance at the end of the reconciliation process (after adjusting journal entries have been made) will equal the cash balance per books. To calculate the unadjusted cash balance at June 30, start with the opening balance at May 31 (adjusted cash balance) and add cash receipts and deduct cash payments.
- To determine the deposits in transit at the end of June, compare the deposits on the bank statement (adjusted for any deposits in transit at the end of May) with the deposits recorded in the books in June. Recall the formula that deposits in transit at the beginning of the period + deposits recorded in the company's books this period − deposits recorded on this period's bank statement = deposits in transit at end of period.
- To determine the outstanding cheques at the end of June, compare the cheques that cleared the bank statement (adjusted for any cheques outstanding at the end of May) with the cheques recorded in the books in June. Recall the formula that outstanding cheques at the beginning of the period + cheques recorded in the company's books this period − cheques recorded on this period's bank statement = outstanding cheques at end of period.
- Identify any items recorded by the bank but not by the company as reconciling items per books (except for bank errors).
- Notify the bank of any bank errors. You cannot correct the bank errors on your own company's books.
- All the journal entries should be based on the reconciling items per books.
- After posting the reconciling items, make sure the Cash ledger account balance agrees with the adjusted cash balance per books.

Solution to Comprehensive Do It!
(a)

			Cash		
May	31	Adj. bal.	34,080		
June cash receipts			34,000	June cash payments	39,520
June	30	Unadj. bal.	28,560		

(b) (1) Deposits in transit: $1,200 + $34,000 − $30,496 = $4,704
    (2) Outstanding cheques: $1,500 + $39,520 − $36,200 = $4,820

(continued)

(c)

WINNIPEG ARTS SOCIETY Bank Reconciliation June 30		
Cash balance per bank statement		$28,342
Add: Deposits in transit		4,704
		33,046
Less: Outstanding cheques	$4,820	
Bank deposit error	70	4,890
Adjusted cash balance per bank		$28,156
Cash balance per books		$28,560
Less: NSF cheque ($310 + $40)	$350	
Bank service charges	24	
Credit card fees	30	404
Adjusted cash balance per books		$28,156

(d)

June 30	Accounts Receivable	350	
	Cash		350
	(To re-establish accounts receivable for Massif Corp. for NSF cheque and related service charge)		
30	Bank Charges Expense	54	
	Cash		54
	(To record bank service charges [$24] and credit card fees [$30])		

Check:

Cash					
June	30	Unadj. bal. 28,560	June	30	350
				30	54
June	30	Adj. bal. 28,156			

the navigator

WileyPLUS   Self-Test, Brief Exercises, Exercises, Problems: Set A, and many more components are available for practice in *WileyPLUS*.

Self-Test Questions

Answers are at the end of the chapter.

Quiz Yourself

(SO 1) 1. Which of the following is not one of the five primary components of internal control?
(a) Control environment
(b) Size of business
(c) Risk assessment
(d) Control activities

(SO 1) 2. Which one of the following is *not* an internal control activity?
(a) Authorization of transactions and activities
(b) Documentation

(c) Cost-benefit constraints
(d) Independent checks of performance

(SO 2) 3. Which of the following items found in a cash register drawer at November 30 is *not* cash?
(a) Debit card slips from sales to customers
(b) Bank credit card slips from sales to customers
(c) A customer cheque dated December 1
(d) A customer cheque dated November 28

(SO 2) 4. Permitting only designated personnel, such as cashiers, to handle cash receipts is an application of which of the following control activities?
(a) Segregation of duties
(b) Authorization of transactions and activities
(c) Independent checks of performance
(d) Human resource controls

(SO 2) 5. The use of prenumbered cheques in disbursing cash is an example of which of the following control activities?
(a) Authorization of transactions and activities
(b) Segregation of duties
(c) Physical controls
(d) Documentation

(SO 3) 6. Davis Corporation had cheques outstanding totalling $5,400 on its June bank reconciliation. In July, Davis Corporation issued cheques totalling $38,900. The July bank statement shows that $26,300 in cheques cleared the bank in July. What is the amount of outstanding cheques on Davis's July bank reconciliation?
(a) $5,400
(b) $7,200
(c) $12,600
(d) $18,000

(SO 3) 7. Terriault Ltée reports an unadjusted cash balance per books of $4,100 at the end of the month and $5,000 on its bank statement. Reconciling items include deposits in transit of $2,500, outstanding

2 500
- 3 500

cheques of $3,500, and service charges of $100. What is the company's adjusted cash balance?
(a) $3,900
(b) $4,000
(c) $4,100
(d) $5,000

(SO 3) 8. Which of the following items on a bank reconciliation would require an adjusting entry on the company's books?
(a) An error by the bank
(b) Outstanding cheques
(c) A bank service charge
(d) A deposit in transit

(SO 4) 9. Which statement correctly describes the reporting of cash?
(a) Restricted cash is listed as the first current asset because it cannot be spent immediately
(b) Restricted cash funds can be combined with cash
(c) Cash is usually listed as the most liquid asset in the current assets section
(d) Compensating balances are reported as a current liability

(SO 4) 10. The principles of cash management do not include:
(a) accelerating the collection of receivables.
(b) accelerating the payment of liabilities.
(c) keeping inventory low.
(d) investing idle cash.

Questions

(SO 1) 1. Identify and describe the five primary components of a good internal control system.

(SO 1) 2. Identify the six control activities that apply to most companies.

(SO 1) 3. How do documentation procedures contribute to good internal control?

(SO 1) 4. Matt Tau is questioning the need for independent checks of performance if the company also segregates duties. What do you think about this?

(SO 1) 5. When faced with labour shortages and high staff turnover, most retail stores do not bother with criminal record checks when hiring employees. Explain what internal control activity is missing from this practice and what kind of problems this could result in.

(SO 1) 6. Kim is trying to design internal control activities so that there is no possibility of errors or theft. Explain to Kim why this may be impractical, and even impossible.

(SO 2) 7. Explain how electronic funds transfers can result in better internal control.

(SO 2) 8. In the corner grocery store, all the clerks make change out of the same cash register drawer. Is this a violation of an internal control activity? Explain.

(SO 2) 9. Dent Department Stores Ltd. has just installed new electronic cash registers with scanners in its stores. How do these cash registers improve control activities over cash receipts?

(SO 2) 10. "To have maximum control over cash payments, all payments should be made by cheque." Is this true? Explain.

(SO 2) 11. At a dental office, the receptionist schedules appointments and can cancel them. She also collects payment from patients (about 10% of them pay cash) and maintains all of the accounting records for the practice. Comment on whether these arrangements can result in a limitation of internal control and give rise to fraud.

(SO 2, 3) 12. Who should be responsible for preparing a bank reconciliation? Why?

(SO 2, 3) 13. "The use of a bank contributes significantly to good internal control over cash." Is this true? Explain.

(SO 3) 14. Paul Pascal is confused about the lack of agreement between the unadjusted cash balance per books and the balance per bank. Explain the possible causes for the lack of agreement to Paul, and give an example of each cause.

(SO 3) 15. Kari Mora asks for your help concerning an NSF cheque. Explain to Kari (a) what an NSF cheque is,

(b) how it is treated in a bank reconciliation, and (c) whether it will require an adjusting entry and, if an adjusting entry is required, what accounts are typically debited and credited.

(SO 3)   16. The Diable Corporation wrote cheque #2375 for $1,325 on March 16. At March 31, the cheque had not cleared the company's bank account and was correctly listed as an outstanding cheque on the March 31 bank reconciliation. If the cheque has still not cleared the bank account on April 30, should it be included in the April bank reconciliation or not? Explain.

(SO 3)   17. Sam Wing is an accounting clerk who has stolen $1,700 in cash from the company he works for. He prepares the bank reconciliation each month. When he performs the reconciliation this month, he knows that the adjusted cash balance will be $1,700 higher than the adjusted bank balance because of his theft. He therefore decides to falsify the amount of outstanding cheques. Why would

he do this and would he overstate or understate the amount?

(SO 4)   18. What account balances are included in cash and cash equivalents?

(SO 4)   19. What is restricted cash? What are compensating balances? How should these items be reported on the statement of financial position?

(SO 4)   20. At the end of its first quarter in the 2015 fiscal year, Brandon Corporation had an undrawn line of credit facility that allowed the company to borrow up to $16 million and pay it down whenever it wants to. How should this line of credit be reported on the statement of financial position?

(SO 4)   21. Describe the six principles of cash management.

(SO 4)   22. Glenn Green owns Green's Groceries Inc. He has been reading about companies having too much cash in the business press but doesn't understand how he can have too much cash. Explain the concept of "too much cash" to Glenn and provide him with some suggestions for the use of his cash.

Brief Exercises

Identify control activities.
(SO 1)

BE7–1   Gina Milan is the new manager of Plenty Parking Ltd., a parking garage. She has heard about internal control but is not clear about its importance for the company. Explain to Gina the six control activities, and give her an example of an application of each control for Plenty Parking.

Match control activities.
(SO 1)

BE7–2   Match each of the following control activities with its appropriate description.

1. Authorization of transactions and activities
2. Segregation of duties
3. Documentation
4. Physical controls
5. Independent checks of performance
6. Human resource controls

(a) _____ All transactions should include original, detailed receipts.
(b) _____ Undeposited cash should be stored in the company safe.
(c) _____ Employees must take their full vacation allotment each year.
(d) _____ Surprise cash counts are performed by internal audit.
(e) _____ Responsibility for related activities should be assigned to specific employees.
(f) _____ Cheque signers are not allowed to record cash transactions.

Identify control activities for cash receipts.
(SO 1, 2)

BE7–3   Tene Ltd. has the following internal controls over cash receipts. Identify the control activity that is applicable to each procedure.

1. All over-the-counter receipts are recorded on cash registers.
2. All cashiers are bonded.
3. Daily cash counts are performed by the accounting supervisor.
4. The duties of receiving cash, recording cash, and maintaining custody of cash are assigned to different individuals.
5. Only cashiers may operate cash registers.
6. All cash is deposited intact in the bank account every day.

Identify control activities for cash payments.
(SO 1, 2)

BE7–4   Rolling Hills Ltd. has the following internal controls over cash payments. Identify the control activity that is applicable to each procedure.

1. Company cheques are prenumbered.
2. The bank statement is reconciled monthly by the assistant controller.
3. Blank cheques are stored in a safe in the controller's office.
4. Both the controller and the assistant controller are required to sign cheques or authorize electronic payments.
5. Cheque signers are not allowed to record cash payments.
6. All payments are made by cheque or electronic transfer.

BE7–5 For each of the items in the following list, identify where it is included on a bank reconciliation. Next to each item write "bank +" for an increase in the bank balance; "bank −" for a decrease in the bank balance; "book +" for an increase in the book balance; "book −" for a decrease in the book balance; or "NA" for not applicable, to indicate that the item is not included in the bank reconciliation.

Identify location of items in bank reconciliation. (SO 3)

_____ 1. Bank service charges
_____ 2. An EFT collection on account
_____ 3. Outstanding cheques from the current month (June)
_____ 4. Outstanding cheques from a prior month (May) that are still outstanding
_____ 5. Outstanding cheques from a prior month (May) that are no longer outstanding
_____ 6. A bank error in recording a company cheque made out for $200 as $290
_____ 7. A bank deposit for interest earned on an investment
_____ 8. A company error in recording a $1,280 deposit as $1,680
_____ 9. A bank service charge for an NSF cheque
_____ 10. A deposit in transit from the current month (June)
_____ 11. A company error in recording a cheque made out for $630 as $360
_____ 12. A bank error in recording a $2,575 deposit as $2,755

BE7–6 For the months of January and February, Monde Ltd. recorded cash deposits in its books of $5,000 and $5,600, respectively. For the same two months, the bank reported deposits totalling $4,000 and $4,600, respectively. Assuming that there were no deposits in transit at the beginning of January, what was the amount of deposits in transit at the end of January and at the end of February?

Analyze deposits in transit. (SO 3)

BE7–7 In the month of November, its first month of operations, Jayasinghe Inc. wrote cheques in the amount of $12,600. In December, cheques in the amount of $9,500 were written. In November, $11,100 of these cheques were presented to the bank for payment and $9,900 were presented in December. What is the amount of outstanding cheques at the end of November and at the end of December?

Analyze outstanding cheques. (SO 3)

BE7–8 Kashechewan Inc. mistakenly recorded a cheque as $68 that was written for $86. In addition, the company noticed the bank had mistakenly deducted a cheque for $125 from its bank account that was written by another company. (a) Explain how each of these errors should be treated on the bank reconciliation. (b) Identify any entries required on Kashechewan's books to correct these errors.

Analyze errors. (SO 3)

BE7–9 The following information relates to Southco Limited's Cash account. The adjusted cash balance from June's bank reconciliation is $18,920. During the month of July, Southco recorded cash receipts of $21,700 and cash payments of $24,300 in the general ledger Cash account. Calculate Southco's unadjusted cash balance at July 31.

Calculate unadjusted cash balance. (SO 3)

BE7–10 Using the data in BE7–9, determine or calculate the unadjusted cash balance for Southco Limited. An examination of the company's July bank statement shows a balance of $15,840 on July 31; outstanding cheques $2,300; deposits in transit $4,300; EFT collections on account $1,960 that were not yet recorded on the books; NSF cheque $290; NSF fee $80; and bank services charges $70. Prepare the bank reconciliation at July 31.

Prepare bank reconciliation. (SO 3)

BE7–11 Using the data in BE7–10, prepare the adjusting entries required on July 31 for Southco.

Prepare adjusting entries. (SO 3)

BE7–12 Ouellette Ltée reports the following items: cash in bank $17,500; payroll bank account $6,000; cash register floats $500; trading investments consisting of term deposits with maturity dates of less than 90 days $5,000; and cash restricted for plant expansion $25,000. Ouellette also maintains a $5,000 compensating bank balance in a separate bank account. Determine which accounts described above would be considered cash, cash equivalents, or other items to be reported on the statement of financial position.

Report cash. (SO 4)

BE7–13 Evergreen Inc. owns these assets at the statement of financial position date:

Calculate cash. (SO 4)

Cash in bank (savings account)	$12,000
Cash on hand	1,700
Income tax refund due from CRA	2,000
Cash in bank (chequing account)	24,000
Bank credit card slips	5,000
Debit card slips	2,400
Postdated cheques	1,000

(a) What amount should be reported as cash and cash equivalents in the statement of financial position? (b) For any item not included in (a), identify where it should be reported.

Exercises

Identify control
activities.
(SO 1)

E7–1   The following situations suggest either a strength or weakness in an internal control activity:

1. At Tingley's, Iryna and Inder work alternate lunch hours. Normally, Iryna works the cash register at the checkout counter, but during her lunch hour Inder takes her place. They both use the same cash drawer and jointly count cash at the end of the day.
2. The Do It Corporation accepts both cash and credit cards for its sales. Due to privacy legislation that requires credit card information to be shredded within three months, it shreds all credit card slips after they are processed.
3. The mail clerk at Genesis Legal Services prepares a daily list of all cash receipts. The cash receipts are forwarded to a staff accountant, who deposits the cash in the company's bank account. The list is sent to the accounts receivable clerk for recording.
4. The Candy Store can only afford a part-time bookkeeper. The bookkeeper's responsibilities include making the bank deposit, recording transactions, and reconciling the bank statement.
5. The Decorator Shoppe counts inventory at the end of each month. Two staff members count the inventory together. It is then priced and totalled by the accounting department and reconciled to the perpetual inventory records. Any variances are investigated.

Instructions
(a) State whether each situation above is a control strength or weakness and explain why.
(b) For each weakness, suggest an improvement.

Identify control
activities to detect and
prevent fraud.
(SO 1)

E7–2   Each of the following situations describes an instance of fraud:

1. A bartender sells drinks to customers and, when they pay cash, he does not record the sale at the cash register and keeps the cash.
2. A bartender knows that there is a special on vodka tonight so he brings his own bottle of vodka to the bar. When a customer orders vodka and pays cash, the bartender pours the vodka from his own bottle, does not record the sale at the cash register, and keeps the cash.
3. The receptionist at a spa enters all appointments into a computerized schedule. After their appointment, the client pays the receptionist for the service received. For about half of the customers who pay with cash, the receptionist keeps the amount and deletes any record of the appointment from the schedule. The receptionist makes the bank deposits and records all sales in the accounting system.
4. The receptionist at a law firm has a key to a cabinet where company cheques are stored. She takes a cheque from the cabinet, makes it payable to herself, and forges the signature of the firm's managing partner on the cheque. She opens the mail every day and when the bank statement is received, she performs the bank reconciliation. She covers the theft by understating the amount of outstanding cheques on the bank reconciliation.

Instructions
(a) Is it possible to detect these types of fraud? Why or why not?
(b) Identify a control activity or activities that could help prevent each instance of fraud described above.

Identify control activi-
ties for cash receipts.
(SO 1, 2)

E7–3   The following control activities are used at Tolan Ltd. for over-the-counter cash receipts:

1. Cashiers are experienced, so they are not bonded.
2. All over-the-counter receipts are received by one of three clerks. The clerks share a cash register with a single cash drawer.
3. To minimize the risk of robbery, cash in excess of $100 is stored in an unlocked strongbox in the stockroom until it is deposited in the bank.
4. At the end of each day, the total receipts are counted by the cashier on duty and reconciled to the cash register total.
5. The company accountant makes the bank deposit and then records the day's receipts.
6. If a customer has the exact change and does not want a receipt, the sale is not entered in the cash register. The money is kept in a loose change box.

Instructions
(a) For each of the above situations, explain the weakness and identify the control activity that is violated.
(b) For each weakness, suggest an improvement.

Identify control activi-
ties for cash payments.
(SO 1, 2)

E7–4   The following control activities are used in Sheera's Boutique Shoppe Ltd. for cash payments:

1. Blank cheques are stored in an unmarked envelope on a shelf behind the cash register.
2. The purchasing manager personally approves payments for purchases and signs the cheques issued to pay suppliers.
3. When the store manager goes away for an extended period of time, she pre-signs cheques to be used in her absence.
4. The company cheques are not prenumbered.
5. The company accountant prepares the bank reconciliation and reports any discrepancies to the store manager.

Instructions

(a) For each of the above situations, explain the weakness and identify the control activity that is violated.
(b) For each weakness, suggest an improvement.

E7–5   The adjusted cash balance from Hudson Corporation's August 31 bank reconciliation was $54,700. Hudson record-ed the following events in the general ledger Cash account during the month of September: (1) cheques totalling $127,492 were issued; (2) salaries of $49,900 deposited to employee accounts; (3) monthly EFT payment of $1,500 for insurance; and (4) deposits totalling $128,658.

Calculate unadjusted cash balance.
(SO 3)

Instructions

(a) Calculate Hudson's unadjusted cash balance in the general ledger Cash account on September 30, prior to the bank reconciliation.
(b) Indicate the effect of items (1) through (4) in the bank reconciliation.

E7–6   Ten items that may or may not be involved in the bank reconciliation process for April are listed in the table shown below:

Indicate effect of items in bank reconcilation.
(SO 3)

Item	Bank		Books		Adjusting Entry Required
	Add (Credit)	Deduct (Debit)	Add (Debit)	Deduct (Credit)	
1. Deposits in transit at the end of April	✓				No
2. Deposits in transit at the beginning of April that cleared the bank in April					
3. Outstanding cheques at the end of April					
4. Outstanding cheques at the beginning of April that cleared the bank in April					
5. Cheque written for $250 recorded in error as $520 on the books					
6. Deposit of $400 made in error by the bank to the company's account					
7. Bank service charges					
8. EFT, collection on account not previously recorded by company					
9. NSF cheque received from customer					
10. Interest earned on bank account					

Instructions

Complete the table shown above, identifying where each item should be included on a bank reconciliation prepared for the month of April. Insert a check mark (✓) in the appropriate column indicating whether the item should be added to, or deducted from, the bank or the books. If the item should not be included in the bank reconciliation, write "NA" for not applicable. Finally, indicate whether the item will require an adjusting entry on the company books by writing "yes" or "no" in the last column. The first item has been done for you as an example.

E7–7   The cash records of Lejeune Inc. show the following situations:

Calculate deposits in transit and outstanding cheques.
(SO 3)

Deposits in transit:

1. The June 30 bank reconciliation indicated that deposits in transit total $2,000. During July, the general ledger account Cash shows deposits of $14,750, but the bank statement indicates that $15,820 in deposits were received during the month.
2. In August, deposits per bank statement totalled $22,500 and deposits per books were $22,900.

Outstanding cheques:

1. The June 30 bank reconciliation reported outstanding cheques of $570. During July, the Lejeune books show that $18,200 of cheques were issued. The bank statement showed that $17,200 of cheques cleared the bank in July.
2. In August, cheques issued were $22,700 and cheques clearing the bank were $23,520.

Instructions

(a) What were the deposits in transit at July 31 and at August 31?
(b) What were the outstanding cheques at July 31 and at August 31?

E7–8   The following information is for Neopolitan Ltd. in July:

Prepare bank recon-ciliation and adjusting entries.
(SO 3)

1. Cash balance per bank, July 31, $8,833
2. Cash balance per books, July 31, $7,190
3. Bank service charge, $24
4. Deposits in transit, $1,575

5. Electronic receipts from customers in payment of their accounts, $883, not previously recorded by the company
6. Outstanding cheques, $2,449
7. Cheque #373 was correctly written and recorded by the company as $672. The bank deducted $762 from the company's account in error. The cheque was written for the purchase of office supplies.

Instructions
(a) Prepare the bank reconciliation at July 31.
(b) Prepare any adjusting journal entries required from the reconciliation.

Calculate cash.
(SO 4)

E7–9　A new accountant at La Maison Ltée is trying to identify which of the following amounts should be reported as cash and cash equivalents in the April 30 year-end statement of financial position:

1. Currency and coin totalling $87 in a locked box used for incidental cash transactions
2. A $10,000 government treasury bill, due the next month, May 31
3. April-dated cheques worth $300 that La Maison has received from customers but not yet deposited
4. An $85 cheque received from a customer in payment of its April account, but postdated to May 1
5. A balance of $2,575 in the Royal Bank chequing account
6. A balance of $4,000 in the Royal Bank savings account
7. Prepaid postage of $75 in the postage meter
8. A $50 IOU from the company receptionist
9. Cash register floats of $250
10. Over-the-counter receipts for April 30 consisting of $550 of currency and coin, $185 of cheques from customers, $685 of debit card slips, and $755 of bank credit card slips. These amounts were processed by the bank on May 1.

Instructions
(a) What amount should La Maison consider to be cash at April 30? What should it consider to be a cash equivalent?
(b) What combined amount would La Maison report as cash and cash equivalents on its year-end statement of financial position?
(c) In which financial statement(s) and in what account(s) should the items not included in (a) be reported?

Discuss cash management.
(SO 4)

E7–10　Tory, Hachey, and Wedunn, three young lawyers who have joined together to open a law practice, are struggling to manage their cash flow. They have not yet built up enough clientele and revenues to support the cost of running their legal practice. Initial costs, such as advertising and renovations to the premises, all result in outgoing cash flow at a time when little is coming in! Tory, Hachey, and Wedunn have not had time to establish a billing system since most of their clients' cases have not yet reached the courts and the lawyers did not think it would be right to bill them until "results were achieved." Unfortunately, Tory, Hachey, and Wedunn's suppliers do not feel the same way. Their suppliers expect them to pay their accounts payable within a few weeks of receiving their bills. So far, there has not even been enough money to pay the three lawyers, and they are not sure how long they can keep practising law without getting some money into their pockets!

Instructions
Provide suggestions for Tory, Hachey, and Wedunn to improve its cash management practices, in particular with respect to accelerating the collection of its receivables and delaying the payment of its liabilities.

Problems: Set A

Identify control activities over cash receipts.
(SO 1, 2)

P7–1A　Red River Theatre has a cashier's booth located near the theatre entrance. There are two cashiers: one works from 1 p.m. to 5 p.m., the other from 5 p.m. to 9 p.m. Each cashier is bonded. The cashiers receive cash from customers and operate a machine that ejects serially numbered tickets. The rolls of tickets are inserted and locked into the machine by the theatre manager at the beginning of each cashier's shift.

After purchasing a ticket, which costs a different amount depending on the day of the week and the customer's age group, the customer takes the ticket to an usher stationed at the entrance to the theatre lobby, a few metres from the cashier's booth. The usher tears the ticket in half, admits the customer, and returns the ticket stub to the customer. The usher drops the other half of the ticket into a locked box.

At the end of each cashier's shift, the theatre manager removes the ticket rolls from the machine and makes a cash count. The cash count sheet is initialled by the cashier. At the end of the day, the manager deposits the total receipts in a bank night deposit slot. In addition, the manager sends copies of the deposit slip and the initialled cash count sheets to the head cashier for verification and to the accounting department for comparison with sales records. Receipts from the first shift are stored in a safe located in the manager's office.

Instructions
(a) Identify the control activities and their application to cash receipts at the theatre.
(b) If the usher and cashier decided to collaborate to steal cash, what actions might they take?

P7-2A High Tech Inc. commenced operations recently. Two friends from university, John Deol and Rehana Gerdman, jointly own the company's shares. John and Rehana have developed a new software application to track shipping. The two friends spend most of their time on the development of new products and the marketing of the current product.

Identify control weaknesses over cash payments.
(SO 1, 2)

John and Rehana hired Fred Glass to be High Tech's controller. Fred has been given overall responsibility for the books and records of High Tech so that John and Rehana can spend their time on development and marketing.

Fred has one assistant, Asmaa. Both Fred and Asmaa have the authority to order goods for High Tech. Asmaa can approve invoices for payment up to $5,000. Fred can approve any invoice for payment. Fred, John, and Rehana are all signing officers on the company's bank account. Only one of the three signing officers needs to sign a cheque under $20,000. For cheques greater than $20,000, two signing officers must sign. Unsigned cheques are kept in the company safe. The safe is kept locked and access to the safe is limited to the signing officers. Fred is responsible for preparing the monthly bank reconciliations and making any necessary journal entries.

Instructions
(a) Identify the control weaknesses over the cash payments and the problems that could occur as a result of these weaknesses.
(b) List the improvements in control activities that High-Tech should consider.

P7-3A Each of the following independent situations has one or more control activity weaknesses:

Identify control weaknesses.
(SO 1, 2)

1. Board Riders Ltd. is a small snowboarding club that offers specialized coaching for snowboarders who want to improve their skills. Group lessons are offered every day. Members who want a lesson pay a $25 fee directly to the instructor at the start of the lesson that day. Most members pay cash. At the end of the lesson, the instructor reports the number of students and turns over the cash to the office manager.
2. Coloroso Agency Corp. offers parenting advice to young single mothers. Most of the agency's revenues are from government grants. The general manager is responsible for all of the accounting work, including approving invoices for payment, preparing and posting all entries into the accounting system, and preparing bank reconciliations.
3. At Nexus Corporation, each salesperson is responsible for deciding on the correct credit policies for his or her customers. For example, the salesperson decides if Nexus should sell to the customer on credit and how high the credit limit should be. Salespeople receive a commission based on their sales.
4. Algorithm Limited is a software company that employs many computer programmers. The company uses accounting software that was created by one of the employees. In order to be more flexible and share the workload, all of the programmers have access to the accounting software program in case changes are needed.
5. The warehouse manager at Orange Wing Distributors Ltd. is well known for running an efficient, cost-saving operation. He has eliminated the requirement for staff to create receiving reports and purchase orders because it was taking too long to prepare them.

Instructions
(a) Identify the control weakness(es) in each of the above situations and the problems that could occur as a result of these weaknesses.
(b) Make recommendations for correcting each situation.

P7-4A Cedar Grove High School wants to raise money for a new sound system for its auditorium. The main fundraising event is a dance at which the famous disc jockey Obnoxious Al will play rap music. Roger DeMaster, the music teacher, has been given the responsibility for coordinating the fundraising efforts. This is Roger's first experience with fundraising. He decides to put the Student Representative Council (SRC) in charge of the event.

Identify control weaknesses over cash receipts and payments.
(SO 1, 2)

Roger had 500 unnumbered tickets printed for the dance. He left the tickets in a locked box on his desk and told the SRC students to take as many tickets as they thought they could sell for $20 each. To ensure that no extra tickets would be floating around, he told the students to get rid of any unsold tickets. When the students received payment for the tickets, they were to bring the cash back to Roger, and he would put it in the locked box on his desk.

Some of the students were responsible for decorating the gymnasium for the dance. Roger gave each of them a key to the locked box and told them that if they took money out to purchase materials, they should put a note in the box saying how much they took and what it was used for. After two weeks, the locked box appeared to be getting full, so Roger asked Praveen Patel to count the money, prepare a deposit slip, and deposit the money in a bank account Roger had opened.

The day of the dance, Roger wrote a cheque from the account to pay Obnoxious Al. Al, however, said that he accepted only cash and did not give receipts. Having no alternative, Roger took $500 out of the locked box and gave it to Al. At the dance, Roger had Sara Wu working at the entrance to the gymnasium, collecting tickets from students and selling tickets to those who had not prepurchased them. Roger estimated that 400 students attended the dance.

The following day, Roger closed out the bank account, which had $750 in it, and gave that amount plus the $1,800 in the locked box to Principal Orlowski. Principal Orlowski seemed surprised that, after generating roughly $8,000 (400 tickets @ $20) in sales, the dance netted only $2,550 in cash. Roger did not know how to respond.

Instructions
(a) Identify the control weaknesses over cash receipts and payments and the problems that could occur because of these weaknesses.
(b) List the improvements in control activities that the school should consider.

Prepare bank recon-
ciliation and adjusting
entries.
(SO 3)

P7–5A On July 31, Beaupré Ltd. had an unadjusted cash balance of $14,786. The bank statement from the Caisse Populaire on that date showed a balance of $21,062. A comparison of the bank statement with the Cash account revealed the following:

— books 1. The bank statement included service charges of $100.

+ books 2. The bank statement included electronic collections from customers on account totalling $4,110. Beaupré had not recorded the EFT.

— bank 3. A deposit of $1,800 made by another company was incorrectly added to Beaupré's account by the Caisse Populaire.

4. Salaries of $4,000 were paid electronically during the month. The company has already recorded these.

— bank 5. Cheques outstanding on June 30 totalled $1,844. Of these, $1,378 worth cleared the bank in July. All cheques written in July cleared the bank in July.

Instructions

(a) Prepare the bank reconciliation at July 31.

(b) Prepare any adjusting journal entries required from the reconciliation.

Prepare bank recon-
ciliation and adjusting
entries.
(SO 3)

P7–6A The bank portion of last month's bank reconciliation for Yap Ltd. at February 28 was as follows:

YAP LTD.
Bank Reconciliation
February 28

Cash balance per bank		$14,368
Add: Deposits in transit		2,530
		16,898
Less: Outstanding cheques		
#3451	$2,260	
#3470	1,535	3,795
Adjusted cash balance		$13,103

The adjusted cash balance per bank agreed with the cash balance per books after the bank reconciliation at February 28. The March bank statement showed the following:

YAP LTD.
Bank Statement
March 31

Date		Description	Amounts Deducted from Account (Debits)	Amounts Added to Account (Credits)	Balance
Feb.	28	Opening balance			14,368
Mar.	1	Cheque, No. 3451	2,260		12,108
	1	Deposit		2,530	14,638
	2	Cheque, No. 3470	1,535		13,103
	4	Deposit		1,221	14,324
	9	Cheque, No. 3471	1,427		12,897
	10	Returned cheque—NSF, R. Aubut	550		12,347
	10	NSF fee	40		12,307
	15	EFT, loan payment	1,062		11,245
	19	Cheque, No. 3472	1,641		9,604
	26	Deposit		2,567	12,171
	31	EFT, collection on account from M. Boudreault		230	12,401
	31	Bank service charges	49		12,352
	31	Debit and credit card fees	65		12,287

Yap's cash receipts and payments for the month of March showed the following:

Cash Receipts			Cash Payments		
Date	Amount		Date	Number	Amount
Mar. 4	$1,221		Mar. 7	3471	$1,427
26	2,567		15	3472	1,461
31	1,025		29	3473	487
	$4,813				$3,375

Additional information:

1. The EFT loan payment should have been recorded by the company on March 15, but this entry was missed. The payment included $62 of interest and a $1,000 payment on the loan principal.
2. The bank made an error processing cheque #3472.
3. The EFT collection was not previously recorded.
4. Bank service charges ($49) and debit and credit card fees ($65) were not previously recorded.

Instructions
(a) Calculate the unadjusted cash balance per books at March 31, prior to reconciliation.
(b) What is the amount of the deposits in transit at March 31?
(c) What is the amount of the outstanding cheques at March 31?
(d) Prepare the bank reconciliation at March 31.
(e) Prepare any adjusting journal entries required from the reconciliation.

P7-7A The bank portion of last month's bank reconciliation for Hamptons Limited at October 31 is shown here:

Prepare bank reconciliation and adjusting entries.
(SO 3)

HAMPTONS LIMITED Bank Reconciliation October 31		
Cash balance per bank		$24,890
Add: Deposits in transit		3,060
		27,950
Less: Outstanding cheques		
#2472	$1,440	
#2473	1,690	
#2474	1,008	4,138
Adjusted cash balance		$23,812

The adjusted cash balance per bank agreed with the cash balance per books after the bank reconciliation at October 31. The November bank statement showed the following:

HAMPTONS LIMITED Bank Statement November 30				
Date	Description	Amounts Deducted from Account (Debits)	Amounts Added to Account (Credits)	Balance
Oct. 31				24,890
Nov. 1	Cheque, No. 2472	1,440		23,450
1	Deposit		3,060	26,510
2	Cheque, No. 2473	1,690		24,820
3	Deposit		2,424	27,244
4	Cheque, No. 2475	3,282		23,962
7	Deposit		1,980	25,942
8	Cheque, No. 2476	5,660		20,282
10	Cheque, No. 2477	1,200		19,082
14	Deposit		5,150	24,232
15	Cheque, No. 2478	3,500		20,732
15	EFT, salaries	6,400		14,332
20	Deposit		5,890	20,222
25	Returned cheque—NSF, Giasson Developments	500		19,722
25	NSF fee	80		19,642
26	Cheque, No. 2479	1,390		18,252
27	Deposit		3,300	21,552
28	EFT, collection of note receivable and interest		5,008	26,560
30	Cheque, No. 2481	1,152		25,408
30	EFT, salaries	6,400		19,008
30	Bank service charges	50		18,958

The cash records per books for November showed the following:

Cash Receipts				Cash Payments		
Date		Amount		Date	Number	Amount
Nov.	3	$ 2,424		Nov.	1	2475	$ 3,282
	7	1,980			2	2476	4,760
	12	5,150			2	2477	1,200
	20	5,908			8	2478	3,500
	27	3,300			15	2479	1,390
	30	2,676			15	EFT, salaries	6,400
		$21,438			18	2480	1,224
					20	2481	1,152
					29	2482	1,660
					30	EFT, salaries	6,400
							$30,968

Additional information:

1. The EFT collection was not previously recorded. The collection of the note on November 28 was for $4,400, plus $608 interest. Interest was not previously accrued.
2. EFT payments are recorded when they occur.
3. The bank did not make any errors.
4. Two errors were made by the company: one in recording a cheque and one in recording a cash receipt. The correction of any errors in the recording of cheques should be made to Accounts Payable. The correction of any errors in the recording of cash receipts should be made to Accounts Receivable.

Instructions

(a) Calculate the unadjusted cash balance per books as at November 30, prior to reconciliation.
(b) Prepare the bank reconciliation at November 30.
(c) Prepare any adjusting journal entries required from the reconciliation.

Calculate cash.
(SO 4)

P7–8A A first-year co-op student is trying to determine the amount of cash and cash equivalents that should be reported on a company's statement of financial position. The following information was provided to the student at year end:

1. Cash on hand in the cash registers totals $5,000.
2. The balance in the commercial bank savings account is $100,000 and in the commercial bank chequing account, $25,000. The company also has a U.S. bank account, which contains the equivalent of $45,000 Canadian at year end.
3. A special bank account holds $150,000 in cash that is restricted for equipment replacement.
4. Amounts due from employees (travel advances) total $12,000.
5. Trading investments held by the company include $32,000 in a term deposit maturing in 120 days, a Government of Canada bond for $75,000 that falls due in 30 days, and $40,000 in shares of Shoppers Drug Mart.
6. The company has a supply of unused postage stamps totalling $150.
7. The company has $1,750 of NSF cheques from customers that were returned by the bank. NSF fees charged by the bank for processing these cheques totalled $80.
8. The company keeps $5,000 as a compensating balance with respect to a long-term loan in a special account.

Instructions

(a) Determine which items listed above would be considered to be cash and which would be considered to be cash equivalents.
(b) What combined amount would the company report as cash and cash equivalents on the year-end statement of financial position?
(c) Identify where any items that were not reported as cash and cash equivalents in (a) should be reported.

Discuss reporting of cash.
(SO 4)

P7–9A Rupert Inc. reports the following selected information (in thousands) in its April 30, 2015, financial statements:

	2015	2014
Cash and cash equivalents	$41,817	$31,525
Restricted cash	5,350	3,100

Additional information: Restricted cash represents monies held for a potential lawsuit settlement.

Instructions

(a) Explain the difference between cash and cash equivalents. Why are they combined for reporting purposes?
(b) In which section of the statement of financial position would the restricted cash most likely be reported? Explain.
(c) Explain why it is necessary to report restricted cash separately when cash equivalents, such as highly liquid trading investments, are included in cash.

P7–10A Bev's Design Services Ltd. commenced operations approximately nine months ago. Bev, the sole shareholder and designer, organizes the hall and table decorations for a variety of functions. Bev has completed 15 contracts so far and, with wedding season coming up, has 20 more signed contracts. However, the company has no cash in its bank account and Bev has had to loan the business money from her personal funds.

    For each signed contract, the company requires a $50 non-refundable deposit. The balance of the account receivable is due three weeks following the function. For the weddings Bev has serviced, receipt of the amount due has occurred on average five weeks after the function. All the decorations must be purchased about two months before the function or once the contract has been signed, whichever is earlier. The company pays for the decorations at the time of purchase. Recently, the company has learned that it can apply for an account, which will permit it to pay 30 days after purchase.

Recommend cash management improvements.
(SO 4)

Instructions
Identify ways the company can improve its cash management practices, in particular with respect to accelerating the collection of its receivables and delaying the payment of its liabilities.

Problems: Set B

P7–1B Segal Office Supply Limited recently changed its control activities over cash payments. The new activities include the following features:

Identify control activities over cash payments.
(SO 1, 2)

1. All cheques are prenumbered and written by an electronic cheque-writing system.
2. Before a cheque or electronic payment can be issued, each invoice must have the approval of Cindy van Bommel, the purchasing agent, and Ray Mills, the receiving department supervisor.
3. Cheques must be signed by either controller François Montpetit or assistant controller Mary Nishiyama. Before signing a cheque, the signer is expected to compare the amount of the cheque with the amount on the invoice.
4. After signing a cheque, the signer stamps the invoice "Paid" and writes in the date, cheque number, and amount of the cheque. The paid invoice is then sent to the accounting department for recording.
5. Blank cheques are stored in a safe in the controller's office. The combination to the safe is known only to the controller and assistant controller.
6. Each month, the bank statement is reconciled by a staff accountant who does not record payments.

Instructions
Identify the control activities and their application to cash payments at Segal Office Supply.

P7–2B You are asked to join the board of elders of a local church to help with the control activities for the offerings collection made at weekly services. At a meeting of the board, you learn the following:

Identify control weaknesses over cash receipts.
(SO 1, 2)

1. The board of elders has delegated responsibility for the financial management and audit of the financial records to the finance committee. This group prepares the annual budget and approves major payments but is not involved in collections or record keeping. No audit has been done in recent years, because the same trusted employee has kept church records and served as financial secretary for 15 years. The church does not carry any fidelity insurance.
2. The collection at the weekly service is taken by a team of ushers who volunteer to serve for one month. The ushers take the collection plates to a basement office at the back of the church. They hand their plates to the head usher and return to the church service. After all plates have been turned in, the head usher counts the cash collected in them. The head usher then places the cash in the church safe along with a note that includes the amount counted. The safe is unlocked because no one can remember the combination, and after all, it is in a church.
3. The morning after the service, the financial secretary goes to the safe and recounts the collection. The secretary withholds $200 to pay for cash purchases for the week, and deposits the remainder of the collection in the bank. To facilitate the deposit, church members who contribute by cheque are asked to make their cheques payable to "Cash."
4. Each month, the financial secretary reconciles the bank statement and submits a copy of the reconciliation to the board of elders. The reconciliations have rarely revealed any bank errors and have never shown any errors per books.

Instructions
(a) Identify the control weaknesses in the handling of collections.
(b) List the improvements in control activities that should be recommended for (1) the head usher, (2) the ushers, (3) the financial secretary, and (4) the finance committee.

P7–3B Each of the following independent situations has one or more control activity weaknesses:

Identify control weaknesses.
(SO 1, 2)

1. Rowena's Cleaning Service Inc. provides home cleaning services for a large number of clients who all pay cash. Rowena collects the cash and keeps it in the glove compartment of her car until the end of the week when she has time to count it and prepare a bank deposit.

2. Hornet's Convenience Store Limited sells a variety of items, including cigarettes, non-alcoholic beverages, and snack foods. A long-term employee is responsible for ordering all merchandise, checking all deliveries, and approving invoices for payment.

3. At Ye Olde Ice Cream Shoppe Ltd., there are three sales clerks on duty during busy times. All three of them use the same cash drawer.

4. Most customers at Better Used Car dealership use the option to pay for their vehicles in 24 equal payments over two years. These customers send the company cheques or cash each month. The office manager opens the mail each day, makes a bank deposit with the cash and cheques received in the mail that day, and prepares and posts a journal entry in the accounting records.

5. Jimmy's Truck Parts Ltd. employs sales staff who visit current and prospective customers. The sales staff keep product samples in their vehicles so they can demonstrate the product to the customers. If a customer has a large order, the order is e-mailed to the warehouse. The warehouse then ships the product to the customer on account. If a customer wishes to purchase one or two sample items, the salesperson can sell these for cash or on account. To obtain more inventory, the salespeople go to the warehouse and restock the vehicle themselves.

Instructions

(a) Identify the control weakness(es) in each of the above situations and the problems that could occur as a result of these weaknesses.

(b) Make recommendations for correcting each situation.

Identify control weaknesses over cash receipts and payments.
(SO 1, 2)

P7–4B The president of a registered charity, the Helping Elderly Low-Income People Foundation (HELP), approaches you for help on a special project to set up the charity's accounting system. HELP is a relatively new organization that is regulated by both the federal and provincial governments. The organization is required to maintain current financial records for the public to scrutinize. In other words, the records must be available to anyone who is interested in reviewing them. It is now the end of the charity's first fiscal year, and HELP has come to you with a shoebox of receipts and bank statements. You notice that the bank statements are still in their envelopes—they have not been opened.

The charity's revenue is mostly from donations. A van driver takes volunteers around the city and they go door to door asking for donations. The volunteers give a donation receipt for amounts over $20. Since volunteering takes a lot of time, the charity has many short-term volunteers and anyone is welcome to be one.

Two car companies generously donated vans to the organization. The van drivers are paid $50 a day, which they take from the donations. Drivers keep a summary of the total donations collected by the volunteers, and at the end of the day the drivers take the money to a bank and deposit it. Drivers also pay for their gas out of the donated funds.

HELP also held a fundraising dance last month. The president said he was disappointed with the project, though, because it did not bring in much money. To keep costs down, the president made the dance tickets by photocopying tickets and cutting them up. He gave them out to volunteers to sell for $25 each. He estimates that he printed 500 tickets, but can only account for about $5,000 (200 tickets @ $25) of revenues turned in by his volunteers.

Instructions

(a) Identify the control weaknesses over cash receipts and payments.

(b) List the improvements in control activities that HELP should consider.

Prepare bank reconciliation and adjusting entries.
(SO 3)

P7–5B On May 31, O'Hearne Limited had an unadjusted cash balance per books of $13,126. The bank statement from Community Bank on that date showed a balance of $15,230. A comparison of the bank statement with the company's Cash account revealed the following:

1. The bank statement included a bank service charge of $80.

2. The bank statement included electronic collections totalling $4,188. These were not previously recorded.

3. Outstanding cheques at April 30 totalled $2,900. Of these, $2,240 worth cleared the bank in May. There were $1,892 of cheques written in May that were still outstanding on May 31.

4. Included with the cancelled cheques was a cheque issued by O'Bearne Inc. for $1,200 that was incorrectly charged to O'Hearne by the bank.

5. On May 31, the bank statement showed a returned (NSF) cheque for $1,350 issued by a customer in payment of its account. In addition, the bank charged an $80 processing fee for this transaction.

6. The May 31 deposit of $1,926 was not included in the deposits on the May bank statement. The deposit had been placed in the bank's night deposit vault on May 31.

Instructions

(a) Prepare the bank reconciliation at May 31.

(b) Prepare any adjusting journal entries required from the reconciliation.

Prepare bank reconciliation and adjusting entries.
(SO 3)

P7–6B The bank portion of last month's bank reconciliation showed the following for River Adventures Ltd.:

RIVER ADVENTURES LTD.
Bank Reconciliation
April 30

Cash balance per bank		$9,009
Add: Deposits in transit		846
		9,855
Less: Outstanding cheques		
#533	$279	
#541	363	642
Adjusted cash balance		$9,213

The adjusted cash balance per bank agreed with the cash balance per books after the bank reconciliation at April 30. The May bank statement showed the following:

RIVER ADVENTURES LTD.
Bank Statement
May 31

Date		Description	Amounts Deducted from Account (Debits)	Amounts Added to Account (Credits)	Balance
Apr.	30	Opening balance			9,009
May	1	Deposit		846	9,855
	3	Cheque, No. 541	363		9,492
	4	Cheque, No. 533	279		9,213
	6	Cheque, No. 542	1,800		7,413
	6	Deposit		1,250	8,663
	10	Cheque, No. 543	1,560		7,103
	18	EFT, collection on account from A. Osborne		650	7,753
	19	Cheque, No. 544	799		6,954
	28	Deposit		1,771	8,725
	28	Returned cheque—NSF, R. Lajeunesse	440		8,285
	28	NSF fee	40		8,245
	30	EFT, prepaid insurance payment	578		7,667
	31	Debit and credit card fees	75		7,592
	31	Bank service charges	25		7,567

River Adventures' cash receipts and payments for the month of May showed the following:

Cash Receipts				Cash Payments			
Date		Amount		Date		Number	Amount
May	6	$1,250		May	5	542	1,800
	28	1,771			7	543	1,650
	31	1,286			15	544	799
		$4,307			31	545	950
							$5,199

Additional information:

1. The bank made an error when processing cheque #543.
2. The EFT collection was not previously recorded.
3. Because the EFT for prepaid insurance payment occurred near the end of the month, it has not been recorded yet.

Instructions
(a) Calculate the unadjusted cash balance per books at May 31, prior to reconciliation.
(b) What is the amount of the deposits in transit at May 31?
(c) What is the amount of the outstanding cheques at May 31?
(d) Prepare the bank reconciliation at May 31.
(e) Prepare any adjusting journal entries required from the reconciliation.

Prepare bank recon-
ciliation and adjusting
entries.
(SO 3)

P7–7B The bank portion of last month's bank reconciliation for Racine Limited at November 30 is shown here:

RACINE LIMITED
Bank Reconciliation
November 30

Cash balance per bank		$14,368
Add: Deposits in transit		2,530
		16,898
Less: Outstanding cheques		
#3451	$2,260	
#3471	845	
#3474	1,050	4,155
Adjusted cash balance		$12,743

The adjusted cash balance per bank agreed with the cash balance per books after the bank reconciliation at November 30. The December bank statement showed the following:

RACINE LIMITED
Bank Statement
December 31

Date		Description	Amounts Deducted from Account (Debits)	Amounts Added to Account (Credits)	Balance
Nov.	30	Opening balance			14,368
Dec.	1	Deposit		2,530	16,898
	1	Cheque, No. 3451	2,260		14,638
	2	Cheque, No. 3471	845		13,793
	3	Deposit		1,212	15,005
	4	Cheque, No. 3475	1,641		13,364
	7	EFT, salaries	1,427		11,937
	8	Cheque, No. 3476	1,300		10,637
	10	Cheque, No. 3477	2,130		8,507
	15	Cheque, No. 3479	3,080		5,427
	15	EFT, collection on account, R. Nishimura		3,145	8,572
	17	Deposit		2,945	11,517
	21	EFT, salaries	1,427		10,090
	24	Returned cheque—NSF, Hilo Holdings	987		9,103
	24	NSF fee	40		9,063
	25	Deposit		2,567	11,630
	27	Cheque, No. 3480	600		11,030
	27	Cheque, No. 3482	1,140		9,890
	30	Deposit		1,025	10,915
	30	Cheque, No. 3481	475		10,440
	31	Bank service charges	45		10,395

The cash records per books for December showed the following:

Cash Receipts				Cash Payments			
Date		Amount		Date		Number	Amount
Dec.	1	$1,212		Dec.	1	3475	$ 1,641
	17	2,954			2	3476	1,300
	27	2,567			2	3477	2,130
	30	1,025			4	3478	538
	31	1,197			7	EFT, salaries	1,427
		$8,955			8	3479	3,080
					10	3480	600
					20	3481	475
					21	EFT, salaries	1,427
					22	3482	1,140
					30	3483	1,390
							$15,148

Additional information:

1. The EFT collection was not previously recorded.
2. EFT payments are recorded when they occur.
3. The bank did not make any errors.
4. One error was made by the company. The correction of any errors in recording cheques should be made to Accounts Payable. The correction of any errors in recording cash receipts should be made to Accounts Receivable.

Instructions
(a) Calculate the unadjusted cash balance per books as at November 30, prior to reconciliation.
(b) Prepare the bank reconciliation at December 31.
(c) Prepare any adjusting journal entries required from the reconciliation.

P7-8B A new accounting student has been asked to determine the balance that should be reported as cash and cash equivalents as at December 31 for one of the firm's clients. The following information is available:

Calculate cash.
(SO 4)

1. Cash on hand in the cash registers on December 31 totals $1,600. Of this amount, $500 is kept on hand as a cash float.
2. At December 31, the company has debit card slips in the cash register totalling $500.
3. At December 31, the company has MasterCard credit card slips in the cash register totalling $975.
4. The balance in the bank chequing account at December 31 is $7,460.
5. Trading investments include $5,000 in a Government of Ontario bond that falls due in 80 days.
6. The company sold $250 of merchandise to a customer late in the day on December 31. The customer had forgotten her wallet and promised to pay the amount on January 2.
7. The company has a U.S. dollar bank account. At December 31, its U.S. funds were the equivalent of $2,241 Canadian.
8. In order to hook up utilities, the company is required to deposit $1,000 in trust with Hydro One. This amount must remain on deposit until a satisfactory credit history has been established. The company expects to have this deposit back within the year.

Instructions
(a) Determine which items listed above would be considered to be cash and which would be considered to be cash equivalents.
(b) What combined amount would the company report as cash and cash equivalents on the year-end statement of financial position?
(c) Identify where any items that were not reported as cash and cash equivalents in (a) should be reported.

P7-9B Boardwalk Real Estate Investment Trust reports the following selected information (in thousands) in its December 31, 2012, financial statements:

Discuss reporting of cash.
(SO 4)

	2012	2011
Cash	$138,656	$255,894
Segregated tenants' security deposits	12,090	11,561

Additional information:

1. Cash consists of bank balances and interest-earning bank accounts.
2. Segregated tenants' security deposits are held on behalf of tenants and are returned at the end of a lease if the apartment rented to the tenant is undamaged. They are considered restricted cash as they are held in trust bank accounts.

Instructions
(a) Why do you think that the security deposits are not reported along with the cash as cash equivalents?
(b) In which section of the statement of financial position would the segregated tenants' security deposits most likely be reported? Explain.

P7-10B Jackie Ledbetter started a business, Jackie's Designs Inc., after finishing her interior design courses eight months ago. Jackie has been fortunate in that the company has already completed six contracts, has four more signed contracts, and has booked three meetings with prospective customers. The prospective customers are referrals from the six contracts she has already completed.

Recommend cash management improvements.
(SO 4)

Jackie is having difficulty understanding why her business has no cash in the bank since it has been so successful. You asked her to explain the terms of the contracts and her system for purchases.

A contract is signed once the customer and Jackie agree on the work to be done. There is no deposit on signing the contract. The contract price is a flat fee for Jackie's work and cost plus a percentage for all items purchased by the company. The fee for Jackie's work is due once the contract is completed.

The amount for items purchased by the company is due three weeks after the items are delivered to the customer, in case the customer wants to return them. To date, an average contract takes four months to complete. The company does not have a formalized system for purchases. If a customer agrees that they would like to purchase certain items, Jackie will purchase the items when she finds them. Generally, she uses cash to pay for the items at the time of purchase. The items are then delivered to the customer within a week.

Instructions

Identify ways the company can improve its cash management practices, in particular with respect to accelerating the collection of its receivables and delaying the payment of its liabilities.

Broadening Your Perspective

Financial Reporting: *Shoppers Drug Mart*

Discuss internal control responsibilities.
(SO 1)

BYP7–1   The financial statements of **Shoppers Drug Mart** are presented in Appendix A at the end of this book. Two reports are presented at the beginning of this appendix: a management report and a report from the independent auditors.

Instructions

(a) What comments, if any, about the company's system of internal control are included in management's report? In the independent auditor's report?

(b) Who is primarily responsible for the system of internal control—management or the auditors? Explain the responsibility of each with regard to internal control.

(c) Who is primarily responsible for the preparation and presentation of the financial statements? In which report(s) are these responsibilities identified?

Comparative Analysis: *Shoppers Drug Mart and Jean Coutu*

Discuss cash and cash equivalents.
(SO 4)

BYP7–2   The financial statements of **Jean Coutu** are presented in Appendix B following the financial statements for **Shoppers Drug Mart** in Appendix A.

Instructions

(a) Jean Coutu reports "cash and cash equivalents"; Shoppers reports only "cash". Refer to Jean Coutu's statement of cash flows. What is the amount of its "cash and cash equivalents" at the end of its most recent fiscal year?

(b) The notes to Jean Coutu's financial statements specify that its cash equivalents consist of temporary investments offset by any bank overdrafts. Refer to Jean Coutu's statement of financial position and identify the amounts of its "cash and cash equivalents" at the end of the most recent fiscal year.

(c) Compare the amount of Jean Coutu's cash and cash equivalents with that reported by Shoppers Drug Mart at the end of the most recent fiscal year. Which company has the better cash position at the end of the most recent fiscal year?

Comparing IFRS and ASPE

Discuss control activities and management's internal control responsibilities.
(SO 1)

BYP7–3   **Nick's Steakhouse and Pizza**, described in the opening feature story of this chapter, is a privately held family-run restaurant located in Calgary. The **Imvescor Restaurant Group Inc.** is a Canadian public company that operates more than 250 Pizza Delight, Mikes, Scores, and Bâton Rouge family restaurants across Canada.

Since Nick's and Imvescor are in the same industry, they have much in common. However, they are also very different. For instance, Nick's is an owner-operated single location, whereas Imvescor has multiple locations and multiple franchise owners. In addition, Nick's is a private company that follows ASPE while Imvescor is a public company that follows IFRS.

Instructions

(a) Do you think that, when a company chooses a particular set of accounting standards to use, this has any impact on its internal controls? If so, how?

(b) Because Imvescor is a public company, management is required to perform an annual in-depth evaluation of the company's internal controls over financial reporting. Imvescor must state in its annual report that the evaluation was performed and state the CEO's and CFO's conclusion on the effectiveness of internal controls. If there were any material weaknesses, this must be reported, along with how management plans to fix these weaknesses. Why do you think public companies are required to report on the effectiveness of their internal controls?

Critical Thinking Case

BYP7–4 Patrick Chen is an entrepreneur who owns several businesses. His most recent acquisition several months ago was the Imperial Hotel, located in a resort community about 300 kilometres from Patrick's residence. Because he is not usually at the hotel, Patrick hired a manager, Kevin Kildare, to run the hotel's operations. Patrick's daughter Vanessa is now studying accounting at university and asked her father if she could work at the hotel during the summer. He agreed and asked her to observe the operations at the hotel and report back to him at the end of her first week of work.

Identify control weaknesses over cash receipts and steps to prevent fraud. (SO 1, 2)

Vanessa Chen's first job was at the front desk working with Megan Kildare, who is Kevin's daughter. One evening Kevin's friends dropped by the hotel to use one of the rooms for a poker party. Vanessa noticed the following day when reviewing room cleaning reports, that even though the room was cleaned by hotel staff, there was no record of a cash or credit card receipt for the use of the room that night that appeared on the daily room sales report.

A couple of days later, Vanessa spent some time in the hotel lounge where Michael Kildare, Kevin's son, was the only bartender on duty during a very busy shift in the early evening. At that time, the lounge had a drink special with tequila on sale. Michael was very busy and sometimes was unable to ring drink sales into the cash register. Vanessa also noticed that he was using tequila bottles from a box under the bar instead of the ones that were on display over the bar. The following morning when the lounge manager, who works only during the day, performed the daily count of inventory, he concluded that tequila sales were not as high as he had hoped they would be given the fact that the tequila inventory had barely fallen over the past 24 hours.

Later that day, Vanessa reviewed a report showing that parking garage receipts had decreased during the past month. Kevin has resisted the installation of any automated payment systems for the parking garage because he is worried that they are not always reliable and prefers instead the more personable approach of having someone, like his nephew Tom, at the parking garage exit to collect the parking fees in cash. When a driver enters the parking garage, they get a ticket with the entry time and then they present this to Tom, who calculates the amount owed when exiting.

Instructions

(a) What internal control weaknesses will Vanessa report to her father?

(b) If Vanessa wanted to determine how much money has been stolen or lost from the hotel, how could she do this? Is it possible?

(c) What steps can the hotel take to avoid the possibility of fraud in the future?

Ethics Case

BYP7–5 Banks charge fees of up to $45 for bounced cheques; that is, NSF cheques that exceed the balance in the payor's account. It has been estimated that processing bounced cheques costs a bank less than $5 per cheque. Thus, the profit margin on bounced cheques is high. Recognizing this, banks process cheques from largest to smallest within the same date range. By doing this, they maximize the number of cheques that bounce if a customer overdraws an account.

Discuss ethical issues related to processing cheques. (SO 3)

Instructions

(a) Who are the stakeholders in this case?

(b) Freeman Corp. had a balance of $1,500 in its chequing account on a day when the bank received the following five cheques for processing against that account:

Cheque Number	Amount
3150	$ 35
3158	1,510
3162	400
3165	890
3169	180

Assuming a $45 fee is charged by the bank for each NSF cheque, how much service charge revenue would the bank generate if it processed cheques (1) from largest to smallest and (2) from smallest to largest?

(c) Do you think that processing cheques from largest to smallest is an ethical business practice?

(d) Besides ethical issues, what else must a bank consider in deciding whether to process cheques from largest to smallest?

(e) If you were managing a bank, what policy would you adopt on bounced cheques?

"All About You" Activity

Determine the cost of
education.
(SO 4)

BYP7-6   The "All About You" feature in this chapter helped you understand the importance of knowing the cost of your education and planning for the amount of debt you are willing to take on. The Investor Education Fund website provides you with information about the cost of your university education. Go to the Fund site, at www.GetSmarterAboutMoney. ca, choose "Tools & Calculators," click on "Calculators," and then follow the links to the University Cost Calculator.

Instructions

(a) Consider all of the expenses that you have had to incur since you started your university education. How do they compare with the costs that are identified in the calculator?

(b) How are you funding your education? How much money do you owe in comparison with the costs that you have incurred? What are the costs that you have left to incur? How are you going to fund what is left of your education?

Serial Case

(*Note*: This is a continuation of the serial case from Chapters 1 through 6).

Identify control
strengths and
weaknesses.
(SO 1, 2)

BYP7-7   Natalie is learning how Koebel's Family Bakery accumulates accounting information. Because Janet and Brian are always busy in the bakery, the accounting for all transactions, especially cash, is sometimes neglected. Because Natalie has taken a few accounting courses, she would like to take a more active role in ensuring that there are effective controls in place at the bakery.

Janet, Brian, and Natalie discuss the accounting process that currently takes place and the following issues come up:

1. There are two employees who work behind the counter and look after customers. There is only one cash register. Each employee has their own password. A customer will come into the bakery, have a look at what baked goods are available behind the counter, and order what they would like from one of the employees. The employee will pull the inventory off the shelf and proceed to the cash register. After inputting a password, the employee will record what has been sold. The cash register calculates the amount owing, records how the customer has paid, and prints a receipt. Sometimes, when the bakery is very busy, the employee will not have a chance to log off a transaction before moving on to the next customer. This will sometimes result in difficulty tracking which sale was made by which employee.

2. A summary of cash, credit card, and debit card receipts is printed daily. Each day, Janet or Brian attempts to reconcile the summary of receipts to cash deposited. (The deposit is done nightly by Janet or Brian.) Lately, the reconciliation is being done once a week and done all at once. Because of the difficulty with passwords, it is difficult to determine who has made the error in processing a sale. Once they have finished reconciling, Janet or Brian enters the amounts into the accounting records.

3. Inventory is usually counted at the end of the day to determine what needs to be available for sale in the bakery at the start of the next day.

4. A work schedule is made at the start of each month and all overtime must be approved by either Janet or Brian. Lately, additional hours are being worked by all staff because of the additional work required to make cupcakes. When Janet completes the payroll, she attempts to reconcile the monthly schedule with the hours worked by each of the staff members. Because Janet and Brian are not writing down which employee was authorized to work overtime, it is difficult to determine whether the overtime was in fact authorized.

5. Cupcakes shipped to Coffee Beans coffee shops are invoiced when the shipment is completed. The invoices are manually prepared by date. A photocopy is made to enable the invoices to be entered in the accounting records.

6. Purchases of inventory occur when one of the bakers alerts Janet or Brian that a particular product is running low. Sometimes this will result in overpurchasing if either Janet or Brian has already recognized a shortage of a particular type of inventory and not told the other that the purchase has already been made.

Instructions

(a) Identify to Natalie the strengths in Koebel's system of internal control. For each strength identified, describe the control activity that is being addressed.

(b) Identify to Natalie the weaknesses in Koebel's system of internal control, and for each weakness identified, suggest an improvement. As well, for each weakness identified, describe the control activity that is violated.

Answers to Self-Test Questions

1. b   2. c   3. c   4. b   5. d
6. d   7. b   8. c   9. c   10. b

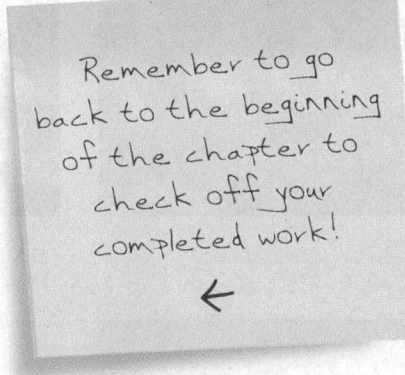

Endnotes

[1] Garry Marr, "Students Have to Be Realistic about the Debt they Take On to Get an Education," *Financial Post Magazine*, March 13, 2012; Chris Martin, "Forty Percent of Graduating Students Have No Debt. Surprised?," *Globe and Mail*, May 8, 2013; Kyle Prevost and Justin Bouchard, *More Money for Beer and Textbooks*, Young and Thrifty Publications, 2013, pp. 8, 29, 93; Rob Carrick, *How Not to Move Back in With Your Parents*, Toronto: Doubleday Canada, 2012, pp. 22, 24; Katherine Marshall, "Employment Patterns of Post-Secondary Students," Statistics Canada, September 2010, www.statcan.gc.ca/pub/75-001-x/2010109/article/11341-eng.htm, accessed June 21, 2013.

CHAPTER 8

Reporting and Analyzing Receivables

The Navigator
Chapter 8

- Scan *Study Objectives*
- Read *Feature Story*
- Read text and answer *Do It!s*
- Review *Comparing IFRS and ASPE*
- Review *Summary of Study Objectives*
- Review *Decision Toolkit—A Summary*
- Work *Using the Decision Toolkit*
- Work *Comprehensive Do It!*
- Answer *Self-Test Questions*
- Complete *assignments*
- Go to *WileyPLUS* for practice and tutorials

study objectives

After studying this chapter, you should be able to:

SO 1 Identify the types of receivables and record accounts receivable transactions.

SO 2 Account for bad debts.

SO 3 Account for notes receivable.

SO 4 Explain the statement presentation of receivables.

SO 5 Apply the principles of sound accounts receivable management.

the navigator

Varying Degrees of Credit

Receivables are generally a company's third-largest asset, after its property, plant, and equipment and inventory. For large retail operations like Canadian Tire, it is essential to manage, and monitor the collection of, its receivables on an ongoing basis.

The 90-year-old Canadian Tire Corporation has more than 1,700 locations across the country, including the iconic Canadian Tire stores and gas bars, as well as clothing retailer Mark's, and sporting goods chains Sport Chek and Sports Experts—part of the former FGL Sports Ltd., which the corporation acquired in 2012.

Canadian Tire's major receivables fall into three broad categories. First, there are the corporation's own credit cards, such as the Canadian Tire Options MasterCard and Sport Chek MasterCard, which it issues to some 4 million customers, representing one in five Canadian households. Second are the receivable accounts created by the 490 Canadian Tire associate dealers and hundreds of franchisees of the other chains across the country that buy merchandise from the company and operate their stores under the company banners. The third category is vendor receivables, which would be money due from vendors in support of various programs such as product launches or new store openings.

The largest receivable amount is Canadian Tire's credit card programs, which represent about $4 billion in receivables. Canadian Tire is one of the few retailers in Canada that has its own financial services division, which manages and finances its credit card receivables. The criteria for issuing a card are similar to any credit card program. Customers apply for new accounts, usually through the hostess program, where someone in the store will invite you to apply. The company assesses applications, does a credit score, and decides whether to issue a card and at what credit limit. It then manages the account, updating the credit score and adjusting the limit, when appropriate.

The credit card processing is outsourced to a company that handles credit card accounts for many companies. Canadian Tire also has a large call centre that deals with customer service collections—although certain collections are outsourced to collection agencies. The decision on when to send an account to an outside agency depends on the individual account, such as how big the balance might be and what the non-payment history has been.

Still, despite efforts to collect its credit card accounts, Canadian Tire writes off well over $300 million per year in bad debts.

Fortunately, the company's dealer and vendor receivables carry virtually no bad debts. Canadian Tire essentially acts as a wholesaler, where dealers and franchisees acquire from Canadian Tire all the merchandise they sell. At any point in time, dealers owe the corporation hundreds of millions of dollars for products that it has shipped to them. Canadian Tire has a dedicated system that tracks shipments to each store, immediately recording the receivable and billing the dealer for the amount owed. It's very unusual for a dealer to not be able to re-pay the money it owes the corporation, and it's also unusual for a vendor not to pay, since the corporation usually owes them money as well.

So, for a large retail operation like Canadian Tire, it pays to have its receivables in more than one category.[1]

the navigator

preview of
CHAPTER | 8

As indicated in our feature story, the management of receivables is important for any company that sells on credit, as Canadian Tire does. In this chapter, we will learn how companies estimate, record, collect receivables when due, and then in some cases collect their uncollectible receivables. We will also discuss how receivables are reported on the financial statements and how they are managed.

The chapter is organized as follows:

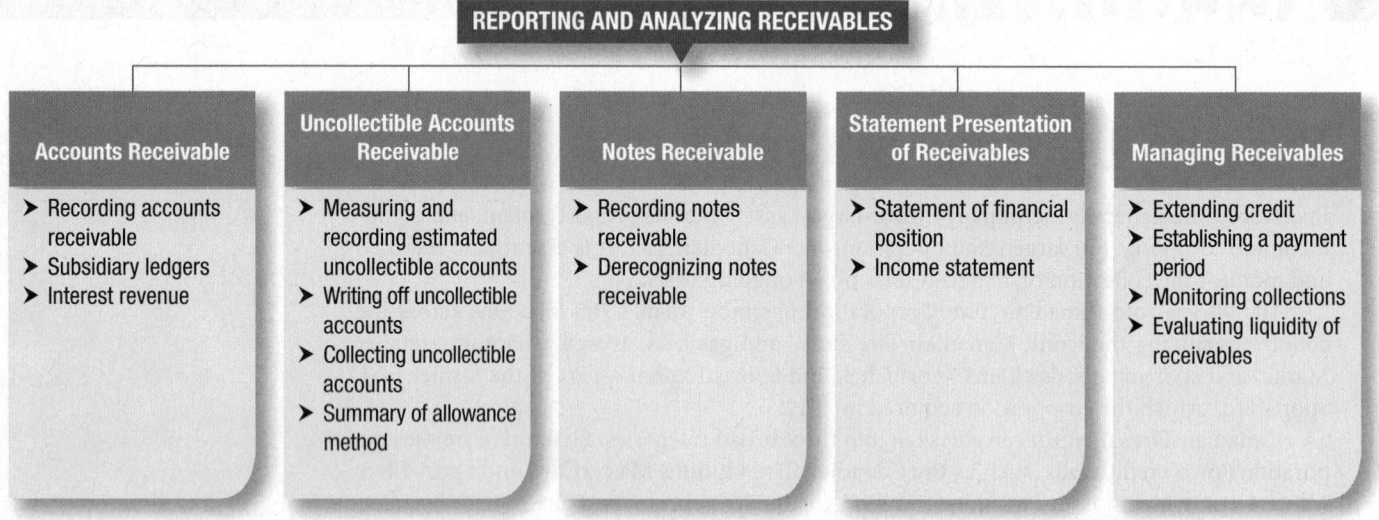

REPORTING AND ANALYZING RECEIVABLES

Accounts Receivable	**Uncollectible Accounts Receivable**	**Notes Receivable**	**Statement Presentation of Receivables**	**Managing Receivables**
➤ Recording accounts receivable ➤ Subsidiary ledgers ➤ Interest revenue	➤ Measuring and recording estimated uncollectible accounts ➤ Writing off uncollectible accounts ➤ Collecting uncollectible accounts ➤ Summary of allowance method	➤ Recording notes receivable ➤ Derecognizing notes receivable	➤ Statement of financial position ➤ Income statement	➤ Extending credit ➤ Establishing a payment period ➤ Monitoring collections ➤ Evaluating liquidity of receivables

Accounts Receivable

STUDY OBJECTIVE 1

Identify the types of receivables and record accounts receivable transactions.

The term *receivables* refers to amounts that are due to a business from its customers or other entities. Receivables are claims that are expected to be collected in cash, and they are frequently classified as (1) accounts receivable, (2) notes receivable, and (3) other receivables. Receivables, along with certain types of investments, are considered **financial assets.** These assets represent a contractual right to receive cash or another financial asset. We will learn more about investments and financial assets in Chapter 12.

Accounts receivable are amounts owed by customers on account. They result from the sale of goods and services. Receivables are generally expected to be collected within 30 days or so, and are classified as current assets.

Notes receivable are claims where formal instruments of credit—a written promise to repay—are issued as evidence of the debt. The credit instrument normally requires the debtor to pay interest and is for time periods of 30 days or longer. Notes receivable may be either current assets or non-current assets, depending on their due dates. Accounts and notes receivable that result from sales transactions are often called **trade receivables**.

Other receivables include nontrade receivables that do not result from the operations of the business. These can include interest receivable, loans to company officers, advances to employees, sales tax recoverable, and income tax receivable, for example.

We will focus our discussion in this section and the next on accounts receivable before turning our attention to notes receivable.

RECORDING ACCOUNTS RECEIVABLE

The first step in recognizing or recording an account receivable is straightforward. For a service company, a receivable is recorded when a service is provided on account. For a merchandising company, a receivable is recorded at the point of sale of merchandise on account. Recall that we learned about revenue recognition criteria in Chapter 4. Revenue (and any related receivable) should be recognized when the performance or sales effort is substantially complete. This normally occurs either when the service is performed or when goods are delivered at the point of sale. In addition, collection must be reasonably certain and measurable.

You will recall from Chapter 5 that the seller may offer terms, such as providing a discount, that encourage early payment. If the buyer chooses to pay within the discount period, the seller's account receivable is reduced in full by the amount of cash received plus the amount of the sales discount. Also, the buyer might find some of the goods unacceptable and choose to return them. This also results in a reduction of the account receivable.

To review, assume that Jordache Corp. sells merchandise on account to Polo Limited for $1,000 on January 2, terms 2/10, n/30. On January 5, Polo returns merchandise worth $100 to Jordache. On January 11, Jordache receives payment from Polo for the balance due. The journal entries to record the receivables portion of these transactions on the books of Jordache are as follows:

Jan. 2	Accounts Receivable	1,000	
	Sales		1,000
	(To record sale of merchandise on account to Polo Limited, terms 2/10, n/30)		
5	Sales Returns and Allowances	100	
	Accounts Receivable		100
	(To record merchandise returned by Polo)		
11	Cash [($1,000 – $100) × 98%]	882	
	Sales Discounts [($1,000 – $100) × 2%]	18	
	Accounts Receivable ($1,000 – $100)		900
	(To record collection of accounts receivable from Polo)		

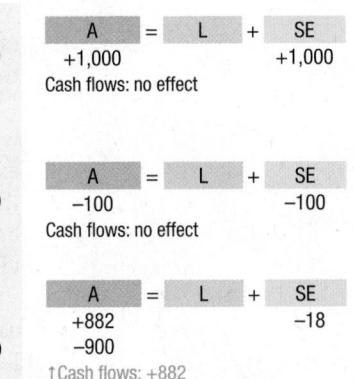

Note that the journal entries to record cost of goods sold for the January 2 and January 5 transactions have been omitted above for simplicity. You will recall that we learned in Chapter 5 that merchandising entries in a perpetual inventory system include both an entry to record the sale (or return) at the sales price and an entry to record the cost of the goods sold (or returned). You may find it helpful to return to Chapter 5 to review merchandising journal entries.

Nonbank Credit Card Receivables

You will recall that in Chapter 7 we learned that, when a customer uses a bank credit card to make a purchase, we record the transaction as a cash sale because banks honour the credit card receipt as cash. However, if the company sponsors its own credit card, as Canadian Tire in our feature story does, such a sale is considered a credit sale, with a debit being recorded to Accounts Receivable rather than Cash. For many companies, including Canadian Tire, nonbank cards are managed independently. As mentioned in our feature story, the processing of Canadian Tire's credit card is outsourced to a company that handles credit card accounts for many companies. Consequently, receipts from nonbank credit card sales such as these are sent to a credit card company for reimbursement rather than deposited at a bank. We will assume this is the case for all company credit card sales illustrated in this text.

To illustrate the accounting for a nonbank credit card sale, assume that Canadian Tire accepts its own Canadian Tire credit card on October 24 for a $500 purchase from Omar Qadri. The entry to record the sale by Canadian Tire is:

Oct. 24	Accounts Receivable	500	
	Sales		500
	(To record company credit card sale)		

The journal entry to record the cost of goods sold has been omitted again for simplicity. You will recall from Chapter 7 that credit card fees for bank cards were deducted directly from the company's bank account and recorded as Bank Charges Expense. There is no credit card fee incurred for a company's own credit card, such as the various Canadian Tire credit cards, although there may be fees for certain types of nonbank cards such as Diner's Club.

The accounts receivable in the journal entry above is from the credit card company, and not from Omar Qadri. This is because Canadian Tire, as we mentioned earlier, outsources the management of its company credit card. In Canadian Tire's case, its receivable is from its financial services division rather than from Omar Qadri.

SUBSIDIARY LEDGERS

In Chapter 3, we learned about the general ledger. Using the Accounts Receivable account in the general ledger works well for companies that do not have many customer accounts. Imagine what would happen, however, if a company like Canadian Tire recorded the accounts receivable for each of its customers in only one general ledger account. If it did, it would be very difficult to determine the balance owed by any one customer at a specific point in time.

Instead, companies like Canadian Tire use a subsidiary ledger in addition to the general ledger. A **subsidiary ledger** is a group of accounts that share a common characteristic (for example, they are all receivable accounts). In addition to accounts receivable, other accounts that are supported by subsidiary ledgers include inventory (to track inventory quantities and balances), accounts payable (to track individual creditor balances), and payroll (to track individual employee pay records).

In the case of an accounts receivable subsidiary ledger, it contains a separate account for each individual customer. The general ledger contains only one receivables account—Accounts Receivable—which acts as a control account for the subsidiary ledger. A **control account** is a general ledger account that summarizes the subsidiary ledger data. At all times, the control account balance must equal the total of all the individual customer receivables balances in the subsidiary ledger. This equality occurs because, when receivables transactions are recorded in the subsidiary ledgers on a customer-by-customer basis, summaries of these transactions are recorded in the general ledger. In this way, the subsidiary ledger provides supporting detail to the general ledger, freeing it from excessive detail.

To illustrate the accounts receivable subsidiary ledger, consider the following simplified example for Jordache Corp.

Accounts Receivable Subsidiary Ledger						General Ledger					
Sych Ltd.						**Accounts Receivable**					
Jan.	5	12,000	Jan.	16	9,000	Jan.	31	24,000	Jan.	31	19,500
Bal.		3,000				Bal.		4,500			
Downey Inc.											
Jan.	9	5,000	Jan.	22	3,500						
Bal.		1,500									
Pawlak Corp.											
Jan.	2	6,000	Jan.	28	6,000						
Bal.		0									
Polo Limited											
Jan.	2	1,000	Jan.	5	100						
				11	900						
Bal.		0									

Jordache posts individual transactions to its subsidiary ledger daily and posts summary transactions to its general ledger monthly. Notice that the debit of $24,000 to the general ledger Accounts Receivable account represents the total of all debits made to customer accounts in the subsidiary ledger in January ($12,000 + $5,000 + $6,000 + $1,000 = $24,000). Likewise, the credit entry of $19,500 represents the total of all credits made to customer accounts in the subsidiary ledger in January ($9,000 + $3,500 + $6,000 + $100 + $900 = $19,500). Because of this, the sum of all customer account balances in the subsidiary ledger is equal to the balance in the Accounts Receivable general ledger account at the end of January.

INTEREST REVENUE

At the end of each month, a company can use the subsidiary ledger to easily determine the transactions in each customer's account and then send the customer a statement of transactions that occurred that month. If the customer does not pay in full within a specified period of time (usually 30 days), an interest (financing) charge may be added to the balance due.

When financing charges are added, the seller recognizes interest revenue and increases the account receivable amount owed by the customer. This can be a substantial amount for some companies.

For example, assume that Jordache Corp. charges 28% interest on the balance due if not paid by the end of the month. If Sych Ltd., in the previous section, does not pay its outstanding balance of $3,000, Jordache would record interest revenue for the month of February of $70 ($3,000 $\times$ 28% $\times$ $\frac{1}{12}$) as follows:

Feb. 28	Accounts Receivable	70	
	Interest Revenue		70
	(To record interest on amount due from Sych Ltd.)		

A	=	L	+	SE
+70				+70

Cash flows: no effect

The above debit to Accounts Receivable would be posted individually to Sych Ltd.'s account in the subsidiary ledger and in total to the Accounts Receivable general ledger control account (likely as a summary entry at the end of the month as described in the previous section). Note that the Accounts Receivable account is debited for the interest due, rather than a separate Interest Receivable account. Interest will be charged on interest the following month (that is, $3,070) if the account continues to be unpaid.

ACCOUNTING MATTERS!

High Cost of Credit Card Debt

A recent study of more than 15,000 Canadian university students found that 9 out of 10 students have at least one credit card. While only 65% of the general population pays their credit card balances off in full each month, 82% of students pay in full each month. These students understand the high cost of carrying credit card debt, especially with interest rates on regular Canadian bank credit cards ranging from 18.5% to 19.9% and interest rates on nonbank cards reaching as high as 28.8%.

For example, the average credit card debt among those students with unpaid balances on their credit cards was $3,444 in 2012. If these students made just the minimum payment every month on their credit card account, it would take 18.5 years to pay off this debt. Of course, on the other hand, the credit card companies are earning lots of interest revenue on these unpaid balances![2]

BEFORE YOU GO ON...

▶Do It! Receivables Transactions

Selected transactions for Holm Corporation follow:

Oct. 29   Sold $10,000 of merchandise to Potter Inc., terms 2/10, n/30. Holm uses a perpetual inventory system and the cost of the goods sold was $6,000.

     31   Added monthly interest charges of 18% per annum (1.5% per month) to various overdue accounts receivable accounts totalling $32,000.

Nov. 1 $500 of merchandise was returned by Potter because it was the wrong size. The cost of the merchandise returned was $300.

     6   Received payment in full from Potter.

     10   Made $5,000 of company credit card sales. The cost of the goods sold was $3,000.

Record the above transactions on Holm's books, including any cost of goods entries.

(continued)

Action Plan

- Remember that two journal entries are required to record sales (or returns) of merchandise: (1) to record the sales price, and (2) to record the cost of the merchandise sold (returned).
- Recall that sales returns and discounts use contra accounts rather than affecting the Sales account directly.
- Calculate interest by multiplying the interest rate by the overdue account balance, adjusted for the appropriate portion of the year (for example, 1/12 for one month).
- Understand the difference between recording a bank credit card sale and a company (nonbank) credit card sale.

Solution

Oct. 29	Accounts Receivable	10,000	
	Sales		10,000
	(To record sales on account to Potter Inc., terms 2/10, n/30)		
29	Cost of Goods Sold	6,000	
	Merchandise Inventory		6,000
	(To record cost of merchandise sold to Potter)		
31	Accounts Receivable	480	
	Interest Revenue ($32,000 × 18% × 1/12)		480
	(To record interest charges on overdue receivables)		
Nov. 1	Sales Returns and Allowances	500	
	Accounts Receivable		500
	(To record sales return by Potter)		
1	Merchandise Inventory	300	
	Cost of Goods Sold		300
	(To record cost of merchandise returned by Potter)		
6	Cash ($10,000 − $500 − $190)	9,310	
	Sales Discounts ($10,000 − $500) × 2%	190	
	Accounts Receivable ($10,000 − $500)		9,500
	(To record collection of account receivable from Potter)		
10	Accounts Receivable	5,000	
	Sales		5,000
	(To record company credit card sales)		
10	Cost of Goods Sold	3,000	
	Merchandise Inventory		3,000
	(To record cost of merchandise sold on company credit cards)		

Related Exercise Material: BE8-1, BE8-2, BE8-3, BE8-4, BE8-10, E8-1, and E8-2.

Uncollectible Accounts Receivable

STUDY OBJECTIVE 2
Account for bad debts.

Once receivables are recorded in the accounts, we need to review them for collectibility in order to determine the amount that they should be measured and reported at in the financial statements, in accordance with the revenue recognition criteria. Although each customer must satisfy the seller's credit requirements before the credit sale is approved, some accounts receivable inevitably become uncollectible. For example, a corporate customer may not be able to pay because of a decline in sales due to a downturn in the economy. Similarly, individuals may be laid off from their jobs or faced with unexpected bills and find themselves unable to pay.

Credit losses from uncollectible receivables are debited to an account called bad debts expense. Note that this new account, Bad Debts Expense, is used instead of debiting a contra sales account as we did for sales returns and allowances because the responsibilities for granting credit and collecting accounts should be separated from sales and marketing. You will recall from Chapter 7 that establishing responsibility to authorize transactions and activities is an important feature of a good internal control system.

The key issue in measuring accounts receivable is when to recognize bad debts expense. If the company waits until it knows for sure that a specific account will not be collected, it could end up recording the bad debts expense in a different period than when the revenue was recorded.

Consider the following example. In 2014, Quick Buck Computer Limited decides it could increase its revenues by offering computers to students without requiring any money down, and with no credit approval process. The promotion is a success and the company sells 100 computers with a selling price of $400 each. This increases Quick Buck Computer's receivables and revenues by $40,000 in 2014. Unfortunately, during 2015, nearly 40% of the student customers default on their accounts. Illustration 8-1 shows that the promotion in 2014 was not such a great success after all.

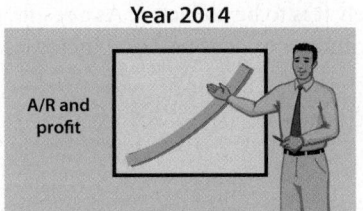

Year 2014	Year 2015
A/R and profit	A/R and profit
Huge sales promotion. Accounts receivable and sales increase dramatically.	Customers default on amounts owed; accounts receivable plummet. Bad debts expense increases dramatically.

▶Illustration 8-1
Effects of mismatching bad debts

Quick Buck Computer Limited's income statement is skewed with an overstatement of profit in 2014 and an understatement of profit in 2015 because of mismatched sales revenue and bad debts expense. In addition, accounts receivable in the statement of financial position are not reported at the amount actually expected to be collected at the end of 2014. Consequently, Quick Buck Computer's receivables are overstated in 2014, misrepresenting its statement of financial position.

The allowance method offers a solution to this problem. The **allowance method** of accounting for bad debts estimates the uncollectible accounts at the end of each period, consistent with the accrual basis of accounting. You will recall that the accrual basis of accounting requires expenses to be recorded in the same period as the revenue they help generate.

To record bad debts, Bad Debts Expense is debited and the Allowance for Doubtful Accounts is credited. This allowance is a contra asset account with a normal credit balance that is deducted from Accounts Receivable. A contra account is used instead of a direct credit to Accounts Receivable for two reasons. First, we do not know which individual customers will not pay. If the company uses a subsidiary ledger, we are unable to credit specific customer accounts to show they are uncollectible. We are also unable to credit the control account itself as this would mean that its balance would not equal the sum of all customer accounts in the subsidiary ledger. Second, the balance in Allowance for Doubtful Accounts is just an estimate. A contra account helps to separate estimates from actual amounts, such as those found in Accounts Receivable.

MEASURING AND RECORDING ESTIMATED UNCOLLECTIBLE ACCOUNTS

While there are several acceptable ways companies can use to calculate an estimate of their uncollectible accounts, the most common is to use a percentage of outstanding receivables to determine the allowance for doubtful accounts.

Under the **percentage of receivables basis**, management estimates what percentage of receivables is likely to be uncollectible. This percentage can be assigned to receivables in total or stratified (divided further) by the ages of the receivables. Stratifying the percentage classifies customer balances by the length of time they have been unpaid, which can improve the reliability of the estimate. Because of its emphasis on time, using stratification is called **aging the accounts receivable.**

To illustrate aging the accounts receivable, assume that Abrams Furniture Ltd. has total accounts receivable of $200,000 at December 31. It reviews the accounts receivable for each of its customers and classifies them by age (number of days outstanding)—this can usually be done easily by the company's accounting software. Based on past experience and factoring in the effects of the current economic climate, Abrams then estimates the likelihood (percentage) of not collecting each category of overdue receivables. Abrams uses five categories to age its receivables ranging from those receivables currently due (outstanding 0–30 days) to those 120 days or more overdue. Other companies may use more or fewer categories, depending on their circumstances.

Abrams presents its aging schedule below in Illustration 8-2. In this schedule, Abrams multiplies the estimated percentage uncollectible by the dollar amount in each aged category of receivables to determine its total estimated uncollectible accounts. Note the uncollectible percentages increasing from 2% to 50% as the receivables become more and more overdue (outstanding). Experience has shown that the longer a receivable is past due, the less likely it is to be collected. As a result, the estimated percentage of uncollectible debts increases as the number of days past due increases.

▶Illustration 8-2
Aging schedule

Number of Days Outstanding	Accounts Receivable	Estimated Percentage Uncollectible	Total Estimated Uncollectible Accounts
0–30 days	$111,500	2%	$ 2,230
31–60 days	41,400	5%	2,070
61–90 days	38,000	10%	3,800
91–120 days	6,600	25%	1,650
Over 120 days	2,500	50%	1,250
Total	$200,000		$11,000

The $11,000 total is the amount of existing receivables that is estimated to become uncollectible in the future. This amount is also the required balance in the account titled Allowance for Doubtful Accounts at the statement of financial position date. Note that this is the amount of the *balance* in the account, and not the amount of the adjustment required.

The amount of the bad debts adjusting entry is determined by calculating the difference between the required balance and the existing unadjusted balance in the allowance account. For example, if Abrams Furniture's trial balance shows Allowance for Doubtful Accounts with an unadjusted credit balance of $1,000, then an adjusting entry for the difference between the desired balance of $11,000 and the existing balance of $1,000, which is $10,000, is recorded as follows:

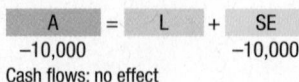

A = L + SE
−10,000   −10,000
Cash flows: no effect

Dec. 31	Bad Debts Expense	10,000	
	Allowance for Doubtful Accounts		10,000
	(To record estimate of uncollectible accounts)		

After the adjusting entry is posted, the accounts of Abrams Furniture will show the following:

Bad Debts Expense					Allowance for Doubtful Accounts			
Dec. 31	Adj.	10,000				Jan. 1	Bal.	1,000
						Dec. 31	Adj.	10,000
						Dec. 31	Bal.	11,000

It's a good idea to stop and check your work after you post the bad debts adjusting entry to the allowance account. The balance in the allowance account, after posting, should equal the total estimated uncollectible accounts, in this case, $11,000. If it equals something different, say $10,000, then your bad debt adjusting entry is incorrect.

Occasionally, the allowance account will have a debit balance before the adjustment. This occurs when write offs during the year exceed previous estimates for bad debts. (We will discuss write offs in the next section.) If there is an opening debit balance, the debit balance is added to the required balance when the adjusting entry is made. That is, if there had been a $1,000 debit balance in Abrams Furniture's allowance account before adjustment, the adjusting entry would have been for $12,000 to arrive at a credit balance in the allowance account of $11,000.

Bad debts expense is reported in the income statement as an operating expense. The balance in Allowance for Doubtful Accounts is deducted from Accounts Receivable in the current assets section of the statement of financial position as shown below:

Accounts receivable	$200,000
Less: Allowance for doubtful accounts	11,000
Net realizable value	$189,000

The $189,000 represents the expected **net realizable value**, or collectible portion, of the accounts receivable at the statement date.

WRITING OFF UNCOLLECTIBLE ACCOUNTS

Companies use various methods of collecting past-due accounts, such as letters, phone calls, collection agencies, and legal action. In the feature story, Canadian Tire mentions that it has a large call centre that it uses to deal with some overdue accounts and it outsources other cases to collection agencies. When all ways of collecting a past-due account have been tried and collection appears unlikely, the account should be written off and removed from the allowance because there is no longer any doubt about its collection. Canadian Tire writes off more than $300 million a year in bad debts.

To prevent premature or unauthorized write offs, each write off should be formally approved in writing by authorized management personnel. To adhere to the appropriate internal control activity, authorization to write off accounts should not be given to someone who also has daily responsibilities related to cash or receivables, in order to prevent them from misappropriating the cash receipt and writing off the account to hide the theft.

To illustrate a receivables write off, assume that on March 1, Abrams Furniture's vice-president of finance authorizes a write off of the $2,500 balance owed by T. Ebbet, a customer. T. Ebbet's account is more than 120 days overdue. The entry to record the write off is:

Mar. 1	Allowance for Doubtful Accounts	2,500	
	Accounts Receivable		2,500
	(Write off of T. Ebbet account)		

A = L + SE
+2,500
−2,500
Cash flows: no effect

Note that bad debts expense is not increased (debited) when the write off occurs. **Under the allowance method, every accounts receivable write off entry is debited to the allowance account and not to bad debts expense.** A debit to bad debts expense would be incorrect because the expense was already recognized when the adjusting entry that estimated the allowance balance was recorded last year.

Notice that the entry to record the write off of an uncollectible account reduces both accounts receivable and allowance for doubtful accounts. After posting, using an assumed Accounts Receivable opening balance of $227,500, the general ledger accounts will appear as follows:

Accounts Receivable					Allowance for Doubtful Accounts				
Feb. 28	Bal.	227,500	Mar. 1	2,500	Mar. 1	2,500	Dec. 31	Bal.	11,000
Mar. 1	Bal.	225,000					Mar. 1	Bal.	8,500

A write off affects only statement of financial position accounts and reduces both Accounts Receivable and Allowance for Doubtful Accounts equally. Net realizable value on the statement of financial position remains the same, as shown below:

	Before Write Off	After Write Off
Accounts receivable	$227,500	$225,000
Less: Allowance for doubtful accounts	11,000	8,500
Net realizable value	$216,500	$216,500

As mentioned earlier, the allowance account can sometimes end up with a debit balance after a write off of an uncollectible account. This occurs if the write offs during the period exceed the opening balance. This is only a temporary situation: it will be corrected when the adjusting entry for estimated uncollectible accounts is made at the end of the period.

ACCOUNTING MATTERS!

Social Media and Debt Collectors

Companies, and collection agencies working on their behalf, go to great lengths to collect amounts owed, including contacting family members and friends of debtors in attempts to locate them. One strategy debt collectors have tried recently has been to set up a fake profile on Facebook, Twitter, or another social media site and use it to try to "friend" or "follow" someone to determine their whereabouts. One woman successfully sued a debt collector who tried to use Facebook to get her to repay her debt. The court ruled that the debt collector had violated the woman's privacy rights when a collection agency sent messages to her and her family on Facebook to have her call the agency about the debt.[3]

COLLECTING UNCOLLECTIBLE ACCOUNTS

Occasionally, a company collects from a customer after the account has been written off as uncollectible. Two entries are required to record the recovery of a bad debt: (1) the entry made in writing off the account is reversed to reinstate the customer's account, and (2) the subsequent collection is recorded in the usual way.

To illustrate, assume that on July 1, T. Ebbet's fortunes have changed and he now wants to restore his credit with Abrams Furniture. In order to do so, he has to pay the $2,500 amount that had been written off on March 1. The entries are as follows:

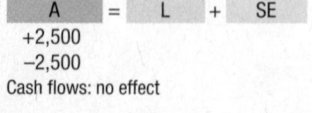

A = L + SE
+2,500
−2,500
Cash flows: no effect

			(1)		
July 1		Accounts Receivable		2,500	
		Allowance for Doubtful Accounts			2,500
		(To reverse write off of T. Ebbet account)			

		(2)		
July 1	Cash		2,500	
	Accounts Receivable			2,500
	(To record collection from T. Ebbet)			

A = L + SE
+2,500
−2,500
↑Cash flows: +2,500

Note that the recovery of a bad debt, like the write off of a bad debt, affects only statement of financial position accounts. The net effect of the two entries is an increase (a debit) to Cash and an increase (a credit) to Allowance for Doubtful Accounts for $2,500. Instead of making one compound journal entry, Accounts Receivable is debited and later credited in a second entry for two reasons. First, the company should reverse the write off as soon as the receivable is considered collectible. Second, T. Ebbet did pay, and the accounts receivable account in the subsidiary and general ledgers should show this collection, as it will need to be considered for future credit purposes.

SUMMARY OF ALLOWANCE METHOD

In summary, there are three types of transactions when accounts receivable are measured and recorded using the allowance method:

1. **Measuring and recording estimated uncollectible accounts**: Estimated uncollectible accounts receivable are determined by using a percentage of total receivables or an aging schedule. They are recorded by an adjusting journal entry that debits Bad Debts Expense and credits Allowance for Doubtful Accounts. Because these adjustments are made at the end of the period, the bad debts expense is recorded in the same period as the related revenue.

2. **Recording the write off of an uncollectible account**: Actual uncollectibles are written off at the time the specific account is determined to be uncollectible. They are debited to Allowance for Doubtful Accounts and credited to Accounts Receivable. This will cause a reduction in the allowance because the account is no longer doubtful as well as a reduction in accounts receivable because the account is not collectible.

3. **Recording the recovery of an uncollectible account**: Later recoveries, if any, are recorded in two separate entries at the time of the recovery. The first reverses the original write off by debiting Accounts Receivable and crediting Allowance for Doubtful Accounts. The second records the collection of the account by debiting Cash and crediting Accounts Receivable. Note that neither the write off nor the subsequent recovery affects the income statement.

Typical receivables transactions and the above entries are summarized and illustrated in the following T accounts:

Cash	
Beginning balance	
(a) Cash sales	
(b) Collections	
of accounts	
receivable	
Ending balance	

Allowance for Doubtful Accounts	
(e) Write offs	Beginning balance
	(d) Subsequent
	recoveries
	Unadjusted balance
	(f) Bad debts expense
	Ending balance

Accounts Receivable	
Beginning balance	
(c) Credit sales	(b) Collections of
	accounts receivable
(d) Subsequent	(e) Write offs
recoveries	
Ending balance	

Bad Debts Expense	
(f) Bad debts expense	

Sales	
	(a) Cash sales
	(c) Credit sales
	Ending balance

DECISION TOOLKIT

Decision Checkpoints	**Info Needed for Decision**	**Tools to Use for Decision**	**How to Evaluate Results**
Is the amount of past-due accounts increasing? Which accounts require management's attention?	List of outstanding receivables and their due dates	Prepare an aging schedule showing the receivables at various stages: outstanding 0–30 days, 31–60 days, 61–90 days, and so on as long as required.	Accounts in the older categories require follow-up: letters, phone calls, e-mails, and possible renegotiation of terms.

BEFORE YOU GO ON...

▶ Do It! Bad Debts

The following information is available for Chang Wholesalers Corporation about the age of its receivables at December 31, its year end:

Number of days outstanding	0–30	31–60	61–90	over 90
Accounts receivable	$200,000	$120,000	$100,000	$40,000
Estimated percentage uncollectible	2%	5%	10%	20%

(a) Using the above information, prepare an aging schedule. (b) Assuming that Allowance for Doubtful Accounts has an unadjusted credit balance of $8,000, prepare the journal entry to record bad debts expense at December 31.

Action Plan

• Apply percentages to outstanding receivables in each age category to determine the total estimated uncollectible accounts.
• The estimated uncollectible accounts is the ending balance amount that should appear in the Allowance for Doubtful Accounts.
• Determine the difference between the desired balance in the allowance account estimated above and the current balance in that account. Be alert to the possibility that the current balance could be either a debit or a credit while the desired balance will always be a credit.
• Stop and check your work. Make sure that the balance in the allowance account equals the total estimated uncollectible accounts after all entries have been posted.

Solution

(a)

Number of Days Outstanding	Accounts Receivable	Estimated Percentage Uncollectible	Total Estimated Uncollectible Accounts
0–30 days	$200,000	2%	$ 4,000
31–60 days	120,000	5%	6,000
61–90 days	100,000	10%	10,000
Over 90 days	40,000	20%	8,000
Total	$460,000		$28,000

(b) An adjusting entry of $20,000 is required to adjust Allowance for Doubtful Accounts from the current credit balance of $8,000 to the desired credit balance of $28,000.

Dec. 31	Bad Debts Expense	20,000	
	Allowance for Doubtful Accounts		20,000
	(To record estimate of uncollectible accounts)		

Allowance for Doubtful Accounts

	Dec.	31		8000
		31	Adj.	20,000
	Dec.	31	Bal.	28,000

Related Exercise Material: BE8-5, BE8-6, BE8-7, BE8-8, E8-3, E8-4, E8-5, and E8-6.

the navigator

Notes Receivable

Instead of accepting an account receivable, credit may also be granted in exchange for a formal credit instrument known as a promissory note. A **promissory note** is a written promise to pay a specified amount of money on demand (as soon as the payee demands repayment) or at a definite time. Promissory notes may be used (1) when individuals and companies lend or borrow money, (2) when the amount of the transaction and the length of the credit period exceed normal limits, and (3) in settlement of accounts receivable.

In a promissory note, the party making the promise to pay is called the **maker**; the party who will be paid is called the **payee**. For the maker of the note, the note would be classified as a note payable. For the payee of the note, the note would be classified as a note receivable. A note receivable and a note payable are accounted for similarly in each company's records except that the payee's note is an asset while the maker's is a liability.

A promissory note details the names of the maker and the payee, the principal amount or face value of the loan, the loan period, the interest rate, and whether interest is payable monthly or at maturity (the note's due date), along with the principal amount. Other details might include whether any security is pledged as collateral for the loan and what happens if the maker defaults (does not pay).

It is easy to confuse accounts and notes receivable as there are many similarities between them. Like accounts receivable, notes receivable are also financial assets because the company will collect cash in the future. Both notes and accounts are credit instruments. And both are valued at their net realizable value.

However, there are also differences between notes and accounts receivable. A note receivable is a formal promise to pay an amount that bears interest from the time it is issued until it is due. An account receivable is an informal promise to pay that bears interest only after its due date. Because it is less formal, it does not have as strong a legal claim as a note receivable. Most accounts receivable are due within a short period of time, usually 30 days, and are classified as current assets. On the other hand, notes receivable can be due over a longer period than accounts receivable and be classified as current or non-current assets depending on their due date.

The basic issues in accounting for notes receivable are the same as those for accounts receivable: recording notes receivable, estimating and writing off uncollectible notes, and collecting notes receivable.

RECORDING NOTES RECEIVABLE

To illustrate the basic accounting for notes receivable, we will assume that on May 1, Tabusintac Inc. (the payee) accepts a note receivable in exchange for an account receivable from Raja Ltd. (the maker). The note is for $10,000, with 6% interest due in four months, on September 1.

STUDY OBJECTIVE 3
Account for notes receivable.

Alternative Terminology
A *note receivable* is sometimes known as a *loan receivable* for the payee of the note, although for the maker of the note it is more common for a *note payable* to be known as a *loan payable*.

We record this entry as follows for the receipt of the note by Tabusintac:

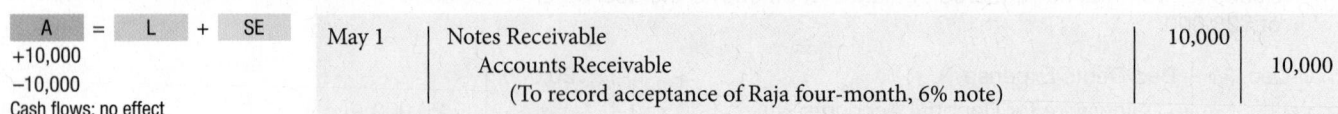

A	=	L	+	SE	May 1	Notes Receivable		10,000	
+10,000						Accounts Receivable			10,000
−10,000						(To record acceptance of Raja four-month, 6% note)			
Cash flows: no effect									

The above note would be considered to be a trade receivable because it was exchanged for an account receivable. If the note had been exchanged for a loan of cash instead, the note would not be a trade receivable and would be recorded as a debit to Notes Receivable and a credit to Cash for the amount of the loan.

As shown above, notes receivable are recorded at their principal amount, the amount owing on the loan (exclusive of interest). You will note that no interest revenue was recorded when the note was accepted on May 1, because, as we learned in Chapter 4, interest revenue is not earned until time passes.

Interest Revenue

When it is time to record interest, the principal amount of the note is multiplied by the appropriate interest rate. You will recall that interest rates are always expressed as an **annual** rate of interest. Interest rates may be set as a fixed rate over the period of the note (such as 6% for the four months' duration of the note) or as a floating (variable) rate that changes over the duration of the note. In the situations we describe in this chapter, it would be common for notes to have a fixed interest rate so you can assume that the interest rate is fixed for the purpose of your assignments in this chapter. The annual interest rate must be adjusted for the fraction of the year that the note is outstanding. As we did in past chapters, for simplicity we will continue to assume that interest is calculated in months, rather than days.

Interest on the Raja note will total $50 ($10,000 × 6% × $\frac{1}{12}$) a month, or $200 for the four-month period. This interest will be recorded as interest revenue for Tabusintac and interest expense for Raja. If Tabusintac's year end was May 31, the following adjusting journal entry would be required to accrue interest for the month of May:

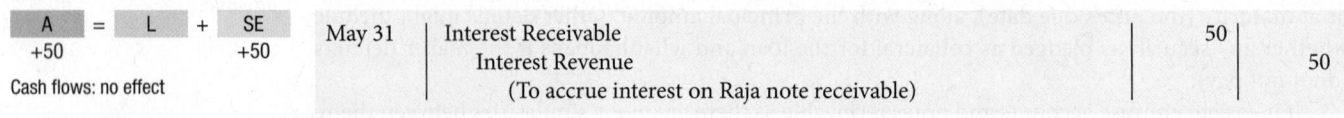

A	=	L	+	SE	May 31	Interest Receivable		50	
+50				+50		Interest Revenue			50
Cash flows: no effect						(To accrue interest on Raja note receivable)			

Note that while interest on an overdue account receivable is debited to Accounts Receivable, interest on a note receivable is *not* debited to the Notes Receivable account. Instead, as we learned in Chapter 4, a separate account for the interest receivable is used. Since the note is a formal credit instrument, its recorded principal amount must remain unchanged.

It is important to know that the calculation of interest as shown above applies only to short-term notes receivable with interest due at maturity. Notes that have a maturity date beyond one year from the statement of financial position date would be classified as non-current. Non-current or long-term notes are generally repayable in instalments rather than at maturity. Although not as common, short-term notes can also be repaid in instalments rather than at maturity. The interest calculations for instalment notes use a method to determine interest revenue called the effective-interest method. This method will be introduced in Chapter 10.

Comparing Notes Receivable and Notes Payable

As we mentioned above, a note receivable is essentially the same as a note payable except that one note is an asset while the other note is a liability. In Illustration 8-3, we compare the journal entries shown above that have been made by Tabusintac, the maker of the note receivable, with those that would be made by Raja, the payee of the note payable.

▶Illustration 8-3
Comparison of notes receivable and payable

		TABUSINTAC INC. (Payee)			RAJA LTD. (Maker)		

Acceptance/ issue of note	May 1	Notes Receivable
		    Accounts Receivable
			10,000	10,000	Accounts Payable
					    Notes Payable
						10,000	10,000

Accrual of interest	31	Interest Receivable
		    Interest Revenue
			50	50	Interest Expense
					    Interest Payable
						50	50

Valuing Notes Receivable

Like accounts receivable, notes receivable are reported at their **net realizable value**. You will recall that net realizable value is the difference between the balance in the receivables account (notes receivable, in this case) and the allowance account. Because companies generally don't have many notes, preparing an aging schedule, as is usually done for accounts receivable, is not the best way to estimate uncollectible notes. Instead, each note should be individually analyzed to determine its probability of collection. If circumstances suggest that eventual collection is in doubt, bad debts expense and an allowance for doubtful notes must be recorded in the same way they are recorded for accounts receivable.

DERECOGNIZING NOTES RECEIVABLE

In the normal course of events, the principal amount of a note receivable and its accrued interest is collected when due and then removed from the books, or **derecognized**. Notes that are collected when due are said to be honoured. In some situations, the maker of the note defaults and an appropriate adjustment must be made. This is known as a dishonoured (not collected) note. Let's look at each of these possibilities in turn.

Honouring Notes Receivable

An **honoured note** is a note that is paid in full at its maturity date. If Raja pays its note when it is due on September 1, the maturity date, the entry by Tabusintac to record the collection is:

Sept. 1	Cash	10,200	
	Notes Receivable		10,000
	Interest Receivable		50
	Interest Revenue		150
	(To record collection of Raja note and interest)		

A	=	L	+	SE
+10,200				+150
−10,000				
−50				

↑Cash flows: +10,200

Recall that one month of interest, $50, was previously accrued on May 31. Consequently, only three months of interest revenue relating to June, July, and August— $150 ($10,000 \times 6\% \times \frac{3}{12}$)—is recorded in the period subsequent to May 31.

Dishonouring Notes Receivable

A **dishonoured note** is a note that is not paid in full at maturity. A dishonoured note receivable is no longer negotiable. However, the payee still has a claim against the maker of the note for both the principal and any unpaid interest. Therefore, if eventual collection is expected, the Notes Receivable account balance and related interest are transferred to an account receivable by debiting Accounts Receivable for the total of the principal amount of the note and the interest due.

As shown below, the journal entry to record this is identical to the one above where the note was honoured, except that the debit to Cash would instead be made to the Accounts Receivable account:

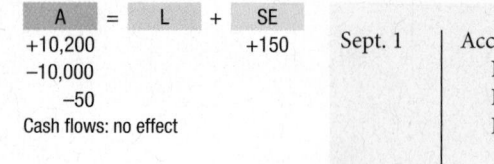

A	=	L	+	SE
+10,200				+150
−10,000				
−50				

Cash flows: no effect

Sept. 1	Accounts Receivable	10,200	
	Notes Receivable		10,000
	Interest Receivable		50
	Interest Revenue		150
	(To record dishonoured Raja note; eventual collection expected)		

If there is no hope of collection, the principal and any accrued interest should be written off. No additional interest revenue would be recorded, because collection will not occur. The entry to write off the amount would be:

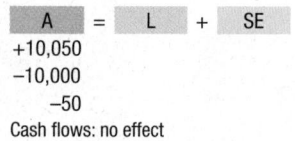

A	=	L	+	SE
+10,050				
−10,000				
−50				

Cash flows: no effect

Sept. 1	Allowance for Doubtful Notes	10,050	
	Notes Receivable		10,000
	Interest Receivable		50
	(To write off dishonoured Raja note)		

BEFORE YOU GO ON...

▶ Do It! Notes Receivable

Sampson Stores Ltd. accepts from Shiraz Corp. a three-month, 6%, $6,800 note dated May 10 in settlement of Shiraz's overdue account.

(a) What journal entries would be made by Sampson on May 10 and on August 10, the maturity date, assuming Shiraz pays the note and interest in full at that time and no interest was previously accrued?

(b) What entry would be made on August 10 if Shiraz could not pay the note but the note is still expected to be collected in the future?

Action Plan

- Calculate the accrued interest. The formula is: principal amount × annual interest rate × time in terms of one year.
- If the note is honoured, record the collection of the note and any interest earned. Use separate accounts for the principal amount of the note and the interest.
- If the note is dishonoured, record the transfer of the note and any interest earned to an accounts receivable account if eventual collection is expected or to an allowance account if collection is not expected.

Solution

(a) Note honoured:

May 10	Notes Receivable	6,800	
	Accounts Receivable		6,800
	(To replace account receivable with a 6% note receivable from Shiraz Corp., due August 10)		

Aug. 10	Cash	6,902	
	Notes Receivable		6,800
	Interest Revenue ($6,800 × 6% × 3/12)		102
	(To record collection of Shiraz note and interest)		

(b) Note dishonoured but collection in future is still likely:

Aug. 10	Accounts Receivable	6,902	
	Notes Receivable		6,800
	Interest Revenue		102
	(To record dishonoured Shiraz note; eventual collection expected)		

Related Exercise Material: BE8-9, BE8-10, BE8-11, BE8-12, BE8-13, E8-7, E8-8, and E8-9.

Statement Presentation of Receivables

Each of the major types of receivables should be identified in the statement of financial position, with supplemental detail included either in the statement or in the supporting notes. In addition, related revenue and expense accounts must be reported in the income statement, as discussed in the following sections.

STUDY OBJECTIVE 4
Explain the statement presentation of receivables.

STATEMENT OF FINANCIAL POSITION

Short-term receivables are reported in the current assets section of the statement of financial position, following cash and trading investments if items are presented from most to least liquid. Trade receivables must be reported separately from other types of receivables. Both the gross amount of receivables and the allowance for doubtful accounts must be reported either in the statement of financial position or in the notes to the financial statements.

Receivables due more than a year from the statement of financial position date must be presented separately in the non-current assets section of the statement. If a company has a significant risk of uncollectible accounts or other problems with its receivables, it is required to discuss this possibility in the notes to the financial statements.

Receivables represent a significant claim for Canadian Tire, making up 38% of its total assets. Illustration 8-4 shows the presentation of receivables for Canadian Tire in its statement of financial position.

▶Illustration 8-4
Presentation of receivables

CANADIAN TIRE CORPORATION Balance Sheet (partial) December 29, 2012 (in millions)		
Current assets		
Trade and other receivables	$ 757.2	
Less: Allowance for credit losses	13.6	$ 743.6
Loans receivable	$4,376.4	
Less: Allowance for credit losses	110.7	4,265.7
Non-current assets		
Loans receivable		608.0
Mortgages receivable		61.1
Other receivables		1.9

The net realizable value of the accounts receivable of $743.6 million and loans receivable of $4,265.7 million was reported in the current assets section of Canadian Tire's statement of financial position, which it calls "balance sheet." The detail was presented in its notes, but is included in the above illustration for ease of reference. Note that Canadian Tire calls its "allowance for doubtful accounts" an "allowance for credit losses" and reports that its allowance for credit losses is determined by considering an aging schedule, the company's past collection history, as well as economic conditions and trends specific to the company.

In the notes to its statements, Canadian Tire also discloses the components of its loans receivable, which includes its credit card loans, dealer loans, and personal loans.

INCOME STATEMENT

Income statement accounts related to receivables can include revenues such as sales or services on account and interest and expenses such as bad debts expense. Sales and service revenue and bad debts expense are reported in the operating expense section of the income statement. Interest revenue is reported separately in the non-operating section.

Canadian Tire reported, on its income statement and in the notes to its statements, revenue of $11,427.2 million and bad debts expense of $265.6 million on loans receivable. It also reported write offs of $331.7 million and recoveries of $58.1 million for the period. Its income statement also included finance income (interest revenue) of $18.1 million.

BEFORE YOU GO ON...

▶ Do It! Statement Presentation

Beau Resources Limited reports the following selected accounts and balances at December 31, 2015:

Accounts receivable	$ 150,000
Advances to employees	5,000
Allowance for doubtful accounts	7,500
Bad debts expense	10,000
Income tax receivable	7,500
Interest receivable	4,000
Interest revenue	6,000
Notes receivable (due in 120 days)	25,000
Notes receivable (due in 3 years)	75,000
Sales	2,000,000
Sales discounts	50,000
Sales tax recoverable	2,500

Beau estimates that all its notes receivable are collectible. Prepare a partial statement of financial position for Beau Resources.

Action Plan

- Determine which accounts are statement of financial position accounts and which are income statement accounts.
- Segregate current and non-current assets. Remember that current assets are turned into cash or used up within one year.
- Contra accounts offset other accounts and when applied against the related account, reduce it to a net balance.

Solution

BEAU RESOURCES LIMITED
Statement of Financial Position (partial)
December 31, 2015

Assets		
Current assets		
Accounts receivable	$150,000	
Less: Allowance for doubtful accounts	7,500	
Net realizable value	142,500	
Notes receivable	25,000	
Advances to employees	5,000	
Income tax receivable	7,500	
Interest receivable	4,000	
Sales tax recoverable	2,500	$186,500
Non-current assets		
Notes receivable		75,000

Related Exercise Material: BE8-14, E8-10, and E8-11.

Managing Receivables

There are four key steps in managing accounts receivable:

1. Determine whom to extend credit to.
2. Establish a payment period.
3. Monitor collections.
4. Evaluate the liquidity of receivables.

STUDY OBJECTIVE 5

Apply the principles of sound accounts receivable management.

EXTENDING CREDIT

A critical part of managing receivables is determining who should receive credit and who should not. If the credit policy is too tight, the company may lose revenue. On the other hand, if the credit policy is too loose, the company may end up extending credit to risky customers who pay late or do not pay at all.

Certain steps can be taken to help minimize losses if credit standards are relaxed. Risky customers might be required to provide letters of credit or bank guarantees. Then, if the customer does not pay, the person or company that provided the guarantee will pay. Particularly risky customers might be required to pay a deposit in advance or cash on delivery. For example, at one time, retailer Linens 'n Things reported that its largest suppliers required cash payment before delivery because it was slow paying its bills after it expanded too rapidly.

In addition, companies should ask potential customers for references from banks and suppliers to determine their payment history. It is important to check these references on potential new customers and to periodically check the financial health of existing customers. Canadian Tire, in our feature story, discusses calculating credit scores before issuing credit cards. A credit score is a measure of risk of a customer defaulting on an account. Many other resources are available for investigating customers and companies. For example, companies such as Equifax provide credit opinions on companies around the world to aid in lending decisions.

ESTABLISHING A PAYMENT PERIOD

Companies that extend credit should determine a required payment period and inform their customers about it. Normally, this period would be similar to the period used by competitors. For example, if you require payment in 30 days but your competitors allow payment in 45 days, you may lose sales to your competitors. If you match your competitors' payment period, the slower receipt of cash from customers may require you to carry higher levels of debt. You might have to consider options such as allowing up to 45 days to pay but offering a sales discount for customers paying within 15 days.

MONITORING COLLECTIONS

As we discussed earlier in this chapter, an accounts receivable aging schedule should be prepared and reviewed often. Almost all accounting software programs can generate an aged listing at any time. In addition to its use in estimating the allowance for doubtful accounts, the aging schedule helps estimate the timing of future cash inflows when preparing a cash budget. It also provides information about the company's overall collection experience, and it identifies problem accounts. As we learned in our feature story, Canadian Tire uses a variety of different strategies to deal with its problem accounts depending on how big the balance might be, what the payment history has been, and so on.

Credit risk can increase during periods of economic downturn. Credit policies and collection experience must always be monitored not only in comparison with past experience, but also in light of current economic conditions.

EVALUATING LIQUIDITY OF RECEIVABLES

Investors and managers keep a watchful eye on the relationship between sales, accounts receivable, and cash collections. If sales increase, then accounts receivable are also expected to increase.

However, if accounts receivable rise faster than sales, this may be an indication of collection problems. Perhaps the company increased its sales by loosening its credit policy, and these receivables may be difficult or impossible to collect, which will impact liquidity. Recall that liquidity is measured by how quickly certain assets can be converted to cash.

The ratio that is used to assess the liquidity of receivables is the **receivables turnover** ratio. This ratio measures the number of times, on average, that receivables are collected during the year. The receivables turnover is calculated by dividing net credit sales by the average gross accounts receivable during the year. Gross accounts receivable is the amount reported in the accounts receivable account (before deducting allowance for doubtful accounts). Unless seasonal factors are significant, average gross accounts receivable can be calculated by adding together the beginning and ending balances and dividing by 2.

Unfortunately, companies seldom report the amount of net credit sales in their financial statements. In such instances, net sales (including both cash and credit sales) can be used as a substitute. As long as one consistently chooses the same component to use in a ratio, the resulting ratio will be useful for comparisons.

The following data (in millions) are available for Canadian Tire's trade receivables:

	2012	2011	2010
Net sales	$10,005.8	$8,997.6	$7,853.8
Accounts receivable (gross)	757.2	813.1	681.6

The receivables turnover for Canadian Tire is shown in Illustration 8-5. Also included in this illustration is the receivables turnover for Sears, one of its competitors, as well as comparative industry data.

▶Illustration 8-5
Receivables turnover

$$\text{RECEIVABLES TURNOVER} = \frac{\text{NET CREDIT SALES}}{\text{AVERAGE GROSS ACCOUNTS RECEIVABLE}}$$

($ in millions)	2012	2011
Canadian Tire	$\frac{\$10,005.8}{(\$757.2 + \$813.1) \div 2} = 12.7$ times	$\frac{\$8,997.6}{(\$813.1 + \$681.6) \div 2} = 12.0$ times
Sears	44.7 times	31.7 times
Industry average	26.7 times	35.6 times

Canadian Tire's receivables turnover was 12.7 times in 2012. The higher the turnover ratio, the more liquid the company's receivables are. This was a slight improvement from its 2011 turnover ratio of 12 times. Despite this improvement, the company is slower than Sears and its industry peers at collecting receivables.

A popular variant of the receivables turnover is to convert it into an **average collection period** in terms of days. This is done by dividing 365 days by the receivables turnover. The average collection period is frequently used to assess the effectiveness of a company's credit and collection policies. The general rule is that the collection period should not greatly exceed the credit term period (the time allowed for payment).

Illustration 8-6 shows the average collection period for Canadian Tire, Sears, and their industry.

▶Illustration 8-6
Average collection period

$$\text{AVERAGE COLLECTION PERIOD} = \frac{\text{365 DAYS}}{\text{RECEIVABLES TURNOVER}}$$

	2012	2011
Canadian Tire	$\frac{365 \text{ days}}{12.7} = 29$ days	$\frac{365 \text{ days}}{12.0} = 30$ days
Sears	8 days	12 days
Industry average	14 days	10 days

This means that, on average, Canadian Tire collected its receivables in approximately 29 days in 2012. The lower the average collection period, the more liquid are a company's receivables. Note that even though Canadian Tire's receivables turnover and collection period are not as good as Sears and the industry, a collection period of 29 days is very good on its own depending on the credit terms granted.

Both the receivables turnover and average collection period are important components of a company's overall liquidity. Ideally, they should be analyzed along with other information about a company's liquidity, including the current ratio and inventory turnover. Recall from earlier chapters that high receivables and inventory balances due to slow-moving accounts and goods can distort a company's current ratio if the appropriate adjustments to reflect a decline in net realizable value have not been made. In general, the faster the turnover, the more reliable the current ratio is for assessing liquidity.

In addition, in some cases, receivables turnover and collection periods can be misleading. Some large retail chains that issue their own credit cards encourage customers to use these cards for purchases. If customers pay slowly, the stores earn a healthy return on the outstanding receivables in terms of interest revenue earned. Consequently, to interpret these ratios correctly, you must know how a company manages its receivables.

Helpful Hint
The higher the receivables turnover and lower the average collection period, the more liquid the company's receivables generally are.

DECISION TOOLKIT

 Decision Checkpoints	 Info Needed for Decision	 Tools to Use for Decision	 How to Evaluate Results
Are collections being made in a timely fashion?	Net credit sales and average gross accounts receivable balance	Receivables turnover = $\dfrac{\text{Net credit sales}}{\text{Average gross accounts receivable}}$ Average collection period = $\dfrac{365 \text{ days}}{\text{Receivables turnover}}$	The average collection period should be consistent with corporate credit policy. An increase may suggest a decline in customers' financial health.

Keeping an Eye on Cash

A company can have strong sales and profits but still have great difficulty paying its liabilities because of poor receivables management. For example, assume that a bank has given your new consulting business an operating line of credit of $20,000 and you have used $15,000 of it to pay for rent, damage deposits, and equipment. After the first month of business, you have earned $18,000 of consulting revenue but have collected only $2,000 cash from your clients. You have to pay your employees tomorrow and you owe them $9,000 for the salaries incurred this month. Although your profit this month is quite healthy ($18,000 − $9,000 − some other expenses), you only have $2,000 in the bank (the amount collected from clients) and you can only borrow another $5,000 on your operating line of credit from the bank to meet your payroll. In situations like this, a cash shortage often comes as a surprise and management does not have time to develop solutions to the problem. Businesses should always remember that profit does not measure cash flow and that they always need to find ways to deal with times when liquidity is tight.

BEFORE YOU GO ON...

▶ Do It! Managing Receivables

The Halifax Discount Store (HDS) Ltd. specializes in selling products at discounted prices. Customers can buy products with cash, debit cards, bank credit cards, or the company's own HDS credit card. The HDS card was introduced six months ago and has helped increase sales considerably. Anyone is eligible to receive an HDS credit card as long as they have valid identification and are over the age of 18. Cardholders have up to four months before they are required to pay any amounts due and many customers take the full amount of time to pay. Others take even longer.

(continued)

HDS has a large outstanding bank loan that has grown this year. The company is concerned that the bank will raise interest rates if the receivables turnover continues to be slow. Consequently, management is looking at ways to speed up the collection of cash and would like you to discuss steps that can be taken to manage receivables more effectively.

Action Plan

Assess the steps this company should take in managing its receivables by reviewing the following four steps: (a) determining whom to extend credit to, (b) establishing a payment period, (c) monitoring collections, (d) evaluating the liquidity of receivables, and any other steps you think the company should consider.

Solution

(a) **Extending credit.** The HDS credit card should not be given to just anyone over the age of 18 years. Credit-granting policies similar to those used by banks when issuing credit cards should be used by the company. Although sales have increased due to issuing this new card, it is likely that bad debts expense has increased even more.

(b) **Payment period.** Allowing HDS cardholders to pay after four months is a credit policy that is too loose. It has slowed the collection of receivables and this in turn has probably caused the company to seek more bank financing to meet cash requirements no longer being met by prompt customer collections.

(c) **Monitor collections.** On a monthly basis, management should review the age of the HDS credit card accounts and identify those cardholders who did not pay on time to determine if their receivables are collectible. It is likely that there are many overdue accounts given the ease with which these cards were issued, which makes frequent monitoring of collections even more important.

(d) **Evaluate liquidity.** The receivables turnover ratio and average collection period should be determined and evaluated each month.

Other steps the company might wish to consider to improve the collection of receivables could include cancelling the company credit card and only accepting bank credit cards, or changing the terms on the HDS card. The advantage of the first option is the immediate receipt of cash because bank credit cards are treated as cash by the bank. The disadvantage is the lost interest revenue that could be earned on the HDS card. Although changing the terms of the HDS card will not bring any immediate cash to the company, it may reduce the level of bad debts in the future and still provide a source of interest revenue on overdue accounts as long as they are collectible. Management will have to calculate the effect of these advantages and disadvantages and consider the effect on the timing of cash flows. The company should discuss these options with the bank to ensure that it realizes that steps are being taken to remedy the liquidity problem.

Related Exercise Material: BE8-15, E8-12, and E8-13.

comparing
IFRS and ASPE

Key Differences	International Financial Reporting Standards (IFRS)	Accounting Standards for Private Enterprises (ASPE)
No significant differences.		

All About You ▶ Should You Be Carrying Plastic?

Smart businesspeople carefully consider their use of credit. They evaluate who they lend to and how they finance their own operations. They know that being overextended on credit can destroy their business.

Students need to evaluate their personal credit positions using the same thought processes and consider carefully if they need a credit card and when to use it. The misuse of credit cards brings financial hardship to many students each year. The best way to avoid credit problems is to be disciplined when using credit cards or to not have them at all. Reduce the number of credit cards you carry and do not accept all the tempting credit card offers that come your way.

Credit cards can make your life easier, as long as they are used properly. They certainly have advantages: (1) they provide interest-free loans on the purchase of goods as long as you pay your bill in full before the end of the grace period; (2) monthly credit card statements provide records of all transactions, payments, and returns; and (3) fraud protection with zero liability is available in cases of fraud. However, credit cards also have disadvantages: (1) if you do not pay for your purchases in full, you can expect to pay a high interest rate on the unpaid balance and you are charged interest back to the date on which you made the purchase; and (2) credit cards are so easy to use that you might start buying items without really thinking about whether you really need them—and can afford them.

Credit cards are also available for cash advances. If you choose to use your credit card for a cash advance, interest will be charged from the date on which you made the cash advance. You will not have an interest-free period on these types of transactions. Credit card companies may also charge a higher interest rate on cash advance transactions.

Credit scoring is used by lenders to assess the credit risk of prospective borrowers. One reason to obtain a credit card is to have a credit score. If you pay off your balance every month, you may ensure a good credit score. If you don't, your credit score will suffer, making it more difficult to obtain a car loan or a mortgage at a competitive interest rate once you graduate.

Some Facts

- The Financial Consumer Agency of Canada summarizes options available when obtaining a student credit card. Most have limits of between $300 to $1,000, have minimum payments required of 2 to 3 percent of the outstanding balance, may have no annual fees, and charge interest rates of approximately 20%.

- A survey compiled by the Canadian University Survey Consortium found that 9 out of 10 university students has a credit card. Approximately 8 out of 10 students pay their outstanding balance in full at the end of each month. For those with unpaid balances, those balances averaged approximately $3,450.

- A cheaper alternative to using a credit card is to obtain a line of credit from your bank. Banks will provide undergraduate students a line of credit of approximately $10,000 per year to a maximum of $40,000 for a four-year program. You pay no monthly or annual fees and you can access that money any time. You have a 12-month grace period once you graduate where you only have to repay interest. After that, you can have up to 20 years to repay your line of credit at a lower rate than a credit card.[4]

What Do You Think?

Should you go plastic-free and get rid of your credit card?

YES—Credit cards encourage unnecessary, spontaneous expenditures. The interest rates on credit cards are very high, so I don't want to end up in debt.

NO—Credit cards are a necessity in today's economy. In fact, many transactions are difficult or impossible to carry out without a credit card. Credit cards are also useful to obtain positive credit scores. People should learn to use credit cards responsibly.

Summary of Study Objectives

1. **Identify the types of receivables and record accounts receivable transactions.** Receivables can include accounts receivable, notes receivable, and other types of receivables. Accounts and notes resulting from sales transactions are called trade receivables. Other receivables include nontrade receivables such as interest receivable, loans to company officers, advances to employees, sales tax recoverable, and income tax receivable.

Accounts receivable arising from sales or services on credit are recorded at the invoice price, and are reduced by any sales returns and allowances and sales discounts. Sales or services using nonbank (company) credit cards result in a receivable from the credit card company. Accounts receivable subsidiary ledgers are used to keep track of individual account balances. When interest is charged on a past-due receivable, interest is added to the accounts receivable balance and is recognized as interest revenue.

2. **Account for bad debts.** The allowance method, using a percentage of receivables, is used to match bad debts expense against revenue, in the period in which the revenue was earned. A percentage of total receivables, or an aging schedule applying percentages to different categories of receivables, is used to estimate the uncollectible accounts or ending balance in the allowance for doubtful accounts. When a specific account receivable is determined to be uncollectible, it is written off and the allowance account reduced. When a previously written-off account is collected, the write off is reversed and the collection recorded. Bad debts expense is the difference between the estimated total uncollectible accounts (required balance in the allowance account) and the unadjusted balance in the allowance account.

3. **Account for notes receivable.** Notes receivable are recorded at their principal amount. Interest is earned from the date the note is issued until it matures and is recorded in a separate interest receivable account. Similar to accounts receivable, estimated uncollectible notes receivable are recorded as an allowance for doubtful notes.

Notes can be held to maturity, at which time the principal plus any unpaid interest is due and the note is removed from the accounts when paid (honoured). In some situations, the maker of the note dishonours the note (defaults). If eventual collection is expected, an account receivable replaces the note receivable and any unpaid interest. If the amount is not expected to be repaid, the note is written off.

4. **Explain the statement presentation of receivables.** Each major type of receivable should be identified in the statement of financial position, with supplemental detail included in the statement or supporting notes. Companies must report the net realizable value of their receivables on the statement of financial position. The gross amount of receivables and allowance for doubtful accounts can be reported directly on the statement or in the notes. Bad debts expense is reported in the income statement as an operating expense, and interest revenue is shown in the non-operating section of the statement.

5. **Apply the principles of sound accounts receivable management.** To properly manage receivables, management must (a) determine whom to extend credit to, (b) establish a payment period, (c) monitor collections, and (d) evaluate the liquidity of receivables by calculating the receivables turnover and average collection period.

The receivables turnover is calculated by dividing net credit sales by average gross accounts receivable. The average collection period converts the receivables turnover into days, dividing 365 days by the receivables turnover ratio.

Glossary

Aging the accounts receivable The analysis of customer balances by the length of time they have been unpaid. (p. 400)

Allowance method A method of accounting for bad debts that involves estimating uncollectible accounts at the end of each period. (p. 399)

Average collection period The average amount of time that a receivable is outstanding. It is calculated by dividing 365 days by the receivables turnover. (p. 412)

Control account An account in the general ledger that summarizes the details for a subsidiary ledger and controls it. (p. 396)

Derecognized A note that is removed from the accounts, either when honoured (collected) or dishonoured (not collected). (p. 407)

Dishonoured note A note that is not paid in full at maturity. (p. 407)

Financial assets Receivables and investments that have a contractual right to receive cash or another financial asset. (p. 394)

Honoured note A note that is paid in full at maturity. (p. 407)

Net realizable value The difference between gross receivables and the allowance for doubtful accounts. Net realizable value measures the net amount expected to be received in cash. (p. 401)

Promissory note A written promise to pay a specified amount of money on demand or at a definite time. (p. 405)

Receivables turnover A measure of the liquidity of receivables. It is calculated by dividing net credit sales by the average gross accounts receivable and is expressed as the number of times per year that the accounts receivable are collected. (p. 412)

Subsidiary ledger A group of accounts that provide details of a control account in the general ledger. (p. 396)

Trade receivables Accounts and notes receivable that result from sales transactions. (p. 394)

DECISION TOOLKIT—A SUMMARY

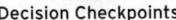Decision Checkpoints	Info Needed for Decision	Tools to Use for Decision	How to Evaluate Results
Is the amount of past-due accounts increasing? Which accounts require management's attention?	List of outstanding receivables and their due dates	Prepare an aging schedule showing the receivables at various stages: outstanding 0–30 days, 31–60 days, 61–90 days, and so on as long as required.	Accounts in the older categories require follow-up: letters, phone calls, e-mails, and possible renegotiation of terms.
Are collections being made in a timely fashion?	Net credit sales and average gross accounts receivable balance	Receivables turnover = $\dfrac{\text{Net credit sales}}{\text{Average gross accounts receivable}}$ Average collection period = $\dfrac{\text{365 days}}{\text{Receivables turnover}}$	The average collection period should be consistent with corporate credit policy. An increase may suggest a decline in customers' financial health.

USING THE DECISION TOOLKIT

There are no direct competitors to Canadian Tire, although Walmart competes in many of the same product lines. Selected financial information for Walmart (in U.S. millions) is shown below and can be compared with the information reported for Canadian Tire, Sears, and the industry shown in Illustrations 8-5 and 8-6:

	2012	2011
Net sales	$466,114	$443,854
Accounts receivable (gross)	6,768	5,937

Instructions

Calculate Walmart's receivables turnover and average collection period for 2012. Assume that all sales are made on credit. Comment on the company's accounts receivable management and liquidity compared with that of Canadian Tire, Sears, and the industry.

Solution

(in U.S. millions)	Walmart	Canadian Tire	Sears	Industry
Receivables turnover	$\dfrac{\$466,114}{(\$6,768+\$5,937) \div 2} = 73.4$ times	12.7 times	44.7 times	26.7 times
Average collection period	$\dfrac{\text{365 days}}{73.4} = 5$ days	29 days	8 days	14 days

Based on the above information, Walmart has a higher (better) receivables turnover and lower (better) collection period than all of its competitors. As this means that the company collects its receivables faster, it can more readily pay its current liabilities. Further analysis, including calculating the current ratio and inventory turnover ratio, would be required before finalizing this assessment.

Comprehensive Do It!

On February 28, Shawinigan Distributors Ltd. had the following balances in its accounts receivable and allowance accounts. Assume all account balances are normal balances.

Accounts Receivable	$500,000
Allowance for Doubtful Accounts	31,000

The following selected transactions occurred throughout the year. Shawinigan's year end is July 31.

Mar. 1 Sold $30,000 of merchandise to Anderson Ltd., terms 2/10, n/30. Shawinigan uses a perpetual inventory system and the cost of goods sold was $18,000.

     10 Received payment in full from Anderson for balance due.

     12 Accepted Dieppe Ltd.'s four-month, 6%, $40,000 note for a balance due from a February transaction (not shown here). Interest is due at maturity.

     13 Made Shawinigan Distributors Ltd. credit card sales for $25,000. The cost of goods sold for these sales totalled $15,000.

     15 Made Visa credit card sales totalling $13,400. The cost of these sales was $8,040. Bank charges of $402 appeared on Shawinigan's bank statement with respect to Visa credit card fees.

Apr. 13 Received collections of $16,000 on Shawinigan credit card sales and added interest charges of 24% per annum (2% per month) to the remaining balances.

May 10 Wrote off as uncollectible $32,000 of accounts receivable.

July 12 Collected Dieppe note (see March 12 transaction).

     16 One of the accounts receivable written off in May was received in full, $8,000.

     31 Using an aging schedule, uncollectible accounts are estimated to be $40,000.

Instructions

(a) Record the above transactions.

(b) Open T accounts for the Accounts Receivable and Allowance for Doubtful Accounts general ledger accounts. Post the opening balances as at February 28 as well as the relevant entries from the transactions recorded above.

(c) Calculate the net realizable value of the accounts receivable at July 31.

Action Plan

- Remember that two journal entries are required to record sales (or returns) of merchandise: (1) to record the sales price, and (2) to record the cost of the merchandise sold (returned).
- Recall that bank credit cards are recorded as a cash sale while nonbank credit cards are recorded as a credit sale.
- Calculate interest by multiplying the interest rate by the principal amount, adjusting for any partial period.
- Consider any existing balance in the allowance account when making the adjustment for uncollectible accounts.
- Record write offs of accounts receivable only in statement of financial position accounts.
- Recall that net realizable value is the difference between the accounts receivable and the allowance accounts.

Solution to Comprehensive Do It!

(a)

Mar.	1	Accounts Receivable	30,000	
		Sales		30,000
		(To record sales on account to Anderson Ltd., terms 2/10, n/30)		
	1	Cost of Goods Sold	18,000	
		Merchandise Inventory		18,000
		(To record cost of merchandise sold to Anderson)		

Mar. 10	Cash	29,400	
	Sales Discounts (2% × $30,000)	600	
	Accounts Receivable		30,000
	(To record collection of account receivable from Anderson)		
12	Notes Receivable	40,000	
	Accounts Receivable		40,000
	(To record acceptance of Dieppe Ltd.'s four-month, 6% note)		
13	Accounts Receivable	25,000	
	Sales		25,000
	(To record company credit card sales)		
13	Cost of Goods Sold	15,000	
	Merchandise Inventory		15,000
	(To record cost of merchandise sold to company credit card customers)		
15	Cash	13,400	
	Sales		13,400
	(To record Visa credit card sales)		
15	Cost of Goods Sold	8,040	
	Merchandise Inventory		8,040
	(To record cost of merchandise sold to credit card customers)		
15	Bank Charges Expense	402	
	Cash		402
	(To record Visa credit card fees)		
Apr. 13	Cash	16,000	
	Accounts Receivable		16,000
	(To record collection of company credit card receivables)		
13	Accounts Receivable [($25,000 − $16,000) × 24% × $\frac{1}{12}$]	180	
	Interest Revenue		180
	(To record interest charges on overdue receivables)		
May 10	Allowance for Doubtful Accounts	32,000	
	Accounts Receivable		32,000
	(To record write off of accounts receivable)		
July 12	Cash	40,800	
	Notes Receivable		40,000
	Interest Revenue ($40,000 × 6% × $\frac{4}{12}$)		800
	(To record collection of note receivable from Dieppe)		
16	Accounts Receivable	8,000	
	Allowance for Doubtful Accounts		8,000
	(To reverse write off of account receivable)		
16	Cash	8,000	
	Accounts Receivable		8,000
	(To record collection of account receivable)		
31	Bad Debts Expense ($40,000 − $7,000)	33,000	
	Allowance for Doubtful Accounts		33,000
	(To record estimate of uncollectible accounts [see Allowance for Doubtful Accounts in part (b) to prove calculations])		

(b)

Accounts Receivable

Feb. 28	Bal.	500,000			
Mar. 1		30,000	Mar. 10		30,000
13		25,000	12		40,000
Apr. 13		180	Apr. 13		16,000
July 16		8,000	May 10		32,000
			July 16		8,000
July 31	Bal.	437,180			

(continued)

Allowance for Doubtful Accounts			
	Feb. 28	Bal.	31,000
May 10 32,000	July 16		8,000
	July 31	Unadj. Bal.	7,000
	31	Adj.	33,000
	July 31	Bal.	40,000

(c) Accounts receivable $437,180
     Less: Allowance for doubtful accounts   40,000
     Net realizable value $397,180

WileyPLUS   Self-Test, Brief Exercises, Exercises, Problems: Set A, and many more components are available for practice in *WileyPLUS*.

Self-Test Questions

dr A/R 1000
cr A/R 300
cr

Answers are at the end of the chapter.

Quiz Yourself

(SO 1) **1.** On June 15, Kersee Corporation sells merchandise on account to Soo Eng Limited for $1,000, terms 2/10, n/30. On June 20, Soo Eng returns merchandise worth $300. On June 24, payment is received from Soo Eng for the balance due. What amount will be credited to the Accounts Receivable account when the collection of this account is recorded on June 24?
(a) $686
(b) $680
(c) $700
(d) $1,000

(SO 1) **2.** Which of the following statements is *not* true about subsidiary ledgers?
(a) Common examples of subsidiary ledgers include accounts receivable, inventory, accounts payable, and payroll.
(b) The total of all individual account balances in the subsidiary ledger must equal the balance in the control account in the general ledger.
(c) Subsidiary ledgers are not generally used by large merchandising companies.
(d) The debit entry to record interest charged on overdue accounts receivable is posted twice—once to the subsidiary ledger account and once to the control account.

(SO 2) **3.** Sanderson Corporation has a debit balance of $5,000 in its Allowance for Doubtful Accounts before any adjustments are made. Based on an aging of its accounts receivable at the end of the period, the company estimates that $60,000 of its receivables are uncollectible at the end of the

period. The adjusting journal entry that would be recorded for bad debts expense at the end of this period would be:

(a)	Bad Debts Expense	55,000	
	Accounts Receivable		55,000
(b)	Bad Debts Expense	55,000	
	Allowance for Doubtful Accounts		55,000
(c)	Bad Debts Expense	65,000	
	Allowance for Doubtful Accounts		65,000
(d)	Bad Debts Expense	60,000	
	Allowance for Doubtful Accounts		60,000

(SO 2) **4.** On January 1, Allowance for Doubtful Accounts had a credit balance of $9,000. During the year, $15,000 of uncollectible accounts receivable were written off. Aging indicates that uncollectible accounts are $10,000 at the end of the year. What is the required adjustment in Bad Debts Expense at December 31?   *dr 6000*
(a) $1,000
(b) $4,000
(c) $10,000
(d) $16,000

(SO 3) 5. Mack Ltd. accepts a three-month, 6%, $2,000 promissory note in settlement of Pandher Ltd.'s account on November 28. The entry to record this transaction on Mack's books on November 28 is:

(a)
Notes Receivable	2,030	
Accounts Receivable		2,000
Interest Revenue		30

(b)
Notes Receivable	2,000	
Accounts Receivable		2,000

(c)
Notes Receivable	2,000	
Cash		2,000

(d)
Notes Receivable	2,120	
Accounts Receivable		2,000
Interest Revenue		120

(SO 3) 6. Schlicht Corp. holds Oleniuk Inc.'s four-month, 9%, $10,000 note. The entry made by Schlicht Corp. when the note is collected, assuming no interest has previously been accrued, is:

(a)
Cash	10,300	
Notes Receivable		10,300

(b)
Cash	10,000	
Notes Receivable		10,000

(c)
Account Receivable	10,300	
Notes Receivable		10,000
Interest Revenue		300

(d)
Cash	10,300	
Notes Receivable		10,000
Interest Revenue		300

(SO 4) 7. The allowance for doubtful accounts is presented in the financial statements as:
(a) a current liability in the statement of financial position.
(b) a contra current asset account in the statement of financial position.
(c) a contra revenue account in the income statement.
(d) an operating expense in the income statement.

(SO 4) 8. Accounts and notes receivable are reported in the assets section of the statement of financial position at their:
(a) net realizable value.
(b) invoice cost.
(c) lower of cost and net realizable value.
(d) carrying amount.

(SO 5) 9. The principles of sound accounts receivable management do *not* include:
(a) instituting a "cash only" policy.
(b) establishing a payment period.
(c) monitoring collections.
(d) evaluating the liquidity of receivables.

(SO 5) 10. Millennium Retailers Corp. has managed to shorten the amount of time that it takes to collect its receivables. Because of this:
(a) The receivables turnover ratio will rise and the average collection period will fall.
(b) The receivables turnover ratio will fall and the average collection period will fall.
(c) The receivables turnover ratio will rise and the average collection period will rise.
(d) The receivables turnover ratio will fall and the average collection period will rise.

Questions

(SO 1) 1. (a) What are the three major types of receivables? (b) Give examples of each type of receivable.

(SO 1) 2. Distinguish between trade receivables and non-trade receivables.

(SO 1) 3. (a) When should a receivable be recorded for a service company? For a merchandising company? (b) Explain how your answer relates to the revenue recognition criteria.

(SO 1) 4. **Canadian Tire** accepts its own company (non-bank) credit card, bank credit cards, and debit cards. (a) What are the advantages of accepting each type of card? (b) Explain how the accounting differs for each type of card.

(SO 1) 5. (a) What are the advantages of using an accounts receivable subsidiary ledger? (b) Describe the relationship between the general ledger control account and the subsidiary ledger.

(SO 2) 6. (a) What is an aging schedule? (b) How is an aging schedule used to determine total estimated uncollectible accounts?

(SO 2) 7. (a) What is the purpose of the account Allowance for Doubtful Accounts? (b) Although the normal balance of this account is a credit balance, it can sometimes have a debit balance. Explain how and when this can happen.

(SO 2) 8. Why is the bad debts expense that is reported in the income statement usually not the same amount as the allowance for doubtful accounts amount reported in the statement of financial position?

(SO 2) 9. Mohamed cannot understand why the net realizable value does not change when an uncollectible account is written off under the allowance method. Clarify this for Mohamed.

(SO 2) 10. When an account receivable that was previously written off is later collected, two separate journal entries are usually made rather than one compound journal entry. Explain why.

(SO 1, 3) 11. (a) How are accounts receivable and notes receivable alike? (b) How do they differ?

(SO 1, 3) 12. (a) Under what circumstances is interest normally recorded for (1) an account receivable and (2) a note receivable? (b) When interest is recorded, is Accounts Receivable or Interest Receivable debited for (1) an account receivable and (2) a note receivable? Explain.

(SO 3)   13. Danielle does not understand why a note receivable is not immediately recorded at its maturity amount (principal plus interest), rather than its principal amount. After all, you know you are going to collect both the principal and the interest and you know how much each will be. Clarify this for Danielle.

(SO 3)   14. Cobden Inc. borrowed money from **Scotiabank**, signing a promissory note. Which company is the maker of the note? The payee? Which company would record a note receivable? A note payable?

(SO 3)   15. What is the difference between honouring a note receivable at maturity and dishonouring a note at maturity?

(SO 3)   16. Athabasca Ltd. has several dozen notes receivable. It expects approximately 10% of these notes to be uncollectible. How should these estimated notes be accounted for?

(SO 4)   17. Indicate how accounts receivable and allowance for doubtful accounts should be presented on the statement of financial position.

(SO 4)   18. Saucier Ltd. has accounts receivable, notes receivable due in three months, notes receivable due in two years, an allowance for doubtful

accounts, an allowance for doubtful short-term notes, sales tax recoverable, and income tax receivable. How should the receivables be reported on the statement of financial position?

(SO 4)   19. (a) Identify three income statement accounts that are related to receivables. (b) Indicate where each account would be reported on the income statement.

(SO 5)   20. What are the four steps in good receivables management?

(SO 5)   21. **Canam Group**'s receivables turnover was 3.1 times in 2012 and 3.3 times in 2011. Based on this information, has Canam's receivables management improved or worsened?

(SO 5)   22. The president of Ho Inc. proudly announces that her company has improved its liquidity since its current ratio has increased substantially. (a) Does an increase in the current ratio always indicate improved liquidity? (b) What other ratio or ratios might you review to determine whether or not the increase in the current ratio indicates an improvement in financial health?

(SO 5)   23. Why should a company not want to have a receivables turnover that is significantly higher than that of its competitors? Why would it not want a receivables turnover that is significantly lower than that of its competitors?

Brief Exercises

Identify types of receivables.
(SO 1)

BE8–1   Presented below are several receivables transactions. For each transaction, indicate whether the receivables should be reported as accounts receivable, notes receivable, or other receivables on a statement of financial position.
(a) Advanced $10,000 to an employee.
(b) Estimated $5,000 of income tax to be refunded.
(c) Received a promissory note of $5,000 for services performed.
(d) Sold merchandise on account to a customer for $6,000.
(e) Sold merchandise for $1,200 to a customer who used a company credit card in payment.
(f) Sales tax (HST) of $2,500 is recoverable at the end of the quarter.
(g) Extended a customer's account for six months by accepting a note in exchange for the amount owed on the account.

Record receivables transactions.
(SO 1)

BE8–2   Record the following transactions on the books of Essex Corp., which uses a perpetual inventory system.
(a) On July 1, Essex Corp. sold merchandise on account to Cambridge Inc. for $42,000, terms 2/10, n/30. The cost of the merchandise sold was $30,000.
(b) On July 8, Cambridge returned merchandise worth $7,200 to Essex. Its original cost was $4,320. The merchandise was restored to inventory.
(c) On July 9, Cambridge paid for the merchandise.
(d) Assume now that Cambridge did not pay on July 9, as indicated in transaction (c). At the end of August, Essex added one month's interest to Cambridge's account for the overdue receivable. Essex charges 24% per year on overdue accounts. Round calculations to the nearest dollar.

Record credit card sales.
(SO 1)

BE8–3   An Ultramar gas station accepted a Visa card in payment of a $100 gas bill. The bank charges a $2 fee. (a) What entries should the Ultramar gas station make to record the sale and the bank charges related to this sale? (b) How would these entries be different if payment had been made with an Ultramar credit card instead of a Visa card?

Prepare subsidiary ledger.
(SO 1)

BE8–4   Information related to Bryant Limited is presented below for its first month of operations.

Credit Sales			Cash Collections		
Jan. 7	Chiu Corp.	$1,800	Jan. 17	Chiu Corp.	$ 700
15	Elbaz Inc.	6,000	24	Elbaz Inc.	2,000
23	Lewis Corp.	3,700	29	Lewis Corp.	3,700

Post the above transactions individually to the accounts receivable subsidiary ledger for each customer, and in summary form at the end of the month to the accounts receivable control account in the general ledger.

BE8–5 At December 31, Canton Imports Ltd. estimates that 4% of total accounts receivable will become uncollectible. Accounts receivable are $600,000 at the end of the year. Allowance for Doubtful Accounts has a credit balance of $3,600 prior to recording any year-end adjusting entries. (a) Prepare the adjusting journal entry to record bad debts expense at December 31. (b) Assuming that Allowance for Doubtful Accounts had a debit balance of $4,000 instead of a credit balance of $3,600, how would the journal entry recorded in part (a) above change?

Record bad debts.
(SO 2)

BE8–6 Refer to BE8–5 and assume that Canton Imports decides to refine its estimate of uncollectible accounts by preparing an aging schedule. (a) Complete the following aging schedule, and (b) prepare the adjusting journal entry at December 31 to record bad debts expense, assuming that the allowance account has a credit balance of $3,600.

Complete aging schedule and record bad debts.
(SO 2)

Number of Days Outstanding	Accounts Receivable	Estimated Percentage Uncollectible	Total Estimated Uncollectible Accounts
0–30 days	$368,000	1%	
31–60 days	120,000	4%	
61–90 days	72,000	10%	
Over 90 days	40,000	20%	
Total	$600,000		

BE8–7 At the end of 2014, Searcy Corp. has accounts receivable of $600,000 and an allowance for doubtful accounts of $36,000. On January 24, 2015, Searcy learns that its $8,000 receivable from Hutley Inc. is not collectible. Management authorizes a write off. (a) Prepare the journal entry to record the write off. (b) What is the net realizable value of the accounts receivable (1) before the write off and (2) after the write off?

Record write off and compare net realizable value.
(SO 2)

BE8–8 Assume the same information as in BE8–7, but that on March 4, 2015, Searcy Corp. receives payment in full of $8,000 from Hutley Inc. after the write off. Prepare the required journal entry(ies) to record this transaction.

Record recovery of bad debts.
(SO 2)

BE8–9 Data on three promissory notes receivable due to Aptara Inc. at December 31, 2014, follow:

Calculate interest.
(SO 3)

Note	Issue Date	Term in Months	Principal	Interest Rate
#1	Apr. 1, 2014	15	$1,800,000	6%
#2	July 2, 2014	9	168,000	5%
#3	Nov. 1, 2014	12	420,000	4%

Aptara's year end is December 31 and it adjusts its books annually. For each of the above notes, calculate the amount of (a) interest revenue to be recorded in 2014, (b) interest revenue to be recorded in 2015, if any, and (c) total interest revenue. Round calculations to the nearest dollar.

BE8–10 On January 2, Kuril Ltd. sold merchandise on account to R. James for $48,000, terms n/30. The company uses a perpetual inventory system and the merchandise originally cost $32,000. On February 1, R. James gave Kuril a five-month, 7% note in settlement of this account. On April 30, Kuril's year-end, annual adjusting entries were made. On July 1, R. James paid the note and accrued interest. Prepare the journal entries for Kuril to record the above transactions.

Record receivables transactions.
(SO 1, 3)

BE8–11 Stratus Ltd. sells merchandise on April 1, 2014, to Red River Enterprises in return for a 12-month, 9%, $10,000 note, with interest due at maturity. The company uses a perpetual inventory system and the cost of the inventory sold was $6,000. Stratus has a December 31 year end and adjusts its accounts annually. Prepare the journal entries that Stratus will record with regard to this note from April 1, 2014, until the note matures on March 31, 2015.

Record note receivable transactions.
(SO 3)

BE8–12 Using the information provided in BE8–11 above, prepare the journal entries that Red River Enterprises will record regarding the issue of the note and the purchase of the merchandise inventory. Red River uses a perpetual inventory system, has a September 30 year end, and adjusts its accounts annually.

Record note payable transactions.
(SO 3)

BE8–13 Xavier Limited accepts a three-month, 6%, $40,000 note receivable in settlement of an account receivable on April 1, 2015. Interest is due at maturity.
(a) Prepare the journal entries required by Xavier Limited to record the issue of the note on April 1, and the settlement of the note on July 1, assuming the note is honoured and that no interest has previously been accrued.
(b) Repeat part (a) assuming that the note is dishonoured, but eventual collection is expected.
(c) Repeat part (a) assuming that the note is dishonoured and eventual collection is not expected.

Record note receivable transactions.
(SO 3)

Prepare current assets section.
(SO 4)

BE8–14 Nias Corporation reported the following selected items at February 28, 2015:

Accounts payable	$938,000	Notes receivable—due November 1, 2015	$300,000
Accounts receivable	· 470,000	Notes receivable—due April 1, 2018	400,000
Allowance for doubtful accounts	30,000	Prepaid rent	8,000
Bad debts expense	24,000	Sales tax recoverable	38,000
Cash	150,000	Trading investments	330,000
Merchandise inventory	380,000	Unearned revenue	5,000

Prepare the current assets section of Nias's statement of financial position.

Calculate ratios.
(SO 5)

BE8–15 **Maple Leaf Foods Inc.** reported the following selected information (in thousands) for the three years ended December 31, 2012, 2011, and 2010:

	2012	2011	2010
Trade receivables (gross)	$ 55,954	$ 81,477	$ 65,084
Allowance for doubtful accounts	204	5,789	6,764
Net sales	4,864,779	4,893,624	4,968,119

(a) Calculate Maple Leaf's receivables turnover and average collection period for 2012 and 2011. (b) Indicate whether each of the receivables turnover and average collection period is better or worse in 2012.

Exercises

Record receivables and payables transactions.
(SO 1)

E8–1 On January 6, Compton Limited sold merchandise on account to Singh Inc. for $24,000, terms 2/10, n/30. The merchandise originally cost Compton $16,000. On January 15, Singh paid the amount due. Both Compton and Singh use a perpetual inventory system.

Instructions
(a) Prepare the entries on Compton's books to record the sale and related collection.
(b) Prepare the entries on Singh's books to record the purchase and related payment.

Record receivables transactions; post to subsidiary and general ledgers.
(SO 1)

E8–2 Selected transactions follow for Discovery Sports Ltd. during the company's first month of business.

Feb.	2	Sold $1,140 of merchandise to Andrew Noren on account, terms n/30.
	4	Andrew Noren returned for credit $140 of the merchandise purchased on February 2.
	5	Sold $760 of merchandise to Dong Corporation on account, terms 2/10, n/30.
	8	Sold $842 of merchandise to Michael Collins for cash.
	10	Sold $920 of merchandise to Rafik Kurji, who paid with a Discovery Sports (company) credit card.
	14	Dong Corporation paid its account in full.
	17	Andrew Noren purchased an additional $696 of merchandise on account, terms n/30.
	22	Sold $1,738 of merchandise to Batstone Corporation, terms 2/10, n/30.
	28	Andrew Noren paid $1,000 on account.

Instructions
(a) Prepare the journal entries to record each of the above transactions. Ignore any cost of goods sold entries in this question. Round calculations to the nearest dollar.
(b) Set up T accounts for the Accounts Receivable general ledger (control) account and for the Accounts Receivable subsidiary ledger accounts. Post the journal entries to these accounts.
(c) Prepare a list of customers and the balances of their accounts from the subsidiary ledger. Prove that the total of the subsidiary ledger balances is equal to the control account balance.

Record bad debts.
(SO 2)

E8–3 Chinook Limited's general ledger reports a balance in Accounts Receivable of $360,000 at the end of December.

Instructions
(a) Assuming that Allowance for Doubtful Accounts has a credit balance of $4,400 and that uncollectible accounts are determined to be $36,000 by aging the accounts, record the adjusting entry at December 31.
(b) Assuming the same information as in part (a) except that uncollectible accounts are expected to be 9% of total accounts receivable, record the adjusting entry at December 31.
(c) Assuming the same information as in part (a) except that the Allowance for Doubtful Accounts has a debit balance of $2,400, record the adjusting entry at December 31.

E8-4 Gemini Ltd. has accounts receivable of $370,000 and an unadjusted credit balance in its allowance for doubtful accounts of $8,800 at March 31. The company's accounts receivable and percentage estimates of its uncollectible accounts are as follows:

Prepare aging schedule; record bad debts.
(SO 2)

Number of Days Outstanding	Accounts Receivable	Estimated Percentage Uncollectible
0–30	$260,000	2%
31–60	50,400	10%
61–90	34,000	30%
Over 90	25,600	50%
Total	$370,000	

Instructions
(a) Prepare an aging schedule to determine the total estimated uncollectibles at March 31.
(b) Prepare the adjusting entry at March 31 to record bad debts expense.
(c) What is the het realizable value of the receivables at March 31?

E8-5 On December 31, 2014, when its accounts receivable were $300,000 and its account Allowance for Doubtful Accounts had an unadjusted debit balance of $2,000, Ceja Corp. estimated that $16,800 of its accounts receivable would become uncollectible, and it recorded the bad debts adjusting entry. On May 11, 2015, Ceja determined that Robert Worthy's account was uncollectible and wrote off $1,900. On November 12, 2015, Worthy paid the amount previously written off.

Record bad debts.
(SO 2)

Instructions
(a) Prepare the required journal entries to record each of the above transactions.
(b) What is the net realizable value of the receivables on (1) December 31, 2014, (2) May 11, 2015, and (3) November 12, 2015, assuming that the total amount of accounts receivable of $300,000 is unchanged on each of these three dates except for any changes recorded in (a).

E8-6 At the beginning of March, Paragon Limited, which records adjusting entries at the end of each month, had accounts receivable of $30,000 and an allowance for doubtful accounts of $5,000. During March, the company had credit sales of $40,000 and collected $35,000 from customers. It also wrote off a certain amount of uncollectible receivables during the month and recorded a certain amount of bad debts expense at the end of the month. No accounts that were written off during the month were subsequently recovered. At the end of March, after all journal entries had been recorded and posted, the balance in Accounts Receivable was $32,000 while Allowance for Doubtful Accounts had a balance of $4,500.

Determine missing amounts and record bad debts.
(SO 2)

Instructions
(a) Prepare T accounts for Accounts Receivable and Allowance for Doubtful Accounts. Post the above transactions and determine the missing amounts for the write off of uncollectible receivables and bad debts expense.
(b) Prepare the journal entry that would have been made by the company to write off uncollectible receivables during March.
(c) Prepare the journal entry that would be made by the company to record bad debts expense for the month of March.

E8-7 Passara Supply Corp. has the following selected transactions for notes receivable.

Record notes receivable transactions.
(SO 3)

Nov.	1	Loaned $48,000 cash to A. Bouchard on a one-year, 8% note.
Dec.	1	Sold goods to Wright, Inc., receiving a two-month, 6%, $8,400 note. The goods cost $5,000.
	15	Received a six-month, 7%, $16,000 note in exchange for an account from Aquilina Corporation.
Feb.	1	Collected the amount owing on the Wright note.
	28	Accrued interest on all notes receivable at year end. Interest is calculated to the nearest half month and is due at maturity.
	28	Analyzed each note and estimated that uncollectible notes at year end totalled $16,000.

Instructions
Record the above transactions for Passara Supply Corp. Round calculations to the nearest dollar.

E8-8 Refer to E8-7 for information about the note between Passara Supply Corp. and Wright, Inc. Round calculations to the nearest dollar.

Record notes payable transactions.
(SO 3)

Instructions
Record the transactions related to the note on Wright's books on December 1, December 31 (Wright's year end), and February 1.

E8-9 The following selected transactions for notes receivable are for Acre Limited.

Record notes receivable transactions.
(SO 3)

May	1	Received a six-month, 5%, $12,000 note on account from Blackstone Limited. Interest is due at maturity.
June	30	Accrued interest on the Blackstone note on this date, which is Acre's year end.
July	31	Lent $10,000 cash to an employee, Noreen Wong, issuing a three-month, 7% note. Interest is due at the end of each month.
Aug.	31	Received the interest due from Ms. Wong.
Sept.	30	Received the interest due from Ms. Wong.
Oct.	31	Received payment in full for the employee note from Ms. Wong.
Nov.	1	Wrote off the Blackstone note as Blackstone defaulted. Future payment is not expected.

Instructions
Record the above transactions for Acre Limited. Round calculations to the nearest dollar.

Show statement
presentation.
(SO 4)

E8-10 **Deere & Company** had the following balances in its short-term receivable accounts at October 31, 2012 (in U.S. millions): Allowance for Doubtful Trade and Notes Receivables $66.0; Allowance for Doubtful Financing Receivables $177.0; Financing Receivables $22,159.1; Other Receivables $1,790.9; and Trade Accounts and Notes Receivable $3,799.1.

Instructions
Show the presentation of Deere & Company's receivables in the current assets section of its statement of financial position at October 31.

Show statement
presentation.
(SO 4)

E8-11 Apollo Corporation reported the following selected accounts and amounts at November 30, 2015:

Accounts payable	$ 22,600
Accounts receivable	18,200
Advances to employees	2,900
Allowance for doubtful accounts	1,300
Allowance for doubtful notes (current)	5,000
Bad debts expense	2,000
Cash	7,500
Interest expense	2,400
Interest revenue	6,000
Merchandise inventory	26,400
Notes receivable (current)	25,000
Notes receivable (non-current)	75,000
Prepaid insurance	1,500
Sales	370,000
Sales discounts	12,000
Sales tax recoverable	3,150

Instructions
(a) Identify which of the above accounts are statement of financial position (SFP) accounts and which are income statement (IS) accounts.
(b) Indicate where each of the income statement accounts would be reported (for example, operating revenue, operating expenses, non-operating expenses, or non-operating revenue).
(c) Prepare the current assets section of Apollo's statement of financial position.

Calculate and evaluate
ratios.
(SO 5)

E8-12 The following information (in millions) was taken from the December 31 financial statements of **Canadian National Railway Company (CN)**:

	2012	2011	2010
Accounts receivable, gross	$ 841	$ 836	$ 796
Allowance for doubtful accounts	10	16	21
Accounts receivable, net	831	820	775
Revenues	9,920	9,028	8,297
Total current assets	1,869	1,848	1,590
Total current liabilities	2,203	1,715	1,906

Instructions
(a) For 2012 and 2011, calculate CN's current ratio, receivables turnover, and average collection period.
(b) Comment on any improvement or deterioration in CN's management of its accounts receivable.

Evaluate liquidity.
(SO 5)

E8-13 The following ratios are for Lin Inc.

	2015	2014
Current ratio	1.5:1	1.3:1
Receivables turnover	10 times	12 times
Inventory turnover	9 times	11 times

Instructions
(a) Is Lin's short-term liquidity improving or deteriorating in 2015? Explain.
(b) Identify any steps Lin might have taken, or wish to take, to improve the management of its accounts receivable and inventory.

Problems: Set A

P8–1A At January 1, 2015, Underwood Imports Inc. reported the following on its statement of financial position:

Accounts receivable	$1,990,000
Allowance for doubtful accounts	124,000

Record receivables and bad debts; show statement presentation. (SO 1, 2, 4)

During 2015, the company had the following summary transactions for receivables:

1. Sales on account, $5,200,000
2. Sales returns and allowances, $80,000
3. Collections of accounts receivable, $5,400,000
4. Interest added to overdue accounts, $400,000
5. Write offs of accounts receivable deemed uncollectible, $150,000
6. Collection of accounts previously written off as uncollectible, $60,000
7. After considering all of the above transactions, total estimated uncollectible accounts, $100,000

Instructions
(a) Prepare journal entries to record each of the above summary transactions.
(b) (1) Prepare T accounts for Accounts Receivable and Allowance for Doubtful Accounts, (2) enter the opening balances, (3) post the above summary entries, and (4) determine the ending balances.
(c) Determine the net realizable value of the accounts receivable as at January 1 and December 31.
(d) Show the statement of financial position presentation of the receivables as at December 31.
(e) Show the income statement presentation of the revenue and expense accounts for the year ended December 31.

P8–2A At the beginning of the current period, Azim Enterprises Ltd. had balances in Accounts Receivable of $1,600,000 and in Allowance for Doubtful Accounts of $88,000 (credit). During the period, Azim had credit sales of $3,800,000 and collections of $4,084,000. It wrote off $116,000 of accounts receivable. However, an $8,000 account written off as uncollectible was recovered before the end of the current period. Uncollectible accounts are estimated to total $72,000 at the end of the period.

Record receivables and bad debts; show statement presentation. (SO 1, 2, 4)

Instructions
(a) Prepare the entries to record sales and collections during the period.
(b) Prepare the entry to record the write off of the $116,000 accounts deemed uncollectible during the period.
(c) Prepare the entry(ies) to record the collection of the $8,000 account written off as part of the uncollectible accounts in part (b).
(d) Prepare the entry to record bad debts expense for the period.
(e) (1) Prepare T accounts for Accounts Receivable and Allowance for Doubtful Accounts, (2) enter the opening balances, (3) post the journal entries prepared in parts (a) through (d), and (4) determine the ending balances.
(f) Show the statement of financial position presentation of the receivables at the end of the period.

P8–3A Wilton Corporation reported the following selected information in its general ledger at December 31:

Determine missing amounts. (SO 2)

Accounts Receivable			Sales	
Beg. bal. 18,000				78,000
	55,000			
(a)	(b)			
End. bal. (c)				

Allowance for Doubtful Accounts			Bad Debts Expense	
	Beg. bal. 1,800		(f)	
1,000				
	Unadj. bal. 800			
	(d)			
	End. bal. (e)			

All sales were on account. Some accounts receivable were collected. One account was written off; there were no subsequent recoveries. At the end of the year, uncollectible accounts were estimated to total $2,000.

Instructions
Using your knowledge of receivables transactions, determine the missing amounts. (*Hint:* You may not be able to solve the above items in alphabetical order. In addition, you may find it helpful to reconstruct the journal entries.)

Prepare aging schedule and record bad debts.
(SO 2)

P8-4A The following selected information is from Richibucto Limited's partial aging schedule at year end:

Number of Days Outstanding	Accounts Receivable	Estimated Percentage Uncollectible
0–30 days	$240,000	1%
31–60 days	120,000	5%
61–90 days	100,000	10%
Over 90 days	60,000	25%
Total	$520,000	

The unadjusted balance in Allowance for Doubtful Accounts is a credit of $20,000.

Instructions

(a) Complete the aging schedule and calculate the total estimated uncollectible accounts from the above information.
(b) (1) Prepare the adjusting journal entry to record the bad debts using the information determined in part (a). (2) Would your journal entry be different if the unadjusted balance in Allowance for Doubtful Accounts were a debit of $20,000?
(c) In the following year, $4,000 of the outstanding receivables is determined to be specifically uncollectible. Prepare the journal entry to write off the uncollectible amount.
(d) Richibucto subsequently collects $1,700 of the $4,000 that was determined to be uncollectible in part (c). Prepare the journal entry(ies) to record the collection.
(e) Comment on how your answers in parts (a) to (d) would change if the company used a percentage of total accounts receivable of 6%, rather than aging the accounts.
(f) What are the advantages to the company of aging the accounts receivable rather than applying a percentage to total accounts receivable?

Prepare aging schedule; record bad debts for two years.
(SO 2)

P8-5A An aging analysis of Yamoto Limited's accounts receivable at December 31, 2015 and 2014, showed the following:

Number of Days Outstanding	Accounts Receivable		Estimated Percentage Uncollectible
	2015	2014	
0–30 days	$300,000	$320,000	3%
31–60 days	64,000	114,000	6%
61–90 days	86,000	76,000	12%
Over 90 days	130,000	50,000	24%
Total	$580,000	$560,000	

Additional information:

1. At December 31, 2014, the unadjusted balance in Allowance for Doubtful Accounts was a credit of $9,000.
2. In 2015, $42,000 of accounts were written off as uncollectible and $3,000 of accounts previously written off were recovered.

Instructions

(a) Prepare an aging schedule to calculate the estimated uncollectible accounts at December 31, 2014 and 2015. Note that the estimated percentages uncollectible are the same for both years. Comment on the results.
(b) Record the adjusting entry relating to bad debts on December 31, 2014.
(c) Record the write off of uncollectible accounts in 2015.
(d) Record the collection of accounts previously written off in 2015.
(e) Prepare the adjusting entry relating to bad debts on December 31, 2015.
(f) Calculate the net realizable value of Yamoto's accounts receivable at December 31, 2014 and 2015.

Record receivables transactions.
(SO 1, 3)

P8-6A The following selected transactions occurred for Bleumortier Corporation. The company uses a perpetual inventory system, has a May 31 year end, and adjusts its accounts annually.

Feb.	1	Sold merchandise for $6,000 to Morgan Ltd., which used a Bleumortier company credit card to pay for it. The cost of goods sold was $4,000.
	3	Sold $13,400 of merchandise costing $8,800 to Gauthier Company and accepted Gauthier's two-month, 6% note in payment. Interest is due at maturity.
	26	Sold $8,000 of merchandise to Mathias Corp., terms n/30. The cost of the merchandise sold was $5,400.
Mar.	6	Sold $4,000 of merchandise that cost $3,000 to Superior Limited. Superior paid using a bank credit card. The bank deducted $120 of service charges (credit card fees) from Bleumortier's bank account with respect to this sale.
	31	Accepted a two-month, 7%, $8,000 note from Mathias for the balance due. Interest is due at maturity. (See February 26 transaction.)
Apr.	3	Collected the Gauthier note in full. (See February 3 transaction.)
May	31	The Mathias note of March 31 was dishonoured. It is expected that Mathias will eventually pay the amount owed.

May   31   Recorded accrued interest for four months on outstanding credit card amount due from Morgan. Interest on unpaid credit card balances is charged at 24% per annum (2% per month). (See February 1 transaction.)

Instructions

Record the above transactions. Round calculations to the nearest dollar.

P8-7A   On November 1, 2015, Sokos Inc. accepted a three-month, 6%, $40,000 note from Malmo Inc. in settlement of its account. Interest is due on the first day of each month, starting December 1. Both companies' year ends are December 31.

Record notes receivable and payable transactions. (SO 3)

Instructions

(a) Prepare all journal entries for Sokos over the term of the note. Assume that the note is collected in full on the maturity date.
(b) Prepare all journal entries for Malmo over the term of the note. Assume that the note is paid in full on the maturity date.
(c) Assume that instead of honouring the note at maturity, Malmo dishonours it. Prepare the necessary journal entry on Sokos's books at the maturity date, February 1, 2016, assuming that eventual collection of the note is (1) expected, and (2) not expected. Interest was last paid by Malmo on January 1.

P8-8A   Tardif Corporation adjusts its books monthly. On September 30, 2015, notes receivable include the following:

Record notes receivable transactions; show statement presentation. (SO 2, 3, 4)

Issue Date	Maker	Principal	Interest	Term
Mar. 31, 2015	RES Inc.	$17,000	6%	7 months
May 31, 2015	Ihara Ltd.	17,500	4%	18 months
Aug. 31, 2015	Dragon Limited	6,000	7%	2 months
Sept. 30, 2015	MGH Corp.	20,500	5%	16 months

Interest is due at maturity for the RES and Dragon notes. Interest is due on the first day of the month for the Ihara and MGH notes. At September 30, the balance in the Allowance for Doubtful Notes account is nil. In October, the following selected transactions were completed.

Oct.   1   Received the interest due from Ihara and MGH.
        31   Received notice that Dragon was unable to pay its note as scheduled. It expects to be able to pay in the future.
        31   The RES note matured and was received in full.
        31   Accrued interest on the Ihara and MGH notes.
        31   Analyzed the remaining notes for collectibility. Estimated that $17,500 of notes may not be collectible in the future because of significant labour issues currently being experienced by Ihara.

Instructions

(a) Calculate the balance in the Interest Receivable and Notes Receivable accounts at September 30, 2015.
(b) Record the October transactions. Round calculations to the nearest dollar.
(c) (1) Prepare T accounts for the Interest Receivable, Notes Receivable, and Allowance for Doubtful Notes accounts, (2) enter the opening balances, (3) post the entries recorded in part (b), and (4) determine the ending balances.
(d) Show the statement of financial position presentation of the receivables accounts at October 31.

P8-9A   Canadiana Corporation reports the following selected accounts (in thousands) at December 31, 2015:

Prepare assets section. (SO 4)

Accounts payable	$1,978	Interest revenue	$ 112
Accounts receivable, gross	1,630	Land	1,077
Accumulated depreciation—buildings	960	Merchandise inventory	1,902
Accumulated depreciation—equipment	488	Notes receivable (current)	2,481
Allowance for doubtful accounts	32	Notes receivable (non-current)	101
Bad debts expense	138	Sales	12,637
Buildings	2,734	Sales discounts	341
Cash	592	Supplies	85
Cost of goods sold	9,741	Trading investments	196
Equipment	737		
Income tax receivable	99		

Instructions

Prepare the assets section of Canadiana's statement of financial position.

P8-10A   Presented here is selected information for **Nike, Inc.** (in U.S. $ millions) and **Adidas AG** (in euro millions):

Calculate and evaluate ratios. (SO 5)

	Nike	Adidas
Net sales	$24,128	€13,344
Allowance for doubtful accounts, beginning of year	74	127
Allowance for doubtful accounts, end of year	50	151
Accounts receivable (gross), beginning of year	3,212	1,794
Accounts receivable (gross), end of year	3,330	1,858

Instructions

(a) Calculate the receivables turnover and average collection period for both companies. The industry average for the receivables turnover was 7.5 times and the average collection period was 49 days.

(b) Comment on the difference in the two companies' collection experiences, and that of their industry counterparts.

Evaluate liquidity.
(SO 5)

P8–11A The following selected ratios are available for Pampered Pets Inc. for the most recent three years:

	2015	2014	2013
Current ratio	2.6:1	2.4:1	2.1:1
Receivables turnover	8.2 times	7.4 times	6.7 times
Inventory turnover	9.9 times	8.7 times	7.5 times

Instructions

(a) Calculate the average collection period and days in inventory for each year.

(b) Is Pampered Pets' liquidity improving or worsening? Explain.

(c) Do changes in turnover ratios affect profitability? Explain.

(d) Do changes in turnover ratios affect cash flow? Explain.

(e) Identify any steps that the company may wish to take in order to improve its management of receivables and inventory.

Problems: Set B

Record receivables and bad debts; show statement presentation.
(SO 1, 2, 4)

P8–1B At January 1, 2015, Bordeaux Inc. reported the following information on its statement of financial position:

Accounts receivable	$480,000
Allowance for doubtful accounts	35,000

During 2015, the company had the following summary transactions for receivables:

1. Sales on account, $1,600,000
2. Sales returns and allowances, $250,000
3. Collections of accounts receivable, $1,500,000
4. Interest added to overdue accounts, $125,000
5. Write offs of accounts receivable deemed uncollectible, $45,000
6. Collection of accounts previously written off as uncollectible, $10,500
7. After considering all of the above transactions, total estimated uncollectible accounts, $25,000

Instructions

(a) Prepare the journal entries to record each of the above summary transactions.

(b) (1) Prepare T accounts for Accounts Receivable and Allowance for Doubtful Accounts, (2) enter the opening balances, (3) post the above summary entries, and (4) determine the ending balances.

(c) Determine the net realizable value of the accounts receivable as at January 1 and December 31.

(d) Show the statement of financial position presentation of the receivables as at December 31.

(e) Show the income statement presentation of the revenue and expense accounts for the year ended December 31.

Record receivables and bad debts; show statement presentation.
(SO 1, 2, 4)

P8–2B At the beginning of the current period, Huang Ltd. had balances in Accounts Receivable of $200,000 and in Allowance for Doubtful Accounts of $14,000 (credit). During the period, Huang had credit sales of $800,000 and collections of $723,000. It wrote off $21,000 of accounts receivable. However, a $3,500 account written off as uncollectible was recovered before the end of the current period. Uncollectible accounts are estimated to total $16,000 at the end of the period.

Instructions

(a) Prepare the entries to record the sales and collections during the period.

(b) Prepare the entry to record the write off of uncollectible accounts during the period.

(c) Prepare the entry(ies) to record the collection of the $3,500 account written off as uncollectible in part (b).

(d) Prepare the entry to record bad debts expense for the period.

(e) (1) Prepare T accounts for Accounts Receivable and Allowance for Doubtful Accounts, (2) enter the opening balances, (3) post the journal entries prepared in parts (a) through (d), and (4) determine the ending balances.

(f) Show the statement of financial position presentation of the receivables at the end of the period.

P8–3B Yasukuni Corporation reported the following selected information in its general ledger at June 30:

Determine missing amounts.
(SO 2)

Accounts Receivable

Accounts Receivable			Sales	
Beg. bal.	(a)		˙|	(e)
		(b)		
	225,000	230,000		
End. bal.	22,500			

Allowance for Doubtful Accounts			Bad Debts Expense	
		Beg. bal.	1,000	(f) |
	250			
		Unadj. bal.	750	
			(c)	
		End. bal.	(d)	

All sales were on account. Some accounts receivable were collected. One account was written off; there were no subsequent recoveries. At the end of the year, uncollectible accounts were estimated to total $1,150.

Instructions
Using your knowledge of receivables transactions, determine the missing amounts. (*Hint:* You may not be able to solve the above items in alphabetical order. In addition, you may find it helpful to reconstruct the journal entries.)

P8–4B The following selected information is from Imagine Corporation's partial aging schedule:

Prepare aging schedule and record bad debts.
(SO 2)

Number of Days Outstanding	Accounts Receivable	Estimated Percentage Uncollectible
0–30 days	$110,000	1%
31–60 days	50,000	5%
61–90 days	20,000	10%
Over 90 days	12,500	20%
Total	$192,500	

The unadjusted balance in Allowance for Doubtful Accounts is a debit of $5,000.

Instructions
(a) Complete the aging schedule and calculate the total estimated uncollectible accounts from the above information.
(b) (1) Prepare the adjusting journal entry to record the bad debts using the information determined in part (a). (2) Would your journal entry be different if the unadjusted balance in Allowance for Doubtful Accounts were a credit of $5,000?
(c) In the following year, $3,000 of the outstanding receivables is determined to be uncollectible. Prepare the journal entry to write off the uncollectible amount.
(d) Imagine Corporation subsequently collects $1,500 of the $3,000 that was determined to be uncollectible in part (c). Prepare the journal entry(ies) to record the collection.
(e) Comment on how your answers in parts (a) to (d) would change if Imagine used a percentage of total accounts receivable of 4%, rather than aging the accounts.
(f) What are the advantages to the company of aging the accounts receivable rather than applying a percentage to total accounts receivable?

P8–5B An aging analysis of Reiko Limited's accounts receivable at December 31, 2015 and 2014 showed the following:

Prepare aging schedule; record bad debts for two years.
(SO 2)

Number of Days Outstanding	Accounts Receivable 2015	Accounts Receivable 2014	Estimated Percentage Uncollectible
0–30 days	$240,000	$220,000	3%
31–60 days	104,000	86,000	6%
61–90 days	62,000	52,000	12%
Over 90 days	34,000	22,000	20%
Total	$440,000	$380,000	

Additional information:

1. At December 31, 2014, the unadjusted balance in Allowance for Doubtful Accounts was a credit of $3,000.
2. In 2015, $28,000 of accounts were written off as uncollectible and $3,000 of accounts previously written off were recovered.

Instructions

(a) Prepare an aging schedule to calculate the estimated uncollectible accounts at December 31, 2014 and 2015. Note that the estimated percentages uncollectible are the same for both years. Comment on the results.

(b) Record the adjusting entry relating to bad debts on December 31, 2014.

(c) Record the write off of uncollectible accounts in 2015.

(d) Record the collection of accounts previously written off in 2015.

(e) Prepare the adjusting entry relating to bad debts on December 31, 2015.

(f) Calculate the net realizable value of Reiko accounts receivable at December 31, 2014 and 2015.

Record receivables transactions.
(SO 1, 3)

P8–6B The following selected transactions occurred for Vu Ltd. The company uses a perpetual inventory system, has a September 30 year end, and adjusts its accounts annually.

Jan.	2	Loaned Emily Collis, an employee, $6,000 on a four-month, 8% note. Interest is due at maturity.
	5	Sold $8,000 of merchandise to Asiz Limited, terms n/15. The merchandise cost $4,800.
	20	Accepted Asiz Limited's two-month, 9%, $8,000 note for its balance due. Interest is due each month on the 20th. (See January 5 transaction.)
Feb.	20	Collected interest on the Asiz note. (See January 20 transaction.)
Mar.	20	Collected the Asiz note in full. (See January 20 and February 20 transactions.)
May	2	Collected the Collis note in full. (See January 2 transaction.)
	25	Accepted Thundercloud Inc.'s three-month, 8%, $3,000 note in settlement of a past-due balance on account. Interest is due at maturity.
Aug.	1	Vu has introduced its own credit card. Pierpont Ltd. used the card to buy merchandise for $6,000 that cost Vu $4,000.
	25	The Thundercloud note was dishonoured. Eventual collection is not expected. (See May 25 transaction.)
Sept.	30	Recorded accrued interest for two months on outstanding credit card amount due from Pierpont. Interest on unpaid balances is charged at 24% per annum (2% per month). (See August 1 transaction.)

Instructions

Record the above transactions. Round calculations to the nearest dollar.

Record notes receivable and payable transactions.
(SO 3)

P8–7B On August 1, 2015, Cappuccitti Limited accepted a two-month, 4%, $30,000 note from Dil-Dil Inc. in settlement of its account. Interest is due on the first day of each month, starting September 1. Both companies' year ends are August 31.

Instructions

(a) Prepare all journal entries for Cappuccitti over the term of the note. Assume that the note is collected in full on the maturity date.

(b) Prepare all journal entries for Dil-Dil over the term of the note. Assume that the note is paid in full on the maturity date.

(c) Assume that instead of honouring the note at maturity, Dil-Dil dishonours it. Prepare the necessary journal entry on Cappuccitti's books at the maturity date, October 1, 2015, assuming that eventual collection of the note is (1) expected, and (2) not expected. Interest was last paid by Dil-Dil on September 1.

Record notes receivable transactions; show statement presentation.
(SO 2, 3, 4)

P8–8B Kitimat Corporation adjusts its books monthly. On November 30, 2015, notes receivable include the following:

Issue Date	Maker	Principal	Interest	Term
Mar. 31, 2015	Kootenay Inc.	$17,000	6%	9 months
May 31, 2015	Cassiar Ltd.	15,000	4%	18 months
Aug. 31, 2015	Namu Limited	6,000	7%	4 months
Sept. 30, 2015	Siska Corp.	20,000	5%	16 months

Interest is due at maturity for the Kootenay and Namu notes. Interest is due on the first day of each month for the Cassiar and Siska notes. At November 30, the balance in the Allowance for Doubtful Notes account is nil. In December, the following selected transactions were completed.

Dec.	1	Received the interest due from Cassiar and Siska.
	31	Received notice that Namu was unable to pay its note as scheduled. It does not expect to be able to pay in the future.
	31	The Kootenay note matured and was received in full.
	31	Accrued interest on the Cassiar and Siska notes.
	31	Analyzed the remaining notes for collectibility. Estimated that $20,000 of notes may not be collectible in the future because of significant economic issues currently being experienced by Siska.

Instructions

(a) Calculate the balance in the Interest Receivable and Notes Receivable accounts at November 30, 2015.
(b) Record the December transactions. Round calculations to the nearest dollar.
(c) (1) Prepare T accounts for the Interest Receivable, Notes Receivable, and Allowance for Doubtful Notes accounts, (2) enter the opening balances, (3) post the entries recorded in part (b), and (4) determine the ending balances.
(d) Show the statement of financial position presentation of the receivables accounts at December 31.

P8-9B Outaouais Inc. reports the following selected accounts (in thousands) at January 31, 2015:

Prepare assets section.
(SO 4)

Accounts payable	$ 2,857	Income tax receivable	$ 20
Accounts receivable, gross	2,468	Interest revenue	35
Accumulated depreciation—buildings	250	Land	200
Accumulated depreciation—equipment	375	Merchandise inventory	3,000
Allowance for doubtful accounts	268	Notes receivable (current)	50
Bank indebtedness	100	Notes receivable (non-current)	300
Bad debts expense	135	Notes payable (current)	1,000
Buildings	1,000	Sales	29,000
Cost of goods sold	19,000	Sales returns and allowances	800
Equipment	750	Supplies	50
Goodwill	100		

Instructions

Prepare the assets section of Outaouais's statement of financial position.

P8-10B Presented here is selected information (in millions) from the most recent financial statements of **Rogers Communications Inc.** and **Shaw Communications Inc.**:

Calculate and evaluate ratios.
(SO 5)

	Rogers	Shaw
Net sales	$12,486	$4,998
Allowance for doubtful accounts, beginning of year	119	29
Allowance for doubtful accounts, end of year	129	28
Accounts receivable (gross), beginning of year	1,693	472
Accounts receivable (gross), end of year	1,665	461

Instructions

(a) Calculate the receivables turnover and average collection period for both companies. The industry average for the receivables turnover was 7.5 times and the average collection period was 49 days.
(b) Comment on the difference in the companies' collection experiences, and that of their industry counterparts.

P8-11B The following selected ratios are available for Tianjin Inc. for the most recent three years:

Evaluate liquidity.
(SO 5)

	2015	2014	2013
Current ratio	1.5:1	1.5:1	1.5:1
Receivables turnover	8 times	7 times	6 times
Inventory turnover	6 times	7 times	8 times

Instructions

(a) Calculate the average collection period and days in inventory for each year.
(b) Is Tianjin's liquidity improving or worsening? Explain.
(c) Do changes in turnover ratios affect profitability? Explain.
(d) Do changes in turnover ratios affect cash flow? Explain.
(e) Identify any steps that the company may wish to consider in order to improve its management of receivables and inventory.

Broadening Your Perspective

Financial Reporting: *Shoppers Drug Mart*

BYP8-1 The financial statements of **Shoppers Drug Mart** are presented in Appendix A at the end of this book.

Identify receivables; calculate and evaluate ratios.
(SO 1, 5)

Instructions

(a) What types of receivables does Shoppers Drug Mart report in its 2012 balance sheet?
(b) Calculate the receivables turnover and average collection period ratios for accounts receivable for 2012 and 2011. Shoppers' accounts receivable were $470,935 thousand at the end of 2010. (Assume all sales were credit sales and use net receivables instead of gross receivables.)
(c) What conclusions can you draw about Shoppers' management of its receivables from your answer to question (b)?

Comparative Analysis: *Shoppers Drug Mart and Jean Coutu*

Calculate and evaluate ratios.
(SO 5)

BYP8–2   The financial statements of **Jean Coutu** are presented in Appendix B following the financial statements for **Shoppers Drug Mart** in Appendix A.

Instructions

(a) Calculate the following for each company for its most recent fiscal year. The industry average is shown in parentheses.
1. Current ratio (1.6:1)
2. Receivables turnover (22.4 times) (Assume all sales were credit sales and use net receivables instead of gross receivables.)
3. Average collection period (16 days)
(b) What conclusions about each company's liquidity and management of its accounts receivable can be drawn from your calculations in part (a)?

Comparing IFRS and ASPE

Understand valuation of accounts receivable and financial statement presentation, and analyze receivables.
(SO 2, 4)

BYP8–3   Assume you are an analyst for Big Bank and you are putting together financial information on two clothing manufacturers, Lava Fashions Inc. and Flow Designs Inc., for your boss, to help her monitor Big Bank's loans with those two companies. Lava Fashions is a public company that follows IFRS and Flow Designs is a private company that follows ASPE.

One of the most significant assets for both companies is the accounts receivable from retailer customers. You know that your boss will be interested in knowing both the receivables' net realizable value and their exposure to credit risk (the risk that some of the customers won't ultimately pay for the goods they purchased).

You look at the financial statements and find that the information provided is considerably different for each company. Lava Fashions reports the following information related to its receivables:

LAVA FASHIONS INC.
Notes to the Financial Statements
December 31
(in thousands)

Note 14: Trade Receivables

	2015	2014
Trade receivables	$1,854	$1,917
Less: allowance for doubtful accounts	(135)	(124)
Net realizable value	$1,719	$1,793

The aging of gross trade receivables at the end of each year was as follows:

($ in thousands)	2015	2014
Current	$1,322	$1,363
Past due 0–30 days	183	192
Past due 31–60 days	170	167
Past due 61–90 days	50	61
Past due 91–180 days	62	70
Past due > 180 days	67	64
Balance at December 31	$1,854	$1,917

Lava is exposed to normal credit risk with respect to its accounts receivable. It has provided for potential credit losses with an allowance for doubtful accounts. It reduces the potential for such losses because it evaluates a potential customer's creditworthiness before extending credit.

Flow Designs reports the following information related to its receivables:

FLOW DESIGNS INC.
Statement of Financial Position (partial)
December 31
(in thousands)

	2015	2014
Current assets		
Trade receivables, net	$1,720	$2,053

Flow provides credit to its customers in the normal course of its operations. It continually conducts credit checks on its customers and has provided for potential credit losses with an allowance for doubtful accounts although it has not disclosed this information in the notes to its financial statements.

Instructions
(a) Which company's financial statement note provides more useful information about the trade receivables? Why?
(b) Why do you think Lava Fashions provides more information on its receivables than Flow Designs?
(c) What additional information do you think Big Bank would want in order to assess the credit risk in trade receivables for Lava Fashions and Flow Designs?

Critical Thinking Case

BYP8–4 Harry's Hamburgers Ltd. (HHL) is a chain of fast-food restaurants. A few years ago, the company decided it didn't want to own any new restaurants. Rather, when a new restaurant opened up, it is owned by a franchisee rather than the company. A franchisee is an individual investor who owns the land, building, furniture, and other assets and operates the restaurant. In return, the franchisee pays HHL a royalty fee, based on a percentage of sales, for the right to use the HHL name and products under a franchise agreement. If the franchisee needs funds to help build the restaurant, they can borrow money from HHL for a one-year period by signing a note receivable to HHL.

Selected items from the 2015 HHL financial statements along with comparative amounts from 2014 are shown below (in thousands of dollars):

Assess adequacy of allowance and impact on ratios. (SO 2, 3, 5)

	2015	2014
Cash	$ 1,300	$ 2,900
Accounts receivable	6,000	5,000
Allowance for doubtful accounts	(400)	(500)
Notes receivable	2,700	2,000
Inventory at company-operated stores	1,000	1,100
Total current assets	10,600	10,500
Current liabilities	6,800	5,100
Net credit sales	60,000	50,000

Accounts receivable consist only of royalties receivable from franchisees. During 2015, accounts receivable amounting to $100,000 were written off.

The notes receivable are from franchisees, and are due within one year. During 2015, notes amounting to $1.5 million were received from new franchise operators and these are still outstanding. Also during 2015, notes of $800,000 were collected in full. A number of notes were dishonoured during the year, but the company's new vice-president of finance believes that all of these are recoverable, so no allowance for doubtful notes was set up. In the past, no dishonoured note has ever been collected.

The company's bank requires HHL to maintain a current ratio of 1.5:1.

Instructions
(a) Based on the above information, calculate the company's current ratio for 2015 and 2014. Does it currently meet the bank's requirement?
(b) Reconstruct the Allowance for Doubtful Accounts and Notes Receivable accounts.
(c) Do you believe the allowance is adequate for accounts receivable? Explain.
(d) Do you think that an allowance should be recorded for notes receivable? Why or why not? If you believe that an allowance should be set up, what amount should be recorded? (*Hint:* Calculate the amount of dishonoured notes).
(e) If an allowance for the doubtful notes was to be recorded based on your answer to (d), recalculate the company's 2015 current ratio. How do you think the bank would react to this?
(f) Based on a review of the information provided above, do you think that the liquidity of HHL has improved or deteriorated in 2015?

Ethics Case

BYP8–5 Sam Wong is the controller of Encounter Limited, a publicly traded company. He has completed an aging schedule and determined that the allowance for doubtful accounts should be $100,000 at the end of the current year. Sam has noticed that the average age of receivables this year is older than in prior years. The president of the company, Suzanne Chen, is nervous because the bank expects the company to maintain a current ratio of 2:1. After recording the adjustment for bad debts this year, the current assets total $2,000,000 while current liabilities total $1,025,000. Suzanne recalls from her accounting studies that estimating uncollectible accounts requires estimates subject to judgement. She has asked that

Identify issues related to estimating uncollectible accounts. (SO 1)

Sam review his estimate percentages to reduce the allowance from $100,000 to $40,000. She believes this will better reflect the "real" liquidity of the company.

Instructions

(a) Who are the stakeholders in this case?

(b) Why did Suzanne request the adjustment?

(c) Does the president's request pose an ethical dilemma for the controller?

(d) Is the president's reason for reducing the allowance a valid one?

"All About You" Activity

Determine cost of credit card.
(SO 1, 5)

BYP8–6   In order to finance your education, you have had to borrow on your credit card. The Financial Consumer Agency of Canada provides you with the ability to determine how long it will take you to pay back your credit card. Go to www.fcac-acfc.gc.ca/iTools-iOutils/CreditCardPaymentCalculator/CreditCardCalculator-eng.aspx. Alternatively, go to www.fcac-acfc.gc.ca. Click on Tools and Calculators, then Credit Card Tools, then Credit Card Payment Calculator.

Instructions

(a) Assume that you have $2,000 outstanding on your credit card and you are making a minimum monthly payment of $60 (or a minimum monthly percentage of 3%). The interest rate on your credit card is 20%. How long will it take you to repay your loan? What if you make the minimum monthly payment and pay an additional $10? What if you make a fixed payment of $100 per month?

(b) If you have a personal credit card, use the same tool as identified in part (a). How long, based on your current conditions, do you expect it will take to pay back your credit card's balance?

(c) Your university friend is about to obtain a credit card. His comment to you is, "The credit card company is giving me money to spend and I am going to purchase that big screen TV that I have always wanted." Based on what you have learned about credit cards, provide some advice to your friend.

Serial Case

(*Note:* This is a continuation of the serial case from Chapters 1 through 7.)

Discuss credit policy.
(SO 5)

BYP8–7   The majority of Koebel's Family Bakery's sales are paid by cash, debit card, or bank credit card. In a few cases, it has extended credit to select customers, including Coffee Beans. To date, Koebel's has been giving Coffee Beans 30 days to pay for the weekly delivery of cupcakes. Generally, Coffee Beans is taking 45 days to pay each invoice issued. As a result, Janet and Brian have had to pay close attention to cash available to purchase additional inventory and pay monthly salaries. Although Janet, Brian, and Natalie are happy to have taken on the additional work, they are reconsidering the credit terms they are prepared to offer Coffee Beans. As well, they are attempting to establish a consistent credit policy as they continue to discuss with Biscuits the possibility of a weekly contractual commitment to sell chocolate chip cookies.

They are meeting with Frank Vosburgh, the president of Coffee Beans, to discuss their ongoing business relationship. Frank has wanted to meet because the demand for cupcakes has increased significantly and it is anticipated that the number of cupcakes required on a weekly basis will double. He would like to continue to have Koebel's prepare the cupcakes on Coffee Beans' behalf and wants to ensure that they can meet the additional demand. Natalie, Janet, and Brian would like to review the terms of sale with Frank and suggest a reduction of the payment period to 15 days. However, before meeting with Frank, they want to consider all of the possible effects of reducing terms of sale from 30 to 15 days.

Instructions

(a) Identify to Natalie, Janet, and Brian some of the advantages and disadvantages of reducing credit terms to Coffee Beans (and other potential customers) from 30 days to 15 days.

(b) If Koebel's Family Bakery decides to continue providing cupcakes to Coffee Beans and doubles the number of cupcakes it produces, what are some of the effects this will have on Koebel's operations and cash flows?

(c) Can you provide other alternatives to Koebel's Family Bakery to encourage Coffee Beans to pay on time?

Answers to Self-Test Questions

1. c	2. c	3. c	4. d	5. b
6. d	7. b	8. a	9. a	10. a

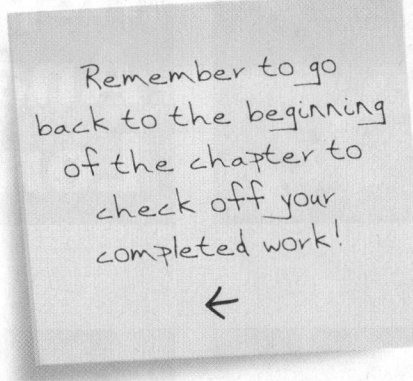

Remember to go back to the beginning of the chapter to check off your completed work! ←

Endnotes

[1]Canadian Tire 2012 Annual Report; "Company Profile" and "Company Facts," corporate website, http://corp.canadiantire.ca.

[2]Rob Carrick, "Students Show Their Smarts on Credit Cards," *The Globe and Mail*, October 25, 2012, page B16; Canadian University Survey Consortium, "2012 Survey of Graduating Undergraduate Students," *Master Report*, June 2012, page 63; "Credit Cards: Statistics and Facts," Canadian Bankers Association, September 27, 2012, available online at www.cbc.ca.

[3]Carter Dougherty, "Debt Collectors Posing as Facebook Friends Spur Watchdogs," Bloomberg, January 24, 2013; Tamara Lush, "Agency Prohibited from Using Facebook to Collect Debt," Associated Press, March 9, 2011; Alexis Madrigal, "Facebook Warns Debt Collectors about Using Its Service," *The Atlantic*, November 19, 2010.

[4]*Rob Carrick, "Students Show Their Smarts on Credit Cards," The Globe and Mail, October 25, 2012; "Best Student Cards 2012," MoneySense, May 10, 2012, www.moneysense.ca/2012/10/05/best-student-cards-2012/, accessed June 23, 2013; Kyle Prevost and Justin Bouchard, "More Money for Beer and Textbooks," Young and Thrifty Publications, 2013, pp. 137-139*; "Student Line of Credit," TD Canada Trust, www.tdcanadatrust.com/products-services/banking/student-life/stline.jsp, accessed June 21, 2013; Canadian Bankers Association, "Credit Cards: Statistics and Facts," www.cba.ca, accessed June 24, 2013; Rob Carrick, *How Not to Move Back in With Your Parents, Toronto:* Doubleday Canada, 2012, p. 46.

CHAPTER 9

Reporting and Analyzing Long-Lived Assets

the navigator

study objectives

After studying this chapter, you should be able to:

SO 1 Determine the cost of property, plant, and equipment.

SO 2 Explain and calculate depreciation.

SO 3 Account for the derecognition of property, plant, and equipment.

SO 4 Identify the basic accounting issues for intangible assets and goodwill.

SO 5 Illustrate how long-lived assets are reported in the financial statements.

SO 6 Describe the methods for evaluating the use of assets.

WestJet's Assets Are for the Long Haul

WestJet took to the skies in 1996, promoting lower-cost flights and a culture that treats its passengers as guests. From its beginnings with three planes, five destinations, and 220 employees—called WestJetters—the Calgary-based airline has grown to include over 100 planes and more than 9,000 WestJetters. The airline takes guests to 85 destinations in Canada, the United States, the Caribbean, and Mexico.

Of the fleet of more than 100 aircraft, WestJet leases 44 planes and owns the rest. The planes it leases are accounted for as operating leases with each lease payment recorded as aircraft rental expense on its income statement. The planes it owns are recorded as property and equipment on its statement of financial position. As at December 31, 2012, WestJet had over $1.9 billion in property and equipment, of which nearly $1.5 billion was aircraft.

The aircraft's purchase price and any costs required to get it into service are capitalized (recorded as property and equipment), as are costs incurred after acquisition to upgrade the aircraft. For example, in 2013, WestJet introduced "premium economy" seats with more legroom in a bid to lure business passengers. The cost to reconfigure its planes for this purpose was capitalized. Meanwhile, costs incurred to maintain the plane but not increase its useful life or add a benefit, such as to repair damages, are expensed.

Depreciation of the aircraft is based on the plane's economic useful life, which WestJet has determined is 20 years. In addition, WestJet separates the parts of a plane into various components—the engine, airframe, landing gear, and satellite television equipment, for example. Each component is depreciated separately. While the aircraft may have a useful life of 20 years, the engine may need to be overhauled every 10 years, in which case the engine would be depreciated over 10 years.

Determining the aircraft's economic useful life involves consultation with the company's technical operations department, observation of the entire industry, and investigation of various external data sources. And although WestJet has been operating for less than 20 years, it has disposed of some older planes that had not been purchased brand new.

In 2013, WestJet expanded its fleet by agreeing to buy 20 new Bombardier Q-400 aircraft over the next three years to service its WestJet Encore regional service to smaller communities in Canada, such as Nanaimo and Fort St. John, B.C. It also committed to purchase thirty 737-700 and five 737-800 aircraft over the next five years. The company bases its decision to acquire new airplanes on several factors, including passenger demand, routes and landing rights, the availability of suitable aircraft, and financing options.

WestJet is also testing the removal of its seatback television sets on some of its flights, replacing them with an option for passengers to rent tablets preloaded with movies and television programs. Removing the seat-back systems will reduce the weight on the aircraft, resulting in better fuel economy and significant cost savings.[1]

the navigator

preview of
CHAPTER | 9

For airlines and many other companies, making the right decisions about long-lived assets such as property, plant, and equipment is critical because these assets determine the company's operating capacity, which in turn affects customer satisfaction. For example, with too few planes, WestJet would lose customers to its competitors. With too many planes, there would be lost revenue from flying planes with empty seats. Management must constantly monitor its needs and adjust the type and number of assets used accordingly. Not doing this can result in lost business opportunities or inefficient use of existing assets, and is a common reason for poor financial results.

In this chapter, we focus our discussion on the following types of long-lived assets: (1) property, plant, and equipment; (2) intangible assets; and (3) goodwill. Long-lived assets can also include natural resources, investment properties, and biological assets. The accounting for these assets can be complex so we will leave any detailed coverage of such assets for another accounting course.

The chapter is organized as follows:

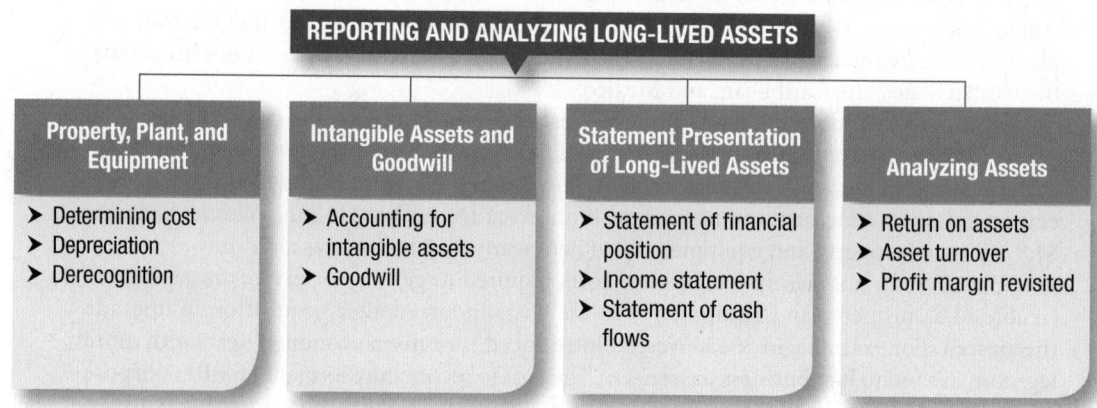

Property, Plant, and Equipment

Alternative Terminology
Property, plant, and equipment are sometimes called *capital assets*; *land, buildings, and equipment*; or *fixed assets.*

Property, plant, and equipment are long-lived resources that a company controls, are tangible (have physical substance), and are not intended for sale to customers. They are used for the production and sale of goods or services to customers, for rental to others, or for administrative purposes. Unlike current assets, which are used or consumed in the current accounting period, property, plant, and equipment provide benefits over many years.

In the following sections, we will learn how to determine the cost of property, plant, and equipment, how to allocate this cost over the asset's useful life, and how to account for its disposal either prior to, or at the end of, its useful life.

DETERMINING COST

STUDY OBJECTIVE 1
Determine the cost of property, plant, and equipment.

As we learned in Chapter 2, most companies record property, plant, and equipment at cost, which includes the following:

1. The purchase price, including certain kinds of non-refundable taxes and duties, less any discounts or rebates
2. The expenditures necessary to bring the asset to its required location and to make it ready for its intended use
3. An estimate of any future obligations related to dismantling, removing, or restoring the asset at the end of its useful life

Determining which costs to include in property, plant, and equipment and which costs not to include is very important and often requires professional judgement. In general, costs that benefit only the current period are expensed. Such costs are called **operating expenditures**. Costs that benefit future periods are capitalized (included) in a long-lived asset account and recorded as either property, plant, or equipment. These are called **capital expenditures**.

For example, the cost to purchase an asset such as equipment should be recorded as a capital expenditure, because the asset will benefit future periods. In addition, the insurance paid to ship that asset to the company should also be capitalized because the insurance during transit is part of the cost of obtaining the asset. Insurance paid to insure the asset against fire or theft after it is situated and in use would be expensed because these costs benefit only the current period. Likewise, any costs incurred to train employees on how to operate the equipment would be expensed and not added to the cost of the equipment because such costs were incurred to get the employees ready and not to get the equipment ready for use.

If there are obligations to dismantle, remove, or restore the long-lived asset when it is retired, these costs must also be estimated and included in the cost of the asset. These capital expenditures are known as **asset retirement costs**. For example, if Encana has a natural gas processing plant on which it expects to incur environmental costs to clean up and restore the property at the end of its useful life, these costs must be estimated and added to the cost of the plant when it is acquired and depreciated over the life of the plant. Accounting for asset retirement costs can be complex and we will leave that discussion to a future accounting course. For simplicity, we will assume that asset retirement costs equal zero in the examples used in this chapter.

Subsequent to acquisition of a long-lived asset, the same distinction exists between operating and capital expenditures. Operating expenditures generally benefit only the current period. They are required to maintain an asset in its normal operating condition and often recur, although not always annually. Examples include repainting a building or replacing the tires on a truck. These costs would be debited to an expense account, such as Repairs and Maintenance Expense, rather than being debited to an asset account.

Capital expenditures after acquisition include costs that increase the life of an asset or its productivity or efficiency. In other words, they are anticipated to provide future economic benefits. These costs are normally larger than operating expenditures and occur less frequently. As was mentioned in our chapter-opening feature story, WestJet capitalizes its reconfiguration and upgrading costs because they improve the planes' service value or extend their useful lives. Other examples for a different type of business might include the cost to replace the roof on a building or to overhaul an engine in a truck.

Property, plant, and equipment are often subdivided into four classes:

1. **Land,** such as a building site
2. **Land improvements,** such as driveways, parking lots, fences, and underground sprinkler systems
3. **Buildings,** such as stores, offices, factories, and warehouses
4. **Equipment,** such as store checkout counters, cash registers, computers, office furniture and equipment, and machinery

How to determine the cost of each of these major classes of property, plant, and equipment is explained in the following sections.

Land

All costs related to the purchase of land, including closing costs such as survey, title search, and legal fees, are added to the Land account. If additional work is required to prepare the land for its intended use, such as clearing, draining, grading, and filling, these costs are also recorded as capital expenditures in the Land account. If the land has a building on it that must be removed to make the site suitable for construction of a new building, all demolition and removal costs, less any proceeds from salvaged materials, are added to the Land account. When land has been purchased to construct a building, all costs that are incurred up to the time of excavation for the new building are considered to be part of the costs that are necessary to prepare the land for its intended use.

To illustrate, assume that Brochu Corporation purchases real estate for $100,000 and that the property contains an old warehouse that is torn down at a net cost of $6,000 ($7,500 in costs less $1,500 in proceeds from salvaged materials). Additional expenditures are also incurred for $1,000 of legal fees related to the purchase of the land. The cost of the land is $107,000, calculated as follows:

Cash price of property	$100,000
Net cost of removing warehouse ($7,500 − $1,500)	6,000
Legal fees	1,000
Cost of land	$107,000

When the acquisition is recorded, Land is debited for $107,000 and Cash is credited for $107,000 (assuming the expenditures were paid in cash). Once the land is ready for its intended use, recurring costs, such as property tax, are recorded as operating expenditures. In other words, these costs are matched against the revenues that the land helps generate.

Land Improvements

Land improvements are structural additions made to land, such as driveways, sidewalks, fences, lighting, and parking lots. Land improvements, unlike land, decline in service potential over time and require maintenance and replacement. Because of this, land improvements are recorded separately from land and are depreciated over their useful lives.

Many students confuse the cost to get land ready for its intended use with land improvements. They think, for example, that removing an old building or grading are "improving" the land, and thus incorrectly reason that these costs should be considered land improvements. When classifying costs, it is important to remember that one-time costs that are required for getting the land ready to use are always charged to the Land account, while land improvements are typically made after acquisition and can be separately distinguished from the land itself.

Buildings

The cost of a building includes all costs that are directly related to its purchase or construction. When a building is purchased, its cost includes the purchase price and any costs incurred to close (complete) the transaction (such as legal fees), in addition to any costs required to make the building ready for its intended use. This can include expenditures for remodelling rooms and offices, and for replacing or repairing the roof, floors, electrical wiring, and plumbing. All of these costs are capitalized to the Buildings account.

When a new building is constructed, its cost consists of the contract price plus payments made for architect fees, building permits, and excavation costs. In addition, interest costs relating to a loan obtained to finance a construction project (that is, interest that could not be avoided) are also included in the cost of the asset but only up to the date that the asset is ready for use. In these circumstances, interest costs are considered as necessary as materials and labour. There are specific rules for determining the amount of interest costs to capitalize; these are not discussed here as they are normally taught in an intermediate accounting course.

If land and a building are purchased together for a single price, as is sometimes the case, the fair (appraised) value of each must be determined and recorded separately.

Equipment

The "equipment" classification is a broad one that can include delivery equipment, office equipment, machinery, vehicles, furniture and fixtures, and other such assets. As with land and buildings, the cost of equipment includes the purchase price and all costs that are necessary to get the equipment ready for its intended use. Thus, freight charges, insurance during transit that is paid by the purchaser, and expenditures that are required to assemble, install, and test the equipment are all charged to the appropriate asset account, such as Equipment or Vehicles.

Because they are recurring expenditures that do not benefit future periods, annual costs such as motor vehicle licences and ongoing insurance are treated as operating expenditures when they are incurred. To illustrate, assume that Perfect Pizzas Ltd. purchases a delivery van for $32,500. Related expenditures are $500 for painting and lettering, $80 for a motor vehicle licence, and $800 for a one-year accident insurance policy. The cost of the delivery van is $33,000, calculated as follows:

Cash price	$32,500
Painting and lettering	500
Cost of delivery van	$33,000

The cost of a motor vehicle licence is treated as a current expense because it is an annual recurring cost. While there are several accounts in which this cost could be recorded, we have chosen to record it in the Vehicles Expense account. Similarly, the cost of the insurance policy is considered a prepaid expense (a current asset). It will be allocated to Insurance Expense throughout the period. The cost of the van and the cost incurred for painting and lettering are capital expenditures because these costs benefit future periods. Painting and lettering are not recorded as separate assets because they are not separate from the van.

The entry to record the purchase of the van and related expenditures, assuming all were paid in cash, is as follows:

Vehicles ($32,500 + $500)	33,000	
Vehicles Expense	80	
Prepaid Insurance	800	
Cash ($33,000 + $80 + $800)		33,880
(To record purchase of delivery van and related expenditures)		

A	=	L	+	SE
+33,000				−80
+800				
−33,880				
↓ Cash flows: −33,880				

To Buy or Lease?

In this chapter, we focus on assets that are purchased, but there is an alternative to purchasing—leasing—that we would like to briefly introduce. In a lease, a party that owns an asset agrees to allow another party to rent the asset for an agreed period of time at an agreed price. The party that is allowing its asset to be leased (rented) is known as the **lessor**, and the party that is paying to use the asset is known as the **lessee**.

Leasing is a common financing practice. Instead of borrowing money to buy an asset, many companies choose to lease it instead. For example, many hotel and motel chains lease their facilities, retail chains lease their retail premises and warehouses, companies lease their photocopiers and other office equipment, and, as indicated in the chapter-opening feature story, companies like WestJet lease their airplanes.

Some advantages of leasing an asset rather than purchasing it include the following:

1. **Reduced risk of obsolescence.** Obsolescence is the process by which an asset becomes out of date before it physically wears out. Frequently, lease terms allow the lessee to exchange the asset for a more modern or technologically capable asset if it becomes outdated. This is much easier than trying to sell an obsolete asset.
2. **100% financing.** If a company borrows to purchase an asset, it is usually required to make a down payment of at least 20%. Leasing an asset does not require any down payment, which helps to conserve cash. In addition, rent payments are often fixed for the term of the lease so they are predictable, unlike other financing, which often has a floating interest rate.
3. **Income tax advantages.** When a company owns a depreciable asset, it can only deduct a certain amount of depreciation expense (called *capital cost allowance* for income tax purposes) on its income tax return. (We will learn more about capital cost allowance later in this chapter.) If the company has borrowed to purchase an asset, it can also deduct the interest expense on the borrowed funds. When a company leases an asset, it simply deducts the rent paid on its income tax return. In some years, this deduction may be greater than the deductions taken if the asset was owned.
4. **Off–balance sheet financing.** Assume that two companies need to use a plane for a three-year period. The first company rents the plane. In this case, the only transaction that the company will

record is some rent expense. The other company buys the plane by taking out a bank loan. On the statement of financial position for this company, the plane is listed as an asset along with the related loan liability. The income statement will show depreciation and interest expense rather than rent expense. The company then sells the plane on the first day of the fourth year. Both companies used the plane for only three years, yet their financial statements at the end of each year look significantly different. The first company, because it is renting the plane and doesn't have to show any liability because it did not take out a bank loan, is using a technique called off-balance sheet financing.

Under IFRS, lease transactions must be accounted for according to their economic substance. That is, if the risks and rewards of ownership are transferred to the lessee, then the leased asset must be treated like a purchase financed with a loan provided by the seller of the asset. How can we determine if the risks and rewards of ownership are transferred or not? Factors such as whether the lease includes a certain type of option for the lessee to purchase the property at the end of the lease term or whether the lease term is long enough to allow the lessee to derive the major part of the benefits offered by the asset are considered, among other criteria. These criteria are reviewed in detail in an intermediate accounting course and are not discussed here.

If the risks and rewards of ownership are *not* transferred to the lessee, then the lease is accounted for as an **operating lease**. Under an operating lease, no asset or liability is recorded; rather, each lease payment is recorded as rent (lease) expense on the income statement. WestJet reported that it leased 44 of its 100 planes in 2012 under operating leases. Because operating leases are accounted for as rentals, these 44 planes are not recorded as assets and liabilities on its statement of financial position. This is known as off-balance sheet financing, similar to the first company discussed in item 4 above, which also accounted for its lease as an operating lease.

If the risks and rewards of ownership of the 44 planes had been transferred to WestJet, then the lease would have been accounted for as a **finance lease**. In other words, WestJet would have had to record these planes as an asset (normally called Assets under Finance Leases), along with a liability relating to future rent payments (normally called Finance Lease Liability). In this case, off-balance sheet financing is not achieved and the financial statements would be identical to those prepared by a company that actually owned and operated the planes. This is similar to the second company discussed in item 4 above. Note that a finance lease is also commonly known as a *capital lease*, especially by private companies reporting under ASPE.

At the time of writing, the Financial Accounting Standards Board in the United States and the International Accounting Standards Board were working together to develop a new leasing standard. The existing standard had been criticized by many for failing to meet the needs of users of financial statements because a faithful representation of leasing transactions did not always occur, especially when operating leases resulted in off-balance sheet financing. Consequently, one of the changes proposed is to eliminate the distinction between operating and finance leases. This change would result in all leases being recorded on the statement of financial position, except for short-term leases of less than 12 months. An effective date for the proposed standard is not expected until deliberations are complete.

Companies often incur costs when they renovate leased property. These costs are charged to a separate account called **Leasehold Improvements**. Since the leasehold improvements are attached to a leased property, they belong to the lessor at the end of the lease. Because the benefits of these improvements to the lessee will end when the lease expires, they are depreciated over the remaining life of the lease (including any renewal options) or the useful life of the improvements, whichever is shorter.

BEFORE YOU GO ON...

▶ Do It! Cost of an Asset

Assume that $50,000 of equipment was purchased on February 4. A $20,000 down payment was made and a bank loan was obtained to pay for the remaining cost of the equipment. Cash expenditures that relate to this purchase include insurance during shipping, $100; an annual insurance policy, $750; installation and testing costs, $500; and staff training costs for the new equipment, $600. (a) What is the cost of the equipment? (b) Record these expenditures.

Action Plan
- Capitalize expenditures that are made to get the equipment ready for its intended use.
- Expense operating costs that benefit only the current period, or that are recurring expenditures.

Solution

(a) The cost of the equipment is $50,600 ($50,000 + $100 + $500).

(b)

Feb. 4	Equipment	50,600	
	Prepaid Insurance	750	
	Salaries Expense	600	
	Cash ($20,000 + $100 + $750 + $500 + $600)		21,950
	Bank Loan Payable ($50,000 − $20,000)		30,000
	(To record purchase of equipment and		
	related expenditures)		

Related Exercise Material: BE9-1, BE9-2, BE9-3, E9-1, and E9-2.

DEPRECIATION

Under International Financial Reporting Standards, companies have two models to choose from when accounting for property, plant, and equipment: the cost model and the revaluation model. The cost model is the most commonly used model under IFRS, and is the only model allowed for use under ASPE. We will cover the cost model in the following sections of the chapter and refer briefly to the revaluation model in a later section.

STUDY OBJECTIVE 2
Explain and calculate depreciation.

The **cost model** records property, plant, and equipment at cost when acquired. Subsequent to acquisition, depreciation is recorded each period and the assets are carried at cost less the accumulated depreciation.

As we learned in Chapter 4, **depreciation is the systematic allocation of the cost of property, plant, and equipment over the asset's useful life.** You will recall that depreciation is recorded in an adjusting journal entry that debits Depreciation Expense and credits Accumulated Depreciation. Depreciation Expense is an income statement account; Accumulated Depreciation appears on the statement of financial position as a contra asset account to the relevant property, plant, or equipment account. The resulting balance, cost less accumulated depreciation, is the carrying amount of a depreciable asset, as was defined in Chapter 4.

Depreciation begins when the asset is available for use and ends when it is derecognized (removed from the accounts). The cost of the asset is allocated to depreciation expense over the asset's useful life so that expenses are properly matched with the expected use of the asset's future economic benefits.

It is important to understand that **depreciation is a process of cost allocation, not a process of determining an asset's fair value.** Under the cost model, an increase in the asset's current fair value is not considered relevant, because property, plant, and equipment are not held for resale. (We will later learn in this chapter that fair values are only relevant if an impairment loss has occurred.) As a result, the carrying amount of property, plant, and equipment may be very different from its fair value. In fact, if an asset is fully depreciated, it can have a carrying amount of zero but may still have a large fair value.

It is also important to understand that **depreciation neither uses up nor provides cash to replace the asset.** The balance in Accumulated Depreciation only represents the total amount of the asset's cost that has been allocated to expense to date: it is not a cash fund. Cash is neither increased nor decreased by the adjusting entry to record depreciation: debit Depreciation Expense; credit Accumulated Depreciation.

■ Keeping an Eye on Cash

Depreciation expense is one of the largest differences between accrual-accounting profit and net cash provided by operating activities that is shown in the statement of cash flows. Depreciation expense reduces profit but does not use up cash. Therefore, to determine net cash provided by operating activities, companies must remove any depreciation from profit. For example, if a company reported profit of $175,000 during the year and had depreciation expense of $40,000, net cash provided by operating activities would be $215,000 ($175,000 + $40,000), assuming no other accrual-accounting differences. Note that depreciation is added to profit in the parenthetical calculation shown here to cancel the non-cash depreciation expense that would originally have been deducted to calculate profit and not because depreciation provides cash.

It is important to understand that, although a business is profitable, it may actually generate more cash flows than the amount of profit shown on the income statement. For this reason, some companies are able to pay out dividends that are greater than profits.

Depreciation applies to only three of the four classes of property, plant, and equipment we discussed in the last section: land improvements, buildings, and equipment. Each of these three classes is considered to be a depreciable asset because the usefulness to the company and revenue-producing ability of each class decline over the asset's useful life. Depreciation does not apply to land because its usefulness and revenue-producing ability generally remain intact as long as the land is owned. In fact, in many cases the usefulness of land increases over time. Thus, land is not a depreciable asset.

Factors in Calculating Depreciation

In Chapter 4, we learned that depreciation expense is calculated by dividing the cost of the depreciable asset by its useful life. At that time, however, we were assuming that the asset's residual value was zero at the end of its useful life. In this chapter, we will now include an actual residual value when calculating depreciation. Thus, there are three factors that affect the calculation of depreciation.

1. **Cost.** The cost of property, plant, and equipment includes the purchase price plus all costs necessary to get the asset ready for use. Cost also includes estimated asset retirement costs, if there are any.
2. **Useful life.** Useful life is expressed as (a) the period of time over which an asset is expected to be available for use or (b) the number of units of production or units of output that are expected to be obtained from an asset. Useful life is an estimate based on such factors as the intended use of the asset and how vulnerable the asset is to wearing out or becoming obsolete. The company's past experience with similar assets is often helpful in estimating a particular asset's useful life.
3. **Residual value.** Residual value is an estimate of the amount that a company would obtain from the disposal of the asset at the end of its useful life. Residual value is not depreciated, since the amount is expected to be recovered at the end of the asset's useful life.

 The difference between a depreciable asset's cost and its residual value is called the **depreciable amount**, which is the total amount to be depreciated over the useful life. Under ASPE, the term *amortization* is often used instead of depreciation, and because of this the depreciable amount is also known as the **amortizable cost.**

Depreciation Methods

Depreciation is generally calculated using one of these three methods:

1. Straight-line
2. Diminishing-balance
3. Units-of-production

While all three methods are used in practice, the majority of Canadian publicly traded companies use the straight-line method of depreciation. WestJet, introduced in our feature story, uses the straight-line method to depreciate its property, plant, and equipment.

How do companies choose which method to use? Management must choose the depreciation method that it believes will best reflect the pattern in which the asset's future economic benefits are expected to be consumed. Once a company chooses the depreciation method, it should apply that method consistently over the useful life of the asset. You will recall from Chapter 2 that comparability is enhanced when the same accounting method is used over multiple years. This does not eliminate the requirement to review the depreciation method, at least annually. And, if the expected pattern of consumption of the future economic benefits has changed, the depreciation method must be changed.

In the sections that follow, the application of each of these depreciation methods is illustrated using the following data for a delivery van purchased by Perfect Pizzas Ltd. on January 1, 2015:

Cost	$33,000
Estimated residual value	$3,000
Estimated useful life (in years)	5
Estimated useful life (in kilometres)	100,000

Straight-Line. The straight-line method of depreciation was originally discussed in Chapter 4. We will discuss it again here, this time including the impact of the residual amount on this method. The **straight-line method** of calculating depreciation has two steps. First, the depreciable amount is determined by deducting the residual value from the cost of the asset. Second, the depreciable amount is divided by the asset's useful life to calculate the annual depreciation expense. The calculation of depreciation expense in the first year for Perfect Pizzas' delivery van is shown in Illustration 9-1.

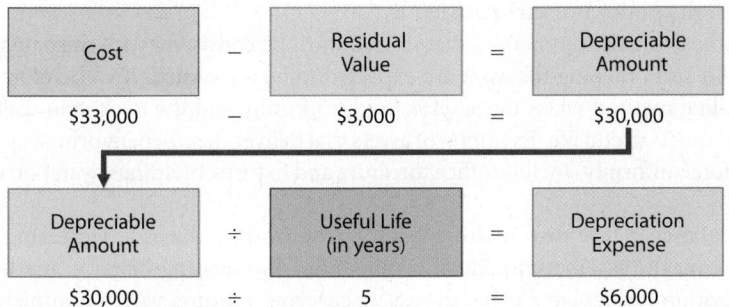

▶Illustration 9-1
Formula for straight-line method

Alternatively, we can calculate a straight-line depreciation rate (expressed as a percentage) to use when determining the delivery van's straight-line annual depreciation expense. First, the depreciation rate is calculated by dividing 100% by the useful life in years.

In Perfect Pizzas' case, the straight-line depreciation rate is 20%. Second, the depreciation expense is calculated by multiplying the asset's depreciable amount by the depreciation rate, as shown in the depreciation schedule in Illustration 9-2.

▶Illustration 9-2

Straight-line depreciation schedule

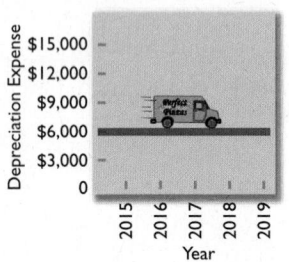

| | | | | | End of Year | |
Year	Depreciable Amount	× Depreciation Rate	= Depreciation Expense		Accumulated Depreciation	Carrying Amount
						$33,000
2015	$30,000	20%	$ 6,000		$ 6,000	27,000
2016	30,000	20%	6,000		12,000	21,000
2017	30,000	20%	6,000		18,000	15,000
2018	30,000	20%	6,000		24,000	9,000
2019	30,000	20%	6,000		30,000	3,000
			$30,000			

PERFECT PIZZAS LTD.
Straight-Line Depreciation Schedule

Note that the depreciation expense of $6,000 is the same each year, and that the carrying amount at the end of the useful life is equal to the estimated $3,000 residual value. Because the depreciation expense is the same each year, a graph showing depreciation per year results in a straight-line pattern, as shown in the margin in Illustration 9-2.

What happens when an asset is purchased during the year, rather than on January 1 as in our example? In such cases, it is necessary **to prorate the annual depreciation for the part of the year when the asset is available for use.** If Perfect Pizzas' delivery van had been purchased on April 1 rather than January 1, the van would be used for nine months in 2015 (April through December). The depreciation for that year would be $4,500 ($30,000 × 20% × 9/12). Note that depreciation is normally calculated to the nearest month. Since depreciation is only an estimate, calculating it to the nearest day gives a false sense of accuracy.

To keep things simple, some companies use a convention for partial-period depreciation rather than calculating depreciation monthly. For example, companies may choose to allocate a full year's depreciation in the year of acquisition and none in the year of disposal. Other companies record a half-year's depreciation in the year of acquisition, and a half-year's depreciation in the year of disposal. Whatever company policy is used for partial-year depreciation, the impact is not significant in the long run if the policy is used consistently.

Recall that the depreciation method that is used must be consistent with the pattern in which the economic benefits from owning the asset are expected to be consumed. It is therefore appropriate to use the straight-line method when the asset is used uniformly and the decline in usefulness is likely constant throughout its useful life. Examples of assets that deliver their benefit primarily as a function of time (and therefore uniformly) include office furniture and fixtures, buildings, warehouses, and the like.

Alternative Terminology
The *diminishing-balance* method is also sometimes called the *declining-balance* method.

Diminishing-Balance.   The **diminishing-balance method** produces a decreasing annual depreciation expense over the asset's useful life. It is called the "diminishing-balance" method because the periodic depreciation is calculated using the asset's carrying amount, which diminishes each year as accumulated depreciation increases. Annual depreciation expense is calculated by multiplying the carrying amount at the beginning of the year by the depreciation rate. The depreciation rate remains constant from year to year, but the carrying amount that the rate is applied to declines each year.

The carrying amount for the first year is the cost of the asset, because the balance in Accumulated Depreciation at the beginning of the asset's useful life is zero. In subsequent years, the carrying amount is the difference between cost and accumulated depreciation at the beginning of the year. Unlike other depreciation methods, the diminishing-balance method uses the asset's carrying amount, not the depreciable amount (cost – residual value), to calculate depreciation. Thus, **residual value is not used in determining the amount that the diminishing-balance rate is applied to.** Residual value does, however, limit the total depreciation that can be recorded. Depreciation stops when the asset's carrying amount equals its expected residual value.

The diminishing-balance method can be applied using different multiples of the straight-line depreciation rate, which result in varying speeds of depreciation. You will find rates such as one time (single), two times (double), and even three times (triple) the straight-line rate of depreciation. A depreciation rate that is often used is double the straight-line rate. This method is referred to as the **double-diminishing-balance method.**

If Perfect Pizzas uses double the straight-line depreciation rate, the depreciation rate is 40% (2 multiplied by the straight-line depreciation rate of 20%). Illustration 9-3 presents the formula and calculation of the first year's depreciation on the delivery van using the diminishing-balance method.

Carrying Amount at Beginning of Year	×	Depreciation Rate (Straight-Line Rate × Multiplier)	=	Depreciation Expense
$33,000	×	20% × 2	=	$13,200

▶Illustration 9-3
Formula for diminishing-balance method

The complete depreciation schedule under this method is shown below in Illustration 9-4.

▶Illustration 9-4
Double-diminishing-balance depreciation schedule

PERFECT PIZZAS LTD.
Double-Diminishing-Balance Depreciation Schedule

Year	Carrying Amount Beginning of Year	×	Depreciation Rate	=	Depreciation Expense	Accumulated Depreciation	Carrying Amount
						End of Year	
							$33,000
2015	$33,000		40%		$13,200	$13,200	19,800
2016	19,800		40%		7,920	21,120	11,880
2017	11,880		40%		4,752	25,872	7,128
2018	7,128		40%		2,851	28,723	4,277
2019	4,277		40%		1,277*	30,000	3,000
					$30,000		

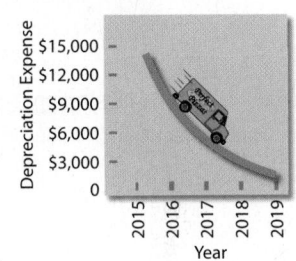

*The calculation of $1,711 ($4,277 × 40%) is adjusted to $1,277 so that the carrying amount will equal the residual value of $3,000.

As explained earlier, depreciation stops in the diminishing-balance method when an asset's carrying amount equals its residual value. Consequently, in 2019, the calculated depreciation expense of $1,711 is restricted to $1,277 ($4,277 − $1,277 = $3,000). This also results in the total amount of depreciation over the life of the delivery van equalling $30,000—the depreciable amount. Note that although we rounded the depreciation rate to two decimal spots (for example, 0.40 or 40%) in the above schedule, we have rounded the depreciation expense to the nearest dollar. We will do the same throughout the text and in your homework assignments.

If you compare the results shown in Illustration 9-4 for the diminishing-balance method with those shown earlier in Illustration 9-2 for the straight-line method, you will see that total depreciation expense is the same regardless of which method is used. However, in the early years, diminishing-balance depreciation expense is higher than straight-line depreciation expense. In later years, the diminishing-balance method will result in less depreciation expense than the straight-line expense.

Methods such as the diminishing-balance method that produce higher depreciation expense in the early years than in the later years are known as *accelerated* depreciation methods. For example, in the above illustration, you can see that the delivery equipment is 64% depreciated ($21,120 ÷ $33,000) at the end of the second year. Under the straight-line method, it would be depreciated 36% ($12,000 ÷ $33,000) at that time.

When an asset is purchased during the year, rather than the beginning of the year as we have illustrated above, it is necessary to prorate the diminishing-balance depreciation in the first year, based on time. For example, if Perfect Pizzas had purchased the delivery van on April 1, 2015, depreciation for 2015 would be $9,900 ($33,000 × 40% × 9/12) if depreciation is calculated based on the number of months in a year that it was used. The carrying amount for calculating depreciation in 2016 then becomes $23,100 ($33,000 − $9,900), and the 2016 depreciation is $9,240 ($23,100 × 40%). Future calculations would follow from these amounts until the carrying amount equalled the residual value.

Managers should choose the diminishing-balance, or another accelerated method, if the company receives more economic benefit in the early years of the asset's useful life than in the later years. That is, this method is used if the asset has a higher revenue-producing ability in its early years, or if the asset is expected to become less useful over time. Some assets require higher repair and maintenance costs in later periods to maintain production capacity, in which case an advantage of the diminishing-balance method is that it will result in a fairly constant total expense (for depreciation plus repairs and maintenance).

Alternative Terminology
The *units-of-production* method is also sometimes called the *units-of-activity* method.

Units-of-Production.   As indicated earlier, useful life can be expressed in ways other than a time period. In the **units-of-production method**, useful life is expressed using a measure of output, such as units produced, or a measure of use, such as machine hours worked, rather than the number of years that the asset is expected to be used. The units-of-production method works well for machinery where production can be measured in terms of units produced or for vehicles where usage can be measured in terms of kilometres driven. The units-of-production method is generally not suitable for such assets as buildings or furniture, because activity levels are less relevant and difficult to measure for these types of assets.

To use the units-of-production method, the units of production in total for the entire useful life are estimated. This amount is divided into the depreciable amount (cost less residual value) to determine the depreciable amount per unit. The depreciable amount per unit is then multiplied by the units of production during the year and the result is the depreciation expense.

To illustrate, assume that Perfect Pizzas' delivery van is driven 15,000 km in the first year of a total estimated useful life of 100,000 km. Using this measure of use, Illustration 9-5 presents the formula and calculation of depreciation expense in the first year.

▶Illustration 9-5
Formula for units-of-production method

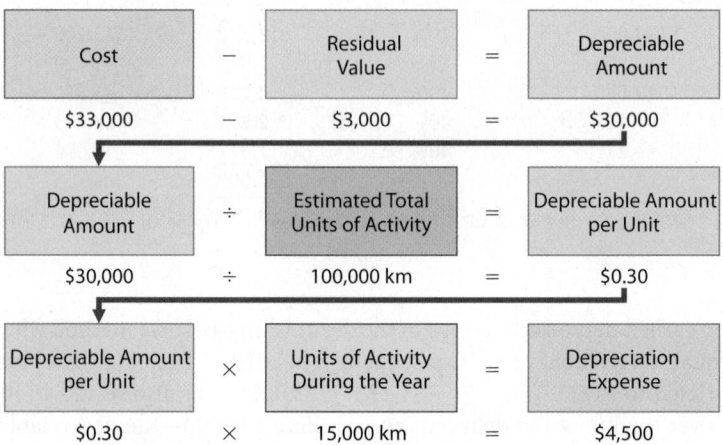

Illustration 9-6 shows the units-of-production depreciation schedule, using assumed distance data for the years 2015–2019.

▶Illustration 9-6
Units-of-production depreciation schedule

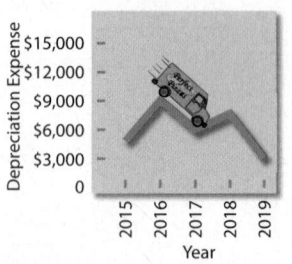

				End of Year	
Year	Units of Production	Depreciable Amount/Unit	Depreciation Expense	Accumulated Depreciation	Carrying Amount
					$33,000
2015	15,000	$0.30	$ 4,500	$ 4,500	28,500
2016	30,000	0.30	9,000	13,500	19,500
2017	20,000	0.30	6,000	19,500	13,500
2018	25,000	0.30	7,500	27,000	6,000
2019	10,000	0.30	3,000	30,000	3,000
	100,000		$30,000		

PERFECT PIZZAS LTD.
Units-of-Production Depreciation Schedule

Similar to our calculations in the diminishing-balance method, we have rounded the depreciable amount per unit to the nearest cent in the above schedule and rounded the depreciation expense to the nearest dollar.

The units-of-production method is easy to apply when assets are purchased during the year. In such cases, the asset's productivity for the partial year is used in calculating depreciation. For example, if Perfect Pizzas had purchased the delivery van on April 1 instead of January 1, and the van was driven 10,000 km in 2015, 10,000 km would be the units of production for the period and not 15,000 km × 9/12.

The units-of-production method, therefore, does not require adjustments for partial periods, as the number of units produced (kilometres driven in this case) already reflects how much the asset was used during the specific period.

Even though it is often difficult to make a reasonable estimate of total activity, this method is useful for long-lived assets whose productivity varies significantly from one period to another. In this situation, the units-of-production method results in depreciation amounts that match the benefits consumed as the asset is used. One area where the units-of-production method is commonly used is in the natural resources industry, which includes oil and gas and mineral deposits. When natural resources are depreciated, the term *depletion* is used instead of depreciation. Further discussion of natural resources is left to an intermediate accounting course.

ACCOUNTING MATTERS!

Why does Morris Formal Wear use the units-of-production method to depreciate its tuxedos? The reason is that the Ottawa-based family business wants to track wear and tear on each of its 5,200 tuxedos individually. Each tuxedo has its own bar code. When a tux is rented, a clerk runs its code across an electronic scanner. At year end, the computer adds up the total rentals for each of the tuxedos, then divides this number by expected total use to calculate the rate. For instance, on a two-button black tux, Morris expects a life of 30 rentals. In one year, the tux was rented 13 times. The depreciation rate for that period was 43% (13 ÷ 30) of the depreciable cost.

Comparison of Depreciation Methods.   The following summarizes the three depreciation methods and calculation of depreciation expense for each method:

Method	Formula
Straight-line	$\frac{\text{Cost} - \text{Residual Value}}{\text{Useful Life}}$
Diminishing-balance	(Cost − Accumulated Depreciation) × Depreciation Rate (Straight-Line Rate × Multiplier)
Units-of-production	$\frac{\text{Cost} - \text{Residual Value}}{\text{Total Estimated Units of Activity}} \times$ Actual Units of Activity During Year

Using each of the above methods and formulas, we calculated annual and total depreciation expense for Perfect Pizzas for a five-year period earlier in this chapter. The following schedule compares the results under the three different depreciation methods. In addition, if we assume that profit, before deducting depreciation expense, was $45,000 for each of the five years, we can clearly see the impact of each method on profit.

| | Straight-Line | | Diminishing-Balance | | Units-of-Production | |
| | Depreciation | | Depreciation | | Depreciation | |
Year	Expense	Profit	Expense	Profit	Expense	Profit
2015	$ 6,000	$ 39,000	$13,200	$ 31,800	$ 4,500	$ 40,500
2016	6,000	39,000	7,920	37,080	9,000	36,000
2017	6,000	39,000	4,752	40,248	6,000	39,000
2018	6,000	39,000	2,851	42,149	7,500	37,500
2019	6,000	39,000	1,277	43,723	3,000	42,000
	$30,000	$195,000	$30,000	$195,000	$30,000	$195,000

As discussed earlier, straight-line depreciation results in the same amount of expense each year on the income statement. Diminishing-balance results in higher expenses, and therefore lower profit, in the early years. It also results in lower expenses and higher profit in later years. Results for the units-of-production method vary, depending on the actual usage each year. While periodic depreciation and profit vary each year under the different methods, total depreciation and total profit are the same for the five-year period.

The statement of financial position is also affected because accumulated depreciation is increased by depreciation expense, and retained earnings is increased by profit. Of course, the choice of depreciation method has no impact on cash flow.

DECISION TOOLKIT

  Decision Checkpoints	 Info Needed for Decision	 Tools to Use for Decision	 How to Evaluate Results
What is the impact of the choice of depreciation method?	Depreciation policy	Income statement, statement of financial position, and accounting policy note to the statements	In the early years, straight-line depreciation results in a lower amount of depreciation expense and higher profit on the income statement than the diminishing-balance method. It also results in higher total assets and higher shareholders' equity on the statement of financial position. The opposite is true in the later years. Results under the units-of-production method will vary. There is no impact on total expense over the life of the asset or cash flow regardless of method used.

Other Depreciation Issues

There are several other issues related to depreciation that we will briefly introduce here. These include how certain assets are separated into their significant components for depreciation purposes, how assets are depreciated for income tax purposes, how the impairment of assets is recorded when the fair value declines, the revaluation model, and under what circumstances depreciation is revised.

Significant Components.   When an item of property, plant, and equipment includes individual components that have different useful lives, the cost of the item should be allocated to each of the asset's significant components. This allows each component to be depreciated separately over different useful lives or even using different depreciation methods if they deliver different patterns of economic benefits. As we learned in our feature story, WestJet records the engine, airframe, landing gear, and satellite television equipment separately from its aircraft. It depreciates its engine, airframe, and landing gear over useful lives ranging from 8 to 15 years, its satellite television equipment over 10 years, and its aircraft over 20 years, all using the straight-line method.

Further discussion of calculating depreciation for the different parts of an asset will be left to a later accounting course. For simplicity, we will assume in this text that all of the components of a depreciable asset have the same useful life and use the same depreciation method, and we will therefore depreciate each asset as a whole.

Depreciation and Income Tax.   For accounting purposes, management determines the method of depreciation to use and estimates the useful life and residual value of assets. The Canada Revenue Agency (CRA) requires that, for income tax purposes, depreciation amounts should be determined not by using management estimates but by using tax regulations. For this reason, when preparing a tax return and determining taxable income, companies cannot deduct the depreciation expense used in the income statement. They must deduct the income tax version of depreciation, which is known as capital cost allowance (CCA). In determining CCA, only the diminishing-balance method of depreciation is permitted. In addition, assets are grouped into various classes and the depreciation rates for each asset class are specified for income tax purposes.

Impairments.   As noted earlier in the chapter, the carrying amount of property, plant, and equipment is rarely the same as its fair value. Remember that the cost model assumes that fair value is not relevant since property, plant, and equipment are not purchased for resale, but rather for use in operations over the long term. While it is accepted that long-lived assets such as property, plant, and equipment may be undervalued on the statement of financial position by reporting a carrying amount lower than fair value, it is not appropriate if assets are overvalued (impaired).

Companies are required to determine if there are indicators of impairment on a regular basis. If there are no indicators, it is not necessary to test the asset for impairment. However, if indicators are present, an impairment test must be done. For example, if a machine has become obsolete, or if the market for a product made by a machine has declined, there is a likelihood that an impairment loss exists. Management is then required to perform an impairment test and this involves determining an estimate of the machine's recoverable amount. The **recoverable amount** can be determined by observing the fair value less selling costs of similar assets in an active market. If this information is not available, the value in use of the asset, which is based on its future cash flows, can be used.

Property, plant, and equipment are considered impaired if the asset's carrying amount exceeds its recoverable amount. When a long-lived asset is impaired, an **impairment loss** is recorded that is equal to the amount by which the asset's carrying amount exceeds its recoverable amount.

Alternative Terminology
An *impairment loss* is also known as a *writedown*.

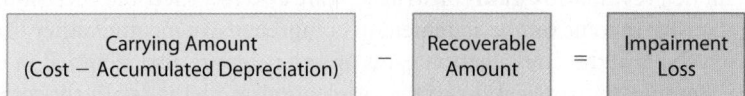

Impairment losses are recorded by debiting an Impairment Loss account, which is reported on the income statement as an operating expense, and by crediting the Accumulated Depreciation account. We previously defined an asset's carrying amount as its cost less accumulated depreciation. This is still the case, but accumulated depreciation can now include more than just the depreciation recorded on the asset to date. It will also include accumulated impairment losses, if there have been any. Certain impairment losses can also be reversed under IFRS, although this does not occur often. Impairment losses are not reversible under ASPE. The rules for determining if an asset is impaired are different under ASPE and IFRS. While the details of these differences are left for a future accounting course, it should be noted that under ASPE, impairments may be recorded less often.

Impairment losses can create problems for users of financial statements. Some companies attempt to record asset impairments in bad years, when they are going to report poor results anyway. This practice is sometimes referred to as "taking a big bath." While asset writedowns must be justified, impairments do involve professional judgement and management can usually provide a reasonable justification for the loss, particularly if the company is not performing well. Critics of such losses note that after a company writes down assets, its depreciation expense will be lower in subsequent periods. When the company later recovers, its results look even better because of lower depreciation expense.

DECISION TOOLKIT

 Decision Checkpoints	 Info Needed for Decision	 Tools to Use for Decision	 How to Evaluate Results
Are the company's long-lived assets over- or undervalued?	Impairment loss; carrying amount of long-lived assets	Compare the carrying and recoverable amounts in light of current business conditions and company performance.	If assets have been adjusted for impairment, expect improved results in subsequent periods, as depreciation will be lower. If assets are substantially undervalued on the statement of financial position, be cautious when interpreting ratios that use carrying amounts, as these ratios may not be comparable with those of other companies.

Revaluation Model.   As previously mentioned, under International Financial Reporting Standards, companies can choose to account for property, plant, and equipment under either the cost model or the revaluation model. We have been describing the cost model in this chapter because it is used by most companies. The revaluation model is used on a limited basis—primarily for companies in certain industries, such as investments or real estate companies, where fair values are more relevant than cost. It is not allowed under ASPE.

Under the **revaluation model**, the carrying amount of property, plant, and equipment is adjusted to reflect its fair value. This model can be applied only to assets whose fair value can be reliably measured. A revaluation is not required each year but must be carried out often enough that the reported carrying amount is not materially different from the asset's fair value.

We saw when using the cost model that impairment losses or writedowns are recorded in the income statement. This is also the case for any allowable reversals of the impairment losses. With the revaluation model, **revaluation gains** or write-ups are also recorded, but these must be recorded in other comprehensive income on the statement of comprehensive income rather than the income statement. Any reversals of these revaluation gains or write-ups are also recorded in other comprehensive income. Because the application of the revaluation model is relatively complex, and few companies use this model, we will leave further discussion of it to a later accounting course.

DECISION TOOLKIT

 Decision Checkpoints	 Info Needed for Decision	 Tools to Use for Decision	 How to Evaluate Results
Should the company use the cost model or the revaluation model?	Cost and fair value of assets	Compare the cost and fair value amounts, as well as the cost of determining the fair value amounts.	If there is a significant difference and the valuation would make a difference to users' decision-making, consider using the revaluation model. Also consider whether the cost of determining the fair value of assets is worth the information provided to users of the financial statements.

Revising Periodic Depreciation. There are several reasons why periodic depreciation may need to be revised during an asset's useful life. These include:

1. **Capital expenditures during the asset's useful life.** While an asset is being used, additional costs relating to it may be incurred. The criteria to determine whether such costs are operating or capital expenditures remain unchanged even if they were not incurred at the acquisition date. As explained earlier in the chapter, if a cost, such as ordinary repairs and maintenance, benefits the company only in the current period, the cost is an operating expenditure and is recorded as an expense in the income statement. If the cost, such as an addition to a building, will benefit future periods, then it is a capital expenditure and is added to the asset's cost. As capital expenditures during the asset's useful life increase the cost of a long-lived asset, the depreciation calculations from that point onward will have to be revised.

2. **Impairment losses.** As described earlier in the chapter, an impairment loss will result in the reduction of the asset's carrying amount. Since the carrying amount is reduced, the future depreciation calculations will also be reduced because the depreciable amount is now lower.

3. **Changes in the estimated useful life or residual value.** Management must review its estimates of useful life and residual value each year. For example, wear and tear or obsolescence might indicate that annual depreciation is not enough. Capital expenditures may increase the asset's useful life and/or its residual value. Impairment losses might signal a reduction in useful life and/or residual value. Regardless of the reason for the change, a change in estimated useful life or residual value will cause a revision to the depreciation calculations.

4. **Changes in the pattern in which the asset's economic benefits are consumed.** As discussed earlier, management must review the choice of depreciation method for a long-lived asset at least annually. If the pattern in which the future benefits will be consumed is expected to change, the depreciation method must change as well. A change in methods will obviously result in a revision to depreciation calculations.

Revising depreciation is known as a change in estimate. **Changes in estimates are made in current and future years but not to prior periods.** Thus, when a change in depreciation is made, (1) there is no correction of previously recorded depreciation expense, and (2) only depreciation expense for current and future years is revised. The rationale for this treatment is that the original calculations were based on the best information known at the time when the asset was purchased. The revision is based on new information that should only affect future periods as that information was not available in the past.

To determine revised depreciation expense, we must first calculate the asset's carrying amount at the time of the change in estimate. This is equal to the asset's original cost less the accumulated depreciation to date plus any capital expenditures. The asset's residual value (either the original amount or a revised amount if appropriate) is deducted from the carrying amount at the time of the change in estimate and the result divided by the remaining estimated useful life. While we will leave a detailed illustration of a change in the depreciation estimate for another accounting course, you should know that many companies need to make revisions to their depreciation. For example, we learned in our feature story that WestJet capitalizes its aircraft reconfiguration costs and any other upgrading costs if they improve the aircraft's service value or extend their useful lives. This will result in extensive revisions to WestJet's depreciation calculations.

BEFORE YOU GO ON...

▶Do It! Depreciation

On October 1, 2014, Mountain Ski Corporation purchased a new snow grooming machine for $52,000. The machine was estimated to have a five-year useful life and a $4,000 residual value. It was also estimated to have a total useful life of 6,000 hours. It is used for 500 hours in the year ended December 31, 2014, and 1,300 hours in the year ended December 31, 2015. How much depreciation expense should Mountain Ski record in each of 2014 and 2015 under each depreciation method: (a) straight-line, (b) diminishing-balance using twice the straight-line rate, and (c) units-of-production?

(continued)

Action Plan

- Under straight-line depreciation, annual depreciation expense is equal to the depreciable amount (cost less residual value) divided by the estimated useful life.
- Under double-diminishing-balance depreciation, annual depreciation expense is equal to twice the straight-line rate of depreciation times the asset's carrying amount at the beginning of the year. Residual values are not used to calculate depreciation in this method, but you must ensure that the carrying amount is not less than residual value.
- Under the straight-line and diminishing-balance methods, the annual depreciation expense must be prorated if the asset is purchased during the year.
- Under units-of-production depreciation, the depreciable amount per unit is equal to the total depreciable amount divided by the total estimated units of production. The annual depreciation expense is equal to the depreciable amount per unit times the actual usage in each year.

Solution

	2014	2015
Straight-line	$2,400	$ 9,600
Diminishing-balance	5,200	18,720
Units-of-production	4,000	10,400

(a) Straight-line: ($52,000 − $4,000) ÷ 5 years = $9,600 per year; for the partial period in 2014: $9,600 × $^3/_{12}$ = $2,400

(b) Diminishing-balance: 100% ÷ 5 years = 20% straight-line depreciation rate; 20% × 2 = 40%

    2014: $52,000 × 40% × $^3/_{12}$ = $5,200
    2015:   ($52,000 − $5,200) × 40% = $18,720

(c) Units-of-production: ($52,000 − $4,000) ÷ 6,000 hours = $8 per hour

    2014:   500 × $8 = $4,000
    2015:   1,300 × $8 = $10,400

Related Exercise Material: BE9-4, BE9-5, BE9-6, BE9-7, BE9-8, BE9-9, E2-2, E9-3, E9-4, E9-5, E9-6, and E9-8.

DERECOGNITION

Property, plant, and equipment is **derecognized**, or removed from the accounts, at the time of disposal. This can be prior to the end of the asset's useful life or at the end of its useful life when an asset is no longer able to provide economic benefits and is sold or retired. There are other methods of disposal when the asset is no longer of use to the company, such as exchanges of property, plant, and equipment where an existing asset is traded for a new asset. Accounting for exchange transactions is complex and discussion of exchanges is left for a future accounting course.

Whether an asset is sold or retired, a company must perform the following four steps to record the derecognition of the property, plant, or equipment. Note that Steps 1 and 2 apply only to depreciable assets and are not required when land is disposed of and derecognized.

Step 1: Update depreciation. Depreciation must be recorded over the entire period of time that an asset is available for use. If the disposal occurs in the middle of an accounting period, depreciation must be updated for the fraction of the year that has passed since the last time adjusting entries were recorded up to the date of disposal. Note that the update period will never exceed one year, since adjusting entries are made at least annually.

Step 2: Calculate the carrying amount. Calculate the carrying amount at the time of disposal after updating the accumulated depreciation for any partial-year depreciation recorded in Step 1:

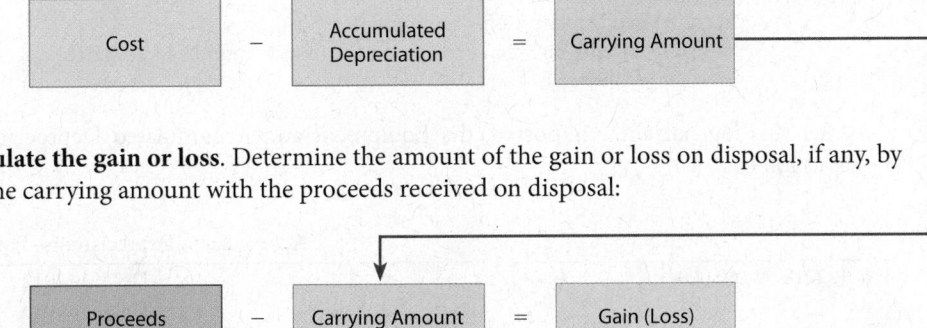

Step 3: Calculate the gain or loss. Determine the amount of the gain or loss on disposal, if any, by comparing the carrying amount with the proceeds received on disposal:

If the proceeds of the sale are more than the carrying amount of the property, plant, or equipment, there is a **gain on disposal**. If the proceeds of the sale are less than the asset's carrying amount, there is a **loss on disposal**.

Step 4: Record the disposal. Record the disposal, removing the cost and accumulated depreciation relating to the disposed-of asset from each affected account. The specific asset account (land, land improvements, buildings, or equipment) is decreased with a credit equal to the cost of the asset disposed of. The Accumulated Depreciation account is decreased with a debit for the portion of the account pertaining to the disposed-of asset, which is the total amount of depreciation (including any impairment losses) that has been recorded for the asset up to its disposal date. Record the proceeds (if any), typically with a debit to Cash. Alternatively, the debit may be to a receivable or other asset account. Record the gain or loss on disposal (if any) by crediting a gain account or debiting a loss account for the difference between the proceeds received and the carrying amount of the asset disposed of. A sample journal entry to record a disposal is illustrated below:

Cash	XX	
Accumulated Depreciation	XX	
Loss on Disposal (or credit Gain on Disposal)	XX	or XX
Specific property, plant, or equipment account		XX

A	=	L	+	SE
+XX				−XX (loss) or
−XX				+XX (gain)
−XX				

↑Cash flows: +XX

Sale of Property, Plant, and Equipment

In the following pages, we will illustrate the recording of a sale of equipment, using the straight-line depreciation method, first at a gain and then at a loss.

Assume that on July 1, 2015, Keystone Ltd. sells equipment for $25,000 cash. The equipment was purchased three and a half years ago, on January 1, 2012, at a cost of $60,000. At that time, it was estimated that the equipment would have a residual value of $5,000 and a useful life of five years. Keystone uses the straight-line method of depreciation and makes adjusting entries annually at its year end, December 31.

The first step in recording the sale is to update any unrecorded depreciation. Annual depreciation using the straight-line method is $11,000 [($60,000 − $5,000) ÷ 5]. Depreciation would have already been recorded along with other adjusting entries for each of the years 2012, 2013, and 2014. Depreciation for 2015 will not yet have been recorded since Keystone only prepares adjusting entries once a year.

The journal entry to record depreciation expense and update the accumulated depreciation for the first six months of 2015 is as follows:

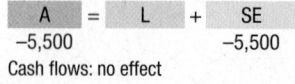

A   =   L   +   SE
−5,500   −5,500
Cash flows: no effect

July 1	Depreciation Expense ($11,000 × ⁶⁄₁₂)	5,500	
	Accumulated Depreciation—Equipment		5,500
	(To record depreciation expense for the first six months of 2015)		

After this journal entry is posted, the Equipment and Accumulated Depreciation accounts appear as follows:

Equipment		Accumulated Depreciation—Equipment	
Jan. 1, 2012 60,000		Dec. 31, 2012	11,000
		Dec. 31, 2013	11,000
		Dec. 31, 2014	11,000
		July 1, 2015	5,500
		Bal.	38,500

Note that the balance in the Accumulated Depreciation account equals 3½ years of depreciation expense ($11,000 × 3.5 = $38,500).

The second step is to calculate the carrying amount on July 1, 2015, the date of disposal:

Cost	−	Accumulated Depreciation	=	Carrying Amount
$60,000	−	$38,500	=	$21,500

The third step is to calculate any gain or loss on disposal. A $3,500 gain is calculated by comparing the proceeds with the carrying amount:

Proceeds	−	Carrying Amount	=	Gain (Loss)
$25,000	−	$21,500	=	$3,500

The fourth step is to record the sale of the equipment, as follows:

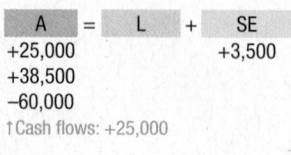

A   =   L   +   SE
+25,000   +3,500
+38,500
−60,000
↑Cash flows: +25,000

July 1	Cash	25,000	
	Accumulated Depreciation—Equipment	38,500	
	Equipment		60,000
	Gain on Disposal		3,500
	(To record sale of equipment at a gain)		

Note that the carrying amount of $21,500 does not appear in the above journal entry. Instead, the equipment's cost ($60,000) and the accumulated depreciation ($38,500) are used. Remember that the carrying amount is simply a number calculated to determine the gain or loss. It is not an account to be debited or credited.

Assume now that, instead of selling the equipment for $25,000, Keystone sells it for $20,000. In this case, a loss of $1,500 results:

Proceeds	−	Carrying Amount	=	Gain (Loss)
$20,000	−	$21,500	=	$(1,500)

The entry to record the sale of the equipment at a loss is:

July 1	Cash	20,000	
	Accumulated Depreciation—Equipment	38,500	
	Loss on Disposal	1,500	
	Equipment		60,000
	(To record sale of equipment at a loss)		

A = L + SE
+20,000   −1,500
+38,500
−60,000
↑Cash flows: +20,000

Retirement of Property, Plant, and Equipment

Companies may choose to retire, rather than sell, some assets at the end of their useful life. For example, some productive assets may have specific uses and consequently have no ready market when the company no longer needs them. In such a case, the asset is simply retired.

Retirement of an asset is recorded just like a sale except that there are usually no, or few, proceeds. Let's continue with the Keystone example introduced in the last section, and assume that the equipment is retired at the end of its useful life, on January 1, 2017. In this scenario, depreciation expense would have been recorded for the full five years of the equipment's useful life. The Equipment and Accumulated Depreciation accounts would be as follows on January 1, 2017:

Equipment		Accumulated Depreciation—Equipment	
Jan. 1, 2012 60,000		Dec. 31, 2012	11,000
		Dec. 31, 2013	11,000
		Dec. 31, 2014	11,000
		Dec. 31, 2015	11,000
		Dec. 31, 2016	11,000
		Bal.	55,000

The equipment is now fully depreciated with a carrying amount of $5,000, as shown below:

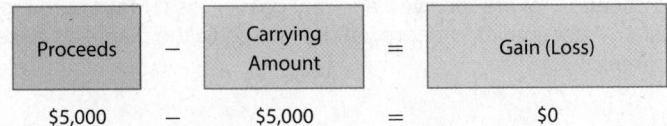

Cost	−	Accumulated Depreciation	=	Carrying Amount
$60,000	−	$55,000	=	$5,000

The carrying amount equals the residual value at the end of the useful life. If we assume that Keystone is able to sell the equipment as scrap for $5,000, as originally estimated, the carrying amount will equal the proceeds and there will be no gain or loss on disposal.

Proceeds	−	Carrying Amount	=	Gain (Loss)
$5,000	−	$5,000	=	$0

The cash received on final disposition of an asset may be greater or less than the estimated residual value, because it would be unusual if the estimate was perfect. In that case, a small gain or loss would result.

The final step that is required is an entry to record the retirement:

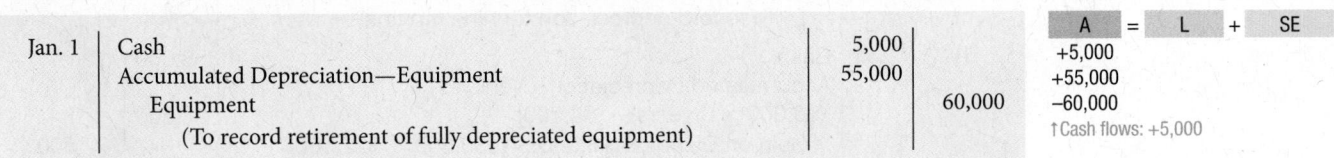

Jan. 1	Cash	5,000	
	Accumulated Depreciation—Equipment	55,000	
	Equipment		60,000
	(To record retirement of fully depreciated equipment)		

A = L + SE
+5,000
+55,000
−60,000
↑Cash flows: +5,000

After this entry is posted, the balance in the Equipment and Accumulated Depreciation—Equipment accounts will be zero.

If no proceeds were received on disposal, rather than $5,000 as we assumed above, a loss on disposal would result. The journal entry to record the retirement would be as follows:

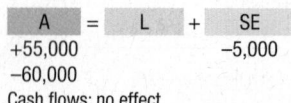

A = L + SE
+55,000   −5,000
−60,000
Cash flows: no effect

Jan. 1	Accumulated Depreciation—Equipment	55,000	
	Loss on Disposal	5,000	
	Equipment		60,000
	(To record retirement of fully depreciated equipment)		

Note that even if there was no residual value and no proceeds received and the carrying amount equalled zero, a journal entry would still be required to remove all accounts related to the retired asset from the books.

What happens if a company is still using a fully depreciated asset? In this case, the asset and its accumulated depreciation are not derecognized and continue to be reported on the statement of financial position, without further depreciation, until the asset is retired. Reporting the asset and related depreciation on the financial statements informs the reader of the financial statements that the asset is still being used by the company. Once an asset is fully depreciated, even if it is still being used, no additional depreciation should be taken. Accumulated depreciation on a piece of property, plant, and equipment can never be more than the asset's cost.

BEFORE YOU GO ON...

▶ Do It! Derecognition of a Vehicle

Overland Trucking Ltd. has a truck that it purchased on January 1, 2012, for $30,000. This purchase was recorded in the Vehicles account at the time. The truck has since been depreciated on a straight-line basis with no residual value and a useful life of five years. Overland has a December 31 year end and prepares adjusting entries annually.

Assume each of the following three independent situations: (a) the truck is sold on October 1, 2015, for $8,000 cash; (b) the truck is sold on October 1, 2015, for $6,500 cash; and (c) the truck is determined to be worthless on January 1, 2017, so the company simply retires it. What journal entry should Overland make to record each scenario?

Action Plan

- Update unrecorded depreciation for any partial period in the current year.
- Calculate the carrying amount.
- Compare the proceeds with the carrying amount to determine whether any gain or loss has occurred.
- Record any proceeds that are received and any gain or loss. Make sure that all accounts (cost and accumulated depreciation) related to the disposed asset are derecognized (removed).

Solution

Annual depreciation expense: $30,000 ÷ 5 years = $6,000

(a) Sale of the truck at a gain:

Oct. 1, 2015	Depreciation Expense ($6,000 × $^{9}/_{12}$)	4,500	
	Accumulated Depreciation—Vehicles		4,500
	(To record depreciation for nine months)		
	Cash	8,000	
	Accumulated Depreciation—Vehicles		
	[($6,000 × 3 years) + $4,500]	22,500	
	Gain on Disposal [$8,000 − ($30,000 − $22,500)]		500
	Vehicles		30,000
	(To record sale of truck at a gain)		

(b) Sale of the truck at a loss:

Oct. 1, 2015	Depreciation Expense ($6,000 × $^{9/12}$)	4,500	
	Accumulated Depreciation—Vehicles		4,500
	(To record depreciation for nine months)		
	Cash	6,500	
	Accumulated Depreciation—Vehicles		
	[($6,000 × 3 years) + $4,500]	22,500	
	Loss on Disposal [$6,500 − ($30,000 − $22,500)]	1,000	
	Vehicles		30,000
	(To record sale of truck at a loss)		

(c) Retirement of the truck:

Jan. 1, 2017	Accumulated Depreciation—Vehicles ($6,000 × 5 years)	30,000	
	Vehicles		30,000
	(To record retirement of truck)		

Related Exercise Material: BE9-10, BE9-11, E9-5, E9-6, and E9-7.

Intangible Assets and Goodwill

STUDY OBJECTIVE 4

Identify the basic accounting issues for intangible assets and goodwill.

Property, plant, and equipment and intangible assets are similar in that both are long-lived resources that are used in the operations of a business, and are not intended for sale to customers. Both provide economic benefits in future periods.

A key distinction between the two is that while property, plant, and equipment are *tangible* assets, which have physical substance, *intangible* assets have no physical substance. In other words, intangible assets involve rights, privileges, and/or competitive advantages that are not physical things. Despite this, they do generate future economic benefits such as revenue from the sale of products or services or cost savings resulting from the company's use of the asset. For some companies, intangible assets are the most valuable assets they have. Some widely known intangibles are Coca-Cola's patents, Tim Hortons' franchises, Apple's trade names, and Google's trademarks.

ACCOUNTING FOR INTANGIBLE ASSETS

An intangible asset must be identifiable, which means it must meet one of the two following criteria: (1) it can be separated from the company and sold, whether or not the company intends to do so, or (2) it is based on contractual or legal rights, regardless of whether or not it can be separated from the company. Since goodwill cannot be separated from a company and sold nor is it based on contractual or legal rights, there are differences in the accounting for goodwill compared with other intangible assets so we will discuss goodwill in the next section.

Similar to property, plant, and equipment, **intangible assets are recorded at cost**. Cost includes all the costs of acquisition and other costs that are needed to make the intangible asset ready for its intended use, including legal fees and similar charges.

As with property, plant, and equipment, companies have a choice of following the cost model or the revaluation model when accounting for an intangible asset subsequent to acquisition. The majority of companies use the cost model so we will leave further study of the revaluation model as it applies to intangible assets for a later accounting course.

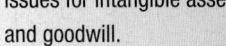

Intangible assets are categorized as having either a **finite (limited) life** or an **indefinite (unlimited) life**. If an intangible asset has a finite life, its cost must be systematically allocated over its useful life. We called this *depreciation* when discussing property, plant, and equipment. With intangible assets, we use the term **amortization** to describe the process of allocating cost to expense. Under ASPE, *amortization* is often the word used to describe depreciation of property, plant, and equipment *or* amortization of intangible assets. Intangible assets with indefinite lives are not amortized.

For an intangible asset with a finite life, its **amortizable amount** (its cost less its residual value) should be allocated over the shorter of (1) the estimated useful life and (2) the legal life. Intangible assets, by their nature, rarely have any residual value, so the amortizable amount is normally equal to the cost. In addition, the useful life of an intangible asset is usually shorter than its legal life, so useful life is most often used as the amortization period. Similar to depreciable assets, the amortization method and useful lives must be disclosed in the notes to the financial statements.

Amortization begins when the intangible asset is ready to be used as intended by management. Similar to depreciation, the company must use the amortization method that best matches the pattern in which the asset's future economic benefits are expected to be consumed. If that pattern cannot be reliably determined, the straight-line method should be used. In the majority of cases, intangible assets are amortized using straight-line.

A sample journal entry to record amortization is as follows:

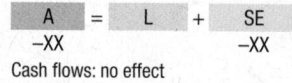

A = L + SE
−XX   −XX
Cash flows: no effect

Amortization Expense	XX	
Accumulated Amortization		XX
(To record amortization)		

As was the case with depreciation, amortization expense is recognized on the income statement as an operating expense. Companies often combine depreciation and amortization expenses in a single amount for reporting purposes. The accumulated amortization account is a contra asset account to the specific intangible asset being amortized, and reported on the statement of financial position.

Recall from earlier in this chapter that an asset is impaired if its recoverable amount falls below its carrying amount. Just as must be done for property, plant, and equipment, companies must determine if there are indicators of impairment on intangible assets with finite lives. If there are indicators, an impairment test is performed. Intangible assets with indefinite lives must be tested annually even if no indications of impairment are present. If any impairment is evident, the asset must be written down to its recoverable amount and an impairment loss recorded and reported in the operating expenses section of the income statement. If the impaired asset is a finite-life intangible asset, the Accumulated Amortization account is credited, similar to our practice of recording impairment losses in the Accumulated Depreciation account for depreciable assets. If the impaired asset is an indefinite-life intangible or goodwill, then the asset account is credited directly since there is no accumulated amortization account available to credit.

Under IFRS, an impairment can be reversed for intangible assets (with the exception of goodwill), just as it can be reversed for property, plant, and equipment. Under ASPE, reversals are not permitted.

Similar to depreciation, amortization is revised if there is a change in cost or useful life, or an impairment loss, and the revision is treated as a change in estimate. At disposal, just as with property, plant, and equipment, the intangible asset's carrying amount is derecognized, and a gain or loss, if any, is recorded.

In the next two sections, we will look in more detail at the accounting for intangibles with finite lives and those with indefinite lives.

Intangible Assets with Finite Lives

Examples of intangible assets with finite lives include patents and copyrights. We also include research and development costs in this section because these costs often lead to the creation of patents and copyrights. WestJet, in our feature story, has intangible assets with limited lives, including software, landing rights, and development costs.

Patents.   A **patent** is an exclusive right issued by the Canadian Intellectual Property Office of Industry Canada that allows the patent holder to manufacture, sell, or otherwise control an invention for a period of 20 years from the date of the application. A patent cannot be renewed, but a patent's legal life can be extended if the patent holder obtains new patents for improvements or other changes in the basic design.

The initial cost of a patent is the price paid to acquire it. Subsequent to acquisition, costs to register the patent, along with legal costs incurred to successfully defend it in any infringement suit, would also be included in the cost of the patent and amortized over time.

The cost of a patent should be amortized over its 20-year legal life or its useful life, whichever is shorter. When a company estimates the useful life of a patent (or any finite-life intangible asset), it must consider factors such as how long the company expects to use the asset, when it may become obsolete, the level of demand for products or services it produces, and other factors that can diminish the economic benefits produced by the patent. For example, suppose a computer hardware manufacturer obtained a patent on a new computer chip that it developed. From experience, we know that the useful life of a computer chip is rarely more than three years because new, superior chips are developed so rapidly that existing chips quickly become obsolete.

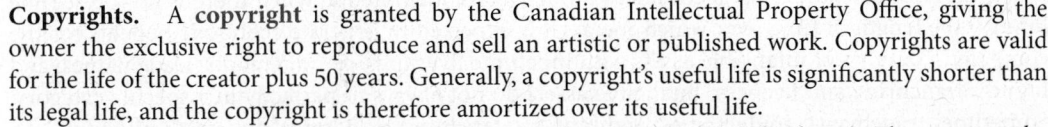

ACCOUNTING MATTERS!

lululemon Sues Calvin Klein for Patent Infringement

Vancouver-based lululemon athletica inc. is well-known for its body accenting yoga pants and it wants to keep it that way. In August 2012, the company sued Calvin Klein and one of its manufacturers, alleging the U.S. apparel giant was selling athletic pants that were remarkably similar to lululemon's own patented clingy design with its stylized waistband. By the end of the year, the two companies had settled the lawsuit out of court for an undisclosed amount.

The lawsuit adds lululemon to a growing list of companies that are engaging in aggressive legal battles over patents. "What lululemon is doing here is staking its turf," said intellectual property expert Jeremy de Beer. "The business strategy is to deter other people from even trying to copy designs, because it's going to cause some legal problems."[2]

Copyrights.   A **copyright** is granted by the Canadian Intellectual Property Office, giving the owner the exclusive right to reproduce and sell an artistic or published work. Copyrights are valid for the life of the creator plus 50 years. Generally, a copyright's useful life is significantly shorter than its legal life, and the copyright is therefore amortized over its useful life.

The cost of the copyright consists of the cost of acquiring and defending it. The cost may be quite low and be composed of only the cost to acquire and register the copyright, or it may amount to a great deal more if a copyright infringement suit is involved. Copyright piracy is a significant issue. For example, according to the Business Software Alliance, more than half the world's personal computer users used pirated software in a recent year.

Research and Development Costs.   Research and development (R&D) costs are not intangible assets on their own, but may lead to patents, copyrights, or other intangible assets. Many companies spend considerable sums of money on research and development in an ongoing effort to develop new products or processes. For example, the Waterloo, Ontario–based BlackBerry company spent more than $1.5 billion on research and development in a recent year.

When a company develops intangible assets internally rather than acquiring them from another party, two accounting problems arise: (1) It is sometimes difficult to determine the costs related to a specific project; and (2) it is hard to know if future benefits will be generated, and if so, when. To help resolve these issues, accounting distinguishes between a research phase and a development phase.

During the research phase, expenditures are made but it is not yet known if these costs will have any future benefit. Consequently, they are expensed and recorded in the account **Research Expenses.**

The development phase begins when certain criteria are met that indicate that the project being developed will have future benefit. All of the following criteria must be met:

1. The project is technically feasible;
2. The company has a desire to complete development;
3. The company is able to complete development; and
4. A market exists for the product.

Once all of the above conditions are met, future expenditures on the project that specifically relate to its development will be capitalized and recorded in the asset account **Development Costs**. During the development phase, if expenditures incurred relate to another specific asset such as equipment or a patent, then those costs are recorded in their respective accounts rather than in Development Costs. After development is complete, such as when commercial production begins, development costs would be amortized over the useful life of the product or process developed.

DECISION TOOLKIT

 Decision Checkpoints	 Info Needed for Decision	 Tools to Use for Decision	 How to Evaluate Results
Is the company's amortization of intangibles reasonable?	The estimated useful lives of intangibles with finite lives from notes to the financial statements of both the company and its competitors	If the company's estimated useful lives are significantly higher than those of its competitors, or do not seem reasonable in light of the circumstances, the reason for the difference should be investigated.	Too high an estimated useful life will result in understating amortization expense and overstating profit and assets.

Intangible Assets with Indefinite Lives

Just as land is considered to have an indefinite life, there are also intangible assets with indefinite lives. An intangible asset is considered to have an indefinite life when there is no foreseeable limit to the length of time over which the asset is expected to generate economic benefits for the company. Examples of intangible assets with indefinite lives include trademarks, trade names, and brands; franchises; and licences. Intangible assets do not always fit perfectly in a specific category. Sometimes trademarks, trade names, and brands; franchises; or licences do have limited lives. In such cases, they would be amortized over the shorter of their legal lives and useful lives. It is more usual, however, for these intangible assets to have indefinite lives and, if so, they are not amortized.

Trademarks (Trade Names).   A **trademark (trade name)** is a word, phrase, jingle, or symbol that distinguishes or identifies a particular business or product. Trade names like Blue Jays, Big Mac, Nike, and CBC create immediate brand recognition and generally help the sale of the product or service. Each year, Interbrand ranks the world's best brands. In 2012, the most valuable Canadian brands were dominated by the banks, in addition to Thomson Reuters, BlackBerry, and Tim Hortons. Coca-Cola and Apple ranked as the two most valuable brands in the world.

A creator or original user may obtain the exclusive legal right to the trademark or trade name by registering it with the Canadian Intellectual Property Office. This registration provides continuous protection and may be renewed every 15 years as long as the trademark or trade name is in use. In most cases, companies continuously renew their trademarks or trade names. Consequently, as long as the trademark or trade name continues to be marketable, it will have an indefinite useful life.

If the trademark or trade name is purchased, the cost is the purchase price. If it is developed internally rather than purchased, it cannot be recognized as an intangible asset on the statement of financial position. The reason is that expenditures on internally developed trademarks cannot be distinguished from the cost of developing the business as a whole and consequently cannot be measured.

Franchises and Licences.   When you purchase a Civic from a Honda dealer, fill up your tank at the corner Irving station, attend an Ottawa Senators hockey game, or order a double-double at Tim Hortons, you are dealing with franchises. A **franchise** is a contractual arrangement under which the franchisor grants the franchisee the right to sell certain products, to provide specific services, or to use certain trademarks or trade names, usually within a designated geographic area.

Another type of franchise, granted by a government body, permits the company to use public property in performing its services. Examples are the use of city streets for a bus line or taxi service; the use of public land for telephone, power, and cable television lines; and the use of airwaves for wireless devices, radio, or TV broadcasting. Such operating rights are referred to as **licences** and can be valuable. For example, the National Hockey League (NHL) currently receives U.S. $2 billion to license its national television rights.

GOODWILL

Goodwill is an asset representing the future economic benefits arising from the purchase of a business that are not individually identified and separately recognized. It symbolizes the value of favourable attributes such as exceptional management, a desirable location, good customer relations, skilled employees, high-quality products, fair pricing policies, and harmonious relations with labour unions. Unlike other assets, which can be sold *individually* in the marketplace, goodwill can be identified only with the business *as a whole*. This is also what differentiates goodwill from other intangible assets. It cannot be separated from the company, nor is it based on legal rights.

If goodwill can only be identified with the business as a whole, how can its value be determined? Certainly a number of businesses have many of the factors cited above (exceptional management, a desirable location, and so on). However, to determine the value of these items would be difficult and subjective, which would not contribute to the reliability of the financial statements. For this reason, internally generated goodwill is not recognized as an asset. Goodwill is only recorded when it can be measured objectively and this only occurs when there is a purchase of an entire business, at which time an independent valuation can be determined.

Goodwill is measured by comparing the amount paid to acquire the business (purchase price) with the fair value of its net identifiable assets (assets less liabilities). Identifiable assets and liabilities are tangible and intangible assets and liabilities that can be specifically identified. If the amount paid to acquire the business is greater than its net identifiable assets, then a transaction has occurred and the cost of the purchased goodwill can be measured and recorded as an asset.

Purchase Price	−	Fair Value of Net Identifiable Assets	=	Goodwill

Because goodwill has an indefinite life, just as the company has an indefinite life, it is not amortized. As mentioned earlier in the chapter, it must be tested for impairment. A recent study noted that in 23 countries, an average amount of 5% of goodwill is recorded as an impairment loss.

DECISION TOOLKIT

 **Decision Checkpoints**

 **Info Needed for Decision**

 **Tools to Use for Decision**

 **How to Evaluate Results**

Decision Checkpoints	Info Needed for Decision	Tools to Use for Decision	How to Evaluate Results
Is the company's goodwill overvalued?	Impairment loss; carrying amount and fair values of the company	Determine if an impairment loss has been recorded and what circumstances led to the impairment.	If goodwill is significant and values are fluctuating, consider excluding goodwill from ratio analysis.

BEFORE YOU GO ON...

▶Do It! Accounting for Intangibles

The Dummies R' Us Corporation purchased a copyright on a new book series for $15,000 cash on August 1, 2014. The books are anticipated to have a saleable life of three years. One year later, the company spent an additional $6,000 cash to successfully defend the copyright in court. The company's year end is July 31 and it prepares adjusting entries

(continued)

annually. Record (a) the purchase of the copyright on August 1, 2014; (b) the amortization at July 31, 2015; and (c) and the legal costs incurred on August 1, 2015.

Action Plan

- Amortize intangible assets with limited lives over the shorter of their useful life and legal life (the legal life of a copyright is the life of the author plus 50 years).
- Treat costs to successfully defend an intangible asset as capital expenditures because they benefit future periods.

Solution

(a)

Aug. 1, 2014	Copyrights	15,000	
	Cash		15,000
	(To record purchase of copyright)		

(b)

July 31, 2015	Amortization Expense ($15,000 ÷ 3)	5,000	
	Accumulated Amortization—Copyrights		5,000
	(To record amortization expense)		

(c)

Aug. 1, 2015	Copyrights	6,000	
	Cash		6,000
	(To record costs incurred to defend copyright)		

Related Exercise Material: BE9-12, BE9-13, E9-8, E9-9, and E9-10.

the navigator

STUDY OBJECTIVE 5
Illustrate how long-lived assets are reported in the financial statements.

Statement Presentation of Long-Lived Assets

In the last few sections we've looked at three categories of long-lived assets: property, plant, and equipment; intangible assets; and goodwill. They are summarized below:

CLASSIFICATION	DEFINITION	EXAMPLES
Property, plant, and equipment	Assets that have physical substance that are used in the operations of a business and are not intended for sale to customers	Land, land improvements, buildings, equipment
Intangible assets	Assets without physical substance that represent rights, privileges, and/or competitive advantages. They are used in the operations of a business and are not intended for sale to customers.	Patents, copyrights, trademarks, trade names, franchises, licences
Goodwill	The value of favourable attributes related to a company as a whole when one business acquires another and pays more than the fair value of the net identifiable assets	Goodwill

The above long-lived assets have an impact on three financial statements: the statement of financial position, income statement, and statement of cash flows. In addition, if a company chooses to use the revaluation model, any valuation gains will affect other comprehensive income on the statement of comprehensive income. This statement will be illustrated in Chapter 12.

STATEMENT OF FINANCIAL POSITION

Long-lived assets are normally reported in the statement of financial position under the headings "Property, Plant, and Equipment," "Intangible Assets," and "Goodwill." Some companies combine property, plant, and equipment and intangible assets under a single heading, such as "Capital Assets." Goodwill must be disclosed separately.

Either on the statement of financial position or in the notes to the financial statements, the cost of each of the major classes of assets must be disclosed, as well as the accumulated depreciation affecting tangible assets and accumulated amortization affecting intangible assets. In addition, the company must specify which depreciation and amortization methods it uses and the useful lives or rates. This is usually done in the summary of significant accounting policies note. Companies must also disclose their policy for testing for impairments as well as any significant changes in methods or rates that result in a revision of depreciation or amortization.

Under International Financial Reporting Standards, companies also have to disclose if they are using the cost or the revaluation model for each class of assets, and include a reconciliation of the carrying amount at the beginning and end of the period for each class of long-lived assets. This means they must show all of the following for each class of long-lived assets: (1) additions, (2) disposals, (3) depreciation or amortization, (4) impairment losses, and (5) reversals of impairment losses. ASPE does not require disclosure of these details.

Illustration 9-7 shows how WestJet reports summary information related to property, plant, and equipment and intangible assets in its statement of financial position. WestJet does not have any goodwill.

WESTJET AIRLINES LTD. Statement of Financial Position (partial) December 31, 2012 (in thousands)	
Non-current assets	
Property and equipment (Note 7)	$1,985,599
Intangible assets (Note 8)	50,808

▶Illustration 9-7
WestJet's statement of financial position

The notes to its financial statements report further detail, as shown in Illustration 9-8.

▶Illustration 9-8
WestJet's notes to the financial statements

WESTJET AIRLINES LTD.
Notes to Financial Statements (partial)
December 31, 2012
(in thousands)

Note 7. Property and equipment	Cost	Accumulated Depreciation	Net Book Value
Aircraft	$2,605,277	$1,127,889	$1,477,388
Ground property and equipment	136,167	79,052	57,115
Spare engines and parts	146,422	44,713	101,709
Buildings	135,924	20,025	115,899
Leasehold improvements	16,538	5,536	11,002
Assets under finance leases	821	821	—
Other	222,486	—	222,486
	$3,263,635	$1,278,036	$1,985,599

Note 8. Intangible assets	Cost	Accumulated Amortization	Net Book Value
Software	$54,519	$35,549	$18,970
Landing rights	17,782	521	17,261
Assets under development	9,621	—	9,621
Other	4,956	—	4,956
	$86,878	$36,070	$50,808

Although only information for 2012 was included in the illustration above, WestJet includes information for 2011 and 2012 in its financial statements, including a detailed reconciliation of the changes between years. WestJet's statement of significant accounting policies note reports that the company uses the cost model. It uses straight-line depreciation and amortization for all of its long-lived assets over periods ranging from five to 40 years for its property and equipment and five to 20 years for its intangible assets. The notes to its financial statements also explain how significant components of property, plant, and equipment are accounted for as well as its policy on testing its long-lived assets for impairment, even though there were no impairments recorded in 2012.

INCOME STATEMENT

Depreciation expense, gains and losses on disposal, and impairment losses are presented in the operating section of the income statement. Why the operating expenses section rather than the other revenues and expenses section of the income statement for the gains and losses? Recall that depreciation expense is an estimate. Gains and losses are basically an adjustment to depreciation expense and should be recorded in the same section of the income statement. Gains would essentially reduce operating expenses, while losses would increase operating expenses.

WestJet reported $185,401 thousand for depreciation and amortization in the operating expenses section of its income statement for the year ended December 31, 2012. It also reported a $469-thousand gain from the disposal of property and equipment. There were no impairment losses.

STATEMENT OF CASH FLOWS

The cash flows from the purchase and sale of long-lived assets are reported in the investing activities section of the statement of cash flows. Illustration 9-9 shows the investing activities section of WestJet's statement of cash flows.

▶Illustration 9-9
WestJet's statement of cash flows

WESTJET AIRLINES LTD. Statement of Cash Flows (partial) Year Ended December 31, 2012 (in thousands)	
Investing activities	
Aircraft additions	$(218,116)
Other property and equipment and intangible additions	(51,191)
Net cash used in investing activities	(269,307)

WestJet is in a growth cycle. It reported purchases of long-lived assets but no significant sale proceeds.

BEFORE YOU GO ON...

▶Do It! Statement Presentation

For each item listed below, state whether it can be found on the income statement (IS) or on the statement of financial position (SFP). Indicate where it would be classified on each statement.

Accumulated Amortization—Patents	Gain on Disposal
Accumulated Depreciation—Buildings	Goodwill
Accumulated Depreciation—Equipment	Impairment Loss
Amortization Expense	Interest Expense
Assets under Finance Leases	Land
Buildings	Loss on Disposal
Depreciation Expense	Patents
Development Costs	Repairs and Maintenance Expense
Equipment	Research Expenses

Action Plan

- Identify which accounts are income statement accounts and which are statement of financial position accounts.
- Review the classifications on the multiple-step income statement and distinguish between operating and non-operating items.
- Review the classifications of long-lived assets among property, plant, and equipment; intangible assets; and goodwill.

Solution

Account Title	Financial Statement	Classification
Accumulated Amórtization—Patents	SFP	Intangible assets: patents (contra asset account)
Accumulated Depreciation—Buildings	SFP	Property, plant, and equipment: buildings (contra asset account)
Accumulated Depreciation—Equipment	SFP	Property, plant, and equipment: equipment (contra asset account)
Amortization Expense	IS	Operating expense
Assets under Finance Leases	SFP	Property, plant, and equipment
Buildings	SFP	Property, plant, and equipment: buildings
Depreciation Expense	IS	Operating expense
Development Costs	SFP	Intangible assets
Equipment	SFP	Property, plant, and equipment: equipment
Gain on Disposal	IS	Operating expenses (reduction)
Goodwill	SFP	Goodwill
Impairment Loss	IS	Operating expenses
Interest Expense	IS	Non-operating expenses (other revenues and expenses)
Land	SFP	Property, plant, and equipment: land
Loss on Disposal	IS	Operating expenses
Patents	SFP	Intangible assets: patents
Repairs and Maintenance Expense	IS	Operating expenses
Research Expenses	IS	Operating expenses

Related Exercise Material: BE9-12, BE9-14, BE9-15, E9-10, and E9-11.

Analyzing Assets

The presentation of financial statement information about long-lived assets allows decision makers to analyze a company's use of its total assets. We will use two ratios to analyze assets: the return on assets and asset turnover. We will also show how the profit margin relates to both.

RETURN ON ASSETS

The **return on assets** ratio measures overall profitability. This ratio is calculated by dividing profit by average total assets. (Recall that average total assets are calculated by adding the beginning and ending amounts of the assets and dividing by 2.) The return on assets ratio indicates the amount of profit generated by each dollar invested in assets. The higher the return on assets, the more profitable the company is.

The following data (in thousands) are provided for WestJet Airlines Ltd. for the fiscal years 2012 and 2011:

STUDY OBJECTIVE 6

Describe the methods for evaluating the use of assets.

	2012	2011	2010
Net sales	$3,427,409	$3,071,540	$2,607,294
Profit	242,392	148,702	90,197
Total assets	3,746,615	3,473,678	3,383,980

The return on assets for WestJet is shown in Illustration 9-10. This illustration also shows this ratio for Air Canada, WestJet's major competitor, as well as the industry average.

▶Illustration 9-10
Return on assets

$$\text{RETURN ON ASSETS} = \frac{\text{PROFIT}}{\text{AVERAGE TOTAL ASSETS}}$$		
($ in thousands)	2012	2011
WestJet	$$\frac{\$242,392}{(\$3,746,615 + \$3,473,678) \div 2} = 6.7\%$$	$$\frac{\$148,702}{(\$3,473,678 + \$3,383,980) \div 2} = 4.3\%$$
Air Canada	2.0%	(2.5)%
Industry average	2.2%	2.3%

As the illustration shows, WestJet's return on assets improved in 2012 compared with 2011. In both years, it was above the industry average, while Air Canada's return on assets, although improving from a negative return in 2011 to a positive return in 2012, was not above the industry average in either year.

ASSET TURNOVER

The **asset turnover** ratio indicates how efficiently a company uses its assets; that is, how many dollars of sales are generated by each dollar invested in assets. It is calculated by dividing net sales by average total assets. When we compare two companies in the same industry, the one with the higher asset turnover ratio is generally perceived to be operating more efficiently because it is generating more sales for every dollar invested in assets.

The asset turnover ratios of WestJet, Air Canada, and their industry for 2012 and 2011 are presented in Illustration 9-11.

▶Illustration 9-11
Asset turnover

$$\text{ASSET TURNOVER} = \frac{\text{NET SALES}}{\text{AVERAGE TOTAL ASSETS}}$$		
($ in thousands)	2012	2011
WestJet	$$\frac{\$3,427,409}{(\$3,746,615 + \$3,473,678) \div 2} = 0.9 \text{ times}$$	$$\frac{\$3,071,540}{(\$3,473,678 + \$3,383,980) \div 2} = 0.9 \text{ times}$$
Air Canada	1.3 times	1.2 times
Industry average	0.9 times	0.9 times

The asset turnover ratios in the illustration indicate that for each dollar invested in assets in 2012, WestJet generated sales of $0.90 and Air Canada $1.30. WestJet's asset turnover was lower than Air Canada's, although the same as that of the industry.

The main reason for WestJet's lower asset turnover ratio was due not to a lower numerator but a higher denominator as WestJet's planes are newer and less depreciated than Air Canada's planes. Note that in calculating the asset turnover ratio we assume that the age of the depreciable assets is about the same for each company. If this assumption is not valid, the company with the newer, less depreciated assets will tend to have a lower turnover ratio, as we found with WestJet. Also, if a company uses operating leases rather than purchasing (or using finance leases for) some of its major assets, this will make the turnover ratio higher because the denominator will have a lower amount for assets.

PROFIT MARGIN REVISITED

For a complete picture of the sales-generating ability of assets, it is also important to look at a company's profit margin ratio. In Chapter 5, you first learned about the profit margin. Profit margin is calculated by dividing profit by net sales. It tells how effective a company is in turning its sales into profits; that is, how much profit is generated by each dollar of sales.

Together, the profit margin and asset turnover explain the return on assets ratio. Illustration 9-12 shows how return on assets can be calculated from the profit margin and asset turnover ratios for WestJet in 2012.

PROFIT MARGIN	×	ASSET TURNOVER	=	RETURN ON ASSETS
$\dfrac{\text{Profit}}{\text{Net Sales}}$	×	$\dfrac{\text{Net Sales}}{\text{Average Total Assets}}$	=	$\dfrac{\text{Profit}}{\text{Average Total Assets}}$
$\dfrac{\$242{,}392}{\$3{,}427{,}409}$		$\dfrac{\$3{,}427{,}409}{(\$3{,}746{,}615 + \$3{,}473{,}678) \div 2}$		$\dfrac{\$242{,}392}{(\$3{,}746{,}615 + \$3{,}473{,}678) \div 2}$
7.1%		0.9 times		6.7%

▶Illustration 9-12
Composition of WestJet's 2012 return on assets (in thousands)

You can see the mathematical connections in the above illustration in that net sales in the denominator of the profit margin calculation cancels the net sales in the numerator of the asset turnover calculation. That said, if you multiply 7.1% by 0.9, you get a result of 6.4% and not 6.7%. This is simply because of rounding differences—we have chosen to present results rounded to one decimal place in this text. If you use unrounded numbers in your calculations, this equation works perfectly.

The relationship of asset turnover and profit margin to the return on assets has important implications for management. From Illustration 9-12, we can see that if a company wants to increase its return on assets, it can do so either by increasing the margin it generates from each dollar of goods that it sells (profit margin), or by trying to increase the volume of goods or services that it sells (asset turnover).

Let's evaluate WestJet's return on assets for 2012 again, but this time by evaluating the ratio's components: the profit margin and asset turnover ratios. WestJet has a profit margin of 7.1%. Compared with an industry average for the profit margin of 2.5%, WestJet is far more profitable. Two possible explanations could be higher ticket prices or better control of costs. Given that WestJet is a discount airline, its superior profitability comes from low costs. This advantage is offset by lower asset turnover. Despite this, WestJet still maintains a higher overall return on assets than its nearest competitor, Air Canada.

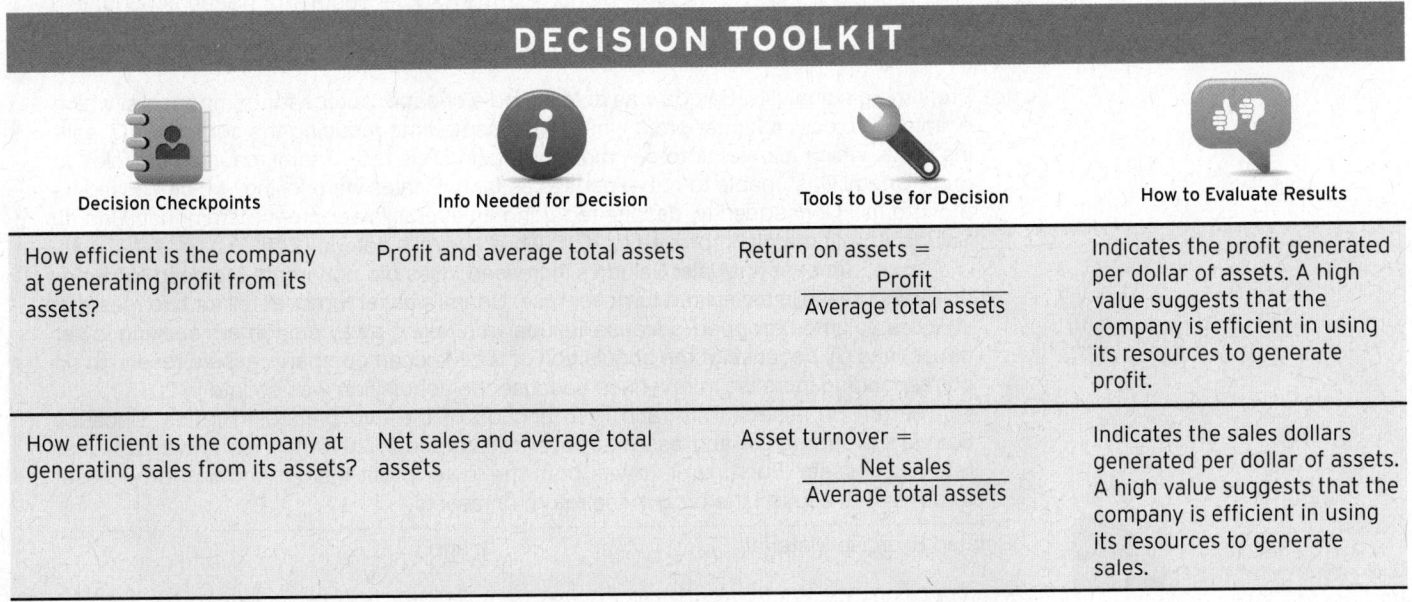

DECISION TOOLKIT

Decision Checkpoints	Info Needed for Decision	Tools to Use for Decision	How to Evaluate Results
How efficient is the company at generating profit from its assets?	Profit and average total assets	$\text{Return on assets} = \dfrac{\text{Profit}}{\text{Average total assets}}$	Indicates the profit generated per dollar of assets. A high value suggests that the company is efficient in using its resources to generate profit.
How efficient is the company at generating sales from its assets?	Net sales and average total assets	$\text{Asset turnover} = \dfrac{\text{Net sales}}{\text{Average total assets}}$	Indicates the sales dollars generated per dollar of assets. A high value suggests that the company is efficient in using its resources to generate sales.

BEFORE YOU GO ON...

▶ Do It! Analyze Assets

Saluda Enterprises Ltd. and Unami Corporation are competitors that manufacture household appliances. Early in 2015, Saluda's management team found a Mexican company that could supply some of the components used in their appliances at a reduced cost. They decided to pass some, but not all, of these savings on to customers so they lowered their prices in an effort to boost the number of appliances sold. Unami reacted to this strategy in late 2015 when it bought the Mexican company.

Listed below are selected amounts taken from the financial statements of these competitors. Calculate the (a) profit margin, (b) asset turnover, and (c) return on assets. (d) Explain why the ratios changed in 2015. Assume that for each company, there was no change in total assets between 2014 and 2013.

($ in thousands)	Saluda		Unami	
	2015	2014	2015	2014
Net sales	$1,200	$1,000	$1,800	$2,000
Profit	100	80	170	200
Total assets	520	500	1,200	800

Action Plan

- Recall the formulas for each ratio: Profit margin = profit ÷ net sales; asset turnover = net sales ÷ average total assets; return on assets = profit ÷ average total assets.
- If the ratio changed compared with the prior year, determine if the change is a result of the numerator or the denominator changing the most.
- Remember how the profit margin and asset turnover ratios relate in order to explain the return on assets ratio.

Solution

	Saluda		Unami	
	2015	2014	2015	2014
(a) Profit margin	$\dfrac{\$100}{\$1,200}$ = 8.3%	$\dfrac{\$80}{\$1,000}$ = 8.0%	$\dfrac{\$170}{\$1,800}$ = 9.4%	$\dfrac{\$200}{\$2,000}$ = 10.0%
(b) Asset turnover	$\dfrac{\$1,200}{(\$520 + \$500) \div 2}$ = 2.4 times	$\dfrac{\$1,000}{(\$500 + \$500) \div 2}$ = 2.0 times	$\dfrac{\$1,800}{(\$1,200 + \$800) \div 2}$ = 1.8 times	$\dfrac{\$2,000}{(\$800 + \$800) \div 2}$ = 2.5 times
(c) Return on assets	$\dfrac{\$100}{(\$520 + \$500) \div 2}$ = 19.6%	$\dfrac{\$80}{(\$500 + \$500) \div 2}$ = 16.0%	$\dfrac{\$170}{(\$1,200 + \$800) \div 2}$ = 17.0%	$\dfrac{\$200}{(\$800 + \$800) \div 2}$ = 25.0%

(d) Profit margin analysis: Saluda was able to find a cheaper source for components, which enabled it to earn a higher profit while at the same time reducing the components' selling price, which allowed it to sell more products. This hurt Unami, causing its sales to drop. Unami was unable to cut expenses as fast as sales were falling, which caused its profit to fall. Consequently, despite reporting an overall lower profit margin than Unami, Saluda's profit margin improved in 2015 while Unami's deteriorated.

Asset turnover analysis: Saluda's increased sales did not create the need for a significant increase in assets, so turnover rose. Unami's asset turnover fell for two reasons: (1) sales volumes dropped because Saluda was taking away customers seeking lower prices, and (2) because of the acquisition of the Mexican company, assets rose with no corresponding increase in revenues because the acquisition was so late in 2015.

Return on assets: This ratio is a function of the two preceding ratios. Because Saluda's profit margin and asset turnover ratios rose in 2015, the result was a higher return on assets. For Unami, it was both the lower profit margin and the lower asset turnover that caused the drop in the return on assets.

the navigator

Related Exercise Material: BE9-16, BE9-17, E9-12, and E9-13.

comparing
IFRS and ASPE

Key Differences	International Financial Reporting Standards (IFRS)	Accounting Standards for Private Enterprises (ASPE)
Terminology	Leases that are essentially the purchase of an asset are called *finance leases*. *Depreciation* is used to describe cost allocation for property, plant, and equipment.	Leases that are essentially the purchase of an asset are known as *capital leases*. *Amortization* may be used instead of *depreciation* for property, plant, and equipment.
Models for valuing property, plant, and equipment	Choice of cost model or revaluation model.	Only cost model allowed.
Impairment requirements for property, plant, and equipment and intangible assets with finite lives	Must determine each year if indicators of impairment are present and, if so, perform an impairment test. Reversals of impairment losses are allowed.	Impairment tests differ between IFRS and ASPE. Reversals of impairment losses are not allowed.
Impairment requirements for intangible assets with indefinite lives and goodwill	Must perform impairment test annually. Impairment losses can be reversed on intangible assets with indefinite lives but cannot be reversed on goodwill.	If indicators of impairment are present, an impairment test must be performed. Reversals of impairment losses are not allowed.
Disclosure	Must provide a reconciliation of the opening and closing carrying amounts of each class of long-lived assets.	Reconciliation not required.

the
navigator

Would you maximize your economic well-being by buying a car? Buying a vehicle—whether new or used—is a fairly straightforward process. You borrow money from a lending institution, pay for the car, and then make monthly payments on the loan. As you pay off the loan, you gain equity in the vehicle until it is all yours. You can keep the vehicle as long as you like and do whatever you want to it.

Should you consider leasing a car instead of buying one? There are many benefits to leasing, including a low or no down payment, driving a new vehicle that's covered by a manufacturer's warranty, and not having to spend a large amount to obtain the use of the vehicle. However, at the end of the lease, you have no equity in the vehicle to put toward a new car.

Monthly lease payments are normally lower than monthly loan payments, assuming the same down payment, costs, and term, because with a lease you are only paying off a portion of the cost of the vehicle plus interest. With a loan, your payments cover the entire cost of the vehicle plus interest. Both lease and loan payments include an interest component.

Should you consider renting a car instead of buying or leasing one? Benefits of renting a vehicle include only incurring the costs of renting the vehicle for the time required, and eliminating the costs of having to purchase or lease a vehicle and all of the related costs of operating the vehicle.

Should you consider car sharing instead of buying, leasing, or renting a car? Car sharing has become popular in many major Canadian cities. Benefits of car sharing include being able to use a vehicle at a moment's notice for a few minutes or a few days, and saving the costs of having to purchase or lease a vehicle and all of the related costs of operating the vehicle. Depending upon the city in which you live, you may also not need to pay for parking.

Some Facts

- If you drive 18,000 km a year in a 2012 Honda Civic LX (4 cylinder), a typical small car, it will cost you on average about 12.9 cents a kilometre plus another $6,440 in fixed costs, according to the Canadian Automobile Association. A 2012 Toyota Camry LE (4 cylinder) would cost you 16.7 cents per kilometre plus $7,450 in additional fixed costs.

- Depreciation is the largest cost of owning a vehicle. Although most car owners sell their vehicles before they are 15 years old, they depreciate at different rates and two cars that have the same purchase price may have different fair values after four years. The Canadian Black Book Company compared the January 1, 2013, values of vehicles purchased in 2009 for 19 different vehicle categories. The cars that retained the highest percentage value of the original purchase price included the Honda Fit for subcompact cars, and the Jeep Wrangler for the compact SUV category.

- Renting a vehicle in Canada for short periods can be relatively inexpensive; for example, $40 a day (before sales taxes). Drivers must be 21 or older and additional fees may apply if the driver is between the ages of 21 to 25. Additional insurance may also have to be purchased for third-party liability and collision. There may be additional fees charged if you don't bring back the car to your original place of rental or if you return it late. Renting a vehicle must be planned in advance as not all car rental companies may have the category of vehicle available that you require.

- One of the newest car-sharing services is in Calgary, where Daimler-owned Car2Go allows members, after paying a one-time sign-up fee of $35, to rent by the minute ($0.38), by the hour ($13.99), or by the day ($72.99). Parking is free if you choose to park in a designated Car2Go parking spot. Drivers must have at least three years of driving experience. You can book on-line 30 minutes before you require the vehicle. There is no additional fee for leaving the car at your destination.[3]

What Do You Think?

To save money, you're renting an apartment on the outskirts of the city where you're going to university, and you need a car to get to campus and to your part-time job. Should you buy a car?

YES I want the convenience of owning my own car and having it available when I need it. I have a part-time job and I am able to meet the loan payments, costs of insurance, maintenance, and fuel.

NO I am a university student and I want to keep my costs down. If I need a car, I would prefer to rent it or use a car sharing service. That is the most economical option.

Summary of Study Objectives

1. **Determine the cost of property, plant, and equipment.** The cost of land, land improvements, buildings, and equipment includes all expenditures that are necessary to acquire these assets and make them ready for their intended use. After acquisition, costs incurred that benefit future periods (capital expenditures) are also included in the cost of the asset. When applicable, cost also includes asset retirement costs.

   If a company leases an asset, depending on whether the risks and rewards of ownership are transferred, it may be accounted for as an operating lease or a finance lease. An operating lease results in rent expense on the income statement. A finance lease results in an asset on the statement of financial position, similar to a purchased asset.

2. **Explain and calculate depreciation.** Depreciation is the process of allocating the cost of a long-lived asset over the asset's useful (service) life in a systematic way. There are three commonly used depreciation methods: straight-line, diminishing-balance, and units-of-production.

Method	Annual Depreciation Pattern	Calculation
Straight-line	Constant amount	(Cost – residual value) ÷ estimated useful life (in years)
Diminishing-balance	Diminishing amount	Carrying amount at beginning of year × depreciation-rate (straight-line rate × multiplier)
Units-of-production	Varying amount	(Cost – residual value) ÷ estimated total units of activity × actual activity during the year

   Other accounting issues related to depreciation include (1) identifying significant components of a long-lived asset for which different depreciation methods or rates may be appropriate; (2) capital cost allowance (CCA) used for income tax purposes; (3) testing long-lived assets for impairment; (4) accounting for property, plant, and equipment using the cost or revaluation model; and (5) circumstances under which a revision of depreciation is required.

3. **Account for the derecognition of property, plant, and equipment.** The procedure for accounting for the disposal of property, plant, and equipment through sale or retirement is:

   Step 1: Update unrecorded depreciation for any partial period.
   Step 2: Calculate the carrying amount.
   Step 3: Calculate any gain (proceeds less carrying amount) or loss (carrying amount less proceeds) on disposal.
   Step 4: Derecognize (remove) the asset and accumulated depreciation accounts related to the sold or retired asset. Record the proceeds received and the gain or loss (if any).

4. **Identify the basic accounting issues for intangible assets and goodwill.** Intangible assets are reported at cost (if the cost model is used), which includes all expenditures that are necessary to prepare the asset for its intended use. An intangible asset with a finite life is amortized over the shorter of its useful life or legal life, usually on a straight-line basis. Like property, plant, and equipment, intangible assets with finite lives are tested for impairment only if indicators of impairment are present. Intangible assets with indefinite lives are not amortized and must be tested for impairment annually under IFRS but only when indicators of impairment are present under ASPE. Impairment losses can be reversed under IFRS but not under ASPE.

   Goodwill, which is the difference between the price paid for a business and the fair value of the identifiable assets less liabilities of the business, is not considered an intangible asset because it is not separately "identifiable." Goodwill has an indefinite life and is not amortized. It is tested for impairment annually under IFRS but under ASPE it is only tested if indicators of impairment are present. Goodwill impairment losses are never reversed.

5. **Illustrate how long-lived assets are reported in the financial statements.** In the statement of financial position, land, land improvements, buildings, and equipment are usually combined and shown under the heading "Property, Plant, and Equipment." Intangible assets with finite and indefinite lives are sometimes combined under the heading "Intangible Assets" or are listed separately. Goodwill must be presented separately.

   Either on the statement of financial position or in the notes to the financial statements, the cost of the major classes of long-lived assets is presented. The depreciation and amortization methods and rates must also be described in the notes to the statements. The accumulated depreciation and amortization of depreciable/amortizable assets and carrying amount by major classes is also disclosed, including a reconciliation of the carrying amount at the beginning and end of each period for companies reporting under IFRS. The company's impairment policy and any impairment losses should be described and reported. The company must disclose whether it is using the cost or revaluation model.

   Depreciation expense, any gain or loss on disposal, and any impairment losses are reported as operating expenses in the income statement. In the statement of cash flows, any cash flows from the purchase or sale of long-lived assets are reported as investing activities.

6. **Describe the methods for evaluating the use of assets.** The use of assets may be analyzed using the return on assets and asset turnover ratios. Return on assets (profit ÷ average total assets) indicates how well assets are used to generate profit. This is really a function of the following two ratios: asset turnover (net sales ÷ average total assets), which indicates how efficiently assets are used to generate revenue, and profit margin (profit ÷ net sales), which measures the profit made on each sale.

the navigator

Glossary

Amortizable amount   The cost of a finite-life intangible asset (for example, patent, copyright) less its residual value, if any. (p. 462)

Amortization   The systematic allocation of the amortizable cost of a finite-life intangible asset over the shorter of the asset's legal or useful life. (p. 461)

Asset retirement costs   The amount added to the cost of a long-lived asset that relates to obligations to dismantle, remove, or restore an asset when it is retired. (p. 441)

Asset turnover   A measure of how efficiently a company uses its total assets to generate sales. It is calculated by dividing net sales by average total assets [(beginning + ending total assets) ÷ 2]. (p. 470)

Capital expenditures   Expenditures that benefit future periods. They are recorded (capitalized) as long-lived assets. (p. 441)

Copyright   An exclusive right granted by the federal government allowing the owner to reproduce and sell an artistic or published work for a period extending over the life of the creator plus 50 years. (p. 463)

Cost model   A model for accounting for a long-lived asset that carries the asset at its cost less any accumulated depreciation or amortization. (p. 445)

Depreciable amount   The cost of a depreciable asset (for example, property, plant, and equipment) less its residual value. (p. 446)

Derecognized   The removal of a long-lived asset from the accounts upon its disposal or when it no longer provides any future benefits. (p. 456)

Development costs   Expenditures related to the application of research to a plan or design for a new or improved product or process for commercial use. These costs are recorded (capitalized) as long-lived assets. (p. 464)

Diminishing-balance method   A depreciation method in which depreciation expense is calculated by multiplying the carrying amount of an asset by a depreciation rate (the straight-line rate, which is 100% divided by the useful life, adjusted for any multiplier effect). This method produces a decreasing periodic depreciation expense over the asset's useful life. (p. 448)

Finance lease (also known as a capital lease)   A long-term agreement allowing one party (the lessee) to use the asset of another party (the lessor). The arrangement is accounted for as a purchase because the risks and rewards of owning the asset have been transferred to the lessee. (p. 444)

Franchise   A contractual arrangement under which the franchisor grants the franchisee the right to sell certain products, to render specific services, or to use certain trademarks or trade names, usually within a designated geographic area. (p. 464)

Goodwill   The value of favourable, unidentifiable attributes related to a company as a whole. It is calculated when one business acquires another and pays more than the fair value of the company's net identifiable assets. (p. 465)

Impairment loss   The amount by which the carrying amount of an asset exceeds its recoverable amount. (p. 453)

Licences   Operating rights to use property that are granted by a government agency to a company. (p. 465)

Operating expenditures   Expenditures that benefit only the current period. They are immediately charged against revenues as an expense. (p. 440)

Operating lease   An arrangement allowing one party (the lessee) to use the asset of another party (the lessor). The arrangement is accounted for as a rental because the risks and rewards of owning the asset have been retained by the lessor. (p. 444)

Patent   An exclusive right issued by the federal government that enables the recipient to manufacture, sell, or otherwise control an invention for a period of 20 years from the date of the application. (p. 462)

Research expenses   Expenditures on an original planned investigation that is done to gain new knowledge and understanding. These costs are expensed because criteria for recording them as assets have not been met. (p. 463)

Residual value   An estimate of the amount that a company would obtain from the disposal of an asset at the end of its useful life. (p. 446)

Return on assets   A profitability measure that indicates the amount of profit generated by each dollar invested in assets. It is calculated as profit divided by average total assets [(beginning + ending total assets) ÷ 2]. It can also be calculated by multiplying profit margin by asset turnover. (p. 469)

Revaluation model   A model of accounting for a long-lived asset that carries the asset at its fair value less accumulated depreciation or amortization. (p. 454)

Straight-line method   A depreciation method in which depreciation expense is calculated by dividing an asset's depreciable amount by its estimated useful life. This method produces the same periodic depreciation expense over the asset's useful life. (p. 447)

Trademark (trade name)   A word, phrase, jingle, or symbol that distinguishes or identifies a particular business or product. (p. 464)

Units-of-production method   A depreciation method in which the useful life is expressed in terms of the total units of production or total use expected from the asset. Depreciation expense is calculated by multiplying the depreciable amount by actual activity during the year divided by the estimated total activity. The method will produce an expense that will vary each period depending on the amount of activity. (p. 450)

DECISION TOOLKIT—A SUMMARY

 Decision Checkpoints	 Info Needed for Decision	 Tools to Use for Decision	 How to Evaluate Results
What is the impact of the choice of depreciation method?	Depreciation policy	Income statement, statement of financial position, and accounting policy note to the statements	In the early years, straight-line depreciation results in a lower amount of depreciation expense and higher profit on the income statement than the diminishing-balance method. It also results in higher total assets and higher shareholders' equity on the statement of financial position. The opposite is true in the later years. Results under the units-of-production method will vary. There is no impact on total expense over the life of the asset or cash flow regardless of method used.
Are the company's long-lived assets over- or undervalued?	Impairment loss; carrying amount of long-lived assets	Compare the carrying and recoverable amounts in light of current business conditions and company performance.	If assets have been adjusted for impairment, expect improved results in subsequent periods, as depreciation will be lower. If assets are substantially undervalued on the statement of financial position, be cautious when interpreting ratios that use carrying amounts, as these ratios may not be comparable with those of other companies.
Should the company use the cost model or the revaluation model?	Cost and fair value of assets	Compare the cost and fair value amounts, as well as the cost of determining the fair value amounts.	If there is a significant difference and the valuation would make a difference to users' decision-making, consider using the revaluation model. Also consider whether the cost of determining the fair value of assets is worth the information provided to users of the financial statements.
Is the company's amortization of intangibles reasonable?	The estimated useful lives of intangibles with finite lives from notes to the financial statements of both the company and its competitors	If the company's estimated useful lives are significantly higher than those of its competitors, or do not seem reasonable in light of the circumstances, the reason for the difference should be investigated.	Too high an estimated useful life will result in understating amortization expense and overstating profit and assets.
Is the company's goodwill overvalued?	Impairment loss; carrying amount and fair values of the company	Determine if an impairment loss has been recorded and what circumstances led to the impairment.	If goodwill is significant and values are fluctuating, consider excluding goodwill from ratio analysis.
How efficient is the company at generating profit from its assets?	Profit and average total assets	Return on assets = $\dfrac{\text{Profit}}{\text{Average total assets}}$	Indicates the profit generated per dollar of assets. A high value suggests that the company is efficient in using its resources to generate profit.
How efficient is the company at generating sales from its assets?	Net sales and average total assets	Asset turnover = $\dfrac{\text{Net sales}}{\text{Average total assets}}$	Indicates the sales dollars generated per dollar of assets. A high value suggests that the company is efficient in using its resources to generate sales.

the navigator

USING THE DECISION TOOLKIT

Transat A.T. Inc. is an international, publicly traded company, headquartered in Canada. It owns an air carrier (Air Transat) and provides holiday travel packages to more than 60 countries. Selected information from its statement of financial position follows:

TRANSAT A.T. INC.
Statement of Financial Position (partial)
October 31, 2012
(in thousands)

Assets	2012	2011
Property, plant and equipment	$ 96,415	$ 86,520
Intangible assets	66,531	52,347
Goodwill	91,494	109,495
Total assets	1,163,301	1,226,570

Selected information from Transat's income statement follows:

	2012	2011
Revenues	$3,714,219	$3,654,167
Depreciation expense	30,820	34,240
Amortization expense	9,575	9,557
Impairment of goodwill	15,000	—
Loss	(13,536)	(11,652)

Instructions

(a) Similar to WestJet, Transat depreciates its property, plant, and equipment using the straight-line method. It also separates its long-lived assets into significant components in the same manner as WestJet. However, where WestJet depreciates its aircraft over 20 years, Transat depreciates its aircraft over seven to 10 years. (1) What is a reason why Transat might use a different useful life than WestJet? (2) Assuming all other factors are equal, what impact would this difference in useful lives have on your comparison of the depreciation expense and profit (or loss) of each company?

(b) Transat reports two different kinds of intangible assets with finite lives: software and customer lists. It amortizes these on a straight-line basis over their useful lives. It also reports trademarks as an intangible asset, which it does not amortize. Why do you think that Transat is not amortizing its trademarks?

(c) Goodwill is not amortized but is tested annually for impairment. In 2012, Transat recorded a $15,000 impairment loss, primarily due to the political and economic climate affecting the performance of its companies in North Africa and Greece. If the financial situation turns around in future, can Transat reverse this impairment loss?

(d) Calculate Transat's return on assets and asset turnover ratios for 2012 and compare them with those of WestJet, Air Canada, and the industry information given in the chapter.

Solution

(a) (1) Transat's planes may have been purchased used, compared with WestJet's, which may have been purchased as new planes. If this was the case, then Transat's remaining useful lives would be shorter.

(2) If we assume that the depreciable cost of the planes for each company is similar, then we would expect Transat to report a higher depreciation expense and lower profit than WestJet simply because of the shorter useful life.

(b) Transat's trademarks likely have an indefinite life. In this case, trademarks are not amortized but are tested for impairment at least annually.

(c) Impairment losses on goodwill cannot be subsequently reversed.

(d)

Ratio	Transat	WestJet	Air Canada	Industry
Return on assets	$\dfrac{\$(13,536)}{(\$1,163,301 + \$1,226,570) \div 2} = (1.1)\%$	6.7%	2.0%	2.2%
Asset turnover	$\dfrac{\$3,714,219}{(\$1,163,301 + \$1,226,570) \div 2} = 3.1 \text{ times}$	0.9 times	1.3 times	0.9 times

Transat's return on assets is negative because of the reported loss. It is interesting to note that if the impairment loss for goodwill had not occurred, Transat would report a small but positive return on assets ratio. Despite its poor return on assets ratio, Transat has a strong asset turnover ratio compared with its competitors. One possible reason for this may be the lower cost of its planes. You will recall that we speculated in (a) (1) above that Transat may be purchasing used planes while WestJet may be purchasing newer planes, which would result in a lower cost of planes for Transat compared to WestJet.

Comprehensive Do It!

Dulcimer Ltd. purchased a piece of equipment at a cost of $35,000 on June 1, 2015. The equipment was expected to have a residual value of $3,000 at the end of its four-year useful life. Dulcimer has a December 31 year end and prepares adjusting entries annually.

During its useful life, the equipment was expected to be used 10,000 hours. Anticipated annual hourly use was as follows: 1,300 hours in 2015, 2,800 hours in 2016, 3,300 hours in 2017, 1,900 hours in 2018, and 700 hours in 2019.

Instructions
(a) Prepare depreciation schedules showing the expected depreciation expense for 2015 to 2019 using the following methods: (1) straight-line, (2) diminishing-balance using double the straight-line rate, and (3) units-of-production.
(b) Prepare the journal entry to record the retirement of the equipment on June 1, 2019, assuming that the straight-line depreciation method was used and the equipment was retired at the end of its useful life for no proceeds.

Action Plan
- To calculate depreciation expense:
  - For straight-line depreciation, determine the depreciable amount (cost less residual value) and divide this by the estimated useful life in years or multiply it by one divided by the useful life in years to determine an annual percentage. For years when the machine is not used throughout the year, do not forget to multiply the annual depreciation by a ratio of months used divided by 12 months in the year.
  - For the diminishing-balance method, determine the straight-line rate by taking one divided by useful life in years and then double this rate. Multiply the rate by the carrying amount at the beginning of the period. For years when the machine is not used throughout the year, do not forget to multiply the annual depreciation by a ratio of months used divided by 12 months in the year. Make sure that you cease depreciating the machine once its carrying amount is equal to the residual value.
  - For the units-of-production method, determine the depreciation rate per unit of production (hours used) by taking the depreciable amount (cost less residual value) and dividing it by the total units that the machine is expected to produce over its useful life. Then multiply that rate by the units produced (hours used). There is no need to prorate this calculation for partial-year use because the proration effect is already reflected in the units produced in the period.

- Stop and check your work. Total depreciation expense (accumulated depreciation) for the total life of the asset should be the same for each method.
- Update any unrecorded depreciation to the date of disposal. Remove the asset's carrying amount at retirement by debiting the Accumulated Depreciation account and crediting the asset account. Compare the proceeds received, if any, to determine and record any gain or loss.

Solution to Comprehensive Do It!

(a)

(1)

				End of Year	
Year	Depreciable Amount	× Depreciation Rate	= Depreciation Expense	Accumulated Depreciation	Carrying Amount
					$35,000
2015	$32,000[a]	25%[b] × 7/12	$4,667	$ 4,667	30,333
2016	32,000	25%	8,000	12,667	22,333
2017	32,000	25%	8,000	20,667	14,333
2018	32,000	25%	8,000	28,667	6,333
2019	32,000	25% × 5/12	3,333	32,000	3,000

DULCIMER LTD.
Straight-Line Depreciation Schedule

[a] $35,000 − $3,000 = $32,000
[b] 100% ÷ 4 years = 25%

(2)

				End of Year	
Year	Carrying Amount Beginning of Year	× Depreciation Rate	= Depreciation Expense	Accumulated Depreciation	Carrying Amount
					$35,000
2015	$35,000	50%[a] × 7/12	$10,208	$10,208	24,792
2016	24,792	50%	12,396	22,604	12,396
2017	12,396	50%	6,198	28,802	6,198
2018	6,198	50%	3,099	31,901	3,099
2019	3,099	50%	99[b]	32,000	3,000

DULCIMER LTD.
Diminishing-Balance Depreciation Schedule

[a] 25% × 2
[b] Adjusted to $99 because the ending carrying amount should not be less than the expected residual value.

(3)

				End of Year	
Year	Units of Activity	× Depreciable Cost/Unit	= Depreciation Expense	Accumulated Depreciation	Carrying Amount
					$35,000
2015	1,300	$3.20[a]	$ 4,160	$ 4,160	30,840
2016	2,800	3.20	8,960	13,120	21,880
2017	3,300	3.20	10,560	23,680	11,320
2018	1,900	3.20	6,080	29,760	5,240
2019	700	3.20	2,240	32,000	3,000

DULCIMER LTD.
Units-of-Production Depreciation Schedule

[a] $35,000 − $3,000 = $32,000 ÷ 10,000 total units = $3.20/unit

(b)

| June 1, 2019 | Depreciation Expense
    Accumulated Depreciation—Equipment
      (To record depreciation for
      January 1–June 1) | 3,333 | 3,333 |
| | Accumulated Depreciation—Equipment
Loss on Disposal
    Equipment
      (To record retirement of equipment) | 32,000
3,000 | 35,000 |

the navigator

WileyPLUS

Self-Test, Brief Exercises, Exercises, Problems: Set A, and many more components are available for practice in *WileyPLUS*.

Self-Test Questions

Answers are at the end of the chapter.

Quiz Yourself

(SO 1)   1. Corrieten Ltd. purchased equipment and incurred these costs:

Invoice price	$24,000
Freight—FOB shipping point	1,000
Insurance during transit	200
Annual insurance policy	350
Training workers on equipment	280
Installation and testing	400
Total costs	$26,230

What amount should be recorded as the cost of the equipment?
(a) $24,000
(b) $24,200
(c) $25,600
(d) $25,950

(SO 1)   2. The advantages of leasing an asset under an operating lease rather than purchasing it do *not* include:
(a) reduced risk of obsolescence.
(b) an increase in total assets.
(c) 100% financing.
(d) off–balance sheet financing.

(SO 2)   3. Kant Enterprises Ltd. purchased a truck for $32,000 on July 1, 2015. The truck has an estimated residual value of $2,000, an estimated useful life of five years, and an estimated total mileage of 300,000 km. If 50,000 km are driven in 2015, what amount of depreciation expense would Kant record at December 31, 2015, assuming it uses the units-of-production method?
(a) $2,500
(b) $3,000
(c) $5,000
(d) $5,333

(SO 2)   4. Refer to the data provided for Kant Enterprises in question 3. If Kant uses the double-diminishing-balance method of depreciation, what amount of depreciation expense would be recorded at December 31, 2015?
(a) $6,000
(b) $6,400
(c) $12,000
(d) $12,800

(SO 3)   5. Oviatt Ltd. sold equipment for $10,000 cash. At the time of disposal, the equipment had a cost of $45,000 and accumulated depreciation of $30,000. Oviatt should record a:
(a) $5,000 loss on disposal
(b) $5,000 gain on disposal
(c) $15,000 loss on disposal
(d) $15,000 gain on disposal

(SO 4)   6. Pierce Inc. incurred $150,000 of development costs in its laboratory in January 2015 to develop a new product. On February 2, 2015, $20,000 was paid to register a patent related to the new product. On July 31, 2015, Pierce paid $15,000 for legal fees in a successful defence of the patent. What is the total amount that should be debited to the Patents account through July 31, 2015?
(a) $20,000
(b) $35,000
(c) $170,000
(d) $185,000

(SO 4)   7. Which of the following statements is *false*?
(a) All intangible assets should be amortized.
(b) Only intangible assets with finite lives should be amortized.
(c) Goodwill is recorded only when a business is purchased.
(d) Intangible assets subject to amortization should be amortized over the shorter of their useful lives and legal lives.

(SO 5)   8. Which of the following statements is *true*?
(a) Since intangible assets lack physical substance, they need to be disclosed only in the notes to the financial statements.
(b) Goodwill should be combined and reported with other intangible assets on the statement of financial position.
(c) Intangible assets are typically combined with property, plant, and equipment and reported in the "Property, Plant, and Equipment" section of the statement of financial position.

(d) Property, plant, and equipment; intangible assets; and goodwill should be separately reported on the statement of financial position.

(SO 6)   9. Which of the following ratios helps determine how efficiently a company uses its assets?
(a) Current ratio
(b) Profit margin
(c) Debt to total assets
(d) Asset turnover

(SO 6)   10. Campbell Corporation reported average total assets of $6.3 million, net sales of $7.6 million, and profit of $1 million. What are the company's return on assets and asset turnover ratios, respectively?
(a) 1.2% and 0.2 times
(b) 1.2% and 1.2 times
(c) 15.9% and 0.2 times
(d) 15.9% and 1.2 times

Questions

(SO 1)   1. (a) Susan Leung is uncertain about how to determine the cost of property, plant, and equipment. Explain this for her. (b) Susan is also wondering what an asset retirement cost is and how that affects the cost of property, plant, and equipment.

(SO 1)   2. Fern Inc. purchases equipment and incurs a number of expenditures before it is ready to use the equipment. Give two examples of operating expenditures and two examples of capital expenditures and explain how these expenditures on new equipment would be recorded and why.

(SO 1)   3. What are land improvements? Should the cost of clearing and grading land be recorded as a land improvement or not? Why or why not?

(SO 1)   4. Explain the difference between an operating lease and a finance lease. What accounts are recorded on the financial statements for each type of lease?

(SO 2)   5. Contrast the effects of the three depreciation methods on (1) depreciation expense, (2) profit, (3) accumulated depreciation, and (4) carrying amount in each of the following: (a) the early years of an asset's life, and (b) over the total life of the asset.

(SO 2)   6. Why is the depreciable amount (the asset's cost less residual value) used in the straight-line and units-of-production methods but not in the diminishing-balance method?

(SO 2)   7. Why must the calculation of depreciation be adjusted for any fraction of a year since the purchase when the straight-line and diminishing-balance methods are used, but no adjustment is needed when the units-of-production method is used?

(SO 2)   8. (a) What factors should a company consider when choosing among the straight-line, diminishing-balance, or units-of-production depreciation methods? (b) When choosing between the cost model or revaluation model?

(SO 2)   9. (a) How is an impairment loss calculated? Recorded? (b) How can impairment losses create problems for users in comparing the financial results of a company over multiple years?

(SO 3)   10. If equipment is sold in the middle of a fiscal year, why does depreciation have to be updated for the partial period? Doesn't the journal entry to record the sale subsequently remove the accumulated depreciation from the books anyway?

(SO 3)   11. How is a gain or loss on the sale of property, plant, or equipment calculated? Is the calculation the same for the retirement of property, plant, or equipment?

(SO 3)   12. Rashid Corporation owns a machine that is fully depreciated but is still being used. How should Rashid account for this asset and report it in the financial statements?

(SO 2, 4) 13. What are the similarities and differences between accounting for tangible and intangible assets?

(SO 4)   14. Why are intangible assets with a finite life amortized, but intangible assets with an indefinite life are not?

(SO 4)   15. Heflin Corporation has been amortizing its finite-life intangible assets over their legal lives. The company's accountant argues that this is appropriate because an intangible asset's legal life is known with certainty, but the useful life of an intangible asset is subjective. (a) Why is this not correct? (b) What impact might using the legal life instead of the useful life have on the company's financial statements?

(SO 4)   16. Two years ago, Pesowski Corp. purchased a patent for $5 million that allows the company to produce and sell a special video game controller. During the year, the company determined that Sucha Ltd. was producing and selling a similar game controller. Pesowski spent $100,000 on legal fees to successfully enforce its rights under the patent. How should Pesowski account for the legal fees and why?

(SO 4) 17. Bob Leno, a business student, is working on a case for one of his classes. The company in the case needs to raise cash to market a new product it has developed. His roommate Saul Cain, an engineering student, takes one look at the company's statement of financial position and says, "This company has an awful lot of goodwill. Why don't you recommend that they sell some of it to raise cash?" How should Bob respond to Saul?

(SO 5) 18. Explain how long-lived assets and transactions relating to them should be reported on the (a) statement of financial position, (b) income statement, and (c) statement of cash flows.

(SO 5) 19. What information about long-lived assets should be disclosed in the notes to the financial statements for a company reporting under IFRS? Under ASPE?

(SO 5) 20. Why are gains and losses on disposal of property, plant, and equipment presented in the operating section of the income statement rather than the non-operating section?

(SO 6) 21. Give an example of an industry that would be characterized by (a) a high asset turnover and low profit margin, and (b) a low asset turnover and high profit margin.

(SO 6) 22. How can the profit margin and asset turnover ratios be used to help explain the return on assets?

(SO 6) 23. In 2012, **Tim Hortons Inc.** reported net sales of $2,226 million, profit of $403 million, and average total assets of $2,244 million. In 2011, its net sales were $2,012 million, profit was $383 million, and average total assets were $2,343 million. Did the company's return on assets and asset turnover ratios improve or deteriorate in 2012.

Brief Exercises

BE9–1   These expenditures were incurred by Shumway Ltd. in purchasing land: cash price $50,000; legal fees $2,500; removal of old building $5,000; cost of clearing and grading $3,500; installation of fence $3,000. What is the cost of the land?

Determine cost.
(SO 1)

BE9–2   Basler Ltd. incurs these expenditures in purchasing a truck: invoice price $42,000; installation of a trailer hitch $1,000; one-year accident insurance policy $900; motor vehicle licence $150; painting and lettering $750. What is the cost of the truck?

Determine cost.
(SO 1)

BE9–3   Indicate whether each of the following items is an operating expenditure (O) or a capital expenditure (C). If the expenditure is neither, write NA for "not applicable" in the space provided.

Identify operating and capital expenditures.
(SO 1)

(a) _____ Repaired building roof, $1,500
(b) _____ Replaced building roof, $27,500
(c) _____ Purchased building, $480,000
(d) _____ Purchased insurance on equipment in transit, $350
(e) _____ Purchased truck, $55,000

(f) _____ Purchased oil and gas for truck, $155
(g) _____ Replaced tires on truck, $500
(h) _____ Anticipated retirement costs for plant, $500,000
(i) _____ Added new wing to building, $250,000
(j) _____ Painted interior of building, $1,500

BE9–4   Buckingham Ltd. purchases a delivery truck on January 1, 2015, at a cost of $86,000. The truck is expected to have a residual value of $6,000 at the end of its four-year useful life. Buckingham has a December 31 year end. Calculate the depreciation using the straight-line method (a) for each year of the truck's life, and (b) in total over the truck's life.

Calculate straight-line depreciation.
(SO 2)

BE9–5   Depreciation information for Buckingham Ltd. is given in BE9–4. Assuming the delivery truck was purchased on May 1 instead of January 1 and that the company records depreciation to the nearest month, calculate the depreciation expense using the straight-line method for 2015 and 2016.

Calculate partial-year straight-line depreciation.
(SO 2)

BE9–6   Depreciation information for Buckingham Ltd. is given in BE9–4. Using the diminishing-balance method and assuming the depreciation rate is equal to one time the straight-line rate, calculate the depreciation (a) for each year of the truck's life, and (b) in total over the truck's life.

Calculate diminishing-balance depreciation.
(SO 2)

BE9–7   Depreciation information for Buckingham Ltd. is given in BE9–4. Assuming the delivery truck was purchased on May 1 instead of January 1, calculate the depreciation expense using the diminishing-balance method for 2015 and 2016. Assume the depreciation rate is equal to one time the straight-line rate.

Calculate partial-year diminishing-balance depreciation.
(SO 2)

BE9–8   Speedy Taxi Service uses the units-of-production method to calculate depreciation on its taxicabs. Each cab is expected to be driven 325,000 km. Taxi 10 was purchased on March 1, 2014, for $33,000 and is expected to have a residual value of $500. Taxi 10 was driven 125,000 km in 2014 and 105,000 km in 2015. Speedy Taxi Service has a December 31 year end. Calculate the depreciation expense on Taxi 10 for 2014 and 2015.

Calculate units-of-production depreciation.
(SO 2)

Calculate carrying amount and impairment loss.
(SO 2)

BE9–9　Tibble Corporation uses straight-line depreciation, prepares adjusting entries annually, and has a December 31 year end. It purchased equipment on January 1, 2014, for $200,000. The equipment had an estimated useful life of five years and a residual value of $20,000. On December 31, 2015, the company tests for impairment and determines that the equipment's recoverable amount is $100,000. (a) Assuming annual depreciation has already been recorded at December 31, calculate the equipment's carrying amount at December 31, 2015. (b) Calculate the amount of the impairment loss, if any.

Record sale of equipment.
(SO 3)

BE9–10　Goo-Yeong Limited sells equipment on September 30, 2015, for $42,000 cash. The equipment originally cost $144,000 when purchased on January 1, 2013. It has an estimated residual value of $4,000 and a useful life of five years. Depreciation was last recorded on December 31, 2014, the company's year end. Prepare the journal entries to (a) update depreciation using the straight-line method to September 30, 2015, and (b) record the sale of the equipment.

Record retirement of equipment.
(SO 3)

BE9–11　Ruiz Ltd. retires equipment that cost $42,000. No proceeds were received. Prepare journal entries to record the transaction if accumulated depreciation is (a) $42,000, and (b) $40,000.

Record patent transactions; show statement presentation.
(SO 4, 5)

BE9–12　Surkis Corporation purchased a patent for $180,000 cash on April 2, 2015. Its legal life is 20 years and its estimated useful life is 5 years. The company's year end is December 31 and it prepares adjusting entries annually. (a) Prepare the journal entry to record the (1) purchase of the patent on April 2, 2015, and (2) amortization for the first year ended December 31, 2015. (b) Show how the patent would be reported on the statement of financial position at December 31.

Record trademark transactions.
(SO 4)

BE9–13　A company manufacturing hockey bags registered trademarks for $1,000 cash for its revolutionary RackDri hockey bags on June 1, 2015. On December 1, 2015, it paid $10,000 cash for legal costs to successfully defend its trademarks in court. (a) Prepare the journal entry to record the (1) registration of the trademarks on June 1, and (2) the legal costs on December 1. (b) Should the cost of the trademarks be amortized? Explain.

Classify long-lived assets.
(SO 5)

BE9–14　Indicate whether each of the following items should be recorded as property, plant, and equipment (PP&E) or an intangible asset (I) on the statement of financial position. If the asset does not fit either of these categories, write NA for "not applicable" in the space provided.

(a) _____ Accumulated amortization	(i) _____ Land
(b) _____ Asset retirement cost for a building	(j) _____ Land improvements
(c) _____ Assets under finance lease	(k) _____ Leasehold improvements
(d) _____ Building	(l) _____ Licence right
(e) _____ Franchise	(m) _____ Operating lease
(f) _____ Merchandise inventory	(n) _____ Patent
(g) _____ Common shares	(o) _____ Research costs
(h) _____ Impairment loss	(p) _____ Trademark

Prepare partial statement of financial position.
(SO 5)

BE9–15　**Canadian Tire Corporation, Limited** reported the following selected information about long-lived assets at December 29, 2012 (in millions):

Accumulated depreciation—buildings	$1,102.9
Accumulated depreciation—fixtures and equipment	591.4
Accumulated amortization—finite-life intangible assets	604.6
Accumulated depreciation—other property and equipment	424.2
Buildings	2,683.7
Fixtures and equipment	880.4
Goodwill	376.9
Indefinite-life intangible assets	385.0
Finite-life intangible assets	932.6
Land	744.2
Other property and equipment	1,153.7

Prepare the long-lived assets section of the statement of financial position for Canadian Tire.

Compare ratios.
(SO 6)

BE9–16　**Coca-Cola** and **Pepsi** reported the following selected ratios:

	Coke	Pepsi
Return on assets	10.9%	8.4%
Asset turnover	0.6 times	0.9 times

(a) Identify which company has the better (1) return on assets ratio and (2) asset turnover ratio. (b) Based on these two ratios, which company would you expect to have the better profit margin?

Calculate and evaluate ratios.
(SO 6)

BE9–17　**Gildan Activewear Inc.** reported the following selected financial information (all in U.S. $ millions): net sales of $1,948 in 2012, $1,726 in 2011, and $1,311 in 2010. The company also reported a profit of $148 in 2012, $234 in 2011, and $198 in 2010. Assets at the end of 2012 were $1,896; at the end of 2011, $1,858; and at the end of 2010, $1,335. (a) Calculate Gildan's (1) asset turnover, (2) profit margin, and (3) return on assets for 2012 and 2011. (b) Comment on whether the return on assets changed primarily due to a changing asset turnover or a changing profit margin.

Exercises

E9–1 The following expenditures relating to property, plant, and equipment were made by Bachinski Ltd.:

1. Paid $600,000 for a plant site.
2. Paid $8,000 of legal fees on the purchase of the plant site.
3. Paid $33,000 to demolish an old building on the plant site; residual materials were sold for $5,000.
4. Paid $35,000 for paving the parking lot on the plant site.
5. Paid $37,600 in architect fees for the design of the new plant.
6. Promised to pay $50,000 in restoration costs when the company is finished using the plant site.
7. Paid $90,000 for a new delivery truck.
8. Paid $5,000 to have the company name and advertising slogan painted on the new truck.
9. Paid a $1,250 motor vehicle licence fee on the new truck.
10. Paid $3,800 for a one-year accident insurance policy on the new truck.

Classify expenditures.
(SO 1)

Instructions
(a) Explain what types of expenditures should be included in determining the cost of property, plant, and equipment.
(b) List the numbers of the above transactions, and beside each number write the account title that the expenditure should be debited to.

E9–2 Hohnberger Enterprises purchased equipment on March 15, 2015, for $75,000. The company also paid the following amounts: $500 for freight charges; $200 for insurance while the equipment was in transit; $1,800 for a one-year insurance policy; $2,100 to train employees to use the new equipment; and $2,800 for testing and installation. The equipment was ready for use on April 1, but the company did not start using it until May 1.

Hohnberger has estimated the equipment will have a 10-year useful life with no residual value. It expects to consume the equipment's future economic benefits evenly over the useful life. The company has a December 31 year end.

Calculate cost and depreciation; recommend method.
(SO 1, 2)

Instructions
(a) Calculate the cost of the equipment.
(b) When should the company begin depreciating the equipment: March 15, April 1, or May 1? Why?
(c) Which depreciation method should the company use? Why?
(d) Using the method chosen in part (c), calculate the depreciation on the equipment for 2015.

E9–3 Cirrus Ltd. purchased a new machine on April 4, 2012, at a cost of $172,000. The company estimated that the machine would have a residual value of $16,000. The machine is expected to be used for 10,000 working hours during its four-year life. Actual machine usage was 1,500 hours in 2012; 2,200 hours in 2013; 2,300 hours in 2014; 2,100 hours in 2015; and 1,900 hours in 2016. Cirrus has a December 31 year end.

Calculate and compare depreciation under different methods.
(SO 2)

Instructions
(a) Calculate depreciation for the machine under each of the following methods: (1) straight-line, (2) diminishing-balance using double the straight-line rate, and (3) units-of-production.
(b) Which method results in the highest depreciation expense over the life of the asset? Highest profit? Highest cash flow?

E9–4 At the beginning of 2015, Lindy Weink, the controller of Lafrenière Inc., reviewed the expected useful life and residual value of two of the company's machines and proposed changes as follows:

Calculate straight-line depreciation; discuss revision of estimate.
(SO 2)

| Machine | Date Acquired | Cost | Useful Life (in years) | | Residual Value | |
			Original	Proposed	Original	Proposed
#1	Jan. 1, 2005	$800,000	20	25	$40,000	$62,000
#2	Jan. 1, 2013	120,000	5	4	5,000	3,600

Instructions
(a) Calculate the annual depreciation for each asset using the straight-line method and the original useful life and residual value.
(b) Calculate the accumulated depreciation and carrying amount of each asset on December 31, 2014.
(c) If the company accepts Lindy's proposed changes in useful life and residual value, will depreciation expense for each asset in 2015 be higher or lower than depreciation expense in 2014? Explain.

E9–5 Shown below are the T accounts relating to equipment that was purchased for cash by a company on the first day of the current year. The equipment was depreciated on a straight-line basis with an estimated useful life of 10 years and a residual value of $100. Part of the equipment was sold on the last day of the current year for cash proceeds while the remaining equipment that was not sold became impaired.

Reconstruct equipment transactions.
(SO 2, 3)

Cash			Equipment			Accumulated Depreciation—Equipment		
	Jan. 1 (a)		Jan. 1 1,100				Dec. 31	100
Dec. 31 450				Dec. 31	440	Dec. 31 40	31	55

Depreciation Expense		Gain on Disposal		Impairment Loss	
Dec. 31 (b)		Dec. 31 (c)		Dec. 31 (d)	

Instructions

Reconstruct the journal entries to record the following and derive the missing amounts:
(a) Purchase of equipment on January 1. What was the cash paid?
(b) Depreciation recorded on December 31. What was the depreciation expense?
(c) Sale of part of the equipment on December 31. What was the gain on disposal?
(d) Impairment loss on the remaining equipment on December 31. What was the impairment loss?

Determine effect of depreciation method over life of asset.
(SO 2, 3)

E9–6   Rahim Corporation purchased a boardroom table for $5,000. The company planned to keep it for four years, after which it was expected to be sold for $500.

Instructions

(a) Calculate the depreciation expense for each of the first three years under (1) the straight-line method, and (2) the double-diminishing-balance method.
(b) Assuming Rahim sold the table for $1,225 at the end of the third year, calculate the gain or loss on disposal under each depreciation method.
(c) Determine the impact on profit (total depreciation of the table plus any loss on disposal or less any gain on disposal) of each method over the entire three-year period.

Record disposal of equipment.
(SO 3)

E9–7   Presented here are selected transactions for Spector Limited for 2015. Spector uses straight-line depreciation and records adjusting entries annually.

Jan.   1   Sold a delivery truck for $18,000 cash. The truck cost $62,000 when it was purchased on January 1, 2012, and was depreciated based on a four-year useful life with a $6,000 residual value.

Sept.   1   Sold computers that were purchased on January 1, 2013. They cost $10,980 and had a useful life of three years with no residual value. The computers were sold for $500 cash.

Dec.   30   Retired equipment that was purchased on January 1, 2006. The equipment cost $150,000 and had a useful life of 10 years with no residual value. No proceeds were received.

Instructions

Record the above transactions.

Apply accounting concepts.
(SO 2, 4)

E9–8   A co-op student, Toni Johnston, encountered the following situations at Chin Corporation, a publicly traded company:

1. Toni learned that Chin is depreciating its buildings and equipment, but not its land. She could not understand why land was omitted, so she prepared journal entries to depreciate all the company's property, plant, and equipment, including land, for the current year.
2. Toni determined that Chin's amortization policy on its intangible assets was wrong. The company was amortizing its patents but not its goodwill. She fixed that for the current year by adding goodwill to her adjusting entry for amortization. She told a fellow student that she felt she had improved the consistency of the company's accounting policies by making these changes.
3. Chin has a building still in use that has a zero carrying amount but a substantial fair value. Toni felt that this practice did not benefit the company's users and so she wrote the building up to its fair value. After all, she reasoned, you can write down assets if fair values are lower. Writing them up if fair value is higher is yet another example of the improved consistency that her employment has brought to the company's accounting practices.

Instructions

Explain whether or not the accounting treatment in each of the above situations is appropriate. If not, explain what the appropriate accounting treatment should be.

Record intangible asset transactions.
(SO 4)

E9–9   Amarista Corporation has the following selected transactions during the year ended December 31, 2015:

Jan.   1   Purchased a copyright for $120,000 cash. The copyright has a useful life of six years and a remaining legal life of 30 years.

Mar.   1   Acquired a franchise with a contract period of nine years for $540,000; the expiration date is March 1, 2024. Paid cash of $40,000 and borrowed the remainder from the bank.

Sept.   1   Purchased a trademark for $75,000 cash. As the purchase was being finalized, spent $35,000 cash in legal fees to successfully defend the trademark in court.

Instructions

(a) Prepare the entries to record the above transactions.

(b) Prepare the entries to record any amortization at December 31.

E9–10   Collins Ltd. has these transactions related to intangible assets and goodwill in 2015, its first year of operations:

Record intangible asset transactions; show statement presentation.
(SO 4, 5)

Jan.	2	Purchased a patent with an estimated useful life of five years and a legal life of 20 years for $40,000.
Apr.	1	Acquired another company and recorded goodwill of $300,000 as part of the purchase.
July	1	Acquired a franchise for $250,000. The franchise agreement is renewable and not expected to expire.
Sept.	1	Incurred research costs of $150,000.
	30	Incurred development costs of $50,000. A marketable product has been identified and production will commence in the near future.
Dec.	31	Recorded annual amortization.
	31	Tested the intangible assets for impairment. Recoverable amounts exceeded carrying amounts in all cases. Also tested goodwill and determined that it had a recoverable amount of $270,000.

Instructions

(a) Prepare the entries to record the above transactions. Assume all costs incurred during January through September were incurred for cash.

(b) Show the presentation of the intangible assets and goodwill on the statement of financial position at December 31.

E9–11   **Reitmans (Canada) Limited** reported the following selected information as at February 2, 2013 (in thousands):

Classify long-lived accounts; prepare partial statement of financial position.
(SO 5)

Accumulated depreciation—buildings	$ 22,467
Accumulated depreciation—fixtures and equipment	85,936
Accumulated depreciation—leasehold improvements	101,961
Accumulated amortization—software	10,191
Amortization expense	5,080
Buildings	53,149
Depreciation expense	53,047
Fixtures and equipment	166,756
Goodwill	42,426
Land	5,860
Impairment loss	2,128
Leasehold improvements	189,730
Operating leases	494,752
Reversal of impairment loss	600
Software (intangible assets)	28,916
Trademarks	499

Instructions

(a) Identify in which financial statement (statement of financial position, income statement, or neither) and which section of the statement each of the above items should be reported.

(b) Prepare the long-lived assets section of the statement of financial position.

E9–12   The following selected ratios have been chosen for two companies in different industries:

Compare ratios.
(SO 6)

	Return on Assets	Asset Turnover	Profit Margin
Company A	6.6%	3.5 times	1.9%
Company B	5.7%	0.8 times	7.2%

One company is Costco Wholesale Corporation in the retail industry; the other is Suncor Energy Inc. in the oil and gas industry.

Instructions

Identify whether Company A or Company B is likely Costco, operating in the retail industry. Explain.

E9–13   Ajax Limited reported the following information (in millions) at December 31, 2015: net sales $14,000; profit $550; total assets at December 31, 2015, $7,200; and total assets at December 31, 2014, $6,800.

Calculate and evaluate ratios.
(SO 6)

Instructions

(a) Calculate the following ratios for the year: (1) return on assets, (2) asset turnover, and (3) profit margin.

(b) By showing the appropriate calculation (using unrounded numbers), prove mathematically how the profit margin and asset turnover work together to explain the return on assets.

(c) On average, the ratio values for Ajax's competitors are return on assets 4.5%, asset turnover 1.5 times, and profit margin 3.0%. Compare these with those of Ajax and determine if Ajax is performing better than the industry.

Problems: Set A

Classify expenditures.
(SO 1)

P9–1A The transactions that follow are expenditures related to property, plant, and equipment:

1. Operator controls on equipment were replaced for $7,000, because the original control devices were not adequate.
2. A total of $4,600 was spent for decorative landscaping (planting flowers and shrubs, etc.).
3. A new air conditioning system for the office was purchased for $16,000.
4. Windows broken in a labour dispute were replaced for $2,400.
5. A fee of $1,500 was paid for adjusting and testing new machinery before its use.
6. Machinery damaged by a forklift was repaired for $5,000.
7. The transmission in a delivery truck was repaired for $2,500.
8. Expenditures totalling $3,000 were incurred to repaint the exterior of the building.
9. Paid $20,000 to convert the company's delivery vehicles from gasoline to propane.
10. Paid $10,000 to convert the company's light bulbs to energy efficient bulbs.

Instructions
For each of the transactions listed above, indicate the title of the account that you think should be debited in recording the transaction. Briefly explain your reasoning.

Determine cost; record
property transactions.
(SO 1, 2)

P9–2A For the year ended December 31, 2015, Westlake Ltd. had the following transactions related to the purchase of property. Assume all transactions are for cash unless otherwise stated.

Feb.	7	Purchased real estate for $550,000, paying $150,000 cash and signing a mortgage payable for the balance. The site had an old building on it and the fair values of the land and building were $500,000 and $50,000, respectively. The old building will be demolished and a new apartment building will be constructed on the site.
	9	Paid legal fees of $11,000 on the real estate purchase of February 7.
	15	Paid $30,000 to demolish the old building and make the land ready for the construction of the apartment building.
	17	Received $8,000 from the sale of material from the demolished building.
	28	Paid $2,000 to grade the land in preparation for the construction of the apartment building.
Mar.	2	Paid architect fees of $36,000 to design the apartment building.
July	2	The full cost for construction of the apartment building was $1.3 million. Paid $340,000 cash and signed a bank loan payable for the balance.
	3	Purchased a one-year insurance policy on the finished building for $5,000.
Aug.	29	Paid $24,000 for the paving of sidewalks and a parking lot for the building.

Instructions
(a) Record the above transactions.
(b) Determine the cost of the land, land improvements, and building that will appear on Westlake's December 31 statement of financial position.
(c) When would depreciation begin on the items recorded above?

Determine cost;
calculate depreciation
under different
methods.
(SO 1, 2)

P9–3A Mazlin Limited purchased a machine on account on April 2, 2015, at an invoice price of $360,000. On April 4, it paid $2,000 for delivery of the machine. A one-year, $4,000 insurance policy on the machine was purchased on April 5. On April 18, Mazlin paid $8,000 for installation and testing of the machine. The machine was ready for use on April 30.
  Mazlin estimates the machine's useful life will be five years with a residual value of $80,000. Mazlin has a December 31 year end.

Instructions
(a) Determine the cost of the machine.
(b) Calculate the annual depreciation and total depreciation over the asset's life using (1) the straight-line method and (2) the double-diminishing-balance method. Which method causes profit to be lower in the early years of the asset's life?
(c) Assume instead that, when Mazlin purchased the machine, there was no residual value and the company had a legal obligation to ensure that the machine would be recycled at the end of its useful life. The cost of the recycling will be significant. Would this have an impact on the answers to parts (a) and (b) above? Explain (calculations are not required).

Calculate and compare
depreciation under
different methods.
(SO 2)

P9–4A Valmont Limited purchased equipment on March 27, 2015, at a cost of $122,000. Management is contemplating the merits of using the diminishing-balance or units-of-production method of depreciation instead of the straight-line method, which it currently uses for other equipment. The new equipment has an estimated residual value of $2,000 and an estimated useful life of either four years or 40,000 units. Demand for the products produced by the equipment is sporadic so the equipment will be used more in some years than in others. Assume the equipment produces the following number of units each year: 7,400 units in 2015; 10,200 units in 2016; 9,900 units in 2017; 10,000 units in 2018; and 2,500 units in 2019. Valmont has a December 31 year end.

Instructions

(a) Prepare separate depreciation schedules for the life of the equipment using (1) the straight-line method, (2) the double-diminishing-balance method, and (3) the units-of-production method.
(b) Compare the total depreciation expense and accumulated depreciation under each of the three methods over the life of the equipment.
(c) How does each method of depreciation affect the company's cash flows?
(d) Which method do you recommend? Why?

P9–5A On January 1, 2013, Penaji Corporation acquired equipment costing $65,000. It was estimated at that time that the equipment would have a useful life of eight years and a residual value of $3,000. The straight-line method of depreciation is used by the company for its equipment, and its year end is December 31.

Calculate depreciation; discuss revision of estimate.
(SO 2)

At the beginning of 2015 (the beginning of the third year of the equipment's life), the company's engineers reconsidered their expectations. They estimated that the equipment's useful life would more likely be six years in total, instead of the previously estimated eight years.

Instructions

(a) Calculate the equipment's accumulated depreciation and carrying amount at the beginning of 2015 immediately before the change in useful life.
(b) Would you expect Penaji's depreciation expense to increase or decrease in 2015 after the change in useful life? Why?
(c) Should the company treat the change in useful life retroactively or only for current and future periods? Explain.
(d) If Penaji had *not* revised the equipment's remaining useful life at the beginning of 2015, what would its total depreciation expense have been over the equipment's life? What would have been the accumulated depreciation and carrying amount at the end of the equipment's useful life?
(e) Would you expect the company's total depreciation expense to change after the useful life has been revised? Would there be changes to the accumulated depreciation and carrying amount at the end of the equipment's useful life?

P9–6A Altona Limited purchased delivery equipment on March 1, 2013, for $130,000 cash. At that time, the equipment was estimated to have a useful life of five years and a residual value of $10,000. The equipment was disposed of on September 30, 2015. Altona uses the diminishing-balance method at one time the straight-line depreciation rate, has an August 31 year end, and makes adjusting entries annually.

Record acquisition, depreciation, and disposal of equipment.
(SO 2, 3)

Instructions

(a) Record the acquisition of equipment on March 1, 2013.
(b) Record depreciation at August 31, 2013, 2014, and 2015.
(c) Record the disposal of the equipment on September 30, 2015, under each of the following independent assumptions:
   1. It was sold for $60,000.
   2. It was sold for $80,000.
   3. It was retired for no proceeds.

P9–7A Yukon Productions Corp. purchased equipment on March 1, 2015, for $70,000. The company estimated the equipment would have a useful life of three years and produce 12,000 units, with a residual value of $10,000. During 2015, the equipment produced 4,900 units. On November 30, 2016, the machine was sold for $18,000 and had produced 5,600 units that year.

Record and determine effect of depreciation method over life of asset.
(SO 2, 3)

Instructions

(a) Record all the necessary journal entries for the years ended December 31, 2015 and 2016, using the following depreciation methods: (1) straight-line, (2) single-diminishing-balance, and (3) units-of-production.
(b) Complete the following schedule for each method of depreciation and compare the total expense over the two-year period.

	Straight-Line	Diminishing-Balance	Units-of-Production
Depreciation expense			
2015			
2016			
Total depreciation expense for two years			
+ Loss (or − gain) on disposal			
= Net expense for two years			

P9–8A At January 1, 2015, Youngstown Limited reported the following property, plant, and equipment accounts:

Record property, plant, and equipment transactions; prepare partial statement of financial position.
(SO 2, 3, 5)

Accumulated depreciation—buildings	$ 62,200,000
Accumulated depreciation—equipment	54,000,000
Buildings	97,400,000
Equipment	150,000,000
Land	20,000,000

The company uses straight-line depreciation for buildings and equipment, its year end is December 31, and it makes adjusting entries annually. The buildings are estimated to have a 40-year useful life and no residual value; the equipment is estimated to have a 10-year useful life and no residual value.

During 2015, the following selected transactions occurred:

Apr.   1   Purchased land for $4.4 million. Paid $1.1 million cash and issued a three-year, 6% mortgage payable for the balance. Interest on the mortgage is payable annually each April 1.

May   1   Sold equipment for $300,000 cash. The equipment cost $2.8 million when originally purchased on January 1, 2007.

June   1   Sold land for $3.6 million. Received $900,000 cash and accepted a three-year, 5% note for the balance. The land cost $1.4 million when purchased on June 1, 2009. Interest on the note is due annually each June 1.

July   1   Purchased equipment for $2.2 million cash.

Dec. 31   Retired equipment that cost $1 million when purchased on December 31, 2005. No proceeds were received.

31   Tested land for impairment and found that its recoverable value was $20 million.

Instructions

(a) Record the above transactions.

(b) Record any adjusting entries required at December 31.

(c) Prepare the property, plant, and equipment section of the company's statement of financial position at December 31.

Identify intangible assets and goodwill.
(SO 4)

P9–9A   The following is a list of items that might or might not be classified as intangible assets and goodwill:

1. Goodwill recorded in the purchase of a business
2. Equipment acquired using a finance lease
3. Cost of purchasing a franchise
4. Cost of purchasing a patent
5. Legal costs incurred to successfully defend a patent (see item 4)
6. Goodwill generated internally
7. Aircraft acquired using an operating lease
8. Cost of purchasing a trademark
9. Legal costs incurred to unsuccessfully defend a trademark (see item 8)
10. Research costs incurred to identify a cure for cancer

Instructions

(a) Identify which of the above items would be reported as intangible assets and goodwill on the statement of financial position.

(b) For those items in part (a) reported as intangible assets and goodwill, identify the specific account title that would be used to record the asset.

(c) For those items in part (a) reported as intangible assets and goodwill, identify which assets would likely be amortized.

(d) For any of the above items that are not intangible assets or goodwill, identify the specific account title, financial statement, and classification under which it would be reported. If it would not be reported on any financial statement, state so.

Record intangible asset transactions; prepare partial statement of financial position.
(SO 4, 5)

P9–10A   The intangible assets and goodwill reported by Ghani Corporation at December 31, 2014, follow:

Copyrights	$36,000	
Less: Accumulated amortization	18,000	$ 18,000
Trademarks		54,000
Goodwill		125,000
Total		$197,000

A copyright (#1) was acquired on January 1, 2013, and has a useful life of four years. The trademarks were acquired on January 1, 2011, and are expected to have an indefinite life. The company has a December 31 year end and prepares adjusting journal entries annually.

The following cash transactions may have affected intangible assets and goodwill during 2015:

Jan.   5   Paid $7,000 in legal costs to successfully defend the trademarks against infringement by another company.

July   1   Developed a new product, incurring $210,000 in research and $50,000 in development costs with probable future benefits. The product is expected to have a useful life of 20 years.

Sept.   1   Paid $60,000 to a popular hockey player to appear in commercials advertising the company's products. The commercials will air in early September.

Oct.   1   Acquired another copyright (#2) for $180,000. The new copyright has a useful life of four years.

Dec. 31   Determined the recoverable amount of the goodwill to be $90,000. There was no indication that the copyrights or trademarks were impaired.

Instructions

(a) Prepare journal entries to record the transactions.

(b) Prepare any adjusting journal entries required at December 31.

(c) Show the presentation of the intangible assets and goodwill on the statement of financial position at December 31, 2015.

P9–11A **The Second Cup Limited** and **Starbucks Corporation** reported the following information in 2012:

Calculate and evaluate ratios.
(SO 4, 6)

	Second Cup (in CAD millions)	Starbucks (in USD millions)
Total assets, 2012	$ 88.7	$ 8,219.2
Total assets, 2011	105.6	7,360.4
Revenue, 2012	26.3	13,299.5
Profit (loss), 2012	(9.4)	1,383.8

Industry averages were as follows: profit margin, 7.7%; asset turnover, 1.1 times; and return on assets, 8.4%.

Instructions

(a) For each company, calculate the (1) profit margin, (2) asset turnover, and (3) return on assets ratios for 2012.

(b) Second Cup reported an impairment loss for goodwill and trademarks of $15.3 million on its 2012 income statement. Had this impairment loss not occurred, it would have reported a profit of $5.9 million and total assets, 2012, of $104 million. Recalculate the profit margin, asset turnover and return on assets ratios for Second Cup, assuming there was no impairment loss. Starbucks did not report any impairment losses in 2012.

(c) Which ratios—those calculated for Second Cup in part (a) or in part (b)—should be used for comparison with Starbucks? Using your chosen ratios, comment on how effectively each company is using its assets to generate sales and produce profit.

P9–12A Delicious Limited competes in the fast food industry with Scrumptious Limited. Delicious embarked on a major expansion in 2015, borrowing a large amount of money and acquiring a small competitor. The acquisition doubled the number of restaurants that Delicious has. Scrumptious, on the other hand, took a more conservative approach and did not buy any new assets, focusing instead on a strategy of making existing operations more efficient.

Calculate and evaluate ratios.
(SO 6)

Data for the two companies are provided below in thousands of dollars:

	2015	2014	2013
Delicious			
Total assets	$2,000	$1,100	$1,000
Net sales	3,100	1,500	1,600
Profit	350	150	140
Scrumptious			
Total assets	800	900	1,000
Net sales	1,900	1,700	2,000
Profit	180	200	210

Instructions

(a) Calculate the (1) profit margin, (2) asset turnover, and (3) return on asset ratios for each company in 2014 and 2015.

(b) Provide an explanation for the year-over-year changes in the ratios calculated in part (a).

Problems: Set B

P9–1B The following expenditures are for a forklift:

Classify expenditures.
(SO 1)

1. Rebuilding of the diesel engine, $10,000
2. New tires, $2,000
3. New safety cab, $5,000
4. Replacement of the windshield, $800
5. Training a new operator, $1,600
6. New paint job, $2,000
7. One-year accident insurance policy, $1,110
8. Payment to an operator to reorganize where items were stored in the warehouse to increase efficiency, $2,400.
9. Added air conditioning for the operator's comfort, $2,000.
10. Completed annual maintenance inspection, $500.

Instructions

For each of the transactions listed above, indicate the title of the account that you think should be debited in recording the transaction. Briefly explain your reasoning.

Determine cost; record property transactions.
(SO 1, 2)

P9–2B   For the year ended December 31, 2015, Kadmen Ltd. incurred the following transactions related to the purchase of a property. Assume all transactions are for cash unless otherwise stated.

Jan.	22	Purchased real estate for a future plant site for $440,000, paying $110,000 cash and signing a mortgage payable for the balance. There was an old building on the site and the fair values of the land and building were $340,000 and $100,000, respectively. The old building will be demolished and a new plant will be constructed on the site.
	24	Paid legal fees of $9,000 on the real estate purchase of January 22.
	31	Paid $50,000 to demolish the old building to make room for the new plant.
Feb.	13	Graded and filled the land at a cost of $16,000 in preparation for the construction.
	28	Received $15,000 from the sale of material from the demolished building.
Mar.	14	Paid $68,000 in architect fees for the building plans.
Apr.	22	Paid excavation costs for the new building of $34,000.
June	15	Received a bill from the building contractor for half of the cost of the new building, $600,000. Paid $150,000 cash and signed a bank loan payable for the balance.
Sept.	29	Received a bill for the remaining $600,000 owed to the building contractor for the completion of the construction of the new building. Paid $200,000 cash and signed a bank loan payable for the balance.
Oct.	1	Paved the parking lots, driveways, and sidewalks for $84,000.

Instructions

(a) Record the above transactions.
(b) Determine the cost of the land, land improvements, and building that will appear on Kadmen's December 31 statement of financial position.
(c) When would depreciation begin on the items recorded above?

Determine cost; calculate depreciation under different methods.
(SO 1, 2)

P9–3B   Mouskori Limited purchased a machine on September 3, 2015, at a cash price of $187,800. On September 4, it paid $1,200 for delivery of the machine. A one-year, $1,950 insurance policy on the machine was purchased on September 6. On September 20, Mouskori paid $7,000 for installation and testing of the machine. The machine was ready for use on September 30.

Mouskori estimates the machine's useful life will be four years, or 40,000 units, with no residual value. Assume the equipment produces the following number of units each year: 2,500 units in 2015; 10,300 units in 2016; 9,900 units in 2017; 8,800 units in 2018; and 8,500 units in 2019. Mouskori has a December 31 year end.

Instructions

(a) Determine the cost of the machine.
(b) Calculate the annual depreciation and the total depreciation over the asset's life using (1) straight-line depreciation, (2) double-diminishing-balance depreciation, and (3) units-of-production depreciation. Which method causes profit to be lower in the early years of the asset's life?
(c) Assume instead that, when Mouskori Corporation purchased the machine, there was no residual value and the company had a legal obligation to ensure that the machine would be recycled at the end of its useful life. The cost of this recycling will be significant. Would this have an impact on the answers to parts (a) and (b) above? Explain (calculations are not required).

Calculate and compare depreciation under different methods.
(SO 2)

P9–4B   Fast Arrow Ltd. purchased a new bus on October 3, 2015, at a total cost of $330,000. Management is contemplating the merits of using the diminishing-balance or units-of-production methods of depreciation instead of the straight-line method, which it currently uses for its other buses. The new bus has an estimated residual value of $30,000, and an estimated useful life of either four years or 600,000 km. Use of the bus will be sporadic so it could be much higher in some years than in other years. Assume the new bus is driven as follows: 15,000 km in 2015; 200,000 km in 2016; 125,000 km in 2017; 190,000 km in 2018; and 70,000 km in 2019. Fast Arrow has an October 31 year end.

Instructions

(a) Prepare separate depreciation schedules for the life of the bus using (1) the straight-line method, (2) the double-diminishing-balance method, and (3) the units-of-production method.
(b) Compare the total depreciation expense and accumulated depreciation under each of the three methods over the life of the bus.
(c) How does each method of depreciation affect the company's cash flows?
(d) Which method do you recommend? Why?

P9-5B On January 1, 2013, Bérubé Ltée acquired equipment costing $60,000. It was estimated at that time that the equipment would have a useful life of five years and a residual value of $4,500. The straight-line method of depreciation is used by Bérubé for its equipment, and its year end is December 31.

Calculate depreciation; discuss revision of estimate.
(SO 2)

At the beginning of 2015 (the beginning of the third year of the equipment's life), the company's engineers reconsidered their expectations. They estimated that the equipment's useful life would more likely be seven years in total, instead of the previously estimated five years.

Instructions

(a) Calculate the equipment's accumulated depreciation and carrying amount at the beginning of 2015, immediately before the change in useful life.
(b) Would you expect the company's depreciation expense to increase or decrease in 2015 after the change in useful life? Why?
(c) Should Bérubé treat the change in the useful life retroactively or only for current and future periods? Explain.
(d) If the company had *not* revised the equipment's remaining useful life at the beginning of 2015, what would its total depreciation expense have been over the equipment's life? What would have been the accumulated depreciation and carrying amount at the end of the equipment's useful life?
(e) Would you expect Bérubé's total depreciation expense to change after the useful life has been revised? Would there be changes to the accumulated depreciation and carrying amount at the end of the equipment's useful life?

P9-6B Balmoral Limited purchased equipment on January 1, 2013, for $170,000 on account. At that time, the equipment was estimated to have a useful life of five years and a $2,000 residual value. The equipment was disposed of on June 1, 2015, when the company relocated to new premises. Balmoral uses the diminishing-balance method at one time the straight-line depreciation rate, has a September 30 year end, and make adjusting entries annually.

Record acquisition, depreciation, and disposal of equipment.
(SO 2, 3)

Instructions

(a) Record the acquisition of the equipment on January 1, 2013.
(b) Record the depreciation at September 30, 2013 and 2014.
(c) Record the disposal of the equipment on June 2, 2015, under each of the following independent assumptions:
   1. It was sold for $105,000.
   2. It was sold for $80,000.
   3. It was retired for no proceeds.

P9-7B PEI Productions Ltd. purchased equipment on February 1, 2015, for $50,000. The company estimated the equipment would have a useful life of three years and would produce 10,000 units, with a residual value of $10,000. During 2015, the equipment produced 4,000 units. On October 31, 2016, the machine was sold for $12,000; it had produced 5,000 units that year.

Record and determine effect of depreciation method over life of asset.
(SO 2, 3)

Instructions

(a) Record all the necessary entries for the years ended December 31, 2015 and 2016, for the following depreciation methods: (1) straight-line, (2) single-diminishing-balance, and (3) units-of-production.
(b) Complete the following schedule for each method of depreciation and compare the total expense over the two-year period.

	Straight-Line	Diminishing-Balance	Units-of-Production
Depreciation expense			
2015			
2016			
Total depreciation expense for two years			
+ Loss (or − gain) on disposal			
= Net expense for two years			

P9-8B At January 1, 2015, Hammersmith Limited reported the following property, plant, and equipment accounts:

Record property, plant, and equipment transactions; prepare partial statement of financial position.
(SO 2, 3, 5)

Accumulated depreciation—buildings	$24,200,000
Accumulated depreciation—equipment	30,000,000
Buildings	57,000,000
Equipment	96,000,000
Land	8,000,000

The company uses straight-line depreciation for buildings and equipment, its year end is December 31, and it makes adjusting entries annually. The buildings are estimated to have a 40-year life and no residual value; the equipment is estimated to have a 10-year useful life and no residual value.

During 2015, the following selected transactions occurred:

Apr. 1	Purchased land for $3.8 million. Paid $950,000 cash and issued a 10-year, 6% mortgage payable for the balance. Interest is payable at maturity.
May 1	Sold equipment for $700,000 cash. The equipment cost $1.5 million when it was originally purchased on January 1, 2011.
June 1	Sold land for $2.4 million. Received $760,000 cash and accepted a 6% note for the balance. The note is due at maturity. The land cost $600,000 when purchased on June 1, 2005.
July 1	Purchased equipment for $2 million on account, terms n/60.
Sept. 2	Paid amount owing on account for purchase of equipment on July 1.
Dec. 31	Retired equipment that cost $940,000 when purchased on December 31, 2005. No proceeds were received.
31	Tested land for impairment and found that its recoverable value was $11 million.

Instructions

(a) Record the above transactions.

(b) Record any adjusting entries required at December 31.

(c) Prepare the property, plant, and equipment section of the company's statement of financial position at December 31.

Identify intangible assets and goodwill.
(SO 4)

P9–9B   The following is a list of items that might or might not be classified as intangible assets and goodwill:

1. Goodwill recorded in the purchase of a business
2. Equipment acquired using a finance lease
3. Cost of purchasing a five-year software licensing agreement
4. Cost of purchasing a patent
5. Legal costs incurred to unsuccessfully defend a patent (see item 4)
6. Goodwill generated internally
7. Vehicles acquired using an operating lease
8. Cost of registering a trade name
9. Legal costs incurred to successfully defend a trade name (see item 8)
10. Research costs incurred to identify a cure for AIDS

Instructions

(a) Identify which of the above items would be reported as intangible assets and goodwill on the statement of financial position.

(b) For those items in part (a) reported as intangible assets and goodwill, identify the specific account title that would be used to record the asset.

(c) For those items in part (a) reported as intangible assets and goodwill, identify which assets would likely be amortized.

(d) For any of the above items that are not intangible assets or goodwill, identify the specific account title, financial statement, and classification under which it would be reported. If it would not be reported on any financial statement, state so.

Record intangible asset transactions; prepare partial statement of financial position.
(SO 4, 5)

P9–10B   The intangible assets and goodwill reported by Ip Corp. at December 31, 2014, follow:

Patents	$70,000	
Less: Accumulated amortization	14,000	$ 56,000
Copyrights	$48,000	
Less: Accumulated amortization	28,800	19,200
Goodwill		210,000
Total		$285,200

The patents were acquired in January 2013 and have a useful life of 10 years. A copyright (#1) was acquired in January 2010 and also has a useful life of 10 years. The company has a December 31 year end and prepares adjusting journal entries annually. The following cash transactions may have affected intangible assets and goodwill during 2015:

Jan. 2	Paid $22,500 in legal costs to successfully defend the patents against infringement by another company. Determined that the revised annual amortization for the patents will be $9,812.
July 1	Developed a new product, incurring $220,000 in research costs and $60,000 in development costs with probable future benefits. The useful life of the new product is equal to 20 years.
Sept. 1	Paid $11,000 to an Olympic rower to appear in commercials advertising the company's products. The commercials will air in September.
Oct. 1	Acquired a second copyright for $16,000. Copyright #2 has a useful life of five years.
Dec. 31	Determined the recoverable amount of the goodwill to be $175,000. There was no indication that the patents or copyrights were impaired.

It is not necessary to prepare an adjusting entry to recognize the current maturities of non-current debt and to have a separate account for the current maturities of non-current debt (although some companies do). We simply recognize the current portion when the statement of financial position is prepared.

PROVISIONS AND CONTINGENT LIABILITIES

Liabilities can be said to be certain (definitely determinable) or uncertain. Liabilities with a known payee, due date, and amount payable are *certain liabilities*. Examples of these include accounts payable, sales tax payable, property tax payable, salaries payable, notes payable, and the other types of liabilities we have covered so far in this section.

Liabilities that are uncertain are those for which we may not know who we owe, when we owe, and/or how much we owe. Such *uncertain liabilities* are known as provisions or contingent liabilities. **Provisions** are defined as liabilities of uncertain timing or amount; however, there is no uncertainty about the fact that a liability will be recorded, only that its value and settlement date are uncertain. A provision has three characteristics: a present obligation that exists as a result of a past event, a probable outflow of resources to settle the obligation, and an ability to estimate the amount of this obligation. An example of a provision is a product warranty. A company knows it will incur an expense for returned products for repair or refund under warranty but it doesn't know exactly when or what it will cost. Provisions are recorded in the accounts using reliable estimates based on past experience and future expectations. As we have learned from past chapters, many liabilities are based on reasonable and probable estimates.

Contingent liabilities are existing or possible obligations arising from past events. The liability is contingent (dependent) on whether or not some uncertain future event occurs that will confirm either its existence or the amount payable, or both. One example of a contingent liability is a loan guarantee. This is when one company (for example, a parent company) guarantees or promises to assume the loan obligation if the other company (for example, a subsidiary company) is unable to repay the loan. The guaranteeing company will have an actual liability and a loss only if the borrower does not make the payments on the loan. However, a contingent liability is simply disclosed in the notes; it is not recorded for two reasons. First of all, the probability of an obligation being settled is only possible, not probable. Under IFRS, probable is defined as "more likely than not," which is normally interpreted to mean more than a 50% probability of occurring. Second, even if the probability is "more likely than not," it may not be possible to estimate the amount of the liability.

Accounting Standards for Private Enterprises use different terminology regarding uncertain liabilities. In the questions and problems in this text, we will use the IFRS terms described above. Under ASPE, the term *provision* is not used. The term *contingent loss* (rather than the terms *provision* or *contingent liability*) is used instead. A contingent loss (along with a related liability) is recorded when two conditions are met: (1) it is likely that a future event will confirm that a liability has been incurred and (2) the amount of the related loss can be estimated. If such a loss is likely to occur but cannot be estimated, note disclosure of this contingent loss is made rather than recording it in the accounts. Similar treatment would occur if the loss was not determinable. If the loss was unlikely to occur, it would not be recorded or disclosed in the notes to the financial statements. Under ASPE, *likely* has a higher degree of probability than the term *probable* used under IFRS.

DECISION TOOLKIT

 Decision Checkpoints	 Info Needed for Decision	 Tools to Use for Decision	 How to Evaluate Results
Does the company have any provisions or contingent liabilities?	Knowledge of events with uncertain but possibly negative outcomes	Financial statements and notes to the financial statements	If negative outcomes are possible, determine the likelihood and amount of the provision, and the potential impact on the financial statements.

BEFORE YOU GO ON...

▶Do It! Current Liabilities

Prepare the journal entries, if required, to record the following transactions:

1. Pre-tax cash sales on April 2 totalled $256,000. The HST rate is 13%. Record the sales and sales tax.

2. A property tax bill for the calendar year of $12,000 is received on May 1 and is due June 30. Record the entries for May 1, for June 30 when the tax is paid, and for December 31, assuming the company has a calendar year end and records adjusting entries annually.

3. A company's gross salary amounts to $10,000 for the week ended July 11. Amounts deducted from the employees' salaries are CPP of $495, EI of $178, income tax of $3,465, and health insurance of $950. The employer's portion of CPP is $495 and of EI, $249. Record the weekly payroll on July 11, assuming cash is paid to the employees but the payroll amounts withheld are still due.

4. Accrue interest on December 31 (the company's year end) for a three-month, 6%, $10,000 bank loan effective November 1. Interest is payable on the first of each month.

5. In November of the current year, a customer sued the company for $10,000. Discussions with legal counsel reveal that the claim is without merit and that it is unlikely that damages will be awarded to the plaintiff.

Action Plan

- Record sales separately from the sales tax. Recall that sales tax is a liability until remitted.
- When the property tax notice is received, record the property tax expense and the property tax payable for the amounts incurred to date. Record the prepaid property tax at the time of payment for any amounts paid in advance.
- Record both the employees' portion of the payroll and the benefits owed by the employer. Employee deductions are not an expense for the employer.
- Remember that interest rates are expressed on an annual basis, so the formula for interest is: principal (face) value × annual interest rate × time.
- Remember that a contingency arises from a past event that then requires an assessment of the likelihood of its eventual outcome and the ability to measure it.

Solution

1.	Apr. 2	Cash ($256,000 + $33,280)	289,280	
		Sales		256,000
		Sales Tax Payable ($256,000 × 13%)		33,280
		(To record sales and sales tax)		
2.	May 1	Property Tax Expense ($12,000 × 4/12)	4,000	
		Property Tax Payable		4,000
		(To record property tax expense for January to April and amount owing)		
	June 30	Property Tax Payable	4,000	
		Property Tax Expense ($12,000 × 2/12)	2,000	
		Prepaid Property Tax ($12,000 × 6/12)	6,000	
		Cash		12,000
		(To record payment of property tax for January through December)		
	Dec. 31	Property Tax Expense	6,000	
		Prepaid Property Tax		6,000
		(To record the expiry of the prepaid and property tax expense for the last six months of the year)		

3.	July 11	Salaries Expense	10,000	
		CPP Payable		495
		EI Payable		178
		Income Tax Payable		3,465
		Health Insurance Payable		950
		Cash		4,912
		(To record payroll and employee deductions)		
	11	Employee Benefits Expense	744	
		CPP Payable		495
		EI Payable		249
		(To record employee benefits)		
4.	Dec. 31	Interest Expense ($10,000 × 6% × 1/12)	50	
		Interest Payable		50
		(To accrue interest for December on bank loan)		
5.		No provision should be recorded or contingent liability disclosed because a loss is not probable or possible.		

Related Exercise Material: BE10-1, BE10-2, BE10-3, BE10-4, BE10-5, E10-1, E10-2, E10-3, and E10-4.

Non-current Liabilities: Instalment Notes Payable

STUDY OBJECTIVE 2

Account for instalment notes payable.

A **non-current liability** is an obligation that is expected to be paid after one year or longer. Common examples of non-current liabilities include instalment notes payable, bonds payable, finance leases, deferred income taxes, and pension liabilities. Instalment notes payable are explained in this section, while bonds payable are explained in Appendix 10A. You will recall that finance leases were briefly introduced in Chapter 9. Discussion of deferred income taxes and pension liabilities is left to an intermediate accounting course.

Many liabilities, including those that are non-current in nature, are often called financial instruments. One type of financial instrument is a **financial liability**. These types of liabilities have contractual obligations to pay cash in the future. While most liabilities are financial liabilities, one example of a liability that is not a financial liability is unearned revenue.

Using long-term notes payable in debt financing is common. Long-term notes payable are similar to short-term notes payable except that the terms of the notes are for more than one year. Long-term notes may have fixed or floating interest rates. In periods of unstable interest rates, it is common for notes to have a floating interest rate that changes as the prime borrowing rate changes. For example, a company may have long-term debt on which it pays interest at the Bank of Canada prime rate plus 1%.

A long-term note may be **secured** or **unsecured**. A secured note pledges title (gives ownership) to specific assets as collateral or security for the loan. Secured notes are also known as mortgages. A **mortgage payable** is widely used by individuals to purchase homes. It is also used by many companies to acquire property, plant, and equipment. Unsecured notes are issued against the general credit of the borrower. There are no assets used as collateral.

ACCOUNTING MATTERS!

Mortgages in Canada

In a 2012 report on the mortgage market, the Canadian Association of Accredited Mortgage Professionals noted that the average house in Canada has a $173,000 mortgage. Of the 9.6 million homes in Canada, nearly 5.9 million have a mortgage. Some homeowners not only have mortgages but they also obtain lines of credit using their homes as collateral, with more than one third of Canadians having a home equity line of credit. For those homeowners who have both a mortgage and a line of credit, the average value of the line of credit is over $52,000. Over 65% of mortgages have a fixed rate and the average homeowner is planning to take 21 years to pay off their mortgage.[3]

While short-term notes are normally repayable in full at maturity, most long-term notes are repayable in a series of periodic payments. These payments are known as **instalments** and are paid monthly, quarterly, semi-annually, or at another defined period.

As with short-term notes, the terms *notes* and *loans* are used interchangeably. Each instalment payment consists of a mix of (1) interest on the unpaid balance of the loan, and (2) a reduction of the loan principal. The actual instalment payments generally take one of two forms: (1) fixed principal payments plus interest, or (2) blended principal and interest payments. Let's look at each of these payment patterns in more detail.

FIXED PRINCIPAL PAYMENTS PLUS INTEREST

Instalment loans with fixed principal payments are repayable in **equal periodic amounts plus interest**. As mentioned earlier, interest rates may be either fixed or floating. For simplicity, we will assume a fixed interest rate. To illustrate, assume that on January 1, 2015, Belanger Ltée borrows $120,000 from the bank for a five-year period at a 7% interest rate to finance a research laboratory. The entry to record the loan is as follows:

A	=	L	+	SE
+120,000		+120,000		

↑Cash flows: +120,000

Jan. 1	Cash	120,000	
	Bank Loan Payable		120,000
	(To record receipt of five-year, 7% bank loan)		

The terms of the loan provide for equal monthly principal payments of $2,000 ($120,000 ÷ 60 monthly periods) on the first of each month, plus interest of 7% on the outstanding principal balance.

Monthly interest expense is calculated by multiplying the outstanding principal balance at the beginning of the period by the interest rate. Because a portion of the principal balance is repaid each month, the outstanding principal balance will change (decrease) each month. This is different from what we observed in the calculation of interest on short-term loans, where the principal balance does not change throughout the term of a short-term loan.

For Belanger, the first payment date is February 1, and the interest expense is $700 ($120,000 × 7% × $\frac{1}{12}$). Similar to short-term loans, the 7% is an annual interest rate and must be adjusted for the monthly time period. The cash payment of $2,700 is the total of the principal payment of $2,000, plus the interest of $700.

The entry to record the first instalment payment on February 1 is as follows:

A	=	L	+	SE
−2,700		−2,000		−700

↓Cash flows: −2,700

Feb. 1	Interest Expense ($120,000 × 7% × $\frac{1}{12}$)	700	
	Bank Loan Payable	2,000	
	Cash ($2,000 + $700)		2,700
	(To record instalment payment on bank loan)		

An instalment payment schedule is a useful tool to help organize this information and to provide information that helps prepare journal entries. A partial instalment payment schedule for the first few months for Belanger Ltée, with amounts rounded to the nearest dollar, is shown in Illustration 10-2.

BELANGER LTÉE			
Instalment Payment Schedule—Fixed Principal Payments			
(A)	(B)	(C)	(D)
Interest Period	Cash Payment (B + C)	Interest Expense (D × 7% × 1/12)	Reduction of Principal ($120,000 ÷ 60)	Principal Balance (D – C)
Jan. 1				$120,000
Feb. 1	$2,700	$700	$2,000	118,000
Mar. 1	2,688	688	2,000	116,000
Apr. 1	2,677	677	2,000	114,000

►Illustration 10-2
Instalment payment schedule principal payments

Column A, the cash payment, is the total of the principal payment, $2,000, plus the interest. The cash payment changes each period because the interest changes. Column B determines the interest expense, which decreases each period because the principal balance, on which interest is calculated, decreases. Column C is the principal repayment amount of $2,000. This payment is constant each period in a "fixed principal payment plus interest" pattern. Column D is the principal balance, which decreases each period by the amount of the principal repayment of $2,000 each period.

In summary, with fixed principal payments, the interest decreases each period as the principal decreases. The portion applied to the reduction of the loan principal stays constant, but because of the decreasing interest, the total cash payment decreases.

BLENDED PRINCIPAL AND INTEREST PAYMENTS

Instalment loan payments can also be made on a blended basis whereby the total payment each period does not change as it does with fixed principal payment arrangements. Blended principal and interest payments are repayable in **equal periodic amounts, including interest**. Blended principal and interest payments result in changing amounts of interest and principal applied to the loan. As with fixed principal payments, the interest decreases each period (as the principal decreases). In contrast to fixed principal payments, the portion applied to the loan principal increases each period. Most consumer and mortgage loans use a blend of principal and interest payments rather than fixed principal payments plus interest.

To illustrate this arrangement, assume that instead of fixed principal payments, Belanger Ltée repays its bank loan in equal monthly blended principal and interest instalments of $2,376. As with the fixed principal payments illustrated above, monthly interest expense is calculated by multiplying the outstanding principal balance by the interest rate. For the first payment date—February 1— interest expense is $700 ($120,000 × 7% × 1/12). The instalment payment of $2,376 is fixed for each month, but the interest and principal components of each payment will vary. In February, the principal balance will be reduced by $1,676, which is the difference between the instalment payment of $2,376 and the interest amount of $700.

The entry to record the borrowing of the money from the bank on January 1 is the same as in the previous section. The entry to record the instalment payment uses the same accounts but different amounts (except that interest expense is the same amount for the first month). The first instalment payment on February 1 is recorded as follows:

Feb. 1	Interest Expense ($120,000 × 7% × 1/12)	700	
	Bank Loan Payable ($2,376 − $700)	1,676	
	Cash		2,376
	(To record instalment payment on bank loan)		

A	=	L	+	SE
−2,376		−1,676		−700

↓Cash flows: −2,376

An instalment payment schedule can also be prepared for blended principal and interest payments. Illustration 10-3 shows a partial instalment payment schedule for the first few months for Belanger Ltée, with amounts rounded to the nearest dollar.

▶Illustration 10-3
Instalment payment schedule—
blended payments

	(A)	(B)	(C)	(D)
		BELANGER LTÉE		
		Instalment Payment Schedule—Blended Payments		
Interest Period	Cash Payment	Interest Expense ($D \times 7\% \times \frac{1}{12}$)	Reduction of Principal ($A - B$)	Principal Balance ($D - C$)
Jan. 1				$120,000
Feb. 1	$2,376	$700	$1,676	118,324
Mar. 1	2,376	690	1,686	116,638
Apr. 1	2,376	680	1,696	114,942

Column A, the cash payment, is specified and is the same for each period. The amount of this cash payment can actually be calculated mathematically. It can also be determined using present value techniques, which are discussed later in Appendix 10A.

Column B determines the interest expense, which decreases each period because the principal balance that the interest is calculated on decreases. Column C shows how much the principal is reduced by. This is the difference between the cash payment of $2,376 and the interest for the period. Consequently, this amount will increase each period. Column D is the principal balance, which decreases each period by a varying amount; that is, by the reduction of the principal amount from Column C. When we prepare this schedule, we determine the interest portion of the payment and then subtract this from the total payment to determine the portion of the payment that relates to the reduction of principal.

In summary, with blended payments, the interest decreases each period as the principal decreases. The total cash payment stays constant, but because of the decreasing interest, the reduction of principal increases.

The following schedule summarizes the differences between the two types of instalment payment patterns:

Instalment Payment Pattern	Principal	Interest	Total Cash Payment
Fixed principal plus interest	Constant: Reduction of principal equal each period	Decreases: Interest expense decreases each period	Decreases: Total cash payment decreases each period
Blended principal and interest	Increases: Reduction of principal increases each period	Decreases: Interest expense decreases each period	Constant: Total cash payment equal each period

CURRENT AND NON-CURRENT PORTIONS

With both types of instalment loans, the principal portion of the loan that will be paid off next year must be reported as a current liability. The remaining unpaid principal is classified as a non-current liability.

For example, consider the following blended payment schedule for a $51,000 loan where payments are made at the end of each year and the interest rate is 4%:

Interest Period	Cash Payment	Interest Expense	Reduction of Principal	Principal Balance
Issue Date				$51,000
2014	$11,456	$2,040	$9.416	41,584
2015	11,456	1,663	9,793	31,791
2016	11,456	1,272	10,184	21,607
2017	11,456	864	10,592	11,015
2018	11,456	441	11,015	0

If financial statements were being prepared at the end of 2015, the company would report $31,791 as its total liability for the bank loan, shown in the principal balance column. Of this, $10,184—the amount of principal to be repaid within the next year (2016), which is highlighted above in red—would be reported as a current liability. Meanwhile, the remaining portion of the loan, which is $21,607, would be reported as a non-current liability. This amount, too, is highlighted in red in the above table. Note that when the current portion ($10,184) and the non-current portion ($21,607) are added together, the amount should agree with the total amount owing at the end of 2015, $31,791. Note as well that, because payments occur at the end of the year, there is no interest payable to report on the financial statements.

BEFORE YOU GO ON...

▶Do It! Instalment Mortgage Payable

On December 31, 2015, Harbin Inc. borrowed $400,000, signing a 10-year, 4% mortgage in return. The terms provide for semi-annual blended instalment payments of $29,433 (principal and interest) on June 30 and December 31. (a) Prepare an instalment payment schedule for the first two years of the mortgage through to December 31, 2017. (b) Prepare the journal entries required to record the receipt of the mortgage loan on December 31, 2015, and the first two instalment payments on June 30, 2016, and December 31, 2016. (c) Show the presentation of the mortgage liability on the statement of financial position at December 31, 2016.

Action Plan

- Prepare an instalment payment schedule. Round all amounts to the nearest dollar.
- Multiply the semi-annual interest rate by the principal balance at the beginning of the period to determine the interest expense. The reduction of principal is the difference between the cash payment and the interest expense.
- Record the instalment payments, recognizing that each payment consists of (1) interest on the unpaid mortgage balance, and (2) a reduction of the mortgage principal.
- The current portion of the mortgage payable as at December 31, 2016, is the amount of principal that will be repaid in the next year (2017). The non-current portion is the total liability as at December 31, 2016, less the current portion.

Solution

(a)

Interest Period	Cash Payment	Interest Expense	Reduction of Principal	Principal Balance
Dec. 31, 2015				$400,000
June 30, 2016	$24,463	$8,000	$16,463	383,537
Dec. 31, 2016	24,463	7,671	16,792	366,745
June 30, 2017	24,463	7,335	17,128	349,617
Dec. 31, 2017	24,463	6,992	17,471	332,146

(b)

2015 Dec. 31	Cash	400,000	
	Mortgage Payable		400,000
	(To record receipt of 10-year, 4% mortgage payable)		
2016 June 30	Interest Expense ($400,000 × 4% × 6/12)	8,000	
	Mortgage Payable ($24,463 – $8,000)	16,463	
	Cash		24,463
	(To record semi-annual instalment payment on mortgage)		
Dec. 31	Interest Expense [($400,000 – $16,463) × 4% × 6/12)]	7,671	
	Mortgage Payable ($24,463– $7,671)	16,792	
	Cash		24,463
	(To record semi-annual instalment payment on mortgage)		

(continued)

(c)

HARBIN INC.
December 31, 2016
Statement of Financial Position (partial)

Current liabilities	
Current portion of mortgage payable ($17,128 + $17,471)	$ 34,599
Non-current liabilities	
Mortgage payable	332,146
Total liabilities	$366,745

Related Exercise Material: BE10-6, BE10-7, BE10-8, BE10-9, E10-5, E10-6, and E10-7.

Statement Presentation and Analysis

STUDY OBJECTIVE 3

Identify the requirements for the financial statement presentation and analysis of liabilities.

Liabilities add up to a significant amount on the financial statements of almost all companies and must be disclosed in detail so they can be properly understood by lenders and other creditors as well as investors. These and other users are very interested in assessing a company's liquidity and solvency in regard to its liabilities. We will look at the presentation and analysis of liabilities in the next sections.

PRESENTATION

The presentation of liability-related accounts in the income statement is fairly straightforward. Interest (finance) expenses are separately reported in the "other revenues and expenses" section of the statement. The presentation in the statement of financial position is a bit more involved, so we will look at this in more detail.

Current Liabilities

Liabilities are usually segregated as current or non-current on the statement of financial position, with current liabilities generally reported as the first category in the liabilities section of the statement of financial position. Each of the primary types of current liabilities can be listed separately within this category or detailed in the notes to the financial statements. In addition, the terms of any operating lines of credit and notes (loans) payable are disclosed in the notes to the financial statements.

Similar to current assets, current liabilities are generally listed in their order of liquidity (by their due date). However, this is not always possible, because of the varying maturity dates that may exist for specific obligations such as short-term notes payable. You will recall from earlier chapters that companies also have the option of presenting current liabilities in order of reverse liquidity. International companies often present their current liabilities following non-current liabilities and order items within each classification in reverse order to what is normally seen in North America. Some international companies also net their current assets and current liabilities.

Illustration 10-4 shows how Canada Post presents its current liabilities in a traditional order in its statement of financial position (which it calls the balance sheet).

Non-current Liabilities

Non-current or long-term liabilities are usually reported separately, immediately following current liabilities if companies follow the traditional North American order, or preceding current liabilities if companies use a reverse-liquidity order. There is no generally prescribed order within the non-current liability classification.

▶Illustration 10-4
Canada Post current liabilities

CANADA POST Balance Sheet (partial) December 31, 2012 (in millions)	
Current liabilities	
Trade and other payables	$ 454
Salaries and benefits payable	771
Provisions	85
Deferred revenue	137
Current portion of long-term debt	20
Total current liabilities	1,467

The presentation of Canada Post's non-current liabilities is shown in Illustration 10-5.

▶Illustration 10-5
Canada Post non-current liabilities

CANADA POST Balance Sheet (partial) December 31, 2012 (in millions)	
Non-current liabilities	
Long-term debt	$1,123
Pension, other post-employment and benefit liabilities	7,054
Provisions	5
Other long-term liabilities	17
Total non-current liabilities	8,199

Generally, non-current liabilities are measured and reported at the amount due when the liability is expected to be paid. There are exceptions to this, but these typically relate to bonds that are reported at their amortized cost. Bonds are covered in Appendix 10A of this chapter. The fair value of the non-current debt should also be disclosed in the notes to the financial statements if it is possible to estimate it. In limited circumstances, there is an option to value financial liabilities at fair value, but this option is used rarely in practice. Valuing financial liabilities at fair value normally applies only to complex financial instruments, which are beyond the scope of an introductory accounting course and are not discussed here.

Full disclosure of non-current debt is very important. Summary data are usually presented in the statement of financial position. Detailed information (such as interest rates, maturity dates, assets pledged as collateral, and fair value, if available) are shown in the notes to the financial statements along with a list showing the amount of non-current debt that is scheduled to be paid off in each of the next five years. Canada Post's disclosure about its non-current liabilities fills 13 pages in the notes to its financial statements.

ANALYSIS

A careful examination of debt obligations makes it easier to assess a company's ability to pay its current obligations. It also helps determine whether a company can obtain long-term financing in order to grow.

Liquidity

Liquidity ratios measure a company's short-term ability to pay its maturing obligations and to meet unexpected needs for cash within the next year. You will recall that we learned about the current ratio (current assets ÷ current liabilities) in Chapter 2, the inventory turnover ratio (cost of goods sold ÷ average inventory) in Chapter 6, and the receivables turnover ratio (net credit sales ÷ average gross accounts receivable) in Chapter 8. We will not illustrate these ratios again here.

In recent years, many companies have intentionally reduced their less liquid current assets (such as accounts receivable and inventory) because these assets cost too much to hold. Companies that keep fewer liquid assets on hand must rely on other sources of liquidity. One such source is an **operating line of credit**, as discussed earlier in this chapter. If a low amount of liquid assets causes a cash shortfall, a company can borrow money on its available short-term lines of credit as necessary. Consequently it is important to interpret a company's liquidity ratios in the context of any unused lines of credit, which add to a company's short-term financing flexibility.

You may recall that we discussed Canada Post's operating line of credit earlier in the chapter. This corporation and its subsidiaries have access to $75 million from a line of credit.

DECISION TOOLKIT

 Decision Checkpoints	 Info Needed for Decision	 Tools to Use for Decision	 How to Evaluate Results
Can the company obtain short-term financing when necessary?	Liquidity ratios, available lines of credit from notes to the financial statements	Compare available lines of credit with current liabilities. Also evaluate liquidity ratios.	If liquidity ratios are low, lines of credit should be high to compensate.

Solvency

Solvency ratios, such as the debt to total assets and times interest earned ratios, measure a company's ability to repay its long-term debt and survive over a long period of time. As the feature story about Canada Post shows, going into debt is often necessary in order to grow a business. However, debt must be carefully monitored to ensure that it does not hurt a company's solvency. We will review the debt to total assets ratio next, and then introduce a related ratio, the times interest earned ratio.

Debt to Total Assets.   In Chapter 2, you learned that one measure of a company's solvency is **debt to total assets**. It is calculated by dividing total liabilities by total assets. This ratio indicates the extent to which a company's assets are financed by debt.

Using the following selected information (in millions) from Canada Post's statement of financial position, the company's debt to total assets ratios for 2012 and 2011 are calculated in Illustration 10-6. The illustration also shows summary ratios for UPS, Canada Post's closest competitor (recall that Canada Post owns Purolator Inc.), as well as industry averages.

	2012	2011
Total assets	$7,018	$6,744
Total liabilities	9,666	8,375

▶Illustration 10-6
Debt to total assets

$$\text{DEBT TO TOTAL ASSETS} = \frac{\text{TOTAL LIABILITIES}}{\text{TOTAL ASSETS}}$$

(in millions)	2012	2011
Canada Post	$\frac{\$9,666}{\$7,018} = 137.7\%$	$\frac{\$8,375}{\$6,744} = 124.2\%$
UPS	87.8%	79.5%
Industry average	39.8%	37.5%

Whereas for liquidity ratios, higher values generally indicate that a company has a greater ability to meet its current obligations, for the debt to total assets ratio, a lower value indicates that the company has not used as much debt to finance its assets and this reduces the risk of not being able to pay back that debt along with the related interest if economic conditions worsen or interest rates rise.

Canada Post's debt to total assets ratio deteriorated in 2012 from 124.2% to 137.7%. This is because its liabilities, especially with the addition of significant long-term debt in 2012, grew faster than its assets.

Canada Post's debt to total assets is, however, much worse (higher) than that of UPS in both 2012 and 2011. The reason why Canada Post's debt to total assets exceeds 100% is because its liabilities are greater than its assets and this has occurred because its equity is negative due to increasing deficits (negative retained earnings). It should be noted that it is difficult to compare Canada Post fully with UPS as the latter does not deliver letter mail. Canada Post is the sole mail provider in Canada. Still, a significant portion of both companies' business consists of package delivery. Both companies' debt to total assets ratios are much worse (higher) than that of the industry.

Debt to total assets varies across industries because different financing options are appropriate for different industries. For example, the average debt to total assets ratio for the major department stores was 41% in 2012. The average debt to total assets ratio for the airline industry for the same period was higher, at 61%.

Times Interest Earned. The **times interest earned** ratio gives an indication of a company's ability to meet interest payments as they come due. The higher this ratio, the more able a company is to pay its interest charges. This ratio should be compared with the debt to total assets ratio because, even if a company has a high debt to total assets ratio, it may still be able to easily cover its interest payments if the times interest earned ratio is also high. Alternatively a company may have a low debt to total assets ratio and struggle to cover its interest payments.

Alternative Terminology
The *times interest earned ratio* is also known as the *interest coverage ratio.*

The times interest earned ratio is calculated by dividing the sum of profit, interest expense, and income tax expense by interest expense. It uses profit or earnings before interest and taxes (often abbreviated as **EBIT**) because this number best represents the amount that is available to cover interest.

EBIT can be found directly on the income statement or calculated by adding interest expense and income tax expense to profit. These are amounts that were originally deducted to determine profit. They are added back now to *remove* them from profit, and give the amount of profit before interest and taxes.

Illustration 10-7 uses the following selected information (in millions) from Canada Post's income statement to calculate its times interest earned ratios for 2012 and 2011. The illustration also shows summary ratios for UPS and industry averages.

	2012	2011
Interest expense	$ 49	$ 46
Income tax (benefit) expense	33	(65)
Profit (loss)	94	(188)

TIMES INTEREST EARNED =	$\dfrac{\text{PROFIT + INTEREST EXPENSE + INCOME TAX EXPENSE (EBIT)}}{\text{INTEREST EXPENSE}}$	
(in millions)	**2012**	**2011**
Canada Post	$\dfrac{\$94 + \$49 + \$33}{\$49} = 3.6$ times	$\dfrac{\$(188) + \$46 - \$65}{\$46} = -4.5$ times
UPS	3.5 times	17.6 times
Industry average	19.6 times	22.3 times

►Illustration 10-7
Times interest earned

Contrary to the debt to total assets ratio, the higher the better for the times interest earned ratio. Although the interest expense changed only slightly in 2012 compared with 2011, Canada Post became profitable in 2012 due to reduced labour costs. Consequently, its times interest earned ratio was positive in 2012 and was approximately the same as that of UPS although still lower than the industry average because of its high debt levels.

Operating Leases.   You will recall that leases were introduced in Chapter 9. For accounting purposes, operating leases are treated as periodic rentals—no assets or liabilities are recorded on the company's books. Finance or capital leases, on the other hand, are treated like a debt-financed purchase—increasing both assets and liabilities.

Operating leases are often short-term, such as the rental of a car or an apartment. If, however, an operating lease covers a long period of time, it may be viewed as "off–balance–sheet financing." Off–balance–sheet financing refers to situations where liabilities are not recorded on the statement of financial position.

Many believe that some companies will choose to structure a lease arrangement as an operating lease rather than a finance lease simply to avoid recording a liability. In their opinion, if an operating lease results in the long-term use of an asset and an unavoidable obligation, it should be recorded as an asset and a liability rather than as a periodic rental expense.

You may also recall from Chapter 9 that standard setters are currently working on a project to reclassify leases. They are suggesting that leases with terms longer than one year be treated as finance leases. Deliberations are not yet finalized.

In the interim, companies are required to report their operating lease obligations in a note to the financial statements. Canada Post reports a total obligation of $885 million of operating leases for its facilities, transportation equipment, and other items in the notes to its financial statements.

This information allows analysts and other financial statement users to adjust a company's ratios for unrecorded debt if they feel that the inclusion of this debt would have a significant effect on the interpretation of a company's solvency. Canada Post's operating leases are about 9% of its total liabilities, so they may be considered to be significant to a user's decision-making. As the adjustments required to remove the effects of operating leases from solvency ratios are complex, they are left to a financial statement analysis course.

Credit Ratings.   Credit-rating agencies, such as the Dominion Bond Rating Service (DBRS), provide opinions about a company's ability to make timely payments (of principal and interest) on its short- and long-term debt. Short-term debt is rated using an "R" scale, with R-1 being the highest credit quality. Within this scale, the rating is further divided as R-1 (high), R-1 (middle), and R-1 (low) to further distinguish between high, superior, and satisfactory credit quality. Short-term debt rated as R-4 or R-5 is considered to be speculative.

Long-term debt is rated using a different letter scale than short-term debt. The highest-quality long-term debt is rated as AAA, superior quality as AA, and good quality as A. The credit scale descends to the D, or default, category. Generally, long-term debt rated below BBB is referred to as speculative and non-investment grade, with a higher risk of default. Canada Post's long-term debt is rated AAA—the highest rating possible by DBRS.

■ Keeping an Eye on Cash

Cash is critical with respect to debt. Companies must not only be able to generate enough cash to pay their interest charges when due but also to repay any principal amounts due annually and/or at maturity. If a company fails to meet any of its due dates, it can have serious consequences for its credit rating.

Debt covenants help companies reduce their risk of default and also help protect lenders. Most borrowing agreements include restrictions called debt covenants that restrict a company's ability to invest, pay dividends, or make other decisions that might adversely affect the company's ability to pay interest and principal.

As well, the statement of cash flows helps provide information about how much cash is being used for debt purposes. Cash paid for interest expense is usually reported in the operating activities section of the cash flow statement. Information on cash inflows and outflows during the year that resulted from the principal portion of debt transactions is reported in the financing activities section of the statement. We will learn about using the statement of cash flows to calculate debt coverage ratios in Chapter 13.

DECISION TOOLKIT

 Decision Checkpoints	 Info Needed for Decision	 Tools to Use for Decision	 How to Evaluate Results
Can the company meet its obligations in the long term?	Total liabilities, total assets, profit, interest expense, and income tax expense	Times interest earned = $\dfrac{\text{Profit} + \text{Interest expense} + \text{Income tax expense (EBIT)}}{\text{Interest expense}}$ Compare the times interest earned ratio with the debt to total assets ratio.	A high times interest earned ratio indicates there is enough profit available to cover annual interest payments. A low debt to total assets ratio is preferable, but a high debt to total assets ratio along with a high times interest earned ratio is acceptable.
Does the company have significant unrecorded obligations, such as operating leases?	Information on unrecorded obligations, such as operating lease payments disclosed in the notes to the financial statements	Compare liquidity and solvency ratios with and without unrecorded obligations included.	If ratios differ significantly after including unrecorded obligations, these obligations should not be ignored in analysis.

BEFORE YOU GO ON...

▶Do It! Liquidity and Solvency

O'Leary Ltd. reported the following information in its financial statements.

O'LEARY LTD.
Statement of Financial Position
December 31

	2015	2014
Assets		
Cash	$ 11,000	$ 10,000
Merchandise inventory	38,000	31,000
Prepaid expenses	6,000	5,000
Equipment	210,000	93,600
Total assets	$265,000	$139,600
Liabilities and shareholders' equity		
Accounts payable	$ 19,400	$ 23,800
Interest payable	6,400	2,800
Bonds payable	160,000	70,000
Common shares	12,000	8,000
Retained earnings	67,200	35,000
Total liabilities and shareholders' equity	$265,000	$139,600
Revenue	$320,000	$180,000
Operating expenses	260,000	151,000
Profit from operations	60,000	29,000
Interest expense	12,800	5,600
Income tax expense	15,000	8,000
Profit	$ 32,200	$ 15,400

(a) Calculate the company's current, debt to total assets, and times interest earned ratios for each year.

(b) Identify if the change in each ratio from 2014 to 2015 is an improvement or a deterioration and provide an explanation for this.

(continued)

Action Plan

- Determine total current assets and total current liabilities. Divide current assets by current liabilities to calculate the current ratio.
- Determine total liabilities. Divide total liabilities by total assets to calculate the debt to total assets ratio.
- Divide the earnings (profit) before interest and income tax expense by the interest expense to calculate the times interest earned ratio. If there are no other revenues or expenses besides interest expense, then EBIT is the same as profit from operations.
- Recall that if the current ratio and interest coverage ratios are higher, then the company's liquidity and ability to make interest payments have improved. If the debt to total asset ratio is higher, the company is undertaking a greater level of risk with regard to its financing.

Solution

	(a)		(b)
	2015	2014	
Current ratio	$\dfrac{\$11{,}000 + \$38{,}000 + \$6{,}000}{\$19{,}400 + \$6{,}400}$ = 2.1:1	$\dfrac{\$10{,}000 + \$31{,}000 + \$5{,}000}{\$23{,}800 + \$2{,}800}$ = 1.7:1	Improvement
Debt to total assets	$\dfrac{\$19{,}400 + \$6{,}400 + \$160{,}000}{\$265{,}000}$ = 70.1%	$\dfrac{\$23{,}800 + \$2{,}800 + \$70{,}000}{\$139{,}600}$ = 69.2%	Deterioration
Times interest earned	$\dfrac{\$32{,}200 + \$12{,}800 + \$15{,}000}{\$12{,}800}$ = 4.7 times	$\dfrac{\$15{,}400 + \$5{,}600 + \$8{,}000}{\$5{,}600}$ = 5.2 times	Deterioration

The company's assets grew considerably in 2015 but so did the debt, resulting in very little change to the debt to total assets ratio. The growth in assets allowed the company to generate more sales and operating profit but this did not grow as fast as the interest expense, so the times interest earned ratio deteriorated. As the company grew, inventory levels increased, but accounts payable were paid down more rapidly and this improved the current ratio.

Related Exercise Material: BE10-10, BE10-11, BE10-12, E10-8, E10-9, E10-10.

APPENDIX 10A—Bonds Payable

STUDY OBJECTIVE 4
Account for bonds payable.

Like other kinds of non-current debt, a **bond** is a promise to repay a specified amount of money (a face value) at a fixed future date in addition to periodic interest payments. A bond is used instead of other types of debt when the amount of financing needed is too large for one lender. A large amount (for example, $1 million) is typically divided into small denominations (usually bonds with a face value of $1,000), which makes it possible for more than one lender to participate in the bond offering. Whereas both small and large corporations issue notes, only large corporations issue bonds.

Accounting for notes and bonds is quite similar. Both have a fixed maturity date and pay interest. Although both can have a fixed or floating interest rate, most bonds have a fixed interest rate. This rate, which determines the amount of interest to pay to bondholders, is known as the **coupon interest rate** and is always quoted as an annual rate. Bond interest is normally paid semi-annually, although some bonds pay interest monthly or quarterly, similar to notes.

Alternative Terminology
The *coupon interest rate* is also known as the *contractual interest rate* or the *stated interest rate.*

Like notes, bonds may be **unsecured** or **secured**. Unsecured bonds are also known as **debentures**. Both notes and bonds can be payable at maturity or in instalments.

BOND TRADING

A significant difference between notes and bonds is that bonds can be traded on a public exchange in the same way that shares trade. Notes are seldom traded on exchanges. **Bond prices are quoted as a percentage of the face value of the bonds, which is usually $1,000.** For example, if the bond price is stated as 100, this means that the bonds will sell at 100% of the face value. If the face value is $1,000, then the bonds will sell for $1,000 ($1,000 × 100%). You can assume that bonds are issued in $1,000 denominations unless you are told otherwise.

However, we need to be aware that the coupon interest rate may differ from the **market interest rate**, which is the rate investors demand to earn for lending their money. This rate is also commonly known as the "effective interest rate."

DETERMINING THE ISSUE PRICE OF BONDS

If you were an investor interested in purchasing a bond, how would you decide how much to pay? To be more specific, assume that Candlestick Inc. issues a zero-interest bond (a bond that pays no interest) with a face value of $1 million due in five years. The face value is a stated value that the bond issuer will pay to the investor on the maturity date of the bond. For this bond, the only cash you receive is $1 million at the end of five years. Would you pay $1 million for this bond? We hope not, because $1 million received five years from now is not the same as $1 million received today.

You should not pay $1 million because of what is called the **time value of money**. If you had $1 million today, you would invest it and earn interest so that after five years your investment could be worth more than $1 million. Thus, if someone is going to pay you $1 million five years from now, you would want to determine its equivalent value today. That amount—how much must be invested today at current interest rates to have $1 million in five years—is called the present value and would be a lower amount than the future or face value of $1 million.

> **Helpful Hint**
> Present value is always less than future value. The difference between present and future value is interest.

The present value of a bond is the amount that it sells for in the marketplace. The issue price (present value), therefore, depends on three factors: (1) the dollar amounts to be received, (2) the length of time until the amounts are received, and (3) the market interest rate. The process of finding the present value is referred to as discounting the future amounts.

To illustrate, assume that on January 1, 2015, Candlestick Inc. issues $1 million of 5% bonds, due in two years, with interest payable semi-annually on January 1 and July 1. Most bonds do not mature in two years, but we are using this shorter time frame for simplicity. The purchaser of the bonds would receive the following two types of cash inflows: (1) the face or principal amount of $1 million to be paid at maturity, and (2) four interest payments of $25,000 ($1,000,000 × 5% × $\frac{6}{12}$ months) over the term of the bonds.

> **Alternative Terminology**
> The *issue price* is also called the *selling price, fair value,* or *market value* of the bonds.

The issue price of a bond is equal to the present value of all the future cash flows relating to the bond, namely the face value of the bond at maturity and periodic interest payments promised by the bond. There are standardized present value tables available that give us factors that can be multiplied by the amount of each type of cash flow (interest and maturity value) relating to a bond to determine its issue price. These are reproduced below for your reference as we outline the procedures for calculating the present value of a bond.

1. Face value: Use Table 1 (the present value of $1) to determine the factor to use to calculate the present value of the principal or face value of the bond. In Candlestick's case, this is a single payment of $1 million to be paid at the end of the bond term, two years from now. Locate the appropriate factor at the intersection of the number of periods (n) and the interest rate (i).

When interest is paid semi-annually, the number of periods and the interest rate must relate to six-month periods of time. In the Candlestick example, the two-year term of the bonds means that there are four semi-annual interest periods. In addition, the annual market interest rate of 5% becomes 2.5% (5% × $\frac{6}{12}$) when adjusted for the semi-annual period. The present value factor to be used for the face value for $n = 4$ and $i = 2.5\%$ is 0.90595.

2. Interest: Use Table 2 (the present value of an annuity of $1) to determine the factor to use to calculate the present value of the bond interest. In Candlestick's case, $25,000 of interest ($1,000,000 $\times$ 2.5%) is to be paid every six months for the next two years, or four semi-annual periods. A series of payments like this is called an annuity. The present value factor to be used for the interest for $n = 4$ and $i = 2.5\%$ is 3.76197.

TABLE 1: PRESENT VALUE OF $1 $\left(PV = \dfrac{1}{(1+i)^n} \right)$

(n) Periods	1%	1.5%	2%	2.5%	3%	3.5%	4%	4.5%	5%	6%	7%	8%	9%	10%
1	0.99010	0.98522	0.98039	0.97561	0.97087	0.96618	0.96154	0.95694	0.95238	0.94340	0.93458	0.92593	0.91743	0.90909
2	0.98030	0.97066	0.96117	0.95181	0.94260	0.93351	0.92456	0.91573	0.90703	0.89000	0.87344	0.85734	0.84168	0.82645
3	0.97059	0.95632	0.94232	0.92860	0.91514	0.90194	0.88900	0.87630	0.86384	0.83962	0.81630	0.79383	077218	0.75131
4	0.96098	0.94218	0.92385	0.90595	0.88849	0.87144	0.85480	0.83856	0.82270	0.79209	0.76290	0.73503	0.70843	0.68301
5	0.95147	0.92826	0.90573	0.88385	0.86261	0.84197	0.82193	0.80245	0.78353	0.74726	0.71299	0.68058	0.64993	0.62092
6	0.94205	0.91454	0.88797	0.86230	0.83748	0.81350	0.79031	0.76790	0.74622	0.70496	0.66634	0.63017	0.59627	0.56447
7	0.93272	0.90103	0.87056	0.84127	0.81309	0.78599	0.75992	0.73483	0.71068	0.66506	0.62275	0.58349	0.54703	0.51316
8	0.92348	0.88771	0.85349	0.82075	0.78941	0.75941	0.73069	0.70319	0.67684	0.62741	0.58201	0.54027	0.50187	0.46651
9	0.91434	0.87459	0.83676	0.80073	0.76642	0.73373	0.70259	0.67290	0.64461	0.59190	0.54393	0.50025	0.46043	0.42410
10	0.90529	0.86167	0.82035	0.78120	0.74409	0.70892	0.67556	0.64393	0.61391	0.55839	0.50835	0.46319	0.42241	0.38554
11	0.89632	0.84893	0.80426	0.76214	0.72242	0.68495	0.64958	0.61620	0.58468	0.52679	0.47509	0.42888	0.38753	0.35049
12	0.88745	0.83639	0.78849	0.74356	0.70138	0.66178	0.62460	0.58966	0.55684	0.49697	0.44401	0.39711	0.35553	0.31863
13	0.87866	0.82403	0.77303	0.72542	0.68095	0.63940	0.60057	0.56427	0.53032	0.46884	0.41496	0.36770	0.32618	0.28966
14	0.86996	0.81185	0.75788	0.70773	0.66112	0.61778	0.57748	0.53997	0.50507	0.44230	0.38782	0.34046	0.29925	0.26333
15	0.86135	0.79985	0.74301	0.69047	0.64186	0.59689	0.55526	0.51672	0.48102	0.41727	0.36245	0.31524	0.27454	0.23939
16	0.85282	0.78803	0.72845	0.67362	0.62317	0.57671	0.53391	0.49447	0.45811	0.39365	0.33873	0.29189	0.25187	0.21763
17	0.84438	0.77639	0.71416	0.65720	0.60502	0.55720	0.51337	0.47318	0.43630	0.37136	0.31657	0.27027	0.23107	0.19784
18	0.83602	0.76491	0.70016	0.64117	0.58739	0.53836	0.49363	0.45280	0.41552	0.35034	0.29586	0.25025	0.21199	0.17986
19	0.82774	0.75361	0.68643	0.62553	0.57029	0.52016	0.47464	0.43330	0.39573	0.33051	0.27651	0.23171	0.19449	0.16351
20	0.81954	0.74247	0.67297	0.61027	0.55368	0.50257	0.45639	0.41464	0.37689	0.31180	0.25842	0.21455	0.17843	0.14864

TABLE 2: PRESENT VALUE OF AN ANNUITY OF $1 $\left(PV = \dfrac{1 - \frac{1}{(1+i)^n}}{i} \right)$

(n) Periods	1%	1.5%	2%	2.5%	3%	3.5%	4%	4.5%	5%	6%	7%	8%	9%	10%
1	0.99010	0.98522	0.98039	0.97561	0.97087	0.96618	0.96154	0.95694	0.95238	0.94340	0.93458	0.92593	0.91743	0.90909
2	1.97040	1.95588	1.94156	1.92742	1.91347	1.89969	1.88609	1.87267	1.85941	1.83339	1.80802	1.78326	1.75911	1.73554
3	2.94099	2.91220	2.88388	2.85602	2.82861	2.80164	2.77509	2.74896	2.72325	2.67301	2.62432	2.57710	2.53129	2.48685
4	3.90197	3.85438	3.80773	3.76197	3.71710	3.67308	3.62990	3.58753	3.54595	3.46511	3.38721	3.31213	3.23972	3.16987
5	4.85343	4.78264	4.71346	4.64583	4.57971	4.51505	4.45182	4.38998	4.32948	4.21236	4.10020	3.99271	3.88965	3.79079
6	5.79548	5.69719	5.60143	5.50813	5.41719	5.32855	5.24214	5.15787	5.07569	4.91732	4.76654	4.62288	4.48592	4.35526
7	6.72819	6.59821	6.47199	6.34939	6.23028	6.11454	6.00205	5.89270	5.78637	5.58238	5.38929	5.20637	5.03295	4.86842
8	7.65168	7.48593	7.32548	7.17014	7.01969	6.87396	6.73274	6.56589	6.46321	6.20979	5.97130	5.74664	5.53482	5.33493
9	8.56602	8.36052	8.16224	7.97087	7.78611	7.60769	7.43533	7.26879	7.10782	6.80169	6.51523	6.24689	5.99525	5.75902
10	9.47130	9.22218	8.98259	8.75206	8.53020	8.31661	8.11090	7.91272	7.72173	7.36009	7.02358	6.71008	6.41766	6.14457
11	10.36763	10.07112	9.78685	9.51421	9.25262	9.00155	8.76048	8.52892	8.30641	7.88687	7.49867	7.13896	6.80519	6.49506
12	11.25508	10.90751	10.57534	10.25776	9.95400	9.66333	9.38507	9.11858	8.86325	8.38384	7.94269	7.53608	7.16073	6.81369
13	12.13374	11.73153	11.34837	10.98318	10.63496	10.30274	9.98565	9.68285	9.39357	8.85268	8.35765	7.90378	7.48690	7.10336
14	13.00370	12.54338	12.10625	11.69091	11.29607	10.92052	10.56312	10.2283	9.89864	9.29498	8.74547	8.24424	7.78615	7.36669
15	13.86505	13.34323	12.84926	12.38138	11.93794	11.51741	11.11839	10.73955	10.37966	9.71225	9.10791	8.55948	8.06069	7.60608
16	14.71787	14.13126	13.57771	13.05500	12.56110	12.09412	11.65230	11.23402	10.83777	10.10590	9.44665	8.85137	8.31256	7.82371
17	15.56225	14.90765	14.29187	13.71220	13.16612	12.65132	12.16567	11.70719	11.27407	10.47726	9.76322	9.12164	8.54363	8.02155
18	16.39827	15.67256	14.99203	14.35336	13.75351	13.18968	12.65930	12.15999	11.68959	10.82760	10.05909	9.37189	8.75563	8.20141
19	17.22601	16.42617	15.67846	14.97889	14.32380	13.70984	13.13394	12.59329	12.08532	11.15812	10.33560	9.60360	8.95011	8.36492
20	18.04555	17.16864	16.35143	15.58916	14.87747	14.21240	13.59033	13.00794	12.46221	11.46992	10.59401	9.81815	9.12855	8.51356

Using the above factors, we can calculate the present values of the face value and the annuity of interest payments as follows:

Present value of $1,000,000 received in 4 periods	
$1,000,000 × 0.90595 ($n = 4, i = 2.5\%$)	$ 905,950
Present value of $25,000 received for each of 4 periods	
$25,000 × 3.76197 ($n = 4, i = 2.5\%$)	94,050
Present value (issue price) of bonds	$1,000,000
Where n = number of interest periods and i = interest rate	

Note that the bonds' face value and the coupon interest rate are always used to calculate the interest payment—$25,000 in this case. However, the market interest rate is always used to determine the appropriate factor to be used for the present value because it clearly has an impact on the bond price. When the present value (issue price) of the bond equals the face value, these two rates are the same (both are 5% per annum), as is the case in our Candlestick example above.

The present value can also be determined mathematically using a financial calculator or spreadsheet program. The same principles are involved as described above, but with a calculator, we can input values relating to both the maturity value and the interest payments and calculate the present value in one step. There are four values to enter: (1) the future value (FV), which is the face value of the bond; (2) the market interest rate per period (i); (3) the number of semi-annual interest periods (n); and (4) the interest payment (PMT).

In the Candlestick example, the future value (FV) is $1 million, the interest rate (i) is 2.5%, the number of periods (n) is 4, and the interest payment (PMT) is $25,000, which is calculated as above by multiplying the future value by the coupon rate. Some calculators may require you to enter the payment and future value amount as a minus (for example, $-25,000$) and you may also have to input the information that the interest payments occur at the end (not the beginning) of each period.

We will not illustrate how to use a financial calculator or spreadsheet program here as the methodology for each can vary. You should be aware that the present value amounts calculated with a financial calculator or spreadsheet program will most likely differ by a few dollars from those calculated using the factors in the present value tables as we have illustrated above. This is because the factors in the present value tables are rounded to five decimal places whereas your own calculations are likely not rounded at all, or are rounded to the number of decimal places you specify.

DISCOUNT OR PREMIUM ON BONDS

Market interest rates change daily. They are influenced by the type of bond issued, the company's financial position and performance, the state of the economy, and current industry conditions, among other factors. As a result, the coupon and market interest rates often differ, and this will cause bonds to sell below or above their face value.

When a bond is issued, the coupon interest rate is stated on the bonds. If an investor wants to purchase bonds that have a coupon rate of 5% when the market interest rate is 6%, they will pay less than the face value of the bond because the coupon rate offered is not as attractive as the market interest rate. By paying less for the bonds, investors can effectively obtain a higher yield, or market interest rate, of 6%. They will actually earn more than the 5% coupon rate because of the difference between what they paid for the bond today and the face value or maturity value they will receive later. When the market interest rate is higher than the coupon interest rate, the bonds are said to sell at a **discount**.

On the other hand, the market interest rate may be lower than the coupon interest rate. In that case, investors will pay more than face value for the bonds. That is, if the market interest rate is 4% but the coupon interest rate on the bonds is 5%, everyone will want to buy the bonds and the price will rise above the bonds' face value. In these cases, the bonds are said to sell at a **premium**.

The relationship between interest rates and a resulting discount, face value, or premium is shown in Illustration 10A-1.

> **Helpful Hint**
> Bond prices vary inversely with changes in the market interest rate. For example, as market interest rates increase, bond prices decrease.

▶Illustration 10A-1
Interest rates and bond prices

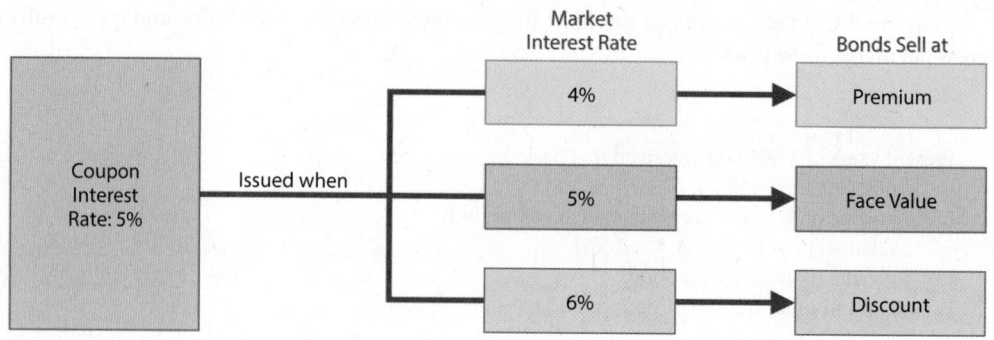

Issuing bonds at an amount different from face value is quite common. By the time a company prints the bond certificates (which provide the legal documentation for the bonds) and markets the bonds, it will be a coincidence if the market interest rate and the coupon rate are the same. Thus, the issue of bonds at a discount does not mean there is doubt about the financial strength of the issuer. Conversely, the sale of bonds at a premium does not indicate that the financial strength of the issuer is exceptional.

ACCOUNTING FOR BOND ISSUES

As we saw above, bonds may be issued at face value, below face value (discount), or above face value (premium).

To illustrate the accounting for bonds issued at face value, let's continue the example discussed in the last section where Candlestick Inc. issues two-year, 5%, $1-million bonds on January 1, 2015, for $1 million (100% of face value). The entry to record the sale is:

A	=	L	+	SE
+1,000,000		+1,000,000		

↑Cash flows: +1,000,000

Jan. 1	Cash		1,000,000	
	Bonds Payable			1,000,000
	(To record issue of two-year, 5% bonds at face value)			

However, if the bonds were issued when the market interest rate was 6%, the bonds would be less attractive and they would sell for a lower amount, as calculated below using factors found in the present value tables or by using a calculator with all of the same input values used before, except that the interest rate used is now 3% instead of 2.5%:

Present value of $1,000,000 received in 4 periods	
$1,000,000 × 0.88849 ($n = 4$, $i = 3\%$)	$888,490
Present value of $25,000 received for each of 4 periods	
$25,000 × 3.7171 ($n = 4$, $i = 3\%$)	92,927
Present value (issue price) of bonds	$981,417

The **carrying amount** of a bond is its face value less any unamortized discount, or plus any unamortized premium. At the date of issue, the carrying amount equals the bond's issue price, which in this case is $981,417. The issue price of $981,417 gives rise to a bond discount of $18,583 ($1,000,000 − $981,417). Note that the carrying amount of the bonds, $981,417, will always be lower than the face value, $1,000,000, when bonds are issued at a discount.

The entry to record the sale is:

A	=	L	+	SE
+981,417		+981,417		

↑Cash flows: +981,417

Jan. 1	Cash		981,417	
	Bonds Payable			981,417
	(To record issue of two-year, 5% bonds at a discount)			

Now let us assume that when these bonds were sold, market interest rates were only 4% rather than the coupon interest rate of 5%. These bonds would be very attractive to investors in the market because the coupon rate is higher than expected, and because of this, Candlestick Inc. will be able to sell these bonds at a premium. The issue price of these bonds can be calculated using factors found in the present value tables or by using a calculator with all of the same input values used before except that the interest rate used is now 2% (4% × ⁶⁄₁₂) instead of 2.5%:

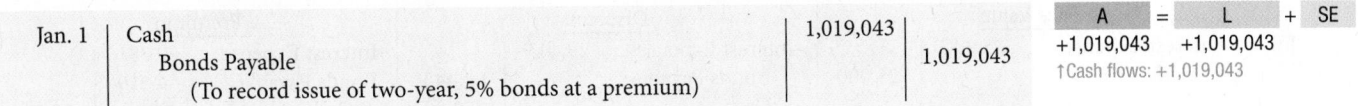

Present value of $1,000,000 received in 4 periods	
$1,000,000 × 0.92385 ($n = 4, i = 2\%$)	$ 923,850
Present value of $25,000 received for each of 4 periods	
$25,000 × 3.80773 ($n = 4, i = 2\%$)	95,193
Present value (issue price) of bonds	$1,019,043

This issue price of $1,019,043 gives rise to a premium of $19,043 ($1,019,043 − $1,000,000). Notice that this time the carrying amount of the bonds, $1,019,043, is greater than their face value, $1,000,000, as will always be the case when bonds are issued at a premium.

The entry to record the sale of the bonds is:

Jan. 1	Cash	1,019,043	
	Bonds Payable		1,019,043
	(To record issue of two-year, 5% bonds at a premium)		

A	=	L	+	SE
+1,019,043		+1,019,043		

↑Cash flows: +1,019,043

ACCOUNTING FOR BOND INTEREST EXPENSE

A discount or premium on a bond is essentially a form of additional interest (in the case of a discount) or interest saving (in the case of a premium). This additional interest or interest saving should be reflected as an increase or decrease in interest expense over the term covered by the bond through a process called amortization, which allocates the discount or premium amount within the bond payable account to interest expense over time. The most common way to do this is by using the **effective-interest method**. In this method, the interest expense is calculated by multiplying the carrying amount of the bonds by the market interest rate when the bonds were sold, as this reflects the reality of the marketplace. This means that interest expense will be different from the interest paid (which is based on the face value and coupon interest rate) if there is a discount or premium on the bonds. The difference between the interest expense and the interest paid is the amount of discount or premium that is being amortized. As amortization occurs, the carrying amount of the bonds will change by the amount amortized and the carrying amount will move closer over time to the face value of the bonds. Because this liability account is changing each period, the interest expense should also change and represent the same proportion of the bond payable every period. This method results in a periodic interest expense that equals a constant percentage (the market or effective interest rate) of the carrying amount of the bond.

The calculation of amortization using the effective-interest method is shown in Illustration 10A-2.

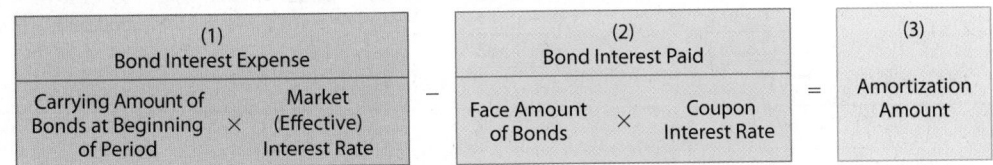

▶Illustration 10A-2
Calculation of amortization using effective-interest method

Returning to our example of Candlestick Inc., if these bonds were issued at face value, the interest expense and interest paid are the same. Interest expense and interest paid are calculated by multiplying $1,000,000 × 5% × 5/12, which equals $25,000.

However, if the bonds, which offer a coupon rate of 5%, were issued when the market interest rate was 6%, they would be issued at a discount for $981,417, as calculated earlier. In this case, the interest expense should reflect market conditions on the issue date and will be based on the market interest rate rather than the coupon rate. Furthermore, the market interest rate will be multiplied by the carrying amount to determine the interest expense, which will be $981,417 × 6% × 5/12 = $29,443. Consequently, interest expense will be higher than the interest paid. This difference, or disadvantage, arises when bonds are issued at a discount because of the market's desire to earn a higher rate than the coupon rate. The disadvantage of this discount is reflected by having higher amounts of interest expense compared with interest paid.

If the Candlestick bonds are instead sold when the market interest rate is 4%, the bonds are more attractive to investors because they offer a 5% coupon rate. The bonds will sell at a premium for $1,019,043, as calculated earlier. Similar to that illustrated earlier for discounts, the interest expense must reflect market conditions that created the premium in the first place. Once again, interest will be calculated by multiplying the carrying amount of the bonds by the market interest rate. Interest expense will be $1,019,043 × 4% × 6/12 = $20,381. The interest payments are still calculated by multiplying the carrying amount by the coupon rate. When there is a premium, the interest expense will be less than the interest paid. Why? An advantage of receiving a premium is that it results in a reduction in interest expense over the term of the bond.

The journal entries required to record interest on bonds selling at face value, at a discount, or at a premium are shown in Illustration 10A-3.

▶Illustration 10A-3

Bond interest payment entries

	Face Value			Discount			Premium	
July 1	Interest Expense 25,000		Interest Expense 29,443			Interest Expense 20,381		
	Cash	25,000	Bonds Payable		4,443	Bonds Payable		4,619
			Cash		25,000	Cash		25,000

From the entries above, we can see that the amortization of the discount to interest expense increases the carrying amount of the bonds and moves it closer to the face value. In contrast, the amortization of the premium to interest expense decreases the carrying amount.

An amortization table can be prepared to show the calculation of interest expense and the amount of discount or premium amortization for each period. Regardless of what period it is, the interest expense is always equal to the carrying amount of the bonds at the beginning of the period times the market interest rate. Tables for Candlestick are shown in Illustration 10A-4.

▶Illustration 10A-4

Amortization tables for bonds issued with discount and premium

CANDLESTICK INC.
Bond Discount Amortization Schedule

Semi-Annual Interest Period	(A) Interest Payment ($1,000,000 × 5% × 6/12)	(B) Interest Expense (Preceding Bond Carrying Amount × 6% × 6/12)	(C) Discount Amortization (B − A)	(D) Unamortized Discount (D − C)	(E) Bond Carrying Amount ($1,000,000 − D)
Issue date (Jan. 1, 2015)				$18,583	$ 981,417
1 (July 1, 2015)	$ 25,000	$ 29,443	$ 4,443	14,140	985,860
2 (Jan. 1, 2016)	25,000	29,576	4,576	9,564	990,436
3 (July 1, 2016)	25,000	29,712	4,712	4,852	995,148
4 (Jan. 1, 2017)	25,000	29,852*	4,852	0	1,000,000
	$100,000	$118,583	$18,583		

*Adjusted for rounding differences.

CANDLESTICK INC.
Bond Premium Amortization Schedule

Semi-Annual Interest Period	(A) Interest Payment ($1,000,000 × 5% × 6/12)	(B) Interest Expense (Preceding Bond Carrying Amount × 4% × 6/12)	(C) Premium Amortization (A − B)	(D) Unamortized Premium (D − C)	(E) Bond Carrying Amount ($1,000,000 + D)
Issue date (Jan. 1, 2015)				$19,043	$1,019,043
1 (July 1, 2015)	$ 25,000	$20,381	$ 4,619	14,424	1,014,423
2 (Jan. 1, 2016)	25,000	20,288	4,712	9,712	1,009,710
3 (July 1, 2016)	25,000	20,194	4,806	4,906	1,004,903
4 (Jan. 1, 2017)	25,000	20,094*	4,906	0	1,000,000
	$100,000	$80,957	$19,043		

*Adjusted for rounding differences.

In the tables above, notice that the carrying amount of a bond is always equal to its present value. Because of this, if you were asked what the carrying amount of the Candlestick bonds would be at the end of a certain period, you could either prepare a schedule as shown in Illustration 10A-4 or calculate the present value of the bond at the end of the specified period, where n is the number of interest periods remaining. Notice that the change in the carrying amount of the bonds is equal to the change in their present value. In other words, the amount of any premium or discount amortized is simply equal to the change in the present value of the bonds.

Using the information from the above tables we can record the adjusting entry needed on December 31, Candlestick's year end, to accrue the interest expense that is due to be paid on January 1, as shown in Illustration 10A-5.

► Illustration 10A-5

Bond interest accrual entries

Face Value			Discount			Premium		
Dec. 31 Interest Expense	25,000		Interest Expense	29,576		Interest Expense	20,288	
Interest Payable		25,000	Bonds Payable		4,576	Bonds Payable	4,712	
			Interest Payable		25,000	Interest Payable		25,000

The interest payable on the bonds is classified as a current liability at December 31, 2015, because it is scheduled for payment within the next year. The bonds payable are reported in the non-current liability section of the statement of financial position because their maturity date is January 1, 2017 (more than one year away). When the interest is paid on January 1, 2016, Interest Payable is decreased (debited) and Cash is also decreased (credited) for $25,000.

The effective-interest method is required for companies reporting under IFRS. Private companies reporting using ASPE can choose to use either the effective-interest method or other methods (usually a straight-line method) if they do not differ materially from the effective-interest method. Because the use of the effective-interest method is prevalent, we focus on this method in the chapter.

ACCOUNTING FOR BOND RETIREMENTS

Bonds are retired either (1) when they mature, or (2) when the issuing corporation purchases them on the open market before they mature. Some bonds have special redemption provisions that allow them to be retired before they mature. Bonds that can be retired at a specified price before maturity at the option of the company (the issuer) are known as **redeemable (or callable) bonds**.

Why would a company want to have the option to retire its bonds early? If interest rates drop, it can be financially advantageous to retire the bond issue and replace it with a new bond issue at a lower interest rate. Or a company may become financially able to repay its debt earlier than expected. In this textbook, we will cover bond retirements only at maturity, leaving coverage of bond retirements prior to maturity for an intermediate accounting course.

Regardless of the issue price of bonds, their carrying amount at maturity will equal their face value because by that time, any discount or premium will have been fully amortized. Assuming that the interest for the last interest payment period is recorded, the entry to record the redemption of the Candlestick bonds at maturity, on January 1, 2017, is:

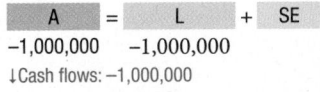

Jan. 1	Bond Payable	1,000,000	
	Cash		1,000,000
	(To record redemption of bond at maturity)		

A = L + SE
−1,000,000   −1,000,000
↓ Cash flows: −1,000,000

BEFORE YOU GO ON...

► Do It! **Bond Transactions**

On January 1, 2015, Selkirk Ltd. issued $800,000 of five-year, 4% bonds to yield a market interest rate of 5%, which resulted in an issue price of 95.62. Interest is paid semi-annually on January 1 and July 1. (a) Using present value factors from Tables 1 and 2 included in this appendix or a financial calculator, prove the bonds' issue price of 95.62. (b) Prepare the entries to record (1) the issue of the bonds on January 1, 2015; (2) the payment of interest and amortization of any bond discount or premium on July 1, 2015; and (3) the final entry that would be made after the last payment of interest when the bonds mature on January 1, 2020. Round all amounts to the nearest dollar.

(continued)

Action Plan

- Identify the key inputs required to determine present value, whether using present value tables or a financial calculator.
- To use present value tables to calculate the present value (issue price), use Table 1 (the present value of $1) to determine the factor to use to calculate the present value of the principal, which is a single sum. Use Table 2 (the present value of an annuity of $1) to calculate the present value of the interest, which recurs periodically (as an annuity). Remember to double the number of periods and halve the annual interest rate when the interest is paid semi-annually.
- Apply the issue price as a percentage, in this case, 95.62%, to the face value of the bonds to determine the proceeds received or use the calculation of the present value.
- Recall that the amortization of a bond discount increases Interest Expense and makes it higher than the cash paid out for interest while the amortization of a bond premium reduces Interest Expense and makes it lower than the cash paid out for interest.
- To record the retirement of the bond at maturity, simply bring the balance in the Bond Payable account, which would now equal its face value, to zero by debiting this account by its carrying amount with an offsetting credit to cash.

Solution

(a) Key inputs: Future value (FV) = $800,000
Market interest rate (i) = 2.5% (5% × $^6/_{12}$)
Interest payment (PMT) = $16,000 ($800,000 × 4% × $^6/_{12}$)
Number of semi-annual periods (n) = 10 (5 years × 2)

Present value of $800,000 received in 10 periods
$800,000 × 0.78120 ($n$ = 10, i = 2.5%) $624,960
Present value of $16,000 received for each of 10 periods
$16,000 × 8.75206 ($n$ × 10, i × 2.5%)   140,033
Present value (issue price) of bonds $764,993

Issue price = $764,993 ÷ $800,000 = 95.62%

(b)

2015			
I. Jan. 1	Cash	764,993	
	Bonds Payable		764,993
	(To record issue of 5-year, 4% bonds at a discount)		
2. July 1	Interest Expense ($764,993 × 5% × $^6/_{12}$)	19,124	
	Bonds Payable ($19,124 − $16,000)		3,124
	Cash ($800,000 × 4% × $^6/_{12}$)		16,000
	(To record semi-annual bond interest payment and amortization of discount)		
2020			
3. Jan. 1	Bonds Payable	800,000	
	Cash		800,000
	(To record redemption of 5-year, 4% bonds at maturity)		

Related Exercise Material: BE10-13, BE10-14, BE10-15, E10-11, E10-12, E10-13, and E10-14.

comparing
IFRS and ASPE

Key Differences	International Financial Reporting Standards (IFRS)	Accounting Standards for Private Enterprises (ASPE)
Contingent liability	The definition of probability used to record a provision is "probable." Under IFRS, a contingent liability is not recorded but disclosed.	The definition of probability used to record a contingent liability is "likely," which is a higher level of certainty needed than the "probable" measure under IFRS. ASPE does not use the term *provision* so a contingent liability could be either recorded or disclosed.
Bonds (Appendix 10A)	Must use the effective-interest method to amortize any bond premium or discount.	Normally will use the effective-interest method to amortize any bond premium or discount but permitted to use alternative methods if the results do not differ materially from the effective-interest method.

the navigator

When companies need money for operations, they go to lenders, other creditors, or investors. As a student, when you need money for school, you must rely on contributions from parents and other relatives, money from summer or part-time jobs, plus grants, bursaries, and scholarships. If these sources do not cover the cost of post-secondary education, you can consider obtaining a student loan. Federal, provincial, and territorial governments offer student loan programs. Private institutions such as banks, trust companies, and credit unions may also offer loan options if you do not qualify for a government student loan.

Student loans are a useful option to consider when you are deciding how to pay for your education. It is important to understand your obligations and responsibilities as a borrower because a student loan is a legal obligation, and you will be required to pay it back. The amount of your student loan is determined based on an assessment of your financial need, which is different for each student. First, your allowable costs (which may include education, living, and transportation costs) and your resources are calculated. The difference between the two is your assessed financial need. For this purpose, and for future personal financial planning, maintenance of your personal financial records is critical. These personal financial records include such records as your income tax return, payroll documents, and other invoices and payments. It is also imperative that you keep your personal financial statements up to date, such as your statement of financial position, which was discussed in the Chapter 2 "All About You."

Financial experts offer the following tips for minimizing the amount of your student loan:

- Understand the loan process; know how much interest you will have to pay, and how long it will take you to pay the loan back.
- Get free money whenever you can; grants, bursaries, and scholarships are tax-exempt and don't have to be paid back.
- If you need help in repaying your loans, repayment assistance programs are available in most provinces.
- Make sure you claim all relevant income tax credits (such as the tuition, education, and textbook credits and interest paid on student loans).

Some Facts

- Canadian full-time students were paying an average of $5,581 in tuition fees for the 2012–13 academic year. Full-time graduate students were paying an average of $5,695.
- Many students are also asked to pay additional compulsory fees: the national average was $750 for the 2012–13 academic year. These fees vary by institution and usually cover items such as athletics, student health services, student associations, and the like.
- A 2010 report from Statistics Canada found that the number of students graduating with outstanding student loans, either government-sponsored or from another source, increased from 49% in the 1990s to 57% in the 2000s. According to the Canadian Council on Learning, the average debt for a student graduating from a Canadian university was $26,680 in 2009.
- For students who have loans, the amount of the student loan has also increased (in constant dollars), from an average of $15,200 in the 1990s to $18,800 in the 2000s. Also, the number of students with loans in excess of $50,000 increased from 2% to 6% over the same time period.[4]

What Do You Think?

Suppose you own a car, but your parents use their car to drop you off at university and pick you up later on their way home. You decide to add your parents' car expenses to your list of expenses when applying for a student loan, because you know that the more expenses you have, the more likely you are to obtain financial aid. To increase your chances of receiving aid, should you overstate your expenses?

YES—You are playing within the rules as you do own a car, and how would the government know that you were not commuting to university in your own car? Even if you can justify the operating costs of running your parents' vehicle, you are going to have to repay all amounts that you have borrowed. It is always better to borrow for only those amounts that are absolutely necessary.

NO—Random audits are conducted each year and, if it were found out that you had lied about your expenses, you would never be able to apply for another government student loan.

Summary of Study Objectives

1. **Account for current liabilities.** A current liability is a debt that will be paid (1) from existing current assets or through the creation of other current liabilities, and (2) within one year or operating cycle. An example of a current liability is an operating line of credit that results in bank indebtedness. Current liabilities also include sales taxes, payroll deductions, and employee benefits, all of which the company collects on behalf of third parties. Other examples include property tax and interest on notes or loans payable, which must be accrued until paid. The portion of non-current debt that is due within the next year must be deducted from the non-current debt and reported as a current liability.

   All of the above are "certain" or determinable liabilities. Contingent liabilities are "uncertain" liabilities awaiting confirmation by a future event that are not recorded unless probable. When recorded, these liabilities are called *provisions*. The terms and nature of each recorded provision and contingent liability should be described in the notes accompanying the financial statements.

2. **Account for instalment notes payable.** Long-term notes payable are usually repayable in a series of instalment payments. Each payment consists of (1) interest on the unpaid balance of the note, and (2) a reduction of the principal balance. These payments can be either (1) fixed principal payments plus interest or (2) blended principal and interest payments. With fixed principal payments plus interest, the reduction of principal is constant but the cash payment and interest expense decrease each period as the principal decreases. With blended principal and interest payments, the reduction of principal increases while the interest expense decreases each period. In total, the cash payment (principal and interest) remains constant each period.

3. **Identify the requirements for the financial statement presentation and analysis of liabilities.** In the income statement, interest expense (finance cost) is reported as "other revenues and expenses." In the statement of financial position, current liabilities are usually reported first, followed by non-current liabilities.

   The liquidity of a company may be analyzed by calculating the current ratio, in addition to the receivables and inventory turnover ratios. The solvency of a company may be analyzed by calculating the debt to total assets and times interest earned ratios. Another factor to consider is unrecorded debt, such as operating lease obligations.

4. **Account for bonds payable (Appendix 10A).** Bonds are issued at their present (market) value. When they are issued, the Cash account is debited and the Bonds Payable account is credited for the issue price of the bonds.

   Bond discounts and bond premiums represent the difference between a bond's face value and present value. They are amortized to interest expense over the life of the bond using the effective-interest method of amortization. Amortization is calculated as the difference between the interest paid and the interest expense. Interest paid is calculated by multiplying the bonds' face value by the coupon interest rate. Interest expense is calculated by multiplying the bonds' carrying amount (which is equal to their present value at that time) at the beginning of the interest period by the market interest rate. The amount of the discount or premium that is amortized is equal to the change in the present value of the bond during that period. The amortization of a bond discount increases interest expense and the bond's carrying amount. The amortization of a bond premium decreases interest expense and the bond's carrying amount.

   When bonds are retired at maturity, Bonds Payable is debited and Cash is credited. There is no gain or loss at retirement.

the navigator

Glossary

Bond A type of long-term debt issued by large corporations, universities, and governments that involves a promise to repay a large amount of money at a fixed future date. (p. 522)

Collateral Assets pledged as security for the payment of a debt. (p. 503)

Contingent liabilities Existing or possible obligations arising from past events. The liability is contingent (dependent) on whether or not some uncertain future event occurs that will confirm either its existence or the amount payable, or both. (p. 509)

Coupon interest rate (also known as the contractual or stated interest rate) The rate stated in a bond certificate used to determine the amount of interest the borrower pays and the investor receives. (p. 522)

Discount The difference between a bond's face value and its issue price when it is sold for less than its face value. This occurs when the market interest rate is higher than the coupon interest rate. (p. 525)

EBIT Earnings (profit) before interest expense and income tax expense. (p. 519)

Effective-interest method A method of amortizing a bond discount or premium that results in a periodic interest expense that equals a constant percentage (the market or effective interest rate) of the bond's carrying amount. Amortization is calculated as the difference between the interest expense and the interest paid. (p. 527)

Employee benefits Payments made by an employer for pension, insurance, health, and/or other benefits paid on behalf of its employees. (p. 505)

Financial liability A form of financial instrument, represented by a contractual obligation to pay cash in the future. (p. 511)

Gross pay The total compensation (such as salaries or wages) earned by an employee. (p. 505)

Market interest rate (also known as the effective interest rate) The rate that investors demand for loaning funds to a corporation. (p. 523)

Net pay Gross pay less payroll deductions. (p. 505)

Operating line of credit (also known as a credit facility) A pre-arranged agreement to borrow money at a bank, up to an agreed-upon amount. (p. 503)

Payroll deductions Deductions from gross pay to determine the amount of a paycheque. (p. 505)

Premium The difference between the issue price and the face value of a bond when a bond is sold for more than its face value. This occurs when the market interest rate is less than the coupon interest rate. (p. 525)

Provisions Liabilities of uncertain timing or amount. They are recorded in the accounts based on reasonable and probable estimates. (p. 509)

Times interest earned A measure of a company's solvency, calculated by dividing profit (earnings) before interest expense and income tax expense (EBIT) by interest expense. (p. 519)

DECISION TOOLKIT—A SUMMARY

 **Decision Checkpoints**  **Info Needed for Decision**  **Tools to Use for Decision**  **How to Evaluate Results**

Decision Checkpoints	Info Needed for Decision	Tools to Use for Decision	How to Evaluate Results
Does the company have any provisions or contingent liabilities?	Knowledge of events with uncertain but possibly negative outcomes	Financial statements and notes to the financial statements	If negative outcomes are possible, determine the likelihood and amount of the provision, and the potential impact on the financial statements.
Can the company obtain short-term financing when necessary?	Liquidity ratios, available lines of credit from notes to the financial statements	Compare available lines of credit with current liabilities. Also evaluate liquidity ratios.	If liquidity ratios are low, lines of credit should be high to compensate.
Can the company meet its obligations in the long term?	Total liabilities, total assets, profit, interest expense, and income tax expense	Times interest earned = $\frac{\text{Profit + Interest expense + Income tax expense (EBIT)}}{\text{Interest expense}}$ Compare the times interest earned ratio with the debt to total assets ratio.	A high times interest earned ratio indicates there is enough profit available to cover annual interest payments. A low debt to total assets ratio is preferable, but a high debt to total assets ratio along with a high times interest earned ratio is acceptable.
Does the company have significant unrecorded obligations, such as operating leases?	Information on unrecorded obligations, such as operating lease payments disclosed in the notes to the financial statements	Compare liquidity and solvency ratios with and without unrecorded obligations included.	If ratios differ significantly after including unrecorded obligations, these obligations should not be ignored in analysis.

USING THE DECISION TOOLKIT

Royal Mail Holdings plc is comparable with Canada Post. Royal Mail is the national postal service in the United Kingdom. It also owns Parcelforce, a parcel delivery company, similar to Canada Post's Purolator.

Selected financial information for Royal Mail follows:

ROYAL MAIL HOLDINGS plc
Selected Financial Information
March 31, 2013
(in £ millions)

Royal Mail

Statement of financial position	
Non-current assets	3,225
Current assets	1,389
Non-current liabilities	1,386
Current liabilities	1,825
Income statement	
Interest expense	104
Income tax expense	246
Profit	570

Additional information:
The company had an unused operating line of credit at March 31, 2013.

Instructions
(a) Canada Post's current ratio is 1.1:1. Calculate Royal Mail's current ratio, and compare its liquidity with that of Canada Post and the industry average of 1.7:1.
(b) Calculate Royal Mail's debt to total assets and times interest earned ratios, and compare its solvency ratios with those of Canada Post, which is 137.7% and 3.6 times respectively, and the industry averages of 39.8% and 19.6 times, respectively.
(c) Because Royal Mail has an unused line of credit, how would that affect the assessment of its liquidity?

Solution

(a) Liquidity:

(in millions)	Royal Mail	Canada Post	Industry Average
Current ratio	$\dfrac{£1,389}{£1,825} = 0.8{:}1$	1.1:1	1.7:1

Royal Mail's current ratio of 0.8:1 means that it has £0.8 of current assets for each £1 of current liabilities. In other words, its current liabilities exceed its current assets. Although its available line of credit improves its liquidity position, the latter is still not good and is significantly below that of Canada Post and the industry. Neither company has inventory nor many receivables, but if they did, these ratios should also be calculated for both companies before reaching a conclusion about the adequacy of their liquidity.

(b) Solvency:

(in millions)	Royal Mail	Canada Post	Industry Average
Debt to total assets	$\dfrac{£1,386 + £1,825}{£3,225 + £1,389} = 69.6\%$	137.7%	39.8%
Times interest earned	$\dfrac{£920 + £236 + £104}{£104} = 8.8 \text{ times}$	3.6 times	19.6 times

Royal Mail's debt to total assets ratio of 69.6% is somewhat better (lower) than that of Canada Post but worse (higher) than the industry average. Royal Mail's times interest earned ratio is also better (higher) than Canada Post's ratio because of its higher profits. However, its times interest earned ratio is worse (lower) than the industry average because of its high debt levels.

(c) Royal Mail's unused operating line of credit improves its liquidity and may help reduce concerns that its short-term lenders and creditors may have.

the navigator

Comprehensive Do It!

Snyder Software Inc. successfully developed a new computer program. To produce and market the program, the company needed to raise $1 million. On December 31, 2014, Snyder borrowed $1 million from the bank for 15 years at 6%. The terms of the bank loan provide for semi-annual blended principal plus interest payments of $51,019 on June 30 and December 31.

Instructions

(a) Prepare an instalment payment schedule for the first four instalment payments. Round all amounts to the nearest dollar.

(b) Record the receipt of the bank loan on December 31, 2014.

(c) Record the first instalment payment on June 30, 2015.

(d) Indicate the current, non-current, and total amounts that would be presented in the statement of financial position for the bank loan payable at December 31, 2015.

(e) Explain how the pattern of payments would change if the instalment payments were based on fixed principal plus interest payments rather than blended principal and interest payments.

Action Plan

- Determine the interest expense for the bank loan by multiplying the semi-annual interest rate by the principal balance at the beginning of the period.
- Determine the principal portion of the payment by subtracting the interest expense from the total amount paid.
- Record the instalment payments, recognizing that each payment consists of (1) interest on the unpaid loan balance, and (2) a reduction of the loan principal.
- The current portion of the bank loan payable is the amount of principal that will be repaid in the next year. The non-current portion is the total liability at the date in question (December 31, 2015) less the current portion.

Solution to Comprehensive Do It!

(a)

Interest Period	(A) Cash Payment	(B) Interest Expense (D × 6% × 6/12)	(C) Reduction of Principal (A − B)	(D) Principal Balance (D − C)
Issue date				$1,000,000
(Dec. 31, 2014)				
1 (June 30, 2015)	$51,019	$30,000	$21,019	978,981
2 (Dec. 31, 2015)	51,019	29,369	21,650	957,331
3 (June 30, 2016)	51,019	28,720	22,299	935,032
4 (Dec. 31, 2016)	51,019	28,051	22,968	912,064

(b)

Dec. 31, 2014	Cash	1,000,000	
	Bank Loan Payable		1,000,000
	(To record receipt of 15-year, 6% bank loan)		

(c)

June 30, 2015	Interest Expense	30,000	
	Bank Loan Payable	21,019	
	Cash		51,019
	(To record semi-annual instalment payment on bank loan)		

(d) The current liability is $45,267 ($22,299 + $22,968). The non-current liability is $912,064. The total liability is the balance of $957,331 at the end of the second period, December 31, 2015.

(e) In a fixed principal plus interest situation, the reduction of the principal is constant while the interest expense and total cash payment decrease. The total cash payment would decrease each period. However, this does not change the nature of the journal entry as the same accounts will be debited and credited; it is just the amounts that will change.

WileyPLUS

Self-Test, Brief Exercises, Exercises, Problems: Set A, and many more components are available for practice in *WileyPLUS*.

Note: All questions, exercises, and problems below with an asterisk (*) relate to material in Appendix 10A.

Self-Test Questions

Answers are at the end of the chapter.

Quiz Yourself

(SO 1)   1. Restouche Ltd. has $4,515 of pre-tax sales. If Restouche collects 13% HST with each sale, what is the amount to be credited to the Sales account?
(a) $587
(b) $3,996
(c) $4,515
(d) $5,102

(SO 1)   2. On January 1, Swift Current Limited received its property tax assessment in the amount of $12,000 for the calendar year. The property tax bill was paid in full on its due date of May 1. If Swift Current prepares quarterly financial statements, how much prepaid property tax should the company report at the end of its second quarter, June 30?
(a) $4,000
(b) $6,000
(c) $8,000
(d) $12,000

(SO 1)   3. Severin works for the Blue Door Corporation at a salary of $550 per week. Canada Pension Plan contributions are $27.23 for the employee and the same for the employer. Income tax is $79.15. Employment insurance premiums are $9.79 for the employee and $13.71 for the employer. How much is Severin's weekly net pay (that is, take-home pay)?
(a) $392.89
(b) $433.83
(c) $470.85
(d) $550.00

(SO 2)   4. Boudreault Ltée issues a three-year, 7%, $497,000 instalment note payable on January 1. The note will be paid in three annual fixed principal payments of $165,667, plus interest, that are payable at the end of each year. What is the amount of interest expense that should be recognized by Boudreault in the second year?
(a) $17,395
(b) $23,193
(c) $23,968
(d) $34,790

(SO 2)   5. Zhang Inc. borrows $497,000 from the bank at 7% for a three-year period on January 1. The bank loan will be repaid in three annual blended principal and interest payments of $189,383 that are due at the end of each year. What is the

amount of interest expense that should be recognized by Zhang in the second year?
(a) $17,395
(b) $23,193
(c) $23,968
(d) $34,790

(SO 2)   6. Which of the following statements is true with regard to the current, non-current, or total amounts for an instalment note payable, with semi-annual payments, as detailed in the instalment payment schedule below?

Interest Period	Cash Payment	Interest Expense	Reduction of Principal	Principal Balance
Issue date				$500,000
1	$31,667	$15,000	$16,667	483,333
2	31,167	14,500	16,667	466,666
3	30,667	14,000	16,667	449,999
4	30,167	13,500	16,667	433,332

(a) The current liability is $16,667 at the end of the first period.
(b) The current liability is $33,334 at the end of the second period.
(c) The non-current liability is $466,666 at the end of the second period.
(d) The total liability is $433,332 at the end of the third period.

(SO 3)   7. Which of the following ratio combinations indicates that a company's solvency is improving?
(a) Debt to total assets ratios of 55% in year 2 and 45% in year 1
(b) Times interest earned ratios of 7 times in year 2 and 10 times in year 1
(c) Debt to total assets ratios of 55% in year 2 and 45% in year 1 and times interest earned ratios of 7 times in year 2 and 10 times in year 1
(d) Debt to total assets ratios of 45% in year 2 and 55% in year 1 and times interest earned ratios of 10 times in year 2 and 7 times in year 1

(SO 3)   8. In a recent year, K-Dough Corporation had profit of $150,000, interest expense of $30,000, and income tax expense of $20,000. What was K-Dough's times interest earned ratio?

(a) 5.0 times
(b) 5.7 times
(c) 6.0 times
(d) 6.7 times

(SO 4) *9. On January 1, Mabuga Corp. issues $200,000 of five-year, 7% bonds at 97. The entry to record the issue of the bonds would include a:
(a) debit to Cash for $200,000.
(b) debit to Interest Expense for $6,000.
(c) debit to Investment in Bonds for $194,000.
(d) credit to Bonds Payable for $194,000.

the navigator

(SO 4) *10. On January 1, 2015, Daigle Corporation issued $2 million of five-year, 7% bonds with interest payable on January 1 and July 1. The bonds sold for $1,918,880 to yield a market interest rate of 8%. The debit entry to the Bond Interest Expense account (rounded to the nearest dollar) on July 1, 2015, is for:
(a) $67,161.
(b) $70,000.
(c) $76,755.
(d) $80,000.

Questions

(SO 1) 1. Identify the similarities and differences between accounts payable and short-term notes payable.

(SO 1) 2. What is the difference between an operating line of credit and a short-term bank loan payable?

(SO 1) 3. Your roommate says, "Sales tax is a part of the cost of doing business and should be reported in the cost of goods sold section of the income statement." Do you agree? Explain.

(SO 1) 4. Explain how recording property tax can result in an expense (property tax expense), a liability (property tax payable), and an asset (prepaid property tax).

(SO 1) 5. What is the difference between (a) gross and net pay, and (b) employee payroll deductions and employee benefits?

(SO 1) 6. What criterion must be met before a contingent liability can be recorded as a provision? How does this criterion differ depending on whether the company is a public company using IFRS or a private company using ASPE?

(SO 1) 7. Review Note 22 to the **Shoppers Drug Mart** financial statements in Appendix A where it reports provisions. Why would the company discuss a claim that is not reasonably determinable? Is such an item considered to be a provision or a contingent liability?

(SO 1, 2) 8. Explain how to determine the current and non-current portions of debt for presentation in the liabilities section of the statement of financial position.

(SO 2) 9. Identify the similarities and differences between short-term notes payable and long-term instalment notes payable.

(SO 2) 10. Distinguish between instalment notes payable with fixed principal payments plus interest and those with blended principal and interest payments.

(SO 2) 11. When students borrow money for their post-secondary education under the Canada Student Loans Program, they sign an instalment note payable. It must be repaid, starting six months after graduation, in equal monthly amounts including principal and interest. Is this a fixed or blended payment pattern?

(SO 2) 12. When students borrow money for their post-secondary education under the Canada Student Loans Program, they can choose a fixed interest rate of prime + 5% or a floating interest rate of prime + 2.5%. (a) Explain the difference between these two types of interest rates. (b) Which interest rate—fixed or variable—do you think you would prefer? Explain.

(SO 2) 13. Doug Bareak, a friend of yours, has recently purchased a home for $200,000. He paid $20,000 down and financed the remainder with a 20-year, 5% mortgage that is payable in blended payments of principal and interest of $1,290 per month. At the end of the first month, Doug received a statement from the bank indicating that only $540 of the principal was paid during the month. At this rate, he calculated that it would take over 28 years to pay off the mortgage. Explain why Doug is incorrect.

(SO 3) 14. In general, what are the requirements for the financial statement presentation of (a) current liabilities and (b) non-current liabilities?

(SO 3) 15. Distinguish between liquidity and solvency. Provide an example of two ratios that can be used to measure each.

(SO 3) 16. Explain how an operating line of credit can help a company's liquidity.

(SO 3) 17. Explain why the debt to total assets ratio should never be interpreted without referring to the times interest earned ratio.

(SO 3) 18. Explain why it is important to know if a company has significant operating lease commitments.

(SO 4) *19. Identify the similarities and differences between bonds payable and (a) instalment notes payable, and (b) common shares.

(SO 4) *20. Ki-Hoon Inc. sold bonds with a face value of $100,000 for $104,000. Was the market interest rate equal to, less than, or greater than the bonds' coupon interest rate? Explain.

(SO 4) *21. Is there a difference between the interest expense recorded in the income statement and the interest paid during the year when a bond is sold (a) at a discount and (b) at a premium? Explain why.

Brief Exercises

BE10-1 Abbotsford Bikes Ltd. reports cash sales of $6,000 on October 1. (a) Record the sales assuming they occurred in Ontario and are subject to 13% HST (charged on selling price only). (b) Record the sales assuming they occurred in Quebec and are subject to 5% GST and 9.975% QST (charged on selling price before GST).

Record sales taxes. (SO 1)

BE10-2 Pierce Corp. has a December 31 year end. It received its property tax assessment of $36,000 for the calendar year on April 30. The property tax bill is payable on July 15. Prepare the journal entries to record the property tax on (a) April 30, (b) July 15, and (c) December 31, assuming the company adjusts its accounts annually.

Record property tax. (SO 1)

BE10-3 Zerbe Consulting Inc.'s gross salaries for the biweekly period ended August 22 were $15,000. Deductions included $743 for CPP, $267 for EI, and $6,258 for income tax. The employer's payroll costs were $743 for CPP and $374 for EI. Prepare journal entries to record (a) the payment of salaries on August 22; (b) the employer payroll costs on August 22, assuming they will not be remitted to the government until September; and (c) the payment to the government on September 1 of all amounts owed.

Record payroll. (SO 1)

BE10-4 Romez Limited borrowed $60,000 from the bank on July 1 for three months; 5% interest is payable the first of each month, starting August 1. Romez's year end is August 31. Prepare journal entries to record (a) the receipt of the bank loan on July 1; (b) (1) the payment of interest on August 1, (2) the accrual of interest on August 31, (3) the payment of interest on September 1, and (4) the payment of interest on October 1; and (c) payment of the bank loan at maturity on October 1.

Record short-term loan. (SO 1)

BE10-5 For each of the following independent situations, indicate whether it should be recorded as a provision or disclosed as a contingent liability for a publicly traded company reporting under IFRS. Indicate if your answer would change if the company were a private company reporting under ASPE.
(a) A pending lawsuit for which a negative outcome has been estimated and determined to be "likely"
(b) A pending lawsuit, about which the outcome cannot be determined
(c) A nuisance lawsuit, which the company is not anticipated to lose
(d) A loan guarantee for a subsidiary company that has a credit rating of AA

Account for contingencies. (SO 1)

BE10-6 Assume that you qualify for a $25,000 loan from the Canada Student Loans Program to help finance your education. You are considering whether to repay this loan on graduation with a fixed interest rate of prime + 5% or a floating interest rate of prime + 2.5%. Assuming you start repaying your loan immediately upon graduation, information related to your loan options follows:

Discuss fixed and floating rates of interest. (SO 2)

	Fixed Interest Rate	Floating Interest Rate
Amount of loan	$25,000	$25,000
Prime interest rate assumed	2.75%	2.75%
Number of months to repay loan	120 months	120 months
Monthly instalment payment	$300	$268
Total interest payable over life of loan	$11,003	$7,188

(a) Identify the advantages and disadvantages of each interest rate option. (b) Explain which option you think is best for you and why.

BE10-7 Assad Inc. issued a five-year, 7% instalment note payable, with fixed principal payments plus interest, due annually. The following instalment payment schedule is partially completed:

Complete instalment payment schedule; identify current and non-current portions. (SO 2)

Interest Period	Cash Payment	Interest Expense	Reduction of Principal	Principal Balance
Issue date				$50,000
1	$13,500	$ [1]	[2]	40,000
2	12,800	2,800	[3]	[4]
3	[5]	2,100	[6]	[7]
4	11,400	1,400	[8]	10,000
5	10,700	700	[9]	[10]

(a) Fill in the missing amounts for items [1] through [10]. Round all amounts to the nearest dollar. (b) What are the current and non-current portions of the note at the end of period 3?

BE10-8 Hyatt Inc. issued a five-year, 7% instalment loan payable, with blended principal and interest payments due annually. The following instalment payment schedule is partially completed:

Complete instalment payment schedule; identify current and non-current portions. (SO 2)

Interest Period	Cash Payment	Interest Expense	Reduction of Principal	Principal Balance
Issue date				$50,000
1	$12,195	$ [1]	$ 8,695	41,305
2	[2]	2,891	[3]	32,001
3	[4]	[5]	9,955	[6]
4	[7]	1,543	[8]	11,394
5	[9]	801*	11,394	[10]

*Adjusted for rounding differences.

(a) Fill in the missing amounts for items [1] to [10]. Round all amounts to the nearest dollar. (b) What are the current and non-current portions of the loan at the end of period 3?

Record mortgage payable.
(SO 2)

BE10–9   Eyre Inc. signs a 10-year, 7%, $300,000 mortgage payable on November 30, 2014, to obtain financing for a new building. The terms provide for payments at the end of each month. Prepare the entries to record the mortgage on November 30, 2014, and the first two payments on December 31, 2014, and January 31, 2015, assuming the payment is (a) a fixed principal payment of $2,500, plus interest, and (b) a blended principal and interest payment of $3,483. Round all amounts to the nearest dollar.

Identify current and non-current liabilities.
(SO 3)

BE10–10   Identify which of the following transactions would be classified as a current liability and which would be classified as a non-current liability. For those that are neither, identify where they should be classified or disclosed.
(a) A bank loan payable due in two years, with principal due at maturity and interest due the first of each month
(b) Cash received in advance by Air Canada for airline tickets
(c) HST collected on sales
(d) Unused amount of operating line of credit
(e) Provision relating to a lawsuit settlement expected to be paid next month
(f) Obligations due under operating leases
(g) Bonds payable, due in 10 years
(h) Payroll deductions withheld from the employees' weekly pay
(i) Prepaid property tax
(j) A $75,000 mortgage payable, of which $5,000 is due in the next year

Calculate liquidity and solvency ratios.
(SO 3)

BE10–11   The **Molson Coors Brewing Company**'s financial statements recently reported the following selected data (in U.S. $ millions):

Total current assets	$ 1,748.0
Total current liabilities	2,598.7
Total assets	16,212.2
Total liabilities	8,220.6
Income tax expense	154.5
Interest expense	185.0
Profit	443.0

Calculate Molson Coors's (a) current ratio, (b) debt to total assets ratio, and (c) times interest earned ratio.

Analyze solvency.
(SO 3)

BE10–12   The following solvency ratios are available for Fromage Corporation:

	2015	2014
Debt to total assets	40%	52%
Times interest earned	7 times	11 times

(a) Identify whether the change in each ratio is an improvement or deterioration. (b) Did the company's overall solvency improve or deteriorate in 2015?

Calculate present value.
(SO 4)

***BE10–13**   On January 1, 2015, Carvel Corp. issued five-year bonds with a face value of $500,000 and a coupon interest rate of 6%, with interest payable semi-annually. How much would Carvel receive from the sale of these bonds if the market interest rate was (a) 5%, (b) 6%, and (c) 7%?

Prepare bond amortization tables.
(SO 4)

***BE10–14**   Using the information from BE10–13, prepare a partial bond amortization table for the first two interest payments assuming that interest is paid on July 1 and January 1 and that the bonds sold when the market interest rate was (a) 5%, (b) 6%, and (c) 7%.

*BE10–15   Using the information from BE10–14, assume that the company has a December 31 year end and records adjusting entries annually. Record the journal entries relating to the bonds on January 1, July 1, and December 31, assuming that when the bonds were sold, the market interest rate was (a) 5%, (b) 6%, and (c) 7%.

Record bond
transactions.
(SO 4)

Exercises

E10–1   A list of transactions follows.

1. Purchased inventory (perpetual system) on account.
2. Extended payment terms of the account payable in item 1 by issuing a nine-month, 5% note payable.
3. Recorded accrued interest on the note payable from item 2.
4. Recorded repayment of the note and accrued interest from items 2 and 3.
5. Recorded cash received from sale of services, plus HST.
6. Recorded salaries expense, employee payroll deductions, and paid employees.
7. Recorded employer's share of employee benefits.
8. Recorded property tax expense and property tax payable when bill was received.
9. Recorded a receipt of cash for services that will be performed in the future.
10. Recorded the performance of services for item 9.

Determine impact
of current liability
transactions.
(SO 1)

Instructions
Set up a table using the format that follows. Indicate the effect of each of the above transactions on the financial statement categories in the table: use "+" for increase, "−" for decrease, and "NE" for no effect. The first one has been done for you as an example.

	Assets	Liabilities	Shareholders' Equity	Revenues	Expenses	Profit
1.	+	+	NE	NE	NE	NE

E10–2   Chen Wholesalers Ltd. incurred the following transactions related to current liabilities.

1. Chen's cash register showed the following totals at the end of the day on March 17: pre-tax sales $50,000; GST $2,500; and PST $3,500.
2. Chen received its property tax bill for the calendar year for $52,800 on May 1, payable July 1.
3. Chen's gross payroll for the week of August 15 was $81,000. The company deducted $4,010 for CPP, $1,442 for EI, $6,400 for pension, and $16,020 for income tax from the employees' pay. Chen's payroll costs for the week were $4,010 for CPP and $2,019 for EI.
4. On October 1, Chen borrowed $100,000 from First Bank for a six-month period; 4% interest on the bank loan is payable the first of each month.

Record current
liabilities.
(SO 1)

Instructions
(a) Record the above transactions.
(b) Assuming that Chen's year end is December 31 and that it makes adjusting entries annually, prepare any adjusting entries required for the property tax in transaction 2 and the interest in transaction 4.

E10–3   Dougald Construction Ltd. borrowed $250,000 from TD Bank on October 1, 2014, for a nine-month period; 5% interest is payable at maturity. Both companies have a December 31 year end and make adjusting entries annually.

Record short-term
loans.
(SO 1)

Instructions
(a) For Dougald Construction, record (1) the receipt of the bank loan on October 1, 2014; (2) the accrual of interest on December 31, 2014; and (3) the payment of the loan on July 1, 2015.
(b) For the TD Bank, record (1) the issue of the bank loan on October 1, 2014; (2) the accrual of interest on December 31, 2014; and (3) the collection of the loan on July 1, 2015. (*Hint:* The TD Bank uses a Notes Receivable account to record its loans. You might find it helpful to review accounting for notes receivable in Chapter 8.)

E10–4   **Walmart Stores, Inc.** is sued about once every two hours every day of the year. These allegations range from falls on icy parking lots to injuries sustained in shoppers' stampedes to a murder with a rifle purchased at one of its stores. The company recently disclosed the following in the notes to its financial statements:

Discuss contingent
liabilities.
(SO 1)

> The Company is involved in a number of legal proceedings. The Company has made accruals with respect to these matters, where appropriate. For some matters, the amount of liability is not probable or the amount cannot be reasonably estimated and therefore accruals have not been made. However, where a liability is reasonably possible and material, such matters have been disclosed.

Instructions
(a) The above states that "the company has made accruals . . . where appropriate." Explain when it would be appropriate for Walmart to accrue a liability as a provision rather than disclose it as a contingent liability.
(b) How might the accrual or disclosure of these legal proceedings change if Walmart were a private company reporting under ASPE?

Record mortgage
payable.
(SO 2)

E10–5 Ste. Anne Corp. issued a 10-year, 5%, $150,000 mortgage payable to finance the construction of a building at December 31, 2014. The terms provide for semi-annual instalment payments on June 30 and December 31.

Instructions

(a) Record the issue of the mortgage payable on December 31, 2014.

(b) Record the first two instalment payments on June 30, 2015, and December 31, 2015, assuming the payment is (1) a fixed principal payment of $7,500, and (2) a blended principal and interest payment of $9,622. Round all amounts to the nearest dollar.

(c) Explain why interest expense is the same regardless of whether the payment is blended or based on fixed principal payments for the six months ending June 30 but different for the six months ended December 31.

Record instalment
note payable; identify
current and non-
current portions.
(SO 2)

E10–6 On July 1, 2014, Granville Ltd. borrowed $9,000 by signing a two-year, 6% note payable. The note is payable in two annual blended principal and interest instalments of $4,909 on June 30. Adjusting journal entries are recorded annually at year end on December 31.

Instructions

(a) Prepare an instalment payment schedule for the term of the note. Round all amounts to the nearest dollar.

(b) Record (1) the issue of the note on July 1, 2014; (2) the accrual of interest on December 31, 2014; and (3) the first payment on June 30, 2015.

(c) What amounts would be reported as current and non-current in the liabilities section of Granville's statement of financial position on December 31, 2015?

Analyze instalment
payment schedule.
(SO 2)

E10–7 The following instalment payment schedule is for a long-term bank loan payable:

Interest Period	Cash Payment	Interest Expense	Reduction of Principal	Principal Balance
Issue date				$100,000.00
1	$23,097.48	$5,000.00	$18,097.48	81,902.52
2	23,097.48	4,095.13	19,002.35	62,900.17
3	23,097.48	3,145.01	19,952.47	42,947.70
4	23,097.48	2,147.38	20,950.10	21,997.60
5	23,097.48	1,099.88	21,997.60	0.00

Instructions

(a) Is the above schedule a fixed principal or blended principal and interest payment schedule?

(b) Assuming payments are made annually, what is the interest rate on the bank loan?

(c) Prepare the journal entry to record the first instalment payment.

(d) What are the current and non-current portions of the bank loan at the end of period 2?

Prepare liabilities
section.
(SO 3)

E10–8 **Shaw Communications Inc.** reported the following liabilities (in thousands) in its August 31, 2012, financial statements:

Accounts payable and accrued liabilities	$ 811		Long-term debt	4,812
			Pension liability	401
Current portion of long-term debt	451		Provisions	27
Deferred income taxes	1,085		Unearned revenue	157
Income taxes payable	156			

Instructions

(a) Identify which of the above liabilities are likely current and which are likely non-current. Say if an item fits in either category. Explain the reasoning for your selections.

(b) Prepare the liabilities section of Shaw Communications Inc.'s statement of financial position.

Analyze liquidity.
(SO 3)

E10–9 The following selected information (in thousands) was taken from Fruition Collections Ltd.'s December 31 statement of financial position:

	2015	2014
Current assets		
Cash	$2,574	$1,021
Accounts receivable	2,147	1,575
Inventories	1,201	1,010
Other current assets	322	192
Total current assets	$6,244	$3,798
Total current liabilities	$4,503	$2,619

Instructions

(a) Calculate the current ratio for each of the two years. (1) Based only on this information, would you say that the company's liquidity is strong or weak? (2) What additional information should you request to complete your assessment of liquidity?

(b) Suppose that Fruition Collections used $1 million of its cash to pay off $1 million of its accounts payable. Would this transaction change the current ratio?

(c) At December 31, 2015, Fruition Collections had an unused operating line of credit of $4 million. Does this information affect the assessment of the company's short-term liquidity that you made in part (a) above?

E10–10 **Buhler Industries Inc.'s** financial statements contain the following selected data (in thousands):

	2012	2011
Total assets	$250,755	$241,733
Total liabilities	89,830	97,171
Profit	16,363	11,917
Income tax expense	3,278	3,623
Interest expense	3,507	3,004

Analyze solvency. (SO 3)

Instructions

(a) Calculate the debt to total assets and times interest earned ratios for 2012 and 2011. Did Buhler's solvency improve or deteriorate in 2012?

(b) The notes to Buhler's financial statements show that the company has an operating line of credit (credit facility) with the Bank of Montreal for $60 million that can be drawn on at any time and repaid at any time. Over $13 million of this credit facility has been drawn on. What does this mean and how is this shown in the financial statements?

*E10–11 The following information about two independent bond issues was reported in the financial press.

1. **BC Provincial** 2.70% bonds, maturing December 18, 2022, were issued at a price of 99.9 to yield a market interest rate of 2.71%.
2. **Bank of Montreal** 5.10% bonds, maturing April 21, 2021, were issued at a price of 108.97 to yield a market interest rate of 2.08%.

Analyze and record bond issue. (SO 4)

Instructions

(a) Were the BC Provincial bonds issued at a premium or a discount?

(b) Were the Bank of Montreal bonds issued at a premium or a discount?

(c) Explain why the market interest rate on the Bank of Montreal bonds is lower than the market interest rate on the BC Provincial bonds.

(d) Record the issue of $100,000 of each of these two bonds.

*E10–12 On October 1, 2015, Spooner Corporation issued $800,000 of 10-year, 5% bonds at 100. Interest is payable semi-annually on October 1 and April 1. Spooner's year end is December 31 and the company records adjusting entries annually.

Record bond transactions; identify current and non-current portions. (SO 4)

Instructions

(a) Prepare journal entries to record the following:
1. The issue of the bonds on October 1, 2015
2. The accrual of interest on December 31, 2015
3. The payment of interest on April 1, 2016

(b) Identify what amounts, if any, would be reported as a current liability and non-current liability with respect to the bond and bond interest accounts on December 31, 2015.

*E10–13 A partial bond amortization schedule follows for Hwee Corporation:

Semi-Annual Interest Period	Interest Payment	Interest Expense	Discount/Premium Amortization	Unamortized Discount/Premium	Bond Carrying Amount
Issue date (Oct. 31)				$74,387	$925,613
1 (Apr. 30)	$25,000	[1]	$2,768	[2]	928,381
2 (Oct. 31)	25,000	$27,851	[3]	68,768	[4]
3 (Apr. 30)	[5]	27,937	[6]	[7]	934,169

Complete amortization schedule; answer questions. (SO 4)

Instructions

(a) Fill in the missing amounts for items [1] to [7].

(b) What is the face value of the bonds?

(c) Were the bonds issued at a discount or at a premium?

(d) What is the coupon interest rate on the bonds? The market interest rate?

(e) Explain why interest expense is greater than interest paid.

(f) Explain why interest expense will increase each period.

(g) What will be the bonds' carrying amount on their maturity date?

Calculate present value; record bond transactions.
(SO 4)

*E10–14　Tarawa Limited issued $1 million of 10-year, 5% bonds on January 1, 2015, at a price to yield a market interest rate of 6%. Interest is payable semi-annually on July 1 and January 1. Tarawa has a December 31 year end.

Instructions
(a) Calculate the bonds' present value (issue price) on January 1.
(b) Record the issue of the bonds on January 1.
(c) Record the payment of interest on July 1.
(d) Record the accrual of interest on December 31.

Problems: Set A

Record and present current liabilities.
(SO 1, 3)

P10–1A　On February 28, 2015, Molega Ltd.'s general ledger contained the following liability accounts:

Accounts payable	$42,500
CPP payable	2,680
EI payable	1,123
Sales tax payable	5,800
Income tax payable	5,515
Unearned revenue	15,000

The following selected transactions occurred during the month:

Mar. 2　Issued a three-month, 6% note payable in exchange for an account payable in the amount of $10,000. Interest is due at maturity.

5　Sold merchandise for cash totalling $40,000, plus 13% HST. The cost of goods sold was $24,000. Molega uses a perpetual inventory system.

9　Received the property tax bill of $18,000 for the calendar year. It is payable on May 1.

12　Provided services for customers who had made advance payments of $11,300 including HST, which is not payable until the related sale occurs.

13　Paid $5,800 HST to the Receiver General for sales tax collected in February.

16　Paid $9,318 to the Receiver General for amounts owing from the February payroll for employee payroll deductions of $7,323 (CPP $1,340, EI $468, and income tax $5,515) and for employee benefits of $1,995 (CPP $1,340 and EI $655).

27　Paid $30,000 to trade creditors on account.

31　Paid employees for the month. Gross salaries totalled $16,000 and payroll deductions included CPP of $792, EI of $285, and income tax of $5,870. Employee benefits included CPP of $792 and EI of $399.

Instructions
(a) Record the above transactions.
(b) Record any required adjusting entries at March 31.
(c) Prepare the current liabilities section of the statement of financial position at March 31.

Record and present short-term notes.
(SO 1, 3)

P10–2A　Cling-on Ltd. sells rock-climbing products and also operates an indoor climbing facility for climbing enthusiasts. On September 1, 2015, the company had a balance of $12,000 in its Bank Loan Payable account, representing a loan from the local credit union on July 1. The loan and 6% interest are both payable at maturity, on September 30. Note that the company records adjusting entries annually at its year end, December 31.

During the next four months, Cling-on incurred the following:

Sept. 1　Purchased inventory on account for $15,000 from Black Diamond, terms n/30. The company uses a perpetual inventory system.

30　Repaid the $12,000 bank loan payable to the credit union (see opening balance), as well as any interest owed.

Oct. 1　Issued a six-month, 7%, $15,000 note payable to Black Diamond in exchange for the account payable (see Sept. 1 transaction). Interest is payable on the first of each month.

2　Borrowed $25,000 from Montpelier Bank for 12 months at 8% to finance the building of a new climbing area for advanced climbers (use the asset account Buildings). Interest is payable monthly on the first of each month.

Nov. 1　Paid interest on the Black Diamond note and Montpelier Bank loan.

Dec. 1　Paid interest on the Black Diamond note and Montpelier Bank loan.

2　Purchased a vehicle for $28,000 from Auto Dealer Ltd. to transport clients to nearby climbing sites. Paid $8,000 as a down payment and borrowed the remainder from the Montpelier Bank for 12 months at 7%. Interest is payable quarterly, at the end of each quarter.

31　Recorded accrued interest for the Black Diamond note and Montpelier Bank loans.

Instructions

(a) Record the above transactions.
(b) Open T accounts for the Interest Expense, Interest Payable, Bank Loans Payable, and Notes Payable accounts and enter any opening balances. Post the above entries.
(c) Assuming there is no other interest expense than that recorded in the transactions above, show the income statement presentation of interest expense for the year ended December 31.
(d) Show the statement of financial position presentation of the bank loans, notes, and interest payable at December 31.

P10-3A On September 30, 2014, Coldwater Corporation purchased equipment for $1.1 million. The equipment was purchased with a $100,000 down payment and a three-year, 8%, $1-million bank loan for the balance. The terms provide for payment of the bank loan with quarterly fixed principal payments of $83,333, plus interest, starting on December 31. Coldwater has a November 30 year end and records adjusting entries annually.

Record instalment note. (SO 2)

Instructions

(a) Record the purchase of equipment on September 30, 2014.
(b) Record the accrual of interest expense on November 30, 2014. Round to the nearest dollar.
(c) Record the first two instalment payments, on December 31, 2014, and March 31, 2015. Round all amounts to the nearest dollar.
(d) Repeat part (b) and (c) assuming that the terms provide for quarterly blended principal and interest payments of $94,560, rather than fixed principal payments of $83,333, plus interest.

P10-4A Starlight Graphics Ltd. signed a 10-year, 6.5%, $700,000 mortgage on June 30, 2014, to help finance a new research laboratory. The mortgage terms provide for semi-annual blended principal and interest payments of $48,145. Payments are due on December 31 and June 30. The company's year end is June 30.

Prepare instalment payment schedule; record and present instalment note. (SO 2, 3)

Instructions

(a) Prepare an instalment payment schedule for the first two years. Round all amounts to the nearest dollar.
(b) Record the receipt of the mortgage loan on June 30, 2014.
(c) Record the first two instalment payments, on December 31, 2014, and June 30, 2015.
(d) Show the statement of financial position presentation of the mortgage payable at June 30, 2015.

P10-5A Peter Furlong has just approached a venture capitalist for financing for his sailing school. The lender is willing to loan the Furlong Sailing School $100,000 at a high-risk interest rate of 12%. The loan is payable over three years in fixed principal payments each quarter of $8,333, plus interest. Peter signs a note payable and receives the loan on April 30, 2015. He makes the first payment on July 31. The company's year end is October 31.

Prepare instalment payment schedule; record and present instalment note. (SO 2, 3)

Instructions

(a) Prepare an instalment payment schedule for the three years. Round all amounts to the nearest dollar.
(b) Record the receipt of the loan on April 30.
(c) Record the first two instalment payments, on July 31 and October 31.
(d) Show the statement of financial position presentation of the note payable at October 31, 2015.
(e) Explain how the quarterly and total cash payments would change if the note had been payable in blended principal and interest payments of $10,046, rather than fixed principal payments plus interest.

P10-6A The following transactions occurred in Wendell Corporation, which has a December 31 year end.

Classify liabilities. (SO 1, 3)

1. Property taxes of $40,000 were assessed on March 1 for the calendar year. They are payable by May 1.
2. Wendell signed a five-year, 7%, $200,000 instalment note payable on July 1. The note requires fixed principal payments of $40,000, plus interest annually on each June 30 for the next five years.
3. Wendell purchased merchandise for $120,000 on December 23 on account, terms n/30, FOB shipping point. The merchandise was shipped on December 28 and received by Wendell on January 2.
4. Wendell received $10,000 from customers on December 21 for services to be performed in January.
5. On December 31, Wendell sold merchandise for $8,000, plus 13% HST. The cost of goods sold was $5,000. The company uses a perpetual inventory system.
6. Weekly salaries of $6,000 are paid every Friday for a five-day workweek (Monday to Friday). This year, December 31 is a Wednesday. Payroll deductions for the three days include CPP of $297, EI of $107, and income tax of $1,300. Employee benefits include CPP of $297 and EI of $150. Payroll deductions will be paid on January 15.
7. Wendell is the defendant in a negligence lawsuit. Wendell's legal counsel estimates that Wendell may suffer a $75,000 loss if it loses the suit. In legal counsel's opinion, it is not possible at this time to determine whether or not the case will be lost.
8. After the preparation of its corporate income tax return at year end, Wendell determined that total income tax payable for the year was $50,000 but $45,000 of this amount was paid during the year when the company paid tax instalments.
9. Wendell reported non-current debt of $250,000 at December 31, of which $30,000 was due within the next year.
10. Wendell has a $100,000 operating line of credit available, on which no funds have yet been drawn.

Instructions

(a) Identify which of the above transactions gave rise to amounts that should be reported in the current liabilities section or the non-current liabilities section of Wendell's statement of financial position on December 31. Identify the account title(s) and amount(s) for each reported liability.

(b) Indicate any information that should be disclosed in the notes to Wendell's financial statements.

Analyze liquidity and solvency.
(SO 3)

P10–7A You have been presented with the following selected information taken from the financial statements of **Magna International Inc.** (in U.S. $ millions):

	2012	2011	2010
Statement of financial position			
Accounts receivable	$ 4,774	$ 4,398	$ 3,543
Inventory	2,512	2,045	1,822
Total current assets	9,135	8,146	7,485
Total assets	17,109	14,679	13,674
Current liabilities	6,684	5,724	4,968
Total liabilities	7,651	6,477	5,648
Income statement			
Net sales	$30,837	$28,748	$23,465
Cost of goods sold	27,010	25,434	20,483
Interest expense	16	0	0
Income tax expense	324	202	194
Profit	1,433	1,018	1,003

Instructions

(a) Calculate each of the following ratios for 2012 and 2011. Industry ratios are shown in parentheses.
   1. Current ratio (2012, 1.5:1; 2011, 1.5:1)
   2. Receivables turnover (2012, 6.7 times; 2011, 6.2 times)
   3. Inventory turnover (2012, 9.0 times; 2011, 11.4 times)
   4. Debt to total assets (2012, 34.6%; 2011, 37.1%)
   5. Times interest earned (2012, 7.6 times; 2011, 8.0 times)

(b) Based on your results in part (a), comment on Magna's liquidity and solvency.

(c) Magna had a U.S. $2.25-billion operating line of credit, all of which was unused at December 31, 2012. Most of the bank debt held by the company was in Brazilian and Chinese currencies, which fell in value relative to the Canadian dollar in 2012. Discuss the implications of this information for your analysis.

(d) Magna had operating lease commitments totalling U.S. $1,634 million in 2012 and U.S. $1,608 million in 2011. Discuss the implications of this information for your analysis.

Analyze liquidity and solvency.
(SO 3)

P10–8A The following selected liquidity and solvency ratios are available for two companies operating in the petroleum industry:

	Petro-Zoom	Sun-Oil	Industry Average
Current ratio	1.3:1	1.2:1	1.4:1
Receivables turnover	12 times	13 times	13 times
Inventory turnover	16 times	10 times	19 times
Debt to total assets	41%	39%	34%
Times interest earned	21 times	24 times	26 times

Instructions

Assume that you are the credit manager of the local bank. Answer the following questions, using relevant ratios to justify your answer.

(a) Both Petro-Zoom and Sun-Oil have applied for a short-term loan from your bank. Which of the two companies is more liquid and should get more consideration for a short-term loan? Explain.

(b) Both Petro-Zoom and Sun-Oil have applied for a long-term loan from your bank. Are you concerned about the solvency of either company? Explain why or why not.

Record bond transactions.
(SO 4)

*P10–9A When market interest rates were 6%, three companies issued bonds on January 1, 2015. Each company has a December 31 year end and each company issued bonds with a face value of $100,000 that pay interest annually on December 31. Able Limited sold its bonds at 100 and offered a coupon interest rate of 6%, while Beta Corp. sold its bonds at 94 and offered a coupon interest rate of 4%. Charles Inc. sold its bonds at 105 and offered a 7% coupon interest rate.

Instructions

(a) Record the issue of the bonds by each company on January 1, 2015.

(b) Prepare the entry that each company would record for the payment of interest on December 31, 2015.

(c) Explain why some of the companies are not recording an interest expense on the bonds that is equal to the interest that was actually paid.

(d) Determine the balance in each company's Bonds Payable account on December 31, 2015.

*P10–10A On July 1, 2014, Global Satellites Corporation issued $1.5 million of 10-year, 7% bonds to yield a market interest rate of 6%. The bonds pay semi-annual interest on July 1 and January 1. Global has a December 31 year end.

Instructions

(a) Calculate the bonds' present value (issue price) on July 1.

(b) Prepare an amortization table through January 1, 2016 (three interest periods) for this bond issue. Round all amounts to the nearest dollar.

(c) Record the issue of the bonds on July 1.

(d) Prepare the adjusting entry on December 31, 2015, to accrue the interest on the bonds.

(e) Show the statement of financial position presentation of the liabilities at December 31, 2015.

(f) Record the payment of interest on January 1, 2016.

Calculate present value; prepare amortization schedule; record and present bond transactions. (SO 3, 4)

Problems: Set B

P10–1B On January 1, 2015, Burlington Inc.'s general ledger contained these opening balances for its liability accounts:

Record and present current liabilities. (SO 1, 3)

Accounts payable	$52,000	Sales tax payable	$18,000
CPP payable	3,810	Income tax payable	7,700
EI payable	1,598	Unearned revenue	16,000

The following selected transactions occurred during the month.

Jan. 5 Sold merchandise for cash totalling $20,000, plus 5% GST and 7% PST. The cost of goods sold was $14,000. Burlington uses a perpetual inventory system.

13 Paid $18,000 ($7,500 GST to the Receiver General and $10,500 PST to the provincial Minister of Finance) for sales taxes collected in December.

14 Paid $13,108 to the Receiver General for amounts owing from the December payroll for the employee payroll deductions of $10,271 (CPP $1,905, EI $666, and income tax $7,700) and employee benefits of $2,837 (CPP $1,905 and EI $932).

15 Borrowed $18,000 from HSBC Bank for three months; 6% interest is payable monthly on the 15th of each month.

19 Provided services for customers who had made advance payments of $11,200. This amount includes applicable GST and PST, which is not payable until the related revenue is earned.

22 Paid $32,000 to trade creditors on account.

28 Received assessment of property taxes of $4,200 for the calendar year. They are payable on March 1.

29 Paid employees for the month. Gross salaries totalled $40,000 and payroll deductions included CPP of $1,980, EI of $712, and income tax of $9,474. Employee benefits included CPP of $1,980 and EI of $997.

Instructions

(a) Record the above transactions.

(b) Record any required adjusting entries at January 31.

(c) Prepare the current liabilities section of the statement of financial position at January 31.

P10–2B Sparky's Mountain Bikes Ltd. markets mountain-bike tours to clients vacationing in various locations in the mountains of British Columbia. On March 1, 2015, the company had a balance of $30,000 in Notes Payable for a six-month, 7% note issued to Easy Finance Corp. on October 1, with interest payable at maturity. Note that the company records adjusting entries annually at its year end, June 30.

Record and present short-term notes. (SO 1, 3)

In preparation for the upcoming summer biking season, Sparky's engaged in the following transactions:

Mar. 2 Purchased Cannondale bikes for use as rentals by borrowing $16,000 from the Western Bank for a three-month period; 8% interest is payable at maturity.

31 Paid the $30,000 note payable to Easy Finance Corp. (see opening balance), as well as any interest owed.

Apr. 1 Issued a nine-month, 6%, $50,000 note to Mountain Real Estate for the purchase of mountain property on which to build bike trails. Interest is payable at the first of each month.

May 1 Paid interest on the Mountain Real Estate note (see April 1 transaction).

2 Borrowed $36,000 from Western Bank for a four-month period. The funds will be used for working capital for the beginning of the season. 7% interest is payable at maturity.

June 1   Paid interest on the Mountain Real Estate note (see April 1 transaction).
      2   Paid principal and interest to the Western Bank (see March 2 transaction).
      29   Purchased trailers for $10,000 to transport the bikes from one location to another. Paid $1,000 as a down payment and borrowed the remainder from the Western Bank for a 12-month period; 6% interest is payable quarterly, at the end of each quarter starting September 30.
      30   Recorded accrued interest for the Mountain Real Estate note and Western Bank loan.

Instructions

(a) Record the above transactions.
(b) Open T accounts for the Interest Expense, Interest Payable, Bank Loans Payable, and Notes Payable accounts and enter any opening balances. Post the above entries.
(c) Assuming there is no other interest expense than that recorded in the transactions above, show the income statement presentation of the interest expense for the year ended June 30.
(d) Show the statement of financial position presentation of the notes, bank loans, and interest payable at June 30.

Record instalment note.
(SO 2)

P10–3B   On July 31, 2015, Myron Corporation purchased equipment for $750,000. The equipment was purchased with a $50,000 down payment and by borrowing a four-year, 6%, $700,000 bank loan payable for the balance. The terms provide for the bank loan to be repaid with monthly blended principal and interest instalment payments of $16,440 starting on August 31. Myron has a September 30 year end.

Instructions

(a) Record the purchase of equipment and the receipt of the bank loan on July 31.
(b) Record the first two instalment payments, on August 31 and September 30. Round all amounts to the nearest dollar.
(c) Repeat part (b) assuming that the terms provide for monthly fixed principal payments of $14,583, plus interest, rather than blended payments of $16,440.

Prepare instalment payment schedule; record and present instalment note.
(SO 2, 3)

P10–4B   Beaumont Building Supplies Limited signed a 10-year, 8%, $1-million mortgage on December 31, 2014, to help finance a plant expansion. The terms of the mortgage provide for semi-annual fixed principal payments of $50,000, plus interest. Payments are due on June 30 and December 31.

Instructions

(a) Prepare an instalment payment schedule for the first two years. Round all amounts to the nearest dollar.
(b) Record the issue of the mortgage payable on December 31, 2014.
(c) Record the first two instalment payments, on June 30, 2015, and December 31, 2015.
(d) Show the statement of financial position presentation of the mortgage payable at December 31, 2015.

Prepare instalment payment schedule; record and present instalment note.
(SO 2, 3)

P10–5B   A local ski hill has just approached a venture capitalist for financing for its new business venture, the development of another local ski hill. On April 1, 2013, the venture capitalist loaned the company $100,000 at an interest rate of 13%. The loan is payable over four years in annual blended principal and interest instalments of $33,619, due each March 31. The first payment is due March 31, 2014. The ski hill's year end is March 31.

Instructions

(a) Prepare an instalment payment schedule for the loan period. Round all amounts to the nearest dollar.
(b) Record the receipt of the loan on April 1, 2013.
(c) Record the first two instalment payments, on March 31, 2014, and March 31, 2015.
(d) Show the statement of financial position presentation of the loan payable as at March 31, 2015.
(e) Explain how the annual and total interest expense would change if the loan had been payable in fixed principal payments of $25,000, plus interest, rather than in blended principal and interest payments.

Classify liabilities.
(SO 1, 3)

P10–6B   The following transactions are for Iqaluit Ltd., which has an April 30 year end.

1. Received property taxes assessment of $12,000 on March 1 for the calendar year. They are payable by May 1.
2. Purchased equipment for $35,000 on April 1 by making a $5,000 down payment and borrowing the remainder from the bank for a six-month period; 6% interest is payable on the first of each month.
3. Purchased merchandise for $7,000 on April 27 on account, terms 2/10, n/30.
4. Sold merchandise on April 28 for $15,000, plus 5% GST. (There is no PST in Nunavut, where Iqaluit Ltd. is based.) The cost of the goods sold was $10,500. The company uses a perpetual inventory system.
5. Received $25,000 from customers on April 29 for services to be performed in May.
6. Weekly salaries of $10,000 are paid every Friday for a five-day workweek (Monday to Friday). This year, April 30 is a Thursday. Payroll deductions for the four days include CPP of $495, EI of $178, and income tax of $3,710. Employee benefits include CPP of $495 and EI of $249. Payroll deductions will be paid on May 15.
7. Iqaluit was named in a lawsuit alleging negligence for an oil spill that leaked into the neighbouring company's water system. Iqaluit's legal counsel estimates that the company will likely lose the suit but the amount of the loss cannot be determined yet.

8. Iqaluit paid income tax instalments of $80,000 throughout the year. After the preparation of its year-end corporate income tax return, it was determined that the total income tax payable for the year was $55,000.
9. Iqaluit reported non-current liabilities of $150,000 at April 30, of which $15,000 was due within the next year.
10. Iqaluit has a $50,000 operating line of credit available, on which no funds have yet been drawn.

Instructions
(a) Identify which of the above transactions give rise to amounts that should be reported in the current liabilities section or the non-current liabilities section of Iqaluit's statement of financial position on April 30. Identify the account title(s) and amount(s) for each reported liability.
(b) Indicate any information that should be disclosed in the notes to Iqaluit's financial statements.

P10–7B The following selected information was taken from **Barrick Gold Corporation**'s financial statements (in U.S. $ millions):

Analyze liquidity and solvency.
(SO 3)

	2012	2011	2010
Statement of financial position			
Accounts receivable	$ 449	$ 426	$ 370
Inventory	2,695	2,498	1,798
Total current assets	5,863	6,545	7,071
Total assets	47,282	48,884	34,637
Current liabilities	4,415	2,911	2,491
Total liabilities	22,774	23,330	13,420
Income statement			
Net sales	$14,547	$14,236	$11,001
Cost of goods sold	7,654	6,240	5,162
Interest expense	177	199	180
Income tax expense (recovery)	(236)	2,287	1,561
Profit (loss)	(677)	4,537	3,630

Instructions
(a) Calculate each of the following ratios for 2012 and 2011. Industry ratios are shown in parentheses.
   1. Current ratio (2012, 2.3:1; 2011, 2.4:1)
   2. Receivables turnover (2012, 19.0 times; 2011, 19.1 times)
   3. Inventory turnover (2012, 3.7 times; 2011, 4.0 times)
   4. Debt to total assets (2012, 20.6%; 2011, 20.6%)
   5. Times interest earned (2012, 17.3 times; 2011, 18.9 times)
(b) Based on your results in part (a), comment on Barrick Gold's liquidity and solvency.
(c) Barrick Gold has three pages of disclosure in the notes to its statements about pending litigation. Discuss the implications of this information for your analysis.

P10–8B The following selected liquidity and solvency ratios are available for two companies operating in the fast food industry:

Analyze liquidity and solvency.
(SO 3)

	Grab 'N Gab	Chick 'N Lick	Industry Average
Current ratio	0.8:1	0.7:1	0.9:1
Receivables turnover	46 times	38 times	34 times
Inventory turnover	39 times	45 times	31 times
Debt to total assets	49%	40%	39%
Times interest earned	10 times	5 times	7 times

Instructions
Assume that you are the credit manager of the local bank. Answer the following questions, using relevant ratios to justify your answer.
(a) Both Grab 'N Gab and Chick 'N Lick have applied for a short-term loan from your bank. Which of the two companies is more liquid and should get more consideration for a short-term loan? Explain.
(b) Both Grab 'N Gab and Chick 'N Lick have applied for a long-term loan from your bank. Are you concerned about the solvency of either company? Explain why or why not.

*P10–9B When market interest rates were 5%, three companies issued bonds on January 1, 2015. Each company has a December 31 year end and each company issued bonds with a face value of $200,000 that pay interest annually on December 31. Delta Limited sold its bonds at 100 and offered a coupon interest rate of 5%, while Founders Corp. sold its bonds at 94 and offered a coupon interest rate of 3%. Grand Inc. sold its bonds at 108 and offered a 7% coupon interest rate.

Record bond transactions.
(SO 4)

Instructions
(a) Record the issue of the bonds by each company on January 1, 2015.
(b) Prepare the entry that each company would record for the payment of interest on December 31, 2015.

(c) Explain why some of the companies are not recording an interest expense on the bonds that is equal to the interest that was actually paid.

(d) Determine the balance in each company's Bonds Payable account on December 31, 2015.

Calculate present value;
prepare amortiza-
tion schedule; record
and present bond
transactions.
(SO 3, 4)

*P10–10B   On July 1, 2014, Ponasis Corporation issued $1 million of 10-year, 6% bonds at a price to yield a market interest rate of 7%. The bonds pay semi-annual interest on July 1 and January 1. Ponasis has a December 31 year end.

Instructions

(a) Calculate the bonds' present value (issue price) on July 1.

(b) Prepare an amortization table through January 1, 2016 (three interest periods) for this bond issue. Round all amounts to the nearest dollar.

(c) Record the issue of the bonds on July 1.

(d) Prepare the adjusting entry on December 31, 2015, to accrue the interest on the bonds.

(e) Show the statement of financial position presentation of the liabilities at December 31, 2015.

(f) Record the payment of interest on January 1, 2016.

Broadening Your Perspective

Financial Reporting: *Shoppers Drug Mart*

Answer questions
about financial
statements.
(SO 1, 2, 3)

BYP10–1   The financial statements of **Shoppers Drug Mart** are presented in Appendix A at the end of the book.

Instructions

(a) What types of current and non-current liabilities were reported in Shoppers' balance sheet at December 29, 2012?

(b) The company has cash reported in the current assets section, and bank indebtedness reported in the current liabilities section, of its balance sheet. Why doesn't the company just use the cash to pay off this liability?

(c) Shoppers issues commercial paper that usually falls due after 90 days and bears interest at a floating rate. Why would this company want to use that type of liability to finance its needs?

Comparative Analysis: *Shoppers Drug Mart* and *Jean Coutu*

Analyze liquidity and
solvency.
(SO 3)

BYP10–2   The financial statements of **Jean Coutu** are presented in Appendix B following the financial statements for **Shoppers Drug Mart** in Appendix A.

Instructions

(a) Based on the information contained in the financial statements, calculate the following ratios for each company for the latest fiscal year. Industry ratios are shown in parentheses.
1. Current ratio (1.4:1)
2. Receivables turnover (22.0 times) (Assume all sales were credit sales and use net receivables instead of gross receivables.)
3. Inventory turnover (7.8 times)
4. Debt to total assets (30.6%)
5. Times interest earned (6.5 times)

(b) What conclusions about the companies' liquidity and solvency can you draw from the ratios calculated in part (a)?

Comparing IFRS and ASPE

Calculate and evaluate
solvency; compare
IFRS and ASPE.
(SO 3, 4)

BYP10–3   Matthew Munk, a venture capitalist, is considering investing in Fly Fast Airlines Limited, a private company that owns and operates a small airline business. Fly Fast Airlines operates out of the major centres in Canada and competes directly with the larger airlines on short-haul flights. One of its major competitors is East Jet Airlines Limited.

Fly Fast prepares its financial statements in accordance with ASPE, while East Jet is a publicly traded company that prepares its financial statements in accordance with IFRS.

The following is an excerpt of selected financial amounts (in thousands) from Fly Fast's and East Jet's financial statements:

	East Jet	Fly Fast
Statement of Financial Position		
Current assets	$1,268,710	$317,178
Non-current assets	2,294,134	573,533
Current liabilities	832,172	120,000
Non-current liabilities	1,222,993	270,000
Income Statement		
Revenue	$2,609,261	$652,315
Profit	136,720	34,180
Income tax expense	59,947	14,986
Interest expense	60,164	9,876

As Matthew considers investing in Fly Fast, he would like to evaluate its solvency and ability to pay interest on its liabilities.

Instructions

(a) Identify two ratios that Matthew can use to assess the solvency of Fly Fast in contrast to that of its main competitor, East Jet. Calculate the recommended ratios for both Fly Fast and East Jet. Which company has better solvency?

(b) In the current liability section of the statement of financial position, East Jet has recorded a provision while Fly Fast has recorded a contingent liability. As these are uncertain liabilities, which company is more likely to recognize this type of liability given the type of accounting standards it uses?

Critical Thinking Case

BYP10-4 Atlas Limited operates a small wholesale private company selling imported foods to grocery retailers on Prince Edward Island. The company began operations on January 1, 2014, and has just completed its second year of operations. In January 2015, the company moved to a new location and now rents a much larger facility. When the move occurred, additional bank loans were taken out to finance the purchase of some new equipment. The CEO of the business, Jim O'Sullivan, negotiated with the bank to have principal payments (not interest) on any bank loan delayed until 2017. Jim has asked you to review information from the company's financial statements shown below and to accompany him to the bank. He wants you to help him convince his banker to give the company an operating line of credit.

The banker has some misgivings. Jim is not sure why, because the current ratio has risen and the debt to total assets ratio has fallen slightly. He did tell you that a contingent liability relating to a lawsuit launched against the company will be disclosed in the financial statements, but it has not been recorded because an estimate could not be determined.

Shown below are amounts extracted from the financial statements (in thousands).

Analyze liquidity and solvency.
(SO 3)

	2015	2014
Statement of Financial Position Information		
Cash	$ 2,000	$10,000
Accounts receivable	20,000	5,000
Merchandise inventory	30,000	7,500
Property, plant, and equipment, net	60,000	50,000
Accounts payable	30,930	16,550
Bank loan, non-current	40,000	30,000
Common shares	13,000	13,000
Retained earnings	28,070	12,950
Income Statement Information		
Sales	$100,000	$50,000
Cost of goods sold	50,000	20,000
Operating expenses	26,000	10,000
Interest expense	2,400	1,500
Income tax expense	6,480	5,550

Instructions

Explain to Jim why his banker may not want to give the company an operating line of credit. Begin your analysis by discussing how ratios that were covered in this chapter have changed in 2015 compared with 2014 and discuss possible underlying reasons for these changes.

Ethics Case

BYP10-5 Crown Point Inc. is in the process of arranging a long-term lease for the company's equipment. The company has dismissed the option of borrowing money from the bank and buying the equipment and is now trying to decide

Discuss impact of lease structure.
(SO 3)

between structuring the lease as an operating lease or a finance lease. Lise Ranier, the company's CEO, strongly urges the controller to structure the lease as an operating lease. "That way," she says, "we won't add debt that might create problems with our existing debt covenants at the bank."

Instructions

(a) Who are the stakeholders in this situation?

(b) Explain generally how an operating lease affects the financial statements of a company, compared with a finance lease.

(c) Is it unethical to deliberately structure a lease as an operating lease just to keep the debt off the financial statements?

(d) Do you think analysts will be able to distinguish among the financial impacts of purchasing equipment by borrowing from a bank compared with leasing it on an operating lease or a finance lease?

"All About You" Activity

Identify options for Canada Student Loan.
(SO 2)

BYP10–6   As indicated in the "All About You" feature in this chapter, a student loan is a loan that must be repaid. Assume that when you have completed your studies you have a student loan of $25,000.

Instructions

Go to the Government of Canada's CanLearn website at www.canlearn.ca and search for the Loan Repayment Estimator. Use the estimator and the information about it to answer the following questions.

(a) What options do you have concerning when you must start to make repayments on your loan and what options do you have regarding the length of time you can take to repay the loan?

(b) What is the monthly loan repayment for each option in part (a) using a fixed interest rate?

(c) What is the monthly loan payment for each option in part (a) using a floating interest rate?

(d) Assume that you want to pay off the loan in five years. How much would that change your payments, assuming (1) a fixed interest rate, and (2) a floating interest rate?

Serial Case

(*Note*: This is a continuation of the serial case from Chapters 1 through 9.)

Prepare instalment payment schedule; record and present an instalment note.
(SO 2, 3)

BYP10–7   The equipment upgrade that Koebel's Family Bakery decided to undertake proved to be a little more expensive than initially budgeted. Natalie, Janet, and Brian had originally thought that the project could be paid for with cash in the bank. Instead, an operating line of credit was obtained. At November 25, 2015, the balance used on the line of credit, and recorded in the Bank Indebtedness account, was $25,000.

At June 25, 2015, the balance of the 5% mortgage payable was $49,050. Monthly blended principal and interest instalment payments are $667 paid on the 25th of each month.

The mortgage is up for renewal on November 25, 2015, and Janet, Brian, and Natalie would like the mortgage term to be five years, instead of the seven years remaining. The current interest rate is 4%. Brian and Natalie are considering transferring the balance of the line of credit onto the mortgage payable balance outstanding instead of trying to pay the balance outstanding from cash generated from operations. The bank is happy to accommodate this request and has estimated the monthly blended principal and interest instalment payments to be $1,320 for the combined amounts, commencing December 25, 2015.

Instructions

(a) If the amount of mortgage owing was $49,050 on June 25, and blended payments are $667 per month as indicated above, what is the amount of the mortgage owing at November 25, 2015, immediately before it is renegotiated? Round all amounts to the nearest dollar.

(b) Assume that the Koebels increase the mortgage payable amount you determined in part (a) by $25,000, the amount of the line of credit outstanding at November 25, 2015. What is the revised amount of the mortgage payable at November 26? Record the increase in the mortgage payable on November 26.

(c) Prepare a revised instalment payment schedule using the blended instalment payments of $1,320, from December 25, 2015, to June 25, 2017. Round all amounts to the nearest dollar.

(d) Record the first two instalment payments for December 25, 2015, and January 25, 2016.

(e) From the information provided in part (c), show the presentation of the current and non-current portions of the mortgage payable on the statement of financial position at June 30, 2016.

Answers to Self-Test Questions

1. c   2. b   3. b   4. b   5. c
6. b   7. d   8. d   9. d   10. c

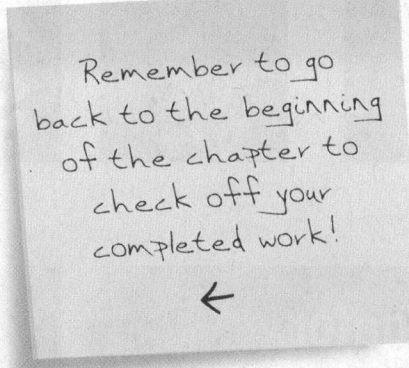

Remember to go back to the beginning of the chapter to check off your completed work!

Endnotes

[1]Canada Post 2012 annual report; "Canada Post Opens New State-of-the-Art Mail Processing Plant," news release, June 4, 2010; *Canada Post: A Blueprint for Change*, Canada Post, September 2008.

[2]Karla Thorpe, "Employee Benefits–The Dragon Will Soon Awake," The Conference Board of Canada, November 2, 2012; www.conferenceboard.ca/topics/humanresource/commentaries/12-11-02/employee_benefits–the_dragon_will_soon_awake.aspx.

[3]Will Dunning, *Confidence in the Canadian Mortgage Market*, Canadian Association of Accredited Mortgage Professionals, May 2012; "Canadians Lack Knowledge About Home Equity Lines of Credit, But Only One-in-Ten Seek Expert Legal Advice, Poll Reveals," LawPRO company news release, November 15, 2011; Roma Luciw, "Canadians Putting Homes at Risk with Lines of Credit," *The Globe and Mail*, November 15, 2011.

[4]Statistics Canada, "The Financial Impact of Student Loans," *The Daily*, January 29, 2010. Statistics Canada, "University Tuition Fees," *The Daily*, September 12, 2012. Postmedia News, "Student Debt More Than Doubled in Last 20 Years," September 24, 2010. Preet Banerjee, "Hey Scholars, Does Your Debt-to-Income Ratio Make the Grade?" *The Globe and Mail*, September 4, 2012.

The Navigator
Chapter 11

- [ ] Scan *Study Objectives*
- [ ] Read *Feature Story*
- [ ] Read text and answer *Do It!s*
- [ ] Review *Comparing IFRS and ASPE*
- [ ] Review *Summary of Study Objectives*
- [ ] Review *Decision Toolkit—A Summary*
- [ ] Work *Using the Decision Toolkit*
- [ ] Work *Comprehensive Do It!*
- [ ] Answer *Self-Test Questions*
- [ ] Complete *assignments*
- [ ] Go to *WileyPLUS* for practice and tutorials

study objectives

After studying this chapter, you should be able to:

SO 1 Identify and discuss the major characteristics of a corporation.

SO 2 Record share transactions.

SO 3 Prepare the entries for cash dividends, stock dividends, and stock splits, and understand their financial impact.

SO 4 Indicate how shareholders' equity is presented in the financial statements.

SO 5 Evaluate dividend and earnings performance.

Brewing Shareholder Return

Public corporations issue shares, but they can buy some of their shares back, as well. When companies do that, they reduce the number of shares that are held by the public, which increases earnings per share and often the share price. For example, Tim Hortons, the iconic quick service restaurant franchise chain, has had several share repurchase programs to create shareholder value.

Tim Hortons began as a privately held company. It started in 1965 with one location in Hamilton, Ontario, and soon expanded with franchises. In 1995, the company was purchased by Wendy's International, Inc. In 2006, Tim Hortons went public and was spun off as a separate company, registered in the United States. In its initial public offering, Tim Hortons issued 29 million common shares at $27 each. Tim Hortons Inc. completed its reorganization as a Canadian public company in September 2009. On that date, Tim Hortons' shares were trading at $30.60 on the Toronto Stock Exchange and $27.99 on the New York Stock Exchange.

Today, there are more than 4,000 Tim Hortons restaurants across Canada, the United States, and in the Arab states of the Persian Gulf. They are mostly owned by franchisees. Tim Hortons' total revenues in 2012 were in excess of $3 billion.

To create value for shareholders, Tim Hortons has to consider the right balance between issuing dividends to existing shareholders and buying back some of its shares. The company has undergone several consecutive major share repurchase programs since it went public in 2006. For example, in early 2013, Tim Hortons announced plans to start a new share repurchase program to buy up to $250 million in common shares, an increase from the previous program. "Our confidence in the strength of our cash flows led us to increase our share repurchase program from $200 million to $250 million as a means of returning capital to our shareholders," said Cynthia Devine, Chief Financial Officer.

Tim Hortons has a dividend policy whereby it commits to paying out a certain percentage of its profit to shareholders every year. The policy is to pay up to 35 to 40% of annual, normalized prior-year profit in dividends in the current year. Since becoming a public company, Tim Hortons increased its quarterly dividend several times, ranging from an 11% increase to a 31% increase.

The company also sets a target that it communicates to shareholders each year to achieve a certain earnings per share for the upcoming year. For 2013, that target is earnings per share of $2.87 to $2.97. If it achieves same-store sales growth and if it delivers the targeted number of new restaurants for the year, then that translates to profits. If the restaurant owners are growing their businesses, then Tim Hortons is too.[1]

the navigator

<table>
<tr><td>preview of
CHAPTER | 11</td><td>Many companies start out small and grow into large corporations, just as Tim Hortons in our feature story has. In this chapter, we look at the essential features of a corporation. The accounting for, and reporting of, the different components that make up shareholders' equity are explained. We conclude by reviewing dividend and earnings measures of performance.</td></tr>
</table>

The chapter is organized as follows:

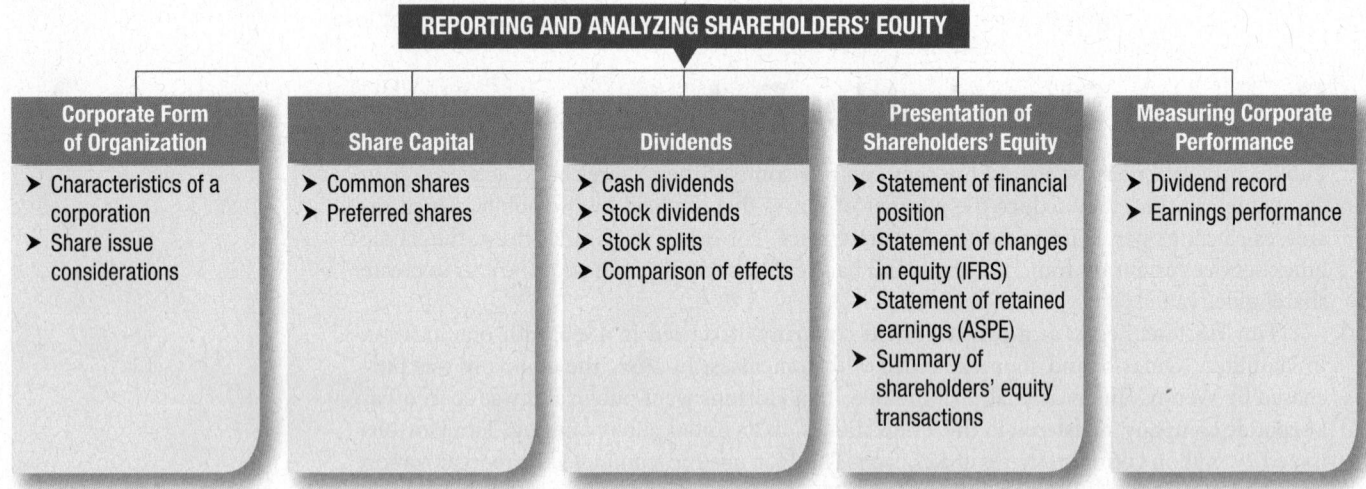

Corporate Form of Organization

STUDY OBJECTIVE 1

Identify and discuss the major characteristics of a corporation.

A **corporation** is a legal entity that is separate and distinct from its owners, who are known as shareholders. You will recall from Chapter 1 that a **public corporation m**ay have thousands of shareholders, and its shares are publicly traded or held. As we have learned in previous chapters, public corporations must follow International Financial Reporting Standards. In contrast, a **private corporation**—often called a privately held corporation—usually has only a few shareholders and does not offer its shares for sale to the general public. A private company has the choice of following International Financial Reporting Standards or Accounting Standards for Private Enterprises. Tim Hortons, in our feature story, was a privately held corporation until it offered its shares for sale to the public in 2006, after which it became a publicly traded company.

CHARACTERISTICS OF A CORPORATION

Many characteristics distinguish corporations—whether public or private—from proprietorships and partnerships. Recall from Chapter 1 that a proprietorship is a business owned by one person, and a partnership is owned by two or more people who are associated as partners. We also discussed some of the distinguishing characteristics of a corporation in Chapter 1, and we review them again here.

Separate Legal Existence

As a legal entity that is separate and distinct from its owners, the corporation acts under its own name rather than in the name of its shareholders. Tim Hortons, for example, may buy, own, and sell property, borrow money, and enter into legally binding contracts in its own name. It may also sue or be sued. And it pays income tax as a separate entity.

In contrast to a proprietorship or partnership, which is bound by the owners' actions, the acts of a corporation's owners (shareholders) do not bind the corporation unless these owners are also agents of the corporation. For example, if you owned Tim Hortons shares, you would not have the right to purchase or lease a new building for the company unless you were designated as an agent of the corporation.

Limited Liability of Shareholders

The liability of shareholders is limited to their investment in the shares of the corporation. This means that creditors have access only to corporate assets to satisfy their claims: in other words, shareholders cannot be made to pay for the company's liabilities out of their personal assets. They may lose the amount that they have invested in the shares of the company, but they will not lose *more* than their investment.

Limited liability is a significant advantage for the corporate form of organization. However, in smaller private corporations, creditors may demand a personal guarantee from the controlling shareholder. This has the effect of making the controlling shareholder's personal assets available, if required, to satisfy the creditor's claim—which, of course, reduces or eliminates the advantage of limited liability.

Transferable Ownership Rights

Ownership of a corporation is held in shares of capital, which are transferable units. Shareholders can dispose of part or all of their interest in a corporation simply by selling their shares. In a public corporation, the transfer of shares is entirely up to the shareholder. It does not require the approval of either the corporation or other shareholders. In contrast, many private corporations impose limitations on the sale or transfer of shares by shareholders.

Whether public or private, the transfer of ownership rights among shareholders has no effect on a corporation's financial position. It does not affect a corporation's assets, liabilities, or shareholders' equity. The transfer of ownership rights is a transaction between individual shareholders. Consequently, when a shareholder sells his or her shares to another investor, the company does not record a journal entry. A journal entry is recorded by the company only at the time of the first offering, or original sale, of the shares. We will discuss how a company records the sale of shares the first time they are offered for sale in the next section.

Ability to Acquire Capital

It is fairly easy for a corporation to obtain capital (cash) by issuing shares. Buying shares in a corporation is often attractive to an investor because a shareholder has limited liability and shares are readily transferable. Also, because only small amounts of money need to be invested, many individuals can become shareholders. A successful corporation's ability to obtain capital is almost unlimited.

Note that the "almost unlimited" ability to acquire capital is only true for large, publicly traded corporations. Small private corporations can have as much difficulty in acquiring capital as do proprietorships or partnerships.

Continuous Life

Corporations have an unlimited life. Since a corporation is a separate legal entity, its continuance as a going concern is not affected by the withdrawal, death, or incapacity of a shareholder, employee, or officer. As a result, a successful corporation can have a very long, if not indefinite, life. For example, there are about 5,500 companies throughout the world that have been in business for more than 200 years. In contrast, proprietorships end if anything happens to the proprietor and partnerships normally re-form if anything happens to one of the partners.

Corporation Management

Shareholders can invest in a corporation without having to manage it personally. Although shareholders legally own the corporation, they manage it indirectly through a board of directors they elect. The board, in turn, sets the broad strategic objectives for the company. The board also selects officers, such as a president and one or more vice-presidents, to execute policy and to perform daily management functions.

Government Regulations

Canadian companies may be incorporated federally, under the terms of the *Canada Business Corporations Act,* or provincially, under the terms of a provincial business corporations act. Federal and provincial laws state the requirements for issuing and reacquiring shares and distributing profits. Similarly, the regulations of provincial securities commissions control the sale of shares to the general public.

There are additional reporting and disclosure requirements by corporations, particularly by publicly traded corporations. When a corporation's shares are listed and traded on foreign securities markets, the corporation must also respect the reporting requirements of these exchanges. For example, Tim Hortons' shares are listed on both the Toronto Stock Exchange in Canada and the New York Stock Exchange in the United States. Complying with federal, provincial, and securities regulations in multiple jurisdictions increases the cost and complexity of the corporate form of organization.

Income Tax

Proprietorships and partnerships do not pay income tax as separate entities. Instead, each owner's (or partner's) share of profit from these organizations is reported on his or her personal income tax return. Income tax is then paid on this amount by the individual. Corporations, on the other hand, must pay federal and provincial income taxes as separate legal entities. Income tax rates vary based on the type of income and by province. In general, however, corporate income tax rates are lower than the rate individuals would pay on the same amount of income, and especially so for small businesses.

The following list summarizes the advantages and disadvantages of the corporate form of business organization:

ADVANTAGES	DISADVANTAGES
• Separate legal entity • Limited liability of shareholders • Ease of transferring ownership rights (shares) • Ability to acquire capital (cash) by issuing shares • Continuous life • Separation of management and ownership • Potential for reduced income tax	• Increased cost and complexity to follow government regulations • Increased reporting and disclosure requirements

The above advantages and disadvantages apply to large, publicly traded corporations. However, as mentioned earlier, not all of them apply to small, privately held corporations.

DECISION TOOLKIT

 Decision Checkpoints	 Info Needed for Decision	 Tools to Use for Decision	 How to Evaluate Results
Should the company incorporate?	Capital needs, growth expectations, type of business, income tax status	Corporations have limited liability, greater ability to raise capital, and professional managers. In addition, there is a potential for reduced income tax. There is increased cost and complexity from additional government regulations.	Carefully weigh the costs and benefits in light of the particular circumstances.

SHARE ISSUE CONSIDERATIONS

After incorporation, a corporation sells ownership rights as shares. The shares of the company are divided into different classes, such as Class A, Class B, and so on. The rights and privileges for each class of shares are stated in articles of incorporation, which form the "constitution" of the company. The different classes are usually identified by the generic terms *common shares* and *preferred shares*. Combined, they form the **share capital** of the company. When a corporation has only one class of shares, that class has the rights and privileges of common shares. As mentioned in Chapter 2, common shares are also known internationally as *ordinary shares*.

Common shareholders are considered to be the "owners" of the corporation. Only common shareholders have the right to vote on certain matters, such as the election of the board of directors and appointment of external auditors. Each shareholder normally has one vote for each common share owned.

Authorized Share Capital

The amount of share capital that a corporation is authorized to sell is indicated in its articles of incorporation. It may be specified as either an unlimited amount or a specific number (for example, 1 million shares authorized). Most companies in Canada have an unlimited amount of **authorized shares**. If a specific number of shares is authorized, the amount normally anticipates a company's initial and later capital needs.

Tim Hortons has an unlimited number of common and preferred shares authorized. The authorization of share capital does not result in a journal entry, because the event has no effect on either corporate assets or shareholders' equity. It is the issue (sale) of shares by the corporation that results in a transaction that must be journalized, and not the authorization of shares. For example, Tim Hortons has never issued preferred shares even though it is authorized to do so. Consequently, no journal entry has been made by Tim Hortons to record the issue of preferred shares.

Issue of Shares

The first time a corporation's shares are offered for sale to the public, the offer is called an **initial public offering (IPO)**. Tim Hortons issued 29 million common shares at $27 each in an IPO in March 2006 when it became a public company. When a company issues shares through an IPO, it receives the cash (less any financing or issue fees) from the sale of the shares. The company's assets (cash) increase, and its shareholders' equity (share capital) also increases; consequently, this transaction requires a journal entry to be made by the company.

Issued shares are authorized shares that have been sold. Tim Hortons had 153 million common shares issued at the end of 2012. Once the shares have been issued and sold by the company through an IPO, they then trade on the secondary market. That is, investors buy and sell shares from each other rather than from the company, using a stock exchange such as the Toronto Stock Exchange. As mentioned earlier in the chapter, when shares are sold among investors, there is no impact on the company's financial position. The company receives no additional assets, and it issues no additional shares. The only change in the company records is the name of the shareholder, not the number of shares issued.

ACCOUNTING MATTERS!

Facebook IPO

In the most heavily anticipated IPO of the year, Mark Zuckerberg, the founder and CEO of Facebook, took Facebook public in 2012. The IPO was one of the biggest in Internet history, raising U.S. $16 billion for the company.

Unfortunately, Facebook's IPO ended up being considered more of a flop than the success everyone had anticipated. The initial share price of U.S. $38 per share fell significantly after the IPO, losing a quarter of its initial value in less than a month and nearly half of its value in three months. The social networking company is now facing lawsuits from shareholders who allege that the company deceived them with misleading growth forecasts during the IPO process.

Fair Value of Shares

After the initial issue of new shares, the share price changes according to the interaction between buyers and sellers. In general, the price follows the trend of a company's profits and dividends. Some factors that are beyond a company's control (such as an embargo on oil, an economic recession, changes in interest rates, the outcome of an election, and war) can also influence share prices. Understanding share prices is complex and the subject of advanced finance courses.

For each listed security, the financial press reports the highest and lowest prices that the shares sold at for the year, the annual dividend rate, the high and low prices for the day, and the net change over the previous day. The total volume of shares traded on a particular day, the dividend yield, and the price-earnings ratio are also reported. A listing for Tim Hortons' common shares on the Toronto Stock Exchange at the end of 2012 follows:

365-day									vol		
high	low	stock	sym	div	high	low	close	chg	(000)	yld	p/e
57.91	45.11	Tim Hortons	THI	0.84	$48.99	$48.40	$48.83	$0.32	168	1.72	18.78

Tim Hortons' shares traded as high as $57.91 and as low as $45.11 during the year. The stock's ticker symbol is "THI." Tim Hortons pays an annual dividend of $0.84 per share, as indicated in the "div" column. The high and low share prices for the date shown were $48.99 and $48.40 per share, respectively. The closing share price was $48.83, an increase of $0.32 from the previous day. The trading volume was 168,000 shares.

The dividend yield ("yld") was 1.72%. The dividend yield reports the rate of return an investor earned from dividends, calculated by dividing the dividend per share by the share price. We will learn more about this ratio later in the chapter. Tim Hortons' shares are currently trading at a price-earnings ("p/e") ratio (share price divided by earnings per share) of 18.78 times earnings. You will recall that the price-earnings ratio was introduced in Chapter 2. The dividend yield and price-earnings ratios are often interpreted together to determine how much investors favour a company.

One commonly reported measure of the fair value of a company's total equity is its market capitalization. The **market capitalization** of a company is calculated by multiplying the number of shares issued by the share price at any given date. Tim Hortons' market capitalization at the end of 2012 was $7.5 billion. The largest market capitalization for any company in Canada was that of the Royal Bank of Canada, whose market capitalization at the time of writing was $88 billion.

Legal Capital

The shareholders' equity section of a corporation's statement of financial position includes both share capital (common shares and preferred shares, if any) and retained earnings, in addition to other items we will discuss later in this chapter. The distinction between retained earnings and share capital is important from both a legal and an economic point of view. Retained earnings can be distributed to shareholders as dividends or retained in the company for operating needs. On the other hand, share capital of most types of shares issued is **legal capital** that cannot be distributed to shareholders. These are commonly known as **no par value shares**, which simply means that the shares have no predetermined value. Rather, all of the proceeds received are considered to be legal capital that must remain invested in the company for the protection of corporate creditors.

Although there are circumstances when other types of shares are issued for which the entire proceeds received do not form the legal capital of the company, these types of shares are rare in Canada and we do not discuss them in this textbook.

BEFORE YOU GO ON...

▶Do It! Corporation Characteristics

Indicate whether each of the following statements is true or false:

_____ 1. Shareholders of a public corporation have unlimited liability.

_____ 2. It is relatively easy for a large, publicly traded corporation to obtain capital through the issue of shares.

_____ 3. The journal entry to record the authorization of share capital includes a credit to the appropriate preferred or common share account.

_____ 4. The journal entry to record the sale of common shares from one shareholder to another involves a credit to the Common Shares account.

_____ 5. The proceeds received from the sale of shares is known as a company's legal capital.

Action Plan

• Review the characteristics of a corporation.
• Understand the difference between authorized and issued share capital.

Solution

1. False. The liability of shareholders is normally limited to their investment in the corporation.

2. True.

3. False. The authorization of share capital does not result in a journal entry; only the actual issue of shares by the company results in a journal entry.

4. False. The company makes no journal entry to record the sale of common shares owned by one shareholder to another.

5. True.

Related Exercise Material: BE11-1 and E11-1.

Share Capital

Contributed capital is the amount shareholders paid, or contributed, to the corporation in exchange for shares of ownership. This includes **share capital**, which can consist of both common and preferred shares. All corporations must issue common shares, whereas they can choose whether or not to issue preferred shares.

Contributed capital can also include other sources of capital as a result of share transactions, known as **additional contributed capital**. We will learn about additional contributed capital in a later section of this chapter.

STUDY OBJECTIVE 2
Record share transactions.

Alternative Terminology
Contributed capital is also known as *contributed surplus*.

COMMON SHARES

Common shares may be issued (sold) to investors, who then become shareholders of the corporation. Common shares can also be reacquired (repurchased) from investors at a later date. We will look at the issue of shares in some detail, and then briefly introduce the concept of reacquiring shares.

Issue of Common Shares

We first learned about issuing common shares in Chapter. 1. To review the accounting for the issue of shares, assume that Hydro-Slide, Inc. is authorized to issue an unlimited number of common shares and that it issues 1,000 of these shares for $2 per share on January 12.

No journal entry is required to record the *authorization* of shares. The entry to record the *issue* of the shares is:

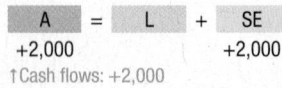

Jan. 12	Cash	2,000	
	Common Shares		2,000
	(To record issue of 1,000 common shares)		

Common shares are most commonly issued in exchange for cash, especially in large corporations. However, they may also be issued for a consideration other than cash, such as services (for example, compensation to lawyers or consultants) or noncash assets (for example, land, buildings, or equipment). **When shares are issued for a noncash consideration, they should be recorded at the fair value of the consideration received** (for example, goods or services). If the fair value of the consideration received cannot be reliably determined, then the fair value of the consideration given up would be used instead.

For example, assume that 5,000 common shares were issued by Hydro-Slide in exchange for a parcel of land on January 27. The shares were trading at $3.50 per share and the land was valued at $20,000 on the date of the acquisition. The transaction is recorded using the value of the land ($20,000)—the consideration received—rather than the value of the common shares ($17,500 = 5,000 × $3.50)—the consideration given up.

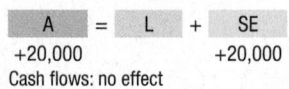

Jan. 27	Land	20,000	
	Common Shares		20,000
	(To record issue of 5,000 common shares in exchange for land)		

Noncash considerations tend to be found more often in private companies than in large publicly traded companies. When shares are issued for a noncash consideration in a private company following ASPE, they should be recorded at the more reliable of the fair value of the consideration received or fair value of the consideration given up. Quite often the fair value of the consideration received is the more reliable value because a private company's shares seldom trade and therefore do not have a ready market value.

Reacquisition of Common Shares

Alternative Terminology
The terms *reacquired* and *repurchased* are used interchangeably with respect to stock purchases.

After shares have been issued, companies may later decide to repurchase their own shares on the open (secondary) market. Why might a company wish to reacquire its own shares? It's to meet one or more of the following objectives, among others:

1. To increase trading of the company's shares in the securities market in the hope of enhancing the company's value. If a company feels that its shares are trading at a price that is less than what they are worth, it may buy back the shares. When the number of shares available for sale in the stock market decreases, the share price should increase in response to changes in supply and demand.
2. To reduce the number of shares issued. By reducing the number of shares issued and reducing the amount recorded in the Common Shares account, earnings per share and return on equity will increase. We first introduced earnings per share in Chapter 2 and will discuss both earnings per share and return on equity later in this chapter.
3. To eliminate hostile shareholders by buying them out.
4. To have additional shares available for issue to employees under bonus and stock compensation plans, or for use in acquiring other companies.

The reacquisition of shares is often called a **normal course issuer bid**. In a normal course issuer bid, a company is allowed to repurchase up to a certain percentage of its shares subject to regulatory approval. It can purchase the shares gradually over a period of time, such as one year. This repurchasing strategy allows the company to buy when its shares are favourably priced.

As mentioned in our feature story, Tim Hortons has repurchased shares under a normal course issuer bid multiple times since it went public in 2006. In its most recent bid, Tim Hortons received approval from the Toronto Stock Exchange to repurchase up to $250 million of its common shares, not to exceed 10 percent (15,239,531) of its shares. The normal course issuer bid commenced February 26, 2013, and expired the earliest of February 25, 2014, or the date the maximum share or dollar amount was reached.

For federally incorporated companies, and most provincially incorporated companies, repurchased shares must be retired (cancelled). This effectively restores the shares to the status of authorized but unissued shares. In some Canadian provinces, in the United States, and internationally, reacquired shares can be held in the "treasury" for subsequent reissue rather than retired. We will not discuss the accounting for reacquired shares in further detail here, but leave it for an intermediate accounting course.

PREFERRED SHARES

To appeal to a larger segment of potential investors, a company may issue an additional class of shares, called preferred shares. **Preferred shares** have contractual provisions that give them a preference, or priority, over common shares in certain areas.

Issue of Preferred Shares

Like common shares, preferred shares may be issued for cash or for noncash considerations. To illustrate, assume that Hydro-Slide, Inc. issues 500 preferred shares for $100 per share for a total consideration of $50,000 (500 × $100) on July 7. The entry to record this transaction is as follows:

July 7	Cash	50,000	
	Preferred Shares		50,000
	(To record issue of 500 preferred shares)		

A	=	L	+	SE
+50,000				+50,000

↑Cash flows: +50,000

Note that when a company has more than one class of shares, separate account titles should be used (for example, Preferred Shares, Common Shares).

Preferred shares can also be issued for noncash considerations. The entry for a noncash transaction is similar to the entry shown earlier for common shares, so it is not illustrated here. Preferred shares can also be reacquired, although it is not as typical to do so as is the case for common shares.

We will discuss the key features of preferred shares, including dividend and liquidation preferences, in the next section.

Preferential Features of Preferred Shares

Typically, preferred shareholders have priority over common shareholders over the distribution of dividends and, in the event of liquidation, over the distribution of assets. However, they do not usually have the voting rights that the common shareholders have. We will discuss these and other contractual provisions that give preferred shares a preference, or priority, over common shares next.

Dividend Preference. Preferred shares are usually issued with a specified dividend rate, which makes them attractive to investors who wish to earn dividend income. In contrast, common shares don't have a specified dividend associated with them, although the company may choose to pay dividends to common shareholders.

A dividend preference simply means that the **preferred shareholders must be paid dividends before any are paid to the common shareholders.** For example, if Hydro-Slide's preferred shares have a $5 annual dividend rate, common shareholders will not receive any dividends in the current year until preferred shareholders have received $5 per share. Preferred shares such as these would be called "$5 preferred," with the $5 indicating the annual dividend rate. Even though the dividend rate is reported as an annual dollar amount per share, it is usual to pay dividends quarterly. For example, in 2012, Tim Hortons had an annual dividend rate of $0.84 on its common shares. This dividend was paid quarterly at a rate of $0.21 ($0.84 ÷ 4) per share.

A preferred claim to dividends does not guarantee that dividends will be paid to the preferred shareholders. The payment of dividends depends on a number of factors, including having sufficient cash in the case of a cash dividend. In addition, all dividends must be formally declared (approved) by the board of directors. We will learn more about these factors in the section on Retained Earnings later in this chapter.

Preferred shares with a dividend preference may contain a **cumulative** dividend feature. This right means that when dividends are declared to be payable, preferred shareholders must be paid both current-year dividends and any unpaid prior-year dividends before common shareholders receive dividends. Preferred shares without this feature are called **noncumulative.** A dividend that is not paid on noncumulative preferred shares in any particular year is lost forever. The majority of preferred shares issued in Canada are noncumulative.

When preferred shares are cumulative, preferred dividends that are not declared in a period are called **dividends in arrears.** No distribution can be made to common shareholders until this entire cumulative preferred dividend is paid. In other words, dividends cannot be paid to common shareholders while any preferred share dividends are in arrears. It is unusual for a company to have any dividends in arrears.

It is important to understand that, if a company does have dividends in arrears, they would *not* be considered a liability. No obligation exists until a dividend is declared by the board of directors. However, the amount of dividends in arrears should be disclosed in the notes to the financial statements. This allows investors to evaluate the potential impact of this commitment on the corporation's financial position.

Even though there is no requirement to pay an annual dividend, companies that are unable to meet their dividend obligations—whether cumulative or noncumulative—are not looked upon favourably by the investment community. As a chief financial officer noted in discussing one company's failure to pay its preferred dividend for a period of time, "Not meeting your obligations on something like that is a major black mark on your record."

Liquidation Preference.   In addition to having a priority claim over common shares on any distribution of dividends, preferred shares also have a priority claim over common shares on corporate assets if the corporation fails. This means that if the company is bankrupt, preferred shareholders will get money back before common shareholders do. The preference on assets may be for the legal value of the shares or for a specified liquidating value. Although creditors rank above all shareholders in terms of preference in liquidations, preferred shareholders rank above common shareholders. This is important as the money usually runs out before everyone gets paid.

Other Preferences.   The attractiveness of preferred shares as an investment is sometimes increased by adding a conversion privilege. **Convertible preferred shares** allow the exchange of preferred shares for common shares at a specified ratio. A significant number of the companies in Canada that have preferred shares also have this conversion privilege. Convertible preferred shares are purchased by investors who want the greater security of preferred shares, but who also desire the option of conversion if the value of the common shares increases significantly.

Most preferred shares are also issued with a redemption or call feature. **Redeemable (or callable) preferred shares** give the issuing corporation the right to purchase the shares from shareholders at specified future dates and prices. The redemption feature offers some flexibility to a corporation by enabling it to eliminate this type of equity security when it is advantageous to do so.

Retractable preferred shares are similar to redeemable or callable preferred shares, except that it is at the *shareholder's* option, rather than the corporation's option, that the shares are redeemed. This usually occurs at an arranged price and date.

When preferred shares are retractable, the distinction between equity and debt is not clear. Similar to debt, retractable preferred shares offer a rate of return (dividend income) to the investor, and with the redemption of the shares, a repayment of the principal investment. Because of this, retractable preferred shares are considered to be an example of a financial liability, which we first discussed in Chapter 10. Consequently, retractable preferred shares are presented in the *liabilities* section of the statement of financial position rather than in the equity section.

Companies are issuing an increasing number of shares with innovative preferences. Some have the attributes of both debt and equity; others have the attributes of both common and preferred shares. Accounting for such financial instruments presents unique challenges for accountants. Further detail is left for an intermediate accounting course.

▶ BEFORE YOU GO ON...

▶ Do It! Share Transactions

At January 1, 2015, MasterMind Corporation, a publicly traded company, had an unlimited number of common shares authorized, of which 120,000 had been issued for $960,000. It also had 100,000 shares of $2, cumulative preferred shares authorized, of which 10,000 shares were issued for $250,000. On July 1, the company issued 1,000 common shares to its lawyers in settlement of their bill for $10,000. At that time, the shares had a fair value of $9 per share. On October 1, the company issued an additional 2,500 preferred shares for $30 per share. (a) Record the issue of the common shares on July 1. (b) Record the issue of the preferred shares on October 1. (c) Calculate the number of preferred and common shares issued at December 31. (d) Assuming dividends are paid quarterly and that all requirements have been met to declare a dividend, calculate the amount of the dividend that MasterMind paid its preferred shareholders for the fourth quarter of 2015.

Action Plan

- Credit the appropriate share account for the entire proceeds received in a share issue.
- When shares are issued for a noncash consideration, record the transaction at the fair value of the consideration received, if available.
- Keep a running total of the number of shares issued to date.
- Recall that the dividend rate given on preferred shares is always expressed as an annual amount. Divide the dividend rate by 4 to determine the quarterly dividend rate.

Solution

(a)

July 1	Legal Fees Expense		10,000	
	Common Shares			10,000
	(To record issue of 1,000 common shares in payment of legal bill)			

(b)

Oct. 1	Cash (2,500 × $30)		75,000	
	Preferred Shares			75,000
	(To record issue of 2,500 preferred shares)			

(c) Preferred shares: 10,000 (Jan. 1) + 2,500 (Oct. 1) = 12,500
Common shares: 120,000 (Jan. 1) + 1,000 (July 1) = 121,000

(d) Oct. 1 – Dec. 31, 2015, dividend = 12,500 × $2 ÷ 4 = $6,250

Related Exercise Material: BE11-2, BE11-3, BE11-4, E11-2, E11-3, E11-4, E11-5, and E11-7.

the navigator

Dividends

A **dividend** is a pro rata (equal) distribution of a portion of a corporation's retained earnings to its shareholders. "Pro rata" means that if you own, say, 10% of the common shares, you will receive 10% of the dividend.

Dividends are discretionary and many high-growth companies, such as Facebook, do not pay dividends. Their policy is to retain all of their profit to make it easier for the company to grow. Investors purchase shares in companies like Facebook with the hope that the share price will increase in value and they will realize a profit when they sell their shares. Other investors purchase shares of established companies with the hope of earning dividends (and maybe also of profiting from some share price appreciation when they sell their shares).

STUDY OBJECTIVE 3
Prepare the entries for cash dividends, stock dividends, and stock splits, and understand their financial impact.

Cash dividends are the most common in practice but stock dividends are also declared on occasion. Stock splits, which are similar to stock dividends, also occur with some frequency. All three of these have varying impacts on a company's share capital and retained earnings, which are discussed in the next sections.

CASH DIVIDENDS

A **cash dividend** is a distribution of cash to shareholders. Cash dividends can be paid to preferred and common shareholders. If dividends are paid to both the preferred and common shareholders, remember that the preferred shareholders have to be paid first.

For a corporation to pay a cash dividend, it must meet a two-part solvency test under the *Canada Business Corporations Act*:

1. It must have sufficient cash or resources to be able to pay its liabilities as they become due after the dividend is declared and paid, and
2. The net realizable value of its assets must exceed the total of its liabilities and share capital.

◼ Keeping an Eye on Cash

If a company has to have sufficient cash in order to pay its liabilities before it can pay a dividend, how much cash is enough? That is hard to say but a company must keep enough cash on hand to pay for its ongoing operations and to pay its bills as they come due. Before paying a cash dividend, a company's board of directors must carefully consider current and future demands on the company's cash resources. In some cases, current (or planned future) liabilities may make a cash dividend inappropriate.

In order to remain in business, companies *must* honour their interest payments to creditors, bankers, and other debt holders. But the payment of dividends to shareholders is discretionary. Consequently, investors must keep an eye on the company's dividend policy and understand what it may mean. For some companies, regular increases in the amount of dividends paid when the company has low cash balances can be a warning signal.

Under some provincial legislation, a company must also have enough retained earnings before it can pay a dividend. You will recall from past chapters that retained earnings are increased by profits and decreased by losses and dividends, as shown below:

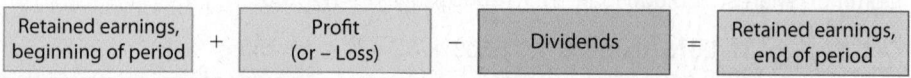

| Retained earnings, beginning of period | + | Profit (or – Loss) | – | Dividends | = | Retained earnings, end of period |

So it makes sense that sufficient retained earnings are required so that the deduction of dividends does not create a deficit (negative retained earnings).

A company cannot pay dividends unless its board of directors decides to do so, at which point the board "declares" (approves and officially states) the dividend to be payable. The date that a dividend is declared, and two other dates, are important for accounting purposes in connection with cash dividends: (1) the declaration date, (2) the record date, and (3) the payment date. Normally, there are several weeks between each date and the next one. For example, on November 8, 2012 (the declaration date), Tim Hortons declared a quarterly dividend of $0.21 per share payable to its common shareholders. These dividends were paid on December 31, 2012 (the payment date), to the shareholders of record at the close of business on November 28, 2012 (the record date).

To illustrate a cash dividend to preferred shareholders, assume that on December 1, 2015, the directors of IBR Inc. declare a $0.50 per share quarterly cash dividend on the company's 100,000 $2 preferred shares, payable on January 20 to shareholders of record on December 22. IBR's dividend is $50,000 (100,000 × $0.50). On the first of the three dates, December 1, which is the **declaration date,** the board of directors formally authorizes the cash dividend and announces it to shareholders.

The declaration of a cash dividend commits the corporation to a binding legal obligation. A journal entry is therefore required to record the declaration of the dividend:

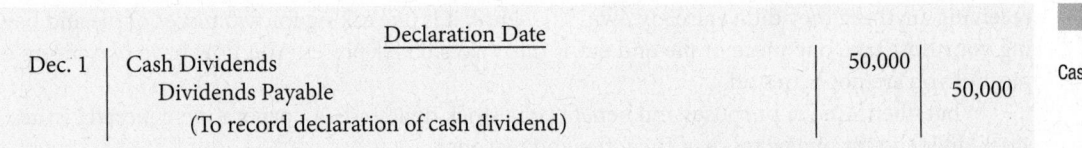

	Declaration Date		
Dec. 1	Cash Dividends	50,000	
	Dividends Payable		50,000
	(To record declaration of cash dividend)		

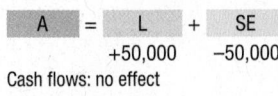

A	=	L	+	SE
		+50,000		−50,000

Cash flows: no effect

In prior chapters, we assumed that the dividend was declared and paid on the same day for simplicity. In this chapter, we illustrate the separation of the declaration of the dividend and the payment of the dividend by recording journal entries on two different dates—the declaration date and the payment date. We also used an account called "Dividends" to record a cash dividend. Here, we use the more specific title "Cash Dividends" to differentiate from other types of dividends, such as stock dividends. As we learned in Chapter 4, the Cash Dividends account will be closed into, and reduce, the Retained Earnings account at the end of the fiscal year. Dividends Payable is a current liability: it will normally be paid within the next month or so—on January 20 in this particular example.

On December 22, which is the **record date,** ownership of the shares is determined. As discussed earlier, individual share owners may change as shares are bought and sold on the secondary market. Although transactions between shareholders do not affect the company's financial position, the company does have to maintain shareholder records identifying individual owners so it knows who to pay the dividend to. In the interval between the declaration date and the record date, the company updates its share ownership record. No journal entry is required on the record date, because the corporation's liability that was recognized on the declaration date is unchanged.

On January 20, which is the **payment date,** dividends are paid to the shareholders. The journal entry is:

	Payment Date		
Jan. 20	Dividends Payable	50,000	
	Cash		50,000
	(To record payment of cash dividend)		

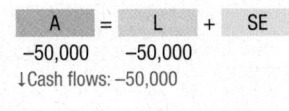

A	=	L	+	SE
−50,000		−50,000		

↓Cash flows: −50,000

As shown below in Illustration 11-1, the declaration of a cash dividend increases liabilities and reduces shareholders' equity (through retained earnings). There is no effect on the record date. The payment of a dividend reduces both assets and liabilities, but it has no effect on shareholders' equity. The cumulative effect of the declaration and payment of a cash dividend on a company's financial statements is to decrease both assets (through cash) and shareholders' equity (through retained earnings). In the illustration below, "+" means increase, "−" means decrease, and "NE" means "no effect."

			Shareholders' Equity	
	Assets	Liabilities	Share Capital	Retained Earnings
Declaration date	NE	+	NE	−
Record date	NE	NE	NE	NE
Payment date	−	−	NE	NE
Cumulative effect of declaration and payment of cash dividend	−	NE	NE	−

▶Illustration 11-1
Effects of cash dividends

STOCK DIVIDENDS

A **stock dividend** is a distribution of the corporation's own shares to shareholders. Whereas a cash dividend is paid in cash, a stock dividend is distributed (paid) in shares. And, while a cash dividend decreases assets (through the Cash account) and shareholders' equity (through the Retained Earnings account), a stock dividend does not change assets, liabilities, or total shareholders' equity. No cash has been paid, and no liabilities have been assumed. Two accounts, share capital and retained earnings, in shareholders' equity are affected, but the changes offset each other. A stock dividend results in a decrease in retained earnings and an increase in share capital but it does not change *total* shareholders' equity.

Because a stock dividend does not result in a distribution of assets, investors are not actually receiving anything they didn't already own. In a sense, it is like asking for two pieces of pie and having your host take one piece of pie and cut it into two smaller pieces. You now have two pieces of pie, but you are not better off.

What, then, are the purposes and benefits of a stock dividend? A corporation generally issues a stock dividend for one or more of the following reasons:

1. To satisfy shareholders' dividend expectations while conserving cash.
2. To increase the marketability of the shares. When the number of shares increases, the share price decreases on the stock market. Decreasing the market price of the shares makes it easier for investors to purchase them.
3. To emphasize that a portion of shareholders' equity has been permanently reinvested in the legal capital of the business and is unavailable for cash dividends. Because of its effects, a stock dividend is often referred to as *capitalizing retained earnings.*

Similar to a cash dividend, stock dividends can be declared for either preferred or common shares, although they are usually done with common shares. Just as cash dividends have three key dates, so too do stock dividends: (1) the declaration date, (2) the record date, and (3) the distribution (payment) date.

To illustrate the accounting for stock dividends, assume that CIS Inc. has 50,000 common shares with a balance of $500,000 in Common Shares and $300,000 in Retained Earnings. On June 30, it declares a 10% stock dividend to shareholders of record at July 20, to be distributed to shareholders on August 5. The share price on June 30 (declaration date) is $15 per share; on July 20 (record date), $16 per share; and on August 5 (distribution date), $14 per share.

The number of shares to be issued is 5,000 (50,000 × 10%). The *Canada Business Corporations Act* requires that stock dividends be recorded at **fair value** (market price per share) because this is what the corporation would have received if the shares had been issued for cash rather than as a stock dividend. So the total amount to be debited to CIS's Stock Dividends account is $75,000 (5,000 × $15). Note that it is the fair value at the declaration date that is relevant for this transaction, and not the fair value on the record date or distribution date.

The entry to record the declaration of the stock dividend on June 30 is as follows:

A	=	L	+	SE
−75,000				
+75,000				

Cash flows: no effect

		Declaration Date		
June 30	Stock Dividends		75,000	
	Stock Dividends Distributable			75,000
	(To record declaration of 10% stock dividend)			

Note that the credit entry uses the word *Distributable*, not *Payable*, in the account title. Stock Dividends Distributable is a shareholders' equity account. It is not a liability, because assets will not be used to pay the dividend. Instead, it will be "paid" with common shares. If a statement of financial position is prepared before the dividend shares are issued, the distributable account is reported along with other share capital in the shareholders' equity section of the statement of financial position. As was the case with cash dividends, the Stock Dividends account will be closed into, and reduce, the Retained Earnings account at the end of the year.

Similar to cash dividends, there is no entry at the record date. When the dividend shares are issued on August 5, the account Stock Dividends Distributable is decreased (debited) and the account Common Shares is increased (credited), as follows:

A	=	L	+	SE
−75,000				
+75,000				

Cash flows: no effect

		Distribution Date		
Aug. 5	Stock Dividends Distributable		75,000	
	Common Shares			75,000
	(To record issue of 5,000 common shares in 10% stock dividend)			

Neither of the above entries changes shareholders' equity in total. However, the composition of shareholders' equity changes because a portion of retained earnings, $75,000, is transferred to the common shares account. The number of shares also increases by 5,000 (50,000 × 10%). These effects are shown below for CIS:

	Before Stock Dividend	Change	After Stock Dividend
Shareholders' equity			
Common shares	$500,000	+$75,000	$575,000
Retained earnings	300,000	−75,000	225,000
Total shareholders' equity	$800,000	$ 0	$800,000
Number of shares	50,000	+5,000	55,000

STOCK SPLITS

Although stock splits are not dividends, we discuss them in this section because of their similarities to stock dividends. A **stock split,** like a stock dividend, involves the issue of additional shares to shareholders according to their percentage ownership. However, a stock split is usually much larger than a stock dividend. For example, a stock dividend might result in an additional 10% of common shares issued, whereas a stock split could result in 100% more common shares issued. This is because the main purpose of a stock split is to increase the marketability of the shares by lowering the share price. Normally it is only common shares that are split as preferred shares are usually purchased primarily for the dividend income.

The effect of a stock split on the share price is generally inversely proportional to the size of the split; that is, in a 2-for-1 stock split, the number of shares will double and the share price will halve. For example, a company that has 100,000 shares trading at $20 per share before the split will issue an additional 100,000 shares and have a total of 200,000 shares (100,000 × 2) trading at about $10 per share ($20 ÷ 2) after the split.

As with a stock dividend, a shareholder is not initially better off after a stock split, although they own more shares to potentially appreciate in value. Quite often, due to increased investor interest, the share price will climb more rapidly than previously. For the company, a stock split does not have any effect on total share capital, retained earnings, or total shareholders' equity. Only the number of shares increases. Because a stock split does not affect the balances in any shareholders' equity accounts, **a stock split is not journalized.** Only a memo entry explaining the effect of the split (that is, the change in the number of shares) is needed.

These effects are shown below for CIS Inc., assuming that instead of issuing a 10% stock dividend, it split its 50,000 common shares on a 2-for-1 basis:

	Before Stock Split	Change	After Stock Split
Shareholders' equity			
Common shares	$500,000	$0	$500,000
Retained earnings	300,000	0	300,000
Total shareholders' equity	$800,000	$0	$800,000
Number of shares	50,000	+50,000	100,000

ACCOUNTING MATTERS!

A Special Split with a Twist

After years of resisting requests to split its shares, Google finally approved a 2-for-1 stock split in June 2012. Many believed it was long past time as Google's shares hit a record trading high of U.S. $756 per share in 2012–far too high a price for an average investor.

However, Google's split came with a twist. Unlike a normal stock split, this split created a new class of non-voting Class C shares. For every Class A share that shareholders owned, they were given a share of Class C stock equal to half of its value before the split. If, for instance, a shareholder held 200 shares worth $756 each, after the split he or she held 400 shares worth about $378 each.

Why did Google decide to split its stock this way? Google's cofounders wanted to keep control of the company so they issued these new shares without voting rights.

COMPARISON OF EFFECTS

A cash dividend, stock dividend, and stock split have differing overall impacts on a company's financial position. The cumulative effect of these differences is shown in Illustration 11-2. In the illustration, "+" means increase, "−" means decrease, and "NE" means "no effect."

▸Illustration 11-2
Effects of cash dividends, stock dividends, and stock splits

	Assets	=	Liabilities	+	Share Capital	+	Retained Earnings	Total Shareholders' Equity	Number of Shares
					Shareholders' Equity				
Cash dividend	−		NE		NE		−	−	NE
Stock dividend	NE		NE		+		−	NE	+
Stock split	NE		NE		NE		NE	NE	+

Cash dividends reduce assets (the Cash account) when paid and reduce retained earnings (the Cash Dividends account) when declared. Stock dividends increase share capital (the Common Shares account) when distributed and decrease retained earnings (the Stock Dividends account) when declared. Stock splits do not affect any of the accounts. However, both a stock dividend and a stock split increase the number of shares issued.

BEFORE YOU GO ON...

▸Do It! Stock Dividend and Split Effects

Sing Corporation has had five years of high profits. Due to this success, the price of its 500,000 common shares tripled from $15 per share to $45. During this period, the Common Shares account remained the same at $2 million. Retained Earnings increased from $1.5 million to $10 million. President John Helston is considering either (1) a 10% stock dividend or (2) a 2-for-1 stock split. He asks you to show the before-and-after effects of each option on shareholders' equity and on the number of shares.

Action Plan

- Calculate the stock dividend effects by multiplying the stock dividend percentage by the number of existing shares to determine the number of new shares to be issued. Multiply the number of new shares by the price (fair value) of each share at the declaration date.
- A stock dividend increases the number of shares and affects both the Common Shares and Retained Earnings accounts.
- A stock split increases the number of shares but does not affect the Common Shares or Retained Earnings accounts.

Solution

1. With a 10% stock dividend, the stock dividend amount is $2,250,000 (500,000 × 10% = 50,000 × $45). The new balance in Common Shares is $4,250,000 ($2,000,000 + $2,250,000) and Retained Earnings is now $7,750,000 ($10,000,000 − $2,250,000). The number of shares is now 550,000 (500,000 + 50,000).

2. With a stock split, the account balances in Common Shares and Retained Earnings after the stock split are the same as they were before: $2 million and $10 million, respectively. The number of shares is now 1,000,000 (500,000 + 500,000).

The effects on the shareholders' equity accounts of each option are as follows:

	Original Balances	After Stock Dividend	After Stock Split
Common shares	$ 2,000,000	$ 4,250,000	$ 2,000,000
Retained earnings	10,000,000	7,750,000	10,000,000
Total shareholders' equity	$12,000,000	$12,000,000	$12,000,000
Number of shares	500,000	550,000	1,000,000

Related Exercise Material: BE11-5, BE11-6, BE11-7, BE11-8, E11-5, E11-6, and E11-7.

the navigator

Presentation of Shareholders' Equity

Shareholders' equity is reported in the statement of financial position and statement of changes in equity for companies using International Financial Reporting Standards. Companies using Accounting Standards for Private Enterprises can prepare a statement of retained earnings rather than a statement of changes in equity. Equity transactions are not reported in the income statement, although the income statement is linked to shareholders' equity through profit or loss, which impacts retained earnings.

STATEMENT OF FINANCIAL POSITION

In the shareholders' equity section of the statement of financial position, the following are reported: (1) contributed capital, (2) retained earnings, and (3) accumulated other comprehensive income, if any. These categories have been introduced previously. We will review each of them briefly here.

Contributed Capital

Contributed capital represents amounts contributed by shareholders. It includes share capital and additional contributed capital, if any:

1. **Share capital.** This category consists of preferred and common shares. Because of the additional rights they give, preferred shares are shown before common shares. Information about the legal capital, number of shares authorized, number of shares issued and amount received for them, and any particular share preferences (such as a dividend rate) is reported for each class of shares either directly in the shareholders' equity section of the statement of financial position or in a note to the financial statements. Note also that any stock dividends distributable that exist at year end are also reported under share capital.
2. **Additional contributed capital.** This category includes amounts contributed by shareholders (in addition to the issue of preferred or common shares reported in the share capital section), or amounts that accrue to shareholders as a result of certain types of transactions, such as reacquiring and retiring shares. The reacquisition of shares was briefly mentioned, but not illustrated, earlier in this chapter. Other situations not discussed in this textbook can also result in additional contributed capital. For many companies, however, there is no additional contributed capital. The caption "share capital" is therefore used more often than "contributed capital."

Alternative Terminology
Additional contributed capital is also known as *contributed surplus*.

Retained Earnings

While contributed capital is provided by the shareholders, retained earnings is often called "earned" capital because it results from the company's (hopefully profitable) operations. You will recall that retained earnings are the cumulative profits (or losses) since incorporation that have been retained in the company (that is, not distributed to shareholders). Each year, profit is added (or a loss is deducted) and any dividends declared are deducted from the opening retained earnings balance to determine the ending retained earnings amount. Note that it is only the amount of dividends *declared* that is deducted from retained earnings, not the amount of dividends *paid*. Dividends can be declared in one year and paid in the next; consequently dividends declared and dividends paid are not always the same amounts.

Other additions to or deductions from retained earnings can also occur, most notably due to changes in accounting policies. We will learn more about this type of adjustment to retained earnings in Chapter 14. Recall that it is only the end-of-period balance of retained earnings that is presented in the shareholders' equity section of the statement of financial position, not the detailed changes that are presented in the statement of changes in equity. We will review the statement of changes in equity in more detail later in this chapter.

Retained Earnings is a shareholders' equity account whose normal balance is a credit. If a deficit (debit balance) exists, it is reported as a deduction from shareholders' equity, rather than as the usual addition.

In some cases, **retained earnings restrictions** make a portion of the balance in the Retained Earnings account unavailable for dividends. For example, a company may have **debt covenants on a loan,** which, among other things, can limit the use of corporate assets for the payment of dividends. Such restrictions make it more likely that a corporation will be able to meet its required loan payments.

Retained earnings are part of the shareholders' claim on the corporation's total assets. The balance in Retained Earnings does not, however, represent a claim on any one specific asset. That means that restricting $100,000 of retained earnings does not necessarily mean that there will be $100,000 of cash set aside. All that a restriction does is inform users that a portion of retained earnings is not available for dividend payments.

No journal entry is necessary to record a retained earnings restriction, but they are disclosed in the notes to the financial statements.

Accumulated Other Comprehensive Income (IFRS)

Most revenues, expenses, gains, and losses are included in profit. However, certain gains and losses bypass profit and are recorded as direct adjustments to shareholders' equity. These are known as **other comprehensive income (OCI).** Other comprehensive income is considered to represent earned capital, similar to retained earnings.

There are several examples of other comprehensive income or loss. One example that we learned about in Chapter 9 is gains or losses on revaluing property, plant, and equipment using the revaluation model. Another example that we will learn about in the next chapter is unrealized gains and losses on certain types of investments. There are also other examples of other comprehensive income that you will learn about in a more advanced accounting course.

Comprehensive income (loss) (which means *total* comprehensive income or loss) includes both profit and other comprehensive income. This means that it includes (1) the revenues, expenses, gains, and losses included in profit, *and* (2) the gains and losses that bypass profit but affect shareholders' equity, as shown in Illustration 11-3.

►Illustration 11-3
Comprehensive income

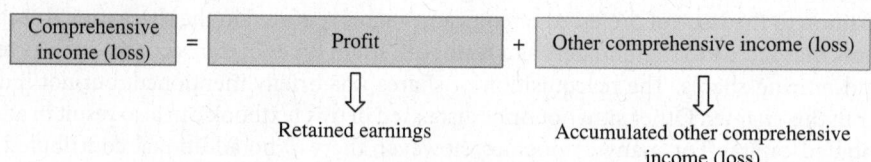

Profit—a period figure—is included in the retained earnings reported on the statement of changes in equity and the ending balance of retained earnings reported on the shareholders' equity section of the statement of financial position. This is because retained earnings is the cumulative total of profits retained in the business. Similarly, other comprehensive income—also a period figure—is included in the accumulated other comprehensive income reported on the same statements. And, just as retained earnings can be negative (in other words, a deficit), other comprehensive income and comprehensive income can also be negative and reported as a loss rather than as income.

Similar to retained earnings, **accumulated other comprehensive income (AOCI)** is the *cumulative* change in shareholders' equity that results from the gains and losses that bypass profit but affect shareholders' equity. In other words, it starts with the balance at the beginning of the period and is increased by other comprehensive income and decreased by other comprehensive losses during the period, to arrive at the ending balance. It is this ending balance that is reported in the shareholders' equity section of the statement of financial position.

You will recall that profit (through each individual revenue and expense account) is closed out to Retained Earnings through the Income Summary account at the end of each period. Similarly, OCI is closed out but not to Retained Earnings; rather it is closed out to various equity accounts that relate to each type of item that is shown in OCI. Further discussion and illustration of closing entries related to other comprehensive income are left to an intermediate accounting course.

Only companies using IFRS have to report other comprehensive income. Companies using ASPE do not. Of course, not all companies using IFRS will have examples of other comprehensive income. However, if they do, they must report comprehensive income in a statement of comprehensive income, and accumulated other comprehensive income in the statement of changes in equity and the shareholders' equity section of the statement of financial position. We will learn about the preparation of the statement of comprehensive income for companies using IFRS in the next chapter.

Illustration of Shareholders' Equity Section

Tim Hortons reports contributed capital comprising common shares and contributed surplus (additional contributed capital) and earned capital comprising retained earnings and accumulated other comprehensive loss in the shareholders' equity section of its balance sheet (statement of financial position), as shown in Illustration 11-4.

TIM HORTONS INC. Balance Sheet (partial) December 30, 2012 (in thousands)		
	2012	2011
Shareholders' equity		
Contributed capital		
Common shares. Authorized: unlimited shares.		
Issued, 153,405 and 157,815, respectively	$ 421,677	$ 437,422
Contributed surplus	10,970	6,375
Total contributed capital	432,647	443,797
Retained earnings	893,619	836,968
Accumulated other comprehensive loss	(139,028)	(128,217)
Other shareholders' equity items	2,853	1,885
	$1,190,091	$1,154,433

▸Illustration 11-4
Tim Hortons statement of financial position—shareholders' equity section

Tim Hortons has an unlimited number of common shares authorized, with 153,405 thousand issued at December 30, 2012 (the end of its 2012 fiscal year) and 157,815 thousand at January 1, 2012 (the end of its 2011 fiscal year). It also has additional contributed capital, which it calls contributed surplus, of $10,970 thousand in 2012 and $6,375 thousand in 2011. Tim Hortons' total contributed capital is $432,647 thousand in 2012, and $443,797 thousand in 2011.

Tim Hortons reported a positive retained earnings balance of $893,619 thousand in 2012, an increase over the retained earnings balance of $836,968 thousand in 2011. The company reported an accumulated other comprehensive loss of $139,028 thousand in 2012 and $128,217 thousand in 2011. In addition, Tim Hortons reported other shareholders' equity items not discussed here, resulting in a total shareholders' equity of $1,190,091 thousand in 2012 and $1,154,433 in 2011.

STATEMENT OF CHANGES IN EQUITY (IFRS)

As we learned in Chapter 1, the **statement of changes in equity** discloses changes in total shareholders' equity for the period, as well as changes in each individual shareholders' equity account, including share capital, additional contributed capital, retained earnings, and accumulated other comprehensive income. It is a required statement for companies reporting under IFRS.

Alternative Terminology
The *statement of changes in equity* is also known as the *statement of shareholders' equity* or *statement of equity*.

A simplified form of Tim Hortons' statement of equity (statement of changes in equity) is shown in Illustration 11-5. Tim Hortons has prepared its statement in long (vertical) form, but other formats that we will illustrate later are also common.

▶Illustration 11-5
Tim Hortons statement of changes in equity

TIM HORTONS INC. Statement of Equity Year Ended December 30, 2012 (in thousands)		
	2012	2011
Common shares		
Balance at beginning of year	$ 437,422	$ 474,508
Repurchase of common shares	(15,745)	(37,086)
Balance at end of year	$ 421,677	$ 437,422
Contributed surplus		
Balance at beginning of year	$ 6,375	$ 0
Stock-based compensation	4,595	6,375
Balance at end of year	$ 10,970	$ 6,375
Retained earnings		
Balance at beginning of year	$ 836,968	$1,105,882
Profit	402,885	382,812
Dividends	(130,509)	(110,187)
Other items affecting retained earnings	(215,725)	(541,539)
Balance at end of year	$ 893,619	$ 836,968
Accumulated other comprehensive loss		
Balance at beginning of year	$ (128,217)	$ (143,589)
Other comprehensive income (loss)	(10,811)	15,372
Balance at end of year	$ (139,028)	$ (128,217)
Other shareholders' equity items		
Balance at beginning of year	$ 1,885	$ 5,641
Changes during year	968	(3,756)
Balance at end of year	$ 2,853	$ 1,885
Total equity	$1,190,091	$1,154,433

Tim Hortons details the changes in each of its equity accounts, starting with the account balances at the beginning of the fiscal year (January 1, 2012) and ending with the account balances at the end of the fiscal year (December 30, 2012). Tim Hortons also includes a separate statement detailing the changes in the number of shares issued (not reproduced here). While we have included the changes for only one year in Illustration 11-5, Tim Hortons actually includes the changes for the three most recent fiscal years in its financial statements.

Note that all of the dollar amounts as at December 30, 2012, that are shown in the above illustration were reported in the shareholders' equity section of Tim Hortons' statement of financial position shown in Illustration 11-4. We recommend that you now trace the opening and ending balances, and the total shareholders' equity amounts, shown in Illustration 11-5 to those shown in Illustration 11-4.

STATEMENT OF RETAINED EARNINGS (ASPE)

Private companies that report using Accounting Standards for Private Enterprises usually have a much simpler capital structure, with few share transactions, which can more easily be disclosed in the notes to the financial statements. Consequently, private companies are not required to prepare a statement of changes in equity but instead prepare a statement of retained earnings. This statement can be prepared as a separate statement or combined with the income statement.

A **statement of retained earnings** shows the amounts and causes of changes in retained earnings during the period. Similar to the statement of changes in equity, a statement of retained earnings must be prepared after the income statement is prepared, as profit is a key component of retained earnings. In contrast to the statement of changes in equity, which shows the amounts and causes of changes in all of the shareholders' equity accounts, the statement of retained earnings shows only the changes in the Retained Earnings account.

The beginning retained earnings amount is shown on the first line of the statement of retained earnings. Then profit is added and dividends (declared) are deducted to calculate the retained earnings at the end of the period. If a company has a loss, it is deducted (rather than added) in the statement of retained earnings. This statement covers the same period of time as the income statement.

A sample statement of retained earnings is shown in Illustration 11-6 for Graber Inc., using assumed data:

▶Illustration 11-6
Statement of retained earnings

GRABER INC. Statement of Retained Earnings Year Ended December 31, 2015	
Balance, January 1	$1,068,000
Add: Profit	262,800
	1,330,800
Less: Cash dividends	58,000
Balance, December 31	$1,272,800

SUMMARY OF SHAREHOLDERS' EQUITY TRANSACTIONS

The table that follows includes a brief overview of some of the common transactions or items that have been discussed in this chapter, indicating which shareholders' equity account is affected, and on which statement the account is reported for public companies following IFRS and private companies following ASPE.

	Statement	
Transaction	IFRS	ASPE
Share capital		
Issue (sale) of share capital	Statement of changes in equity	Disclosed in the notes
Ending balance of share capital	Statement of changes in equity; Statement of financial position	Statement of financial position
Retained earnings		
Profit (loss)	Statement of changes in equity	Statement of retained earnings
Cash dividends declared and paid	Statement of changes in equity	Statement of retained earnings
Stock dividends declared and distributed	Statement of changes in equity	Statement of retained earnings
Stock split	Disclosed in notes	Disclosed in notes
Dividends in arrears	Disclosed in notes	Disclosed in notes
Ending balance of retained earnings	Statement of changes in equity; Statement of financial position	Statement of retained earnings; Statement of financial position
Restriction of retained earnings	Disclosed in notes	Disclosed in notes
Accumulated other comprehensive income		
Other comprehensive income (loss)	Statement of changes in equity	Not reported
Ending balance of accumulated other comprehensive income (loss)	Statement of changes in equity; statement of financial position	Not reported

BEFORE YOU GO ON...

►Do It! Statement of Changes in Equity

Grand Lake Corporation had the following shareholders' equity balances at January 1, 2015:

Common shares, unlimited number authorized, 500,000 issued	$1,000,000
Retained earnings	600,000
Accumulated other comprehensive income	100,000

The following selected information is available for the year ended December 31, 2015:

1. Issued 100,000 common shares for $300,000 on January 1.

2. Declared and paid dividends of $0.10 per share in December.

3. Reported profit of $360,000 for the year.

4. Reported other comprehensive income of $25,000 for the year.

Prepare a statement of changes in equity.

Action Plan

- The statement of changes in equity covers a period of time, starting with the opening balances and ending with the ending balances for the period.
- Explain the changes in each shareholders' equity account, as well as total shareholders' equity.

Solution

GRAND LAKE CORPORATION
Statement of Changes in Equity
Year Ended December 31, 2015

	Common Shares	Retained Earnings	Accumulated Other Comprehensive Income	Total
Balance, January 1	$1,000,000	$600,000	$100,000	$1,700,000
Issued common shares	300,000			300,000
Cash dividends		(60,000)*		(60,000)
Comprehensive income				
Profit		360,000		360,000
Other comprehensive income			25,000	25,000
Balance, December 31	$1,300,000	$900,000	$125,000	$2,325,000

*(500,000 + 100,000) × $0.10 = $60,000

Related Exercise Material: BE11-9, BE11-10, BE11-11, E11-7, E11-8, E11-9, E11-10, and E11-11.

Measuring Corporate Performance

STUDY OBJECTIVE 5

Evaluate dividend and earnings performance.

Investors are interested in both a company's dividend record and its earnings performance. Although they are often parallel, sometimes they are not. Each item should therefore be investigated separately.

The information in Illustration 11-7 will be used throughout this section to calculate the payout ratio, dividend yield, earnings per share, and return on common shareholders' equity for Tim Hortons in 2012 and 2011:

(in thousands, except for per share information)	2012	2011
Profit	$ 402,885	$ 382,812
Shareholders' equity	1,190,091	1,154,433
Cash dividends	130,509	110,187
Weighted average number of common shares	155,160	162,145
Dividends per common share	0.84	0.68
Market price per common share	48.83	49.36

▶Illustration 11-7
Selected information for Tim Hortons

Tim Hortons has no preferred shares issued.

DIVIDEND RECORD

One way that companies reward investors for their investment is to pay them dividends. The **payout ratio** measures the percentage of a company's profit distributed as cash dividends. It is calculated by dividing the cash dividends by profit. It can also be calculated using per share information rather than total information. In that case, dividends per share would be divided by earnings per share (which will be discussed in the next section).

Using selected information from Illustration 11-7, Tim Hortons' payout ratio follows in Illustration 11-8. We have also included the payout ratios for Second Cup, one of Tim Hortons' competitors, and their industry in this illustration for comparative purposes.

▶Illustration 11-8
Payout ratio

$$\text{PAYOUT RATIO} = \frac{\text{CASH DIVIDENDS}}{\text{PROFIT}}$$

($ in thousands)	2012	2011
Tim Hortons	$\dfrac{\$130,509}{\$402,885} = 32.4\%$	$\dfrac{\$110,187}{\$382,812} = 28.8\%$
Second Cup	n/a	33.5%
Industry average	31.0%	32.3%

In 2012, Tim Hortons paid 32.4% of its profit back to its common shareholders, an increase from 2011 when it paid 28.8%, and higher in 2012 than the industry average. As mentioned in the feature story, Tim Hortons sets specific targets each year to pay out a certain proportion of its profit in dividends. Second Cup reported a loss in 2012 compared to a profit in 2011, which resulted in a negative payout ratio. Negative payout ratios aren't meaningful so it has not been included in Illustration 11-8.

Another dividend measure that interests shareholders is the dividend yield. The **dividend yield** is calculated by dividing the dividend per share by the market price per share. Using selected information from Illustration 11-7, the dividend yield is shown in Illustration 11-9 for Tim Hortons. Second Cup and the industry average have been included for comparative purposes.

▶Illustration 11-9
Dividend yield

$$\text{DIVIDEND YIELD} = \frac{\text{DIVIDEND PER SHARE}}{\text{MARKET PRICE PER SHARE}}$$

($ in thousands)	2012	2011
Tim Hortons	$\dfrac{\$0.84}{\$48.83} = 1.7\%$	$\dfrac{\$0.68}{\$49.36} = 1.4\%$
Second Cup	6.6%	9.7%
Industry average	1.2%	1.6%

Tim Hortons' dividend yield was 1.7% at the end of 2012, an improvement over its yield of 1.4% at the end of 2011 and higher than the industry average in 2012. It is still significantly lower than Second Cup's dividend yield, although it is notable that Second Cup's yield declined in 2012 at a time when Tim Hortons' yield increased.

The dividend yield is, in essence, a measure of a shareholder's return on his or her investment. In Tim Hortons' case, an investor who purchased common shares at the end of 2012 paid $48.83 to purchase each share. Based on the annual dividend of $0.84 per share, the investor earned a return of 1.7% on this investment.

Of course, dividend income is only one part of an investor's return on an investment in shares. Investors hope to also earn a return from increases in the market price of their shares when they are ready to sell them. In general, however, investors tend to buy shares with high payout ratios and dividend yields if they are looking to earn a regular income (dividend). They tend to buy shares with low payout ratios and dividend yields if they are looking for more capital appreciation (growth) from their shares.

Illustration 11-10 shows the payout ratios and dividend yields of selected companies in a recent year.

▶Illustration 11-10
Payout ratios and dividend yields

	Payout Ratio	Dividend Yield
BCE (Bell Canada Enterprises)	70.0%	5.4%
Costco	26.1%	1.1%
lululemon athletica	0.0%	0.0%
Royal Bank of Canada	48.2%	4.0%
WestJet	15.6%	1.6%

Companies that have high growth rates tend to be characterized by low payout ratios and dividend yields because they reinvest most of the profit back into the business. For example, lululemon's payout ratio and dividend yield are zero in Illustration 11-10. The company comments on its dividend policy in its annual report: "We have never declared or paid any cash dividends on our common stock and do not anticipate paying any cash dividends on our common stock in the foreseeable future. We anticipate that we will retain all of our available funds for use in the operation and expansion of our business."

DECISION TOOLKIT

Decision Checkpoints	Info Needed for Decision	Tools to Use for Decision	How to Evaluate Results
What portion of its profit does the company pay out in dividends?	Profit and total cash dividends	$\text{Payout ratio} = \dfrac{\text{Cash dividends}}{\text{Profit}}$	A high payout ratio is considered desirable for investors seeking income. A low ratio suggests that the company is retaining its profit for investment in future growth.
What percentage of the share price is the company paying in dividends?	Dividends and share price	$\text{Dividend yield} = \dfrac{\text{Dividend per share}}{\text{Market price per share}}$	A high dividend yield is considered desirable for investors. It also means that the company is paying out, rather than retaining, its profit.

EARNINGS PERFORMANCE

The earnings performance, or profitability, of a company is measured in several different ways. In Chapter 2, we learned about the earnings per share ratio. In this section, we will revisit the calculation of this ratio and introduce a new profitability ratio, the return on common shareholders' equity.

Earnings per Share

Using selected information shown earlier in Illustration 11-7, Tim Hortons' earnings per share ratio is illustrated below. Comparative information for Second Cup and the industry has not been included because earnings per share are not comparable between companies because of differing capital structures.

▶Illustration 11-11
Earnings per share

	PROFIT AVAILABLE TO COMMON SHAREHOLDERS (PROFIT − PREFERRED DIVIDENDS)	
EARNINGS PER SHARE =	WEIGHTED AVERAGE NUMBER OF COMMON SHARES	
(in thousands)	**2012**	**2011**
Tim Hortons	$\dfrac{\$402,885 - \$0}{155,160} = \$2.60$	$\dfrac{\$382,812 - \$0}{162,145} = \$2.36$
Second Cup	n/a	n/a
Industry average	n/a	n/a

In Chapter 2, we gave the information for you to calculate the earnings per share and said that you would learn how to calculate the numerator (profit available to common shareholders) and the denominator (weighted average number of common shares) in this chapter. The numerator, **profit available to common shareholders,** is calculated by subtracting any preferred dividends from profit. This is because preferred shareholders have preferential rights to receive these dividends before the common shareholders can share in any remaining amounts. Note that cumulative preferred dividends are deducted from profit whether declared or not; noncumulative preferred dividends are deducted only if declared. In Tim Hortons' case, no preferred shares have been issued so its profit available to common shareholders is the same as its profit.

For the denominator of the earnings per share calculation, the weighted average number of shares is used. It is important to understand that Tim Hortons' weighted average number of common shares, 155,160 thousand in 2012 and 162,145 thousand in 2011, is not the same as the ending balance of its common shares, which was 153,405 thousand in 2012 and 157,815 thousand in 2011. You will recall that, whenever we calculate a ratio with a period figure (such as profit) and an end-of-period figure (such as the number of common shares), we always average the end-of-period figure so that the numerator and denominator in the calculation are for the same period of time. However, we do not use a straight average in the calculation of the number of common shares as we do in some other ratio calculations. For example, we do not take the beginning and ending balances of the number of common shares, add them together, and divide the result by two.

Instead, we use a **weighted average number of common shares** as this considers the impact of shares issued at different times throughout the year. This is done because the issue of shares changes the amount of assets on which profit can be generated. Consequently, shares issued or repurchased during each current period must be weighted by the fraction of the year (or period) that they have been issued. If there is no change in the number of common shares during the year, the weighted average number of shares will be the same as the ending balance. If new shares are issued or existing shares are reacquired throughout the year, then these shares are adjusted for the fraction of the year they are outstanding to determine the weighted average number of shares.

To illustrate the calculation of the weighted average number of common shares, assume that a company had 100,000 common shares on January 1. It issued an additional 7,500 shares on July 1 and 10,000 shares on October 1. The weighted average number of shares for the year would be calculated as follows:

Date	Actual Number		Weighted Average
Jan. 1	100,000	$\times\ ^{12}/_{12} =$	100,000
July 1	7,500	$\times\ ^{6}/_{12} =$	3,750
Oct. 1	10,000	$\times\ ^{3}/_{12} =$	2,500
	117,500		106,250

As indicated in the "Actual Number" column shown on the previous page, 117,500 shares were actually issued by the end of the year. Of these, 100,000 were issued for the full year and are allocated a full weight, or 12 months of 12 months. The 7,500 new shares issued on July 1 have only been issued for six months (from July 1 to December 31) and are weighted for $^6/_{12}$ of the year, to result in 3,750 weighted shares. The other 10,000 shares have been issued for three months (from October 1 to December 31) and are weighted for $^3/_{12}$ of the year, to result in 2,500 weighted shares. In total, the company's weighted average number of shares is 106,250 for the year. In the next calendar year, the 106,250 shares would receive full weight because all 106,250 shares would be issued for the entire year.

When a corporation has securities that may be converted into common shares, it has what is called a complex capital structure. One example of a convertible security is convertible preferred shares. When the preferred shares are converted into common shares, the additional common shares will result in a reduced, or diluted, earnings per share figure.

Two earnings per share figures are calculated when a corporation has a complex capital structure. The first earnings per share figure is called **basic earnings per share.** The earnings per share amounts we calculated in Illustration 11-11, $2.60 in 2012 and $2.36 in 2011, are basic earnings per share. The second earnings per share figure is called **diluted earnings per share.** The calculation of diluted earnings per share is complex. We focus only on basic earnings per share in this chapter and leave further discussion of diluted earnings per share and other complexities to an intermediate accounting course.

The disclosure of earnings per share is required for companies reporting using IFRS. This ratio is considered to be so important that it must be reported directly on the income statement (or the statement of comprehensive income, which will be illustrated in the next chapter). As we mentioned in Chapter 2, companies reporting using ASPE do not have to report earnings per share.

Return on Equity

A widely used ratio that measures profitability from the common shareholders' viewpoint is the **return on common shareholders' equity.** This ratio shows how many dollars were earned for each dollar invested by common shareholders. It is calculated by dividing profit available to common shareholders by average common shareholders' equity. As we just learned, the profit available to common shareholders is profit less preferred dividends. Common shareholders' equity is total shareholders' equity less the legal capital of any preferred shares. Recall that everything else belongs to the common, or residual, shareholders.

We can calculate a return on common shareholders' equity for Tim Hortons using the information shown in Illustration 11-7. In addition, we will require the shareholders' equity amount for 2010, which was $1,442,442 thousand, in order to calculate average common shareholders' equity for 2011. As we mentioned earlier, Tim Hortons' common shareholders' equity is the same as its total shareholders' equity since it does not have any preferred shares.

Tim Hortons' return on common shareholders' equity ratios are calculated for 2012 and 2011 in Illustration 11-12, with comparative information included for Second Cup and the industry.

▶Illustration 11-12

Return on common shareholders' equity

RETURN ON COMMON SHAREHOLDERS' EQUITY =	PROFIT AVAILABLE TO COMMON SHAREHOLDERS (PROFIT − PREFERRED DIVIDENDS)	
	AVERAGE COMMON SHAREHOLDERS' EQUITY	
(in thousands)	2012	2011
Tim Hortons	$\dfrac{\$402,885 - \$0}{(\$1,190,091 + \$1,154,433) \div 2} = 34.4\%$	$\dfrac{\$382,812 - \$0}{(\$1,154,433 + \$1,442,442) \div 2} = 29.5\%$
Second Cup	(14.7)%	19.9%
Industry average	17.3%	9.4%

In 2012, Tim Hortons' return on common shareholders' equity was 34,4%, an improvement over 2012. Both years' returns exceeded that of Second Cup and the industry average by quite a margin.

DECISION TOOLKIT

 Decision Checkpoints	 Info Needed for Decision	 Tools to Use for Decision	 How to Evaluate Results
How does the company's profit compare with previous years?	Profit available to common shareholders and weighted average number of common shares	Earnings per share = $$\frac{\text{Profit} - \text{Preferred dividends}}{\text{Weighted average number of common shares}}$$	A higher measure suggests improved performance. Values should not be compared across companies.
What is the company's return on its common shareholders' investment?	Profit available to common shareholders and average common shareholders' equity	Return on common shareholders' equity = $$\frac{\text{Profit} - \text{Preferred dividends}}{\text{Average common shareholders' equity}}$$	A high measure suggests a strong earnings performance from the common shareholders' perspective.

BEFORE YOU GO ON...

▶ Do It! Earnings Per Share

The Shoten Corporation reported profit of $249,750 for the year ended October 31, 2015. The shareholders' equity section of its statement of financial position reported 3,000 $2 cumulative preferred shares and 60,000 common shares issued. Of the common shares, 40,000 had been issued since the beginning of the year, 15,000 were issued on March 1, and 5,000 were issued on August 1. Calculate Shoten's earnings per share.

Action Plan

- Subtract any preferred dividends from profit to determine the profit available for common shareholders.
- Note that cumulative preferred dividends are deducted from profit whether declared or not; noncumulative preferred dividends are deducted only if declared.
- Adjust the shares for the fraction of the year issued to determine the weighted average number of common shares.
- Divide the profit available for common shareholders by the weighted average number of common shares to calculate earnings per share.

Solution

Preferred dividends: 3,000 × $2 = $6,000
Weighted average number of common shares:

Date	Actual Number		Weighted Average
Nov. 1	40,000	× 12/12 =	40,000
Mar. 1	15,000	× 8/12 =	10,000
Aug. 1	5,000	× 3/12 =	1,250
	60,000		51,250

Earnings per share $\dfrac{\$249{,}750 - \$6{,}000}{51{,}250} = \$4.76$

Related Exercise Material: BE11-12, BE11-13, BE11-14, BE11-15, BE11-16, BE11-17, E11-12, E11-13, E11-14, and E11-15.

comparing
IFRS and ASPE

Key Differences	International Financial Reporting Standards (IFRS)	Accounting Standards for Private Enterprises (ASPE)
Issue of shares for a noncash consideration	When shares are issued for a noncash consideration, they should be recorded at the fair value of the consideration (for example, goods or services) received. If the fair value of the consideration received cannot be reliably determined, then the fair value of the consideration given up would be used instead.	When shares are issued for a noncash consideration, they should be recorded at the most reliable of the two values—the fair value of the consideration (for example, goods or services) received or the fair value of the consideration given up.
Comprehensive income	Must present accumulated other comprehensive income in the statement of financial position and detail changes in other comprehensive income in the statement of changes in equity.	Disclosure of comprehensive income is not required.
Statement of changes in equity/retained earnings	Changes in all shareholders' equity accounts are presented in a statement of changes in equity.	Changes in retained earnings are presented in a statement of retained earnings. Changes in share capital and other accounts are presented in the notes to the financial statements.
Earnings per share	Required to present in the income statement (or statement of comprehensive income).	Not required to present in the income statement.

All About You ▶ Should I Play the Market?

When companies need additional financing, they raise this money by issuing shares (equity financing) or borrowing money (debt financing).

Suppose you have some extra cash and would like to buy some shares (equity) in a public company. An equity investment carries neither a promise that your investment will be returned to you nor a guarantee that your investment will earn income. Buying a company's common shares rather than preferred shares represents a decision to take a greater risk. With preferred shares, a shareholder will often receive dividend income. While a common shareholder can also receive dividend income, dividends are not always part of common shares. Common shareholders earn income if they can sell their shares at a price higher than what they paid for them (which is known as share price appreciation).

Share prices are determined by the interaction of buyers and sellers. Share prices can be influenced by both objective factors, such as a company's profits, and subjective factors, such as future expectations, including unverified information or rumours. Nevertheless, if a company prospers, the price of its common shares will typically rise. If the company doesn't prosper, or if external factors such as the economy or the Canadian dollar exchange rate are negative or expected to be negative, the share price will likely decline.

If you plan to invest in shares, you need to consider the following:

- How will you decide which companies to invest in? Do you plan to purchase shares for dividend income or for growth (share price appreciation)?
- How will you manage your investment portfolio? What is your time frame, how will you evaluate performance, and how will you determine the right time to sell and the right time to buy?

Some Facts

- The largest stock exchange in Canada is the Toronto Stock Exchange (TSX). It was established in 1852 and is owned by TMX Group Inc.
- Canadian markets are small compared with the number of listed companies in the world. In January 2013, there were 45,405 listed companies worldwide, of which 3,973 were listed with the TMX Group.
- Research is ongoing to establish whether men and women have different investing styles. Some studies have suggested that men of all ages have higher levels of financial literacy than women of the same age. But men are more prone to overconfidence than women, and their stock market behaviour is riskier, resulting in higher trading costs and lower returns. Women tend to prefer a slow and steady approach.
- A recent poll conducted for BMO Nesbitt Burns found that 28% of Canadians do not hold any investments. The poll also found that men were more likely than women to invest in equities (a practice found among 25% of men and 13% women), to know the specific investments they hold (67% of men and 51% of women), and to be optimistic about the future of the stock market (69% of men and 55% of women).[2]

What Do You Think?

Jemima Djeric has a good salary with excellent potential for advancement in the newly listed public company where she works. She has accumulated $10,000 in savings, which is sitting in a bank savings account earning very little interest. She has decided to use $5,000 of her savings to buy shares in her employer's company. Should Jemima make this investment?

YES She has a good income, and purchasing shares will align her interests with those of the company she works for. She will also have an opportunity to earn dividends if any are paid, as well as sell her shares for more than she paid for them if the price increases in the future.

NO There is more risk with a stock investment. She might make money if the share price increases but she could also lose her savings if the share price decreases and she has to sell her shares before it recovers.

Summary of Study Objectives

1. **Identify and discuss the major characteristics of a corporation.** The major characteristics of a corporation are separate legal existence, limited liability of shareholders, transferable ownership rights, the ability to acquire capital, a continuous life, separation of corporation management from ownership, increased cost and complexity of government regulations, and the possibility of reduced corporate income tax.

    Corporations issue shares for sale to investors. The proceeds received from the issue of shares become the company's legal capital. Shares then trade among investors on the secondary stock market and do not affect the company's financial position.

2. **Record share transactions.** If only one class of shares is issued, they are considered to be common shares. When shares are issued for noncash goods or services in a company using IFRS, the fair value of the goods or services received is used to record the transaction if it can be reliably determined. If not, the fair value of the common shares is used. For a private company following ASPE, the more reliable of the two fair values should be used, which is usually also the fair value of the goods or services received.

    The accounting for preferred shares is similar to the accounting for common shares. Preferred shares have contractual provisions that give them preference over common shares for dividends and assets in the event of liquidation. Dividends are quoted as an annual rate (such as $5 preferred), but are normally paid quarterly.

    In addition, preferred shares may have other preferences, such as the right to convert, redeem, and/or retract. However, preferred shares do not have the right to vote—only common shares have voting rights.

3. **Prepare the entries for cash dividends, stock dividends, and stock splits, and understand their financial impact.** Entries for both cash and stock dividends are required at the declaration date and the payment or distribution date. There is no entry (other than a memo entry) for a stock split. The overall impact of a cash dividend is to reduce assets (cash) and shareholders' equity (retained earnings). Stock dividends increase common shares and decrease retained earnings but do not affect assets, liabilities, or shareholders' equity in total. Stock splits also have no impact on assets, liabilities, or shareholders' equity. The number of shares increases with both stock dividends and stock splits.

4. **Indicate how shareholders' equity is presented in the financial statements.** In the shareholders' equity section of the statement of financial position for companies using IFRS, share capital, retained earnings, and accumulated other comprehensive income, if any, are reported separately. If additional contributed capital exists, then the caption "Contributed capital" is used for share capital (preferred and common shares) and additional contributed capital that may have been created from various sources. A statement of changes in equity explains the changes in each shareholders' equity account, and in total, for the reporting period. Notes to the financial statements explain details about authorized and issued shares, restrictions on retained earnings, and dividends in arrears, if there are any.

    For private companies reporting using ASPE, comprehensive income is not reported and a statement of changes in equity is not required. Instead, a statement of retained earnings is prepared that explains the changes in the retained earnings account for the reporting period. Changes to share capital and any other equity items are disclosed in the notes to the statements.

5. **Evaluate dividend and earnings performance.** A company's dividend record can be evaluated by looking at what percentage of profit it chooses to pay out in dividends, as measured by the dividend payout ratio (dividends divided by profit) and the dividend yield ratio (dividends per share divided by the share price).

    Earnings performance can be measured by two profitability ratios: earnings per share (profit less preferred dividends divided by the weighted average number of common shares) and the return on common shareholders' equity ratio (profit less preferred dividends divided by average common shareholders' equity).

Glossary

Accumulated other comprehensive income (AOCI)   The cumulative change in shareholders' equity that results from the gains and losses that bypass profit (recorded in OCI) but affect shareholders' equity. (p. 572)

Authorized shares   The amount of share capital that a corporation is authorized to sell. The amount may be unlimited or specified. (p. 559)

Cash dividend   A pro rata (proportional) distribution of cash to shareholders. (p. 566)

Contributed capital   The total amount paid or contributed by shareholders in exchange for shares of ownership. It consists of share capital and additional contributed capital, if any. (p. 561)

Corporation   A company organized as a separate legal entity, with most of the rights and privileges of a person. Shares are evidence of ownership. (p. 556)

Cumulative   A feature of preferred shares that entitles the shareholder to receive current-year and unpaid prior-year dividends when dividends are declared before common shareholders receive any dividends. (p. 564)

Declaration date   The date the board of directors formally declares (approves) a dividend and announces it to shareholders. (p. 566)

Dividend yield   A measure of the percentage of the share price that is paid in dividends. It is calculated by dividing dividends per share by the share price. (p. 577)

Dividends in arrears   Dividends that were not declared on cumulative preferred shares during a period. (p. 564)

Initial public offering (IPO)   The initial offering of a corporation's shares to the public. (p. 559)

Issued shares   The portion of authorized shares that has been sold. (p. 559)

Legal capital   The amount per share that must be retained in the business for the protection of corporate creditors. Equal to the proceeds received from the issue of most shares. (p. 560)

Market capitalization   A measure of the fair value of a company's equity. It is calculated by multiplying the number of shares by the share price at any given date. (p. 560)

Noncumulative   Preferred shares that are entitled to the current dividend, if declared, but not to any undeclared and unpaid amounts from prior years. (p. 564)

Normal course issuer bid   The reacquisition of a specified percentage of a company's own shares from the general public for a predetermined price and period, subject to regulatory approval. (p. 562)

Other comprehensive income (OCI)   Gains and losses that affect shareholders' equity but are not shown in profit or loss. They relate to complex transactions such as certain types of gains and losses on investments. (p. 572)

Payment (distribution) date   The date dividends are paid or distributed to shareholders. (p. 567)

Payout ratio   A measure of the percentage of the profit distributed in the form of cash dividends to common shareholders. It is calculated by dividing cash dividends by profit. (p. 577)

Preferred shares   Share capital that has contractual preferences over common shares in certain areas. (p. 563)

Profit available to common shareholders   Profit less the annual preferred dividend for cumulative preferred shares. The dividend is deducted for noncumulative preferred shares only if declared. (p. 579)

Record date   The date when ownership of shares is determined for dividend purposes. (p. 567)

Retained earnings restrictions   Circumstances that make a portion of retained earnings currently unavailable for dividends. (p. 572)

Return on common shareholders' equity   A measure of profitability from the shareholders' point of view. It is calculated by dividing profit minus preferred dividends by average common shareholders' equity (total shareholders' equity minus preferred shares). (p. 580)

Statement of retained earnings   A statement that summarizes the changes in the Retained Earnings account during the period. This statement is issued only by private companies reporting using ASPE. (p. 574)

Stock dividend   A pro rata (proportional) distribution of the corporation's own shares to shareholders. (p. 567)

Stock split   The issue of additional shares to shareholders accompanied by a reduction in the legal capital per share. (p. 569)

Weighted average number of common shares   A weighted average of the number of common shares issued during the year. Shares issued or repurchased during the year are weighted by the fraction of the year for which they have been issued. (p. 579)

DECISION TOOLKIT—A SUMMARY

 Decision Checkpoints	 Info Needed for Decision	 Tools to Use for Decision	 How to Evaluate Results
Should the company incorporate?	Capital needs, growth expectations, type of business, income tax status	Corporations have limited liability, greater ability to raise capital, and professional managers. In addition, there is a potential for reduced income tax. There is increased cost and complexity from additional government regulations.	Carefully weigh the costs and benefits in light of the particular circumstances.
What portion of its profit does the company pay out in dividends?	Profit and total cash dividends	$\text{Payout ratio} = \dfrac{\text{Cash dividends}}{\text{Profit}}$	A high payout ratio is considered desirable for investors seeking income. A low ratio suggests that the company is retaining its profit for investment in future growth.
What percentage of the share price is the company paying in dividends?	Dividends and share price	$\text{Dividend yield} = \dfrac{\text{Dividend per share}}{\text{Market price per share}}$	A high dividend yield is considered desirable for investors. It also means that the company is paying out, rather than retaining, its profit.

(continued)

How does the company's profit compare with previous years?	Profit available to common shareholders and weighted average number of common shares	Earnings per share = $\dfrac{\text{Profit} - \text{Preferred dividends}}{\text{Weighted average number of common shares}}$	A higher measure suggests improved performance. Values should not be compared across companies.
What is the company's return on its common shareholders' investment?	Profit available to common shareholders and average common shareholders' equity	Return on common shareholders' equity = $\dfrac{\text{Profit} - \text{Preferred dividends}}{\text{Average common shareholders' equity}}$	A high measure suggests a strong earnings performance from the common shareholders' perspective.

USING THE DECISION TOOLKIT

The following selected information (in U.S. millions, except per share information) is available for Starbucks Corporation, one of Tim Hortons' competitors. Note that Starbucks has no preferred shares.

	2012	2011
Profit	$1,383.8	$1,245.7
Cash dividends	543.7	419.5
Shareholders' equity	5,114.5	4,387.3
Weighted average number of common shares	754.4	748.3
Dividends per share	0.72	0.56
Market price per share	45.71	41.58

Instructions

(a) Using the above information, calculate the (1) payout ratio, (2) dividend yield, (3) earnings per share, and (4) return on common shareholders' equity for Starbucks for 2012.

(b) Contrast the company's (1) dividend record and (2) earnings performance with that of Tim Hortons and the industry, which is given in the chapter.

Solution

(a)

(in U.S. millions, except per share information)	Starbucks	Tim Hortons	Industry
1. Payout ratio	$\dfrac{\$543.7}{\$1,383.8} = 39.3\%$	32.4%	31.0%
2. Dividend yield	$\dfrac{\$0.72}{\$45.71} = 1.6\%$	1.7%	1.2%
3. Earnings per share	$\dfrac{\$1,383.8 - \$0}{\$754.4} = \$1.83$	$2.60	n/a
4. Return on common shareholders' equity	$\dfrac{\$1,383.8 - \$0}{(\$5,114.5 + \$4,387.3) \div 2} = 29.1\%$	34.4%	17.3%

(b) 1. Dividend record: Starbucks' payout ratio is higher than that of both Tim Hortons and its competitors in the industry. Yet its dividend yield is marginally lower than that of Tim Hortons, while still higher than that of the industry. Investors would likely favour Tim Hortons over Starbucks for dividend income because of its higher dividend yield. Tim Hortons' payout ratio is not all that much lower than that of Starbucks and will vary depending on the profit for a particular year.

2. Earnings performance: It is not possible to compare earnings per share between companies, because of the differing capital structures. Starbucks' return on common shareholders' equity is lower than that of Tim Hortons, but still significantly above that of its industry counterparts.

Comprehensive Do It!

Rolman Corporation is authorized to issue an unlimited number of common shares and 100,000 $6 cumulative preferred shares. At January 1, 2015, it had the following opening equity balances: Preferred shares, nil; Common Shares, 300,000 shares issued, $1.8 million; Additional Contributed Capital, $50,000; Retained Earnings, $1,150,000; and Accumulated Other Comprehensive Income, $50,000.

During the year ended December 31, 2015, the company had the following share transactions:

Jan.	10	Issued 100,000 common shares at $8 per share.
July	1	Issued 20,000 preferred shares at $50 per share.
Sept.	1	Declared a 5% stock dividend to common shareholders of record on September 15, distributable September 30. The price of the common shares was $10 per share on September 1, $12 per share on September 15, and $11 per share on September 30.
Nov.	1	Issued 5,000 preferred shares at $40 per share.
Dec.	24	Declared an annual preferred cash dividend to shareholders of record on January 15, payable January 31.
	31	A loan agreement entered into on December 31 contains a restrictive covenant that limits the payment of future dividends to 15% of profit.

In addition, Rolman reported profit of $392,000 for the year.

Instructions

(a) Record the above transactions, including any entries required to close dividends and profit (Income Summary) to Retained Earnings.

(b) Prepare the statement of changes in equity and the shareholders' equity section of the statement of financial position, including any required note disclosure.

Action Plan

- Keep a running total of the number of shares issued to date.
- Apply the stock dividend percentage to the number of common shares issued. Multiply the new shares to be issued by the fair value of the shares at the declaration date.
- Recall that the statement of changes in equity explains the changes for the period in the beginning and ending balances of each shareholders' equity account.
- The statement of financial position reports shareholders' equity at the end of the period. Disclose the share details in the shareholders' equity section of the statement of financial position.

Solution to Comprehensive Do It!

(a)

Jan.	10	Cash (100,000 × $8)	800,000	
		Common Shares		800,000
		(To record issue of 100,000 common shares)		
July	1	Cash (20,000 × $50)	1,000,000	
		Preferred Shares		1,000,000
		(To record issue of 20,000 preferred shares)		
Sept.	1	Stock Dividends (300,000 + 100,000 = 400,000 × 5% = 20,000 × $10)	200,000	
		Stock Dividends Distributable		200,000
		(To record declaration of 5% stock dividend)		
	15	Record date—no entry required		
	30	Stock Dividends Distributable	200,000	
		Common Shares		200,000
		(To record issue of 20,000 common shares in a 5% stock dividend)		
Nov.	1	Cash (5,000 × $40)	200,000	
		Preferred Shares		200,000
		(To record issue of 5,000 preferred shares)		

(*continued*)

(a) (*continued*)

Dec.	24	Cash Dividends (20,000 + 5,000 = 25,000 × $6)	150,000	
		Dividends Payable		150,000
		(To record declaration of annual preferred cash dividend)		
	31	No entry required for restriction of retained earnings—disclosure only		
	31	Retained Earnings	350,000	
		Stock Dividends		200,000
		Cash Dividends		150,000
		(To close dividends)		
	31	Income Summary	392,000	
		Retained Earnings		392,000
		(To close profit)		

(b)

ROLMAN CORPORATION
Statement of Changes in Equity
Year Ended December 31, 2015

	Share Capital		Additional Contributed Capital	Retained Earnings	Accumulated Other Comprehensive Income	Total
	Preferred Shares	Common Shares				
Balance, Jan. 1		$1,800,000	$50,000	$1,150,000	$50,000	$3,050,000
Issued preferred shares	$1,200,000[1]					1,200,000
Issued common shares		800,000				800,000
Profit				392,000		392,000
Declared and issued stock dividend		200,000		(200,000)		0
Declared cash dividend				(150,000)		(150,000)
Balance, Dec. 31	$1,200,000	$2,800,000	$50,000	$1,192,000	$50,000	$5,292,000

ROLMAN CORPORATION
Statement of Financial Position (partial)
December 31, 2015

Shareholders' equity			
Contributed capital			
Share capital			
Preferred shares, 100,000 $6 cumulative authorized, 25,000[2] shares issued		$1,200,000	
Common shares, unlimited number of shares authorized, 420,000[3] shares issued		2,800,000	$4,000,000
Additional contributed capital			50,000
Total contributed capital			4,050,000
Retained earnings (Note x)			1,192,000
Accumulated other comprehensive income			50,000
Total shareholders' equity			$5,292,000

Note x: A loan agreement contains a restrictive covenant that limits the payment of future dividends to 15% of profit.

[1]$1,000,000 + $200,000 = $1,200,000
[2]20,000 + 5,000 = 25,000
[3]300,000 + 100,000 + 20,000 = 420,000

Self-Test Questions

Answers are at the end of the chapter.

Quiz Yourself

(SO 1)   1. Which of the following advantages of a publicly traded corporation might not be an advantage to a private corporation?
(a) Separate legal existence
(b) Continuous life
(c) Potential for reduced income tax
(d) Ability to acquire capital

(SO 1)   2. Which of the following statements is *false?*
(a) Ownership of common shares gives the owner a voting right.
(b) If a company's shares are sold by one shareholder to another, this transaction must be recorded by the company.
(c) The authorization of share capital does not result in a transaction that is recorded by the company.
(d) Legal capital cannot be distributed to shareholders.

(SO 2)   3. Simeon Corporation, a publicly traded company, issues 10,000 common shares in exchange for a piece of land. At the time of the transaction, the common shares were trading at $5 per share and the land was valued at $45,000. To record this transaction:
(a) Land should be debited $45,000, Loss on Sale of Common Shares debited $5,000, and Common Shares credited $50,000.
(b) Land should be debited $45,000 and Common Shares credited $45,000.
(c) Land should be debited $50,000 and Common Shares credited $50,000.
(d) This transaction would not be recorded since it is a noncash transaction.

(SO 2)   4. ABC Corporation issues 1,000 preferred shares at $12 per share. In recording the transaction, a credit of $12,000 is made to:
(a) Investment in ABC Corporation.
(b) Preferred Shares.
(c) Accumulated Other Comprehensive Income.
(d) Additional Contributed Capital.

(SO 3)   5. Entries for cash dividends are required on the:
(a) declaration date and record date.
(b) record date and payment date.
(c) declaration date, record date, and payment date.
(d) declaration date and payment date.

(SO 3)   6. Which of the following statements about stock dividends and stock splits is *true?*
(a) A stock dividend and stock split increase total shareholders' equity.
(b) A stock dividend and stock split decrease total shareholders' equity.
(c) A stock dividend and stock split have no effect on total shareholders' equity.
(d) A stock dividend and stock split have no effect on the number of common shares.

(SO 4)   7. Which of the following is *not* reported in a public company's statement of changes in equity?
(a) Legal capital of common shares
(b) Fair value of common shares
(c) Dividends
(d) Accumulated other comprehensive income

(SO 4)   8. Which of the following is *not* a required financial statement for a private company reporting under ASPE?
(a) Income statement
(b) Statement of changes in equity
(c) Statement of retained earnings
(d) Statement of financial position

(SO 5)   9. If a company's net sales is $800,000, profit $60,000, preferred dividends $10,000, total assets $1 million, and average common shareholders' equity $500,000, its return on common shareholders' equity is:
(a) 0.8%.
(b) 10.0%.
(c) 12.0%.
(d) 160.0%

(SO 5) 10. For the year ended June 30, 2015, Dupuis Inc. reported profit of $90,000. It had 5,000 common shares issued since the beginning of the year, July 1, 2014, and 2,000 shares issued on January 1, 2015. In addition, it paid dividends of $3 per common share at the end of the year and had a share price of $60. It had no preferred shares. What were its earnings per share and dividend yield?
(a) $12.86 and 5%
(b) $12.86 and 23%
(c) $15 and 5%
(d) $15 and 20%

the navigator

Questions

(SO 1)   1. Pat Kabza, a student, asks for your help in understanding the different corporation characteristics. (a) Explain the following characteristics to Pat and identify whether they are an advantage or a disadvantage for a large, publicly traded corporation: (1) separate legal existence, (2) limited liability of shareholders, (3) transferable ownership rights, (4) ability to acquire capital, (5) continuous life, (6) separation of management and ownership, (7) government regulations, and (8) income tax. (b) Would your answers to part (a) change if you were commenting about the advantages and disadvantages for a small, private corporation rather than a large, publicly traded corporation? Explain.

(SO 1)   2. Letson Corporation is authorized to issue 100,000 common shares. During its first two years of operation, Letson issued 60,000 shares. (a) After this transaction, how many more shares is Letson able to issue? (b) Are both authorized and issued shares recorded in the general journal?

(SO 1)   3. Richard Boudreault purchased 100 **lululemon athletica** common shares for $18 a share from the company's initial public offering. A few years later, Richard purchased 200 more lululemon shares for $71 each on the Toronto Stock Exchange. Explain the impact of each of these transactions on lululemon's assets, liabilities, and shareholders' equity.

(SO 1)   4. The market capitalization of **Plazacorp Retail Properties Limited** was $278 million at the end of 2011 and $317 million at the end of 2012. Explain what "market capitalization" means and describe the effect of this increase in market capitalization between 2011 and 2012 on Plazacorp's assets, liabilities, and shareholders' equity.

(SO 1)   5. What is legal capital? How is the value of the legal capital determined? Why is legal capital reported separately from retained earnings in the shareholders' equity section of the statement of financial position?

(SO 2)   6. Compare the rights of preferred shareholders with those of common shareholders. Include in your answer the areas in which preferred shares are given priority over common shares.

(SO 2)   7. When common and preferred shares are issued for a consideration other than cash (for example, goods or services), at what value should the shares be recorded for a publicly traded company using IFRS? Would your answer change if it were a private company using ASPE?

(SO 2)   8. (a) What is a normal course issuer bid? (b) Why might a company wish to reacquire some of its own shares?

(SO 2)   9. The **Royal Bank of Canada** has a noncumulative class of preferred shares with an annual dividend rate of $1.125. Assad David owns 1,000 of these shares. If the Royal Bank declares and pays a quarterly dividend on these shares, how much dividend can Assad expect to receive for the quarter?

(SO 2)   10. What is the difference between cumulative and noncumulative preferred shares? Can dividends in arrears arise for both types of preferred shares? Explain.

(SO 3)   11. What conditions must be met before a cash dividend can be paid?

(SO 3)   12. Contrast the effects of the (a) declaration date, (b) record date, and (c) payment date for a cash dividend on a company's (1) assets, (2) liabilities, (3) share capital, (4) retained earnings, (5) total shareholders' equity, and (6) number of shares.

(SO 3)   13. Contrast the effects of a (a) cash dividend, (b) stock dividend, and (c) stock split on a company's (1) assets, (2) liabilities, (3) share capital, (4) retained earnings, (5) total shareholders' equity, and (6) number of shares.

(SO 3)   14. Bella Corporation has 10,000 common shares issued when it announces a 3-for-1 split. Before the split, the shares were trading for $120 per share. (a) After the split, how many shares will be issued? (b) After the split, what will be the likely share price?

(SO 3)   15. Why are cash and stock dividends recorded in the general journal but stock splits are not?

(SO 4)   16. Indicate how each of the following should be reported in (a) the statement of changes in equity and (b) the shareholders' equity section of the statement of financial position: (1) preferred shares, (2) common shares, (3) stock dividends distributable, (4) additional contributed capital, (5) retained earnings, and (6) accumulated other comprehensive income.

(SO 4)   17. For what reason might a company restrict its retained earnings? How is a restriction reported in the financial statements?

(SO 4)   18. Distinguish between other comprehensive income and accumulated other comprehensive income. Include in your answer how and where each is reported in the financial statements.

(SO 4)   19. (a) What is the difference between a statement of changes in equity and statement of retained earnings? (b) How do each of these relate to the shareholders' equity section of the statement of financial position?

(SO 4)   20. Distinguish between the content of the (a) shareholders' equity sections and (b) financial statements of a publicly traded company using IFRS and a private company using ASPE.

(SO 5)   21. Indicate whether each of the following is generally considered favourable or unfavourable by a potential investor:
(a) A decrease in the payout ratio
(b) An increase in the dividend yield
(c) A decrease in the return on common shareholders' equity
(d) An increase in earnings per share

(SO 5) 22. **Coca-Cola** recently reported dividends per share of U.S. $1.00 and a dividend yield of 1.5%. **Pepsi** reported dividends per share of U.S. $2.15 and a dividend yield of 3.0% for the same period. Can you figure out which company had the higher share price?

(SO 5) 23. In the calculation of earnings per share, why is the weighted average number of common shares used instead of the number of common shares at the end of the year?

(SO 5) 24. Why do the earnings per share and return on common shareholders' equity ratios use profit available to common shareholders in their numerator rather than profit?

(SO 5) 25. Company A has a payout ratio of 30% and a dividend yield of 2%. Company B has a payout ratio of 50% and a dividend yield of 3%. Which company's shares would be of more interest to an investor wanting a steady dividend income?

Brief Exercises

BE11–1 In November 2012, the **Hudson's Bay Company** issued an IPO on the Toronto Stock Exchange. Shares purchased under the IPO were sold at $17 per share. If a shareholder purchased Hudson's Bay's shares in January 2013, they would have paid $16.81 per share. Explain the impact on Hudson's Bay's financial position of the shares sold (a) under the IPO in November 2012 for $17 and (b) on the Toronto Stock Exchange in January 2013 for $16.81.

Evaluate impact of share issue. (SO 1)

BE11–2 On May 1, Armada Corporation incorporated and authorized 100,000 preferred shares and an unlimited number of common shares. On May 2, Armada issued 1,000 common shares for $15 per share. On June 15, it issued an additional 500 common shares for $17 per share. On November 1, Armada issued 100 preferred shares for $30 per share. On December 15, it issued an additional 100 preferred shares for $35 per share. (a) Record the share transactions. (b) Indicate how many shares are authorized and how many are issued at the end of the year for the (1) preferred shares and (2) common shares.

Record issue of shares. (SO 2)

BE11–3 On March 8, Daschen Inc., a publicly traded company, issued 5,000 preferred shares for cash of $30 per share. On April 20, when the shares were trading at $35, the company issued an additional 3,000 preferred shares in exchange for land with a fair value of $110,000. (a) Prepare the journal entries for each transaction. (b) Would your answer change if you were unable to determine the land's fair value on April 20?

Record issue of shares for cash and noncash. (SO 2)

BE11–4 Canaan Limited had 20,000 $2 cumulative preferred shares issued. It was unable to pay any dividend to the preferred shareholders in the current year. (a) What are the dividends in arrears? (b) How would the dividends in arrears be reported in the financial statements? (c) Would your answer to part (a) change if the preferred shares were noncumulative rather than cumulative?

Determine dividends in arrears. (SO 2)

BE11–5 The Seabee Corporation has 30,000 $2 noncumulative preferred shares. It declares a quarterly cash dividend on November 15 to shareholders of record on December 10. The dividend is paid on December 31. Prepare the entries on the appropriate dates to record the cash dividend.

Record cash dividend. (SO 3)

BE11–6 Satina Corporation has 100,000 common shares. It declares a 5% stock dividend on December 1 to shareholders of record on December 20. The shares are issued on January 10. The share price is $15 on December 1, $14.50 on December 20, and $14.75 on January 10. Prepare the entries on the appropriate dates to record the stock dividend.

Record stock dividend. (SO 3)

BE11–7 In January 2013, **Lorillard, Inc.** completed a 3-for-1 stock split. Immediately before the split, Lorillard had 129 million common shares trading at U.S. $117 per share. (a) How many shares did it have after the stock split? (b) What was the most likely price of the shares after the stock split? (c) How would Lorillard record or report this stock split?

Analyze impact of stock split. (SO 3)

BE11–8 Indicate whether each of the following transactions would increase (+), decrease (–), or have no effect (NE) on total assets, total liabilities, total shareholders' equity, and the number of shares:

Compare cash dividend, stock dividend, and stock split. (SO 3)

	Assets	Liabilities	Shareholders' Equity	Number of Shares

(a) Declared cash dividend.
(b) Paid cash dividend declared in (a).
(c) Declared stock dividend.
(d) Distributed stock dividend declared in (c).
(e) Split stock 2-for-1.

Determine missing amounts in statement of changes in equity.
(SO 4)

BE11–9 Luxat Corporation reported the following statement of changes in equity accounts for the year ended December 31, 2015.

LUXAT CORPORATION
Statement of Changes in Equity
Year Ended December 31, 2015

	Common Shares	Additional Contributed Capital	Retained Earnings	Accumulated Other Comprehensive Income	Total
Bal., Jan. 1	$1,500,000	$500,000	$3,000,000	$100,000	$5,100,000
Issued common shares	[1]				[2]
Declared and issued stock dividend	110,000		[3]		[4]
Declared cash dividends			(135,000)		(135,000)
Comprehensive income					
Profit			750,000		[5]
Other comprehensive income				[6]	25,000
Bal., Dec. 31	$2,050,000	$ [7]	$3,505,000	$125,000	$ [8]

Determine the missing amounts for items [1] to [8].

Prepare shareholders' equity section.
(SO 4)

BE11–10 Refer to the data given in BE11–9 for Luxat Corporation. Luxat had an unlimited number of common shares authorized and 550,000 shares issued at December 31. Prepare the shareholders' equity section of its statement of financial position at December 31, 2015.

Prepare statement of retained earnings.
(SO 4)

BE11–11 For the year ended December 31, 2015, Stirling Farms Limited, a private company, reported a profit of $150,000. The company declared cash dividends of $90,000 and paid $80,000 of these dividends during the year. (a) Prepare a statement of retained earnings for the year, assuming the balance in Retained Earnings on January 1, 2015, was $490,000. (b) How would this statement change if Stirling Farms were a publicly traded company?

Evaluate payout ratio.
(SO 5)

BE11–12 Paul Schwartz, president of Schwartz Corporation, believes that it is good practice to maintain a constant payout of dividends relative to profit. Last year, profit was $600,000, and the company paid $60,000 in dividends. This year, due to some unusual circumstances, the company had a profit of $2 million. Paul expects next year's profit to be about $700,000. (a) What was Schwartz Corporation's payout ratio last year? (b) If it is to maintain the same payout ratio, what amount of dividends would it pay this year? (c) Is this a good idea? In other words, what are the pros and cons of maintaining a constant payout ratio?

Calculate dividend yield.
(SO 5)

BE11–13 **Canadian National Railway** and **Canadian Pacific Railway** have a dividend of $1.50 per common share and $1.40 per common share, respectively. The market price of their shares is $93.72 per share and $108.55 per share, respectively. (a) Calculate the dividend yield for each company. (b) Which company would investors prefer if they wish to purchase shares for the purpose of dividend income?

Calculate weighted average number of shares.
(SO 5)

BE11–14 Messier Inc. had 34,000 common shares on January 1, 2015. On August 31 and November 30, 9,000 and 6,000 common shares were issued, respectively. Calculate (a) the number of common shares issued at December 31, 2015, and (b) the weighted average number of common shares for 2015.

Calculate earnings per share.
(SO 5)

BE11–15 Refer to the data for Messier Inc. given in BE11–14. Messier reported a profit of $370,000. Messier also had 10,000 $2 cumulative preferred shares, on which the dividend for the current year was declared and paid. Calculate the earnings per share.

Calculate earnings per share.
(SO 5)

BE11–16 Castera Inc. reported a profit of $500,000 and a weighted average number of common shares of 200,000 for the year. It also had 25,000 $2 preferred shares. Calculate earnings per share assuming (a) the preferred shares are cumulative and the dividend was not paid, (b) the preferred shares are noncumulative and the dividend was paid, and (c) the preferred shares are noncumulative and the dividend was not paid.

Calculate return on common shareholders' equity.
(SO 5)

BE11–17 Salliq Ltd. reported the following selected information for the year ended January 31, 2015: profit, $14,000; beginning shareholders' equity, $104,000; and ending shareholders' equity, $122,000. Salliq has no preferred shares. (a) Calculate the return on common shareholders' equity. (b) Explain how your calculation in part (a) would change if Salliq had preferred shares and had paid the preferred shareholders a dividend.

Exercises

E11–1 The following is a recent stock market listing for **Bombardier Inc.** Class B (common) shares:

Interpret stock market
listing.
(SO 1)

365-day		stock	sym	div	high	low	close	chg	vol (000)	yld	p/e ratio
high	low										
4.93	2.97	Bombardier	BBD.B	0.10	4.10	4.02	4.02	−0.08	12,260	2.53	9.14

Instructions
(a) What is the highest price Bombardier's shares traded for during the year? The lowest?
(b) What is the annual per share dividend paid on these shares?
(c) If you had purchased 1,000 common shares at Bombardier's closing price of the day in the above listing, what would be the total cost of your share purchase?
(d) What was the closing price of Bombardier's common shares on the previous day?
(e) How many Bombardier common shares were sold on the trading day of the listing?

E11–2 Santiago Corp., a publicly traded company, had 2,500 preferred shares issued with a balance of $55,000 and 140,000 common shares issued with a balance of $700,000 at the beginning of the year. The following share transactions occurred during the year:

Record issue of shares.
(SO 2)

June	12	Issued 50,000 common shares for $6 per share.
July	11	Issued 1,000 preferred shares for $25 per share.
Oct.	1	Issued 10,000 common shares in exchange for land. The common shares were trading for $7 per share on that date. The fair value of the land was estimated to be $75,000.
Nov.	15	Issued 25,000 preferred shares for $28 per share.

Instructions
(a) Record the above transactions.
(b) Calculate the number of shares and balance in the account for each of the preferred and common shares at the end of the year.

E11–3 Moosonee Ltd. was incorporated as a private company on January 2, 2015, and is authorized to issue an unlimited number of common shares and $1 preferred shares. The company had the following share transactions in its first month of operations:

Record issue of shares.
(SO 2)

Jan.	6	Issued 200,000 common shares for $1.50 per share.
	12	Issued 50,000 common shares for $1.75 per share.
	18	Issued 10,000 preferred shares for $25 per share.
	31	Issued 10,000 common shares in exchange for $15,000 of legal services.

Instructions
(a) Record the above transactions.
(b) What is the number of preferred and common shares at the end of January?
(c) If Moosonee were a publicly traded company, how might the journal entry to record the noncash transaction on January 31 change?

E11–4 Marsh Corporation issued 400,000 $1 cumulative preferred shares. In its first year of operations, it paid $300,000 of dividends to its preferred shareholders. In its second year, the company paid dividends of $400,000 to its preferred shareholders.

Determine dividends
in arrears.
(SO 2)

Instructions
(a) What is the total annual preferred dividend supposed to be for the preferred shareholders?
(b) Calculate any dividends in arrears in years 1 and 2.
(c) Explain how dividends in arrears should be reported in the financial statements.
(d) If the preferred shares were noncumulative rather than cumulative, how much dividend would the company have been obligated to pay its preferred shareholders in each year?

Record and post share and dividend transactions.
(SO 2, 3)

E11-5 On January 1, 2015, Tarow Corporation had 80,000 common shares, recorded at $600,000, and retained earnings of $1,000,000. During the year, the following transactions occurred:

Apr. 1	Issued 5,000 common shares at $20 per share.
June 15	Declared a cash dividend of $0.25 per share to common shareholders of record on June 30, payable on July 10.
Aug. 21	Declared a 5% stock dividend to common shareholders of record on September 5, distributable on September 20. The shares were trading for $22 a share on August 21, $24 on September 5, and $26 on September 20.
Nov. 1	Issued 3,000 common shares at $25 per share.
Dec. 20	Declared a cash dividend of $0.30 per share to common shareholders of record on December 31, payable on January 10.

Instructions

(a) Record the above transactions for 2015. (*Note:* Closing entries are not required.)

(b) Open T accounts and post to the shareholders' equity accounts journalized in (a).

(c) What is the number of common shares at the end of the year?

Compare cash dividend, stock dividend, and stock split.
(SO 3)

E11-6 Laine Inc. is considering one of three following courses of action: (1) paying a $0.50 cash dividend, (2) distributing a 5% stock dividend, or (3) effecting a 2-for-1 stock split. The current share price is $14 per share.

Instructions

Help Laine make its decision by completing the following chart (treat each possibility independently):

	Before Action	(1) After Cash Dividend	(2) After Stock Dividend	(3) After Stock Split
Total assets	$1,250,000			
Total liabilities	$ 250,000			
Shareholders' equity				
Common shares	600,000			
Retained earnings	400,000			
Total shareholders' equity	1,000,000			
Total liabilities and shareholders' equity	$1,250,000			
Number of common shares	100,000			

Indicate impact of transactions on shareholders' equity.
(SO 2, 3, 4)

E11-7 Milford Corporation had the following transactions and events:

1. Issued preferred shares for cash.
2. Declared a cash dividend on the preferred shares.
3. Paid the cash dividend declared in (2).
4. Issued common shares for cash.
5. Issued common shares for a noncash exchange of assets.
6. Completed a 2-for-1 stock split of the common shares.
7. Declared a stock dividend on the common shares.
8. Distributed the stock dividend declared in (7).
9. Restricted retained earnings.
10. Reported other comprehensive income from an unrealized gain on investments.

Instructions

Indicate whether each of the above transactions would increase (+), decrease (−), or have no effect (NE) on assets, liabilities, and key categories within shareholders' equity, as shown in the following table. The first one has been done for you as an example.

			Shareholders' Equity			
	Assets	Liabilities	Share Capital	Retained Earnings	Accumulated Other Comprehensive Income	Total Shareholders' Equity
1.	+	NE	+	NE	NE	+

E11–8 The general ledger of Val d'Or Corporation contains the following selected accounts and information:

Classify accounts.
(SO 4)

1. Cash
2. Common shares
3. Other comprehensive income—Revaluation gain from revaluing property, plant, and equipment to fair value
4. Long-term investments
5. Preferred shares
6. Retained earnings
7. Gain on disposal
8. Cash dividends
9. Stock split
10. Stock dividends distributable

Instructions

Indicate whether each of the above accounts should be reported in the statement of changes in equity. If yes, indicate whether the account should be reported in the share capital, retained earnings, or accumulated other comprehensive income section of the statement. If not, indicate in which financial statement (statement of financial position or income statement) and in which section the account should be reported or write NE (no effect), if the statement is not affected. The first account has been done for you as an example.

| | | Statement of Changes in Equity | | | | |
	Account	Share Capital	Retained Earnings	Accumulated Other Comprehensive Income	Other Financial Statement	Classification
1.	Cash	NE	NE	NE	Statement of financial position	Current assets

E11–9 The following accounts appear in the ledger of Ozabal Inc. after the books are closed at December 31, 2015:

Prepare shareholders' equity section.
(SO 4)

Accumulated other comprehensive loss	$ 50,000
Common shares (unlimited number of shares authorized, 250,000 shares issued)	500,000
Stock dividends distributable	50,000
Additional contributed capital	25,000
Preferred shares ($1.25 noncumulative, 100,000 shares authorized, 10,000 shares issued)	250,000
Retained earnings (of which $100,000 is restricted for a plant expansion)	900,000

Instructions

Prepare the shareholders' equity section of Ozabal's statement of financial position, including any required note disclosure.

E11–10 The Blue Canoe Limited reported the following changes to its shareholders' equity accounts for the year ended December 31, 2015.

Prepare statement of changes in equity and shareholders' equity section.
(SO 4)

Accumulated other comprehensive income:		Retained earnings:	
Balance, Jan. 1	$ 90,000	Balance, Jan. 1	$1,500,000
Other comprehensive income	(25,000)	Profit	400,000
Balance, Dec. 31	$ 65,000	Cash dividends	(70,000)
Additional contributed capital:		Balance, Dec. 31	$1,830,000
Balance, Jan. 1	$540,000	Common shares:	
Balance, Dec. 31	$540,000	Balance, Jan. 1	$ 800,000
		Shares issued	180,000
		Balance, Dec. 31	$ 980,000

Instructions

(a) Prepare a statement of changes in equity for the year.
(b) Prepare the shareholders' equity section of the balance sheet at December 31.

E11–11 **Sobeys Inc.** is a private company. It reported beginning retained earnings at May 7, 2011, of $1,362.8 million. During the year ended May 5, 2012, it reported a profit of $322.5 million and declared and paid dividends on its common shares of $70.5 million. It also reported other deductions to retained earnings of $47.5 million.

Prepare statement of retained earnings.
(SO 4)

Instructions

(a) Prepare a statement of retained earnings for the year ended May 5, 2012.

(b) If Sobeys were a publicly traded company, would it still have to prepare a statement of retained earnings? Explain.

Calculate and evaluate dividend record.
(SO 5)

E11–12   The following selected information is available for two competitors, **Nike, Inc.** and **Adidas AG:**

(in millions, except for per share information)	Nike (in U.S. $)	Adidas (in euros)
Market price per share	$53.68	€67.33
Total cash dividends	619	282
Dividends per share	1.565	1.35
Profit	2,223	791

Instructions

(a) Calculate the (1) payout and (2) dividend yield ratios for each company.

(b) Which company would investors favour for dividend income purposes? Explain.

Calculate earnings per share.
(SO 5)

E11–13   Chinook Corporation started the year ended November 30, 2015, with 60,000 common shares and no preferred shares issued. The following changes in share capital occurred during the year:

Feb. 28   Issued 15,000 common shares for $225,000.

Sept. 1   Issued 20,000 $1 cumulative preferred shares for $500,000.

Nov. 1   Issued 6,000 common shares in exchange for land. The shares were trading for $20 on this date and the fair value of the land was $115,000.

 30   Reported profit of $351,250.

 30   Declared the quarterly cash dividend to the preferred shareholders of record on December 16, payable on December 31.

Instructions

(a) Calculate the profit available for the common shareholders.

(b) Calculate the weighted average number of common shares for the year.

(c) Calculate the earnings per share for the year.

Calculate and evaluate ratios.
(SO 5)

E11–14   Selected financial information (in millions, except per share information) is available for **CIBC** at October 31:

	2012	2011	2010
Total cash dividends paid to common shareholders	$ 1,470	$ 1,391	$ 1,350
Cash dividends per common share	$ 3.64	$ 3.51	$ 3.48
Profit available to common shareholders	$ 3,173	$ 2,690	$ 2,114
Common shareholders' equity	$15,332	$13,335	$11,643
Market price per common share	$ 78.56	$ 73.96	$ 78.23
Weighted average number of common shares	404	396	388

Instructions

(a) Calculate the (1) payout, (2) dividend yield, (3) earnings per share, and (4) return on common shareholders' equity ratios for the common shareholders for 2012 and 2011.

(b) Using the information in part (a), comment on CIBC's dividend record and earnings performance over the two-year period.

Evaluate ratios.
(SO 5)

E11–15   Selected ratios are shown below for two competing toolmakers, **Stanley Black & Decker, Inc.** and **Snap-On Incorporated.**

	Stanley Black & Decker	Snap-On
Payout ratio	2.4%	1.7%
Dividend yield	2.6%	1.9%
Earnings per share (in U.S. dollars)	$3.42	$5.03
Return on common shareholders' equity	8.3%	17.9%

Instructions

Which of the two companies' shares would you prefer to purchase if you were looking for an income-oriented investment to supplement your income? Explain which ratios you used to support your answer.

Problems: Set A

P11–1A The following shareholders' equity accounts are reported by Talty Inc. on January 1, 2015:

Show impact of
transactions on
accounts.
(SO 2, 3, 4)

Preferred shares ($6 cumulative, 6,000 issued)	$ 600,000
Common shares (500,000 issued)	4,000,000
Retained earnings	1,958,000
Accumulated other comprehensive income	25,000

The following selected transactions, given in chronological order, occurred during the year:

1. Issued 10,000 common shares for $14 per share.
2. Issued 5,000 common shares in exchange for equipment. The fair value of the shares was $14 per share. The fair value of the equipment could not be reliably determined.
3. Issued 1,000 preferred shares for $100 per share.
4. The annual preferred share cash dividend was declared and paid during the year.
5. Determined that the company had an other comprehensive loss of $5,000 from the revaluation of land.

Instructions
For each of the above transactions, indicate its impact on the items in the table that follows. Indicate if the item will increase (+) or decrease (−), and by how much, or if there will be no effect (NE). The first transaction has been done for you as an example.

			Shareholders' Equity			
	Assets	Liabilities	Preferred Shares	Common Shares	Retained Earnings	Accumulated Other Comprehensive Income
1.	+$140,000	NE	NE	+$140,000	NE	NE

P11–2A Remmers Corporation, a publicly traded company, was organized on January 1, 2015. It is authorized to issue an unlimited number of $3 noncumulative preferred shares and an unlimited number of common shares. The following share transactions were completed during the company's first year of operations:

Record and post equity
transactions; prepare
shareholders' equity
section.
(SO 2, 3, 4)

Jan.	10	Issued 500,000 common shares for $2 per share.
Mar.	1	Issued 10,000 preferred shares for $50 per share.
May	1	Issued 50,000 common shares for $3 per share.
July	24	Issued 16,800 common shares for $60,000 cash and used equipment. The equipment originally cost $15,000. It now has a carrying amount of $7,500 and a fair value of $8,000. The common shares were trading for $4 per share on this date.
Sept.	1	Issued 5,000 common shares for $5 per share.
Nov.	1	Issued 2,000 preferred shares for $50 per share.
Dec.	15	Declared a $36,000 cash dividend to the preferred shareholders, to shareholders of record on December 31, payable on January 10.
	31	Reported profit of $650,000 for the year.

Instructions
(a) Record the above transactions for 2015, including any required entries to close dividends and profit to Retained Earnings.
(b) Open T accounts and post to the shareholders' equity accounts.
(c) Prepare the shareholders' equity section of the statement of financial position at December 31.

P11–3A Largent Corporation, a publicly traded company, is authorized to issue 200,000 $4 cumulative preferred shares and an unlimited number of common shares. On January 1, 2015, the general ledger contained the following shareholders' equity accounts:

Record and post equity
transactions; prepare
statements.
(SO 2, 3, 4)

Preferred shares (8,000 shares issued)	$ 440,000
Common shares (70,000 shares issued)	1,050,000
Additional contributed capital	25,000
Retained earnings	800,000
Accumulated other comprehensive income	10,000

The following equity transactions occurred in 2015:

Feb.	6	Issued 10,000 preferred shares for $600,000.
Apr.	6	Issued 20,000 common shares for $560,000.
May	29	Declared a semi-annual cash dividend to the preferred shareholders of record at June 12, payable July 1.
Aug.	22	Issued 5,000 common shares in exchange for a building. At the time of the exchange, the building was valued at $165,000 and the common shares at $150,000.
Dec.	15	The board decided there were insufficient funds to declare the semi-annual dividend to the preferred shareholders.
	31	Profit for the year was $582,000.

Instructions

(a) Record the above transactions, including any entries required to close dividends and profit to Retained Earnings.
(b) Open T accounts and post to the shareholders' equity accounts.
(c) Prepare the statement of changes in equity for the year.
(d) Prepare the shareholders' equity section of the statement of financial position at December 31, including any required note disclosure.

Record and post equity transactions; prepare statements under ASPE.
(SO 2, 3, 4)

P11–4A   On January 1, 2015, Conway Ltd., a private company, had the following shareholders' equity accounts:

Preferred shares, $5 noncumulative, unlimited number authorized, none issued	
Common shares, unlimited number authorized, 1.5 million issued	$1,500,000
Retained earnings	1,900,000

The following selected transactions occurred during 2015:

Jan.	2	Issued 100,000 preferred shares at $100 per share.
Feb.	8	Issued 50,000 common shares in exchange for land. On this date, the value of the land was $105,000. The common shares have not recently traded but the last time they traded, they sold for $2.50 per share.
Mar.	5	Declared the quarterly cash dividend to preferred shareholders of record on March 20, payable April 1.
Apr.	18	Issued 200,000 common shares at $3 per share.
June	5	Declared the quarterly cash dividend to preferred shareholders of record on June 20, payable July 1.
Sept.	5	Declared the quarterly cash dividend to preferred shareholders of record on September 20, payable October 1.
Dec.	5	Declared the quarterly cash dividend to preferred shareholders of record on December 20, payable January 1.
	14	Declared a cash dividend of $0.50 per share to the common shareholders of record on December 29, payable January 10.
	31	Profit for the year was $1 million.

Instructions

(a) Record the above transactions for 2015, including any entries required to close dividends and profit to Retained Earnings.
(b) Open T accounts and post to the shareholders' equity accounts.
(c) Prepare a statement of retained earnings for the year.
(d) Prepare the shareholders' equity section of the statement of financial position at December 31.
(e) Conway is a private company following ASPE. If it followed IFRS instead, how might your answers in parts (a) through (d) change?

Reproduce equity accounts; prepare shareholders' equity section.
(SO 2, 3, 4)

P11–5A   The general ledger of Robichaud Corporation, a publicly traded company, contained the following shareholders' equity accounts in 2015:

	January 1	December 31
Preferred shares (10,000 and 20,000 shares issued, respectively)	$ 500,000	$1,000,000
Common shares (320,000 and 370,000 shares issued, respectively)	2,700,000	3,700,000
Stock dividends distributable	0	407,000
Retained earnings	2,980,000	3,345,000

A review of the accounting records for the year ended December 31, 2015, reveals the following information:

1. On January 1, 10,000 $5 noncumulative preferred shares were issued for $50 each. An unlimited number are authorized.
2. On October 1, 50,000 common shares were sold for cash at $20 per share. An unlimited number are authorized.
3. The annual preferred shareholders' cash dividend was declared and paid during the year.
4. On December 31, a 5% stock dividend was declared on common shares when the share price was $22. The stock dividend is distributable on January 20.
5. Profit for the year was $872,000.
6. On December 31, the board of directors authorized a $500,000 restriction on retained earnings for a plant expansion.

Instructions

(a) Reproduce the Preferred Shares, Common Shares, Stock Dividends, Stock Dividends Distributable, and Retained Earnings general ledger accounts for the year. (*Hint:* Although not required, you may find it helpful to prepare journal entries.)
(b) Prepare the shareholders' equity section of the statement of financial position at December 31, including any required note disclosure.

P11-6A The condensed statement of financial position of Laporte Corporation reports the following amounts:

Compare impact of cash dividend, stock dividend, and stock split.
(SO 3)

LAPORTE CORPORATION		
Statement of Financial Position (partial)		
June 30, 2015		
Total assets		$16,000,000
Total liabilities		$ 6,000,000
Shareholders' equity		
Common shares, unlimited number authorized, 400,000 issued	$2,000,000	
Retained earnings	8,000,000	10,000,000
Total liabilities and shareholders' equity		$16,000,000

The common shares are currently trading for $30 per share. Laporte wants to assess the impact of three possible alternatives:

1. Payment of a $1.50 per share cash dividend
2. Distribution of a 5% stock dividend
3. A 3-for-2 stock split

Instructions

(a) Determine the impact of each alternative on (1) assets, (2) liabilities, (3) common shares, (4) retained earnings, (5) total shareholders' equity, and (6) the number of shares.
(b) Identify the advantages and disadvantages of each alternative for the company.

P11-7A On January 1, 2015, Wirth Corporation, a publicly traded company, had these shareholders' equity accounts:

Record and post dividend transactions; prepare statements.
(SO 3, 4)

Common shares (unlimited number of shares authorized, 110,000 shares issued)	$1,100,000
Retained earnings	540,000
Accumulated other comprehensive income	60,000

During the year, the following transactions occurred:

Jan.	15	Declared a $1 per share cash dividend to shareholders of record on January 31, payable February 15.
Apr.	15	Declared a 10% stock dividend to shareholders of record on April 30, distributable May 15. On April 15, April 30, and May 15, the share prices were $15, $13.50, and $14, respectively.
Oct.	1	Effected a 2-for-1 stock split. On October 1, the share price was $20.
Dec.	31	Determined that profit for the year was $350,000.

Instructions

(a) Record the above transactions, including any required entries to close dividends and profit to Retained Earnings.
(b) Open T accounts as required and post to the shareholders' equity accounts.
(c) Prepare a statement of changes in equity for the year.
(d) Prepare the shareholders' equity section of the statement of financial position at December 31.

Calculate earnings
per share.
(SO 5)

P11–8A Gualtieri Inc.'s shareholders' equity accounts were as follows at the beginning of the current fiscal year, August 1, 2015:

$5 noncumulative preferred shares (25,000 shares issued)	$2,500,000
Common shares (350,000 shares issued)	3,750,000
Retained earnings	2,250,000
Total shareholders' equity	$8,500,000

During the year, the following selected transactions occurred:

Dec.	1	Issued 60,000 common shares for $25 per share.
Feb.	1	Issued 10,000 common shares for $26 per share.
June	20	Declared the annual preferred cash dividend to shareholders of record on July 10, payable on July 31.
July	31	Profit for the year ended July 31, 2015, was $1,280,000.

Instructions

(a) Calculate the weighted average number of common shares for the year.
(b) Calculate the earnings per share.
(c) Why is it important to use a weighted average number of shares in the calculation of earnings per share? Why not just use the number of shares issued at year end?
(d) Would your answer to part (b) change if the preferred share dividend had not been declared on June 20? Explain.

Evaluate ratios.
(SO 5)

P11–9A The following summary of the payout, dividend yield, and earnings per share (in U.S. $) ratios is available for five years ended December 31 for **Barrick Gold Corporation**:

	Payout Ratio	Dividend Yield	Earnings per Share
2008	44%	1.1%	$0.96
2009	n/a	1.1	(4.73)
2010	14	1.0	3.50
2011	11	1.0	4.49
2012	n/a	2.2	(0.66)

Instructions

(a) What are some possible reasons that Barrick Gold's dividend payout ratio declined from 44% in 2008 to 14% in 2010, while its dividend yield ratio changed very little—from 1.1% in 2008 to 1.0% in 2010? Note that there is no payout ratio available in 2009 or 2012 because of the loss incurred in those years.
(b) Why do you think Barrick Gold's dividend yield increased from 1% in 2011 to 2.2% in 2012, despite the fact that the company reported a loss in 2012?
(c) If you were one of Barrick Gold's creditors, what would you think about the company continuing to pay dividends (such as in 2009 and 2012) regardless of whether it reports a profit or a loss? Explain.

Calculate and evaluate
ratios.
(SO 5)

P11–10A The following selected information (in millions, except for per share information) is available for the **National Bank of Canada** for the year ended October 31:

	2012	2011
Weighted average number of common shares	161.4	162.4
Profit available to common shareholders	$1,518	$1,137
Common cash dividends per share	3.08	2.74
Total common cash dividends	485	437
Average common shareholders' equity	6,089	5,535
Market price per common share	77.18	69.61
Industry averages were as follows:		
Payout ratio	30.0%	40.0%
Dividend yield	4.3	3.8
Earnings per share	n/a	n/a
Return on common shareholders' equity	24.4	17.7

Instructions

(a) Calculate the following ratios for the common shareholders for each fiscal year:
1. Payout ratio
2. Dividend yield
3. Earnings per share
4. Return on common shareholders' equity
(b) Comment on the above ratios for 2012 in comparison with the prior year, and in comparison with the industry.

P11–11A Selected ratios for two companies operating in the petroleum industry follow, along with the industry averages:

Evaluate profitability ratios.
(SO 5)

Ratio	Petro-Boost	World Oil	Industry Average
Profit margin	10.0%	8.4%	10.9%
Return on common shareholders' equity	15.1%	29.6%	11.3%
Return on assets	11.0%	12.6%	6.2%
Asset turnover	1.1 times	1.5 times	0.5 times
Earnings per share	$4.06	$4.38	n/a
Price-earnings ratio	14.2 times	17.1 times	13.0 times
Payout ratio	12.3%	9.9%	0.2%
Dividend yield	1.9%	0.7%	1.2%

Instructions

(a) Compare the profitability of Petro-Boost with that of World Oil, and with the industry average. Which company is more profitable? Explain.
(b) You would like to invest in the shares of one of the two companies. Your goal is to have regular income from your investment that will help pay your tuition fees for the next few years. Which of the companies is a better choice for you? Explain.
(c) Assume that instead of looking for regular income, you are looking for growth in the share value so that you can resell the shares at a gain in the future. Now which of the two companies is better for you? Explain.

Problems: Set B

P11–1B The following shareholders' equity accounts are reported by Branch Inc. on January 1, 2015:

Show impact of transactions on accounts.
(SO 2, 3, 4)

Preferred shares ($4 noncumulative, 35,000 issued)	$ 350,000
Common shares (150,000 issued)	2,400,000
Retained earnings	1,276,000
Accumulated other comprehensive income	15,000

The following selected transactions, given in chronological order, occurred during the year:

1. Issued 10,000 common shares for $30 per share.
2. Issued 500 preferred shares for $100 per share.
3. Issued 1,000 common shares in exchange for land. The fair value of the shares was $30 per share. The fair value of the land was $29,000.
4. Declared and paid the preferred shareholders a $2 per share cash dividend.
5. Determined that the company had other comprehensive income of $5,000 from the revaluation of land.

Instructions

For each of the above transactions, indicate its impact on the items in the table below. Indicate if the item will increase (+) or decrease (–), and by how much, or if there will be no effect (NE). The first transaction has been done for you as an example.

			Shareholders' Equity		
Assets	Liabilities	Preferred Shares	Common Shares	Retained Earnings	Accumulated Other Comprehensive Income
1. +$300,000	NE	NE	+$300,000	NE	NE

Record and post equity transactions; prepare shareholders' equity section.
(SO 2, 3, 4)

P11–2B   Wetland Corporation, a publicly traded company, was organized on June 1, 2014. It is authorized to issue an unlimited number of $4 cumulative preferred shares and an unlimited number of common shares. The following share transactions were completed during the company's first year of operations:

June	5	Issued 80,000 common shares for $4 per share.
Aug.	21	Issued 5,000 preferred shares for $100 per share.
Sept.	15	Issued 22,000 common shares in exchange for land. The asking price of the land was $100,000 and the fair value was $95,000. The common shares were trading for $4.25 per share on this date.
Nov.	20	Issued 78,000 common shares for $4.50 per share.
Mar.	9	Issued 10,000 common shares for $5 per share.
Apr.	16	Issued 2,000 preferred shares for $100 per share.
May	15	Declared the annual preferred cash dividend to the preferred shareholders, to shareholders of record on May 30, payable on June 10.
	31	Reported profit of $250,000 for the year.

Instructions
(a) Record the above transactions for the year ended May 31, 2015, including any required entries to close dividends and profit to Retained Earnings.
(b) Open T accounts and post to the shareholders' equity accounts.
(c) Prepare the shareholders' equity section of the statement of financial position at May 31.

Record and post equity transactions; prepare statements.
(SO 2, 3, 4)

P11–3B   Ujjal Corporation, a publicly traded company, is authorized to issue an unlimited number of $5 noncumulative preferred shares and an unlimited number of common shares. On February 1, 2015, the general ledger contained the following shareholders' equity accounts:

Preferred shares (44,000 shares issued)	$ 440,000
Common shares (70,000 shares issued)	1,050,000
Additional contributed capital	75,000
Retained earnings	1,000,000
Accumulated other comprehensive income	65,000

The following equity transactions occurred during the year ended January 31, 2016:

Feb.	28	Issued 1,500 preferred shares for $150,000.
Apr.	12	Issued 100,000 common shares for $3.5 million.
May	25	Issued 2,500 common shares in exchange for land. At the time of the exchange, the land was valued at $85,000 and the common shares at $87,500.
Dec.	29	Declared a $2.50 per share cash dividend to the preferred shareholders of record at January 15, payable February 1.
Jan.	31	A loss of $5,000 was incurred for the year.

Instructions
(a) Record the above transactions for the year ended January 31, 2016, including any entries required to close dividends and loss to Retained Earnings.
(b) Open T accounts and post to the shareholders' equity accounts.
(c) Prepare the statement of changes in equity for the year.
(d) Prepare the shareholders' equity section of the statement of financial position at January 31, 2016.

Record and post equity transactions; prepare statements under ASPE.
(SO 2, 3, 4)

P11–4B   On January 1, 2015, Schipper Ltd., a private company, had the following shareholders' equity accounts:

Preferred shares, $2 noncumulative, unlimited number authorized, none issued	
Common shares, unlimited number authorized, 100,000 issued	$150,000
Retained earnings	580,000

The following selected transactions occurred during 2015:

Jan. 2 Issued 10,000 preferred shares for $50 per share.

Mar. 10 Declared the quarterly cash dividend to preferred shareholders of record on March 22, payable April 1.

June 10 Declared the quarterly cash dividend to preferred shareholders of record on June 22, payable July 1.

Aug. 12 Issued 10,000 common shares for $7.30 per share.

Sept. 1 Declared the quarterly cash dividend to preferred shareholders of record on September 22, payable October 1.

Oct. 15 Issued 2,000 common shares in exchange for equipment. The common shares had not traded recently but were valued at $7.60 per share on the last date they had traded. The value of the equipment was $15,000 on October 15.

Dec. 1 The fourth quarter cash dividend to preferred shareholders was not declared or paid.

31 A loss of $50,000 was reported for the year.

Instructions

(a) Record the above transactions for 2015, including any required entries to close dividends and loss to Retained Earnings.

(b) Open T accounts and post to the shareholders' equity accounts.

(c) Prepare a statement of retained earnings for the year.

(d) Prepare the shareholders' equity section of the statement of financial position at December 31.

(e) Schipper is a private company following ASPE. If it followed IFRS instead, how might your answers in parts (a) through (d) change?

P11–5B The general ledger of Maggio Corporation, a publicly traded company, contained the following shareholders' equity accounts in 2015:

	January 1	December 31
Preferred shares (15,000 and 15,000 shares issued, respectively)	$ 750,000	$ 750,000
Common shares (255,000 and 291,500 shares issued, respectively)	3,210,000	3,857,000
Retained earnings	980,000	1,373,000

Reproduce equity accounts; prepare shareholders' equity section.
(SO 2, 3, 4)

A review of the accounting records for the year ended December 31, 2015, reveals the following information:

1. On March 1, 20,000 common shares were sold for $17.50 per share. An unlimited number are authorized.
2. On August 18, a 6% stock dividend was declared for 16,500 common shares when the share price was $18. The stock dividend was distributed on September 25.
3. The preferred shares are $4 cumulative. An unlimited number of preferred shares are authorized. The quarterly preferred shareholders' cash dividend was declared and paid in each quarter.
4. Profit for the year was $750,000.
5. On December 31, the directors authorized a $200,000 restriction on retained earnings in accordance with a debt covenant.

Instructions

(a) Reproduce the Preferred Shares, Common Shares, Stock Dividends, Stock Dividends Distributable, and Retained Earnings general ledger accounts for the year. (*Hint*: Although not required, you may find it helpful to prepare journal entries.)

(b) Prepare the shareholders' equity section of the statement of financial position at December 31, including any required note disclosure.

P11–6B The condensed statement of financial position of Erickson Corporation reports the following amounts:

Compare impact of cash dividend, stock dividend, and stock split.
(SO 3)

ERICKSON CORPORATION
Statement of Financial Position (partial)
January 31, 2015

Total assets		$9,000,000
Total liabilities		$2,500,000
Shareholders' equity		
Common shares, unlimited number authorized, 500,000 issued	$3,000,000	
Retained earnings	3,500,000	6,500,000
Total liabilities and shareholders' equity		$9,000,000

The common shares are currently trading for $15 per share. Erickson wants to assess the impact of three possible alternatives on the corporation and its shareholders:

1. Payment of a $1 per share cash dividend
2. Distribution of a 5% stock dividend
3. A 2-for-1 stock split

Instructions

(a) Determine the impact of each alternative on (1) assets, (2) liabilities, (3) common shares, (4) retained earnings, (5) total shareholders' equity, and (6) the number of shares.
(b) Identify the advantages and disadvantages of each alternative for the company.

Record and post dividend transactions; prepare statements.
(SO 3, 4)

P11–7B On January 1, 2015, Stengel Corporation, a publicly traded company, had these shareholders' equity accounts:

Common shares (unlimited number of shares authorized, 75,000 issued)	$1,700,000
Retained earnings	900,000
Accumulated other comprehensive loss	125,000

During the year, the following transactions occurred:

Feb.	1	Declared a $1 per share cash dividend to shareholders of record on February 15, payable March 1.
Apr.	1	Effected a 3-for-1 stock split. On April 1, the share price was $36.
July	1	Declared a 5% stock dividend to shareholders of record on July 15, distributable July 31. On July 1, July 15, and July 31, the share prices were $14, $13.50, and $13.75, respectively.
Dec.	31	Determined that profit for the year was $400,000.

Instructions

(a) Record the above transactions, including any entries required to close dividends and profit to Retained Earnings.
(b) Open T accounts as required and post to the shareholders' equity accounts.
(c) Prepare a statement of changes in equity for the year.
(d) Prepare the shareholders' equity section of the statement of financial position at December 31.

Calculate earnings per share.
(SO 5)

P11–8B Blue Bay Logistics Ltd.'s shareholders' equity accounts were as follows at the beginning of the current fiscal year, April 1, 2014:

$5 cumulative preferred shares (20,000 shares issued)	$1,950,000
Common shares (500,000 shares issued)	3,750,000
Retained earnings	1,500,000
Total shareholders' equity	$7,200,000

During the year, the following selected transactions occurred:

June	1	Issued 2,000 common shares for $12 per share.
July	1	Issued 50,000 common shares for $13 per share.
Feb.	28	Declared the annual preferred cash dividend to shareholders of record on March 12, payable on April 1.
Mar.	31	Profit for the year ended March 31, 2015, was $1,016,750.

Instructions

(a) Calculate the weighted average number of common shares for the year.
(b) Calculate the earnings per share.
(c) Why is it important to use profit available to common shareholders in the calculation of earnings per share? Why not just use profit?
(d) Would your answer to part (b) change if the preferred share dividend had not been declared on February 28? Explain.

Evaluate ratios.
(SO 5)

P11–9B The following summary of the payout, dividend yield, and earnings per share ratios is available for five years ended December 31 for **TransAlta Corporation**:

	Payout Ratio	Dividend Yield	Earnings per Share
2008	91.5%	4.4%	$1.18
2009	129.8%	4.9	0.90
2010	125.1%	5.5	1.16
2011	66.9%	5.5	1.31
2012	n/a	7.7	(2.61)

Instructions

(a) What are some possible reasons that TransAlta's dividend payout ratio increased from 91.5% in 2008 to 129.8% in 2009 at a time when the earnings per share fell from $1.18 per share to $0.90 per share?
(b) Why do you think that TransAlta continued to pay dividends in 2012 in a year when it reported a loss per share? Note there is no payout ratio available in 2012 because of the loss incurred that year.

(c) Why do you think that TransAlta's dividend yield increased from 5.5% in 2011 to 7.7% in 2012 at a time when the earnings per share fell from a profit of $1.31 per share to a loss of $2.61 per share?

(d) If you were an investor looking for dividend income, would you be happy with TransAlta's dividend policy? Explain.

P11–10B The following selected information (in millions, except for per share information) is available for **Scotiabank** for the year ended October 31:

Calculate and evaluate ratios.
(SO 5)

	2012	2011
Weighted average number of common shares	1,133	1,072
Profit available to common shareholders	$6,023	$4,965
Common cash dividends per share	2.19	2.05
Total common cash dividends	2,493	2,200
Average common shareholders' equity	30,804	24,042
Market price per common share	54.25	52.53
Industry averages were as follows:		
Payout ratio	30.0%	40.0%
Dividend yield	4.3	3.8
Earnings per share	n/a	n/a
Return on common shareholders' equity	24.4	17.7

Instructions

(a) Calculate the following ratios for the common shareholders for each fiscal year:
1. Payout ratio
2. Dividend yield
3. Earnings per share
4. Return on common shareholders' equity

(b) Comment on the above ratios for 2012 in comparison with the prior year and in comparison with the industry.

P11–11B Selected ratios for two retailers follow, along with the industry averages:

Evaluate profitability ratios.
(SO 5)

	Bargain Hunters	Discount Paradise	Industry Average
Profit margin	6.8%	3.5%	3.7%
Return on common shareholders' equity	24.9%	22.4%	20.8%
Return on assets	10.2%	8.8%	9.2%
Asset turnover	1.5 times	2.5 times	2.5 times
Earnings per share	$3.30	$2.49	n/a
Price-earnings ratio	12.3 times	17.0 times	16.3 times
Payout ratio	9.4%	25.0%	19.3%
Dividend yield	0.8%	2.5%	1.2%

Instructions

(a) Compare the profitability of Bargain Hunters with that of Discount Paradise, and with the industry average. Which company is more profitable? Explain.

(b) You would like to invest in the shares of one of the two companies. Your goal is to have regular income from your investment that will help pay your tuition fees for the next few years. Which of the two companies is a better choice for you? Explain.

(c) Assume that instead of looking for regular income, you are looking for growth in the share value so that you can resell the shares at a gain in the future. Now which of the two companies is better for you? Explain.

Broadening Your Perspective

Financial Reporting: *Shoppers Drug Mart*

BYP11–1 The financial statements of **Shoppers Drug Mart** are presented in Appendix A at the end of this book.

Answer questions about shareholders' equity.
(SO 1, 2, 3, 4)

Instructions

(a) Using the statement of earnings, answer the following questions:
1. What amount did Shoppers report as basic earnings per share in 2012 and 2011?
2. What was its weighted average number of shares for each year?

(b) Review Note 24: Share Capital and answer the following questions:
1. How many common shares and preferred shares has Shoppers authorized?

2. How many common and preferred shares did Shoppers have issued at the end of 2012 and 2011? How does the number of issued shares compare with the weighted average number of shares determined in (a) (2) above?

3. Did Shoppers have a normal course issuer bid in 2012? If so, how many common shares did it repurchase and for what cost?

(c) Using the statement of changes in shareholders' equity, answer the following questions:

1. Did Shoppers report other comprehensive income or loss in 2012 and 2011? If so, how much?

2. Did Shoppers declare any dividends in 2012 and 2011? If so, how much?

Comparative Analysis: *Shoppers Drug Mart and Jean Coutu*

Calculate ratios and comment on liquidity, solvency, and profitability.
(SO 5)

BYP11–2   The financial statements of **Jean Coutu** are presented in Appendix B following the financial statements for **Shoppers Drug Mart** in Appendix A.

Instructions

(a) Refer to the statement of earnings for Shoppers and the statement of income for Jean Coutu and find the earnings per share for each company for the most recent fiscal year. Is there a difference between basic and diluted earnings per share for either company?

(b) Calculate the payout ratio, dividend yield, and price-earnings ratios for each company for the most recent fiscal year. To determine the amount of cash dividends paid for the payout ratio calculation, look at the retained earnings section of the statement of changes in equity. The dividend per share for the dividend yield ratio calculation was $0.28 for Jean Coutu and $1.08 for Shoppers. At the end of each company's fiscal year, Jean Coutu's share price was $15.78 and Shoppers' share price was $42.80.

(c) Can you determine which company investors interested in dividend income might favour based on your answers in (a) and (b)? Identify which ratios you used to come to your conclusion.

Comparing IFRS and ASPE

Compare ownership structure, issue of shares, and earnings per share for public and private company.
(SO 1, 2, 5)

BYP11–3   Boston Pizza Royalties Income Fund is a public company that has over 340 Boston Pizza locations in Canada. **Pizza Pizza Limited** is a privately held company that has over 500 locations in Canada.

Instructions

(a) Although the companies are similar, Boston Pizza is a public company while Pizza Pizza is privately held. Why do you think the two companies chose different types of ownership structure?

(b) When Boston Pizza or Pizza Pizza purchases new restaurants, part of the payment may be in shares of the company. How would Boston Pizza determine the fair value of its shares (which it calls units) for this purpose? How would Pizza Pizza determine the fair value of its shares? Which fair value measure would be the more reliable?

(c) Since Boston Pizza is a public company, it uses IFRS and is required to disclose earnings per share. Pizza Pizza uses ASPE and is not required to report earnings per share. Why do you think the standard setters do not require private companies to disclose their earnings per share?

Critical Thinking Case

Calculate and evaluate debt and equity alternatives.
(SO 2, 5)

BYP11–4   Depinder Singh is a friend of yours who has worked at a number of restaurants. He has always wanted to own his own business and his dream can now come true because he just won $1 million in a lottery. There are two restaurants (one is small and one is large) currently operating that are available for purchase on January 1. Regardless of which one he buys, Depinder will set up a business that will have a December 31 year end. The business will be financed with his winnings from the lottery and the business will then buy all of the assets of one of the two restaurants. Depinder is not sure if the money he puts into the business should consist completely of debt or equity. He believes that the assets will cost $1 million for the small restaurant or $2 million for the large restaurant. Revenues for the first year are expected to be equal to the value of the assets purchased. Operating expenses are expected to be 85% of sales, and the corporate income tax rate calculated at 25% of profit before income tax. Interest on any loans (whether from Depinder or from the bank) will be 6% and any profit earned by the corporation will be paid out as dividends.

Depinder needs your help in assessing the following three options:

1. His business is formed as a corporation with $1 million of common shares and no debt. The assets of the small restaurant are then purchased by the business.

2. His business is formed as a corporation with $1 of common shares and a $999,999 loan from Depinder. The assets of the small restaurant are then purchased by the business.

3. His business is formed as a corporation with $1 million of common shares and a $1-million loan from the bank. The assets of the large restaurant are then purchased.

Instructions

(a) For each of the three options listed above, prepare the income statement that you would expect to see for the first year of the company's operations.

(b) Calculate the return on common shareholders' equity for the first year for each option above. Which option results in the best return? Explain why.

(c) Based on your results in part (a) above, how much cash (before personal income tax) would Depinder have personally (not in the corporation) under each option if all of the profit earned by the company is paid out to him at the end of the year as a dividend?

(d) Without calculating any amounts, what do you think would happen to the return on common shareholders' equity if the operating expenses were 110% of revenue and the company suffered a loss? Would the return be better or worse if the company had more debt?

(e) Without calculating any amounts, how would the income statement change if Depinder did not borrow $1 million from the bank, but obtained those funds from an uncle who bought preferred shares in the corporation and wanted a 5% dividend yield?

(f) Following from part (e) above, if the uncle insisted on being able to sell the preferred shares back to the company at a time of his (the uncle's) choosing, would the preferred shares be classified as debt or equity on the statement of financial position?

(g) Without doing any calculations, if Depinder bought the small restaurant, operated it as a proprietorship rather than in-corporating it, and did not borrow any money, how would the projected income statement change from that indicated in your answer to Option 1 in part (a) above?

Ethics Case

BYP11–5   Flambeau Corporation has paid 60 consecutive quarterly cash dividends (15 years' worth). The last six months have been a real cash drain on the company, however, as profit margins have been greatly narrowed by increasing competition. With a cash balance that is only enough to meet day-to-day operating needs, the president, Vince Ramsey, has decided that a stock dividend instead of a cash dividend should be declared. He tells Flambeau's financial vice-president, Janice Rahn, to issue a press release stating that the company is extending its consecutive dividend record with the declaration of a 5% stock dividend. "Write the press release convincing the shareholders that the stock dividend is just as good as a cash dividend," he orders. "Just watch our share price rise when we announce the stock dividend; it must be a good thing if that happens."

Discuss impact of stock dividend.
(SO 3)

Instructions
(a) Who are the stakeholders in this situation?
(b) What is the effect of a stock dividend on a corporation's shareholders' equity accounts?
(c) Will the share price rise if a stock dividend is declared, as the president expects?
(d) Is there anything unethical about President Ramsey's intentions or actions?

"All About You" Activity

BYP11–6   In this chapter, you learned about equity financing and in Chapter 10 you learned about debt financing.
     You are evaluating the financial statements of a private company that is considering purchasing equipment. You have prepared projected year-end financial statements using three different alternatives: (1) borrow $50,000 at the beginning of the year with repayment terms of $10,000 per year and interest at 6% per year; (2) issue 500 common shares for $100 per share ($50,000 in total) at the beginning of the year; and (3) issue 500 $6 noncumulative preferred shares for $100 per share ($50,000 in total) at the beginning of the year.
     Selected information related to each of these three alternatives follows:

Calculate and evaluate debt and equity invest-ment alternatives.
(SO 5)

	Alternative 1 (Borrow $50,000)	Alternative 2 (Issue $50,000 common shares)	Alternative 3 (Issue $50,000 preferred shares)
Total assets, end of year	$195,280	$207,680	$204,680
Total liabilities, end of year	$ 71,980	$ 31,980	$ 31,980
Total shareholders' equity			
Preferred shares, beg. of year	$ 0	$ 0	$ 0
Issue of 500 shares			50,000
Preferred shares, end of year	0	0	50,000
Common shares, beg. of year	50,000	50,000	50,000
Issue of 500 shares	0	50,000	0
Common shares, end of year	50,000	100,000	50,000
Retained earnings, beg. of year	51,700	51,700	51,700
Add: Profit	21,600	24,000	24,000
Less: Preferred dividends	0	0	3,000
Retained earnings, end of year	73,300	75,700	72,700

Instructions
(a) Using the information provided above, calculate the debt to total assets, return on common shareholders' equity, and earnings per share ratios for each alternative at the end of year.
(b) Based upon your calculations in part (a), which alternative(s) provides for the least amount of debt? Why?
(c) Which alternative provides for the highest return on common shareholders' equity? The highest earnings per share?
(d) If you were a shareholder at the beginning of the year, which alternative would you choose? Why?

Serial Case

(*Note:* This is a continuation of the serial case from Chapters 1 through 10.)

Record equity transactions; prepare shareholders' equity section.

(SO 2, 3, 4)

BYP11–7   Natalie, Janet, and Brian are thrilled with the success of Koebel's Family Bakery Ltd. That success, however, has meant that the Koebels have had no time to enjoy personal interests. When Natalie was hired, Janet and Brian believed that they would have a little more time to take a holiday, leaving Natalie in charge. Because of the weekly cupcake contract with Coffee Beans, that has not happened.

Coffee Beans has increased the volume of cupcakes required on a weekly basis, and the bakery is trying to keep up with the demand. Natalie, Janet, and Brian recognize that more help is needed with running the business. Currently, each of them owns 100 shares of the 300 common shares issued.

Natalie's brother, Daniel, has been operating a trucking business in a major Canadian city for a number of years. After being away for over a decade, he has returned with a keen interest in helping his family out at the bakery. He believes that the experience he has obtained operating his trucking business will prove to be a great resource that Koebel's can rely upon as it continues to experience significant growth. Daniel would like to purchase a 25% interest in the company in exchange for cash and one of the delivery trucks he has kept.

The share capital and retained earnings of Koebel's Family Bakery Ltd. at July 1, 2014, are as follows:

Share capital	
$6 cumulative preferred shares, 10,000 shares authorized, none issued	
Common shares, unlimited number of shares authorized, 300 shares issued	$ 300
Retained earnings	182,601

Profit for the year ended June 30, was $216,069. In addition, a dividend of $75,000 was declared on June 15, to common shareholders of record on June 20, payable on June 30.

Based on the bakery's success, the Koebels would like to issue 100 common shares to Daniel for $1,075 per share. The fair value of the delivery truck is estimated at $45,000. The sale of shares to Daniel is expected to take place on June 30. After the sale of the shares to Daniel, each member of the Koebel family will hold a 25% interest in the common shares of Koebel's Family Bakery.

Instructions

(a) Prepare the journal entries required for the dividend declared on June 15 and paid on June 30. Who will receive the dividend to be paid on June 30, and for what amount?

(b) Assume Daniel purchases a total of 100 common shares on June 30, in exchange for his delivery truck and cash of $62,500. Prepare the journal entry required.

(c) Prepare a statement of retained earnings for the year ended June 30, 2015. If Koebel's followed IFRS rather than ASPE, would it still have to prepare a statement of retained earnings?

(d) Prepare the shareholders' equity section of the statement of financial position at June 30, 2015.

Answers to Self-Test Questions

1. d	2. b	3. b	4. b	5. d
6. c	7. b	8. b	9. b	10. c

Remember to go back to the beginning of the chapter to check off your completed work!
←

Endnotes

[1]"The Story of Tim Hortons," company website, www.timhortons.com; "Tim Hortons Inc. Announces New Share Repurchase Program for Up to $250 Million in Common Shares," company news release, February 21, 2013; "Tim Hortons Inc. Increases Quarterly Dividend by 23.8% and Declares a Dividend of $0.26 per Common Share," company news release, February 21, 2013; Tim Hortons 2011 Annual Report.

[2]World Federation of Exchanges, "Statistics: Number of Listed Companies," www.world-exchanges.org, accessed June 24, 2013. World Federation of Exchanges, "Top 10 Stock Exchanges in the World," www.world-exchanges.org, accessed June 24, 2013. *TMX: A Capital Opportunity*, TMX Group, no date, available at www.tmx.com/en/pdf/Guide_to_Listing.pdf, accessed June 24, 2013. "Warren Buffet's Investing Style: Invest like a Girl," www.charteredclub.com/warren-buffet's-investing-style-invest-like-a-girl/, accessed June 24, 2013. Noreen Rasbach, "Invest Like a Man or a Woman?," *Globe and Mail*, August 23, 2012. Jonathan Chevreau, "Albertans Canada's Savviest Investors," *Financial Post*, July 19, 2011.

Comprehensive Case: Chapters 3–11

Hampton Corporation's statement of financial position at December 31, 2014, is presented below.

HAMPTON CORPORATION Statement of Financial Position December 31, 2014			
Cash	$ 24,000	Accounts payable	$ 55,600
Accounts receivable	45,500	Mortgage payable	80,000
Allowance for doubtful accounts	(1,500)	Common shares, unlimited number	
Merchandise inventory	70,000	authorized, 3,000 issued	30,000
Supplies	4,400	Retained earnings	127,400
Land	40,000	Accumulated other comprehensive	
Buildings	142,000	income	9,400
Accumulated depreciation	(22,000)		
	$302,400		$302,400

Prepare and post transaction, adjusting, and closing entries; prepare adjusted trial balance; prepare financial statements. (SO 2, 3, 4)

During 2015, the following transactions occurred.

1. Hampton issued 500 shares of $2.80 cumulative preferred shares for $50,000. Hampton is authorized to issue 50,000 preferred shares.
2. Hampton also issued 500 common shares for $30,000.
3. Hampton sold merchandise for $320,000 on account and $100,000 on bank credit cards. Hampton uses a perpetual inventory system and its cost of goods sold for this total transaction was $250,000.
4. Hampton collected $296,000 from customers on account.
5. Hampton bought $35,100 of supplies on account.
6. Purchased $330,000 of merchandise inventory on account, terms 2/10, n/30.
7. Hampton paid $322,000 on accounts payable related to purchases of merchandise in transaction 6, within the 10-day discount period.
8. Paid salaries of $88,200.
9. An account receivable of $1,700, which originated in 2014, was written off as uncollectible.
10. Paid $2,000 on the mortgage principal during the year, and $4,000 of interest.
11. Near the end of the current fiscal year, Hampton declared the annual preferred share cash dividend of $1,400 and a $4,200 common share cash dividend, to shareholders of record on January 13, 2016, payable on January 31, 2016.

Adjustment data:

1. A count of supplies indicates that $5,900 of supplies remain unused at year end.
2. Estimated uncollectible accounts were $3,500 at year end.
3. Depreciation is recorded on the building on a straight-line basis based on a 30-year life and a residual value of $10,000.
4. Interest of $350 is owed on the mortgage at year end. The current portion of the mortgage due is $2,500.
5. The bank statement included a service charge of $3,000 for bank credit card fees.
6. Income tax of $6,000 is estimated to be due.

Instructions

(a) Record the above summary transactions and adjusting journal entries.
(b) Open T accounts and enter the opening balances at January 1, 2015. Post the above general and adjusting journal entries to T accounts, adding new ones as required.
(c) Prepare an adjusted trial balance as at December 31.
(d) Prepare (1) an income statement, (2) a statement of changes in equity, and (3) a statement of financial position.
(e) Prepare and post closing journal entries to the relevant T accounts set up in part (b).

CHAPTER 12

Reporting and Analyzing Investments

The Navigator
Chapter 12

- Scan *Study Objectives*
- Read *Feature Story*
- Read text and answer *Do It!s*
- Review *Comparing IFRS and ASPE*
- Review *Summary of Study Objectives*
- Review *Decision Toolkit—A Summary*
- Work *Using the Decision Toolkit*
- Work *Comprehensive Do It!*
- Answer *Self-Test Questions*
- Complete *assignments*
- Go to *WileyPLUS* for practice and tutorials

study objectives

After studying this chapter, you should be able to:

SO 1 Identify reasons to invest, and classify investments.

SO 2 Account for non-strategic investments.

SO 3 Account for strategic investments.

SO 4 Explain how investments are reported in the financial statements.

SO 5 Compare the accounting for a bond investment and a bond payable (Appendix 12A).

Managing Money for Clients and the Company

Like all large organizations, Scotiabank manages its money through a number of investment vehicles. It has two main areas of investments: its regular banking operations and strategic acquisitions.

"In banks, we're always changing the mix of financial assets, looking for different opportunities," says Sean McGuckin, Executive Vice-President and Chief Financial Officer, "whereas for non-financial institutions, financial assets may not be their primary assets. It could be property, plant, and equipment, oil in the ground, what have you. So they may take a longer-term view on some of their investments." Scotiabank is like an individual investor who reviews and rebalances his or her portfolio regularly, rather than one who buys stocks and holds them over time with little adjustment.

In its regular banking operations, Scotiabank holds investments in trading portfolios and treasury portfolios. In its trading environment, Scotiabank buys and sells securities primarily to facilitate customer requests and invests in certain securities to adjust its trading risk profile. These may be debt instruments such as bonds, or equity instruments such as common and preferred shares. Scotiabank's treasury investments strengthen the organization's liquidity profile by having some assets on hand that it could quickly convert into cash if needed. The bank also uses various investments in fixed-term securities or variable-rate securities to help adjust its interest rate exposure. These investments can be held for a few days or longer. As well, the bank may also invest in long-term instruments, for example, five-year government bonds.

Scotiabank also invests strategically by acquiring all or a portion of other companies. "Our strategy, like most companies, is to grow," Mr. McGuckin explains. "You can grow either organically over time by continuing to build out your business, or you can acquire growth by buying a company." If a business fits within Scotiabank's overall strategy, it may buy shares in that company.

For example, several years ago Scotiabank bought 19% of the shares in DundeeWealth Inc. Then, in 2011, it bought all the remaining common shares that it did not already own. In 2012, Scotiabank purchased ING Bank of Canada (ING DIRECT) from Netherlands-based parent ING Group for $3.1 billion in cash. "ING DIRECT will benefit from the backing of a strong, stable Canadian shareholder with the additional resources to enable it to expand and grow. This in turn will provide our shareholders with a new source of incremental earnings beginning in year one, and a new deposit base to further diversify our funding," said Scotiabank President and CEO Rick Waugh, at the time the acquisition was announced.

These strategic investments have additional benefits in allowing Scotiabank to diversify into different revenue streams and leverage its existing business since the acquired company may have products that would be of interest to existing customers.

In fact, there are many reasons and ways by which organizations make investments, whether they are non-strategic investments to earn a higher return on extra cash than from a bank account, or strategic investments to influence or control another company, such as a competitor, supplier, or complementary business that their customers may benefit from.[1]

the
navigator

Investments can be made by purchasing equity securities issued by corporations or by purchasing debt securities issued by corporations or governments. Investments can be either non-strategic, where the goal is to generate investment income, or strategic, where the goal is to influence the decisions made by the company invested in. As you will see in the chapter, the way in which a company accounts for each of its investments is determined by several factors, including whether the investment is non-strategic or strategic.

The chapter is organized as follows:

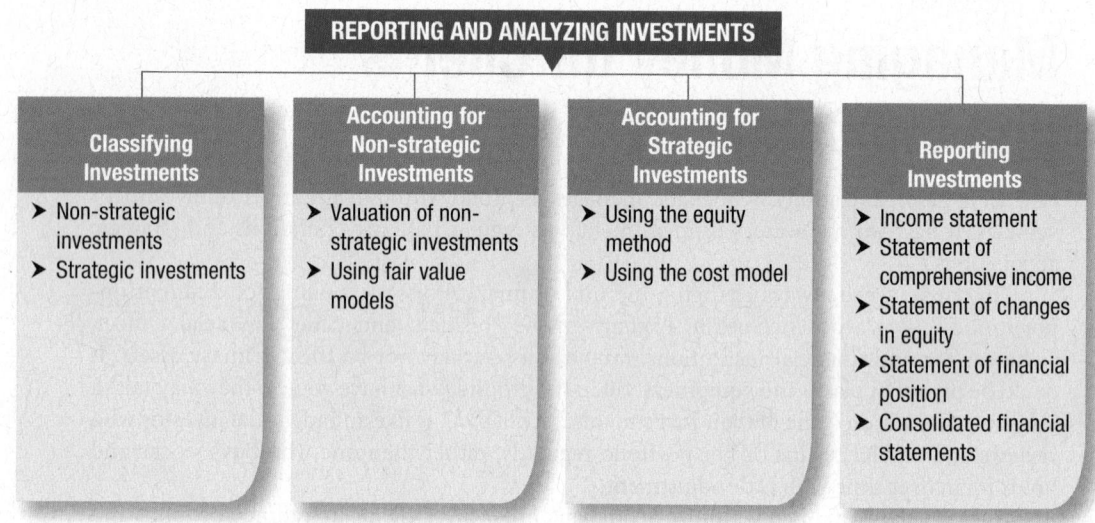

Classifying Investments

Recall that in Chapter 8 you were introduced to the concept of financial assets. These are assets that consist of cash and other assets such as receivables and investments that have a contractual right to receive cash. It is common practice for corporations to purchase financial assets, such as debt and equity investments, for investment purposes. **Debt investments** are made by purchasing low-risk guaranteed investment certificates or term deposits, as well as investments in bonds, commercial paper, and a large variety of other debt securities available for purchase. They earn interest revenue over time, and in most cases, the borrower has an obligation to return the original amount (principal) of the investment on a fixed maturity date. **Equity investments** are usually made by buying either preferred or common shares of other corporations in the expectation of generating revenue from dividend income or a gain on future sale. Equity investments are riskier than debt investments as there is no requirement to receive any form of revenue through dividends over time or to receive a return of the original amount invested.

Investments may be made for one of two reasons: as a **non-strategic investment** to generate investment income from interest, dividends, or gains upon sale of the investment, or as a **strategic investment** to influence or control the operations of another company in some way. We will discuss each of these reasons in the next two sections.

NON-STRATEGIC INVESTMENTS

There are several reasons for a company to purchase debt or equity securities of another company as a non-strategic investment. A corporation may have **excess cash** that it does not immediately need. For example, many companies have seasonal fluctuations in their sales levels, which can lead to idle cash until purchases are made for the next busy season. Until the cash is needed, the excess funds may be invested to earn a greater return than would be realized by just holding the funds in the company's chequing account.

When investing excess cash for short periods of time, corporations generally invest in debt securities that have low risk and high liquidity. Examples include guaranteed investment certificates, bankers' acceptances, term deposits, and treasury bills. It is usually not wise to invest short-term excess cash in equity securities. If the share price drops just before the company needs the cash again, the company will be forced to sell its investment at a loss. Most debt securities do not change significantly in value and are purchased for the interest they generate.

If a company has excess cash for a prolonged period of time, and wants a low-risk investment, bonds or preferred shares may be purchased as their values do not fluctuate very much. Although a company is not required to pay out a dividend, as discussed in Chapter 11, it is common to do so for preferred shares. Investments of this nature usually generate steady amounts of dividend revenue over time.

A company can also invest in debt and equity securities with the hope of selling them later at a higher price and benefiting from their price appreciation. The resulting gain is called a capital gain, which receives preferential income tax treatment in Canada because only half of the gain is usually taxed. Non-strategic investments that are held for the purpose of earning capital gains are called **trading investments**.

Non-strategic investments can be further classified as **short-term investments** or **long-term investments**, depending on how liquid the investment is and how long management wants to hold it. Later in this chapter, we will learn about the classification and methods of accounting for non-strategic investments.

STRATEGIC INVESTMENTS

Although both debt and equity securities can be purchased as non-strategic investments, only equity securities (normally common shares) can be purchased for the strategic purpose of influencing relationships between companies. This is because, for most companies, only common shareholders have voting rights and the ability to influence or control the company's major decisions. Preferred shareholders generally do not have voting rights, and therefore they have no influence or control.

The degree of influence determines how a strategic investment is classified. More details about the degree of influence and how it affects the accounting for that investment will be discussed later in this chapter. Note also that, while non-strategic investments can be either short- or long-term, strategic investments are usually long-term.

To summarize, the reasons corporations make non-strategic and strategic investments are shown in Illustration 12-1.

► Illustration 12-1
Why corporations invest

Reason	Purpose	Type of Investment
Non-strategic investment *(I need 1,000 treasury bills by tonight.)*	To generate investment income (interest, dividends, appreciation in share prices)	Debt securities (guaranteed investment certificates, term deposits, bonds, commercial paper) and equity securities (preferred and common shares)
Strategic investment	To influence or control another company	Equity securities (common shares)

BEFORE YOU GO ON...

▶ Do It! Investment Classifications

For each investment below, determine:

(a) whether the investment is a debt or equity instrument.

(b) whether the investment is non-strategic or strategic.

(c) the purpose for making the investment.

1. Investment in 120-day treasury bills, purchased with excess cash after the Christmas season

2. Investment in Canadian Pacific common shares, intended to be sold when the price rises 10% above cost

3. Investment in Royal Bank 20-year bonds, intended to be held for 20 years

4. Investment in 40% of the shares of Ajax Limited, a supplier

Action Plan

- Distinguish between debt and equity investments:
  - Debt investments are securities that have fixed due dates to receive interest revenue and a maturity date on which the investment's original amount (principal) is returned.
  - Equity investments give the owner a portion of equity in a company and are usually made by buying preferred or common shares.
- Distinguish between non-strategic and strategic investments:
  - Non-strategic investments are debt or equity investments that are purchased to earn interest or dividend revenue and/or to earn gains from the appreciation in the value of the investment.
  - Strategic investments are equity investments that represent a sizable amount of a company's common shares so that the investor can influence or control the decisions made by that company.

Solution

	(a)	(b)	(c)
1.	Debt	Non-strategic	Interest revenue for 120 days
2.	Equity	Non-strategic	Share price appreciation (capital gain)
3.	Debt	Non-strategic	Interest revenue over the long term
4.	Equity	Strategic	Influence the company or other shareholders with a large block of voting common shares

Related Exercise Material: BE12-1, E12-1, and E12-2.

Accounting for Non-strategic Investments

STUDY OBJECTIVE 2
Account for non-strategic investments.

At acquisition, debt and equity investments are recorded at their purchase cost. Although the investment's fair value is equal to its cost when purchased, this value may rise and fall greatly during the time debt and equity investments are held. Bond and share prices may jump dramatically with favourable economic events and drop drastically with unfavourable conditions. For example, when Netflix began making its own productions like *House of Cards* available, its share price rose from $100 in late January 2013 to over $240 by May 2013. Scotiabank, which was mentioned in our feature story, often invests in companies like Netflix for the purpose of trading their shares for a profit.

Volatility of share prices presents investors with an opportunity for trading profits. If prices can change so much, an important question arises: should non-strategic investments be valued at the statement of financial position date at fair value or at cost or at some other value? The next sections will discuss the valuation models for non-strategic investments.

ACCOUNTING MATTERS!

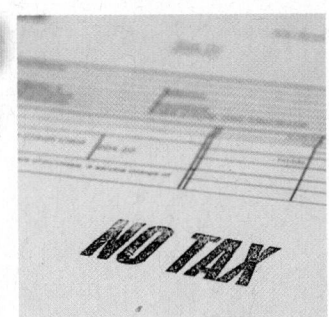

Non-strategic Investments for Individuals

Most Canadians, when they invest in the shares of public companies, are buying non-strategic investments rather than strategic ones. These individuals may trade these shares frequently or not, depending on their investment strategies. Studies have shown that investors with smaller portfolios of non-strategic investments usually have a higher return on their investments if they resist the urge to frequently trade them. One reason for this is the cost of commissions, which increase with trading activity. Another reason is the fact that income tax is paid on gains only once the investment is sold, so delaying the sale of an investment also delays the payment of any income tax on these gains.

In another form of non-strategic investment, since 2009, Canadians over the age of 18 have been allowed to contribute to a tax-free savings account (TFSA). Currently, the limit that can be paid into this account each year is $5,500. Any income earned in this account is not taxed. Let's assume someone opens up a TFSA when they are 18 years old and contributes $5,500 each year into the account for the next 42 years until they are 60 years old. Let's also assume that the investments made by the funds placed in the account earn 7% per year. By the time that person is 60 years old, the value of the account would be $1.2 million. If no more contributions were made into the account but it continued to grow by 8% per year until the person was 85 years old, the value of the account would be over $4.9 million ... quite a nest egg to spend or to leave to their family, even accounting for inflation.

VALUATION OF NON-STRATEGIC INVESTMENTS

There are four major models that can be used for valuing non-strategic investments, as outlined below:

1. **Fair value through profit or loss model.** Under this model, investments are adjusted upwards or downwards to reflect their fair value at the end of an accounting period. Fair value, for this purpose, means the price that would be received to sell an asset in an orderly transaction between market participants at the measurement date. This adjustment (the difference between the investment's fair value and carrying amount) to reflect fair value is known as an **unrealized gain or loss**. It is recorded in the income statement along with any interest or dividend revenue. When the investment is sold, any resulting gain or loss is known as a **realized gain or loss** and is also shown in the income statement.

2. **Fair value through other comprehensive income (OCI) model.** This is a variation of the fair value through profit or loss model and is exactly the same as that model except for the recording of unrealized and realized gains and losses in other comprehensive income rather than in the income statement. This is done if these types of gains and losses are not critical to the evaluation of management and therefore do not need to be reflected in profit. This model is used only for equity investments, not for debt investments.

3. **Amortized cost model.** Under this model, which applies only to debt investments, the investment's carrying amount is not adjusted to reflect fair value (unless it is impaired, similar to the way we would record an impairment loss on property). Consequently, no unrealized gains and losses are recorded. The term *amortized* is used because, if the investment was purchased at a discount or a premium, as is often the case when purchasing bond investments, the discount

or premium would be gradually amortized over the period of time until the bond matures. You learned about bond premium and discount amortization in the appendix to Chapter 10 when accounting for bond liabilities and you will review this concept again with regard to bond investments in Appendix 12A in this chapter. Because this model requires amortization over the remaining term of the investment, it is used for debt investments rather than equity investments. Any interest revenue or realized gains or losses on this type of investment are reported in the income statement.

4. **Cost model**. This model (often referred to as the *cost method*) is very similar to the amortized cost model except that it is used for equity investments. Again, no adjustments are made to the investments to record them at fair value. Because this type of investment does not give rise to a discount or premium (because there is no period to maturity for an equity investment) the concept of amortization does not apply to this model. Investment revenue under this model arises from dividend revenue along with realized gains and losses that would be reported in the income statement. Although the name is identical to the cost model used when accounting for depreciation in Chapter 9, its use in this chapter is different and it relates only to investments.

A summary of these models is shown in Illustration 12-2.

▶Illustration 12-2

Summary of valuation models for non-strategic investments

	Fair Value Through Profit or Loss	Fair Value Through OCI	Amortized Cost	Cost
Used for	Debt or equity investments	Equity investments	Debt investments	Equity investments
Investment valued at	Fair value	Fair value	Amortized cost	Cost
Interest revenue	Income statement	Not applicable	Income statement	Not applicable
Dividend revenue	Income statement	Income statement	Not applicable	Income statement
Unrealized gains and losses	Income statement	Other comprehensive income	Not recorded	Not recorded
Realized gains and losses	Income statement	Other comprehensive income	Income statement	Income statement

The items listed above that are shown on the income statement are typically listed as other revenues and expenses below profit from operations.

We will look at the fair value models (the first two models described above) in the next section. We will look at the third model, the amortized cost model, in the appendix to this chapter and the fourth model, the cost model, later in the chapter when we discuss strategic investments. We will also review when these models are used under both IFRS and ASPE in the Reporting Investments section of the chapter.

USING FAIR VALUE MODELS

We will now look in greater detail at how each of the fair value models described earlier is used.

Fair Value Through Profit or Loss

As mentioned earlier, because this model requires an adjustment to the investment to reflect it at fair value, a corresponding unrealized gain or loss is recorded when the investment is adjusted upwards or downwards, respectively. An unrealized gain or loss is recorded rather than a realized gain or loss because the investment has not actually been sold and the gain or loss "realized."

To illustrate the valuation of trading investments accounted for under the fair value through profit or loss model, assume that on December 31, 2015, Plano Corporation has the following costs and fair values for its debt and equity securities:

Trading Investments	Cost	Fair Value	Unrealized Gain (Loss)
BCE shares	$ 50,000	$ 48,000	$(2,000)
Norbord bonds	90,000	95,000	5,000
Total	$140,000	$143,000	$ 3,000

Plano has an overall unrealized gain of $3,000 because the total fair value of $143,000 is $3,000 greater than the total cost of $140,000. Its trading investments would be reported at $143,000 at December 31 in the current assets section of the statement of financial position. In addition, Plano would report a net unrealized gain of $3,000 in its income statement. **Note that unrealized gains and losses for trading investments under the fair value through profit or loss model are reported in exactly the same way as realized gains and losses.**

The adjustment of the trading investments to fair value and the recognition of any unrealized gain or loss are usually done through an adjusting journal entry. The adjusting entry for Plano is:

Dec. 31	Trading Investments ($5,000 − $2,000)	3,000	
	Unrealized Gain on Trading Investments		3,000
	(To record unrealized net gain on trading investments)		

A	=	L	+	SE
+3,000				+3,000

Cash flows: no effect

We have combined the BCE shares and Norbord bonds into a single Trading Investments account in the above journal entry and maintain a subsidiary ledger containing the details of individual investments. This entry also nets an unrealized loss of $2,000 on the BCE shares with an unrealized gain of $5,000 on the Norbord bonds. Although we have chosen to net the two trading investment securities and their respective gains and losses here, it would also be correct to record them separately.

If, early in January, Plano sells its BCE shares for $48,000, the following journal entry would be recorded:

Jan. 5	Cash	48,000	
	Trading Investments		48,000
	(To record sale of BCE shares)		

A	=	L	+	SE
+48,000				
−48,000				

↑Cash flows: +48,000

The BCE shares originally cost $50,000, but because they were written down to their fair value of $48,000 on December 31, the new carrying amount is $48,000. Consequently, the investment account is credited for that amount. Although it could be argued that the $2,000 unrealized loss recorded in the prior year has now been realized, for simplicity we are not going to reclassify an unrealized loss from one period into a realized loss in another period. As such, a reclassification has no impact on the profit reported in either period.

If the shares had been sold for $47,000 instead of $48,000, then a realized loss of $1,000 ($48,000 − $47,000) would have been recorded, representing the difference between the carrying amount of the investment on the date of sale and the proceeds received from that sale. This would be done as follows:

Jan. 5	Cash	47,000	
	Realized Loss on Trading Investments	1,000	
	Trading Investments		48,000
	(To record a realized loss on BCE shares)		

A	=	L	+	SE
+47,000				−1,000
−48,000				

↑Cash flows: +47,000

Fair Value Through Other Comprehensive Income

When we use fair value models, we attempt to show users of the financial statements relevant information regarding the value of investments. Under the fair value through profit or loss model, as the investments fluctuate in value, any corresponding unrealized gains or losses are shown in the income statement because we are trying to evaluate the company's ability to manage these investments. However, if management does not place a great deal of importance on measuring gains and losses because they are not intending to trade the investments frequently or use them to evaluate management, it may not make much sense to record these gains and losses in the income statement. In this case, they are recorded in other comprehensive income. When such an investment is sold, any realized gain or loss arising from the sale is also recorded in other comprehensive income.

Companies have to make a specific election to use the fair value through OCI model on an investment-by-investment basis. Otherwise the fair value through profit or loss model is used. Once an investment is accounted for under this approach, it cannot be changed. Furthermore, this model can be used only for equity investments. Because fair value through OCI is not used widely, detailed coverage of this topic is left for an intermediate accounting course.

BEFORE YOU GO ON...

▶ Do It! Non-strategic Investments

Wang Corporation had the following transactions:

Sept.	2	Purchased an investment in Hillary Corp. shares for $30,400 with the intention of trading it soon.
Oct.	12	Received a dividend on the Hillary shares, $750.
	22	Sold half of the investment in Hillary shares for $14,250.
Dec.	31	The remaining Hillary shares are worth $15,000 on this date.

(a) Record the above transactions.

(b) Prepare the adjusting entry for the valuation of the investment on December 31, Wang's year end.

(c) Identify where each account would be reported and on what financial statement.

Action Plan

- Use the fair value through profit or loss model for trading investments.
- Record the trading investment initially at cost and adjust for changes in fair value.
- When the investment is adjusted for any change in value, record any difference between the shares' carrying amount and fair value as an unrealized gain or loss.
- Report dividend revenue and both realized and unrealized gains (losses) in the income statement.
- When the investment is sold, record any difference between the carrying amount of the shares and the proceeds as a realized gain or loss.

Solution

(a)

Sept.	2	Trading Investments	30,400	
		Cash		30,400
		(To record purchase of Hillary Corp. shares)		
Oct.	12	Cash	750	
		Dividend Revenue		750
		(To record receipt of dividend on Hillary shares)		
	22	Cash	14,250	
		Realized Loss on Trading Investments	950	
		Trading Investments ($30,400 × ½)		15,200
		(To record sale of half of Hillary shares)		

(b)

| Dec. 31 | Unrealized Loss on Trading Investments
($15,200 − $15,000)
    Trading Investments
    (To record unrealized loss on Hilary shares) | 200 | 200 |

(c) The Cash and Trading Investments accounts would be reported as current assets on the statement of financial position. Dividend Revenue and Realized Loss and Unrealized Loss accounts would be reported as other revenues and expenses on the income statement.

Related Exercise Material: BE12-2, BE12-3, BE12-4, BE12-5, BE12-8, E12-3, E12-4, E12-5, E12-6, and E12-8.

the navigator

Accounting for Strategic Investments

A company that purchases (owns) securities is known as the **investor**, whereas the company that issues (sells) the securities is known as the **investee**. An investor that owns common shares has the potential to strategically influence the investee if enough shares are owned. The accounting for equity investments in common shares is based on how much influence the investor has over the investee's operating, investing, and financial affairs.

STUDY OBJECTIVE 3
Account for strategic investments.

Investor's Ownership Interest in Investee's Common Shares	Presumed Influence over Investee	Method to Account for Investment
Less than 20%	Insignificant	Fair value
20% to 50%	Significant	Equity method
More than 50%	Control	Consolidation of financial statements

▶Illustration 12-3
Accounting guidelines for strategic investments

As noted in Illustration 12-3, we assume that if the investor owns less than 20% of the investee's common shares, the investment is accounted for using one of the fair value models. Remember that, although this usually means the fair value through profit or loss model, an election can be made to account for the investment using the fair value through OCI model, as discussed earlier in this chapter. When an investor owns 20% or more of the common shares of another company but does not have control, the investor is generally presumed to have a **significant influence** over the decisions of the investee company. When an investee can be significantly influenced, it is known as an **associate**.

The presumption of significant influence may not be valid if other evidence exists to refute it. For example, a company that purchases a 25% interest in another company in a "hostile" acquisition may not have any significant influence over the investee. If less than 20% ownership is held, there is a presumption that significant influence does not exist but evidence could suggest otherwise. For example, if a highly respected investor with 18% ownership has board membership and plays a key role in forming company strategy, then significant influence could exist.

Among the questions that should be considered in determining an investor's influence are (1) whether the investor has representation on the investee's board of directors, (2) whether the investor participates in the investee's policy-making process, (3) whether there are material transactions between the investor and the investee, (4) whether the investor and investee are exchanging managerial personnel, and (5) whether the investor is providing key technical information to the investee. Companies are required to use judgement instead of blindly following the guidelines.

ACCOUNTING MATTERS!

Pershing Square Changes CP Board and CEO

In September 2011, Pershing Square Capital Management, Inc. began acquiring common shares of Canadian Pacific Railway Limited (CP). After obtaining more than 14% of the outstanding common shares, Pershing made it clear that it wanted individuals nominated by Pershing to replace a number of CP board members. Because it became obvious that other shareholders were about to support Pershing, the board took action and by June 2012, eight of the 15 positions on the board of directors were held by Pershing nominees and a new CEO supported by Pershing was running the company. Although Pershing did not hold more than the 20% level of ownership often used as a guide to measure significant influence, it is clear that Pershing had significant influence over CP because of its successful efforts to change both the board and upper management. By May 2013, the CP stock price was three times greater than it was when Pershing first began investing in the company.[2]

If the investor has more than 50% of the investee's voting shares, we generally consider that investee to be a **subsidiary company** of the investor. In this case, the investor is referred to as the **parent company**. Even though the investee is a separate legal entity, it is part of a group of corporations controlled by the parent. In order to show shareholders and other users of the parent's financial statements the full extent of the group's operations, the financial statements of all entities within the group are combined, resulting in **consolidated financial statements**. The process of consolidating financial statements is quite complex and will be left for an advanced accounting course, but in essence, the investment account is replaced with the subsidiary's assets and liabilities.

USING THE EQUITY METHOD

When an investor exercises significant influence over an associate, the investee company, to some extent, becomes an extension of the investor company. Consequently, such an investment is recorded using the equity method.

Under the **equity method**, the investment is initially recorded at cost in an account called Investment in Associates. After that, the Investment in Associates account is adjusted annually to show how the investor's equity in the associate has changed. In this way, the movement in the investment account reflects the changes that are occurring to the associate's retained earnings. When the associate has a profit, the investor will increase the investment account for its share of the profit. When the associate declares a dividend, resulting in the reduction of its retained earnings, the investor's investment account will be decreased. It would be wrong to delay recognizing the investor's share of profit until a cash dividend is received or declared, as that approach would ignore the fact that the investor and associate are, in some sense, one company, and that the investor therefore benefits from, and can influence the timing of, the distribution of the associate's profit.

To keep its records up to date, each year the investor adjusts the investment account to:

> **Helpful Hint**
> Under the equity method, revenue is recognized on the accrual basis, so when it is earned by the investee, it is also earned by the investor.

1. **Record its share of the associate's profit (loss)**: When the associate has a profit, the investor records its share of the profit by increasing (debiting) the investment account and increasing (crediting) a revenue account. Conversely, when the associate has a loss, the investor increases (debits) a loss account and decreases (credits) the investment account for its share of the associate's loss.
2. **Record the dividends received**: This is done by decreasing (crediting) the investment account for the amount of any dividends received. The investment account is reduced for dividends received because the associate's net assets are decreased when a dividend is paid.

We will now illustrate the equity method, using two fictitious companies, Milar Corporation and Beck Inc.

Recording Acquisition of Shares

Beck Inc. has 10,000 common shares issued in total. Assume that on January 1, 2015, Milar Corporation (the investor) acquires 30%, or 3,000 common shares, of Beck (the associate) for $120,000 cash or $40 per share. Milar is assumed to have significant influence over Beck and will use the equity method to account for this transaction. If Milar had more than one associate, we would add the associate's name to the investment account name, or maintain a subsidiary ledger of associates similar to that discussed earlier in the Using Fair Value Models section with respect to trading investments. The entry to record this investment is:

Jan. 1	Investment in Associates	120,000	
	Cash		120,000
	(To record purchase of Beck common shares)		

A = L + SE
+120,000
−120,000
↓Cash flows: −120,000

Recording Investment Revenue

Now assume that for the year ended December 31, 2015, Beck reports profit of $100,000 and declares and pays a $40,000 cash dividend. At December 31, 2015, Beck's common shares were trading at $42 each. Milar is required to record (1) its share of Beck's profit, $30,000 (30% × $100,000), and (2) the reduction in the investment account for the dividends received, $12,000 ($40,000 × 30%). If Milar had owned the Beck shares for only a portion of the year, the revenue recorded from the Beck investment would be prorated for that portion. The entries are as follows:

	(1)		
Dec. 31	Investment in Associates	30,000	
	Revenue from Investment in Associates		30,000
	(To record 30% equity in Beck's profit)		

A = L + SE
+30,000   +30,000
Cash flows: no effect

	(2)		
Dec. 31	Cash	12,000	
	Investment in Associates		12,000
	(To record dividends received from Beck)		

A = L + SE
+12,000
−12,000
↑Cash flows: +12,000

No entry is required under the equity method for the increase in the shares' fair value (from $40 to $42 per share). After the above transactions are posted, the investment and revenue accounts show the following:

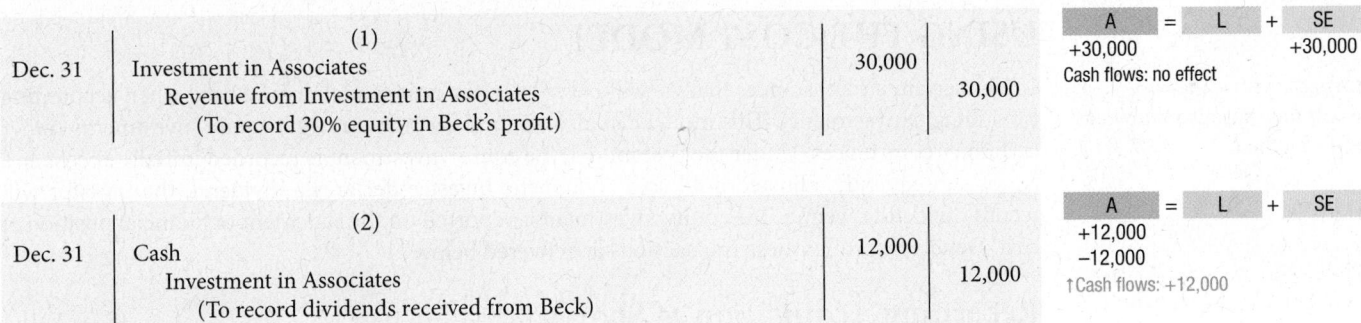

Investment in Associates				Revenue from Investment in Associates	
Jan. 1	120,000	Dec. 31	12,000	Dec. 31	30,000
Dec. 31	30,000				
Bal. Dec. 31	138,000				

During the year, the investment account has increased by $18,000 ($30,000 − $12,000). This $18,000 is Milar's 30% share of the $60,000 increase in Beck's retained earnings ($100,000 − $40,000). In addition, Milar will report $30,000 of revenue from its investment, which is 30% of Beck's profit of $100,000.

The revenue recorded under the equity method can be significant. Illustration 12-4 compares the journal entries recorded above under the equity method with the journal entries that would have been recorded if significant influence did not exist and the fair value through profit or loss model were used to account for the investment, assuming that it was held for trading. This is done on the left-hand side of the illustration. On the right-hand side of the illustration, we assume that Milar did have significant influence over Beck and used the equity method (as just illustrated in this section).

▶Illustration 12-4

Comparison of fair value through profit or loss and equity methods

Fair Value Through Profit or Loss Model			Equity Method		
Acquisition			*Acquisition*		
Trading Investments	120,000		Investment in Associates	120,000	
Cash		120,000	Cash		120,000
Investee reports profit			*Associate reports profit*		
No entry			Investment in Associates	30,000	
			Revenue from Investment in Associates		30,000
Investee pays dividends			*Associate pays dividends*		
Cash	12,000		Cash	12,000	
Dividend Revenue		12,000	Investment in Associates		12,000
Adjustment to fair value			*Adjustment to fair value*		
Trading Investments	6,000		No entry		
Unrealized Gain on Trading Investments		6,000			

Using the fair value through profit or loss model, the investment is reported as a trading investment of $120,000. Dividend revenue of $12,000 is recognized in the income statement, as is an unrealized gain of $6,000 (3,000 shares × $2 [$42 fair value less $40 purchase price] per share). Using the equity method of accounting, the investment account is reported as $138,000 and revenue of $30,000 is recognized on the income statement. Notice how the use of different methods can affect profit and the carrying amount of investments. The decision as to whether an investee can be significantly influenced is therefore a very critical one.

USING THE COST MODEL

Alternative Terminology
The *cost model* is also known as the *cost method*.

Under certain circumstances that we will cover later, the cost model may be used when accounting for strategic investments. This model can also be used for non-strategic equity investments under certain circumstances. Under the cost model, the equity investment is recorded initially at cost and is not subsequently adjusted until sold. When the investee declares a dividend, the investor will record dividend revenue. The equity investment is reported on the statement of financial position at cost. Details regarding these transactions are covered below.

Recording Acquisition of Shares

At acquisition, the cost of the investment is the price paid to acquire the equity securities. Assume, for example, that on July 1, 2015, Passera Corporation (the investor) acquires 1,000 common shares of Beal Corporation (the investee) at $40 per share. Beal is a private corporation and its shares are held by only two individuals and Passera. If Beal has a total of 10,000 common shares, then Passera has a 10% (1,000 ÷ 10,000) ownership interest in Beal. When a company uses the cost model, it is usually not for investments that are held for trading or investments in which there is significant influence. Consequently, the investment account when using this method is often just referred to as Long-Term Investments. The assumption here is that the Beal shares are the only long-term investment held by Passera. If there were others, we would distinguish them by adding the name of the investee to the account name or maintaining a subsidiary ledger.

The entry to record the acquisition of the Beal shares is as follows:

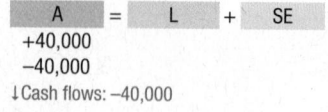

A = L + SE
+40,000
−40,000
↓Cash flows: −40,000

July 1	Long-Term Investments	40,000	
	Cash		40,000
	(To record purchase of 1,000 common shares of Beal)		

This investment would be reported as a non-current asset on the statement of financial position.

Recording Dividend Revenue

During the time the shares are held, entries are required for any cash dividends that the investee declares. If a $2-per-share dividend is declared and paid by Beal Corporation on October 1, the entry that Passera would record is:

Oct. 1	Cash (1,000 × $2)	2,000	
	Dividend Revenue		2,000
	(To record receipt of cash dividend)		

A	=	L	+	SE
+2,000				+2,000

↑Cash flows: +2,000

Recording Sales of Shares

When shares are sold, the difference between the net proceeds from the sale and the cost of the shares is recognized as a realized gain or realized loss. Assume that Passera Corporation receives net proceeds of $39,000 on the sale of its Beal Corporation shares on December 10. Because the shares cost $40,000, a loss of $1,000 has been realized. The entry to record the sale is:

Dec. 10	Cash	39,000	
	Realized Loss on Long-Term Investments	1,000	
	Long-Term Investments		40,000
	(To record sale of Beal common shares)		

A	=	L	+	SE
+39,000				−1,000
−40,000				

↑Cash flows: +39,000

BEFORE YOU GO ON...

▶ Do It! Strategic Investments

CJW Inc. purchased 20% of North Sails Ltd.'s 60,000 common shares for $10 per share on January 2, 2015. On April 15, North Sails paid a cash dividend of $45,000. On December 31, North Sails reported profit of $120,000 for the year and had a share value of $10.25. Prepare all necessary journal entries assuming (a) CJW plans to trade the investment and uses the fair value through profit or loss model; (b) this is a strategic investment with significant influence accounted for using the equity method; and (c) this is neither a trading investment nor one that has given CJW significant influence so the company has used the cost model.

Action Plan

- Fair value through profit or loss model
  - Recognize dividend revenue when dividends are declared.
  - Adjust the investment's carrying amount to fair value, thereby recognizing an unrealized gain or unrealized loss at year end that is recorded in the income statement.
- Equity method
  - Under the equity method, recognize revenue when the associate reports profit. The declaration of dividends is not revenue; rather, it reduces the equity investment.
- Cost model
  - Under the cost model, only dividend revenue and realized gains and losses are recognized in the income statement.

Solution

(a) Fair value through profit or loss model

Jan. 2	Trading Investments (20% × 60,000 × $10)	120,000	
	Cash		120,000
	(To record purchase of 12,000		
	[20% × 60,000] North Sails shares)		

(continued)

Apr. 15	Cash	9,000	
	Dividend Revenue (20% × $45,000)		9,000
	(To record receipt of cash dividend)		
Dec. 31	Trading Investments	3,000	
	Unrealized Gain on Trading Investments		3,000
	(12,000 × $0.25 [$10.25 − $10])		
	(To record unrealized gain on North Sails shares)		

(b) Equity method

Jan. 2	Investment in Associates (20% × 60,000 × $10)	120,000	
	Cash		120,000
	(To record purchase of 12,000		
	[20% × 60,000] North Sails shares)		
Apr. 15	Cash	9,000	
	Investment in Associates (20% × $45,000)		9,000
	(To record receipt of cash dividend)		
Dec. 31	Investment in Associates (20% × $120,000)	24,000	
	Revenue from Investment in Associates		24,000
	(To record 20% equity in North Sails' profit)		

(c) Cost model

Jan. 2	Long-Term Investments (20% × 60,000 × $10)	120,000	
	Cash		120,000
	(To record purchase of 12,000		
	[20% × 60,000] North Sails shares)		
Apr. 15	Cash	9,000	
	Dividend Revenue (20% × $45,000)		9,000
	(To record receipt of cash dividend)		
Dec. 31	No entry		

Related Exercise Material: BE12-6, BE12-7, BE12-8, E12-6, E12-7, and E12-8.

Reporting Investments

STUDY OBJECTIVE 4
Explain how investments are reported in the financial statements.

This section will explain when the valuation models we have covered are used under both IFRS and ASPE. This will be done as we cover the presentation of investments in the income statement, statement of comprehensive income, statement of changes in equity, and statement of financial position.

INCOME STATEMENT

Under most models, if applicable, all gains and losses along with dividend and interest revenue and revenue from investment in associates are shown in the "other revenues and expenses" section of the income statement. There are two exceptions to this treatment. The first occurs when using the fair value through OCI model whereby realized and unrealized gains and losses are recorded in other comprehensive income. Note, however, that because OCI is not used under ASPE, neither is the fair value through OCI model. The second exception relates to dividend revenue under the equity method, which is shown as a reduction in the investment rather than in the income statement. Illustration 12-5 summarizes the above.

▶Illustration 12-5
Treatment of investment income items under valuation models

Item Earned	Fair Value Through Profit or Loss (Debt or Equity Investments)	Fair Value Through OCI (Equity Investments)	Equity (Equity Investments)	Amortized Cost (Debt Investments)	Cost (Equity Investments)
Realized gains and losses	Income statement	OCI	Income statement	Income statement	Income statement
Unrealized gains and losses	Income statement	OCI	Not recorded	Not recorded	Not recorded
Interest revenue	Income statement	Not applicable	Not applicable	Income statement	Not applicable
Dividend revenue	Income statement	Income statement	Reduces investment	Not applicable	Income statement
Revenue from investment in associates	Not recorded	Not recorded	Income statement	Not applicable	Not recorded

Scotiabank, introduced in our chapter-opening feature story, reported various types of income from investments totalling $2,984 million in its income statement for the year ended October 31, 2012, as shown in Illustration 12-6.

▶Illustration 12-6
Income statement

BANK OF NOVA SCOTIA
Income Statement (partial)
Year Ended October 31, 2012
(in millions)

Other operating income	
Trading revenues (primarily unrealized gains and losses)	$1,316
Net realized gain on sale of investments	185
Revenue from investment in associates	442
Interest revenue	1,041
	$2,984

STATEMENT OF COMPREHENSIVE INCOME

You learned in Chapter 11 that the **statement of comprehensive income** includes not only profit reported on the income statement but also "other comprehensive income" transactions. You learned about other comprehensive income in past chapters. You will recall that one source of other comprehensive income is revaluations of property, plant, and equipment under the revaluation model. A new source of other comprehensive income introduced in this chapter occurs when unrealized gains and losses are recorded using the fair value through OCI model.

Companies can present the items included in other comprehensive income in a separate statement or at the bottom of the income statement in a combined statement of comprehensive income.

Scotiabank presents its profit in an income statement and then prepares a separate statement of comprehensive income by listing profit and then adding other comprehensive income (or subtracting other comprehensive loss) elements to profit to arrive at comprehensive income, as Illustration 12-7 shows.

►Illustration 12-7
Statement of comprehensive income

BANK OF NOVA SCOTIA Statement of Comprehensive Income (partial) Year Ended October 31, 2012 (in millions)		
Profit		$6,023
Other comprehensive income (loss), net of tax		
Change in unrealized loss on investments using the fair value through OCI model	$151	
Unrealized foreign currency losses	149	
Other	176	476
Comprehensive income		$6,499

The bank's profit of $6,023 million was increased by the other comprehensive income of $476 million, resulting in overall comprehensive income of $6,499 million. Note that adjustments to comprehensive income are reported net of income tax. For simplicity, we are ignoring the income tax implications of comprehensive income in this chapter.

STATEMENT OF CHANGES IN EQUITY

As you learned in prior chapters, the statement of changes in equity presents the changes in each component of shareholders' equity each period. This includes changes in share capital, retained earnings, accumulated other comprehensive income (loss), and any other equity items that a company might report. While profit increases retained earnings, other comprehensive income (loss) increases (decreases) accumulated other comprehensive income.

An extract from the bank's statement of changes in equity, detailing the determination of accumulated other comprehensive income, is shown below in Illustration 12-8. Note that detailed calculations of the changes in share capital have been omitted in the following illustration for simplicity. Shown below are the movements in retained earnings and accumulated other comprehensive income only.

►Illustration 12-8
Statement of changes in equity

BANK OF NOVA SCOTIA Statement of Changes in Equity (partial) Year Ended October 31, 2012 (in millions)		
Share capital (not detailed)		$17,523
Retained earnings		
Balance at beginning of year	$18,421	
Profit	6,023	
Other	27	
Dividends	(2,493)	
Balance at end of year		21,978
Accumulated other comprehensive loss		
Balance at beginning of year	$ (507)	
Other comprehensive income	476	
Balance at end of year		(31)
Other (not detailed)		1,909
Total shareholders' equity		$41,379

It is important to understand that the other comprehensive income of $476 million shown above in Illustration 12-8 is not the same amount reported as the ending comprehensive income amount on the bank's statement of comprehensive income, which was $6,499 million. This is because comprehensive income shown in Illustration 12-7 comprises both profit ($6,023 million) and the other comprehensive income ($476 million). Similar to how ending retained earnings is determined, the current period's other comprehensive income of $476 million is added to the opening accumulated other comprehensive loss balance to determine the ending balance. This resulted in an ending accumulated other comprehensive loss of $31 million, as shown above. It is this amount that is reported in the shareholders' equity section of the statement of financial position.

Closing Entries for Other Comprehensive Income

As we saw in Chapter 4, revenues and expenses are closed to the Retained Earnings account through the Income Summary account. This was done because we wanted to add the profit earned (or loss incurred) during the year to update retained earnings. Just as profit or loss for the year is used to update retained earnings, other comprehensive income must be closed out into the Accumulated Other Comprehensive Income account at the end of the year. For Scotiabank this would be done by decreasing Other Comprehensive Income with a debit of $476 million and recording an offsetting credit to Accumulated Other Comprehensive Income.

STATEMENT OF FINANCIAL POSITION

Before we look at the ways investments are reported on the statement of financial position, we need to determine when the various models we have been covering are used under both IFRS and ASPE.

Accounting for Investments under IFRS

With regard to non-strategic investments, under current IFRS, a company determines how an investment is accounted for based on its business model and the nature of the investment's cash flows. If the business model is not based on trading investments, and the investment is held to earn contractual cash flows relating to principal and interest payments rather than price appreciation, the investment (which is usually a debt investment) is accounted for using the amortized cost model, although an option to use fair value is allowed. If, instead, the investment is a trading investment and not held to earn contractual cash flows, then it is accounted for using the fair value model. The version of the fair value model that should be used is fair value through profit or loss, although an election can be made to use the fair value through OCI model. IFRS assumes that a fair value for an investment can always be obtained.

For strategic investments, IFRS requires the preparation of consolidated financial statements if control over the investee has been achieved. If significant influence but no control exists, then the investment is accounted for using the equity method. If neither control nor significant influence exists, then the investment is likely non-strategic.

Illustration 12-9 summarizes the above. Notice that the cost model is not listed in Illustration 12-9 as IFRS does not anticipate a situation where the fair value of an investment cannot be determined.

▶Illustration 12-9

Accounting for investments on the statement of financial position under IFRS

ACCOUNTING FOR INVESTMENTS UNDER IFRS				
	Criteria	Valuation Model	Statement of Financial Position Classification	Name of Account Used in This Text
Non-strategic investments	Investment purchased to earn contractual cash flows	Amortized cost model but option exists to use fair value through profit or loss	Current or non-current based on when the contract to receive cash ends	If current, usually a specific name is used, such as Note Receivable (see Chapter 8), and if non-current, Long-Term Investments
	Investment not purchased to earn contractual cash flows (for example, a trading investment)	Fair value through profit or loss model with some exceptions allowed for fair value through OCI	Usually current assets but could be non-current	Trading Investments
Strategic investments	Investor has control	Consolidation	Because consolidated financial statements are prepared, the investment account is not shown. It is replaced with the specific assets and liabilities of the subsidiary.	Not applicable
	Investor has significant influence but not control	Equity method	Non-current	Investment in Associates

DECISION TOOLKIT

Decision Checkpoints

Info Needed for Decision

Tools to Use for Decision

How to Evaluate Results

Decision Checkpoints	Info Needed for Decision	Tools to Use for Decision	How to Evaluate Results
Should a company reporting under IFRS elect to use the fair value through OCI model for non-strategic equity investments? Should the company elect to use fair value through profit or loss on investments with contractual cash flows?	Need to know how management is evaluated on the performance of an investment and whether the investment is to be held on a short- or long-term basis.	If an investment is to be held on a longer-term basis, or held only for the purposes of earning cash flows like interest payments, management is less likely to be evaluated on unrealized gains. Excluding unrealized items from the income statement makes sense, especially if management receives bonuses based on profit.	Review the financial statements to see the extent to which investments are recorded using the fair value through OCI model and whether debt investments are valued at fair value through profit or loss. This will give an indication of how the company views the importance of measuring short-term fluctuations in the fair value of investments in the income statement and may provide some insight into the relationship between investment performance and bonus calculations.

Accounting for Investments under ASPE

Under ASPE, for non-strategic investments, one first determines if an investment is an equity investment that has a quoted price in an active market. An example of this would be shares in a public company that trade on a stock exchange. For these investments, the fair value through profit or loss model is used. For all other non-strategic investments, the amortized cost (for debt) or cost model (for equities) would be used. However, if a debt investment had a quoted price in an active market, an option to use fair value through profit or loss can be taken. Because, under ASPE, other comprehensive income is not measured, the fair value through OCI model is not applicable at any time.

► Illustration 12-10
Accounting for investments under ASPE

For strategic investments, if control is exercised, the investor can prepare consolidated financial statements or choose not to consolidate and use instead the fair value through profit or loss model or the equity method. The cost model can also be used if there is no quoted price in an active market. If control is not achieved but significant influence can be exercised, then the equity method or fair value through profit or loss model can be used. However, the cost model can be used if a quoted value of the associate's shares cannot be obtained. Illustration 12-10 summarizes the above.

	ACCOUNTING FOR INVESTMENTS UNDER ASPE			
	Criteria	**Valuation Model**	**Statement of Financial Position Classification**	**Name of Account Used in This Text**
Non-strategic investments	Equity investment has a quoted price in an active market	Fair value through profit or loss	Current or non-current based on management's intentions	Trading Investments or Long-Term Investments
	Investment is not an equity investment, or it is but there is no quoted price in an active market	Amortized cost if debt or cost model if equity (can choose fair value through profit or loss on debt investment)	Current or non-current based on management's intentions	Trading Investments or Long-Term Investments
Strategic investments	Investor has control	(a) Consolidation, or (b) if fair value is known, can choose equity method or fair value through profit or loss, or (c) if fair value is not known, can choose equity method or cost model	If consolidated financial statements are prepared, the investment account is not shown as it is replaced with the specific assets and liabilities of the subsidiary. However, under ASPE, consolidation is not mandatory.	Not applicable if consolidation takes place. If no consolidation, then Long-Term Investments
	Investor has significant influence but not control	If fair value is known, can choose equity method or fair value through profit or loss. If fair value is not known, can choose equity method or cost model.	Non-current	Investment in Associates

DECISION TOOLKIT

 Decision Checkpoints	 Info Needed for Decision	 Tools to Use for Decision	 How to Evaluate Results
Given the options that are available under ASPE when accounting for investments, what model should be used?	Need to know what the users of the financial statements are using the information regarding these investments for. Also need to know if the fair value of the investment can be determined from an active market.	If the shareholders of the parent company want detailed information about the assets and liabilities of subsidiaries, then statements will be consolidated. If not, then determine if recording a share of the investee's income is needed to evaluate the performance of the subsidiary. A similar question would be asked of associates. If it is needed, then the equity method should be used. If it is not needed, then the fair value through profit or loss model must be used unless fair value cannot be determined, in which case the cost model would be used. For debt investments, fair value would be used if it was considered more relevant to users than amortized cost.	Review the financial statements to see the extent to which subsidiaries have been consolidated. Then determine if revenue from associates or subsidiaries is being reported on the income statement. This will give an indication of how the company views the importance of measuring the performance of subsidiaries and associates. Then determine if any strategic investments are carried at fair value or cost as this will give an indication of how actively the shares of the investee are traded.

Classifying Investments on the Statement of Financial Position

Many companies, including Scotiabank view highly liquid investments that are near maturity (usually less than three months) as cash equivalents.

Other short-term investments rank next in order of liquidity. As you learned earlier, trading investments are always classified as current assets, whereas non-strategic investments that are not held for trading may be either current or non-current, depending on whether the investment is capable of reasonably prompt liquidation and when management intends to sell it. Regardless of their classification, these types of investments are carried at fair value if this can be determined.

Illustration 12-11 shows how Scotiabank reports its trading investments, and for illustration purposes only we are showing the amounts that appeared in the notes to the financial statements.

BANK OF NOVA SCOTIA Statement of Financial Position (partial) October 31, 2012 (in millions)	
Current assets	
Trading securities—equity	$30,417
Trading securities—debt	44,222
	$74,639

▶Illustration 12-11
Presentation of short-term investments

No distinction is usually made between debt and equity securities on the face of the statement of financial position. These securities are often combined and reported as one portfolio amount on that statement. Most companies will then provide further details in notes to the financial statements.

Long-term investments include debt securities held to earn interest revenue until they mature, and consequently they are reported at amortized cost. Any portion that is expected to mature within the year is classified as a current asset. Long-term investments also include equity securities that are purchased to have significant influence or control. If an investment is not large enough to exercise either significant influence or control, but is still being held for long-term purposes, it will typically be accounted for using the fair value through profit or loss model unless the option to use the fair value through other comprehensive income model is taken. Investments recorded using the latter approach are currently called *available-for-sale securities* but this term will soon be discontinued. Under IFRS, it is possible to report long-term debt investments using the fair value through profit or loss model even though they would normally be accounted for using the amortized cost model. Scotiabank did this with some of its debt investments.

Scotiabank reports its long-term investments as shown in Illustration 12-12.

►Illustration 12-12
Presentation of long-term investments

BANK OF NOVA SCOTIA Statement of Financial Position (partial) October 31, 2012 (in millions)	
Assets	
Non-current assets	
Available-for-sale investments	$33,171
Investment in associates	4,760
Investments at fair value through profit or loss	197
Debt investments held using amortized cost	190
	$38,318

In the notes to its financial statements, Scotiabank provides further details about these investments.

Accumulated Other Comprehensive Income (Loss)

Accumulated other comprehensive income (or loss) is presented in the shareholders' equity section of the statement of financial position. Scotiabank reports an accumulated other comprehensive loss of $31 million, as shown earlier in Illustration 12-8.

Illustration 12-13 reviews the interrelationships among the income statement, statement of comprehensive income, statement of changes in equity, and statement of financial position. Note that changes in share capital have not been detailed in the illustration but the statement of changes

►Illustration 12-13
Financial statement interrelationships

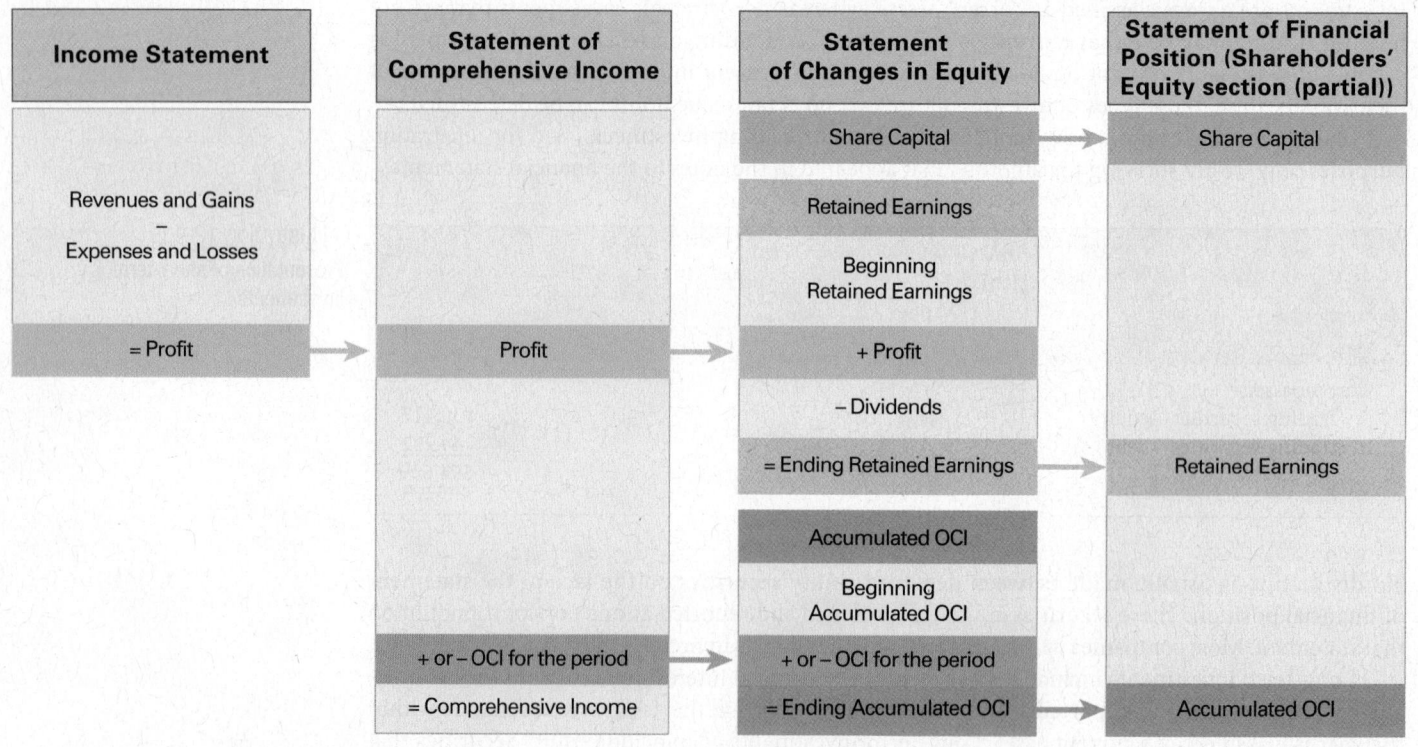

in equity would include this information as well as changes in retained earnings, accumulated other comprehensive income, and any other equity items.

Although we have chosen not to illustrate the statement of cash flows, you will recall from earlier chapters that the purchase and sale of investments are generally reported in the investing activities section of the statement. You will learn more about this in the next chapter.

■ Keeping an Eye on Cash

You have seen so far how various transactions relating to investments affect the statement of financial position and the income statement, but how do these transactions affect the statement of cash flows? The table below shows items arising from investment transactions and how they are shown on the statement of cash flows. You will learn more about the preparation of the statement of cash flows in Chapter 13.

Transaction	Impact on Statement of Cash Flows
Purchase of investment	Investing cash outflow, unless the investment purchased was a trading investment, in which case the payment is treated as an operating item since the investment is treated like inventory.
Dividends and interest received recorded as revenue	Operating or investing cash receipt (under ASPE shown only as an operating cash flow)
Dividends recorded under the equity method as a reduction in the investment account	Operating or investing cash receipt (under ASPE shown only as an operating cash flow)
Realized and unrealized gains and losses	Not shown because gains and losses do not constitute a cash flow
Proceeds received from the sale of an investment	Investing cash receipt, unless the investment sold was a trading investment, in which case the receipt is treated as an operating item since the investment is treated like inventory.

CONSOLIDATED FINANCIAL STATEMENTS

Earlier in the chapter, you learned that when one company controls another, **consolidated financial statements** are prepared that show the combined assets and liabilities of both the parent and subsidiary companies. For example, Scotiabank accounts for its investment in DundeeWealth using the equity method and then consolidates its financial statements into its own.

Consolidating financial statements is a complex topic that is usually dealt with in advanced accounting courses. However, under ASPE, companies can choose not to consolidate subsidiaries and instead use the equity method or the cost model unless the fair value of the subsidiary's shares is available, in which case the fair value through profit or loss method would be used rather than the cost model.

BEFORE YOU GO ON...

▶ Do It! Reporting Investments

Zaboschuk Corporation has the following selected accounts:

Accumulated other comprehensive income

Cash

Common shares

Dividends

Dividend revenue

Interest revenue

Investment in associates

Realized gain or loss on sale of investment using the fair value through profit or loss model

Revenue from investment in associates

Trading investments

Unrealized gain or loss under fair value through profit or loss model

Unrealized gain or loss under fair value through OCI model

(continued)

Identify the financial statement on which each of the above accounts would be reported and its classification in the statement. Assume that Zaboschuk reports profit and other comprehensive income in separate statements.

Action Plan

- Determine whether each account belongs on the income statement, statement of other comprehensive income, statement of changes in equity, and/or statement of financial position.
- Organize each account into its proper classification on each statement.

Solution

Account	Financial Statement	Classification
Accumulated other comprehensive income	Statement of changes in equity; statement of financial position	Accumulated OCI; shareholders' equity
Cash	Statement of financial position	Current assets
Common shares	Statement of changes in equity; statement of financial position	Share capital; shareholders' equity
Dividends	Statement of changes in equity	Retained earnings section (deduction from retained earnings)
Dividend revenue	Income statement	Other revenues and expenses
Interest revenue	Income statement	Other revenues and expenses
Investment in associates	Statement of financial position	Non-current assets
Realized gain or loss under the fair value through profit or loss model	Income statement	Other revenues and expenses
Revenue from investment in associates	Income statement	Other revenues and expenses
Trading investments	Statement of financial position	Current assets
Unrealized gain or loss under fair value through profit or loss model	Income statement	Other revenues and expenses
Unrealized gain or loss under fair value through OCI model	Statement of other comprehensive income	Other comprehensive income

Related Exercise Material: BE12-8, BE12-9, BE12-10, BE12-11, BE12-12, E12-2, E12-5, E12-8, and E12-9.

the navigator

Appendix 12A—Investments in Bonds with Discounts and Premiums

STUDY OBJECTIVE 5
Compare the accounting for a bond investment and a bond payable.

Chapter 10 covered bonds from the issuer's perspective where the bonds were liabilities. Corporations and governments are the major issuers of bonds that are purchased by investors. The issuer of the bonds is known as the investee. The purchaser of the bonds, or the bondholder, is known as the investor. For the investor, short-term investments in bonds, because they are not held for the purposes of earning interest until the bond matures, are accounted for using the fair value through profit or loss model as they are considered trading investments. Long-term investments in bonds, on the other hand, are typically accounted for using the amortized cost model.

You will recall from Chapter 10 that premiums or discounts on long-term bonds payable must be amortized using the effective-interest method of amortization. Similarly, premiums or discounts on bond investments must be amortized using the effective-interest method. However, under ASPE, companies have the choice of amortizing premiums and discounts on a straight-line basis over the period to maturity if the results do not differ materially from the effective-interest method. The effective interest rate method will be illustrated in this chapter.

If a bond investment is held for trading purposes, there is no requirement to amortize any premium or discount because it is not held to earn interest. Any misstatement of interest that might result would not be significant.

While the amortization of discounts and premiums on bonds payable was recorded in an Interest Expense account, the amortization of discounts and premiums on a bond investment is recorded in an Interest Revenue account. If there is a bond premium on a long-term bond investment, the Interest Revenue account and carrying amount of the investment are *reduced* by the amortization amount. If there is a bond discount, the Interest Revenue account and carrying amount of the investment are *increased* by the amortization amount.

RECORDING A BOND INVESTMENT FOR THE INVESTOR

This section will illustrate the recording of a bond investment using an example for Kuhl Corporation (the bond purchaser). It will then compare Kuhl's recording with Doan Inc.'s (the bond issuer's) recording of its bond liability. Assume that Kuhl Corporation acquires $50,000 of Doan 10-year, 6% bonds on January 1, 2015, for $49,000. This means that the bonds sold at a discount of $1,000 ($50,000 − $49,000). The price of $49,000 was based on a market, or effective, rate of interest of 6.272%. The bonds pay interest semi-annually, on July 1 and January 1. We will use the account Long-Term Investments because this investment is not held for trading purposes nor is it an investment in an associate. If more than one such investment were held, we would add the company's specific name to the end of the account name or use a subsidiary ledger to track each individual investment. Assuming that Kuhl is intending to hold these bonds until maturity and is therefore using the amortized cost model, the entry to record the investment is as follows:

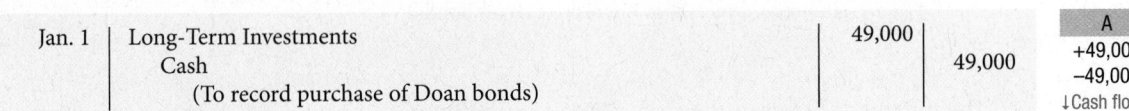

Jan. 1	Long-Term Investments	49,000	
	Cash		49,000
	(To record purchase of Doan bonds)		

A	=	L	+	SE
+49,000				
−49,000				

↓Cash flows: −49,000

In the above entry, the bonds are recorded at their acquisition cost of $49,000. Similar to a bond liability, the $1,000 discount on the bonds is not recorded separately but rather is netted with the cost in the investment account. Therefore the balance in the Long-Term Investments account really consists of a credit relating to the discount of $1,000 and a debit relating to the bond's maturity value of $50,000. Over time, the credit pertaining to the discount will be amortized. This process transfers a portion of this credit into the Interest Revenue account in the income statement each period and increases it to reflect the benefit of buying the bond at a discount.

Interest to be received in cash is calculated by multiplying the face value of the bond investment by the coupon (stated) interest rate per semi-annual period. Kuhl will collect interest of $1,500 ($50,000 × 6% × $^6/_{12}$) semi-annually on July 1 and January 1.

Interest revenue will differ from the cash received by the amount of discount that is to be amortized. The interest revenue is calculated by multiplying the carrying amount of the bond investment by the market (effective) rate of interest per semi-annual interest period. Kuhl's interest revenue is $1,537 ($49,000 × 6.272% × $^6/_{12}$) for the first interest period. Interest revenue is then compared with the interest received to determine the amount by which to amortize the discount, in this case, the portion of the $1,000 discount that is amortized in this six-month period. The amortization is

$37 ($1,537 − $1,500) in this case, and is debited to the bond investment account. Notice that the interest revenue of $1,537 is higher than the interest received in cash of $1,500 because the company is recognizing the benefit of purchasing the bond at a discount over the period that it intends to hold the bond.

The entry to record the receipt of interest on July 1 is:

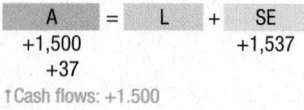

July 1	Cash ($50,000 × 6% × $^6/_{12}$)	1,500	
	Long-Term Investments	37	
	Interest Revenue ($49,000 × 6.272% × $^6/_{12}$)		1,537
	(To record of interest on Doan bonds)		

After amortization, the investment's carrying amount will increase to $49,037, which is the bond's present value on July 1. This is shown in the following T account:

Long-Term Investments			
Jan. 1	49,000		
July 1	37		
Bal. July 1	49,037		

If the bonds are later sold before their maturity date, it is necessary to (1) update any unrecorded interest, (2) debit Cash for the proceeds received, (3) credit the investment account for the cost of the bonds, and (4) record any gain or loss realized on the sale. Any difference between the proceeds from the sale and their original cost is recorded as a realized gain or loss.

Assume, for example, that Kuhl receives proceeds of $50,500 plus accrued interest on the sale of the Doan bonds on September 1, 2015. First, record the interest entry for the two months from July 1 to September 1.

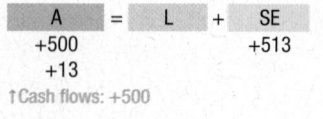

Sept. 1	Cash ($50,000 × 6% × $^2/_{12}$)	500	
	Long-Term Investments	13	
	Interest Revenue ($49,037 × 6.272% × $^2/_{12}$)		513
	(To record receipt of interest on Doan bonds)		

The difference between the cash, $500, and the interest revenue, $513, is the amortization of the discount, $13 ($513 − $500). The investment's carrying amount is now $49,050, as shown here:

Long-Term Investments			
Jan. 1	49,000		
July 1	37		
Sept. 1	13		
Bal. Sept. 1	49,050		

Since the investment has been sold for $50,500, a gain of $1,450 has been realized ($50,500 − $49,050). The entry to record the sale is:

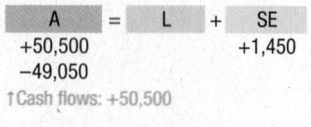

Sept. 1	Cash	50,500	
	Long-Term Investments		49,050
	Realized Gain on Long-Term Investments		1,450
	(To record sale of Doan bonds)		

RECORDING A BOND FOR INVESTOR AND INVESTEE

With a few exceptions, recording a debt investment in bonds (an asset) for an investor is essentially the opposite of recording bonds payable (a liability) for an investee, which was discussed in Chapter 10. Using the Kuhl Corporation example, Illustration 12A-1 compares the recording of the bonds as an investment for Kuhl and as a liability for Doan.

Kuhl Corporation (Investor)		
Acquisition of bonds		
Jan. 1 Long-Term Investments	49,000	
Cash		49,000
Receipt of interest and amortization of discount		
July 1 Cash	1,500	
Long-Term Investments	37	
Interest Revenue		1,537
Sale of investment		
Sept. 1 Cash	500	
Long-Term Investments	13	
Interest Revenue		513
1 Cash	50,500	
Long-Term Investments		49,050
Realized Gain on Long-Term Investments		1,450

Doan Inc. (Investee)		
Issue of bonds		
Cash	49,000	
Bonds Payable		49,000
Payment of interest and amortization of discount		
Interest Expense	1,537	
Bonds Payable		37
Cash		1,500
No entry as the interest that Kuhl receives is paid by the party that purchases the bond from Kuhl		

► Illustration 12A-1

Comparison of a bond investment using the amortized cost model and a bond liability

Recording an investment in bonds (an asset) for an investor differs from the recording of bonds payable (a liability) for an investee in the following two ways. First, any premium or discount is not amortized by the investor, as it is by the investee, if the bonds are held for trading purposes and accounted for under the fair value through profit or loss model. Second, assuming that Kuhl sold its bonds on the open market, the issuer, Doan, is not affected by this transaction because it took place between Kuhl and another company. Doan would only be affected if that company decided to buy back (redeem) its bonds from Kuhl.

BEFORE YOU GO ON...

► Do It! Investments in Bonds with Discounts and Premiums

Apollo Limited purchased a 6%, 5-year, $500,000 Genstar bond on January 1, 2015, for $520,000 with the intention of holding it until maturity. At that time, market interest rates were 5.08%. The bond matures on December 31, 2019, and pays interest on June 30 and December 31 each year. Apollo has a December 31 year end.

(a) Explain why the bond was purchased by Apollo Limited at a premium.

(b) Record the journal entries that Apollo would make on January 1, June 30, and December 31, 2015.

(c) Explain why a different amount of interest revenue is recorded on June 30 and December 31, 2015.

(d) If market interest rates rise, will bond prices fall? Why or why not?

(e) Assume that the market value of the bond on December 31, 2015, was $525,000 and because of this, Apollo decided to sell the bond immediately after receiving the interest payment that day. Record the journal entry that the company would make to record this sale.

(continued)

Action Plan

- Record bond investments at their cost when acquired.
- Calculate the interest revenue on a bond by multiplying the carrying amount of the bond at the beginning of the period by the market interest rate when the bond was purchased.
- Calculate the cash payment received for interest on the bond by multiplying the face or maturity value of the bond by the coupon interest rate.
- If the bond is to be held until maturity, any premium or discount is amortized over time. The amount to be amortized is the difference between the interest revenue earned and the interest revenue received. Over time, the carrying amount of a bond investment will move toward its maturity value as the discount or premium on the bond is amortized.
- When a bond investment is sold, the difference between its carrying amount and the proceeds received from its sale is the gain or loss on the sale of the bond.

Solution

(a) A bond will typically sell at a price that is equal to its present value determined by using market interest rates on the date that the investment is acquired. In this case, since the bond offers a coupon interest rate that is greater than the market interest rate, the bond is more attractive to investors, who will bid the price of the bond up to a value where its effective interest rate will then be equal to the market rate. A bond premium can be considered an additional cost to obtain the investment, which is amortized over time until maturity through reductions in interest revenue.

(b) Journal entries for the events described above are shown below:

Jan. 1	Long-Term Investments	520,000	
	Cash		520,000
	(To record purchase of Genstar bond)		
June 30	Cash (6% × $500,000 × $^6/_{12}$)	15,000	
	Long-Term Investments		1,792
	Interest Revenue (5.08% × $520,000 × $^6/_{12}$)		13,208
	(To record interest revenue on Genstar bond)		
Dec. 31	Cash (6% × $500,000 × $^6/_{12}$)	15,000	
	Long-Term Investments		1,838
	Interest Revenue (5.08% × ($520,000 − $1,792) × $^6/_{12}$)		13,162
	(To record interest revenue on Genstar bond)		

(c) Every time interest revenue is recorded, the premium on the bond is amortized. This in turn reduces the bond's carrying amount, as a portion of the bond's cost is allocated to interest revenue. Since the interest revenue earned is a function of the carrying amount, which is declining each period, the interest revenue in turn will decline each period.

(d) If market interest rates rise, the bond becomes less attractive to potential investors as its interest rate is locked in at 6%. Consequently, the bond price will fall. Therefore, bond prices are inversely related to changes in market interest rates.

(e) The journal entry that would be recorded for the sale of this bond would be:

Dec. 31	Cash	525,000	
	Long-Term Investments ($520,000 − $1,792 − $1,838)		516,370
	Realized Gain on Long-Term Investments		8,630
	(To record sale of Genstar bond)		

the navigator

Related Exercise Material: *BE12-13 and *E12-10.

comparing
IFRS and ASPE

Key Differences	International Financial Reporting Standards (IFRS)	Accounting Standards for Private Enterprises (ASPE)
Fair value through OCI	Allowed	Not allowed because other comprehensive income is not reported
Accounting for investments in associates	Must use the equity method	Choice of using the equity method or cost model if shares do not have quoted prices. If they are quoted, the equity method or the fair value through profit or loss model can be chosen
Investments in bonds	Must use the effective-interest method to amortize any bond premium or discount	Normally will use the effective-interest method to amortize any bond premium or discount but permitted to use alternative methods if the results do not differ materially from the effective-interest method
Consolidation of financial statements	Consolidation required if investor controls investee	Consolidation is optional. If consolidation is not used, there is a choice of using the equity method or cost model if shares do not have quoted prices. If share prices are quoted, the equity method or the fair value through profit or loss model can be chosen

the navigator

Savings are an essential part of personal financial planning. Without savings you cannot purchase investments, buy a house, deal with emergencies, or retire in comfort. To become a successful saver, you should: (1) set a goal for saving a certain amount each month, (2) make a plan for accomplishing this goal, and (3) save regularly.

Some people may be good savers but have little idea how to invest. There are two basic ways to invest: (1) by lending money to others or buying debt instruments such as Canada Savings Bonds or guaranteed investment certificates (GICs), or (2) by investing in equity instruments such as shares of a publicly traded company. A debt investment is usually safer and the goal is to earn interest revenue over a period of time. An equity investment is riskier and the goal is to earn a gain from the appreciation in value of the investment and perhaps some dividend revenue.

Canadians aged 18 and older are allowed to put up to $5,500 of their savings each year into a tax-free savings account (TFSA). Interest income, dividend revenue, and capital gains earned by investments in a TFSA are not taxed, which can save you thousands of dollars. You can set up a TFSA at most financial institutions.

Experts recommend that, if you will need to access your savings in the near future, you should have more debt investments because of their lower risk. If you do not need cash from your investments, consider investing in equities.

Some Facts

- Canadians planned to save an average of $9,859 in 2013 according to a BMO Household Savings Report. One half of those surveyed who are savers have a TFSA. One half of those surveyed say they are not saving enough, blaming high expenses, low income, and debt repayment.
- TFSAs were introduced in 2009. Anyone over 18 can contribute to a TFSA. The annual contribution started at $5,000 and increased to $5,500 in 2013. If you began contributing in 2009 and contributed the maximum allowable amount each year, you would have set aside $25,500. If you miss a year, you have "unused contribution room," which means you can make up the difference at any time. If you take money out of your TFSA, there is no penalty. You can replace the amount that you withdrew as long as you do it in the year following the withdrawal.
- Experts suggest that if you don't start saving until you are in your 40s, you will have to save 15% to 20% of your income for retirement. If you start saving in your 20s, you will have to save 3% to 5% of your income each year.[3]

What Do You Think?

You are entering the first year of university and have recently inherited $30,000. This $30,000 will help you fund your education. Your parents want you to invest some of the money in a TFSA and GICs but you know you could get a greater return by purchasing shares in a public company. What should you do?

YES You know that you will use all of this money for your education, so it should be invested in a low-risk savings vehicle with a steady predictable return. If the money goes into a TFSA account where bonds are held or a GIC or some combination, you know it will be there when you need it.

NO Savings accounts and GICs pay very little interest and you can earn a higher return by buying shares in a public company. You are very young and have plenty of time to recover any losses in the long term if you lose money on the shares.

Summary of Study Objectives

1. **Identify reasons to invest, and classify investments.** Corporations generally purchase investments in debt and equity securities for a variety of reasons. The investment may be purchased as a non-strategic investment to generate investment income or it might be purchased as a strategic investment to influence or control the operations of another company. Non-strategic investments may include debt securities that are purchased to earn investment income through the receipt of interest payments. Sometimes, though, a debt security may be held for trading purposes. Non-strategic equity investments can be held for trading purposes or to earn dividend revenue and can be held for any length of time.

2. **Account for non-strategic investments.** Non-strategic investments include investments in debt and equity securities. There are four major models that can be used to account for some of these investments. The fair value through profit or loss model reports debt or equity investments at their fair values on the statement of financial position while all related investment income, such as interest, dividends, and both unrealized and realized gains and losses, are reported in the income statement under other revenues and expenses. The fair value through other comprehensive income model is very similar to the above except that both unrealized and realized gains and losses are reported in other comprehensive income rather than on the income statement. Furthermore, this model is used for equity, not debt-related investments. The amortized cost model is used for debt investments that have premiums or discounts that need to be amortized over time. Under this model, if interest is received, it is recorded in the income statement, as is the effect of any amortization. The investment is not adjusted to reflect fair value so no unrealized gains or losses are recorded. Any realized gains and losses arising on the sale of the investment are recorded in the income statement. The cost model is identical to the amortized cost model but would not be used on an investment with a discount or premium.

3. **Account for strategic investments.** When an investor company makes a strategic investment, it is usually done to influence or control the investee. Significant influence is usually achieved when at least 20% of the investee's shares are acquired, although qualitative factors should also be evaluated to determine the existence of significant influence. If the investor is not able to exert significant influence over the investee company, the investment is accounted for as if it were a non-strategic equity investment. When significant influence exists (there is share ownership of usually 20% or more along with qualitative evidence of influence), the equity method can be used. The equity method records investment revenue from an associate (a significantly influenced investee) based on the investor's proportion of the associate's income. If the investor receives dividends from the associate, they reduce the carrying amount of the investment account because that company's equity has fallen.

   When the investor obtains control (usually more than 50% of the shares) of the investee, the subsidiary's financial statements are normally consolidated into those of the parent company.

4. **Explain how investments are reported in the financial statements.** Realized gains and losses, unrealized gains and losses, dividend revenue, and interest revenue are shown in the income statement as other revenues and expenses, with two exceptions. The first exception applies to equity investments accounted for under the fair value through OCI model, where unrealized and realized gains and losses are not shown in the income statement but are instead reported in OCI. The second exception arises when using the equity method, where dividend revenue is not recorded in the income statement but is instead shown as a reduction to the investment account.

   Under both IFRS and ASPE, non-strategic equity investments are usually held for trading purposes and would be shown in the current assets section of the statement of financial position using the fair value through profit or loss model. If a non-strategic equity investment is not held for trading, it may be shown as a long-term investment on the statement of financial position. These non-trading, non-strategic investments can be accounted for using the fair value through OCI model under IFRS, but because ASPE does not use other comprehensive income, this option is not available under ASPE. Debt investments that are held to earn interest revenue until maturity may be shown as current assets or long-term investments, depending on their maturity date. Under both IFRS and ASPE, these debt investments would be accounted for under the amortized cost model, although under IFRS, there is an option to use fair value through profit or loss. Under ASPE, if fair value cannot be measured, the cost model for equity investments or the amortized cost model for debt investments would be used.

   Strategic investments in significantly influenced associates are shown as long-term investments. Under IFRS, they are accounted for using the equity method. Under ASPE, if fair value is known, they are accounted for using the equity method or fair value through profit or loss method, and if fair value is not known, they can be accounted for using the equity method or cost model.

   Strategic investments in subsidiaries where control has been obtained would require the preparation of consolidated financial statements by the parent company under IFRS. In this case, the investment account is replaced by the specific assets and liabilities of the subsidiary. Under ASPE, parent companies can choose to use consolidation or can account for the investment using the equity method or the cost model, but if a fair value for the investment can be determined, the fair value through profit or loss model rather than the cost model must be used.

   Accumulated other comprehensive income is presented in the shareholders' equity section of the statement of financial position. Other comprehensive income is closed out at the end of the year into accumulated other comprehensive income.

Changes in share capital, retained earnings, and accumulated comprehensive income are shown in the statement of changes in equity.

5. **Compare the accounting for a bond investment and a bond payable (Appendix 12A).** The accounting for a bond investment is similar to that of a bond payable in that any premium or discount is amortized using the effective-interest method of amortization. Companies using ASPE can choose to use the straight-line method instead if the results do not materially differ from the effective-interest method. Premiums and discounts are not amortized for non-strategic investments that are held for trading purposes and would normally be accounted for under the fair value through profit or loss model.

Glossary

Amortized cost model   A method of valuing debt investments that are held to earn cash flows with specified payment dates in a contract in which the carrying value is adjusted only to the extent that discounts and premiums are amortized and not for the effect of changes in fair value. (p. 615)

Associate   An investee that is significantly influenced by an investor. (p. 619)

Consolidated financial statements   Financial statements that present the assets and liabilities controlled by the parent company and the total profitability of the combined companies (the parent company and the subsidiary companies). (p. 620)

Cost model (also known as the cost method)   An accounting model in which an equity investment is recorded at cost because a fair value for the investment cannot be readily determined. This model is also a choice allowed under ASPE for investments in associates. Investment revenue is recognized only when cash dividends are earned. This model should not be confused with the cost model that is used when accounting for property, plant, and equipment in Chapter 9. (p. 616)

Debt investments   Investments in money-market instruments, bonds, commercial paper, or similar items. (p.612)

Equity investments   Investments in the share capital (common and/or preferred shares) of other corporations. (p. 612)

Equity method   An accounting method in which the investment in common shares is initially recorded at cost. The investment account is then adjusted (increased for the investor's share of the investee's profit and decreased for dividends received) to show the investor's equity in the investee. (p. 620)

Fair value through profit or loss model   A valuation method that reports non-strategic debt or equity investments that are held for trading at their fair values, resulting in the recording of unrealized gains and losses in the income statement. (p. 615)

Fair value through other comprehensive income (OCI) model   A fair value model for equity investments that can be used only with an election under IFRS (not used under ASPE). It allows investors to record realized and unrealized gains and losses in other comprehensive income rather than in profit. (p. 615)

Investee   The corporation that issues (sells) the debt or equity securities. (p. 619)

Investor   The corporation that buys (owns) the debt or equity securities. (p. 619)

Non-strategic investment   A debt or equity investment that is purchased mainly to generate investment income. (p. 612)

Parent company   A company that controls (usually owns more than 50% of) the common shares of another company. (p. 620)

Realized gain or loss   The difference between fair value and cost (carrying amount) when an investment is actually sold. (p. 615)

Significant influence   An investor's ability to influence decisions made by an investee, which is assumed to exist when more than 20% but less than 50% of an investee's shares are owned. (p. 619)

Statement of comprehensive income   A financial statement that presents the profit (loss) and other comprehensive income (loss) for a specific period of time. Other comprehensive income items, such as realized and unrealized gains and losses from investments accounted for using the fair value through OCI model, are not reported on the income statement because they are not considered critical to the evaluation of management's performance, but are included in comprehensive income. (p. 625)

Strategic investment   An equity investment that is purchased to influence or control another company. (p. 612)

Subsidiary company   A company whose common shares are controlled (usually more than 50% of the common shares are owned) by another company. (p. 620)

Unrealized gain or loss   The difference between the fair value and cost (carrying amount) of an investment still held (owned) by the investor. (p. 615)

DECISION TOOLKIT—A SUMMARY

Decision Checkpoints

Info Needed for Decision

Tools to Use for Decision

How to Evaluate Results

Decision Checkpoints	Info Needed for Decision	Tools to Use for Decision	How to Evaluate Results
Should a company reporting under IFRS elect to use the fair value through OCI model for non-strategic equity investments? Should the company elect to use fair value through profit or loss on investments with contractual cash flows?	Need to know how management is evaluated on the performance of an investment and whether the investment is to be held on a short- or long-term basis.	If an investment is to be held on a longer-term basis, or held only for the purposes of earning cash flows like interest payments, management is less likely to be evaluated on unrealized gains. Excluding unrealized items from the income statement makes sense, especially if management receives bonuses based on profit.	Review the financial statements to see the extent to which investments are recorded using the fair value through OCI model and whether debt investments are valued at fair value through profit or loss. This will give an indication of how the company views the importance of measuring short-term fluctuations in the fair value of investments in the income statement and may provide some insight into the relationship between investment performance and bonus calculations.
Given the options that are available under ASPE when accounting for strategic investments, what model should be used?	Need to know what the users of the financial statements are using the information regarding these investments for. Also need to know if the fair value of the investment can be determined from an active market.	If the shareholders of the parent company want detailed information about the assets and liabilities of subsidiaries, then statements will be consolidated. If not, then determine if recording a share of the investee's income is needed to evaluate the performance of the subsidiary. A similar question would be asked of associates. If it is needed, then the equity method should be used. If it is not needed, then the fair value through profit or loss model must be used unless fair value cannot be determined, in which case the cost model would be used. For debt investments, fair value would be used if it was considered more relevant to users than amortized cost.	Review the financial statements to see the extent to which subsidiaries have been consolidated. Then determine if revenue from associates or subsidiaries is being reported on the income statement. This will give an indication of how the company views the importance of measuring the performance of subsidiaries and associates. Then determine if any strategic investments are carried at fair value or cost as this will give an indication of how actively the shares of the investee are traded.

USING THE DECISION TOOLKIT

the navigator

The Simmons Foundation was established to hold a number of investments on behalf of a publicly funded university and allocate the investment income to a number of worthy projects undertaken by the university. The foundation reports under IFRS, given its high public profile, and consults with several financial advisors who ensure that it has an appropriate mix of debt and equity investments in its portfolio. Some of the debt investments mature in less than a few years while others mature in 10 or 20 years. All of the debt investments are typically held to maturity in order to earn interest revenue. Other investments include non-strategic equity investments, which are actively traded.

Instructions

(a) What reasons does the foundation have for purchasing both debt and equity investments?

(b) Why would debt investments with different maturities be purchased?

(c) Given the criteria for evaluating performance, how should each type of investment be accounted for?

(d) The foundation is considering a strategic investment without achieving control. How would this be accounted for and presented on the statement of financial position? How would the profit and dividends relating to this investment be reported?

(e) If the foundation were using ASPE instead of IFRS, would it have more or less choice when it came to presenting information in its financial statements?

Solution

(a) When the foundation purchases debt investments, they are held to maturity and this is done for the purpose of earning interest revenue. These types of investments on average are less risky than equity investments and typically earn a lower return. The equity investments are held for trading purposes so as to earn dividend income and realize gains on the sale of these investments.

(b) Debt investments, such as bonds, with shorter periods to maturity are chosen so that, if interest rates change, the foundation will not be "locked in" and earn a specific interest rate that may now be too low. Debt investments, such as bonds, with longer terms are purchased so that interest revenue will be stable for a number of years, which makes it easier to prepare budgets.

(c) If the criterion to measure the performance of a debt investment is the interest revenue it will earn to maturity, the amortized cost model should be used when accounting for such an investment. This model does not measure unrealized gains and losses, as these are not relevant to the objectives for investing in such a security. On the other hand, if the investment was purchased for its potential price appreciation, then the fair value through profit or loss model should be used, as this model recognizes unrealized gains and losses directly in the income statement and carries the investment at its fair value. Knowing this information allows users of the financial statements to better evaluate the investment's performance.

(d) A strategic investment is an equity investment where the investor obtains a significant portion of the voting shares of an investee or associate, usually 20% or more of the shares. Undertaking such an investment requires the investor's commitment to become more involved with the associate's operations and the foundation must take this into consideration before making the investment. If 20% to 50% of the shares are purchased, it is likely that significant influence is achieved, although other qualitative factors may have to be considered. Given that the foundation uses IFRS, an investment of this size would be accounted for using the equity method. It would be reported as a non-current asset that would be increased by the foundation's share of the associate's profit (with a corresponding increase in investment revenue) and decreased by its share of the associate's dividends (with a corresponding increase in cash).

(e) Under IFRS, an election could be made to use the fair value through OCI approach rather than the fair value through profit or loss approach for non-strategic, non-trading investments. Furthermore, an election to use the fair value through profit or loss model on debt investments is also allowed. These alternatives are not available under ASPE, so there is less choice with respect to this type of investment. On the other hand, if the investment was large enough to attain significant influence over the investee, IFRS would allow only the equity method to be used while ASPE would allow a choice between the equity method and fair value through profit or loss. If fair value could not be obtained, the choice would be the equity method or the cost model.

Comprehensive Do It!

In 2015, its first year of operations, Northstar Finance Corporation, which reports under IFRS, had the following transactions regarding its investments:

May	1	Purchased 600 Sandburg Ltd. common shares for $60 per share. This investment is held for trading purposes.
June	1	Purchased 1,000 bonds of Gladstone Inc. at $100 each. These bonds bear interest at 6%, which is paid semi-annually on November 30 and May 31 each year. They were also purchased for trading purposes.
July	1	Purchased 4,000 Cey Corporation common shares for $70 per share. This represents 25% of the issued common shares. Because of this investment, the directors of Cey have invited a Northstar executive to sit on their board.
Sept.	1	Received a $1-per-share cash dividend from Cey.
Nov.	1	Sold 200 Sandburg common shares for $63 per share.
	30	Interest on the Gladstone bonds was received.
Dec.	15	Received a $0.50-per-share cash dividend on Sandburg common shares.
	31	On this date, the fair values per share were $55 for Sandburg and $73 for Cey. The fair value of the Gladstone bonds was $101 each. Cey reported a profit for the year ended December 31, 2015, of $100,000.

Instructions

(a) Record the above transactions.

(b) Prepare the adjusting entries required to report the investments at their fair value and accrue any investment revenue.

(c) Show the presentation of each investment and the related investment income in the statement of financial position and income statement.

(d) Without recording any entries or presenting financial statements, discuss how your answer could change if Northstar used ASPE.

Action Plan

- Keep a running balance of the number of shares and bonds purchased and sold for each investment.
- Calculate the realized gains or losses by subtracting the cost of any investments sold from the proceeds received from their sale.
- Determine the adjustment to fair value based on the difference between the carrying amount (cost) and fair value of the securities.

Solution to Comprehensive Do It!

(a)

May 1	Trading Investments		36,000	
		Cash (600 × $60)		36,000
		(To record purchase of 600 Sandburg common shares)		
June 1	Trading Investments		100,000	
		Cash (1,000 × $100)		100,000
		(To record purchase of 1,000 Gladstone bonds)		
July 1	Investment in Associates		280,000	
		Cash (4,000 × $70)		280,000
		(To record purchase of Cey common shares)		
Sept. 1	Cash (4,000 × $1)		4,000	
		Investment in Associates		4,000
		(To record dividend received from associate, Cey, of $1 per share)		
Nov. 1	Cash (200 × $63)		12,600	
		Trading Investments (200 × $60)		12,000
		Realized Gain on Trading Investments		600
		(To record sale of 200 Sandburg shares)		
30	Cash (6% × $100,000 × $^6/_{12}$)		3,000	
		Interest Revenue		3,000
		(To record interest received on Gladstone bonds)		
Dec. 15	Cash [(600 − 200) × $0.50]		200	
		Dividend Revenue		200
		(To record dividend received of $0.50 per share from Sandburg)		

(b)

Dec. 31	Unrealized Loss on Trading Investments		1,000	
		Trading Investments [400 × ($55 − $60)] − [1,000 × ($101 − $100)]		1,000
		(To record net unrealized loss on Sandburg shares and Gladstone bonds)		

(continued)

Dec. 31	No entry is made for the change in the fair value of Cey shares as the equity method is used for this investment.		
31	Interest Receivable (6% × $100,000 × $^1/_{12}$)		500	
	Interest Revenue			500
	(To accrue interest revenue on Gladstone bonds for December)		
31	Investment in Associates		12,500	
	Revenue from Investment in Associates		
	(25% × $100,000 × $^6/_{12}$)			12,500
	(To record Northstar's share of Cey's profit since the date of acquisition of July 1, which was six months ago)		

Supporting calculations:

	Trading Investment— Sandburg Shares	Trading Investment— Gladstone Bonds	Total Trading Investments	Investment in Associates
At acquisition	$36,000	$100,000	$136,000	$280,000
Dividends received				(4,000)
Carrying amount of shares sold	(12,000)		(12,000)	
Adjustment to fair value	(2,000)	1,000	(1,000)	
Share of associate's profit				12,500
Carrying amount, December	$22,000	$101,000	$123,000	$288,500

(c)

NORTHSTAR FINANCE CORPORATION
Statement of Financial Position (partial)
December 31, 2015

Assets	
Current assets	
Trading investments	$123,000
Interest receivable	500
Non-current assets	
Investment in associates	288,500

NORTHSTAR FINANCE CORPORATION
Income Statement (partial)
Year Ended December 31, 2012

Other revenues and expenses	
Revenue from investment in associates	$12,500
Interest revenue	3,500
Realized gain on trading investments	600
Dividend revenue	200
Unrealized loss on trading investments	1,000

(d) If Northstar reported using ASPE, it could account for the investment in Cey Corporation using either the equity method or the fair value through profit or loss model (because a fair value for Cey shares can be obtained). If the fair value through profit or loss model were used, other revenue would be increased from the $12,500 share of Cey's income to $16,000, consisting of dividend revenue of $4,000 and an unrealized gain of $12,000 arising from the difference in the fair value of the investment of $292,000 (4,000 shares at $73 each) and the carrying amount of $280,000. Therefore the total change in profit would be an increase of $3,500. On the statement of financial position, the investment would be shown at its fair value of $292,000 rather than the amount shown above of $288,500 under the equity method. So in summary, both profit and the carrying amount of the investment account would be higher by $3,500.

the navigator

WileyPLUS Self-Test, Brief Exercises, Exercises, Problems: Set A, and many more components are available for practice in *WileyPLUS*.

Note: All questions, exercises, and problems below with an asterisk (*) relate to material in Appendix 12A.

Self-Test Questions

Answers are at the end of the chapter.

Quiz Yourself

(SO 1) 1. Which of the following is the best reason for a corporation's managers to purchase equity securities as a strategic investment?
   (a) They want to exert influence over the decisions of the investee company.
   (b) They want to invest excess cash for short periods of time to earn a greater return (interest revenue) than would be earned if the funds were simply held in the company's chequing account.
   (c) They want to invest excess cash for the long term to generate investment income.
   (d) They speculate that the investment will increase in value in the short term and result in a gain when sold.

(SO 1) 2. Which of the following is a strategic investment?
   (a) Equity investment held for the purpose of trading
   (b) Debt investment held for the purpose of trading
   (c) Debt investment intended to be held to maturity
   (d) Equity investment representing 30% of the issued common shares

(SO 1) 3. Which statement does *not* apply to a debt investment that is being held until it matures in three years?
   (a) The company is speculating that a debt investment will increase in value and it will therefore be able to sell it at a gain.
   (b) The company is more interested in earning interest revenue than in realizing gains from short-term price fluctuation in the value of the investment.
   (c) The company has the ability to hold the investment to maturity.
   (d) The investment is classified as a non-current asset.

(SO 2) 4. Which statement is *incorrect* with respect to the valuation models used for non-strategic investments?
   (a) Unrealized gains and losses are not reported when the amortized cost model is used.
   (b) Realized gains and losses are reported in the income statement when using the fair value through other comprehensive income model.

   (c) Both unrealized and realized gains and losses are reported in the income statement under the fair value through profit or loss model.
   (d) The cost model is used only for equity investments.

(SO 2) 5. Boisclair Ltée sells investments reported under the fair value through profit or loss model that cost $28,000 for $26,000 in the same year as they were purchased. The entry to record this sale would include a:
   (a) debit to a realized loss account of $2,000.
   (b) debit to an unrealized loss account of $2,000.
   (c) debit to OCI of $2,000.
   (d) debit to a Trading Investments account of $26,000.

(SO 2) 6. A company purchased an equity investment for trading purposes for $20,000 in April 2014 and determined that its fair value was $23,000 on its year-end date of December 31, 2014. In 2015, the investment was sold for $24,000. Based on these facts, the company will record:
   (a) a realized gain of $3,000 in 2014 and a realized gain of $1,000 in 2015.
   (b) no gain or loss in 2014 and a $1,000 realized gain in 2015.
   (c) an unrealized gain of $3,000 in 2014 and a realized gain of $1,000 in 2015.
   (d) no gain or loss in 2014 and a $3,000 realized gain in 2015.

(SO 3) 7. The equity method of accounting for strategic equity investments could be used when the investor:
   (a) owns less than 20% of the investee's common shares, because there is no significant influence.
   (b) owns more than 20% of the investee's common shares but not more than 50%, because this indicates that significant influence has been achieved.
   (c) owns more than 20% of the investee's common shares but has not yet achieved either significant influence or control.
   (d) has purchased debt investments that will be held until maturity.

(SO 3)   8. Big K Ranch owns 20% of Little L Ranch. Little L Ranch reported profit of $150,000 and paid dividends of $40,000 this year. How much investment revenue would Big K Ranch report if it used the equity method to account for this investment?
(a) $8,000
(b) $22,000
(c) $30,000
(d) $110,000

(SO 4)   9. Athabasca Holdings Ltd. has owned 40% of the shares of Mackenzie Ltd. for a number of years. Athabasca reports under ASPE and uses the cost model. For the year just ended, Mackenzie earned $100,000 of profit and declared and paid dividends of $20,000. Athabasca would report how much investment revenue for the year from its investment in Mackenzie?
(a) $8,000
(b) $20,000
(c) $32,000
(d) $40,000

(SO 4)   10. Accumulated other comprehensive income is reported on which of the following statements?
(a) Income statement
(b) Statement of financial position
(c) Statement of changes in equity
(d) Both (b) and (c)

the navigator

(SO 5) *11. Which of the following statements is *incorrect* with regard to recording bonds under the amortized cost model?
(a) Unrealized gains and losses are recorded through adjusting entries at the end of the period.
(b) A bond purchased at a premium will result in the amount of interest received exceeding the amount of interest revenue recorded.
(c) Premiums and discounts are usually not recorded separately for the investor.
(d) The investor records the bonds initially at acquisition cost rather than at their maturity value.

(SO 5) *12. Bonds with a face value of $100,000 were purchased for $90,000 with the intention of holding the bonds to maturity. The following entry would be made by the investor when the semi-annual interest is received (assuming no previous accrual of interest):
(a) Debit Cash, Credit Interest Revenue
(b) Debit Cash, Credit Long-Term Investment, Credit Interest Revenue
(c) Debit Cash, Debit Long-Term Investment, Credit Interest Revenue
(d) Debit Cash, Debit Interest Revenue, Credit Long-Term Investment

Questions

(SO 1)   1. What are the reasons why corporations invest in debt and equity securities?

(SO 1)   2. Explain the differences between non-strategic and strategic investments.

(SO 1, 4) 3. Cumby Corporation is a golf equipment retailer that owns 1,000 common shares of Suncor Energy Inc. It intends to sell these shares if it needs cash. (a) Is the investment in Suncor considered a non-strategic investment or a strategic investment? Explain your reasoning. (b) Would the investment be classified as a current asset or a non-current asset on Cumby's statement of financial position?

(SO 2, 4) 4. At what amount—cost, amortized cost, or fair value—are each of the following most likely to be reported at on a statement of financial position: (a) common shares in a publicly traded company that will probably be sold within a year, (b) bond investments that will be held until maturity, and (c) shares in a private company that do not have a determinable fair value?

(SO 2)   5. What is the difference between realized gains/losses and unrealized gains/losses?

(SO 2)   6. Communications Inc. reported trading investments at their fair value of $255 million on its year-end statement of financial position. These securities were purchased earlier in the year at a cost of $245 million. (a) How should the

difference between these two amounts be recorded and reported? (b) Would your answer differ if the fair value of these securities could not be determined?

(SO 2)   7. Timmerman Ltd. purchased $1 million of 10-year bonds at face value (100) in 2015. The bonds were trading at 105 (recall that a bond price in this case means that the bond trades at 105% of its maturity value) on December 31, 2015. (a) At what amount would the bonds be reported in the December 31, 2015, statement of financial position if management accounted for the bonds using the fair value through profit or loss model? (b) How would any related interest revenue be reported?

(SO 2)   8. Music Makers Ltd. reported trading investments with an original cost of $115,000 and a fair value of $130,000 at December 31, 2014. It also reported an unrealized gain of $15,000 relating to the investment. During 2015, the investment was sold for $125,000. Describe how the sale of the investment would be recorded and reported in the 2015 financial statements.

(SO 3)   9. What constitutes "significant influence"? Is it safe to conclude that there is significant influence when a company owns 20% of the common shares of another company?

(SO 3)   10. Identify what is included in the carrying amount of a strategic equity investment using the (a) cost model and (b) equity method.

(SO 3)   11. Explain how, and why, the investment revenue differs when a strategic long-term equity investment is accounted for using the (a) cost model and (b) equity method.

(SO 4)   12. Indicate how (a) trading investments, (b) investment in associates, and (c) debt investments held to maturity are classified on the statement of financial position.

(SO 4)   13. Identify the proper statement presentation of the following accounts: (a) Unrealized Gain on Trading Investments, (b) Realized Loss on Trading Investments, (c) Revenue from Investment in Associates, and (d) Dividends received from an investment accounted for using the equity method.

(SO 4)   14. Distinguish between other comprehensive income and accumulated other comprehensive income. Indicate how each is reported in the financial statements. Explain how closing entries for other comprehensive income differ from closing entries for profit.

(SO 4)   15. Explain how the income statement, statement of comprehensive income, statement of changes in equity, and statement of financial position are interrelated.

(SO 3, 4) 16. **George Weston Ltd.** owns 63% of the common shares of **Loblaw Companies Ltd.** (a) What method should George Weston Ltd. use to account for this investment? (b) Which company is the parent? The subsidiary? (c) What kind of financial statements should George Weston Ltd. prepare to properly present this investment?

(SO 5) *17. Compare the accounting for a debt investment in bonds with the accounting for a bond liability.

(SO 2, 5) *18. Explain why premiums and discounts on bond investments must be amortized when using the amortized cost model and why no amortization occurs when using the fair value through profit or loss model.

(SO 5) *19. When bonds mature, a journal entry is recorded on the books of both the investor and the investee (issuer). However, when bonds are sold by the investor prior to maturity on the open market, the sale of the bond investment results in a journal entry on the books of the investor, but not on the books of the investee (issuer). Explain why.

Brief Exercises

BE12–1   Identify whether each of the following is most likely (a) a debt or equity investment, and (b) a non-strategic or strategic investment. (c) Identify the most likely reason (such as earning gains, interest, dividends, obtaining influence or control) for making the investment.

Classify investments.
(SO 1)

	(a) Debt or Equity Investment?	(b) Non-strategic or Strategic Investment?	(c) Reason for Making the Investment?
1. 120-day treasury bill			
2. A few common shares of a small oil company purchased with a temporary surplus of cash			
3. 30% of the common shares of a company purchased in order to obtain a position on the board of directors			
4. Bonds purchased with a temporary cash surplus			
5. 100% of the common shares of a company purchased to amalgamate its operations with those of the investor			
6. Five-year bonds intended to be held for the entire term of the bonds			

BE12–2   On January 1, 2015, Columbia Ltd. purchased $200,000 of 10%, 10-year bonds at face value (100) with the intention of selling the bonds early next year. Interest is received semi-annually on July 1 and January 1. At December 31, 2015, which is the company's fiscal year end, the bonds were trading in the market at 97 (this means 97% of maturity value). Using the fair value through profit or loss model, prepare the journal entries to record (a) the purchase of the bonds on January 1, (b) the receipt of the interest on July 1, and (c) any adjusting entries required at December 31.

Record trading investment.
(SO 2)

BE12–3   Using the data presented in BE12–2, assume that the bonds were sold for $194,000 on January 2, 2016. Record the sale of the bonds.

Record trading investment.
(SO 2)

Record trading investment.
(SO 2)

BE12–4   On August 1, 2015, McLellan Ltd. purchased 1,000 Datawave common shares for $45,000 cash with the intention of trading the shares and using the fair value through profit or loss model. On December 31, 2015, McLellan's year end, the shares' fair value was $49,000. Prepare the journal entry to record (a) the purchase of this investment on August 1, and (b) any adjusting journal entry required at December 31.

Record trading investment.
(SO 2)

BE12–5   Using the data presented in BE12–4, assume that the shares were sold for $47,000 on February 1, 2016. Record the sale.

Record strategic investment.
(SO 3)

BE12–6   On January 1, Rook Corporation, a publicly traded company, purchased 25% of Hook Ltd. common shares for $400,000. At December 31, Hook paid a $32,000 dividend (Rook received its share that day) and reported profit of $800,000. The shares' fair value at December 31 was $420,000. Record each of these transactions, assuming Rook has significant influence over Hook and is using the equity method to account for this investment. How much revenue would be reported by Rook because of its share of Hook?

Record strategic investment.
(SO 3)

BE12–7   Using the data presented in BE12–6, assume that Rook Corporation reports under ASPE and has chosen to account for its investment in Hook Ltd. using the cost model because the shares do not trade in an active market. Record each of the transactions and any necessary adjusting journal entries under this assumption. How much revenue would be reported by Rook in this situation? Explain why this differs from your answer in BE12–6.

Determine investment account balances and indicate statement presentation.
(SO 2, 3, 4)

BE12–8   Chan Inc., a publicly traded company, purchased 20% of Dong Ltd.'s common shares for $225,000 on January 1. During the year, Dong reported profit of $350,000 and paid a dividend of $40,000. The investment's fair value at December 31 was $275,000. (a) Assuming there is significant influence, indicate the balance in the investment account at year end and where it would be reported in the statement of financial position if Chan uses the equity method. (b) Assuming Chan does not have significant influence, determine the balance in the investment account at year end and where it would be reported in the statement of financial position if the fair value through profit or loss model is used. (c) Assuming Chan reports under ASPE and chooses the cost model because fair value cannot be determined on December 31, determine the balance in the investment account at year end and where it would be reported in the statement of financial position.

Indicate statement presentation.
(SO 4)

BE12–9   Indicate on which financial statement (the statement of financial position, income statement, or statement of changes in equity) each of the following accounts would be reported. Also give the appropriate financial statement classification (such as current assets, non-current assets, shareholders' equity, and other revenues and expenses). Assume all trading investments are accounted for using the fair value through profit or loss model.

	Financial Statement	Classification
A bond investment that will mature next year	_____	_____
Dividend revenue from a trading investment	_____	_____
Investment in associate	_____	_____
Investment of a few hundred common shares in a large publicly traded company that is held for trading purposes	_____	_____
A bond investment that management intends to hold for 10 years	_____	_____
Realized gain on a trading investment	_____	_____
Unrealized gain on a trading investment	_____	_____
Dividends received from a strategic investment accounted for using the equity method	_____	_____
Interest earned on a trading investment	_____	_____

Classify items as profit or OCI.
(SO 4)

BE12–10   Rosewater Corporation, a publicly traded company, reported a realized gain in the year ended April 30, 2015, on the sale of a long-term bond investment that was held to earn interest revenue. For the same year, the company also had an unrealized loss of $28,000 on its equity trading investments and $17,000 of revenue relating to its share of the profit of an associate. The accountant was not sure if these items should have been included in profit or in other comprehensive income. Identify whether each of the above items should be included in profit or OCI. Would your answer change if Rosewater made an election under IFRS to use fair value through OCI for the trading investments?

Prepare partial statement of financial position.
(SO 4)

BE12–11   Sabre Corporation, which reports under IFRS, has the following investments at December 31, 2015:

1. Trading investments: common shares of National Bank, cost $25,000, fair value $29,000.
2. Investment in an associate (40% ownership): common shares of Sword Corp., cost $110,000, fair value cannot be determined as the shares do not trade publicly. Investment was purchased on January 1, 2015. For the year ended December 31, 2015, Sword Corp. reported profit of $25,000 and paid out dividends of $8,000.

3. Equity investment: common shares of Epee Inc. (18% ownership) purchased on July 1, 2015, cost $210,000, fair value at December 31, 2015, $275,000. Management intends to purchase more shares of Epee in two years. Epee earned $21,000 for the year ended December 31, 2015, and paid out dividends of $1,000, which were received at the end of each quarter in 2015.
4. Bond investment that is to be held to maturity: bonds of Ghoti Ltd., purchased at a cost equal to its maturity value of $160,000, fair value $172,000.

Prepare a partial statement of financial position for Sabre Corporation at December 31, 2015.

BE12–12 Brookfield Asset Management Inc., a publicly traded company, reported in its financial statements for the year ended December 31, 2012, the following information: purchases of investments in associates, $1,232 million; share of profit of associates, $1,243 million; dividends received from associates, $375 million; investment in associates at year end, $11,689 million. Explain how each of these amounts should be reported in Brookfield's financial statements.

Indicate statement presentation.
(SO 4)

*BE12–13 On June 30, $150,000 of five-year, 10% Orbite bonds are issued at $138,960 to yield a market interest rate of 12%. Interest is payable semi-annually each June 30 and December 31. (a) Record the purchase of these bonds on June 30 and the receipt of the first interest payment on December 31 on the books of the investor assuming the bonds are to be held to maturity. (b) Record the issue of the bonds on June 30 and the first interest payment on December 31 on the books of the investee (issuer).

Record bonds for investor and investee.
(SO 5)

Exercises

E12–1 Gleason Telecommunications Ltd. has several investments in debt and equity securities of other companies:

Classify investments.
(SO 1)

1. 15% of the common shares of Morrison Telecommunications Inc., with the intent of purchasing at least 10% more of the common shares because Gleason has already been allowed to appoint one of its executives to a seat on Morrison's board of directors
2. 100% of the 15-year bonds issued by Li Internet Ltd., intended to be held for 15 years
3. 95% of the common shares of Barlow Internet Services Inc.
4. 120-day treasury bills, purchased for interest income
5. 10% of the common shares of Talk to Us Ltd., to be sold if the share price increases

Instructions
Indicate whether each of the above investments is a (a) debt or equity investment, and (b) non-strategic or strategic investment.

E12–2 Kroshka Holdings Corporation has several investments in debt and equity securities of other companies:

Classify investments.
(SO 1, 4)

1. 10-year BCE bonds, intended to be held until the bonds mature
2. 10-year GE bonds, intended to be sold if interest rates go down
3. 5-year Government of Canada bonds, intended to be sold if cash is needed, which is likely
4. 180-day treasury bill
5. Bank of Montreal preferred shares, purchased for the dividend income
6. TMX common shares, purchased to sell in the near term at a profit. These shares are part of an investment portfolio that is actively traded.

Instructions
(a) Indicate whether each of the above investments is a non-strategic or strategic investment.
(b) For each investment that you classified as non-strategic in part (a), indicate whether it is a trading investment, an investment that will be held until maturity to earn interest, or an investment that does not relate to these two categories.
(c) Indicate whether each of the above investments would be classified as a current or non-current asset on Kroshka Holdings' statement of financial position.

E12–3 Matthews Ltd. purchased $700,000 of 10-year, 10% bonds on July 1, 2015, at 106.5 (this means 106.5% of maturity value). The purchase price was based on a market interest rate of 9%. Interest is received semi-annually on January 1 and July 1. The bonds were trading at 107 at December 31, 2015. Matthews intends to trade the bonds in the near future and is using the fair value through profit or loss model.

Record trading investment.
(SO 2)

Instructions
(a) Record the purchase of the bonds.
(b) Record any required adjusting journal entries at December 31.

Record trading
investment.
(SO 2)

E12–4   During the year ended December 31, 2015, McCormick Inc. had the following transactions for its trading investments:

Jan.	1	Purchased 2,000 Starr Corporation $5, preferred shares for $210,000 cash.
Apr.	1	Received quarterly cash dividend.
July	1	Received quarterly cash dividend.
	2	Sold 500 Starr shares for $57,000 cash.
Oct.	1	Received quarterly cash dividend.
Nov.	22	Starr declared the quarterly dividend on November 22, to preferred shareholders of record on December 15, payable on January 1.
Dec.	31	Starr's shares were trading at $115 per share.

Instructions
(a) Record the above transactions, using the fair value through profit or loss model.
(b) Prepare any required adjusting entries at December 31. If no adjusting entries are required, explain why.
(c) On February 15, 2016, McCormick sold 500 Starr shares for $117 per share. Record the sale of the shares.

Record trading
investments; indicate
statement presentation.
(SO 2, 4)

E12–5   At December 31, 2015, the trading investments for Yanik Inc. are as follows:

Security	Cost	Fair Value
A	$18,500	$21,000
B	12,500	14,000
C	21,000	19,000
Totals	$52,000	$54,000

Instructions
(a) Prepare the adjusting entry at December 31 to report the trading investment portfolio at fair value.
(b) Show the financial statement presentation of the trading investments and any related accounts at December 31, 2015.
(c) On March 22, 2016, Yanik sold security A for $22,000 cash. Record the sale of the security.

Record investments.
(SO 2, 3)

E12–6   Aurora Cosmetics Ltd. acquired 40% of Diner Corporation's 30,000 common shares for $16 per share on January 1, 2015. On June 15, Diner paid a cash dividend of $70,000 and Aurora received its share of the dividend on the same day. On December 31, Diner reported profit of $150,000 for the year. At December 31, Diner's shares were trading at $20 per share. Aurora accounts for this investment using the equity method.

Aurora Cosmetics also acquired 15% of the 200,000 common shares of Bell Fashion Ltd. for $28 per share on March 18, 2015. On June 30, Bell paid a $150,000 dividend. On December 31, Bell reported profit of $320,000 for the year. At December 31, Bell's shares were trading at $26 per share. Aurora intends to hold onto the Bell shares as a long-term investment for the dividend income. Aurora uses the fair value through profit or loss model for this investment.

Instructions
Record the above transactions for the year ended December 31, 2015.

Record strategic
investments.
(SO 3)

E12–7   Lovell Corporation purchased 200,000 of the 1 million common shares of Abacus Ltd. on October 1, 2015, at $2.50 per share. Near the end of the fourth quarter, Abacus declared and paid dividends on its common shares of $80,000. Lovell received its share of the dividends on December 29. Abacus also announced that it had profit for the quarter ending December 31, 2015, of $200,000.

Instructions
Record the journal entries that Lovell would make during the last quarter ending December 31, 2015, under the following assumptions:
(a) Lowell has significant influence over Abacus and uses the equity method to account for this investment.
(b) Lowell does not have significant influence over Abacus and uses the cost model to account for this investment.

Determine investment
account balances and
indicate statement
presentation.
(SO 2, 3, 4)

E12–8   Grimsby Holdings Ltd., a publicly traded company, has two portfolios of investments: trading investments using the fair value through profit or loss model and investments in associates using the equity method. Information regarding these two portfolios is shown below:

	Trading Investments	Investment in Associates
Balance, beginning of year	$100,000	$300,000
Purchases of investments during the year	30,000	40,000
Proceeds from sale of investments during the year	55,000	32,000
Realized gain (loss) on sale of investments	12,000	(10,000)
Dividends received	3,000	8,000
Share of associates' profit		43,000
Fair value of portfolio, end of year	94,000	350,000

Instructions

(a) Calculate the ending balance for each investment category at the end of the year.

(b) Record the journal entries for each event described in the table above.

(c) Present the amounts that would be reported on the income statement and statement of financial position at year end.

E12–9   Cameco Corp., a publicly traded company and the world's largest producer of uranium concentrates, has several long-term investments, including a 100% investment in Cameco Europe, a 23.3% investment in UEX Corporation (a publicly traded company that Cameco does not want to trade), and a 24% interest in GE-Hitachi Global Laser Enrichment LLC (a private corporation with no determinable fair value that Cameco does not wish to trade).

Identify method of accounting for strategic investments under IFRS.
(SO 4)

Instructions

(a) Indicate whether each of the above investments should be accounted for using the cost model, the fair value through profit or loss model, or the equity method, and explain why.

(b) Which of the above investments, if any, should be consolidated with Cameco's operations?

*E12–10   On June 30, 2015, Imperial Inc. purchased $500,000 of Acme Corp. 5% bonds at a price to yield a market interest rate of 6%. The bonds pay interest semi-annually on June 30 and December 31, and mature on June 30, 2025. Imperial plans to hold this investment until it matures. At December 31, 2015, which is the year end for both companies, the bonds were trading at 93 (this means 93% of maturity value).

Record bonds for investor and investee.
(SO 5)

Instructions

(a) Calculate the present value (issue price) of the bonds on June 30, 2015.

(b) For Imperial, the investor, record

    1. the purchase of the bonds on June 30, 2015,

    2. the receipt of interest on December 31, 2015, and

    3. the receipt of interest on June 30, 2016.

(c) For Acme, the investee (issuer), record

    1. the issue of the bonds on June 30, 2015,

    2. the payment of interest on December 31, 2015, and

    3. the payment of interest on June 30, 2016.

(d) Explain how your responses to parts (a) and (b) would differ if Imperial classified the bond investment as a trading investment instead of one that would be held until maturity.

Problems: Set A

P12–1A   The following Givarz Corporation transactions are for bonds that were purchased as trading investments for the year ended December 31, 2015:

Record trading investments; show statement presentation.
(SO 2, 4)

Feb.	1	Purchased $100,000 of Leslye Corporation 9% bonds at 104 (this means 104% of maturity value). Interest is received semi-annually on August 1 and February 1. The bonds mature on February 1, 2017.
Aug.	1	Received interest on Leslye bonds.
	2	Sold $40,000 of the Leslye bonds at 102.
Dec. 31		Accrued interest on the remaining bonds.
	31	The fair value of the remaining bonds was 100 on this date.

Instructions

(a) Record the above transactions, using the fair value through profit or loss model including required adjusting entries (if any).

(b) Show how the investments would be presented on the statement of financial position at December 31, 2015.

(c) Determine the balance in each of the income statement accounts that are affected in the transactions above and indicate how they would be presented on the income statement for the year ended December 31, 2015.

P12–2A   During 2015, Kakisa Financial Corporation had the following trading investment transactions:

Record trading investments; show statement presentation.
(SO 2, 4)

Feb.	1	Purchased 600 CBF common shares for $36,000.
Mar.	1	Purchased 800 RSD common shares for $24,000.
Apr.	1	Purchased 7% MRT bonds at face value, for $60,000. Interest is received semi-annually on April 1 and October 1.
July	1	Received a cash dividend of $3 per share on the CBF common shares.
Aug.	1	Sold 200 CBF common shares at $58 per share.
Sept.	1	Received a cash dividend of $1.50 per share on the RSD common shares.
Oct.	1	Received the semi-annual interest on the MRT bonds.
	1	Sold the MRT bonds for $62,000.
Dec. 31		The market prices of the CBF and RSD common shares were $55 and $31 per share, respectively.

Instructions

(a) Record the above transactions, including any required adjusting entries, using the fair value through profit or loss model.

(b) Show how the investments would be presented on the statement of financial position at December 31, 2015.

(c) Determine the balance in each of the income statement accounts that are affected in the transactions above and indicate how they would be presented on the income statement for the year ended December 31, 2015.

Record trading investments; show statement presentation.
(SO 2, 4)

P12–3A   Data for Kakisa Financial's trading investments in 2015 are presented in P12–2A. Kakisa had the following trading investment transactions in 2016:

Mar. 1   Sold 400 CBF common shares for $23,600.

June 1   Purchased 2,000 KEF common shares for $28,000.

Sept. 1   Received a cash dividend of $1.50 per share on the RSD common shares.

Oct. 1   Sold 400 RSD common shares for $12,500.

Dec. 1   The market prices of the RSD and KEF common shares were $33 and $11 per share, respectively.

Instructions

(a) Record the above transactions including any required adjusting entries, continuing the use of the fair value through profit or loss model.

(b) Show how the investments would be presented on the statement of financial position at December 31, 2016.

(c) Determine the balance in each of the income statement accounts that are affected in the transactions above and indicate how they would be presented on the income statement for the year ended December 31, 2016.

Determine valuation of investments; indicate statement presentation.
(SO 2, 4)

P12–4A   On December 31, 2015, Val d'Or Ltée held the following debt and equity investments:

	Quantity	Cost per Unit	Fair Value per Unit
Debt Securities			
Dominion bonds	2,000	$100	$ 97
Government of Canada bonds	1,000	100	135
Equity Securities			
Bank of Calgary	2,000	55	61
Matco Inc.	5,000	29	32
Argenta Corp.	5,000	36	40

Instructions

(a) Calculate the cost and fair value of Val d'Or's investment portfolio at December 31.

(b) If Val d'Or considers its entire portfolio to be trading investments, at what value should the investments be reported on the statement of financial position at December 31 if it uses the fair value through profit or loss model? At what amount, and where, should any unrealized gains or losses on the debt securities be reported?

(c) If Val d'Or intends to hold the debt securities until maturity and uses the amortized cost model, at what value should the debt investments be reported on the statement of financial position at December 31? At what amount, and where, should any unrealized gains or losses be reported?

(d) If all of the investments held by Val d'Or related to private companies and no fair value information relating to these securities could be obtained, what would be the impact on the income statement and on the statement of financial position?

Identify impact of investment transactions.
(SO 2, 3, 4)

P12–5A   Lai Inc. had the following investment transactions:

1. Purchased Chang Corporation preferred shares as a trading investment and accounts for them using the fair value through profit or loss model.

2. Received a cash dividend on the Chang preferred shares.

3. Purchased Government of Canada bonds for cash, intending to hold them until maturity and account for them using the amortized cost model.

4. Accrued interest on the Government of Canada bonds.

5. Sold half of the Chang preferred shares at a price less than originally paid.

6. On the first day of the year, purchased 25% of Xing Ltd.'s common shares, which was enough to achieve significant influence and account for the investment using the equity method.

7. Received Xing's financial statements, which reported a net loss for the year.

8. Received a cash dividend from Xing.

9. The fair value of Chang's preferred shares was lower than cost at year end.

10. The fair value of the Government of Canada bonds was higher than amortized cost at year end and the fair value of Xing Ltd.'s common shares is unknown.

Instructions

(a) Using the following table format, indicate whether each of the above transactions would result in an increase (+), a decrease (−), or have no effect (NE) on the specific element in the statement. The first one has been done for you as an example.

Statement of Financial Position			Income Statement		
Assets	Liabilities	Shareholders' Equity	Revenues and Gains	Expenses and Losses	Profit
1. (+/−) NE	NE	NE	NE	NE	NE

(b) If the company were reporting under IFRS, would any alternative(s) to the models chosen be allowed? Explain.

(c) If the company were reporting under ASPE, would any alternative(s) to the models that were initially chosen be allowed? Explain.

P12–6A Drummond Services Ltd. acquired 25% of the common shares of Bella Roma Ltd. on January 1, 2015, by paying $1.8 million for 100,000 shares. Bella Roma paid a $0.50-per-share cash dividend in each quarter that was received on March 15, June 15, September 15, and December 15. Bella Roma reported profit of $1.1 million for the year. At December 31, the market price of the Bella Roma shares was $17 per share.

Record strategic investment.
(SO 2, 3, 4)

Instructions

(a) Prepare the journal entries for Drummond Services for 2015, assuming Drummond cannot exercise significant influence over Bella Roma and uses the fair value through profit or loss model.

(b) Prepare the journal entries for Drummond Services for 2015, assuming Drummond can exercise significant influence over Bella Roma and uses the equity method.

(c) What factors help determine whether a company has significant influence over another company?

(d) Prepare the journal entries for Drummond Services for 2015, assuming that the company reports under ASPE and has chosen to account for its investment using the cost model.

(e) Under ASPE, why do you think companies can choose to use the cost model?

(f) For parts (a), (b), and (d) above, track the movement in all accounts affected by this investment throughout 2015 in columnar format, showing the balance in the accounts at the beginning of the year and the amount of each transaction affecting the accounts during the year to arrive at the balance in the accounts at the end of the year.

P12–7A Hat Limited has a total of 200,000 common shares issued. On October 3, 2014, CT Inc. purchased a block of these shares in the open market at $50 per share to hold as a long-term equity investment. Hat reported profit of $575,000 for the year ended September 30, 2015, and CT received a $0.25-per-share dividend on that date. Hat's shares were trading at $53 per share at September 30, 2015.

This problem assumes three independent situations related to the accounting for this investment by CT:

Record investments; indicate statement presentation.
(SO 2, 3, 4)

Situation 1: CT purchased 25,000 Hat common shares.
Situation 2: CT purchased 70,000 Hat common shares.
Situation 3: CT purchased 200,000 Hat common shares.

Instructions

(a) For situation 1, is it likely that significant influence has been achieved? If it has not been achieved, record all journal entries relating to the investment for the year ended September 30, 2015, using the fair value through profit or loss model. If significant influence is met, use the equity method to record these transactions. Track the movement throughout the year in the investment account and any related investment revenue accounts in columnar format beginning with the balance in these accounts at the beginning of the fiscal year and then listing transactions relating to these accounts to arrive at the balance in these accounts at the end of the fiscal year.

(b) For situation 2, is it likely that significant influence has been achieved? If it has not been achieved, record all journal entries relating to the investment for the year ended September 30, 2015, using the fair value through profit or loss model. If significant influence is met, use the equity method to record these transactions. Track the movement throughout the year in the investment account and any related investment revenue accounts in columnar format beginning with the balance in these accounts at the beginning of the fiscal year and then listing transactions relating to these accounts to arrive at the balance in these accounts at the end of the fiscal year.

(c) When significant influence is achieved, does the investment have to be accounted for using the equity method if the investor is reporting under IFRS? Does this change if the investor is reporting under ASPE?

(d) For situation 3, is consolidation required? Why or why not? Do options to consolidation exist under IFRS? Do options exist under ASPE?

(e) What does consolidation mean? What happens to the investment account when consolidation occurs? Whose name will be on the consolidated financial statements?

(f) What accounting models would most likely be used for each of the situations listed above if CT Inc. reported under ASPE and the fair value of the Hat shares was unknown?

Analyze strategic
investment.
(SO 2, 3, 4)

P12–8A Sandhu Travel Agency Ltd. has 400,000 common shares authorized and 120,000 shares issued on December 31, 2014. On January 2, 2015, Kang Inc. purchased shares of Sandhu Travel Agency for $40 per share. Kang intends to hold these shares as a long-term investment.

Kang's accountant prepared a trial balance as at December 31, 2015, under the assumption that Kang could not exercise significant influence over Sandhu Travel Agency. Under this assumption, the trial balance included the following accounts and amounts related to the Sandhu investment:

Long-term investment	$1,320,000
Dividend revenue	90,000
Unrealized gain on long-term investment	120,000

Instructions

(a) How many shares of Sandhu Travel Agency did Kang purchase on January 2? (*Hint:* Subtract the unrealized gain from the investment account.)

(b) What percentage of Sandhu Travel Agency's shares does Kang own?

(c) What was the amount of the cash dividend per share that Kang received from Sandhu Travel Agency in 2015?

(d) What was the fair value per share of the Sandhu Travel Agency shares at December 31, 2015?

(e) Assume that, after closely examining the situation, Kang's auditors determine that Kang does have significant influence over Sandhu Travel Agency and the equity method should be used. Accordingly, the investment account balance is adjusted to $1.4 million at December 31, 2015. What was the profit reported by Sandhu Travel Agency for the year ended December 31, 2015?

(f) Assuming that Kang does use the equity method, what amount will Kang report on its income statement for 2015 with regard to this investment?

(g) How would your answer to part (f) change if Kang reported under ASPE and chose to use the cost model when accounting for its investment in Sandhu because the shares did not trade in an active market?

Record bond investment;
show statement
presentation.
(SO 5)

*P12–9A On January 1, 2015, Jackson Corp. purchased $1.6 million of 10-year, 7% bonds for $1,658,157. The purchase price was based on a market interest rate of 6.5%. Interest is received semi-annually on July 1 and January 1. Jackson's year end is September 30. Jackson intends to hold the bonds until January 1, 2025, the date the bonds mature. The bonds' trading value was $1,660,000 on September 30, 2015.

Instructions

(a) Record the purchase of the bonds on January 1, 2015.

(b) Prepare a bond amortization schedule for the term of the bonds.

(c) Prepare the entry to record the receipt of interest on July 1, 2015.

(d) Prepare any adjusting entries required at September 30, 2015.

(e) Prepare the entry to record the repayment of the bonds on January 1, 2025.

(f) Show the financial statement presentation of the bonds at September 30, 2015.

Record bonds for
investor and investee.
(SO 5)

*P12–10A The following bond transactions occurred during 2015 for the University of Higher Learning (UHL) and Otutye Ltd.:

Feb. 1 UHL issued $10 million of five-year, 8% bonds at 98 (this means 98% of maturity value). The bonds pay interest semi-annually on August 1 and February 1 and were sold at a discount because the market interest rate was 8.5%.

   1 Otutye Ltd. purchased $3 million of UHL's bonds at 98 as a long-term investment that was to be held to maturity.

Aug. 1 The semi-annual interest on the bonds was paid.

   1 After paying the semi-annual interest on the bonds on this date, UHL decided to repurchase $3 million of its bonds and retire them. UHL repurchased all $3 million of the bonds from Otutye at 99.

Instructions

(a) Prepare all required journal entries for Otutye Ltd., the investor, to record the above transactions.

(b) How would the journal entries for Otutye Ltd. change if the investment had been purchased for trading purposes?

(c) Prepare all required entries for UHL, the investee, to record the above transactions.

(d) Comment on the differences in recording that you observe between the investor and the investee.

Problems: Set B

P12–1B The following Liu Corporation transactions are for bonds that were purchased as trading investments for the year ended December 31, 2015:

Record trading investments; show statement presentation. (SO 2, 4)

Jan.	1	Purchased $100,000 of RAM Corporation 8% bonds at 96 (this means 96% of maturity value). Interest is received semi-annually on July 1 and January 1. The bonds mature on January 1, 2017.
July	1	Received interest on the RAM bonds.
	2	Sold $25,000 of RAM bonds at 100.
Dec.	31	Accrued interest on the remaining bonds.
	31	The fair value of the remaining bonds was 101 on this date.

Instructions
(a) Record the above transactions, including any required adjusting entries, using the fair value through profit or loss model.
(b) Show how the investments would be presented on the statement of financial position at December 31, 2015.
(c) Determine the balance in each of the income statement accounts that are affected in the transactions above and indicate how they would be presented on the income statement for the year ended December 31, 2015.

P12–2B During 2015, Cheque Mart Ltd. had the following trading investment transactions:

Record trading investments; show statement presentation. (SO 2, 4)

Feb.	1	Purchased 1,000 IBF common shares for $30,000.
Mar.	1	Purchased 500 RST common shares for $29,000.
Apr.	1	Purchased 6% CRT bonds at face value, for $90,000. Interest is received semi-annually on April 1 and October 1.
July	1	Received a cash dividend of $2 per share on the IBF common shares.
Aug.	1	Sold 350 IBF common shares at $33 per share.
Sept.	1	Received a cash dividend of $1.50 per share on the RST common shares.
Oct.	1	Received the semi-annual interest on the CRT bonds.
	1	Sold the CRT bonds for $86,000.
Dec.	31	The market prices of the IBF and RST common shares were $28 and $62 per share, respectively.

Instructions
(a) Record the above transactions, including any required adjusting entries, using the fair value through profit or loss model.
(b) Show how the investments would be presented on the statement of financial position at December 31, 2015.
(c) Determine the balance in each of the income statement accounts that are affected in the transactions above and indicate how they would be presented on the income statement for the year ended December 31, 2015.

P12–3B Data for Cheque Mart's trading investments in 2015 are presented in P12–2B. Cheque Mart had the following trading investment transactions in 2016:

Record trading investments; show statement presentation. (SO 2, 4)

Mar.	1	Sold 650 IBF common shares for $22,100.
June	1	Purchased 2,000 DEF common shares for $18,000.
Sept.	1	Received a cash dividend of $1.50 per share on the RST common shares.
Oct.	1	Sold 250 RST common shares for $14,250.
Dec.	31	The market prices of the RST and DEF common shares were $56 and $12 per share, respectively.

Instructions
(a) Record the above transactions, including any required adjusting journal entries, continuing the use of the fair value through profit or loss model.
(b) Show how the investments would be presented on the statement of financial position at December 31, 2016.
(c) Determine the balance in each of the income statement accounts that are affected in the transactions above and indicate how they would be presented on the income statement for the year ended December 31, 2016.

P12–4B On January 1, 2015, Sturge Enterprises Inc. held the following debt and equity investments:

Determine valuation of investments; indicate statement presentation. (SO 2, 4)

Security	Quantity	Cost per Unit
Ajax Ltd. shares	1,500	$12
Beta Corp. shares	2,000	7

During the year, Sturge made the following purchases:

Security	Quantity	Cost per Unit
Ajax Ltd. shares	1,200	$ 11
Ajax Ltd. shares	1,000	9
Ajax Ltd. shares	1,000	10
Beta Corp. shares	500	8
Citrus Inc. bonds	300	100

There were no differences between cost and fair value at January 1, 2015. The market prices of the various securities at year end, December 31, 2015, were as follows: Ajax shares $6; Beta shares $9; and Citrus bonds $107 (this means 107% of maturity value).

Instructions
(a) Calculate the cost and fair value of Sturge Enterprises' investment portfolio at December 31.
(b) If Sturge Enterprises considers its entire portfolio to be trading investments and uses the fair value through profit or loss model, at what value should these investments be reported on the statement of financial position at December 31? At what amount, and where, should any unrealized gains or losses be reported?
(c) If Sturge Enterprises intends to hold the Citrus bonds until they mature and uses the amortized cost model, at what value should these bonds be reported on the statement of financial position at December 31? At what amount, and where, should any unrealized gains or losses on the bonds be reported?
(d) If all of the investments held by Sturge Enterprises related to private companies and no fair value information related to these securities could be obtained, what would be the impact on the income statement and on the statement of financial position?

Identify impact of investment transactions.
(SO 2, 3, 4)

P12–5B   Olsztyn Inc. had the following investment transactions:

1. Purchased Arichat Corporation common shares as a trading investment and accounts for them using the fair value through profit or loss model.
2. Received a cash dividend on Arichat common shares.
3. Purchased Bombardier bonds intending to hold them to maturity and account for them using the amortized cost model.
4. Received interest on Bombardier bonds.
5. Sold half of the Bombardier bonds at a price greater than originally paid.
6. On the first day of the year, purchased 40% of LaHave Ltd.'s common shares, which was enough to achieve significant influence and account for the investment using the equity method.
7. Received LaHave's financial statements, which reported profit for the year.
8. Received a cash dividend from LaHave.
9. The fair value of Arichat's common shares was higher than cost at year end.
10. The fair value of Bombardier's bonds was lower than their amortized cost at year end and the fair value of LaHave Ltd.'s common shares is unknown.

Instructions
(a) Using the following table format, indicate whether each of the above transactions would result in an increase (+), a decrease (−), or have no effect (NE) on the specific element on the statement. The first one has been done for you as an example.

Statement of Financial Position			Income Statement		
Assets	Liabilities	Shareholders' Equity	Revenues and Gains	Expenses and Losses	Profit
1. (+/−) NE	NE	NE	NE	NE	NE

(b) If the company were reporting under IFRS, would any alternative(s) to the models chosen above be allowed? Explain.
(c) If the company were reporting under ASPE, would any alternative(s) to the models that were initially chosen be allowed? Explain.

Record strategic investment.
(SO 2, 3, 4)

P12–6B   Cassidy Concrete Corp. acquired 20% of Enda Inc.'s common shares on January 1, 2015, by paying $3 million for 100,000 shares. Enda paid a $0.50-per-share cash dividend, which Cassidy received on June 30 and again on December 31. Enda reported profit of $1,680,000 for the year. At December 31, the market price of the Enda shares was $31 per share.

Instructions

(a) Prepare the journal entries for Cassidy Concrete for 2015, assuming Cassidy cannot exercise significant influence over Enda and uses the fair value through profit or loss model.

(b) Prepare the journal entries for Cassidy Concrete for 2015, assuming Cassidy can exercise significant influence over Enda and uses the equity method.

(c) What factors help determine whether a company has significant influence over another company?

(d) Prepare the journal entries for Cassidy Concrete for 2015, assuming that the company reports under ASPE and has chosen to account for its investment using the cost model because the shares did not trade in an active market.

(e) Under ASPE, why do you think companies can choose to use the cost model?

(f) For parts (a), (b), and (d) above, track the movement in all accounts affected by this investment throughout 2015 in columnar format, showing the balance in the accounts at the beginning of the year and the amount of each transaction affecting the accounts during the year to arrive at the balance in the accounts at the end of the year.

P12–7B Sub Corporation has a total of 500,000 common shares issued. On January 2, 2015, Partridge Inc. purchased a block of these shares in the open market at $10 per share to hold as a long-term equity investment. At the end of 2015, Sub Corporation reported profit of $350,000 and Partridge received a $0.50-per-share dividend from Sub. Sub Corporation's shares were trading at $12 per share at December 31, 2015.

Record investment; indicate statement presentation. (SO 2, 3, 4)

This problem assumes three independent situations related to the accounting for this investment by Partridge:

Situation 1: Partridge purchased 60,000 Sub common shares.
Situation 2: Partridge purchased 125,000 Sub common shares.
Situation 3: Partridge purchased 500,000 Sub common shares.

Instructions

(a) For situation 1, is it likely that significant influence has been achieved? If it has not been achieved, record all journal entries relating to the investment for the year ended December 31, 2015, using the fair value through profit or loss model. If significant influence is met, use the equity method to record these transactions. Track the movement throughout the year in the investment account and any related investment revenue accounts in columnar format beginning with the balance in these accounts at the beginning of the fiscal year and then listing transactions relating to these accounts to arrive at the balance in these accounts at the end of the fiscal year.

(b) For situation 2, is it likely that significant influence has been achieved? If it has not been achieved, record all journal entries relating to the investment for the year ended December 31, 2015, using the fair value through profit or loss model. If significant influence is met, use the equity method to record these transactions. Track the movement throughout the year in the investment account and any related investment revenue accounts in columnar format beginning with the balance in these accounts at the beginning of the fiscal year and then listing transactions relating to these accounts to arrive at the balance in these accounts at the end of the fiscal year.

(c) When significant influence is achieved, does the investment have to be accounted for using the equity method if the investor is reporting under IFRS? Does this change if the investor is reporting under ASPE?

(d) For situation 3, is consolidation required? Why or why not? Do options to consolidation exist under IFRS? Do options exist under ASPE?

(e) What does consolidation mean? What happens to the investment account when consolidation occurs? Whose name will be on the consolidated financial statements?

(f) What accounting models would most likely be used for each of the situations listed above if Partridge Corporation reported under ASPE and the fair value of the Sub shares was unknown?

P12–8B On January 2, 2015, Hadley Inc. purchased shares of Letourneau Cycles Corp. for $10 per share. Hadley intends to hold these shares as a long-term investment. During 2015, Letourneau Cycles reported profit of $1 million and paid cash dividends of $200,000. The investment's fair value at December 31, 2015, was $950,000.

Analyze strategic investment. (SO 2, 3, 4)

Hadley's accountant prepared a trial balance as at December 31, 2015, under the assumption that Hadley should use the equity method because it could exercise significant influence over Letourneau Cycles. Under this assumption, the trial balance included the following accounts and amounts:

Investment in associates	$960,000
Investment revenue	200,000

Instructions

(a) What percentage of the Letourneau Cycles shares does Hadley own? (*Hint:* The ownership percentage can be determined using the investment revenue and Letourneau's profit.)

(b) What was the amount of the cash dividend that Hadley received from Letourneau Cycles during 2015?

(c) How many shares of Letourneau Cycles did Hadley purchase on January 2?

(d) What questions need to be asked to determine if Hadley has significant influence over Letourneau Cycles?

(e) Assume that, after closely examining the situation, Hadley's auditors determine that Hadley does not have significant influence over Letourneau Cycles. What amount should be reported on Hadley's statement of financial position at December 31 for its investment in Letourneau Cycles assuming that the fair value through profit and loss model was used? What will be reported on Hadley's income statement for 2015?

(f) How would your answer to part (e) change if Hadley reported under ASPE and chose to use the cost model when accounting for its investment in Letourneau assuming that the shares did not trade in an active market?

Record bond investment; show statement presentation.
(SO 5)

*P12–9B On January 1, 2015, Morissette Inc. purchased $800,000 of 10-year, 6% bonds for $770,921. The purchase price was based on a market interest rate of 6.5%. Interest is received semi-annually on July 1 and January 1. Morissette's year end is October 31. Morissette intends to hold the bonds until January 1, 2025, the date the bonds mature. The bonds' fair value on October 31, 2015, was $790,000.

Instructions

(a) Record the purchase of the bonds on January 1, 2015.

(b) Prepare a bond amortization schedule for the term of the bonds.

(c) Prepare the entry to record the receipt of interest on July 1, 2015.

(d) Prepare any adjusting entries required at October 31, 2015.

(e) Prepare the entry to record the repayment of the bonds on January 1, 2025.

(f) Show the financial statement presentation of the bonds at October 31, 2015.

Record bonds for investor and investee.
(SO 5)

*P12–10B On January 1, 2015, CASB Incorporated issued $1 million of 10-year, 8% bonds at 102 (this means 102% of maturity value). They were sold at a premium because the market interest rate was 7.7%. The bonds pay interest semi-annually on June 30 and December 31. On January 1, Densmore Consulting Ltd. purchased $200,000 of CASB bonds at 102 as a trading investment. On July 1, after receiving the bond interest, Densmore Consulting sold its CASB bonds at 103. Both companies have a December 31 year end.

Instructions

(a) Prepare all required entries for Densmore Consulting, the investor, to record the above transactions.

(b) How would the journal entries for Densmore Consulting change if the investment had been purchased with the intent of holding it to maturity?

(c) Prepare all required entries for CASB, the investee, to record the above transactions.

(d) Comment on the differences in recording that you observe between the investor and the investee.

Broadening Your Perspective

Financial Reporting: *Shoppers Drug Mart*

Identify investments.
(SO 1, 4)

BYP12–1 The financial statements of **Shoppers Drug Mart** are presented in Appendix A at the end of this textbook.

Instructions

(a) Does Shoppers Drug Mart report any investments on its statement of financial position? If so, are they debt or equity investments? Are they current or non-current?

(b) Does Shoppers Drug Mart report any investment income on its income statement? On its statement of comprehensive income? Indicate what type of investment income is reported, if any.

(c) Note 29 to the financial statements lists a number of subsidiaries owned by the company. Why aren't investment accounts relating to these subsidiaries shown on the statement of financial position?

(d) What section of the statement of cash flows would you look at to determine if investments were purchased or sold? In conjunction with this statement, also look at Note 8. When Shoppers Drug Mart acquired a business in 2012, did the company buy the shares of the business or did it acquire the business in another way?

Comparative Analysis: *Shoppers Drug Mart and Jean Coutu*

BYP12–2   The financial statements of **Jean Coutu** are presented in Appendix B, following the financial statements for **Shoppers Drug Mart** in Appendix A.

Compare investments.
(SO 1, 2, 3, 4)

Instructions

(a) Compare the statements of financial positions of the two companies. Which one tends to have more investments? What is the most common type of investment? What is the most likely reason for this?

(b) Compare the income statements of each company. How did each company's investments affect its income statement?

(c) In July 2013, it was announced that Loblaw Companies Ltd. was purchasing all of the shares of Shoppers Drug Mart. How do you think Loblaw will account for this investment?

Comparing IFRS and ASPE

BYP12–3   Two brothers, Adam and Robert Merkle, began A&R Plumbing Ltd. (ARP), a private company, approximately five years ago. Adam performs all administrative tasks (inventory ordering, accounting, payroll, and so on) while Robert provides the skills of the trade. In January 2015, ARP purchased 20,000 common shares of Canadian Plumbing Supplies Ltd (CPS). CPS is a plumbing supply distributor and its shares were acquired for $100,000. The shares represent a 20% ownership holding of CPS and the shares are traded actively on the Toronto Stock Exchange. Since the purchase, neither Adam nor Robert has been actively involved in any decisions related to CPS's operations. However, next year when Robert has more free time, he plans on using ARP's 20% share to obtain a seat on the CPS board of directors. He wants to use his board position to develop a referral system whereby CPS will refer customers to ARP for plumbing services. At the same time, he hopes to obtain additional financing from his bank to expand ARP further. The banker is very interested in ARP's profitability. At December 31, 2015, CPS's shares were trading for $4.50 each.

Compare strategic investment under IFRS and ASPE.
(SO 3, 4)

CPS's year end is December 31. For the year ended December 31, 2015, CPS reported a loss of $30,000. CPS did not declare any dividends. Adam had accounted for the investment in ARP using the cost model.

Instructions

(a) Robert has come to you, an independent public accountant, for advice. He would like you to assess the accounting choice that Adam has made for the investment in CPS.

   1. Describe the acceptable accounting policy choices available under ASPE to account for ARP's investment in CPS. Is the cost model an acceptable method under ASPE for this investment?

   2. Which accounting policy choice do you think Robert would prefer? Why?

(b) Explain how the accounting policy choices available to ARP for its investment in CPS might be different if it reported its financial results in accordance with IFRS.

Critical Thinking Case

BYP12–4   At the beginning of 2015, Bering Limited purchased three investments: Government of Alberta bonds, which are to be held to maturity; common shares in Atlas Inc., representing only 1% of the outstanding shares of this company, that are expected to be traded soon; and 40% of the common shares in CH Resources Ltd. The cost and the fair value at December 31, 2015, for each of these investments is shown below:

Choose models of accounting for investments.
(SO 2, 3, 4)

Security	Cost	Fair Value
Government of Alberta bonds	$100,000	$ 90,000
Atlas Inc. common shares	100,000	105,000
CH Resources Ltd. common shares	100,000	111,000

During 2015, interest revenue of $3,000 was earned and received on the Government of Alberta bonds and CH Resources Ltd., which had a profit in 2015 of $10,000, declared and paid dividends of $2,000 to all of its common shareholders. No dividends were received on the Atlas Inc. shares.

Instructions

(a) The board of directors of Bering Limited is considering the use of IFRS and is aware that there are choices that can be made when accounting for investments using these standards. The board would like you to choose the appropriate model for each type of investment that will maximize Bering's financial position and profitability and determine the amounts that would appear on the December 31, 2015, financial statements given these choices.

(b) Assuming that the company may prefer to use ASPE rather than IFRS, address the issues raised in part (a) above but do this in an ASPE context.

Ethics Case

Compare valuation
models; identify impact
on statements.
(SO 2, 3, 4)

BYP12–5 Kreiter Financial Services Ltd. recently purchased a portfolio of debt and equity securities. Financial vice-president Vicki Lemke and controller Ula Greenwood are in the process of classifying the securities in the portfolio.

Lemke suggests accounting for both debt and equity securities expected to increase in value during the year using the fair value through profit and loss model in order to increase profit. She wants to account for all securities that are expected to decline in value using the cost model for equity securities and the amortized cost model for debt securities so that no decline in the value of the investment will ever be shown.

Greenwood disagrees. She recommends accounting for all equity securities that are expected to increase in value using the equity method and using the amortized cost model for all debt securities and the cost model for equity securities expected to fall in value to avoid recording the decline. Greenwood argues that the fair value of an equity investment is more volatile and, if the equity method were used instead, there would be a "smoother" buildup in the value of the investment.

Instructions

(a) Prepare arguments against the position taken by Lemke. What flaws are there in her arguments? Are any of her proposals reasonable? Does she understand the implications that each method has for the financial statements?

(b) Prepare arguments against the position taken by Greenwood. What flaws are there in her arguments? Are any of her proposals reasonable? Does she understand the implications that each method has for the financial statements?

(c) Assume that Lemke and Greenwood classify the portfolio properly. If Kreiter sold all of its trading investments that had risen in value just prior to year end and sold all of its trading investments that declined in value immediately after year end, would these decisions allow the company to manipulate profit?

"All About You" Activity

Compare personal
savings options.
(SO 1)

BYP12–6   In this chapter, you learned that saving is an important part of personal financial planning and that without savings you cannot make investments. One way to invest your savings is to open a tax-free savings account (TFSA) and make a contribution. Let's assume that you have $5,000 to invest and are considering a high-interest savings account or a guaranteed investment certificate (GIC) to be placed in your TFSA.

Instructions

(a) Go to the website of your Canadian financial institution and find the current rates of return that each investment—a savings account or a GIC—is providing.

(b) If you invested the $5,000 in a savings account or a GIC, how much would each of these alternatives be worth after two years if the current rate of return continued? Assume that the contribution is made through monthly payments of $416.67.

(c) Assume that you continue to invest $5,000 every year for 40 years. What rate of return would you require to reach $1 million? How does this compare with the rate of return provided in a savings account or a GIC?

Hint: Use the investment savings calculator under Tools at www.ingdirect.ca or an equivalent site.

Serial Case

(*Note*: This is a continuation of the serial case from Chapters 1 through 11.)

Compare strategic
equity investments.
(SO 3)

BYP 12–7   The year ended June 30, 2016, has been another successful year for Koebel's Family Bakery Ltd. The success, however, has meant that Natalie, Daniel, Janet, and Brian have spent many long hours in the bakery accommodating their customers, both large and small. Janet and Brian have still not had time to enjoy any of their successes and are considering retiring from the bakery.

The Koebel family has come to know the executives at Biscuits, a public corporation, and Coffee Beans, a private corporation. Both of these organizations have been thrilled with the products that Koebel's Family Bakery has provided over the year. Frank Vosburgh, the president of Biscuits, wishes to strengthen the relationship between Koebel's Family Bakery and Biscuits. He recognizes that Janet and Brian are considering retirement. He has put forward an offer for Biscuits to purchase all of the shares that are currently held by the Koebel family. He has also guaranteed employment to both Natalie and Daniel for the next two years.

Bruce Anderson, the president of Coffee Beans, has found out about the offer put forward by Biscuits and is concerned that the great relationship he has developed with Koebel's Bakery will be not be maintained if Koebel's is taken over by Biscuits. As a result, he has also offered to purchase the shares held by Janet and Brian, leaving Natalie and Daniel with their 50% ownership interest and the responsibility for running the bakery. Natalie and Daniel would maintain control of the company. You will recall from Chapter 11 that 100 common shares are owned by each family member, for a total of 400 common shares.

Instructions

(a) If Biscuits were to succeed in the offer to purchase all of the outstanding shares of Koebel's Family Bakery Ltd., describe how this investment would be accounted for in the accounting records of Biscuits. Would a change in the manner in which Koebel's accounting records are maintained have to be undertaken? Why or why not?

(b) If Coffee Beans were to succeed in the offer to purchase Janet and Brian's shares (50%) of Koebel's Family Bakery Ltd., describe how this investment would be accounted for in the accounting records of Coffee Beans. Would a change in the manner in which Koebel's accounting records are maintained have to be undertaken? Why or why not?

(c) Identify some of the advantages and disadvantages to Janet, Brian, Natalie, and Daniel of each of these offers.

Answers to Self-Test Questions

1. a	2. d	3. a	4. b	5. a
6. c	7. b	8. c	9. a	10. d
*11. a	*12. c			

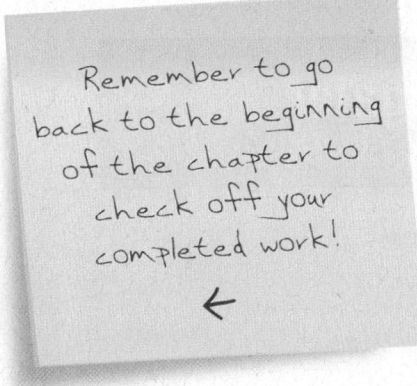

Remember to go back to the beginning of the chapter to check off your completed work! ←

Endnotes

[1]"Scotiabank Completes Acquisition of ING Bank of Canada (ING DIRECT)," Scotiabank news release, November 15, 2012; "Scotiabank Reaches Agreement to Acquire ING Bank of Canada and Announces Common Share Offering," Scotiabank news release, August 29, 2012; Sunny Freeman, "Scotiabank to Buy ING Bank of Canada for $3.13 Billion in Cash," Canada.com, August 29, 2012.

[2]Brent Jang and Jacquie McNish, "Activist Hedge Fund Takes Major Stake in CP Rail," *The Globe and Mail*, October 28, 2011; Susan Taylor and Allison Martell, "Pershing Presses for New CP Boss in Filing." *Reuters*, April 5, 2012; Steven Davidoff, "How Ackman Won in the Fight for Canadian Pacific," *New York Times*, May 17, 2012.

[3]Rob Carrick, *How Not to Move Back in With Your Parents*, Toronto: Doubleday Canada, 2012, p. 103; "BMO Household Savings Report: Canadians Plan to Boost Annual Savings in 2013 to $10,000," BMO news release, February 4, 2013; Melissa Leong, "Extreme Saving: Setting a Retirement Goal of Age 35," *Financial Post*, June 3, 2013.

The Navigator
Chapter 13

- ☐ Scan *Study Objectives*
- ☐ Read *Feature Story*
- ☐ Read text and answer *Do It!s*
- ☐ Review *Comparing IFRS and ASPE*
- ☐ Review *Summary of Study Objectives*
- ☐ Review *Decision Toolkit—A Summary*
- ☐ Work *Using the Decision Toolkit*
- ☐ Work *Comprehensive Do It!*
- ☐ Answer *Self-Test Questions*
- ☐ Complete *assignments*
- ☐ Go to *WileyPLUS* for practice and tutorials

the navigator

study objectives

After studying this chapter, you should be able to:

SO 1 Describe the purpose and content of the statement of cash flows.

SO 2 Prepare the operating activities section of a statement of cash flows using one of two approaches: (a) the indirect method or (b) the direct method.

SO 3 Prepare the investing activities section of a statement of cash flows.

SO 4 Prepare the financing activities section of a statement of cash flows.

SO 5 Complete the statement of cash flows.

SO 6 Use the statement of cash flows to evaluate a company's liquidity and solvency.

Cash Flow Can Be a Rocky Road

What a difference a few years can make! In 2006, metal prices were riding high, creating a swell of cash for mining companies like Teck Resources, headquartered in Vancouver. At the time Teck, a world leader in the production of zinc and metallurgical coal, as well as a significant producer of copper, gold, and specialty metals, was busy trying to decide how best to spend its money. It took part in a bidding war for Inco Ltd., which it lost, then invested a significant amount of cash in the purchase of Aur Resources Inc. in 2007. The first eight months of 2008 were also quite good for the company. In July, it announced plans to acquire the assets of the Fording Canadian Coal Trust, taking on $11.2 billion of debt to finance the acquisition. But by late 2008, the global financial crisis was in full swing, resulting in "unprecedented volatility for the world economy and for the mining sector," according to Don Lindsay, Teck President and CEO. Because of this, the timing of the Fording transaction created "very significant short-term challenges," Mr. Lindsay said.

During this economic turmoil in late 2008 and early 2009, Teck had to implement a multi-step program to manage its debt. This included suspending dividends, reducing planned capital expenditures, withdrawing from a copper project in Panama, reducing refined zinc production, selling its interest in a gold property in Chile, selling other assets, and reducing its global workforce by 13%.

Any free cash flow went toward servicing the company's debt. Teck was able to repay a bridge loan for the Fording project in July 2009 entirely from cash flow generated by its operating activities. By the end of 2009, Teck's cash flow had returned to 2006 levels at $5 billion.

Teck's financial position continued to be volatile in the following years. In 2010, stronger commodity markets resulted in a profit of $4.4 billion. The company reinstated its dividend and the major credit-rating agencies upgraded Teck's credit rating to "BBB"—an investment-grade rating—from what was previously considered to be a junk rating. In 2011, Teck saw record revenues and a record gross profit of $5.8 billion as there was strong demand for its products and it had good output from its mines and other facilities. The next year, though, several factors—including lower commodity prices (particularly for coal), a tough European economy, and slower growth in China—meant that Teck had lower earnings and cash flow, as did most other companies in that industry. Teck's 2012 gross profit fell to $4.0 billion.

With the global economy still uncertain in 2012, Teck continued to develop strategies to improve its financial position, including deferring about $1.5 billion in capital spending. It also retired the remaining portion of the high-yield debt it issued in 2009. Teck increased its dividend by 12.5% to $0.90 per share in 2012. The company planned to reduce operating costs by approximately $200 million in 2013 while meeting or exceeding its planned production for all operations. "This allows us to respond in the short term to changing market conditions while remaining poised for future growth," Mr. Lindsay told shareholders in Teck's 2012 annual report. Keeping a close eye on cash flow is key to Teck's future.[1]

the navigator

preview of CHAPTER **13**

The statement of financial position, income statement, statement of comprehensive income, and statement of changes in equity do not show the whole picture of a company's financial condition. In fact, looking at the financial statements of some organizations, a thoughtful investor might ask questions like these: How can a company purchase equipment in a year when it had no cash but only bank indebtedness? Why did the students' union at a university spend $632,000 of cash in a year in which it earned only $345,000? Where did Loblaw Companies Limited get the $12.4 billion to purchase Shoppers Drug Mart? This chapter presents the statement of cash flows, which answers these and similar questions.

The chapter is organized as follows:

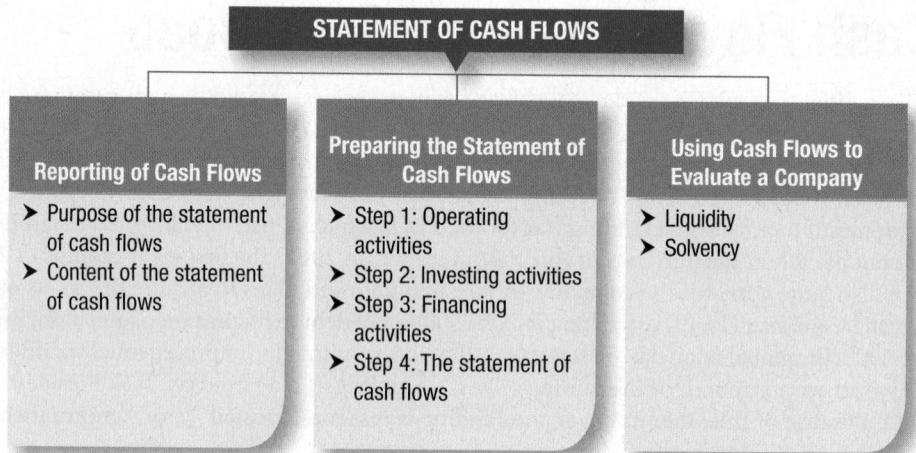

the navigator

Reporting of Cash Flows

STUDY OBJECTIVE 1
Describe the purpose and content of the statement of cash flows.

The financial statements that we have studied so far present only partial information about a company's cash flows because these statements are prepared on an accrual basis rather than a cash basis. For example, comparative statements of financial position show the increase in property, plant, and equipment during the year, but they do not show how the additions were financed or paid for. The income statement reports profit for the year, but it does not indicate the amount of cash generated or used by operating activities. The statement of changes in equity shows cash dividends declared, but not the cash dividends paid during the year.

As our chapter-opening feature story about Teck demonstrates, it is essential to understand a company's cash flows in order to determine its financial capabilities and options to wisely use (or obtain) cash. In order to do so, we will begin by examining the purpose and content of the statement of cash flows.

PURPOSE OF THE STATEMENT OF CASH FLOWS

Alternative Terminology
The *statement of cash flows* is also commonly known as the *cash flow statement.*

The main purpose of the statement of cash flows is to provide information that enables users to assess a company's ability to generate cash, and to assess what the company did with that cash. For example, a statement of cash flows, when used in conjunction with the other financial statements, provides information about a company's investing and financing activities that will enable users to evaluate the changes in a company's assets and liabilities and in its financial structure (including its liquidity and solvency). Cash flow information about historical events is also useful in assessing a company's ability to generate future cash flows. The statement of cash flows can also enhance the comparability of different companies because it eliminates the accrual-based effects of using different accounting treatments for similar transactions and events.

Because of the importance of this information to users, the statement of cash flows is a required financial statement for both publicly traded and private corporations.

CONTENT OF THE STATEMENT OF CASH FLOWS

Before we can prepare the statement of cash flows, we must first understand what it includes and why. We will begin by reviewing the definition of cash used in the statement of cash flows and then discuss how cash receipts and payments are classified within the statement.

Definition of Cash

The statement of cash flows is often prepared using **cash and cash equivalents** as its basis rather than just cash. You will recall from Chapter 7 that cash equivalents are short-term, highly liquid trading investments that are readily convertible to cash within a very short period of time. Generally, only debt investments due within three months qualify by this definition. Bank overdrafts that are repayable on demand are included in (deducted from) cash and cash equivalents.

Classification of Cash Flows

The statement of cash flows classifies cash receipts and cash payments into three types of activities: (1) operating, (2) investing, and (3) financing. The transactions that are found within each type of activity include the following:

1. **Operating activities** include a company's principal revenue-producing activities and all other activities that are not investing or financing activities. They arise from the cash effects of transactions that create revenues and expenses.
2. **Investing activities** include the acquisition and disposal of non-current assets. This would include (a) purchasing and disposing of long-lived assets and investments not held for trading and (b) lending money and collecting the loans.
3. **Financing activities** are those that result in changes in the size and composition of the equity and borrowings of a company. They include (a) obtaining cash from issuing debt and repaying the amounts borrowed and (b) obtaining cash from shareholders and paying dividends to them. Financing activities generally affect non-current liability and shareholders' equity accounts.

Illustration 13-1 lists typical cash receipts and cash payments in each of the three activities.

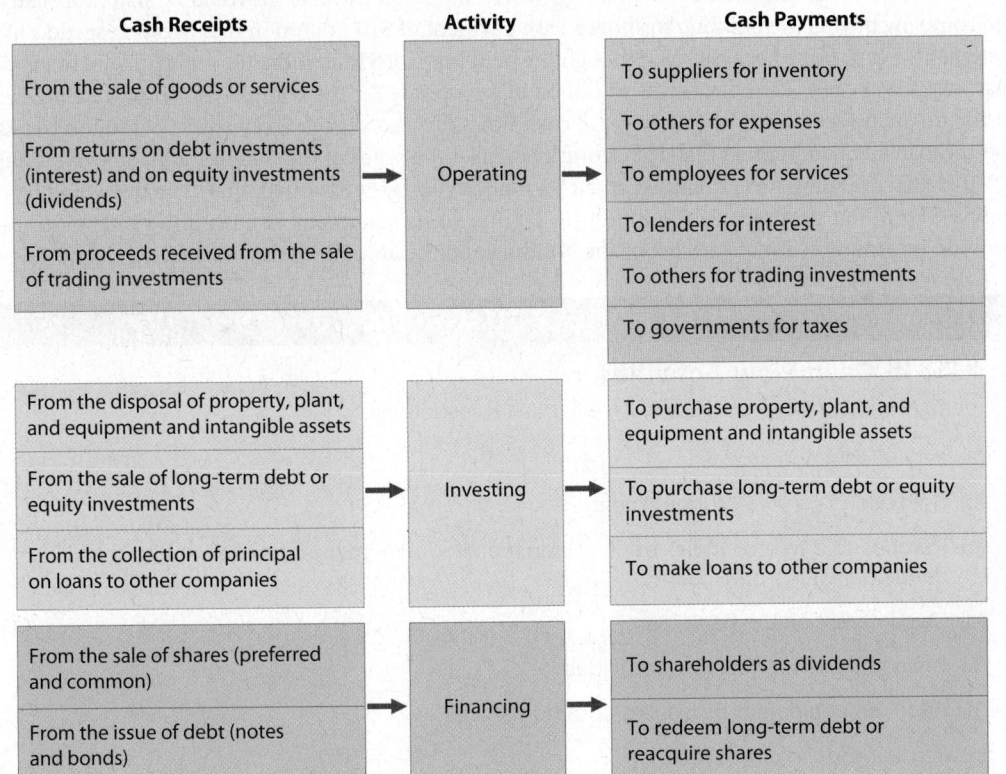

▶Illustration 13-1

Cash receipts and payments classified by activity

As you can see above, some cash flows that an average person may consider to be investing or financing activities are actually shown as operating activities. For example, receipts of investment revenue (interest and dividends) are classified in the above illustration as operating activities. So are payments of interest to lenders. Why are these considered operating activities? It is because these items are reported in the income statement where results of operations are shown.

 Private companies reporting under ASPE classify interest received and paid and dividends received as operating activities because they are shown on the income statement. Dividends paid, which are reported on the statement of changes in equity rather than in the income statement, are shown as financing activities. Companies reporting under IFRS, however, have more flexibility and can choose to show interest and dividends received and paid in more than one section of the statement of cash flows. For example, interest and dividends received may be classified as either an operating or investing activity. Interest and dividends paid may be classified as either an operating or financing activity. Once the choice is made, it must be applied consistently. Most North American companies, whether they follow IFRS or ASPE, will usually classify any dividends received or interest received or paid as operating activities. Because of this, this classification is the one illustrated above in Illustration 13-1 and the one we recommend you use when completing assignments in this text.

Significant Noncash Activities

It is important to recognize that not all of a company's significant investing and financing activities involve cash. Because of this, **significant investing and financing activities that do not affect cash are not reported in the body of the statement of cash flows**. However, because they are significant, details about these activities are disclosed in notes to the financial statements. These types of noncash investing and financing activities involve changes in non-current assets, non-current liabilities, and equity and include the following examples:

1. Issue of debt to purchase assets
2. Issue of shares to purchase assets
3. Conversion of debt into equity
4. Exchange of property, plant, and equipment

For example, assume that a building is purchased for $10 million. A $1-million down payment was paid in cash and the remainder was financed with a mortgage payable. It would be inappropriate for the company buying the building to show a cash payment of $10 million in the investing section of its statement of cash flows because, even though the building cost $10 million, the company did not spend that amount of cash. Furthermore, it would be inappropriate for the company to show a cash receipt in the financing section of its statement of cash flows for a mortgage received of $9 million because the company did not receive that cash from the bank—the seller of the building did. So even though a $10-million building was purchased and a $9-million mortgage assumed, the company would report only a $1-million payment in the investing section of its statement of cash flows but would also provide information about the cost of the building and the amount of the mortgage in its notes.

BEFORE YOU GO ON...

▶ Do It! Cash Flow Activities

Plano Moulding Corp. had the following cash transactions:

(a) Issued common shares.

(b) Sold a long-term debt investment.

(c) Purchased a tractor-trailer truck. Made a cash down payment and financed the remainder with a bank loan.

(d) Paid interest on the bank loan.

(e) Collected cash for services provided.

(f) Acquired equipment by issuing common shares.

(g) Paid salaries to employees.

Classify each of these transactions by type of cash flow activity. Indicate whether the transaction would be reported as a cash receipt or cash payment, or as a noncash activity.

Action Plan

- Report as operating activities the cash effects of transactions that create revenues and expenses and are used to determine profit.
- Report as investing activities the transactions that (a) acquire and dispose of long-lived assets, and (b) lend money and collect loans.
- Report as financing activities the transactions that (a) obtain cash by issuing debt or repay the amounts borrowed, and (b) obtain cash from shareholders or pay them dividends or amounts for the buyback of their shares.

Solution

(a) Financing activity, cash receipt

(b) Investing activity, cash receipt

(c) Investing activity, cash payment for down payment. The remainder is a noncash investing activity for the truck and a noncash financing activity for the bank loan payable that would be disclosed in a note

(d) Operating activity, cash payment

(e) Operating activity, cash receipt

(f) Noncash activity (noncash investing activity for equipment and noncash financing activity for common shares) so not shown on statement, just in a note

(g) Operating activity, cash payment

Related Exercise Material: BE13-1, BE13-2, BE13-3, E13-1, and E13-2.

Preparing the Statement of Cash Flows

We first introduced the statement of cash flows in Chapter 1. You will recall that the general format of the statement is as shown in Illustration 13-2.

The statement covers the same period of time as the income statement, statement of comprehensive income, and statement of changes in equity (such as for the year ended). Cash receipts and payments are reported in three separate sections: operating, investing, and financing. The section that reports cash flows from operating activities usually appears first. When we introduced the statement of cash flows in Chapter 1, we used the direct method of preparing the operating activities section for simplicity although we did not call it the "direct method" at the time. As we will learn,

▶Illustration 13-2

Format of the statement of cash flows

COMPANY NAME Statement of Cash Flows Period Covered		
Operating activities		
(Prepared using indirect or direct method)	XX	
Net cash provided (used) by operating activities		XXX
Investing activities		
(List of individual receipts and payments)	XX	
Net cash provided (used) by investing activities		XXX
Financing activities		
(List of individual receipts and payments)	XX	
Net cash provided (used) by financing activities		XXX
Net increase (decrease) in cash		XXX
Cash, beginning of period		XXX
Cash, end of period		XXX

there are two acceptable ways to prepare the operating activities section: the indirect method and the direct method.

The operating activities section is followed by the investing activities section and then the financing activities section. Each of these sections reports a subtotal showing net cash either provided from or used by each activity. These subtotals are totalled to determine the net increase or decrease in cash for the period. This amount is then added to (if a net increase) or subtracted from (if a net decrease) the beginning-of-period cash balance to obtain the end-of-period cash balance. The end-of-period cash balance should agree with the cash balance reported on the statement of financial position.

When we illustrated the statement of cash flows in Chapter 1, and in subsequent chapters, we did so without explaining how to prepare it. Let's return to basics now and learn how to prepare the statement of cash flows. Where do we find the information to prepare this statement?

There are no specific accounts in the general ledger for the types of operating activities, investing activities, or financing activities shown in Illustration 13-1. This is because the statement of cash flows is prepared differently from the other financial statements in that it is not prepared from an adjusted trial balance. The statement of cash flows requires detailed information about the changes in account balances that occurred over a period of time. An adjusted trial balance will not provide the necessary data. The information to prepare this statement usually comes from three sources:

1. The **comparative statement of financial position** is examined to determine the amounts of the changes in assets, liabilities, and shareholders' equity from the beginning of the period to its end.
2. The **income statement** and related noncash current asset and current liability accounts from the statement of financial position are used to determine the amount of cash provided or used by operating activities during the period.
3. **Additional information** includes transaction data that are needed to determine how cash was provided or used during the period. We will also use selected information from the statement of changes in equity to help us complete the statement of cash flows and the notes to the financial statements.

There are four steps to prepare the statement of cash flows from these data sources, as shown in Illustration 13-3.

▶Illustration 13-3

Steps in preparing the statement of cash flows

Step 1: Prepare operating activities section.
Determine the net cash provided (used) by operating activities by converting profit from an accrual basis to a cash basis. To do this, analyze the current year's income statement, relevant current asset and current liability accounts from the comparative statement of financial position, and selected information.

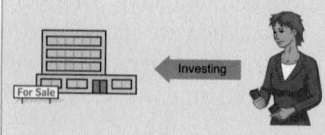

Step 2: Prepare investing activities section.
Determine the net cash provided (used) by investing activities by analyzing changes in non-current asset accounts from the comparative statement of financial position, and selected information.

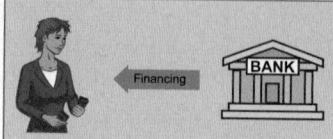

Step 3: Prepare financing activities section.
Determine the net cash provided (used) by financing activities by analyzing changes in non-current liability and equity accounts from the comparative statement of financial position, and selected information.

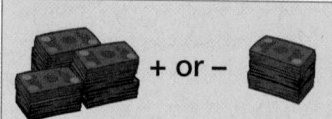

Step 4: Complete the statement of cash flows.
Determine the net increase (decrease) in cash. Compare the net change in cash reported on the statement of cash flows with the change in cash reported on the statement of financial position to make sure the amounts agree.

To explain and illustrate the preparation of a statement of cash flows, we will use financial information from Computer Services Corporation. Illustration 13-4 presents Computer Services' current- and previous-year statement of financial position, its current-year income statement, and related financial information.

COMPUTER SERVICES CORPORATION Statement of Financial Position December 31			
	2015	2014	Increase (Decrease)
Assets			
Current assets			
Cash	$ 55,000	$ 33,000	$ 22,000
Accounts receivable	20,000	30,000	(10,000)
Merchandise inventory	15,000	10,000	5,000
Prepaid expenses	5,000	1,000	4,000
Property, plant, and equipment			
Land	140,000	30,000	110,000
Building	160,000	40,000	120,000
Accumulated depreciation—building	(11,000)	(5,000)	6,000
Equipment	27,000	10,000	17,000
Accumulated depreciation—equipment	(3,000)	(1,000)	2,000
Total assets	$408,000	$148,000	
Liabilities and Shareholders' Equity			
Liabilities			
Current liabilities			
Accounts payable	28,000	$ 12,000	16,000
Income tax payable	6,000	8,000	(2,000)
Non-current liabilities			
Mortgage payable	130,000	20,000	110,000
Shareholders' equity			
Common shares	70,000	50,000	20,000
Retained earnings	164,000	48,000	116,000
Accumulated other comprehensive income	10,000	10,000	0
Total liabilities and shareholders' equity	$408,000	$148,000	

COMPUTER SERVICES CORPORATION Income Statement Year Ended December 31, 2015		
Sales revenue		$507,000
Cost of goods sold		150,000
Gross profit		357,000
Operating expenses		
Other operating expenses	$141,000	
Depreciation expense	9,000	
Loss on disposal of equipment	3,000	153,000
Profit from operations		204,000
Interest expense		12,000
Profit before income tax		192,000
Income tax expense		47,000
Profit		$145,000

Additional information for 2015:

1. The company uses a perpetual inventory system.
2. Assume that prepaid expenses relate to other operating expenses and accounts payable relate to purchases of merchandise inventory on account.
3. The company acquired land by obtaining a $110,000 mortgage from the bank.
4. Equipment costing $25,000 was purchased for cash.
5. The company sold equipment with a carrying amount of $7,000 (cost of $8,000, less accumulated depreciation of $1,000) for $4,000 cash.
6. Depreciation expense consists of $6,000 for the building and $3,000 for equipment.
7. The company paid a $29,000 cash dividend.
8. There was no other comprehensive income reported in 2015.

Before we even begin to prepare the statement of cash flows, we can determine what the company's cash flow for the year is by simply looking at how its cash and equivalents have changed during the year. For Computer Services Corporation, the cash flow for 2015 is $22,000 because cash increased from $33,000 to $55,000. If we know this, why don't we prepare the statement of cash flows by simply listing this single amount of $22,000? Because we need to know *why* the cash flow for the year is $22,000. Notice that if the change in the cash account was $22,000, the changes in all of the other accounts listed on the statement of financial position would also have to add up to $22,000. If we listed the changes in all of these accounts, other than cash, we would in essence be preparing a statement of cash flows, the total of which would be $22,000. By explaining the changes in all of these noncash accounts and then totalling them to equal $22,000, we will have in essence prepared a statement of cash flows.

We will now apply the four steps shown in Illustration 13-3 using the above information for Computer Services Corporation, starting with the operating activities section.

STEP 1: OPERATING ACTIVITIES

STUDY OBJECTIVE 2

Prepare the operating activities section of a statement of cash flows using one of two approaches: (a) the indirect method or (b) the direct method.

Determine the Net Cash Provided (Used) by Operating Activities by Converting Profit from an Accrual Basis to a Cash Basis

There are two ways to prepare the operating activity section of the statement of cash flows. One way is to use the **indirect method**, which converts total profit from an accrual basis to a cash basis. As mentioned earlier in this chapter, since operating cash flows are those that relate to revenue-producing activities, we could calculate operating cash flows by starting first with profit, because most revenues and expenses that generate profit will also generate operating cash flows. This is the approach taken with the indirect method. However, if we start our determination of operating cash flows with profit as we do under this method, we have to understand that the profit amount is flawed for two major reasons.

First of all, some items included in profit will not be received or paid in cash and should be completely excluded from our determination of operating cash flows. Consider these items: depreciation expense and gains and losses from the disposal of assets. Depreciation is not an expense that is paid; it is simply an allocation of the cost of an asset to periods of time over which the asset is used. The related asset may have been purchased years ago. Any cash paid at that time would have been shown as an investing activity payment. Likewise gains and losses from the disposal of an asset do not represent cash receipts but are simply the difference between the cash received from the disposal and the carrying amount of the asset. Like depreciation, these items should be excluded from the statement of cash flows even though they are part of profit.

Second, most amounts reported in profit were determined using accrual accounting concepts, not cash basis concepts. Because of this, many revenues and expenses on the income statement consist of two parts: one representing a cash flow and one representing a noncash event that changed the balance in a noncash current asset or current liability.

When the indirect method is used, we take profit and adjust it for depreciation, gains and losses, and changes in noncash current assets and current liabilities as described above. An alternative to the indirect method of presentation is the **direct method**. With this method, rather than listing profit and then adjusting it for noncash items, we simply make the operating section look like a cash basis income statement. It will therefore list first not revenues but cash from customers, followed not by expenses but cash paid for various operating activities.

To expand on the general format of the statement of cash flows shown in Illustration 13-2, the indirect and direct methods would look somewhat like the following:

Indirect Method			Direct Method		
Operating activities			Operating activities		
Profit		XX	Cash receipts from customers		XX
Adjustments to reconcile profit to net cash provided (used) by operating activities			Cash payments		
			To suppliers	XX	
(List of individual adjustments)	XX	XX	For operating expenses	XX	
Net cash provided (used) by operating activities			To employees	XX	
		XX	For interest	XX	
			For income tax	XX	XX
			Net cash provided (used) by operating activities		XX

While both the indirect and direct methods are acceptable choices to determine cash flows from operating activities, the direct method is preferred by standard setters. It is considered to be more informative for users and is easier to compare with other financial statements. Despite this preference, most companies use the indirect method because it is easier to prepare and reveals less company information to competitors. For example, more than 90% of international companies use the indirect method including Teck, which was introduced in our chapter-opening story.

On this and subsequent pages, in two separate sections, we describe the use of the two methods. Section 1 explains the indirect method. Section 2 explains the direct method. Both methods are included because they are acceptable choices for both publicly traded and private companies. These sections are independent of each other in case your instructor wishes to assign only one section. When you have finished the section(s) assigned by your instructor, turn to the next topic after these sections, "Step 2: Investing Activities."

Section 1: Indirect Method

To determine the net cash provided (used) by operating activities under the indirect method, profit is adjusted for items that did not affect cash. Illustration 13-5 shows three common types of adjustments that are made to adjust profit for items that affect accrual-based profit but do not affect cash. The first two types of adjustments—noncash expenses and revenues and losses and gains—are found on the income statement. The last type of adjustment—changes (increases or decreases) in certain current asset and current liability accounts—is found on the statement of financial position.

STUDY OBJECTIVE 2(a)

Prepare the operating activities section of the statement of cash flows using the indirect method.

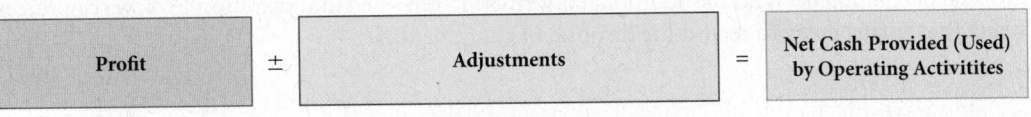

▶Illustration 13-5
Adjustments to convert profit to net cash provided (used) by operating activities

The next three sections explain each type of adjustment.

NONCASH EXPENSES AND REVENUES

The income statement includes expenses that do not use cash, such as depreciation and amortization expense. For example, Computer Services' income statement reports depreciation expense of $9,000. Although depreciation expense reduces profit, it does not reduce cash. Recall that the entry to record depreciation is:

This entry has no effect on cash, so although it reduced profit, it did not reduce cash. Since the indirect method starts with profit, depreciation expense is added back to profit in order to arrive at net cash provided (used) by operating activities. It is important to understand that depreciation expense is not added to operating activities as if it were a source of cash. As shown in the journal entry above, depreciation does not involve cash. It is simply added to profit to cancel out the effect it has on that amount.

The following is a partial operating activities section of the statement of cash flows for Computer Services. The addition of the noncash expense to profit is highlighted in red.

Operating activities	
Profit	$145,000
Adjustments to reconcile profit to net cash provided (used) by operating activities	
Depreciation expense	9,000

Similar to depreciation expense, amortization expense for intangible assets is also added to profit to arrive at net cash provided (used) by operating activities. Another example of a noncash expense is the amortization of bond discounts and premiums. Since this topic was covered in the appendices to Chapters 10 and 12, we will not cover them in this chapter.

LOSSES AND GAINS

Cash received from the disposal of long-lived assets should be reported in the investing activities section of the statement of cash flows. Since these cash receipts are recorded in the investing section, any amounts relating to the disposal of these assets must be excluded from other sections of the statement of cash flows. Since the operating section lists profit as its starting amount, all losses and gains from asset disposal must be eliminated from profit. To understand this more fully, we review the accounting for the disposal of property, plant, and equipment.

The disposal of property, plant, and equipment is recorded by (1) recognizing the cash proceeds that are received, (2) removing the asset and accumulated depreciation accounts from the books, and (3) recognizing any loss or gain on the disposal.

To illustrate, recall that Computer Services' income statement reported a $3,000 loss on the disposal of equipment. With the additional information provided in Illustration 13-4, we can reconstruct the journal entry to record the disposal of equipment:

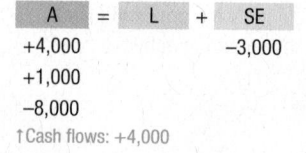

Cash	4,000	
Accumulated Depreciation	1,000	
Loss on Disposal	3,000	
Equipment		8,000

The cash proceeds of $4,000 that are received are not considered part of operating activities; rather, they are part of investing activities. Selling equipment is not part of the company's primary activities. **There is therefore no cash receipt (or payment) from operating activities.** Logically, then, to calculate the net cash provided (used) by operating activities, we have to eliminate the loss or gain on the disposal of an asset from profit.

To eliminate the $3,000 loss on the disposal of the equipment, we have to add the loss back to profit to cancel the original deduction made for this loss in the income statement. We can then arrive at net cash provided (used) by operating activities, as shown in the following partial statement of cash flows for Computer Services:

Operating activities	
Profit	$145,000
Adjustments to reconcile profit to net cash provided (used) by operating activities	
Depreciation expense	9,000
Loss on disposal of equipment	3,000

If a gain on disposal occurs, the gain is deducted from profit in order to determine net cash provided (used) by operating activities. For both a loss and a gain, the actual amount of cash received from the sale is reported as a cash receipt in the investing activities section of the statement of cash flows.

Gains and losses can arise in other circumstances and will always result in an adjustment to profit if the gain or loss was recorded in the income statement. Examples include unrealized gains and losses on investments that are recorded when the carrying amount of an investment is adjusted to fair value but it is not sold. Other examples include realized gains and losses on investments and the early settlement of debt. Again, these gains and losses, which would have been recorded on the income statement, would cause profit to be adjusted on the statement of cash flows.

CHANGES IN CURRENT ASSET AND CURRENT LIABILITY ACCOUNTS

Another type of adjustment in converting profit to net cash provided (used) by operating activities involves examining the changes (increases or decreases) in certain noncash current asset and current liability accounts, also known as noncash working capital accounts. You will recall that working capital is the difference between current assets and current liabilities.

Not all noncash working capital accounts affect operating activities, however. One such example is short-term loans or notes receivable that have been issued for lending purposes rather than for trade. The issue and repayment of loans or notes such as these are shown instead in the investing section of the statement of cash flows. Similarly, the receipt and repayment of short-term loans or notes payable that have been incurred for lending purposes rather than trade are shown in the financing section of the statement of cash flows. Furthermore, the declaration and payment of dividends affects the dividend payable account, but these activities are financing in nature rather than operating in nature.

So what types of noncash working capital accounts affect operating activities? In this course you will find that all of them—other than those referred to above relating to loans, notes, and dividends—will affect operating activities. As we discussed earlier, portions of some revenue and expense accounts arose not because of a cash transaction but because of noncash events such as a credit sale or the incurring of an expense on credit. Even though these events are reflected in the income statement, they do not affect cash. Instead they affect noncash working capital accounts, such as accounts receivable and accounts payable. To the extent that these balances exist, they pertain to the noncash portion of their related revenue and expense accounts and so they will be adjusted out of profit as we determine operating cash flows. On the other hand, some working capital accounts relating to prepayments, such as prepaid insurance and unearned revenue, are created when cash is paid or received, yet these operating cash receipts are not reflected in profit. To the extent that we have balances in these prepayment-related accounts, we need to reflect the related cash flow by adjusting profit for these items.

In addition, cash paid to purchase trading investments and cash received upon the sale of these investments would be considered operating activities.

Changes in Current Assets

We will analyze the changes in Computer Services' current asset accounts to determine each change's impact on profit and cash. The adjustments that are required for changes in noncash current asset accounts that affect operating activities are as follows: increases in current asset accounts are deducted from profit, and decreases in current asset accounts are added to profit, to arrive at net cash provided (used) by operating activities.

Accounts Receivable.   Computer Services' accounts receivable decreased by $10,000 (from $30,000 to $20,000) during the year. When accounts receivable decrease during the year, revenues on an accrual basis are lower than revenues on a cash basis. In other words, more cash was collected during the period than was recorded as revenue. For Computer Services, this means that cash receipts were $10,000 higher than revenues.

Illustration 13-4 shows that Computer Services had $507,000 in sales revenue reported on its income statement. To determine how much cash was collected in connection with this revenue, it is useful to analyze the Accounts Receivable account:

Accounts Receivable					
Jan.	1	Balance	30,000		
		Sales on account	507,000	Receipts from customers	517,000
Dec.	31	Balance	20,000		

$10,000 net decrease (add to profit)

If sales revenue (assumed to be sales on account) recorded during the period was $507,000 (Dr. Accounts Receivable; Cr. Sales Revenue), and the change in Accounts Receivable during the period was a decrease of $10,000, then cash receipts from customers must have been $517,000 (Dr. Cash; Cr. Accounts Receivable).

When we use the indirect method, we first list profit, which would include the $507,000 sales on account amount seen above. However, because the cash received from customers was actually

$10,000 higher than this—as indicated by the decrease in accounts receivable—this amount would have to be added to profit to determine net cash provided by operating cash flows.

What happens if accounts receivable increase rather than decrease? When the Accounts Receivable account increases during the year, this means that revenues on an accrual basis are higher than cash receipts. Therefore, the amount of the increase in accounts receivable is deducted from profit to arrive at net cash provided (used) by operating activities. Notice how an increase in an asset like accounts receivable results in a reduction to profit in arriving at net cash provided by operations. All increases to noncash current assets related to operating activities would have the same effect. Conversely, decreases in these assets would result in additions made to profit.

Merchandise Inventory.   Computer Services' merchandise inventory increased by $5,000 (from $10,000 to $15,000) during the year. When inventory increases during the year, the cost of goods purchased is greater than the cost of goods sold expense recorded in the income statement. In other words, Computer Services must have purchased $5,000 more inventory than it sold in order for inventory levels to increase. To determine how much cash it paid for merchandise purchases, it is useful to analyze the Merchandise Inventory account:

Merchandise Inventory					
Jan.	1	Balance	10,000		
		Purchases	155,000	Cost of goods sold	150,000
Dec.	31	Balance	15,000		

$5,000 net increase (deduct from profit)

In a perpetual inventory system, the Merchandise Inventory account is increased by the cost of goods purchased (debit Merchandise Inventory and credit Accounts Payable) and decreased by the cost of goods sold (debit Cost of Goods Sold and credit Merchandise Inventory). Because Computer Services reported $150,000 of cost of goods sold on its income statement (as shown in Illustration 13-4), purchases of merchandise during the year must have been $155,000.

To convert profit to net cash provided (used) by operating activities, the $5,000 increase in the Merchandise Inventory must be deducted from profit. As explained above, the increase in inventory means that the cash-based expense must be increased and we do this by deducting this increase from profit in arriving at net cash provided by operating activities.

The deduction of an increase in inventory from profit does not completely convert an accrual-based figure to a cash-based figure. It does not tell us how much cash was paid for the goods purchased. It just converts the cost of goods sold to the cost of goods purchased during the year. The analysis of accounts payable—shown later in this section—completes this analysis by converting the cost of goods purchased from an accrual basis to a cash basis.

Prepaid Expenses.   Computer Services' prepaid expenses increased by $4,000 (from $1,000 to $5,000) during the year. When prepaid expenses increase during the year, it means that these prepayments have reduced cash flows. It also means that expenses reported on the accrual-based income statement are lower than what expenses would be on a cash basis.

Computer Services' other operating expenses, other than its depreciation expense and loss from the disposal of equipment, have been combined in one summary account in Illustration 13-4. These other operating expenses would include administrative and selling expenses, among other types of expenses. To determine how much cash was paid relative to these expenses, the Prepaid Expenses account must be analyzed. Other operating expenses, as reported on the income statement, are $141,000. Accordingly, payments for expenses must have been $145,000:

Prepaid Expenses					
Jan.	1	Balance	1,000		
		Payments for expenses	145,000	Other operating expenses	141,000
Dec.	31	Balance	5,000		

$4,000 net increase (deduct from profit)

To adjust profit to net cash provided (used) by operating activities, the $4,000 increase in prepaid expenses must be deducted from profit to determine the cash paid for expenses.

If prepaid expenses decrease during the year, rather than increase, expenses reported on an accrual-based income statement would be higher than expenses on a cash basis. Decreases in prepaid expenses would be added to profit rather than deducted as we did above for an increase in prepaid expenses.

If Computer Services Corporation had any accrued liabilities, such as for property tax or utility bills, these would also have to be considered before we could completely determine the amount of cash paid for other operating expenses.

Changes in Current Liabilities

We will now look at the changes in Computer Services' current liability accounts to determine each change's impact on profit and cash. The adjustments that are required for changes in current liability accounts are as follows: increases in current liability accounts are added to profit. An increase in a liability means that the company has not paid it and this improves operating cash flows. Likewise, decreases in current liability accounts are deducted from profit, to arrive at net cash provided (used) by operating activities. A decrease in a liability means that it was paid down and this decreases operating cash flows.

Accounts Payable. In some companies, the Accounts Payable account is used only to record purchases of merchandise on account. Other payable accounts are used to record the credit entries for other expenditures made on account. In other companies, the Accounts Payable account is used to record all credit purchases. For simplicity in this chapter, we have assumed that Accounts Payable is used only to record purchases of merchandise on account.

Computer Services' accounts payable increased by $16,000 (from $12,000 to $28,000) during the year. When accounts payable increase during the year, expenses on an accrual basis are higher than expenses on a cash basis. For Computer Services, this means that it received $16,000 more in goods than it actually paid for.

To illustrate, recall that Computer Services' Accounts Payable account is increased by purchases of merchandise (Dr. Merchandise Inventory; Cr. Accounts Payable) and decreased by payments to suppliers (Dr. Accounts Payable; Cr. Cash). We determined the amount of purchases made by Computer Services in the analysis of the Merchandise Inventory account earlier: $155,000. Using this figure, we can now determine that payments to suppliers must have been $139,000.

Accounts Payable						
		Jan.	1	Balance	12,000	
Payments to suppliers	139,000			Purchases	155,000	$16,000 net increase (add to profit)
		Dec.	31	Balance	28,000	

To convert profit to net cash provided (used) by operating activities, the $16,000 increase in accounts payable must be added to profit. The increase in accounts payable means that less cash was paid for the purchases than was deducted in the accrual-based expenses section of the income statement. The addition of $16,000 completes the adjustment required to convert the cost of goods purchased to the cash paid for these goods.

Decreases in accounts payable mean that more cash was paid for purchases than recorded as an expense. As a result, decreases in accounts payable are deducted from profit.

In summary, the conversion of the cost of goods sold on the accrual-based income statement to the cash paid for goods purchased involves two steps: (1) The change in the Merchandise Inventory account adjusts the cost of goods sold to the accrual-based cost of goods purchased. (2) The change in the Accounts Payable account adjusts the accrual-based cost of goods purchased to the cash-based payments to suppliers.

Income Tax Payable. A change in the Income Tax Payable account reflects the difference between the income tax expense incurred and the income tax actually paid during the year.

Computer Services' Income Tax Payable account has decreased by $2,000 (from $8,000 to $6,000) during the year. This means that the $47,000 of income tax expense reported on the income statement in Illustration 13-4 was $2,000 less than the $49,000 of taxes paid during the period, as shown in the following T account:

	Income Tax Payable			
	Jan.	1	Balance	8,000
Payments for income tax 49,000			Income tax expense	47,000
	Dec.	31	Balance	6,000

$2,000 net decrease (deduct from profit)

To adjust profit to net cash provided (used) by operating activities, the $2,000 decrease in income tax payable must be deducted from profit. If the amount of income tax payable had increased during the year, the increase would be added to profit to reflect the fact that income tax expense deducted on the accrual-based income statement was higher than the cash paid during the period.

The partial statement of cash flows in Illustration 13-6 shows the impact on operating activities of the changes in the current asset and current liability accounts (the changes are highlighted in red). It also shows the adjustments that were described earlier for noncash expenses and revenues and losses and gains. The operating activities section of the statement of cash flows is now complete.

▶ Illustration 13-6

Net cash provided (used) by operating activities—indirect method

COMPUTER SERVICES CORPORATION		
Statement of Cash Flows—Indirect Method (partial)		
Year Ended December 31, 2015		
Operating activities		
Profit		$145,000
Adjustments to reconcile profit to net cash provided (used) by operating activities		
Depreciation expense	$ 9,000	
Loss on disposal of equipment	3,000	
Decrease in accounts receivable	10,000	
Increase in merchandise inventory	(5,000)	
Increase in prepaid expenses	(4,000)	
Increase in accounts payable	16,000	
Decrease in income tax payable	(2,000)	27,000
Net cash provided by operating activities		172,000

Helpful Hint
Whether the indirect or direct method is used, net cash provided (used) by operating activities will be the same.

In summary, the operating activities section of Computer Services' statement of cash flows shows that the accrual-based profit of $145,000 resulted in net cash provided by operating activities of $172,000, after adjustments for noncash items.

SUMMARY OF CONVERSION TO NET CASH PROVIDED (USED) BY OPERATING ACTIVITIES—INDIRECT METHOD

As shown in the previous pages, the statement of cash flows prepared by the indirect method starts with profit. It then adds or deducts items from profit to arrive at net cash provided (used) by operating activities. Selected adjustments to profit to determine cash provided (used) by operating activities are summarized here:

Noncash expenses	Depreciation expense (property and equipment)	Add
	Amortization expense (intangible assets)	Add

Losses and gains	Losses including impairment losses	Add
	Gains and reversal of impairment losses	Deduct
Changes in certain noncash current asset and current liability accounts	Increase in current asset account	Deduct
	Decrease in current asset account	Add
	Increase in current liability account	Add
	Decrease in current liability account	Deduct

BEFORE YOU GO ON...

▼

▶ Do It! Net Cash Provided (Used) by Operating Activities

Selected financial information follows for Denham Ltd. at December 31. Prepare the operating activities section of the statement of cash flows using the indirect method.

	2015	2014	Increase (Decrease)
Current assets			
Cash	$61,000	$37,000	$24,000
Accounts receivable	68,000	26,000	42,000
Merchandise inventory	54,000	10,000	44,000
Prepaid expenses	4,000	6,000	(2,000)
Current liabilities			
Accounts payable	35,000	55,000	(20,000)
Accrued liabilities	4,000	5,000	(1,000)
Salaries payable	6,000	4,000	2,000
Income tax payable	20,000	10,000	10,000

DENHAM LTD.
Income Statement
Year Ended December 31, 2015

Sales revenue		$890,000
Cost of goods sold		465,000
Gross profit		425,000
Operating expenses		
Salaries expense	$150,000	
Administrative expenses	46,000	
Depreciation expense	33,000	
Loss on disposal of equipment	4,000	233,000
Profit from operations		192,000
Other expenses and losses		
Interest expense		12,000
Profit before income tax		180,000
Income tax expense		36,000
Profit		$144,000

Action Plan

- Start with profit to determine the net cash provided (used) by operating activities.
- Examine the income statement: Add back noncash expenses and losses because although these items are included in profit, they have no effect on cash flows and must therefore be removed from our determination of cash flow. For the same reasons, we would deduct any gains recorded in profit.
- Analyze the noncash current assets and liabilities on the statement of financial position: Add decreases in related noncash current asset accounts and increases in related noncash current liability accounts. Deduct increases in related noncash current asset accounts and decreases in related noncash current liability accounts.

(continued)

Solution

DENHAM LTD. Statement of Cash Flows (partial) Year Ended December 31, 2015		
Operating activities		
Profit		$144,000
Adjustments to reconcile profit to net cash provided (used) by operating activities		
Depreciation expense	$33,000	
Loss on disposal of equipment	4,000	
Increase in accounts receivable	(42,000)	
Increase in merchandise inventory	(44,000)	
Decrease in prepaid expenses	2,000	
Decrease in accounts payable	(20,000)	
Decrease in accrued liabilities	(1,000)	
Increase in salaries payable	2,000	
Increase in income tax payable	10,000	(56,000)
Net cash provided by operating activities		88,000

Related Exercise Material: BE13-3, BE13-4, BE13-5, E13-3, E13-4, E13-5, E13-8, E13-9, E13-12, and E13-13.

Section 2: Direct Method

STUDY OBJECTIVE 2(b)

Prepare the operating activities section of the statement of cash flows using the direct method.

Similar to the indirect method, net cash provided (used) by operating activities using the direct method is determined by adjusting the income statement from the accrual basis of accounting to the cash basis of accounting. Whereas the indirect method adjusts total profit, the direct method adjusts each individual revenue and expense item in the income statement.

We will analyze the accrual-based revenues and expenses reported in Computer Services' income statement in the following sections. The cash receipts and cash payments that relate to these revenues and expenses will be determined by adjusting for changes (increases or decreases) in the related current asset and current liability accounts.

To simplify and condense the operating activities section, only major classes of operating cash receipts and cash payments are reported. The difference between the cash receipts and cash payments for these major classes is the net cash provided (used) by operating activities.

These relationships are shown in Illustration 13-7 on the following page.

CASH RECEIPTS

We will now look at Computer Services' cash receipts. Note that it has only one source of cash receipts: from the sale of goods to its customers.

Cash Receipts from Customers

The income statement shown in Illustration 13-4 for Computer Services reported sales revenue from customers of $507,000. How much of that was received in cash? To answer that, we need to look at the change in accounts receivable during the year.

Computer Services' accounts receivable decreased by $10,000 (from $30,000 to $20,000) during the year. When accounts receivable decrease during the year, this means that the company has collected more cash during the year than the amount of revenues earned. In this case, accrual-basis revenues are lower than cash-basis revenues. In other words, more cash was collected during the year than was recorded as revenue and this caused accounts receivable to decrease. To determine the amount of cash receipts, the decrease in accounts receivable is added to sales revenue.

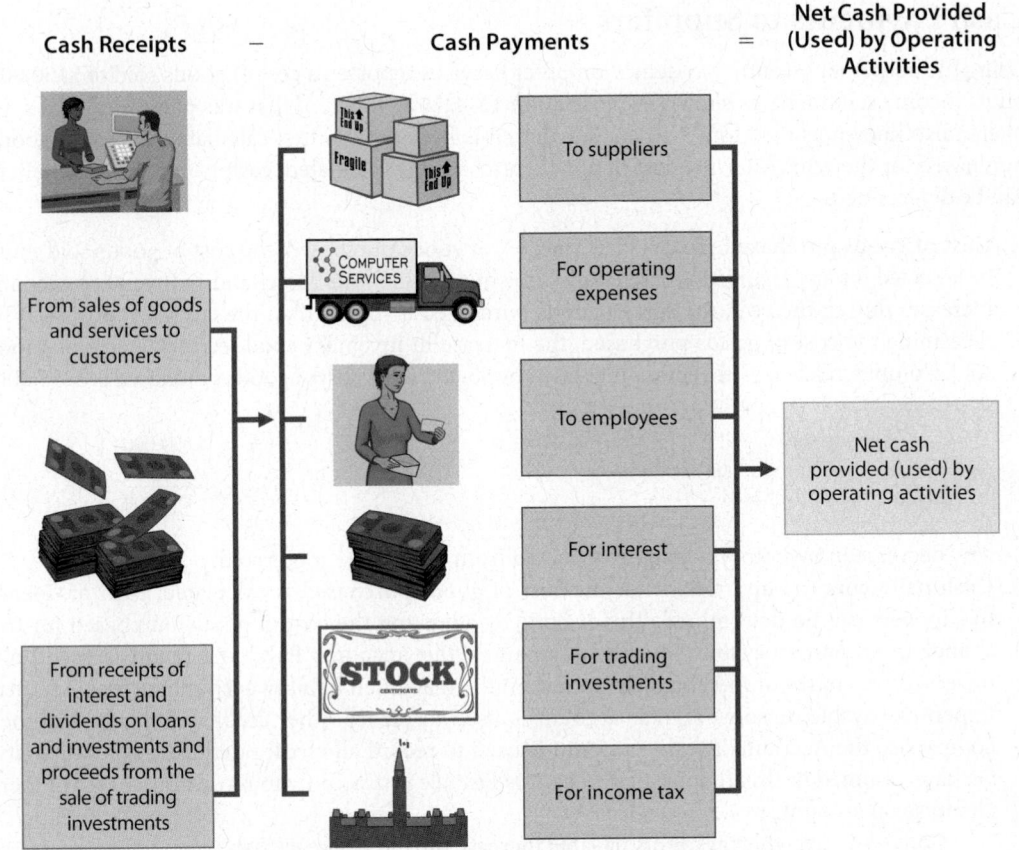

▶Illustration 13-7
Major classes of cash receipts and payments

For Computer Services, cash receipts from customers were $517,000, or $10,000 higher than revenues, as shown in Illustration 13-8.

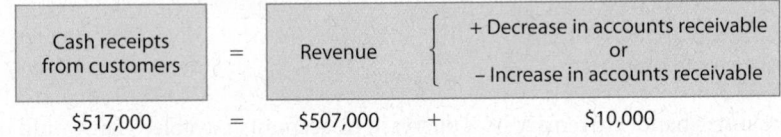

▶Illustration 13-8
Formula to calculate cash receipts from customers

Alternatively, when the Accounts Receivable account balance increases during the year, revenues on an accrual basis are higher than cash receipts. In other words, revenues have increased, but not all of these revenues resulted in cash receipts. Therefore, the amount of the increase in accounts receivable is deducted from sales revenues to arrive at cash receipts from customers.

Cash Receipts from Interest

Computer Services does not have cash receipts from any source other than customers. If an income statement details other revenue, such as interest revenue, these amounts must be adjusted for the change in interest receivable amounts to determine the actual cash receipts.

Interest is the most common source of other revenue. Similar to the adjustments shown in Illustration 13-8, decreases in interest receivable would be added to interest revenue. This is done as the decrease in the receivable happened because interest was collected this year that was earned last period, which caused the decline in the receivable. Increases in interest receivable would be deducted from interest revenue.

CASH PAYMENTS

Computer Services has many kinds of cash payments: suppliers, operating expenses, interest, and income taxes. We will analyze each of these in the next sections.

Cash Payments to Suppliers

Using the perpetual inventory system, Computer Services reported a cost of goods sold of $150,000 on its income statement, as shown in Illustration 13-4. How much of that was paid in cash to suppliers (also known as creditors)? To answer that, it is necessary to first calculate the cost of goods purchased for the year. After the cost of goods purchased is calculated, cash payments to suppliers can be determined.

1. **Cost of goods purchased:** To calculate the cost of goods purchased, the cost of goods sold must be adjusted for any change in merchandise inventory. When the Merchandise Inventory account increases during the year, the cost of goods purchased is higher than the cost of goods sold. To determine the cost of goods purchased, the increase in inventory is added to the cost of goods sold. Computer Services' inventory increased by $5,000 so its cost of goods purchased is $155,000.

Cost of goods sold	$150,000
Add: Increase in merchandise inventory	5,000
Cost of goods purchased	155,000

Any decrease in inventory would be deducted from the cost of goods sold.

2. **Cash payments to suppliers:** After the cost of goods purchased is calculated, cash payments to suppliers can be determined. This is done by adjusting the cost of goods purchased for the change in accounts payable. In some companies, the Accounts Payable account is used only to record purchases of merchandise on account. An accrued liability account such as Accrued Expenses Payable or some similar account is used to record other credit purchases. In other companies, the Accounts Payable account is used to record all credit purchases. For simplicity, we have assumed in this chapter that Accounts Payable is used only to record purchases of merchandise on account.

    Consequently, when accounts payable increase during the year, cash payments to suppliers will be lower than the cost of goods purchased. To determine cash payments to suppliers, an increase in accounts payable is deducted from the cost of goods purchased. For Computer Services, cash payments to suppliers were $139,000.

Cost of goods purchased (from item 1 above)	$155,000
Less: Increase in accounts payable	16,000
Cash payments to suppliers	139,000

On the other hand, there may be a decrease in accounts payable. That would occur if cash payments to suppliers amounted to more than purchases. In that case, the decrease in accounts payable is added to the cost of goods purchased.

The narrative above is shown in formula format in Illustration 13-9.

▶Illustration 13-9
Formula to calculate cash payments to suppliers

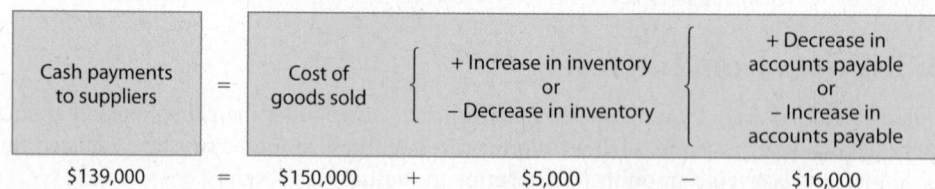

Cash Payments for Operating Expenses

Computer Services' income statement shown in Illustration 13-4 includes $141,000 of other operating expenses. In this particular case, other operating expenses are total operating expenses exclusive of the noncash depreciation expense and loss on the disposal of equipment, which have been reported separately for our convenience. If these amounts had been combined, we would have first had to remove the noncash expenses before determining how much of the $141,000 of other operating expenses was paid in cash. Then, this amount would be adjusted for any changes in prepaid expenses and accrued liabilities.

If prepaid expenses increase during the year, the cash paid for operating expenses will be higher than the operating expenses reported on the income statement because cash was spent not only to pay for the related expense but also to build up the prepaid balance. To adjust operating expenses to cash payments for services, any increase in prepaid expenses must be added to operating expenses. On the other hand, if prepaid expenses decrease during the year, the decrease must be deducted from operating expenses, because the expense that arose when the prepaid expense expired was not paid in cash.

Operating expenses must also be adjusted for changes in other liability accounts such as accrued expenses payable. While for simplicity we have assumed in this chapter that accrued liabilities are recorded separately from accounts payable, some companies do combine them with accounts payable. This is one reason that using the direct method can be difficult in real life. If accrued liabilities and accounts payable are combined and recorded in one account, you have to determine what proportion of accounts payable relate to purchases of merchandise, and what relates to other payables, in order to determine the cash payments to suppliers and cash payments for operating expenses.

At this time, Computer Services does not have any accrued liabilities related to its operating expenses. If it did, any changes in these accounts would affect operating expenses as follows: When an accrued liability account increases during the year, operating expenses on an accrual basis are higher than they are on a cash basis. This happens because some of the operating expenses have not yet been paid, which is why the liability increased. To determine cash payments for operating expenses, an increase in the accrued liability account is deducted from operating expenses. On the other hand, a decrease in an accrued liability account is added to operating expenses because the cash payments are greater than the operating expenses.

Computer Services' cash payments for operating expenses were $145,000, calculated as in Illustration 13-10.

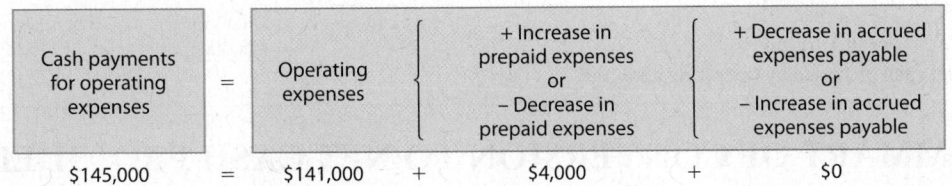

$145,000   = $141,000   + $4,000   + $0

▶Illustration 13-10
Formula to calculate cash payments for operating expenses

Cash Payments to Employees

Some companies report payments to employees separately, removing these payments from their operating expenses. To determine payments to employees, you would have to know the salaries expense amount on the income statement and any salaries payable on the comparative statement of financial position. Cash payments to employees would equal the salaries expense plus any decrease (or less any increase) during the period in the amount of salaries payable.

Other companies condense their income statement in such a way that cash payments to suppliers and employees cannot be separated from cash payments for operating expenses. (For example, they do not disclose their salaries expense separately.) Although this presentation will not be as informative, for reporting purposes it is acceptable to combine these sources of cash payments.

Cash Payments for Interest

Computer Services reported $12,000 of interest expense on its income statement in Illustration 13-4. This amount equals the cash paid, since the comparative statement of financial position indicated no interest payable at the beginning or end of the year. If there was any interest payable, decreases in the interest payable account would be added to, or increases would be deducted from, the interest expense account to determine cash payments for interest.

Cash Payments for Income Tax

Computer Services reported income tax expense of $47,000 on its income statement shown in Illustration 13-4. Income tax payable, however, decreased by $2,000 (from $8,000 to $6,000) during the year. This means that income tax paid was more than the income tax reported in the income statement; otherwise, the income tax payable would not have fallen. Decreases in income tax payable are added to income tax expense, to determine the cash payments for income tax. This would be $49,000 for Computer Services.

The relationship among cash payments for income tax, income tax expense, and changes in income tax payable is shown in Illustration 13-11.

► Illustration 13-11
Formula to calculate cash payments for income tax

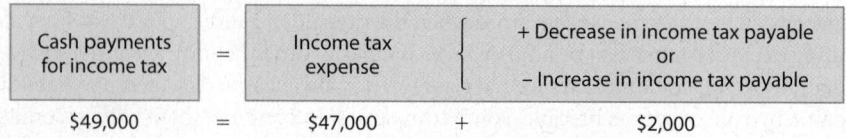

Cash payments for income tax	=	Income tax expense	{	+ Decrease in income tax payable or − Increase in income tax payable
$49,000	=	$47,000	+	$2,000

All of the revenues and expenses in Computer Services' income statement have now been adjusted to a cash basis. The operating activities section of the statement of cash flows is shown in Illustration 13-12. Note that positive numbers in the statement of cash flows prepared using the direct method indicate cash receipts (inflows) and that negative numbers, shown in parentheses, indicate cash payments (outflows).

► Illustration 13-12

Net cash provided (used) by operating activities—direct method

Helpful Hint
Whether the direct or indirect method is used, net cash provided (used) by operating activities will be the same.

COMPUTER SERVICES CORPORATION
Statement of Cash Flows (partial)
Year Ended December 31, 2015

Operating activities		
Cash receipts from customers		$517,000
Cash payments		
To suppliers	$(139,000)	
For operating expenses	(145,000)	
For interest	(12,000)	
For income tax	(49,000)	(345,000)
Net cash provided by operating activities		172,000

SUMMARY OF CONVERSION TO NET CASH PROVIDED (USED) BY OPERATING ACTIVITIES—DIRECT METHOD

As shown on the previous pages, revenues and expenses reported on the income statement are reviewed to determine if any cash receipts and cash payments relate to them. Noncash revenues and expenses are excluded. Any revenue and expense accounts with cash effects are included, after adjusting them for changes (increases or decreases) in the related current asset and current liability accounts to determine cash receipts and cash payments in the operating activities section.

The adjustments that are required to convert individual revenues and expenses from an accrual basis of accounting to a cash basis of accounting are summarized here:

	Cash Receipts (Revenues)	Cash Payments (Expenses)
Current assets		
Increase in account balance	Deduct (−)	Add (+)
Decrease in account balance	Add (+)	Deduct (−)
Current liabilities		
Increase in account balance	Add (+)	Deduct (−)
Decrease in account balance	Deduct (−)	Add (+)

Note that while the adjustments to revenues shown above are in the same direction as those we discussed in the indirect section, the adjustments to expenses move in the opposite direction. This is because in the indirect method, we are adjusting profit (in which expenses are deductions). In the direct method, we are adjusting each expense account, which will later be deducted in the calculation of operating activities.

Before we move on, let's revisit the relationship between the amounts shown in the income statement and the effect they have on assets and liabilities to review our understanding of the cash flow effect of these items. This is done below in Illustration 13-13.

►Illustration 13-13
Comparison of indirect and direct methods

	Income Statement Account—Cash Flow Effect	Components of Income Statement Accounts Not Reflected in Cash	Amount of Adjustment Needed (Shown in Indirect Method)	Net Cash Flow (Shown in Direct Method)
Sales	$507,000	Decrease in accounts receivable	$10,000	$517,000
Cost of goods sold	(150,000)	Increase in merchandise inventory	(5,000)	(139,000)
		Increase in accounts payable	16,000	
Other operating expenses	(141,000)	Increase in prepaid expenses	(4,000)	(145,000)
Depreciation expense	(9,000)	Entire amount is noncash	9,000	0
Loss on disposal of equipment	(3,000)	Entire amount is noncash	3,000	0
Interest expense	(12,000)	No change		(12,000)
Income tax expense	(47,000)	Decrease in income tax payable	(2,000)	(49,000)
Profit	$145,000			
Net cash provided by operating activities			$27,000	$172,000

We know that the amounts shown in red above are the amounts that appeared on the statement of cash flows when using the indirect method and that these amounts totalled $172,000 ($145,000 + $27,000) for the net cash provided by operating activities. However, if we were to take a different approach and use individual items from the income statement rather than the total profit amount and then make adjustments to each of these items to arrive at cash flows (the items shown in blue above), we would be preparing the operating activities section of the statement of cash flows using the direct method. Regardless of method used, the net cash provided by operating activities is $172,000.

ACCOUNTING MATTERS!

Why Does the Indirect Method Persist?

Both IFRS and ASPE recommend that companies prepare the statement of cash flows using the direct method rather than the indirect method. Standard setters prefer the direct method because its presentation is easier to understand for the average financial statement user. Despite this, the vast majority of companies continue to use the indirect method. The primary reason for this is that it is easier to prepare. Changes in noncash current asset and liability accounts do not have to be split up to relate to inventory purchases and other administrative expenses. However, some analysts prefer the use of the indirect method because users can see in one place how management of noncash working capital can affect cash flow. Furthermore, users can also see to what extent profit has been created by noncash items. For most companies, when preparing the statement using the indirect method, after adding back depreciation to profit, operating cash flow is higher than profit. Taking into consideration the changes in noncash working capital, there may be a slight decrease in operating cash flows as the rise in accounts receivable and merchandise inventory may be higher than the increase in accounts payable for a healthy growing company. However, the effect of the noncash working capital is usually not significant. Consider the following information relating to the first six months of a fiscal year for a Canadian company:

	Current Period	Prior Period
Profit	$ 31,183	$ 6,341
Depreciation and other noncash expenses	8,224	9,627
Operating cash flow before the following	39,407	15,968
Changes in noncash working capital	(31,467)	(3,878)
Net cash from operating activities	$ 7,940	$12,090

(continued)

When we use the indirect method, we can see very clearly that the change in the noncash working capital, which represented a 24% ($3,878 ÷ $15,968) decline in operating cash flows (before considering changes in noncash working capital) in the prior period, grew to represent an 80% decline in the current year. Despite profit rising almost fivefold, net cash from operating activities declined. Why? It is because of the changes in noncash working capital. If you dug deeper into the reason for this, you would have discovered a very large increase in accounts receivable as this company was having difficulty collecting receivables. Consequently, the company, Poseidon Concepts, which supplied storage tanks to the oil and gas sector, later declared bankruptcy.

BEFORE YOU GO ON...

▶ Do It! Net Cash Provided (Used) by Operating Activities

Selected financial information follows for Denham Ltd. at December 31. Prepare the operating activities section of the statement of cash flows using the indirect method.

	2015	2014	Increase (Decrease)
Current assets			
Cash	$61,000	$37,000	$24,000
Accounts receivable	68,000	26,000	42,000
Merchandise inventory	54,000	10,000	44,000
Prepaid expenses	4,000	6,000	(2,000)
Current liabilities			
Accounts payable	35,000	55,000	(20,000)
Accrued expenses payable	4,000	5,000	(1,000)
Salaries payable	6,000	4,000	2,000
Income tax payable	20,000	10,000	10,000

DENHAM LTD.
Income Statement
Year Ended December 31, 2015

Sales revenue		$890,000
Cost of goods sold		465,000
Gross profit		425,000
Operating expenses		
Salaries expense	$150,000	
Administrative expenses	46,000	
Depreciation expense	33,000	
Loss on disposal of equipment	4,000	233,000
Profit from operations		192,000
Interest expense		12,000
Profit before income tax		180,000
Income tax expense		36,000
Profit		$144,000

Action Plan

- Determine the net cash provided (used) by operating activities by adjusting each revenue and expense item for changes in the related current asset and current liability account.
- Remove any noncash revenues and expenses.
- To adjust revenues for changes in related noncash working capital accounts, add decreases in noncash current asset accounts and increases in noncash current liability accounts. Deduct increases in these asset accounts and decreases in these liability accounts. To adjust expenses, add increases in these asset accounts and decreases in these liability accounts. Deduct decreases in these asset accounts and increases in these liability accounts.

- Assume that the accounts payable relate to suppliers.
- Assume that the prepaid expenses and accrued payables relate to administrative expenses.
- Report cash receipts and cash payments by major sources and uses: (1) cash receipts from customers, and (2) cash payments to suppliers, for administrative expenses, to employees, for interest, and for income tax.

Solution

DENHAM LTD. Statement of Cash Flows (partial) Year Ended December 31, 2015		
Operating activities		
Cash receipts from customers		$848,000[1]
Cash payments		
To suppliers	$(529,000)[2]	
For administrative expenses	(45,000)[3]	
To employees	(148,000)[4]	
For interest	(12,000)	
For income tax	(26,000)[5]	(760,000)
Net cash provided by operating activities		88,000

Calculations:

[1] Cash receipts from customers: $890,000 − $42,000 (accounts receivable) = $848,000

[2] Payments to suppliers: $465,000 + $44,000 (inventory) + $20,000 (accounts payable) = $529,000

[3] Payments for administrative expenses: $46,000 − $2,000 (prepaid expenses) + $1,000 (accrued expenses payable) = $45,000

[4] Payments to employees: $150,000 − $2,000 (salaries payable) = $148,000

[5] Payments for income tax: $36,000 − $10,000 (income tax payable) = $26,000

Related Exercise Material: BE13-6, BE13-7, BE13-8, BE13-9, BE13-10, E13-6, E13-7, E13-10, E13-12, and E13-13.

the navigator

STEP 2: INVESTING ACTIVITIES

Determine the Net Cash Provided (Used) by Investing Activities by Analyzing Changes in Non-Current Asset Accounts

STUDY OBJECTIVE 3
Prepare the investing activities section of a statement of cash flows.

Regardless of whether the indirect or direct method is used, both methods are identical when preparing the investing and financing activities section of the statement of cash flows. We will look first at investing activities in this section, and financing activities in the next section.

Investing activities measure cash flows relating to non-current asset accounts, such as long-term investments; property, plant, and equipment; and intangible assets. Note that not all types of investments relate to investing activities, only cash flows from the purchase and sale of investments not held for trading purposes. For example, cash flows relating to investments in debt or equity securities that are held specifically for trading purposes are classified as operating activities rather than as investing activities. This is because they relate to revenue-producing activities of the company, similar to inventory purchased for resale. You will recall that trading investments were discussed in Chapter 12.

Although it is primarily non-current asset accounts that give rise to investing activities, there are some current asset account transactions that may also be classified as investing activities.

For example, short-term notes receivable issued for loans rather than for trade transactions would be classified as an investing activity rather than an operating activity. The point of mentioning exceptions such as this is to advocate caution about applying general guidelines too widely.

We will use the statement of financial position and additional information provided in Illustration 13-4 to determine what effect, if any, the change in each relevant current asset and non-current asset account had on investing activities. Computer Services did not have any affected current asset accounts but does have three non-current asset accounts that must be analyzed: Land, Building, and Equipment.

LAND

Land increased by $110,000 during the year, as reported in Computer Services' statement of financial position in Illustration 13-4. The additional information provided states that this land was purchased by obtaining an additional mortgage. Obtaining a mortgage for land has no effect on the company's cash because it is using cash from a lender, but it is a significant noncash investing activity (acquisition of land), as well as a noncash financing activity (obtaining mortgage), that must be disclosed in a note to the statement of cash flows even though these amounts are not listed in the actual statement of cash flows.

BUILDING

The Building account increased by $120,000 during the year, as reported in Illustration 13-4. What caused this increase? No additional information has been provided regarding this change. Whenever unexplained differences in non-current accounts occur, we assume the transaction was for cash. That is, we would assume in this case that a building was acquired, or expanded, for $120,000 cash and report this cash payment as an investing activity.

Accumulated Depreciation—Building

Accumulated Depreciation increased by $6,000 during the year, as shown in Illustration 13-4. As explained in the additional information, this increase resulted from the $9,000 of depreciation expense reported on the income statement, of which $6,000 related to the building:

$6,000 net increase

Accumulated Depreciation—Building				
	Jan.	1	Balance	5,000
			Depreciation expense	6,000
	Dec.	31	Balance	11,000

Depreciation expense is a noncash charge and does not affect the statement of cash flows. Adding it back to profit in the operating section of the statement when we used the indirect method or just ignoring depreciation expense when using the direct method means that we have recognized its noncash nature. Therefore, it does not need to be dealt with in the investing activity section.

EQUIPMENT

Computer Services' Equipment account increased by $17,000, as reported in Illustration 13-4. The additional information provided in this illustration explains that this was a net increase resulting from two different transactions: (1) a purchase of equipment for $25,000 cash, and (2) a disposal of equipment that cost $8,000 for $4,000 cash. The following entries reproduce these two equipment transactions:

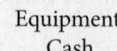

A = L + SE
+25,000
−25,000
↓ Cash flows: −25,000

| Equipment | 25,000 | |
| Cash | | 25,000 |

Cash		4,000		
Accumulated Depreciation		1,000		
Loss on Disposal		3,000		
Equipment			8,000	

A	=	L	+	SE
+4,000				−3,000
+1,000				
−8,000				

↑Cash flows: +4,000

The T account that follows summarizes the changes in the Equipment account during the year:

Equipment					
Jan.	1	Balance	10,000		
		Purchase of equipment	25,000	Cost of equipment sold	8,000
Dec.	31	Balance	27,000		

} $17,000 net increase

In the above example, you were given information about both the purchase and the disposal of equipment. Often, in analyzing accounts, you will not be given all of the information needed to determine what caused the change in an account balance. You need to know four things about a non-current asset account when preparing the investing section. They are: the opening and closing balances, and the upward and downward movement in the account. If you know three of these four amounts, you can always derive the fourth and usually it will be an upward or downward movement that you will have to determine. For example, if you knew the beginning and ending balances of the Equipment account were $10,000 and $27,000 respectively as well as the fact that the cost of the equipment sold was $8,000, you could determine that the cost of the equipment purchased must have been $25,000.

Each upward or downward movement in an applicable account should be reported separately in the investing section even though the net movement is often reported for accounts applicable to the operating section. In this particular case, the purchase of equipment should be reported as a $25,000 cash payment. The disposal of equipment should be reported as a $4,000 cash receipt. We do not net these two amounts together but show them separately because this information is useful. This treatment differs from the operating section, where the net change in each noncash working capital account like accounts receivable or accounts payable is shown rather than the increase and decrease in each account.

Accumulated Depreciation—Equipment

The accumulated depreciation for equipment increased during the year by $2,000. This change does not represent the overall depreciation expense for the year. This is important to remember: the change in the accumulated depreciation account is only equal to depreciation expense if there were no disposals of related assets during the period, and this is very rare. The additional information in Illustration 13-4 reported that depreciation expense was $9,000 in total, of which $3,000 related to the equipment.

We can use the journal entry shown earlier for the disposal of the equipment and the information about the amount of the depreciation expense recorded for the year to help us understand why the Accumulated Depreciation account increased by $2,000, and not $3,000:

Accumulated Depreciation—Equipment					
		Jan.	1	Balance	1,000
Disposal of equipment	1,000			Depreciation expense	3,000
		Dec.	31	Balance	3,000

} $2,000 net increase

The $2,000 net increase is composed of two different amounts: (1) a reduction in accumulated depreciation of $1,000 as a result of the disposal of equipment described above, and (2) an increase in accumulated depreciation of $3,000 as a result of depreciation expense for the current period. Neither of these amounts, however, is shown on the statement of cash flows because they do not represent an amount of cash received or paid.

As we have seen, the disposal of the equipment affected a number of accounts: one account on Computer Services' income statement (Loss on Sale of Equipment) and three accounts on its statement of financial position (Cash, Equipment, and Accumulated Depreciation). In the statement of cash flows, it is important to combine the effects of this disposal in one place: the investing activities section. The overall result, then, is that the loss on the disposal of the equipment is removed from profit in the operating activities section of the statement of cash flows and the cash proceeds received from the disposal of the equipment are shown in their entirety in the investing activities section.

INVESTMENTS

Although Computer Services has no investment accounts, it is important to remember to remove any noncash transactions when analyzing changes in any long-term investment and investment-related accounts. Similar to the disposal of equipment discussed above, items reported for investments in a statement of cash flows should consist only of amounts paid when purchasing the investments and amounts received when selling investments. These amounts are not netted together but are shown separately.

The investing activities section of Computer Services' statement of cash flows is shown in Illustration 13-14. It reports the purchase of a building as well as the purchase and disposal of equipment.

▶Illustration 13-14
Net cash provided (used) by investing activities

COMPUTER SERVICES CORPORATION Statement of Cash Flows (partial) Year Ended December 31, 2015		
Investing activities		
Purchase of building	$(120,000)	
Purchase of equipment	(25,000)	
Disposal of equipment	4,000	
Net cash used by investing activities		$(141,000)
Note x: Significant noncash investing and financing activities		
Mortgage received to purchase land		$110,000

Computer Services also reports in the accompanying notes to the statement the significant noncash investing and financing activity.

As a company grows, you can expect to see it *use* cash for its investing activities as it purchases property, plant, and equipment. Typically, you do not see cash *provided* by investing activities unless a company sells off excess assets. Obtaining cash by selling off non-current assets could mean that a company may be in the midst of restructuring its business activities, or even in financial difficulty. Understanding the pattern of a company's cash flows over time can provide important information for users.

BEFORE YOU GO ON...

▶ Do It! Net Cash Provided (Used) by Investing Activities

In its Equipment account, Umiujaq Corporation reported an opening balance of $146,000 and an ending balance of $135,000 while the Accumulated Depreciation—Equipment account had an opening balance of $47,000 and an ending balance of $62,000. During the year, it sold for cash some equipment with a cost of $21,000 and a carrying amount of $5,000, for a gain on the disposal of $1,000. It also purchased equipment for cash. It recorded depreciation expense on the equipment of $31,000. Calculate the cash received from the disposal of equipment and the cash paid for equipment. Circle the entries in the T accounts that represent cash receipts and cash payments that would appear in the investing section of the statement of cash flows.

Action Plan

• Use journal entries and T accounts, and your knowledge of account relationships, to reconstruct the transactions affecting the Equipment account. Fill in the information given and use this to determine any missing information (for example, the cost of equipment purchased).

- Use journal entries and T accounts, and your knowledge of account relationships, to reconstruct the transactions affecting the Accumulated Depreciation account. Fill in the information given and use this to determine any missing information (such as the accumulated depreciation on the equipment that was disposed).
- Remember that the carrying amount of equipment is its cost less accumulated depreciation and that gains result when the cash proceeds exceed the carrying amount.

Solution

Cash received from disposal of equipment = $6,000

Cash	6,000	
Accumulated Depreciation ($21,000 – $5,000)	16,000	
Gain on Disposal		1,000
Equipment		21,000

Cash paid for equipment = $10,000

Equipment	10,000	
Cash		10,000

Equipment

Opening balance	146,000		
Purchase of equipment	⟨10,000⟩	Disposal of equipment	21,000
Ending balance	135,000		

Accumulated Depreciation—Equipment

		Opening balance	47,000
Sale of equipment	⟨16,000⟩	Depreciation expense	31,000
		Ending balance	62,000

Related Exercise Material: BE13-11, BE13-12, E13-8, E13-9, E13-11, E13-12, and E13-13.

the navigator

STEP 3: FINANCING ACTIVITIES

Determine the Net Cash Provided (Used) by Financing Activities by Analyzing Changes in Non-Current Liability and Equity Accounts

The third step in preparing a statement of cash flows is to analyze the changes in non-current liability and equity accounts. In addition, changes involving short-term loans (including notes) payable should also be reported in the financing activities section if they have been incurred for lending purposes rather than for trade. Computer Services has one non-current liability account (Mortgage Payable) and three shareholders' equity accounts (Common Shares, Retained Earnings, and Accumulated Other Comprehensive Income), as shown in Illustration 13-4.

STUDY OBJECTIVE 4
Prepare the financing activities section of a statement of cash flows.

BANK LOAN AND MORTGAGE PAYABLE

Computer Services does not have any bank loans, but it has a mortgage payable, which was increased by $110,000 during the year when land for the same amount was purchased. In other words, the purchase of the land was fully financed with a mortgage. Because the cash from the mortgage was transferred from the bank to the seller of the land and not received directly by Computer Services, even though the Mortgage Payable account increased, this would be considered a noncash transaction and not shown on the actual statement of cash flows but in a note accompanying this statement. If cash had been borrowed directly, the loan principal received would be shown as a cash receipt in the financing section. As the principal is repaid, this would be shown as a cash payment in the financing section. Note that any interest paid would be recorded in the operating section as covered earlier. As we see with many investing and financing activities, we disclose separately the increases and decreases in cash pertaining to a particular asset or liability. We do not net these movements together, which is why you will see both the receipts of cash from loans and their repayment in the financing section.

Given the nature of bank loans and mortgages, it is common to have these items split into current and non-current liabilities. When disclosing the movement in these items, they should be combined. Thus we show the total loan received regardless of whether it affected the current or non-current portion of the loan and the total loan principal payment made regardless of which portion, current or non-current, changed as a result of this payment.

BONDS PAYABLE

Movements in the Bonds Payable account are treated in a similar manner to bank loans, with cash received from issuing the bonds and cash paid to redeem them shown as receipts and payments in the financing section.

SHARE CAPITAL

Share capital can include both preferred and common shares. Computer Services does not have any preferred shares, but does have a balance of $70,000 in common shares at the end of 2015. According to Illustration 13-4, the company's Common Shares account increased by $20,000. Since no additional information is provided about any reacquisition of shares, we assume that this change relates solely to the issue of additional common shares for cash. However, just as we did with investing activities, if we are aware of what caused an account to rise and fall, we would show both movements separately rather than netting them together. The cash receipt from the issue of shares is reported in the financing activities section of the statement of cash flows.

If the company had reacquired shares, the amount of cash paid to reacquire the shares would be reported as a cash payment in the financing activities section of the statement of cash flows.

RETAINED EARNINGS

What caused the net increase of $116,000 in Retained Earnings reported in Illustration 13-4? This increase can be explained by two factors. First, profit increased retained earnings by $145,000. Second, the additional information provided in Illustration 13-4 indicates that a cash dividend of $29,000 was paid.

This information could also have been determined by analyzing the T account:

					Retained Earnings		
			Jan.	1	Balance		48,000
Cash dividend	29,000				Profit		145,000
			Dec.	31	Balance		164,000

$116,000 net increase {

As we noted in the investing activities section, these two changes must be reported separately. The profit is therefore reported, albeit indirectly, in the operating activities section of the statement of cash flows (after the revenue and expense components have been adjusted to a cash basis using either the indirect or direct method).

The cash dividends paid are reported as cash payments in the financing activities section of the statement. Note that the Retained Earnings account above only reports the dividends declared. We need to report the dividends paid. This will differ from the dividends declared if there is a change in the Dividends Payable account. For example, if the Dividends Payable increased, then the dividends declared were not fully paid and the dividends paid amount on the statement would be lower than the dividends declared. Computer Services did not have any dividends payable, so the dividends declared are equal to the dividends paid.

ACCUMULATED OTHER COMPREHENSIVE INCOME

Computer Services had no changes in its accumulated other comprehensive income during 2015. That is why it did not prepare a statement of comprehensive income, only an income statement for that year. If accumulated other comprehensive income had increased or decreased in the current year, it would not affect the statement of cash flows as there are no cash effects in any of the sources of other comprehensive income. That is why the starting point for the operating activities of the statement of cash flows is profit and not comprehensive income.

The financing activities section of Computer Services' statement of cash flows is shown in Illustration 13-15 and reports the issue of common shares and payment of a dividend. It also reports in the accompanying notes to the statement the significant noncash investing and financing activity. This is the same note shown in Illustration 13-14. It is not a new note; it has been included here for completeness only.

▶Illustration 13-15

Net cash provided (used) by financing activities

COMPUTER SERVICES CORPORATION Statement of Cash Flows (partial) Year Ended December 31, 2015		
Financing activities		
Issue of common shares	$20,000	
Payment of cash dividend	(29,000)	
Net cash used by financing activities		$ (9,000)
Note x: Significant noncash investing and financing activities		
Mortgage received to purchase land		$110,000

As a company grows, you can expect to see cash *provided* by its financing activities. When they are growing, most companies are not able to generate sufficient cash from their operating activities to pay for their investing activities, so they have to borrow for any shortfall. Growing companies must invest in productive assets, such as buildings and equipment. To finance these purchases, the company will have to issue debt or shares.

Typically you do not see cash *used* by financing activities, as we see in Illustration 13-15 for Computer Services, unless a company is mature and is repaying its debt. As we mentioned in the investing activities section, understanding the pattern of a company's cash flows over time can provide important information for users.

BEFORE YOU GO ON...

▶Do It! Net Cash Provided (Used) by Financing Activities

Selected financial information for La Tuque Ltd. at December 31 is shown below.

	2015	2014
Current liabilities		
Dividends payable	$ 2,000	$ 1,000
Current portion of bank loan	5,000	4,000
Non-current liabilities		
Bank loan payable	55,000	48,000
Shareholders' equity		
Common shares	121,000	103,000
Retained earnings	72,000	57,000

During the year, the company had a profit of $27,000. It received bank loans of $17,000 and repaid others. It issued new common shares and did not reacquire any. Calculate and present the net cash provided by financing activities for 2015.

Action Plan

- Use journal entries and T accounts, and your knowledge of account relationships, to reconstruct the transactions affecting the accounts listed above. Fill in the information given and use this to determine any missing information (such as the average cost of the reacquired shares).
- Based on the journal entries and T accounts used above, list the amounts that would appear in the financing section of the statement of cash flows.

(continued)

Solution

Bank loans received would have been recorded as follows:

Cash	17,000	
Bank Loan Payable		17,000

We will combine both accounts relating to the bank loan and analyze the movement in these accounts in one T account. The opening balance is therefore $52,000 ($4,000 + $48,000) while the ending balance is $60,000 ($5,000 + $55,000). We know that the amount of new loans received is $17,000 so we can derive the loan payments as follows:

Current and Non-Current Bank Loan Payable

		Opening balance	52,000
Loan payments	9,000	Loans received	17,000
		Ending balance	60,000

The entry that would have been recorded for the bank loan payments would have been:

Bank Loan Payable	9,000	
Cash		9,000

Since we know the opening and closing balance in the Common Shares account and that only one transaction (the issue of shares) affected the account during the year, we can determine the amount for which the shares were issued.

Common Shares

	Opening balance	103,000
	Shares issued	18,000
	Ending balance	121,000

The entry to record the issue of common shares would have been:

Cash	18,000	
Common Shares		18,000

Because we know the profit and the opening and ending Retained Earnings account balances, we can determine the dividends declared as follows:

Retained Earnings

		Opening balance	57,000
Dividends	12,000	Profit	27,000
		Ending balance	72,000

The journal entry to record the declaration of these dividends would have been:

Dividends	12,000	
Dividends Payable		12,000

Knowing what dividends were declared, we can now determine the amount of dividends that were paid by analyzing the movement in the Dividends Payable account as follows:

Dividends Payable

		Opening balance	1,000
Dividends paid	11,000	Dividends	12,000
		Ending balance	2,000

The entry to record dividends paid would be:

Dividends Payable	11,000	
Cash		11,000

LA TUQUE LTD.
Statement of Cash Flows (partial)
Year Ended December 31, 2015

Financing activities	
Bank loans received	$17,000
Bank loan payments	(9,000)
Issue of common shares	18,000
Payment of dividend	(11,000)
Net cash provided by financing activities	15,000

Related Exercise Material: BE13-13, BE13-14, E13-8, E13-9, E13-11, E13-12, and E13-13.

STEP 4: THE STATEMENT OF CASH FLOWS

Complete the Statement of Cash Flows and Determine the Net Increase (Decrease) in Cash

Using the partial information shown in Illustration 13-12 for operating activities, in Illustration 13-14 for investing activities, and in Illustration 13-15 for financing activities, we can now combine the sections and present a complete statement of cash flows for Computer Services Corporation, as shown in Illustration 13-16.

The statement of cash flows starts with the operating activities section. Because it is preferred by standard setters, we have chosen to illustrate the direct method of preparing the operating activities section in Illustration 13-16. The operating activities section prepared using the indirect method was shown in Illustration 13-6, and could be substituted in this illustration if desired. Both methods report cash provided by operating activities of $172,000. As mentioned earlier in the chapter, while the operating activities sections differ in format between the indirect and direct methods, the investing and financing activities sections are exactly the same.

STUDY OBJECTIVE 5
Complete the statement of cash flows.

▶Illustration 13-16
Statement of cash flows—direct method

COMPUTER SERVICES CORPORATION
Statement of Cash Flows
Year Ended December 31, 2015

Operating activities		
Cash receipts from customers		$517,000
Cash payments		
To suppliers	$(139,000)	
For operating expenses	(145,000)	
For interest	(12,000)	
For income tax	(49,000)	(345,000)
Net cash provided by operating activities		172,000
Investing activities		
Purchase of building	$(120,000)	
Purchase of equipment	(25,000)	
Disposal of equipment	4,000	
Net cash used by investing activities		(141,000)
Financing activities		
Issue of common shares	$ 20,000	
Payment of cash dividend	(29,000)	
Net cash used by financing activities		(9,000)
Net increase in cash		22,000
Cash, January 1		33,000
Cash, December 31		$ 55,000
Note x: Significant noncash investing and financing activities		
Mortgage received to purchase land		$110,000

The statement continues with investing activities, reporting that investing activities used $141,000 of cash. Financing activities follow, and used $9,000 of cash. The statement concludes with the net change in cash, reconciled to the beginning- and end-of-period cash balances. The comparative statement of financial position in Illustration 13-4 indicates that the net change in cash during the period was an increase of $22,000. The $22,000 net increase in cash reported in the statement of cash flows above agrees with this change.

Additional disclosures are required to complete the statement of cash flows. As we previously discussed, significant noncash investing and financing activities must be reported in the notes to the financial statements. In addition, if a company has combined cash equivalents with its cash, it must disclose the components of its cash equivalents along with a reconciliation of the amounts reported on the statement of cash flows with those reported on the statement of financial position. There are other disclosures required, but we will leave discussion of these to a future accounting course.

■ Keeping an Eye on Cash

Just as products have a life cycle, so too do companies. The "corporate" life cycle can be said to consist of four phases: introductory, growth, maturity, and decline. Each phase, as indicated in the following graph, can help us understand what to expect for a company's cash flow from its operating, investing, and financing activities.

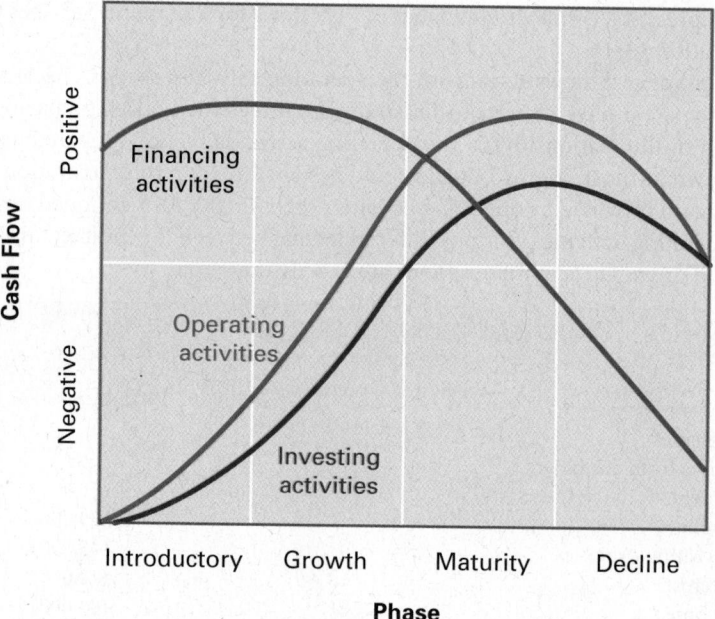

In the introductory and growth phases, we don't usually expect to see a company generate positive cash from its operating activities. Because the company is making significant investments in its long-lived assets, cash generated by investing activities is also negative. In contrast, cash generated by financing activities is usually positive as debt and equity are issued to pay for the investments and cover the operating activities shortfall.

As companies move to the maturity and decline phases of their life cycle, these patterns tend to reverse. The company is usually able to generate positive cash from its operating activities as it reaches maturity, which is used to cover its investing activities. At this point in their life cycle, companies can start to pay dividends, retire debt, and/or buy back shares so their cash flows from financing activities move toward the negative. In the decline phase, cash from operating activities decreases. Cash from investing activities is positive as the company sells off its excess assets, before starting to decline. Cash is used for financing activities as the company continues to pay off its debt.

BEFORE YOU GO ON...

▶ Do It! Statement of Cash Flows:

Selected information follows for Denham Ltd. at December 31:

	2015	2014	Increase (Decrease)
Cash	$ 61,000	$ 37,000	$24,000
Property, plant, and equipment			
Land	45,000	70,000	(25,000)
Buildings	200,000	200,000	0
Accumulated depreciation—buildings	(21,000)	(11,000)	10,000
Equipment	193,000	68,000	125,000
Accumulated depreciation—equipment	(28,000)	(10,000)	18,000
Liabilities and shareholders' equity			
Bank loan payable	110,000	150,000	(40,000)
Common shares	200,000	60,000	140,000
Retained earnings	201,000	112,000	89,000

Additional information:

1. Cash provided by operating activities was $88,000 for the year, whether calculated using the indirect or direct method, as shown in the Before You Go On—Do It! examples in the Step 1: Operating Activities section of the chapter.

2. Equipment was purchased for cash. Equipment with a cost of $41,000 and a carrying amount of $36,000 was sold at a loss of $4,000. Land was sold for an amount equal to its cost.

3. Bank loans amounting to $65,000 were paid off this year while some new loans were obtained.

4. Common shares were issued for cash; no shares were reacquired during the year.

5. Profit was $144,000.

6. A cash dividend was paid.

Prepare a statement of cash flows, excluding the detail normally required for the operating activities section.

Action Plan

- Begin with the operating activities section.
- Determine the net cash provided (used) by investing activities. Investing activities generally relate to changes in non-current asset accounts.
- Determine the net cash provided (used) by financing activities. Financing activities generally relate to changes in non-current liabilities and shareholders' equity accounts.
- Determine the net increase (decrease) in cash. Reconcile to the end-of-period cash balance reported on the statement of financial position ($61,000 in this case).

Solution

DENHAM LTD.		
Statement of Cash Flows		
Year Ended December 31, 2015		
Operating activities		
Net cash provided by operating activities		$ 88,000
Investing activities		
Disposal of land	$ 25,000	
Disposal of equipment	32,000[1]	
Purchase of equipment	(166,000)[2]	
Net cash used by investing activities		(109,000)

(continued)

Financing activities

Bank loan payments made	$(65,000)	
New bank loans received	25,000[3]	
Issue of common shares	140,000	
Payment of dividends	(55,000)[4]	
Net cash provided by financing activities		45,000
Net increase in cash		24,000
Cash, January 1		37,000
Cash, December 31		$ 61,000

[1] Proceeds on disposal of equipment: $36,000 (carrying amount) − $4,000 (loss) = $32,000

[2] Purchase of equipment: $68,000 (opening account balance) − $41,000 (disposal of equipment) + $166,000 (purchase of equipment) = $193,000 (ending account balance)

[3] New loans received: $150,000 (opening account balance) − $65,000 (loan payments made) + $25,000 (new loans received) = $110,000 (ending account balance)

[4] Payment of dividends: $112,000 (opening account balance) + $144,000 (profit) − $55,000 (dividends) = $201,000 (ending account balance)

the navigator

Related Exercise Material: E13-8, E13-9, and E13-12.

Using Cash Flows to Evaluate a Company

STUDY OBJECTIVE 6

Use the statement of cash flows to evaluate a company's liquidity and solvency.

Previous chapters have presented ratios that are used to analyze a company's liquidity and solvency. Most of those ratios used accrual-based numbers from the income statement and statement of financial position. In this section, we focus on ratios that are *cash-based* rather than accrual-based. That is, instead of using numbers only from the income statement and statement of financial position, these ratios also use numbers from the statement of cash flows. Analysts often find it helpful to supplement and compare accrual-based measures with cash-based measures.

In this section, we will use the following selected information (in millions) to introduce cash-based liquidity and solvency ratios for Teck, featured in our chapter-opening story:

	2012	2011
Net cash provided by operating activities	$ 2,795	$ 3,957
Net capital expenditures	2,516	1,410
Cash dividends	469	354
Current assets	6,573	7,389
Total assets	34,617	34,219
Current liabilities	1,820	2,122
Total liabilities	16,640	16,326

LIQUIDITY

Liquidity is the ability of a company to pay obligations expected to become due within the next year. In Chapter 2, you learned that one measure of liquidity is the current ratio (current assets divided by current liabilities). One disadvantage of the current ratio is that it uses year-end balances of current asset and current liability accounts. These year-end balances may not be representative of the company's position during most of the year. Another disadvantage is that current assets and current liabilities include accrual-based numbers so they may change in value without any impact on cash flow.

A ratio that partially addresses these disadvantages is the **cash current debt coverage** ratio. It is calculated by dividing net cash provided or used by operating activities by average current liabilities. We say "partially" because, even though the numerator uses cash-based numbers, the denominator, current liabilities, does not.

The cash current debt coverage ratio for Teck is shown in Illustration 13-17 for 2012, along with comparative results for Freeport-McMoRan Copper & Gold Inc. Freeport-McMoRan, a key competitor to Teck, is an international mining company headquartered in Arizona. We have also provided each company's current ratio for comparative purposes. Unfortunately, although there are industry averages for the more commonly used accrual-based measures, no industry averages are available for cash-based measures.

▶Illustration 13-17
Cash current debt coverage ratio

CASH CURRENT DEBT COVERAGE =	$\dfrac{\text{NET CASH PROVIDED (USED) BY OPERATING ACTIVITIES}}{\text{AVERAGE CURRENT LIABILITIES}}$	
(in millions)	Cash Current Debt Coverage Ratio	Current Ratio
Teck	$\dfrac{\$2,795}{(\$1,820 + \$2,122) \div 2} = 1.4$ times	$\dfrac{\$6,573}{\$1,820} = 3.6{:}1$
Freeport-McMoRan	1.2 times	3.1:1

Teck's cash provided by operating activities is 1.4 times more than its average current liabilities. In other words, it is generating $1.40 of cash flow from operating activities to cover each dollar of current liabilities. The higher the cash current debt coverage ratio, the better a company's liquidity is.

Teck's current ratio is much higher than its cash current debt coverage ratio because it is likely that Teck's current assets include some amount of accruals from revenue billed but not yet collected (accounts receivable) or from merchandise purchased on account. This is not a problem, however, as long as the receivables are collectible and the inventory is saleable.

Teck's cash current debt coverage ratio is slightly higher than that of Freeport-McMoRan, as is its current ratio. This is due to a decrease in the current portion of bank loans by Teck when it restructured some of its debt.

ACCOUNTING MATTERS!

Analyze Statement of Cash Flows with Care

When one prepares an income statement, estimates are used such as the useful life of a building or the amount of the allowance for doubtful accounts. Furthermore, due to accrual accounting concepts, revenue is recorded even though the related cash from that activity may not yet have been received. Because of these estimates and uncertainty regarding the collection of revenue, some analysts believe that cash flow from operating activities is a better indicator of a company's success than profit. They believe that, because cash flow measures what has actually happened and is not based on estimates or accruals, it is a superior indicator of performance.

Although this viewpoint certainly has some merit, we have to be careful when analyzing the statement of cash flows. Some operating cash flows are nonrecurring, and although they cause an immediate increase in cash flow, this is not sustainable. For example, what would happen if a company, just prior to the end of the year, sold its accounts receivable? There would be an immediate jump in operating cash flows. However, one year later, if the accounts receivable that existed at that time were not sold, the increase in accounts receivable over that year would cause a large drop in operating cash flows, reversing out the increase recorded in the prior year. Although overall cash flows are hard to manipulate, their classification within the statement can sometimes be distorted. For example, assume that a company had a major repair on a building and there was some doubt about whether the expenditure should be expensed or capitalized. If the company wanted to maximize its operating cash flows, the decision would be made to capitalize the amount spent on the building as this would be treated as a cash payment in the investing section rather than the operating section. In summary, as with all financial statements, we need to understand and question the decisions that were made regarding the underlying events that affect amounts recorded on the statement.

DECISION TOOLKIT

 Decision Checkpoints	 Info Needed for Decision	 Tools to Use for Decision	 How to Evaluate Results
Is the company generating sufficient cash from operating activities to meet its current obligations?	Net cash provided or used by operating activities and average current liabilities	Cash current debt coverage = $\dfrac{\text{Net cash provided (used) by operating activities}}{\text{Average current liabilities}}$	A high value suggests good liquidity. Since the numerator contains a cash flow measure, it provides a useful supplement to the current ratio.

SOLVENCY

Solvency is the ability of a company to survive over the long term by having enough assets to settle its liabilities as they fall due. We will introduce two cash-based measures of solvency: the cash total debt coverage ratio and free cash flow.

Cash Total Debt Coverage

The cash total debt coverage ratio is similar to the cash current debt coverage ratio except that it uses total liabilities instead of current liabilities. The **cash total debt coverage** ratio is calculated by dividing net cash provided or used by operating activities by average total liabilities. This ratio indicates a company's ability to repay its liabilities from cash generated from operating activities; that is, without having to liquidate productive assets such as property, plant, and equipment. The higher the cash total debt coverage ratio is, the more solvent a company is.

The cash total debt coverage ratios for Teck and Freeport-McMoRan are given in Illustration 13-18 for 2012. For comparative purposes, the accrual-based counterpart, the debt to total assets ratio, is also provided for each company. You will recall from Chapter 2 that the debt to total assets ratio is calculated by dividing total liabilities by total assets.

▶Illustration 13-18
Cash total debt coverage ratio

CASH TOTAL DEBT COVERAGE =	$\dfrac{\text{NET CASH PROVIDED (USED) BY OPERATING ACTIVITIES}}{\text{AVERAGE TOTAL LIABILITIES}}$	
(in millions)	Cash Total Debt Coverage Ratio	Debt to Total Assets
Teck	$\dfrac{\$2{,}795}{(\$16{,}640 + \$16{,}326) \div 2} = 0.2$ times	$\dfrac{\$16{,}640}{\$34{,}617} = 48.1\%$
Freeport-McMoRan	0.3 times	39.9%

Teck's cash total debt coverage ratio of 0.2 times means that it is generating $0.20 every year through its operations to cover each dollar of total liabilities. This ratio is significantly less than its cash current debt coverage ratio of 1.4 times, so we know that Teck has a considerable amount of non-current liabilities.

Notice that Freeport-McMoRan's cash total debt coverage ratio is better than Teck's, and this is also true for the debt to total assets ratio. Since this company has less debt than Teck, it makes sense that its cash provided by operating activities relative to total debt would be larger. This may not always be the case. If a company increased its debt levels but this improved profit and cash provided by operating activities even more significantly, the debt to total assets ratio could rise along with the cash total debt coverage ratio.

It is difficult to reach a conclusion about either company's solvency position without also knowing more about each company's ability to handle its debt (for example, its times interest earned ratio). However, a low cash total debt coverage ratio could signal a long-term solvency problem if the company is not able to generate enough cash internally to repay its debt.

Free Cash Flow

Free cash flow is a solvency-based measure that helps creditors and investors understand how much discretionary cash flow a company has left from its operating activities that can be used to expand operations, reduce debt, or pay additional dividends. You may recall that free cash flow was briefly introduced in Chapter 2 in the Keeping an Eye on Cash feature.

Although there are different definitions of free cash flow, a commonly used one is to deduct net capital expenditures and dividends from cash provided or used by operating activities to determine **free cash flow.** Net capital expenditures—representing amounts paid for the acquisition of property, plant, and equipment less any recoveries from the disposal of these assets—can be found in the investing activities section of the statement of cash flows. Dividends paid, if any, are reported in the financing activities section of the statement of cash flows.

Illustration 13-19 presents the free cash flow numbers for Teck and Freeport-McMoRan for both 2012 and 2011.

▶Illustration 13-19
Free cash flow

FREE CASH FLOW =	NET CASH PROVIDED (USED) BY OPERATING ACTIVITIES	− NET CAPITAL EXPENDITURES	− DIVIDENDS PAID
(in millions)	2012		2011
Teck (in C$ millions)	$2,795 − $2,516 − $469 = $(190)		$3,957 − $1,410 − $354 = $2,193
Freeport-McMoRan (in U.S. $ millions)	$(931)		$2,271

The free cash flow for both of these companies declined in 2012 and became negative. This was due to two things: (1) a decline in cash flow from operating activities, which dropped because copper and gold prices fell, and (2) both companies increasing their capital expenditures as assets from less profitable companies became available due to lower metals prices. Freeport-McMoRan's free cash flow fell more significantly than Teck's because of increases in these capital expenditures.

DECISION TOOLKIT

Decision Checkpoints	Info Needed for Decision	Tools to Use for Decision	How to Evaluate Results
Is the company generating sufficient cash from operating activities to meet its total obligations?	Net cash provided or used by operating activities and average total liabilities	$$\text{Cash total debt coverage} = \frac{\text{Net cash provided (used) by operating activities}}{\text{Average total liabilities}}$$	A high value suggests the company is solvent; that is, it will meet its obligations in the long term. Since the numerator contains a cash flow measure, it provides a useful supplement to the debt to total assets ratio.
Can the company meet its long-term obligations?	Net cash provided or used by operating activities, net capital expenditures, and cash dividends	Free cash flow = Net cash provided (used) by operating activities − Net capital expenditures − Dividends paid	Free cash flow indicates the potential to finance new investments, reduce debt, or pay more dividends.

BEFORE YOU GO ON...

▶**Do It! Cash-Based Measures**

Speyside Inc. reported the following selected information:

	2015	2014	2013
Net cash provided by operating activities	$ 72,000	$ 62,000	$ 50,000
Net capital expenditures	24,000	20,000	17,000
Cash dividends	10,000	10,000	10,000
Current liabilities	32,000	30,000	34,000
Total liabilities	240,000	220,000	250,000

(continued)

(a) Calculate the company's cash current debt coverage ratio, cash total debt coverage ratio, and free cash flow for 2015 and 2014. (b) Indicate whether the company's liquidity and solvency have improved, deteriorated, or did not change in 2015 based on these three measures.

Action Plan

- Recall the formula for cash current debt coverage, a measure of liquidity: Net cash provided (used) by operating activities ÷ average current liabilities.
- Recall the formula for cash total debt coverage, a measure of solvency: Net cash provided (used) by operating activities ÷ average total liabilities.
- Recall the formula for free cash flow, a measure of solvency: Net cash provided (used) by operating activities − net capital expenditures − cash dividends.

Solution

	(a) 2015	2014	(b)
Cash current debt coverage	$\dfrac{\$72{,}000}{(\$32{,}000 + \$30{,}000) \div 2}$ = 2.3 times	$\dfrac{\$62{,}000}{(\$30{,}000 + \$34{,}000) \div 2}$ = 1.9 times	Improvement
Cash total debt coverage	$\dfrac{\$72{,}000}{(\$240{,}000 + \$220{,}000) \div 2}$ = 0.3 times	$\dfrac{\$62{,}000}{(\$220{,}000 + \$250{,}000) \div 2}$ = 0.3 times	Unchanged
Free cash flow	$72{,}000 − $24{,}000 − $10{,}000 = $38{,}000	$62{,}000 − $20{,}000 − $10{,}000 = $32{,}000	Improvement

Related Exercise Material: BE13-15, BE13-16, BE13-17, E13-8, E13-9, E13-13, and E13-14.

comparing
IFRS and ASPE

Key Differences	International Financial Reporting Standards (IFRS)	Accounting Standards for Private Enterprises (ASPE)
Classification of activities	Interest and dividends received may be classified as operating or investing activities.	Interest and dividends received are classified as operating activities.
	Interest and dividends paid may be classified as operating or financing activities.	Interest paid is classified as an operating activity. Dividends paid are classified as a financing activity.
	Once the choice is made, it must be applied consistently.	

Just as a company has three major categories of cash flows, so do students. Operating activities for students include cash received from work and cash payments for transportation, clothing, accommodations, food, and personal expenses. Most students would have negative operating cash flows.

Amounts spent on books, tuition, computers, and a car would be typical investing activities for a student and these all pertain to payments. How then can a student continue to live if his or her operating and investing cash flows are both negative? Easy (maybe) . . . they obtain financing, usually from the government, a bank, or relatives.

Before obtaining funds from a bank, consider the costs of any transaction, such as the cost of writing a cheque, paying bills, or transferring funds. Determine how many transactions during the course of a month are "free." Ask about credit card fees, reward points, and interest charged on the card. Find out if the bank will provide you with free overdraft protection up to a specific amount and whether you can get a student loan at a competitive rate.

Once you have graduated, you will begin to pay off loans and you may be saving some money. At that point you may invest in a tax-free account like an RRSP (registered retirement savings plan) or TFSA (tax free savings account) that can be used to buy shares or bond investments or you may invest in a house. Since a house is very costly, you will probably need a mortgage loan from your bank to help you do this.

Some Facts

- Banks will generally require you to prove your status by showing them your student ID card so you can continue with your student fee status.
- Generally, all bank savings deposits are protected for up to $100,000 by the Canada Deposit Insurance Corporation (CDIC). If a bank is offering a significantly higher interest rate than any other, always make sure that the bank is protected under CDIC.
- Once you start working, experts recommend that you should always have six months' worth of spending on hand in case you lose your job. The amount that you have set aside should never be used unless it is for an emergency.[2]

What Do You Think?

Your friend has just started working for a stockbroker. He is working on commission. He has approached you with the "next great investment," an investment in a new public company that has no track record. You have just started working and have set aside savings in an emergency fund to ensure that if you ever lose your job, you will have enough to pay your rent, your utilities, your car loan, and your student loan. Your friend is telling you that this investment is a sure thing and your money will double in the next 12 months. Should you use the savings from your emergency fund to invest?

YES Your friend is working for a reputable stockbrokerage and would not provide you with this information unless he truly believed that your investment would double in the next 12 months. Worst-case scenario is that you could access this money at any time by selling the shares that you hold in this investment.

NO There is always risk when investing in shares of a public company. As well, the risk is not only that you will lose the investment that you have made in these shares, but that you will have no savings to access if you need funds for emergency purposes.

Summary of Study Objectives

1. **Describe the purpose and content of the statement of cash flows.** The statement of cash flows provides information about the cash receipts and cash payments resulting from the operating, investing, and financing activities of a company during a specific period.

   Operating activities include the cash effects of transactions that create revenues and expenses used in the determination of profit. Operating activities are affected by noncash items in the income statement and changes in certain noncash current asset and current liability accounts in the statement of financial position. Investing activities involve cash flows resulting from changes in non-current asset items. Financing activities involve cash flows resulting from changes in non-current liabilities and shareholders' equity items. These are general guidelines, to which there are a few exceptions.

2. **Prepare the operating activities section of a statement of cash flows using one of two approaches: (a) the indirect method or (b) the direct method.** The first step in the preparation of a statement of cash flows is to determine the net cash provided (used) by operating activities using either the indirect or direct method (preferred). In the indirect method, we convert profit from an accrual basis to a cash basis. In the direct method, we convert each individual revenue and expense account from an accrual basis to a cash basis.

3. **Prepare the investing activities section of a statement of cash flows.** The second step in the preparation of a statement of

cash flows is to analyze the changes in non-current asset accounts and record them as investing activities, or disclose them as significant noncash transactions.

4. **Prepare the financing activities section of a statement of cash flows.** The third step in the preparation of a statement of cash flows is to analyze the changes in non-current liability and equity accounts and record them as financing activities, or disclose them as significant noncash transactions.

5. **Complete the statement of cash flows.** The fourth and final step in the preparation of a statement of cash flows is to determine the overall cash flow for the year and add it to the opening amount of cash and cash equivalents to determine the ending amount of cash and cash equivalents.

6. **Use the statement of cash flows to evaluate a company's liquidity and solvency.** Liquidity can be measured by the cash-based cash current debt coverage ratio (net cash provided or used by operating activities divided by average current liabilities) and compared with the accrual-based current ratio (current assets divided by current liabilities). Solvency can be measured by the cash-based cash total debt coverage ratio (net cash provided or used by operating activities divided by average total liabilities) and compared with the accrual-based debt to total assets ratio (total liabilities divided by total assets). Free cash flow (net cash provided or used by operating activities minus net capital expenditures minus dividends) is another measure of solvency.

Glossary

Cash current debt coverage   A cash-based ratio used to evaluate liquidity. It is calculated by dividing net cash provided (used) by operating activities by average current liabilities. (p. 696)

Cash total debt coverage   A cash-based ratio used to evaluate solvency. It is calculated by dividing net cash provided (used) by operating activities by average total liabilities. (p. 698)

Direct method   A method of determining net cash provided (used) by operating activities by adjusting each item in the income statement from the accrual basis to the cash basis. (p. 670)

Financing activities   Cash flow activities that result in changes in the size and composition of the equity and borrowings of a company. (p. 665)

Free cash flow   A cash-based measure used to evaluate solvency. It is calculated by deducting net capital expenditures and cash dividends from net cash provided (used) by operating activities. (p. 699)

Indirect method   A method of determining net cash provided (used) by operating activities in which profit is adjusted for items that do not affect cash. (p. 670)

Investing activities   Cash flow activities from the acquisition and disposal of non-current assets. (p. 665)

Operating activities   Cash flow activities arising from a company's principal revenue-producing activities and all other activities that are not investing or financing activities. (p. 665)

DECISION TOOLKIT—A SUMMARY

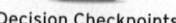
Decision Checkpoints

Info Needed for Decision

Tools to Use for Decision

How to Evaluate Results

Decision Checkpoints	Info Needed for Decision	Tools to Use for Decision	How to Evaluate Results
Is the company generating sufficient cash from operating activities to meet its current obligations?	Net cash provided or used by operating activities and average current liabilities	$$\text{Cash current debt coverage} = \frac{\text{Net cash provided (used) by operating activities}}{\text{Average current liabilities}}$$	A high value suggests good liquidity. Since the numerator contains a cash flow measure, it provides a useful supplement to the current ratio.

| Is the company generating sufficient cash from operating activities to meet its total obligations? | Net cash provided or used by operating activities and average total liabilities | Cash total debt coverage = $$\frac{\text{Net cash provided (used) by operating activities}}{\text{Average total liabilities}}$$ | A high value suggests the company is solvent; that is, it will meet its obligations in the long term. Since the numerator contains a cash flow measure, it provides a useful supplement to the debt to total assets ratio. |
| Can the company meet its long-term obligations? | Net cash provided or used by operating activities, net capital expenditures, and cash dividends | Free cash flow = Net cash provided (used) by operating activities − Net capital expenditures − Dividends paid | Free cash flow indicates the potential to finance new investments, reduce debt, or pay more dividends. |

USING THE DECISION TOOLKIT

Stantec Inc., headquartered in Edmonton, is a professional consulting services company with employees in more than 160 offices throughout North America. Stantec's statement of cash flows for the most recent three years follows:

STANTEC INC.
Statement of Cash Flows
Years Ended December 31
(in thousands)

	2012	2011	2010
Operating activities			
Cash receipts from clients	$1,885,600	$1,611,974	$1,499,392
Cash paid to suppliers	(597,185)	(496,270)	(510,410)
Cash paid to employees	(1,063,256)	(943,439)	(821,360)
Dividends received	—	—	2,852
Interest received	1,910	1,953	3,111
Interest and finance costs paid	(16,010)	(19,150)	(16,775)
Interest taxes paid	(37,760)	(50,282)	(51,548)
Income taxes recovered	7,239	9,800	9,522
Net cash provided by operating activities	180,538	114,586	114,784
Investing activities			
Business acquisitions	(102,019)	(76,434)	(66,989)
Dividends from equity investments	630	175	—
Increase in investments held for self-insured liabilities	(12,594)	(8,393)	(7,301)
Decrease in investments and other assets	2,176	10,767	11,263
Purchase of intangible assets	(9,065)	(3,958)	(3,262)
Purchase of property and equipment	(22,684)	(21,832)	(25,725)
Proceeds on disposition of property and equipment	215	291	412
Net cash used by investing activities	(143,341)	(99,384)	(91,602)
Financing activities			
Repayment of bank debt	(98,195)	(232,838)	(183,301)
Proceeds from bank debt	83,751	80,736	216,948
Net proceeds from notes payable	—	123,885	—
Repayment of finance lease obligations	(6,434)	(5,449)	(5,356)
Repurchase of shares for cancellation	—	(11,074)	(4,887)
Proceeds from issue of share capital	10,205	2,867	3,044
Payment of dividends to shareholders	(20,601)	—	—
Net cash provided (used) by financing activities	(31,274)	(41,873)	26,448
Other (foreign exchange gain [loss])	(281)	51	(1,589)
Net increase (decrease) in cash and cash equivalents	5,642	(26,620)	48,041
Cash and cash equivalents, beginning of the year	36,111	62,731	14,690
Cash and cash equivalents, end of the year	$ 41,753	$ 36,111	$ 62,731

Additional information:

1. Current liabilities were $345,158 thousand, $327,516 thousand, and $331,342 thousand at the end of 2012, 2011, and 2010, respectively.
2. Total liabilities were $741,487 thousand, $700,205 thousand, and $697,930 thousand at the end of 2012, 2011, and 2010, respectively.
3. Profit was $120,902 thousand, $12,662 thousand, and $93,595 thousand in 2012, 2011, and 2010, respectively. The lower profit in 2011 arose primarily from the impairment of goodwill, which does not affect cash flow.

Instructions

(a) Does Stantec use the indirect or direct method to prepare its operating activities section?
(b) Calculate Stantec's cash current debt coverage ratio, cash total debt coverage ratio, and free cash flow for 2012 and 2011.
(c) Comment on any significant changes in Stantec's cash flows over the last three years.

Solution

(a) Stantec uses the direct method to prepare the operating activities section of its statement of cash flows.
(b) (in thousands)

	2012	2011
Cash current debt coverage	$\dfrac{\$180,538}{(\$345,158 + \$327,516) \div 2}$ = 0.5 times	$\dfrac{\$114,586}{(\$327,516 + \$331,342) \div 2}$ = 0.3 times
Cash total debt coverage	$\dfrac{\$180,538}{(\$741,487 + \$700,205) \div 2}$ = 0.3 times	$\dfrac{\$114,586}{(\$700,205 + \$697,930) \div 2}$ = 0.2 times
Free cash flow	$180,538 − ($22,684 − $215) − $20,601 = $137,468	$114,586 − ($21,832 − $291) − $0 = $93,045

(c) Even though there was an increase in cash from customers in 2011 compared with 2010, cash paid to employees increased even more and this held net cash from operating activities at approximately the same level. In 2012, net cash from operating activities rose as cash from customers increased. During that year, cash paid to employees did not rise to the same extent and cash paid for other items such as interest and income taxes fell. Stantec's cash current debt coverage increased in 2012 because of improved cash flow provided by operating activities. The cash total debt coverage in 2012 was not significantly different from 2011 because, even though cash provided by operating activities increased, so did total liabilities as the company did not pay off as much of its bank loans as it did in 2011.

During the past three years, Stantec spent increasing amounts of cash on business acquisitions, with the largest increase in 2012. In each of the three years, cash provided by operating activities was greater than the cash used for investing activities, so the excess cash generated could be used to pay down bank debt and start paying dividends in 2012. Even after paying out dividends in 2012, the company's free cash flow rose.

the
navigator

Comprehensive Do It!

The income statement for Kosinski Inc. contains the following condensed information:

KOSINSKI INC.
Income Statement
Year Ended December 31, 2015

Sales	$6,583,000
Cost of goods sold	3,427,000
Gross profit	3,156,000
Operating expenses	2,349,000
Profit from operations	807,000
Interest expense	124,000
Profit before income tax	683,000
Income tax expense	203,000
Profit	$ 480,000

The following selected current asset and current liability balances are reported on Kosinski's comparative statement of financial position at December 31:

	2015	2014	Increase (Decrease)
Cash	$150,000	$ 30,000	$120,000
Accounts receivable	775,000	610,000	165,000
Merchandise inventory	834,000	867,000	(33,000)
Accounts payable	521,000	501,000	20,000
Income tax payable	53,000	25,000	28,000

Additional information:

1. The company uses a perpetual inventory system.
2. Operating expenses include salaries expense of $1 million, depreciation expense of $300,000, amortization expense of $80,000, and a loss on the disposal of machinery of $24,000.
3. Machinery was sold for $270,000, at a loss of $24,000.
4. New machinery was purchased during the year for $1,250,000. It was partially financed by a bank loan payable issued for $400,000.
5. Dividends paid in 2015 totalled $100,000.

Instructions

(a) Prepare the statement of cash flows using the indirect method.
(b) Prepare the statement of cash flows using the direct method.
(c) Identify the similarities and differences between your answers in parts (a) and (b).

Action Plan

- Determine the net cash provided (used) by operating activities. Operating activities generally relate to revenues and expenses shown on the income statement, which are affected by noncash items in the income statement and changes in noncash current assets and current liabilities in the statement of financial position.
- Recall that profit is used to determine the net cash provided (used) by operating activities and not total comprehensive income.
- Determine the net cash provided (used) by investing activities. Investing activities generally relate to changes in non-current asset accounts.
- Determine the net cash provided (used) by financing activities. Financing activities generally relate to changes in non-current liability and shareholders' equity accounts.
- Determine the net increase (decrease) in cash. Verify that this amount agrees with the end-of-period cash balance reported on the statement of financial position.

Solution to Comprehensive Do It!

(a)

KOSINSKI INC.		
Statement of Cash Flows—Indirect Method		
Year Ended December 31, 2015		
Operating activities		
Profit		$480,000
Adjustments to reconcile profit to net cash		
provided by operating activities		
Depreciation expense	$ 300,000	
Amortization expense	80,000	
Loss on disposal of machinery	24,000	
Increase in accounts receivable	(165,000)	
Decrease in merchandise inventory	33,000	
Increase in accounts payable	20,000	
Increase in income tax payable	28,000	320,000
Net cash provided by operating activities		800,000

(continued)

Investing activities

Disposal of machinery	$ 270,000	
Purchase of machinery (see Note x)	(850,000)	
Net cash used by investing activities		(580,000)

Financing activities

Payment of dividends	$(100,000)	
Net cash used by financing activities		(100,000)
Net increase in cash		120,000
Cash, January 1		30,000
Cash, December 31		$150,000

Note x: Machinery was purchased for $1,250,000 and partially financed by the issue of a $400,000 bank loan payable.

(b)

KOSINSKI INC.
Statement of Cash Flows—Direct Method
Year Ended December 31, 2015

Operating activities

Cash receipts from customers	$6,418,000[1]	
Cash payments		
To suppliers	(3,374,000)[2]	
For operating expenses	(945,000)[3]	
To employees	(1,000,000)	
For interest	(124,000)	
For income tax	(175,000)[4]	
Net cash provided by operating activities		$800,000

Investing activities

Disposal of machinery	$ 270,000	
Purchase of machinery (see Note x)	(850,000)	
Net cash used by investing activities		(580,000)

Financing activities

Payment of dividends	$ (100,000)	
Net cash used by financing activities		(100,000)
Net increase in cash		120,000
Cash, January 1		30,000
Cash, December 31		$150,000

Note x: Machinery was purchased for $1,250,000 and partially financed by the issue of a $400,000 bank loan payable.

Calculations:

[1] Cash receipts from customers: $6,583,000 − $165,000 (accounts receivable) = $6,418,000

[2] Cash payments to suppliers: $3,427,000 − $33,000 (merchandise inventory) − $20,000 (accounts payable) = $3,374,000

[3] Cash payments for operating expenses: $2,349,000 − $1,000,000 (salaries: shown separately as cash payments to employees) − $300,000 (depreciation) − $80,000 (amortization) − $24,000 (loss) = $945,000

[4] Cash payments for income tax: $203,000 − $28,000 (income tax payable) = $175,000

(c) Both the indirect and direct methods report the same net cash provided by operating activities, but they report different detail within each section. Both methods report the same totals and detail for the investing and financing activities section. Both methods arrive at the same change in cash for the period and ending cash balances.

the navigator

WileyPLUS

Self-Test, Brief Exercises, Exercises, Problems: Set A, and many more components are available for practice in *WileyPLUS*.

Self-Test Questions

Answers are at the end of the chapter.

Quiz Yourself

(SO 1, 2) 1. Which is an example of a cash flow from an operating activity?
  (a) A payment of cash to lenders for interest
  (b) A receipt of cash from the sale of common shares
  (c) A payment of dividends to shareholders
  (d) A purchase of merchandise inventory on account

(SO 1, 3) 2. Which is an example of a cash flow from an investing activity?
  (a) A payment of cash to repay a bank loan
  (b) A receipt of cash from issuing common shares
  (c) A receipt of cash from the disposal of equipment
  (d) A purchase of a building, fully financed by a mortgage payable

(SO 1, 4) 3. Which is an example of a cash flow related to a financing activity?
  (a) A receipt of cash from the disposal of land
  (b) A payment of dividends to shareholders
  (c) A payment of cash for income tax
  (d) A receipt of cash for interest on an investment

(SO 2a) 4. Profit for the year is $132,000. During the year, accounts payable increased by $10,000, merchandise inventory decreased by $6,000, and accounts receivable increased by $12,000. Under the indirect method, what is the net cash provided (used) by operating activities?
  (a) $116,000
  (b) $128,000
  (c) $136,000
  (d) $148,000

(SO 2a) 5. In determining net cash provided (used) by operating activities under the indirect method, noncash items that are added back to profit do *not* include:
  (a) depreciation expense.
  (b) impairment loss on equipment.
  (c) a gain on the disposal of equipment.
  (d) a loss on the disposal of equipment.

(SO 2b) 6. The beginning balance in Accounts Receivable is $44,000. The ending balance is $42,000. Sales on account during the period are $129,000. What are the cash receipts from customers?
  (a) $127,000
  (b) $129,000
  (c) $131,000
  (d) $141,000

(SO 2b) 7. Which of the following items is reported in the operating activities section of a statement of cash flows prepared by the direct method?
  (a) A loss on the disposal of a building
  (b) An increase in accounts receivable
  (c) Depreciation expense
  (d) Cash payments to suppliers

(SO 3, 4) 8. The following data relate to cash received or paid from various transactions for Orange Corporation:

Disposal of land	$100,000
Issue of common shares	70,000
Disposal of a long-term investment	50,000
Payment of cash dividends	40,000
Purchase of equipment	30,000

Orange's net cash provided by investing and financing activities is as follows:
  (a) $120,000 provided by investing activities and $30,000 provided by financing activities.
  (b) $70,000 provided by investing activities and $80,000 provided by financing activities.
  (c) $50,000 provided by investing activities and $100,000 provided by financing activities.
  (d) $180,000 provided by investing activities and $110,000 provided by financing activities.

(SO 6) 9. Which of the following statements is *not* true?
  (a) The higher the cash current debt coverage and current ratios, the better.
  (b) The higher the cash total debt coverage and debt to total assets ratios, the better.
  (c) The higher the free cash flow, the better.
  (d) The cash current debt coverage ratio is a liquidity ratio.

(SO 6) 10. The cash current debt coverage ratio is a cash-based counterpart to the accrual-based:
  (a) current ratio.
  (b) receivables turnover.
  (c) debt to total assets.
  (d) free cash flow.

Questions

(SO 1) 1. What is a statement of cash flows and why is it useful?

(SO 1) 2. What are "cash equivalents"? Should a company combine cash equivalents with cash when preparing the statement of cash flows? Explain why or why not.

(SO 1) 3. Explain the differences among the three categories of activities—operating, investing, and financing—reported in the statement of cash flows.

(SO 1) 4. Private companies following ASPE can classify interest and dividends differently than can companies following IFRS. Explain how these classifications can differ and identify the most commonly used classification(s).

(SO 1) 5. Masood and Adriana were discussing where they should report significant noncash investing and financing transactions in Rock Candy Corp.'s statement of cash flows. Give two examples of these transactions and describe where they should be reported.

(SO 2) 6. (a) Identify whether each of the following is used in the preparation of a statement of cash flows: (1) the adjusted trial balance, (2) the statement of financial position, (3) the income statement, (4) the statement of comprehensive income, and (5) the statement of changes in equity. (b) Explain how each of the items identified in part (a) is used in the preparation of the statement of cash flows.

(SO 2) 7. Goh Corporation changed its method of reporting operating activities from the indirect method to the direct method in order to make its statement of cash flows more informative to its readers. Will this change increase, decrease, or not affect the net cash provided (used) by operating activities?

(SO 2) 8. In 2012, **Clearwater Seafoods Incorporated,** one of Canada's largest seafood companies, reported $22,704 thousand of profit. During the same period of time, its cash provided by operating activities, of $48,141 thousand, was more than twice the amount of profit. Explain how this could occur.

(SO 2a) 9. Describe the indirect method for determining net cash provided (used) by operating activities.

(SO 2a) 10. Why and how is depreciation and amortization expense reported in the operating activities section of a statement of cash flows prepared using the indirect method?

(SO 2a) 11. The gain on the disposal of equipment is deducted from profit when calculating net cash provided (used) by operating activities in the indirect method. Jacques doesn't understand why gains aren't added, rather than deducted, on the statement of cash flows since they result in an increase in profit on the income statement. He also doesn't understand why only the gain and not the proceeds from the entire disposal of the equipment is reported in the operating activities section. Help Jacques understand the reporting of the disposal of equipment on the statement of cash flows.

(SO 2b) 12. Describe the direct method for determining net cash provided (used) by operating activities.

(SO 2b) 13. Under the direct method, why is depreciation and amortization expense not reported in the operating activities section?

(SO 2, 3) 14. Denis says, "I understand that operating activities are affected by changes in current asset and current liability accounts. I also know that trading investments are current assets and that the purchase and sale of trading investments are recorded as operating activities. What I don't understand is why the purchase and sale of investments that are not held for trading are usually classified as investing activities." Help Denis understand the classification of investments.

(SO 2b, 3, 4) 15. Explain how (a) the disposal of equipment at a gain, and (b) the loss on disposal of land are reported on a statement of cash flows using the direct method.

(SO 2, 4) 16. Laurel says, "I understand that operating activities are affected by changes in current asset and current liability accounts. I also know that short-term loans payable are current liabilities. What I don't understand is why short-term loans are not always classified as operating activities. Occasionally they are classified as operating activities but mostly they are classified as financing activities." Help Laurel understand the classification of short-term loans payable.

(SO 2, 3, 4) 17. In general, would you expect a growing company to report positive or negative cash flows from its operating, investing, and financing activities? Explain.

(SO 5) 18. Explain how the statement of cash flows interrelates with the other financial statements.

(SO 6) 19. Give examples of cash- and accrual-based ratios that measure (a) liquidity, and (b) solvency.

(SO 6) 20. In 2012, **Leon's Furniture Limited** reported a current ratio of 2.9:1 and a cash current debt coverage ratio of 0.4 times. Explain why Leon's cash current debt coverage is likely so much lower than its current ratio.

(SO 6) 21. In 2012, **Rogers Communications Inc.** reported a debt to total assets ratio of 81% and a cash total debt coverage ratio of 0.2 times. Its competitor, **Shaw Communications Inc.,** reported a debt to total assets ratio of 68% and a cash total debt coverage ratio of 0.1 times in the same year. Based only on this information, which company is more solvent?

(SO 6) 22. A company's cash total debt coverage ratio and free cash flow have been declining steadily over the last five years. What does this decline likely mean to creditors and investors?

(SO 6) 23. How is it possible for a company to report positive net cash provided by operating activities but have a negative free cash flow?

Brief Exercises

BE13–1 For each of the following transactions, indicate whether it will result in an increase (+), decrease (−), or have no effect (NE) on cash flows:

(a) _____ Repayment of mortgage payable
(b) _____ Payment of interest on mortgage
(c) _____ Purchase of land in exchange for common shares
(d) _____ Issue of preferred shares
(e) _____ Purchase of a trading investment that is not a cash equivalent

(f) _____ Collection of accounts receivable
(g) _____ Declaration of cash dividend
(h) _____ Payment of cash dividend (see item [g] above)
(i) _____ Purchase of merchandise inventory
(j) _____ Recording of depreciation expense

Indicate impact of transactions on cash.
(SO 1)

BE13–2 Classify each of the transactions listed in BE13–1 as an operating (O), investing (I), financing (F), or significant noncash investing and financing (NC) activity. If a transaction does not belong in any of these classifications, explain why.

Classify activities.
(SO 1)

BE13–3 **Mega Brands Inc.** reported the following items on its statement of cash flows:

1. _____ Repayment of long-term debt
2. _____ Depreciation expense
3. _____ Acquisition of property, plant, and equipment
4. _____ Issue of common shares

5. _____ Repayment of debentures (bonds)
6. _____ Changes in noncash operating working capital items

Classify activities.
(SO 1, 2a)

(a) Indicate in which section each of the above items was reported in Mega Brands' statement of cash flows—operating activity (O), investing activity (I), or financing activity (F). (b) Does Mega Brands use the indirect or direct method of preparing the operating activities section of its statement of cash flow? Explain how you came to your conclusion.

BE13–4 Indicate whether each of the following transactions would be added to (+) or subtracted from (−) profit to calculate net cash provided (used) by operating activities using the indirect method. If a transaction is not an operating activity, indicate that it is NA (not applicable).

(a) _____ Depreciation expense
(b) _____ Increase in accounts receivable
(c) _____ Decrease in merchandise inventory in the perpetual inventory system
(d) _____ Increase in accounts payable

(e) _____ Decrease in income tax payable
(f) _____ Gain on disposal of equipment
(g) _____ Loss on sale of long-term investment
(h) _____ Decrease in dividend payable
(i) _____ Impairment loss for goodwill

Indicate impact on operating activities—indirect method.
(SO 2a)

BE13–5 The comparative statement of financial position for Dupigne Corporation shows the following noncash current asset and liability accounts at March 31:

	2015	2014
Accounts receivable	$60,000	$40,000
Merchandise inventory	75,000	70,000
Prepaid expenses	6,000	4,000
Accounts payable	35,000	40,000
Interest payable	5,000	7,500
Income tax payable	17,000	12,000

Calculate operating activities—indirect method.
(SO 2a)

Dupigne's income statement reported the following selected information for the year ended March 31, 2015: profit was $275,000, depreciation expense was $60,000, and a loss on the disposal of land was $15,000. Dupigne uses a perpetual inventory system. Calculate net cash provided (used) by operating activities using the indirect method.

BE13–6 Idol Corporation has accounts receivable of $14,000 at January 1, and of $24,000 at December 31. Sales revenues were $170,000 for the year. What amount of cash was received from customers?

Calculate cash receipts from customers—direct method.
(SO 2b)

BE13–7 **Columbia Sportswear Company** reported cost of goods sold of U.S. $953,169 thousand on its 2012 income statement. It also reported a decrease in merchandise inventory of U.S. $1,874 thousand and a decrease in accounts payable of U.S. $6,733 thousand. What amount of cash was paid to suppliers, assuming that the company uses a perpetual inventory system and that accounts payable relate to merchandise creditors?

Calculate cash payments to suppliers—direct method.
(SO 2b)

BE13–8 Excellence Corporation reports operating expenses of $100,000, including depreciation expense of $15,000, amortization expense of $2,500, and a gain of $500 on the disposal of equipment during the current year. During this same period, prepaid expenses increased by $6,600 and accrued expenses payable decreased by $2,400. Calculate the cash payments for operating expenses.

Calculate cash payments for operating expenses—direct method.
(SO 2b)

BE13–9 Home Grocery Limited reported income tax expense of $90,000 for the year. (a) Calculate the cash payments for income tax assuming income tax payable increased by $2,000 during the year. (b) Repeat part (a), assuming income tax payable decreased by $2,000 during the year.

Calculate cash payments for income tax—direct method.
(SO 2b)

Calculate operating activities—direct method.
(SO 2b)

BE13–10 The comparative statement of financial position for Baird Corporation shows the following noncash current asset and liability accounts at March 31:

	2015	2014
Accounts receivable	$60,000	$40,000
Merchandise inventory	64,000	70,000
Prepaid expenses	6,000	4,000
Accounts payable	35,000	40,000
Interest payable	4,000	5,000
Income tax payable	10,000	5,000

Baird's income statement reported the following selected information for the year ended March 31, 2015: sales were $850,000, cost of goods sold was $475,000, operating expenses were $230,000 (which included depreciation expense of $20,000), interest expense was $50,000, and income tax expense was $15,000. Calculate net cash provided (used) by operating activities using the direct method.

Calculate cash received from disposal of equipment.
(SO 3)

BE13–11 The T accounts for equipment and accumulated depreciation for Trevis Ltd. are shown here:

Equipment				Accumulated Depreciation—Equipment		
Beg. bal.	80,000	Disposals	20,000	Disposals	5,500	Beg. bal. 44,500
Acquisitions	40,000					Depreciation 20,000
End bal.	100,000					End bal. 59,000

In addition, Trevis's income statement reported a $1,500 loss on the disposal of equipment. (a) What amount was reported on the statement of cash flows as "cash provided by disposal of equipment"? (b) In what section of the statement of cash flows would this transaction be reported?

Prepare investing activities section.
(SO 3)

BE13–12 Holmes Corporation reported the following information (in thousands) at December 31, 2015:

	2015	2014
Long-term investments	$150	$100
Land	200	200
Buildings	300	300
Accumulated depreciation—buildings	90	75
Equipment	500	400
Accumulated depreciation—equipment	200	200

Additional information:

1. Long-term investments were purchased during the year; none were sold.
2. Equipment was purchased during the year. In addition, equipment with a cost of $100 and a carrying amount of $50 was sold at a gain of $10.

Prepare the investing activities section of Holmes's statement of cash flows for the year.

Calculate cash paid for dividends.
(SO 4)

BE13–13 **Canadian Tire Corporation, Limited** reported a profit of $499.2 million for the year ended December 29, 2012. Its retained earnings were $3,686.4 million at the beginning of the year and $4,074.4 million at the end of the year. It had no dividends payable at the beginning or end of the year. Assuming no other changes to retained earnings, what amount of dividends did Canadian Tire pay during the year? Would your answer change if you knew that the Dividends Payable account increased during the year?

Prepare financing activities section.
(SO 4)

BE13–14 Nicoloff Corporation reported the following information (in thousands) at December 31, 2015:

	2015	2014
Dividends payable	$ 15	$ 10
Bank loan payable—current portion	200	200
Bank loan payable—non-current portion	400	300
Common shares	600	400
Retained earnings	700	500

Additional information:

1. The bank loan was increased by additional borrowings of $300 to partially finance the purchase of new equipment that cost $500. The bank loan was decreased by repayments.
2. Common shares were issued during the year. None were reacquired.
3. Dividends were paid during the year.
4. Profit for the year was $400.

Prepare the financing activities section of Nicoloff's statement of cash flows for the year.

Calculate cash-based ratios.
(SO 6)

BE13–15 Jain Corporation reported net cash provided by operating activities of $325,000, net cash used by investing activities of $250,000, and net cash provided by financing activities of $70,000. In addition, cash spent for net capital expenditures during the period was $200,000, and $25,000 of dividends were paid. Average current liabilities were $215,000 and average total liabilities were $360,000. Calculate these values: (a) cash current debt coverage, (b) cash total debt coverage, and (c) free cash flow.

BE13–16   **Big Rock Brewery** reported the following selected liquidity ratios:

	2012	2011
Current ratio	1.7:1	1.1:1
Cash current debt coverage	1.8 times	1.2 times

Both the current and cash current debt coverage ratios increased in 2012. What does this mean?

Evaluate liquidity.
(SO 6)

BE13–17   **Bombardier Inc.** reported the following selected solvency ratios:

	2012	2011
Debt to total assets	94.7%	97.2%
Cash total debt coverage	0.1 times	0.0 times

Based on the above, has Bombardier's solvency improved or deteriorated? Explain.

Evaluate solvency.
(SO 6)

Exercises

E13–1   Eng Corporation had the following transactions:

Classify activities.
(SO 1)

	(a) Cash Effect	(b) Classification
1. Issued common shares for $50,000.		
2. Purchased a machine for $30,000. Made a $5,000 down payment and issued a long-term note payable for the remainder.		
3. Collected $16,000 of accounts receivable.		
4. Paid a $25,000 cash dividend.		
5. Sold a long-term investment with a carrying amount of $15,000 for $18,000.		
6. Sold merchandise inventory for $1,000.		
7. Paid $18,000 on accounts payable.		
8. Purchased a trading investment (equity securities) for $100,000.		
9. Purchased merchandise inventory for $28,000 on account.		
10. Collected $1,000 in advance from customers.		

Instructions

(a) In the above table, indicate by how much each transaction increases (+) or decreases (−) cash. If the transaction has no effect (NE) on cash, say so.

(b) Identify whether the transaction should be classified as an operating activity (O), investing activity (I), financing activity (F), or noncash investing and financing activity (NC).

E13–2   Crown Point Limited reports the following noncash transactions:

Discuss noncash items.
(SO 1)

1. Recorded an impairment loss on goodwill
2. Recorded depreciation expense
3. Recorded an unrealized gain on a trading investment carried at fair value through profit or loss
4. Purchased a new vehicle by signing a bank loan payable
5. Declared and distributed a stock dividend
6. Effected a 2-for-1 stock split
7. Converted an account receivable to a note receivable
8. Acquired equipment by issuing common shares

Instructions

For each of the above transactions, explain why it does not involve cash and where it should be reported, if at all, on the statement of cash flows or accompanying notes.

E13–3   He Corporation had the following transactions:

Indicate impact of transactions on profit and operating activities.
(SO 2)

	(a) Profit	(b) Cash Provided (Used) by Operating Activities
1. Sold merchandise inventory for cash at a higher price than its cost.	+	+
2. Collected cash in advance from a customer for a service to be provided in the future.		
3. Purchased merchandise inventory on account in a perpetual inventory system.		
4. Declared and paid dividends.		
5. Recorded and paid salaries.		

(continued)

	(a)	(b)
		Cash Provided (Used)
	Profit	by Operating Activities

6. Recorded income tax payable.
7. Accrued interest receivable.
8. Recorded depreciation expense.
9. Paid an amount owing on account to a supplier.
10. Collected an amount owing from a customer.

Instructions

Complete the above table indicating whether each transaction will increase (+), decrease (−), or have no effect (NE) on (a) profit and (b) cash provided (used) by operating activities. The first one has been done for you as an example.

Classify activities—
indirect method.
(SO 2a)

E13–4 The following is a list of transactions that occurred during the year.

	Operating Activities	Investing Activities	Financing Activities	Noncash Activities
1. Purchased merchandise inventory for cash.	−	NE	NE	NE
2. Sold merchandise inventory on account.				
3. Sold equipment for cash at a loss.				
4. Recorded depreciation on equipment.				
5. Paid dividends.				
6. Recorded an unrealized loss on a long-term equity investment carried at fair value through profit or loss.				
7. Collected an account from a customer.				
8. Signed and received a mortgage payable.				
9. Paid, in full, the current portion of a mortgage payable.				
10. Purchased land by issuing common shares.				

Instructions

Complete the above table, indicating in which classification(s) each transaction would appear in a statement of cash flows prepared using the indirect method, and whether the transaction would be added to (+), deducted from (−), or have no effect (NE) on the category you have chosen. The first one has been done for you as an example.

Prepare operating
activities section—
indirect method.
(SO 2a)

E13–5 Selected information from Juno Ltd.'s statement of financial position and income statement is shown on the following page:

JUNO LTD.
Statement of Financial Position (partial)
December 31

	2015	2014
Current assets		
Accounts receivable	$7,000	$12,000
Merchandise inventory	5,900	4,500
Prepaid expenses	3,000	2,500
Current liabilities		
Accounts payable	3,750	2,500
Income tax payable	1,200	800
Accrued liabilities	2,500	1,500
Bank loan payable—current portion	5,000	10,000

JUNO LTD.
Income Statement
Year Ended December 31, 2015

Net sales	$190,000
Cost of goods sold	114,000
Gross profit	76,000
Operating expenses	50,000
Profit from operations	26,000
Interest expense	1,200
Profit before income tax	24,800
Income tax expense	3,800
Profit	$ 21,000

Additional information:

1. The bank loan was issued to finance the purchase of equipment.
2. Operating expenses included depreciation expense of $11,000 and a loss of $5,000 on the disposal of equipment.

Instructions

Prepare the operating activities section of the statement of cash flows, using the indirect method.

E13–6 The following is a list of income statement accounts that must be converted from the accrual basis to the cash basis in order to calculate cash provided (used) by operating activities using the direct method:

Convert operating activities from accrual to cash basis—direct method.
(SO 2b)

Income Statement Account	Change in Current Asset/ Current Liability Account	(a) Add to (+) or Deduct from (−) Income Statement Account	(b) Related Cash Receipt or Payment
1. Sales revenue	Increase in accounts receivable	−	Cash receipts from customers
2. Dividend revenue	Decrease in dividends receivable		
3. Interest revenue	Increase in interest receivable		
4. Rent revenue	Increase in unearned rent		
5. Cost of goods sold	Increase in merchandise inventory		
6. Cost of goods sold	Increase in accounts payable		
7. Insurance expense	Increase in prepaid insurance		
8. Salaries expense	Increase in salaries payable		
9. Interest expense	Decrease in interest payable		
10. Income tax expense	Increase in income tax payable		

Instructions

For each of the above changes in a current asset or current liability account listed beside the related income statement account, identify if (a) the change should be added to (+) or deducted from (−) the income statement account in order to convert the accrual-based number to a cash-based number; and (b) the title of the resulting cash receipt or payment on the statement of cash flows. The first one has been done for you as an example.

E13–7 The following selected information is taken from the general ledger of Carnival Limited:

Calculate cash flows—direct method.
(SO 2b)

(a)	Sales revenue	$160,000	(c)	Salaries expense	$35,000
	Accounts receivable, January 1	16,000		Salaries payable, January 1	500
	Accounts receivable, December 31	14,000		Salaries payable, December 31	675
(b)	Cost of goods sold	$96,000	(d)	Operating expenses	$50,000
	Merchandise inventory, January 1	9,200		Accrued expenses payable, January 1	4,200
	Merchandise inventory, December 31	10,900		Accrued expenses payable, December 31	3,900
	Accounts payable, January 1	11,500		Prepaid expenses, January 1	2,600
	Accounts payable, December 31	10,700		Prepaid expenses, December 31	2,150

Instructions

Using the above information and the direct method, calculate the (a) cash receipts from customers, (b) cash payments to suppliers, (c) cash payments to employees, and (d) cash payments for operating expenses.

E13–8 The comparative statement of financial position for Charmaine Retailers Ltd. follows:

Prepare statement of cash flows—indirect method.
(SO 2a, 3, 4, 5, 6)

CHARMAINE RETAILERS LTD.
Statement of Financial Position
December 31

	2015	2014
Assets		
Cash	$ 18,000	$ 9,000
Accounts receivable	50,000	42,000
Merchandise inventory	168,000	143,000
Furniture	163,000	80,000
Accumulated depreciation	(45,000)	(24,000)
Total assets	$354,000	$250,000
Liabilities and Shareholders' Equity		
Accounts payable	$ 45,000	$ 35,000
Bank loan payable (noncurrent)	103,000	76,000
Common shares	60,000	55,000
Retained earnings	146,000	84,000
Total liabilities and shareholders' equity	$354,000	$250,000

Additional information:

1. Profit was $62,000 in 2015.
2. Depreciation expense was $21,000 in 2015.
3. Payments made to the bank pertaining to the bank loan were $10,000 in 2015. Some new loans were obtained that year.
4. Common shares were issued in 2015 and no shares have been bought back by the company.
5. In 2015, no furniture was sold.

Instructions

Prepare a statement of cash flows using the indirect method for 2015. Assess the strength of the company's cash flows for that year.

Prepare statement of cash flows—indirect method.
(SO 2a, 3, 4, 5, 6)

E13-9   The comparative statement of financial position for Dagenais Retailers Ltd. follows:

DAGENAIS RETAILERS LTD.
Statement of Financial Position
December 31

	2015	2014
Assets		
Cash	$ 1,000	$ 18,000
Accounts receivable	76,000	50,000
Merchandise inventory	219,000	168,000
Furniture	130,000	163,000
Accumulated depreciation	(35,000)	(45,000)
Total assets	$391,000	$354,000
Liabilities and Shareholders' Equity		
Accounts payable	$ 58,000	$ 45,000
Bank loan payable (noncurrent)	100,000	103,000
Common shares	60,000	60,000
Retained earnings	173,000	146,000
Total liabilities and shareholders' equity	$391,000	$354,000

Additional information:

1. Profit was $32,000 in 2015.
2. Depreciation expense was $19,000 in 2015.
3. In 2015, no new bank loans were received.
4. In 2015, no furniture was purchased, but some furniture was sold for $6,000, which resulted in a gain on this disposal of $2,000.
5. In 2015, dividends were declared and paid.

Instructions

Prepare a statement of cash flows using the indirect method for 2015. Assess the strength of the company's cash flows for that year.

Prepare operating activities section—direct method.
(SO 2b)

E13-10   Selected information from Juno Ltd.'s statement of financial position and income statement is found in E13-5. In addition to the information contained in these statements, note the following:

1. Prepaid expenses and accrued liabilities relate to operating expenses.
2. Accounts payable relate to purchases of merchandise.
3. Operating expenses included depreciation expense of $11,000 and a loss of $5,000 on the disposal of equipment.

Instructions

Prepare the operating activities section of the statement of cash flows, using the direct method.

Calculate investing and financing activities.
(SO 3, 4)

E13-11   The following selected accounts are from Dupré Corp.'s general ledger:

Land

Jan.	1	Bal.	500,000		
Dec.	1		6,000		
Dec.	31	Bal.	506,000		

Equipment

Jan.	1	Bal.	160,000		
July	31		70,000		
Sept.	2		53,000	Nov. 10	39,000
Dec.	31	Bal.	244,000		

Accumulated Depreciation—Equipment

		Jan. 1	Bal.	71,000
Nov. 10	30,000	Dec. 31		48,000
		Dec. 31	Bal.	89,000

Bank Loan Payable

		Jan. 1	Bal.	0
		Sept. 2		43,000
		Dec. 31	Bal.	43,000

Retained Earnings

		Jan. 1	Bal.	105,000
Aug. 23	4,000	Dec. 31		60,000
		Dec. 31	Bal.	161,000

Additional information:

July 31	Equipment with a cost of $70,000 was purchased for cash.
Sept. 2	Equipment with a cost of $53,000 was purchased and partially financed through the issue of a long-term bank loan payable.
Aug. 23	A $4,000 cash dividend was paid.
Nov. 10	A loss of $3,000 was incurred on the disposal of equipment.
Dec. 1	Acquired a small parcel of adjoining land.
31	Depreciation expense of $48,000 was recorded for the year.
31	Profit for the year was $60,000.

Instructions

From the postings in the above accounts and additional information provided, indicate what information would be reported in the investing and/or financing activities sections of, and notes to, the statement of cash flows.

E13–12 The comparative unclassified statement of financial position for Puffy Ltd. follows:

Prepare statement of cash flows—indirect and direct methods.
(SO 2a, 2b, 3, 4, 5)

PUFFY LTD.
Statement of Financial Position
December 31

	2015	2014
Assets		
Cash	$ 53,000	$ 22,000
Accounts receivable	80,000	76,000
Merchandise inventory	185,000	189,000
Land	70,000	100,000
Equipment	265,000	200,000
Accumulated depreciation	(66,000)	(32,000)
Total assets	$587,000	$555,000
Liabilities and Shareholders' Equity		
Accounts payable	$ 39,000	$ 47,000
Bank loan payable	150,000	200,000
Common shares	199,000	174,000
Retained earnings	199,000	134,000
Total liabilities and shareholders' equity	$587,000	$555,000

Additional information:

1. Profit was $115,000.
2. Sales were $978,000.
3. Cost of goods sold was $751,000.
4. Operating expenses were $43,000, exclusive of depreciation expense.
5. Depreciation expense was $34,000.
6. Interest expense was $14,000.
7. Income tax expense was $26,000.
8. Land was sold at a gain of $5,000.
9. No equipment was sold during the year.
10. $50,000 of the bank loan was repaid during the year.
11. Common shares were issued for $25,000.

Instructions

Prepare a statement of cash flows using (a) the indirect method, or (b) the direct method, as assigned by your instructor.

Compare cash flows for three companies.
(SO 2, 3, 4, 6)

E13–13 Condensed profit and cash flow information follow for three companies operating in the same industry:

	Company A	Company B	Company C
Profit	$ 75,000	$ 25,000	$(50,000)
Net cash provided (used) by operating activities	100,000	(25,000)	(25,000)
Net cash provided (used) by investing activities	(50,000)	(25,000)	35,000
Net cash provided (used) by financing activities	(25,000)	75,000	15,000
Net increase in cash	25,000	25,000	25,000

Instructions

Which company is in better financial condition? Explain the reasoning behind your decision.

Calculate and evaluate liquidity and solvency.
(SO 6)

E13–14 Information for two companies in the same industry, Ria Corporation and Les Corporation, is presented here:

	Ria Corporation	Les Corporation
Net cash provided by operating activities	$200,000	$200,000
Average current liabilities	50,000	150,000
Average total liabilities	200,000	200,000
Net capital expenditures	20,000	35,000
Dividends paid	24,000	18,000

Instructions

(a) Calculate the cash current debt coverage ratio, cash total debt coverage ratio, and free cash flow for each company.
(b) Compare the liquidity and solvency of the two companies.

Problems: Set A

Classify activities.
(SO 1)

P13–1A The following is a list of transactions that took place during the year:

	(a) Classification	(b) Cash Flow	(c) Profit
1. Paid salaries to employees.	O	–	–
2. Sold land for cash, at a gain.			
3. Purchased a building by making a down payment in cash and signing a mortgage payable for the balance.			
4. Made a principal repayment on the mortgage.			
5. Paid interest on the mortgage.			
6. Issued common shares for cash.			
7. Purchased shares of another company to be held as a long-term non-strategic investment.			
8. Paid dividends to shareholders.			
9. Sold merchandise inventory on account, at a price greater than cost. The company uses a perpetual inventory system.			
10. Wrote down the cost of the remaining inventory to its net realizable value.			

Instructions

(a) Classify each of the above transactions as an operating activity (O), investing activity (I), financing activity (F), or noncash investing and financing activity (NC). If it does not fit into one of these classifications, indicate that there is no effect (NE). The first one has been done for you as an example.
(b) Specify if the transaction will result in a cash receipt (+), cash payment (−), or have no effect on cash (NE).
(c) Indicate if the transaction will increase (+), decrease (−), or have no effect (NE) on profit.
(d) Explain how it is possible for the same transaction to affect cash and profit differently.

Prepare operating activities section—indirect and direct methods.
(SO 2a, 2b)

P13–2A The income statement for Whistler Ltd., a publicly traded company following IFRS, is presented here:

WHISTLER LTD.
Income Statement
Year Ended November 30, 2015

Sales	$8,000,000
Cost of goods sold	5,000,000
Gross profit	3,000,000
Operating expenses	2,000,000
Profit from operations	1,000,000
Interest expense	100,000
Profit before income tax	900,000
Income tax expense	300,000
Profit	$ 600,000

Additional information:

1. Operating expenses include $75,000 of depreciation expense and a $100,000 impairment loss on property, plant, and equipment.
2. Accounts receivable increased by $190,000.
3. Merchandise inventory decreased by $50,000.
4. Prepaid expenses related to operating expenses increased by $40,000.
5. Accounts payable to suppliers of merchandise decreased by $180,000.

6. Accrued liabilities related to operating expenses decreased by $90,000.
7. Interest payable decreased by $10,000.
8. Unearned revenue that was received from customers decreased by $17,000.
9. Income tax payable increased by $20,000.

Instructions

(a) Prepare the operating activities section of the statement of cash flows, using either (1) the indirect method or (2) the direct method, as assigned by your instructor.

(b) Would your answer in part (a) change if Whistler were a private company following ASPE?

P13–3A The income statement for Tremblant Limited is presented here:

Prepare operating activities section— indirect and direct methods—and discuss methods.
(SO 2a, 2b)

TREMBLANT LIMITED	
Income Statement	
Year Ended December 31, 2015	
Service revenue	$925,000
Operating expenses	701,000
Profit from operations	224,000
Interest expense	75,000
Profit before income tax	149,000
Income tax expense	37,250
Profit	$111,750

Tremblant's statement of financial position contained these comparative data at December 31:

	2015	2014
Accounts receivable	$57,000	$47,000
Prepaid expenses	12,000	15,000
Accounts payable	36,000	41,000
Salaries payable	19,500	20,000
Unearned revenue	12,000	9,000
Interest payable	6,250	5,000
Income tax payable	4,000	9,250

Additional information:

1. Operating expenses include depreciation expense, $50,000; amortization expense, $15,000; administrative expenses, $110,000; salaries expense, $500,000; and loss on the disposal of equipment, $26,000.
2. Unearned revenue is received from customers.
3. Prepaid expenses and accounts payable relate to operating (administrative) expenses.

Instructions

(a) Prepare the operating activities section of the statement of cash flows, using either (1) the indirect method or (2) the direct method, as assigned by your instructor.

(b) Which method—indirect or direct—do you recommend that this company use to prepare its operating activities section? Explain your reasoning.

P13–4A The following selected account balances relate to the property, plant, and equipment accounts of Katewill Inc.:

Calculate and classify cash flows for property, plant, and equipment.
(SO 3)

	2015	2014
Accumulated depreciation—buildings	$337,500	$300,000
Accumulated depreciation—equipment	144,000	96,000
Depreciation expense—buildings	37,500	37,500
Depreciation expense—equipment	60,000	48,000
Land	100,000	60,000
Buildings	750,000	750,000
Equipment	300,000	240,000
Gain on disposal of equipment	5,000	0

Additional information:

1. Purchased $40,000 of land for cash.
2. Purchased $75,000 of equipment for a $10,000 down payment, financing the remainder with a bank loan. Equipment was also sold during the year.

Instructions

(a) Calculate any cash receipts or payments related to the property, plant, and equipment accounts in 2015.

(b) Indicate where each of the cash receipts or payments identified in part (a) would be classified on the statement of cash flows or accompanying notes.

(c) Would you expect a growing company to be generating or using cash for its investing activities? Explain.

Calculate and classify cash flows for shareholders' equity.
(SO 4)

P13–5A   The following selected account balances relate to the shareholders' equity accounts of Valerio Corp.:

	2015	2014
Preferred shares, 3,250 shares in 2015; 2,750 in 2014	$325,000	$275,000
Common shares, 50,000 shares in 2015; 40,000 in 2014	600,000	400,000
Retained earnings	500,000	300,000
Cash dividends—preferred	11,250	13,750
Dividends payable	2,812	3,438

Additional information:

1. During the year, 500 preferred shares were issued. No preferred shares were repurchased.
2. During the year, 10,000 common shares were issued. No common shares were repurchased.

Instructions

(a) Determine the amounts of any cash receipts or payments related to the shareholders' equity accounts in 2015.

(b) Indicate where each of the cash receipts or payments identified in part (a) would be classified on the statement of cash flows or accompanying notes.

(c) Would you expect a growing company to be generating or using cash for its financing activities? Explain.

Prepare statement of cash flows—indirect and direct methods.
(SO 2a, 2b, 3, 4, 5)

P13–6A   Financial statements for E-Perform, Inc. follow:

E-PERFORM, INC.
Statement of Financial Position
December 31

	2015	2014
Assets		
Cash	$ 97,800	$ 48,400
Trading investments	128,000	114,000
Accounts receivable	75,800	43,000
Inventories	122,500	92,850
Prepaid expenses	18,400	26,000
Property, plant, and equipment	270,000	242,500
Accumulated depreciation	(50,000)	(52,000)
Total assets	$662,500	$514,750
Liabilities and Shareholders' Equity		
Accounts payable	$ 93,000	$ 77,300
Accrued liabilities	11,500	7,000
Bank loan payable	110,000	150,000
Common shares	200,000	175,000
Retained earnings	248,000	105,450
Total liabilities and shareholders' equity	$662,500	$514,750

E-PERFORM, INC.
Income Statement
Year Ended December 31, 2015

Sales		$492,780
Cost of goods sold		185,460
Gross profit		307,320
Operating expenses		116,410
Profit from operations		190,910
Other revenues and expenses		
Unrealized gain on trading investments	$14,000	
Interest expense	(4,730)	9,270
Profit before income tax		200,180
Income tax expense		45,000
Profit		$155,180

Additional information:

1. Prepaid expenses and accrued liabilities relate to operating expenses.
2. An unrealized gain on trading investments of $14,000 was recorded.
3. New equipment costing $85,000 was purchased for $25,000 cash and a $60,000 long-term bank loan payable.
4. Old equipment having an original cost of $57,500 was sold for $1,500.
5. Accounts payable relate to merchandise creditors.
6. Some of the bank loan was repaid during the year.
7. A dividend was paid during the year.
8. Operating expenses include $46,500 of depreciation expense and a $7,500 loss on disposal of equipment.

Instructions

(a) Prepare the statement of cash flows, using either (1) the indirect method or (2) the direct method, as assigned by your instructor.
(b) E-Perform's cash position doubled between 2014 and 2015. Identify the primary reason(s) for this significant increase.

P13–7A The financial statements of Resolute Inc. are presented here:

Prepare statement of cash flows—indirect and direct methods. (SO 2a, 2b, 3, 4, 5)

RESOLUTE INC.
Statement of Financial Position
December 31

	2015	2014
Assets		
Cash	$ 13,000	$ 5,000
Accounts receivable	38,000	24,000
Merchandise inventory	27,000	20,000
Property, plant, and equipment	80,000	78,000
Accumulated depreciation	(30,000)	(24,000)
Goodwill	5,000	16,000
Total assets	$133,000	$119,000
Liabilities and Shareholders' Equity		
Accounts payable	$ 17,000	$ 15,000
Salaries payable	1,900	2,100
Income tax payable	1,000	4,000
Bank loan payable	34,100	50,650
Common shares	18,000	14,000
Retained earnings	56,000	28,250
Accumulated other comprehensive income	5,000	5,000
Total liabilities and shareholders' equity	$133,000	$119,000

RESOLUTE INC.
Income Statement
Year Ended December 31, 2015

Sales	$256,000
Cost of goods sold	140,000
Gross profit	116,000
Operating expenses	78,250
Profit from operations	37,750
Interest expense	4,000
Profit before income tax	33,750
Income tax expense	6,000
Profit	$ 27,750

Cash 8500
Accumulated 6000

Additional information:

1. Equipment was sold during the year for $8,500 cash. The equipment originally cost $12,000 and had a carrying amount of $8,500 at the time of sale.
2. Equipment costing $14,000 was purchased in exchange for $4,000 cash and a $10,000 long-term bank loan.
3. Accounts payable relate to merchandise creditors.
4. Some of the bank loan was repaid during the year.
5. Operating expenses are composed of $9,500 of depreciation expense, $7,750 of administrative expenses, $50,000 of salaries expense, and an $11,000 impairment loss on goodwill.

Instructions

(a) Prepare the statement of cash flows, using either (1) the indirect method or (2) the direct method, as assigned by your instructor.

(b) Resolute's cash position more than doubled between 2014 and 2015. Identify the primary reason(s) for this significant increase.

Prepare statement of cash flows (indirect method) and answer questions.
(SO 2a, 3, 4, 5)

P13–8A   The comparative statement of financial position for Sylvester Ltd. shows the following balances at December 31:

	2015	2014
Assets		
Cash	$ 23,000	$ 6,000
Accounts receivable	25,000	30,000
Merchandise inventory	34,000	55,000
Land	100,000	110,000
Buildings	527,000	263,000
Accumulated depreciation—buildings	(67,000)	(100,000)
Equipment	85,000	40,000
Accumulated depreciation—equipment	(18,000)	(10,000)
Total assets	$709,000	$394,000
Liabilities and Shareholders' Equity		
Accounts payable	$ 46,000	$ 35,000
Income tax payable	3,000	2,000
Interest payable	6,000	7,000
Bank loan payable—current portion	26,000	20,000
Bank loan payable—non-current portion	380,000	212,000
Common shares	198,000	88,000
Retained earnings	50,000	30,000
Total liabilities and shareholders' equity	$709,000	$394,000

Additional information regarding 2015:

1. Profit was $57,000.
2. A gain of $7,000 was recorded on the disposal of a small parcel of land. No land was purchased during the year.
3. A gain on the disposal of an old building of $38,000 was recorded when it was sold for $50,000 cash. A new building was purchased for $364,000 and depreciation expense on buildings for the year was $55,000.
4. Equipment costing $65,000 was purchased while a loss of $4,000 was recorded on equipment that was sold for $5,000. The equipment that was sold late in the year had accumulated depreciation of $11,000.
5. The company took out $210,000 of new bank loans during the year.
6. Dividends were declared and paid and no common shares were bought back by the company.

Instructions

(a) Prepare the statement of cash flows using the indirect approach.
(b) Did the company manage its noncash working capital effectively?
(c) How could the company afford to buy a new building?

Calculate and evaluate liquidity and solvency.
(SO 6)

P13–9A   Selected information (in thousands) for **Reitmans (Canada) Limited** and **Le Château Inc.** for fiscal 2012 follows:

	Reitmans	Le Château
Net cash provided by operating activities	$ 51,797	$ 6,602
Average current liabilities	95,474	44,871
Average total liabilities	147,724	85,550
Net capital expenditures	84,433	8,723
Dividends paid	52,068	0

Instructions

(a) Calculate the cash current debt coverage ratio, cash total debt coverage ratio, and free cash flow for each company.
(b) Using the ratios calculated in part (a), compare the liquidity and solvency of the two companies.

Evaluate liquidity and solvency.
(SO 6)

P13–10A   Selected ratios for two companies are as follows:

	Grenville	Portage
Current ratio	1.7:1	1.2:1
Receivables turnover	10 times	20 times
Inventory turnover	4 times	2 times
Cash current debt coverage	0.4 times	0.3 times
Debt to total assets	60%	20%
Times interest earned	5 times	20 times
Cash total debt coverage	0.2 times	0.1 times

Instructions

(a) Which company is more liquid? Explain.

(b) Which company is more solvent? Explain.

P13–11A Condensed profit and cash flow information follow for a recent year for three coffee companies, **Tim Hortons Inc.**, **The Second Cup Ltd.**, and **Starbucks Corporation**:

Compare cash flows for three companies.
(SO 2, 3, 4, 5)

	Tim Hortons (in C$ millions)	Second Cup (in C$ millions)	Starbucks (in U.S. $ millions)
Profit (loss)	$407.8	$ (9.4)	$1,383.8
Net cash provided by operating activities	$ 559.3	$ 5.1	$ 1,750.3
Net cash used by investing activities	(242.2)	(1.3)	(974.0)
Net cash used by financing activities	(323.5)	(5.4)	(735.8)
Net increase (decrease) in cash	(6.4)	(1.6)	40.5
Cash, beginning of year	126.5	5.5	1,148.1
Cash, end of year	$120.1	$ 3.9	$1,188.6

Instructions

(a) Compare the provision and use of cash in each of the three activities by each company.

(b) Based on the information provided above, which company appears to be in the strongest position? Explain the reasoning behind your decision.

Problems: Set B

P13–1B The following is a list of transactions that took place during the year:

Classify activities.
(SO 1)

	(a) Classification O	(b) Cash Flow +	(c) Profit NE
1. Collected an account receivable.			
2. Sold equipment for cash, at a loss.			
3. Recorded an unrealized gain on a trading investment.			
4. Acquired land by issuing common shares.			
5. Expired prepaid insurance.			
6. Paid dividends to preferred shareholders.			
7. Recorded depreciation expense.			
8. Issued preferred shares for cash.			
9. Purchased inventory for cash. The company uses a perpetual inventory system.			
10. Provided services on account.			

Instructions

(a) Classify each of the above transactions as an operating activity (O), investing activity (I), financing activity (F), or noncash investing and financing activity (NC). If it does not fit into one of these classifications, indicate that there is no effect (NE). The first one has been done for you as an example.

(b) Specify if the transaction will result in a cash receipt (+), cash payment (−), or have no effect on cash (NE).

(c) Indicate if the transaction will increase (+), decrease (−), or have no effect (NE) on profit.

(d) Explain how it is possible for the same transaction to affect cash and profit differently.

P13–2B The income statement for Gum San Ltd., a publicly traded company following IFRS, is presented here:

Prepare operating activities section—indirect and direct methods.
(SO 2a, 2b)

GUM SAN LTD. Income Statement Year Ended December 31, 2015	
Sales	$4,500,000
Cost of goods sold	2,390,000
Gross profit	2,110,000
Operating expenses	1,070,000
Profit from operations	1,040,000
Interest	12,000
Profit before income tax	1,028,000
Income tax expense	260,000
Profit	$ 768,000

Additional information:

1. Operating expenses include $150,000 of depreciation expense and a $12,000 gain on disposal of equipment.
2. Accounts receivable increased by $500,000.
3. Merchandise inventory decreased by $220,000.
4. Prepaid expenses related to operating expenses increased by $170,000.
5. Accounts payable to suppliers of merchandise increased by $50,000.
6. Accrued liabilities related to operating expenses decreased by $165,000.
7. Interest payable increased by $5,000.
8. Unearned revenue that is received from customers increased by $8,000.
9. Income tax payable decreased by $16,000.

Instructions

(a) Prepare the operating activities section of the statement of cash flows, using either (1) the indirect method or (2) the direct method, as assigned by your instructor.

(b) Would your answer in part (a) change if Gum San were a private company following ASPE?

Prepare operating activities section— indirect and direct methods—and discuss methods.
(SO 2a, 2b)

P13–3B   The income statement for Hanalei International Inc. is presented here:

HANALEI INTERNATIONAL INC. Income Statement Year Ended December 31, 2015	
Fee revenue	$565,000
Operating expenses	365,000
Profit from operations	200,000
Interest expense	10,000
Profit before income tax	190,000
Income tax expense	47,500
Profit	$142,500

Hanalei's statement of financial position contained the following account balances:

	2015	2014
Accounts receivable	$50,000	$60,000
Prepaid insurance	5,000	8,000
Accounts payable	40,000	31,000
Unearned revenue	10,000	14,000
Salaries payable	10,000	7,000
Interest payable	1,000	1,000
Income tax payable	4,000	3,000

Additional information:

1. Operating expenses include depreciation expense, $45,000; amortization expense, $5,000; administrative expenses, $40,000; salaries expense, $300,000; and gain on disposal of equipment, $25,000.
2. Unearned revenue is received from customers.
3. Prepaid insurance and accounts payable relate to operating (administrative) expenses.

Instructions

(a) Prepare the operating activities section of the statement of cash flows, using either (1) the indirect method or (2) the direct method, as assigned by your instructor.

(b) Which method—indirect or direct—do you recommend that this company use to prepare its operating activities section? Explain your reasoning.

Calculate and classify cash flows for property, plant, and equipment.
(SO 3)

P13–4B   The following selected account balances relate to the property, plant, and equipment accounts of Bird Corp.

	2015	2014
Accumulated depreciation—buildings	$ 675,000	$ 600,000
Accumulated depreciation—equipment	288,000	192,000
Depreciation expense—buildings	75,000	75,000
Depreciation expense—equipment	128,000	96,000
Land	250,000	200,000
Buildings	1,250,000	1,250,000
Equipment	500,000	480,000
Loss on disposal of equipment	4,000	0

Additional information:

1. Purchased land for $50,000, making a $20,000 down payment and financing the remainder with a mortgage payable.
2. Equipment was purchased for $80,000 cash. Equipment was also sold during the year.

Instructions

(a) Calculate any cash receipts or payments related to the property, plant, and equipment accounts in 2015.

(b) Indicate where each of the cash receipts or payments identified in part (a) would be classified on the statement of cash flows or accompanying notes.

(c) Would you expect a growing company to be generating or using cash for its investing activities? Explain.

P13–5B The following selected account balances relate to the shareholders' equity accounts of Mathur Corp. at year end:

Calculate and classify cash flows for shareholders' equity.
(SO 4)

	2015	2014
Preferred shares, 6,000 shares in 2015, 5,000 shares in 2014	$150,000	$125,000
Common shares, 10,000 shares in 2015, 9,000 in 2014	176,000	136,000
Retained earnings	240,000	250,000
Cash dividends—preferred	7,500	6,250
Stock dividends—common	40,000	0

Additional information:

1. During 2015, the company sold 1,000 preferred shares. No shares were reacquired by the company.
2. All cash dividends were declared and paid during the same year. There were no dividends payable at the end of 2014 or 2015.
3. During the year, 1,000 common shares were issued as a stock dividend. The fair value of the shares at the time of declaration was $40 per share.
4. Profit was $37,500 in 2015.

Instructions

(a) Determine the amounts of any cash receipts or payments related to the shareholders' equity accounts in 2015.

(b) Indicate where each of the cash receipts or payments identified in part (a) would be classified on the statement of cash flows or accompanying notes.

(c) Would you expect a growing company to be generating or using cash for its financing activities? Explain.

P13–6B Financial statements for Nackawic Inc. follow:

Prepare statement of cash flows—indirect and direct methods.
(SO 2a, 2b, 3, 4, 5)

NACKAWIC INC.
Statement of Financial Position
December 31

	2015	2014
Assets		
Cash	$ 82,700	$ 47,250
Accounts receivable	80,800	37,000
Inventories	131,900	102,650
Long-term investments	94,500	107,000
Property, plant, and equipment	290,000	205,000
Accumulated depreciation	(49,500)	(40,000)
Total assets	$630,400	$458,900
Liabilities and Shareholders' Equity		
Accounts payable	$ 62,700	$ 48,280
Accrued liabilities	12,100	18,830
Bank loan payable	140,000	70,000
Common shares	240,000	200,000
Retained earnings	175,600	121,790
Total liabilities and shareholders' equity	$630,400	$458,900

NACKAWIC INC.
Income Statement
Year Ended December 31, 2015

Sales		$317,500
Cost of goods sold		99,460
Gross profit		218,040
Operating expenses		82,120
Profit from operations		135,920
Other revenues and expenses		
Interest expense	$12,940	
Realized loss on sale of long-term investments	7,500	20,440
Profit before income tax		115,480
Income tax expense		27,670
Profit		$ 87,810

Additional information:

1. Long-term investments were sold for $5,000, resulting in a realized loss of $7,500.
2. New equipment costing $141,000 was purchased for $71,000 cash and a $70,000 bank loan payable.
3. Equipment costing $56,000 was sold for $15,550, resulting in a gain of $8,750.
4. Accounts payable relate to merchandise creditors; accrued liabilities relate to operating expenses.
5. A dividend was paid during the year.
6. Operating expenses include $58,700 of depreciation expense and an $8,750 gain on disposal of equipment.

Instructions

(a) Prepare the statement of cash flows, using either (1) the indirect method or (2) the direct method, as assigned by your instructor.

(b) Nackawic's cash position increased by 75% between 2014 and 2015. Identify the primary reason(s) for this significant increase.

Prepare statement of cash flows—indirect and direct methods.
(SO 2a, 2b, 3, 4, 5)

P13–7B The financial statements of Wetaskiwin Limited are presented here:

WETASKIWIN LIMITED
Statement of Financial Position
December 31

	2015	2014
Assets		
Cash	$ 9,000	$ 10,000
Trading investments	14,000	23,000
Accounts receivable	28,000	14,000
Merchandise inventory	29,000	25,000
Property, plant, and equipment	73,000	78,000
Accumulated depreciation	(30,000)	(24,000)
Total assets	$123,000	$126,000
Liabilities and Shareholders' Equity		
Accounts payable	$ 32,000	$ 58,000
Income tax payable	2,000	10,000
Bank loan payable	15,000	20,000
Common shares	25,000	25,000
Retained earnings	64,000	28,000
Accumulated other comprehensive loss	(15,000)	(15,000)
Total liabilities and shareholders' equity	$123,000	$126,000

WETASKIWIN LIMITED
Income Statement
Year Ended December 31, 2015

Sales		$286,000
Cost of goods sold		154,000
Gross profit		132,000
Operating expenses		74,000
Profit from operations		58,000
Other revenues and expenses		
Unrealized loss on trading investments	$9,000	
Interest expense	3,000	12,000
Profit before income tax		46,000
Income tax expense		10,000
Profit		$ 36,000

Additional information:

1. Recorded an unrealized loss of $9,000 on trading investments.
2. Equipment was sold during the year for $8,000 cash. This equipment originally cost $15,000 and had a carrying amount of $10,000 at the time of sale.

3. Equipment costing $10,000 was purchased in exchange for $5,000 cash and a bank loan for the balance.
4. Accounts payable relate to merchandise creditors.
5. Operating expenses are composed of $11,000 of depreciation expense, $12,000 of administrative expenses, $49,000 of salaries expense, and a $2,000 loss on the disposal of equipment.

Instructions

(a) Prepare the statement of cash flows, using either (1) the indirect method or (2) the direct method, as assigned by your instructor.
(b) Wetaskiwin's cash position declined by $1,000 between 2014 and 2015. Identify the reason(s) for this decrease.

P13–8B The comparative statement of financial position for Anderson Ltd. shows the following balances at December 31:

Prepare statement of cash flows (indirect method) and answer questions.
(SO 2a, 3, 4, 5)

	2015	2014
Assets		
Cash	$ 3,000	$ 36,000
Accounts receivable	35,000	20,000
Merchandise inventory	49,000	35,000
Land	95,000	110,000
Building	477,000	263,000
Accumulated depreciation—building	(67,000)	(100,000)
Equipment	135,000	40,000
Accumulated depreciation—equipment	(18,000)	(10,000)
Total assets	$709,000	$394,000
Liabilities and Shareholders' Equity		
Accounts payable	$ 14,000	$ 35,000
Income tax payable	3,000	2,000
Interest payable	6,000	7,000
Bank loan payable—current portion	26,000	20,000
Bank loan payable—non-current portion	520,000	212,000
Common shares	90,000	88,000
Retained earnings	50,000	30,000
Total liabilities and shareholders' equity	$709,000	$394,000

Additional information regarding 2015:

1. Profit was $53,000.
2. A gain of $14,000 was recorded on the disposal of a small parcel of land. No land was purchased during the year.
3. A gain on the disposal of an old building of $28,000 was recorded when it was sold for $40,000 cash. A new building was purchased for $304,000 and depreciation expense on buildings for the year was $45,000.
4. Equipment costing $125,000 was purchased while a loss of $5,000 was recorded on equipment that originally cost $30,000 and was sold for $4,000.
5. The company took out $350,000 of new bank loans during the year.
6. Dividends were declared and paid and common shares were issued during the year.

Instructions

(a) Prepare the statement of cash flows using the indirect approach.
(b) Did the company manage its noncash working capital effectively?
(c) The company's banker is worried. Why?

P13–9B Selected information (in U.S. $ millions) for **Google Inc.** and **Yahoo! Inc.** for 2012 follows:

Calculate and evaluate liquidity and solvency.
(SO 6)

	Google	Yahoo!
Net cash provided (used) by operating activities	$16,619	$(281.6)
Average current liabilities	11,625	1,248.8
Average total liabilities	18,256	2,349.5
Net capital expenditures	3,273	505.5
Dividends paid	0	0

Instructions

(a) Calculate the cash current debt coverage ratio, cash total debt coverage ratio, and free cash flow for each company.
(b) Using the ratios calculated in part (a), compare the liquidity and solvency of the two companies.

Evaluate liquidity and solvency.
(SO 6)

P13–10B   Selected ratios for two companies are as follows:

	Barrington	Ste-Croix
Current ratio	1:1	0.8:1
Receivables turnover	6 times	4 times
Inventory turnover	5 times	4 times
Cash current debt coverage	0.5 times	0.4 times
Debt to total assets	75%	50%
Times interest earned	6 times	2 times
Cash total debt coverage	0.4 times	0.3 times

Instructions
(a) Which company is more liquid? Explain.
(b) Which company is more solvent? Explain.

Compare cash flows for three companies.
(SO 2, 3, 4, 5)

P13–11B   Condensed profit and cash flow information (in U.S. $ millions) for a recent year follow for three fast food companies: **McDonald's Corporation, Burger King Holdings, Inc.,** and **Wendy's/Arby's Group, Inc.:**

	McDonald's	Burger King	Wendy's
Profit	$5,464.8	$117.7	$ 9.5
Net cash provided by operating activities	$6,966.1	$224.4	$190.4
Net cash provided (used) by investing activities	(3,167.3)	33.6	(189.4)
Net cash used by financing activities	(3,849.8)	(174.6)	(24.1)
Other (foreign exchange gain [loss])	51.4	4.3	1.2
Net increase in cash and cash equivalents	0.4	87.7	(21.9)
Cash and cash equivalents, beginning of year	2,335.7	459.0	475.2
Cash and cash equivalents, end of year	$2,336.1	$546.7	$ 453.3

Instructions
(a) Compare the provision and use of cash in each of the three activities by each company.
(b) Based on the information provided above, which company appears to be in the strongest position? Explain.

Broadening Your Perspective

Financial Reporting: *Shoppers Drug Mart*

Answer questions about the statement of cash flows.
(SO 1, 2, 3, 4, 5)

BYP13–1   The financial statements of **Shoppers Drug Mart** are presented in Appendix A at the end of this book.

Instructions
(a) Does Shoppers use the indirect or direct method of calculating operating activities?
(b) What was the amount of net operating cash flows reported for 2012? For 2011?
(c) From your analysis of the 2012 statement of cash flows, what was the most significant investing activity? Financing activity?
(d) What amount was reported as the increase or decrease in cash and cash equivalents on the statement of cash flows for 2012? 2011?
(e) Did Shoppers grow during 2012 by purchasing other drugstores or did it just open up new locations or both?
(f) By comparing operating, investing, and financing cash flows for 2012, describe how Shoppers spent its operating cash flows. Was this a different approach than the one taken in 2011?

Comparative Analysis: *Shoppers Drug Mart and Jean Coutu*

Calculate and evaluate liquidity and solvency.
(SO 6)

BYP13–2   The financial statements of **Jean Coutu** are presented in Appendix B, following the financial statements for **Shoppers Drug Mart** in Appendix A.

Instructions
(a) Calculate the following ratios for Jean Coutu and Shoppers Drug Mart for 2012:
    1. Cash current debt coverage   4. Debt to total assets
    2. Current ratio   5. Times interest earned
    3. Cash total debt coverage   6. Free cash flow
(b) Compare the liquidity and solvency of each company from the ratios calculated in part (a).
(c) By reviewing the statement of cash flows for each company, which one is more committed to growth? Which one is more committed to paying down debt? Which one spends more of its operating cash flows on dividends?

Comparing IFRS and ASPE

BYP13–3   Action Carpets Ltd. recently became publicly traded. A few years ago, the company reported under ASPE and it did not really change the way that it presented the statement of cash flows when it adopted IFRS upon going public. The CEO of Action has just read a newspaper article comparing her company with Discount Carpets Ltd., which is another public company. She is angry because the article claimed that Discount was "better" because it had higher net cash flows from operating activities. As the CFO of Action, you have been asked to explain to your boss how the author of the newspaper article may be mistaken because he is unaware of the choices that can made under IFRS when presenting the statement of cash flows. You are pretty sure that the choices made by Discount were ones that would maximize its operating cash flow.

Adjust and compare liquidity and solvency with different classifications.
(SO 1, 6)

Instructions
(a) Using your understanding of the differences between IFRS and ASPE with regard to the presentation of information on the statement of cash flows, explain the choices that Discount Ltd. management probably made when preparing this statement for their company.
(b) Based on your answer to part (a) above, explain how each difference you covered would affect the cash current debt coverage, cash total debt coverage, and free cash flow ratios.

Critical Thinking Case

BYP13–4   Listed below are statements of cash flows for three companies in millions of dollars. Each company went public in 2014 and then commenced operations by acquiring a number of restaurants. Despite the identical profits and cash flows of each company, there are some differences in the way that each company manages its cash flows.

Analyze statement of cash flows.
(SO 6)

	A Limited		B Limited		C Limited	
	2015	2014	2015	2014	2015	2014
Operating activities						
Profit	$ 800	$ 800	$ 800	$ 800	$ 800	$ 800
Depreciation	300	200	220	200	210	200
Loss (gain) on disposal of non-current assets	(10)	—	(20)	—	70	—
	1,090	1,000	1,000	1,000	1,080	1,000
Increase in accounts receivable	(50)	(80)	(20)	(80)	(150)	(80)
Increase in inventory	(50)	(50)	(10)	(50)	(200)	(50)
Increase in accounts payable	40	60	10	60	90	60
Net cash provided by operating activities	1,030	930	980	930	820	930
Investing activities						
Disposal of property, plant, and equipment	50	—	50	—	120	—
Purchases of property, plant, and equipment	(2,350)	(2,000)	(830)	(2,000)	(430)	(2,000)
Net cash used by investing activities	(2,300)	(2,000)	(780)	(2,000)	(310)	(2,000)
Financing activities						
Bank loans received	—	700	—	—	0	1,050
Bank loan payments made	(50)	(50)	—	—	(425)	(115)
Common share sale proceeds	1,500	500	—	1,200	0	200
Dividends paid	(100)	(20)	(120)	(70)	(5)	(5)
Net cash provided (used) by financing activities	1,350	1,130	(120)	1,130	(430)	1,130
Cash flow for the year	80	60	80	60	80	60
Cash, January 1	60	—	60	—	60	—
Cash, December 31	$ 140	$ 60	$ 140	$ 60	$ 140	$ 60

Instructions

(a) Which company may have too much debt?

(b) Which company probably has the highest cash total debt coverage? (You cannot calculate this; just use logic.)

(c) Which company has some problems with its operating cash flows? What is causing these problems?

(d) Why do you think that C Limited had to pay down its bank loans so much in 2015?

(e) If you were a shareholder wanting to receive dividends but were not too interested in owning shares for a long time, which company's shares might you consider buying?

(f) Which company is the most committed to growth? Do you think that this company is growing too quickly?

(g) Which company has the highest free cash flow?

(h) Based on the above, which company would you like to own or lend cash to?

Ethics Case

Discuss dividend policy and classification of interest.
(SO 1)

BYP13–5   Onwards and Upwards Corporation has paid cash dividends to its shareholders for eight consecutive years. The board of directors' policy requires that in order for a dividend to be declared, cash provided by operating activities as reported in the current year's statement of cash flows must exceed $1 million. The job of president Phil Monat is secure so long as Phil produces annual operating cash flows to support the usual dividend.

At the end of the current year, controller Leland Yee informs president Monat of some disappointing news. The net cash provided by operating activities is only $970,000. The president says to Leland, "We must get that amount above $1 million. Isn't there some way to increase this amount?" Leland answers, "These figures were prepared by my assistant. I'll go back to my office and see what I can do." The president replies, "I know you won't let me down, Leland."

Upon close scrutiny of the statement of cash flows, Leland concludes that he can get net cash provided by operating activities above $1 million by reclassifying interest paid from the operating activities section, where it has been classified in the past, to the financing activities section. The company is a publicly traded company using IFRS. Leland knows that sometimes a major repair can be recorded as an asset rather than an expense. He returns to the president and exclaims, "You can tell the board to declare their usual dividend. Our cash flow provided by operating activities is $1,030,000." Excited, the president exclaims, "Good job, Leland! I knew I could count on you."

Instructions

(a) Should any other factors, besides net cash provided by operating activities, be considered by the board in setting the company's dividend policy?

(b) Who are the stakeholders in this situation?

(c) Was there anything unethical about the president's actions? Was there anything unethical about the controller's actions?

(d) Because the company reported under IFRS, could there be other ways to change the cash flow provided by operating activities? Are these options available under ASPE?

"All About You" Activity

Calculate and assess cash flow.
(SO 2b, 5)

BYP 13–6   Your friend and colleague has been working for about a year since graduating from university. He has come to you for advice on his saving and spending habits. You have accumulated the following information on his savings and spending that has occurred over the past year:

Salary received over the last year, net of income tax	$45,000
Rent and utilities paid	16,600
Car expenses paid	4,800
Credit card debt at the start of the year	1,000
Food, entertainment, recreation paid	6,000
Credit card debt at the end of the year	2,500
Line of credit at the start of the year	2,500
Line of credit at the end of the year	1,200
Purchase of car	20,000
Car loan at the end of the year	15,000
Cash account, beginning of year	500
Cash received from disposal of motorcycle	1,000
Cash received from disposal of computer	100
Cash account, end of year	1,000
Purchase of investments	5,500
Student loan at the beginning of the year	15,000
Student loan at the end of the year	10,000
Purchase of new computer	1,500
Interest expense paid	1,400

Instructions

(a) Prepare a statement of cash flow from information provided above using the direct method.

(b) Can you provide some advice to your friend on how he could improve his cash flow strategies, such as managing debt levels and terms of payment?

Serial Case

This is a continuation of the serial case from Chapters 1 through 12.

BYP13–7 The Koebels have met with representatives of Biscuits, a public company, and Coffee Beans, a private company. Both companies have offered to purchase the shares of Koebel's Family Bakery Ltd. The financial statements, including the statement of cash flows, for Koebel's Family Bakery have been prepared for analysis and the Koebels are meeting to discuss the results of these financial statements with representatives of both of these companies. These meetings will enable Janet and Brian to decide upon the best alternative as they move forward with their decision to sell their shares. Natalie and Daniel have been offered employment at each of these organizations and want to ensure these companies have the ability to continue to operate.

Compare cash flows for three companies, evaluate liquidity and solvency. (SO 2, 3, 4, 5, 6)

Selected information for Koebel's Family Bakery, Biscuits, and Coffee Beans for 2016 follow:

	Koebel's Family Bakery Ltd.	Biscuits Ltd.	Coffee Beans Ltd.
Profit	$199,629	$ 2,628,000	$ 699,000
Net cash provided by operating activities	$235,279	$ 6,821,000	$1,594,000
Net cash used by investing activities	(157,833)	(3,397,000)	(1,448,000)
Net cash used by financing activities	(37,071)	(1,762,000)	(890,000)
Net (decrease) increase in cash	40,375	1,662,000	(744,000)
Cash, beginning of year	159,068	2,252,000	776,000
Cash, end of year	$199,443	$ 3,914,000	$ 32,000
Average current liabilities	$ 31,121	$16,233,000	$3,759,000
Average total liabilities	81,551	27,758,500	8,879,000
Net capital expenditures	144,000	3,414,000	1,448,000
Dividends paid	120,000	580,000	0

Instructions

(a) Calculate the cash current debt coverage ratio, cash total debt coverage ratio, and free cash flow for each company.

(b) Compare the provision and use of cash in each of the three activities by each company.

(c) Based on the information provided in parts (a) and (b), identify why Biscuits Ltd. and Coffee Beans Ltd. are likely pursuing an investment in Koebel's Family Bakery Ltd.

(d) Based on the information provided in parts (a) and (b), identify to the Koebels some of the issues they should consider before making the decision to sell their shares and/or to be employed by one of these companies.

Answers to Self-Test Questions

1. a	2. c	3. b	4. c	5. c
6. c	7. d	8. a	9. b	10. a

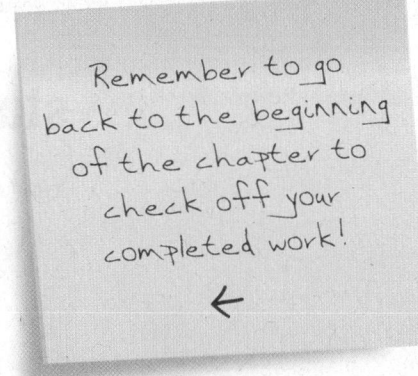

Remember to go back to the beginning of the chapter to check off your completed work!

←

Endnotes

[1] Teck Resources Limited 2009, 2010, 2011, and 2012 annual reports.

[2] Rob Carrick, *How Not to Move Back In with Your Parents*, Toronto: Doubleday Canada, 2012, pages 60–72; Kevin O'Leary, *Cold Hard Truth on Men, Women and Money*, Toronto: Doubleday Canada, 2012, page 80; Gail Vaz-Oxlade, *Money Rules*, Toronto: Harper Collins, 2012, page 52.

The Navigator
Chapter 14

the navigator

study objectives

After studying this chapter, you should be able to:

SO 1 Understand the concept of sustainable income and indicate how discontinued items are presented.

SO 2 Explain and apply horizontal analysis.

SO 3 Explain and apply vertical analysis.

SO 4 Identify and calculate ratios that are used to analyze liquidity.

SO 5 Identify and calculate ratios that are used to analyze solvency.

SO 6 Identify and calculate ratios that are used to analyze profitability.

SO 7 Understand the limitations of financial analysis.

From the Fur Trade to Fifth Avenue

In its first two centuries, the Hudson's Bay Company, created by a royal charter from King Charles II in 1670, was largely a fur trader. The company had outposts in the interior of what would not become Canada for another 200 years, where it bartered with its customers trading goods such as kettles and blankets for furs. Employees in charge of the trading posts sent an annual letter to the headquarters in London, England, tallying the year's activities and enclosing their financial account books. With only a yearly update, head office did not have the financial information needed to react quickly to changing market conditions and opportunities. Its business strategy was mostly to expand its trading territory, which eventually stretched from sea to sea to sea.

After leaving the fur trading business and evolving into a department store in the late 1800s, today the Hudson's Bay Company or HBC, the oldest continuing corporation in North America, uses the modern currency of cash, and electronically tracks its accounts daily. Its head office, now in Toronto, has instant access to financial information and uses it for decision-making, including decisions about how to position itself in the highly competitive retail industry.

In recent years, HBC's ownership has changed hands several times. In 2006, the company was purchased by American businessman Jerry Zucker, who died in 2008. Shortly after Zucker's death, the company was bought by a U.S. equity group owned by U.S. real estate investor Richard Baker. In 2012, HBC became a publicly traded corporation with a $365-million initial public offering to raise money to pay down debt and return some ownership to Canadian hands.

HBC's recent strategy has been to specialize in the high-end market. Two years before buying HBC, Mr. Baker purchased U.S. luxury department store Lord & Taylor, which is now part of Hudson's Bay Company. In 2011, HBC started moving away from the discount retail business by announcing it would sell the leases for most of its Zellers and Fields discount stores for $1.8 billion to U.S.-based Target Corporation.

In mid-2013, HBC announced a deal to purchase iconic American luxury retailer Saks Inc. for U.S. $2.9 billion. An attractive asset is Saks's valuable real estate, since it owns about two thirds of its stores, including its flagship location on Fifth Avenue in New York City. HBC expected to operate some half dozen Saks stores and 25 Saks Off Fifth discount luxury stores in Canada. "This acquisition will increase our growth potential both in the U.S. and Canada, generate significant efficiencies of scale, add to our powerful real estate portfolio and deliver substantial value to our shareholders," said Mr. Baker, who is HBC Chairman and CEO.

HBC has 90 Hudson's Bay department stores across Canada, along with 69 Home Outfitters stores that sell home decor items. With its planned opening of Saks and Lord & Taylor stores in Canada, HBC plans to compete in the high-end market with competitors such as U.S. department store Nordstrom, which was set to open stores in Canada in 2014. Hudson's Bay Company and its shareholders and potential investors will be relying on financial information to measure its performance in the changing retail landscape.[1]

the navigator

An important lesson can be learned from the Hudson's Bay Company, described in our feature story. It is essential to understand a company's business strategy before its financial information can be used effectively for decision-making. The purpose of this chapter is to give you a comprehensive review of the financial analysis tools a company's stakeholders use to help them make decisions. We will also examine the impact of certain irregular items on financial results and analyses. In addition, we will identify factors that can impose limits on the analysis of financial information.

The chapter is organized as follows:

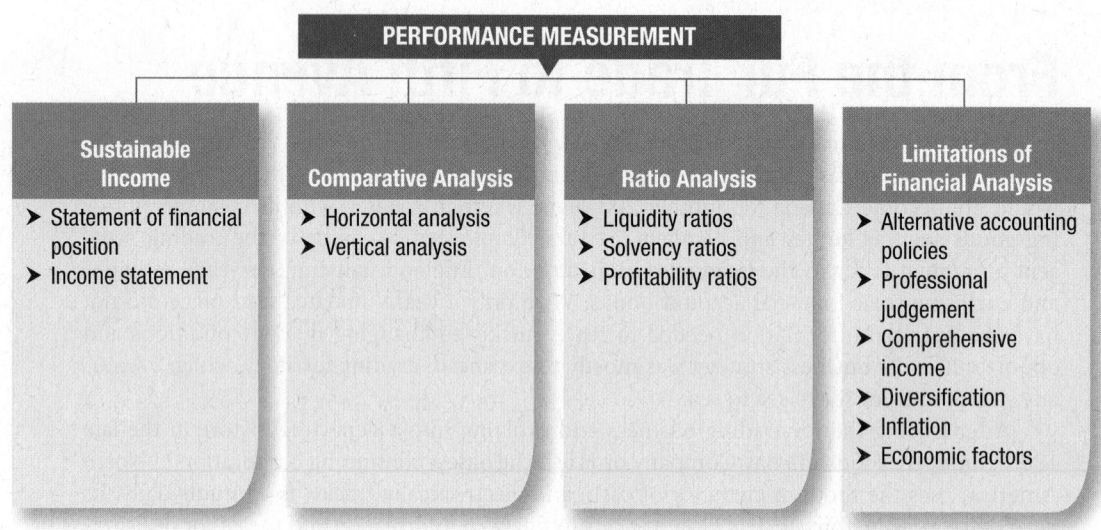

Sustainable Income

STUDY OBJECTIVE 1

Understand the concept of sustainable income and indicate how discontinued items are presented.

We learned about the objective of financial reporting in Chapter 2: to provide information about a company that is useful to existing and potential investors, lenders, and other creditors in making decisions about providing resources to the company. This financial information is provided by general purpose financial statements, which are used to assess the financial position and performance—past, current, and future—of a company. For example, investors, lenders, and other creditors often use profit reported on the income statement to help estimate future cash flows and profits and, in particular, their timing and certainty. When they do this, they must make sure that profit does not include irregular (out of the ordinary) items that are not likely to recur.

Profit adjusted for irregular items is known as **sustainable income**—the level of profit that is most likely to be obtained in the future. Sustainable income differs from actual profit by the amount of irregular revenues, expenses, gains, and losses that are included in profit. For example, suppose Rye Corporation reports that this year's profit is $500,000, but this amount includes a once-in-a-lifetime gain of $400,000. In estimating next year's profit for Rye Corporation, we would likely ignore this $400,000 gain and estimate that next year's profit will be closer to $100,000, plus or minus any expected changes. That is, based on this year's results, the company's sustainable income is roughly $100,000.

We will discuss one type of irregular item that occurs with some frequency—discontinued operations—in more detail. The term **discontinued operations** refers to the disposal, or availability for sale, of a component of an entity. A **component of an entity**, for the purpose of discontinued operations, represents a separate major line of business or major geographical area of operations that has been disposed of or is held for sale. It must be clearly distinguishable operationally and financially from the rest of the company.

Most large corporations have a few major lines of business, many in different geographic areas. For example, Hudson's Bay operates stores under several names or banners: Hudson's Bay

Company and Home Outfitters stores in Canada and Lord & Taylor stores in the United States. As mentioned in the feature story, the company used to operate Zellers and Fields stores in Canada but decided to sell or shut down many of these locations in 2011. The decision to discontinue these businesses was made as part of a shift in the strategic direction of the company to enter the segment of the retail market that sells higher-priced products. The strategy was implemented in several stages:

1. The company sold its leasehold interests (the right to use store locations) in most Zellers locations to Target Corporation during the fiscal 2011 year. The Zellers stores, however, did not begin to close until 2012. This created a large gain in 2011 and losses due to shutting down stores in 2012.
2. With the cash received from Target, Hudson's Bay paid down a large part of its bank debt and also used some of the proceeds to reorganize its share structure, to pay a special dividend, and to buy back some of its shares in 2011. This strengthened the financial position of the company, allowing it to sell shares to the public and become listed on the Toronto Stock Exchange in November 2012.
3. The Fields stores were either sold or shut down in fiscal 2012, although the decision to do so was announced in 2011.
4. In July 2013, the company announced that it would acquire Saks, a high-end department store in the United States, financing the deal with cash raised through a proposed private offering of shares and debt and the sale of its real estate assets.

To help determine sustainable income, discontinued operations are reported separately on the financial statements. We will review the presentation of this type of irregular item on the statement of financial position and income statement in the next sections.

STATEMENT OF FINANCIAL POSITION

Assets and liabilities of a discontinued operation that are held for sale are reported separately on the statement of financial position. They are valued and reported at the lower of their carrying amount and fair value (less any anticipated costs of selling) as current assets or liabilities. Of course, assets or liabilities that have already been disposed of are no longer recorded or reported on the statement of financial position.

Illustration 14-1 shows how the Hudson's Bay Company presented discontinued operations on its fiscal 2012 (year ended February 2, 2013) and 2011 (year ended January 28, 2012) statement of financial position (which it calls balance sheet).

HUDSON'S BAY COMPANY Balance Sheet (partial) February 2, 2013, and January 28, 2012 (in millions)		
	2012	2011
Current assets of discontinued operations held for sale (Note 4)	$273.6	$1,096.1
Current liabilities of discontinued operations held for sale (Note 4)	361.5	781.3

▶Illustration 14-1
Presentation of discontinued operations on statement of financial position

In Note 4 to its financial statements, HBC explains the details of the decision to discontinue its operation of Zellers and Fields stores. Because assets relating to these businesses are now held for sale, they are shown as current assets and shown separately so readers of the financial statements can understand that these assets will not likely be on the financial statements in the future. For the same reason, any liabilities relating to these businesses are also shown separately. These liabilities are current in nature because they will be settled as soon as the businesses are closed or sold, which is expected to occur within a year.

INCOME STATEMENT

On the income statement, items relating to discontinued operations are segregated from continuing operations. Because companies want readers of the financial statements to understand that discontinued operations are not likely to recur, they are shown near the bottom of the income statement immediately following the profit or loss from continuing operations. Any income tax relating to discontinued operations is also segregated from the income tax expense relating to continuing operations and shown within the discontinued operations section of the income statement.

Discontinued operations on the income statement can consist of two parts: (1) the profit (loss) earned from the discontinued operations during the period, net of any income tax expense or savings, and (2) the gain (loss) on the disposal of the component, net of any income tax expense or savings. Of course, if the component of an entity has not yet been disposed of but is being held for sale, only the first part (the profit or loss from the discontinued operations) will be reported on the income statement until the actual disposal occurs.

Illustration 14-2 shows the information pertaining to discontinued operations that HBC reported on its income statement (which it calls statement of earnings) in fiscal 2012 and 2011.

▶Illustration 14-2

Presentation of discontinued operations on income statement

HUDSON'S BAY COMPANY Statement of Earnings (partial) Years Ended February 2, 2013, and January 28, 2012 (in millions)		
	2012	2011
Profit from continuing operations before income tax	$ 23.5	$ 53.5
Income tax recovery	8.0	3.8
Profit from continuing operations	31.5	57.3
Discontinued operations (Note 4)		
Profit (loss) from discontinued operations, net of income tax	(257.8)	74.1
Gain on disposal of discontinued operations, net of income tax	181.5	1,317.6
Profit (loss) from discontinued operations, net of income tax	(76.3)	1,391.7
Profit (loss)	$(44.8)	$1,449.0

Expenses are deducted from revenues on the company's income statement to calculate profit or loss from continuing operations before income tax, although it is not detailed in the above illustration. Income tax expense applicable to continuing operations is then deducted (or added in this case because the company received a refund of income tax paid in prior years) to arrive at profit or loss from continuing operations. Note that the caption "profit (loss) from continuing operations" is used and "discontinued operations" are separately reported. Within the discontinued operations section, both the profit (loss) and the gain on disposal related to the discontinued operations are reported net of applicable income tax.

Notice that in fiscal 2011 a large gain of $1,317.6 million on the disposal of assets was reported, followed by a smaller gain of $181.5 million in 2012. These gains arose primarily from the sale of leasehold interests in the Zellers and Fields stores. These stores operated in 2011 with a profit of $74.1 million compared with 2012, when they operated at a loss of $257.8 million, which is one of the reasons why management made the decision to sell these stores.

In addition, although not illustrated here, earnings per share must be reported separately for continuing operations and for discontinued operations so that investors can clearly see the impact of this decision on the company. The impact of the discontinued operations on cash flows must also be reported separately on the statement of cash flows.

Discontinued operations are not uncommon and can have a significant impact on a company's financial position and profit. In general, in evaluating a company, it makes sense to eliminate irregular items such as discontinued operations from the analysis.

DECISION TOOLKIT

Decision Checkpoints

Info Needed for Decision

Tools to Use for Decision

How to Evaluate Results

Decision Checkpoints	Info Needed for Decision	Tools to Use for Decision	How to Evaluate Results
Has the company sold, or is it holding for sale, a component of an entity?	Discontinuation of, or plans to discontinue, a component of an entity	Discontinued operations section of the statement of financial position, income statement, and/or statement of cash flows	If a component of an entity has been discontinued, its results in the current period should not be included in assessing the company's financial position or in estimating its future profit or cash flows.

BEFORE YOU GO ON...

▶ Do It! Discontinued Operations

AIR Corporation reported profit from continuing operations before income tax of $150,000 thousand and a loss on disposal of a paper facility (considered a discontinued business) of $99,000 thousand before income tax for the year ended October 31, 2015. The company had an income tax rate of 25% and a weighted average of 85,000 thousand common shares. Prepare a partial income statement, starting with profit from continuing operations before income tax, including earnings per share information.

Action Plan

- Separately calculate and report the income tax effect of continuing operations and discontinued operations.
- Separately calculate and report earnings per share for continuing operations and discontinued operations.

Solution

AIR CORPORATION
Income Statement (partial)
Year Ended October 31, 2015
(in thousands)

Profit from continuing operations before income tax	$150,000
Income tax expense	37,500[1]
Profit from continuing operations	112,500
Loss on disposal of paper facility, net of $24,750[2] income tax savings	74,250[3]
Profit	$ 38,250
Earnings per share from continuing operations	$1.32[4]
Loss per share from discontinued operations	(0.87)[5]

Calculations:
[1] $150,000 × 25% = $37,500
[2] $99,000 × 25% = $24,750
[3] $99,000 − $24,750 = $74,250
[4] $112,500 ÷ 85,000 = $1.32
[5] $(74,250) ÷ 85,000 = $(0.87)

Related Exercise Material: BE14-1, BE14-2, E14-1, and E14-4.

Comparative Analysis

STUDY OBJECTIVE 2
Explain and apply horizontal analysis.

As mentioned earlier, investors, lenders, and other creditors are interested in a company's sustainable income. They will use this information, in addition to information found in the other financial statements, to make comparisons in order to evaluate a company's past and current financial performance and position, and help determine future expectations.

Various tools are available to help users make comparisons of a company's financial data. In the following two sections, we will explain and illustrate horizontal and vertical analysis, two commonly used tools in comparative analysis. But first, we should note that, while a company's financial statement data are usually the starting point in any analysis, it is important to review nonfinancial information as well. Nonfinancial information includes information found in a company's annual report, such as its mission, strategy, goals and objectives, and management discussion and analysis (MD&A). Understanding a company's business strategy and its goals and objectives is important when interpreting financial performance, as we learned in our feature story about HBC.

HORIZONTAL ANALYSIS

Helpful Hint
The term *horizontal analysis* means that we view financial statement data from left to right (or right to left) across time.

Horizontal analysis, also called **trend analysis**, is a technique to determine the change (increase or decrease) that has taken place in a series of financial statement data over time. This change can be expressed as either an amount or a percentage.

Horizontal analysis is used in intracompany comparisons. You will recall from earlier chapters that intracompany comparisons involve financial data *within* a company, comparing current financial data with those of one or more prior years. Comparisons within a company are often useful to detect significant trends. For example, net sales for the last four years for HBC are shown in Illustration 14-3 in dollars (in millions) and percentages.

▶Illustration 14-3
Horizontal analysis for Hudson's Bay Company sales

	2012	2011	2010	2009
Net sales	$4,077.0	$3,849.6	$3,718.2	$3,619.7
% of base-year (2009) amount	112.6%	106.4%	102.7%	100.0%
% change for the year	5.9%	3.5%	2.7%	—

If we assume that 2009 is the base year, we can express net sales in each year as a percentage of the base-year (or period if less than a year) amount shown on the second line of the above illustration. We call this a **horizontal percentage of a base-period amount**. This percentage is calculated by dividing the amount for the specific year (or period) we are analyzing by the base-year (or period) amount, as shown in Illustration 14-4.

▶Illustration 14-4
Horizontal percentage of a base-period amount formula

Horizontal Percentage of Base-Period Amount	=	Analysis-Period Amount	÷	Base-Period Amount

We can use horizontal analysis on the Hudson's Bay Company's sales shown in Illustration 14-3 to determine that net sales in 2012 are 112.6% of net sales in 2009 by dividing $4,077.0 million by $3,619.7 million. In other words, sales in 2012 are 12.6% greater than sales four years earlier in 2009.

Reviewing the percentages of base-year amounts shown in the second row of Illustration 14-3, we can easily see the trend of the company's net sales, which steadily improved as the economy recovered from the recession. It must be remembered, however, that these net sales amounts pertain to continuing business operations and reflect the sales of the Hudson's Bay and Lord & Taylor stores but not the sales of Zellers and Fields stores. It would be difficult to properly interpret the company's past performance over this time period without fully understanding the strategic decisions made by the company and the underlying economic environment.

We can also use horizontal analysis to measure the percentage change for the year or period (between any two periods of time) by calculating a **horizontal percentage change for the period**. This is calculated by dividing the dollar amount of the change between the specific year (or period) under analysis and the prior year (or period) by the prior-year (or period) amount, as shown in Illustration 14-5.

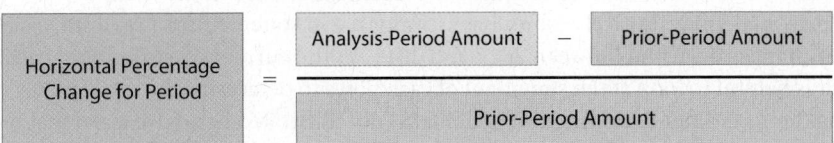

For example, we can determine that Hudson's Bay's sales increased by $227.4 million ($4,077.0 − $3,849.6) in 2012 compared to 2011. This increase can then be expressed as a percentage by dividing the amount of the change between the two years of $227.4 million by the amount in the prior year, the 2011 net sales of $3,849.6 million. Thus, in 2012, sales increased by 5.9% compared with 2011. The horizontal percentage change in sales for each of the last four years is presented in the last row of Illustration 14-3. Note that no change can be calculated for the first year in our example, 2009, since 2008 data were not included.

We will apply horizontal analysis, calculating the percentage change for each year to compare HBC's statement of financial position and income statement in the next sections. We will also use other financial and nonfinancial information found in the company's annual report to help us understand some of the reasons for the changes we will observe by comparing these statements.

Statement of Financial Position

Condensed statements of financial position, which the company chooses to call the balance sheet, for fiscal 2012 (as at February 2, 2013) and for fiscal 2011 (as at January 28, 2012), showing dollar and percentage changes for the two-year period, are shown in Illustration 14-6.

HUDSON'S BAY COMPANY
Balance Sheet
February 2, 2013, and January 28, 2012
(in millions)

	2012	2011	Increase (Decrease) Amount	Increase (Decrease) Percentage
Assets				
Current assets				
Cash	$ 48.3	$ 42.4	$ 5.9	13.9%
Trade and other receivables	74.3	68.0	6.3	9.3%
Inventories	994.3	970.0	24.3	2.5%
Other current assets	34.2	25.6	8.6	33.6%
Assets of discontinued operations held for sale	273.6	1,096.1	(822.5)	(75.0)%
Total current assets	1,424.7	2,202.1	(777.4)	(35.3)%
Property, plant, and equipment	1,335.0	1,270.5	64.5	5.1%
Intangible assets	233.0	224.6	8.4	3.7%
Other assets	259.9	296.3	(36.4)	(12.3)%
Total assets	$3,252.6	$3,993.5	$(740.9)	(18.6)%
Liabilities and Shareholders' Equity				
Liabilities				
Current liabilities				
Loans and borrowings	$ 132.1	$ 291.0	$(158.9)	(54.6)%
Trade payables and accrued liabilities	670.1	715.5	(45.4)	(6.3)%
Unearned revenue	109.9	101.4	8.5	8.4%
Provisions and other	89.9	86.3	3.6	4.2%
Liabilities of discontinued operations held for sale	361.5	781.3	(419.8)	(53.7)%
Total current liabilities	1,363.5	1,975.5	(612.0)	(31.0)%
Non-current liabilities	891.1	1,062.1	(171.0)	(16.1)%
Total liabilities	2,254.6	3,037.6	(783.0)	(25.8)%
Shareholders' equity	998.0	955.9	42.1	4.4%
Total liabilities and shareholders' equity	$3,252.6	$3,993.5	$(740.9)	(18.6)%

Note that in a horizontal analysis, while the amount column of the increase or decrease is additive (the total change in assets is a decrease of $740.9 million), the percentage column is not additive. That is, 18.6% is not a total but just the percentage change in the total.

The horizontal analysis of Hudson's Bay's comparative statement of financial position shows that several changes occurred between 2012 and 2011. In the current assets section, cash increased by 13.9%. It is helpful to look at the statement of cash flows to determine the cause of key changes in cash during the year. After reviewing this statement (not illustrated here), we learn that the increase in cash is primarily because of cash received from the sale of discontinued businesses and from improved cash flow from operating activities.

The analysis also shows that accounts receivable increased by $6.3 million, or 9.3%. We will look at the income statement in the next section to determine if sales and accounts receivable changed by the same percentage. Inventories increased by $24.3 million, or 2.5%. Similar to accounts receivable, we will look at the income statement to determine if cost of goods sold and inventory increased by the same percentage. We will also review the receivables and inventory turnover ratios in later sections to assess the company's ability to collect its receivables and sell its merchandise.

The most significant change in current assets was caused by the decline in the assets of discontinued operations that were held for sale. These decreased by $822.5 million (a 75.0% decline) as these were sold off due to the sale or closures of Zellers and Fields operations. Overall, current assets decreased by $777.4 million, or 35.3%.

With respect to non-current assets, there were no significant changes. Property, plant, and equipment increased by $64.5 million, or 5.1% as funds were spent to upgrade stores and purchase new computer hardware. Intangible assets rose by $8.4 million, or 3.7%, due to software purchases. Other assets, which consisted of several different types of assets including deferred tax assets and pension-related assets, declined by $36.4 million or 12.3% as the benefits relating to these assets were used up over time.

In 2012, Hudson's Bay's total current liabilities decreased by $612.0 million, or 31.0%, primarily because liabilities relating to Zellers and Fields were paid off with the proceeds received from the sale of the assets relating to these stores. The proceeds were also used to pay off current bank borrowings, which fell by $158.9 million or 54.6%. Furthermore, the additional cash on hand allowed the company to pay down trade payables and accrued liabilities more promptly, as these fell by $45.4 million or 6.3%. The company's non-current liabilities were reduced by $171 million or 16.1%, as funds from the sale of discontinued operations and the public issue of shares were used to pay down these liabilities.

The company's total shareholders' equity changed very little in 2012, increasing by only $42.1 million or 4.4%. Although shares were issued to the public when the company became listed on the Toronto Stock Exchange, some of the proceeds from that issue were used to buy back shares that were previously outstanding and this meant that there was very little change in this section of the statement of financial position.

Income Statement

Illustration 14-7 presents a horizontal analysis of HBC's condensed income statement for the fiscal years 2012 and 2011.

A horizontal analysis of the income statement shows that net sales increased by $227.4 million, or 5.9%. Notice, however, that the cost of goods sold (or cost of sales as HBC calls it) increased by $181.0 million or 7.8%, which was more than the increase in net sales in percentage terms. When this occurs, the gross profit will not rise by as much as net sales, which we can see. The gross profit rose by only $46.4 million or 3.0%. Hudson's Bay noted in its management discussion and analysis that the lower gross profit was a result of a hurricane in the United States. Hurricane Sandy caused many Lord & Taylor stores to close for up to a week and sales prices were discounted to ensure that merchandise levels did not rise due to the slowdown caused by this hurricane.

HBC's selling, general, and administrative expenses increased by $122.0 million, or 9.1%. One of the reasons for this increase was the fact that the 2012 fiscal year is one week longer than the 2011 fiscal year because the company's year end falls on the Sunday closest to the end of January. Interest expense was down by $45.6 million, or 31.9%, because a significant amount of bank loans were paid down in mid to late fiscal 2011. Nonetheless, despite the decline in interest expenses, the lower gross

►Illustration 14-7
Horizontal analysis of income
statement (percentage change
for year)

HUDSON'S BAY COMPANY
Statement of Earnings
Years Ended February 2, 2013, and January 28, 2012
(in millions)

	2012	2011	Increase (Decrease) Amount	Increase (Decrease) Percentage
Net sales	$4,077.0	$3,849.6	$ 227.4	5.9%
Cost of sales	2,487.0	2,306.0	181.0	7.8%
Gross profit	1,590.0	1,543.6	46.4	3.0%
Selling, general, and administrative expenses	1,469.2	1,347.2	122.0	9.1%
Profit from operations	120.8	196.4	(75.6)	(38.5)%
Interest expense	97.3	142.9	(45.6)	(31.9)%
Profit from continuing operations before income tax	23.5	53.5	(30.0)	(56.1)%
Income tax recovery	8.0	3.8	4.2	110.5%
Profit from continuing operations	31.5	57.3	(25.8)	(45.0)%
Profit (loss) from discontinued operations, net of income tax	(76.3)	1,391.7	(1,468.0)	(105.5)%
Profit (loss)	$ (44.8)	$1,449.0	$(1,493.8)	(103.1)%

profit and higher selling, general, and administrative expenses caused a decrease in profit from continuing operations before income tax of $30 million or 56.1%. Because the company is not taxable and received income tax refunds in both 2012 and 2011, the profit from continuing operations rose after taking income tax into effect. The most significant change on the income statement in terms of dollar amounts is the large decrease in the profit from discontinued businesses, which fell by $1,468.0 million or 105.5% into a loss position. It is normal for a discontinued business to show a loss. The reason for the large profit in 2011 was the sale of Zellers leaseholds.

The measurement of changes in percentages from period to period is fairly straightforward and quite useful. However, the calculations can be affected by complications. For example, if an item has a small value in a base year and a large value in the next year, the percentage change, although large, may not be meaningful. Look at the 110.5% increase in income tax recovery in Illustration 14-7. This is because the base year amount was relatively low. In addition, if an item has no value in a base year and a value in the next year, no percentage change can be determined. Finally, if a negative amount appears in the base year and a positive amount in the following year, or vice versa, the percentage change will exceed 100% and in many cases should not be calculated, although we did so above for illustration purposes only.

We have not done a horizontal analysis of the Hudson's Bay Company statement of comprehensive income (which it presents separately from its income statement), statement of changes in equity, and statement of cash flows because analyses of these statements are not as useful as horizontal analyses pertaining to the statement of financial position and income statement. The amounts presented in these other statements already give details of the changes between two periods.

DECISION TOOLKIT

Decision Checkpoints

Info Needed for Decision

Tools to Use for Decision

How to Evaluate Results

Decision Checkpoints	Info Needed for Decision	Tools to Use for Decision	How to Evaluate Results
How do the company's financial position and operating results compare with those of previous periods?	Statement of financial position and income statement	Comparative financial statements should be prepared over at least two years, with the first year reported as the base year. Changes in each line item relative to the base year should be presented both by amount and by percentage. This is called horizontal analysis.	A significant change should be investigated to determine what caused it.

BEFORE YOU GO ON...

▶ Do It! Horizontal Analysis

Selected condensed information (in thousands) from Bonora Ltd.'s income statement for four years ended June 30 follows:

	2015	2014	2013	2012
Net sales	$37,600	$36,500	$38,700	$40,500
Cost of goods sold	14,900	14,200	13,800	15,300
Gross profit	22,700	22,300	24,900	25,200
Operating expenses	18,500	17,400	16,200	17,600
Profit from operations	4,200	4,900	8,700	7,600
Income tax expense	1,050	1,225	2,175	1,900
Profit	$ 3,150	$ 3,675	$ 6,525	$ 5,700

Using horizontal analysis, calculate (a) the percentage of the base-year amount for each year, assuming that 2012 is the base year, and (b) the percentage change for each year (that is, between each of the following sets of years: 2015 and 2014, 2014 and 2013, and 2013 and 2012).

Action Plan

- Horizontal percentage of the base-year amount: Set the base-year (2012) dollar amounts at 100%. Express each subsequent year's amount as a percentage of the base period by dividing the dollar amount for the year under analysis by the base-year amount.
- Horizontal percentage change for year: Divide the dollar amount of the change between the current and prior year by the prior-year amount.

Solution

(a) Horizontal percentage of base-year amount

	2015	2014	2013	2012
Net sales	92.8%	90.1%	95.6%	100.0%
Cost of goods sold	97.4%	92.8%	90.2%	100.0%
Gross profit	90.1%	88.5%	98.8%	100.0%
Operating expenses	105.1%	98.9%	92.0%	100.0%
Profit from operations	55.3%	64.5%	114.5%	100.0%
Income tax expense	55.3%	64.5%	114.5%	100.0%
Profit	55.3%	64.5%	114.5%	100.0%

(b) Horizontal percentage change for year

	2015	2014	2013	2012
Net sales	3.0%	(5.7)%	(4.4)%	—
Cost of goods sold	4.9%	2.9%	(9.8)%	—
Gross profit	1.8%	(10.4)%	(1.2)%	—
Operating expenses	6.3%	7.4%	(8.0)%	—
Profit from operations	(14.3)%	(43.7)%	14.5%	—
Income tax expense	(14.3)%	(43.7)%	14.5%	—
Profit	(14.3)%	(43.7)%	14.5%	—

Related Exercise Material: BE14-3, BE14-4, BE14-5, BE14-6, E14-2, and E14-4.

VERTICAL ANALYSIS

STUDY OBJECTIVE 3

Explain and apply vertical analysis.

Vertical analysis, also called **common size analysis**, is a technique that expresses each item in a financial statement as a percentage of a total (base) amount within the same financial statement. Note that while horizontal analysis compares data across more than one year, vertical analysis compares data within the same year.

Vertical analysis expresses account balances in percentage terms known as the **vertical percentage of a base amount**. These percentages are calculated by dividing the financial statement amount under analysis by the base amount in that particular financial statement, as shown in Illustration 14-8.

Vertical Percentage of Base Amount	=	Analysis Amount	÷	Base Amount

▸Illustration 14-8
Vertical percentage of a base amount formula

The base amount commonly used for the statement of financial position is *total assets* (or total liabilities and shareholders' equity, which equals total assets) as that is the largest amount on the statement. For example, we might say that current assets are 43.8% of total assets (total assets being the base amount). The base amount for the income statement is usually *revenues* for a service company and *net sales* for a merchandising company, again, because that is usually the largest amount on that statement. Because of this, we might say that cost of goods sold is 61.0% of net sales (net sales being the base amount).

Vertical analysis is used in both intracompany and intercompany comparisons. Vertical analysis is helpful to compare financial data both *within* a company and *between* one or more competitor companies. We will use vertical analysis to compare HBC's statement of financial position and income statement for two years as well as with one of its competitors, Sears Canada, in the next sections.

> **Helpful Hint**
> The term *vertical analysis* means that we view rows of financial statement data from up to down (or down to up) within the same period of time.

Statement of Financial Position

Illustration 14-9 presents a vertical analysis of HBC's comparative statement of financial position.

▸Illustration 14-9
Vertical analysis of statement of financial position

	2012 Amount	2012 Percentage	2011 Amount	2011 Percentage
HUDSON'S BAY COMPANY Balance Sheet February 2, 2013, and January 28, 2012 (in millions)				
Assets				
Current assets				
Cash	$ 48.3	1.5%	$ 42.4	1.1%
Trade and other receivables	74.3	2.3%	68.0	1.7%
Inventories	994.3	30.6%	970.0	24.3%
Other current assets	34.2	1.1%	25.6	0.6%
Assets of discontinued operations held for sale	273.6	8.4%	1,096.1	27.4%
Total current assets	1,424.7	43.8%	2,202.1	55.1%
Property, plant, and equipment	1,335.0	41.0%	1,270.5	31.8%
Intangible assets	233.0	7.2%	224.6	5.6%
Other assets	259.9	8.0%	296.3	7.4%
Total assets	$3,252.6	100.0%	$3,993.5	100.0%
Liabilities and Shareholders' Equity				
Liabilities				
Current liabilities				
Loans and borrowings	$ 132.1	4.1%	$ 291.0	7.3%
Trade payables and accrued liabilities	670.1	20.6%	715.5	17.9%
Unearned revenue	109.9	3.4%	101.4	2.5%
Provisions and other	89.9	2.8%	86.3	2.2%
Liabilities of discontinued operations held for sale	361.5	11.1%	781.3	19.6%
Total current liabilities	1,363.5	41.9%	1,975.5	49.5%
Non-current liabilities	891.1	27.4%	1,062.1	26.6%
Total liabilities	2,254.6	69.3%	3,037.6	76.1%
Shareholders' equity	998.0	30.7%	955.9	23.9%
Total liabilities and shareholders' equity	$3,252.6	100.0%	$3,993.5	100.0%

In contrast to the percentage changes shown in the horizontal analysis section, the percentage changes in the vertical analysis are additive. That is, if you add the vertical percentages in the 2012 and 2011 columns above, they should sum to 100.0%. However, because the percentage changes shown above have been rounded to one decimal spot, not all the percentage columns add perfectly. This is due solely to rounding discrepancies.

Vertical analysis shows the relative size of each item in the statement of financial position compared with a base amount. It can be prepared for one or more years, as we've shown in Illustration 14-9. It is also useful to compare vertically prepared information for multiple periods with similar information provided earlier in our horizontal analysis. In 2012, the most significant change affecting Hudson's Bay's current assets was a drop in the assets of the discontinued operations for sale, which fell from 27.4% to 8.4%.

We also see that liabilities relating to discontinued operations, which represented 19.6% of total liabilities and shareholders' equity in fiscal 2011, had fallen to 11.1% by 2012. This was due to the fact that these were paid down from the proceeds of the sale of assets from these discontinued operations. Loans and borrowings were also reduced with these proceeds, causing the percentage of these to fall from 7.3% to 4.1% of total liabilities and shareholders' equity. Even though non-current liabilities decreased in absolute dollar terms, the percentage that they represent of total liabilities and shareholders' equity actually rose slightly, from 26.6% to 27.4%.

Notice that shareholders' equity at the end of the fiscal 2012 year had risen to 30.7% from 23.9% in 2011 of total liabilities and shareholders' equity. This was caused not by an increase in shareholders' equity but a decrease in liabilities, which was part of the company's strategy to create a stronger statement of financial position with lower liabilities before going public in late 2012.

Income Statement

Illustration 14-10 presents a vertical analysis of Hudson's Bay's comparative income statement for fiscal 2012 and 2011.

▶Illustration 14-10

Vertical analysis of income
lstatement

	2012		2011	
HUDSON'S BAY COMPANY Statement of Earnings (partial) Years Ended February 2, 2013, and January 28, 2012 (in millions)				
	Amount	Percentage	Amount	Percentage
Net sales	$4,077.0	100.0%	$3,849.6	100.0%
Cost of sales	2,487.0	61.0%	2,306.0	59.9%
Gross profit	1,590.0	39.0%	1,543.6	40.1%
Selling, general, and administrative expenses	1,469.2	36.0%	1,347.2	35.0%
Profit from operations	120.8	3.0%	196.4	5.1%
Interest expense	97.3	2.4%	142.9	3.7%
Profit from continuing operations before income tax	23.5	0.6%	53.5	1.4%
Income tax recovery	8.0	0.2%	3.8	0.1%
Profit from continuing operations	31.5	0.8%	57.3	1.5%
Profit (loss) from discontinued operations, net of income tax	(76.3)	(1.9)%	1,391.7	36.2%
Profit (loss)	$ (44.8)	(1.1)%	$1,449.0	37.6%

Percentage changes in horizontal analysis tend to be larger than percentage changes in vertical analysis but often reflect the same events. As we saw in our horizontal analysis shown in Illustration 14-7, both net sales and cost of sales rose in 2012 by 5.9% and 7.8%, respectively, and since net sales growth was lower, gross profit rose by only 3.0%. In the vertical analysis above, we can see that the gross profit as a percentage of sales fell from 40.1% to 39.0%, explaining the same events but with a different base for comparison.

Similar to the vertical percentages shown in Illustration 14-9, the percentages shown in Illustration 14-10 should add vertically. However, minor rounding discrepancies may prevent this from occurring in some cases. For example, in 2011, profit from continuing operations of 1.5% and profit from discontinued operations, net of income tax of 36.2% do not add to profit of 37.6%.

Although vertical analysis can also be performed on the other period statements—comprehensive income, changes in equity, and cash flows—this is seldom done. As mentioned earlier, these statements, by their very nature, provide an analysis of changes during the year.

■ Keeping an Eye on Cash

While a common size analysis of the statement of cash flows is not always productive, a detailed review of this statement is a useful starting point to understand where the company's cash comes from and what it is used for. When reviewing the contents of the operating, investing, and financing activities sections, it may be helpful to calculate the total of the major sources and uses of cash over several years since annual reporting periods are often too short for decision-making. For example, financing of asset replacements, major expansions, or business acquisitions often spans several years.

The types of questions that analyzing the statement of cash flows can help us to answer include the following:

- Is cash generated from, or used by, each classification of activity growing or declining?
- Is the company generating enough cash from its operating activities to pay for asset replacements or is it relying on debt to finance them?
- What is the company's dependence on debt financing versus equity financing?
- What types of cash sources are available for financing activities?
- Does the company pay dividends using cash generated from operating activities, from selling assets (investing activities), or from issuing debt (financing activities)?
- What is the company's cash flexibility to meet unexpected demands?

By looking at the relationships between the three types of activities on a statement of cash flows, we can begin to gain an overall understanding of the company's strategy. Management at Hudson's Bay felt strongly about this and included the following table in its annual report:

	2012	2011	2010
Operating activities – continuing operations	$ 80.8	$ 29.3	$ 55.4
Investing activities – continuing operations	(197.3)	(222.6)	(89.7)
Financing activities – continuing operations	(232.1)	(1,679.5)	(52.1)
Cash flow from continuing operations	(348.6)	(1,872.8)	(86.4)
Cash from discontinued operations	354.5	1,858.0	92.6
Total cash flow	$ 5.9	$ (14.8)	$ 6.2

We can see from above that, as the company implemented its strategy of exiting from the operation of discount stores, cash flows from operating activities improved. Investing expenditures were made by the company to renovate remaining stores. A significant receipt of cash from the sale of discontinued operations was used in part to pay down debt, thereby reducing risk, which made the sale of shares to the public more viable.

Intercompany Comparisons

Vertical analysis also makes it easier to compare different companies. As we mentioned earlier, one of Hudson's Bay's competitors is Sears. Using vertical analysis, we can make a more meaningful comparison of the condensed income statements of both of these companies, as shown in Illustration 14-11, because it reduces each financial statement item to a percentage that can be compared more easily than large differences in dollar amounts.

Despite the lower gross profit experienced by Hudson's Bay in 2012 compared with 2011, this company still had a higher gross profit percentage of 39.0% compared with Sears at 36.1%. Recall that HBC tends to operate in the "high-end" retail market, so we would expect the goods it sells to have a higher gross profit, whereas Sears does not operate in this segment of the market.

It is interesting to note that Hudson's Bay's selling, general, and administrative expenses are lower than Sears's, representing only 36% of sales compared with Sears's 38%. Management of Sears seems to be aware of this as they mention in their annual report that they are trying to reduce advertising expenses. Sears's expenses also included severance costs for employees at stores that were closed.

Unlike HBC, when Sears closed stores in 2012, they did not constitute an entire business like Zellers and, as such, these stores were not considered a discontinued operation. Consequently, any gains (or

Illustration 14-11
Intercompany comparison
by vertical analysis

HUDSON'S BAY COMPANY AND SEARS CANADA INC.
Statements of Earnings
Year Ended February 2, 2013
(in millions)

	Hudson's Bay		Sears	
	Amount	Percentage	Amount	Percentage
Net sales	$4,077.0	100.0%	$4,300.7	100.0%
Cost of sales	2,487.0	61.0%	2,749.2	63.9%
Gross profit	1,590.0	39.0%	1,551.5	36.1%
Selling, general, and administrative expenses	1,469.2	36.0%	1,634.4	38.0%
Profit from operations	120.8	3.0%	(82.9)	(1.9)%
Other revenues and expenses				
Interest expense	97.3	2.4%	13.3	0.3%
Gain from sale of stores	—	0.0%	210.4	4.9%
Profit from continuing operations before income tax	23.5	0.6%	114.2	2.7%
Income tax recovery (expense)	8.0	0.2%	(13.0)	(0.3)%
Profit from continuing operations	31.5	0.8%	101.2	2.4%
Profit (loss) from discontinued operations,				
net of income tax	(76.3)	(1.9)%	—	0.0%
Profit (loss)	$ (44.8)	(1.1)%	$ 101.2	2.4%

losses) from the sale of these Sears stores were shown within profit from continuing operations. These gains represented 4.9% of Sears's net sales, and without these gains the company would not have had a profit from continuing operations. It is important to note that, although this did not qualify as a discontinued operation, it is a nonrecurring item and we will need to remember that when doing our analysis.

Interest expense for Hudson's Bay was 2.4% of net sales compared with Sears at 0.3%, because Sears has very few interest-bearing liabilities. Sears's largest liability relates to its underfunded employee pension fund and not bank loans.

As we saw earlier, HBC received a small income tax refund and the above shows that Sears incurred income tax expense. As a percentage of net sales, these are not that significant. Finally, we can see that the discontinued business loss for Hudson's Bay was only 1.9% of net sales but it was twice as large as the profit from continuing operations, resulting in the company having a loss for the year.

In summary, we can conclude from our comparative vertical analysis of these two companies that Hudson's Bay was able to generate a higher gross profit. Furthermore, that company controlled its selling, general, and administrative expenses, giving it a much higher profit from operations than that generated by Sears (a negative 1.9%). However, when other revenues and expenses are considered, including the nonrecurring gain generated from the sale of stores by Sears, Sears's profit from continuing operations exceeded HBC's, as did its final profit figure once HBC's loss from discontinued operations was deducted.

DECISION TOOLKIT

Decision Checkpoints	 Info Needed for Decision	 Tools to Use for Decision	 How to Evaluate Results
How do the relationships between items in this year's financial statements compare with last year's relationships or those of competitors?	Statement of financial position and income statement	Each line item on the statement of financial position should be presented as a percentage of total assets (total liabilities and shareholders' equity). Each line item on the income statement should be presented as a percentage of revenues (or net sales). This is called vertical analysis.	Any difference, either across years or between companies, should be investigated to determine the cause.

Vertical analysis can also be used to compare two companies' statements of financial position, in addition to the income statement as we did above. We have not done so here as the information that would be obtained from doing this can also be derived from ratio analysis, which we will cover next.

BEFORE YOU GO ON...

▶ Do It! Vertical Analysis

Selected condensed information (in thousands) from Bonora Ltd.'s income statement for four years ended June 30 follows:

	2015	2014	2013	2012
Net sales	$37,600	$36,500	$38,700	$40,500
Cost of goods sold	14,900	14,200	13,800	15,300
Gross profit	22,700	22,300	24,900	25,200
Operating expenses	18,500	17,400	16,200	17,600
Profit from operations	4,200	4,900	8,700	7,600
Income tax expense	1,050	1,225	2,175	1,900
Profit	$ 3,150	$ 3,675	$ 6,525	$ 5,700

Using vertical analysis, calculate the percentage of a base amount for each year.

Action Plan

- Set the base amount as net sales in an income statement.
- Vertical percentage of a base amount: Find the relative percentage by dividing the specific income statement amount by the base amount (net sales) for each year. Round your results to one decimal spot. Recall that although the vertical percentage columns should add, minor rounding discrepancies may prevent this from happening.

Solution

	2015	2014	2013	2012
Net sales	100.0%	100.0%	100.0%	100.0%
Cost of goods sold	39.6%	38.9%	35.7%	37.8%
Gross profit	60.4%	61.1%	64.3%	62.2%
Operating expenses	49.2%	47.7%	41.9%	43.5%
Profit from operations	11.2%	13.4%	22.5%	18.8%
Income tax expense	2.8%	3.4%	5.6%	4.7%
Profit	8.4%	10.1%	16.9%	14.1%

Related Exercise Material: BE14-5, BE14-6, BE14-7, BE14-8, E14-3, and E14-4.

Ratio Analysis

The first step in any comprehensive analysis is to perform a horizontal and vertical analysis. This helps users understand some of the reasons for changes in financial position and performance, as well as identify further areas for investigation. Calculating and interpreting the meaning of ratios completes our overall analysis. Similar to horizontal and vertical analyses, ratio analysis is also a comparative tool used to evaluate the significance of financial data for a company. However, ratio analysis is much broader than the other tools, as it can be used in all three types of comparisons (intracompany, intercompany, and industry) discussed in this text.

In the next three sections, we provide an example of comprehensive ratio analysis using the liquidity, solvency, and profitability ratios presented in past chapters. This analysis uses three categories of comparisons: (1) intracompany, comparing two years of data for Hudson's Bay Company for 2012 and 2011; (2) intercompany, comparing Hudson's Bay Company and Sears Canada Inc. for 2012 and 2011; and (3) industry, comparing both companies with industry averages for 2012 and 2011.

As we analyze each ratio for these two companies and compare them with industry averages, each ratio will be determined based on the exact interpretation of the formula provided. For example, if the ratio requires the use of profit, we will use that exact amount. However, as was explained earlier, to properly understand the performance of a company, we need to focus on sustainable income and ignore irregular items such as discontinued business losses and nonrecurring gains. If these items have a major impact on the meaning of a ratio, we will cover this so that you can see the effect on a ratio when irregular items are considered and when they are ignored.

You will recall that Hudson's Bay's statement of financial position was presented earlier in the chapter in Illustration 14-6 and its income statement in Illustration 14-7. We will use the information in these two financial statements, in addition to the following data, to calculate the Hudson's Bay Company's ratios:

(in millions)	2012	2011
Net cash provided by operating activities	$353.6	$ 68.8
Net capital expenditures	$159.3	$144.0
Total cash dividends	$101.1	$321.4
Dividend per share	$ 0.94	$ 3.07
Market price per share	$16.80	Not traded
Weighted average number of shares	107.5	104.7

Note that HBC does not have any preferred shares.

Detailed calculations of the ratios are not shown in the ratios that follow, but you can use the above data and the statement of financial position and income statement data shown earlier in the chapter to recalculate the ratios for Hudson's Bay to make sure you understand where the numbers came from.

LIQUIDITY RATIOS

STUDY OBJECTIVE 4
Identify and calculate ratios that are used to analyze liquidity.

Liquidity ratios measure a company's short-term ability to pay its maturing obligations and to meet unexpected needs for cash. Short-term lenders and other creditors, such as bankers and suppliers, are particularly interested in assessing liquidity. Liquidity ratios include working capital, the current ratio, cash current debt coverage, receivables turnover, average collection period, inventory turnover, and days in inventory. Cash provided by operating activities, reported on the statement of cash flows, is also useful in assessing liquidity.

Working Capital

Working capital is the difference between current assets and current liabilities. It is one measure of liquidity. However, as we learned in Chapter 2, the current ratio—which expresses current assets and current liabilities as a ratio rather than as an amount—is a more useful indicator of liquidity. Consequently, we will not illustrate working capital again here, and will focus instead on the current ratio.

Current Ratio

The current ratio expresses the relationship of current assets to current liabilities, and is calculated by dividing current assets by current liabilities. It is widely used for evaluating a company's liquidity and short-term debt-paying ability.

The 2012 and 2011 current ratios for HBC, Sears, and the industry are shown below. Note that in the following ratio comparison, and in all ratios that follow, there is a column titled "Comparison with Prior Year," indicating whether the 2012 result is better or worse than the 2011 result shown for each of HBC, Sears, and the industry.

$$\text{CURRENT RATIO} = \frac{\text{CURRENT ASSETS}}{\text{CURRENT LIABILITIES}}$$		
	2012	2011	Comparison with Prior Year
Hudson's Bay	1.0:1	1.1:1	Worse
Sears	1.5:1	1.5:1	Same
Industry average	1.4:1	1.5:1	Worse

What does the current ratio actually mean? The 2012 ratio of 1.0:1 means that for every dollar of current liabilities, Hudson's Bay has $1.00 of current assets. Hudson's Bay's current ratio declined marginally between 2012 and 2011. The sale of current assets relating to discontinued businesses caused a drop in current assets but this was offset by a corresponding decrease in current liabilities when the proceeds from this sale were used to pay down current liabilities.

Hudson's Bay's current ratio is less than that of both Sears and the industry. However, it is too early in our analysis to draw any conclusions about HBC's liquidity, because the current ratio is only one measure of liquidity. It does not take into account the composition of the company's current assets or operating cash flows.

ACCOUNTING MATTERS!

How to Manage the Current Ratio

The apparent simplicity of the current ratio can have real-world limitations because adding equal amounts to both the numerator and the denominator causes the ratio to decrease.

Assume, for example, that a company has $2 million of current assets and $1 million of current liabilities. Its current ratio is 2:1. If it purchases $1 million of inventory on account, it will have $3 million of current assets and $2 million of current liabilities. Its current ratio decreases to 1.5:1. If, instead, the company pays off $500,000 of its current liabilities, it will have $1.5 million of current assets and $500,000 of current liabilities. Its current ratio increases to 3:1. Thus, any horizontal or ratio analysis should be done with care because the ratio is susceptible to sudden changes and is easily influenced by management's decisions.

Cash Current Debt Coverage

One disadvantage of the current ratio is that it uses year-end balances of current asset and current liability accounts. These year-end balances may not reflect the company's position during most of the year. A ratio that partially corrects this problem is the cash current debt coverage ratio. It is calculated by dividing net cash provided (or used) by operating activities (from the statement of cash flows) by average current liabilities. Because it uses cash provided (or used) by operating activities from the statement of cash flows that covers a period of time, in conjunction with the average current assets from that period, the cash current debt coverage ratio may be a better indicator of liquidity.

The 2012 and 2011 cash current debt coverage ratios for Hudson's Bay and Sears are shown below. Industry averages are not available (n/a) for cash-based ratios.

CASH CURRENT DEBT COVERAGE = $\dfrac{\text{NET CASH PROVIDED (USED) BY OPERATING ACTIVITIES}}{\text{AVERAGE CURRENT LIABILITIES}}$			
	2012	2011	Comparison with Prior Year
Hudson's Bay	0.2:1	0.0:1	Better
Sears	n/a	0.1:1	Worse
Industry average	n/a	n/a	n/a

In the retail industry, the value of the cash current debt coverage ratio is usually quite low because inventory, which is a significant asset for these companies, is often financed with short-term bank loans or through accounts payable, both of which are current liabilities. Because these current liabilities are quite significant, this tends to make this ratio quite low, as we can see above.

During 2012, HBC's cash provided by operating activities increased significantly due to the sale of current assets relating to discontinued businesses, while for Sears, cash provided by operating activities was negative in 2012. Recall that although Sears had a profit that year, it arose primarily because of the sale of some stores. Without that sale, Sears would have had a loss in 2012. Since the proceeds on this sale are from an investing activity, Sears actually had negative operating cash flows because its selling, general, and administrative expenses exceeded gross profit. Therefore, we have shown its cash current debt ratio for 2012 as not applicable.

Receivables Turnover

We mentioned earlier that a high current ratio is not always a good indication of liquidity. A high current ratio can exist because of increased receivables resulting from uncollectible accounts. The ratio that is used to assess the liquidity of the receivables is the receivables turnover. It measures the number of times, on average, that receivables are collected during the period. The receivables turnover is calculated by dividing net credit sales (sales on account less sales returns and allowances and discounts) by average gross accounts receivable (before the allowance for doubtful accounts is deducted) during the year.

The 2012 and 2011 receivables turnover ratios for Hudson's Bay, Sears, and the industry are shown below.

RECEIVABLES TURNOVER = $\dfrac{\text{NET CREDIT SALES}}{\text{AVERAGE GROSS ACCOUNTS RECEIVABLE}}$			
	2012	2011	Comparison with Prior Year
Hudson's Bay	57.3 times	38.5 times	Better
Sears	44.7 times	35.5 times	Better
Industry average	107.8 times	125.6 times	Worse

Since companies do not normally disclose the proportion of their sales that were made for cash and for credit, we normally assume that all sales are credit sales. In addition, not all companies report gross and net accounts receivable separately. In such cases, it is appropriate to use net accounts receivable. The important thing is to be consistent in your input data to ensure that the resulting ratios are comparable.

Since many sales made by retailers are not on credit, the receivables turnover for the companies we are analyzing will be quite high given the low level of accounts receivable that these companies have. Hudson's Bay's receivables turnover improved substantially in 2012, from 38.5 times to 57.3 times. This was due in part to the disposal of receivables relating to discontinued operations. Sears also improved its receivables collection because an amount receivable from a financial institution that the company uses for its credit card services decreased. Because receivables represent a small portion of the assets of most retailers (most sales are not on credit), we usually do not place a great deal of emphasis on this ratio for this type of business. The industry average is higher than the ratio value for both of our companies because the industry average includes retailers that do not use their own credit cards to offer credit to customers.

Average Collection Period.   A variant of the receivables turnover is calculated by converting it into a collection period stated in days. This is done by dividing 365 days by the receivables turnover. The 2012 and 2011 average collection period for Hudson's Bay, Sears, and the industry are shown below.

AVERAGE COLLECTION PERIOD = $\dfrac{\text{365 DAYS}}{\text{RECEIVABLES TURNOVER}}$			
	2012	2011	Comparison with Prior Year
Hudson's Bay	6 days	9 days	Better
Sears	8 days	10 days	Better
Industry average	3 days	3 days	Same

Analysts frequently use the average collection period to assess the effectiveness of a company's credit and collection policies. The general rule is that the collection period should not greatly exceed the credit period (the time allowed for payment). While we do not know Hudson's Bay's credit period, it appears to have been much better at collecting its accounts receivable in 2012 than in 2011, and the same holds true for Sears. The average collection period for both of these companies is worse than the industry average because they have receivables from credit card companies that they have partnered with. Please note that although the industry average appears unchanged at three days, it is actually slightly worse if we ignore rounding. This finding is consistent with the results from the receivables turnover ratio.

It is important to understand that although we have indicated that HBC, Sears, and the industry average collection periods were better or the same, any collection period of less than 10 days is excellent. Both Hudson's Bay and Sears have excellent collection periods regardless of the comparison above.

Inventory Turnover

Slow-moving inventory can also distort the current ratio. The liquidity of a company's inventory is measured by the inventory turnover ratio. This ratio measures the number of times on average that the inventory is sold during the period, and is calculated by dividing the cost of goods sold by the average inventory.

The 2012 and 2011 inventory turnover ratios for Hudson's Bay, Sears, and the industry are shown below.

$$\text{INVENTORY TURNOVER} = \frac{\text{COST OF GOODS SOLD}}{\text{AVERAGE INVENTORY}}$$			
	2012	2011	Comparison with Prior Year
Hudson's Bay	2.5 times	1.7 times	Better
Sears	3.3 times	3.3 times	Same
Industry average	2.7 times	3.4 times	Worse

HBC's inventory turnover improved in 2012 as excess inventories from discontinued operations were sold off or reclassified out of inventory on the statement of financial position and put into a separate current asset account relating to assets from discontinued operations. Nonetheless, Hudson's Bay is still slower at moving inventory than Sears, which experienced no change in its inventory turnover in 2012 compared with 2011. Management at Hudson's Bay would attribute this to slower turnover in Lord & Taylor stores because of the effects of Hurricane Sandy. The lower turnover may also be attributable to the higher-end nature of HBC's inventory, which generally does not turn over as rapidly as discount-priced products. The industry average fell in 2012, moving closer to the Hudson's Bay turnover value and becoming worse than Sears's turnover for that year.

Days in Inventory.   A variant of the inventory turnover ratio is days in inventory, which measures the average number of days it takes to sell the inventory. It is calculated by dividing 365 days by the inventory turnover.

The 2012 and 2011 days in inventory for Hudson's Bay, Sears, and the industry are shown below.

$$\text{DAYS IN INVENTORY} = \frac{365 \text{ DAYS}}{\text{INVENTORY TURNOVER}}$$			
	2012	2011	Comparison with Prior Year
Hudson's Bay	146 days	215 days	Better
Sears	111 days	111 days	Same
Industry average	135 days	107 days	Worse

Hudson's Bay's 146 days in inventory means that in 2012, on average, it took Hudson's Bay 146 days to sell merchandise. Sears, on the other hand, sells its inventory faster. Generally, the faster inventory is sold, the less cash there is tied up in inventory and the less chance there is of inventory becoming obsolete.

If we relate the current ratio to the receivables and inventory turnover ratios, we must first understand that for retailers like HBC and Sears, the effect of receivables turnover is insignificant given that receivables, unlike inventory, represent a small percentage of current assets. For Sears, the days in inventory did not change and neither did the current ratio. For Hudson's Bay, the days in inventory declined yet the current ratio rose. We can conclude that this increase was not caused by slow-moving or obsolete inventory.

It is worth noting here that the above interpretations are based not only on the financial data, but also on the knowledge gained from an understanding of the underlying nature of these companies and of the significant events that occurred during the year, all of which are disclosed in annual reports and other publicly available information. As mentioned earlier in the chapter, nonfinancial information is important in interpreting the financial results.

Liquidity Conclusion

In an intracompany comparison, except for the current ratio, all of Hudson's Bay's liquidity ratios improved between 2011 and 2012, as would be expected given the company's strategy to sell off less profitable business units.

In an intercompany and industry comparison, Hudson's Bay's liquidity ratios are generally worse than those of Sears and the industry average except for receivables turnover, which is probably the least important ratio we have examined given the fact that receivables account for a very low percentage of total assets. This, however, may change when HBC sells off its discontinued business assets and settles the related liabilities. We also see that HBC is managing its inventory more effectively and improving turnover. Although not considered in this ratio analysis, it is worth nothing that Hudson's Bay also has access to an unused credit facility (operating line of credit) of several hundred million dollars, which gives it a source of additional liquidity if needed.

Summary of Liquidity Ratios

Illustration 14-12 summarizes the liquidity ratios we have used in this chapter, and throughout the textbook. We have included the chapter number where each ratio was discussed in detail for your review. In addition to the ratio formula and what it measures, the desired direction (higher or lower) of the ratio result is included.

▶ Illustration 14-12

Liquidity ratios

Chapter	Ratio	Formula	What the Ratio Measures	Desired Result
2	Working capital	Current assets − Current liabilities	Short-term debt-paying ability	Higher
2	Current ratio	$\dfrac{\text{Current assets}}{\text{Current liabilities}}$	Short-term debt-paying ability	Higher
13	Cash current debt coverage	$\dfrac{\text{Net cash provided (used) by operating activities}}{\text{Average current liabilities}}$	Short-term debt-paying ability (cash basis)	Higher
8	Receivables turnover	$\dfrac{\text{Net credit sales}}{\text{Average gross accounts receivable}}$	Liquidity of receivables	Higher
8	Average collection period	$\dfrac{365 \text{ days}}{\text{Receivables turnover}}$	Number of days receivables are outstanding	Lower
6	Inventory Turnover	$\dfrac{\text{Cost of goods sold}}{\text{Average inventory}}$	Liquidity of inventory	Higher
6	Days in inventory	$\dfrac{365 \text{ days}}{\text{Inventory turnover}}$	Number of days inventory is on hand	Lower

To summarize, a higher result is generally considered to be better for the working capital, current, cash current debt coverage, receivables turnover, and inventory turnover ratios. For those ratios that use turnover ratios in their denominators—the average collection period and days in inventory—a lower result is better. That is, you want to take fewer days to collect receivables and have fewer days of inventory on hand.

Of course, there are exceptions. A current ratio can be high at times because of higher balances of receivables and inventory included in current assets that are the result of uncollectible receivables or slow-moving inventory. This is why it is important never to conclude an assessment of liquidity based only on one ratio. In the case of the current ratio, it should always be interpreted along with the receivables and inventory turnover ratios. Furthermore, we also have to assess the significance of each item in a turnover ratio. As we saw with these companies, inventory was much more significant than receivables.

BEFORE YOU GO ON...

▶ Do It! Liquidity Analysis

Liquidity ratios for two companies follow:

	Wasis Corporation	Rita Limited
Current ratio	1.6:1	1.9:1
Receivables turnover	27.0 times	22.6 times
Inventory turnover	6.8 times	5.6 times

(a) For each company, calculate the average collection period and days in inventory ratios.

(b) Identify whether Wasis or Rita has the "better" current ratio, receivables turnover ratio, average collection period, inventory turnover ratio, and days in inventory.

(c) Which company is more liquid? Explain.

Action Plan

- Review the formula for each ratio so you understand how it is calculated and how to interpret it.
- The current ratio should always be interpreted along with the receivables and inventory turnover ratios.
- Remember that for liquidity ratios, a higher result is usually better unless the current ratio has been artificially inflated by slow-moving receivables or inventory.

Solution

(a)

Wasis	Rita

Average collection period

$$\frac{365 \text{ days}}{27.0} = 14 \text{ days} \qquad \frac{365 \text{ days}}{22.6} = 16 \text{ days}$$

Days in inventory

$$\frac{365 \text{ days}}{6.8} = 54 \text{ days} \qquad \frac{365 \text{ days}}{5.6} = 65 \text{ days}$$

(b) Rita has the better (higher) current ratio, ignoring any potential inflation due to slow-moving receivables and inventory. Wasis has the better (higher) receivables and inventory turnover ratios. It also has the better (lower) average collection period and days in inventory ratios.

(c) Wasis is the more liquid of the two companies, as it collects its receivables and sells its inventory sooner than does Rita. This could help explain Rita's higher current ratio, although this is unlikely given the small differential between both companies' liquidity ratios. In addition, it is noteworthy that, even though Wasis has a better receivables turnover and average collection period than Rita, both companies are collecting their receivables in a very timely fashion—far less than 30 days. It is safe to assume that neither company has a large proportion of receivables and they most likely sell their goods for cash more often than on account.

Related Exercise Material: BE14-9, BE14-10, E14-5, E14-6, E14-7, and E14-13.

the navigator

SOLVENCY RATIOS

STUDY OBJECTIVE 5
Identify and calculate ratios that are used to analyze solvency.

While liquidity ratios measure a company's ability to pay its current liabilities, solvency ratios measure the ability to pay total liabilities. The debt to total assets, times interest earned, and cash total debt coverage ratios give information about debt-paying ability. In addition, free cash flow gives information about the company's discretionary cash flow that is available to expand operations, go after new opportunities, or pay additional dividends, among other alternatives.

Debt to Total Assets

The debt to total assets ratio measures the percentage of the total assets that is provided by creditors. It is calculated by dividing total liabilities (both current and non-current) by total assets. This ratio indicates the company's reliance on debt as it measures the proportion of total liabilities relative to total assets. When this ratio is high, the company has a high level of debt and there is greater risk that it will be unable to pay its maturing obligations. If the debt to total assets ratio is low, the company has less debt and there is less concern about being able to pay it off. So, from the creditors' point of view, a low ratio of debt to total assets is good. However, if the ratio is too low, it may indicate that management is not trying to grow the business by obtaining financing from lenders.

The 2012 and 2011 debt to total assets ratios for Hudson's Bay, Sears, and the industry are shown below.

$$\text{DEBT TO TOTAL ASSETS} = \frac{\text{TOTAL LIABILITIES}}{\text{TOTAL ASSETS}}$$

	2012	2011	Comparison with Prior Year
Hudson's Bay	69.3%	76.1%	Better
Sears	56.6%	60.0%	Better
Industry average	50.0%	48.2%	Worse

HBC's debt to total assets ratio of 69.3% in 2012 means that creditors have provided financing that covers 69.3% of the company's total assets. The inverse means that shareholders have provided financing to cover 30.7% (100% − 69.3%) of the company's total assets.

Hudson's Bay's solvency, as measured by the debt to total assets ratio, improved between 2012 and 2011, decreasing from 76.1% to 69.3%. According to Illustration 14-6, presented earlier in the chapter, total assets decreased by 18.6% in 2012 and total liabilities decreased by 25.8%. Consequently, liabilities have fallen faster than assets and the debt to total assets ratio has fallen. As was mentioned earlier in the chapter, HBC sold off assets in 2012 pertaining to the Zellers and Fields stores and used the proceeds to pay down debt, buy back shares, and pay out dividends. The company also raised funds when it went public and used them to reduce debt further. Nonetheless, these measures to reduce debt were not enough to lower the ratio to a level comparable with those of Sears or the industry average, which are still much lower.

Sears also reduced its liabilities in 2012, improving its debt to total assets ratio. During 2012, many companies reduced debt in anticipation of rising interest rates while others increased debt and locked in the low interest rates that were prevailing at that time. Many companies in the industry followed the latter approach, which is why there was a slight increase in the industry average for the debt to total assets ratio in 2012.

Another ratio with a similar meaning to the debt to total assets ratio is the debt to equity ratio. It shows the use of borrowed funds relative to the investments by shareholders. The debt to equity ratio is calculated by dividing total liabilities by total shareholders' equity. When the debt to total assets ratio equals 50%, the debt to equity ratio is 100% (because total liabilities plus shareholders' equity equals total assets).

Using this definition, Hudson's Bay's debt to equity ratio for 2012 is 225.9% ($2,254.6 million ÷ $998.0 million). This means that Hudson's Bay has financed its operations with 2.3 times as much debt as equity, which is quite high compared with Sears and the industry.

Times Interest Earned

While a company's debt level is important, its ability to service the debt—that is, pay the interest—is of equal or greater importance. The times interest earned ratio (also called interest coverage) indicates the company's ability to meet interest payments as they come due. The numerator in this ratio consists of profit (earnings) before interest expense and income tax. This is often abbreviated as EBIT, which stands for earnings before interest and tax. EBIT is then divided by interest expense to determine this ratio's value. The ratio therefore measures how many times higher EBIT is than interest expense. The higher the ratio, the more EBIT there is available to cover interest.

The 2012 and 2011 times interest earned ratios for Hudson's Bay, Sears, and the industry are shown below.

TIMES INTEREST EARNED = $\dfrac{\text{PROFIT} + \text{INTEREST EXPENSE} + \text{INCOME TAX EXPENSE (EBIT)}}{\text{INTEREST EXPENSE}}$		
	2012	2011	Comparison with Prior Year
Hudson's Bay	0.5 times	11.1 times	Worse
Sears	9.6 times	n/a	Better
Industry average	3.0 times	3.2 times	Worse

Sears's times interest earned ratio was not determinable for 2011 because the company did not have a profit that year that exceeded interest and income tax. HBC's 2012 times interest earned was very low at 0.5 times. That is, its profit before interest and taxes was 0.5 times the amount needed to pay its interest expense. We must remember, however, that this company had lower profits in 2012 because of discontinued business losses and considerably higher profits in 2011 when there were gains from discontinued operations, which is why the times interest earned was so much higher that year. If we were to calculate this ratio using profit from just continuing operations, the times interest earned would have been 1.2 in 2012 and 1.4 in 2011. As long as this ratio is above a value of one, it means that the company is generating sufficient EBIT to pay its interest expense. However, even excluding the effects of discontinued operations, it seems that Hudson's Bay's times interest earned is sufficient but considerably below those of Sears and the industry average.

Times interest earned should always be interpreted along with the debt to total assets ratio. We saw earlier that HBC's debt to total assets ratio is higher than those of Sears and the industry average, even though it did fall in 2012. This high debt level increases interest expense relative to other companies, and causes the times interest earned ratio to fall. Furthermore, unlike Sears, which has many non-current liabilities that do not bear interest (pension liabilities), most of HBC's non-current liabilities do bear interest. This causes a lower times interest earned ratio for this company.

Cash Total Debt Coverage

A cash-based equivalent to assess solvency is the cash total debt coverage ratio. This ratio indicates a company's ability to repay its liabilities from cash provided by operating activities, without having to liquidate the assets used in its operations. It is calculated by dividing net cash provided (or used) by operating activities (from the statement of cash flows) by average total liabilities.

The 2012 and 2011 cash total debt coverage ratios for Hudson's Bay and Sears are shown below.

CASH TOTAL DEBT COVERAGE = $\dfrac{\text{NET CASH PROVIDED (USED) BY OPERATING ACTIVITIES}}{\text{AVERAGE TOTAL LIABILITIES}}$		
	2012	2011	Comparison with Prior Year
Hudson's Bay	0.1 times	0.0 times	Better
Sears	n/a	0.1 times	Worse
Industry average	n/a	n/a	n/a

An industry ratio for this measure is not available. No ratio for Sears was calculated for 2012 because the company did not have a positive amount of cash provided by operating activities. The Hudson's Bay ratio improved in 2012 because cash provided by operating activities rose as the current assets relating to discontinued operations were sold. One way of interpreting the cash total debt coverage ratio is to say that cash provided by HBC's 2012 operating activities would be enough to pay off 10% of its total liabilities. If 10% of liabilities were retired each year, it would take approximately 10 years to retire all debt.

Free Cash Flow

Another indication of a company's solvency is the amount of free cash flow that it generates. Free cash flow is measured as the amount of cash left over from operating cash flows after investing some of this to maintain its current productive capacity and after paying current dividends.

Free cash flow for 2012 and 2011 for Hudson's Bay and Sears is shown below.

FREE CASH FLOW =	NET CASH PROVIDED (USED) BY OPERATING ACTIVITIES − NET CAPITAL EXPENDITURES − DIVIDENDS PAID		
(in millions)	2012	2011	Comparison with Prior Year
Hudson's Bay	$93.2	$(396.6)	Better
Sears	$(279.3)	$0.7	Worse
Industry average	n/a	n/a	n/a

There are no industry average amounts available. Hudson's Bay's free cash flow improved considerably in 2012 compared with 2011. This happened for two reasons. Operating cash flows improved because a large portion of the working capital of discontinued operations was sold during the year and because the company, after going public, reduced the amount of dividends that were paid out to shareholders. It should be noted that the sale of assets from discontinued operations will probably not occur to the same extent in future years, so the improvement we see in HBC's free cash flow may not be sustainable. Sears's free cash flow has fallen because of lower net cash flow from operating activities.

Solvency Conclusion

In an intracompany comparison, except for the times interest earned ratio, Hudson's Bay's solvency ratios improved in 2012. The company clearly took steps to reduce the amount of debt that it had. The times interest earned ratio fell because of lower profit, which in turn occurred because sales of discontinued business operations did not yield the large gains that were made in 2011.

Compared with Sears, HBC had lower profit but higher net cash flows from operating activities in 2012. During that year, Sears had a large gain on the sale of some stores. Without that gain, Sears would have had a loss in 2012 rather than a profit. As we know, a gain is not a cash flow, so when we ignore it in determining net cash flow from operations, Sears's cash flow from that source is actually negative. This is why, when we look at ratios involving net cash flow from operating activities such as cash total debt coverage and free cash flow, Hudson's Bay has better results. However, when using ratios based on profit rather than net cash flow from operating activities, like the times interest earned ratio, Sears has a better result. The debt to total assets ratio indicates that Hudson's Bay is worse because of its higher debt levels, which was likely a concern for management, as they did reduce debt levels in 2012, but the company still has more of its assets financed with debt than Sears does.

Summary of Solvency Ratios

Illustration 14-13 summarizes the solvency ratios discussed above, and throughout this textbook.

Chapter	Ratio	Formula	What the Ratio Measures	Desired Result
2, 10	Debt to total assets	$\dfrac{\text{Total liabilities}}{\text{Total assets}}$	Percentage of total assets provided by creditors	Lower
10	Times interest earned	$\dfrac{\text{Profit + Interest expense + Income tax expense (EBIT)}}{\text{Interest expense}}$	Ability to meet interest payments	Higher
13	Cash total debt coverage	$\dfrac{\text{Net cash provided (used) by operating activities}}{\text{Average total liabilities}}$	Long-term debt-paying ability (cash basis)	Higher
13	Free cash flow	Net cash provided (used) by operating activities − Net capital expenditures − Dividends paid	Cash available from operating activities for discretionary purposes	Higher

For the debt to total assets ratio, a lower result is generally considered to be better. Having less debt reduces a company's dependence on debt financing and offers more flexibility for future financing alternatives. For times interest earned, cash total debt coverage, and free cash flow, a higher result is better.

It is important to interpret the debt to total assets and times interest earned ratios together. For example, assume that a company goes further into debt and borrows more money. It uses that money to invest in a new venture that is incredibly profitable. Because of this, the times interest earned ratio will rise because of the increased profit even though the debt to total assets ratio has also increased. In this case, taking on more leverage was the appropriate strategy to follow. On the other hand, if after raising the debt to total assets ratio, a company finds that its times interest earned ratio is falling, it means that the interest incurred to obtain that extra debt has decreased the profitability of the company. In this case the company should take steps to reduce its debt. Consequently, one should always interpret a company's solvency after considering the interrelationship of these two ratios.

BEFORE YOU GO ON...

▶Do It! Solvency Analysis

Selected information from the financial statement of the Home Affairs Corporation follows:

	2015	2014
Total assets	$1,000,000	$1,015,000
Total liabilities	737,700	809,000
Interest expense	59,000	40,500
Income tax expense	48,400	50,500
Profit	193,600	202,000

(a) For each company, calculate the debt to total assets and times interest earned ratios.

(b) Comment on whether Home Affairs' overall solvency has improved or deteriorated in 2015.

Action Plan

• Review the formula for each ratio so you understand how it is calculated and how to interpret it.
• The debt to total assets ratio should always be interpreted together with the times interest earned ratio.
• Remember that for debt to total assets, a lower result is better. For other solvency ratios, a higher result is better.

(continued)

Solution

(a)

	2015	2014	Comparison with Prior Year
Debt to total assets			
	$\dfrac{\$737,700}{\$1,000,000} = 73.8\%$	$\dfrac{\$809,000}{\$1,015,000} = 79.7\%$	Better
Times interest earned			
	$\dfrac{\$193,600 + \$59,000 + \$48,400}{\$59,000}$	$\dfrac{\$202,000 + \$40,500 + \$50,500}{\$40,500}$	Worse
	= 5.1 times	= 7.2 times	

(b) Overall, solvency has deteriorated in 2015. While the debt to total assets ratio has improved in 2015, total liabilities are still a very high percentage of total assets. Of greater concern is the proportionally greater decline in the times interest earned ratio in 2015. The company is no longer able to handle its interest payments as well as in the past, even though it is still able to cover its interest payments 5.1 times. Taken together, this leads us to conclude that overall solvency has deteriorated.

Related Exercise Material: BE14-11, E14-5, E14-8, E14-9, and E14-13.

the navigator

PROFITABILITY RATIOS

STUDY OBJECTIVE 6

Identify and calculate ratios that are used to analyze profitability.

Profitability ratios measure the company's operating success for a specific period of time. To be successful, assets must be used efficiently and generate enough sales at an appropriate price to cover all of the company's expenses. Consequently, profitability ratios focus mainly on the relationships between income statement items and statement of financial position items. Understanding these relationships can help management determine where to focus efforts on improving profitability.

Illustration 14-14 diagrams these relationships and will guide our discussion of Hudson's Bay's profitability. Profitability ratios include the gross profit margin, profit margin, asset turnover, return on assets, and return on common shareholders' equity ratios, as shown in Illustration 14-14.

▶Illustration 14-14

Relationship among profitability measures

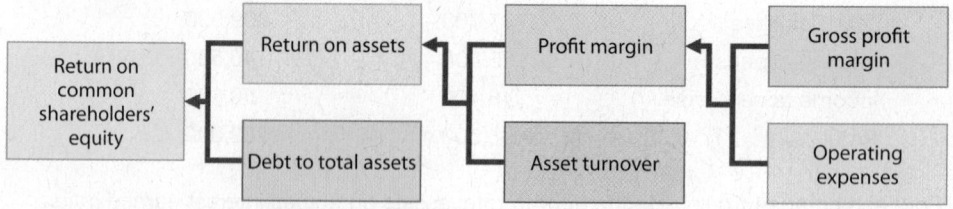

As shown in the above illustration, the return on common shareholders' equity ratio is affected by the return on assets and debt to total assets ratios. If a company wants to increase its return on common shareholders' equity, it can either increase its return on assets or increase its reliance on debt financing. In fact, as long as the return on assets is higher than the interest rate paid on debt, the return on common shareholders' equity will always be increased by the use of debt.

For example, if you bought a house and did not borrow any money to do it, your house, which is an asset, would be equal to the equity you had in the house. If you sold the house one year later at a 15% gain, your return on both your asset and your equity would be the same (15%) because your asset is equal to your equity. Now consider what would happen if you bought two houses instead of one, and purchased the second house completely with money that you borrowed at 5%. Now your assets are twice the amount of your equity because you now have debt. Using debt like this is called leverage.

When you later sell the houses, you will earn 15% on the first house but this time you will earn a return on the second house of 15% less 5% interest which is equal to 10%. Your return on your equity is now 25% (15% on the first house and 10% on the second house) because the borrowed money, which cost you 5% in interest, earned you a return of 15% and you got to keep the spread (the difference between 15% and 5%). However, if house prices did not rise and you only bought one house, you would have no profit or loss. On the other hand, if you bought two houses, you would still have to pay the bank 5% interest on the money that was borrowed and you would have a negative 5% return on your equity. This is why taking on debt is risky.

The return on assets ratio is affected by the profit margin and asset turnover. If a company wants to increase its return on assets, it can do this by either increasing its return (profit margin) or trying to increase its asset utilization (asset turnover). It is very rare for a company to do both, however. For example, years ago Hudson's Bay acquired discount stores like Zellers in an effort to boost its asset turnover. Discount stores operate on a low-price, high-volume basis, which means in effect that they are prepared to reduce profit margins in order to improve turnover. They feel that the trade-off is an effective strategy that will boost overall return on assets. With new ownership and management, Hudson's Bay is now reversing that strategy and trying to boost return on assets with higher profit margins that come with the sale of higher-quality goods. Hudson's Bay's acquisition of Lord & Taylor and Saks will allow it to compete in the high-end market for luxury goods, as discussed in the chapter-opening feature story.

The profit margin is in turn affected by the gross profit margin and the amount, or percentage, of operating expenses (assuming there are no other revenues or expenses). If a company wants to increase its profit margin, it can increase its gross profit margin (by either raising selling prices or reducing its cost of goods sold), or reduce its operating expenses.

We will now look at each of these ratios in turn and examine their relationships. In addition, before we conclude this section, we will also review the earnings per share, price-earnings, payout, and dividend yield ratios.

Gross Profit Margin

The gross profit margin is calculated by dividing gross profit (net sales less cost of goods sold) by net sales. This ratio indicates a company's ability to maintain an adequate selling price above its cost of goods sold. The 2012 and 2011 gross profit margin ratios for Hudson's Bay, Sears, and the industry are shown below.

GROSS PROFIT MARGIN = $\dfrac{\text{GROSS PROFIT}}{\text{NET SALES}}$		
	2012	2011	Comparison with Prior Year
Hudson's Bay	39.0%	40.1%	Worse
Sears	36.1%	36.5%	Worse
Industry average	33.5%	33.7%	Worse

Hudson's Bay's gross profit margin decreased slightly in 2012 due to price decreases on merchandise sold by Lord & Taylor stores in areas affected by Hurricane Sandy. In both years, however, HBC's gross profit margin was higher than Sears's gross profit margin and the industry average. This is due in part to the higher-end nature of the products sold.

ACCOUNTING MATTERS!

Apple's Gross Profit

The cellular phone market is very competitive. The iPhone by Apple Inc. dominated the smartphone market until competition from Samsung and Google began to cut into its market share. To combat this competition, Apple needed not only to be more innovative but also to be more price-competitive while at the same time trying to maintain the healthy gross profits that investors had come to expect.

Listed below are the sales, cost of goods sold, gross profit, gross profit margin, and share price for all Apple products for five consecutive quarters:

(in U.S. $ millions, except for share price)	June 30, 2013	Mar. 31, 2013	Dec. 31, 2012	Oct. 31, 2012	June 30, 2012
Sales	$35,323	$43,603	$54,512	$35,966	$35,023
Cost of goods sold	22,299	27,254	33,452	21,565	20,029
Gross profit	13,024	16,349	21,060	14,401	14,994
Gross profit margin	36.9%	37.5%	38.6%	40.0%	42.8%
Share price	$397	$443	$549	$661	$584

As Apple's quarterly results were released, investors noticed that sales rose and peaked during the Christmas season but then dropped off in the first quarter of the calendar year as expected. However, when the June 30, 2013, quarterly results came out, everyone had expected sales to continue to rise as they always had done for Apple—but this time they did not.

When investors noticed the steady decline in gross profits caused by price competition with Samsung and other competitors, Apple's share price began to fall, as shown above. The share price recovered somewhat during the summer of 2013 as some investors felt that the decline in the share price was too drastic and would recover. Only time will tell if they were right, but this case clearly illustrates the importance of gross profit margins to share prices.

Profit Margin

The profit margin is calculated by dividing profit by net sales for the period. This ratio is significantly affected by the gross profit margin ratio as gross profit is a major component of profit. The profit margin ratio, in addition to measuring the effect of the gross profit margin, also indicates how effective the company is at controlling operating expenses and how interest expense and income tax expense have affected profit.

The 2012 and 2011 profit margin ratios for Hudson's Bay, Sears, and the industry are shown below.

$$\text{PROFIT MARGIN} = \frac{\text{PROFIT}}{\text{NET SALES}}$$			
	2012	2011	Comparison with Prior Year
Hudson's Bay	(1.1)%	37.6%	Worse
Sears	2.4%	(1.1)%	Better
Industry average	0.1%	0.3%	Worse

We know that Hudson's Bay has a higher gross profit margin. Because of this, we would expect to see this company with a higher profit margin ratio as well. This would certainly be true in a "normal" year, but 2012 was not a normal year for this company. Although the company did a good job of controlling its operating expenses, it incurred losses from the sale of discontinued operations and this caused the profit margin ratio to become negative. In 2011, the opposite had occurred when a large gain was recorded on the sale of Zellers' leaseholds and this made the decrease in the profit margin from 2011 to 2012 seem even larger.

In 2012, Sears had a higher profit margin than HBC because it sold some stores. Both Sears and Hudson's Bay's profits have therefore been affected by these nonrecurring events. If we removed the effect of the loss from discontinued operations from the Hudson's Bay profit margin, the ratio would be 0.8% in 2012 and 1.5% in 2011, both of which are higher than the industry average. If we removed the effect of the store sales from Sears's ratio in 2012, it would again show a negative profit margin, just as in 2011, but in 2012 it would be a negative 2.0%. We can therefore conclude, after taking out the effect of store closures and sales, that HBC has a higher profit margin than both Sears and the industry average.

Asset Turnover

The asset turnover ratio measures how efficiently a company uses its assets to generate sales. It is calculated by dividing net sales by average total assets for the period. The resulting number shows the dollars of sales produced by each dollar invested in assets.

The 2012 and 2011 asset turnover ratios for Hudson's Bay, Sears, and the industry are shown below.

ASSET TURNOVER = $\dfrac{\text{NET SALES}}{\text{AVERAGE TOTAL ASSETS}}$			
	2012	2011	Comparison with Prior Year
Hudson's Bay	1.1 times	1.0 times	Better
Sears	1.7 times	1.6 times	Better
Industry average	1.4 times	1.5 times	Worse

The asset turnover ratio shows that HBC generated $1.10 of sales in 2012 for each dollar it had invested in assets. The asset turnover was up slightly from 2011; however, it is lower than Sears's asset turnover and that of the industry. We normally believe that the higher this ratio is, the more efficient a company is at generating sales with a certain amount of assets. However, we can only draw that conclusion if the assets are comparable.

Since the largest asset for these two companies is property, plant, and equipment, we have to be careful when analyzing this ratio. Why? Consider our two retailers. Sears has operated in a number of locations across Canada for years. It has not purchased any companies recently but Hudson's Bay has. Consequently, Sears's depreciable assets have been depreciated for a longer period of time. If we look carefully at the notes to its financial statements, we see that accumulated depreciation at the end of fiscal 2012 represented 68% of the cost of Sears's depreciable assets. For HBC, this amount was only 23%. Consequently, the denominator in this ratio is much lower for Sears because that company's assets have been depreciated to a greater extent, and because of this, the asset turnover is higher.

Return on Assets

Return on assets measures the overall profitability of assets in terms of how much is earned on each dollar invested in assets. You may recall that we first learned that the return on assets ratio is affected by the profit margin and asset turnover in Chapter 9. By multiplying the profit margin and asset turnover ratios, we can calculate the return on assets ratio as illustrated below:

$$\text{Return on Assets} = \text{Profit Margin} \times \text{Asset Turnover}$$

$$\frac{\text{Profit}}{\text{Average Total Assets}} = \frac{\text{Profit}}{\text{Net Sales}} \times \frac{\text{Net Sales}}{\text{Average Total Assets}}$$

Notice that when we cancel out the net sales term in the profit margin and asset turnover ratios, we have the return on assets ratio, which is profit divided by average total assets.

The 2012 and 2011 return on assets ratios for Hudson's Bay, Sears, and the industry are shown below.

RETURN ON ASSETS = $\dfrac{\text{PROFIT}}{\text{AVERAGE TOTAL ASSETS}}$			
	2012	2011	Comparison with Prior Year
Hudson's Bay	(1.2)%	36.8%	Worse
Sears	4.0%	(1.7)%	Better
Industry average	0.2%	0.4%	Worse

The return on asset ratio for Hudson's Bay can also be calculated by multiplying the profit margin by the asset turnover. For 2012 this is (1.1)% × 1.1 times = (1.2)%. For Sears, the corresponding amounts are 2.4% × 1.7 times = 4.0%. Notice how the higher asset turnover experienced by Sears "boosts" the return on assets higher.

We know that in 2012, the asset turnover for HBC and Sears changed very little, so the major reason for the change in the return on assets ratio for each company was caused by changes in the profit margin. This means that profitability was the primary driver in each company's return on assets rather than asset utilization (turnover). We can therefore understand the reasons for the change in the return on assets ratio by understanding the reasons for the changes to the profit margin ratio.

Return on Common Shareholders' Equity

A widely used measure of profitability from the common shareholders' viewpoint is the return on common shareholders' equity. This ratio shows how many dollars of profit were earned for each dollar invested by the common shareholders. It is calculated by dividing profit available to common shareholders (profit − preferred dividends) by average common shareholders' equity (total shareholders' equity − preferred shares).

The 2012 and 2011 return on common shareholders' equity ratios for Hudson's Bay, Sears, and the industry are shown below.

RETURN ON COMMON SHAREHOLDERS' EQUITY = $\dfrac{\text{PROFIT} - \text{PREFERRED DIVIDENDS}}{\text{AVERAGE COMMON SHAREHOLDERS' EQUITY}}$			
	2012	2011	Comparison with Prior Year
Hudson's Bay	(4.6)%	245.2%	Worse
Sears	9.3%	(3.8)%	Better
Industry average	0.6%	1.2%	Worse

The return on common shareholders' equity is a ratio that is affected by other ratios as discussed above. It is determined in part by the company's use of leverage (the debt to total assets ratio) and the return on assets, which in turn is determined by the profit margin and the asset turnover. We know from examining solvency ratios that Hudson's Bay has more interest-bearing liabilities and is using leverage to a greater extent than Sears. As long as the profit made on these borrowed funds exceeds the interest incurred on the funds, then the return on common shareholders' equity will rise.

We can see the effect of this leverage by comparing the company's return on assets with its return on equity. In 2011, the return on assets was 36.8%, but because a large amount of the company's assets were financed with debt, the equity was much smaller than assets. As a result, when we take the profit and divide it by a smaller average common shareholders' equity amount compared with average total assets, we get a much higher return on common shareholders' equity of 245.2%. This shows the advantage of leverage, which, as it increases, magnifies the difference between the return on common shareholders' equity and the return on assets. In 2012, this effect was felt in the opposite direction when the return on assets was a negative 1.2% while the return on common shareholders' equity was a negative 4.6%.

We know from our discussion of other ratios that the large decrease in profitability in 2012 was due to the fact that there were large gains from discontinued businesses in 2011 followed by discontinued business losses in 2012. If we ignored the effects of these gains and losses, the return on common shareholders' equity in 2012 would have been 3.2% and in 2011 it would have been 9.7%. These exceed the industry average in both of these years, and Sears's return in 2011. If Sears had not had a gain from the sale of some of its stores in 2012, its return on common shareholders' equity would have been negative and therefore lower than Hudson's Bay's return. Therefore, we can conclude that HBC appears to be a more successful company at this time if we exclude the effect of discontinued business operations.

Earnings per Share

Earnings per share is a measure of the profit realized on each common share. It is calculated by dividing profit available to common shareholders (profit − preferred dividends) by the weighted average number of common shares. Earnings per share is widely used by current and potential investors. It is the only ratio that must be presented on the income statement or statement of comprehensive income by companies following IFRS. As we mentioned earlier in this text, earnings per share is not required to be reported by companies following ASPE.

Earnings per share for 2012 and 2011 for Hudson's Bay, Sears, and the industry are shown below.

EARNINGS PER SHARE = $\dfrac{\text{PROFIT} - \text{PREFERRED DIVIDENDS}}{\text{WEIGHTED AVERAGE NUMBER OF COMMON SHARES}}$			
	2012	2011	Comparison with Prior Year
Hudson's Bay	$(0.42)	$13.84	Worse
Sears	$0.99	$(0.48)	Better
Industry average	n/a	n/a	n/a

Note that no industry average is included above. Comparisons with the industry average, or with Sears's earnings per share, are not meaningful, because of the different financing structures. For example, one company could have more debt than the other. Furthermore, there are wide variations in numbers of shares issued by companies. The only meaningful earnings per share comparison would be an intracompany one. Hudson's Bay's earnings per share decreased significantly, from $13.84 in 2011 to a loss per share of $0.42 in 2012. This was due to a large gain in 2011 when the Zellers' leaseholds were sold, followed by a loss in 2012 when the Fields' and Zellers' locations were shut down.

Price-Earnings (P-E) Ratio

The price-earnings ratio is often quoted as a measure of the relationship of the market price of each common share to the earnings per share. It is commonly known as a market measure because it uses a company's share price, which reflects the stock market's (investors') expectations for the company.

The 2012 and 2011 price-earnings ratios for Hudson's Bay, Sears, and the industry are shown below.

PRICE-EARNINGS = $\dfrac{\text{MARKET PRICE PER SHARE}}{\text{EARNINGS PER SHARE}}$			
	2012	2011	Comparison with Prior Year
Hudson's Bay	n/a	n/a	n/a
Sears	9.6 times	n/a	Better
Industry average	21.1 times	17.3 times	Better

Typically, if a company has incurred a loss, the price-earnings ratio is not calculated, which is why no ratio is shown for Hudson's Bay in 2012 or for Sears in 2011. Furthermore, in 2011, Hudson's Bay's shares were not listed on a stock exchange so no publicly available information on its share price can be obtained for that year.

When HBC went public in late November 2012, its shares were offered at the price of $17 per share. By the end of fiscal 2012 (February 2, 2013), the company's shares were trading for $16.80—a price very close to the original issue price of $17 per share. We know that the loss incurred by Hudson's Bay in 2012 was due to discontinued operations. When investors discovered this, how did they react? Clearly, the share price did not fall significantly, even though a loss was incurred. Investors seemed to ignore the loss either because they knew it would not happen again or because they expected such a loss to occur when they bought the shares. If we ignore the effect of the discontinued business loss, the earnings per share would have been $0.29 per share for fiscal 2012. With shares trading at $16.80, the price-earnings ratio based on these amounts would be quite high, at 57.9 times earnings.

Since the average P-E ratio for the industry is 21.1 times earnings, we can conclude that either the shares are overpriced or the market thinks that profit will rise in the future, which will result in this ratio falling to more normal levels.

Throughout 2012, Sears's share price declined from $11.63 to $9.50. Despite the fact that the company reported a profit in 2012 after recording a loss in 2011, investors seemed to have dismissed the good news, because without the sale of stores, the company would also have had a loss in 2012. Because of these results, the P-E ratio for this company was below the industry average.

Some investors carefully study price-earnings ratios over time to help them determine when to buy or sell shares. They will buy shares when the P-E ratio is low in the belief that this indicates that the price of the shares is inexpensive. However, a low P-E ratio may also indicate that the market believes that the company will be less profitable in the future. Investors should be very cautious when interpreting price-earnings ratios.

Payout Ratio

The payout ratio measures the percentage of profit that is distributed as cash dividends. It is calculated by dividing cash dividends by profit. Companies that have high growth rates usually have low payout ratios because they reinvest most of their profit back into the company, spending funds on new assets rather than paying out dividends to shareholders.

The 2012 and 2011 payout ratios for Hudson's Bay, Sears, and the industry are shown below.

PAYOUT RATIO $= \dfrac{\text{CASH DIVIDENDS}}{\text{PROFIT}}$			
	2012	2011	Comparison with Prior Year
Hudson's Bay	n/a	22.2%	Worse
Sears	9.6%	n/a	Better
Industry average	n/a	n/a	n/a

If a company does not have a profit, determining a payout ratio is not possible. Therefore no ratio was calculated for Hudson's Bay in 2012 or for Sears in 2011. The amount of dividends that a company will declare each year is at the discretion of the board of directors. They are generally reluctant to reduce a dividend below the amount paid in a previous year. Prior to going public, Hudson's Bay paid a very large dividend in 2011 to shareholders, some of whom then sold their shares back to the company. When HBC made its public offering of shares in late November 2012, the company stated that the board would attempt to have a 20% to 25% payout ratio, which was estimated to be $0.33 to $0.41 per share per year. This commitment was met until plans were announced to acquire Saks. To help pay for this acquisition, the board announced that the dividend would be cut in half.

Sears did not pay any dividends in 2011 and paid out a large special dividend in the fourth quarter of the 2012 fiscal year. The cash for this came from the sale of stores. If a company is keeping dividends stable, the payout ratio will actually decrease if a company's profit increases and increase if profit falls.

Dividend Yield

The dividend yield supplements the payout ratio. The dividend yield reports the rate of return a shareholder earned from dividends during the year as percentage of the share price. It is calculated by dividing the dividend per share by the market price per share. Similar to the price-earnings ratio, this ratio is also known as a market measure, because of the use of the share price in its calculation.

The dividend yields for 2012 and 2011 for Hudson's Bay, Sears, and the industry are shown below.

$$\text{DIVIDEND YIELD} = \frac{\text{DIVIDEND PER SHARE}}{\text{MARKET PRICE PER SHARE}}$$			
	2012	2011	Comparison with Prior Year
Hudson's Bay	5.6%	n/a	Better
Sears	10.4%	0.0%	Better
Industry average	3.1%	3.3%	Worse

Hudson's Bay's share price cannot be obtained for 2011 as the company's shares did not start trading publicly until 2012, so the dividend yield was not able to be calculated for that year. The 5.6% dividend yield in 2012 is above the industry average. However, as mentioned previously, the company has since reduced its dividend payments. This was expected given the company's plan to expand and buy other retailers like Saks. Sears suspended its dividends several years ago and paid out its first dividend since then in 2012, when a special dividend was paid, because cash was available from the sale of some of its stores. It did not seem at the time this text was being prepared that the company was planning to pay out a dividend on a regular basis.

Profitability Conclusion

In an intracompany comparison, Hudson's Bay's profitability measures all decreased from 2011 to 2012, with one exception: its asset turnover increased as some unproductive assets were sold. The lower profitability ratios were caused by losses from discontinued operations in 2012, which followed a year when there were gains from these discontinued operations. If we were to exclude the effects of these losses in 2012 and gains in 2011, HBC would have shown a profit in 2012 but it would have been lower than in 2011 because of the effects of Hurricane Sandy. We cannot assess if the HBC dividend yield improved in 2012 since its shares were not publicly traded until 2012.

In an intercompany comparison, HBC profitability in 2012 was lower than that of Sears, again because of the losses incurred from the discontinued operations. Sears, on the other hand, had a large gain in 2012 from the sale of some stores, which boosted its profitability. If we were to ignore that event, Sears would not have been profitable in 2012. Hudson's Bay's asset turnover ratio is lower than that of Sears and this also contributed to lower profitability ratios. Its dividend yield is also lower than those of Sears and the industry.

Although we could not calculate a price-earnings ratio for HBC in 2012 because the company did not report a profit, knowing that the share price was relatively unchanged after the company reported a loss in 2012 and given the fact that Sears's share price fell throughout 2012 even though that company had a profit, would seem to indicate that the market is favouring Hudson's Bay over Sears. Investors are likely intrigued by its strategic plans, which many consider to be quite bold and aggressive.

Summary of Profitability Ratios

Illustration 14-15 summarizes the profitability ratios discussed above, and throughout this textbook.

▶Illustration 14-15
Profitability ratios

Chapter	Ratio	Formula	What the Ratio Measures	Desired Result
5	Gross profit margin	$\dfrac{\text{Gross profit}}{\text{Net sales}}$	Margin between selling price and cost of goods sold	Higher
5	Profit margin	$\dfrac{\text{Profit}}{\text{Net sales}}$	Profit generated by each dollar of sales	Higher
9	Asset turnover	$\dfrac{\text{Net sales}}{\text{Average total assets}}$	How efficiently assets are used to generate sales	Higher
9	Return on assets	$\dfrac{\text{Profit}}{\text{Average total assets}}$	Overall profitability of assets	Higher
11	Return on common shareholders' equity	$\dfrac{\text{Profit} - \text{Preferred dividends}}{\text{Average common shareholders' equity}}$	Profitability of shareholders' investment	Higher
2, 11	Earnings per share	$\dfrac{\text{Profit} - \text{Preferred dividends}}{\text{Weighted average number of common shares}}$	Profit earned on each common share	Higher
2	Price-earnings ratio	$\dfrac{\text{Market price per share}}{\text{Earnings per share}}$	Relationship between market price per share and earnings per share	Higher
11	Payout ratio	$\dfrac{\text{Cash dividends}}{\text{Profit}}$	Percentage of profit distributed as cash dividends	Higher
11	Dividend yield	$\dfrac{\text{Dividend per share}}{\text{Market price per share}}$	Income generated for the shareholder by each share, based on the market price per share	Higher

For the profitability ratios shown above, a higher result is generally considered to be better. However, there are some user-related considerations with respect to the price-earnings and payout ratios that must be understood. A higher price-earnings ratio generally means that investors favour that company and have high expectations of future profitability.

Investors interested in purchasing a company's shares for income purposes (in the form of a dividend) are interested in companies with a high dividend yield. Investors more interested in purchasing a company's shares for growth purposes (for the share price's appreciation) are interested in a low payout ratio. They would prefer to see the company retain its profit rather than pay it out.

We have shown liquidity, solvency, and profitability ratios in separate sections above. However, it is important to recognize that analysis should not focus on one type of ratio without considering the others. Liquidity, solvency, and profitability are closely interrelated in most companies. For example, a company's profitability is affected by the availability of financing and its liquidity. Similarly, a company's solvency not only requires satisfactory liquidity but is also affected by its profitability.

It is also important to recognize that the ratios shown in Illustrations 14-12, 14-13, and 14-15 are only examples of commonly used ratios. There are many different and additional ratios and groupings that financial analysts use. Users should therefore determine which ratios best suit the decisions they need to make. Analysts often use ratios that are specific to an industry. For example, in the retail sector, because growing companies open new stores every year, growing sales are expected, so looking at sales growth is not as important as same-store sales and sales per square foot of retail space.

Finally, it is important to remember that ratios give clues about underlying conditions that may not be seen from an inspection of the individual components of a particular ratio. A single ratio by itself is not very meaningful. Accordingly, ratios must be interpreted in conjunction with information that has been gained from a detailed review of the financial information, including horizontal and vertical analyses, as well as relevant nonfinancial information.

This ends our comprehensive analysis illustration using Hudson's Bay Company. What can be practically covered in a textbook shows only the tip of the iceberg when it comes to the types of financial information available and the ratios that are used by various industries. The availability of information is not a problem. The real challenge is to be discriminating enough to choose relevant data for comparisons and analyses.

BEFORE YOU GO ON...

▶ Do It! Profitability Analysis

Selected information from the financial statements of two companies competing in the same industry follows:

	De Marchi Corporation	Bear Limited
Total assets, beginning of year	$388,000	$372,000
Total assets, end of year	434,000	536,000
Total liabilities, beginning of year	119,000	76,000
Total liabilities, end of year	97,000	135,000
Total common shareholders' equity, beginning of year	269,000	296,000
Total common shareholders' equity, end of year	337,000	401,000
Net sales	660,000	780,000
Gross profit	175,000	248,000
Profit	68,000	105,000

(a) For each company, calculate the following ratios: debt to total assets, gross profit margin, profit margin, asset turnover, return on assets, and return on common shareholders' equity.

(b) Which company is more profitable? Explain.

(c) What is the key driver of Bear Limited's return on common shareholders' equity ratio, when compared with that of De Marchi Corporation?

Action Plan

- Review the formula for each ratio so you understand how it is calculated and how to interpret it.
- Recall that averages must be used for statement of financial position figures when compared with an income statement figure in a ratio. Averages are calculated by adding together the beginning and ending balances and dividing the result by 2.
- Remember that for profitability ratios, a higher result is usually better.
- Recall that the profit margin and the asset turnover ratios combine to explain the return on assets ratio. The return on assets and debt to total assets ratios combine to explain the return on common shareholders' equity ratio.

Solution

(a)

De Marchi	Bear
Debt to total assets	
$\dfrac{\$97,000}{\$434,000} = 22.4\%$	$\dfrac{\$135,000}{\$536,000} = 25.2\%$
Gross profit margin	
$\dfrac{\$175,000}{\$660,000} = 26.5\%$	$\dfrac{\$248,000}{\$780,000} = 31.8\%$

(continued)

	De Marchi	Bear
Profit margin		
	$\dfrac{\$68,000}{\$660,000} = 10.3\%$	$\dfrac{\$105,000}{\$780,000} = 13.5\%$
Asset turnover		
	$\dfrac{\$660,000}{(\$388,000 + \$434,000) \div 2} = 1.6 \text{ times}$	$\dfrac{\$780,000}{(\$372,000 + \$536,000) \div 2} = 1.7 \text{ times}$
Return on assets		
	$\dfrac{\$68,000}{(\$388,000 + \$434,000) \div 2} = 16.5\%$	$\dfrac{\$105,000}{(\$372,000 + \$536,000) \div 2} = 23.1\%$
Return on common shareholders' equity		
	$\dfrac{\$68,000}{(\$269,000 + \$337,000) \div 2} = 22.4\%$	$\dfrac{\$105,000}{(\$296,000 + \$401,000) \div 2} = 30.1\%$

(b) Bear is more profitable than De Marchi on all profitability ratios.

(c) The factor most influencing the higher return on assets ratio is the profit margin. Bear has the higher profit margin of the two companies, much higher than its asset turnover. Drilling down, this particular ratio—profit margin—is the key driver of Bear's significantly higher return on common shareholders' equity ratio. Bear has the higher return on common shareholders' equity ratio, primarily because of its higher return on assets ratio as there is not a large difference between the two companies' debt to total assets ratios.

Related Exercise Material: BE14-12, BE14-14, BE14-15, E14-5, E14-10, E14-11, E14-12, and E14-13.

Limitations of Financial Analysis

STUDY OBJECTIVE 7
Understand the limitations of financial analysis.

Before relying on the information you have gathered through your horizontal, vertical, and ratio analyses, you must understand the limitations of these tools and of the financial statements they are based on. Some of the factors that can limit the usefulness of your analysis include alternative accounting policies, professional judgement, comprehensive income, diversification, inflation, and economic factors.

ALTERNATIVE ACCOUNTING POLICIES

Variations among companies in their use of generally accepted accounting principles may lessen the comparability of their statements. Companies may choose from a large number of acceptable accounting policies, such as different inventory cost determination methods (for example, FIFO or average). Different choices can result in differing financial positions, which again affect how easily their results can be compared.

Although Hudson's Bay and Sears both use the average method for determining the cost of their inventory, this is not true of all retailers. If we tried to compare Hudson's Bay's inventory balances and cost of goods sold with those of a company that used FIFO instead of average, we would need to adjust one of the company's amounts to make them comparable with the other. Note that although cost of goods sold may be different because of the use of a different policy, this is really just an "artificial," or timing, difference. While there may be differences year by year, in total, over time, there is no difference.

In more and more industries, competition is global and this, too, can present a challenge. In this chapter we compared the financial statements of two Canadian companies that both use IFRS. However, if we wanted to compare the performance of Hudson's Bay with Walmart, this would be more difficult, as Walmart prepares its financial statements using U.S. GAAP. And what if we wanted to compare Hudson's Bay with a private company using ASPE rather than IFRS? Although differences in accounting policies might be detectable from reading the notes to the financial statements, adjusting the financial data to compensate for the different policies is difficult, if not impossible, in some cases.

PROFESSIONAL JUDGEMENT

We must accept that management has to use professional judgement in choosing the most appropriate accounting policy for the circumstances. Because judgement is required, management's choices may be biased in favour of a presentation that furthers certain company objectives. In addition, many estimates are required in preparing financial information. Estimates are used, for example, in determining the allowance for doubtful accounts estimated useful lives and residual values for depreciation, and fair values of certain investment securities and properties. To the extent that these estimates are inaccurate or biased, ratios and percentages that are based on such information will also be inaccurate or biased. Even if these estimates are unbiased, they can still yield different results. For example, HBC depreciates some of its buildings over a 70-year period, whereas the longest period used by Sears is 50 years.

To help ensure that the quality of information is as high as possible, boards of directors form audit committees that are held responsible for quizzing management on the degree of aggressiveness or conservatism that has been used when determining accounting policies, estimates, and judgements. In addition, CEOs and CFOs of Canadian public companies are required to certify that the financial statements, together with other financial information, "present fairly" and do not misrepresent in any material respects the company's financial condition, financial performance, and cash flows.

COMPREHENSIVE INCOME

Most financial ratios exclude total comprehensive income, or other comprehensive income, from the analysis. Profitability ratios, including industry averages, generally use data from the income statement and not from the statement of comprehensive income, which includes both profit and other comprehensive income. In addition, there are no standard ratio formulas incorporating comprehensive income.

Nonetheless, it is important to review a company's sources of comprehensive income in any financial analysis. For example, Hudson's Bay reported a loss of $44.8 million for the year ended February 2, 2013. During the same year, it reported other comprehensive losses of $27.8 million, which resulted in total comprehensive loss of $72.6 million ($44.8 + $27.8). Losses occurring within the company's pension plan were the cause of the other comprehensive loss. They are not reported on the income statement as they do not deal directly with the company's operations.

HBC's profit margin, illustrated earlier in the chapter, was $(44.8) million ÷ $4,077.0 million = (1.1)%. However, if the other comprehensive loss had been included in this ratio as well as the other profitability ratios we covered in this chapter, those ratios would have indicated much worse performance than originally shown. For example, Hudson's Bay's profit margin would have been ($72.6 million) ÷ $4,077.0 million = (1.8)%.

In cases like this, where other comprehensive income is significant, and depending on the source of the income, some analysts will adjust profitability ratios to incorporate the effect of total comprehensive income. Of course, you will recall from past chapters that private companies following ASPE do not report comprehensive income, so this limitation would apply only to private and public companies following IFRS.

DIVERSIFICATION

Diversification in Canadian industry can also limit the usefulness of financial analysis. Many companies today are so diversified that they cannot be classified by industry. Canadian Tire, for example, sells selected grocery, home, car, clothing, sports, and leisure products. In addition, it is the country's largest independent gasoline retailer. Consequently, deciding what industry a company like Canadian Tire is in can be one of the main challenges to effectively evaluating its results.

Other companies may appear to be comparable but are not. McCain Foods and Irving-owned Cavendish Farms compete in the frozen potato product category. Yet McCain produces other food products besides french fries, and Irving has many other interests, including oil, newspapers, tissue products, transportation, and shipbuilding.

Because of this diversification, analysts must be careful in interpreting consolidated financial statements. You will recall that we learned about consolidated financial statements in Chapter 12. Consolidated statements include financial information about the parent company and each of its subsidiaries. The parent company may have a strong debt to total assets ratio, and the subsidiary a weak one. However, because these statements are consolidated, the combined results may show that the debt to total assets ratio is close to the industry average. The fact that the subsidiary may have solvency problems is hidden from the general public because of the consolidated reporting of the financial information. Of course, such a situation would not be hidden from management as it has access to the individual statements of each subsidiary company even though the general public does not.

When companies have significant operations in different lines of business, they are required to report additional disclosures in a segmented information note to their financial statements. IFRS has specific revenue, profit, and asset tests to determine if a company is required to report segmented information or not. (You will learn more about this in an intermediate accounting course.) If a company has reportable operating segments, it must disclose relevant information about revenues, operating income, and/or identifiable assets by products and services, by geographic area, and by major customer.

Note that segments are not as common in private companies as they are in large public companies and consequently there are no requirements for the disclosure of segments in ASPE.

INFLATION

Our accounting information system does not adjust data for inflation or price-level changes. For example, a four-year comparison of HBC's net sales shows growth of 112.6%. But this growth trend would be misleading if the general price level had increased or decreased greatly during the same period. The inflation rate over this same time period was 7.0%, so while Hudson's Bay's sales have indeed increased, they have not increased as much as it first appears. Still, our comparisons are relevant because the data from neither company that we analyzed had been adjusted for inflation.

In Canada, inflation was not very significant at the time of writing. In 2012, Canada's inflation rate was quite low, averaging just under 1%. Today, the Bank of Canada tries to maintain an inflation rate within the 1% to 3% range.

ECONOMIC FACTORS

We cannot properly interpret a financial analysis without also considering the economic circumstances in which a company operates. Economic measures such as the rate of interest, unemployment, and changes in demand and supply can have a significant impact on a company's performance.

For example, much of the industrialized world entered into a global recession in late 2008 and 2009. In 2011 and 2012, many companies restructured or downsized their operations, as we saw with Hudson's Bay Company. During times like these, horizontal analyses and ratios compared across years can lose much of their relevance. When losses result in negative numbers, it is difficult to calculate percentages and ratios, much less interpret them. Vertical analyses become more useful in such times. If a company has losses, they must be assessed based on the factors driving the loss in the current period. Less attention should be paid to comparing the losses with results from prior periods.

One must use this information, along with nonfinancial information, to try to assess what changes relate to the economic situation and what changes relate to factors that management can, or should be able to, control. For example, have operating expenses increased faster than revenues? Why? Are consumers not spending? Are prices too high? Have expenses not been adequately controlled or adjusted for the current marketplace? Particular attention must be paid to the company's results compared with those of its competitors and the entire industry.

DECISION TOOLKIT

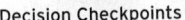 **Decision Checkpoints**

 **Info Needed for Decision**

 **Tools to Use for Decision**

 **How to Evaluate Results**

Decision Checkpoints	Info Needed for Decision	Tools to Use for Decision	How to Evaluate Results
Does the company report other comprehensive income?	Statement of income and comprehensive Income	Determine source and amount of other comprehensive income	If other comprehensive income is significant, selected profitability ratios should be recalculated using total comprehensive income rather than profit.
Are efforts to evaluate the company hampered by alternative accounting policies, professional judgement, diversification, inflation, or economic factors?	Financial statements as well as other information that is disclosed	Review accounting policies and estimates for comparability and reasonableness. Assess the strength of corporate governance processes. Review segmented information. Check that inflation is in a reasonable range. Understand significant economic factors.	If there are any comparability issues or irregularities, the analysis should be relied on with caution.

BEFORE YOU GO ON...

▶ Do It! Other Comprehensive Income

HSBC Bank Canada reported the following selected information (in millions) for the year ended December 31, 2012:

Average total assets	$80,391
Total revenue	2,236
Profit	761
Other comprehensive loss	(197)
Total comprehensive income	564

(a) Calculate the profit margin and return on assets ratios using (1) profit as the numerator, and (2) total comprehensive income as the numerator.

(b) Do you think other comprehensive income is a significant factor in the analysis of HSBC Bank's profitability?

Action Plan

- Recall the formula for profit margin: Profit ÷ Net sales. Substitute total comprehensive income instead of profit to determine the impact of other comprehensive income on profitability.
- Recall the formula for return on assets: Profit ÷ Average total assets. Substitute total comprehensive income instead of profit to determine the impact of other comprehensive income on profitability.
- To determine the significance of other comprehensive income, compare the ratios with and without other comprehensive income and assess whether the change in the ratio is significant enough to affect decision-making.

(continued)

Solution

(a)

($ in millions)	(1)	(2)
Profit margin	$\dfrac{\$761}{\$2,236} = 34.0\%$	$\dfrac{\$564}{\$2,236} = 25.2\%$
Return on assets	$\dfrac{\$761}{\$80,391} = 0.9\%$	$\dfrac{\$564}{\$80,391} = 0.7\%$

(b) The inclusion of other comprehensive income in the calculation of the profitability ratios is most likely significant enough to make a difference in a user's decision-making.

Related Exercise Material: BE14-14.

comparing
IFRS and ASPE

Key Differences	International Financial Reporting Standards (IFRS)	Accounting Standards for Private Enterprises (ASPE)
Earnings per share	Must be reported on the face of the income statement or statement of comprehensive income.	Earnings per share is not required to be reported.
Comprehensive income	If other comprehensive income is significant, selected profitability ratios should be recalculated using total comprehensive income rather than profit.	Comprehensive income is not reported.
Segmented reporting	There are specific revenue, profit, and asset tests to determine if information must be reported in the notes to the financial statements for segments.	There are no disclosure requirements for reporting segment information.

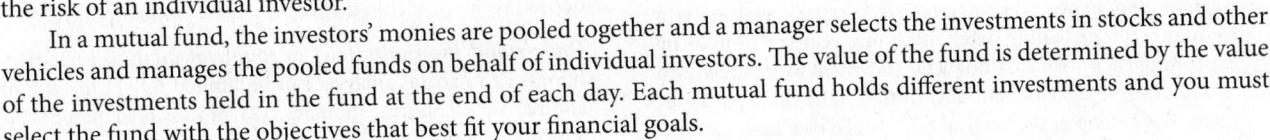

As you have seen throughout this textbook, both individuals and companies use ratios to help them make decisions about investing in the stock market. Some of the ratios they use to make decisions include the earnings per share, price earnings, payout, and dividend yield ratios. The motive for investing can be either to have a steady source of income through dividends or to have the possibility of the investment appreciating in value over time as the share price increases.

Financial planners recommend that, before you make personal investments in the stock market, you first ensure that you are in control of your personal finances by not spending more money than you are making and by eliminating any student loan and credit card debt. Personal financial planning goals will help you set your priorities.

The type of savings or investment vehicle to use will likely vary according to your age and family situation, income, and savings goals. In addition, you should try to take advantage of any tax-free savings opportunities by holding investments in a Tax Free Savings Account (TFSA) or Registered Retirement Savings Plan (RRSP) where possible.

If you decide that now is the time to invest in the market, how do you start? Most investors start by buying units of a mutual fund, rather than purchasing shares in an individual company. Both of these investment vehicles will help diversify the risk of an individual investor.

In a mutual fund, the investors' monies are pooled together and a manager selects the investments in stocks and other vehicles and manages the pooled funds on behalf of individual investors. The value of the fund is determined by the value of the investments held in the fund at the end of each day. Each mutual fund holds different investments and you must select the fund with the objectives that best fit your financial goals.

Some Facts

- Experts suggest that until your savings have reached $50,000 you should consider guaranteed investment certificates (GIC), low-cost mutual funds, or other similar investments. You should not be investing in shares of publicly traded corporations.
- The cost of purchasing a mutual fund can range from 0% to 2% of the amount you are investing. In some cases, you must purchase a minimum investment. The cost of owning the investment in a mutual fund will reduce your return by approximately 1.5% to 2.5%. Mutual fund companies pay themselves first by charging you a fee to operate the fund. When you see a published return on a mutual fund, generally the return is net of the value of the fee that has been charged.[2]

What Do You Think?

Your grandparents have given you $50,000 to put toward your post-secondary education. You would like to invest the $50,000 in a dividend income mutual fund. Is this a good idea?

YES—A dividend income fund will likely include shares with high payout ratios and dividend yield ratios, so you will earn regular income. High dividend yielding shares held within mutual fund units usually do not fluctuate a great deal in value so your reward will come primarily from dividend income rather than unit price appreciation.

NO—Just because a company within a fund declared dividends in the past, that does not guarantee dividends will be distributed at the same rate in the future. There is also a risk that the unit value may decline. If loss of capital (your original investment) is an issue, you may want to consider a less risky investment such as a GIC.

Summary of Study Objectives

1. **Understand the concept of sustainable income and indicate how discontinued items are presented.** Sustainable income is the level of profit likely to be obtained in the future. It excludes irregular revenues and expenses that may be included in profit. Discontinued items are presented separately from continuing operations on the statement of financial position, income statement, and statement of cash flows, net of income tax, to highlight their infrequent nature.

2. **Explain and apply horizontal analysis.** Horizontal analysis is a technique for evaluating a series of data, such as line items in a company's financial statements, by expressing them as percentage increases or decreases over two or more years (or periods of time). The horizontal percentage of a base-period amount is calculated by dividing the amount in a specific year (period) by a base-year (period) amount. This percentage calculation normally covers multiple years (periods).

   The horizontal percentage change for the period is calculated by dividing the dollar amount of the change between two years (or periods) by the prior-year (period) amount. This percentage calculation normally covers two years (or periods) only.

3. **Explain and apply vertical analysis.** Vertical analysis is a technique for evaluating data within one year (or period) by expressing each item in a financial statement as a percentage of a relevant total (base amount) in that same financial statement. For example, the vertical percentage of a base amount can be determined by expressing each item on the income statement as a percentage of revenue (or net sales) or each item on the statement of financial position as a percentage of

total assets by dividing the financial statement amount under analysis by the base amount for that particular financial statement.

4. **Identify and calculate ratios that are used to analyze liquidity.** Liquidity ratios include working capital, the current ratio, cash current debt coverage, receivables turnover and average collection period, and inventory turnover and days in inventory. The formula, what it measures, and desired result of each ratio are presented in Illustration 14-12.

5. **Identify and calculate ratios that are used to analyze solvency.** Solvency ratios include debt to total assets, times interest earned, cash total debt coverage, and free cash flow. The formula, what it measures, and desired result of each ratio are presented in Illustration 14-13.

6. **Identify and calculate ratios that are used to analyze profitability.** Profitability ratios include gross profit margin, profit margin, asset turnover, return on assets, return on common shareholders' equity, earnings per share, price-earnings, payout, and dividend yield. The formula, what it measures, and desired result of each ratio are presented in Illustration 14-15.

7. **Understand the limitations of financial analysis.** The usefulness of financial analysis can be limited by (1) the use of alternative accounting policies, (2) professional judgement affecting the quality of the information, (3) the existence of a large amount of other comprehensive income, (4) diversification within a company or industry, (5) significant inflation, and (6) variable economic factors.

Glossary

Component of an entity   A separate major line of business or major geographic area of operations that can be clearly distinguished operationally and financially from the rest of the company. (p. 732)

Discontinued operations   The disposal, or availability for sale, of a separate component of an entity. (p. 732)

Horizontal analysis   (also known as trend analysis) A technique for evaluating a series of financial statement data over a period of time to determine the increase (decrease) that has taken place. This increase (decrease) is expressed as either an amount or a percentage. (p. 736)

Horizontal percentage change for the period   (also known as the horizontal percentage change between periods) A percentage measuring the change from one year (or period) to the next year (or period). It is calculated by dividing the dollar amount of the change between the specific year (or period) under analysis and the prior year (or period) by the prior-year amount. (p. 736)

Horizontal percentage of a base-period amount   A percentage measuring the change since a base year (or period), normally

involving more than one year (or period). It is calculated by dividing the amount for the specific year (or period) under analysis by the base-year (period) amount. (p. 736)

Sustainable income   The most likely level of profit to be obtained in the future, determined by adjusting profit for irregular items such as discontinued operations. (p. 732)

Vertical analysis   (also known as common size analysis) A technique for evaluating financial statement data that expresses each item in a financial statement as a percentage of a base amount. The base amount is usually net sales in the income statement and total assets in the statement of financial position. (p. 740)

Vertical percentage of a base amount   A percentage measuring the proportion of an amount in a financial statement within a year (or period). It is calculated by dividing the financial statement amount under analysis by the base amount for that particular financial statement (such as net sales for the income statement or total assets for the statement of financial position). (p. 741)

DECISION TOOLKIT—A SUMMARY

Decision Checkpoints

Info Needed for Decision

Tools to Use for Decision

How to Evaluate Results

Decision Checkpoints	Info Needed for Decision	Tools to Use for Decision	How to Evaluate Results
Has the company sold, or is it holding for sale, a component of an entity?	Discontinuation of, or plans to discontinue, a component of an entity	Discontinued operations section of the statement of financial position, income statement, and/or statement of cash flows	If a component of an entity has been discontinued, its results in the current period should not be included in assessing the company's financial position or in estimating its future profit or cash flows.
How do the company's financial position and operating results compare with those of previous periods?	Statement of financial position and income statement	Comparative financial statements should be prepared over at least two years, with the first year reported as the base year. Changes in each line item relative to the base year should be presented both by amount and by percentage. This is called horizontal analysis.	A significant change should be investigated to determine what caused it.
How do the relationships between items in this year's financial statements compare with last year's relationships or those of competitors?	Statement of financial position and income statement	Each line item on the statement of financial position should be presented as a percentage of total assets (total liabilities and shareholders' equity). Each line item on the income statement should be presented as a percentage of revenues (or net sales). This is called vertical analysis.	Any difference, either across years or between companies, should be investigated to determine the cause.
Does the company report other comprehensive income?	Statement of income and comprehensive income	Determine source and amount of other comprehensive income	If other comprehensive income is significant, selected profitability ratios should be recalculated using total comprehensive income rather than profit.
Are efforts to evaluate the company hampered by alternative accounting policies, professional judgement, diversification, inflation, or economic factors?	Financial statements as well as other information that is disclosed	Review accounting policies and estimates for comparability and reasonableness. Assess the strength of corporate governance processes. Review segmented information. Check that inflation is in a reasonable range. Understand significant economic factors.	If there are any comparability issues or irregularities, the analysis should be relied on with caution.

the navigator

USING THE DECISION TOOLKIT

Goldcorp Inc. and Yamana Gold Inc. are two Canadian competitors in the gold industry. Selected liquidity, solvency, and profitability ratios follow for the two companies and their industry for a recent year:

	Goldcorp	Yamana Gold	Industry
Liquidity			
Current ratio	2.2:1	1.4:1	2.6:1
Average collection period	40 days	30 days	34 days
Days in inventory	101 days	86 days	130 days
Solvency			
Debt to total assets	26.5%	33.4%	25.4%
Times interest earned	76.1 times	15.1 times	(4.3) times
Profitability			
Gross profit margin	57.0%	64.4%	29.7%
Profit margin	32.2%	18.9%	6.6%
Asset turnover	0.2 times	0.2 times	0.2 times
Return on assets	6.4%	3.8%	1.3%
Return on common shareholders' equity	7.9%	5.8%	10.9%

Instructions

(a) Which company is more liquid? Explain.

(b) Which company is more solvent? Explain.

(c) Which company is more profitable? Explain.

Solution

(a) Despite having a lower current ratio, Yamana Gold's current assets exceed its current liabilities by 1.4 times. It can also be argued that Yamana Gold is more liquid than Goldcorp because it collects its receivables and sells its inventory faster, as indicated by its lower collection period and lower days in inventory.

   Compared with the industry, both Yamana Gold and Goldcorp have a lower (worse) current ratio but are better at managing their inventory. The higher inventory indicated by the low days in inventory for the industry may be artificially increasing the industry's current ratio, making it appear better than it really is. In addition, Yamana Gold is faster at collecting its receivables than its industry counterparts, while Goldcorp is somewhat slower.

(b) Goldcorp would be considered to be more solvent than Yamana Gold because of its lower debt to total assets and higher times interest earned ratios.

   Both companies would be considered to be more solvent than the industry. Even though the industry's debt to total assets ratio is better (lower) than that of both companies, their times interest earned ratios and consequent ability to service their debt is far superior to the industry, which reports a negative times interest earned ratio.

(c) Goldcorp is more profitable than Yamana Gold on all profitability measures except for the gross profit margin, which is higher (better) for Yamana Gold, and the asset turnover ratio, which is the same for each company.

   Both companies are generally ahead of the industry averages, with the exception of the return on common shareholders' equity ratios, which are lower than that of the industry, and the asset turnover ratios, which are the same as the industry.

   Note that neither company has used debt in a significant way to take advantage of leverage, which is why the return on common shareholders' equity is closer to the return on assets for both of these companies when compared to the industry average.

the
navigator

Comprehensive Do It!

A vertical analysis of the condensed financial statements of Mukhin Inc. for the years 2012 to 2015 follows:

MUKHIN INC. Vertical Analysis of Statement of Financial Position May 31				
	2015	2014	2013	2012
Assets				
Current assets	11.1%	11.1%	13.9%	11.4%
Current assets of discontinued operations	0.2%	2.1%	0.6%	4.2%
Non-current assets	88.0%	77.0%	84.8%	81.2%
Non-current assets of discontinued operations	0.7%	9.8%	0.7%	3.2%
Total assets	100.0%	100.0%	100.0%	100.0%
Liabilities and Shareholders' Equity				
Liabilities				
Current liabilities	19.3%	17.5%	19.0%	15.0%
Current liabilities of discontinued operations	0.0%	1.4%	0.2%	4.1%
Non-current liabilities	52.4%	52.1%	46.0%	45.3%
Non-current liabilities of discontinued operations	2.3%	4.8%	1.8%	3.4%
Total liabilities	74.0%	75.8%	67.0%	67.8%
Shareholders' equity	26.0%	24.2%	33.0%	32.2%
Total liabilities and shareholders' equity	100.0%	100.0%	100.0%	100.0%

MUKHIN INC. Vertical Analysis of Income Statement Year Ended May 31				
	2015	2014	2013	2012
Revenues	100.0%	100.0%	100.0%	100.0%
Expenses	87.8%	89.5%	104.0%	96.0%
Profit (loss) from continuing operations before income tax	12.2%	10.5%	(4.0%)	4.0%
Income tax expense (recovery)	3.8%	3.1%	(0.3%)	2.3%
Profit (loss) from continuing operations	8.4%	7.4%	(3.7%)	1.7%
Profit (loss) from discontinued operations	0.0%	(0.2%)	1.4%	9.0%
Profit (loss)	8.4%	7.2%	(2.3%)	10.7%

Instructions

(a) How should discontinued operations be treated in a financial analysis?

(b) Discuss the significant changes between 2012 and 2015 for the company with and without the impact of discontinued operations.

Action Plan

- Exclude the impact of irregular items in your analysis.
- Look at the percentage comparisons both vertically (within the year) and horizontally (across the years).

Solution to Comprehensive Do It!

(a) Irregular items, such as discontinued operations, should be excluded from any comparative analysis because these items are not expected to recur and do not represent sustainable income going forward.

(b) Current assets increased in 2013, declined in 2014, and remained stable in 2015. Mukhin's current liabilities are a higher percentage of total assets than are its current assets. Current

(continued)

liabilities have generally been increasing, except for in 2014. Except for during that same year, 2014, Mukhin's non-current assets have also been increasing as a percentage of total assets. Non-current liabilities have been increasing steadily. The company likely increased its long-term liabilities to help finance increasing purchases of non-current assets.

Mukhin's liquidity and solvency appear to be declining over recent years, with increasing percentages of liabilities (exclusive of discontinued operations). We would have to perform further analyses, such as calculating and interpreting ratios, to determine the reasons for this decline.

In terms of profitability, Mukhin appears to be controlling its expenses, which have declined, except in 2013. Except for this same year, its profitability (based on profit from continuing operations) also appears to be on the increase.

It is interesting to note the impact that discontinued operations have on Mukhin's financial position. These should be excluded from our comparative analysis. However, except in 2012, the discontinued operations have not significantly affected Mukhin's profitability.

the navigator

WileyPLUS   **Self-Test, Brief Exercises, Exercises, Problems: Set A, and many more components are available for practice in *WileyPLUS*.**

Self-Test Questions

Answers are at the end of the chapter.

Quiz Yourself

(SO 1)   1. Sustainable income is calculated:
    (a) by determining the average of profit for the last five years.
    (b) by projecting average profit for the next five years.
    (c) by subtracting irregular revenues, expenses, gains, and losses from profit.
    (d) by subtracting dividends from profit.

(SO 1)   2. The income effect of discontinued operations:
    (a) is reported as part of other revenues and expenses on the income statement.
    (b) is segregated and reported on the income statement after profit from continuing operations.
    (c) is segregated and reported on the statement of changes in equity as an adjustment to opening retained earnings.
    (d) is disclosed only in the notes to the financial statements.

(SO 2)   3. Inlet Corporation reported profit of $300,000, $330,000, and $360,000 in the years 2013, 2014, and 2015, respectively. If 2013 is the base year, what is the horizontal percentage of the base-year amount for 2015?
    (a) 36%
    (b) 100%
    (c) 110%
    (d) 120%

(SO 2)   4. As indicated in Question 3 above, Inlet Corporation reported profit of $300,000,

$330,000, and $360,000 in the years 2013, 2014, and 2015, respectively. What is the horizontal percentage change between each year?
    (a) 10% for 2013 to 2014 and 9% for 2014 to 2015
    (b) 110% for 2013 to 2014 and 109% for 2014 to 2015
    (c) 10% for 2013 to 2014 and 20% for 2014 to 2015
    (d) 110% for 2013 to 2014 and 120% for 2014 to 2015

(SO 3)   5. What type of analysis does the following schedule show?

	Amount	Percentage
Current assets	$200,000	25%
Non-current assets	600,000	75%
Total assets	$800,000	100%

    (a) Horizontal analysis
    (b) Vertical analysis
    (c) Ratio analysis
    (d) Intercompany comparison

(SO 3)   6. In a vertical analysis, the base amount used for depreciation expense in the income statement is generally:
    (a) net sales.
    (b) depreciation expense in the prior year.
    (c) total assets.
    (d) total property, plant, and equipment.

(SO 4)   7. A company reported an increasing current ratio and decreasing inventory turnover and receivables turnover ratios. This means the
(a) company may be experiencing liquidity problems.
(b) company has improved its overall liquidity position.
(c) company's sales of its inventory are improving while its collection of receivables is deteriorating.
(d) company has fewer current assets.

(SO 5)   8. Which of the following situations would be the most likely indicator that Wang Corporation might have a solvency problem?
(a) Increasing debt to total assets and times interest earned ratios
(b) Increasing debt to total assets and decreasing times interest earned ratios
(c) Decreasing debt to total assets and times interest earned ratios
(d) Decreasing debt to total assets and increasing times interest earned ratios

(SO 6)   9. Which of the following situations is the most likely indicator of profitability?
(a) Increasing price-earnings ratio and decreasing earnings per share
(b) Increasing return on assets, asset turnover, and profit margin ratios
(c) Decreasing return on common shareholders' equity and increasing asset turnover
(d) Decreasing gross profit margin and increasing profit margin

(SO 7)   10. Which of the following situations might indicate that a financial analysis should be used with caution?
(a) Different inventory cost determination methods are being used by competing companies with similar types of inventory.
(b) A company had no reportable segments.
(c) The company has no other comprehensive income.
(d) Inflation is low.

Questions

(SO 1)   1. Explain the concept of sustainable income.
(SO 1)   2. (a) What are discontinued operations? (b) What is a component of an entity?
(SO 1)   3. Explain how discontinued operations are reported on the (a) statement of financial position, and (b) income statement.
(SO 2)   4. Explain how a horizontal analysis is affected if an account (a) has no value in a base year and a value in the next year, or (b) has a negative value in the base year and a positive value in the next year.
(SO 2, 3)   5. Two methods of financial statement analysis are horizontal analysis and vertical analysis. Explain how these two methods are similar, and how they differ.
(SO 2, 3)   6. Explain how the (a) horizontal percentage of a base-period amount, (b) horizontal percentage change for a period, and (c) vertical percentage of a base amount is calculated.
(SO 2, 3)   7. **Facebook** became a public corporation in May 2012. Can a meaningful horizontal and vertical analysis be prepared for its first two years of operations as a public company, the years ended December 31, 2012 and 2013? Why or why not?
(SO 3)   8. What base amount is usually assigned a 100% value in a vertical analysis of the (a) statement of financial position and (b) income statement?
(SO 3)   9. Can vertical analysis be used to compare two companies of different sizes and using different currencies, such as **Anheuser-Busch InBev SA/NV**, the world's largest brewer, headquartered in Belgium, and **SABMiller plc**, the second-largest brewer, headquartered in the United Kingdom? Explain.

(SO 2, 3, 4)   10. (a) Distinguish among the following bases of comparison: intracompany, intercompany, and industry average. (b) Explain which analysis technique(s)—horizontal analysis, vertical analysis, or ratio analysis—is normally used with each base of comparison.
(SO 4)   11. Is a high current ratio always a good indicator of a company's liquidity? Describe two situations in which a high current ratio might be hiding liquidity problems.
(SO 4)   12. Identify for which liquidity ratios a lower result might be better, and explain why.
(SO 5)   13. Identify for which solvency ratios a lower result might be better, and explain why.
(SO 5)   14. **Tim Hortons Inc.** reported a debt to total assets ratio of 32.2% and times interest earned ratio of 41.1 times at the end of its second quarter in 2013. The industry averages at the time were 39.3% and 55.6 times, respectively. Is Tim Hortons' solvency better or worse than that of the industry?
(SO 4, 5, 6)   15. Which ratio(s) should be used to help answer each of these questions?
(a) How efficient is the company in using its assets to produce sales?
(b) How near to sale is the inventory on hand?
(c) How profitable was the company relative to the amount invested by shareholders?
(d) How able is the company to pay interest charges as they come due?
(e) How able is the company to repay a short-term loan?

(SO 6)   16. **CIBC's** return on assets was 0.8%. During the same year, CIBC reported a return on common shareholders' equity of 21.8%. Has CIBC made effective use of leverage? Explain.

(SO 6)   17. Explain how the profit margin, asset turnover, and debt to total assets ratios help explain the return on common shareholders' equity ratio.

(SO 1, 6) 18. In 2014, Lai Inc. reported a profit margin of 5% before discontinued operations and a profit margin of 8% after discontinued operations. In 2015, the company had no discontinued operations and reported a profit margin of 6.5%. Has Lai's profitability improved or weakened? Explain.

(SO 6)   19. (a) If you were an investor interested in buying the shares of a company with growth potential, what ratio(s) would you primarily look at to help you make your decision? (b) How would your answer change if you were interested in buying shares with an income potential?

(SO 6, 7) 20. In 2012, **Yum Brands Inc.** reported a profit margin of 11.8% using profit in the numerator.

Had the profit margin been based on total comprehensive income, instead of profit, the revised profit margin would have increased to 12.6%. In 2011, its profit margin was 10.6% using profit and 10.5% using total comprehensive income. (a) Has Yum Brands' profitability improved or deteriorated in 2012? (b) Which profit margin—without other comprehensive income or with other comprehensive income—is the most appropriate ratio to use in this particular case for analysis purposes? Explain.

(SO 7)   21. Identify and explain the factors that can limit the usefulness of financial analysis.

(SO 7)   22. Explain how management must use professional judgement in financial reporting and how this can affect financial analysis.

(SO 7)   23. **McCain Foods** and **Cavendish Farms** are both private companies. McCain Foods uses IFRS and Cavendish Farms uses ASPE. What impact do these differing standards have on financial analysis?

Brief Exercises

Calculate sustainable income.
(SO 1)

BE14–1   Avondale Inc. reported the following information from its income statement for the current year:

Profit from continuing operations before income tax	$1,040,000
Interest expense	125,000
Income tax expense	260,000
Loss on operations of discontinued chemical division, net of $60,000 income tax savings	140,000
Loss on disposal of chemical division, net of $30,000 income tax savings	70,000

Based on the above information, what is Avondale's sustainable income?

Classify regular and irregular income statement items.
(SO 1)

BE14–2   A numbered list of income statement classifications for a merchandising company follows. Write the number of the appropriate classification beside each item in the lettered list below to show in what section the item would be reported.

1. Gross profit section
2. Operating expenses section
3. Other revenues and expenses section
4. Discontinued operations section
5. Not reported on income statement

(a) _____ A realized gain on the sale of trading investments
(b) _____ Sales revenue
(c) _____ Salaries expense
(d) _____ Cost of goods sold
(e) _____ Dividend revenue
(f) _____ A loss from operations of a discontinued wholesale business
(g) _____ Interest expense
(h) _____ A writedown of obsolete inventory
(i) _____ A gain on the disposal of assets of a discontinued wholesale business

Prepare horizontal analysis.
(SO 2)

BE14–3   Selected data from the comparative statement of financial position of Rioux Ltd. are shown below:

	2015	2014	2013
Cash	$ 150,000	$ 175,000	$ 75,000
Accounts receivable	600,000	400,000	450,000
Inventory	780,000	600,000	700,000
Property, plant, and equipment	3,130,000	2,800,000	2,850,000
Intangible assets	90,000	100,000	0
Total assets	$4,750,000	$4,075,000	$4,075,000

(a) Using horizontal analysis, calculate the percentage of a base-year amount, assuming 2013 is the base year.

(b) Using horizontal analysis, calculate the percentage change for each year.

BE14–4 Selected horizontal percentages of a base-year amount from Coastal Ltd.'s income statement are listed here:

Use horizontal analysis to determine change in profit.
(SO 2)

	2015	2014	2013
Net sales	110%	101%	100%
Cost of goods sold	105%	111%	100%
Operating expenses	99%	112%	100%
Income tax expense	136%	60%	100%

Assuming that Coastal did not have any non-operating or irregular items, did its profit increase, decrease, or remain unchanged over the period 2013 to 2015? Explain.

BE14–5 Identify the appropriate basis of comparison—intracompany or intercompany—and better tool of analysis—horizontal or vertical—to use for each of the following financial situations.

Identify comparisons and tools.
(SO 2, 3)

	Basis of Comparison	Tool of Analysis
(a) Analysis of a company's dividend history		
(b) Comparison of different-sized companies		
(c) Comparison of gross profit to net sales among competitors		
(d) Calculation of a company's sales growth over time		

BE14–6 Comparative data from the statement of financial position of Elke Ltd. are shown below. (a) Using horizontal analysis, calculate the percentage of the base-year amount, using 2013 as the base year. (b) Using vertical analysis, calculate the percentage of the base amount for each year.

Prepare horizontal and vertical analyses.
(SO 2, 3)

	2015	2014	2013
Current assets	$1,530,000	$1,175,000	$1,225,000
Property, plant, and equipment	3,130,000	2,800,000	2,850,000
Goodwill	90,000	100,000	0
Total assets	$4,750,000	$4,075,000	$4,075,000

BE14–7 Selected data (in thousands) from the income statement of JTI Inc. are shown below. Using vertical analysis, calculate the percentage of the base amount for each year.

Prepare vertical analysis.
(SO 3)

	2015	2014
Net sales	$1,914	$2,073
Cost of goods sold	1,612	1,674
Gross profit	302	399
Operating expenses	218	210
Profit before income tax	84	189
Income tax expense	17	38
Profit	$ 67	$ 151

BE14–8 Vertical analysis percentages from Waubon Corp.'s income statement are listed here:

Use vertical analysis to determine change in profit.
(SO 3)

	2015	2014	2013
Net sales	100.0%	100.0%	100.0%
Cost of goods sold	59.4%	60.5%	60.0%
Operating expenses	19.6%	20.4%	20.0%
Income tax expense	4.2%	3.8%	4.0%

Assuming that Waubon did not have any non-operating or irregular items, did its profit as a percentage of sales increase, decrease, or remain unchanged over the three-year period? Explain.

Calculate and evaluate
liquidity.
(SO 4)

BE14–9   Selected financial data for Shumway Ltd. are shown below. (a) Calculate for each of 2015 and 2014 the (1) current ratio, (2) receivables turnover ratio, and (3) inventory turnover ratio. (b) Based on these ratios, what conclusion(s) can be drawn about the company's liquidity?

	2015	2014	2013
Accounts receivable (gross)	$ 850,000	$ 750,000	$ 650,000
Merchandise inventory	1,020,000	980,000	840,000
Total current assets	2,100,000	2,000,000	1,700,000
Total current liabilities	1,000,000	1,100,000	1,250,000
Net credit sales	6,420,000	6,240,000	5,430,000
Cost of goods sold	4,540,000	4,550,000	3,950,000

Evaluate liquidity.
(SO 4)

BE14–10   Holysh Inc. reported a current ratio of 1.5:1 in the current fiscal year, which is higher than its current ratio last year of 1.2:1. It also reported a receivables turnover of 9 times, which is less than last year's receivables turnover of 12 times, and an inventory turnover of 6 times, which is less than last year's inventory turnover of 9 times. Is Holysh's liquidity improving or deteriorating? Explain.

Evaluate solvency.
(SO 5)

BE14–11   **Manulife Financial Corporation** reported the following measures for 2012 and 2011:

	2012	2011
Debt to total assets	94.6%	94.6%
Times interest earned	0.8 times	1.0 times
Cash total debt coverage	0.2 times	0.2 times
Free cash flow (in millions)	$10,347	$10,151

Is Manulife's solvency improving or deteriorating? Explain.

Evaluate profitability.
(SO 6)

BE14–12   Wolastoq Corp. reported the following ratios for 2015 and 2014:

	2015	2014
Return on common shareholders' equity	8.6%	13.6%
Return on assets	7.4%	11.8%
Debt to total assets	13.8%	13.8%
Profit margin	37.0%	58.8%
Asset turnover	0.2 times	0.2 times

(a) Is Wolastoq's profitability improving or deteriorating? (b) What is the key reason driving the change in Wolastoq's return on common shareholders' equity in 2015? Explain.

Evaluate market
measures.
(SO 6)

BE14–13   Recently, the price-earnings ratio of **Loblaw Companies Limited** was 17.9 times, and the price-earnings ratio of **Bank of Montreal** was 10.9 times. The dividend yield of each company was 2.1% and 4.5%, respectively. Which company's shares would you purchase for growth? For income? Explain.

Calculate impact of
other comprehensive
income on profit
margin.
(SO 6, 7)

BE14–14   **Thomson Reuters Corporation** reported the following selected information (in U.S. $ millions):

	2012	2011	2010
Revenues	$13,278	$13,807	$13,070
Profit	2,123	(1,392)	933
Other comprehensive loss	(255)	(298)	(117)
Total comprehensive income (loss)	1,868	(1,690)	816

(a) Calculate the profit margin with and without the other comprehensive loss for each year. (b) Which of the two profit margin ratios that you calculated in part (a) should you rely upon for your financial analysis? Explain.

Exercises

Indicate reporting of
regular and irregular
items.
(SO 1)

E14–1   The following independent events occurred at Ike Inc. during the year:

1. A realized gain on the sale of long-term investments
2. A loss caused by a labour strike
3. Current assets of a discontinued component of an entity being held for immediate and probable sale
4. An operating loss from a discontinued component of an entity, held for immediate and probable sale
5. An impairment loss on goodwill

Instructions

(a) Identify which of the above items are sustainable (regular) items and which are irregular items.
(b) Indicate on which financial statement each of the above items would be reported, and where.

E14–2 Condensed data from the comparative statement of financial position of Dressaire Inc. follow:

Prepare horizontal analysis.
(SO 2)

	2015	2014	2013
Current assets	$120,000	$ 80,000	$100,000
Non-current assets	400,000	350,000	300,000
Current liabilities	70,000	90,000	65,000
Non-current liabilities	165,000	105,000	150,000
Common shares	150,000	115,000	100,000
Retained earnings	135,000	120,000	85,000

Instructions

(a) Using horizontal analysis, calculate the percentage of a base-year amount, using 2013 as the base year.
(b) Using horizontal analysis, calculate the percentage change for each year.

E14–3 Condensed data from the income statement for Fleetwood Corporation follow:

Prepare vertical analysis.
(SO 3)

	2015	2014
Net sales	$800,000	$600,000
Cost of goods sold	550,000	375,000
Gross profit	250,000	225,000
Operating expenses	175,000	125,000
Profit before income tax	75,000	100,000
Income tax expense	15,000	20,000
Profit	$ 60,000	$ 80,000

Instructions

Using vertical analysis, calculate the percentage of the base amount for each year.

E14–4 The income statement for **Postmedia Network Canada Corp.** follows:

Prepare horizontal and vertical analyses of income statement.
(SO 1, 2, 3)

POSTMEDIA NETWORK CANADA CORP.
Income Statement
Year Ended August 31
(in thousands)

	2012	2011	2010
Revenues	$831,877	$898,888	$122,094
Operating expenses	792,619	819,921	133,650
Other expenses	76,533	91,121	33,062
Loss from continuing operations before income tax	(37,275)	(12,154)	(44,618)
Income tax expense	—	—	—
Loss from continuing operations	(37,275)	(12,154)	(44,618)
Income from discontinued operations, net of income tax	14,053	2,565	—
Loss	$(23,222)	$ (9,589)	$(44,618)

Instructions

(a) Using horizontal analysis, calculate the horizontal percentage of a base-year amount, assuming 2010 is the base year.
(b) Using vertical analysis, calculate the percentage of the base amount for each year.
(c) Identify any significant changes from 2010 to 2012, including the impact of discontinued operations on your analysis.

E14–5 The following is a list of the ratios and values we have calculated in this text:

Classify ratios.
(SO 4, 5, 6)

(a)	(b)	
_____	_____	Asset turnover
_____	_____	Average collection period
_____	_____	Cash current debt coverage
_____	_____	Cash total debt coverage
_____	_____	Current ratio

(a)	(b)	
_____	_____	Days in inventory
_____	_____	Debt to total assets
_____	_____	Dividend yield
_____	_____	Earnings per share
_____	_____	Free cash flow
_____	_____	Gross profit margin
_____	_____	Inventory turnover
_____	_____	Payout ratio
_____	_____	Price-earnings ratio
_____	_____	Profit margin
_____	_____	Receivables turnover
_____	_____	Return on assets
_____	_____	Return on common shareholders' equity
_____	_____	Times interest earned
_____	_____	Working capital

Instructions

(a) Classify each of the above ratios as a liquidity (L), solvency (S), or profitability (P) ratio.

(b) For each of the above ratios, indicate whether a higher result is generally considered better (B) or worse (W).

**Calculate and compare liquidity ratios.
(SO 4)**

E14–6   Selected comparative financial statement data for Kigio Inc. are shown below.

KIGIO INC.
Statement of Financial Position (partial)
December 31
(in thousands)

	2015	2014	2013
Current assets			
Cash	$ 30	$ 91	$ 60
Trading investments	55	60	40
Accounts receivable, net	676	586	496
Inventory	628	525	575
Prepaid expenses	41	52	29
Total current assets	$1,430	$1,314	$1,200
Total current liabilities	$ 890	$ 825	$ 750

Additional information:

(in thousands)	2015	2014	2013
Allowance for doubtful accounts	$ 50	$ 45	$ 40
Net credit sales	4,190	3,940	3,700
Cost of goods sold	2,900	2,650	2,350

Instructions

(a) Calculate all possible liquidity ratios for 2015 and 2014.

(b) Indicate whether each of the liquidity ratios calculated in part (a) is better or worse in 2015.

**Evaluate liquidity.
(SO 4)**

E14–7   The following selected ratios are available for Pampered Pets Inc. for the three most recent years:

	2015	2014	2013
Current ratio	2.7:1	2.4:1	2.1:1
Receivables turnover	6.7 times	7.4 times	8.2 times
Inventory turnover	7.7 times	8.6 times	9.9 times

Instructions

(a) Has the company's collection of its receivables improved or deteriorated over the last three years?

(b) Is the company selling its inventory faster or slower than in past years?

(c) Overall, has the company's liquidity improved or deteriorated over the last three years? Explain.

E14-8 The following selected information (in thousands) is available for Tukai Limited:

Calculate and compare solvency ratios. (SO 5)

	2015	2014
Total assets	$3,890	$3,700
Total liabilities	2,175	1,960
Interest expense	15	25
Income tax expense	175	150
Profit	405	375
Cash provided by operating activities	850	580
Cash used by investing activities	400	300

Instructions
(a) Calculate all possible solvency ratios for 2015 and 2014.
(b) Indicate whether each of the solvency ratios calculated in part (a) is better or worse in 2015.

E14-9 The following selected ratios are available for Ackabe Inc. for the three most recent years:

Evaluate solvency. (SO 5)

	2015	2014	2013
Debt to total assets	50.0%	45.5%	40.3%
Times interest earned	1.8 times	1.4 times	1.0 times
Cash total debt coverage	0.7 times	0.5 times	0.3 times

Instructions
(a) Has the debt to total assets improved or deteriorated over the last three years?
(b) Has the times interest earned improved or deteriorated over the last three years?
(c) Overall, has the company's solvency improved or deteriorated over the last three years? Explain.

E14-10 The following selected information is for Karatu Corporation:

Calculate and compare profitability ratios. (SO 6)

	2015	2014	2013
Total assets	$350,000	$275,000	$274,000
Total shareholders' equity	133,500	100,000	50,000
Net sales	500,000	400,000	300,000
Cost of goods sold	375,000	290,000	180,000
Profit	33,500	30,000	20,000

Karatu had no preferred shares.

Instructions
(a) Calculate the gross profit margin, profit margin, asset turnover, return on assets, and return on common shareholders' equity ratios for 2015 and 2014.
(b) Indicate whether each of the profitability ratios calculated in part (a) is better or worse in 2015.

E14-11 The following selected profitability ratios are available for two companies, BetaCom Corporation and Top Corporation, for a recent fiscal year:

Evaluate profitability. (SO 6)

	BetaCom	Top	Industry
Gross profit margin	37.5%	48.2%	37.9%
Profit margin	5.2%	4.9%	4.8%
Asset turnover	1.1 times	1.1 times	1.0 times
Return on assets	5.7%	5.4%	4.8%
Return on common shareholders' equity	9.5%	6.4%	6.0%

Instructions
Which company is more profitable? Explain, making sure to refer to the industry ratios where appropriate.

E14-12 Selected information for **Teck Resources Limited** for the most recent three years is as follows:

Identify drivers of profitability. (SO 6)

	2012	2011	2010
Return on common shareholders' equity	4.6%	15.8%	12.2%
Return on assets	2.5%	7.2%	6.3%
Debt to total assets	28.6%	28.6%	23.7%
Asset turnover	0.3 times	0.3 times	0.3 times
Profit margin	8.4%	24.0%	21.1%

Instructions
(a) What was the main driver of the company's return on assets over the last three years? Explain.
(b) What was the main driver of the company's return on common shareholders' equity over the last three years? Explain.

Evaluate liquidity, solvency, and profitability.
(SO 4, 5, 6)

E14–13   The following selected ratios are available for a recent year for Archers Post Limited and Nyarboro Corporation:

	Archers Post	Nyarboro	Industry Average
Liquidity			
Current ratio	0.8:1	0.6:1	1.0:1
Receivables turnover	8.7 times	10.4 times	15.2 times
Inventory turnover	6.7 times	29.9 times	65.3 times
Solvency			
Debt to total assets	66.7%	59.0%	68.9%
Times interest earned	4.1 times	3.4 times	3.6 times
Profitability			
Gross profit margin	88.2%	45.2%	55.8%
Profit margin	12.6%	11.2%	2.0%
Return on assets	8.7%	3.9%	1.0%
Return on common shareholders' equity	32.8%	16.2%	4.6%
Price-earnings ratio	13.8 times	20.6 times	26.5 times

Instructions
(a) Which company is more liquid? Explain.
(b) Which company is more solvent? Explain.
(c) Which company is more profitable? Explain.
(d) Which company do investors favour? Is this consistent with your findings in parts (a) to (c)? Investors would be more interested in buying the shares of which company?

Problems: Set A

Prepare horizontal analysis.
(SO 2)

P14–1A   ClubLink Enterprises Limited is Canada's largest golf course and resort owner. The following selected information is available for three recent fiscal years:

CLUBLINK ENTERPRISES LIMITED
Statement of Financial Position
December 31
(in thousands)

	2012	2011	2010
Assets			
Current assets	$ 9,530	$ 13,891	$ 11,731
Non-current assets	643,059	648,241	599,681
Total assets	$652,589	$662,132	$611,412
Liabilities and Shareholders' Equity			
Liabilities			
Current liabilities	$ 51,194	$ 61,488	$ 48,631
Non-current liabilities	419,123	411,102	406,984
Total liabilities	470,317	472,590	455,615
Shareholders' equity	182,272	189,542	155,797
Total liabilities and shareholders' equity	$652,589	$662,132	$611,412

CLUBLINK ENTERPRISES LIMITED
Income Statement
Year Ended December 31
(in thousands)

	2012	2011	2010
Revenue	$215,160	$216,254	$205,195
Operating expenses	174,795	179,289	167,630
Profit from operations	40,635	36,965	37,565
Other revenues and expenses			
Interest expense	21,189	21,709	22,108
Other	427	(6,777)	(344)
Profit before income tax	18,749	22,033	15,801
Income tax expense	4,198	5,645	3,959
Profit	$ 14,551	$ 16,388	$ 11,842

ClubLink had 18,192, 18,939, and 18,917 golf club members as at December 31, 2012, 2011, and 2010, respectively.

Instructions

(a) Using horizontal analysis, calculate the percentage of the base-year amount for each of the statement of financial position and income statement items, assuming 2010 is the base year.

(b) Identify the key components in Club Link's statement of financial position and income statement that are primarily responsible for the change in the company's financial position and performance over the three-year period.

P14–2A The following condensed information is available for **Big Rock Brewery Inc.**:

Prepare vertical
analysis.
(SO 3)

BIG ROCK BREWERY INC.
Statement of Financial Position
December 31
(in thousands)

	2012	2011	2010
Assets			
Current assets	$10,895	$ 8,089	$ 7,426
Non-current assets	35,405	37,081	27,035
Total assets	$46,300	$45,170	$34,461
Liabilities and Shareholders' Equity			
Liabilities			
Current liabilities	$ 6,318	$ 5,575	$ 4,322
Non-current liabilities	7,911	7,146	4,786
Total liabilities	14,229	12,721	9,108
Shareholders' equity	32,071	32,449	25,353
Total liabilities and shareholders' equity	$46,300	$45,170	$34,461

BIG ROCK BREWERY INC.
Income Statement
December 31
(in thousands)

	2012	2011	2010
Net sales	$46,057	$45,183	$45,130
Cost of goods sold	21,149	21,385	19,418
Gross profit	24,908	23,798	25,712
Operating expenses	19,290	20,455	20,054
Profit from operations	5,618	3,343	5,658
Other revenues and expenses			
Interest expense	93	141	147
Other income	(204)	(288)	(327)
Profit before income tax	5,729	3,490	5,838
Income tax expense (recovery)	1,594	957	(279)
Profit	$ 4,135	$ 2,533	$ 6,117

Instructions

(a) Using vertical analysis, calculate the percentage of the base amount for the statement of financial position and income statement for each year.

(b) Identify the key components in Big Rock's statement of financial position and income statement that are primarily responsible for the change in the company's financial position and performance over the three-year period.

(c) How has Big Rock primarily financed its assets—through debt or equity—over the last three years?

P14–3A A horizontal and vertical analysis of the income statement for a service company providing consulting services is shown below:

SERVICE CORPORATION
Horizontal Income Statement
Year Ended December 31

	2015	2014	2013	2012
Revenue	120.0%	110.0%	114.0%	100.0%
Operating expenses	118.6%	111.4%	114.3%	100.0%
Profit from operations	123.3%	106.7%	113.3%	100.0%
Other revenues and expenses				
Interest expense	40.0%	60.0%	80.0%	100.0%
Other revenue	240.0%	140.0%	140.0%	100.0%
Profit before income tax	166.8%	130.2%	131.7%	100.0%
Income tax expense	166.8%	130.2%	131.7%	100.0%
Profit	166.8%	130.2%	131.7%	100.0%

SERVICE CORPORATION
Vertical Income Statement
Year Ended December 31

	2015	2014	2013	2012
Revenue	100.0%	100.0%	100.0%	100.0%
Operating expenses	69.2%	70.9%	70.2%	70.0%
Profit from operations	30.8%	29.1%	29.8%	30.0%
Other revenues and expenses				
Interest expense	3.3%	5.4%	7.0%	10.0%
Other revenue	(1.0)%	(0.6)%	(0.9)%	(0.5)%
Profit before income tax	28.5%	24.3%	23.7%	20.5%
Income tax expense	5.7%	4.9%	4.8%	4.1%
Profit	22.8%	19.4%	18.9%	16.4%

Instructions

(a) How effectively has the company controlled its operating expenses over the four-year period?

(b) In a horizontal analysis, the company's income tax expense has changed exactly the same as profit (66.8%) over the four-year period. Yet, in a vertical analysis, the income tax percentage is different than the profit percentage in each period. Explain how this is possible.

(c) Identify any other key financial statement components that have changed over the four-year period for the company.

(d) Identify any additional information that might be helpful to you in your analysis of this company over the four-year period.

P14–4A **Nexen Inc.** reported the following selected information for the last five years (in millions, except earnings per share):

	2012	2011	2010	2009	2008
Net sales	$ 6,430	$ 6,169	$ 5,411	$ 4,203	$ 6,576
Average common shareholders' equity	8,589	8,094	8,218	7,418	6,374
Average total assets	20,302	19,858	22,404	22,528	20,115
Average total assets (excluding discontinued assets held for sale)	20,302	19,493	22,030	22,528	20,115
Profit from continuing operations	333	395	572	512	1,602
Profit from discontinued operations	—	302	625	24	113
Profit	333	697	1,197	536	1,715
Earnings per share from continuing operations	0.61	0.75	1.09	0.98	3.05
Total earnings per share	0.61	1.32	2.28	1.03	3.26

Instructions

(a) Calculate Nexen's profit margin, return on assets, and return on common shareholders' equity (for this calculation, note that the company has no preferred shares) before and after discontinued operations for each of the last five years.

(b) Evaluate Nexen's profitability over the last five years before and after discontinued operations.

(c) Which analysis—before or after discontinued operations—is more relevant to investors? Explain.

P14–5A Condensed statement of financial position and income statement data for Pitka Corporation follow:

Calculate and evaluate ratios.
(SO 4, 5, 6)

PITKA CORPORATION
Statement of Financial Position
December 31

	2015	2014	2013
Assets			
Current assets			
Cash	$ 25,000	$ 20,000	$ 18,000
Accounts receivable (net)	55,000	45,000	48,000
Inventory	100,000	85,000	64,000
Total current assets	180,000	150,000	130,000
Long-term investments	55,000	70,000	45,000
Property, plant, and equipment (net)	500,000	370,000	258,000
Total assets	$735,000	$590,000	$433,000
Liabilities and Shareholders' Equity			
Liabilities			
Current liabilities	$ 85,000	$ 80,000	$ 30,000
Non-current liabilities	155,000	85,000	20,000
Total liabilities	240,000	165,000	50,000
Shareholders' equity			
Common shares	330,000	300,000	300,000
Retained earnings	165,000	125,000	83,000
Total shareholders' equity	495,000	425,000	383,000
Total liabilities and shareholders' equity	$735,000	$590,000	$433,000

PITKA CORPORATION
Income Statement
Year Ended December 31

	2015	2014
Sales	$740,000	$500,000
Less: Sales returns and allowances	40,000	50,000
Net sales	700,000	450,000
Cost of goods sold	450,000	300,000
Gross profit	250,000	150,000
Operating expenses	150,000	84,000
Profit from operations	100,000	66,000
Interest expense	10,000	4,000
Profit before income tax	90,000	62,000
Income tax expense	18,000	12,400
Profit	$ 72,000	$ 49,600

Additional information:

1. The allowance for doubtful accounts was $4,800 in 2013, $4,500 in 2014, and $5,000 in 2015.
2. All sales were credit sales.
3. Net cash provided by operating activities was $119,600 in 2014 and $102,000 in 2015.

Instructions

(a) Calculate the following ratios for each of 2014 and 2015:

1. Current ratio
2. Receivables turnover
3. Inventory turnover
4. Debt to total assets
5. Times interest earned
6. Cash total debt coverage
7. Gross profit margin
8. Profit margin
9. Asset turnover
10. Return on assets

(b) Identify whether the change in each ratio calculated in part (a) was favourable, unfavourable, or unchanged between 2014 and 2015.

(c) Explain whether overall (1) liquidity, (2) solvency, and (3) profitability improved, deteriorated, or remained the same between 2014 and 2015.

Calculate and evaluate ratios.
(SO 4, 5, 6)

P14–6A Condensed statement of financial position and comprehensive income statement data for Clack Ltd. follow:

CLACK LTD.
Statement of Financial Position
December 31

	2015	2014
Assets		
Cash	$ 70,000	$ 65,000
Accounts receivable (net)	95,000	90,000
Merchandise inventory	130,000	125,000
Prepaid expenses	24,000	23,000
Long-term investments	45,000	40,000
Property, plant, and equipment (net)	390,000	305,000
Total assets	$754,000	$648,000
Liabilities and Shareholders' Equity		
Liabilities		
Accounts payable	$ 45,000	$ 42,000
Accrued liabilities	30,000	40,000
Bank loan payable (current)	110,000	100,000
Bonds payable, due 2022	200,000	150,000
Total liabilities	385,000	332,000
Shareholders' equity		
Common shares (20,000 shares issued)	200,000	200,000
Retained earnings	172,000	116,000
Accumulated other comprehensive loss	(3,000)	
Total shareholders' equity	369,000	316,000
Total liabilities and shareholders' equity	$754,000	$648,000

CLACK LTD.
Statement of Comprehensive Income
Year Ended December 31

	2015	2014
Sales	$900,000	$840,000
Cost of goods sold	600,000	575,000
Gross profit	300,000	265,000
Operating expenses	184,000	160,000
Profit from operations	116,000	105,000
Interest expense	30,000	20,000
Profit before income tax	86,000	85,000
Income tax expense	22,000	20,000
Profit	64,000	65,000
Other comprehensive loss	(3,000)	—
Total comprehensive income	$ 61,000	$ 65,000

Additional information:

1. The allowance for doubtful accounts was $4,000 in 2014 and $5,000 in 2015.
2. Accounts receivable at the beginning of 2014 were $88,000, net of an allowance for doubtful accounts of $3,000.
3. Merchandise inventory at the beginning of 2014 was $115,000.
4. Total assets at the beginning of 2014 were $630,000.
5. Total current liabilities at the beginning of 2014 were $180,000.
6. Total liabilities at the beginning of 2014 were $371,000.
7. Shareholders' equity at the beginning of 2014 was $259,000.
8. Seventy-five percent of the sales were on account.
9. Net cash provided by operating activities was $85,000 in 2014 and $96,000 in 2015.
10. Net capital expenditures were $50,000 in 2014 and $125,000 in 2015.
11. In each of 2014 and 2015, $8,000 of dividends were paid to the common shareholders.

Instructions

(a) Calculate all possible liquidity, solvency, and profitability ratios for each of 2014 and 2015.

(b) Identify whether the change in each ratio calculated in part (a) was favourable, unfavourable, or unchanged between 2014 and 2015.

(c) Explain whether overall (1) liquidity, (2) solvency, and (3) profitability improved, deteriorated, or remained the same between 2014 and 2015.

P14-7A Selected ratios for the current year for two companies in the office supplies industry, Bureau Nouveau Inc. and Supplies Unlimited Corp., follow:

Evaluate ratios.
(SO 4, 5, 6)

	Bureau Nouveau	Supplies Unlimited
Asset turnover	2.6 times	2.2 times
Average collection period	31 days	35 days
Cash current debt coverage	0.3 times	0.1 times
Current ratio	1.7:1	2.0:1
Days in inventory	61 days	122 days
Debt to total assets	45.5%	30.8%
Dividend yield	0.3%	0.5%
Earnings per share	$3.50	$2.40
Gross profit margin	22.6%	30.7%
Payout ratio	8.0%	19.2%
Price-earnings ratio	29 times	45 times
Profit margin	5.5%	4.7%
Return on assets	14.3%	10.3%
Return on common shareholders' equity	26.1%	12.9%
Times interest earned	4.2 times	8.6 times

Instructions

(a) Both companies offer their customers credit terms of net 30 days. Indicate which ratio(s) should be used to assess how well the accounts receivable are managed. Comment on how well each company appears to be managing its accounts receivable.

(b) Indicate the ratio(s) used to assess inventory management. Which company is managing its inventory better?

(c) Supplies Unlimited's current ratio is higher than that of Bureau Nouveau. Identify two possible reasons for this.

(d) Which company is more solvent? Identify the ratio(s) used to determine this, and defend your choice.

(e) You notice that Supplies Unlimited's gross profit margin is higher and its profit margin lower than those of Bureau Nouveau. Identify two possible reasons for this.

(f) What is mostly responsible for Bureau Nouveau's higher return on assets: profit margin or asset turnover? Explain.

(g) What is mostly responsible for Bureau Nouveau's higher return on common shareholders' equity: return on assets or use of debt? Explain.

(h) Bureau Nouveau's payout ratio is lower than Supplies Unlimited's. Indicate one possible reason for this.

(i) What is the market price per share of each company's common shares?

(j) Which company do investors appear to believe has greater prospects for growing in future? Indicate the ratio(s) you used to reach this conclusion, and explain your reasoning.

P14-8A The following ratios are available for fast-food competitors and their industry, for a recent year:

Evaluate liquidity, solvency, and profitability.
(SO 4, 5, 6)

	Mac's Burgers	King's Burgers	Industry Average
Liquidity			
Current ratio	1.5:1	0.9:1	1.2:1
Receivables turnover	21.5 times	28.3 times	34.8 times
Inventory turnover	33.6 times	42.3 times	35.2 times
Solvency			
Debt to total assets	44.6%	40.1%	44.8%
Times interest earned	16.5 times	6.7 times	11.4 times
Profitability			
Gross profit margin	40.0%	33.1%	36.9%
Profit margin	20.6%	7.5%	10.8%
Asset turnover	0.8 times	0.9 times	1.2 times
Return on assets	16.5%	6.8%	13.0%
Return on common shareholders' equity	34.5%	17.8%	22.4%
Price-earnings ratio	19.6 times	17.6 times	19.9 times
Dividend yield	3.0%	1.0%	1.6%

Instructions

(a) Which company is more liquid? Explain.

(b) Which company is more solvent? Explain.

(c) Which company is more profitable? Explain.

(d) Which company do investors favour? Is your answer consistent with your findings in parts (a) to (c)?

Discuss impact of accounting policies and estimates on financial analysis. (SO 4, 5, 6, 7)

P14–9A   You are in the process of analyzing two similar companies in the same industry. You learn that they have different accounting practices and policies, as follows:

1. Company A, which has the same type of inventory as Company B, uses the FIFO cost method while Company B uses average. Prices have generally been rising in this industry.

2. Company A uses the double-diminishing balance depreciation method for most of its buildings, while Company B uses the straight-line method for its buildings.

Instructions

(a) Considering only the impact of the choice of inventory cost method, determine which company will report a higher (1) current ratio, (2) debt to total assets ratio, and (3) profit margin ratio, or whether the choice of cost method will have no impact This is the first year of operations for both companies.

(b) Considering only the impact of the choice of depreciation method, determine which company will report a higher (1) current ratio, (2) debt to total assets ratio, and (3) profit margin ratio, or whether the choice of depreciation method will have no impact. This is the first year of operations for both companies.

(c) Will the use of different accounting estimates and policies affect your analysis? Explain.

(d) Identify two other limitations of financial analysis that an analyst should watch for when analyzing financial statements.

Problems: Set B

Prepare horizontal analysis. (SO 2)

P14–1B   **lululemon athletica inc.** has seen a significant amount of growth over the last three years. The following selected information is available for three recent fiscal years:

LULULEMON ATHLETICA INC.
Statement of Financial Position
January 31
(in U.S. thousands)

	2013	2012	2011
Assets			
Current assets	$ 787,053	$527,093	$389,279
Non-current assets	264,025	207,541	110,023
Total assets	$1,051,078	$734,634	$499,302
Liabilities and Shareholders' Equity			
Liabilities			
Current liabilities	$ 133,357	$103,439	$ 85,364
Non-current liabilities	30,422	25,014	19,645
Total liabilities	163,779	128,453	105,009
Shareholders' equity	887,299	606,181	394,293
Total liabilities and shareholders' equity	$1,051,078	$734,634	$499,302

LULULEMON ATHLETICA INC.
Income Statement
Year Ended January 31
(in U.S. thousands)

	2013	2012	2011
Net revenue	$1,370,358	$1,000,839	$711,704
Cost of goods sold	607,532	431,488	316,757
Gross profit	762,826	569,351	394,947
Operating expenses	386,387	282,393	214,556
Profit from operations	376,439	286,958	180,391
Other income	4,082	1,599	2,536
Profit before income tax	380,521	288,557	182,927
Income tax expense	109,965	104,494	61,080
Profit	$ 270,556	$ 184,063	$121,847

Instructions
(a) Using horizontal analysis, calculate the percentage of the base-year amount for each of the statement of financial position and income statement, assuming 2011 is the base year.
(b) Identify the key components in lululemon's statement of financial position and income statement that are primarily responsible for the change in the company's financial position and performance over the three-year period.

P14–2B The following condensed information is available for **Yellow Media Inc.**, Canada's largest Internet media and marketing company:

Prepare vertical analysis, with discontinued operations.
(SO 1, 3)

YELLOW MEDIA INC.
Statement of Financial Position
December 31
(in thousands)

	2012	2011	2010
Assets			
Current assets	$ 369,361	$ 350,559	$ 443,370
Fixed assets	27,414	46,496	112,445
Intangible assets	1,312,148	1,658,051	2,123,776
Goodwill	—	2,967,847	6,508,984
Other assets	47,553	25,979	111,673
Total assets	$1,756,476	$5,048,932	$9,300,248
Liabilities and Shareholders' Equity			
Liabilities			
Current liabilities	$ 326,923	$ 634,613	$ 478,562
Non-current liabilities	1,143,393	2,329,292	2,871,617
Total liabilities	1,470,316	2,963,905	3,350,179
Shareholders' equity	286,160	2,085,027	5,950,069
Total liabilities and shareholders' equity	$1,756,476	$5,048,932	$9,300,248

YELLOW MEDIA INC.
Income Statement
Year Ended December 31
(in thousands)

	2012	2011	2010
Revenues	$ 1,107,715	$ 1,328,866	$1,679,860
Operating expenses	686,331	843,950	1,164,104
Goodwill impairment	3,267,847	2,900,000	—
Profit (loss) from operations	(2,846,463)	(2,415,084)	515,756
Other revenues and expenses			
Interest expense	(146,265)	(130,582)	(144,796)
Other	962,788	(75,307)	(36,398)
Profit (loss) from continuing operations before income tax	(2,029,940)	(2,620,973)	334,562
Income tax expense (recovery)	(75,935)	87,149	60,527
Profit (loss) from continuing operations	(1,954,005)	(2,708,122)	274,035
Discontinued business loss	—	120,877	—
Profit (loss)	$(1,954,005)	$(2,828,999)	$ 274,035

Instructions
(a) Using vertical analysis, calculate the percentage of the base amount for the statement of financial position and income statement for each year.
(b) Identify the key components in Yellow Media's statement of financial position and income statement that are primarily responsible for the change in the company's financial position and performance over the three-year period. Include in your answer a specific comment on the impact the company's discontinued operations had on your analysis.
(c) How has Yellow Media primarily financed its assets—through debt or equity—over the last three years?

Interpret horizontal and vertical analysis.
(SO 2, 3)

P14–3B A horizontal and vertical analysis of the income statement for a retail company selling a wide variety of general merchandise is shown below:

RETAIL CORPORATION
Horizontal Income Statement
Year Ended January 31

	2015	2014	2013	2012
Revenue	140.0%	111.0%	114.0%	100.0%
Cost of goods sold	148.3%	113.3%	116.7%	100.0%
Gross profit	127.5%	107.5%	110.0%	100.0%
Operating expenses	171.4%	133.1%	126.9%	100.0%
Profit from operations	93.3%	87.6%	96.9%	100.0%
Interest expense	40.0%	60.0%	80.0%	100.0%
Other revenue	240.0%	140.0%	200.0%	100.0%
Profit before income tax	140.0%	110.8%	113.8%	100.0%
Income tax expense	160.0%	116.0%	124.0%	100.0%
Profit	135.2%	109.5%	111.4%	100.0%

RETAIL CORPORATION
Vertical Income Statement
Year Ended January 31

	2015	2014	2013	2012
Revenue	100.0%	100.0%	100.0%	100.0%
Cost of goods sold	63.6%	61.2%	61.4%	60.0%
Gross profit	36.4%	38.8%	38.6%	40.0%
Operating expenses	21.4%	21.0%	19.5%	17.5%
Profit from operations	15.0%	17.8%	19.1%	22.5%
Interest expense	(2.9%)	(5.4%)	(7.0%)	(10.0%)
Other revenue	0.9%	0.6%	0.9%	0.5%
Profit before income tax	13.0%	13.0%	13.0%	13.0%
Income tax expense	2.9%	2.6%	2.7%	2.5%
Profit	10.1%	10.4%	10.3%	10.5%

Instructions

(a) How effectively has the company controlled its cost of goods sold over the four-year period?

(b) In a vertical analysis, the company's profit before income tax has remained unchanged at 13% of revenue over the four-year period. Yet, in a horizontal analysis, profit before income tax has grown 40% over that period of time. Explain how this is possible.

(c) Identify any other key financial statement components that have changed over the four-year period for the company.

(d) Identify any additional information that might be helpful to you in your analysis of this company over the four-year period.

Calculate and evaluate profitability ratios with discontinued operations.
(SO 1, 6)

P14–4B **The Home Depot Inc.** reported the following selected information for the last five years ending on the Saturday closest to January 31 (in U.S. $ millions, except earnings per share):

	2013	2012	2011	2010	2009
Net sales	$74,754	$70,395	$67,997	$66,176	$71,288
Average common shareholders' equity	17,837	18,394	19,141	18,585	17,746
Average total assets	40,801	40,321	40,501	41,020	42,744
Profit from continuing operations	4,535	3,883	3,338	2,620	2,312
Net loss (gain) from discontinued operations	—	—	—	41	(52)
Profit	4,535	3,883	3,338	2,661	2,260
Earnings per share from continuing operations	3.03	2.49	2.01	1.55	1.37
Total earnings per share	3.03	2.49	2.01	1.57	1.34

Instructions

(a) Calculate Home Depot's return on common shareholders' equity (for this calculation, note that the company has no preferred shares), return on assets, and profit margin ratios before and after discontinued operations for each of the last five years.

(b) Evaluate Home Depot's profitability over the last five years before and after discontinued operations.

(c) Which analysis—before or after discontinued operations—is more relevant to investors? Explain.

P14–5B   Condensed statement of financial position and income statement data for Colinas Corporation follow:

COLINAS CORPORATION
Statement of Financial Position
December 31

	2015	2014	2013
Assets			
Cash	$ 30,000	$ 24,000	$ 10,000
Accounts receivable (net)	80,000	50,000	53,000
Inventory	85,000	45,000	50,000
Other current assets	70,000	75,000	62,000
Long-term investments	100,000	76,000	50,000
Property, plant, and equipment (net)	595,000	345,000	315,000
Total assets	$960,000	$615,000	$540,000
Liabilities and Shareholders' Equity			
Liabilities			
Current liabilities	$ 63,500	$ 51,000	$ 65,000
Non-current liabilities	245,000	65,000	70,000
Total liabilities	308,500	116,000	135,000
Shareholders' equity			
Common shares	416,500	319,000	275,000
Retained earnings	235,000	180,000	130,000
Total shareholders' equity	651,500	499,000	405,000
Total liabilities and shareholders' equity	$960,000	$615,000	$540,000

COLINAS CORPORATION
Income Statement
Year Ended December 31

	2015	2014
Sales	$950,000	$840,000
Less: Sales returns and allowances	60,000	40,000
Net sales	890,000	800,000
Cost of goods sold	490,000	450,000
Gross profit	400,000	350,000
Operating expenses	266,000	260,000
Profit from operations	134,000	90,000
Interest expense	27,750	8,750
Profit before income tax	106,250	81,250
Income tax expense	21,250	16,250
Profit	$ 85,000	$ 65,000

Additional information:

1. The allowance for doubtful accounts was $2,400 in 2013, $2,750 in 2014, and $3,650 in 2015.
2. Assume all sales were credit sales.
3. Net cash provided by operating activities was $91,000 in 2014 and $107,500 in 2015.

Instructions

(a) Calculate the following ratios for each of 2014 and 2015:
   1. Current ratio
   2. Receivables turnover
   3. Inventory turnover
   4. Debt to total assets
   5. Times interest earned
   6. Cash total debt coverage
   7. Gross profit margin
   8. Profit margin
   9. Asset turnover
   10. Return on assets
(b) Indicate whether the change in each ratio calculated in part (a) was favourable, unfavourable, or unchanged between 2014 and 2015.

Calculate and evaluate ratios.
(SO 4, 5, 6)

P14–6B Condensed statement of financial position and comprehensive income statement data for Track Ltd. follow:

TRACK LTD.
Statement of Financial Position
December 31

	2015	2014
Assets		
Cash	$ 50,000	$ 42,000
Accounts receivable (net)	100,000	87,000
Inventories	400,000	300,000
Prepaid expenses	25,000	31,000
Long-term investments	80,000	50,000
Land	125,000	75,000
Buildings and equipment (net)	560,000	400,000
Total assets	$1,340,000	$985,000
Liabilities and Shareholders' Equity		
Liabilities		
Notes payable	$ 150,000	$ 50,000
Accounts payable	245,000	190,000
Current portion of mortgage payable	48,750	25,000
Mortgage payable, due 2022	200,000	125,000
Total liabilities	643,750	390,000
Shareholders' equity		
Common shares (100,000 shares issued)	400,000	400,000
Retained earnings	292,250	195,000
Accumulated other comprehensive income	4,000	—
Total shareholders' equity	696,250	595,000
Total liabilities and shareholders' equity	$1,340,000	$985,000

TRACK LTD.
Statement of Comprehensive Income
Year Ended December 31

	2015	2014
Net sales	$1,100,000	$950,000
Cost of goods sold	650,000	635,000
Gross profit	450,000	315,000
Operating expenses	285,000	215,000
Profit from operations	165,000	100,000
Interest expense	30,000	10,000
Profit before income tax	135,000	90,000
Income tax expense	33,750	22,500
Profit	101,250	67,500
Other comprehensive income	4,000	—
Total comprehensive income	$ 105,250	$ 67,500

Additional information:

1. The allowance for doubtful accounts was $5,000 in 2014 and $10,000 in 2015.
2. Accounts receivable at the beginning of 2014 were $80,000, net of an allowance for doubtful accounts of $3,000.
3. Inventories at the beginning of 2014 were $320,000.
4. Total assets at the beginning of 2014 were $1,075,000.
5. Current liabilities at the beginning of 2014 were $250,000.
6. Total liabilities at the beginning of 2014 were $543,500.
7. Total shareholders' equity at the beginning of 2014 was $531,500.
8. All sales were on account.
9. Net cash provided by operating activities was $135,500 in 2014 and $223,000 in 2015.
10. Net capital expenditures were $50,000 in 2014 and $92,000 in 2015.
11. In each of 2014 and 2015, $4,000 of dividends were paid to the common shareholders.

Instructions

(a) Calculate all possible liquidity, solvency, and profitability ratios for each of 2014 and 2015.
(b) Indicate whether the change in each ratio calculated in part (a) was favourable, unfavourable, or unchanged between 2014 and 2015.

(c) Explain whether Track's overall (1) liquidity, (2) solvency, and (3) profitability improved, deteriorated, or remained the same between 2014 to 2015.

P14–7B Selected ratios for the current year for two companies in the beverage industry, Refresh Corp. and Flavour Limited, follow:

Evaluate ratios.
(SO 4, 5, 6)

	Refresh	Flavour
Asset turnover	1.0 times	1.0 times
Cash total debt coverage	30.2%	22.4%
Current ratio	2.2:1	1.6:1
Debt to total assets	56%	72%
Dividend yield	0.2%	1.1%
Earnings per share	$0.98	$1.37
Gross profit margin	73.8%	60.0%
Inventory turnover	5.8 times	9.9 times
Payout ratio	10.0%	20.5%
Price-earnings ratio	14.3 times	20.3 times
Profit margin	9.3%	10.2%
Receivables turnover	9.8 times	10.4 times
Return on assets	9.3%	10.2%
Return on common shareholders' equity	25.7%	29.8%
Times interest earned	12.3 times	6.9 times

Instructions

(a) Both companies offer their customers credit terms of net 30 days. Indicate which ratio(s) should be used to assess how well the accounts receivable are managed. Comment on how well each company appears to be managing its accounts receivable.
(b) Indicate the ratio(s) used to assess inventory management. Which company is managing its inventory better?
(c) Refresh's current ratio is higher than that of Flavour. Identify two possible reasons for this.
(d) Which company, Refresh or Flavour, is more solvent? Identify the ratio(s) used to determine this, and defend your choice.
(e) You notice that Refresh's gross profit margin is higher and its profit margin lower than those of Flavour. Identify two possible reasons for this.
(f) What is mostly responsible for Flavour's higher return on assets: profit margin or asset turnover? Explain.
(g) What is mostly responsible for Flavour's higher return on common shareholders' equity: return on assets or use of debt? Explain.
(h) Refresh's payout ratio is significantly lower than that of Flavour. Indicate one possible reason for this.
(i) What is the market price per share of each company's common shares?
(j) Which company, Refresh or Flavour, do investors appear to believe has greater prospects for future growth? Indicate the ratio(s) you used to reach this conclusion, and explain your reasoning.

P14–8B The following ratios are available for toolmakers Best Tools, Inc. and Snappy Tools Incorporated, and their industry, for a recent year:

Evaluate liquidity, solvency, and profitability.
(SO 4, 5, 6)

	Best Tools	Snappy Tools	Industry Average
Liquidity			
Current ratio	1.8:1	2:1	2.6:1
Receivables turnover	8.7 times	6.1 times	7.4 times
Inventory turnover	6.7 times	4.8 times	3.9 times
Solvency			
Debt to total assets	32.9%	45.7%	22.5%
Times interest earned	3.2 times	6.1 times	7.6 times
Profitability			
Gross profit margin	35.1%	45.7%	33.3%
Profit margin	2.4%	7.0%	3.0%
Asset turnover	0.8 times	0.7 times	0.9 times
Return on assets	1.9%	4.9%	2.7%
Return on common shareholders' equity	4.4%	13.9%	4.9%
Price-earnings ratio	8.1 times	19.2 times	15.4 times
Payout ratio	11.5%	38.2%	17.4%
Dividend yield	0.8%	2.0%	1.2%

Instructions

(a) Which company is more liquid? Explain.
(b) Which company is more solvent? Explain.
(c) Which company is more profitable? Explain.
(d) Which company do investors favour? Is your answer consistent with your findings in parts (a) to (c)? Explain.

Discuss impact of accounting policies on financial analysis.
(SO 4, 5, 6, 7)

P14–9B You are in the process of analyzing two similar companies in the same industry. You learn that they have different accounting practices and policies, as follows:

1. Company A, which has the same type of equipment as Company B, uses the straight-line method of depreciation while Company B uses diminishing-balance. This is the first year of operations for both companies.
2. Company A is a private company and does not report other comprehensive income. Company B is a publicly traded company that generates and reports other comprehensive income from the revaluation of property, plant, and equipment.

Instructions

(a) Considering only the impact of the choice of depreciation method, determine which company will report a higher (1) current ratio, (2) debt to total assets ratio, and (3) profit margin ratio, or if the depreciation method will have no impact.
(b) Considering only the impact of total comprehensive income, determine which company will report a higher (1) current ratio, (2) debt to total assets ratio, and (3) profit margin ratio, or if the other comprehensive income will have no impact.
(c) Will the use of different accounting practices and policies affect your analysis? Explain.
(d) Identify two other limitations of financial analysis that an analyst should watch for when analyzing financial statements.

Broadening Your Perspective

Financial Reporting: *Shoppers Drug Mart*

Prepare horizontal and vertical analysis.
(SO 2, 3)

BYP14–1 The financial statements of **Shoppers Drug Mart** are presented in Appendix A at the end of this book. The following selected condensed information (in thousands) has been taken from these, and the prior years', financial statements:

	2012	2011	2010
Income statement			
Sales	$10,781,848	$10,458,652	$10,192,714
Cost of goods sold	6,609,229	6,416,208	6,283,634
Gross profit	4,172,619	4,042,444	3,909,080
Operating expenses	3,291,698	3,131,539	3,011,758
Profit from operations	880,921	910,905	897,322
Interest expense	57,595	64,038	60,633
Income tax expense	214,845	232,933	244,838
Profit	608,481	613,934	591,851
Statement of financial position			
Current assets	$2,764,997	$2,695,647	$2,542,820
Non-current assets	4,708,724	4,604,663	4,501,377
Current liabilities	2,334,917	1,776,238	1,527,567
Non-current liabilities	815,477	1,256,242	1,413,995
Shareholders' equity	4,323,327	4,267,830	4,102,635

Instructions

(a) Using horizontal analysis, calculate the percentage of the base-year amount for the information shown above, assuming 2010 is the base year.
(b) Using vertical analysis, calculate the percentage of a base amount for each of the (1) income statement and (2) statement of financial position, shown above for each year.
(c) Comment on any significant changes you observe from your calculations in parts (a) and (b).

Comparative Analysis: *Shoppers Drug Mart and Jean Coutu*

Calculate and evaluate liquidity, solvency, and profitability.
(SO 4, 5, 6)

BYP14–2 The financial statements of **Jean Coutu** are presented in Appendix B following the financial statements for **Shoppers Drug Mart** in Appendix A.

Instructions

(a) Calculate the liquidity ratios for 2012 that you believe are relevant for each company. Which company is more liquid?
(b) Calculate the solvency ratios for 2012 that you believe are relevant for each company. Which company is more solvent?

Specimen Financial Statements: Shoppers Drug Mart Corporation

In this appendix and the next, we illustrate current financial reporting with two different sets of corporate financial statements that are prepared in accordance with Canadian generally accepted accounting principles applicable to publicly accountable companies. We are grateful for permission to use the actual financial statements of Shoppers Drug Mart Corporation in Appendix A and The Jean Coutu Group (PJC) Inc. in Appendix B.

The financial statement package for Shoppers Drug Mart includes the statement of earnings, statement of comprehensive income, balance sheet, statement of changes in shareholders' equity, and statement of cash flows. The financial statements are preceded by two reports: management's responsibility for the financial statements and the auditors' report on these statements.

Only selected notes to the financial statements related to the topics included in this textbook have been included in this appendix. The complete set of financial statements and annual report for Shoppers Drug Mart can be found on *WileyPLUS* and the companion website to this textbook. In addition, material about working with annual reports, including the financial statements, is included on both sites.

We encourage you to scan Shoppers Drug Mart's financial statements to familiarize yourself with the contents of this appendix. You will also have the opportunity to use these financial statements in conjunction with relevant chapter material in the textbook. As well, these statements can be used to solve the Financial Reporting and Comparative Analysis cases in the Broadening Your Perspective section of the end of chapter material. As you near the end of your financial accounting course, we challenge you to reread Shoppers Drug Mart's financial statements to see how much greater your understanding of them has become.

We would like to mention, that at the time of writing, Loblaw Companies Limited had entered into an agreement to purchase Shoppers Drug Mart Corporation. This transaction was still in progress when this text was published and is expected to be complete early in 2014. It is anticipated that Shoppers will continue to operate under its own name after this acquisition but will no longer be a publicly traded company in 2014. Rather, it will operate as a private company that will be 100% owned by Loblaw. Consequently, we can expect to see one more year (for the year ended December 28, 2013) of financial statements published for Shoppers, after which its financial statements may not be widely available, as is the case with most private companies.

Management's Report

Management's Responsibility for Financial Statements

Management is responsible for the preparation and presentation of the accompanying consolidated financial statements and all other information in the Annual Report. This responsibility includes the selection and consistent application of appropriate accounting principles and methods in addition to making the estimates, judgements and assumptions necessary to prepare the consolidated financial statements in accordance with Canadian generally accepted accounting principles applicable to publicly accountable enterprises, which comply with International Financial Reporting Standards. It also includes ensuring that the financial information presented elsewhere in the Annual Report is consistent with the consolidated financial statements.

In fulfilling its responsibilities, management has established and maintains systems of internal controls. Although no cost-effective system of internal controls will prevent or detect all errors and irregularities, these systems are designed to provide reasonable assurance regarding the reliability of the Company's financial reporting and preparation of the financial statements in accordance with Canadian generally accepted accounting principles. These systems include controls to provide reasonable assurance that resources are safeguarded from material loss or inappropriate use, that transactions are authorized, recorded and reported properly and that financial records are reliable for preparing the consolidated financial statements. Internal auditors, who are employees of the Company, review and evaluate internal controls on management's behalf. The consolidated financial statements have been audited by the independent auditors, Deloitte LLP, in accordance with generally accepted auditing standards. Their report follows.

The Board of Directors, acting through an Audit Committee which is comprised solely of directors who are not employees of the Company, is responsible for determining that management fulfils its responsibility for financial reporting and internal control. This responsibility is carried out through periodic meetings with senior officers, financial management, internal audit and the independent auditors to discuss audit activities, the adequacy of internal financial controls and financial reporting matters. The Audit Committee has reviewed these consolidated financial statements and the Management's Discussion and Analysis and has recommended their approval by the Board of Directors prior to their inclusion in this Annual Report.

Domenic Pilla
President and Chief Executive Officer

TORONTO, ONTARIO
FEBRUARY 7, 2013

Brad Lukow
Executive Vice-President and Chief Financial Officer

Independent Auditor's Report

To the Shareholders of Shoppers Drug Mart Corporation

We have audited the accompanying consolidated financial statements of Shoppers Drug Mart Corporation, which comprise the consolidated balance sheets as at December 29, 2012 and December 31, 2011, and the consolidated statements of earnings, consolidated statements of comprehensive income, consolidated statements of changes in shareholders' equity and consolidated statements of cash flows for the 52 week periods ended December 29, 2012 and December 31, 2011, and a summary of significant accounting policies and other explanatory information.

Management's Responsibility for the Consolidated Financial Statements

Management is responsible for the preparation and fair presentation of these consolidated financial statements in accordance with International Financial Reporting Standards, and for such internal control as management determines is necessary to enable the preparation of consolidated financial statements that are free from material misstatement, whether due to fraud or error.

Auditor's Responsibility

Our responsibility is to express an opinion on these consolidated financial statements based on our audits. We conducted our audits in accordance with Canadian generally accepted auditing standards. Those standards require that we comply with ethical requirements and plan and perform the audit to obtain reasonable assurance about whether the consolidated financial statements are free from material misstatement.

An audit involves performing procedures to obtain audit evidence about the amounts and disclosures in the consolidated financial statements. The procedures selected depend on the auditor's judgment, including the assessment of the risks of material misstatement of the consolidated financial statements, whether due to fraud or error. In making those risk assessments, the auditor considers internal control relevant to the entity's preparation and fair presentation of the consolidated financial statements in order to design audit procedures that are appropriate in the circumstances, but not for the purpose of expressing an opinion on the effectiveness of the entity's internal control. An audit also includes evaluating the appropriateness of accounting policies used and the reasonableness of accounting estimates made by management, as well as evaluating the overall presentation of the consolidated financial statements.

We believe that the audit evidence we have obtained in our audits is sufficient and appropriate to provide a basis for our audit opinion.

Opinion

In our opinion, the consolidated financial statements present fairly, in all material respects, the financial position of Shoppers Drug Mart Corporation as at December 29, 2012 and December 31, 2011 and its financial performance and its cash flows for the 52 week periods ended December 29, 2012 and December 31, 2011 in accordance with International Financial Reporting Standards.

Deloitte LLP

Chartered Accountants,
Licensed Public Accountants

FEBRUARY 7, 2013
TORONTO, ONTARIO

Consolidated Statements of Earnings

For the 52 weeks ended December 29, 2012 and December 31, 2011
(in thousands of Canadian dollars, except per share amounts)

	Note	2012	2011
Sales		$ 10,781,848	$ 10,458,652
Cost of goods sold	9	(6,609,229)	(6,416,208)
Gross profit		4,172,619	4,042,444
Operating and administrative expenses	10, 11, 13	(3,291,698)	(3,131,539)
Operating income		880,921	910,905
Finance expenses	12	(57,595)	(64,038)
Earnings before income taxes		823,326	846,867
Income taxes	14		
Current		(235,791)	(208,696)
Deferred		20,946	(24,237)
		(214,845)	(232,933)
Net earnings		$ 608,481	$ 613,934
Net earnings per common share			
Basic	25	$ 2.92	$ 2.84
Diluted	25	$ 2.92	$ 2.84
Weighted average common shares outstanding (millions)			
Basic	25	208.4	216.4
Diluted	25	208.5	216.5
Actual common shares outstanding (millions)	24	204.5	212.5

The accompanying notes are an integral part of these consolidated financial statements.

Consolidated Statements of Comprehensive Income

For the 52 weeks ended December 29, 2012 and December 31, 2011
(in thousands of Canadian dollars, except per share amounts)

	Note	2012	2011
Net earnings		$ 608,481	$ 613,934
Other comprehensive income (loss), net of tax			
Effective portion of changes in fair value of hedges on equity forward derivatives (net of tax of $11 (2011: $12))	18	35	(39)
Net change in fair value of hedges on equity forward derivatives transferred to earnings (net of tax of $38 (2011: $163))	18	102	411
Retirement benefit obligations actuarial losses (net of tax of $2,310 (2011: $7,433))	21	(5,115)	(21,943)
Other comprehensive loss, net of tax		(4,978)	(21,571)
Total comprehensive income		$ 603,503	$ 592,363

The accompanying notes are an integral part of these consolidated financial statements.

Consolidated Balance Sheets

As at December 29, 2012 and December 31, 2011
(in thousands of Canadian dollars)

	Note	December 29, 2012	December 31, 2011
Current assets			
Cash		$ 104,529	$ 118,566
Accounts receivable		469,683	493,338
Inventory		2,148,484	2,042,302
Prepaid expenses and deposits		42,301	41,441
Total current assets		2,764,997	2,695,647
Non-current assets			
Property and equipment	15	1,717,993	1,767,543
Investment property	15	16,379	16,372
Goodwill	16	2,572,707	2,499,722
Intangible assets	17	339,972	281,737
Other assets	18	22,824	18,214
Deferred tax assets	14	38,849	21,075
Total non-current assets		4,708,724	4,604,663
Total assets		$ 7,473,721	$ 7,300,310
Liabilities			
Bank indebtedness	19	$ 170,927	$ 172,262
Commercial paper	19	249,977	–
Accounts payable and accrued liabilities	18	1,206,748	1,109,444
Income taxes payable		17,994	26,538
Dividends payable	24	54,180	53,119
Current portion of long-term debt	20	449,798	249,971
Provisions	22	10,926	12,024
Associate interest		174,367	152,880
Total current liabilities		2,334,917	1,776,238
Long-term debt	20	247,009	695,675
Other long-term liabilities	23	517,323	520,188
Provisions	22	4,273	1,701
Deferred tax liabilities	14	46,872	38,678
Total long-term liabilities		815,477	1,256,242
Total liabilities		3,150,394	3,032,480
Shareholders' equity			
Share capital	24	1,431,315	1,486,455
Treasury shares	24	–	(4,735)
Contributed surplus	26	10,856	10,246
Accumulated other comprehensive loss	7	(35,192)	(30,214)
Retained earnings		2,916,348	2,806,078
Total shareholders' equity		4,323,327	4,267,830
Total liabilities and shareholders' equity		$ 7,473,721	$ 7,300,310

The accompanying notes are an integral part of these consolidated financial statements.

On behalf of the Board of Directors:

Domenic Pilla
Director

Holger Kluge
Director

Consolidated Statements of Changes in Shareholders' Equity

For the 52 weeks ended December 29, 2012 and December 31, 2011
(in thousands of Canadian dollars)

	Note	Share Capital	Treasury Shares	Contributed Surplus	Accumulated Other Comprehensive Loss (Notes 7, 18 and 21)	Retained Earnings	Total
Balance as at December 31, 2011		$ 1,486,455	$ (4,735)	$ 10,246	$ (30,214)	$ 2,806,078	$ 4,267,830
Total comprehensive income		–	–	–	(4,978)	608,481	603,503
Dividends	24	–	–	–	–	(219,793)	(219,793)
Share repurchases	24	(55,635)	–	–	–	(274,493)	(330,128)
Treasury shares cancelled	24	(810)	4,735	–	–	(3,925)	–
Share-based payments	26	–	–	789	–	–	789
Share options exercised	26	1,295	–	(179)	–	–	1,116
Repayment of share-purchase loans		10	–	–	–	–	10
Balance as at December 29, 2012		**$ 1,431,315**	**$ –**	**$ 10,856**	**$ (35,192)**	**$ 2,916,348**	**$ 4,323,327**
Balance as at January 1, 2011		$ 1,520,558	$ –	$ 11,702	$ (8,643)	$ 2,579,018	$ 4,102,635
Total comprehensive income		–	–	–	(21,571)	613,934	592,363
Dividends	24	–	–	–	–	(215,671)	(215,671)
Share repurchases	24	(35,576)	(4,735)	–	–	(171,203)	(211,514)
Share-based payments	26	–	–	(1,210)	–	–	(1,210)
Share options exercised	26	1,466	–	(246)	–	–	1,220
Repayment of share-purchase loans		7	–	–	–	–	7
Balance as at December 31, 2011		$ 1,486,455	$ (4,735)	$ 10,246	$ (30,214)	$ 2,806,078	$ 4,267,830

The accompanying notes are an integral part of these consolidated financial statements.

Consolidated Statements of Cash Flows

For the 52 weeks ended December 29, 2012 and December 31, 2011 (in thousands of Canadian dollars)	Note	2012	2011
Cash flows from operating activities			
Net earnings		$ 608,481	$ 613,934
Adjustments for:			
Depreciation and amortization	13	318,341	296,464
Finance expenses	12	57,595	64,038
(Gain) loss on sale or disposal of property and equipment and intangible assets	13	(5,746)	2,015
Share-based payment transactions	26	789	(1,210)
Recognition and reversal of provisions, net	22	17,419	9,218
Other long-term liabilities	23	(1,298)	296
Income tax expense	14	214,845	232,933
		1,210,426	1,217,688
Net change in non-cash working capital balances	27	15,458	32,166
Provisions used	22	(15,945)	(9,907)
Interest paid		(62,712)	(63,853)
Income tax paid		(230,411)	(202,256)
Net cash from operating activities		916,816	973,838
Cash flows from investing activities			
Proceeds from disposition of property and equipment		50,724	55,459
Business acquisitions	8	(129,454)	(10,496)
Deposits		(8,217)	105
Acquisition and development of property and equipment	15	(254,259)	(341,868)
Acquisition and development of intangible assets	17	(54,385)	(53,836)
Other assets		517	1,464
Net cash used in investing activities		(395,074)	(349,172)
Cash flows from financing activities			
Repurchase of own shares	24	(334,863)	(206,779)
Proceeds from exercise of share options	26	1,116	1,220
Repayment of share-purchase loans	24	10	7
Bank indebtedness, net	19	(1,372)	(36,714)
Issuance (repayment) of commercial paper, net	19	250,000	(128,000)
Repayment of long-term debt	20	(250,000)	–
Revolving term debt, net	20	(152)	152
Payment of transaction costs for debt refinancing	20	(380)	(575)
Repayment of financing lease obligations	23	(2,893)	(2,173)
Associate interest		21,487	13,887
Dividends paid	24	(218,732)	(211,479)
Net cash used in financing activities		(535,779)	(570,454)
Net (decrease) increase in cash		(14,037)	54,212
Cash, beginning of period		118,566	64,354
Cash, end of period		$ 104,529	$ 118,566

The accompanying notes are an integral part of these consolidated financial statements.

Notes to the Consolidated Financial Statements

December 29, 2012 and December 31, 2011 (in thousands of Canadian dollars, except per share data)

1. GENERAL INFORMATION

Shoppers Drug Mart Corporation (the "Company") is a public company incorporated and domiciled in Canada, whose shares are publicly traded on the Toronto Stock Exchange. The Company's registered address is 243 Consumers Road, Toronto, Ontario, M2J 4W8, Canada.

The Company is a licensor of 1,240 Shoppers Drug Mart®/Pharmaprix® full-service retail drug stores across Canada. The Shoppers Drug Mart®/Pharmaprix® stores are licensed to corporations owned by pharmacists ("Associates"). The Company also licenses or owns 55 Shoppers Simply Pharmacy®/Pharmaprix Simplement Santé® medical clinic pharmacies and six Murale™ beauty stores. In addition, the Company owns and operates 62 Shoppers Home Health Care® stores. In addition to its store network, the Company owns Shoppers Drug Mart Specialty Health Network Inc., a provider of specialty drug distribution, pharmacy and comprehensive patient support services, and MediSystem Technologies Inc., a provider of pharmaceutical products and services to long-term care facilities.

The majority of the Company's sales are generated from the Shoppers Drug Mart®/Pharmaprix® full-service retail drug stores and the majority of the Company's assets are used in the operations of these stores. As such, the Company presents one operating segment in its consolidated financial statement disclosures. The revenue generated by Shoppers Simply Pharmacy®/Pharmaprix Simplement Santé®, MediSystem Technologies Inc. and Shoppers Drug Mart Specialty Health Network Inc. is included with prescription sales of the Company's retail drug stores. The revenue generated by Shoppers Home Health Care® and Murale™ is included with the front store sales of the Company's retail drug stores.

These consolidated financial statements of the Company as at and for the financial year ended December 29, 2012 include the accounts of Shoppers Drug Mart Corporation, its subsidiaries, and the Associate-owned stores that comprise the majority of the Company's store network. The financial year of the Company consists of a 52 or 53 week period ending on the Saturday closest to December 31. The current financial year is the 52 weeks ended December 29, 2012. The comparative financial year is the 52 weeks ended December 31, 2011.

2. BASIS OF PREPARATION

(a) Statement of Compliance

These consolidated financial statements have been prepared in accordance with Canadian generally accepted accounting principles applicable to publicly accountable enterprises ("Canadian GAAP"). These consolidated financial statements also comply with International Financial Reporting Standards ("IFRS") as issued by the International Accounting Standards Board ("IASB").

These consolidated financial statements were authorized for issuance by the Board of Directors of the Company on February 7, 2013.

(b) Use of Estimates and Judgements

The preparation of these consolidated financial statements in conformity with Canadian GAAP requires management to make certain judgements, estimates and assumptions that affect the application of accounting policies and the reported amounts of assets and liabilities and disclosure of contingent assets and liabilities at the date of these consolidated financial statements and the reported amounts of revenues and expenses during the reporting period.

Judgement is commonly used in determining whether a balance or transaction should be recognized in the consolidated financial statements and estimates and assumptions are more commonly used in determining the measurement of recognized transactions and balances. However, judgements and estimates are often interrelated.

The Company has applied judgement in its assessment of the appropriateness of the consolidation of the Associate-owned stores, classification of items such as leases and financial instruments, recognition of tax losses and provisions, determination of the tax rates used for measuring deferred taxes, determination of cash-generating units, identification of the indicators of impairment for property and equipment and intangible assets with finite useful lives, and the level of componentization of property and equipment. Further information on these judgements can be found in the significant accounting policies and relevant notes.

Estimates are used when determining the useful lives of property and equipment and intangible assets for the purpose of depreciation and amortization, when accounting for or measuring items such as inventory provisions, Shoppers Optimum® Loyalty Card Program deferred revenue, assumptions underlying the actuarial determination of retirement benefit obligations, income and other taxes, provisions, certain fair value measures including those related to the valuation of business combinations, share-based payments and financial instruments and when testing goodwill, indefinite useful life intangible assets and other assets for impairment. Actual results may differ from these estimates.

Management does not believe that any reasonable deviation from these judgements and estimates would have a material impact on these consolidated financial statements. Estimates and underlying assumptions are reviewed on an ongoing basis. Revisions to accounting estimates are recognized in the period in which the estimates are revised and in any future periods affected.

3. SIGNIFICANT ACCOUNTING POLICIES

The accounting policies set out in these consolidated financial statements have been applied consistently to all periods presented in these consolidated financial statements.

(a) Basis of Consolidation

(i) Subsidiaries

Subsidiaries are entities controlled by the Company. Control exists where the Company has the power to govern the financial and operating policies of an entity so as to obtain benefits from its activities. All of the Company's subsidiaries are wholly owned. The financial statements of subsidiaries are included in the Company's consolidated financial statements from the date that control commences until the date that control ceases.

(ii) Associate-owned Stores

Associate-owned stores comprise the majority of the Company's store network. The Company does not have any direct or indirect shareholdings in the corporations (the "Associates' corporations") that operate the Associate-owned stores. The Associates' corporations remain separate legal entities. The Company consolidates the Associate-owned stores under IAS 27, "Consolidated and Separate Financial Statements" ("IAS 27"). The consolidation of the stores under IAS 27 was determined based on the concept of control under IAS 27 and determined primarily through the Company's agreements with Associates that govern the relationship between the Company and the Associates.

(iii) Transactions Eliminated on Consolidation

Intra-company balances and transactions and any unrealized earnings and expenses arising from intra-company transactions, including those of the Associate-owned stores, are eliminated in preparing the consolidated financial statements.

(b) Basis of Measurement

These consolidated financial statements have been prepared on the historical cost basis except for certain financial instruments, deferred revenue related to the Shoppers Optimum® Loyalty Card Program and the liability for the Company's restricted share unit plan, which are measured at fair value (see Note 26 to these consolidated financial statements for further information on the restricted share unit plan). Any recognized impairment losses will also impact the historical cost of certain balances.

The methods used to measure fair values are discussed further in Note 4 to these consolidated financial statements.

(c) Revenue

(i) Sale of Goods and Services

Revenue is comprised primarily of retail sales, including prescription sales. Retail sales are recognized as revenue when the goods are sold to the customer. Revenue is net of returns and amounts deferred related to the issuance of points under the Shoppers Optimum® Loyalty Card Program (the "Program"). Where a sales transaction includes points awarded under the Program, revenue allocated to the Program points is deferred based on the fair value of the awards and recognized as revenue when the Program points are redeemed and the Company fulfills its obligations to supply the awards.

Revenue is measured at the fair value of the consideration received or receivable from the customer for products sold or services supplied.

(ii) Shoppers Optimum® Loyalty Card Program

The Shoppers Optimum® Loyalty Card Program allows members to earn points on their purchases in Shoppers Drug Mart®, Pharmaprix®, Shoppers Simply Pharmacy®, Pharmaprix Simplement Santé®, Shoppers Home Health Care® and Murale™ stores at a rate of 10 points for each dollar spent on eligible products and services, plus any applicable bonus points. Members can then redeem points, in accordance with the Program rewards schedule or other offers, for qualifying merchandise at the time of a future purchase transaction.

When points are earned by Program members, the Company defers revenue equal to the fair value of the awards. The Program's deferred revenue is recognized within accounts payable and accrued liabilities in the Company's consolidated balance sheets. When awards are redeemed by Program members, the redemption value of the awards is charged against the deferred revenue balance and recognized as revenue.

The estimated fair value per point is determined based on the expected weighted average redemption levels for future redemptions based on the Program reward schedule, including special redemption events. The trends in redemption rates (points redeemed as a percentage of points issued) are reviewed on an ongoing basis and the estimated fair value per point is adjusted based upon expected future activity.

(d) Vendor Rebates

The Company classifies rebates and other consideration received from vendors as a reduction to the cost of inventory. These amounts are recognized in cost of goods sold when the associated inventory is sold. Certain exceptions apply where the consideration received from the vendor is a reimbursement of a selling cost or a payment for services delivered to the vendor, in which case the consideration is reflected in cost of goods sold or operating and administrative expenses depending on where the related expenses are recorded.

(e) Finance Expenses

Finance expenses are comprised of interest expense on borrowings, net of amounts capitalized, and the amortization of transaction costs incurred in conjunction with debt transactions. All borrowing costs are recognized in earnings on an accrual basis using the effective interest method, net of amounts capitalized as part of the cost of qualifying property and equipment.

The Company's finance income is not significant.

(f) Borrowing Costs

Borrowing costs that are directly attributable to the acquisition, construction or development of a qualifying asset are recognized as part of the cost of that asset. Qualifying assets are those that require a substantial period of time to prepare for their intended use. All other borrowing costs are recognized as finance expenses in the period in which they are incurred.

The Company capitalizes borrowing costs at the weighted average interest rate on borrowings outstanding for the period. The Company commences capitalization of borrowing costs as part of the cost of a qualifying asset when activities are undertaken to prepare the asset for its intended use and when expenditures, including borrowing costs, are incurred for the asset. Capitalization of borrowing costs ceases when substantially all of the activities necessary to prepare the asset for its intended use are complete.

(g) Income Taxes

Income tax expense is comprised of taxes currently payable on earnings and changes in deferred tax balances, excluding those changes related to business acquisitions. Income tax expense is recognized in net earnings except to the extent that it relates to items recognized either in other comprehensive income (loss) or directly in equity, in which case it is recognized in other comprehensive income (loss) or in equity, respectively.

Current tax expense is comprised of the tax payable on the taxable income for the current financial year based on tax standards and using tax rates that have been enacted or substantively enacted at the reporting date, and any adjustment to income taxes payable in respect of previous years.

Deferred tax is recognized using the balance sheet method in respect of taxable temporary differences arising from differences between the carrying amount of assets and liabilities for tax purposes and their carrying amounts in the financial statements. Deferred tax is calculated based on tax standards and using tax rates that are expected to apply to temporary differences in the year they are expected to reverse, and are based on the tax legislation that has been enacted or substantively enacted by the reporting date. Deferred tax is not recognized for the following temporary differences: the initial recognition of goodwill and the initial recognition of assets or liabilities in a transaction that is not a business acquisition and that affects neither accounting nor taxable earnings; and differences relating to investments in subsidiaries to the extent that it is probable that they will not reverse in the foreseeable future. Deferred tax assets and liabilities are offset if there is a legally enforceable right to offset the recognized amounts and the Company intends to settle on a net basis or to realize the asset and settle the liability simultaneously.

A deferred tax asset is recognized to the extent that it is probable that future taxable earnings will be available against which the temporary difference can be utilized. Deferred tax assets are reviewed at each reporting date and are reduced to the extent that it is no longer probable that all or part of the related tax benefit will be realized.

(h) Earnings per Common Share

The Company presents basic and diluted earnings per share ("EPS") amounts for its common shares. Basic EPS is calculated by dividing the net earnings attributable to common shareholders of the Company by the weighted average number of common shares outstanding during the period. Diluted EPS is determined by dividing the net earnings attributable to common shareholders of the Company by the weighted average number of common shares outstanding after adjusting both amounts for the effects of all potential dilutive common shares, which are comprised of share options granted to employees. Anti-dilutive options are not included in the calculation of diluted EPS.

(i) Financial Instruments

(i) Classification of Financial Instruments

Financial instruments are recognized when the Company becomes a party to the contractual provisions of a financial instrument. Financial instruments are classified into one of the following categories: held for trading, held-to-maturity investments, loans and receivables, available-for-sale financial assets, or financial liabilities. The classification determines the accounting treatment of the instrument. The classification is determined by the Company when the financial instrument is initially recorded, based on the underlying purpose of the instrument.

The Company's financial instruments are classified and measured as follows:

Financial Asset/Liability	Category	Measurement
Cash	Loans and receivables	Amortized cost
Accounts receivable	Loans and receivables	Amortized cost
Deposits[1]	Loans and receivables	Amortized cost
Long-term receivables[2]	Loans and receivables	Amortized cost
Bank indebtedness	Financial liabilities	Amortized cost
Commercial paper	Financial liabilities	Amortized cost
Accounts payable and accrued liabilities	Financial liabilities	Amortized cost
Dividends payable	Financial liabilities	Amortized cost
Long-term debt	Financial liabilities	Amortized cost
Other long-term liabilities	Financial liabilities	Amortized cost

Derivatives	Classification	Measurement
Equity forward derivatives[3][4]	Derivative financial instrument	Fair value through earnings
Equity forward derivatives[3][4]	Effective cash flow hedge	Fair value through other comprehensive income (loss)

[1] The carrying value of deposits is recognized within prepaid expenses and deposits in the consolidated balance sheets.
[2] The carrying value of long-term receivables is recognized within other assets in the consolidated balance sheets.
[3] The carrying values of the Company's derivatives are recognized within other assets, accounts payable and accrued liabilities and other long-term liabilities in the consolidated balance sheets.
[4] The portion of the equity forward derivative agreements relating to the earned restricted share unit plan units is considered a derivative financial instrument. The portion of the equity forward derivative agreements relating to the unearned restricted share unit plan units is considered an effective cash flow hedge. See Note 26 to these consolidated financial statements for further discussion of the restricted share unit plan.

Financial instruments measured at amortized cost are initially recognized at fair value and then subsequently at amortized cost using the effective interest method, less any impairment losses, with gains and losses recognized in earnings in the period in which the gain or loss occurs. Changes in the fair value of the Company's derivative instruments designated as effective cash flow hedges are recognized in other comprehensive income (loss) and changes in derivative instruments not designated as effective hedges are recognized within operating and administrative expenses in the Company's consolidated statements of earnings in the period of the change.

The Company categorizes its financial assets and financial liabilities that are recognized in the consolidated balance sheets at fair value using the fair value hierarchy. The fair value hierarchy has the following levels:

• Level 1 – quoted market prices in active markets for identical assets or liabilities;

• Level 2 – inputs other than quoted market prices included in Level 1 that are observable for the asset or liability, either directly (as prices) or indirectly (derived from prices); and

• Level 3 – unobservable inputs such as inputs for the asset or liability that are not based on observable market data.

The level in the fair value hierarchy within which the fair value measurement is categorized in its entirety is determined on the basis of the lowest level input that is significant to the fair value measurement in its entirety.

(ii) Transaction Costs

Transaction costs are added to the initial fair value of financial assets and liabilities when those financial assets and liabilities are not measured at fair value subsequent to initial measurement. Transaction costs are amortized to net earnings, within finance expenses, using the effective interest method.

(iii) Derivative Financial Instruments and Hedge Accounting

The Company is exposed to fluctuations in interest rates by virtue of its borrowings under its bank credit facilities, commercial paper program and financing programs available to its Associates. Increases and decreases in interest rates will negatively or positively impact the financial performance of the Company. The Company may use, from time to time, interest rate derivatives to manage this exposure. The earnings or expense arising from the use of these instruments are recognized within finance expenses for the financial year.

The Company uses cash-settled equity forward agreements to limit its exposure to future price changes in the Company's share price for share unit awards under the Company's restricted share unit plan ("RSU Plan"). The earnings or expense arising from the use of these instruments are included in other comprehensive income (loss) and in operating and administrative expenses, based on the amounts considered to be an effective hedge or a derivative, respectively, for the financial year. See Note 26 to these consolidated financial statements for further discussion of the RSU Plan.

The Company formally identifies, designates, and documents all relationships between hedging instruments and hedged items, as well as its risk assessment objective and strategy for undertaking various hedge transactions. The Company assesses, both at the inception of the hedge and on an ongoing basis, including on re-designation, whether the derivatives that are used in hedging transactions are highly effective in offsetting changes in fair values or cash flows of hedged items. When such derivative instruments cease to exist or to be effective as hedges, or when designation of a hedging relationship is terminated, any associated deferred gains or losses are recognized in earnings in the same period as the corresponding gains or losses associated with the hedged item. When a hedged item ceases to exist, any associated deferred gains or losses are recognized in earnings in the period the hedged item ceases to exist.

(iv) Embedded Derivatives

Embedded derivatives (elements of contracts whose cash flows move independently from the host contract) are required to be separated and measured at their respective fair values unless certain criteria are met. The Company does not have any significant embedded features in contractual arrangements that require separate accounting or presentation from the related host contracts.

(v) Share Capital

Common Shares   Common shares issued by the Company are recorded in the amount of the proceeds received, net of direct issue costs.

Repurchase of Share Capital   The Company, from time to time, will repurchase its common shares under a normal course issuer bid. When common shares are repurchased, the amount of the consideration paid, which includes directly attributable costs, is recognized as a deduction from share capital. Any repurchased common shares are cancelled. The premium paid over the average book value of the common shares repurchased is charged to retained earnings. At the end of a reporting period, if there are shares that have not yet been cancelled, they are recognized as treasury shares at the purchase price of the transaction.

(j) Business Combinations

The Company applies the acquisition method in accounting for business combinations.

On acquisition, the assets, including intangible assets, and any liabilities assumed are measured at their fair value. Purchase price allocations may be preliminary when initially recognized and may change pending finalization of the valuation of the assets acquired. Purchase price allocations are finalized within one year of the acquisition and prior periods are restated to reflect any adjustments to the purchase price allocation made subsequent to the initial recognition.

The determination of fair values, particularly for intangible assets, is based on management's estimates and includes assumptions on the timing and amount of future cash flows. The Company recognizes as goodwill the excess of the purchase price of an acquired business over the fair value of the underlying net assets, including intangible assets, at the date of acquisition. Transaction costs are expensed as incurred. The date of acquisition is the date on which the Company obtains control over the acquired business.

(k) Inventory

Inventory is comprised of merchandise inventory, which includes prescription inventory, and is valued at the lower of cost and estimated net realizable value. Cost is determined on the first-in, first-out basis. Cost includes all direct expenditures and other appropriate costs incurred in bringing inventory to its present location and condition. The Company classifies rebates and other consideration received from a vendor as a reduction to the cost of inventory unless the rebate relates to the reimbursement of a selling cost or a payment for services.

Net realizable value is the estimated selling price in the ordinary course of business, less the estimated selling expenses.

(l) Property and Equipment and Investment Property

(i) Recognition and Measurement

Items of property and equipment are carried at cost less accumulated depreciation and any recognized impairment losses (see (p) Impairment).

Cost includes expenditures that are directly attributable to the acquisition of the asset. The cost of self-constructed assets includes the cost of materials and direct labour, any other costs directly attributable to bringing the assets to a working condition for their intended use, and, where applicable, the costs of dismantling and removing the items and restoring the site on which they are located. Borrowing costs are recognized as part of the cost of an asset, where appropriate.

Purchased software that is integral to the functionality of the related equipment is capitalized as part of that equipment.

When components of property and equipment have different useful lives, they are accounted for as separate items of property and equipment.

Gains and losses on disposal of an item of property and equipment are determined by comparing the proceeds from disposal with the carrying amount of property and equipment and are recognized net, within operating and administrative expenses, in net earnings.

Fully depreciated items of property and equipment that are still in use continue to be recognized in cost and accumulated depreciation.

(iii) Subsequent Costs

The cost of replacing part of an item of property and equipment is recognized in the carrying amount of the item if it is probable that the future economic benefits embodied within the part will flow to the Company and its cost can be measured reliably. The carrying amount of the replaced part is de-recognized. The costs of repairs and maintenance of property and equipment are recognized in earnings as incurred.

(iii) Depreciation

Depreciation is recognized in earnings on a straight-line basis over the estimated useful lives of each component of an item of property and equipment. Land is not depreciated. The Company commences recognition of depreciation in earnings when the item of property and equipment is ready for its intended use.

The estimated useful lives for the current and comparative periods are as follows:

Buildings and their components	10 to 40 years
Equipment and fixtures	3 to 10 years
Computer equipment	2 to 10 years
Leasehold improvements	Lesser of term of the lease and useful life
Assets under financing leases	Lesser of term of the lease and useful life

Depreciation methods and useful lives are reviewed at each reporting date.

(iv) Investment Property

Investment property is carried at cost less accumulated depreciation and any recognized impairment losses.

(m) Goodwill

(i) Recognition and Measurement

The Company recognizes goodwill as the excess amount of the purchase price of an acquired business over the fair value of the underlying net assets, including intangible assets, at the date of acquisition. Goodwill is not amortized but is tested for impairment on an annual basis or more frequently if there are indicators that goodwill may be impaired (see (p) Impairment).

(ii) Acquisitions Prior to January 3, 2010

As part of its transition to IFRS, the Company elected to apply IFRS 3, "Business Combinations" ("IFRS 3"), only to those business combinations that occurred on or after January 3, 2010. In respect of acquisitions prior to January 3, 2010, goodwill represents the amount recognized under previous Canadian GAAP.

(iii) Subsequent Measurement

Goodwill is measured at cost less any accumulated impairment losses.

(n) Intangible Assets

(i) Computer Software

The Company acquires computer software through purchases from vendors and internal development. Computer software that is an integral part of computer equipment is presented in property and equipment. All other computer software is treated as an intangible asset. The Company includes computer software under development in intangible assets. The assessment of whether computer software is an integral part of computer hardware is made when the software development project is complete and placed into use. Costs for internally developed computer software include directly attributable costs including direct labour and overheads associated with the software development project. Expenditures on research activities as part of internally developed computer software are recognized in earnings when incurred.

(ii) Other Intangible Assets

Other intangible assets that are acquired by the Company, other than as a result of a business acquisition, which have finite useful lives, are measured at cost less accumulated amortization and any accumulated impairment losses (see (p) Impairment). Other intangible assets that are acquired by the Company as a result of a business acquisition are measured at their fair values as at the date of acquisition.

(iii) Amortization

Amortization is recognized in earnings on a straight-line basis over the estimated useful lives of intangible assets from the date that they are available for their intended use. The estimated useful lives are as follows:

Prescription files	7 to 12 years
Customer relationships	5 to 25 years
Computer software	3 to 10 years
Other	Term of the lease or 3 years

Computer software under development is not amortized. Amortization methods and useful lives are reviewed at each reporting date.

(o) Leases

The Company leases most of its store locations and office space. Terms vary in length and typically permit renewal for additional periods. Leases for which substantially all the benefits and risks of ownership are transferred to the Company, based on certain criteria, are recorded as financing leases and classified as property and equipment, accounts payable and accrued liabilities and other long-term liabilities. All other leases are classified as operating leases, under which minimum rent, including scheduled escalations, is expensed on a straight-line basis over the term of the lease, including any rent-free periods. Landlord inducements are deferred and amortized as reductions to rent expense on a straight-line basis over the same period.

In the normal course of business, the Company sells certain real estate properties and enters into leaseback arrangements for the area occupied by the Associate-owned stores. The leases are assessed as financing or operating in nature, as applicable, and are accounted for accordingly. The gains realized on the disposal of the real estate properties related to sale-leaseback transactions, which are financing in nature, are deferred and amortized on a straight-line basis over the shorter of the lease term and the estimated useful life of the leased asset. The gains realized on the disposal of real estate properties related to sale-leaseback transactions, which are transacted at fair value and are operating in nature, are recognized within operating and administrative expenses in the consolidated statements of earnings. In the event that the fair value of the asset at the time of the sale-leaseback transaction is less than its carrying value, the difference would be recognized within operating and administrative expenses in the consolidated statements of earnings.

Leases may include additional payments for real estate taxes, maintenance and insurance. These amounts are expensed in the period to which they relate.

(p) Impairment

(i) Financial Assets

A financial asset is assessed at each reporting date to determine whether there is any objective evidence that it is impaired. A financial asset is considered to be impaired if objective evidence indicates that one or more events, which have a negative effect on the estimated future cash flows of that asset, have occurred.

An impairment loss in respect of a financial asset measured at amortized cost is calculated as the difference between its carrying amount and the present value of the estimated future cash flows, discounted at the original effective interest rate.

Individually significant financial assets are tested for impairment on an individual basis. The remaining financial assets are assessed collectively in groups that share similar credit risk characteristics.

All impairment losses are recognized in the consolidated statements of earnings.

An impairment loss is reversed if the reversal can be objectively related to an event occurring after the impairment loss was recognized. For financial assets measured at amortized cost, the reversal is recognized in earnings.

(ii) Property and Equipment and Intangible Assets with Finite Useful Lives

The carrying amount of property and equipment and intangible assets with finite useful lives is reviewed at each reporting date to determine whether there are any indicators of impairment. If any such indicators exist, then the recoverable amount of the asset is estimated as the higher of the fair value of the asset, less costs to sell, or value-in-use. An impairment loss is recognized in net earnings for the amount by which the carrying amount of the asset exceeds its recoverable amount. For the purposes of assessing impairment, when an individual asset does not generate cash flows in and of itself, assets are then grouped and tested at the lowest level for which there are separately identifiable cash flows, called a cash-generating unit. The Company has determined that its cash-generating units are primarily its retail stores.

(iii) Goodwill and Intangible Assets with Indefinite Useful Lives

For goodwill and intangible assets that have indefinite useful lives or that are not yet available for use, the carrying value is reviewed for impairment on an annual basis, or more frequently if there are indicators that impairment may exist.

Goodwill allocated to cash-generating units that are expected to benefit from the synergies created from a business combination and to the lowest level at which management monitors goodwill. To review for impairment, the recoverable amount of each cash-generating unit to which goodwill is allocated is compared to its carrying value, including goodwill.

(iv) Recoverable Amount

The recoverable amount of an asset or cash-generating unit is the greater of its value-in-use and its fair value less costs to sell. In assessing value-in-use, the estimated future cash flows are discounted to their present value using a pre-tax discount rate that reflects current market assessments of the time value of money and the risks specific to the asset.

(v) Impairment Losses

An impairment loss is recognized if the carrying amount of an asset or its cash-generating unit exceeds its estimated recoverable amount. Impairment losses are recognized in operating and administrative expenses in the consolidated statements of earnings. Impairment losses recognized in respect of cash-generating units are allocated first to reduce the carrying amount of any goodwill allocated to the cash-generating units and, then, to reduce the carrying amounts of the other assets in the cash-generating unit (group of cash-generating units) on a pro rata basis.

An impairment loss in respect of goodwill is not reversed. In respect of other assets, impairment losses recognized in prior periods are assessed at each reporting date for any indicators that the loss has decreased or no longer exists. An impairment loss is reversed if there has been a change in the estimates used to determine the recoverable amount. An impairment loss is reversed only to the extent to which the carrying amount of the asset does not exceed the carrying amount that would have been determined, net of depreciation or amortization, if no impairment loss had been recognized.

(q) Bank Indebtedness

Bank indebtedness is comprised of corporate bank overdraft balances, corporate and Associate-owned store bank lines of credit and outstanding cheques.

(r) Employee Benefits

(i) Defined Benefit Plans

The Company maintains registered defined benefit pension plans under which benefits are available to certain employee groups. The Company also makes supplementary retirement benefits available to certain employees under a non-registered defined benefit pension plan.

The Company accrues for its defined benefit plans under the following policies:

• The cost of pensions and other retirement benefits earned by employees is actuarially determined using the projected unit credit method (also known as the projected benefit method pro-rated on service) and management's best estimate of expected plan investment performance, salary escalation, retirement ages of employees and their expected future longevity.

• For the purposes of calculating the expected return on plan assets, those assets are valued at fair value.

• The Company recognizes actuarial gains and losses in other comprehensive income (loss) in the period in which those gains and losses occur.

The pension plans are funded through contributions based on actuarial cost methods as permitted by applicable pension regulatory bodies. Benefits under these plans are based on the employees' years of service and final average earnings.

(ii) Defined Contribution Plan

The Company maintains a defined contribution plan for a small number of employees. Required contributions are recognized as an expense when the employees have rendered service.

(iii) Other Long-term Employee Benefits

The Company maintains post-employment benefit plans, other than pensions, covering benefits such as health and life insurance for certain retirees. The cost of these plans is charged to earnings as benefits are earned by employees on the basis of service rendered.

(s) Share-based Payment Transactions

The grant-date fair value of stock options granted to employees is recognized as employee compensation expense, with a corresponding increase in equity, over the period that the employees become unconditionally entitled to the options. Fair value is measured using the Black-Scholes option-pricing model. The amount expensed is adjusted for estimated future forfeitures of all options. For amounts that have been recognized related to options not yet vested that are subsequently forfeited, the amounts recognized as expenses and equity are reversed.

The fair value of the amount payable to employees in respect of cash-settled share-based payments is recognized as an expense, with a corresponding increase in liabilities, over the period that the employees become unconditionally entitled to payment. The fair value of the liability is re-measured at each reporting date and at settlement date. Any changes in the fair value of the liability are recognized within operating and administrative expenses in the consolidated statements of earnings.

(t) Provisions

Provisions are recognized when there is a present legal or constructive obligation as a result of a past event, it is probable that an outflow of economic benefits will be required to settle the obligation, and that obligation can be measured reliably. If the effect of the time value of money is material, provisions are discounted using a current pre-tax rate that reflects the risks specific to the liability. Provisions are reviewed on a regular basis and adjusted to reflect management's best current estimates. Due to the judgemental nature of these items, future settlements may differ from amounts recognized. Provisions are comprised of estimated insurance claims, litigation settlements and store closing costs.

(i) Insurance Claims

The insurance claim provision is management's best estimate of future payments for current insurance claims that are below the Company's deductible limits and is based on determinations made by an independent insurance adjuster. The timing of utilization of the provision will vary according to the individual claims.

(ii) Litigation Claims

A provision for legal claims is recognized when it is probable that a settlement will be made in respect of a claim.

(iii) Store Closing Costs

The Company records a provision for store closings when it vacates current leased-store locations and relocates.

(u) Associate Interest

Associate interest reflects the investment the Associates have in the net assets of their businesses. Under the terms of the Company's agreements with Associates (the "Associate Agreements"), the Company agrees to purchase the assets that the Associates use in store operations, primarily at the carrying value to the Associate, when Associate Agreements are terminated by either party.

(v) New Accounting Standards and Interpretations

The Company adopted the following new standards in preparing these annual financial statements:

(i) Financial Instruments – Disclosures

The IASB issued an amendment to IFRS 7, "Financial Instruments: Disclosures" ("IFRS 7 amendment"), requiring incremental disclosures regarding transfers of financial assets. This amendment is effective for annual periods beginning on or after July 1, 2011. The application of this amendment did not have a significant impact on the Company's disclosures.

(ii) Deferred Taxes – Recovery of Underlying Assets

The IASB issued an amendment to IAS 12, "Income Taxes" ("IAS 12 amendment"), which introduced an exception to the general measurement requirements of IAS 12 with respect to investment properties measured at fair value. The IAS 12 amendment is effective for annual periods beginning on or after January 1, 2012. The application of this amendment did not have a significant impact on the Company's results of operations, financial position and disclosures.

(w) New Accounting Standards and Interpretations Not Yet Adopted

A number of new standards, amendments to standards and interpretations have been issued but are not yet effective for the financial year ended December 29, 2012, and, accordingly, have not been applied in preparing these consolidated financial statements:

(i) Fair Value Measurement

The IASB has issued a new standard, IFRS 13, "Fair Value Measurement" ("IFRS 13"), which provides a standard definition of fair value, sets out a framework for measuring fair value and provides for specific disclosures about fair value measurements. IFRS 13 applies to all International Financial Reporting Standards that require or permit fair value measurements or disclosures. IFRS 13 defines fair value as the price that would be received to sell an asset or paid to transfer a liability in an orderly transaction between market participants at the measurement date. IFRS 13 is effective for annual periods beginning on or after January 1, 2013 and must be applied retrospectively. The Company is assessing the impact of IFRS 13 on its results of operations, financial position and disclosures.

(ii) Consolidated Financial Statements

The IASB has issued a new standard, IFRS 10, "Consolidated Financial Statements" ("IFRS 10"), which establishes the principles for the presentation and preparation of consolidated financial statements when an entity controls one or more other entities. IFRS 10 establishes control as the basis for consolidation and defines the principle of control. An investor controls an investee if the investor has power over the investee, exposure or rights to variable returns from its involvement with the investee and the ability to use its power over the investee to affect the amount of the investor's returns. IFRS 10 was issued as part of the IASB's broader project on interests in all types of entities. This project also resulted in the issuance of additional standards as described in (iii) to (vi) below. IFRS 10 is effective for annual periods beginning on or after January 1, 2013 and must be applied retrospectively. The Company is assessing the impact of IFRS 10 on its results of operations, financial position and disclosures.

(iii) Joint Arrangements

The IASB has issued a new standard, IFRS 11, "Joint Arrangements" ("IFRS 11"), which establishes the principles for financial reporting by parties to a joint arrangement. IFRS 11 supersedes IAS 31, "Interests in Joint Ventures", and SIC Interpretation 13, "Jointly Controlled Entities – Non-Monetary Contributions by Venturers". The standard defines a joint arrangement as an arrangement where two or more parties have joint control, with joint control being defined as the contractually agreed sharing of control where decisions about relevant activities require unanimous consent of the parties sharing control. The standard classifies joint arrangements as either joint operations or joint investments, and the classification determines the accounting treatment. IFRS 11 is effective for annual periods beginning on or after January 1, 2013 and must be applied retrospectively. The Company is assessing the impact of IFRS 11 on its results of operations, financial position and disclosures.

(iv) Disclosure of Interests in Other Entities

The IASB has issued a new standard, IFRS 12, "Disclosure of Interests in Other Entities" ("IFRS 12"), which integrates and provides consistent disclosure requirements for all interests in other entities such as subsidiaries, joint arrangements, associates and unconsolidated structured entities. IFRS 12 is effective for annual periods beginning on or after January 1, 2013 and must be applied retrospectively. The Company is assessing the impact of IFRS 12 on its disclosures.

(v) Separate Financial Statements

The IASB has issued a revised standard, IAS 27, "Separate Financial Statements" ("IAS 27"), which contains the accounting and disclosure requirements for investments in subsidiaries, joint ventures and associates when an entity prepares separate (non-consolidated) financial statements. IAS 27 is effective for annual periods beginning on or after January 1, 2013 and must be applied retrospectively. IAS 27 will not have an impact on the Company's consolidated results of operations, financial position and disclosures.

(vi) Investments in Associates and Joint Ventures

The IASB has issued a revised standard, IAS 28, "Investments in Associates and Joint Ventures" ("IAS 28"), which prescribes the accounting for investments in associates and sets out the requirements for the application of the equity method when accounting for investments in associates and joint ventures. IAS 28 is effective for annual periods beginning on or after January 1, 2013 and must be applied retrospectively. The Company is assessing the impact of IAS 28 on its results of operations, financial position and disclosures.

(vii) Presentation of Financial Statements – Other Comprehensive Income

The IASB has issued an amendment to IAS 1, "Presentation of Financial Statements" ("IAS 1 amendment"), to improve consistency and clarity of the presentation of items of other comprehensive income. A requirement has been added to present items in other comprehensive income grouped on the basis of whether they may be subsequently reclassified to earnings in order to more clearly show the effects the items of other comprehensive income may have on future earnings. The IAS 1 amendment is effective for annual periods beginning on or after July 1, 2012 and must be applied retrospectively. The Company is assessing the impact of the IAS 1 amendment on its presentation of other comprehensive income.

(viii) Post-employment Benefits

The IASB has issued amendments to IAS 19, "Employee Benefits" ("IAS 19"), which eliminate the option to defer the recognition of actuarial gains and losses through the "corridor" approach, revise the presentation of changes in assets and liabilities arising from defined benefit plans and enhance the disclosures for defined benefit plans. IAS 19 is effective for annual periods beginning on or after January 1, 2013 and must be applied retrospectively. The Company is assessing the impact of IAS 19 on its results of operations, financial position and disclosures.

(ix) Financial Instruments

The IASB has issued a new standard, IFRS 9, "Financial Instruments" ("IFRS 9"), which will ultimately replace IAS 39, "Financial Instruments: Recognition and Measurement" ("IAS 39"). The replacement of IAS 39 is a multi-phase project with the objective of improving and simplifying the reporting for financial instruments, and the issuance of IFRS 9 is part of the first phase of this project. IFRS 9 uses a single approach to determine whether a financial asset or liability is measured at amortized cost or fair value, replacing the multiple rules in IAS 39. For financial assets, the approach in IFRS 9 is based on how an entity manages its financial instruments in the context of its business model and the contractual cash flow characteristics of the financial assets. IFRS 9 requires a single impairment method to be used, replacing multiple impairment methods in IAS 39. For financial liabilities measured at fair value, fair value changes due to changes in an entity's credit risk are presented in other comprehensive income. IFRS 9 is effective for annual periods beginning on or after January 1, 2015 and must be applied retrospectively. The Company is assessing the impact of IFRS 9 on its results of operations, financial position and disclosures.

(x) Financial Instruments – Asset and Liability Offsetting

The IASB has issued amendments to IFRS 7, "Financial Instruments: Disclosures" ("IFRS 7"), and IAS 32, "Financial Instruments: Presentation" ("IAS 32"), which clarify the requirements for offsetting financial instruments and require new disclosures on the effect of offsetting arrangements on an entity's financial position. The amendments to IFRS 7 are effective for annual periods beginning on or after January 1, 2013 and must be applied retrospectively. The amendments to IAS 32 are effective for annual periods beginning on or after January 1, 2014 and must be applied retrospectively. The Company is assessing the impact of the amendments to IFRS 7 and IAS 32 on its results of operations, financial position and disclosures.

8. BUSINESS ACQUISITIONS

Paragon Pharmacies Limited

On August 1, 2012, the Company acquired substantially all of the assets of Paragon Pharmacies Limited ("Paragon") for a cash purchase price of $72,059. The acquisition included 19 retail pharmacies and three central fill pharmacies in British Columbia, Alberta, and Manitoba.

The acquisition of Paragon will increase the Company's retail presence in Western Canada and provide a platform for the Company's MediSystem Technologies Inc. ("MediSystem") business to enter the British Columbia and Manitoba markets. In addition, this acquisition is consistent with the Company's stated growth objectives in retail pharmacy and long-term care.

The following table summarizes the consideration paid for Paragon, and the amounts recognized for the assets acquired and liabilities assumed at the acquisition date.

Fair value of net assets acquired as at acquisition date

Cash	$ 43
Accounts receivable (gross amount of $4,751, net of allowance of $430)	4,321
Inventory	7,906
Prepaid expenses	611
Property and equipment	4,929
Prescription files	20,000
Customer relationships	8,000
Accounts payable and accrued liabilities	(1,245)
Net assets acquired	44,565
Goodwill, net of deferred taxes	27,494
Total cash purchase price	72,059
Cash acquired	(43)
Purchase price, net of cash acquired	$ 72,016

The goodwill arising from this acquisition reflects the expected future growth potential arising from increased prescription script counts and the synergies expected following the integration of Paragon, as well as the opportunity to introduce the MediSystem business into two new provinces. The Company expects that $20,620 of the acquired goodwill will be deductible for tax purposes.

The Company has incurred acquisition costs of $797 relating primarily to external legal fees, consulting fees, and due diligence costs. These costs have been recognized within operating and administrative expenses in the consolidated statements of earnings.

The results of operations of Paragon have been included in the consolidated financial statements from August 1, 2012, the date of acquisition. The acquisition has added approximately $27,800 to the Company's sales since acquisition. If the acquisition had occurred on January 1, 2012, the Company estimates that for the 52 weeks ended December 29, 2012, sales would have increased by approximately $68,800.

Other Business Acquisitions

In the normal course of business, the Company acquires the assets or shares of pharmacies. The total cost of these acquisitions during the financial year ended December 29, 2012 was $57,438 (2011: $10,496).

The following table summarizes the consideration paid, and the amounts recognized for the assets acquired and liabilities assumed at the acquisition date.

Fair value of net assets acquired as at acquisition date

Accounts receivable	$ 205
Inventory	3,193
Prepaid expenses	12
Property and equipment	3,361
Prescription files	18,959
Other assets	456
Accounts payable and accrued liabilities	(610)
Net assets acquired	25,576
Goodwill, net of deferred taxes	31,862
Total purchase price	$ 57,438

The goodwill acquired represents the benefits the Company expects to receive from the acquisitions. See Note 16 to these consolidated financial statements for further details on goodwill.

The assets acquired and liabilities assumed have been valued at the acquisition date using fair values. See Note 4 to these consolidated financial statements for the methods used in determining fair values, except as discussed below. In determining the fair value of prescription files acquired, the Company applied a pre-tax discount rate of 9.0% (2011: 9.0%) to the estimated expected future cash flows.

The results of operations of the acquired pharmacies have been included in the Company's results of operations from the dates of acquisition. These acquisitions have added approximately $14,600 to the Company's sales since acquisition. If these acquisitions had occurred on January 1, 2012, the Company estimates that sales for the full year would have increased by approximately $54,300.

Funds Held in Escrow

As at December 29, 2012, the Company had amounts held in escrow of $8,217 (2011: $nil) with respect to a number of offers to acquire certain pharmacies. These amounts are recognized within the prepaid expenses and deposits balance in the consolidated balance sheets.

9. COST OF GOODS SOLD

During the current financial year, the Company recorded $44,334 (2011: $39,943) as an expense for the write-down of inventory as a result of net realizable value being lower than cost in cost of goods sold in the consolidated statements of earnings.

During the financial years ended December 29, 2012 and December 31, 2011, the Company did not reverse any significant inventory write-downs recognized in previous years.

13. DEPRECIATION AND AMORTIZATION EXPENSE

The components of the Company's depreciation and amortization expense, recognized within operating and administrative expenses, are as follows:

	Note	2012	2011
Property and equipment amortization	15	$ 263,134	$ 249,467
(Gain) loss on disposal of property and equipment	15	(6,508)	1,498
Investment property	15	336	325
Loss on disposal of investment property	15	85	–
Amortization of intangible assets	17	54,369	46,368
(Gain) loss on disposal of intangible assets	17	(8)	24
Depreciation and amortization expense		$ 311,408	$ 297,682
Depreciation and amortization expense		$ 311,408	$ 297,682
Amortization of intangible assets included separately in operating and administrative expenses	17	1,187	797
Amortization of deferred gains		(685)	(493)
Less: (Gain) loss on disposal		6,431	(1,522)
Depreciation and amortization for cash flow purposes		$ 318,341	$ 296,464
(Gain) loss on disposal		$ (6,431)	$ 1,522
Amortization of deferred gains		685	493
(Gain) loss on disposal for cash flow purposes		$ (5,746)	$ 2,015

During the financial years ended December 29, 2012 and December 31, 2011, the Company did not recognize any impairment losses on property and equipment, investment property, or intangible assets.

15. PROPERTY AND EQUIPMENT AND INVESTMENT PROPERTY

	Properties under Development	Land	Buildings	Equipment, Fixtures and Computer Equipment	Leasehold Improvements	Assets under Financing Leases (Note 23)	Total
Cost							
Balance at December 31, 2011	$ 71,342	$ 65,478	$ 214,043	$ 1,283,062	$ 1,291,445	$ 127,034	$ 3,052,404
Additions:							
– Business acquisitions	10,135	112	485	2,210	5,483	—	8,290
– Asset acquisitions						8,296	18,431
– Development	14,315	8,331	23,790	90,555	107,066		244,057
Transfers	(34,898)	15,098	16,319		3,481		—
Properties transferred to investment properties		(859)	(1,352)				(2,211)
Transfers (to) from intangible assets				902	(33,750)		(32,848)
Disposals		(18,555)	(19,750)	(57,919)	(18,135)	(625)	(114,984)
Retirements				192			192
Balance at December 29, 2012	$ 60,894	$ 69,605	$ 233,535	$ 1,319,002	$ 1,355,590	$ 134,705	$ 3,173,331
Depreciation							
Balance at December 31, 2011	$ —	$ —	$ 24,325	$ 776,387	$ 436,016	$ 16,411	$ 1,253,139
Depreciation for the financial year		11,542	145,408	99,416	6,768		263,134
Transfers							
Properties transferred to investment properties			(210)				(210)
Transfers (to) from intangible assets					(20,250)		(20,250)
Disposals			(2,915)	(49,596)	(11,125)		(63,636)
Retirements				(39)			(39)
Balance at December 29, 2012	$ —	$ —	$ 32,742	$ 872,160	$ 504,057	$ 23,179	$ 1,432,138
Impairment losses							
Balance at December 31, 2011	$ —	$ —	$ —	$ 16,257	$ 15,465	$ —	$ 31,722
Reduction of impairment loss associated with disposed assets				(3,947)	(4,575)		(8,522)
Balance at December 29, 2012	$ —	$ —	$ —	$ 12,310	$ 10,890	$ —	$ 23,200
Net book value at December 29, 2012	$ 60,894	$ 69,605	$ 200,793	$ 434,532	$ 840,643	$ 111,526	$ 1,717,993

	Properties under Development	Land	Buildings	Equipment, Fixtures and Computer Equipment	Leasehold Improvements	Assets under Financing Leases (Note 23)	Total
Cost							
Balance at January 1, 2011	$ 72,035	$ 70,411	$ 206,472	$ 1,135,805	$ 1,179,795	$ 83,082	$ 2,747,600
Additions:							
– Asset acquisitions	9,979					43,952	53,931
– Development	9,990	3,688	25,738	168,204	131,667		339,287
Transfers	(20,662)	6,147	8,791	752	320		(4,652)
Computer software transfers from intangible assets				1,330			1,330
Disposals		(14,768)	(26,958)	(23,563)	(20,337)		(85,626)
Retirements				534			534
Balance at December 31, 2011	$ 71,342	$ 65,478	$ 214,043	$ 1,283,062	$ 1,291,445	$ 127,034	$ 3,052,404
Depreciation							
Balance at January 1, 2011	$ —	$ —	$ 16,102	$ 655,467	$ 355,523	$ 11,446	$ 1,038,538
Depreciation for the financial year			11,542	140,537	92,423	4,965	249,467
Transfers			(216)	375	(123)		36
Computer software transfers from intangible assets				(18)			(18)
Disposals			(3,103)	(19,792)	(11,807)		(34,702)
Retirements				(182)			(182)
Balance at December 31, 2011	$ —	$ —	$ 24,325	$ 776,387	$ 436,016	$ 16,411	$ 1,253,139
Impairment losses							
Balance at January 1, 2011 and December 31, 2011	$ —	$ —	$ —	$ 16,257	$ 15,465	$ —	$ 31,722
Net book value at December 31, 2011	$ 71,342	$ 65,478	$ 189,718	$ 490,418	$ 839,964	$ 110,623	$ 1,767,543

Impairment Loss

During the financial years ended December 29, 2012 and December 31, 2011, the Company reviewed its long-lived assets for indicators of impairment at the cash-generating unit level and determined that an impairment test was not necessary.

During the financial years ended December 29, 2012 and December 31, 2011, the Company did not record any reversals of previously recorded impairment charges.

During the financial year ended December 29, 2012, the Company disposed of assets that had been previously impaired. As a result, the Company reduced the impairment loss associated with these assets by $8,522.

Property under Development

During the financial year ended December 29, 2012, the Company acquired properties with the intention of developing retail stores on the sites. The cost of acquisition was $10,135 (2011: $9,979).

Investment Property

Cost	2012			2011		
	Land	Buildings	Total	Land	Buildings	Total
Balance, beginning of financial year	$ 11,686	$ 6,320	$ 18,006	$ 8,084	$ 5,995	$ 14,079
Additions	63	7	70		327	
Transfers	859	1,352	2,211	4,325		4,652
Disposals	(1,507)	(271)	(1,778)	(723)	(2)	(725)
Balance, end of financial year	$ 11,101	$ 7,408	$ 18,509	$ 11,686	$ 6,320	$ 18,006
Amortization						
Balance, beginning of financial year	$ —	$ 1,634	$ 1,634	$ —	$ 1,309	$ 1,309
Amortization for the financial year	—	336	336	—	325	325
Disposals	—	(50)	(50)			
Transfers	—	210	210			
Balance, end of financial year	$ —	$ 2,130	$ 2,130	$ —	$ 1,634	$ 1,634
Net book value, end of financial year			$ 16,379			$ 16,372

The fair value of investment property approximates its carrying value.

16. GOODWILL

Cost	2012	2011
Balance, beginning of the financial year	$ 2,499,722	$ 2,493,108
Additions	72,985	10,496
Transfers		(3,882)
Balance, end of the financial year	$ 2,572,707	$ 2,499,722

Impairment Testing of Goodwill

For the purpose of impairment testing, goodwill is allocated to the group of cash-generating units which represent the lowest level within the group at which the goodwill is monitored for internal management purposes.

The aggregate carrying amounts of goodwill allocated to each unit are as follows:

	December 29, 2012	December 31, 2011
Goodwill allocated to the store network	$ 2,547,525	$ 2,474,540
Goodwill allocated to Shoppers Home Health Care®	25,182	25,182
	$ 2,572,707	$ 2,499,722

During the financial years ended December 29, 2012 and December 31, 2011, the Company performed impairment testing of goodwill in accordance with the Company's accounting policy. No impairment was identified.

The Company uses the value-in-use method for determining the recoverable amount of the group of cash-generating units to which goodwill is allocated. The values assigned to the key assumptions represent management's assessment of future trends in the retail and drug industry and are based on both external sources and internal sources (historical data). Key assumptions include comparable store sales growth, gross margin rates, changes in employee wages and benefits, occupancy cost changes and other operating expense changes. The Company has projected cash flows based on the most recent three-year budgets and forecasts. For the purposes of the impairment test, the Company has adjusted budgets and forecasts to reflect a steady growth assumption at the time the test was performed. Years four and five of the projection continue to reflect a steady growth rate, and terminal value growth of two percent after the fifth year is used for the present value calculation.

The Company has used a pre-tax discount rate of 9.0% (2011: 9.0%), which is based on the Company's weighted average cost of capital with appropriate adjustments for the risks associated with the group of cash-generating units to which goodwill is allocated and market data from a comparable industry grouping. Cash flow projections are discounted over a five-year period.

17. INTANGIBLE ASSETS

Cost	Note	Prescription Files	Customer Relationships	Computer Software	Computer Software under Development	Other	Total
Balance at December 31, 2011		$ 133,987	$ 50,736	$ 286,803	$ 21,675	$ 9,267	$ 502,468
Additions							
– Purchases		—	5,967	3,162	—	1,336	10,465
– Development		—	—	—	43,920	—	43,920
– Business acquisitions	8, 15	38,959	8,000	—	—	—	46,959
Transfers		—	33,750	40,740	(41,642)	—	32,848
Disposals	16	—	—	(159)	—	—	(159)
Balance at December 29, 2012		$ 172,946	$ 98,453	$ 330,546	$ 23,953	$ 10,603	$ 636,501
Amortization							
Balance at December 31, 2011	13	64,372	13,691	136,406	—	6,262	220,731
Amortization for the financial year		15,961	4,704	33,700	—	1,191	55,556
Transfers		—	20,250	—	—	—	20,250
Disposals		—	—	(8)	—	—	(8)
Balance at December 29, 2012		$ 80,333	$ 38,645	$ 170,098	$ —	$ 7,453	$ 296,529
Net book value at December 29, 2012		$ 92,613	$ 59,808	$ 160,448	$ 23,953	$ 3,150	$ 339,972

Cost	Note	Prescription Files	Customer Relationships	Computer Software	Computer Software under Development	Other	Total
Balance at January 1, 2011		$ 129,803	$ 43,600	$ 211,162	$ 52,412	$ 8,824	$ 445,801
Additions							
– Purchases		—	7,136	1,381	—	696	9,213
– Development		—	—	—	44,624	—	44,624
– Business acquisitions	8, 15	4,184	—	—	—	—	4,184
Transfers		—	—	74,260	(75,337)	(253)	(1,330)
Disposals	16	—	—	—	(24)	—	(24)
Balance at December 31, 2011		$ 133,987	$ 50,736	$ 286,803	$ 21,675	$ 9,267	$ 502,468
Amortization							
Balance at January 1, 2011	13	49,675	9,959	108,463	—	5,487	173,584
Amortization for the financial year		14,697	3,732	27,932	—	804	47,165
Transfers		—	—	11	—	(29)	(18)
Balance at December 31, 2011		$ 64,372	$ 13,691	$ 136,406	$ —	$ 6,262	$ 220,731
Net book value at December 31, 2011		$ 69,615	$ 37,045	$ 150,397	$ 21,675	$ 3,005	$ 281,737

The holders of common shares are entitled to receive dividends as declared from time to time and are entitled to one vote per share at meetings of the Company.

Normal Course Issuer Bid

On February 9, 2012, the Company renewed its normal course issuer bid providing for the repurchase, for cancellation, of up to 10,600,000 of its common shares, representing approximately 5.0% of the Company's then outstanding common shares. Repurchases will be effected through the facilities of the Toronto Stock Exchange (the "TSX") and may take place over a 12-month period ending no later than February 14, 2013. Repurchases will be made at market prices in accordance with the requirements of the TSX. The Company has entered into an automatic purchase plan with its designated broker to allow for purchases of its common shares during certain pre-determined black-out periods, subject to certain parameters as to price and number of shares. Outside of these pre-determined black-out periods, shares will be purchased at the Company's discretion, subject to applicable law. The Company's previous normal course issuer bid, which was implemented on February 10, 2011 and expired on February 14, 2012, provided for the repurchase, for cancellation, of up to 8,700,000 of its common shares, representing approximately 4.0% of the Company's then outstanding common shares.

During the financial year ended December 29, 2012, the Company purchased and cancelled 7,949,400 (2011: 5,086,200) common shares under its normal course issuer bid programs at a cost of $330,128 (2011: $206,779). The premium paid over the average book value of the shares repurchased of $274,493 (2011: $171,203) has been charged to retained earnings. During the financial year ended December 31, 2011, the Company purchased an additional 115,900 shares at a cost of $4,735. The cost of these latter purchases was recorded as treasury shares in shareholders' equity as at December 31, 2011 and the shares were cancelled subsequent to the end of the financial year.

Dividends

The following table provides a summary of the dividends declared by the Company:

Declaration Date	Record Date	Payment Date	Dividend per Common Share
February 9, 2012	March 30, 2012	April 13, 2012	$ 0.265
April 26, 2012	June 29, 2012	July 13, 2012	0.265
July 19, 2012	September 28, 2012	October 15, 2012	0.265
November 13, 2012	December 31, 2012	January 15, 2013	0.265
February 10, 2011	March 31, 2011	April 15, 2011	$ 0.250
April 27, 2011	June 30, 2011	July 15, 2011	0.250
July 21, 2011	September 30, 2011	October 14, 2011	0.250
November 9, 2011	December 30, 2011	January 13, 2012	0.250

On February 7, 2013, the Board of Directors declared a dividend of 28.5 cents per common share payable April 15, 2013 to shareholders of record as of the close of business on March 28, 2013.

Impairment Loss

During the financial years ended December 29, 2012 and December 31, 2011, the Company reviewed its finite life intangible assets for indicators of impairment at the cash-generating unit level and determined that an impairment test was not necessary. An impairment loss and any subsequent reversals, if any, are recognized within operating and administrative expenses in the consolidated statements of earnings.

---

19. BANK INDEBTEDNESS AND COMMERCIAL PAPER

Bank Indebtedness

The Associate-owned stores borrow under their bank line of credit agreements guaranteed by the Company. The Company has entered into agreements with banks to guarantee a total of $540,000 (2011: $520,000) of lines of credit. At December 29, 2012, the Associate-owned stores utilized $173,372 (2011: $166,592) of the available lines of credit.

Commercial Paper

Commercial paper is issued with maturities from overnight to 90 days at floating interest rates based on bankers' acceptance rates. On November 16, 2012, the Company amended its commercial paper program, increasing the amount available under the program from $500,000 to $600,000. The commercial paper program retained its rating of R-1(low) from DBRS Limited following this increase. No incremental debt was incurred by the Company as a result of this amendment.

24. SHARE CAPITAL

Share Capital and Contributed Surplus

Authorized

Unlimited number of common shares

Unlimited number of preferred shares, issuable in series without nominal or par value

Outstanding

	2012		2011	
	Number of Common Shares	Stated Value	Number of Common Shares	Stated Value
Beginning balance	212,475,597	$ 1,486,455	217,452,068	$ 1,520,558
Treasury shares cancelled	(115,900)	(810)	—	—
Share options exercised	41,491	1,295	109,729	1,466
Shares repurchased in cash	(7,949,400)	(55,635)	(5,086,200)	(35,576)
Repayment of share purchase loans	—	10	—	7
Ending balance	204,451,788	$ 1,431,315	212,475,597	$ 1,486,455

The Company also has issued share options. See Note 26 to these consolidated financial statements for further details on the Company's issued share options.

Individual shareholder agreements address matters related to the transfer of certain shares issued to the Company's management and Associates, including shares issued under certain options granted to management. In particular, each provides, subject to certain exceptions, for a general prohibition on any transfer of a member of management's or Associates' shares for a period of five years from the date that the individual entered into the shareholder agreement.

27. NET CHANGE IN NON-CASH WORKING CAPITAL BALANCES

	2012	2011
Accounts receivable	$ 36,818	$ (36,242)
Inventory	(93,842)	(84,242)
Prepaid expenses	(5,708)	32,759
Accounts payable and accrued liabilities	78,190	119,891
	$ 15,458	$ 32,166

28. CONTINGENCIES, COMMITMENTS AND GUARANTEES

Obligations under Operating Leases

As at December 29, 2012, the minimum lease payments (exclusive of taxes, insurance and other occupancy charges) on a calendar year basis under long-term leases for store locations and office space are as follows:

	2013	2014	2015	2016	2017	Thereafter	Total
Minimum lease payments	$ 423,332	$ 419,854	$ 409,497	$ 398,209	$ 383,488	$ 2,218,963	$ 4,253,343
Less: sub-lease revenue	4,321	3,531	2,799	2,280	1,806	6,884	21,621
Total operating lease obligations	$ 419,011	$ 416,323	$ 406,698	$ 395,929	$ 381,682	$ 2,212,079	$ 4,231,722

Obligations under Financing Leases

As at December 29, 2012, the minimum lease payments on a calendar year basis for the Company's assets under financing leases are as follows:

	2013	2014	2015	2016	2017	Thereafter	Total
Minimum lease payments	$ 12,283	$ 12,460	$ 12,592	$ 12,917	$ 13,215	$ 161,499	$ 224,966
Less: financing expenses included in minimum lease payments	9,048	8,820	8,562	8,274	7,942	56,546	99,192
Total financing lease obligations	$ 3,235	$ 3,640	$ 4,030	$ 4,643	$ 5,273	$ 104,953	$ 125,774

The Company has financing lease obligations for buildings. The leases have an average interest rate of 7.3% (2011: 7.3%) and an average remaining term of approximately 16 years (2011: 17 years).

Distribution Services

The Company has entered into an agreement with a third party to provide inventory distribution services to the Company's locations to December 31, 2015. Under the terms of this agreement, the third party will charge the Company specified costs incurred to provide the distribution services, plus an annual management fee.

Information Services

The Company has entered into agreements with several third parties to provide information services to the Company. These agreements have remaining terms of 4 to 9 years. The Company has committed to annual payments over the next five years as follows:

Minimum commitment

2013	$ 9,108
2014	8,135
2015	5,182
2016	2,768
2017	1,064
Thereafter	4,702
Total	$ 30,959

Litigation

See Note 22 to these consolidated financial statements for a discussion of the Company's exposure to litigation claims.

Other

In the normal course of business, the Company enters into significant commitments for the purchase of goods and services, such as the purchase of inventory or capital assets, most of which are short-term in nature and are settled under normal trade terms. The Company is involved in and could potentially be subject to various claims by third parties arising out of its business including, but not limited to, contract, product liability, labour and employment, regulatory and environmental claims. In addition, the Company is subject to regular audits from federal and provincial tax authorities relating to income, capital and commodity taxes, and as a result of these audits, may receive reassessments. While income, capital and commodity tax filings are subject to audits and reassessments, management believes that adequate provisions have been made for all income and other tax obligations. However, changes in the interpretations or judgements may result in an increase or decrease in the Company's income, capital, or commodity tax provisions in the future. The amount of any such increase or decrease cannot be reasonably estimated.

29. RELATED PARTY TRANSACTIONS

Key Management Personnel Compensation

Key management personnel are those individuals having authority and responsibility for planning, directing and controlling the activities of the Company including the Company's Board of Directors. The Company considers key management to be the members of the Board of Directors, the Chief Executive Officer and the executive team (in 2011, the Company considered key management to be the members of the Board of Directors and the Chief Executive Officer).

Key management personnel may also participate in the Company's stock-based compensation plans and the Company's RSU Plan. See Note 26 to these consolidated financial statements for further details on the Company's share-based payment plans.

Key management personnel compensation is comprised of:

	2012	2011
Salaries and directors' fees	$ 9,036	$ 5,134
Statutory deductions	192	104
Expense related to pension and other post-employment benefits	1,910	293
Share-based payment transactions	5,011	(734)
	$ 16,149	$ 4,797

Key management personnel may purchase goods for personal and family use from the Company on the same terms as those available to all other employees of the Company.

Principal Subsidiaries

All of the Company's subsidiaries are wholly-owned. Intra-company balances and transactions and any unrealized earnings and expenses arising from intra-company transactions are eliminated in preparing the consolidated financial statements. Principal subsidiary companies as at December 29, 2012 were as follows:

Shoppers Home Health Care (Canada) Inc.
Shoppers Drug Mart Specialty Health Network Inc.
MediSystem Technologies Inc.
Shoppers Drug Mart Inc.
Shoppers Drug Mart (London) Limited
Pharmaprix Inc.
911979 Alberta Ltd.
Shoppers Realty Inc.
Sanis Health Inc.

The list excludes non-trading companies that have no material effect on the accounts of the Company.

The Associate-owned stores are each operated through a corporation owned by the Associates. See Note 3(a)(iii) to these consolidated financial statements for further discussion.

Earnings Coverage Exhibit to the Consolidated Financial Statements (unaudited)

52 weeks ended December 29, 2012	
Earnings coverage ratio	14.94 times

The earnings coverage ratio is equal to earnings (before finance expenses and income taxes) divided by finance expenses. Finance expenses include finance expense capitalized to property and equipment.

Specimen Financial Statements:
The Jean Coutu Group (PJC) Inc.

In this appendix, we illustrate current financial reporting using the financial statements of Jean Coutu, one of Canada's leading drugstore chains.

The financial statement package includes the management's report with respect to the financial statements, the auditor's report, statement of income, statement of comprehensive income, statement of changes in equity, statement of financial position, and statement of cash flows. The complete set of financial statements, including the notes, as well as the annual report for Jean Coutu can be found on *WileyPLUS* and the companion website to this textbook.

We encourage you to use these financial statements in conjunction with relevant chapter material in the textbook, and to solve the Comparative Analysis cases in the Broadening Your Perspective section at the end of every chapter.

MANAGEMENT'S REPORT WITH RESPECT TO FINANCIAL STATEMENTS

The financial statements of The Jean Coutu Group (PJC) Inc. and the financial information contained in the annual report are the responsibility of management. This responsibility is applied through an appropriate choice of accounting policies, the application of which requires the informed judgment of management. Management is also responsible for all other information in this report and for ensuring that this information is consistent, where appropriate, with the information and data included in the consolidated financial statements. The consolidated financial statements have been prepared in accordance with the International Financial Reporting Standards.

To discharge its responsibility, management maintains a system of internal controls to provide reasonable assurance as to the reliability of financial information and the safeguarding of assets.

The Board of Directors carries out its responsibility relative to the consolidated financial statements principally through its Audit Committee, consisting solely of independent directors, which reviews the consolidated financial statements and reports thereon to the Board. The Committee meets periodically with the independent auditors, internal auditor and management to review their respective activities and the discharge by each of their responsibilities. Both the independent auditors and the internal auditor have free access to the Committee, with or without the presence of management, to discuss the scope of their audits, the adequacy of the system of internal controls and the adequacy of financial reporting.

The consolidated financial statements have been reviewed by the Audit Committee and approved by the Board of Directors. In addition, the Corporation's independent auditors, Deloitte LLP, are responsible for auditing the consolidated financial statements and providing an opinion thereon. Their report is provided hereafter.

/s/ François J. Coutu

President and Chief Executive Officer
April 30, 2013

/s/ André Belzile

Senior Vice-President, Finances and Corporate Affairs

INDEPENDENT AUDITOR'S REPORT

Deloitte LLP
1, Place Ville Marie
Bureau 3000
Montréal QC H3B 4T9
Canada

Tél. : 514-393-7115
Téléc. : 514-390-4113
www.deloitte.ca

To the Shareholders of The Jean Coutu Group (PJC) Inc.

We have audited the accompanying consolidated financial statements of The Jean Coutu Group (PJC) Inc., which comprise the consolidated statements of financial position as at March 2, 2013 and March 3, 2012 and the consolidated statements of income, the consolidated statements of comprehensive income, the consolidated statements of changes in equity and the consolidated statements of cash flows for the years then ended, and a summary of significant accounting policies and other explanatory information.

Management's Responsibility for the Consolidated Financial Statements

Management is responsible for the preparation and fair presentation of these consolidated financial statements in accordance with International Financial Reporting Standards, and for such internal control as management determines is necessary to enable the preparation of consolidated financial statements that are free from material misstatement, whether due to fraud or error.

Auditor's Responsibility

Our responsibility is to express an opinion on these consolidated financial statements based on our audits. We conducted our audits in accordance with Canadian generally accepted auditing standards. Those standards require that we comply with ethical requirements and plan and perform the audit to obtain reasonable assurance about whether the consolidated financial statements are free from material misstatement.

An audit involves performing procedures to obtain audit evidence about the amounts and disclosures in the consolidated financial statements. The procedures selected depend on the auditor's judgment, including the assessment of the risks of material misstatement of the consolidated financial statements, whether due to fraud or error. In making those risk assessments, the auditor considers internal control relevant to the entity's preparation and fair presentation of the consolidated financial statements in order to design audit procedures that are appropriate in the circumstances, but not for the purpose of expressing an opinion on the effectiveness of the entity's internal control. An audit also includes evaluating the appropriateness of accounting policies used and the reasonableness of accounting estimates made by management, as well as evaluating the overall presentation of the consolidated financial statements.

We believe that the audit evidence we have obtained in our audits is sufficient and appropriate to provide a basis for our audit opinion.

Opinion

In our opinion, the consolidated financial statements present fairly, in all material respects, the financial position of The Jean Coutu Group (PJC) Inc. as at March 2, 2013 and March 3, 2012 and its financial performance and its cash flows for the years then ended in accordance with International Financial Reporting Standards.

/s/ Deloitte LLP[1]

April 30, 2013
Montréal (Québec)

---
[1] CPA auditor, CA, public accountancy permit No. A119522

THE JEAN COUTU GROUP (PJC) INC.

Consolidated statements of income

For the fiscal years ended March 2, 2013 and March 3, 2012	2013	2012
(in millions of Canadian dollars, unless otherwise noted)	$	$
		(Note 2b)
Sales	**2,468.0**	2,463.2
Other revenues (Note 5)	**271.5**	269.9
	2,739.5	2,733.1
Operating expenses		
Cost of sales	**2,169.0**	2,184.3
General and operating expenses (Note 6)	**247.5**	237.6
Operating income before depreciation and amortization	**323.0**	311.2
Depreciation and amortization (Note 7)	**31.7**	30.4
Operating income	**291.3**	280.8
Financing expenses (Note 8)	**2.0**	1.0
Profit before the following items	**289.3**	279.8
Gains on sales of investment in Rite Aid (Note 14)	**82.8**	22.0
Unrealized gain related to the investment in Rite Aid (Note 14)	**265.2**	-
Profit before income taxes	**637.3**	301.8
Income taxes (Note 9)	**78.9**	71.8
Net profit	**558.4**	230.0
Basic and diluted profit per share, in dollars (Note 10)	**2.57**	1.03

Consolidated statements of comprehensive income

For the fiscal years ended March 2, 2013 and March 3, 2012	2013	2012
(in millions of Canadian dollars)	$	$
		(Note 2b)
Net profit	**558.4**	230.0
Other comprehensive income		
Defined benefit pension plans (Note 28) :		
Actuarial losses	**(0.2)**	(3.3)
Pension plan asset limitation	**-**	1.1
Available-for-sale financial asset (Note 14) :		
Change in fair value of investment in Rite Aid	**40.8**	-
Income taxes on the above items (Note 9)	**-**	0.6
	40.6	(1.6)
Total comprehensive income	**599.0**	228.4

The accompanying notes are an integral part of these consolidated financial statements.

THE JEAN COUTU GROUP (PJC) INC.

Consolidated statements of changes in equity

For the fiscal years ended March 2, 2013 and March 3, 2012

(in millions of Canadian dollars)

	Capital stock	Treasury stock	Contributed surplus	Change in fair value of the investment in Rite Aid	Retained earnings (deficit)	Total equity
	$	$	$	$	$	$
Balance at February 26, 2011	614.4	-	1.4	-	(17.5)	598.3
Net profit	-	-	-	-	230.0	230.0
Other comprehensive income	-	-	-	-	(1.6)	(1.6)
Total comprehensive income	-	-	-	-	228.4	228.4
Redemption of capital stock (Note 23)	(55.5)	(1.0)	-	-	(68.6)	(125.1)
Dividends (Note 23)	-	-	-	-	(53.8)	(53.8)
Share-based compensation cost (Note 25)	-	-	0.6	-	0.1	0.7
Options exercised (Note 25)	0.8	-	(0.1)	-	-	0.7
Balance at March 3, 2012	559.7	(1.0)	1.9	-	88.6	649.2
Net profit	-	-	-	-	558.4	558.4
Other comprehensive income	-	-	-	40.8	(0.2)	40.6
Total comprehensive income	-	-	-	40.8	558.2	599.0
Redemption of capital stock (Note 23)	(29.1)	(1.2)	-	-	(52.6)	(82.9)
Dividends (Note 23)	-	-	-	-	(60.8)	(60.8)
Share-based compensation cost (Note 25)	-	-	0.8	-	-	0.8
Options exercised (Note 25)	6.5	-	(1.0)	-	-	5.5
Balance at March 2, 2013	**537.1**	**(2.2)**	**1.7**	**40.8**	**533.4**	**1,110.8**

The accompanying notes are an integral part of these consolidated financial statements.

THE JEAN COUTU GROUP (PJC) INC.

Consolidated statements of financial position

	As at March 2, 2013	As at March 3, 2012
(in millions of Canadian dollars)	$	$
Current assets		
Temporary investment	20.0	-
Trade and other receivables	199.6	206.5
Inventories (Note 11)	190.1	166.2
Income taxes recoverable	-	0.2
Prepaid expenses	12.2	12.9
	421.9	385.8
Non-current assets		
Long-term receivables from franchisees (Note 12)	24.9	33.4
Other financial assets (Note 13)	-	19.0
Investment in Rite Aid (Note 14)	306.0	-
Investment in associates and joint venture	8.3	6.9
Property and equipment (Note 15)	359.5	361.1
Investment property (Note 16)	17.4	20.5
Intangible assets (Note 17)	195.0	186.9
Goodwill (Note 18)	36.0	36.0
Deferred tax (Note 9)	11.2	12.6
Other long-term assets (Note 19)	12.5	10.6
Total assets	1,392.7	1,072.8
Current liabilities		
Bank overdraft	21.6	5.0
Trade and other payables (Note 20)	225.2	230.6
Income taxes payable	18.5	23.2
Short term portion of long-term debt (Note 21)	-	149.9
	265.3	408.7
Non-current liabilities		
Deferred tax (Note 9)	0.8	1.0
Other long-term liabilities (Note 22)	15.8	13.9
Total liabilities	281.9	423.6
Guarantees, contingencies and commitments (Notes 26 and 27)		
Equity	1,110.8	649.2
Total liabilities and equity	1,392.7	1,072.8

The accompanying notes are an integral part of these consolidated financial statements.

Approved by the Board

/s/ François J. Coutu
François J. Coutu
Director and President and Chief Executive Officer

/s/ L. Denis Desautels
L. Denis Desautels
Director

THE JEAN COUTU GROUP (PJC) INC.

Consolidated statements of cash flows

For the fiscal years ended March 2, 2013 and March 3, 2012	2013	2012
(in millions of Canadian dollars)	$	$
		(Note 2b)
Operating activities		
Net profit	**558.4**	230.0
Adjustments for:		
Depreciation and amortization	**31.7**	30.4
Change in fair value of other financial assets (Note 13)	**1.1**	(1.9)
Gains on sales of investment in Rite Aid	**(82.8)**	(22.0)
Unrealized gain related to the investment in Rite Aid	**(265.2)**	-
Interest on long-term debt	**0.7**	2.8
Income taxes	**78.9**	71.8
Others	**5.9**	3.8
	328.7	314.9
Net changes in non-cash asset and liability items (Note 31)	**(21.9)**	16.7
Interest paid on long term debt	**(0.8)**	(2.8)
Income taxes paid	**(82.2)**	(83.8)
Cash flow related to operating activities	**223.8**	245.0
Investing activities		
Receipts from other financial assets (Note 13)	**17.9**	5.9
Proceeds from disposal of investment in Rite Aid	**82.8**	22.0
Purchase of property and equipment	**(20.9)**	(24.9)
Proceeds from disposal of property and equipment	**1.1**	2.2
Purchase of investment property	**(0.1)**	(0.3)
Proceeds from disposal of investment property	**4.1**	2.7
Net change in long-term receivables from franchisees	**(0.1)**	(3.4)
Purchase of intangible assets	**(16.1)**	(22.7)
Others	**(2.7)**	1.6
Cash flow related to investing activities	**66.0**	(16.9)
Financing activities		
Net change in revolving credit facility	**(149.8)**	(34.9)
Financing fees	**(0.3)**	(1.3)
Issuance of capital stock	**5.5**	0.7
Redemption of capital stock and treasury stock	**(81.0)**	(127.3)
Dividends paid	**(60.8)**	(53.8)
Cash flow related to financing activities	**(286.4)**	(216.6)
Net change in cash and cash equivalents	**3.4**	11.5
Cash and cash equivalents, beginning of year	**(5.0)**	(16.5)
Cash and cash equivalents, end of year	**(1.6)**	(5.0)

The accompanying notes are an integral part of these consolidated financial statements. See supplemental cash flow information in Note 31.

Company Index

Subject Index

Photo Credits

Chapter 1: Page 2: © istock.com/Julie Marshall. Page 14: © istock/Alex Slobodkin. Page 27 (All About You feature): © istock.com/ Skip ODonnell. **Chapter 2:** Page 52: Courtesy Plazacorp Retail Properties Ltd. Page 70: © istock.com/EdStock. **Chapter 3:** Page 104: Courtesy of BeaverTails Canada Inc. Page 107: © istock.com/Walik. Page 122: © istock.com/Johnny Kurtz. **Chapter 4:** Page 160: Courtesy of Western University. Page 166: © istock.com/cotesebastien. **Chapter 5:** Page 220: © istock.com/YvanDubé. Page 226: © istock.com/ Richard Goerg. Page 243: © istock.com/WILLSIE. **Chapter 6:** Page 284: © istock.com/Mlenny Photography. Page 287: © istock.com/ GrzegorzMalec. Page 305: © istock.com/vesilvio. **Chapter 7:** Page 340: Courtesy of Nick's Steakhouse and Pizza. Page 350: © istock.com/ audioundwerbung. Page 356: istock.com/Sparky2000. **Chapter 8:** Page 392: © istock.com/Anthony Seebaran. Page 397: © istock.com/ Sturti. Page 402: © istock.com/DNY59. **Chapter 9:** Page 438: © istock.com/tomeng. Page 451: © istock.com/DNY59. Page 463: © istock. com/labelled. **Chapter 10:** Page 500: Copied with the permission of Canada Post Corporation. Page 507: © istock.com/Igor Dimovski. Page 512: © istock.com/Pgiam. Page 535: Royal Mail cruciform © and Trade Mark of Royal Mail Group Ltd. Reproduced by kind permission of Royal Mail Group Ltd. All rights reserved. **Chapter 11:** Page 554: © istock.com/Shane Shaw. Page 559: © istock.com/EdStock. Page 569: © istock.com/leezsnow. **Chapter 12:** Page 610: Kevin Frayer/The Canadian Press. Page 615: © istock.com/Maria Toutoudaki. Page 620: © istock.com/KathrynHatashitaLee. **Chapter 13:** Page 662: Courtesy of Teck Resources Limited. Page 697: © istock.com/LastSax. **Chapter 14:** Page 730: The Canadian Press Images/Francis Vachon. Page 758: © istock.com/Lya_Cattel.

SHAREHOLDERS' EQUITY   (Chapter 11)

Equity Transactions

Transaction	Journal Entry
Issue of shares	Dr. Cash Cr. Common/Preferred Shares

Cash dividends (declaration and payment)	Dr. Cash Dividends
	    Cr. Dividends Payable
	Dr. Dividends Payable
	    Cr. Cash

Stock dividends (declaration and distribution)	Dr. Stock Dividends
	    Cr. Stock Dividends Distributable
	Dr. Stock Dividends Distributable
	    Cr. Common Shares

Comparison of Dividend Effects

	Assets	=	Liabilities	+	Share Capital	+	Retained Earnings	Number of Shares
					Shareholders' Equity			
Cash dividend	−		NE		NE		−	NE
Stock dividend	NE		NE		+		−	+
Stock split	NE		NE		NE		NE	+

Note: "+" means increase, "−" means decrease, "NE" means no effect.

Comprehensive Income

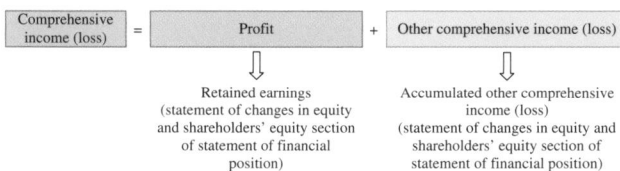

Comprehensive income (loss)	=	Profit	+	Other comprehensive income (loss)

Retained earnings (statement of changes in equity and shareholders' equity section of statement of financial position)

Accumulated other comprehensive income (loss) (statement of changes in equity and shareholders' equity section of statement of financial position)

INVESTMENTS   (Chapter 12)

Reporting and Valuation of Investments

Statement of Financial Position Classification	Strategy	Type of Investment	Valuation Model
Trading investments (current assets)	Non-strategic	Trading investments (debt or equity)	Fair value through profit or loss
Long-term investments (non-current assets)	Non-strategic	Equity investments without significant influence or control, with determinable fair values	Fair value through profit or loss (with option under IFRS to use fair value through OCI)
		Debt investments held to earn interest revenue	Amortized cost
	Strategic	Investments in associates (equity investments with significant influence)	Equity method (with option to use cost or fair value model under ASPE. Consolidation required if control exists (with option to use equity, cost, or fair value under ASPE).

Comparison of Fair Value through Profit or Loss Model and Equity Method of Accounting for Equity Investments

Transaction	Fair Value (no significant influence)	Equity (significant influence)

Acquisition	Dr. Trading Investments
	    Cr. Cash
		Dr. Investment in Associates
		    Cr. Cash

Investee reports profit	No entry	Dr. Investment in Associates
		    Cr. Revenue from
		        Investment in Associates

Investee pays dividends	Dr. Cash
	    Cr. Dividend Revenue
		Dr. Cash
		    Cr. Investment in Associates

Adjustment for increase in fair value (entry is opposite for decrease)	Dr. Trading Investments
	    Cr. Unrealized Gain on
	        Trading Investments
		No entry

Note: The unrealized gain (or loss) on trading investments is reported as other revenues and expenses in the income statement.

Comparison of Long-Term Bond Investment and Liability Journal Entries

Transaction	Investor (amortized cost model)	Investee

Purchase/issue of bonds	Dr. Long-Term Investments
	    Cr. Cash
		Dr. Cash
		    Cr. Bonds Payable

Interest receipt/payment and amortization of discount or premium	Dr. Cash
	Dr. Long-Term Investments (dr. for discount; cr. for premium)
	    Cr. Interest Revenue
		Dr. Interest Expense
		    Cr. Bonds Payable
		        (dr. for premium;
		        cr. for discount)
		    Cr. Cash

Sale of investment	Dr. Cash Dr. Realized Loss (or cr. Realized Gain) Cr. Long-Term Investments	No entry

STATEMENT OF CASH FLOWS   (Chapter 13)

Business Activities

1. Operating activities: Include cash effects of transactions that create revenues and expenses. They affect profit.
2. Investing activities: Include (a) purchasing and disposing of long-term investments and long-lived assets and (b) lending money and collecting the loans. Investing activities generally affect non-current asset accounts.
3. Financing activities: Include (a) obtaining cash from issuing debt and repaying the amounts borrowed and (b) obtaining cash from shareholders and paying them dividends. Financing activities generally affect non-current liability and shareholders' equity accounts.

Steps in Preparing the Statement of Cash Flows

1. Prepare operating activities section: Determine net cash provided (used) by operating activities by converting profit from accrual basis to cash basis using either indirect or direct method (preferred). To do this, analyze the current year's income statement, relevant current asset and current liability accounts from comparative statement of financial position, and selected information. In the indirect method, this is done by converting total profit from accrual basis to cash basis. In the direct method, this is done by converting each individual revenue and expense account from accrual basis to cash basis.
2. Prepare investing activities section: Determine net cash provided (used) by investing activities by analyzing changes in non-current asset accounts from comparative statement of financial position and selected information.
3. Prepare financing activities section: Determine net cash provided (used) by financing activities by analyzing changes in non-current liability and equity accounts from comparative statement of financial position and selected information.
4. Complete statement of cash flows: Determine net increase (decrease) in cash. Compare net change in cash reported on statement of cash flows with change in cash reported on statement of financial position to make sure amounts agree.

PERFORMANCE MEASUREMENT   (Chapter 14)

Discontinued Operations

- Disposal, or availability for sale, of a component of an entity
- Statement of financial position: assets and liabilities held for sale reported separately
- Income statement: gains (losses) and/or profit (loss) from discontinued operations presented separately, net of income tax, after profit (loss) from continuing operations

Horizontal (Trend) Analysis

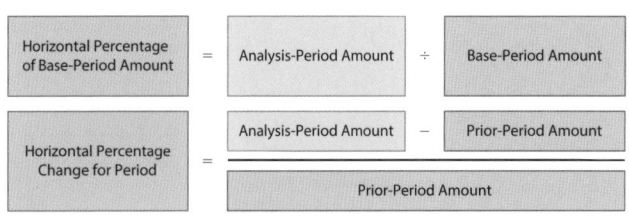

Horizontal Percentage of Base-Period Amount	=	Analysis-Period Amount	÷	Base-Period Amount

Horizontal Percentage Change for Period = (Analysis-Period Amount − Prior-Period Amount) / Prior-Period Amount

Vertical (Common-Size) Analysis

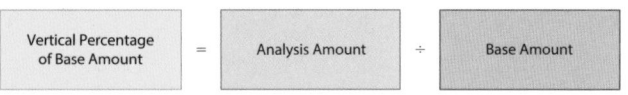

| Vertical Percentage of Base Amount | = | Analysis Amount | ÷ | Base Amount |

Liquidity Ratios

Chapter	Ratio	Formula	What the Ratio Measures	Desired Result
2	Working capital	Current assets − Current liabilities	Short-term debt-paying ability	Higher
2	Current ratio	$\dfrac{\text{Current assets}}{\text{Current liabilities}}$	Short-term debt-paying ability	Higher
13	Cash current debt coverage	$\dfrac{\text{Net cash provided (used) by operating activities}}{\text{Average current liabilities}}$	Short-term debt-paying ability (cash basis)	Higher
8	Receivables turnover	$\dfrac{\text{Net credit sales}}{\text{Average gross accounts receivable}}$	Liquidity of receivables	Higher
8	Average collection period	$\dfrac{365 \text{ days}}{\text{Receivables turnover}}$	Number of days receivables are outstanding	Lower
6	Inventory turnover	$\dfrac{\text{Cost of goods sold}}{\text{Average inventory}}$	Liquidity of inventory	Higher
6	Days in inventory	$\dfrac{365 \text{ days}}{\text{Inventory turnover}}$	Number of days inventory is on hand	Lower

Solvency Ratios

Chapter	Ratio	Formula	What the Ratio Measures	Desired Result
2, 10	Debt to total assets	$\dfrac{\text{Total liabilities}}{\text{Total assets}}$	Percentage of total assets provided by creditors	Lower
10	Times interest earned	$\dfrac{\text{Profit + Interest expense + Income tax expense (EBIT)}}{\text{Interest expense}}$	Ability to meet interest payments	Higher
13	Cash total debt coverage	$\dfrac{\text{Net cash provided (used) by operating activities}}{\text{Average total liabilities}}$	Long-term debt-paying ability (cash basis)	Higher
13	Free cash flow	Net cash provided (used) by operating activities − Net capital expenditures − Dividends paid	Cash available from operating activities for discretionary purposes	Higher

Profitability Ratios

Chapter	Ratio	Formula	What the Ratio Measures	Desired Result
11	Return on common shareholders' equity	$\dfrac{\text{Profit − Preferred dividends}}{\text{Average common shareholders' equity}}$	Profitability of shareholders' investment	Higher
9	Return on assets	$\dfrac{\text{Profit}}{\text{Average total assets}}$	Overall profitability of assets	Higher
5	Profit margin	$\dfrac{\text{Profit}}{\text{Net sales}}$	Profit generated by each dollar of sales	Higher
9	Asset turnover	$\dfrac{\text{Net sales}}{\text{Average total assets}}$	How efficiently assets are used to generate sales	Higher
5	Gross profit margin	$\dfrac{\text{Gross profit}}{\text{Net sales}}$	Margin between selling price and cost of goods sold	Higher
2, 11	Earnings per share	$\dfrac{\text{Profit − Preferred dividends}}{\text{Weighted average number of common shares}}$	Profit earned on each common share	Higher
2	Price-earnings ratio	$\dfrac{\text{Market price per share}}{\text{Earnings per share}}$	Relationship between market price per share and earnings per share	Higher
11	Payout ratio	$\dfrac{\text{Cash dividends}}{\text{Profit}}$	Percentage of profit distributed as cash dividends	Higher
11	Dividend yield	$\dfrac{\text{Dividend per share}}{\text{Market price per share}}$	Income generated for the shareholder by each share, based on the market price per share	Higher

SAMPLE FINANCIAL STATEMENTS

Multiple-Step Income Statement (perpetual inventory system)

Name of Company Income Statement Period Ended		
Sales revenues		
Sales		$X
Less: Sales returns and allowances	$X	
Sales discounts	X	X
Net sales		X
Cost of goods sold		X
Gross profit		X
Operating expenses		
(Examples: salaries, advertising, freight, rent, depreciation, utilities, insurance)		X
Profit from operations		X
Other revenues and expenses		
(Example: interest)		X
Profit before income tax		X
Income tax expense		X
Profit		$X

Income Statement (cost of goods sold detail in periodic inventory system—Appendix 5A)

Cost of goods sold		
Beginning inventory		$X
Purchases	$X	
Less: Purchase returns and allowances	X	
Net purchases	X	
Add: Freight in	X	
Cost of goods purchased		X
Cost of goods available for sale		X
Less: Ending inventory		X
Cost of goods sold		$X

Statement of Comprehensive Income

Name of Company Statement of Comprehensive Income Period Ended	
Profit	$X
Other comprehensive income (loss)	
(Example: revaluations of property, plant, and equipment)	X
Comprehensive income (loss)	$X

Statement of Changes in Equity

	Common Shares	Additional Contributed Capital	Retained Earnings	Accumulated Other Comprehensive Income (Loss)	Total
Balance, beginning of period	$X	$X	$X	$X	$X
Issued shares	X				X
Cash dividends			(X)		(X)
Stock dividends	X		(X)		
Comprehensive income					
Profit			X		X
Other comprehensive income (loss)				X	X
Balance, end of period	$X	$X	$X	$X	$X

Financial management involves the analysis of financial data, as well as the determination of how to obtain and use funds. Chapter 15 explains how a financial analysis of a firm can be conducted to determine how it is performing, and why. This type of analysis is used to detect a firm's deficiencies so that they can be corrected.

Finance is the means by which firms obtain funds (financing) and invest funds in business projects. Firms may obtain funds to build a new factory, purchase new machinery, purchase more supplies, or even purchase an existing business owned by another company. Chapter 16 describes the common financing methods that firms use and also identifies the types of financial institutions that provide financing. It also explains the factors that influence the ideal type of financing. Chapter 17 describes the tasks that are necessary when a firm determines whether to invest in a particular business project. In addition, it explains why firms sometimes use their funds to acquire other firms. The chapters on financing and business investment are closely related because financing supports the firm's investment in new business projects.

Accounting and Financial Analysis (Chapter 15)	→	• Identify Deficiencies and Correct Them			
Financing (Chapter 16)	→	• How to Obtain Funds? • Where to Obtain Funds?	→	Firm's Revenue and Expenses	→ Firm's Performance (and Value)
Expanding the Business (Chapter 17)	→	• Whether to Invest in New Business Projects? • Whether to Acquire New Businesses? • How Much to Invest in Accounts Receivable? • How Much to Invest in Inventory?			

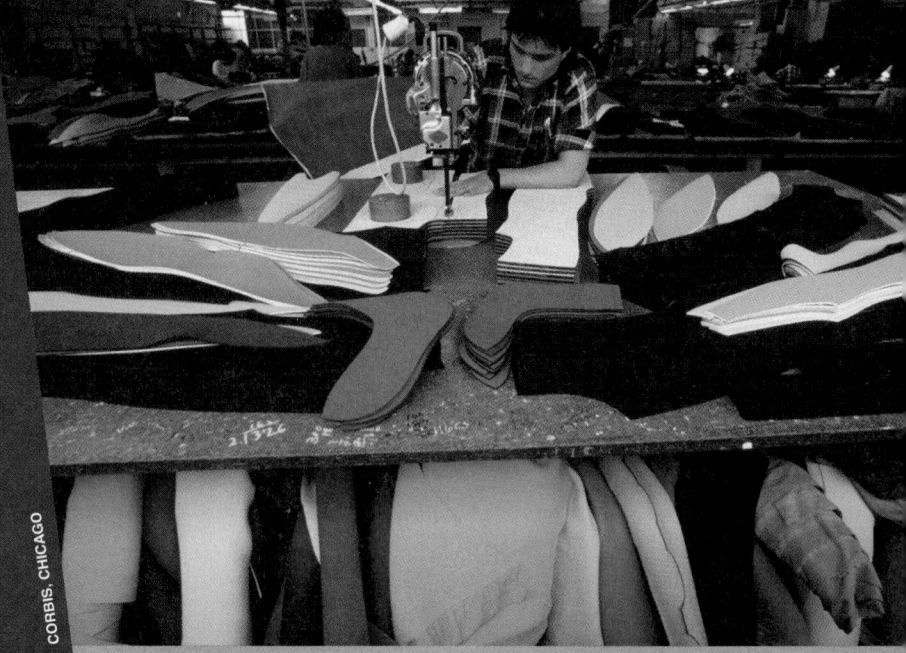

CORBIS, CHICAGO

Chapter

15

Surf Clothing Company relies on recent accounting statements to monitor its performance over time.

Accounting and Financial Analysis

Accounting is the summary and analysis of a firm's financial condition. The accounting process generates financial statements, which provide detailed information about a firm's recent performance and its financial condition. Managers of all types of firms use financial statements to assess their performance and to make business decisions. Consider the situation of Surf Clothing Company, which produces clothing that it sells in its retail stores. Surf Clothing wants to monitor its business performance so that it can detect any deficiencies that need to be corrected. It also wants to determine whether its financial condi-

tion is adequate to support the expansion of its business in the near future. Surf Clothing Company must decide:

▶ How can it measure its recent performance?

▶ How can it ensure that its financial statements are accurate?

▶ How can it assess its present financial condition?

▶ How can it apply ratio analysis?

Surf Clothing Company can assess its financial statements to determine how its revenue, expenses, and earnings changed in response

to specific strategies that it used in the past. Its financial statements allow Surf to monitor its recent performance so that it can detect any weakness in time to revise its strategies. Surf can also ensure that its present financial condition is strong enough to allow for expansion.

The types of decisions described above are necessary for all businesses. This chapter explains how the accounting and financial analysis functions described here can be used by Surf Clothing Company or by any other firm in a manner that maximizes its value.

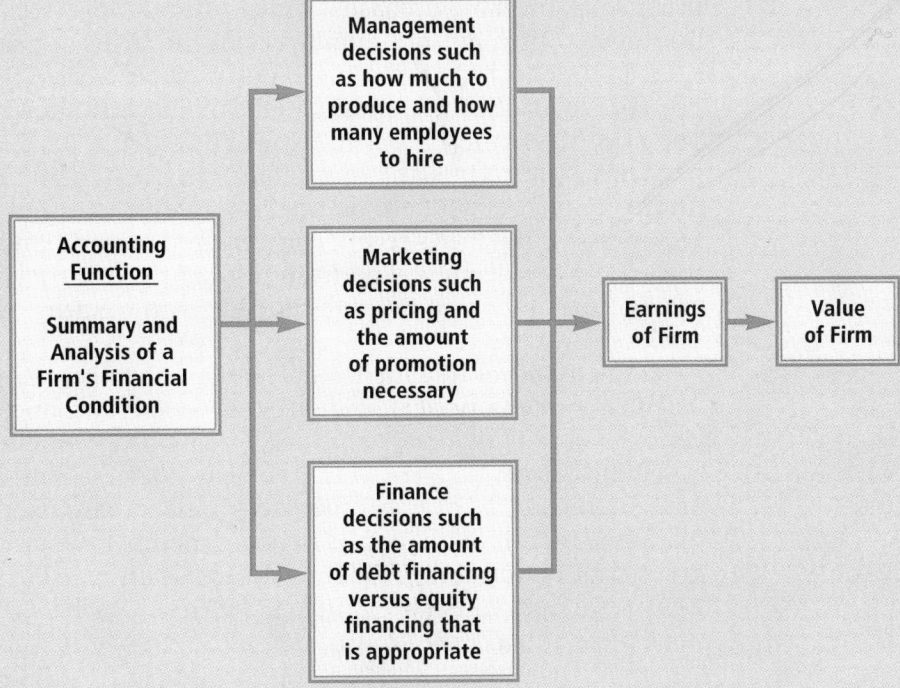

567

How Firms Use Accounting

1

Explain how firms use accounting.

accounting
the summary and analysis of a firm's financial condition

public accountants
accountants who provide accounting services for a variety of firms for a fee

certified public accountants (CPAs)
accountants who meet specific educational requirements and pass a national examination

bookkeeping
the recording of a firm's financial transactions

financial accounting
accounting performed for reporting purposes

Firms use **accounting** to report their financial condition, support decisions, and control business operations, as explained in this order next. The accounting process itself is performed by accountants who may be private or public accountants. Private accountants provide accounting services for the firms where they are employed. Although they usually have an accounting degree, they do not have to be certified.

Public accountants provide accounting services for a variety of firms for a fee. A license is required to practice public accounting. Accountants who meet specific educational requirements and pass a national examination are referred to as **certified public accountants (CPAs)**.

Reporting

One accounting task is to report accurate financial data. **Bookkeeping** is the recording of a firm's financial transactions. For example, the recording of daily or weekly revenue and expenses is part of the bookkeeping process.

Firms are required to periodically report their revenue, expenses, and earnings to the Internal Revenue Service (IRS) so that their taxes can be determined. The type of accounting performed for reporting purposes is called **financial accounting**.

Financial accounting must be conducted in accordance with generally accepted accounting principles (GAAP) that explain how financial information should be reported. The Financial Accounting Standards Board (FASB), Securities and Exchange Commission (SEC), and IRS establish the accounting guidelines. The use of a common set of guidelines allows for more consistency in reporting practices among firms. Consequently, a comparison of financial statements between two or more different firms may be more meaningful.

Reporting to Investors   Publicly owned firms are required to periodically report their financial condition for investors who either already own the firm's stock or may purchase it in the future. Most shareholders of a publicly owned firm are not employees of the firm, but simply invest in its stock in an effort to earn a high return on their investment. The market price of the firm's stock tends to move in line with the firm's performance. The price rises when the firm performs well, but declines when the firm performs poorly. Thus, the return on an investment in the firm's stock in a future period is dependent on the firm's performance over that period. Investors assess the firm's recent earnings and other financial information to predict how the firm will perform in the future. If they conclude that the price of the stock will rise substantially in the future, they may buy the stock.

If the financial statements indicate that the firm has performed poorly and do not offer any clear evidence that the performance will improve, investors will not buy the firm's stock, and existing shareholders may decide to sell their stock. Alternatively, if they own a large amount of shares, they may attempt to join with other disgruntled shareholders in demanding that some high-level managers or board members be fired as a result of the firm's poor performance. This activist role is intended to result in more effective management of the firm in the future, which would lead to a higher stock price and a decent return on their investment.

Responsibility for Financial Reporting

In a recent National Small Business poll conducted for the NFIB Research Foundation, small business owners were asked who is responsible for their financial reporting. Their responses are shown below:

Businesses with 1–9 employees

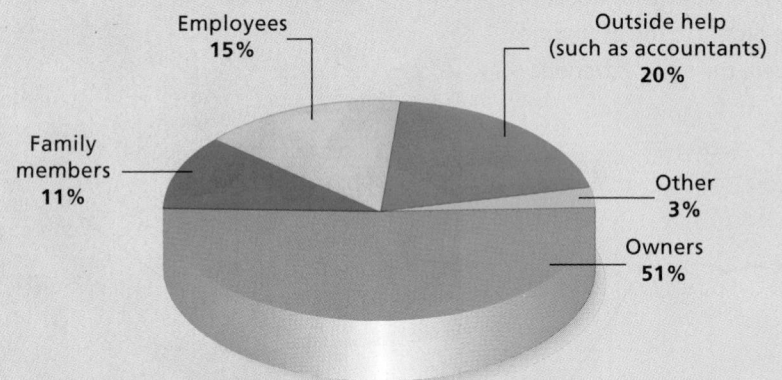

Employees
15%

Outside help
(such as accountants)
20%

Family
members
11%

Other
3%

Owners
51%

Businesses with 10–19 employees

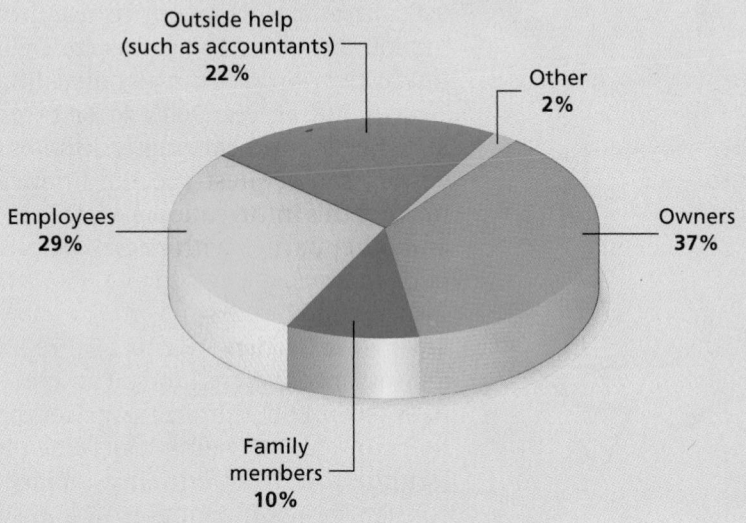

Outside help
(such as accountants)
22%

Other
2%

Employees
29%

Owners
37%

Family
members
10%

Businesses with 20–249 employees

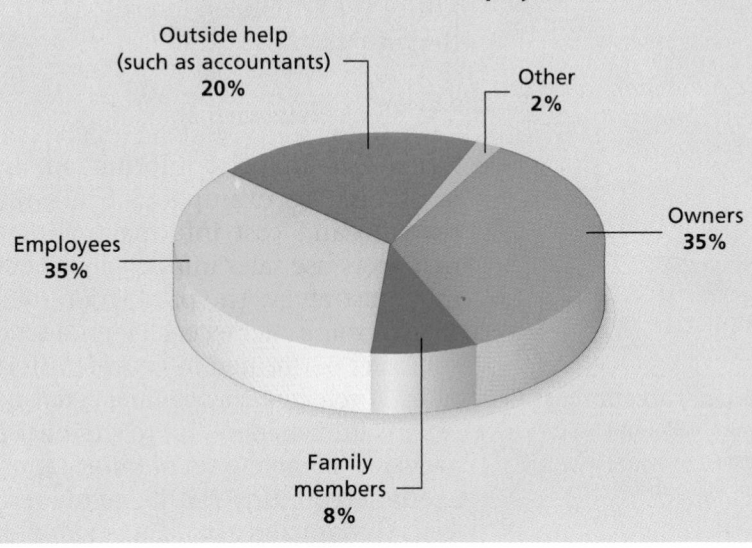

Outside help
(such as accountants)
20%

Other
2%

Employees
35%

Owners
35%

Family
members
8%

Stocks are traded on stock exchanges such as the New York Stock Exchange, shown here. Investors can buy or sell stocks by placing orders with stock brokers who transmit the orders to the exchange where the stock is traded.

GETTY IMAGES

Online Reporting   Many firms use the Internet to make their financial information available. For example, Dell, Inc., provides its investors and other interested parties with detailed financial information via its website. Investors can access Dell's most recent annual report, quarterly "financial fact sheets," and earnings estimates for the coming year. Furthermore, investors can request specific financial information using the website. By making this information available over the Internet, Dell provides investors and other parties with current, up-to-the-minute feedback on its financial performance.

Reporting to Creditors   Firms also report their financial condition to existing and prospective creditors. The creditors assess firms' financial statements to determine the probability that the firms will default on loans. Creditors that consider providing short-term loans assess financial statements to determine the firm's liquidity (ability to sell existing assets). Creditors that consider providing long-term loans may assess the financial statements to determine whether the firm is capable of generating sufficient income in future years to make interest and principal payments on the loan far into the future.

Decision Support

Firms use financial information developed by accountants to support decisions. For example, a firm's financial managers may use historical revenue and cost information for budgeting decisions. The marketing managers use sales information to evaluate the impact of a particular promotion strategy. The production managers use seasonal sales information to determine the necessary production level in the future. The type of accounting performed to provide information to help managers make decisions is referred to as **managerial accounting**. Financial accounting also reports information, but to shareholders and the IRS (outside the firm). To provide a complete set of information, the information generated by managerial accounting can be combined with other information (such as industry characteristics). For example, Blockbuster maintains information

managerial accounting
accounting performed to provide information to help managers of the firm make decisions

on revenue, current and historical sales and rental activity, demographics of store customers, and rental patterns. It can use this information to predict the types of DVDs and videos that may be popular in the future.

Control

In addition to providing information to support decisions, managerial accounting helps managers maintain control. By reviewing financial information, managers monitor the performance of individuals, divisions, and products. Accounting information on sales is used to monitor the performance of various products and the salespeople who sell them. Information on operating expenses is used to monitor production efficiency.

Managers evaluate their firm's financial statements to monitor operations and to identify the firm's strengths and weaknesses. Financial statements can be generated and analyzed as frequently as necessary to identify problems and resolve them quickly before they become serious.

Another accounting task used for control is **auditing,** which is an assessment of the records that were used to prepare the firm's financial statements. **Internal auditors** specialize in evaluating various divisions within a firm to ensure that they are operating efficiently.

auditing
an assessment of the records that were used to prepare a firm's financial statements

internal auditors
specialize in evaluating various divisions of a business to ensure that they are operating efficiently

Decision Making

Using Financial Reports to Detect Deficiencies

Surf Clothing Company relies on its accountants to keep track of its revenue and expenses. First, the company's revenue and expenses are summed up across all stores to provide an overall report. Second, Surf's revenue and expenses are reported per retail store so that individual store performance can be monitored. Third, Surf's revenue and expenses are reported per category of clothing (segmented by age group and gender) so that the performance of each clothing category can be monitored. In this way, Surf can identify the underlying reasons for its overall performance.

1. Why do you think that Surf's revenue may vary across its individual retail stores?
2. How could financial reports be used when deciding which stores should be allowed to grow over time and which stores (if any) should be closed down?

ANSWERS: 1. Revenue is based on demand by the local customers who shop at a particular store. The demand may be higher for stores when the income of local customers is high, when the competition is low, and when the local customers have preferences for the type of clothing produced by Surf Clothing Company. 2. Financial reports disclose the earnings of each store. Therefore, the stores with strong earnings may be allowed to expand because they could possibly increase their profits. Conversely, the stores with weak or negative earnings may be closed down because they are not providing an adequate return on the funds invested by the owners of Surf Clothing Company.

Responsible Financial Reporting

2

Discuss how firms can ensure proper financial reporting.

Firms have some flexibility when accounting for their financial condition. Some firms tend to use whatever method of accounting will inflate their earnings because they know that their stockholders will be better satisfied if earnings are high. Moreover, some of a firm's top managers who own the firm's stock may want a favorable financial report to ensure that the stock value stays high until they sell their stock holdings. Enron, Inc., used accounting gimmicks to inflate its revenue and its earnings until 2001 when

Out of
Business

investors finally realized that the financial statements were distorted. Enron filed for bankruptcy in November 2001. WorldCom used accounting gimmicks to reduce its expenses. In June 2002, it admitted that its expenses over the previous five quarters were underestimated by $3.9 billion. In July 2002, it went bankrupt.

A firm should use whatever method of accounting provides the most accurate indication of its financial condition. By doing so, the firm may benefit in two ways. First, it may gain some credibility with existing and prospective stockholders by providing clear and consistent reports that are easily understood. Second, using an understandable and logical accounting method makes it easier for the firm's managers to detect and correct deficiencies.

The Role of Auditors in Ensuring Proper Reporting

Publicly traded firms are required to have their annual financial reports audited by an independent accounting firm of public accountants, known as an independent auditor. The auditor's role is to certify that the financial reports are accurate and within the generally accepted reporting guidelines. An auditor's stamp of approval does not imply anything about a firm's performance; the auditor is certifying only that the information contained within the financial statements is accurate. Nevertheless, some auditors have certified financial reports that were misleading. Perhaps the best-known example was the audit of Enron by the accounting firm Arthur Andersen in the year 2000. Andersen certified some of Enron's financial reports that were very questionable. Auditors are sometimes tempted to certify financial reports because they want to be hired by the firm again in the future. In 2000, Arthur Andersen earned more than $50 million in fees for its auditing and other work provided to Enron. The auditors knew that if they did not certify the financial reports, Enron would hire another accounting firm instead. This ethical dilemma does not absolve Arthur Andersen from blame, but it does explain why auditors sometimes certify financial reports that should not be certified. Arthur

Andersen was also the auditor of WorldCom during the period when WorldCom's expenses were underestimated.

Given the conflict of interest that may arise, auditors cannot always be trusted to ensure that a firm properly reports financial information to its stockholders. The publicity surrounding the demise of Enron and World-Com has caused investors to be more cautious when interpreting financial statements. Some firms have responded by disclosing more details about their financial condition to demonstrate that they have nothing to hide.

The Role of the Board of Directors in Ensuring Proper Reporting

Since a firm's board of directors represents the shareholders, it can try to prevent the firm from providing misleading financial reports. However, some boards do not effectively represent the stockholders. For example, a problem may arise when board members are compensated with the firm's stock. Like the firm's top managers who own its stock, the board members might benefit from misleading financial reporting that artificially inflates the stock's price because they too could sell their shares while the stock is priced artificially high. The board members may be more willing to enforce proper disclosure if they cannot sell any of their stock holdings while serving on the board. If forced to hold on to their shares for a long-term period, directors may be more likely to make decisions that benefit the long-term performance of the firm.

The Role of the Sarbanes-Oxley Act

In response to the accounting fraud at Enron and other firms, regulators are attempting to ensure more accurate financial disclosure by firms. Stock exchanges have instituted new regulations for the firms that list on the exchange. The Securities and Exchange Commission has been granted more resources and power to monitor financial reporting.

Dennis Kozlowski, the former CEO of Tyco, was found guilty of fraud. The financial statements of Tyco did not fully disclose all financial information, causing some investors to pay a higher price for Tyco stock than what Tyco was really worth.

LANDOV LLC

Walt Disney Company's board of directors is introduced at a recent annual meeting for its shareholders.

Perhaps the most important regulatory changes to ensure accurate financial disclosure are the result of the Sarbanes-Oxley Act of 2002. Some of the act's more important provisions are summarized here.

▶ An auditing firm is allowed to provide nonaudit services when auditing a client only if the client's audit committee preapproves these services before the audit begins. This provision is intended to prevent a firm from requesting extra nonaudit work in an attempt to entice the auditor to approve its financial statements.

▶ Auditing firms may not audit companies whose chief executive officer (CEO), chief financial officer (CFO), or other managers in similar roles were employed by the auditing firm in the one-year period prior to the audit. This provision prevents an audit by auditors who may still have close ties to the firm.

▶ Those board members of the firm who are assigned to oversee the audit to ensure that it is done properly should not receive consulting or advising fees or other compensation from the auditing firm. This provision prevents audit committee members from being paid off to ignore their oversight duties.

▶ The CFO and other managers of the firm must file an internal control report along with each annual report. The internal control report must explain the controls that the firm has established to ensure that its financial reporting is accurate.

▶ The CEO and CFO must certify that the audited statements fairly represent the operations and financial condition of the firm. This prevents them from later saying that they were unaware of accounting gimmicks that were used to inflate earnings.

▶ Major fines or prison terms are imposed on employees who mislead investors or hide evidence. This provision attempts to ensure that a firm's employees will be penalized for their role in distorting the accounting statements.

The act should result in more accurate accounting. However, it requires publicly traded firms to complete substantial paperwork and increases their reporting costs. For some firms, the cost to ensure that they are following the guidelines of the Sarbanes-Oxley Act will exceed $1 million per year. Consequently, some small publicly traded firms have decided to revert back to privately held ownership to avoid the substantial costs of reporting. In addition, some firms will likely continue to use creative accounting methods (within the guidelines) that mislead investors. Therefore, investors will still have to be cautious when making investment decisions based on the financial information provided by firms.

Decision Making

Ensuring Accurate Financial Reporting

Surf Clothing Company employs accountants to report the financial condition of the firm on a quarterly basis. Many of the high-level managers who oversee the accounting function receive a bonus that is tied to the company's profits. Thus, these managers might be tempted to pressure the accountants to either overstate Surf's revenue or understate its expenses so that the profits will appear higher and their bonus will be bigger. To prevent such behavior, Surf Clothing Company (and all other publicly traded firms) has a set of guidelines that it uses to ensure accurate financial reporting. Most importantly, its top executives sign off on the financial statements to verify that they have seen the financial statements and pledge that the statements are accurate (as a result of the Sarbanes-Oxley Act).

1. Explain how Surf Clothing Company might incur higher expenses from compensating its employees if its financial reporting is not properly monitored.

2. How can Surf's internal controls ensure that its financial reporting to investors is accurate?

ANSWERS: 1. The profits might be overstated; if so, Surf would have to pay higher compensation to its managers. 2. Surf's internal controls can be matched to the financial reporting to ensure there are no discrepancies.

3

Explain how to interpret financial statements.

income statement
indicates the revenue, costs, and earnings of a firm over a period of time

balance sheet
reports the book value of all assets, liabilities, and owner's equity of a firm at a given point in time

Interpreting Financial Statements

The most important financial statements are the income statement and the balance sheet. The **income statement** indicates the firm's revenue, costs, and earnings over a period of time (such as a quarter or year), and the **balance sheet** reports the book value of all the firm's assets, liabilities, and owner's equity at a given point in time.

It is possible for a firm to show high earnings on its income statement while being financially weak according to its balance sheet. It is also possible for a firm to show low earnings or even losses on its income statement while being financially strong according to its balance sheet. Because the two statements reveal different financial characteristics, both financial statements must be analyzed along with other information to perform a complete evaluation.

Understanding the information reported on income statements and balance sheets is a necessary part of financial analysis. These financial statements are explained briefly next.

Income Statement

The annual income statement for Taylor, Inc., a manufacturing firm, is presented in Exhibit 15.1. The income statement items shown in Exhibit 15.1 are disclosed in the income statements of most manufacturing firms. **Net sales** reflect the total sales adjusted for any discounts. **Cost of goods sold** is the cost of the materials used to produce the goods that were sold. For example, the cost of steel used to produce automobiles is part of the cost of goods sold for Ford Motor Company. **Gross profit** is equal to net sales minus the cost of goods sold. Thus, gross profit measures the degree to which the revenue from selling products exceeded the cost of the materials used to produce them.

Operating expenses are composed of selling expenses and general and administrative expenses. For example, the cost of labor and utilities and advertising expenses at Ford Motor Company are part of operating expenses. Gross profit minus a firm's operating expenses equals **earnings before interest and taxes (EBIT)**. Earnings before interest and taxes minus interest expenses equals **earnings before taxes.** Finally, earnings before taxes minus taxes equals **net income** (sometimes referred to as **earnings after taxes**).

Firms commonly measure each income statement item as a percentage of total sales, as illustrated in Exhibit 15.2 for Taylor, Inc. The exhibit shows how each dollar of sales is used to cover various expenses that were incurred to generate the sales. Notice that 80 cents of every dollar of sales is used to cover the cost of the goods sold, while 12.5 cents of every dollar of sales is needed to cover operating expenses; 2.5 cents of every dollar of sales is needed to cover interest expense, and 1.5 cents of every dollar of sales is needed to pay taxes. That leaves 3.5 cents of every dollar of sales as net income. This breakdown for a firm can be compared with other firms in the industry. Based on this information, the firm may notice that it is using too much of its revenue to cover the cost of goods sold (relative to other firms in the industry). Therefore, it may search for ways to reduce the cost of producing its goods.

Balance Sheet

Anything owned by a firm is an **asset.** Anything owed by a firm is a **liability.** Firms normally support a portion of their assets with funds of the

---

net sales
total sales adjusted for any discounts

cost of goods sold
the cost of materials used to produce the goods that were sold

gross profit
net sales minus the cost of goods sold

operating expenses
composed of selling expenses and general and administrative expenses

earnings before interest and taxes (EBIT)
gross profit minus operating expenses

earnings before taxes
earnings before interest and taxes minus interest expenses

net income (earnings after taxes)
earnings before taxes minus taxes

asset
anything owned by a firm

liability
anything owed by a firm

Exhibit 15.1

Example of Income Statement: Taylor, Inc.

Net Sales		$20,000,000
Cost of Goods Sold		16,000,000
Gross Profit		$4,000,000
Selling Expense	$1,500,000	
General & Administrative Expenses	1,000,000	
Total Operating Expenses		2,500,000
Earnings before Interest and Taxes (EBIT)		$1,500,000
Interest Expense		500,000
Earnings before Taxes		$1,000,000
Income Taxes (at 30%)		300,000
Net Income		$700,000

Exhibit 15.2

Income Statement Items as a Percentage of Net Sales for Taylor, Inc.

Net Sales		100.0%
Cost of Goods Sold		80.0%
Gross Profit		20.0%
Selling Expense	7.5%	
General & Administrative Expenses	5.0%	
Total Operating Expenses		12.5%
Earnings before Interest and Taxes (EBIT)		7.5%
Interest Expense		2.5%
Earnings before Taxes		5.0%
Income Taxes (at 30%)		1.5%
Net Income		3.5%

owners, called "owner's equity" (also called "stockholder's equity"). The remaining portion is supported with borrowed funds, which creates a liability. This relationship is described by the following **basic accounting equation**:

basic accounting equation
Assets = Liabilities + Owner's Equity

$$\text{Assets} = \text{Liabilities} + \text{Owner's Equity}$$

For example, consider a person who purchases a car repair shop for $200,000. Assume that the person uses $40,000 of savings for the purchase and borrows the remaining $160,000 from a local bank. The accounting statement for this business will show assets of $200,000, liabilities of $160,000, and owner's equity of $40,000. As the business acquires equipment and machinery, its total asset value will increase. The funds used to purchase more assets will be obtained through either additional borrowing or additional support from the owner. Any increase in assets will therefore be matched by an equal increase in liabilities and owner's equity.

The balance sheet for Taylor, Inc., as of the end of the year, is shown in Exhibit 15.3. The assets listed on a balance sheet are separated into current assets and fixed assets. **Current assets** are assets that will be converted into cash within one year. They include cash, marketable securities, accounts receivable, and inventories. Cash typically represents checking account balances. Marketable securities are short-term securities that can easily be sold and quickly converted to cash if additional funds are needed. Marketable securities earn interest for the firm until they are sold or redeemed at maturity. Accounts receivable reflect sales that have been made but for which payment has not yet been received. Inventories are composed of raw materials, partially completed products, and finished products that have not yet been sold.

current assets
assets that will be converted into cash within one year

Fixed assets are assets that the firm will use for more than one year. They include the firm's plant and equipment. In Exhibit 15.3, depreciation is subtracted from plant and equipment to arrive at net fixed assets. **Depreciation** represents a reduction in the value of fixed assets to reflect deterioration in the assets over time. Specific accounting rules are used to measure the depreciation of fixed assets.

fixed assets
assets that will be used by a firm for more than one year

depreciation
a reduction in the value of fixed assets to reflect deterioration in the assets over time

Liabilities and owner's equity are also shown in Exhibit 15.3. Current (short-term) liabilities include accounts payable and notes payable. **Accounts payable** represent money owed by the firm for the purchase of

accounts payable
money owed by a firm for the purchase of materials

Exhibit 15.3

Example of Balance Sheet for Taylor, Inc.

Taylor, Inc.

Assets

Current Assets:	
Cash	$200,000
Marketable Securities	300,000
Accounts Receivable	500,000
Inventory	1,000,000
Total Current Assets	$2,000,000
Fixed Assets:	
Plant and Equipment	$10,000,000
Less: Accumulated Depreciation	2,000,000
Net Fixed Assets	$8,000,000
Total Assets	$10,000,000

Liabilities & Owner's Equity

Current Liabilities:	
Accounts Payable	$600,000
Notes Payable	400,000
Total Current Liabilities	$1,000,000
Long-Term Debt	$5,000,000
Owner's Equity:	
Common Stock ($5 par value, 200,000 shares)	$1,000,000
Additional Paid-In Capital	2,000,000
Retained Earnings	1,000,000
Total Owner's Equity	$4,000,000
Total Liabilities and Owner's Equity	$10,000,000

notes payable
short-term loans to a firm made by creditors such as banks

owner's equity
includes the par (or stated) value of all common stock issued, additional paid-in capital, and retained earnings

materials. **Notes payable** represent short-term loans to the firm made by creditors such as banks. Long-term liabilities (debt) are liabilities that will not be repaid within one year. These liabilities commonly include long-term loans provided by banks and the issuance of bonds.

Owner's equity includes the par (or stated) value of all common stock issued, additional paid-in capital, and retained earnings. Additional paid-in capital represents the dollar amount received from issuing common stock that exceeds par value. Retained earnings represent the accumulation of the firm's earnings that are reinvested in the firm's assets rather than distributed as dividends to shareholders.

A firm can use its balance sheet to determine the percentage of its investment in each type of asset. An example is provided in Exhibit 15.4. Notice that 80 percent of the firm's assets are allocated to net fixed assets. Most manufacturing firms allocate a large portion of their funds to net fixed assets because these are the assets used in the production process.

The liabilities and owner's equity can also be broken down to determine where the firm is obtaining most of its financial support. Notice that the firm obtained 50 percent of its funds by issuing long-term debt and another 30 percent from issuing stock. Retained earnings made up 10 percent of the firm's funds.

Exhibit 15.4

Breakdown of Balance Sheet
for Taylor, Inc.

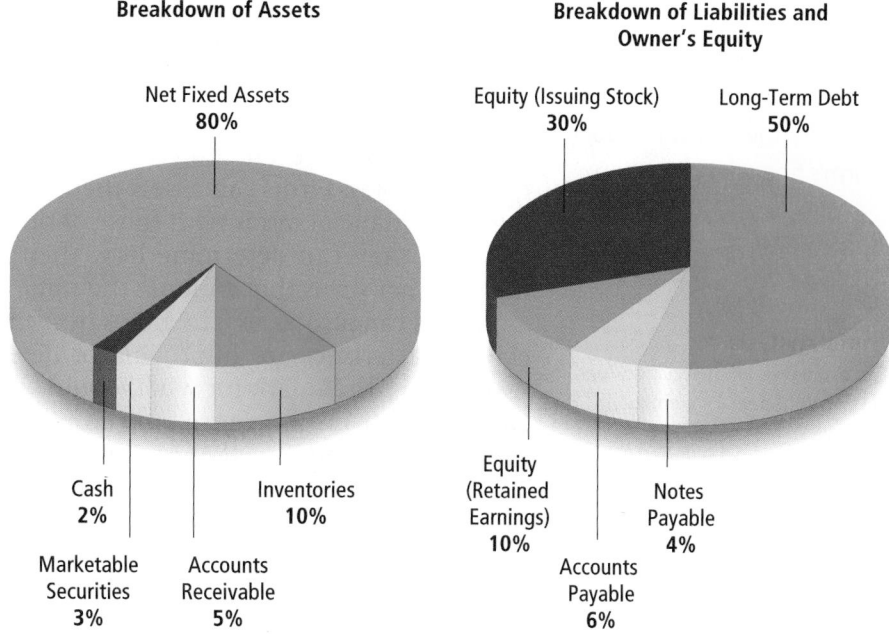

Breakdown of Assets

Net Fixed Assets
80%

Cash
2%

Marketable
Securities
3%

Accounts
Receivable
5%

Inventories
10%

**Breakdown of Liabilities and
Owner's Equity**

Equity (Issuing Stock)
30%

Long-Term Debt
50%

Equity
(Retained
Earnings)
10%

Accounts
Payable
6%

Notes
Payable
4%

Decision Making

Interpreting Financial Information to Make Business Decisions

The high-level managers of Surf Clothing Company are planning to establish new clothing stores, but first they want to assess the performance of two stores that they opened earlier this year. In general, the new stores have not performed as well as expected, so the managers want to detect deficiencies in those stores that could be avoided in the new stores. Their accountants compile financial information for each individual store that can be used by the high-level managers to assess the performance of these stores. Each store sells clothes for three different target markets: (1) children, (2) teenagers, and (3) customers in the 20 to 35 age range.

The sales and cost information for the new stores shows that revenue was much higher than expenses for clothing targeted for teenagers and customers in the 20 to 35 age range, but that revenue was lower than expenses for children's clothing. Based on this financial information, the managers of Surf Clothing decide that the new stores will not carry children's clothing and will instead focus on clothing only for teenagers and for customers in the 20 to 35 age range. Since the new stores will not carry children's clothing, they will have space to offer a wide variety of clothing for the other target markets. As a result of this strategy, the managers decide that Surf's production plant should increase its production of clothing targeted toward teenagers and reduce its production of children's clothing. Thus, by relying on accounting information, Surf Clothing Company revises its business focus so that it can increase its performance.

1. How could Surf Clothing Company use the accounting information to make changes in its existing retail stores?

2. Explain how the accounting information used by Surf could lead to the wrong decisions for a new store that is established in a different city.

ANSWERS: 1. It could change its existing stores to increase space for the clothing targeted toward teenagers and the 20 to 35 age group, while reducing space for the children's clothing.   2. The revenue and expense information in its existing stores will not necessarily reflect the future results in the new stores. It is possible that children's clothing revenue could be higher in those new stores, especially if there are fewer stores selling children's clothes (competition) in those locations.

Explain how to evaluate a firm's financial condition.

ratio analysis
an evaluation of the relationships between financial statement variables

Ratio Analysis

A firm's financial managers can use the financial statements to assess the financial condition of the firm. An important part of this assessment is **ratio analysis,** an evaluation of the relationships between financial statement variables. Firms can assess their financial characteristics by comparing their financial ratios with those of other firms in the same industry. In this way, they can determine how their financial condition differs from that of other firms that conduct the same type of business.

Firms can also assess the ratios over time to determine whether financial characteristics are improving or deteriorating. The industry average serves as a benchmark for what would be considered normal for the firm. Differences from the norm can be favorable or unfavorable, depending upon the size and direction of the difference.

Financial ratios are commonly classified according to the characteristics they measure. These include the following:

▶ Measures of liquidity

▶ Measures of efficiency

▶ Measures of financial leverage

▶ Measures of profitability

The ratios that are used to assess each of these characteristics are defined and discussed next. Each ratio is computed for Taylor, Inc., based on its financial statements in Exhibits 15.1 and 15.3.

Measures of Liquidity

liquidity
a firm's ability to meet short-term obligations

Liquidity refers to a firm's ability to meet short-term obligations. Since short-term assets are commonly used to pay short-term obligations (which are current liabilities), most liquidity measures compare current assets with current liabilities. The greater the level of current assets available relative to current liabilities, the greater the firm's liquidity.

A high degree of liquidity can enhance the firm's safety, but an excessive degree of liquidity can reduce the firm's return. For example, holding an excessive amount of cash is a waste and can reduce a firm's returns. Firms that have excessive cash, marketable securities, accounts receivable, and inventories could have invested more funds in assets such as machinery or buildings (fixed assets) that are used for production. Firms attempt to maintain sufficient liquidity to be safe, but not excessive liquidity. Two common liquidity measures are identified next.

Current Ratio   The current ratio compares current assets with current liabilities in ratio form. It is defined as:

$$\text{Current Ratio} = \frac{\text{Current Assets}}{\text{Current Liabilities}}$$

For Taylor:

$$\text{Current Ratio} = \frac{\$2,000,000}{\$1,000,000}$$

$$= 2.00$$

For most manufacturing firms, the current ratio is between 1.0 and 2.0. For Taylor, current assets are twice the amount of its current liabilities. A more detailed comparison of Taylor's liquidity and other financial ratios to the industry norms is conducted later in this chapter after all financial ratios have been discussed.

Quick Ratio   The quick ratio requires a slight adjustment in the current ratio. Inventory may not be easily converted into cash and therefore may be excluded when assessing liquidity. To get a more conservative indication of a firm's liquidity, the quick ratio does not include inventory in the numerator:

$$\text{Quick Ratio} = \frac{\text{Cash} + \text{Marketable Securities} + \text{Accounts Receivable}}{\text{Current Liabilities}}$$

For Taylor:

$$\text{Quick Ratio} = \frac{\$1,000,000}{\$1,000,000}$$

$$= 1.00$$

Since the quick ratio does not include inventory in the numerator, it is smaller than the current ratio for any firm that has some inventory. The larger the firm's quick ratio, the greater its liquidity.

Measures of Efficiency

Efficiency ratios measure how efficiently a firm manages its assets. Two of the more popular efficiency ratios are described next.

Inventory Turnover   Firms prefer to generate a high level of sales with a low investment in inventory because fewer funds are tied up. However, very low levels of inventory can also be unfavorable because they can result in shortages, which can reduce sales. To assess the relationship between a firm's inventory level and sales, the inventory turnover ratio can be used:

$$\text{Inventory Turnover} = \frac{\text{Cost of Goods Sold}}{\text{Inventory}}$$

For Taylor:

$$\text{Inventory Turnover} = \frac{\$16,000,000}{\$1,000,000}$$

$$= 16.00$$

This ratio suggests that Taylor turns its inventory over 16 times during the year. The cost of goods sold is used instead of sales in the numerator to exclude the markup that is reflected in sales.

The average inventory over the period of concern should be used in the denominator when it is available, since inventory can change substantially during that period. When the average inventory is not available, the year-end inventory is used.

Asset Turnover   Firms prefer to support a high level of sales with a relatively small amount of assets so that they efficiently utilize the assets they invest in. Firms that maintain excess assets are not investing their funds wisely. To measure the efficiency with which firms use their assets, the asset turnover ratio can be calculated. It is defined and computed for Taylor as follows:

$$\text{Asset Turnover} = \frac{\text{Net Sales}}{\text{Total Assets}}$$

$$= \frac{\$20,000,000}{\$10,000,000}$$

$$= 2.00$$

Taylor's sales during the year were two times the level of its total assets. Like all other financial ratios, the asset turnover should be evaluated over time and in comparison with the industry norm.

Measures of Financial Leverage

Financial leverage represents the degree to which a firm uses borrowed funds to finance its assets. Firms that borrow a large proportion of their funds have a high degree of financial leverage. This can favorably affect the firm's owners when the firm performs well, because the earnings generated by the firm can be spread among a relatively small group of owners. When the firm experiences poor performance, however, a high degree of financial leverage is dangerous. Firms with a high degree of financial leverage incur higher fixed financial costs (interest expenses) that must be paid regardless of their levels of sales. These firms are more likely to experience debt repayment problems and therefore are perceived as having more risk. Conversely, firms that obtain a larger proportion of funds from equity financing incur smaller debt payments and therefore have less risk.

Although a high proportion of equity financing reduces risk, it may also force earnings to be widely distributed among many shareholders. Firms that rely heavily on equity typically have a large number of shareholders who share the firm's earnings. This may dilute the earnings that are distributed to each shareholder as dividends.

debt-to-equity ratio
a measure of the amount of long-term financing provided by debt relative to equity

Debt-to-Equity Ratio   A measure of the amount of long-term financing provided by debt relative to equity is called the **debt-to-equity ratio.** This ratio is defined and computed for Taylor as follows:

$$\text{Debt-to-Equity Ratio} = \frac{\text{Long-Term Debt}}{\text{Owner's Equity}}$$

$$= \frac{\$5,000,000}{\$4,000,000}$$

$$= 1.25$$

For Taylor, long-term debt is 1.25 times the amount of owner's equity.

times interest earned ratio
measures the ability of a firm to cover its interest payments

Times Interest Earned   The **times interest earned ratio** measures a firm's ability to cover its interest payments. If a firm has a low level of earnings before interest and taxes (EBIT) relative to the size of its interest expense, a small decrease in EBIT in the future could force the firm to default on the loan. Conversely, a high level of EBIT relative to the annual interest expense suggests that even if next year's EBIT declines substantially, the firm will still be able to cover the interest expense. The times interest earned ratio is defined and computed for Taylor as follows:

$$\text{Times Interest Earned} = \frac{\text{Earnings before Interest and Taxes (EBIT)}}{\text{Annual Interest Expense}}$$

$$= \frac{\$1,500,000}{\$500,000}$$

$$= 3.0$$

A times interest earned ratio of 3.0 indicates that Taylor's earnings before interest and taxes were three times its interest expense.

Measures of Profitability

Profitability measures indicate the performance of a firm's operations during a given period. The dollar amount of profit generated by the firm can be measured relative to the firm's level of sales, assets, or equity. The ratios that measure these relationships are discussed next.

net profit margin
a measure of net income as a percentage of sales

Net Profit Margin   The **net profit margin** is a measure of net income as a percentage of sales. This ratio measures the proportion of every dollar of sales that ultimately becomes net income. The net profit margin is computed for Taylor as follows:

$$\text{Net Profit Margin} = \frac{\text{Net Income}}{\text{Net Sales}}$$

$$= \frac{\$700,000}{\$20,000,000}$$

$$= 3.50\%$$

Even with a low profit margin, firms with a high volume of sales can generate a reasonable return for their shareholders. However, firms with a low volume of sales may need a higher profit margin to generate a reasonable return for their shareholders.

return on assets (ROA)
measures a firm's net income as a percentage of the total amount of assets utilized by the firm

Return on Assets   A firm's **return on assets (ROA)** measures the return (net income) of the firm as a percentage of the total amount of assets utilized by the firm. It is defined and computed for Taylor as follows:

$$\text{Return on Assets} = \frac{\text{Net Income}}{\text{Total Assets}}$$

$$= \frac{\$700,000}{\$10,000,000}$$

$$= 7.00\%$$

The ROA provides a broad measure of a firm's performance. The higher the ROA, the more efficiently the firm utilized its assets to generate net income.

return on equity (ROE)
measures the return to the common stockholders (net income) as a percentage of their investment in the firm; earnings as a proportion of the firm's equity

Return on Equity   The **return on equity (ROE)** measures the return to the common stockholders as a percentage of their investment in the firm. Existing and potential investors monitor this ratio closely because it indicates the recent return on the investment of the existing shareholders. The ROE measures the firm's performance from using the equity provided. The return on equity is defined and computed for Taylor as follows:

$$\text{Return on Equity} = \frac{\text{Net Income}}{\text{Owner's Equity}}$$

$$= \frac{\$700,000}{\$4,000,000}$$

$$= 17.50\%$$

Stockholders prefer ROE to be very high because a high ROE indicates a high return relative to the size of their investment. Using high levels of financial leverage can increase ROE (because less equity is used), so the net income is distributed among fewer shareholders, but high levels of financial leverage increase the firm's exposure to risk.

Comparison of Ratios with Those of Other Firms

Exhibit 15.5 provides the common interpretations for ratios that deviate substantially from what is normal in the industry. Note, however, that there may be a perfectly acceptable reason why a ratio deviates from the norm. For example, consider a firm that has an abnormally large amount

Exhibit 15.5

Interpretation of Financial Ratios That Differ from the Industry Norm

Ratios	Common Interpretation If Ratio Is Significantly Lower than Normal	Common Interpretation If Ratio Is Significantly Higher than Normal
Liquidity Ratios		
Current ratio	Insufficient liquidity	Excessive liquidity
Quick ratio	Insufficient liquidity	Excessive liquidity
Efficiency Ratios		
Inventory turnover	Excessive inventory	Insufficient inventory
Asset turnover	Excessive level of assets relative to sales	Insufficient assets based on existing sales
Leverage Ratios		
Debt-to-equity ratio	Low level of long-term debt	Excessive long-term debt
Times interest earned	Potential cash flow problems because required interest payments are high relative to the earnings available to pay interest	The firm can easily make its debt payments.
Profitability Ratios		
Net profit margin	Expenses are high relative to sales.	Expenses are low relative to sales.
Return on assets	Net income is low relative to the amount of assets maintained by the firm.	Net income is high relative to the amount of assets maintained by the firm.
Return on equity	Net income is low relative to the amount of equity invested in the firm.	Net income is high relative to the amount of equity invested in the firm.

Exhibit 15.6

Evaluation of Taylor, Inc., Based on Ratio Analysis

Ratio	Calculation	Ratio for Taylor	Average for Industry	Evaluation of Taylor Based on the Ratio
Liquidity				
Current	$\dfrac{\text{Current Assets}}{\text{Current Liabilities}}$	2.00	1.60	Too high
Quick	$\dfrac{\text{Cash + Marketable Securities + Accts. Receivable}}{\text{Current Liabilities}}$	1.00	0.90	Too high
Efficiency				
Inventory Turnover	$\dfrac{\text{Cost of Goods Sold}}{\text{Inventory}}$	16.00	16.22	OK, unless shortages are occurring
Asset Turnover	$\dfrac{\text{Net Sales}}{\text{Total Assets}}$	2.00	4.11	Too low
Financial Leverage				
Debt-to-Equity Ratio	$\dfrac{\text{Long-Term Debt}}{\text{Owner's Equity}}$	1.25	0.60	Too high
Times Interest Earned	$\dfrac{\text{Earnings before Interest and Taxes}}{\text{Annual Interest Expense}}$	3.0	7.4	Too low
Profitability				
Net Profit Margin	$\dfrac{\text{Net Income}}{\text{Net Sales}}$	3.5%	4.00%	Too low
Return on Assets	$\dfrac{\text{Net Income}}{\text{Total Assets}}$	7.00%	16.44%	Too low
Return on Equity	$\dfrac{\text{Net Income}}{\text{Owner's Equity}}$	17.50%	26.30%	Too low

of cash according to a comparison with the industry average. Common stockholders may interpret this as evidence of inefficient use of assets. However, further investigation may reveal that the firm has built up its cash because it plans to purchase machinery in the near future. Financial analysis based on an assessment of financial ratios does not necessarily lead to immediate conclusions, but it does lead to questions about a firm that deserve further investigation.

Exhibit 15.6 provides a general summary of the financial ratios commonly used for ratio analysis. Comparing a firm's ratios with an industry average can help identify the firm's strengths and weaknesses. Columns 1 and 2 of Exhibit 15.6 identify and define the financial ratios presented in this chapter. Column 3 lists Taylor's ratios, and the industry averages are provided in column 4. Column 5 uses the information in columns 3 and 4 to provide an evaluation of Taylor's ratios relative to those of the industry average.

In terms of liquidity, Taylor's current and quick ratios are above the industry average. This suggests that although Taylor probably has sufficient liquidity, it may have an excessive amount of current assets.

Taylor's inventory turnover ratio is similar to the industry average. This suggests that Taylor maintains the normal amount of inventory.

Taylor's asset turnover ratio is below the industry average. This suggests that Taylor is not using all of its assets efficiently. That is, it has an excessive investment in assets, given the level of sales. Taylor might consider either taking steps to increase sales (which would force more production from its assets) or selling some of its assets.

Global Business

Effect of Exchange Rate Movements on Earnings

A U.S. firm that has subsidiaries (including offices and factories) in foreign countries typically generates earnings in the local currencies of the countries where those subsidiaries are located. Any firm with foreign subsidiaries must consolidate the financial data from all subsidiaries when preparing its financial statements. Because of the consolidation process, changes in exchange rates can have an impact on the firm's reported earnings, as illustrated next.

Consider a U.S. firm that has a subsidiary in the United Kingdom that generated £10 million in earnings last year. Also assume that the firm's U.S. operations generated $12 million in earnings. The firm must consolidate the £10 million with the $12 million when preparing its income statement. The £10 million cannot simply be added to the $12 million because the British and U.S. currencies have different values. Therefore, the British earnings must be "translated" by determining the dollar amount of those earnings. The average exchange rate of the currency of concern over the period in which income was generated is used to translate the foreign earnings. For example, if the average exchange rate of the British pound during the last year was $2.00, the British earnings would be converted into $20 million (computed as £10 million × $2.00 per pound). In this case, the firm would report total earnings of $32 million (computed as $20 million translated from the British subsidiary plus the $12 million of earnings generated in the United States).

To recognize how the firm's reported earnings are affected by the exchange rate, assume that the average exchange rate during the last year was $1.70 per pound instead of $2.00 per pound. Based on this assumption, the British earnings are translated into $17 million (£10 million × $1.70 per pound). Thus, the British earnings are translated into a smaller amount of dollar earnings. The firm's consolidated earnings in this example are $29 million (computed as $17 million from the British operations plus $12 million from the U.S. operations), which is $3 million less than in the first example. This illustrates how the reported amount of earnings is affected by the average exchange rate over the period of concern.

If the foreign currency has a high value over the period of concern, the foreign earnings will be translated into a higher amount of dollar earnings reported on the income statement. Many U.S. firms with foreign subsidiaries may report unusually high earnings when the values of foreign currencies are high in that period (when the dollar is weak). Under these conditions, the foreign earnings are translated into a large amount of dollar earnings on the income statement. If the values of foreign currencies decline over a particular year (when the dollar strengthens), the foreign earnings will translate into a smaller amount of dollar earnings, which will reduce the level of consolidated earnings reported on the firm's income statement.

With regard to financial leverage, the debt-to-equity ratio is higher than the industry average. This suggests that Taylor has a relatively high proportion of long-term financing provided by debt relative to equity. The times interest earned ratio for Taylor is lower than the industry norm. Other firms of the same size and in the same industry have lower interest expenses (because they use a lower proportion of debt financing). Since Taylor already has a relatively high proportion of debt, it may be less able to borrow additional funds.

Regarding profitability, Taylor's net profit margin is lower than the industry norm, which suggests that Taylor is not generating adequate net income based on its level of sales. Also, its return on assets is too low, which is partially attributed to its inefficient use of assets. Since Taylor is not using its assets efficiently to generate sufficient sales, it cannot generate a sufficient amount of net income.

Taylor's ROE is too low, which means that it is not generating an adequate net income, given the size of the equity investment in the firm. If Taylor could more efficiently utilize its assets, it could increase its net income and therefore increase its ROE.

Exhibit 15.7

Example of How
Management, Marketing,
and Finance Deficiencies
Can Be Detected with
Ratio Analysis

Management Decisions

One of a firm's relevant management decisions is the production process used to produce products. An efficient production process can result in a relatively higher amount of production and sales with a given level of assets. The asset turnover ratio is an indicator of the efficiency of production because it measures the level of sales generated with a given level of assets. Taylor has a low asset turnover ratio, implying an inefficient use of assets.

Marketing Decisions

Since Taylor's asset turnover ratio is low, it should either eliminate those assets that are not efficiently utilized or maintain its assets but produce and sell a higher volume of products. If it decides to maintain its assets and increase production, it will need effective marketing strategies to sell the extra amount of products produced. Thus, proper marketing strategies may help Taylor to improve its asset turnover ratio.

Finance Decisions

Taylor's debt-to-equity ratio is higher than the norm, which reflects its high degree of financial leverage. Its high proportion of debt financing may make it difficult for Taylor to cover its interest payments. Taylor may use more equity financing in the future, but this will reduce its return on equity. Given its poor utilization of assets, Taylor might consider selling some of its assets and using the proceeds to reduce its debt level. This would allow for a more acceptable degree of financial leverage.

Exhibit 15.7 illustrates how the financial analysis identifies different business functions that may need improvement. Taylor's management, marketing, and finance functions may need to be reassessed to improve its performance. In general, management strategies may be revised to improve production efficiency, marketing strategies may be revised to increase sales, and financing strategies may be revised to establish a more appropriate degree of financial leverage.

Limitations of Ratio Analysis

Ratio analysis is useful for detecting a firm's strengths and weaknesses. Nevertheless, it has some limitations, which can result in misleading conclusions. The major limitations of ratio analysis are as follows:

1. Comparing some firms with an industry average can be difficult because the firms operate in more than one industry. Consider a firm that produces gas grills, machinery, and aluminum panels. The firm's ratios may deviate from a specific industry norm as a result of the characteristics of the other industries in which the firm operates. Also, the industry used as a benchmark for comparison may include firms that are involved in a variety of other businesses. This distorts the average ratios for the industry.

2. Accounting practices vary among firms. A firm's financial ratios can deviate from the norm because of differences in accounting methods rather than differences in operations. For example, one firm may have used an accounting method that inflates its revenue or defers the reporting of some expenses until the following quarter. Consequently, this quarter's earnings will be inflated, and ratios such as ROA or ROE will be inflated. The firm's performance is essentially exaggerated in the quarter because of the accounting method used. Investors may overvalue a firm when its reported earnings are inflated.

3. Firms with seasonal swings in sales may show large deviations from the norm at certain times but not at others. Normally, however, the seasonal swings should not distort annual financial statements.

Sources of Information for Ratio Analysis

To help perform ratio analysis, industry data can be obtained from a variety of sources. The following are two of the more common sources:

▶ **Robert Morris Associates** The booklet *Annual Statement Studies,* published by Robert Morris Associates, provides financial ratios for many different industries. Ratios for firms of various sizes are included so that a firm's ratios can be compared with those of similar-sized firms in the same industry.

▶ **Dun and Bradstreet** Dun and Bradstreet provides financial ratios for industries and for groups of firms within industries classified by size.

Decision Making

Using Ratio Analysis for Business Decisions

Surf Clothing Company attempts to monitor its performance and financial condition so that it can detect any deficiencies in its business. Various managers at Surf rely on financial statements created by its accountants to make business decisions:

▶ Financial managers measure liquidity ratios to determine whether Surf has sufficient funds to cover upcoming bills.

▶ Managers in the production department measure efficiency ratios to determine whether the inventory level is excessive and whether Surf's sales are sufficient, given the size of its business.

▶ Financial managers measure financial leverage ratios to determine whether Surf can afford to cover its future debt payments.

▶ Financial managers measure profitability ratios to determine Surf's recent profitability.

  1. Explain how Surf's ratio analysis may affect its decision regarding how much to produce in the future.

  2. Explain how Surf's ratio analysis may affect its marketing decisions.

ANSWERS: 1. Surf can use ratio analysis to determine its inventory, which will influence its decision regarding how much to produce in the future. 2. Surf can use ratio analysis to determine its inventory, which will influence its decision regarding how much advertising will be needed to sell the inventory or whether it should lower prices in order to sell its inventory.

COLLEGE HEALTH CLUB: FINANCIAL CONDITION OF CHC

Sue Kramer is conducting a financial analysis of College Health Club (CHC). Her analysis raises two concerns. First, her expenses may exceed her income for several months, which will result in a loss (negative profits) over that period. Sue realizes, however, that as CHC's memberships increase, its revenue will increase. In addition, many of CHC's expenses are fixed and should not change significantly. Thus, CHC's revenue should exceed its expenses once the memberships increase.

Sue is also concerned that CHC's financial leverage (based on the debt-to-equity ratio) is high. Since Sue is investing $20,000 of her own money (equity) and is borrowing an additional $40,000 (debt), CHC's initial debt-to-equity ratio is 2.0, indicating that its debt is twice its equity. Since Sue plans to reinvest any profits back into the business, CHC's equity will increase over time as profits accumulate. By increasing the equity over time without borrowing additional funds, she will be able to reduce CHC's degree of financial leverage.

Overall, Sue's financial analysis helps her realize that her concerns about CHC's profitability and its financial leverage should be alleviated over time. If CHC's memberships increase as expected, its profitability and financial leverage ratios will improve.

Summary

1 A firm's financial condition is important to financial managers, to the firm's creditors, and to investors. Financial managers evaluate the firm to detect weaknesses that can be corrected and strengths that can be exploited. Creditors evaluate the firm with a view toward determining its creditworthiness, and investors evaluate the firm's performance to determine whether they should buy or sell the firm's stock.

A firm's existing shareholders and other investors use financial statements to make investment decisions. Most existing shareholders of a publicly owned firm are not employees of the firm. They simply invested in the firm's stock in an effort to earn a high return on their investment. They rely on financial statements to serve as an indicator of the firm's recent and future performance. Thus, they may decide whether to sell the stock they are holding based on a review of the firm's financial statements.

When investors consider buying a stock, they may rely on financial statements to determine the firm's financial condition. Based on a review of the firm's financial statements, they derive an estimate of the firm's stock price. If the existing market price of the firm's stock is below the value that they derive from the financial statements, they may conclude that the stock is currently undervalued by the market, which may encourage them to buy the stock.

2 Firms are responsible for reporting accurate financial information to their existing shareholders, prospective investors, and creditors. Unfortunately, managers are sometimes tempted to exaggerate their firm's financial performance by distorting its financial statements. This may result in a strong demand for the stock, which drives the price higher. Once the price increases, some managers who own some of the stock may sell their stock before other investors recognize the firm's true financial condition. Under the Sarbanes-Oxley Act (SOX), any managers or auditors who were responsible for a firm's misleading financial statements are subject to more severe penalties. The act was intended to protect the interests of investors who may make investment decisions based on information disclosed in financial statements.

3 The key financial statements necessary to perform a thorough evaluation are the income statement and balance sheet. The income statement reports costs, revenue, and earnings over a specified period. The balance sheet reports the book value of assets, liabilities, and owner's equity at a given point in time.

4 Most financial ratios help evaluate one of four characteristics: liquidity, efficiency, financial leverage, and profitability. The liquidity ratios measure a firm's ability to meet its short-term obligations. Efficiency ratios measure how efficiently a firm utilizes its assets. Financial leverage ratios measure the firm's relative use of debt financing versus equity financing and indicate the firm's ability to repay its debt. Profitability ratios measure the firm's net income relative to various size levels. In evaluating a firm's financial ratios, it is useful to compare them with an industry norm. This approach can help detect any deficiencies that exist so that corrective action can be taken. Furthermore, it provides useful input for implementing new policies.

How the Chapter Concepts Affect Business Performance

A firm's managers use accounting and financial analysis to make decisions. These functions provide information that is needed to identify existing deficiencies that need to be corrected and to assess the potential benefits of proposed business ideas.

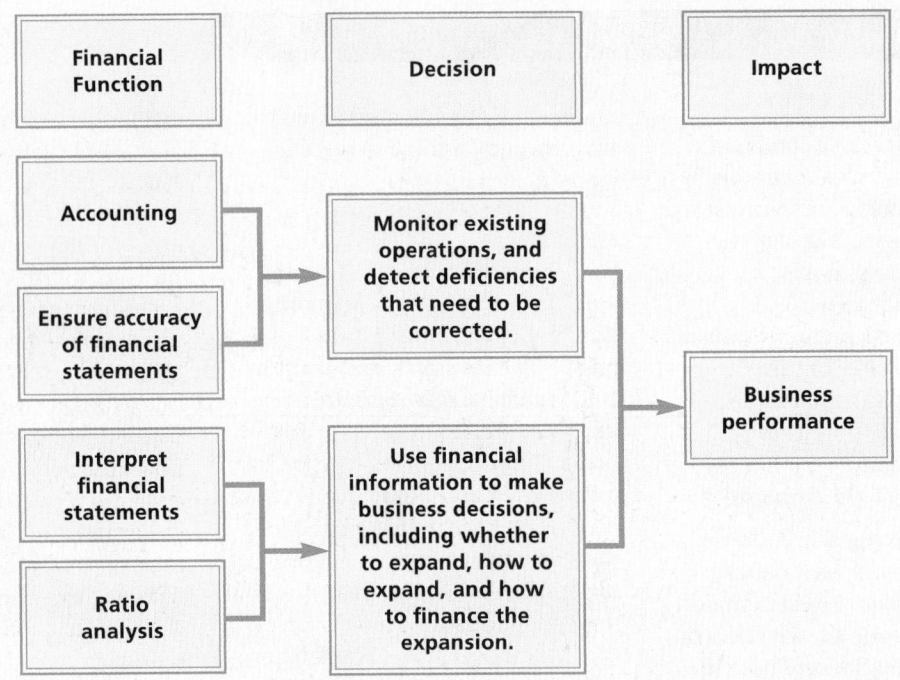

Key Terms

accounting 568
accounts payable 577
asset 576
auditing 571
balance sheet 575
basic accounting equation 577
bookkeeping 568
certified public accountants (CPAs) 568
cost of goods sold 576
current assets 577
debt-to-equity ratio 582

depreciation 577
earnings before interest and taxes (EBIT) 576
earnings before taxes 576
financial accounting 568
fixed assets 577
gross profit 576
income statement 575
internal auditors 571
liability 576
liquidity 580
managerial accounting 570

net income 576
net profit margin 583
net sales 576
notes payable 578
operating expenses 576
owner's equity 578
public accountants 568
ratio analysis 580
return on assets (ROA) 583
return on equity (ROE) 584
times interest earned ratio 582

Review & Critical Thinking Questions

1. What is accounting? Why is accounting important for a firm?

2. List the parties that would be interested in a firm's financial condition. How would each use financial information about the firm?

3. What is a public accountant? What is an important job of public accountants?

4. What is the difference between a balance sheet and an income statement?

5. What is the difference between current assets and fixed assets? Provide examples of each type of asset.

6. Discuss how assets can be financed by a firm.

7. Why is responsible financial reporting important?

8. What role does a firm's board of directors play in ensuring proper financial reporting? If board members are being compensated with shares of the firm's stock, how could they be forced to act in the long-term interests of the company?

9. Discuss the pros and cons of financial leverage for a firm.

10. Why is profitability relevant for a firm? How can profitability be measured?

11. What are the limitations of ratio analysis?

12. Discuss the effect of exchange rates on the earnings of a foreign subsidiary whose parent corporation is located in the United States.

13. Why do firms have to follow GAAP, SEC regulations, and IRS regulations when they report financial information?

14. Why do publicly owned firms have to hire public accountants when reporting their financial statements?

15. How did the Sarbanes-Oxley Act of 2002 affect auditors' relationships with the firms they audit?

16. What kinds of disincentives does the Sarbanes-Oxley Act impose to discourage managers from falsifying financial statements?

17. What is the difference between assets and liabilities?

18. Why do manufacturing firms hold relatively little cash compared to net fixed assets?

19. What is meant by "responsible" financial reporting?

Discussion Questions

1. Discuss the concept of short-term financing for short-term assets and long-term financing for long-term assets.

2. How can a firm use the Internet to provide information about its financial performance?

3. Indicate the ratio that measures each of the following and classify it as a measure of liquidity, efficiency, financial leverage, or profitability: (a) the return of profits to owners, (b) the amount of debt financing relative to the owner's investment, and (c) the ratio of the firm's short-term assets to its short-term liabilities.

4. Discuss the difference between gross profit and earnings before interest and taxes.

5. Assume that you are planning to invest in a corporation. Before you do this, however, you would like to examine its financial statements. Which statements would you want to review and why?

6. You are ready to invest in a company, primarily because its financial statements have recently been audited by a reputable accounting firm. Those statements show that the company had a very strong financial performance recently. Why might you conduct some additional research before investing in this firm?

7. Why is financial reporting important for firms? What impact might financial reporting have on a firm's stock price?

8. Describe the Sarbanes-Oxley Act of 2002. How did it affect auditors and managers of publicly owned firms?

9. Explain the basic accounting equation. What does each component represent? What is owner's equity?

10. Describe the interaction between (a) auditors, (b) managers, and (c) the board of directors in ensuring accurate financial reporting.

IT's YOUR DECISION: FINANCIAL MANAGEMENT AT CHC

1. Explain why the current ratio is important to CHC.

2. Explain how CHC's financial leverage can be measured. If the leverage is too high, what is the danger to CHC?

3. Explain how Sue Kramer can monitor CHC's performance by comparing its net income to the amount of equity invested in CHC.

4. If Sue decides to expand CHC's existing facilities, explain why its earnings may be lower initially.

5. A health club differs from manufacturing firms in that it produces a service rather than products. Manufacturing firms tend to require more machinery than service firms. Explain why manufacturing firms may need more financing than service firms.

Investing in a Business

Using the annual report of the firm in which you would like to invest, complete the following:

1. Review the income statement and balance sheet in the firm's annual report. Determine the return on equity that the firm generated last year for its investors. Do you believe that this return is satisfactory? What was the firm's return on equity in the previous year? Did the firm's performance improve last year?

2. Use the balance sheet to determine the firm's liquidity ratio as of the end of last year. Interpret that ratio.

3. Use the balance sheet to determine the firm's debt-to-equity ratio. Interpret that ratio.

4. Explain how the business uses technology to publicize its financial performance. For example, does it use the Internet to provide information about its financial performance? Does it provide information regarding the methods used to assess its financial performance and to improve it in the future?

5. Go to http://hoovers.com and locate the NEWS SEARCH. Type in the name of the firm in the space provided, and review the recent news stories about the firm. Summarize any (at least one) recent news story about the firm that applies to one or more of the key concepts in this chapter.

Case: Using an Accounting System

Sue Williams is an artist who creates drawings that are purchased by individuals. She displays her drawings at various art fairs, where she has obtained many orders. She has also received many referrals from her previous customers, and her business continues to grow. Sue maintains her own financial records, which include a separate checking account for the business and two notebooks.

In one notebook, Sue records her sales. When she sells a drawing to a customer, Sue records the date, amount, customer name, and a brief description of the drawing.

In the second notebook, Sue enters similar information for each purchase of art supplies that she makes. She is planning to meet with her accountant and is not sure if she has all the accounting data regarding the transactions of her business.

Questions

1. If Sue wants to assess her firm's performance, what type of firms should she use for purposes of comparison?

2. Explain how the two notebooks that Sue uses could be used to develop an income statement.

3. Sue notices that her asset turnover is low. Interpret this situation.

4. How will a low asset turnover ratio affect the profits at Sue's firm?

5. Considering this is a sole proprietorship without shareholders, do you think responsible financial reporting still applies to Sue's business? Why or why not?

Video Case: Reporting Information at Archway

Archway Cookies, a leading cookie producer, was founded in 1936. Archway's managers had difficulty obtaining cost information quickly because its business information systems were not integrated. Archway now employs a very sophisticated business information system that allows it to integrate its information packages and avoid manual recording of information. Archway's managers recognize the importance of timely and accurate information when making decisions. Higher-level executives need to have general information in a sum-

mary format and also need to be able to screen large amounts of data to identify exceptions to normal operations. Archway's managers are now able to estimate the costs of specific operations. The managers anticipate that the new information system will generate great operating cost savings for the firm. Nevertheless, the managers understand that implementing the new system will present challenges; in particular, employees will have to learn how to use the integrated information system.

Questions

1 Why was Archway's management concerned about its old information system?

2 What kinds of problems was Archway having with coordinating information?

3 Why do Archway's higher-level managers need a global, summarized set of information rather than specific details about the company's production and stores?

4 What kinds of problems may Archway encounter as it implements the new information system?

Internet Applications

1. http://www.aicpa.org/index.htm

Click on "About AICPA." What is this organization? What kinds of information regarding accounting can be found at this website? Click on "AICPA Antifraud & Corporate Responsibility Resource Center." What are some ways to detect and prevent accounting fraud?

2. http://www.sec.gov

What organization does this website belong to? What is the SEC? Click on "Corporation Finance" and then on

"Statements Made by CEOs and CFOs." Which CEOs certified their financial statements on time? Which CEOs were late in certifying their financial statements?

3. http://www.sci-corp.com

Enter the Service Corporation International website. What kinds of information for investors are available at the website? Click on "Investors" and then on "Annual Report." What kinds of information are reported in the Annual Report?

Dell's Secret to Success

DELL™

Go to http://www.reportgallery.com and review Dell's most recent annual report. Also, go to Dell's website (http://www.dell.com) and in the section "about Dell," review the background material about Dell that relates to this chapter.

Questions

1 Based on Dell's focus, what items on the income statement would Dell closely monitor to ensure that it was achieving its goals?

2 What balance sheet items would be very important to Dell?

3 Review Dell's comments on its website about its financial reporting. Notice how it emphasizes the integrity of its reporting process and how it implements systems, controls, and processes so that it can summarize timely and accurate information. Why do you think that Dell emphasizes its integrity when discussing financial reporting?

In-Text Study Guide

Answers are in Appendix C at the back of book.

True or False

1. Accounting is the summary and analysis of a firm's financial condition.

2. Financial accounting is primarily used to help managers make decisions.

3. Bookkeeping is the recording of a firm's financial transactions.

4. An accountant working for Microsoft, a publicly owned corporation, is an example of a public accountant.

5. The two primary financial statements for a firm are the balance sheet and the bookkeeping statement.

6. Inventory and accounts receivables are shown as fixed assets on a firm's financial statements.

7. A balance sheet reports the book value of a firm's assets, liabilities, and owner's equity.

8. Firms are encouraged to design their financial accounting reports to best satisfy their managers' need for information.

9. Independent auditors are sometimes tempted to certify questionable financial reports because the auditors usually sit on the board of directors of the firm.

10. The debt-to-equity ratio measures the liquidity of a firm.

11. Financial leverage represents the degree to which a firm uses borrowed funds to finance its assets.

Multiple Choice

12. Publicly owned firms are required to periodically report their financial condition for existing or potential:
    a) suppliers.
    b) customers.
    c) employees.
    d) shareholders.
    e) unions.

13. The type of accounting performed for reporting purposes is referred to as:
    a) ratio analysis.
    b) financial accounting.
    c) managerial accounting.
    d) cost accounting.
    e) payroll accounting.

14. Which of the following groups are primarily concerned with the risk of default on a loan?
    a) owners
    b) certified public accountants
    c) creditors
    d) auditors
    e) stockholders

15. Firms use financial information developed by accountants to:
    a) support financial data.
    b) analyze job descriptions.
    c) support decisions.
    d) prepare job specifications.
    e) analyze working conditions.

In-Text Study Guide

Answers are in Appendix C at the back of book.

16. Individuals who provide accounting services to a variety of firms for a fee are:
    a) master accountants.
    b) managerial accountants.
    c) internal auditors.
    d) corporate controllers.
    e) public accountants.

17. The type of accounting performed to provide information to help managers of the firm make decisions is referred to as:
    a) certified public accounting.
    b) external auditing.
    c) public accounting.
    d) government accounting.
    e) managerial accounting.

18. Which of the following financial statements summarizes a firm's revenues, costs, and earnings for a specific period of time?
    a) balance sheet.
    b) income statement.
    c) cash budget.
    d) retained earnings statement.
    e) sources and uses of funds statement.

19. The statement that reports the book value of all assets, liabilities, and owner's equity of firms at a given point in time is the:
    a) income statement.
    b) cash budget.
    c) profit and loss statement.
    d) revenue statement.
    e) balance sheet.

20. A firm's operating expenses are subtracted from gross profit to determine its:
    a) net sales.
    b) cost of goods sold.
    c) profit or loss.
    d) balance sheet.
    e) earnings before interest and taxes (EBIT).

21. The value of materials used in the production of goods that are then sold is called:
    a) net sales.
    b) cost of goods sold.
    c) sales return and allowances.
    d) gross profit.
    e) net income.

22. Which of the following represents funds provided by the owners of a business?
    a) revenue.
    b) cost of goods sold.
    c) gross profit.
    d) net income.
    e) owner's equity.

23. The firm's assets are financed with its:
    a) cost of goods sold.
    b) earnings before interest and taxes.
    c) liabilities and owner's equity.
    d) plant and equipment.
    e) net sales.

24. If a firm has $1,000 in assets and $300 in liabilities, the owner's equity must be:
    a) $700.
    b) $333.
    c) $1,300.
    d) $3,000.
    e) $0.30.

25. Assets that will be converted into cash within one year are:
    a) fixed assets.
    b) current assets.
    c) plant and equipment.
    d) owner's equity.
    e) liabilities.

In-Text Study Guide

Answers are in Appendix C at the back of book.

26. A reduction in the value of the assets to reflect deterioration in assets over time is:
    a) cost of goods sold.
    b) gross profit.
    c) sales revenue.
    d) depreciation.
    e) owner's equity.

27. In order to encourage board members to enforce proper financial disclosures:
    a) all board members should be certified public accountants or financial analysts.
    b) all board members should be outside members.
    c) board members should not be allowed to own the firm's stock.
    d) all board members should be officers of the corporation.
    e) board members should not be able to sell the firm's stock while serving on the board.

28. An evaluation of the relationship between financial statement variables is called:
    a) ratio analysis.
    b) asset turnover.
    c) cost of goods sold.
    d) operating expenses.
    e) gross profit.

29. All of the following are characteristics commonly used to classify financial ratios except for:
    a) revenue.
    b) liquidity.
    c) efficiency.
    d) leverage.
    e) profitability.

30. Which of the following categories of financial ratios measures how well management uses its assets to generate sales?
    a) liquidity.
    b) profitability.
    c) efficiency.
    d) financial leverage.
    e) sales leverage.

31. Long-term borrowing undertaken by a firm can be assessed through:
    a) liquidity ratios.
    b) profitability ratios.
    c) current ratios.
    d) efficiency ratios.
    e) leverage ratios.

32. A ratio that measures net income as a percentage of sales is the:
    a) net profit margin.
    b) leverage ratio.
    c) liquidity ratio.
    d) activity ratio.
    e) asset turnover.

33. A ratio that measures the firm's dollar amount of profit relative to sales, assets, or equity is a(n):
    a) current ratio.
    b) liquidity ratio.
    c) profitability ratio.
    d) activity ratio.
    e) leverage ratio.

34. All of the following are limitations of ratio analysis except:
    a) the identification of a comparable firm.
    b) the firm operates in more than one industry.
    c) accounting practices may vary between firms.
    d) firms are too much alike.
    e) firms may have large seasonal swings in sales.

In-Text Study Guide

Answers are in Appendix C at the back of book.

35. Any firm with foreign subsidiaries must consolidate the financial data from all subsidiaries when preparing its:
    a) mission statement.
    b) foreign exchange.
    c) balance of payment.
    d) financial statements.
    e) domestic policy.

36. A U.S. firm will report the earnings of its foreign subsidiaries in:
    a) the currencies of the countries where the subsidiaries exist.
    b) U.S. dollars.
    c) units of the product sold.
    d) the consolidated balance sheet of the firm.
    e) the annual liquidity report.

Chapter 16

The performance of Rock-On Company is dependent on whether it can obtain funds to support its expansion, and the cost of the funds that it obtains.

The Learning Goals of this chapter are to:

Identify the common methods of debt financing for firms. *1*

Identify the common methods of equity financing for firms. *2*

Explain how firms issue securities to obtain funds. *3*

Explain how firms may obtain financing through suppliers or leasing. *4*

Describe how firms determine the composition of their financing. *5*

Describe the remedies for firms that are unable to repay their debts. *6*

Financing

Firms obtain capital (long-term funds) in the form of debt or equity. With debt financing, the firm borrows funds. With equity financing, the firm receives investment from owners (by issuing stock or retaining earnings). The manner in which a firm decides to finance its business can affect its financing costs and thus can affect its value. Consider the situation of the Rock-On Company, which produces musical instruments and is planning to expand. Before undertaking the expansion, Rock-On Company will address the following questions:

▶ What are some common methods of debt financing that it could use to finance its expansion?

▶ What are some common methods of equity financing that it could use to finance its expansion?

▶ How could it issue securities to obtain funds?

▶ Should it lease its facilities to avoid borrowing money?

▶ What is the optimal composition of the financing for its expansion?

The debt-financing decisions affect the firm's interest expenses. Equity financing decisions determine the number of owners and therefore determine how the earnings will be spread among owners. The decision to issue securities will affect the amount of funds that a business can attract and therefore the degree to which it can grow. The decision about the composition of financing will affect the firm's financing costs and its degree of risk.

The types of decisions described here are necessary for all businesses. This chapter explains how Rock-On Company or any other firm can make financing decisions in a manner that maximizes its value.

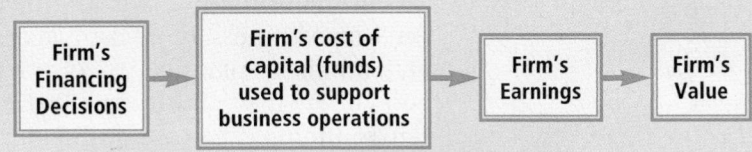

Methods of Debt Financing

1

Identify the common methods of debt financing for firms.

debt financing
the act of borrowing funds

Businesses commonly rely on **debt financing** as a means of funding business operations. Most businesses rely on debt financing to some degree at most stages of their life. The disadvantage of debt financing, however, is that interest must be paid on the loan. An interest payment on a loan is like any other expense. The higher the interest paid in a given month, the higher are the firm's expenses, and the lower are its profits. Thus, it is important for a firm to rely on debt financing only to the degree that it is necessary. In addition, the firm should understand the various sources of debt financing so that it can obtain funding at the lowest possible interest rate.

When a business is first established, its owners may rely on their savings to finance the operations. They may borrow from family members or friends or from a credit card. Or they may allow family members or friends to become part-owners by investing in the firm as a form of equity. At some point, though, the business will likely need more funding than can be provided by family members or friends. It may need funds to invest in assets.

Firms borrow funds to invest in assets such as buildings, machinery, and equipment. Those firms that invest in more assets typically need to borrow more funds. Service firms spend more money on employees and less on machinery and factories. Thus, they may not need to borrow as much because they do not have to purchase machinery for production purposes. In contrast, industrial firms tend to have large investments in assets such as buildings and machinery and therefore need to obtain more **capital.** The common methods of debt financing are described next.

capital
long-term funds

Borrowing from Financial Institutions

Firms commonly attempt to obtain financing from financial institutions such as commercial banks, savings institutions, and finance companies (the different financial institutions will be discussed in more detail later in the chapter). Commercial banks are the biggest lenders to businesses. They are known for their low loan rates and their useful advice to businesses that borrow from them. Before a commercial bank will provide a loan, however, it will want to be certain that the business is capable of generating enough cash each month to cover its loan payments. Therefore, when a firm applies for a loan, it must present a detailed financial plan that includes specific projections of future revenue and expenses. The plan should demonstrate how the firm will generate sufficient revenue over time to repay the loan. Newly established businesses may not be able to obtain a commercial loan because they do not have a business history to demonstrate that they will have sufficient cash to make monthly loan payments.

Because many loans are for three years or longer, lenders assess the creditworthiness of a firm according to several factors. These include (1) the firm's planned use of the borrowed funds, (2) the financial condition of the firm's business, (3) the outlook for the industry or environment surrounding the firm's business, and (4) available collateral of the business that can be used to back the loan. To perform this assessment and determine whether the firm will be able to repay its loan on schedule, the lender will want to examine the firm's financial statements. In addition, the lender will want to assess the firm's business plan so that it can determine whether the firm has a reasonable strategy for expanding its market share in the future or at least for preventing competitors from taking its market share.

If the lender determines that the firm is creditworthy, it will attempt to establish terms of the loan that are acceptable to the firm. The terms of the loan specify the amount to be borrowed, the maturity, the collateral, and the rate of interest on the loan. Several different types of loans are generally available.

Pledging Collateral   Firms that need to borrow may be asked to pledge a portion of their assets as collateral to back the loan. Lenders are more comfortable providing loans when the loans are backed by collateral. A common form of collateral is the asset for which the borrowed funds will be used. For example, a firm that is borrowing funds to purchase a machine may offer that machine as collateral. If the lender expects that it could sell the machine for 70 percent of its existing value, the lender may finance 70 percent of the purchase and require the machine to be used as collateral. If the firm defaults on the loan, the lender can sell the machine for an amount that covers the loan.

A firm may also pledge its accounts receivable (payments owed to the firm for previous sales of products) as collateral. If the firm defaults on the loan, the lender takes control of the accounts receivable. To ensure that the accounts receivable collateral sufficiently covers the loan balance, the lender will provide a loan amount that is just a fraction (say, 65 percent) of the required collateral. Thus, even if some customers never pay off their accounts receivable, the collateral may still cover the full amount of the loan.

Loan Rate   When setting the loan rate, banks determine the average rate of interest that they pay on their deposits (which represents their cost of funds) and add on a premium. Since deposit rates change over time in response to general interest rate movements, loan rates change as well.

The premium is dependent on the credit risk of the loan or the probability of default. If the firm appears to be in good financial condition and the collateral covers the loan amount, the premium may be about 4 percentage points. For example, if the lender's cost of funds is 6 percent, the loan rate may be 10 percent. If the borrowing firm is perceived to have more credit risk, however, the premium may be more than 4 percentage points. The rate of interest typically charged on loans to the most creditworthy firms that borrow is called the **prime rate.**

prime rate
the rate of interest typically charged on loans to the most creditworthy firms that borrow

Fixed-Rate versus Floating-Rate Loans   When firms need funds, they must choose between a fixed-rate loan and a floating-rate loan. Most commercial loans charge floating interest rates that move in tandem with market interest rates. Consider a firm that can obtain a five-year floating-rate loan with an interest rate that is adjusted by the bank once a year according to changes in the prime rate. Assume that the initial loan rate of interest is 8 percent (based on the prevailing prime rate) and will be adjusted once a year. Alternatively, the firm can obtain a fixed-rate loan of 10 percent. Which loan is preferable? The answer depends on future interest rate movements, which are uncertain. Firms that expect interest rates to rise consistently over the five-year period will prefer a fixed-rate loan so that they can avoid the upward adjustments on a floating-rate loan. Firms that expect interest rates to decline or remain stable over the five-year period will prefer a floating-rate loan.

Exhibit 16.1 shows the interest rates that would be charged under three different scenarios. If the firm has a fixed-rate loan, the interest rate charged on its loan is I_1, regardless of how market interest rates move over time. If the firm has a floating-rate loan, the interest rate charged on its loan will be I_2 if market interest rates increase over time, or I_3 if market interest rates decrease over time. Rising interest rates adversely affect firms that obtain floating-rate loans because the interest rate on their loans will increase.

The interest rate charged on a new loan is based on the general level of interest rates at that time. The top part of Exhibit 16.2 shows how the prime rate has changed over time. The lower part of the exhibit shows the

Exhibit 16.1

Interest Rate Charged on Loans under Three Different Scenarios

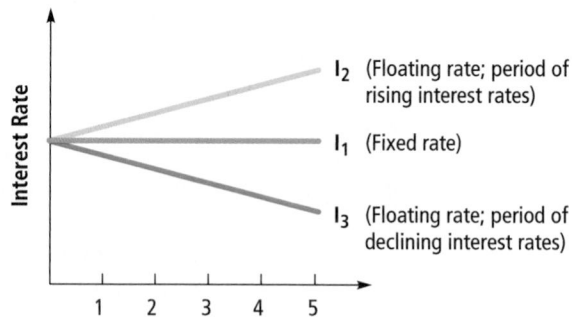

Exhibit 16.2

Effect of Interest Rates on Interest Expenses Incurred by Firms

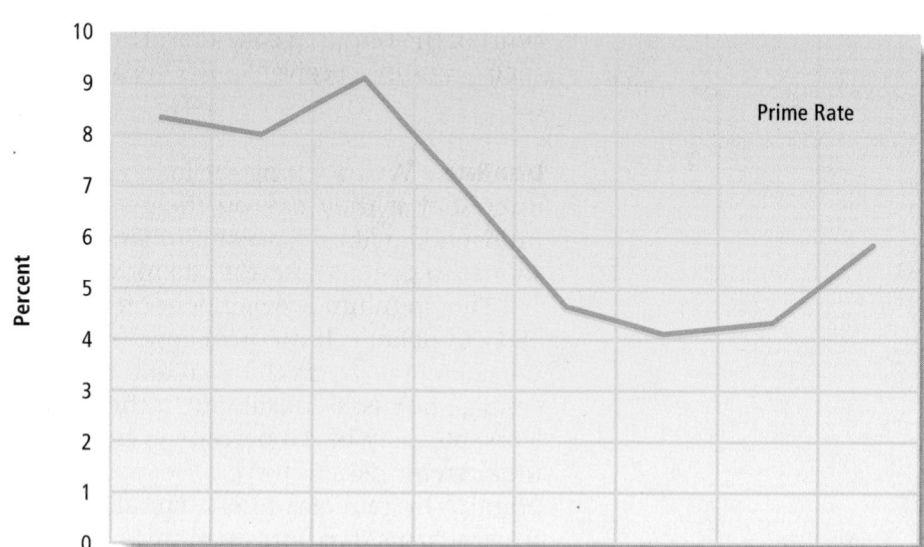

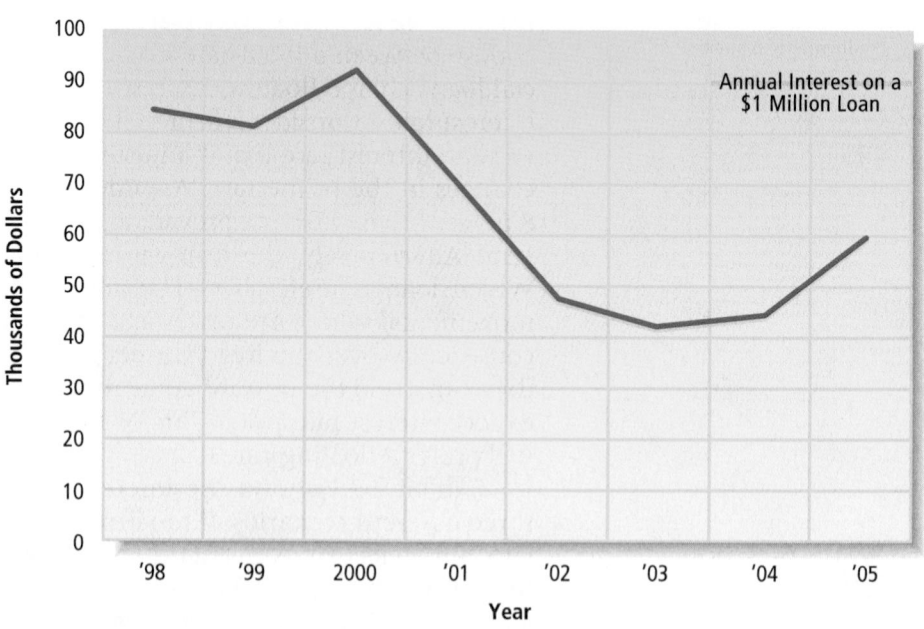

interest expense that a firm would have incurred if it was charged the prime rate on a $1 million loan at that time.

Types of Business Loans   Several different types of business loans are generally available. The specific type of loan that a firm obtains may depend on its reasons for needing funding or the length of time the funds are required. A common type of business loan is intended to support ongoing business operations. There is a lag between the time when a firm incurs costs for producing and marketing a product and the time when the firm receives revenue from selling the product. The loan can provide necessary funding to cover expenses until the product is sold and cash is received.

Another type of business loan is a term loan, which is used to finance the purchase of fixed assets such as machinery. The maturity on a term loan is typically between 3 and 10 years.

A more flexible lending arrangement is a line of credit, which allows the firm to borrow up to a specified amount of money within a specified period of time. For example, a line of credit may allow a firm to borrow up to $100,000, but it would have to pay off the credit within one year. A line of credit is especially useful when a firm expects that it will need funding in the future, but does not know exactly when it will need funds or how much it will need.

Loans Backed by the U.S. Government   The Small Business Administration (SBA) backs loans provided by lenders to small businesses under various programs. When a loan is backed by the SBA, a financial institution is more willing to lend because it is less exposed to the risk that the business will be unable to repay the loan. The SBA guarantees that a large portion (such as 75 percent) of the loan will be repaid, so the lender has less to lose if the business is unable to repay the loan.

The most popular loan program sponsored by the SBA is the 7(a) program, which can be used for a wide variety of purposes, including the start-up of business. To qualify for this program, the business must show that it

This salon located in Union, New Jersey, received assistance from the Small Business Administration. The SBA not only offers funding for some small businesses, but also provides guidance about business planning and operations.

AP/WIDE WORLD PHOTOS

should be capable of repaying the loan and must also make a down payment with nonborrowed funds to partially cover the funding. This down payment may amount to about 25 percent of the total funds needed. In this way, the owners demonstrate their belief that the investment is worthwhile. A financial institution such as a commercial bank agrees to finance the remainder of the project. The average size of this type of loan is about $167,000.

The SBA also has a program to finance the purchase of fixed assets such as land and buildings. As with the 7(a) program, the business must provide a down payment toward the purchase. The size of these loans is between $200,000 and $10 million.

For very small businesses, the SBA offers a microloan program. These businesses usually have fewer than five employees, and the business owner qualifies as low income, minority, or disabled. These loans are made by nonprofit community groups that are granted funds by the SBA. The average microloan is about $14,000.

Issuing Bonds

bonds
long-term debt securities (IOUs) purchased by investors

Large firms may obtain funds by issuing **bonds,** which are long-term debt securities (IOUs) purchased by investors. Some large firms prefer to issue bonds rather than obtain loans from financial institutions because the interest rate may be lower. Bondholders are creditors, not owners, of the firm that issued the bonds.

Small firms that are not well known are unable to issue bonds. Even if they could issue their own bonds, a bond issuance typically raises more funds than a small firm would need.

par value
the amount that bondholders receive at maturity

The **par value** of a bond is the amount that the bondholders receive at maturity. Most bonds have a maturity of between 10 and 30 years. The coupon (interest) payments paid per year are determined by applying the so-called coupon rate to the par value. If the coupon rate is 10 percent, the coupon payments paid per year will be $100 for every $1,000 of par value. The coupon payments are normally paid semiannually and are fixed over the life of the bond. The coupon rate of bonds is influenced by the general level of interest rates at the time the bonds are issued. Firms typically prefer to issue bonds at a time when interest rates are relatively low. By doing so, they can lock in a relatively low coupon rate over the life of the bond. Forecasting interest rates is difficult, however, so firms cannot easily time a bond issue to take place when interest rates have hit their bottom. Also, firms that need funds immediately cannot wait until interest rates are at a more desirable level.

indenture
a legal document that explains the firm's obligations to bondholders

secured bonds
bonds backed by collateral

unsecured bonds
bonds that are not backed by collateral

call feature
provides the issuing firm with the right to repurchase its bonds before maturity

When a firm plans to issue bonds, it creates an **indenture,** which is a legal document that explains its obligations to bondholders. For example, the indenture will state what collateral (if any) is backing the bonds. **Secured bonds** are backed by collateral, whereas **unsecured bonds** are not backed by collateral. The indenture also states whether the bonds have a **call feature,** which provides the issuing firm with the right to repurchase the bonds before maturity. To recognize the benefits of a call feature, consider a firm that issued bonds when interest rates were very high. If interest rates decline a few years later, the firm could issue new bonds at the lower interest rate and use the proceeds to repay the old bonds. Thus, the call feature gives the firm the flexibility to replace old bonds with new bonds that have a lower interest rate. Bonds that have a call feature typically need to pay a higher rate of interest.

Exhibit 16.3

Summary of Risk Ratings Assigned by Bond Rating Agencies

	Rating Assigned by:	
	Moody's	**Standard & Poor's**
Highest quality	Aaa	AAA
High quality	Aa	AA
High-medium quality	A	A
Medium quality	Baa	BBB
Medium-low quality	Ba	BB
Low quality (speculative)	B	B
Poor quality	Caa	CCC
Very poor quality	Ca	CC
Lowest quality (in default)	C	DDD,D

Default Risk of Bonds   The interest rate paid on bonds is influenced not only by prevailing interest rates but also by the issuing firm's risk level. Firms that have more risk of default must provide higher interest to bondholders to compensate for the risk involved. Rating agencies such as Moody's Investor Service and Standard & Poor's Corporation rate the bonds according to their quality (safety). The rating agencies assign ratings after evaluating the financial condition of each firm. They closely assess the amount of debt that a firm has and the firm's ability to cover interest payments on its existing debt. Firms are periodically reevaluated since their ability to repay debt can change in response to economic or industry conditions, or even conditions unique to the firm.

Exhibit 16.3 provides a summary of the different ratings that can be assigned. Although each rating agency uses its own criteria for rating bonds, most bonds are rated within a similar risk level by the agencies. Investors may prefer to rely on the rating agencies rather than develop their own evaluations of the firms that issue bonds. At a given point in time, firms with higher ratings will be able to issue bonds with lower interest rates.

If a firm's financial condition weakens, the rating agencies may lower their ratings on the bonds it has issued. As a firm's bond ratings decline, it is less able to issue new bonds because investors will be concerned about the lower rating (higher risk).

protective covenants
restrictions imposed on specific financial policies of a firm that has issued bonds

Bondholders may attempt to limit the risk of default by enforcing **protective covenants,** which are restrictions imposed on specific financial policies of the firm. The purpose of these covenants is to ensure that managers do not make decisions that could increase the firm's risk and therefore increase the probability of default. For example, some protective covenants may restrict the firm from borrowing beyond some specified debt limit until the existing bonds are paid off.

Issuing Commercial Paper

commercial paper
a short-term debt security normally issued by firms in good financial condition

Many firms also issue **commercial paper,** which is a short-term debt security normally issued by firms in good financial condition. Its normal maturity is between three and six months. Thus, the issuance of commercial paper is an alternative to obtaining loans directly from financial institutions. The minimum denomination of commercial paper is usually $100,000. Typically, denominations are in multiples of $1 million. Various

Like most companies, Dell incurs the cost of its production before it sells the products it produces. It commonly uses debt financing so that it can cover its cost of production, and part of the subsequent revenue from selling the products can be used to make the interest payments.

DELL INC.

financial institutions commonly purchase commercial paper. The interest rate on commercial paper is influenced by the general market interest rates at the time of issuance.

Impact of the Debt Financing Level on Interest Expenses

To illustrate how the level of debt financing (whether by borrowing from financial institutions or by issuing IOUs) affects interest expenses, consider a firm that borrows $1 million for a five-year period at an interest rate of 9 percent. This firm will pay $90,000 in interest in each of the next five years (computed as $1,000,000 \times 9\%$). Thus, the firm will need sufficient revenue to cover not only its operating expenses (such as salaries) but also its interest expenses. If the firm had borrowed $2 million, it would have to pay $180,000 in annual interest (computed as $2,000,000 \times 9\%$). When firms borrow money excessively, they have large annual interest payments that are difficult to cover. For this reason, the firms have a higher probability of defaulting on the loans than they would if they had borrowed less funds.

Common Creditors That Provide Debt Financing

commercial banks

financial institutions that obtain deposits from individuals and use the funds primarily to provide business loans

savings institutions

financial institutions that obtain deposits from individuals and use the deposited funds primarily to provide mortgage loans

finance companies

financial institutions that typically obtain funds by issuing debt securities (IOUs) and lend most of their funds to firms

pension funds

receive employee and firm contributions toward pensions and invest the proceeds for the employees until the funds are needed

insurance companies

receive insurance premiums from selling insurance to customers and invest the proceeds until the funds are needed to pay insurance claims

Various types of creditors can provide debt financing to firms. **Commercial banks** obtain deposits from individuals and use the funds primarily to provide business loans. **Savings institutions** (also called "thrift institutions") also obtain deposits from individuals and use some of the deposited funds to provide business loans. Although savings institutions lend most of their funds to individuals who need mortgage loans, they have increased their amount of business loans in recent years.

Finance companies typically obtain funds by issuing debt securities (IOUs) and lend most of their funds to firms. In general, finance companies tend to focus on loans to less established firms that have a higher risk of loan default. The finance companies charge a higher rate of interest on these loans to compensate for the higher degree of risk.

Pension funds receive employee and firm contributions toward pensions and invest the proceeds for the employees until the funds are needed. They commonly invest part of their funds in bonds issued by firms.

Insurance companies receive insurance premiums from selling insurance to customers and invest the proceeds until the funds are needed to

mutual funds
investment companies that receive funds from individual investors and then pool and invest those funds in securities

bond mutual funds
investment companies that invest the funds received from investors in bonds

pay insurance claims. They also commonly invest part of their funds in bonds issued by firms.

Mutual funds are investment companies that receive funds from individual investors; the mutual funds pool the amounts and invest them in securities. Mutual funds can be classified by the type of investments that they make. Some mutual funds (called **bond mutual funds**) invest the funds received from investors in bonds that are issued by firms.

Decision Making

Whether to Borrow Funds

Rock-On Company (which was introduced at the beginning of the chapter) produces musical instruments, including guitars and drum sets, and sells them to retail stores in North Carolina. It currently has 30 owners who have already invested a total of $4 million in the firm. Rock-On has used the equity to invest in its operations. Now it wants to purchase an additional manufacturing plant that will cost about $4 million. Rock-On has about $1 million in cash, so it needs to borrow the remaining $3 million to purchase this plant. If it obtains a loan, it will have to make loan payments of about $300,000 per year. It revises its business plan to include the manner in which it will use the funds. For the loan to be worthwhile, it needs to use the funds in a manner that will generate profits after repaying the loan. Rock-On Company decides that it definitely wants to purchase the manufacturing plant, but before it pursues a loan, it will consider the alternative financing methods discussed later in this chapter.

1. Assume that Rock-On decides to pursue a loan. Explain why a lender would require Rock-On to provide a business plan showing how the funds would be used.

2. Why would the interest rate on a loan to Rock-On be dependent on its financial condition?

ANSWERS: 1. The lender would want to know how Rock-On will use the loan and how it will generate revenue from the use of the funds so that it will be able to repay the loan. 2. Rock-On's financial condition affects its ability to repay the loan. If its financial condition is poor, the lender will charge a higher interest rate to compensate for the risk that the loan may not be repaid. If the risk is too high, the lender will not provide a loan at all.

Methods of Equity Financing

2

Identify the common methods of equity financing for firms.

equity financing
the act of receiving investment from owners (by issuing stock or retaining earnings)

dividend policy
the decision regarding how much of the firm's quarterly earnings should be retained (reinvested in the firm) versus distributed as dividends to owners

The common methods of **equity financing** are retaining earnings and issuing stock, as explained next.

Retaining Earnings

A firm can obtain equity financing by retaining earnings rather than by distributing the earnings to its owners. The board of directors of each firm decides how much of the firm's quarterly earnings should be retained (reinvested in the firm) versus distributed as dividends to owners. This decision, referred to as the firm's **dividend policy,** is important because it influences the amount of additional financing the firm must obtain. For example, consider a firm that earned $30 million after taxes. Assume that it will need $40 million for various expenses in the near future. If it retains all of the earnings, it will need an additional $10 million. At the other extreme, if it pays out the entire $30 million as dividends, it will need to obtain an additional $40 million.

Managers may retain earnings to provide financial support for the firm's expansion. For example, if a firm needs $10 million for expansion and has just earned $6 million after taxes, it may retain the $6 million as equity financing and borrow the remaining $4 million. Many small firms retain most of their earnings to support expansion. Larger corporations tend to pay out a portion of their earnings as dividends and retain only part of what they earned. Large firms can more easily obtain debt financing, so they can afford to pay out a portion of their earnings as dividends.

Factors That Affect a Firm's Dividend Policy   There is no optimal dividend policy to be used by all firms. Some firms establish their dividend payment as a percentage of future earnings. For example, General Mills sets a dividend target of 50 percent of earnings, while Goodyear Tire sets a dividend target of between 20 and 25 percent of earnings. Each firm's unique characteristics may influence its dividend policy. Two characteristics that can influence the dividend policy are shareholder expectations and the firm's financing needs:

▶ **Shareholder Expectations** A firm's shareholders may expect to receive dividends if they have historically been receiving them. If the firm discontinues or reduces the dividend payment, shareholders could become dissatisfied. Thus, many firms such as ConAgra and Campbell's Soup make an effort to either maintain or increase dividends from year to year.

▶ **Firm's Financing Needs** A firm that has no need for additional funds may distribute most of its earnings as dividends. However, it may be concerned that if it pays high dividends, shareholders will come to expect them. Thus, instead of trying to maintain its high dividend payment, the firm may decide to use a portion of the earnings for another purpose. For example, it may consider replacing old assets or expanding part of its business.

Issuing Stock

common stock
a security that represents partial ownership of a particular firm

A firm can also obtain equity financing by issuing stock. **Common stock** is a security that represents partial ownership of a particular firm. Only the owners of common stock are permitted to vote on certain key matters concerning the firm, such as the election of the board of directors, whether to issue new shares of common stock, and whether to accept a merger proposal. Firms can issue common stock to obtain funds. When new shares of stock are issued, the number of shareholders who own the firm increases.

preferred stock
a security that represents partial ownership of a particular firm and offers specific priorities over common stock

Preferred stock is a security that represents partial ownership of a particular firm and offers specific priorities over common stock. If a firm does not pay dividends over a period, it must pay preferred stockholders all dividends that were omitted before paying any dividends to common stockholders. Also, if the firm goes bankrupt, the preferred stockholders have priority claim to the firm's assets over common stockholders. If a firm goes bankrupt, however, there may not be any assets left for preferred stockholders, because creditors (such as lenders or bondholders) have first claim. Preferred stockholders normally do not have voting rights. Firms issue common stock more frequently than preferred stock.

venture capital firm
a firm composed of individuals who invest in small businesses

Issuing Stock to Venture Capital Firms   Firms can issue stock privately to a **venture capital firm,** which is a firm composed of individuals who invest in

Common stock certificates represent ownership in a firm. Investors invest in stocks so that they can earn a return on their investment if the value of the company (and therefore of the corresponding stock) increases.

CORBIS, CHICAGO

small businesses. These individuals act as investors in firms rather than as creditors. They expect a share of the businesses in which they invest. Their investments typically support projects that have potential for high returns but also have high risk.

Entrepreneurs who need equity financing can attend venture capital forums, where they are allowed a short time (15 minutes or so) to convince the venture capital firms to provide them with equity financing. If an entrepreneur's presentation is impressive, venture capital firms may arrange for a longer meeting with the entrepreneur to learn more about the business that needs financing.

Providers of venture capital recognize that some of the businesses they invest in may generate little or no return. They hope that the successful businesses will more than make up for any unsuccessful ones. Venture capital firms commonly assess businesses that require an equity investment of between $200,000 and $2 million. Small projects are not popular because their potential return is not worth the time required to assess their feasibility.

initial public offering (IPO)
the first issue of stock to the public

Going Public   If a small privately held business desires to obtain additional funds, it may consider an **initial public offering (IPO)** of stock (also called "going public"), which is the first issue of stock to the public. Firms such as Google, Yahoo!, and Amazon.com went public so that they would have sufficient funds to support their expansion.

stock mutual funds
investment companies that invest funds received from individual investors in stocks

Insurance companies and pension funds commonly purchase large amounts of stocks issued by firms. In addition, **stock mutual funds** (investment companies that invest pooled funds received from individual investors in stocks) purchase large amounts of stocks issued by firms. An IPO allows a firm to obtain additional funds without boosting its existing debt level and without relying on retained earnings. Firms can obtain a large amount of funds by going public without increasing future interest payments to creditors.

Along with the advantages, IPOs have some disadvantages. First, firms that go public are responsible for informing shareholders of their financial condition. All firms that issue stock to the public must file periodic financial reports with the Securities and Exchange Commission, and preparing these reports can be expensive. Furthermore, the financial information then is accessible to investors. Some firms may prefer not to disclose information that would reveal the success (and perhaps the wealth) of the owners.

Google engaged in an initial public offering in order to obtain funds to finance its expansion.

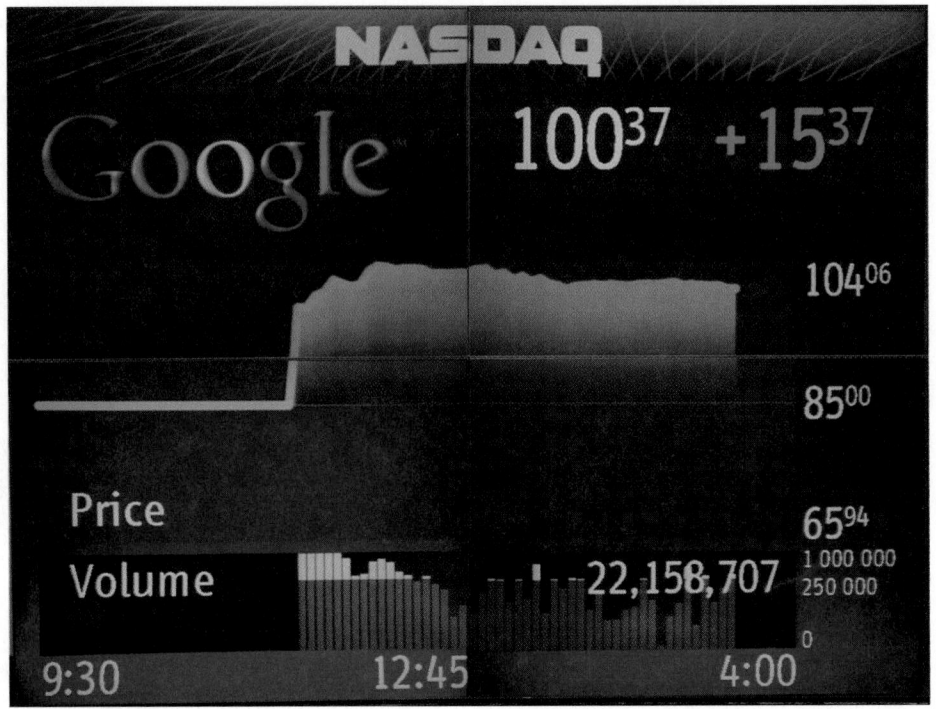

Out of
Business

A second disadvantage is that when a small business attempts to obtain funding from the public, it may have difficulty convincing investors that its business plans are feasible. This limits the amount of funding that can be obtained from an IPO. It also forces the firm to sell part of the ownership at a relatively low cost. If a firm goes public and cannot obtain funding at a reasonable price, its original owners may feel that they gave away part of the firm for nothing.

A third disadvantage of an IPO is that the firm's ownership structure is diluted. Once shares are sold to the public, the proportion of the firm owned by the original owners is reduced. Thus, the original owners have less control of the firm, and other investors have more influence on the firm's board of directors and therefore on major decisions. Also, the profits earned by the firm that are distributed among owners as dividends must be allocated among more owners.

A fourth disadvantage of an IPO is that investment banks charge high fees for advising and placing the stock with investors. The firm also incurs legal fees, accounting fees, and printing fees. The fees may be about 10 percent of the total amount of funds received from the IPO. Thus, an IPO of $20 million may result in fees of $2 million.

IPOs are generally more popular when most stock prices are high, as firms may receive a higher price for their newly issued stock under these conditions. For example, stock prices were very high in the late 1990s, and there were numerous IPOs in that period.

Listing the Stock Once a firm has issued stock to the public, it lists its stock on a stock exchange. This allows the investors to sell the stock they purchased from the firm to other investors over time. The stock exchange serves as a **secondary market,** or a market where existing securities can be traded among investors. Thus, investors have the flexibility to sell stocks that they no longer wish to hold.

The most popular stock exchanges in the United States are the New York Stock Exchange (NYSE), the American Stock Exchange (AMEX), and the over-the-counter (OTC) market. Stocks in the OTC market trade via an electronic network known as the National Association of Securities Dealers Automated Quotations (Nasdaq). Each exchange has a set of listing requirements that firms must satisfy to have their stocks listed on that exchange.

secondary market
a market where existing securities can be traded among investors

The New York Stock Exchange (NYSE) shown here facilitates the trading of stock in the secondary market. The NYSE enables investors to buy or sell shares of any firm that is listed on its exchange.

GETTY IMAGES

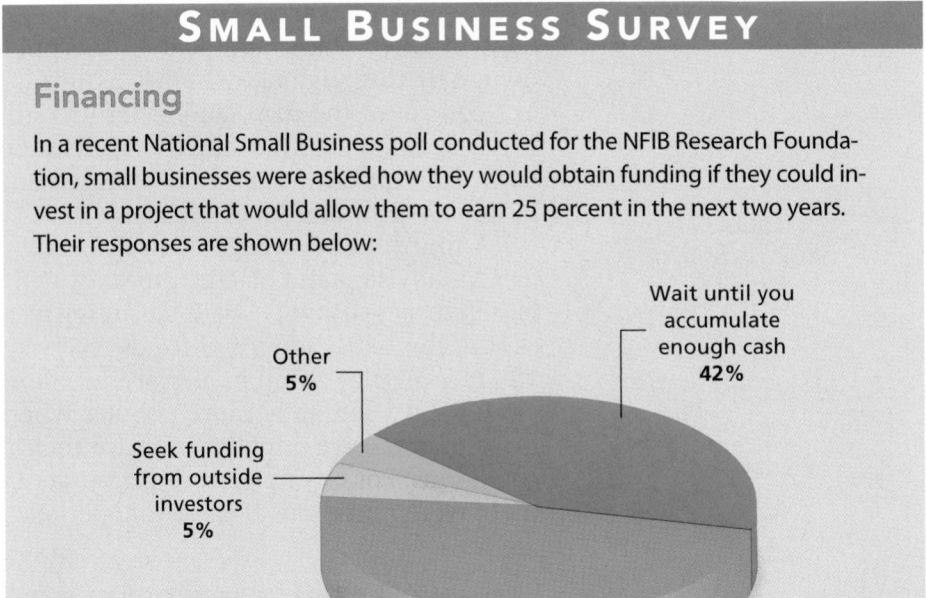

SMALL BUSINESS SURVEY

Financing

In a recent National Small Business poll conducted for the NFIB Research Foundation, small businesses were asked how they would obtain funding if they could invest in a project that would allow them to earn 25 percent in the next two years. Their responses are shown below:

Other
5%

Seek funding
from outside
investors
5%

Wait until you
accumulate
enough cash
42%

Borrow
money
48%

Comparison of Equity Financing with Debt Financing

Equity financing and debt financing are compared in Exhibit 16.4. Notice from the exhibit that the forms of debt financing (loans and bonds) require the firm to make interest and principal payments. Conversely, the forms of equity financing (retained earnings and stock) do not require any payments. Financing with stock may result in dividend payments, but only if the firm can afford them. Also, there are no principal payments to the stockholders, as the stock has no maturity.

Exhibit 16.4

Summary of Firm's Debt and
Equity Financing Methods

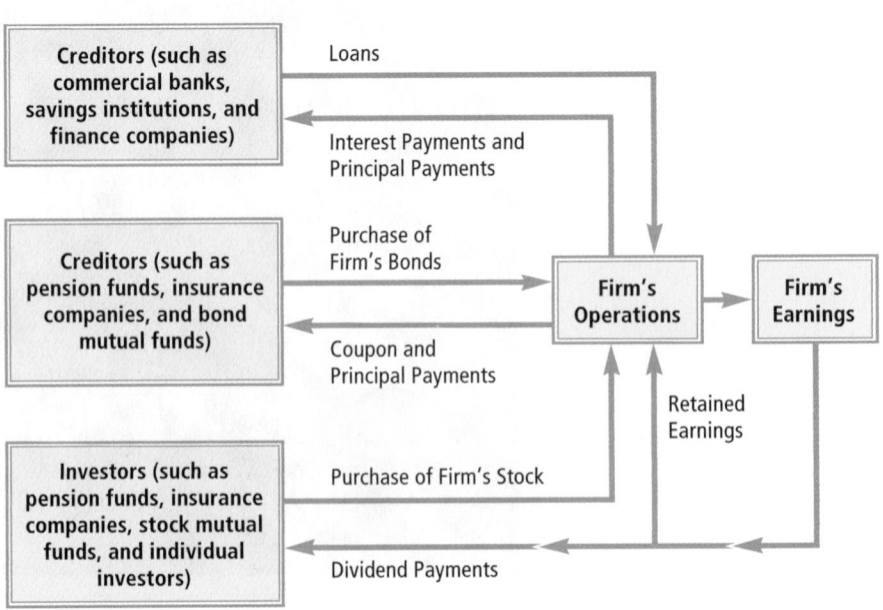

Firms typically use a variety of financing methods to obtain funds. General Motors, Ford Motor Company, Motorola, and many other firms frequently obtain funds by borrowing from banks, issuing bonds, and issuing new stock.

Deciding Whether to Obtain Equity Funding

Recall that Rock-On Company wants to purchase an additional manufacturing plant for about $4 million. It could borrow funds, but it wants to consider equity financing. Its existing owners cannot afford to invest more equity in the firm at this point. Rock-On could obtain more equity from a venture capital firm, but then the existing owners would have to give up part of their ownership of the firm. Consequently, if the business is ever sold, the existing owners would have to share the proceeds with the venture capital firm. The owners decide that the best way to increase equity financing over time is to retain earnings so that the profits are reinvested in the business. This allows them to maintain the existing ownership structure, but it also means that they cannot rely on equity financing to purchase the manufacturing plant at this time.

1.   What is a possible advantage for Rock-On of obtaining equity from a venture capital firm rather than borrowing funds?
2.   Why will Rock-On's strategy of retaining earnings limit the amount of funds that will be invested in the business?

ANSWERS: 1. Because an investment from a venture capital firm represents equity, it does not require interest payments. 2. If Rock-On does not use any new equity financing, it will have to rely on more debt, and its interest payments on debt will rise. Lenders will limit the amount that they will lend to Rock-On because they may worry that it will not be able to make the interest payments.

How Firms Issue Securities

Explain how firms issue securities to obtain funds.

A **public offering** of securities (such as bonds or stocks) represents the selling of securities to the public. Public offerings include both IPOs and offerings of additional securities by firms that went public earlier. A firm that plans a public offering of securities can receive help from investment banks, which originate, underwrite, and distribute the securities.

Origination

Investment banks advise firms on the amount of stocks or bonds they can issue. The issuance of an excessive amount of securities can cause a decline in the market price because the supply of securities issued may exceed the demand. Also, the issuance of bonds requires the determination of a maturity date, a coupon rate, and collateral.

Underwriting

When securities offerings are **underwritten,** the investment bank guarantees a price to the issuing firm, no matter what price the securities are sold for. In this way, the investment bank bears the risk that the securities may be sold only at low prices. Alternatively, the investment bank may attempt to sell the securities on a **best-efforts basis;** in this case, it does not guarantee a price to the issuing firm.

public offering
the selling of securities to the public

underwritten
the investment bank guarantees a price to the issuing firm, no matter what price the securities are sold for

best-efforts basis
the investment bank does not guarantee a price to the firm issuing securities

underwriting syndicate
a group of investment banks that
share the obligations of underwriting securities

prospectus
a document that discloses relevant
financial information about
securities and about the firm
issuing them

private placement
the selling of securities to one
or a few investors

flotation costs
costs of issuing securities; include
fees paid to investment banks for
their advice and efforts to sell the
securities, printing expenses, and
registration fees

For large issues of securities, the investment bank may create an **underwriting syndicate,** which is a group of investment banks that share the obligations of underwriting the securities. Each investment bank in the syndicate is allocated a portion of the securities and is responsible for selling that portion.

Distribution

The issuing firm must register the issue with the Securities and Exchange Commission (SEC). It provides the SEC with a **prospectus,** which is a document that discloses relevant financial information about the securities (such as the amount) and about the firm.

Once the SEC approves the registration, the prospectus is distributed to investors who may purchase the securities. Some of the more likely investors are pension funds and insurance companies that have large amounts of funds to invest. Some issues are completely sold within hours. When an issue does not sell well, the investment bank may lower the price of the securities to increase demand.

Some firms may prefer to use a **private placement,** in which the securities are sold to one or a few investors. An investment bank may still be used for advisory purposes and for help in identifying a financial institution (such as an insurance company) that may purchase the entire issue. The selling costs are lower with a private placement because only one or a few investors are involved. A disadvantage, however, is that many investors cannot afford to purchase an entire issue. Consequently, privately placing the securities may be difficult.

Firms that issue securities incur **flotation costs,** which include fees paid to investment banks for advice and for selling the securities, printing expenses, and registration fees.

Decision Making

Deciding Whether to Issue Stock

Recall that Rock-On Company is currently owned by 30 owners. While its owners were deciding how to finance an investment in an additional manufacturing plant, they also considered a much more ambitious long-term plan to expand their business throughout the United States. Rock-On could afford to expand to that degree only if it engaged in an initial public offering (IPO) of stock, as it would need about $40 million. Though Rock-On has been successful in selling its musical instruments in its home state of North Carolina, it does not have name recognition outside that state. Thus, its musical instruments may not necessarily attract as much demand in other parts of the United States. Investors would likely be skeptical as well and would not be willing to pay a high price for the stock at this time. Because a stock offering would not be appealing to the public at this time, Rock-On's owners decided to scale down their growth plans. Before considering a stock offering to support expansion throughout the United States, they will think about expanding their business to the states neighboring North Carolina.

1. How would the ownership structure of Rock-On Company change if it pursued an IPO?
2. Why would Rock-On possibly benefit from an IPO in the future?

ANSWERS: 1. The original owners of Rock-On would give up much of their ownership. 2. An IPO would allow Rock-On to expand its business, and the business expansion could lead to much higher profits (but it could also lead to failure if the business growth is not properly managed).

Explain how firms may obtain financing through suppliers or leasing.

Other Methods of Obtaining Funds

In addition to debt financing and equity financing, firms may obtain funds in other ways, as discussed next.

Financing from Suppliers

When a firm obtains supplies, it may be given a specific period to pay its bill. The supplier is essentially financing the firm's investment over that period. If the firm is able to generate adequate revenue over that time to pay the bill, it will not need any more financing. Even if it needs more financing, the supplier's willingness to wait for payment saves the firm some financing costs.

Exhibit 16.5 shows the benefits of supplier financing. In the top diagram, the firm receives supplies on March 1, but does not have to pay its bill until August 1. By August 1, the firm will have sold the product that required the use of the supplies. Thus, it can use a portion of the revenue received from selling the product to pay the supplier.

The lower diagram shows that with no supplier financing, the firm must obtain funds from another source. For example, it may borrow funds from a commercial bank on March 1 to pay the supplier at that time. When the firm receives its payment for the product on August 1, it can use a portion of the revenue received to pay off the debt. In this case, the firm had to borrow funds for five months and incurred interest expenses over that period. The difference between these two scenarios is that the firm incurs only the expense of the supplies when it obtains supplier financing, but it incurs the expense of supplies plus interest expenses if supplier financing is not available.

Exhibit 16.5

How Firms Can Benefit from Supplier Financing

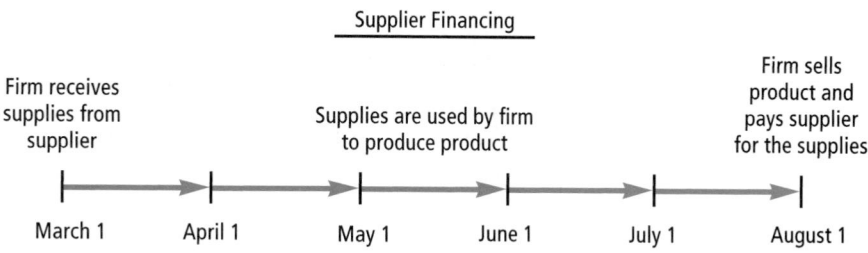

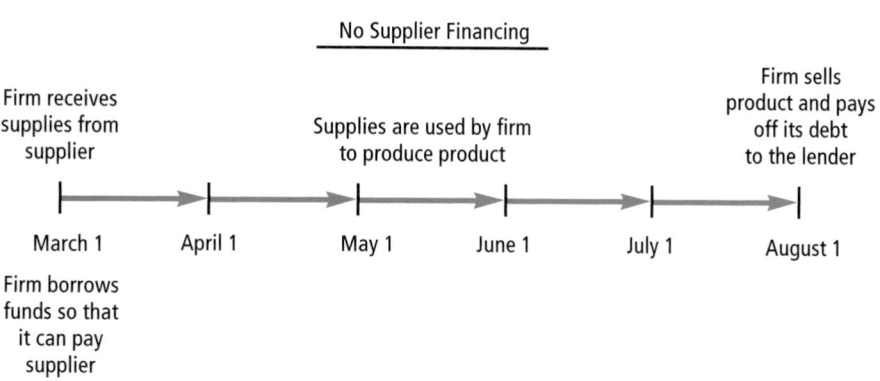

Leasing

leasing
renting assets for a specified
period of time

Some firms prefer to finance the use of assets by **leasing,** or renting the assets for a specified period of time. These firms rent the assets and have full control over them over a particular period. They return the assets at the time specified in the lease contract. Many firms that lease assets cannot afford to purchase them. By leasing, they must make periodic lease payments but do not need to make a large initial outlay.

Some firms prefer to lease rather than purchase when they may need the assets for only a short period of time. For example, consider a new firm that does not know how much factory space it will need until it can assess the demand for its product. This firm may initially lease factory space so that it can switch factories without having to sell its existing factory if it needs more space.

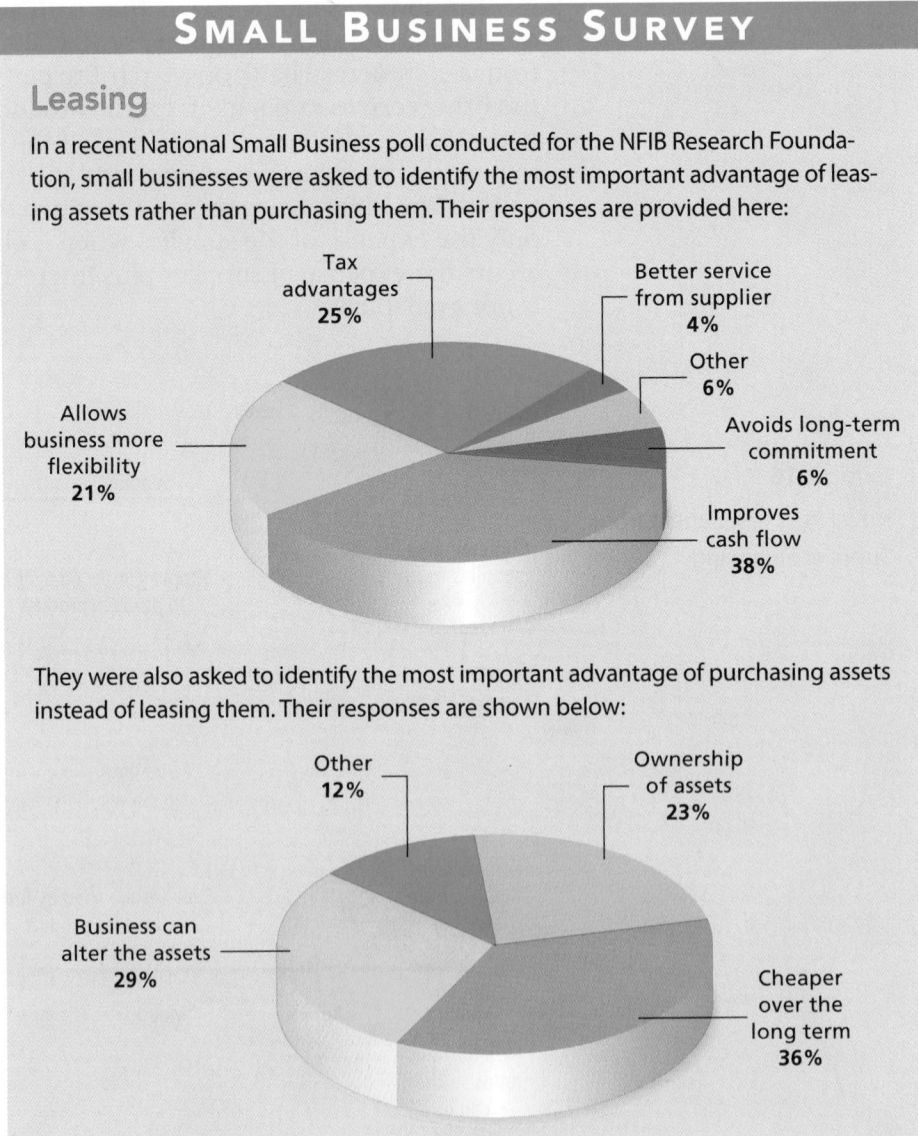

SMALL BUSINESS SURVEY

Leasing

In a recent National Small Business poll conducted for the NFIB Research Foundation, small businesses were asked to identify the most important advantage of leasing assets rather than purchasing them. Their responses are provided here:

Tax advantages 25%
Better service from supplier 4%
Other 6%
Allows business more flexibility 21%
Avoids long-term commitment 6%
Improves cash flow 38%

They were also asked to identify the most important advantage of purchasing assets instead of leasing them. Their responses are shown below:

Other 12%
Ownership of assets 23%
Business can alter the assets 29%
Cheaper over the long term 36%

Decision Making

Deciding Whether to Lease as a Financing Method

Recall that Rock-On Company is planning to purchase an additional manufacturing plant for $4 million. It will need to borrow most of the money to finance this investment. Rather than purchase the plant, Rock-On could lease a manufacturing facility that is owned by another firm. The advantage of leasing is that Rock-On would not need $4 million to make the purchase. Instead, it would make periodic lease payments. The disadvantage of leasing is that it would not own the plant and would have to shift its production to another facility when the lease period ends. Rock-On would prefer to avoid borrowing a large amount of funds at this time because it is concerned that it may not generate enough revenue to cover its interest payments. It decides that the best solution at this time is to lease the manufacturing plant for the next three years. If it determines that the facility is too large relative to the quantity of instruments it can sell, it can shift to a smaller facility. Alternatively, if the demand for its instruments increases substantially, it may need to purchase a larger facility. Thus, leasing gives Rock-On the flexibility it desires for the next few years until it is better able to determine the size of the production plant that it will need.

1. If Rock-On wants the flexibility to expand the specific facility it is using, would it prefer to purchase (own) or lease the facility?

2. If Rock-On expects that the value of the specific facility it is using will rise substantially over the next few years, would it prefer to purchase (own) or lease the facility today?

ANSWERS: 1. Rock-On would prefer to own the facility so that it would be able to expand the plant as needed. 2. Rock-On would prefer to own the facility because it could be sold in the future at a much higher price than Rock-On paid for it. If Rock-On leases the facility, it does not benefit from the increase in the price.

Deciding the Capital Structure

Describe how firms determine the composition of their financing.

capital structure
the amount of debt versus equity financing

All firms must decide on a **capital structure,** or the amount of debt versus equity financing. No particular capital structure is perfect for all firms. However, some characteristics should be considered when determining the appropriate capital structure. The use of debt (such as bank loans or bonds) as a source of funds is desirable because the interest payments made by the firm on its debt are tax-deductible. Firms can claim their interest payments during the year as an expense, thereby reducing their reported earnings and their taxes. When firms use equity as a source of funds, they do not benefit in this way.

Although debt offers the advantage of tax deductibility, too much debt can increase the firm's risk of default on its debt. A higher level of debt results in a higher level of interest payments each year, which can make it difficult for a firm to cover all its debt payments. When creditors are concerned about the firm's ability to make future interest payments, they are less willing to provide additional credit. A firm's ability to increase its debt level is also constrained by the amount of collateral available.

Cross Functional Teamwork

Relationship between Pricing and Financing Strategies

A firm's financing decisions will be dependent on its pricing decisions. If the firm is using a pricing strategy that will result in a relatively low level of sales (and therefore a low level of production), it will need a small amount of funds to support that production level. If the firm uses a pricing strategy that will result in a high level of sales (and therefore a high level of production), however, it will need a much larger amount of funds to support that production level. If the firm needs a relatively small amount of funds, it may decide to borrow from a commercial bank. If it needs a large amount of funds, it may issue bonds. It may also need to consider using some equity financing if the amount of funds needed will exceed its debt capacity.

Firms tend to retain some earnings as an easy and continual form of equity financing. When they need additional funds to support their operations, they typically use debt financing if they have the flexibility to do so. When they approach their debt capacity, however, they may have to retain more earnings or issue stock to obtain additional capital.

Revising the Capital Structure

Many firms revise their capital structure in response to changes in economic conditions, such as economic growth and interest rates. If economic growth declines and their earnings decline, they may reduce their debt because it is more difficult to cover interest payments. When interest rates decline, firms may increase their debt because the interest payments will be relatively low.

To reduce the strain of meeting high interest payments in the 1990s, many firms reduced their debt levels by hundreds of millions of dollars. Conversely, other firms such as IBM increased their debt because they anticipated that they could easily cover future interest payments resulting from the additional debt.

Sometimes firms revise their capital structure by changing the amount of stock they have outstanding. As described earlier, a firm can obtain equity financing by issuing additional shares of stock. Firms may also decrease the amount of stock outstanding by repurchasing shares issued previously. This strategy may have a favorable impact on the firm's stock price. To illustrate how the repurchasing of stock can improve a firm's value (and therefore its stock price), consider the following statements from a recent annual report of Wal-Mart:

"In a move to improve shareholder value, the Board of Directors authorized a $2 billion share repurchase program. . . . We started buying [when the stock price was] in the low 20s, and the stock ended up rising 73 percent in the last calendar year."

How the Capital Structure Affects the Return on Equity

A firm's earnings performance (as measured by its return on equity) can be significantly influenced by the capital structure decision. Consider a firm that had earnings of $1 million last year and has $10 million in assets. The firm's return on equity (measured as earnings divided by owner's equity) depends on the amount of the firm's assets that was financed with equity versus debt. Exhibit 16.6 shows how the firm's return on equity is dependent on its financial leverage. If the firm used all equity to finance its $10 million in assets, its return on equity (ROE) would be:

$$\text{ROE} = \frac{\$1,000,000}{\$10,000,000}$$

$$= 10\%$$

At the other extreme, if the firm used only 20 percent equity ($2 million) to finance its assets, its ROE would be:

$$\text{ROE} = \frac{\$1,000,000}{\$2,000,000}$$

$$= 50\%$$

Although using little equity (mostly debt) can achieve a higher return on equity, it exposes a firm to the risk of being unable to cover its interest payments. To illustrate the risk, Exhibit 16.7 shows how the annual interest expense incurred by a firm (with $10 million in assets) is dependent on the firm's degree of financial leverage. This exhibit assumes a 10 percent interest rate. For example, if the firm uses all equity, it does not incur any interest expenses. At the other extreme, if it uses only 20 percent ($2 million) of equity financing and relies on 80 percent ($8 million) of debt financing, it will incur an interest expense of $800,000 per year.

The relationship shown in Exhibit 16.7 is intended simply to illustrate how a high degree of financial leverage can result in high interest expenses. In reality, the impact of high financial leverage may be even more

Exhibit 16.6

How a Firm's Return on Equity Is Dependent on Financial Leverage
Note: Assume that the firm had a net income of $1 million last year and has $10 million in assets.

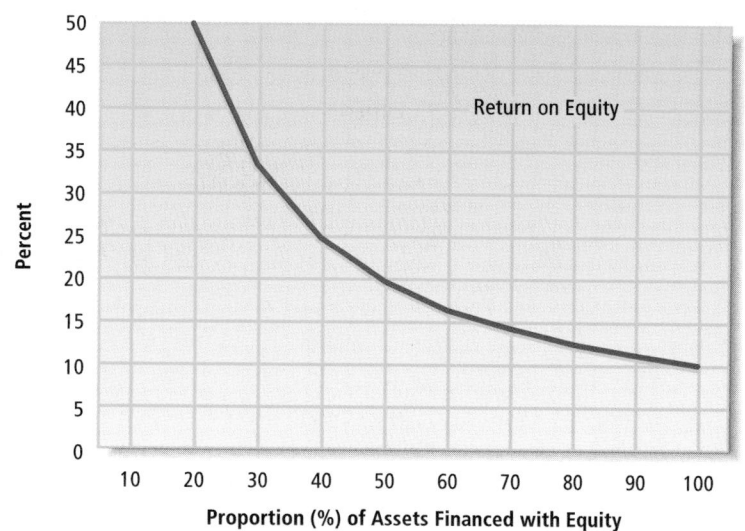

Exhibit 16.7

How a Firm's Interest Expense Is Dependent on Financial Leverage
Note: Assume that the firm has $10 million in assets; also assume a 10 percent interest rate on debt.

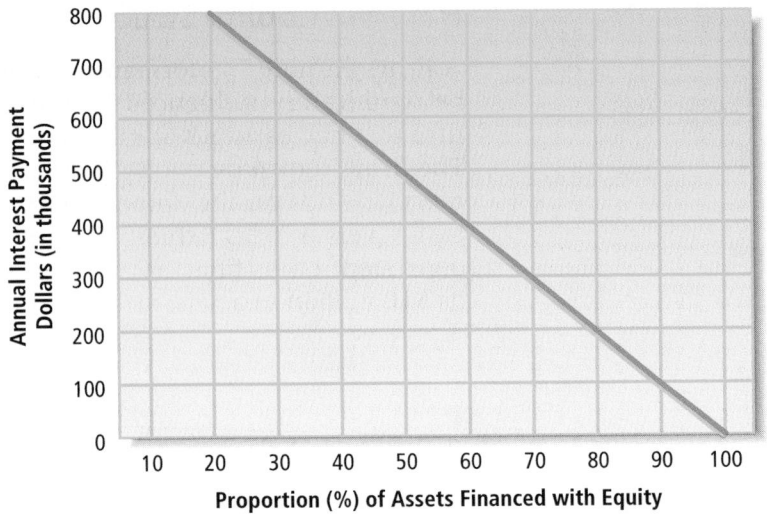

SMALL BUSINESS SURVEY

Financing Choices of Small Firms

A recent survey asked small firms how they are financing their businesses, with the results as shown:

	Proportion of Firms That Recently Used This Type of Financing
Commercial bank loans	36%
Credit cards	27
Retained earnings	24
Private loans	18
Personal bank loans	17
Supplier credit	14
Leasing	10
Other	13

The results of this survey show that small firms use a wide variety of methods to obtain funds. The commercial bank loans, credit cards, and private loans reflect debt financing, while the use of retained earnings reflects equity financing.

Global Business

Global Financing

When U.S. firms establish businesses in foreign countries (called "foreign subsidiaries"), they must obtain sufficient funds to support them. Foreign subsidiaries must decide not only whether to use debt or equity but also what currency to use. A common method is for the subsidiary to borrow funds locally. This financing strategy allows the interest expense to be in the same currency as the revenue. Consequently, the subsidiary does not need to exchange its local currency into another currency to pay off the debt.

Cross Functional Teamwork

Interaction between Financing Decisions and Other Business Decisions

When financial managers make financing decisions, they rely on input from other managers. The amount of financing is dependent on the difference between the amount of cash outflows resulting from the payment of expenses and the cash inflows resulting from sales. The larger the difference, the more financing will be needed. Financial managers can ask production managers to estimate the salaries and other production expenses that will be incurred by the firm in the future. They can ask marketing managers to estimate the marketing expenses to be incurred by the firm. They can also ask marketing managers to estimate the future demand for each of the firm's products; this information can be used to estimate the firm's future revenue.

When financial managers decide whether to finance with debt or equity, they rely on input from marketing managers. If the future revenue to be received by the firm is somewhat stable over time, the firm may be willing to finance with debt because cash inflows each month will be sufficient to cover its interest payments on debt. If the monthly revenue is expected to be erratic, however, cash inflows each month may not be sufficient to make interest payments. In this case, the firm may use equity financing instead of debt financing. The marketing managers can offer useful input on this topic because they should know whether the demand for the product will be somewhat stable over time.

pronounced than in Exhibit 16.7, because lenders may charge a higher interest rate to firms that wish to borrow an excessive amount. The extra premium on the interest rate compensates the lenders for the risk that the firm may be unable to repay its debt.

Firms weigh the potential higher return on equity that results from using mostly debt financing against the risk resulting from high interest payments. Many firms compromise by balancing their amounts of equity and debt financing. For example, a firm might finance its $10 million in assets by using $5 million of equity and the remaining $5 million of debt. Assuming an interest rate of 10 percent on debt, the interest expense would be $500,000 (computed as 10% × $5,000,000), as shown in Exhibit 16.7.

Decision Making

Deciding on the Capital Structure

The capital structure used by a firm is dependent on its specific characteristics. To illustrate, reconsider the case of Rock-On Company, which produces musical instruments. Its capital structure is mostly equity, which was obtained from its original owners. Now Rock-On wants to decide how it should obtain financing if it expands in the future. Its decision will affect its capital structure. Rock-On's lease requires it to make monthly payments, but it always generates enough revenue each month to easily cover its expenses. Since the company can afford to make loan (debt) payments each month, it can rely on debt to finance its future expansion. Therefore, when it needs more funding, Rock-On plans to revise its capital structure to increase its debt level.

1. Suppose that Rock-On's monthly revenue was very unstable. How might this affect its capital structure decision?
2. Why would Rock-On prefer not to use more equity to support future expansion?

ANSWERS: 1. Rock-On might not have sufficient revenue in some months to cover its debt payments, so it might prefer to avoid debt. 2. Its existing owners would prefer to maintain the ownership structure so that they do not have to share the business with other owners.

Describe the remedies for firms that are unable to repay their debts.

Remedies for Debt Problems

The ultimate danger to taking on too much debt is that the firm may be unable to make its payments to its creditors. The extreme consequence of this situation is business failure, in which the firm's assets are sold to pay creditors part of what they are owed. In this case, a formal bankruptcy process is necessary. First, however, the firm should consider alternative informal remedies, which could avoid some legal expenses. Common remedies include the following:

▶ Extension

▶ Composition

▶ Private liquidation

▶ Formal remedies

Extension

extension

provides additional time for a firm to generate the necessary cash to cover its payments to its creditors

If a firm is having difficulty covering the payments it owes, its creditors may allow an **extension,** which provides additional time for the firm to generate the necessary cash to cover its payments. An extension is feasible only if the creditors believe that the firm's financial problems are temporary. If formal bankruptcy is inevitable, an extension may only delay the liquidation process and possibly reduce the liquidation value of the firm's assets.

If creditors allow an extension, they may require that the firm abide by various provisions. For example, they may prohibit the firm from making dividend payments until the firm retains enough funds to repay its loans. The firm will likely agree to any reasonable provisions because the extension gives the firm a chance to survive.

A creditor cannot be forced to go along with an extension. Creditors who prefer some alternative action must be paid off in full if an extension is to be allowed. If too many creditors disapprove, an extension will not be feasible, as the firm would first have to pay all disapproving creditors what they are owed.

Composition

composition
specifies that a firm will provide its creditors with a portion of what they are owed

If the failing firm and its creditors do not agree on an extension, they may attempt to negotiate a **composition** agreement, which specifies that the firm will provide its creditors with a portion of what they are owed. For example, the agreement may call for creditors to receive 40 cents on every dollar owed to them. This partial repayment may be as much as or more than the creditors would receive from formal bankruptcy proceedings. In addition, the firm may be able to survive, since its future interest payments will be eliminated after paying off the creditors. As with an extension, creditors cannot be forced to go along with a composition agreement. Any dissenting creditors must be paid in full.

Private Liquidation

If an extension or composition is not possible, the creditors may informally request that the failing firm liquidate (sell) its assets and distribute the funds received from liquidation to them. Although this can be achieved through formal bankruptcy proceedings, it can also be accomplished informally outside the court system. An informal agreement will typically be accomplished more quickly than formal bankruptcy proceedings and is less expensive as it avoids excessive legal fees. All creditors must agree to this so-called **private liquidation,** or an alternative remedy will be necessary.

private liquidation
creditors may informally request that a failing firm liquidate (sell) its assets and distribute the funds received from liquidation to them

To carry out a private liquidation, a law firm with expertise in liquidation will normally be hired to liquidate the debtor firm's assets. Once the assets are liquidated, the remaining funds are distributed to the creditors on a pro rata basis.

Formal Remedies

If creditors cannot agree to any of the informal remedies, the solution to the firm's financial problems will be worked out formally in the court system. The formal remedies are either reorganization or liquidation under bankruptcy. Whether a firm should reorganize or liquidate depends on its estimated value under each alternative.

liquidation value
the amount of funds that would be received as a result of the liquidation of a firm.

Reorganization   Reorganization of a firm can include the termination of some of its businesses, an increased focus on its other businesses, revisions of the organizational structure, and downsizing. Consider a firm whose value as a "going concern" (a continuing business) would be $20 million after it reorganizes. Now consider the **liquidation value** of that firm, which is the amount of funds that would be received from liquidating all of the firm's assets. If the firm's liquidation value exceeds $20 million, it should be liquidated. The creditors would receive more funds from liquidation than they would expect to receive if the firm were reorganized. Conversely, if its liquidation value is less than $20 million, the firm should be reorganized.

In the case of reorganization, the firm or the creditors must file a petition. The bankruptcy court then appoints a committee of creditors to work with the firm in restructuring its operations. The firm is protected against any legal action that would interrupt its operations. The firm may revise its capital structure by using less debt so that it can reduce its periodic interest payments owed to creditors. Once the restructuring plan is completed, it is submitted to the court and must be approved by the creditors.

Liquidation under Bankruptcy   If the firm and its creditors cannot agree on some informal agreement, and if reorganization is not feasible, the firm will file for bankruptcy. A petition for bankruptcy may be filed by either the failing firm or the creditors.

The failing firm is obligated to file a list of creditors along with up-to-date financial statements. A law firm is appointed to sell off the existing assets and allocate the funds received to the creditors. Secured creditors are paid with the proceeds from selling off any assets serving as their collateral.

COLLEGE HEALTH CLUB: FINANCING AT CHC

One of the decisions that Sue Kramer needs to make as part of her business plan for College Health Club (CHC) is how to finance the business. Sue has obtained a loan for $40,000 to finance CHC. One advantage of using debt rather than obtaining additional equity is that the interest payments are tax-deductible. A second advantage is that since Sue has not accepted an equity investment from another person, she has full control over the business. The disadvantage of using debt rather than equity financing is that CHC will incur an interest expense each month as long as the loan exists. Sue expects that the annual interest expense will be $4,000, which means that CHC's earnings before taxes will be $4,000 less than if it had no debt. Sue decided to use debt financing rather than additional equity financing because she prefers to be the sole owner and feels confident that CHC can afford the $4,000 interest payment.

Sue also has to decide whether to purchase the land and facilities for the health club or lease the space. The advantage of owning assets such as the weight and exercise machines and the facilities is that they would be hers to keep, unless she sold them. In addition, she would not have to make lease payments. The disadvantage, however, is the expense associated with purchasing the equipment and facilities. To purchase them, she would need a very large loan. Creditors might not be willing to extend such a large amount. Even if they did, her interest payments would be much higher because of the large loan. Also, leasing gives her flexibility. If Sue decides to discontinue the business, for example, she will not need to find a buyer for the equipment or facilities. Given the advantages of leasing, Sue has decided to lease the equipment and the facilities. If she accumulates substantial funds in the future, she will reconsider whether to purchase these assets.

Summary

1 The common sources of debt financing are obtaining bank loans, issuing bonds, or issuing commercial paper.

The financial institutions that provide loans to firms are commercial banks, savings institutions, and finance companies. The financial institutions that commonly purchase the corporate bonds issued by firms are insurance companies, pension funds, and bond mutual funds.

2 The common sources of equity financing are retaining earnings and issuing stock. The financial institutions that purchase stocks issued by firms are insurance companies, pension funds, and stock mutual funds.

3 When firms issue debt securities or stocks, they normally hire an investment bank. The investment bank may provide advice on the amount of securities the firm should issue (origination), underwrite the securities, and find buyers of the securities that the firm issues (distribution).

4 In addition to debt financing and equity financing, firms may also obtain financing from suppliers. A firm may be given a period of time to make payment after the supplies are delivered. Since the firm is not required to pay for the supplies immediately, it is essentially receiving funding from the supplier. The firm may be given only a short-term period such as one month to make payment, however, so such an arrangement with a supplier does not provide long-term financing.

Firms may also be able to finance investments in their business by leasing. In this case, they rent (rather than own) buildings, machinery, or other assets that they need for operations. By leasing assets rather than buying then, a firm does not need to obtain funding. It only needs to make the monthly lease payment for the use of those assets.

5 Firms may prefer to use debt financing over equity financing because the interest payments are tax-deductible. This can allow debt to be a relatively cheap form of financing. However, a high level of debt financing results in a high level of interest payments, which could make it difficult for the firm to make those payments. Therefore, firms may prefer to avoid such a risk by using some equity financing as well. With equity financing, the firm does not have to make periodic payments.

6 When a firm performs poorly, it may not have sufficient funds to repay its debt. It may need to sell all of its assets and use the proceeds to pay off part of the debt. Alternatively, it could attempt to obtain an extension from its creditors; an extension allows additional time for the firm to cover its debt payments. Another possibility is to negotiate a composition agreement, in which the creditors accept a portion of what they are owed, and the firm may be able to stay in business.

How the Chapter Concepts Affect Business Performance

A firm's decisions regarding the financing concepts summarized here can affect its performance. Several methods of financing can be used, and no method is perfect for every situation. The firm must recognize the tradeoffs involved. The use of debt is especially desirable when the firm can borrow at a low interest rate and when it can easily afford to cover its interest payments. Equity financing may be more appropriate when the firm cannot afford interest payments. However, equity financing typically results in more owners of the business, so the profits are ultimately shared among more investors. Thus, the return on equity could decline as a result of an increase in equity financing.

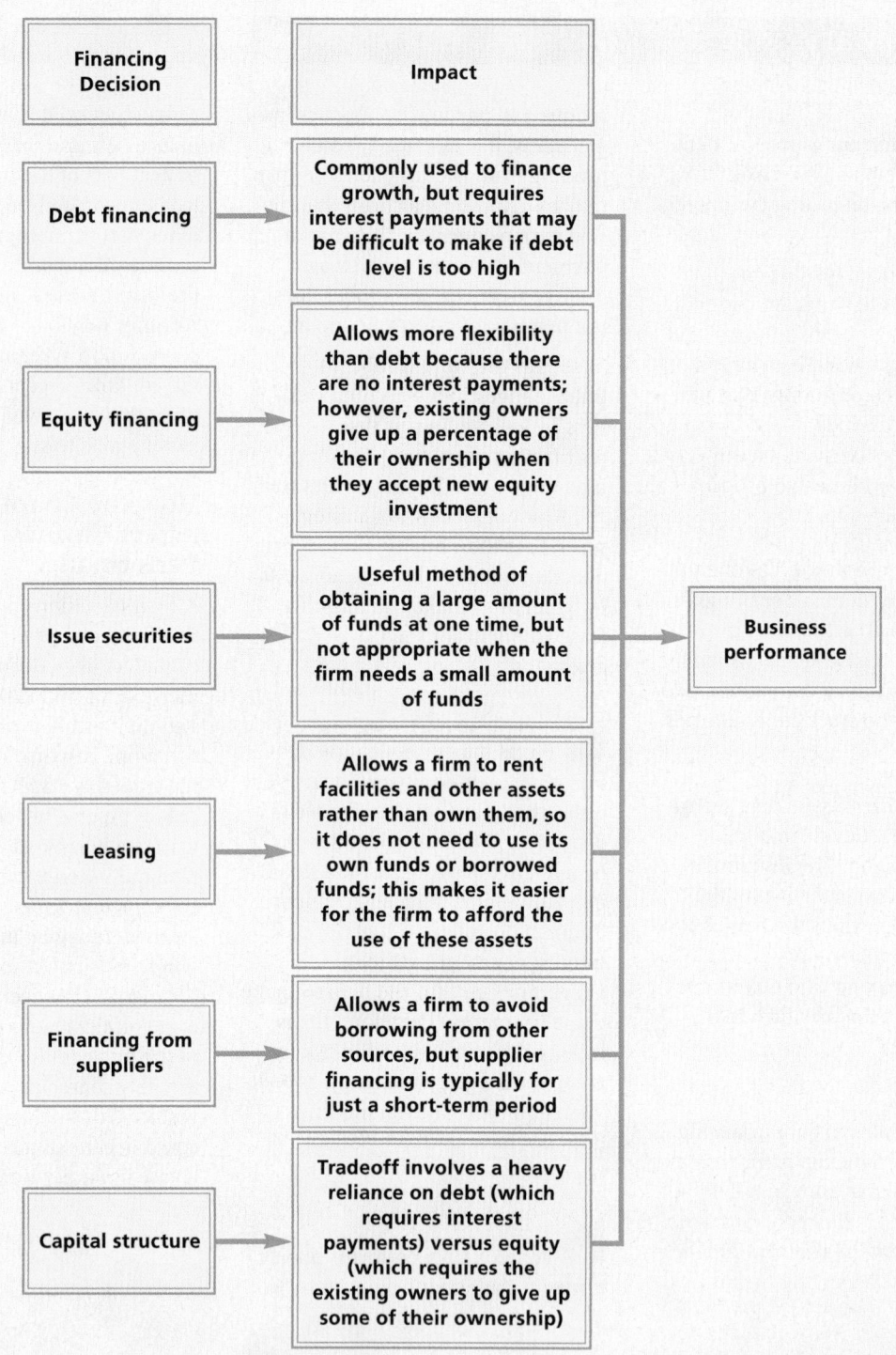

Financing Decision	Impact
Debt financing	**Commonly used to finance growth, but requires interest payments that may be difficult to make if debt level is too high**
Equity financing	**Allows more flexibility than debt because there are no interest payments; however, existing owners give up a percentage of their ownership when they accept new equity investment**
Issue securities	**Useful method of obtaining a large amount of funds at one time, but not appropriate when the firm needs a small amount of funds**
Leasing	**Allows a firm to rent facilities and other assets rather than own them, so it does not need to use its own funds or borrowed funds; this makes it easier for the firm to afford the use of these assets**
Financing from suppliers	**Allows a firm to avoid borrowing from other sources, but supplier financing is typically for just a short-term period**
Capital structure	**Tradeoff involves a heavy reliance on debt (which requires interest payments) versus equity (which requires the existing owners to give up some of their ownership)**

Business performance

Key Terms

Review & Critical Thinking Questions

1. Compare the use of funds required by a service firm with the use of funds required by an industrial firm.

2. What factors do lenders use to assess the creditworthiness of firms?

3. What determines the loan rate a business could obtain?

4. When would a firm obtain a floating-rate loan rather than a fixed-rate loan?

5. When a firm plans to issue bonds, what legal document is created by the firm, and what is included in this document?

6. What is the call feature associated with bonds? Do callable bonds have higher or lower interest rates than noncallable bonds?

7. List the common types of creditors that can provide debt financing to firms.

8. Briefly describe the common methods of equity financing for a firm.

9. What are the advantages and disadvantages of IPOs (initial public offerings)?

10. What is the difference between debt financing and equity financing?

11. Identify and explain other methods of obtaining funds that a firm can use in addition to debt financing and equity financing.

12. What factors influence a firm's choice of financing?

13. List and briefly describe the factors that affect a firm's dividend policy.

14. What services do investment banks provide to clients that are doing an IPO?

15. Why might the amount of funds a firm needs to raise affect its willingness to do an IPO?

16. What are the informal remedies for business failure? What are the formal remedies?

17. What does the term *liquidation value* mean? What is *value as a going concern*?

18. What services do venture capital firms provide in addition to their capital investment in the firm?

19. What are the benefits to investors of owning preferred stock? What are the benefits to holding common stock?

Discussion Questions

1. You are a financial manager. Why would you want to use a very high degree of financial leverage for your firm?

2. You are a business entrepreneur who is starting a business that requires a $100,000 investment. You have very little cash; however, you own your own home that is appraised at $220,000, and you own a car valued at $10,000. Both of these assets are free and clear from any indebtedness. Offer opinions on how you might negotiate a loan with the bank.

3. How can a firm use the Internet and technology to research financing alternatives?

4. You are a vice-president of finance for a large privately held corporation and you must raise $20 million for a project. Discuss why you might consider an IPO.

5. Why do you think stockholders of a firm that is performing very well would prefer that the firm pay only a low percentage of its earnings as dividends?

6. Why might the owners of a firm prefer debt financing to equity financing?

7. You are the owner of a small florist business. You need to raise $50,000 to buy new showcases for your flowers. What alterna-tives for raising the funds are available to you?

8. Why might a creditor prefer informal remedies to formal remedies in the event of a business failure?

9. What are the differences be-tween the IPO market and the secondary market?

10. Why is a firm more likely to be able to get a loan from a bank if it can provide collateral?

It's Your Decision: Financing Decisions at CHC

1. If CHC expands by creating three new health clubs, should Sue Kramer (CHC's presi-dent) finance the expansion with an initial public offering?

2. How can CHC obtain additional funds if Sue does not want to borrow any more funds?

3. What is a disadvantage of CHC obtaining additional financing with borrowed funds?

4. If Sue decides to expand CHC's existing facilities, why must she first consider its finan-cial situation?

5. Recall that Sue expects total expenses of $142,000 in CHC's first year. She will price memberships at $500 and expects to attract 300 members in the first year. She can re-duce CHC's debt by $3,600 if she does not spend any money on marketing this year. However, the expected membership in the first year would be only 280 rather than 300 if no marketing is conducted.

   a. What is the expected level of earnings in the first year if Sue decides to reduce CHC's debt as described here?

   b. Should CHC's debt level be reduced in the manner described here? Explain.

6. A health club differs from manufacturing firms in that it produces a service rather than products. Why are manufacturing firms more likely to go public than service firms? When service firms go public, how do you think they expand? By expanding one or a few facilities? Or by creating a large number of smaller facilities around the United States?

Investing in a Business

Using the annual report of the firm in which you would like to invest, complete the following:

1. Has the firm obtained new funding over the last year? If so, how?

2. When the firm borrows funds, does it rely mostly on loans from commercial banks, or does it issue bonds?

3. Has the firm's degree of financial leverage changed in the last year because of new financing? If so, has the degree of financial leverage increased or decreased?

4. Explain how the business uses technology to pro-vide information on its financing alternatives and decisions. For example, does it use the Internet to provide information on interest rates on debt in-struments that it issues? Does it provide informa-tion on the stock price received when issuing stock?

5. Go to http://hoovers.com and locate the NEWS SEARCH. Type in the name of the firm in the space provided, and review the recent news stories about the firm. Summarize any (at least one) re-cent news story about the firm that applies to one or more of the key concepts in this chapter.

Exhibit 16A.4

Summary of Key Factors
That Affect Interest Rates

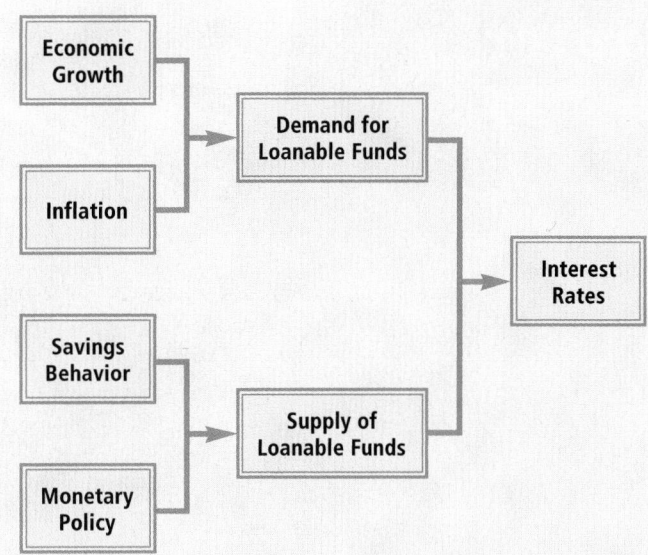

of funds that can be loaned out by banks to borrowers has increased, a surplus of funds is available at the previous equilibrium interest rate. Therefore, the new equilibrium interest rate will decline to the level at which the quantity of funds supplied equals the quantity of funds demanded.

Summary of Factors That Affect Interest Rates

Four factors that influence interest rates have been identified and are illustrated in Exhibit 16A.4. The main effects of economic growth and inflation on interest rates occur as a result of influencing the demand for loanable funds. The main effects of savings behavior and monetary policy on interest rates occur as a result of influencing the supply of loanable funds.

The factors that affect interest rates can all change at the same time. One factor may be pushing interest rates up while the others are pushing interest rates down. The final effect on interest rates may depend on which factor has the biggest impact.

Chapter

17

PHOTOEDIT, INC.

Tropical Cruise Line's performance is highly dependent on how it invests its funds. Its investment decisions determine the type of cruise ships that it should build, the number of cruise ships that it should build, and the cruise journeys that it should offer. For any cruise ship that it builds, it needs to generate substantial cash flows over time for the investment to be feasible.

The Learning Goals of this chapter are to:

Explain capital budgeting and identify the types of investment decisions that a firm may make. *1*

Describe the capital budgeting tasks that are necessary to make business investment decisions. *2*

Describe the motive for investing in other firms (acquisitions), explain the merger process, and identify other types of restructuring that firms may use. *3*

Explain how firms make decisions for investing in short-term assets. *4*

640

Expanding the Business

Whereas the previous chapter focused on how firms obtain funds (financing), this chapter focuses on how firms utilize funds (business investment). A firm makes short-term investment decisions when it considers investing in accounts receivable and inventory. It makes long-term investment decisions when it considers investing in long-term assets. Consider the situation of Tropical Cruise Line, which provides cruises from Miami to the Caribbean islands. It wants to expand its cruise business and must decide:

▶ What types of investments should it consider?

▶ What tasks are necessary to make business investment decisions?

▶ How can it conduct an analysis of proposed investments to decide whether they are feasible?

▶ How should it make decisions to invest in short-term assets?

If Tropical Cruise Line can make investment decisions properly, it will use its funds in a manner that is beneficial to its owners. That is, the benefits from expansion will exceed the costs. Its decisions on investing in short-term assets are also intended to enhance its business performance by using funds in an efficient manner.

The types of decisions described above are necessary for all businesses. This chapter explains how Tropical Cruise Line or any other firm can make investment decisions in a manner that maximizes the firm's value.

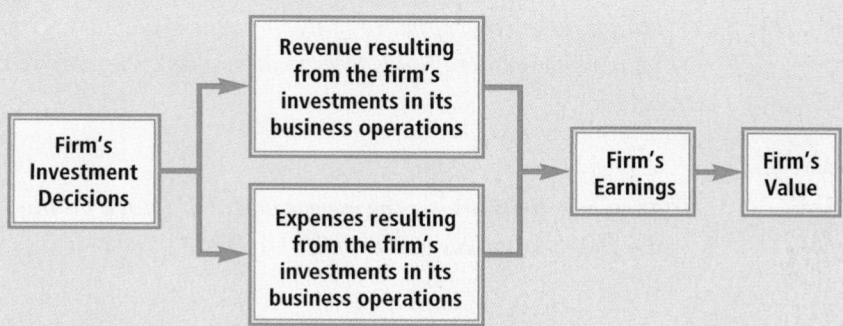

641

1

Explain capital budgeting and identify the types of investment decisions that a firm may make.

capital budgeting
a comparison of the costs and benefits of a proposed project to determine whether it is feasible

Investment Decisions

Firms continually evaluate potential projects in which they may invest, such as the construction of a new building or the purchase of a machine. Many firms plan for growth every year. DuPont, IBM, and 3M Company expand by continually creating new products. Retailers such as The Gap and Abercrombie & Fitch expand by establishing new stores. To decide whether proposed projects should be implemented, firms such as The Gap conduct **capital budgeting,** which is a comparison of the costs and benefits of a proposed project to determine whether it is feasible. The costs of a project include the initial outlay (payment) for the project, along with the periodic costs of maintaining the project. The benefits of a project are the revenue it generates.

For example, when McDonald's establishes a new restaurant, the initial outlay includes the construction of the building, the furniture needed, utensils, and cooking facilities. It also includes costs of food as well as labor. The benefits of this project are the revenue that the restaurant will generate over time. In most cases, the precise amounts of a project's costs and benefits are not known in advance and can only be estimated.

Many decisions that result from capital budgeting are irreversible. That is, if the project does not generate the benefits expected, it is too late to reverse the decision. For example, if a restaurant is unsuccessful, its selling price will likely be much lower than the cost of establishing it.

To illustrate how an inaccurate budgeting analysis can affect the firm, consider the case of Converse, which invested in a company called Apex One. Unfortunately, Converse underestimated the expenses involved in this project and overestimated the revenue. Consequently, just three months after the initial outlay, Converse terminated the project and incurred a $41.6 million loss. As an illustration of how firms focus on each project's return versus its cost, consider the following statements from recent annual reports:

"Our goal is to achieve a return on invested capital over the course of each business cycle that exceeds the company's cost of capital."

—Boise Cascade

"With a return on capital roughly three times our cost of capital, this strategy [of borrowing more funds to expand] makes even more sense now than before."

—The Coca-Cola Company

"All of our divisions use the measurement of return on invested capital relative to the cost of capital as their standard."

—Textron

How Interest Rates Affect Investment Decisions

Interest rates determine the cost of borrowed funds. A change in interest rates can affect the cost of borrowing as well as the project's feasibility. Firms require a return on projects that exceeds their cost of funds. If they use borrowed funds to finance a project and pay 15 percent on those funds, they would require a return of at least 15 percent on that project.

Before PepsiCo decided to establish a large plant in Beijing, China (shown here), it needed to conduct capital budgeting to determine whether the large investment would be worthwhile.

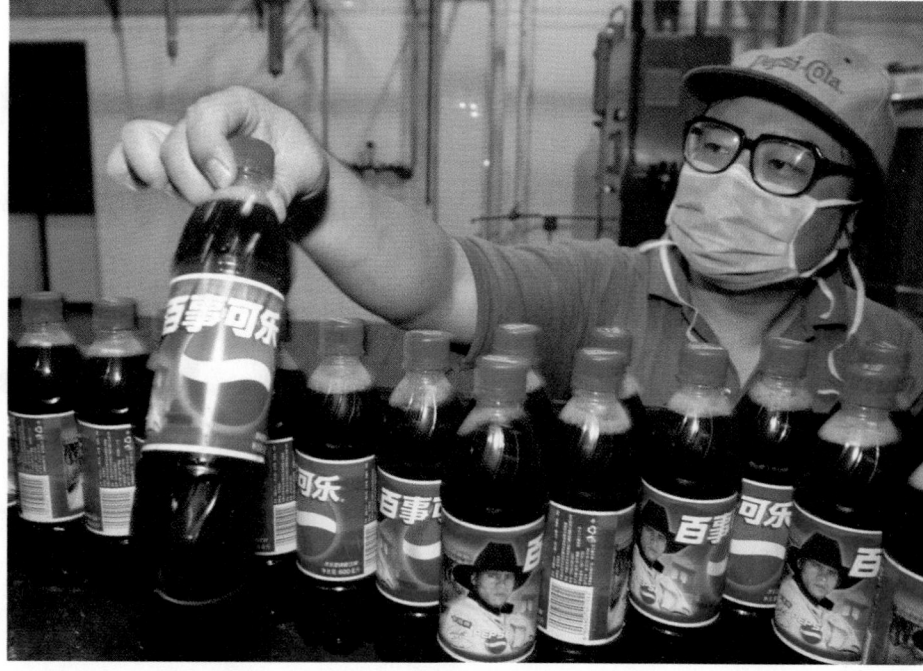

LANDOV LLC

If interest rates decrease, the cost of financing decreases, and the firm's required rate of return decreases. Thus, a project once perceived by the firm as unfeasible may be feasible once the firm's required rate of return is lowered.

Capital Budget

capital budget
a targeted amount of funds to be used for purchasing assets such as buildings, machinery, and equipment that are needed for long-term projects

Firms plan a **capital budget,** or a targeted amount of funds to be used for purchasing assets such as buildings, machinery, and equipment that are needed for long-term projects. The annual capital budget for firms such as PepsiCo, The Coca-Cola Company, IBM, and ExxonMobil commonly exceeds $1 billion. The size of a firm's capital budget is influenced by the amount and size of feasible business projects.

A firm's capital budget can be allocated across its various businesses. PepsiCo distributes its capital budget across snack foods and beverages.

A capital budget can also be segmented by geographic markets. PepsiCo allocates its capital budget for projects in the United States and for projects in foreign countries.

Classification of Capital Expenditures

The types of potential capital expenditures considered by a firm can be broadly classified into the following three categories.

Expansion of Current Business   If the demand for a firm's products increases, a firm invests in additional assets (such as machinery or equipment) to produce a large enough volume of products to accommodate the increased demand. For example, many health-care firms have increased their capital budgets as they anticipate an increase in demand for their products.

Development of New Business   When firms expand the line of products that they produce and sell, they need new facilities for production. They may also need to hire employees to produce and sell the new products. Car

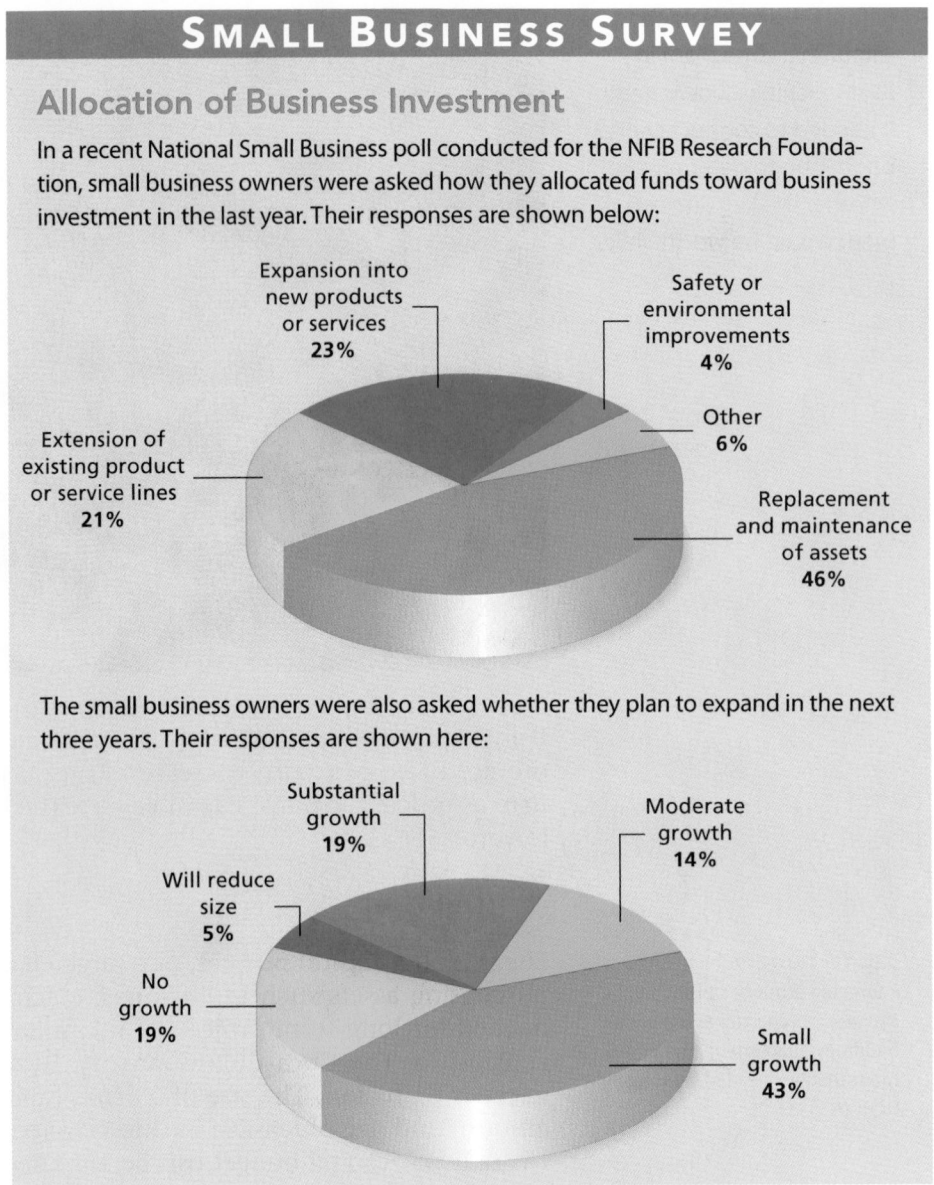

SMALL BUSINESS SURVEY

Allocation of Business Investment

In a recent National Small Business poll conducted for the NFIB Research Foundation, small business owners were asked how they allocated funds toward business investment in the last year. Their responses are shown below:

Expansion into new products or services **23%**

Safety or environmental improvements **4%**

Other **6%**

Replacement and maintenance of assets **46%**

Extension of existing product or service lines **21%**

The small business owners were also asked whether they plan to expand in the next three years. Their responses are shown here:

Substantial growth **19%**

Moderate growth **14%**

Will reduce size **5%**

No growth **19%**

Small growth **43%**

---

manufacturers frequently invest millions of dollars per year to expand their product line and to improve their exporting capabilities.

Investment in Assets That Will Reduce Expenses Machines and equipment wear out or become technologically obsolete over time. Firms replace old machines and equipment to capitalize on new technology, which may allow for lower expenses over time. For example, a new computer may be able to generate a firm's financial reports more economically than an older computer. The benefits of lower expenses may outweigh the initial outlay needed to purchase the new computer.

Firms also purchase machines that can perform the work of employees. For example, machines rather than employees could be used on an assembly line to package a product. The benefits of these machines are the cost savings that result from employing fewer workers. To determine whether the machines are feasible for this purpose, the cost savings must be compared with the price of the machines.

Factories like this automobile manufacturing facility commonly rely on robotic equipment to produce products. The investment in robotic equipment is expensive and is only feasible if it will ultimately generate substantial cash flow for the firm over time.

INDEX STOCK IMAGERY

Decision Making

Business Investment Decisions

Tropical Cruise Line (introduced at the beginning of the chapter) offers cruises from Miami to various islands in the Caribbean Sea. The demand for its cruises is so high that its future cruises are fully booked through the winter months. It wants to build another cruise ship that will sail from Miami to the islands once a week. This is an important investment decision because the ship may cost $200 million or more. Tropical Cruise Line does not want to make such a large investment unless it is confident that the benefits of the new ship outweigh the costs.

1. How can Tropical's investment decision regarding a new ship influence its decision about how much financing it needs?

2. How can Tropical's investment decision regarding a new ship influence its marketing decisions?

ANSWERS: 1. Tropical's decision to invest in a ship would require a specific amount of funds. Tropical must decide how much cash to allocate toward the investment; the remainder is the amount of funding it must obtain. 2. Tropical's decision to invest in a ship will force it to do additional marketing to attract customers to reserve cruises on the new ship.

2

Describe the capital budgeting tasks that are necessary to make business investment decisions.

Capital Budgeting Tasks

The process of capital budgeting involves five tasks:

▶ Proposing new projects

▶ Estimating cash flows of projects

▶ Determining whether projects are feasible

▶ Implementing feasible projects

▶ Monitoring projects that were implemented

Cross Functional Teamwork

Cross Functional Relationships Involved in Business Investment Decisions

When financial managers make capital budgeting decisions, they rely on information from the production and marketing departments, as shown in the diagram below. The expected cash inflows resulting from a project are dependent on the expected sales to be generated by the project, which are normally forecasted by the marketing department. The expected cash outflows resulting from a project are dependent on the expected expenses incurred by the project. The marketing department can forecast the expenses that would be incurred by marketing (such as promotion expenses). The production department can forecast the expenses that would be incurred by production (such as labor expenses). The financial manager's ability to estimate a project's net present value is dependent on the input provided by marketing and production

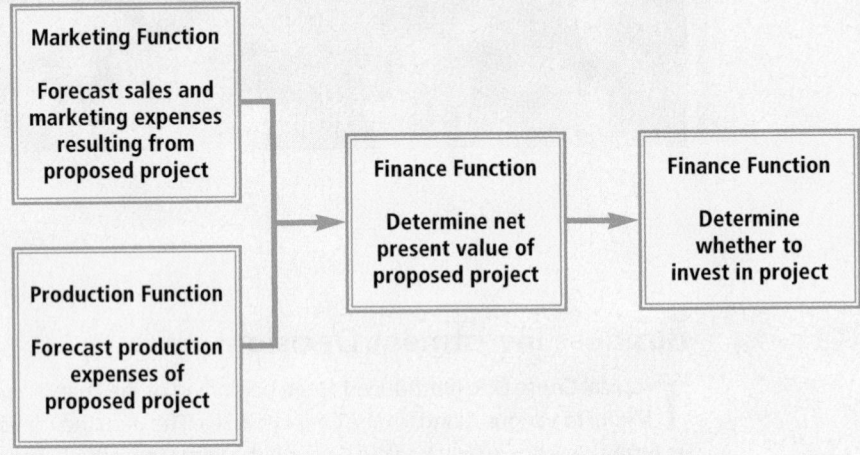

Proposing New Projects

New projects are continually proposed within the firm as various departments or divisions offer input on new projects to consider.

Estimating Cash Flows of Projects

Each potential project affects the cash flows of the firm. Estimating the cash flows that will result from the project is a critical part of the capital budgeting process. Revenue received from the project represents cash inflows, while payments to cover the project's expenses represent cash outflows. The decision whether to make a capital expenditure is based on the size of the periodic cash flows (defined as cash inflows minus cash outflows per period) that are expected to occur as a result of the project.

Determining Whether Projects Are Feasible

Once potential projects are proposed and their cash flows estimated, the projects must be evaluated to determine whether they are feasible. Specific techniques are available to assess the feasibility of projects. One popular method is the net present value technique, which compares the expected periodic cash flows resulting from the project with the initial outlay needed to finance the project. This process is discussed in more detail in an appendix to this chapter. If the present value of the project's expected cash flows is above or equal to the initial outlay, the project is feasible. Conversely, if the present value of the project's expected cash flows is below the initial outlay, the project is not feasible.

In some cases, the evaluation involves deciding between two projects designed for the same purpose. When only one of the projects can be accepted, such projects are referred to as **mutually exclusive.** For example, a firm may be considering two machines that perform the same task. The two alternative machines are mutually exclusive because the purchase of one machine precludes the purchase of the other.

When the decision of whether to adopt one project has no bearing on the adoption of other projects, the project is said to be **independent.** For example, the purchase of a truck to enhance delivery capabilities and the purchase of a large computer system to handle payroll processing are independent projects. That is, the acceptance (or rejection) of one project does not influence the acceptance (or rejection) of the other project.

The authority to evaluate the feasibility of projects may be dependent on the types of projects evaluated. Larger capital expenditures normally are reviewed by high-level managers. Smaller capital expenditures may be made by other managers.

mutually exclusive
the situation in which only one of two projects designed for the same purpose can be accepted

independent project
a project whose feasibility can be assessed without consideration of any others

Implementing Feasible Projects

Once the firm has determined which projects are feasible, it must focus on implementing those projects. All feasible projects should be given a priority status so that those projects that fulfill immediate needs can be implemented first. As part of the implementation process, the firm must obtain the necessary funds to finance the projects.

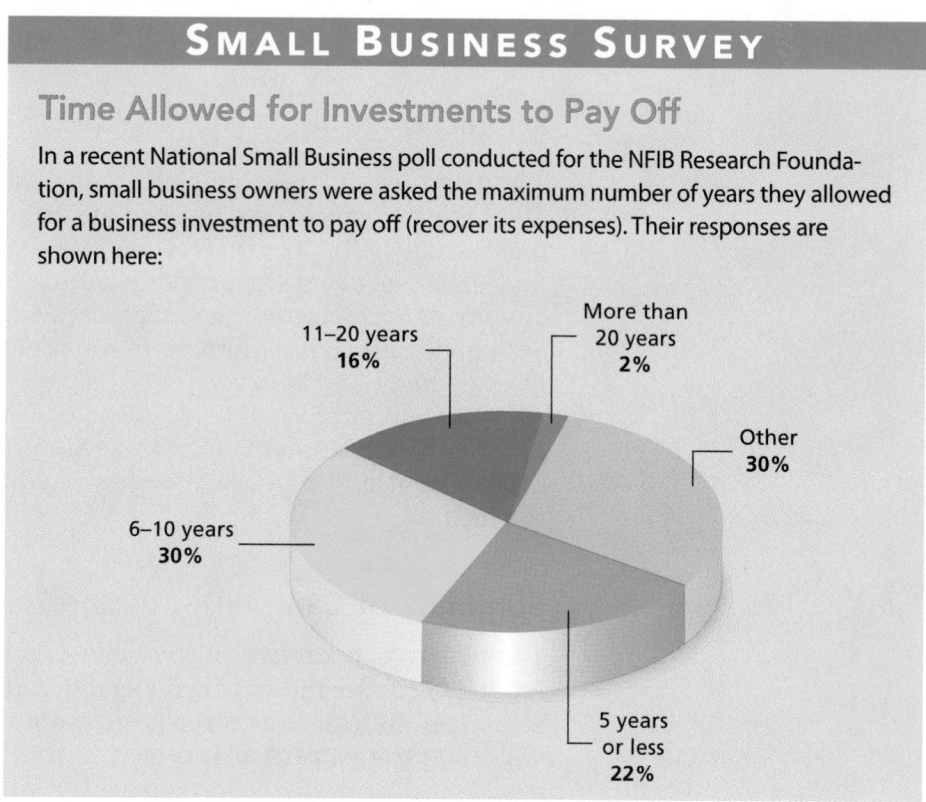

SMALL BUSINESS SURVEY

Time Allowed for Investments to Pay Off

In a recent National Small Business poll conducted for the NFIB Research Foundation, small business owners were asked the maximum number of years they allowed for a business investment to pay off (recover its expenses). Their responses are shown here:

11–20 years 16%
More than 20 years 2%
Other 30%
6–10 years 30%
5 years or less 22%

Global Business

Global Investing

U.S. firms frequently consider investing funds in foreign projects. The Coca-Cola Company commonly invests more than $1 billion per year to expand its worldwide business. The Coca-Cola Company typically invests the bulk of its capital budget overseas, because international markets offer more opportunities for the company.

When U.S. firms such as Coca-Cola consider the purchase of a foreign company, they conduct a capital budgeting analysis to determine whether this type of project is feasible. The capital budgeting analysis required to assess a foreign project is more complex than the analysis for a domestic project because of the need to assess specific characteristics of the foreign country. First, the initial outlay required to purchase the foreign firm will depend on the exchange rate at that time. The lower the value of the foreign currency needed, the lower the initial outlay needed by the U.S. firm to invest in the foreign country. Firms prefer to invest in foreign companies (or any other foreign projects) under these conditions.

Firms that consider foreign projects must also determine the required rate of return for the foreign project to be feasible. Many foreign projects are considered to be more risky than domestic projects, so U.S. firms require higher rates of return on foreign projects than on domestic projects. A higher rate of return is required to compensate for the higher risk. Foreign projects in developing countries are especially risky because of the high probability that these projects could be terminated by the governments of those countries. This point is especially important in light of recent trends by U.S. firms to invest in large projects based in developing countries. General Motors typically invests more than $100 million per year in developing countries. The large amount of investment by General Motors in these countries suggests that it expects the projects to generate very high returns, making them worthwhile even though they are riskier than projects in the United States.

Monitoring Projects That Were Implemented

After a project has been implemented, it should be monitored over time. The project's actual costs and benefits should be compared with the estimates made before the project was implemented. The monitoring process may detect errors in the previous estimation of the project's cash flows. If any errors are detected, the employees who were responsible for project evaluation should be informed of the problem so that future projects can be evaluated more accurately.

A second purpose of monitoring is to detect and correct inefficiencies in the current operation of the project. Furthermore, monitoring can help determine if and when a project should be abandoned (liquidated) by the firm.

Summary of Capital Budgeting Tasks

The five tasks necessary to conduct capital budgeting are summarized in Exhibit 17.1. The most challenging task is the estimation of cash flows, because it is difficult to accurately measure the revenue and expenses that will result from a particular project.

Exhibit 17.1

Summary of Capital
Budgeting Tasks

Task	Description
Propose new projects.	Propose new projects that require expenditures necessary to support expansion of existing businesses, development of new businesses, or replacement of old assets.
Estimate cash flows of projects.	Cash flows in each period can be estimated as the cash inflows (such as revenue) resulting from the project minus cash outflows (expenses) resulting from the project.
Determine whether projects are feasible.	A project is feasible if the present value of its future cash flows exceeds the initial outlay needed to purchase the project.
Implement feasible projects.	Feasible projects should be implemented, with priority given to those projects that fulfill immediate needs.
Monitor projects that were implemented.	Projects that have been implemented need to be monitored to determine whether their cash flows were estimated properly. Monitoring may also detect inefficiencies in the project and can help determine when a project should be abandoned.

Decision Making

Capital Budgeting Tasks

Recall that Tropical Cruise Line plans to build a new ship. Its financial managers consider the revenue that could be generated from a weekly cruise. The revenue is primarily determined by the price charged for a cruise and the number of customers who pay the price each week. The life of the cruise ship is expected to be 15 years, so it will generate revenue over that period. Next, the managers must estimate the cost of building the ship. They also need to estimate the cost of operating the ship, which includes food and other services on the ship as well as maintenance.

1. Explain why the expected life of the cruise ship affects the firm's estimate of the revenue that will result from building the ship.

2. What are some obvious factors that Tropical Cruise Line would consider when it attempts to estimate the revenue that would be generated by the cruise ship each month?

ANSWERS: 1. The longer the expected life, the longer the ship can provide revenue. 2. The revenue for each month is dependent on the number of passengers and the price charged for a cruise. The size of the ship would dictate the amount of passengers that would be on the ship at a given time. However, Tropical must consider that some cruises will not sell out, so there will be fewer passengers in some months.

Mergers and Other Forms of Restructuring

3

Describe the motives for investing in other firms (acquisitions), explain the merger process, and identify other restructurings that firms may use.

merger
two firms are merged (or combined) to become a single firm owned by the same owners (shareholders)

horizontal merger
the combination of firms that engage in the same types of business

vertical merger
the combination of a firm with a potential supplier or customer

conglomerate merger
the combination of two firms in unrelated businesses

Among the most expensive projects that a firm may consider are investments in other firms through acquistions. The different types of mergers that firms may engage in are described here, followed by an examination of the motives for mergers and the merger process. Firms may also engage in other forms of restructuring including leveraged buyouts and divestitures, and those are described as well.

Types of Mergers

A firm may invest in another company by purchasing all the stock of that company. This results in a **merger,** in which two firms are merged (or combined) to become a single firm owned by the same owners (shareholders). A merger may be feasible if it can increase a firm's value either by increasing the return to the firm's owners or by reducing the firm's risk without a reduction in return.

Mergers can be classified as one of three general types. A **horizontal merger** is the combination of firms that engage in the same types of business. For example, the merger between First Union Corporation and Wachovia Corporation was a horizontal merger, as it combined two large commercial banks. A **vertical merger** is the combination of a firm with a potential supplier or customer, such as General Motors' acquisition of a battery manufacturer that could produce the batteries for many of its automobiles. A **conglomerate merger** is the combination of two firms in unrelated businesses. For example, a merger between a book publisher and a steel manufacturer would be a conglomerate merger. The term *conglomerate* is sometimes used to describe a firm that is engaged in a variety of unrelated businesses.

Corporate Motives for Mergers

Mergers are normally initiated as a result of one or more of the following motives.

Immediate Growth A firm that plans for growth may prefer to achieve its objective immediately through a merger. Consider a firm whose production capacity cannot fully satisfy demand for its product. The firm would need two years to build additional production facilities. To achieve an immediate increase in production, the firm may search for a company that owns the appropriate facilities. By acquiring either part or all of such a company, the firm can achieve immediate growth in its production capacity, thereby allowing for growth in its sales. When Walt Disney Company purchased Capital Cities/ABC, it created more growth potential than if it had simply attempted to expand its existing businesses.

Economies of Scale Growth may also be desirable to reduce the production cost per unit. Products that exhibit economies of scale can be produced at a much lower cost per unit if a large amount is produced. A merger may allow a firm to combine two production facilities and thereby achieve a lower production cost per unit.

For example, assume that Firm A and Firm B produce a similar product. Also assume that each firm uses an assembly-line operation for about

Exhibit 17.2

Illustration of How an Acquisition Can Generate Economies of Scale

Firm	Total Output Produced	Variable Cost per Unit	Variable Cost	Fixed Cost (Rent)	Total Cost	Average Cost per Unit
A	500 units	$10	$5,000	$6,000	$11,000	($11,000/500) = $22.00
B	400 units	$10	$4,000	$6,000	$10,000	($10,000/400) = $25.00
A & B Combined	900 units	$10	$9,000	$6,000	$15,000	($15,000/900) = $16.67

eight hours per day and sells its product to its own set of customers. Firm A sells 500 units per month, while Firm B sells 400 units per month. The variable cost per unit is $10 for each firm. Each firm pays $6,000 per month to rent its own factory. This rent is a fixed cost because it is not affected by the amount of the product produced. If Firm A acquires Firm B, it will be able to serve both sets of customers, which will result in a higher production level. The factory can be used for 16 hours a day by running a second shift for the assembly line.

Based on the initial assumptions, the average cost per unit for each firm is shown in Exhibit 17.2. Notice that when Firm A acquires Firm B, the average cost per unit is lower than it was for either individual firm. This occurs because only one factory is needed when the firms are merged. Thus, the average cost per unit declines when Firm A makes more efficient use of the factory.

There may be additional ways for the combination of firms to reduce costs, beyond the savings resulting from renting only one factory. For example, assume each firm has its own accountant. Each firm pays a salary for this position, which reflects a fixed cost. However, Firm A's accountant may be able to cover all the accounting duties for the combined firm, which means that it need not incur the cost of Firm B's accountant. Therefore, it can further reduce costs by removing any job positions in Firm B that can be handled by Firm A's existing employees.

Horizontal mergers are more likely to achieve economies of scale than vertical or conglomerate mergers because they involve firms that produce similar products. Firms with similar operations can eliminate similar positions once the firms are combined.

Managerial Expertise   The performance of a firm is highly dependent on the managers who make the decisions for the firm. Since the firm's value is influenced by its performance, its value is influenced by its managers. To illustrate this point, consider a firm called "Weakfirm" that has had weak performance recently because of its managers. This firm's value should be low if its performance has been weak and is not expected to improve.

Also assume, however, that another firm in the same industry, called "Strongfirm," has more competent managers. If the managers of Strongfirm had been managing the operations of Weakfirm, the performance of Weakfirm might have been much higher. Given this information, Strongfirm may consider purchasing Weakfirm. The price for Weakfirm should be relatively low because of its recent performance. Yet, once Strongfirm purchases Weakfirm, it can improve Weakfirm's performance. The owners (shareholders) of Strongfirm will benefit because their firm is able to acquire another firm at a relatively low price and turn it into something more valuable. In other words, the additional earnings generated by Strongfirm following the acquisition may exceed the cost of the acquisition.

When an acquirer firm purchases a target, the success of the merger is dependent on its management. Its managers may be able to improve upon the operations of the target or motivate the employees of the target, so that the target's performance improves after the acquisition.

GETTY IMAGES

The example just described occurs frequently. Some firms that have had relatively weak performance (compared with other firms in the industry) become targets. Consequently, weak firms are always in danger of being acquired.

Some mergers can be beneficial when each firm relies on the other firm for specific managerial expertise. For example, consider Disney's acquisition of the ABC television network. Disney produced movies that were sold to television networks. When television networks began to produce their own movies, Disney could have had difficulty selling its movies to various networks. By acquiring the ABC network, Disney could rely on the network to show some of its movies, while the ABC network was assured that it would be supplied with various popular Disney movies. Disney had expertise as the producer of the product (movies), and ABC had expertise as the distributor of that product. Both firms benefited as a result of the acquisition.

Tax Benefits   Firms that incur negative earnings (losses) are sometimes attractive candidates for mergers because of potential tax advantages. The previous losses incurred by the company prior to the merger can be carried forward to offset positive earnings of the acquiring firm. Although the losses of the acquired firm have occurred prior to the acquisition, they reduce the taxable earnings of the newly merged corporation. To illustrate the potential tax benefits, consider an acquisition in which the acquiring firm applies a $1 million loss of the acquired firm to partially offset its earnings. If the acquiring firm is subject to a 30 percent tax rate, it can reduce its taxes by $300,000 (computed as 30 percent times the $1 million in earnings that is no longer subject to tax because of applying the $1 million loss).

Merger Analysis

When a firm plans to engage in a merger or acquisition, it must conduct the following tasks:

▶   Identify potential merger prospects.

▶   Evaluate potential merger prospects.

▶   Make the merger decision.

Identify Potential Merger Prospects   Firms attempt to identify potential merger prospects that may help them achieve their strategic plan. If the firm plans for growth in its current line of products, it will consider purchasing (or "acquiring") companies in the same business. If it needs to restructure its production process, it may attempt to acquire a supplier. If it desires a more diversified product line, it may attempt to acquire companies in unrelated businesses. The firm's long-run objectives influence the selection of merger prospects that are worthy of evaluation.

The size of the firm is also a relevant criterion, as some firms may be too small to achieve the desired objectives while others may be too large to acquire. The location is another possible criterion because a firm's product demand and production costs are dependent on its location.

Evaluate Potential Merger Prospects   Once merger prospects have been identified, they must be analyzed thoroughly, using publicly available financial statements. The financial analysis may detect problems that will eliminate some prospects from further consideration. Prospects with deficiencies that can be corrected should still be considered, however. Along with the firm's financial condition, additional characteristics of each prospect must be assessed, including its reputation and labor-management relations. From this assessment, potential problems that may not be disclosed on financial statements can be detected.

The firm planning the acquisition needs to evaluate the prospect's specific characteristics, such as its facilities, its dependence on suppliers, and pending lawsuits. Unfortunately, a full evaluation of such specific characteristics may not be possible unless the prospect provides the information. The firm planning the acquisition may contact the prospect to request more detailed information. The prospect may comply if it is willing to consider the possibility of a merger.

Make the Merger Decision   Once the firm has identified a specific prospect it wishes to acquire, it can assess the feasibility of acquiring that prospect

Sprint and Nextel merged their companies in an effort to improve their businesses.

by using capital budgeting analysis. Thus, the acquisition prospect can be evaluated just like any other project. The cost of this project is the outlay necessary to purchase the firm. The benefits are the extra cash flows that will be generated over time as a result of the acquisition. If the present value of the future cash flows to be received by the acquiring firm exceeds the initial outlay, the acquisition is feasible.

Merger Procedures

If an attempt is made to acquire a prospect, that prospect becomes the "target." It is set apart from all the other prospects that were considered. To carry out the acquisition, firms will normally hire an investment bank (such as Morgan Stanley or Goldman Sachs) for guidance. Some firms that continuously acquire or sell businesses may employ their own investment banking department to handle many of the necessary tasks. Most tasks can be classified into one of the following:

▶ Financing the merger

▶ Tender offer

▶ Integrating the businesses

▶ Postmerger evaluation

Financing the Merger A merger normally requires a substantial amount of long-term funds, as one firm may purchase the existing stock of another firm. In a common method of financing a merger, a firm issues more of its own stock to the public. As new stock is sold to the public, the proceeds are used to purchase the target's stock. Alternatively, the acquiring firm may trade its new stock to the shareholders of the target firm in exchange for their stock. Instead of issuing new stock, the acquiring firm may also borrow the necessary funds to purchase the target's stock from its shareholders.

Tender Offer The acquiring firm first contacts the management of the target firm to negotiate a merger. The acquiring firm normally pays a premium on the target firm's stock to make the deal worthwhile to the target firm's stockholders.

When two firms cannot come to terms, the acquiring firm may attempt a **tender offer.** This is a direct bid by the acquiring firm for the shares of the target firm. It does not require prior approval of the target firm's management. Thus, a tender offer could accomplish a merger even if the management of the target firm disapproves.

The acquiring firm must decide the price at which it is willing to purchase the target firm's shares and then officially extend this tender offer to the shareholders. The tender offer normally represents a premium of 20 percent or more above the prevailing market price, which may be necessary to encourage the shareholders of the target firm to sell their shares. The acquiring firm can achieve control of the target firm only if enough of the target firm's shareholders are willing to sell.

Integrating the Businesses If a merger is achieved, various departments within the two companies may need to be restructured. The key to successfully integrating the management of two companies is to clearly communicate the strategic plan of the firm. In addition, the organizational

tender offer
a direct bid by an acquiring firm for the shares of a target firm

structure should be communicated to clarify the roles of each department and position. This includes identifying to whom each position will report and who is accountable for various tasks. If the roles are not clearly defined up front, the newly integrated management will not function properly. Tensions are especially high in the beginning stages of a merger, as the employees of the acquired firm are not fully aware of the acquiring firm's plans. Once the merger has occurred, the personnel involved in the initial evaluation of the target firm should guide the integration of the two firms. For example, if the primary reason for a horizontal merger was to reduce the duplication of some managerial functions (to increase production efficiency), management of the newly formed firm should make sure that these reasons for initiating the merger are realized.

A newly formed merger typically requires a period in which the production, financing, inventory management, capital structure, and dividend policies are reevaluated. Policies are commonly revised to conform to the newly formed firm's characteristics. For example, to deal with the larger volume of sales, inventory of the combined firm may need to be larger than for either original business (although perhaps not as large as the sum of both businesses).

Although identifying ways in which a merger could be beneficial is often easy, it may not be as easy to achieve those benefits without creating any new problems. As a final point, the process of creating the merger can also be much more expensive than originally anticipated and can often impose a financial strain on the acquiring company (especially when the target fights the takeover effort). Therefore, firms that are considering acquisitions should attempt to anticipate all types of expenses that may be incurred as a result of the acquisitions.

Postmerger Evaluation   After the merger, the firm should periodically assess the merger's costs and benefits. Were the benefits as high as expected? Did the merger involve unanticipated costs? Was the analysis of the target firm too optimistic? Once the merger takes place, it cannot easily be reversed. Thus, any errors detected from the analysis that led to the merger cannot be washed away. Nevertheless, the firm can learn lessons from any errors so that it will be able to evaluate future merger prospects more accurately.

Defense against Takeover Attempts

In some cases, managers of a target firm may not approve of the takeover attempt by the acquiring firm. They may believe that the price offered for their firm is less than it is worth or that their firm has higher potential if it is not acquired. They may view the potential acquiring firm as a shark approaching for the kill (takeover). Under such conditions, management of the target firm can choose from a variety of "shark repellents" to defend it against the hostile takeover attempt.

A common defensive tactic against a takeover attempt is to try to convince shareholders to retain their shares. Another tactic to avoid a merger is a private placement of stock. By selling shares directly (privately) to specific institutions, the target firm can reduce the acquiring firm's chances of obtaining enough shares to gain a controlling interest. The more shares outstanding, the larger the amount of shares that must be purchased by the acquiring firm to gain a controlling interest.

white knight
a more suitable company that
is willing to acquire a firm and
rescue it from the hostile takeover
efforts of some other firm

A third defensive tactic is for the target firm to find a more suitable company (called a **white knight**) that is willing to acquire the firm and rescue it from the hostile takeover efforts of some other firm. The white knight rescues the target firm by acquiring the target firm itself. Although the target firm no longer retains its independence, it may prefer being acquired by the white knight firm.

Leveraged Buyouts

leveraged buyout (LBO)
the purchase of a company (or
a subsidiary of a company) by a
group of investors with borrowed
funds

In a **leveraged buyout,** or **LBO,** a group of investors purchase a company (or a subsidiary of a company) with borrowed funds. In many cases, the investors are the previous managers of the business. For example, consider a diversified firm that plans to sell off its financial services division to obtain cash. The management of this division may attempt to borrow the necessary funds to purchase the division themselves and become the owners. The newly owned business would be supported with mostly borrowed funds.

Any business with characteristics that enable it to operate adequately with a large amount of borrowed funds is a potential candidate for an LBO. Such characteristics include established product lines, stable cash flow, and no need for additional fixed assets. These characteristics increase the probability that a sufficient amount of cash flows will consistently be forthcoming to cover periodic interest payments on the debt. Growth normally is not a primary goal, since the firm does not have excess cash to expand and may have already borrowed up to its capacity.

Although an LBO can place a strain on cash, it does offer an advantage. The ownership of the business is restricted to a small group of people. All earnings can be allocated to this group, creating the potential for high returns to the owners (although most earnings will likely be reinvested in the business in the early years). However, since businesses that experience LBOs have a debt-intensive capital structure (high degree of financial leverage), they are risky.

Divestitures

divestiture
the sale of an existing business by
a firm

A **divestiture** is the sale of an existing business by a firm. It is the reverse of investing in new assets. Firms may have several motives for divestitures. First, a firm may divest (sell) businesses that are not part of its core operations so that it can focus on what it does best. For example, Eastman Kodak, Ford Motor Company, and many other firms have sold various businesses that were not closely related to their core businesses. A second motive for divestitures is to obtain funds. Divestitures generate funds for the firm because it is selling one of its businesses in exchange for cash. For example, CSX Corporation made divestitures to focus on its core railroad business and also to obtain funds so that it could pay off some of its existing debt.

A third motive for divesting is that a firm's "break-up" value is sometimes believed to be greater than the value of the firm as a whole. In other words, the sum of a firm's individual asset liquidation values exceeds the market value of the firm's combined assets. This encourages firms to sell off what would be worth more when liquidated than when retained.

Some firms are using technology to facilitate the process of divesting some divisions. They post the information about any division that they wish to sell on their website so that it is available to any firm that may be interested in buying the division. For example, Alcoa has established an online showroom of the divisions that are for sale. By communicating the information online, Alcoa has reduced its hotel, travel, and meeting expenses.

Decision Making

Deciding Whether to Acquire a Business

To understand the potential benefits of mergers, consider Tropical Cruise Line, which provides cruises from Miami to the Caribbean islands. It is considering the acquisition of a casino on a small island. The casino is not easily accessible to tourists because the island does not have an airport. If Tropical acquires the casino, some of its cruise ships would add the island to their scheduled stops. The ships would stop at the island each day of the week to drop off tourists who want to visit the casino. Thus, the acquisition would allow the casino to perform much better than it has performed in the past. If Tropical becomes the owner of the casino, it will benefit from the casino's improved performance.

1. Explain how Tropical's decision to acquire a business affects its decision regarding the amount of funds that it needs to borrow.

2. Explain how Tropical's decision to acquire a business may affect its marketing decisions.

ANSWERS: 1. If Tropical decides to acquire a business, it will need sufficient funds to buy that business.   2. If Tropical decides to acquire a business, it may need to apply marketing to that business.

Short-Term Investment Decisions

Explain how firms make decisions for investing in short-term assets.

working capital management
the management of a firm's short-term assets and liabilities

liquid
having access to funds to pay bills when they come due

liquidity management
the management of short-term assets and liabilities to ensure adequate liquidity

Treasury bills
short-term debt securities issued by the U.S. Treasury

Working capital management involves the management of a firm's short-term assets and liabilities. A firm's short-term assets include cash, short-term securities, accounts receivable, and inventory. Its short-term liabilities include accounts payable and short-term loans. Working capital management is typically focused on the proper amount of investment in a firm's cash, short-term securities, accounts receivable, and inventory. All of these strategies can be classified as a firm's investment strategies. Working capital management can be segmented into liquidity management, accounts receivable management, and inventory management.

Liquidity Management

Firms that are **liquid** have adequate access to funds to pay bills when they come due. **Liquidity management** involves the management of short-term assets and liabilities to ensure adequate liquidity. To remain liquid, firms may maintain cash and short-term securities. For example, they may invest in **Treasury bills,** which are short-term debt securities issued by the U.S. Treasury. Treasury bills have maturities of 13 weeks, 26 weeks, and one year. Treasury bills offer a relatively low return. They provide a firm with easy access to funds because they can easily be sold to other investors. When firms need funds to cover expenses, they sell the Treasury bills and

Out of Business

use the proceeds to pay expenses. Firms such as DuPont and The Coca-Cola Company hold hundreds of millions of dollars worth of short-term securities to maintain liquidity.

Firms normally attempt to limit their holdings of cash and short-term securities so that they can use their funds for other purposes that generate higher returns. They can be liquid without holding cash and short-term securities if they have easy access to borrowed funds. Most firms have a **line of credit** with one or more banks, which is an agreement that allows access to borrowed funds upon demand over some specified period (usually one year). If a firm experiences a temporary shortage of funds, it can use its line of credit to obtain a short-term loan immediately. The interest charged by the banks on the loan is normally tied to some specified market-determined interest rate. Thus, the interest rate will be consistent with existing market rates at the time of the loan. Firms with a line of credit do not need to go through the loan application process. They can normally reapply for a new line of credit each year.

Because of its line of credit, its cash, and its short-term securities, The Coca-Cola Company always has access to a sufficient amount of funds to pay its bills.

When firms build up an excessive amount of cash, they search for ways to use the excess. For example, they commonly use excess cash to repurchase some of their existing stock. Alternatively, they may use excess cash to pay off some of their existing debt.

Accounts Receivable Management

Firms have accounts receivable when they grant credit to customers. By granting credit, firms may generate more sales than if they required an immediate cash payment. Allowing credit has two potential disadvantages, however. The first is that the customers may not pay the credit balance for a long time. Thus, the firm does not have use of the cash until several

line of credit
an agreement with a bank that allows a firm access to borrowed funds upon demand over some specified period

SMALL BUSINESS SURVEY

Investment Decisions by Small Businesses

About 300 Entrepreneur of the Year award winners were surveyed by the accounting firm Ernst & Young to determine how they would invest funds if they received the ideal level of financing. The respondents were allowed to select more than one type of investment. Their responses are shown in the following chart:

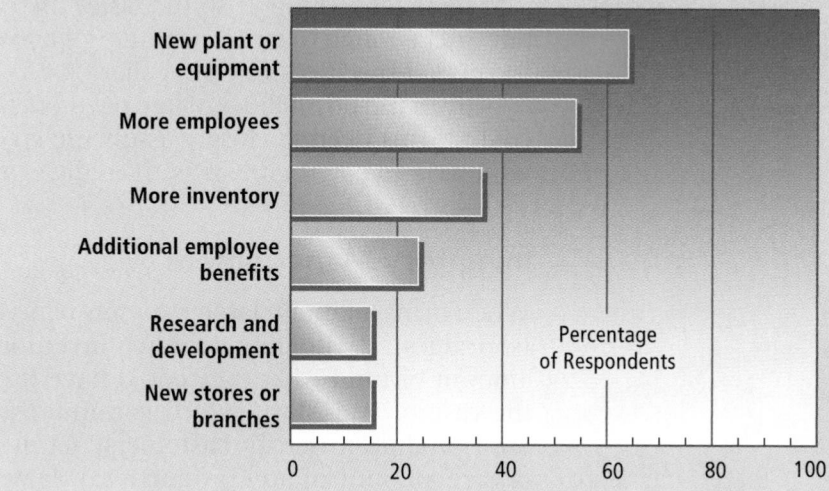

SMALL BUSINESS SURVEY

Extending Credit

In a recent National Small Business poll conducted for the NFIB Research Foundation, small businesses were asked if they extend credit to business customers, to individual customers, or to both types of customers. Their responses are shown here:

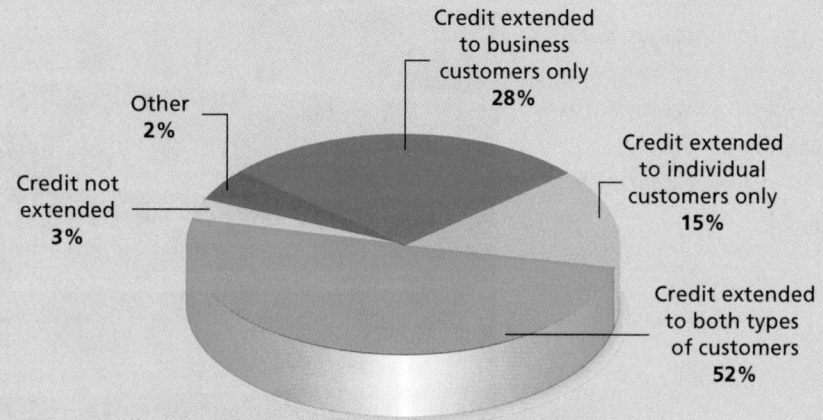

Clearly, businesses recognize that they need to provide credit in order to attract customers.

months after the sale was made. Consequently, the firm may have to borrow funds until the cash is received and will have to pay interest on those funds.

The second potential disadvantage of extending credit to customers is that the customers may default on the credit provided. In this case, the firm never receives payment for the products it sold to customers.

accounts receivable management
sets the limits on credit available to customers and the length of the period in which payment is due

Accounts receivable management sets the limits on credit available to customers and the length of the period in which payment is due. The goal is to be flexible enough so that sales increase as a result of credit granted but strict enough to avoid customers who would pay their bills late (beyond the period specified) or not at all.

Given the possibilities of late payments or no payments (default) on the credit, firms need to closely assess the creditworthiness of any customers who wish to pay their bills with credit.

Inventory Management

When firms maintain large amounts of inventory, they can avoid stockouts (shortages). By holding so much inventory, however, they invest a large amount of funds that they could have used for other purposes. Consider the case of Wal-Mart, which continuously attempts to order enough of each product to satisfy customers. Yet, it does not want to order an excessive amount of any product, which would be an inefficient use of its funds.

inventory management
determines the amount of inventory that is held

Inventory management determines the amount of inventory that is held. Managers attempt to hold just enough inventory to avoid stockouts, without tying up funds in excess inventories. This task is complicated because it requires forecasts of future sales levels, which can be erratic. If sales are more than expected, stockouts may occur unless the firm has excess inventory.

Wal-Mart attempts to have sufficient inventory so that it can satisfy customer demand and avoid shortages, but it also wants to avoid having an excessive investment in inventory because it is costly to finance excessive inventory.

LANDOV LLC

Decision Making

Deciding How Much Liquidity Is Needed

To understand the importance of liquidity management, reconsider Tropical Cruise Line. In the winter months, its cruises are sold out, but in the summer months when cruises to the Caribbean islands are not as popular, some of its ships may be only half full. Tropical's cash inflows during the summer months may not be sufficient to cover all of its expenses. It prepares for this situation by investing some of its cash in Treasury bills. If it experiences a cash shortage, it can easily sell its holdings of Treasury bills to obtain cash. In addition, Tropical maintains a line of credit so that it has quick access to borrowed funds if needed.

1. Why doesn't Tropical Cruise Line maintain a large amount of cash at all times in order to avoid potential cash shortages?

2. Tropical Cruise Line could increase the demand for its cruises if it extended credit to its customers by allowing them to delay payment until three months after the cruise is over. What is the disadvantage of this type of credit policy?

Answers: 1. Tropical prefers to put its cash to a better use, such as using it for investments that will earn a high return.
2. If Tropical used such a liberal credit policy, some of its customers would never make their payments.

COLLEGE HEALTH CLUB: ACCOUNTS RECEIVABLE MANAGEMENT AT CHC

One of the decisions that Sue Kramer needs to make as part of her business plan for College Health Club (CHC) is whether to implement a credit policy for her members. Recall that she expects that CHC will attract 300 members in its first year. Sue knows that some students who may want to become members cannot afford CHC's annual membership fee. She thinks that by implementing a credit policy that would allow members to pay later in the year, she could increase the membership to 330 members in the first year. However, Sue also thinks that 40 of those members would never pay their membership fee if they were not required to pay when they first joined the club. Her analysis of the impact of a credit policy on CHC's first-year performance is shown in the following table:

	CHC's Performance If . . .	
	Credit Is Not Offered	**Credit Is Offered**
(1) Price per membership	$500	$500
(2) Number of members in first year	300	330
(3) Number of members who pay their fees	300	290
(4) Revenue = (1) × (3)	$150,000	$145,000
(5) Total operating expenses	$138,000	$138,000
(6) Interest expenses	$4,000	$4,000
(7) Earnings before Taxes = (4) − (5) − (6)	$8,000	$3,000

Although the number of members would be higher if Sue allows credit, fewer members would pay their fees. Based on this analysis, Sue decides not to allow credit. However, she will consider an alternative plan that would allow a student to purchase a four-month membership for $110. This price is slightly higher (on a monthly basis) than the annual membership fee. This plan would attract students who could not afford the annual membership. In addition, it does not involve an extension of credit, as these students will not be allowed to continue receiving health club services unless they renew their membership.

The entire business plan developed throughout this text by Sue Kramer is shown in Appendix B of this chapter. Among other things, the plans for the business determine how funds are to be invested, which influences the amount of financing that is needed.

Summary

1 Capital budgeting involves a comparison of the costs and benefits of a proposed project to determine whether it is feasible. A capital budget is a targeted amount of funds to be used for purchasing assets that are needed for long-term projects. Firms consider three types of potential capital expenditures: expansion of a current business, development of a new business, and investment in assets that will reduce expenses.

2 The process of capital budgeting involves five tasks:

▶ Proposing new projects that deserve to be assessed.

▶ Estimating cash flows of projects, which represent the cash inflows (derived from revenue) minus the cash outflows (derived from expenses) per period.

▶ Determining which projects are feasible, which can be accomplished by comparing the present value of the project's cash flows with the project's initial outlay.

▶ Implementing feasible projects based on a priority status.

▶ Monitoring projects that were implemented, so that any errors from estimating project cash flows are recognized and may be avoided when assessing projects in the future.

3 Firms consider investing funds to acquire other companies based on one or more of the following motives:

▶ A firm can achieve immediate growth by acquiring another firm, whereas growth without a merger will be slower.

▶ Mergers can create a higher volume of sales for a firm, which allows it to spread its fixed cost across more units, thereby reducing costs (economies of scale).

▶ Mergers can allow firms to combine resources and contribute those resources in which they have the most managerial expertise.

▶ Mergers can allow the acquiring firm to reduce its taxable earnings when it acquires a company that recently incurred a loss.

In addition to mergers, firms engage in other forms of restructuring. In a leveraged buyout (LBO), a group of investors acquire a company (or a company's subsidiary) with mostly borrowed funds. A divestiture is a sale of assets owned by a business. Many firms sell off some assets such as buildings, factories, and divisions when they can obtain a higher price for an asset than what it would be worth if retained.

4 Firms invest in short-term assets such as cash, short-term securities, accounts receivable, and inventory. They invest in a sufficient amount of cash and short-term securities to maintain adequate liquidity. However, excessive investment in cash and short-term securities represents an inefficient use of funds.

Firms desire to invest in sufficient accounts receivable so that they can increase revenue over time. They must impose adequate credit standards, however, so that they can avoid excessive defaults on credit they have provided.

Firms desire to invest in a sufficient amount of inventory so that they can avoid stockouts. However, excessive investment in inventory represents an inefficient use of funds.

How the Chapter Concepts Affect Business Performance

A firm's decisions regarding the business investment concepts summarized here affect its performance. It conducts analysis to assess a variety of projects that it considers for expanding its business. Proper capital budgeting analysis allows it to select the projects that will enhance its business performance.

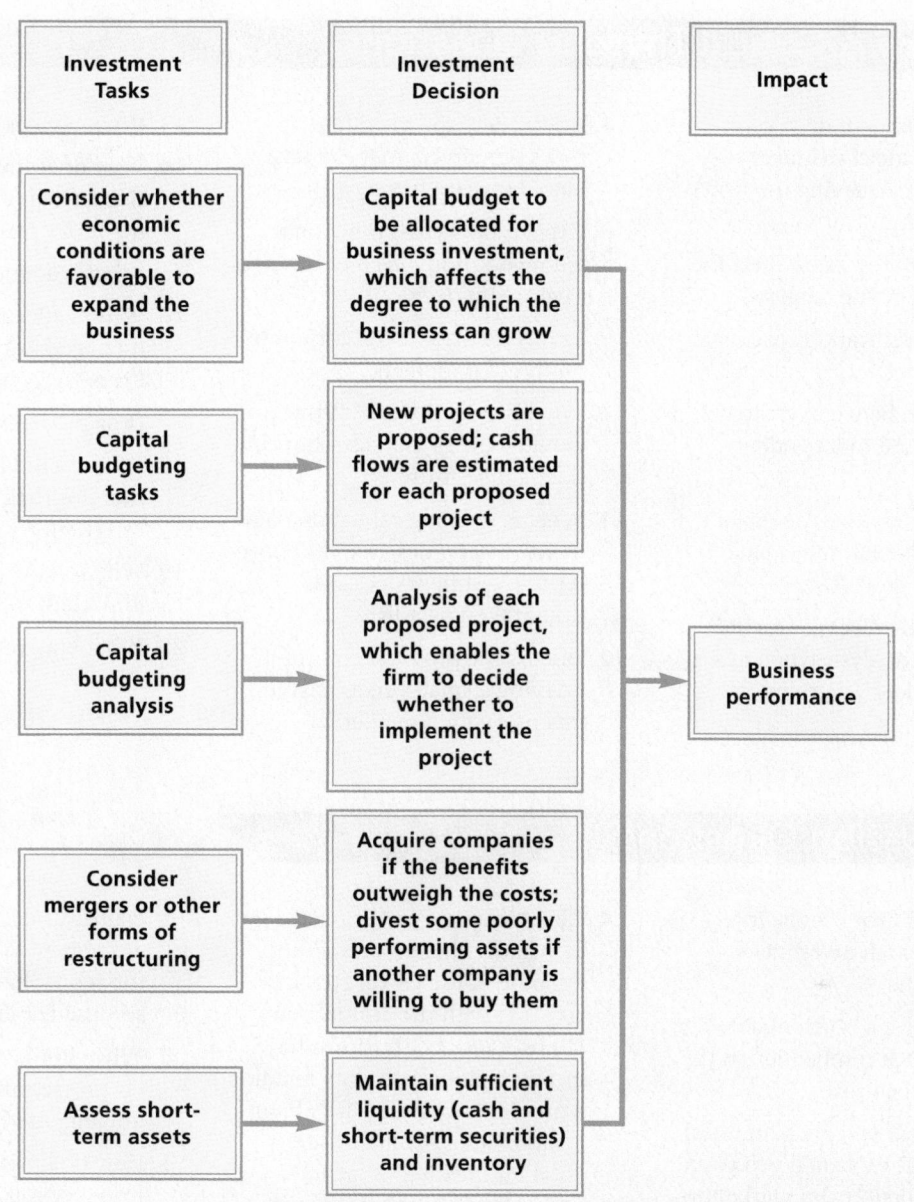

Key Terms

Review & Critical Thinking Questions

1. What investment decisions should financial managers consider in achieving the firm's objectives?

2. How do interest rates affect the capital budgeting analysis?

3. List the classifications of capital expenditures.

4. Distinguish between mutually exclusive and independent projects.

5. Briefly summarize the major tasks involved in the capital budgeting process.

6. Discuss the process of capital budgeting analysis when a firm assesses a foreign project.

7. Briefly describe the different types of mergers that can take place between firms.

8. Explain how cross functional teamwork is involved in business investment decisions.

9. Briefly describe some corporate motives for mergers.

10. What is a divestiture? Why would a firm's management consider a divestiture?

11. What is working capital management? Briefly describe the short-term investment decisions undertaken by a firm.

12. Discuss the pros and cons of carrying a small versus a large inventory for a retailer.

13. What are conglomerate mergers?

14. Why does the threat of an acquisition result in better management of firms?

15. What is a tender offer?

16. Why is effective working capital management important for firms?

17. How do firms use lines of credit?

18. Why should firms continually monitor their accounts receivable?

19. Why is good inventory control important to firms?

20. What is a "white knight"?

Discussion Questions

1. How can a firm use the Internet to research investment opportunities?

2. Explain why a horizontal merger could reduce competition in the automobile industry?

3. Assume that you are a financial manager. How would you work with production and marketing managers in making capital budgeting decisions to introduce a new product? What must the product generate to make it economically feasible?

4. Kim Aiken has just opened a go-cart track. She has timed the opening of the go-cart track to coincide with the annual county fair. Because her business has grown rapidly, cash flow remains a problem. Analyze Kim's financial problems. Could this be a good business?

5. Why might a horizontal merger achieve economies of scale?

6. Over lunch, you are listening to your firm's chief financial officer. He is telling you that he just undertook a capital budgeting proj-

ect because it "looked good and attractive." What steps should the officer have followed to assess the feasibility of this project?

7. Why should managers monitor projects that have been implemented?

8. How do horizontal mergers differ from vertical mergers?

9. What might be a drawback to a conglomerate merger?

10. What are some techniques that allow a firm to defend against a takeover attempt?

It's Your Decision: Investment Decisions at CHC

1. Recall that Sue Kramer expects total expenses of $142,000 in CHC's first year. She will price a membership at $500 and expects to attract 300 members in the first year. Sue is considering ways to boost CHC's potential membership. She thinks that if she allows members to pay their membership fees later in the year, the number of members will increase to 320. The expected number of paid memberships is equal to the total number of memberships minus the expected number of memberships that are never paid. Determine the expected earnings of CHC based on the following possible scenarios if Sue implements a credit policy.

Number of Members Who Never Pay Their Fee	CHC's Earnings before Taxes in the First Year
10	
20	
30	
40	

a. Explain the relationship between the number of members who do not pay their fee and CHC's earnings.

b. Describe the tradeoff between offering credit for members versus not offering credit. Would you recommend that Sue allow credit for her members?

2. A health club differs from manufacturing firms in that it produces a service rather than products. When a service firm such as a health club considers the creation of a new facility, it must forecast demand for services there. When a manufacturing firm considers the creation of a new facility to produce more of its product, it must forecast its demand. Is it generally easier for a service or a manufacturing firm to forecast demand?

Investing in a Business

Using the annual report of the firm in which you would like to invest, complete the following:

1. What is the firm's capital budget for this year? Is this budget higher or lower than last year's?

2. What types of new projects has the firm invested in recently?

3. Has the firm divested any of its operations? If so, did it divest to focus more on its core business?

4. Has the firm been involved in any recent merger activity? If so, what is its justification for this action?

5. Explain how the business uses technology to promote its capital budgeting activities. For example, does it use the Internet to provide information about recent investment projects? Does it use the Internet to provide information on planned future capital budgeting activities?

6. Go to http://hoovers.com and locate the NEWS SEARCH. Type in the name of the firm in the space provided, and review the recent news stories about the firm. Summarize any (at least one) recent news story about the firm that applies to one or more of the key concepts in this chapter.

Case: Deciding Whether to Acquire a Business

Benson, Inc., is a publisher of books that it sells to retail bookstores in the United States. Judith Benson, the owner of Benson, Inc., is concerned because its suppliers continue to increase the price of paper and other materials that Benson purchases from them weekly. One supplier to Benson, Inc., is Hill Company, which provides high-quality supplies but has experienced financial problems recently because of inefficient management.

Judith believes that Benson could benefit from merging with Hill Company. She believes that she could acquire (purchase) Hill at a low price because it has performed poorly in the past. She also believes that she could improve Hill's performance by reorganizing its business. In addition, the merger with Hill would give

Benson, Inc., more control over the cost of its supplies. It could obtain supplies from Hill, which would now be part of Benson, Inc. Therefore, it would not be subjected to increased prices by other suppliers. Meanwhile, Hill would not only produce supplies for Benson, Inc., but would also sell them to other customers, as it did in the past.

Questions

1. What type of merger is Judith considering?

2. Explain how Judith might decide on a purchase price for Hill Company.

3. How could the purchase of Hill Company backfire?

Video Case: Investing and Financing at Timbuk2

Timbuk2 is a manufacturer and retailer of backpacks, laptop bags, and accessories such as cell phone holders and protective strap pouches. Several years ago, the firm was experiencing a decline in sales and had to reorganize in terms of its management and objectives. Top-line growth (increased sales) became the new objective for the firm, given that the company needed an infusion of cash. Timbuk2 needed to expand through increased sales in new product lines (a product portfolio) and new markets in order to generate cash. The firm's original goal was to generate $25 million in revenue in five years. It not only achieved that goal but surpassed it. The company has now revised its growth estimates. Timbuk2's management recognizes the importance of business funding to facilitate growth. It also emphasizes forecasts. The controller of Timbuk2 says that everyone has to be on the same page with fore-

casts. This is accomplished through meetings between management and staff, where successes and shortcomings are recognized. The company also focuses on daily numbers. More information on Timbuk2 is available at http://www.timbuk2.com.

Questions

1. Why did the new managers of Timbuk2 decide to finance growth with increased sales, rather than by borrowing more funds?

2. How does a reputation for excellence in its market help Timbuk2 improve top-line growth and bottom-line performance?

3. Why do all divisions of Timbuk2 have to agree on business forecasts?

Internet Applications

1. http://www.invoicefinancial.com

What services are offered by this firm? What is factoring? Why might a firm find factoring services useful?

2. http://biz.yahoo.com/me

What kind of information does this site offer? Which firms are engaging in mergers and acquisitions? Click

on "News" for one transaction. What kind of information can you find regarding whether acquisitions are vertical or horizontal?

3. http://www.legalcenter.com/lc/hostile-takeovers.html

What is a "hostile" takeover? What kinds of strategies can firms use to avoid hostile takeovers?

Dell's Secret to Success

Go to http://www.reportgallery.com and review Dell's most recent annual report. Also, go to Dell's website (http://www.dell.com) in the section "about Dell," review the background material about Dell that relates to this chapter.

Questions

1. Dell has expanded its operations in recent years. Review how the size of Dell's assets has increased over time.

2. Why do you think Dell has been able to grow at a much faster rate than other firms in its industry?

3. Do you think Dell is reaching its peak level, or does it have more potential for growth?

In-Text Study Guide

True or False

1. Capital budgeting involves the comparison of assets and revenue.

2. Many decisions that result from capital budgeting decisions are irreversible.

3. One of the most popular methods available to assess the feasibility of projects is the net present value (NPV) technique.

4. A payment received by a firm at a future point in time has more value than the exact payment received today.

5. A payment of $1,000 received two years from today has a higher present value than a payment of $1,000 received one year from today.

6. A firm should invest in a project only if its net present value is less than zero.

7. The amount of money that a firm can receive from selling a project is referred to as the net present value.

8. Capital budgeting analysis for investment projects in foreign countries tends to be more complex than analysis for domestic projects.

9. Firms can merge only if they are producing similar products.

10. Firms can be liquid even if they are not holding large amounts of cash and short-term securities.

Multiple Choice

11. A capital budgeting project is considered to be feasible if:
    a) the sum of future cash flows from the project is greater than the initial outlay.
    b) the sum of the present values of all future cash flows from the project is greater than the initial outlay.
    c) no other projects have a higher initial outlay.
    d) the initial outlay is greater than the sum of all discounted future cash flows that result from the project.
    e) the discount rate used to compute present values is less than the rate of inflation.

12. When interest rates rise, a firm will:
    a) require a higher discount rate when it evaluates capital budgeting proposals.
    b) find that more of its capital budgeting proposals are feasible.
    c) find that present values of future cash flows are unaffected.
    d) want to borrow more funds.
    e) find that cash flows in the early years of a project will be discounted more heavily than cash flows that occur during later years.

13. A firm's _____ is a targeted amount of funds to be used for purchasing assets such as buildings, machinery, and equipment that are needed for long-term projects.
    a) master budget
    b) capital budget
    c) working capital projection
    d) escrow account
    e) sinking fund

In-Text Study Guide

Answers are in Appendix C at the back of book.

14. All of the following are motives for capital budgeting expenditures except:
    a) expansion of current business.
    b) development of new business.
    c) acquisition of assets that will reduce expenses.
    d) acquisition of liabilities.

15. If the adoption of investment A has no bearing on whether other investments should be adopted, investment A is said to be:
    a) redundant.
    b) irrelevant.
    c) independent.
    d) expedient.
    e) unrestricted.

16. All of the following are tasks involved in capital budgeting except:
    a) estimating cash flows from the investment.
    b) determining which projects are feasible.
    c) monitoring projects that are implemented.
    d) determining the appropriate size of the line of credit.
    e) implementing feasible projects.

17. The discount rate used to compute the present values of future cash flows from an investment should be equal to the:
    a) rate of inflation expected to exist over the life of the investment.
    b) tax rate applied to the earnings from the investment.
    c) rate of return the firm could have earned on an alternative project of similar risk.
    d) rate at which the assets purchased to make the investment will depreciate.
    e) rate of interest the government pays on Treasury bills of the same duration as the investment project.

18. If the discount rate is 12 percent, the present value of a $20,000 payment received three years from today would be found by:
    a) dividing $20,000 by 3 and dividing the result by .12.
    b) multiplying $20,000 by .12 and dividing the result by 3.
    c) dividing $20,000 by $(1 + .12)^3$.
    d) multiplying $20,000 by $(1 + .12)^3$.
    e) multiplying $20,000 by 3 and dividing the result by $(1 + .12)$.

19. The _____ of an investment is computed by subtracting the initial outlay for the investment from the present value of all future cash flows that result from the investment.
    a) net present value
    b) capitalization factor
    c) discount value
    d) investment premium
    e) gross cash position

20. A merger between a tire manufacturer and a firm that produces clocks and watches is:
    a) illegal.
    b) a horizontal merger.
    c) a diagonal merger.
    d) a vertical merger.
    e) a conglomerate merger.

21. The three general types of mergers are horizontal, conglomerate, and:
    a) cooperative.
    b) vertical.
    c) divestiture.
    d) bureaucratic.
    e) parallel.

In-Text Study Guide

Answers are in Appendix C at the back of book.

22. Which of the following is the best example of a vertical merger?
    a) A chain of fast-food restaurants merges with a firm that produces electronic components for computers.
    b) A small book publisher that specializes in travel and history books merges with a larger book publisher that specializes in biographies and popular fiction.
    c) A golf club manufacturer merges with a firm that helps people prepare their income taxes.
    d) A firm that publishes a newspaper in the St. Louis area merges with a firm that publishes a newspaper in the Chicago area.
    e) A firm that sells flour, sugar, and spices merges with a firm that bakes pies and cakes.

23. The result of a firm investing in another company by purchasing all the stock of that company is a(n):
    a) divestiture.
    b) net present value.
    c) economies of scale.
    d) line of credit.
    e) merger.

24. If the per unit cost of producing a good decreases as a greater quantity is produced, the production process exhibits:
    a) economies of scale.
    b) diminishing returns.
    c) higher fixed costs than variable costs.
    d) an exception to the law of supply.
    e) a very high break-even point.

25. Economies of scale are more likely to be achieved by:
    a) vertical mergers.
    b) horizontal mergers.
    c) conglomerate mergers.
    d) divestitures.
    e) accounts receivable management.

26. Firms that incur negative earnings are sometimes attractive candidates for mergers because of potential:
    a) tax advantages.
    b) cash advantages.
    c) profit exploitation.
    d) retained earnings.
    e) divestitures.

27. A purchase of a company (or the subsidiary of the company) by a group of investors with borrowed funds is a(n):
    a) common stock purchase.
    b) purchase from retained earnings.
    c) equity purchase.
    d) preferred stock purchase.
    e) leveraged buyout.

28. When a firm sells off one of its existing businesses, the process is known as a:
    a) reverse merger.
    b) leveraged buyout.
    c) corporate downsizing.
    d) conglomeration strategy.
    e) divestiture.

29. A firm's short-term assets include all of the following except:
    a) cash.
    b) accounts receivable.
    c) machinery.
    d) inventory.
    e) short-term securities.

30. Firms are said to be _____ if they have adequate access to funds so that they can pay their bills as they come due.
    a) leveraged
    b) fully endowed
    c) vested
    d) bonded
    e) liquid

In-Text Study Guide

Answers are in Appendix C at the back of book.

31. _____ are short-term debt securities offered by the U.S. Treasury that provide firms with easy access to funds since they can be sold to other investors.
    a) Federal warrants
    b) Treasury trust certificates
    c) Treasury stock
    d) Treasury bills
    e) Federal Reserve notes

32. The management of a firm's short-term assets and liabilities is:
    a) accounts receivable management.
    b) working capital management.
    c) sales management.
    d) plant and equipment management.
    e) fixed asset management.

33. An agreement that allows a firm access to borrowed funds upon demand over some specified period of time is a:
    a) bond indenture.
    b) stock flotation.
    c) note receivable.
    d) line of credit.
    e) note payable.

34. The goal of _____ management is to be flexible enough to increase sales to credit customers while being strict enough to limit losses due to customers who pay their bills late or not at all.
    a) leverage
    b) accounts receivable
    c) trade credit
    d) accounts payable
    e) invoice

35. Firms try to maintain a large enough inventory to avoid:
    a) stockouts.
    b) the need for trade credit.
    c) leveraged financing.
    d) default on bonds.
    e) undiversified portfolios.

Chapter 17 Appendix A
Capital Budgeting Analysis

PHOTOEDIT, INC.

A firm performs a capital budgeting analysis of each project by comparing the project's initial outlay with the project's expected benefits. The benefits represent the cash flows generated by the project. Before providing an example of a firm's capital budgeting analysis, the procedure for estimating the present value of future cash flows is described.

Background on Present Value

Because money has a time value, a payment received by a firm at a future point in time has less value than the same payment received today. For this reason, future payments are commonly discounted to determine their present value. For example, if a payment of $50,000 is received in one year, it can be discounted to determine its present value. Assume that the firm can achieve a return of 10 percent over the next year on funds available today. It will use this interest rate to discount the $50,000 payment to be received in one year.

$$\text{Present Value } (PV) \text{ of } \$50{,}000 \text{ Payment} = \frac{\$50{,}000}{(1 + .10)}$$

$$= \$45{,}455$$

This means that the $50,000 payment to be received in one year has a present value of $45,455. If the firm received $45,455 today (instead of $50,000 in one year) and invested the funds at 10 percent, the funds would accumulate to $50,000 at the end of the year.

Capital budgeting analysis compares future cash flows resulting from the project with the initial outlay needed to purchase the project. The initial outlay is made immediately (if the project is implemented), but the cash flows resulting from the project may be received over several years. Since the timing of the cash flows differs from that of the initial outlay, the cash flows must be converted to a present value so that they can be compared with the initial outlay.

The present value of a project's future cash flows is determined by discounting the cash flows at the rate of return that the firm could have earned on the funds if it had used them for an alternative project with similar risk. That is, the discount rate reflects the return that the firm would require to make the investment. The firm must earn at least that return, or it would simply invest the funds in the alternative project.

For example, assume a firm can invest in a project today that would generate a lump-sum cash flow (*CF*) of $10,000 from the investment in one year. If the firm has a required return (r) on this investment of 12 percent, the present value (PV) of the cash flow is as follows:

$$PV = \frac{CF \text{ at End of Year 1}}{(1 + r)}$$

$$= \frac{\$10,000}{(1 + .12)^1}$$

$$= \$8,929$$

This indicates that if the firm had the cash amount of $8,929 available today and could invest it at 12 percent, the investment would be worth $10,000 in one year. Therefore, if the initial outlay is more than $8,929, the firm should not invest in the project, because the initial outlay would exceed the present value of the cash flow generated by the investment.

Now adjust the example to determine the present value of the $10,000 cash flow if it is received at the end of the second year instead of the first year. The present value of this project based on a required return of 12 percent is as follows:

$$PV = \frac{CF \text{ at End of Year 2}}{(1 + r)^2}$$

$$= \frac{\$10,000}{(1 + .12)^2}$$

$$= \$7,972$$

The exponent of the denominator is adjusted to discount the amount based on a period of two years instead of one year. Notice that the present value of cash flows in Year 2 is less than the present value of cash flows in Year 1. The further out the time when a given amount is received, the lower the present value.

The present value of a cash amount in any year can be estimated by adjusting the exponent to reflect the number of years in the future. As one final example, the present value of a $10,000 cash flow to be received three years from now is estimated as follows (assuming the required return is 12 percent):

$$PV = \frac{CF \text{ at End of Year 3}}{(1 + r)^3}$$

$$= \frac{\$10,000}{(1 + .12)^3}$$

$$= \$7,118$$

Now consider a project that generates a cash flow of $10,000 for the firm in Years 1, 2, and 3. Each cash flow can be discounted separately to derive its present value; then, the discounted cash flows are added to de-

Exhibit 17A.1

Example of Discounting
Cash Flows

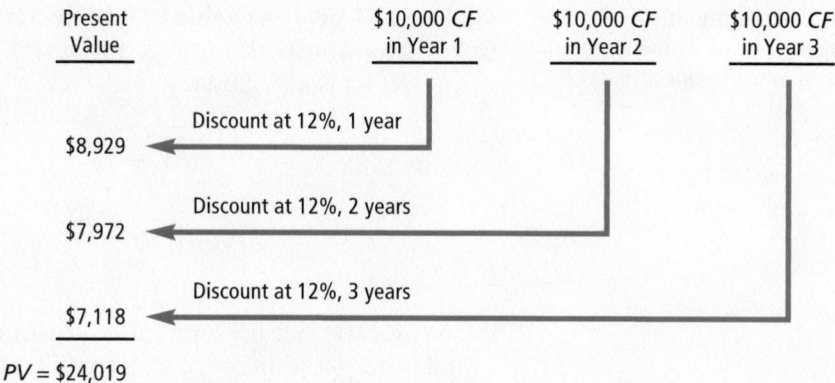

termine the present value of the investment. The present value of these cash flows is estimated as follows:

$$PV = \frac{CF \text{ at End of Year } 1}{(1 + r)^1} + \frac{CF \text{ at End of Year } 2}{(1 + r)^2} + \frac{CF \text{ at End of Year } 3}{(1 + r)^3}$$

$$= \frac{\$10,000}{(1 + .12)^1} + \frac{\$10,000}{(1 + .12)^2} + \frac{\$10,000}{(1 + .12)^3}$$

$$= \$8,929 + \$7,972 + \$7,118$$

$$= \$24,019$$

This example is illustrated in Exhibit 17A.1. It shows how the present value of cash flows is determined by discounting the cash flows in each year at the firm's required rate of return. Then, those discounted cash flows are added together to determine the present value of the cash flows. If the initial outlay necessary to purchase this project is less than $24,019, the project is feasible and should be implemented. If the initial outlay necessary to purchase the project is more than $24,019, the project is not feasible and should not be implemented.

Estimating the Net Present Value

To reinforce the use of capital budgeting analysis, consider a firm that decides to purchase a used delivery truck for $15,000 that will be used to make extra deliveries and will last only two years. By having this truck, the firm estimates that it will generate an extra $8,000 in cash flow at the end of next year and an extra $12,000 at the end of the following year. Assume that the firm requires a return of 15 percent on this project. The present value of these cash flows is estimated as follows:

$$PV = \frac{\$8,000}{(1 + .15)^1} + \frac{\$12,000}{(1 + .15)^2}$$

$$= \$6,957 + \$9,074$$

$$= \$16,031$$

net present value

equal to the present value of cash flows minus the initial outlay

The **net present value** of a project is equal to the present value (PV) of cash flows minus the initial outlay (I). In our example, the net present value (NPV) is as follows:

$$NPV = PV - I$$
$$= \$16,031 - \$15,000$$
$$= \$1,031$$

When the net present value is positive, the present value exceeds the initial outlay, and the project is feasible. When the net present value is negative, the present value of cash flows is less than the initial outlay, and the project is not feasible. Projects are undertaken only when they are expected to generate benefits (present value of cash flows) that exceed the cost (initial outlay).

Now let's progress to larger-scale decisions by firms. Assume that a firm considers opening up a new store, which would require an initial outlay of $2 million. The firm has estimated its revenue and expenses as shown in the first three columns of Exhibit 17A.2 over a four-year period. To simplify the example, assume that the firm conducts all transactions on a cash basis (no accounts payable or receivable). At the end of four years, the firm expects to sell the store for $1 million (after paying taxes on the proceeds of the sale). The amount of money that a firm can receive from selling a project is referred to as the **salvage value.** Assume that the firm requires a 20 percent rate of return on this project. Assume a tax rate of 30 percent charged on earnings generated by the project.

salvage value

the amount of money that a firm can receive from selling a project

Exhibit 17A.2

Capital Budgeting Example

(1) End of Year	(2) Revenue	(3) Expenses	(4) Earnings	(5) Tax (30%)	(6) After-Tax Cash Flow	(7) Discounted Value of Cash Flow
1	$4,000,000	$4,000,000	0	0	0	0
2	5,000,000	4,000,000	$1,000,000	$300,000	$700,000	$486,111
3	6,000,000	5,000,000	1,000,000	300,000	700,000	405,093
4	7,000,000	5,000,000	2,000,000	600,000	1,400,000	675,154
Salvage Value					1,000,000	482,253
					PV =	$2,048,611
					I =	2,000,000
					NPV = $	48,611

Steps

1. Subtract expenses (in column 3) from revenue (in column 2) to derive earnings (shown in column 4) each year.

2. Apply the 30 percent tax rate on earnings to determine the tax on earnings each year (as shown in column 5).

3. Subtract the taxes from earnings to determine the after-tax cash flow each year (as shown in column 6).

4. Discount the after-tax cash flow each year, as shown in column 7.

To determine whether this project is feasible, the firm takes the following steps:

1. The earnings are derived by subtracting expenses from revenue, as shown in column 4 of Exhibit 17A.2.

2. The tax on the earnings is estimated as 30 percent of each year's earnings, as shown in column 5.

3. The taxes are subtracted from earnings to derive the cash flows shown in column 6.

4. The firm discounts the cash flows received (including the salvage value) using its required rate of return (20 percent) as the discount rate.

5. The discounted cash flows for each year (shown in column 7) are then added at the bottom of column 7 to determine the present value (*PV*) of future cash flows.

The process of discounting the project's cash flows to derive its present value is illustrated in Exhibit 17A.3. In this example, the cash flows had to be determined before they could be discounted. Notice that because of the time value of money, the $700,000 cash flow in Year 3 has a much lower present value than the $700,000 cash flow in Year 2.

The present value is equal to $2,048,611 in our example. To derive the project's net present value (*NPV*), the project's initial outlay (*I*) of $2,000,000 is subtracted from the present value. In our example, the *NPV* = $48,611. This means that the present value of future cash flows resulting from the project is expected to exceed the project's initial outlay (*I*) by $48,611. Since the *NPV* is positive, the proposed project should be undertaken. When the present value of the project's cash flows exceeds the initial outlay (cost) of the project, the return of the project is expected to exceed the cost of capital used to support the project.

Exhibit 17A.3

Deriving a Project's
Net Present Value

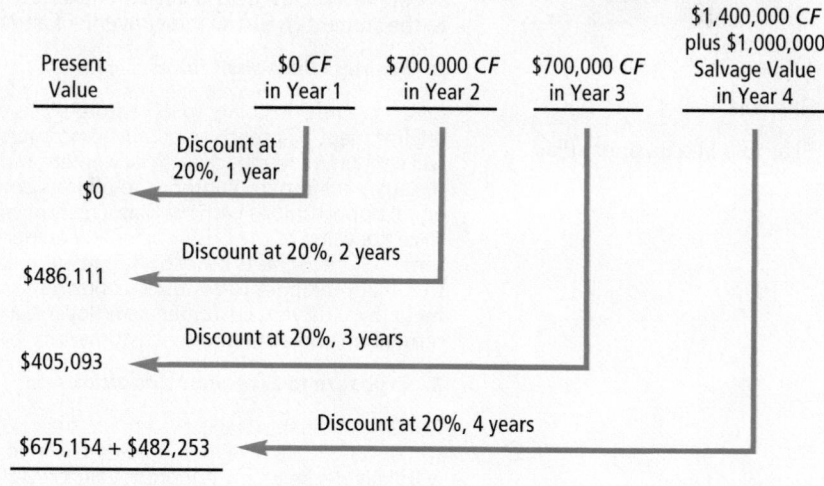

Chapter 17 Appendix B
Consolidating All Major Strategies in the Business Plan

PHOTOEDIT, INC.

Exhibit 17B.1

Example of a Business Plan

Each chapter of the text has explained specific strategies, each of which represents a portion of the business plan. A complete business plan consolidates all of the firm's major strategies. Exhibit 17B.1 shows the complete business plan for College Health Club (CHC), which consolidates the various business plan segments that were discussed in each chapter. Notice that every major business function is covered, in the order that it was discussed in the text. As time passes, Sue Kramer may change various strategies in CHC's business plan, and each change could affect other parts of the business plan. If Sue decides on an investment plan of expanding the club, she will have to revise the financial plan to finance the additional investment. If CHC needs additional financing, Sue will have a better chance of obtaining funds from a creditor if she can present a revised business plan showing how CHC will efficiently use those funds.

Business Plan for College Health Club (CHC)

Part I. Business Environment

1. *Business Idea*

The business is a health club called College Health Club (CHC) that will be located in a shopping mall just across from the Texas College campus. The health club should appeal to the students because it is convenient and will be affordable to them.

2. *Business Responsibilities*

CHC has a responsibility to its customers, its employees, its owners, its creditors, and the environment. It intends to offer its customers excellent service at reasonable prices. It will encourage feedback from customers and attempt to continually improve its services to satisfy customers. It intends to offer its employees a safe working environment and equal opportunities without bias. The firm will be managed in a manner that will maximize the value of the business for any owners who are invited to invest in the firm over time. CHC recognizes its responsibility to make timely payments on debt owed to creditors. It also pledges to conduct its business in a manner that will not harm the environment. By satisfying customers, employees, and creditors, CHC should establish a good reputation and attract more customers in the future.

3. *Exposure to Economic Conditions*

CHC's membership is exposed to local economic conditions. If a weaker economy causes some students to lose their part-time jobs in the local area, the number of memberships will likely decline. Consequently, CHC's revenue and its earnings will also decline. A stronger economy will allow for more part-time jobs and will result in more memberships at CHC. Consequently, CHC's revenue and earnings will increase.

4. *Exposure to Global Conditions*

CHC serves the local community and is not directly affected by global conditions. It will sell vitamin supplements (which are imported from Mexico), and the cost of the supplements will rise when the dollar weakens against the Mexican peso. Since vitamins are not expected to be a primary source of revenue, CHC's exposure to global conditions is negligible.

Part II. Business Ownership and Plan

5. *Business Ownership*

CHC is structured as a proprietorship, with Sue Kramer as the sole proprietor. She will invest $20,000 in the business. An additional $40,000 is needed and will be obtained in the form of a loan.

The business is expected to incur a small level of earnings in the first year, but earnings should increase over the years as the number of memberships increases. The main source of risk of the firm is uncertainty regarding the number of future memberships, which is the key to the success of the business. However, given the strong interest by the local students in joining a health club, the membership level is expected to increase rapidly over time.

6. *Exposure to Competition*

Currently, no other health clubs are convenient to the Texas College campus. New health clubs may be established over time and could pull some of CHC's customers away. Nevertheless, because most of CHC's business is expected to come from students at the college, CHC should not be significantly affected by other health clubs that focus on customers who have full-time jobs and are not currently enrolled at the college. CHC needs to develop a strategy for retaining its members over time. The overall demand for health club services is expected to remain strong because of the desire by people to stay in shape.

Part III. Management

7. *Strategic Plan*

CHC must attract a large number of members to fully utilize the health club space and achieve high performance. As memberships increase, CHC's earnings will increase.

A longer-term objective is to expand over time by capitalizing on the same business concept by establishing other health clubs near college campuses. CHC will assess other college campuses to determine whether there is sufficient demand for health club services. If students appear to want these services and no health club is located nearby, CHC will conduct a more thorough analysis of the expenses and potential revenue associated with establishing a new health club near that campus. CHC will open additional health clubs near other college campuses only if and when it is feasible to do so.

8. *Organizational Structure*

CHC uses a wide span of control, as all employees report directly to Sue Kramer. Tasks at CHC are departmentalized: some employees conduct aerobics classes in one part of the club while others assist members with the exercise and weight machines. Sue Kramer sets up a weekly aerobics schedule and assigns a specific employee (or herself) to lead each class. When employees are not leading an aerobics class, they are assigned to help members use the exercise and weight machines.

If CHC expands by opening new health clubs over the long term, it will departmentalize by location. A manager will be hired for each new health club and will be responsible for managing all of its operations. The manager of each new health club will be trained by Sue Kramer, so that she can ensure that the manager is trained in the procedures that have made CHC successful.

9. *Production*

Resources Used at CHC
CHC's resources are combined to produce health club services. First, human resources are used to lead aerobics classes and interact with customers. Second, equipment such as exercise and weight machines is provided for customers' use. A health club facility is available to the customers. The main expenses of providing these resources are salaries to the human resources and the rental cost of equipment and the facilities.

Site
CHC is located in a shopping mall across the street from the Texas College campus. Since the goal of the business is to target students at this college who want to join a health club, the site selection serves those students. The rent at this facility is reasonable. The health club has easy access to labor because it hires exercise science majors on internships to work part-time.

Design and Layout
The production of health club services is organized by type of service. Aerobics classes are offered in one part of the health club, and exercise and weight machines are avail-

able in another part. While Sue Kramer leads aerobics classes, another employee is responsible for overseeing the machines in case the members need any assistance. The facilities are large enough to allow for some expansion. The layout of the facilities allows flexibility so that the exercise and weight machines can be rearranged.

Production Control
CHC engages in production control to ensure that its services are provided in a timely manner and achieve the desired level of quality. CHC purchases vitamin supplements from its supplier every month and attempts to have a sufficient number of jars of each type of supplement available for its customers. Since the jars are inexpensive and do not take up much space, CHC maintains a large inventory of all of its supplements.

Routing for CHC involves the sequence of tasks necessary to complete the production of health club services. Sue Kramer has a daily schedule of aerobics classes that she teaches. She also posts a weekly schedule of aerobics classes so that members know when they are offered. The main preparation is to ensure that equipment (e.g., a step for step aerobics) and towels are available for the participants. The exercise and weight machines are always available to members.

Production Quality and Efficiency
Total quality management is needed to ensure customer satisfaction. Survey cards will be periodically distributed to members to obtain their feedback about the services. In particular, members will be asked to rate the aerobics classes they take at CHC and the quality of the exercise and weight machines. They will also be asked for suggestions on any other services that they would like CHC to provide.

Production efficiency is needed for CHC to achieve a high level of earnings. Many of its expenses are fixed. Therefore, CHC needs a large number of members to achieve production efficiency. To the extent that CHC offers a membership at an attractive price and provides the types of health club services that students desire, it should attract a large number of members. With a large number of members, CHC's revenue will be high, and since many of its expenses are fixed, they will not be affected by the high membership level.

Part IV. Managing Employees

10. *Motivating Employees*

Part time employees tend to like working in a health club. CHC can easily find qualified part-time employees by recruiting students who are majoring in exercise science at Texas College. CHC offers compensation that is slightly higher than other local employers of part-time college students. It allows flexible work schedules so that students can work fewer hours in a particular week if they have a major exam or class project. CHC welcomes employee involvement.

11. *Human Resource Planning*

CHC's part-time staffing needs are filled by hiring students who are currently majoring in exercise science at the Texas College. Ads are posted in that department to recruit new applicants. The typical tasks of part-time employees include leading aerobics classes, helping members use the weight and exercise machines, washing towels, and responding to phone inquiries. Students submit applications online.

Developing Employees Skills
When part-time employees are hired at CHC, they are told that the focus is on safety in using the weight and exercise machines. Although all members are given a booklet on safety, employees should understand the safety features in case they see a member who is not using the machines properly. Second, employees are trained on the importance of customer relations. Third, employees are trained to work together.

Employee Evaluation
Part-time employees are evaluated according to their customer relations and their employee relations. The survey forms that request feedback from members ask if they have any comments about the individual part-time employees.

Part V. Marketing

12. *Product and Pricing*

Product Mix
CHC's product mix includes the provision of aerobics classes, weight machines, and exercise machines. All of these services are provided at no charge to customers who pay an annual membership fee. In addition, CHC sells vitamin supplements to members. It may expand its product mix over time by selling workout clothing.

Target Market
The target market is the set of students enrolled at Texas College who want to join a health club. CHC also wants to retain the students as members after they graduate if they continue to live in the local area. Since the health club is not on the campus but in a shopping mall across the street from the campus, CHC should also be able to attract local people who are not affiliated with the college.

Product Differentiation
The main appeal of CHC to the students at Texas College is its location. It is located across from the college campus, so students can walk to the club. Since many of them do not have a car, this location is ideal and separates CHC from all other health clubs.

Pricing Policy
The membership fee is influenced by the cost of production and by competitors' prices. CHC's annual expenses are expected to be about $142,000. Assuming that CHC can attract 300 members, an annual membership fee of $500 will be sufficient to cover the cost of production and will also be competitive. The number of members is expected to grow over time.

13. *Distribution*

Since CHC provides its services directly to members, channels of distribution are not needed. However, CHC does serve as a retailer for vitamin supplements and may serve as a retailer for a limited amount of exercise clothing CHC purchases its vitamin supplements from a vitamin wholesaler and may purchase exercise clothing from a clothing wholesaler.

14. *Promotion*

Advertising
CHC reaches its target market by advertising in the college's school newspaper. This weekly newspaper is free to students, and most students read it or at least skim it.

Personal Selling
CHC offers presentations about exercise and health to students at the auditorium on one Friday afternoon each month. The presentations do not directly advertise CHC's services, but they provide some name recognition for CHC.

Sales Promotion Strategy
CHC distributes coupons for the vitamin supplements in the Texas College newspaper. The intent is to attract nonmember students who will come to CHC to buy the vitamin supplements at a discounted price (with the coupon) and will look at the health club facilities while they are there. CHC also distributes coupons in the student newspaper that allow a free pass for a day to try out an aerobics class or the weight machines. These coupons may entice some students who will try out the facilities and later become members. A display of the vitamin supplements is set up near the door of CHC so that they are visible to anyone who walks into the health club.

Promotion Mix
CHC uses a promotion mix consisting of (1) advertising in the Texas College newspaper, (2) a sales promotion of coupons for vitamin supplements and a free day pass in the Texas College newspaper, and (3) personal selling through monthly presentations about exercise and health to students on campus. All three parts of the promotion mix are focused on the students.

Evaluating the Effects of Promotion
The membership application requests information about what caused the person to purchase a membership. The choices are (1) referral from a friend, (2) advertising in the student newspaper, (3) coupons in the student newspaper, (4) the exercise and health presentations on campus, or (5) other. A review of the information provided by applicants indicates what promotion strategy was effective. This information will be considered when deciding what sales promotion strategies should be used in the future.

Part VI. Financial Plan

15. *Financial Plan at CHC*

Revenue from annual memberships, sales of vitamin supplements, and sales of exercise clothing is expected to be about $150,000 at the end of the first year. CHC's expenses in the first year are expected to be $142,000, as shown below. Its main expenses are the rent for the facilities ($60,000 per year), salaries ($48,000), rental expenses for the weight and exercise machines ($7,200), and marketing expenses ($3,600). Other expenses are expected to be $23,200 over the first year.

Operating Expenses	Monthly Expenses	Total Expenses in First Year
Rent of facilities	$5,000	$60,000
Salaries	4,000	48,000
Utilities	700	8,400
Rent of exercise and weight machines	600	7,200
Marketing expenses	300	3,600
Liability insurance	800	9,600
Miscellaneous	100	1,200
Total operating expenses		$138,000
Interest expenses		4,000
Total Expenses		$142,000

Given the estimated revenue of $150,000 and total expenses of $142,000, CHC's estimated earning before taxes are $8,000 in the first year. In the following years, the expenses are expected to be about the same, but memberships are expected to increase, so revenue should be higher. In addition, sales of vitamin supplements and exercise clothing are expected to increase.

16. *Financing*

Equity Financing
Sue Kramer, president of CHC, invests $20,000 of her own money as an equity investment in CHC. She will reinvest any earnings in the business over time. Sue has no plans to rely on additional equity funding from venture capital firms.

Debt Financing
CHC needs a loan for $40,000 to finance this business. The prevailing interest rate for small business loans is about 10 percent. The desired loan maturity is seven years. At the end of seven years. CHC will repay the loan. Given a 10 percent interest rate on the loan amount of $40,000, CHC's annual interest expense is $4,000.

Leasing
The exercise and weight machines will be leased. The facilities for the health club will also be leased. Thus, in the event that the business is discontinued, there will be no need to find a buyer for the machines or the facilities. This flexibility makes CHC a more favorable opportunity for lenders because they are less exposed to the possibility of failure by the business. If CHC has substantial funds in the future, it will reconsider whether to purchase these assets.

Dividend Policy
Once CHC begins to generate positive earnings, it will retain the earnings and reinvest them rather than pay dividends. This will allow for more expansion.

17. *Business Investment and Expansion*

Investment of Funds
CHC will lease its equipment and facilities rather than purchase them, so it does not need funds to make such purchase. However, CHC needs to have sufficient funds on hand to cover the monthly lease payments. It will initially use its funds to cover operating expenses such as salaries, utility expenses, insurance, and marketing expenses. As time passes. CHC should generate sufficient revenue to cover these operating expenses.

   If CHC accumulates substantial funds over time, it may purchase the exercise and weight machines that it leases. Second, it may purchase the facilities that it currently leases. Third, it may acquire an existing health club as a means of expanding its business. It would likely need some additional financing if it purchases its present facilities or acquires another health club.

Credit Policy
CHC will not extend credit to its members. To make its membership more affordable to students who want credit, it will offer shorter-term memberships, such as a three-month membership for $110.

Summary/Part VI

Financial Management

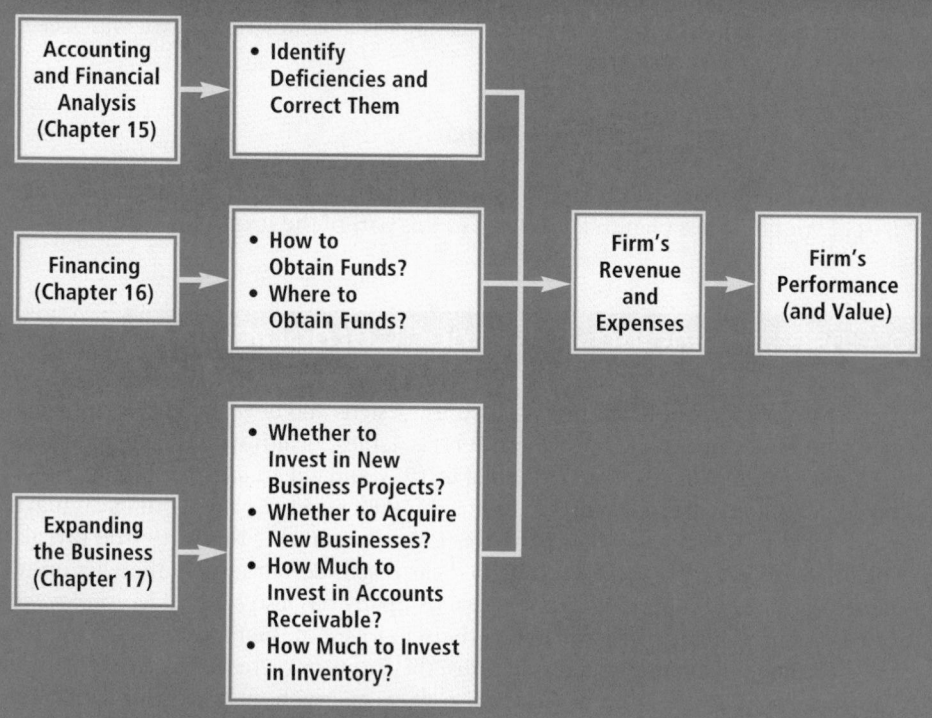

Developing the Financial Plan for Campus.com

Monitoring Performance (related to Chapter 15)

In your business plan for Campus.com, explain how the firm will monitor its performance over time. That is, describe the specific financial ratios that it can monitor to measure its performance and its efficiency.

Financing Business Expansion (related to Chapter 16)

In your business plan for Campus.com, identify the alternative choices you have to obtain funds to support additional expansion. Which alternative is the best choice for you? Does the financing method that you selected have any disadvantages?

Business Investment (related to Chapter 17)

In your business plan for Campus.com, briefly explain how Campus.com will determine whether future expansion is feasible. That is, describe how it will decide whether to pursue a specific project.

Communication and Teamwork

You (or your team) may be asked by your instructor to hand in and/or present the part of your business plan that is related to this part of the text.

Integrative Video Case: Financing at Cerner Corporation

Cerner Corporation of Kansas City, Missouri, designs and develops clinical information systems for health-care providers. It is the largest health-care consultancy business in the United States. It was founded in 1979 and did an initial public offering to become a publicly traded company in March 1990, raising $14 million. Its annual revenues have grown at a very fast pace over time. Cerner CEO Neal Patterson says that the best equity is what you earn (retained earnings). Cerner frequently relies on retained earnings to support its growth. The company has also allowed its employees to provide equity financing by permitting them to invest in the firm, and some of them have become millionaires as a result. Thus, the firm was increased its equity without the need for financing from new outside owners and without borrowing funds. Patterson observes that businesses need to take risks to be successful, but he also admits that he has not lost all fear when making business decisions. More information about Cerner Corporation is available at http://www.cerner.com/public.

Questions:

1. Explain how Cerner's financing decisions can affect its performance. Specifically, how can the financing decision to share equity with employees affect their motivation and performance?

2. Cerner has commonly used retained earnings to support the growth of its business. How does this form of financing affect the firm's capital structure? Why does this give Cerner more flexibility to borrow funds in the future?

3. Explain how the growth of Cerner's business is related to its financing decisions.

4. Neal Patterson, the CEO of Cerner, says that although his business needs to take risks, he does not want to ever lose all fear when making business decisions. What does this mean?

The Stock Market Game

Check the performance of your stock.

Check Your Performance

1. What is the value of your stock today?

2. What is your return on your investment?

3. How did your return compare to those of other students? (This comparison tells you whether your stock performance is relatively high or low.)

Explaining Your Stock Performance

Stock prices are frequently influenced by changes in a firm's financial strategies, including new financing policies and new investment strategies (such as acquisitions). A stock's price may increase if investors expect the new financial strategies to improve the performance of the firm. A stock's price can also decrease if the financial strategies are expected to reduce the firm's performance. Review the latest news about your stock.

1. Determine how your stock's price was affected (since you purchased it) by changes in the firm's financial strategies (the main topic in this part of the text).

2. Identify the specific type of financial policies that caused the stock price to change.

3. Did the stock price increase or decrease in response to the announcement of new financial policies?

Running Your Own Business

1. Forecast the revenue of your business in the first year. (Multiply the amount you expect to sell over the year times the price charged.)

2. Forecast the expenses of your business in the first year. Include the cost of materials and supplies, administrative (management) expenses, marketing expenses, rent expenses, and interest expenses.

3. Forecast the earnings (before taxes) of your business. (This is the difference between the forecasted revenue and the forecasted expenses.)

4. Assuming a tax rate of 20 percent, forecast your taxes. (You can apply a different tax rate if you know what your tax rate would be.)

5. Forecast your earnings after taxes. (This is the difference between your earnings before taxes and the amount of taxes you expect to pay.)

6. State how much of your own money you will invest as a form of equity investment in the business.

7. Indicate whether you will have any co-owners in this business and how much money they will have to invest.

8. State how much money you will need to start your business. (To determine this amount, compare expected expenses with expected revenue. Having a cushion is helpful in case the expenses turn out to be higher than expected or revenue turns out to be less than expected.)

9 State how much money you will need to borrow. (You can estimate this amount by comparing the amount of money you will need to start your business with the amount of equity that will be invested in your business.)

10 Indicate where you plan to obtain borrowed funds. For example, do you plan to obtain a loan from a regular commercial bank or from an Internet bank?

11 State the interest rate that you expect to pay on the borrowed funds.

12 Describe how long you expect to need the borrowed funds before you can pay back the loan.

13 Forecast your return on equity over the first year based on your forecast of earnings after taxes and the amount of equity invested in your business.

14 Describe any big purchases (such as a computer or a machine) that you may need to make for your business someday. What factors would be a part of a cost-benefit analysis of this purchase?

15 Explain how much inventory you would have to maintain to avoid shortages.

16 Would your business generate accounts receivable? If so, how would you manage this asset?

Your Career in Business: *Pursuing a Major and a Career in Accounting and Finance*

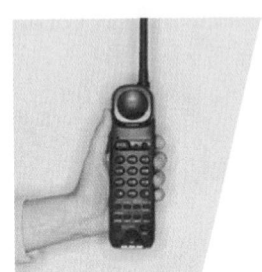

If you are very interested in the topics covered in this section, you may want to consider a major in Accounting or Finance. Some of the more common courses taken by Accounting and Finance majors are summarized here.

Common Courses for Accounting Majors

▶ *Principles of Accounting*—Focuses on the creation and interpretation of the income statement and the balance sheet.

▶ *Intermediate Accounting*—Deals with the accounting for inventory, fixed assets, and operating expenses.

▶ *Cost Accounting*—Focuses on internal accounting related to management decisions.

▶ *Accounting Information Systems*—Deals with the design and application of information systems used to facilitate accounting.

▶ *Auditing*—Provides an overview of the concepts and methods used to ensure the accuracy of accounting reports and financial statements.

▶ *Internal Auditing*—Focuses on the evaluation of internal tasks, procedures, and guidelines.

Common Courses for Finance Majors

▶ *Financial Management*—Emphasizes managerial decisions about financing and investing.

▶ *Personal Finance*—Focuses on individuals' financial decisions about budgeting, the use of credit, insurance, investments, and retirement planning.

▶ *Financial Institutions*—Examines the sources and uses of funds of financial institutions; also covers the management, performance, and regulation of financial institutions.

▶ *Financial Management of Institutions*—Discusses decision making by financial institutions, exposure of institutions to risk, and how the risk can be managed.

▶ *Financial Markets*—Provides an overview of securities that are traded in financial markets, with emphasis on how financial markets facilitate security transactions.

▶ *Advanced Financial Management*—Provides an in-depth analysis of decisions by financial managers, including dividend policy, capital structure, and capital budgeting.

▶ *Investment Analysis*—Focuses on valuation of securities, investment strategies, and managing the risk of investment portfolios.

▶ *International Financial Management*—Discusses financial management from the perspective of a firm in an international environment, with emphasis on how financial decisions account for exchange rate movements.

▶ *Real Estate*—Provides a survey of real estate investments, the valuation of real estate, and the risk of real estate investments.

Careers in Accounting and Finance

The following websites provide information about job positions, salaries, and careers for students who major in Accounting or Finance:

▶ Job position websites:

http://jobsearch.monster.com	Accounting/Auditing, Banking, Finance, Insurance, and Real Estate
http://careers.yahoo.com	Accounting/Finance, Banking/Mortgage, Insurance, and Real Estate

▶ Salary website:

http://collegejournal.com/salarydata	Accounting, Banking, Consulting, Insurance, and Real Estate

Appendix A
Using Information Technology

An information system (IS) collects and processes data into information that is provided to users for use in strategic planning, decision making, performance monitoring, and production. These systems give both firms and consumers access to vast amounts of information and also facilitate communication within and between all parties. Consequently, they can help firms increase their revenue and reduce their expenses. They have also enabled new firms to compete in various product markets, which has forced firms to be very efficient in order to survive. Virtually all firms use some type of IS to store, access, and analyze information; improve communication with customers; and improve communication among employees.

If a firm determines how to use information technology to improve its efficiency, it can reduce its expenses and increase its earnings. If it can use information technology to attract more customers or offer additional products, it can increase revenue and increase its earnings. An IS can be expensive, however, so firms should also recognize the danger of investing in technologies that will not provide a positive return on investment within their potentially short useful lives.

What Is an Information System?

A complete IS usually includes hardware, software, and telecommunications as well as people and the data themselves.

Hardware

hardware
the physical components of a computer

system architecture
the basic logical organization of a computer

The physical components of a computer are collectively called **hardware.** Although computer hardware is constantly changing, the basic logical organization of computers, often referred to as **system architecture,** has been relatively stable since the mid-1950s. From laptops to mainframes, nearly all computers are built around four key components: the central processing unit, primary storage, secondary-storage, and peripherals.

Central Processing Unit

clock rate
the rate at which a central processing unit can perform its most basic functions

hertz
a unit of frequency equal to one cycle per second

The central processing unit (CPU) is a microprocessor that performs most calculations and moves information between the computer's other components. More than any other single component, the CPU determines the basic behavior and capabilities of a particular computer. CPUs commonly seen in consumer products include Intel's Pentium line and Advanced Micro Devices' Athlon line. Traditionally, CPUs have been marketed by their clock rate. **Clock rate** is the rate, measured in cycles per second, or **hertz,** at which the CPU can perform its most basic functions. This can be misleading as different processors do different amounts and different kinds of work with each cycle.